Reference and Information Services

London Borough of Bromley Library Service

MIDDLE EAST CONTEMPORARY SURVEY
Volume Two: 1977-78

Also available

MIDDLE EAST CONTEMPORARY SURVEY, Volume 1, 1976–77

MIDDLE EAST CONTEMPORARY SURVEY

Volume Two
1977–78

COLIN LEGUM, Editor

HAIM SHAKED, Academic Editor

Daniel Dishon, Shiloah Center Editor

Jacqueline Dyck, Executive Editor

**The Shiloah Center
for Middle Eastern and African Studies
Tel Aviv University**

Holmes & Meier Publishers, Inc.
New York and London

Published in the United States of America 1979 by
Holmes & Meier Publishers, Inc
30 Irving Place
New York, NY 10003

and in Great Britain by
Holmes & Meier Publishers, Ltd
Hillview House
1, Hallswelle Parade
Finchley Road
London NW11 ODL

Copyright © 1979 Holmes & Meier Publishers, Inc

International Standard Book Number: 0–8419–0398–0
International Standard Serial Number: 0163–5476
Library of Congress Catalog Card Number:78–648245

Manufactured in the United States of America

Preface

The *Middle East Contemporary Survey* (MECS) is an annual record and analysis of political, economic, military and international developments in the Middle East and its peripheral regions. It complements the respected *Middle East Record* which has been prepared by the Shiloah Center for Middle Eastern and African Studies of Tel Aviv University since 1962 and to date covers events up to 1970. The present volume is the second in a series which provides scholars, diplomats, students and informed laymen with a continuing up-to-date reference work recording the rapidly changing events in an exceptionally complex part of the world. Every attempt has again been made to use the widest range of source material and maintain the highest possible academic standards.

MECS is a joint publishing venture between the Shiloah Center and Holmes & Meier Publishers. Most of the essays have been researched and written by the staff of the Shiloah Center; other contributions have been made by distinguished academics and experts mainly from the United States and the United Kingdom.

The material in this volume is arranged in two parts. The first comprises a series of essays which study developments relating to internal and external issues, both regionally and internationally. Subjects explored in detail include the Israeli-Arab conflict, inter-Arab relations, and the international dimensions of the contending forces in the region. The second part comprises a country-by-country survey of each of the Middle Eastern entities, excluding the three North African states of Tunisia, Algeria and Morocco. The prospects for the signing of an Egyptian-Israeli peace treaty and its implications are analysed in the introductory essay, "The Middle East in Perspective."

The period surveyed in this volume, unless otherwise specifically indicated, is generally from October 1977 to October 1978, but a number of chapters deal with events to the end of 1978 and even early 1979. In order to avoid excessive repetition while at the same time achieving a comprehensive survey of the affairs of each country individually, extensive cross-references have been used.

We feel it necessary to alert the reader to two problems which affect the economic analyses contained in this volume. The first is that official sources for economic data are often incomplete or of questionable accuracy, or both. The second is that arms procurement from foreign sources are important components of the economies of most Middle East countries, but by their very nature tend to be kept secret by both supplier and recipient. As such, they may be disguised in the published itemized national budgetary accounts, or may even be excluded entirely. Unpublished arms sales have therefore been treated as unknown quantities and thus, unless otherwise indicated, have not been incorporated in the economics affairs sections.

Similar problems arise in trying to provide accurate information about the balance of military power in the Middle East. Unless specifically stated to the contrary, all the statistical data relating to military forces are derived from the *Military Balance* of the International Institute for Strategic Studies, London, to which we are indebted.

Acknowledgements

As editors we are indebted to a large number of contributors who have made this volume possible. First and foremost we recognize the work of the staff of the Shiloah Center for Middle Eastern and African Studies at Tel Aviv University whose individual contributions are separately acknowledged.

The economic sections of the countries surveyed in Part II, together with the accompanying statistical tables, have been prepared by Ira E. Hoffman.

Jacqueline Dyck's role as executive editor has again been indispensable. She has been assisted in copy-editing by Lalit Adolphus.

Jutta Hinrichs and Jo Palmer, editorial assistants in London, have given valiant service. The exacting work of indexing has been carried out by Mrs H. M. Pearson of Cambridge.

Among those at the Shiloah Center who must be singled out for special thanks are Edna Liftman, who has been responsible for co-ordinating the flow of material between Tel Aviv, London and New York; and the Shiloah Center's Director, Elie Rekhess, who fulfilled with meticulous care and great perseverance a variety of executive tasks. Steven Frieder has been of great help to those in the Center whose native language is not English. Special thanks are also due to the Shiloah Documentation System headed by Amikam Salant, as well as Amira Margalith. We are particularly indebted to Terry Walz, Associate Editor of Holmes & Meier, who has been responsible for co-ordinating our work in New York.

Finally, we would like to mention Max Holmes who, from the inception of MECS, has viewed this work not simply as another publishing venture, but more imaginatively, as a serious contribution towards widening knowledge and understanding of Middle Eastern affairs.

C.L.
H.S.

Table of Contents

PART ONE: CURRENT ISSUES

x

List of Maps

Transliteration

The Arabic alphabet has been transliterated as follows:

b	for	ب	n	for	ن	
d	for	ض،د	q	for	ق	
dh	for	ذ	r	for	ر	
f	for	ف	s	for	ص،س	
gh	for	غ	sh	for	ش	
h	for	ه	t	for	ط،ت	
ḥ	for	ح	th	for	ث	
j	for	ج	w (or ū)	for	و	
k	for	ك	y (or ī)	for	ي	
kh	for	خ	z	for	ظ،ز	
l	for	ل	'	for	ا،ء	
m	for	م	'	for	ع	

In addition,
- Long vowels have been distinguished from short ones by a stroke over the letters
- The *hamza* is shown only in the middle of a word
- The *shadda* is rendered by doubling the consonant containing it
- The *ta marbuta* is not shown
- The definite article is always shown as "al-" regardless of whether or not it is assimilated to the following letter
- No distinction is made between the ordinary and emphatic d, s, t or z
- Exceptions to the above are those Lebanese and North African personalities who have adopted a French spelling for their names

Abbreviations

ABEDA	Arab Bank for African Economic Development (or BADEA)
ACP	Africa, the Caribbean and the Pacific (Lomé Convention)
ADF	Arab Deterrent Force (in Lebanon)
ADNOC	Abu Dhabi National Oil Company
AFAED	Abu Dhabi Fund for Arab Economic Development
AFESD	Arab Fund for Economic and Social Development (Kuwaiti-based)
AGOIC	Arabian Gulf Organization for Industrial Consulting
ALF	Arab Liberation Front (Iraqi-directed organization in PLO)
ALO	Arab Labour Organization
AMIO	Arab Military Industries Organization
AMOCO	American Oil Company
ANM	Arab Nationalist Movement
Aramco	Arabian-American Oil Company
AS	Arab Socialists (Syria)
ASPE	Arab Socialist Party of Egypt (Centrist)
ASU	Arab Socialist Union (Syria, Egypt)
CD	Chamber of Deputies (Lebanon)
CEMA	Council of Mutual Economic Assistance
CENTO	Central Treaty Organization
CIEC	Conference on International Economic Co-operation (North/South Dialogue)
cif	cost, insurance and freight
CPA	Constituent People's Assembly (YAR)
CSCE	Conference on Security and Co-operation in Europe (Helsinki)
DCA	Defence Co-operation Agreement (Turkey and the US)
DISK	Revolutionary Trade Union Confederation (Turkey)
DMC	Democratic Movement for Change (Israel)
DP	Democratic Party (Turkey)
EEC	European Economic Community
EIB	European Investment Bank (EEC)
ELF	Eritrean Liberation Front
ELF-PLF	Eritrean Liberation Front—Popular Liberation Forces
EPC	European Political Co-operation
EPLF	Eritrean People's Liberation Front
EUA	EEC Unit of Account
FAO	Food and Agriculture Organization (UN)
FLOSY	Front for the Liberation of Occupied South Yemen
fob	free on board
Frolinat	*Front de Libération Nationale* (Chad)
GA	General Assembly (UN, or UNGA)
GDP	Gross Domestic Product
GNP	Gross National Product

GODE	Gulf Organization for the Development of Egypt
IAJ	Iranian Association of Jurists
IATUC	International Arab Trade Union Confederation
ICP	Iraqi Communist Party
IDF	Israel Defence Forces
IEA	International Energy Agency
IMF	International Monetary Fund
JCP	Jordanian Communist Party
JP	Justice Party (Turkey)
KFAED	Kuwait Fund for Arab Economic Development
LAA	Lebanon's Arab Army
MCC	Military Command Council (YAR)
MIT	Turkish Intelligence Service
NA	National Assembly
NAP	Nationalist Action Party (Turkey)
NATO	North Atlantic Treaty Organization
NC	National Command (Iraqi Ba'th Party, Syrian Ba'th Party)
NCC	National Consultative Council (Jordan)
NDF	National Democratic Front (YAR)
NDP	National Democratic Party (Egypt)
nes	not elsewhere specified
NF	National Front (Sudan, Turkey)
nie	not included elsewhere
NLP	National Liberal Party (Lebanon)
NPF	National Progressive Front (Syria)
NRP	National Religious Party (Israel)
NSC	National Security Council (Turkey)
NSP	National Salvation Party (Turkey)
OAPEC	Organization of Arab Petroleum Exporting Countries
OECD	Organization for Economic Co-operation and Development
OPEC	Organization of Petroleum Exporting Countries
pa	per annum
PA	People's Assembly (Egypt)
PC	Presidential Council (YAR)
PDFLP	Popular Democratic Front for the Liberation of Palestine
PDFLP-GC	Popular Democratic Front for the Liberation of Palestine—General Command
PDRY	People's Democratic Republic of Yemen (South Yemen)
PFLO	Popular Front for the Liberation of Oman
PFLOAG	Popular Front for the Liberation of Oman and the Arab Gulf
PFLP	Popular Front for the Liberation of Palestine—General Command
PLA	Palestine Liberation Army
PLF	Popular Liberation Front (PLO)
PLO	Palestine Liberation Organization
PNA	People's National Assembly (Sudan)
PNC	Palestine National Council

PNF	Palestine National Front
Polisario	Front for the Liberation of Saquiet al-Hamra and Rio de Oro
PPNF	Progressive Patriotic and Nationalist Front (Iraq)
PRA	People's Regional Assembly (Southern Sudan)
PSF	Popular Struggle Front
PUK	Patriotic Union of Kurdistan
PUSA	Progressive Unionist Socialist Alignment Party (Egypt, Left-wing)
RC	Regional Command (Ba'th Party, Iraq, Syria)
RCD	Regional Co-operation for Development (Turkey-Iran-Pakistan)
RPP	Republican People's Party (Turkey)
RRP	Republican Reliance Party (Turkey)
SADR	Saharan Arab Democratic Republic
SALT	Strategic Arms Limitation Talks
SAMA	Saudi Arabia Monetary Agency
SANU	Sudan African National Union
SAVAK	State Intelligence and Security Organization (Iran)
SC	Security Council (UN, or UNSC)
SCP	Syrian Communist Party
SDF	Saudi Development Fund
SDRs	Special Drawing Rights (IMF)
SITC	Standard International Trade Classification
SLP	Socialist Liberal Party (Egypt, Right-wing)
SPO	State Planning Organization (Turkey)
SSU	Sudanese Socialist Union
SU	Socialist Unionists (Syria)
Tapline	Trans-Arabian Pipeline
TFSC	Turkish Federated State of Cyprus
UAE	United Arab Emirates
UNDOF	United Nations Disengagement Observation Force
UNEF	United Nations Emergency Force
UNIFIL	United Nations Interim Force in Lebanon
UNRWA	United Nations Relief and Works Agency (for Palestine Refugees)
UNTSO	United Nations Truce Supervision Organization
UPONF	Unified Political Organization—The National Front (PDRY)
USFP	*Union Socialiste des Forces Populaires* (Morocco)
WIZO	Women's International Zionist Organization
YAR	Yemen Arab Republic (North Yemen)

List of Sources

Newspapers, Periodicals, Yearly, Irregular and Single Publications

Name *(Place, frequency of publication)*	Abbreviation	Notes
Africa (London, monthly)		
Africa Contemporary Record (London, yearbook)	ACR	
Afro-Asian Affairs (London, monthly)		
Al-Ahālī (Cairo, weekly)		Organ of the Progressive Unionist Socialist Alignment Party (PUSA)
Al-Ahrām (Cairo, daily)		
Al-Ahrām al-Iqtisādī (Cairo, fortnightly)		Published by al-Ahrām; dealing mainly with economic issues
Al-Ahrār (Cairo, weekly)		Organ of the Socialist Liberal Party (SLP)
Al-Akhbār (Amman, daily)		
Al-Akhbār (Cairo, daily)		
Akhbār al-Khalīj (Manāma, daily)		
Akhbār 'Umān (Muscat, weekly)		
Akhbār al-Usbū' (Amman, weekly)		
Akhbār al-Yawm (Cairo, weekly)		Weekly edition of the Cairene al-Akhbār
Ākhir Sā'a (Cairo, weekly)		
'Al Hamishmar (Tel Aviv, daily)		Organ of the United Workers' Party (Mapam)
Al-'Amal (Beirut, daily)		Organ of the Lebanese Phalanges
Al-'Amal (Tunis, daily)		Organ of the Socialist Dustūr Party
Amnesty International (London, irregular)		
Al-Anbā (Beirut, weekly)		Organ of Junblāt's Socialist Progressive Party
Al-Anbā (Jerusalem, daily)		Published by the Israeli Trade Union Federation (Histadrut)
Al-Anbā (Kuwait, daily)		
Al-Anbā (Rabat, daily)		Published by the Ministry of Information
Annual Report and Balance Sheet 25 35 (Tehran, Yearly)		Published by Bank Markazi Iran

Al-Da'wa (Cairo, monthly)		Organ of the Muslim Brethren
Department of State Bulletin (Washington, weekly)	DSB	
Department of State Press Release (Washington, irregular)	DSPR	
Diplomat (Ankara, weekly)		
Direction of Trade (Washington, monthly)		Published by the International Monetary Fund (IMF). Includes an annual supplement
Al-Diyār (Beirut, weekly)		
Al-Dustūr (Amman, daily)		
Al-Dustūr (London, weekly)		Pro-Iraqi. Originally a Beirut weekly reflecting the Iraqi Ba'th views. Closed down in Beirut by the Syrians (December 1976). Published in Paris (until July 1977), then in London
Economic and Political Weekly (Bombay, weekly)		
The Economist (London, weekly)		
The Egyptian Gazette (Cairo, daily)		
L'Espresso (Rome, weekly)		
Ettela'at (Tehran, daily)		
Events (London, weekly)		Published in English by the owner of al-Ḥawādith, Beirut
Al-Fajr (East Jerusalem, daily)		Sympathetic to the PLO
Al-Fajr al-Jadīd (Tripoli, daily)		
Al-Fātih (Tripoli, weekly)		
Le Figaro (Paris, daily)		
Filastīn al-Muhtalla (Beirut, weekly)		Published by al-Fath
The Financial Times (London, daily)	FT	
Foreign Affairs (New York, quarterly)		
Foreign Report (London, weekly)		
Fourteenth October (Aden, daily)		Organ of the UPONF
France Soir (Paris, daily)		
Die Frankfurter Allgemeine Zeitung (Frankfurt, daily)	FAZ	
The Guardian (London, daily)		

Güneydin
(Istanbul, daily)

Ha'aretz
(Tel Aviv, daily)

Al-Hadaf
(Beirut, weekly)

Ceased to appear

Ha-Olam ha-zeh
(Tel Aviv, weekly)

Al-Hawādith
(Beirut, weekly)

Pro-Phalanges tendencies

Al-Hurriyya
(Beirut, weekly)

Organ of PDFLP

Information: European Economic
Community
(Brussels, irregular)

International Financial
Statistics
(Washington, monthly)

IFS

Published by the International
Monetary Fund

International Herald Tribune
(Paris and Zürich, daily)

IHT

Iran Economic Service
(Tehran, weekly)

IES

English-language review of
Iranian press on economic
affairs. Published by Echo of
Iran

Issues and Studies
(Taipei, monthly)

Al-Ittihād
(Abu Dhabi, daily)

Al-Ittihād
(Haifa, twice a week)

Organ of Communist Party

Izvestiia
(Moscow, daily)

Organ of the Government of
the USSR

Jamāhiriyya Mail
(Valleta, daily)

Published by the Libyan
information services

Al-Jarīda
(Beirut, weekly)

Al-Jarīda al-Rasmiyya
Damascus, weekly)

Official Gazette of Syria

Jarīdat Misr
(Cairo, weekly)

Organ of the Arab Socialist
Party of Egypt (ASPE)

Al-Jazīra
(Riyadh, daily)

The Jerusalem Post
(Jerusalem, daily)

JP

Jeune Afrique
(Paris, weekly)

Reflects views of Tunisian
expatriates

Al-Jihād
(Tripoli, daily)

Jīl al-Thawra
(Damascus, monthly)

Organ of the Executive
Bureau of the National Union
of Students in Syria

Jordan Times
(Amman, daily)

JT

Al-Jumhūr
(Beirut, weekly)

Al-Jumhūriyya
(Baghdad, daily)

Semi-official

Al-Jumhūriyya
(Cairo, daily)

Kayhan (Tehran, daily)		
Kayhan International (Tehran, daily)	KI	English-language edition of the Kayhan
Khwandaniha (Tehran, weekly)		
Al-Kifāh al-'Arabī (Beirut, daily)		Reflects Leftist views
Al-Liwā (Beirut, daily)		
Los Angeles Times (Los Angeles, daily)	LAT	
Lugano Review (Lugano, bi-monthly)		
Lumea (Bucharest, daily)		Foreign affairs weekly of the Socialist Republic of Romania. Published in Romanian, English and French editions
Ma'ariv (Tel Aviv, daily)		
Al-Madīna (Jidda, daily)		
Al-Manar (London, weekly)		Hostile to the present Egyptian regime
Le Matin (Casablanca, daily)		
Le Matin (Paris, daily)		
Al-Mawāqif (Manāma, weekly)		
Mezhdunarodnaia Zhizn' (Moscow, monthly)		
The Middle East (London, monthly)		
Middle East Economic Digest (London, weekly)	MEED	
Middle East Intelligence Survey (Tel Aviv, fortnightly)	MEIS	
Middle East International (London, monthly)	MEI	
Middle East Record (Tel Aviv, yearbook)	MER	
Mideast Markets (New York, fortnightly)	MM	
Migvan (Tel Aviv, monthly)		Published by the Israeli Labour Party
The Military Balance 1978–79 (London, yearly)		Published by the International Institute for Strategic Studies
Milliyet (Istanbul, daily)		
Monday Morning (Beirut, weekly)		
Le Monde (Paris, daily)		
Monthly Statistical Bulletin (New York, monthly)	MSB	
Al-Muharrir (Beirut, daily)		Pro-Iraqi, pro-PLO

Al-Munādil (Damascus, monthly)		Internal organ of the Syrian Ba'th Party. Distributed mainly among party members, but frequently quoted by Syrian media and occasionally available to the public at large
Al-Musawwar (Cairo, weekly)		
Al-Mustaqbal (Paris, weekly)		Pro-Saudi
Al-Nahār (Beirut, daily)		Rightist
Al-Nahār al-'Arabī wal-Duwalī (Paris and Zurich, weekly)	NAD	Weekly international edition of al-Nahār
An-Nahar Arab Report and Memo (Beirut and Zürich, weekly)		English language political and economic report published by al-Nahār
Near East Report (Washington, weekly)		
New African (London, monthly)		
Newsweek (New York, weekly)		
New York Times (New York, daily)	NYT	
Nidāl al-Fallāhīn (Damascus, weekly)		Organ of the Syrian Peasant Federation
Novoe Vremia (Moscow, weekly)		
The Observer (London, weekly)		
October (Cairo, weekly)		
Outlook (Ankara, weekly)		
Paris Match (Paris, weekly)		
Peking Review (Peking, weekly)	PR	
Petroleum Economist (London, monthly)		
Philadelphia Inquirer (Philadelphia, daily)		
Political Digest (Tehran, weekly)		English-language review of Iranian press on political affairs published by Echo of Iran
Pravda (Moscow, daily)		Organ of the Central Committee of the CPSU
Die Presse (Vienna, daily)		
Pulse (Ankara, daily)		English-language summary of Turkish press
Al-Qabas (Kuwait, daily)		Sympathetic to the Palestinian cause
Quarterly Bulletin (Damascus, quarterly)		Published by the Central Bank of Syria

Quarterly Economic Review (London, quarterly)	QER	Published by the Economist Intelligence Unit
Al-Quds (East Jerusalem, daily)		Known for favourable views towards Jordan
Rastakhiz (Tehran, daily)		Organ of Rastakhiz party
Al-Ra'y (Amman, daily)		
Al-Ra'y al-'Amm (Kuwait, daily)		
Review of Economic Conditions (Ankara, quarterly)	REC	Published by Türkie Is Bank
Al-Riyād (Riyadh, daily)		
Rūz al-Yūsuf (Cairo, weekly)		
Al-Safīr (Beirut, daily)		Reflects Libyan views
Al-Saḥāfa (Khartoum, daily)		
Saudi Arabian Monetary Agency (Jidda, annual)	SAMA	Also biannual Statistical Summary
The Saudi Gazette (Jidda, daily)		Published by 'Ukāz publishing house
Sawt al-Talī'a (Damascus, monthly)		Internal organ of the United Palestinian Organization of the Syrian Ba'th Party. Distributed mainly among Palestinian party members, but frequently quoted by Syrian media and occasionally available to the public at large.
Al-Sayyād (Beirut, weekly)		
Scintea (Bucharest, daily)		Organ of the Romanian Communist Party (RCP)
Al-Sha'b (Algiers, daily)		
Al-Sha'b (East Jerusalem, daily)		Sympathetic to PLO
Al-Sharq al-Jadīd (London, monthly)		
Shu'ūn Filastīniyya (Beirut, monthly)		Issued by the PLO Research Institute
Al-Siyāsa (Kuwait, daily)		
Al-Siyāsa al-Dawliyya (Cairo, quarterly)		Published by the Al-Ahrām Center for Political and Strategic Studies
Le Soir (Brussels, daily)		
Son Havadıs (Istanbul, daily)		Organ of the Justice Party
Sovetskaia Rossiia (Moscow, daily)		
Der Spiegel (Hamburg, weekly)		

La Stampa
(Milan, daily)

Strategic Middle Eastern Affairs
(Washington, weekly)

Sudanow
(Khartoum, monthly)

The Sunday Telegraph
(London, weekly)

Sunday Times
(London, weekly)

The Swiss Review of World Affairs
(Zürich, monthly)

Syrie et Monde Arabe
(Damascus, monthly)

Published by the Office Arabe de Presse et de Documentation

Al-Talā'i'
(Damascus, weekly)

Organ of al-Sā'iqa, the Syrian-run organization belonging to the PLO

Al-Talī'a
(East Jerusalem, weekly)

Reflects views of Communists in the West Bank

Tarīq al-Sha'b
(Baghdad, daily

Organ of the Communist Party (ICP)

Tehran Journal
(Tehran, daily)

Tercüman
(Istanbul, daily)

Conservative

Al-Thawra
(Baghdad, daily)

Organ of the Iraqi Ba'th Party

Al-Thawra
(Damascus, daily)

Al-Thawra
(San'ā, daily)

Semi-official

Al-Thawra Mustamirra
(Damascus, weekly)

Organ of PFLP

Al-Thawrī
(Aden, weekly)

Organ of UPONF

Thirteenth June
(San'ā, weekly)

Organ of the Yemeni Armed Forces

Time
(New York, weekly)

The Times
(London, daily)

Tishrīn
(Damascus, daily)

Trouw
(Amsterdam, daily)

'Ukāz
(Jidda, daily)

United Nations Monthly Chronicle
(New York, monthly)

Al-Usbū' al-'Arabī
(Beirut, weekly)

Al-Usbū' al-Siyāsī
(Tripoli, weekly)

US Information Service
(Tel Aviv, irregular)

USIS

Press releases by the USIS branch in Israel

US International Communication Agency
(Tel Aviv, irregular)

USICA

The new name of USIS beginning April 1978

US News and World Report
(Washington, weekly)

Wall Street Journal
(New York, daily)

Washington Post   WP
(Washington, daily)

Washington Star
(Washington, daily)

Al-Watan
(Kuwait, daily)

Al-Watan al-'Arabī
(Paris, weekly)

Al-Wathba
(Abu Dhabi, daily)

Weekly Compilation of Presidential   WCPD
Documents
(Washington, weekly)

The White House Press Release   WHPR
(Washington, irregular)

The World Today
(London, monthly)

Al-Yamāma
(Riyadh, weekly)

Al-Yaqza   Reflects Pan-Arab tendencies
(Kuwait, weekly)

Al-Yasār al-'Arabī   Produced by a group of
(Paris, monthly)   Leftist expatriates from Egypt
                                   and Lebanon; strongly critical
                                   of Sādāt's regime

Yedi'ot Aharonot
(Tel Aviv, daily)

Die Zeit
(Hamburg, weekly)

News Agencies

Full Name	Abbreviation
Agence France Presse	AFP
Agenţia Română di Presă	Agerpres
Algérie Presse-Service	APS
Anatolia (Ankara)	
Arab Press Service (Beirut)	
Arab Revolution News Agency (Tripoli)	ARNA (Changed its name, see below†)
Associated Press	AP
Associazione Nazionale Stampa Associata	ANSA
Deutsche Presse Agentur	DPA
Gulf News Agency	
Inter Press Service (Beirut)	IPS
Iraqi News Agency	INA
Jamāhiriyya Arab News Agency (Tripoli)	JANA†
Jewish Telegraphic Agency	JTA
Maghreb Arabe Presse	MAP
Middle East News Agency (Cairo)	MENA
New China News Agency	NCNA
Pars (Tehran)	
Qatari News Agency	QNA
Reuter	

Syrian Arab News Agency	SANA
The Saudi News Agency	SNA
Sudanese News Agency	SUNA
Telegraofnoe Agentstvo Sovetskovo Soiuza	TASS
UAE news agency	
United Press	UP
United Press International	UPI

Radio Stations and Monitoring Services

(Radio stations known by the location of their principal transmitter are not listed—their names being self-explanatory.)

Name	Abbreviation	Notes
British Broadcasting Corporation Summary of World Broadcasts;		
The ME and Africa	BBC	Monitoring reports published in
The USSR	BBC/SU	English translations
Daily Report;		
Middle East and North Africa	DR	Monitoring reports published in
Eastern Europe	DR/EE	English translation by the US
Soviet Union	DR/SU	Foreign Broadcast Information Service
Israel Broadcasting Authority	IBA	
Israel Defence Forces Radio	R IDF	
Joint Publication Research Service;	JPRS	English language translations from foreign press and occasionally
Near East and North Africa		monitoring reports published in English by the US Joint Publication Research Service
R Bayrak		Transmitter of the FTSC
R Cairo, Voice of Palestine	VOP	Run by PLO under the supervision of R Cairo
R Cyprus		Greek-Cypriot transmitter in Turkish
R Nicosia		Greek-Cypriot transmitter in Greek
R of the Phalanges		Transmissions of the Phalanges Party, Lebanon
Voice of America	VoA	
Voice of the Arab Homeland	R Tripoli, VoAH	Libyan transmitter to Arab audiences outside Libya
Voice of the Arabs	R Cairo, VoA	Cairo transmitter to Arab audiences outside Egypt
Voice of Arab Syria	VoAS	Iraqi-operated station, pretends to transmit from Syrian territory
Voice of Lebanon	VoL	Radio station operated by the Lebanese Phalanges
Voice of Oman Revolution		Run by the PFLO under the supervision of R Aden
Voice of Palestine	VoP	PLO clandestine station transmitting from Lebanon
Voice of the Palestinian Revolution— Voice of the Central Committee	VoCC	Baghdad transmitter to Palestinian audiences

Note: Hebrew translation of transcripts of radio stations or news agency copy are available at the Shiloah Center Archives.

Notes on Contributors

ISRAEL ALTMAN, Ph.D. (University of California, Los Angeles, 1976). Research Associate at the Shiloah Center. Fields of specialization: Egypt, Palestinian organizations, modern Islamic movements. Published papers on Egypt and on the Palestinian organizations.

DAN AVIDAN, M.A. (University of California, Los Angeles, 1975). Junior Research Associate at the Shiloah Center. Fields of specialization: the West Bank and the Gaza Strip.

OFRA BENGIO, B.A. (Tel Aviv University, 1966). Junior Research Associate at the Shiloah Center. Fields of specialization: history and politics of Iraq. Contributed chapters to the *Middle East Record*.

VARDA BEN-ZVI, B.A. (Hebrew University, Jerusalem, 1966). Junior Research Associate at the Shiloah Center. Field of specialization: inter-Arab relations. Published papers and contributed chapters to the *Middle East Record*.

ALVIN J. COTTRELL, Ph.D. (University of Pennsylvania). Executive Director, International Research Council, CSIS. Graduated from the National War College, where he was Professor of Foreign Affairs. Publications include: *Soviet Shadow Over Africa* (1976); *Indian Ocean Naval Limitations* (1976); *The Indian Ocean: Its Political, Economic and Military Importance (1972)*; and "The Armed Forces Under the Pahlavis," in *Iran Under the Pahlavis* (1978).

URIEL DANN, Ph.D. (Jerusalem, 1966). Associate Professor of Modern Middle Eastern History and Senior Research Fellow at the Shiloah Center. Published *Iraq Under Qassem* and articles.

DANIEL DISHON (Hebrew University, Jerusalem, 1938–40). Senior Research Fellow at the Shiloah Center. Fields of specialization: contemporary Middle Eastern history and politics and inter-Arab relations. Publications: Editor of the *Middle East Record* volumes III, IV, V, VI (1967, 1968, 1969–1970, 1971). Published papers on inter-Arab relations.

MOSHE GAMMER, B.A. (Tel Aviv University, 1977). Research Assistant at the Shiloah Center. Fields of specialization: history of the modern Middle East and the Arab-Israeli conflict. Contributed chapters to the *Middle East Record*.

GIDEON GERA, recently completed Ph.D. dissertation (Tel Aviv University). Senior Research Fellow at the Shiloah Center. Fields of specialization: the modern Middle East, history and politics of Libya. Published papers on Libya.

JACOB GOLDBERG, Ph.D. (Harvard University, 1978). Lecturer, Department of Middle Eastern and African History, Tel Aviv University. Fields of specialization: history and politics of Saudi Arabia. Contributed chapters to the *Middle East Record*.

REAR-ADMIRAL ROBERT J. HANKS, USN (Ret) Director, Strategic Plans, Policy, Nuclear Systems and NSC Affairs Division, Office of the Chief of Naval Operations, at the time of his retirement in September 1977. Earlier assignments included service as Director, Security Assistance Division, Office of the Chief of Naval Operations; Commander, Middle East Force; and Deputy Director for Nuclear Planning Affairs, Office of the Assistant Secretary of Defense (International Security Affairs). Research Fellow at the Center for International Affairs, Harvard University (1970–71).

IRA E. HOFFMAN, M.Sc. (Econ; London School of Economics, 1975). Junior Research Associate at the Shiloah Center. Fields of specialization: economics of the Middle East; relations of the European Community with the Middle East. Contributed economic chapters to the *Africa Contemporary Record*.

ELIYAHU KANOVSKY, Ph.D. (Columbia University, 1961). Associate Professor, Department of Economics at Bar Ilan University; Senior Research Fellow at the Shiloah Center. Fields of specialization: Middle East economics. Published books and articles on economic affairs in the Middle East.

DINA KEHAT, B.A. (Tel Aviv University, 1975). Junior Research Associate at the Shiloah Center. Fields of specialization: history and politics of Syria and inter-Arab relations. Contributed chapters to the *Middle East Record*.

GEOFFREY KEMP, Ph.D. (Massachusetts Institute of Technology). Associate Professor of International Politics at The Fletcher School of Law and Diplomacy, Tufts University. Written extensively on Middle East military affairs.

AARON KLIEMAN, Ph.D. (John Hopkins University, School of Advanced International Affairs, 1969). Senior Lecturer and Chairman, Political Science Department, Tel Aviv University. Fields of specialization: international and Middle Eastern affairs; Israeli foreign policy. Author of *Foundations of British Policy in the Arab World; Soviet Russia and the Middle East.*

COLIN LEGUM, Associate Editor of *The Observer* and Editor of the *Africa Contemporary Record*. Published works include *Must We Lose Africa?* (W. H. Allen); *Bandung, Cairo and Accra* (Africa Bureau); *Attitude to Africa* (Penguin, 1953) with others; *Congo Disaster* (Penguin); *Pan-Africanism* (1962); *South Africa: Crisis for the West* (1964) with his wife; *The Bitter Choice* (World Publishers) with his wife; Editor of the *Africa Handbook*; *After Angola* (1976); *The Fall of Haile Selassie's Empire* (1976); *Vorster's Gamble for Africa* (1977); *The Year of the Whirlwind* (1977); *Conflict in the Horn of Africa* (1978); *The Continuing Conflict in the Horn of Africa* (1979); *The Challenge to the West in Southern Africa* (1979).

ESTHER LIDZBARSKI-TAL, B.A. (Tel Aviv University, 1972). Research Assistant at the Shiloah Center. Field of specialization: the history and politics of Turkey.

DAVID MENASHRI, M.A. (Tel Aviv University, 1973). Junior Research Associate at the Shiloah Center. Field of specialization: the history and politics of Iran. Contributed chapters to the *Middle East Record*.

DAVID MORISON, Director of the Central Asian Research Centre, London; Editor of *USSR and the Third World*, a periodical which surveys the development of Soviet and Chinese relations with the countries of Asia, Africa and Latin America.

ITAMAR RABINOVICH, Ph.D. (University of California, Los Angeles, 1971). Chairman and Associate Professor, the Department of Middle Eastern and African History, Tel Aviv University; Senior Research Fellow at the Shiloah Center. Fields of specialization: the modern and contemporary history of the Arab world with particular reference to Syria, Lebanon and inter-Arab affairs. Publications: *Syria under the Ba'th 1963–66: The Army Party Symbiosis* and *The Lebanese Civil War: A Documented History* (Hebrew); co-editor of *From June to October: The ME between 1967–73.*

R. K. RAMAZANI, Edward R. Stettinius Professor and Chairman at the Woodrow Wilson Department of Government and Foreign Affairs, University of Virginia. Associate Editor of *Journal of South Asia and Middle Eastern Studies*; Advisory Editor of the *Middle East Journal*, and consultant to the Rockefeller Foundation and Institute for Foreign Policy Analysis. Author of *The Middle East and the European Common Market*; *The Northern Tier: Afghanistan, Iran and Turkey*; *The Foreign Policy of Iran, 1500–1941: A Developing Nation in World Affairs*; *Iran's Foreign Policy 1941–1973: A Study of Foreign Policy in Modernizing Nations*; *The Persian Gulf: Iran's Role*; *Beyond the Arab-Israeli Settlement: New Directions for US Policy in the Middle East*; and numerous articles and reviews.

JACQUES REINICH, M.A. (Tel Aviv University, 1977). Fields of specialization: the modern Middle East and Egypt.

ELIE REKHESS, M.A. (Tel Aviv University, 1977). Director of Shiloah Center for Middle Eastern and African Studies. Fields of specialization: the Israeli Arabs and the Arabs in the West Bank and Gaza Strip. Published papers and studies on the Arab intelligentsia in Israel and in the West Bank; political trends and socio-economic change within the Arab population in Israel, the West Bank and Gaza.

YEHUDIT RONEN, B.A. (Tel Aviv University, 1977). Research Assistant at the Shiloah Center. Fields of specialization: Sudan and Libya.

DANKWART A. RUSTOW, Ph.D. (Yale, 1951). Distinguished Professor of Political Science at the City University of New York. Taught at Princeton (1952–59) and Columbia (1959–70). Publications include: *A World of Nations* (1967), *Philosophers and Kings: Studies in Leadership* (1968), *Middle Eastern Political Systems* (1971), *OPEC: Success and Prospects* (with J. F. Mugno, 1976). Vice-President of the Middle Eastern Studies Association of North America (1969–70) and the American Political Science Association (1973–74).

HAIM SHAKED, Ph.D. (School of Oriental and African Studies, University of London, 1969). Associate Professor, Department of Middle Eastern and African History, Tel Aviv University. Head of the Shiloah Center; Dean of the Faculty of Humanities, Tel Aviv University. Fields of specialization: modern and contemporary history of the ME; Sudan, Saudi Arabia, Yemen and South Yemen. Author of *The Life of the Sudanese Mahdi* and co-editor of *From June to October: The ME Between 1967–1973*. Co-editor of *Middle East Record*; Chairman, Editorial Board of the Shiloah Center Monograph Series.

SHIMON SHAMIR, Ph.D. (Princeton University, 1960). Associate Professor, Department of Middle Eastern and African History, Tel Aviv University, and Senior Research Fellow at Shiloah Center. In 1966, established the Shiloah Center at Tel Aviv University, which he directed until 1973. Has published books on the modern history of the Arabs and contemporary Egypt and various articles on Ottoman Syria and Palestine. Co-editor of *USSR and the ME*; Editor of *Decline of Nasserism*.

ARYEH SHMUELEVITZ, M.A. (Hebrew University, 1960). Senior Lecturer, Department of Middle Eastern History, Tel Aviv University, and Senior Research Fellow at Shiloah Center. One of the founders of the Shiloah Center in 1959 and of the *Middle East Record*. Fields of specialization: history of the Ottomans and the Persians; contemporary history of Turkey, Iran and the Persian Gulf. Publications: articles on the Middle East in general and on the history of the Ottoman Empire; Co-editor of *Middle East Record*; Departmental Editor of *Encyclopedia Judaica*; Chairman, Editorial Board of the Shiloah Center Research and Teaching Aids Series.

UDO STEINBACH, Ph.D. in Oriental Studies (Freiburg University, Germany). Director of Deutsches Orient-Institut, Hamburg. Editor of *Orient—Deutsche Zeitschrift fuer Politik und Wirtschaft des Orients*. Consultant to the Volkswagen Foundation. Author of numerous articles on Middle East politics, focusing on Turkish and Iranian foreign policy and international aspects of ME policy.

ASHER SUSSER, B.A. (Tel Aviv University, 1972). Junior Research Associate at the Shiloah Center. Fields of specialization: history and politics of Jordan and the Palestinians. Published papers on Jordanian politics and contributed chapters to the *Middle East Record*.

MICHAEL YAHUDA, M.Sc. (Econ; University of London, 1966). Lecturer in International Relations, LSE, and frequent broadcaster for the BBC. Author of *China's Role in World Affairs* (Croom Helm, 1978) and articles.

TAMAR YEGNES, B.A. (Tel Aviv University, 1977). Junior Research Associate at the Shiloah Center. Fields of specialization: history and politics of Saudi Arabia, Yemen Arab Republic and the People's Democratic Republic of Yemen. Published papers and contributed chapters to the *Middle East Record.*

HANNA ZAMIR, B.A. (Hebrew University, Jerusalem, 1968). Junior Research Associate at the Shiloah Center. Fields of specialization: contemporary history of Lebanon. Co-author of the book *The Lebanese Civil War: A Documented History*. Contributed chapters to the *Middle East Record.*

PART I
CURRENT ISSUES

The Middle East in Perspective:
A Review of 1978

Two chains of events dominated the Middle Eastern scene from late 1977 and throughout 1978: the Egyptian-Israeli negotiations and the near-collapse of the Iranian regime. Both were perceived as marking new departures. Both overturned long-entrenched views, held within the area as well as outside it, on fundamental aspects of regional politics. Both sent out ripples spreading across the entire ME. Both affected the standing of the great powers in the ME and their policies towards it. Yet both left untouched and unchanged many basic political, social, economic and cultural problems of the region whose potential tensions made themselves felt as undercurrents—less dramatic, less conspicuous, less commented upon, but no less significant for the area's future.

THE NEGOTIATING PROCESS

Throughout 1978, the mere fact of direct negotiations being conducted between Israel and an Arab country for the conclusion of a full-fledged peace treaty hardly lost anything of its overwhelming innovative impact on the contracting parties and on the Arab world at large—notwithstanding the major and minor crises which marked their course and the frequent reversals of public mood in both Israel and Egypt. In fact, many of the occasions on which either side disregarded the other's special sensitivities and caused old fears to be revived or mutual good faith to be questioned stemmed from the sheer lack of experience in dealing with each other directly.

From its inception, the negotiating process had been bedevilled by one inherent contradiction: Egypt's desire (fully shared by the US, less so by Israel) to seek a comprehensive ME settlement was set against the fact that no additional Arab interlocutor was ready to join the political process. On the contrary, Arab opinion against participation hardened during the course of the year, both among Arab governments and in the PLO, as well as among West Bank and Gaza Palestinians, culminating in the almost universal rejection of the Camp David accords. The accords themselves had been drawn up in acknowledgement of the logic of the situation: their very division into one bilateral Egyptian-Israeli "framework agreement" and another dealing with the West Bank and the Gaza Strip was evidence of a realistic reading of political circumstances. So was the marked difference between the two parts in their language and approach: the bilateral "framework" being firm, clear, fairly detailed, and definite in laying down a timetable for the next phase; the West Bank and Gaza "framework" being vague on many points, including the time element, and open to conflicting interpretations. It allotted specific roles in subsequent negotiations both to Jordan and to Palestinian representatives, but did so with insufficient grounds for the assumption that they would indeed join in. By the end of 1978, neither had come forward.

Consistent with the nature of the Camp David accords, the subsequent negotiations were successful in rapidly converting the bilateral provisions of the "framework" into the language of a treaty. What eventually prevented the treaty's signature by the date laid down at Camp David (17 December 1978) were two issues transcending the bilateral plane—issues which made the difference between a separate peace, pure and simple, and a bilateral peace containing elements of an eventual comprehensive or somewhat more comprehensive settlement. These were the status of Egypt's obligations under existing inter-Arab pacts, and the interrelationship, or "linkage," between the two parts of the Camp David accords.

On the bilateral plane, the only major substantive issue left unresolved at the conclusion of the Camp David summit was the future of the Israeli settlements in Sinai. This was removed ten days later when an overwhelming majority of the Knesset (in an acknowledgement of realities comparable to the support of partition in 1947 by the majority of the then Jewish *yishuv* in Palestine) voted to dismantle them, provided all other outstanding issues were settled. As far as the future of direct Israeli-Egyptian relations were concerned, the Knesset vote was the final and complete vindication of the policy Sādāt had launched in November 1977: within less than a year, his offer of contractual peace and of security arrangements in Sinai had ranged the US alongside Egypt and led Israel to agree to the complete restoration to Egypt of what Sādāt had referred to in his Jerusalem press conference as "my sacred soil." By contrast, at the end of 1978, Egypt and Israel remained sharply divided not only on the exact character of the "linkage" between bilateral Egyptian-Israeli relations and the West Bank/Gaza plan, but also in their understanding of the very nature of the autonomy to be applied to these territories.

In Israel, alongside security considerations and ideological commitments inherited from the past, domestic politics played a part in shaping government attitudes on the West Bank. Opposition to the strictly bilateral aspects of the Camp David accords had proved manageable—as shown by the Knesset vote. Against these aspects were the "new opposition" which had sprung up on the Right wing ("outflanking Begin on the Right," as local political language had it) and the Communist List which took its cue from Moscow's rejection of the Camp David agreements, together with a few abstentions from other quarters of the house. However, opposition to the autonomy—whether as originally proposed or as modified at Camp David—was gaining some strength. There were indications that larger sections of the government coalition might oppose the autonomy scheme if they came to perceive it—in its post-Camp David form—as the kernel of an independent Palestinian state, and that they would have significant support from the ranks of Labour (the principal opposition party).

Conversely, the concept of autonomy being only a step on the road to Palestinian self-determination was precisely the concept Egypt felt it needed to foster, although not primarily for domestic reasons. Domestic opposition to Sādāt's policy towards Israel, though not entirely lacking, had surprisingly little weight in 1978. The main motive governing Sādāt's attitude on the West Bank and Gaza scheme was that of Egypt's inter-Arab standing. Domestic consideration entered through Sādāt's wish to reassure the more pan-Arab oriented parts of the Egyptian establishment and political public that his peace policy was not going to dissociate Egypt from the Arab cause. As Jordan, let alone Syria, showed less and less inclination to join the negotiating process, Egyptian insistence on "linkage" between its own peace treaty with Israel and the future of the West Bank and Gaza became the only way to prevent the proposed settlement from being altogether "separate." Egypt's ability to set into motion a process for the solution of the Palestinian problem became the touchstone Sādāt needed to acquit himself of the charge levelled against him by the majority of the Arab states and by the PLO: that of seeking Egypt's own, narrow and particular interests at the expense of the Arab cause.

THE BAGHDAD CONFERENCE

The accusation that Egypt was out for a separate deal had been at the core of Arab criticism of Sādāt since the launching of his initiative in 1977. Yet until the Camp

4

David summit, there had been a clear division between the radical states, vocal and emphatic in their criticism of Sādāt and unrestrained in their appeals to overthrow him, and a conservative camp critical of Sādāt's policy but anxious not to destabilize his regime. The Camp David accords brought about a decisive change in this constellation. Both camps interpreted the accords to mean that a separate peace had now become an established fact; both dismissed the ensuing negotiations as merely a search for the proper wording of agreements already conclusively entered upon.

It was this shift in Arab alignments in the wake of the Camp David conference which made possible the convening of the ninth Arab summit conference at Baghdad (2–5 November 1978). At the end of 1977, Jordan, Saudi Arabia and the minor Peninsular states following the Saudi line had refused to attend an Arab summit from which Egypt might possibly absent itself. Now they consented to participate in a summit conference to which Egypt was not even invited. The fact that every single Arab League member except Egypt took part in the Baghdad meeting turned its very convention into the most resounding demonstration yet of anti-Sādāt Arab sentiment. This registered all the more strongly with the Arab political public since the very institution (in 1964) of Arab summit meetings had been an Egyptian invention, designed to reassert Egypt's ascendancy. The first six summit conferences had all been convened on Egypt's initiative. The seventh (Rabat, 1974) had been promoted mainly by Syria and Saudi Arabia, the eighth (see *MECS 1976–77*, pp. 148–49) by Saudi Arabia alone. None of them had met without Egypt's active participation. The ninth, by contrast, turned into an all-Arab court trying Egypt *in absentia* and unanimously finding it guilty of having acted "outside the framework of collective Arab responsibility." It rejected the Camp David accords and "all effects resulting from them," and called on Cairo to "abrogate" them and not to sign "any reconciliation treaty with the enemy."

True, the all-inclusive anti-Sādāt unanimity achieved at Baghdad did not last very long: Morocco, Sudan and Oman, who had supported Sādāt in November 1977, gradually and with a great deal of caution dissociated themselves from the harsh tenor of the Baghdad resolutions. But the summit's principal result—bringing Jordan and Saudi Arabia closer to Iraq and the Syrian-led Tripoli bloc than at any time since the beginning of Sādāt's initiative—was still clearly in evidence at the end of 1978. The two groups were not only united in rejecting the Camp David accords, but had also found common ground in redefining their attitude on the fundamentals of the Arab-Israeli conflict. On the one hand, Iraq dropped its earlier insistence on a public and immediate disavowal of Security Council Resolutions 242 and 338 and on proclaiming "the road to armed struggle" as the only admissible policy. On the other hand, Saudi Arabia, Jordan and the other participants from the conservative camp gave evidence of increased militancy by putting their signatures to resolutions bearing all the marks of Syria's concept of the nature, and future, of the conflict. In language more suitable to the early 1960s (the peak period of Nasserist and Ba'thi ideological fervour) rather than the 1970s, the resolutions stressed that "the struggle for the restoration of Arab rights in Palestine and the occupied Arab territories is a *pan-Arab* responsibility"; they reaffirmed, in terms which had almost gone out of fashion, the all-embracing nature of the "Zionist challenge" as constituting a "military, political, economic and cultural danger . . . to the entire Arab nation and its vital national interests, its culture and its fate"; they reiterated support for the PLO; and, by warning Egypt that a settlement must not take the form of a "reconciliation treaty," they implied the adoption of Syria's vision of an open-ended conflict not to be terminated by the withdrawal from the occupied territories and the establishment of a Palestinian state. (A Syrian statement on the

Camp David agreements issued before the Baghdad conference had stipulated that Israel's withdrawal to the former borders must be 'unconditional.'') Finally, the future state of the Palestinians was not described as being limited to the West Bank and Gaza Strip: it was to be established "on their national soil."

Unanimity in rejecting the Camp David accords and the establishment of a broader consensus on basic attitudes towards Israel had gone hand in hand with a series of reconciliations among quarrelling members of the Arab League. The most spectacular was that between Syria and Iraq. A meeting between Presidents Ḥāfiz al-Asad and Ahmad Ḥasan al-Bakr (24–26 October 1978) led to the signature of a joint "Charter for National Action" pledging both sides "to seek arduously" for the "closest form of ties of unity" between their countries. The understanding reached between them sufficed to enable both to co-operate in the course of the Baghdad conference and contributed to the formulation of its resolutions. However, by the end of 1978 there were few signs that the decade-old dispute between the two rival Ba'th parties had become a thing of the past. Hostile propaganda had indeed been stopped, mutual subversive activities called off, and irksome restrictions on traffic dropped. However, until the end of 1978, the work done by a variety of joint committees instituted under the Charter related only to marginal issues, leaving major policy problems untouched. In particular, the question of stationing Iraqi troops on Syrian soil was left open. Yet two points need to be made: the October meeting reversed Iraq's earlier policy of giving priority to its dispute with Syria over its attempts to counteract Sādāt's policy; and Syria's interest in "redressing the military balance" to compensate for Egypt's "defection" made it imperative that matters of military co-ordination would figure—sooner or later—in the new Syrian-Iraqi relationship.

Syria and Iraq did not provide the only example of settling, or toning down, Arab disputes under the impact of the Camp David accords. The general *rapprochement* between the conservative bloc led by Saudi Arabia and the radical Arab states has already been mentioned. In addition, Iraq took steps to improve relations with Jordan. Jordan for its part opened a dialogue with the PLO. Even though conducted at arm's length, as it were, this contrasted with the unconcealed hostility of previous years. Although it evolved against an entirely different background, the earlier improvement of Libyan-Sudanese relations is also worth mentioning as complementing an overall picture of receding internal disputes in the Arab world, which reversed the trends of 1976 and 1977. (The exceptions were the PDRY's relations with its three neighbours and relations between Morocco and Algeria; both situations remained tense.)

For all the unanimity at Baghdad in rejecting the Camp David accords and condemning Sādāt, the consensus achieved there did not extend to one point: how best to deal with Egypt in order to deter Sādāt from concluding peace, and what action to take if he did. Beyond tactical questions of the carrot-and-stick kind, larger issues loomed. Was Egypt on the point of relapsing into what Arabs call "regionalism," i.e. an "Egypt-first" policy? If so, what could be done to "rescue" Egypt for Arabism? Need Sādāt be overthrown for this purpose, as Syria, Libya and Iraq believed, or could he be coaxed back into the Arab fold, as Saudi Arabia seemed to assume? If there was going to be a separate Egyptian-Israeli peace, what would the Arab world be like with its central inter-continental link missing; would it be weakened in its "Arabism"? Could the Arab League, steered by an Egyptian secretary-general ever since its establishment in 1945, be removed from its Cairo headquarters and resuscitated elśewhere? Could Arab solidarity be restructured without Egypt? Was "Arab solidarity" in any sense still valid under the circumstances evolving during the year and particularly after the Camp David summit? No answers were forthcoming in 1978. But the fact that these questions were being asked in so probing a manner marked the year off from any other since the establishment of the State of Israel.

TORPEDOING AUTONOMY

Neither the anti-Egyptian tenor of the Baghdad resolutions nor their emphatic rejection of the Camp David agreements lessened Egypt's determination to continue with the negotiations. Their only immediate effect was in hardening anti-autonomy opinion in the West Bank (less so in the Gaza Strip with its special longstanding links with Egypt). In the West Bank, the division between PLO supporters and pro-Jordanians, which had dominated local politics for a decade, became blurred. After the PLO and Jordan had joined in condemning autonomy at Baghdad, their respective sympathizers in the West Bank could more easily co-operate in adopting and propagating an anti-autonomy stand. The PLO's post-Baghdad slogan of "Autonomy is Slavery" may have seemed too strident for the customary style of the pro-Hashimites, but it did not contradict their basic attitude towards the scheme. The Baghdad summit participants had thus located the weak spot in Egypt's policy: while Cairo was pressing for visible "linkage" and for speedy implementation of autonomy as a sign of its continued commitment to the Arab cause, the outside Arab world did not want autonomy *quickly*: rather, it wanted autonomy *scrapped* altogether, along with the rest of the Camp David accords. The Baghdad conference participants had sensed that if they had one remaining hold over Egypt's future conduct it was through their ability to torpedo the autonomy project by urging West Bank leaders to turn it down. Therefore, if Cairo continued to hold out for "linkage," it was no longer in the expectation of an immediate improvement of its standing in the Arab world: it was to provide a "clean bill" of Arab loyalty to those in the Egyptian establishment to whom Egypt's Arabism mattered; and it was to prepare evidence for the day—now perceived to have receded into the somewhat more distant future, but still confidently expected to arrive—when all Arabs would recognize the wisdom of Sādāt's policy, acknowledge his success and again admit Egypt to its rightful place at the centre of the Arab world.

IRAN: A CRISIS AND ITS REVERBERATIONS

For 15 years, the Shah had succeeded in projecting an image of Iran as a bastion of stability; of his regime as a "success story" of reform, modernization and industrialization; and of the country as being well on the way to becoming a major regional power in its own right, with armed forces strong enough not only to defend the Gulf, but to radiate Iranian power far into the Indian Ocean. In 1978, that image collapsed entirely, and the regime very nearly did so too.

Many factors were at work and many strata of Iranian society combined to produce the year's upheavals. A rapidly growing middle class clamoured for participation in politics commensurate with its wealth, sophistication and contribution to the country's development. Gestures of liberalization and experiments with democratization had raised, but not fulfilled, their expectations. Most of them would have regarded a genuinely constitutional monarchy as a satisfactory solution. However, intellectuals and students, rebelling against the autocratic character of the regime, had come to believe that only the removal of the Shah or even the abolition of the monarchy could produce the change they wanted. The economically weaker classes perceived themselves as being caught in the vice of inflation, as victims of shortages, deficient public services and over-accelerated urbanization, and as helpless witnesses of economic changes which, incomprehensibly, had enriched their neighbours but not themselves. Among all classes, the strictly traditionally minded, led by the Shī'ī clerics, regarded modernization as godless, the government as anti-Islamic, and the spread of foreign influence and alien *mores* as the ultimate danger to their values and beliefs. They held that only an "Islamic Republic" governed according to the *sharī'a* (the canonical law of Islam) could save Iran.

Religious ferment eventually became the dominant characteristic of the outwardly visible course of events. Liberals, Leftists and malcontents of every hue were content to be carried along by the tide of Shī'ī protest; the share of each could not be isolated. Nor could even a guess be ventured as to how these disparate groupings might have conducted themselves or how they would have related to each other had their combined efforts brought the Shah down in 1978. In the event, the Iranian army, loyal to its Imperial commander-in-chief, saved the day. The year's history offered no clue to the twofold question of whether army loyalty was of unlimited durability, and of how long a military government could hold the combination of hostile forces at bay.

Outside Iran, the effects of the regime's convulsions were felt in three widening circles: in the Persian Gulf, in other parts of the ME, and in the field of great power relations. Among the Arab littorals of the Gulf, events in Iran had a decidedly unsettling influence, though their anxiety related to potential future dangers rather than to actual developments in 1978. All shared the fear that a prolonged domestic crisis might incapacitate Iran in its role of guardian of the oil shipping lanes. All Gulf producers had relied on Iran's capability to protect the flow of oil against local or regional disturbances and to at least discourage foreign interference with tanker movements in the Gulf and its maritime approaches. Should Iran's armed forces, and particularly its navy and air force, fall victim in one way or another to domestic complications, Iraq would be next in line to inherit Iran's place as the Gulf's most powerful littoral in terms of military strength. This was not a happy prospect for the conservative Gulf emirates and for Saudi Arabia who, despite Iraq's restrained policy in the Gulf ever since its reconciliation with Iran in 1975, distrusted the Iraqi Ba'th regime's potentially radical tendencies. Iraq, for its part, having succeeded late in 1978 in ending its relative isolation in the Arab world by hosting and steering the Baghdad summit and by its reconciliation with Syria, was likely to welcome such a prospect of added prestige and wider influence. There was speculation that a consideration in Saudi Arabia's decision to participate in the Baghdad summit was that its best interest might be served by improving its standing with the major Gulf power of tomorrow. There was no definite evidence to this effect, but the point was arguable.

Iraq had no reason to gloat over the Shah's misfortunes, however. A breakdown of the central government in Tehran might spell dangers to Iraq which the preservation of the status quo was better suited to guard against. The Kurds in Iraq were likely to be influenced by developments affecting their kinsmen in Iran. Unrest among Arab-speaking tribes in south-western Iran could drag Iraq into unwanted confrontations. Most of all, the possible success of a Shī'ī protest movement in Iran could prove contagious among Iraq's own Shī'īs (the country's largest community—roughly half the population—and largely alienated from Iraq's Sunnī establishment and its politics). Fear of a Shī'ī upsurge was shared by those Gulf emirates with a proportion of Shī'īs among their own local inhabitants, mainly Bahrain, the UAE and Oman. Saudi Arabia had no need to share this preoccupation, as there was no sizeable group of Shī'īs among its population. Yet the prospect of a religious grassroots movement overturning an established regime could but displease the Saudi Court which believed in its own—but not in any other—form of combining strong religious sentiment with personalized political power. The Libyan example had taught Riyadh the dangers which even a highly

"Islamicized" type of radicalism could hold: Qadhdhāfī's Libya had always been one of the bitterest and most consistent critics of the Saudi dynasty.

All Gulf states feared the effects on their internal security should the Iranian coast of the Gulf become a jumping-off ground for subversive movements, radical or terrorist elements, or clandestine Communist groups. The network of bilateral police and security service co-ordination which had been built up during 1977 and 1978 would lose its effectiveness should the Iranian side no longer co-operate. Iraq, which had trouble with its own Communist party in 1978, and which in any case objected to any kind of radicalism not specifically fostered by its own Ba'th party, seemed fully to share these anxieties. Finally, all Gulf littorals (again including Iraq) feared the possibility of increased Soviet influence in the Gulf—a point to be taken up again presently. Therefore, in one way or another, all expressed support for the Shah.

Further afield, Egypt felt the loss of support from a leading ME Head of State who had given unqualified backing to Sādāt's initiative in its early stages, but whose voice had fallen silent under the pressure of domestic unrest. Beyond that, however, Egyptians could hardly fail to perceive the many parallels between their own present situation and that in Iran on the eve of the storm there. The tribulations of modernization; the discontent of a new middle class; frustration with the kind of political pluralism which remained limited in scope and firmly controlled from above; the ills of inflation, corruption, shortages and inefficient public services; the alienation of large sections of the population who felt their traditions and faith being threatened by liberalization and Westernization; and finally the ultimate dependence of the establishment on the support, or at least the benevolent toleration, of the officer corps—all these were common to Egypt in 1978 and Iran in 1976. (It was not without good reason that outside observers repeatedly attempted to probe the Egyptian army's stand on the process of negotiations with Israel. The matter turned crucial when, immediately after the Camp David summit, Sādāt dismissed the country's two highest-ranking generals. No crisis ensued, perhaps because at the same time the status of another general, now the country's Vice-President, was considerably enhanced.) An essential difference was that, in keeping with Sunnī tradition in general and Egyptian Sunnī tradition in particular, the bulk of Egypt's 'ulamā were loyal to the regime. Egypt had no parallel to Iran's militant Shī'ī clerics. Radical Islam was certainly part of Egypt's political scene, but operated outside the recognized religious establishment.

In Israel, the malaise created by the Iranian object-lesson in ME instability and unpredictability and in the irrepressible power of Islam was aggravated by specifically Israeli anxieties: most of the anti-Western and xenophobic sentiment in Iran contained expressly anti-Israeli motifs. Israel's ties with one of the few all-Muslim countries with which it had relations at all were unlikely to survive a change of regime. Israel's oil supplies came mainly from Iran—a source all the more vital as the Sinai offshore oilfields were due to be returned to Egypt during the first phase of the projected withdrawal. Israel's air links to the Far East passed through Tehran. The future of the Jewish community in Iran had come to look uncertain.

In wider terms, both Egyptian and Israeli leaders seemed at one time or another to have considered the potential benefits of turning their countries' special relationship with the US into a broader framework, sometimes referred to as a potential "Cairo-Jerusalem-Amman-Riyadh-Tehran axis." During the second half of 1978, however, Saudi-US and Jordanian-US relations became cooler, and Tehran's place along such an axis more than doubtful. Generally speaking, the concept seemed a great deal less feasible at the end of 1978 than had been thought earlier. During the first few days of the year, for instance, the Shah had been in touch with all other parties along the "axis"—hosting President Carter and King Ḥusayn in Tehran (and reportedly Israeli Foreign Minister Moshe Dayan as well), and then proceeding to visit President Sādāt and King Khālid. At year's end, there was no longer any basis for contacts on such a pattern.

THE GREAT POWERS

Over the year, the US moved steadily towards a position of increasing identification with Egyptian positions in the negotiating process and with Egyptian ME policies in general. Like Egypt, and at times more than Egypt, it emphasized that the sought-for settlement must be comprehensive rather than separate. As the year passed, the US thus found itself caught in a paradox similar to the one noted above with regard to Egypt's policies: in the interests of its future relations with pro-Western, conservative and (mostly) oil-exporting states, notably Saudi Arabia and Jordan, it promoted a comprehensive approach to the negotiating process; but because these states objected in increasing measure to US support for Egypt in that process, it actually alienated them. As with many of the trends noted above, these developments came to a head in the period between the Camp David conference in September 1978 and the Baghdad summit in November. As the negative attitude of Jordan and Saudi Arabia towards the Camp David accords emerged more clearly, their relations with the US became strained. The rejection of the Camp David accords by *all* the participants of the Baghdad summit created an anti-US alignment broader perhaps than any since Washington's entry into active ME politics. However, the degree of anti-American sentiment and the sharpness of its expression varied throughout the year—even at the time of the Baghdad summit. While the Tripoli bloc (Syria, Algeria, Libya, the PDRY and the PLO) spoke of the "US-Egyptian-Zionist conspiracy," the conservative camp refrained from direct criticism of the US other than that so strongly implied in its rejection of the Camp David accords. The promotion by the US of the autonomy scheme (in an interpretation a great deal more pro-Palestinian than that accepted by the Israeli government) did not contribute to improve American relations with those who totally rejected autonomy—just as Egypt's insistence on "linkage" did not restore Egypt's standing with them. As soon as the first effects of Baghdad had worn off, Morocco and Sudan again moderated their stand towards Egypt and also avoided being drawn into an anti-US stance. In the Arab world, the US thus found that developments during the year had enabled it to reach an unprecedented degree of closeness and co-operation with Egypt, but had, for the time being, narrowed down the number of Arab states whose policies it could influence significantly. In the non-Arab ME, some successful fence-mending with Turkey was more than offset by the uncertainty overhanging the immediate future of US-Iranian relations.

America's losses or difficulties were not, however, the Soviet Union's immediate gain. The USSR has hardly made any progress among Arab states since a limited upsurge of Soviet influence late in 1977, when the establishment of the Tripoli bloc provided a common framework for the Soviet-oriented Arab countries. Their enmity towards Sādāt and their rejection of his initiative from its first stage onwards provided common threads in their policies and those of the USSR. The results of the Camp David conference seemed to prepare the ground for a new leap forward by Moscow in the ME, but no such leap in fact occurred. None of the traditionally pro-Western states now disappointed with the US turned to the USSR instead. More than that: Soviet relations with its two major Arab allies—Syria and Iraq—were not free of tensions during 1978. In the case of Iraq, they stemmed mainly from suspicions of Soviet interference in its internal affairs through the Iraqi Communist party; in the case of Syria, apparently from a heavy-handed Soviet attempt to exploit the post-Camp David situation in order to place it in a position of more clearly marked dependence on the USSR.

As regards Iran, Soviet policy did not assume an unequivocal form during 1978. Aware of the possibly deleterious effect of anarchy in a neighbouring country; aware perhaps of the potential effect of a political victory of Islam close to the concentration of Muslims in the USSR; uncertain of the character and policy of an alternative Iranian regime; above all, uncertain whether a new regime would be pro-Soviet—Moscow preferred a cautious stance. Yet the prospect of seeing US influence cut back in a major territory bordering on their own was too tempting for the Soviets to remain altogether passive. Overt support of the opposition (mainly by means of Persian-language broadcasts from transmitters on Soviet or Eastern European soil) stressed the social, economic and anti-American motivations of the Iranian opposition, playing down the religious theme. Towards the end of 1978, after the installation of the military government in Tehran in October, Soviet propaganda support of the opposition was stepped up significantly.

But the greatest effect of Soviet influence on the ME was produced by Soviet actions or policies close to, but *outside*, the area itself—in Afghanistan, the Indian Ocean, Ethiopia, Chad, Zaïre and Angola (in addition to Libya and the PDRY). These points of impact could also be interpreted as being directed *outwards*: towards the Indian sub-continent, even the Far East, and towards the southern half of Africa. However, the Shah, King Khālid and Crown Prince Fahd, and Presidents Sādāt and Numayrī were all united in interpreting the thrust of Soviet policy as being directed *inwards*: towards the Persian Gulf and the Red Sea, and towards the encirclement of Iran, Saudi Arabia and the Nile Valley by hostile regimes. Events in 1978 provided no clue of sufficient clarity to assess the accuracy of either interpretation. A third one—that of keeping options open with the intent of moving as opportunity permitted—could not be ruled out.

LEBANON

A focus of violence and instability tangentially touched by the two main chains of events referred to above, yet divorced from them by the unique character of the forces involved, persisted throughout 1978 in Lebanon. The timing of the peak periods of violence in Beirut and in South Lebanon was in some cases linked to the Egyptian-Israeli negotiating process. But the basic issues were Lebanon's own and, for yet another year, were mainly characterized by their apparent insolubility. The central government failed to re-establish its authority or to recreate a Lebanese army. This was part of a larger Syrian failure in attempting to let the Lebanese do Syria's work for it and to set up a Lebanese administration sufficiently reliable and loyal to the Syrian cause for Damascus to consider diminishing its physical presence without endangering its ultimate overlordship. The maintenance of a large expeditionary force in Lebanon was becoming a burden for Syria in military terms (extended lines, spread-out forces, operational duties interfering with training, doubtful effects on troop morale) as well as economically, and possibly also in terms of domestic politics. Yet the considerations of future strategic benefits, combined with fear of the results of a renewed outbreak of civil war, precluded even a partial withdrawal as long as the survival of a totally pro-Syrian administration could not be assured. In 1978, it could not.

Within Lebanon, a new reversal of alliances was in progress. The two major Maronite groups, the Phalanges and the National Liberals—Syria's allies in 1976—became its main opponents in 1978. A third, smaller Maronite group under Sulaymān Faranjiyya sided with Syria and was embroiled in sporadic clashes with the other two. The PLO, Syria's foe of 1976, by and large co-operated with it in

1978, partly under physical pressure from Syria and partly as a result of their joint stand against Sādāt. Israeli ties with the Maronites (other than those of the enclaves in the South) seemed to weaken during the year. The Maronite leadership in Beirut assessed that the progress of the Egyptian-Israeli negotiations was making Israel more reluctant to intervene against Syria. Accordingly, they sought other ties. An attempt was made to revive traditional Maronite links with France. A tentative approach to some quarters in the PLO was made by Maronite leaders, partly to signal disappointment with Israel, partly to explore possible PLO-Maronite co-operation against Syria, and partly to reaffirm the common Lebanese-Palestinian interest in the latters' "right of return." Both moves remained inconclusive. Lebanon as a whole, and Beirut in particular, remained suspended between the absence of any conceivable practical political solution and the reluctance of the two major protagonists to risk the ultimate test of all-out violence.

MIDDLE EASTERN REGIMES: DOCTRINE AND PERFORMANCE

The events which caught the headlines were not, however, the only significant ones in the ME. Regimes of many different kinds faced problems of surprising similarity; these stemmed from underlying long-term trends which were not, on the whole, specific to 1978. A brief survey of how and where they surfaced is at least as relevant to the year's story as the centre-stage political drama. One such undercurrent was the struggle for legitimacy and popular acceptance in which ME regimes have long been engaged. This came to the fore in Iran from two directions: in the claim for a greater share of political power by a new middle class which the process of modernization had created; and in the regime's attempt to at least partially replace the traditional religious value-system by linking the legitimacy of the regime to the imperial history of Persia, thus stressing its pre-Islamic era as much as or more than its Islamic period. Elsewhere, the clamour for greater democratization was loudest in Egypt. Sādāt had proclaimed in 1974 that the October War had proved that Egypt now possessed the maturity needed for democracy. Press censorship had officially been lifted and an experiment in launching a multiparty system was made, proceeding by stages, from "platforms" within the single political organization (the Arab Socialist Union, inherited from the Nasserist period), to a system of three recognized parties, and finally to a removal of the ceiling on the number of political parties. In 1978, the contradiction between this process and the essentially autocratic character of the Egyptian presidential regime came to a head. As criticism became less restrained and the party system less and less amenable to control and guidance (particularly with the re-emergence of the Wafd party as a focus of power and influence genuinely independent of the government), Sādāt reversed the process sharply: press freedom was all but rescinded by means of a referendum in May; the Wafd and the "legal" Leftist party were repressed. A new party, headed by President Sādāt, was set up, destined from the start to be the new ruling party and to indicate to the political public what views "right-thinking" Egyptians ought to hold. A new "constructive" opposition was to serve as its foil, so as to alleviate the impression of a return to a single-party system. But in its essentials, Sādāt's new party was a throwback to the various experiments of 'Abd al-Nāsir's period of instituting a political organization by official *fiat* from the top.

In large measure, Sādāt's domestic difficulties stemmed from the fact that on assuming power he had taken over a regime which had started out as an ideologically motivated one, but whose ideology had been eroded over the years. Conservative Arab regimes, based on traditional authority and Islam, had no secular ideology to lose and therefore fared better. In Saudi Arabia, Kuwait and other Peninsular emirates, new classes of technocrats, managers and independent businessmen were rising; yet in 1978 political dynamics were still confined to relations within the ruling families, or (as in the UAE) to rivalries between such families. Although the new potential élites did not take any action, their presence was felt in the precautions rulers took to guard against their intrusion into the political process. Though more liberal in its political style, Jordan also succeeded in preserving the unquestioned predominance of King and Court. The establishment of a National Consultative Council to exercise some, but certainly not all, the functions of parliament (dissolved in 1974) was entirely palliative in character, but passed unchallenged. By contrast, the year's really significant event in domestic politics was the settling of the royal succession. The only challenge to the regime was a short-lived restiveness among Jordan's Palestinian inhabitants. The new middle class, though undoubtedly burgeoning, remained politically quiescent.

At the other end of the spectrum, the regimes which had succeeded in retaining some of the ideological fervour of their early days did equally well in keeping at bay demands for political participation from outside their own élite groups. Much as in the most conservative regimes, political struggles took the form of infighting within the ruling group. This was best illustrated in 1978 by the fate of Nājī Jamīl who fell from grace in Syria's "inner circle." Iraq demonstrated the strength of its regime by pursuing pragmatic policies, inconsistent with a strict application of Ba'th ideology, both in its *de facto* support of the Shah and in its deviation—however slight—from longstanding ideological positions with regard to the Arab-Israeli conflict. It seems to have been able to explain away such inconsistencies to the party rank and file with comparative ease. In Libya, Qadhdhāfī's new social policies and his partial revision of the bodies representing "People's Power" were accepted with no public sign of opposition. In Algeria, Boumedienne's death in December 1978 left the regime facing a major test of its strength and cohesion.

Neither North nor South Yemen (the YAR and the PDRY) fitted into any classification of Arab regimes. In the North, instability resulted from unresolved conflicts between tribesmen and townspeople, tribal warriors and regular officers, with Shī'ī-Sunnī tensions superimposed upon them. In the South, ideological factionalism and personal power struggles were at the core of political events. A party militia was pitted against regular army forces. Yet to ensure cohesion among their followers, individual leaders, factions and armed units often fell back on tribal loyalties—supposedly a thing of the colonial past.

As noted above, the clash between the process of modernization and the traditional system of beliefs and values had been a major factor influencing events in Iran. Though the Shah frequently proclaimed his personal devotion, the Shī'ī clerics and their followers discounted his type of piety as meaningless, negated—as it was in their view—by his policies of reform which they perceived as plainly anti-Islamic. Again, the closest parallel, not in the course of events but in the assessment of underlying factors, was with Egypt: many tradition-oriented people in Egypt believed that state and society had deviated too much from the fundamentals of the *sharī'a*. While there were no outbursts of violence in 1978 on the part of the radical Islamic fringe groups, the Muslim Brethren grew in strength. Their strictly religious activities were permitted, but their forays into politics (including criticism of the regime's domestic policies as well as of its reliance on the US and on its negotiations with Israel) were frowned upon though not suppressed. The potential danger to the regime from these quarters was demonstrated by the sweeping victory of Islamic lists in elections to various student associations during 1978. This was in the nature of a protest vote—muted, non-violent, but a protest all the same.

13

In Saudi Arabia, as well as in some of the Gulf states, a deliberate policy of protecting the traditional way of life was noticeable. It was directed against erosion or any adverse consequences which the process of modernization and the growth of an indigenous but Western-oriented technocratic élite might have on the observance of Islamic law as applied by Saudi Arabia's Wahhābī *'ulamā*. The most emphatic thurst of this policy, however, was to prevent the presence of the vast numbers of foreigners from impinging on Islamic faith and practice. Aliens were expected to conform strictly to the standards of behaviour of their Muslim environment and, particularly in Saudi Arabia, such conformity was enforced with increasing vigour. In Syria, Sunnī resentment of 'Alāwī ascendancy persisted but as an undercurrent. The reconciliation between Numayrī and some of his opponents brought representatives of traditional Islamic views in their particular Sudanese (Mahdist) garb closer to the seats of power. It was clearly noticeable, however, that for all his readiness to pursue conciliation on the political plane, Numayrī took special care not to let the latent strength of Sudanese Islam assert itself or disrupt relations with the sizeable non-Muslim population in Southern Sudan. In Libya, Qadhdhāfī's career as a religious leader took a new turn in 1978 when, in a programmatic speech on the Prophet's birthday, he came out both against the religious establishment and against the traditional forms of exegesis, extolling instead direct inspiration drawn from the Qur'ān. What influence this could have on Qadhdhāfī's regime, on Islam in Libya, and possibly on Islam elsewhere could not yet be assessed. Also of note is that the parties advocating Islamic revival in Turkey lost a great deal of popular support in 1977 and 1978.

In as far as purely political ideologies (rather than the application to politics of Islamic tenets) figured in Arab politics, little change was noted during 1978. The rise and fall of the Egyptian Wafd counted for little in this respect, the Wafd (both old and new) being a rather unideological movement. Sādāt's attempts to have an ideology tailored to fit his own new party remained ineffectual. However, two trends towards a reassertion of ideology became noticeable late in 1978 and contained possible pointers for 1979. One has been touched upon above in the context of the Baghdad summit conference: the tendency among those who rejected Sādāt's policies to "re-ideologize" their concept of the Arab-Israeli conflict as a clash of irreconcilable entities, contrasting with the much more pragmatic perception which had become current since 1973. The other trend was closely connected with the first: the Arab Left seemed to have found a rallying point in its opposition to the Camp David accords. In the wake of the 1973 war, Leftist arguments had lost much of their conviction and Leftist movements much of their self-confidence. In complete contrast to what their doctrines had led them to expect, the 1973 war had been conducted by one "Rightist" regime (Egypt) supported by a "reactionary" one (Saudi Arabia) in co-operation with Syria, which many of them would have classed as "petit-bourgeois." The "progressive" regimes had played a secondary role. Moreover, in the post-war period, the "reactionaries" had done more by their oil wealth to lead the Arabs back to a position of strength in world affairs than the "progressives" had been able to do at any time. Now the outcome of the Camp David conference provided a rallying cry and made the old slogans of a "US-Zionist-reactionary global conspiracy" viable again. The countries of the radical camp— Algeria, Libya, Syria, Iraq and the PDRY—naturally fostered this incipient and still very tentative revival, but it was also shared by opposition groupings elsewhere.

However, ME regimes did not move solely in the somewhat abstract spheres of legitimacy, value-systems and political doctrine. Arguably, these had greater influence on political stability than was the case in other regions of the world. But performance was no less of a yardstick, and performance for most ME countries meant successful development. In this respect, few governments did well. The backlash of rising but unfulfilled expectations caught up with Iran and Egypt in the most spectacular manner, but was felt in countries as diverse as Algeria, Tunisia, Sudan and Turkey. Signs of economic discontent were also evident in Syria, and possibly in Jordan too, despite the latter's considerable prosperity. Inflation afflicted all of them, as it did Israel (for different reasons).

The main thrust of development programmes was still infrastructure; in the oil states, attempts at diversification in non-oil industries were not carried very far and industrial development was largely directed towards oil-related projects such as petrochemicals. Greater emphasis than in the past was placed on investment in downstream operations. Manpower problems, both with respect to skilled labour and at the managerial level, continued to be a limiting factor. Local graduates returning from abroad successfully reinforced the managerial class in the oil industry, in banking and in financial management, but not in other economic sectors.

The oil-producing countries were affected by the world-wide oil glut that existed at least until mid-1978 and created a measure of economic difficulty. Most major producers sold less oil and, as a consequence, some found themselves anxious about liquidity. Throughout the year, the Saudis believed that the turn towards the restoration of a buyers' market was but a short-term trend. What eventually re-established a sellers' market before the end of 1978 was the sharp reduction in Iranian oil output caused by strikes due to domestic unrest, as well as by stockpiling on the part of the oil companies in anticipation of a price rise. A price increase of 14–15% during 1979 was indeed imposed by OPEC at the Abu Dhabi meeting in December 1978, justified by the need for compensation following the drop in the value of the dollar. The impact of this decision could not yet be ascertained.

CONCLUSION

In conclusion, changes in the ME political map during 1978 concerning the relative standing of major states in the region can be assessed as follows:

Iran's rise to the position of a regional power was stopped short.

Turkey, beset by economic difficulties, struggling to cope with increasing political violence, and with a foreign policy focused on the great powers, had a diminishing impact on regional developments.

Saudi Arabia was not able to assert itself as the fulcrum of Arab affairs which it had very nearly become in 1976 and 1977. Its repeated attempts in 1978 to act as the catalyst for reuniting Arab ranks failed. The position it occupied towards the end of the year as (temporary?) partner to a consensus embracing Iraq, Syria and Jordan was less congenial to its regime and its general outlook than the role of arbiter it had frequently exercised in previous years.

Iraq entered the year in almost total, mostly self-inflicted, isolation in the Arab world. By the end of 1978, it had moved to the centre of the Arab stage: a summit convened in Baghdad at its initiative ended in a consensus largely authored by the Iraqi president. In addition, its reconciliation with Syria removed the chief obstacle which had previously prevented it from resuming a major role in the all-Arab arena. For the first time, Iraq seemed on the verge of assuming a position commensurate with its rapidly increasing military strength.

The PLO, compelled to toe the Syrian line on most issues, came to count for less in Arab councils. However, in the West Bank, the PLO line seemed to have gained wider acceptance, particularly towards the end of the year.

Egypt remained confident throughout the year that it could combine the conclusion of a peace treaty with Israel with a resumption of its focal position in the Arab world. But at the end of 1978, it was assured of neither.

15

Israel entered the year expecting a breakthrough which would totally change the nature of its relations with Egypt and point the way towards its acceptance as an integral part of the ME. It ended the year with the negotiations completed on bilateral issues but deadlocked on their "comprehensive" aspects, with the negotiating process interrupted and Israeli-US relations strained.

Daniel Dishon

THE MIDDLE EAST AND WORLD AFFAIRS

The United States and the Middle East: The Peace Process

The Sādāt-Begin peace negotiations, initiated by the Egyptian leader's historic visit to Jerusalem in November 1977, appeared at first to eclipse the central role previously occupied by the US in the Middle East peace process. As seen from Tel Aviv, the opening of direct negotiations between Israel and Egypt downgraded the role of extra-regional intermediaries; and in Cairo, Egypt and Israel were perceived as "now holding the cards."[1] That Washington described itself as "supportive" of the Egyptian-Israeli initiatives indicated a belief in its own diminished role. The Secretary of State, Cyrus Vance, said that the two ME leaders had themselves broken through "psychological barriers" and set in motion an "irreversible process" toward peace.[2]

While supporting the direct Egyptian-Israeli peace initiative, the US was concerned lest Israel's interest in making a separate peace with Egypt on the one hand, and Sādāt's break with Syria on the other, militated against the American objective of a "comprehensive settlement"; namely, one that would include all of Israel's neighbours and resolve all the essential issues of the conflict, including the Palestinian problem. Thus, the relatively tardy American response to Sādāt's call for a conference in Cairo was primarily for the purpose of consulting with other interested parties. Washington also hoped that the Cairo conference would produce a comprehensive framework within which substantive matters could be dealt with, and that it would ultimately lead to a Geneva conference. In fact, the US National Security Adviser, Zbigniew Brzezinski, envisaged the peace process in terms of expanding concentric circles. The first circle encompassed Egyptian-Israeli negotiations; the second, the "moderate Arabs"—including Jordan and "moderate Palestinians," with the support of Saudi Arabia; and the third, the Syrians, the Soviet Union and implicitly "radical Arabs." It was understood that this last stage of negotiations would take place in Geneva.

The failure of the Sādāt-Begin summit at Ismā'īliyya (24–25 December 1977) pointed to a resumption by the US of its pivotal role as the key intermediary power in the peace process. Although the summit failed to achieve its objective of a declaration of principles for a ME settlement, the two leaders did agree to maintain the "momentum" towards peace by establishing Political and Military Committees. (For details, see essay, "The Egyptian-Israeli Negotiations.") Considering the complexity of the issues facing the Political Committee (including the Palestinian question and the future of Israeli settlements in Sinai, the West Bank and the Gaza Strip), it was obvious that if direct talks broke down, the American role could soon change from supporting the negotiations to active mediation. Such a breakdown occurred on 18 January 1978 when Sādāt recalled the Egyptian delegation from the Political Committee's meeting in Jerusalem; this marked the second major setback for the 1978 peace process. The first involved differences over how to resolve the Palestinian problem.

The texts of the following documents and statements are printed as appendices at the end of the essay entitled "The Egyptian-Israeli Negotiations": speeches by Sādāt and Begin to the Knesset; Israel's Peace Plan for Self-Rule in the West Bank and Gaza Strip; principles agreed to at the Ismā'īliyya summit; speeches at the Political Committee; Egypt's Six-Point Peace Plan; and the Camp David Agreement.

THE ASWĀN FORMULA

Just before embarking on his first foreign tour (which did not initially include a visit to Egypt), President Carter praised the Begin plan as a "long step forward" and strongly reaffirmed US opposition to the creation of an independent Palestinian state. In spite of insisting that he was only expressing a "preference" and not dictating the terms of a settlement, his remarks—particularly their timing—disappointed and "embarrassed" Sādāt. After his visits to Iran (where he failed to persuade King Husayn to join the Cairo negotiations) and to Riyadh (where he briefed the Saudi leaders on his talks with Begin, Husayn and the Shah), he stopped over briefly in Aswān on 4 January, presumably to assure Sādāt of America's impartiality in the peace process.[3]

Just before Carter's arrival, it was believed in Cairo that Sādāt would take a "moderate and flexible approach" to the Palestinian problem in the talks; indeed, it became clear afterwards that privately at least, Egypt had steered away from insisting on the concept of a Palestinian "state." In return, Sādāt succeeded in drawing the US closer to the concept of "self-determination." In his Aswān statement, Carter agreed with Egypt that "certain principles" had to be observed before a comprehensive ME peace could be achieved. These included the need for "normal relations" among the parties to the conflict; Israeli withdrawal from territories occupied in 1967; and agreement on "secure and recognized borders" in accordance with UN Resolutions 242 and 338. But the principles went further: "There must be a resolution of the Palestinian problem in all its aspects." Carter emphasized that "the problem must recognize the *legitimate rights* of the Palestinian people, and enable the Palestinians to participate in *the determination* of their own future."[4]

American acceptance of the concept of "the legitimate rights"—rather than the "legitimate interests"—of the Palestinian people had already been expressed in the joint US-USSR declaration of 1 October 1977,[5] but the phrase of Palestinian "participation in the determination of their own future" was a crucial new departure in US thinking. American officials believed that Carter had come "within a hair's breadth" of calling for outright self-determination; while some Egyptians felt that Sādāt had "got the concept of self-determination now, all but the actual term."[6] However, as far as the US Administration was concerned, Carter's statement was meant as a first step in bridging the gap between Israel's proposal for Palestinian "self-rule" on the West Bank and in the Gaza Strip, and the Egyptian insistence on "self-determination," which carried with it the possibility of an independent state. Sādāt himself strongly favoured close organic links between a Palestinian "entity" and Jordan.

Cyrus Vance explained Carter's Aswān statement in these terms: "The Palestinians must participate in determining their future because it's their future at stake; on the other hand, the Israelis have an interest in this question and the Jordanians have an interest. So that when one talks about participation, we're talking about the process in which all three of the interested parties to that question have a chance to participate."[7]

Israeli officials stressed that in the working paper agreed in New York in October 1977 between Israel's Foreign Minister, Moshe Dayan, and President Carter,[8] Palestinians were entitled to join the Geneva peace talks and to participate in a working group with Egypt, Jordan and Israel to discuss the West Bank and the Gaza Strip. This agreement had followed Israel's rejection in August 1977 of the concept, privately proposed by the US, of Palestinian "self-determination."

To the extent that the Aswān statement propounded the concept of "self-determination," it was unacceptable to Israel. So was the phrase "legitimate rights" of the Palestinians, which had been rejected by Israel when it was first used in the US-Soviet declaration of October 1977.

THE ABORTIVE JERUSALEM TALKS

The second major development in the 1978 ME peace process that actively involved the US was the breakdown of the Jerusalem talks. The immediate hurdle was the adoption of an agenda, but as a result of Vance's strenuous efforts, Egypt and Israel finally agreed that it would include: (1) a declaration of principles governing the negotiations for a comprehensive peace settlement in the ME; (2) guidelines for negotiations relating to the issues of the West Bank and the Gaza Strip (the West Bank was referred to as Judea and Samaria in the Israeli version); and (3) the elements of peace treaties between Israel and its neighbours according to the principles of Security Council Resolution 242. [9]

The wide gap between the positions of Egypt and Israel surfaced on 17 January in their Foreign Ministers' opening remarks. Ibrāhīm Kāmil spoke of the Palestinians' struggle "to end their subjugation and their diaspora, to express their national rights in accordance with the most sacred principles of equal rights and self-determination of peoples"; Moshe Dayan stated that "the only way to make progress in our joint task is to explore the various problems including, presumably, the Palestinian problem, but obviously excluding the principle of self-determination." Taking the middle ground, Vance stated that "there must be a resolution of the Palestinian problem in all its aspects. The solution must recognize the legitimate rights of the Palestinian people and enable the Palestinians to participate in the determination of their future." [10] This was, of course, a reiteration of the Aswān formula, but it was intended to bridge the gap between Egypt's insistence on the principle of "self-determination" and Israel's concept of "self-rule." Vance's statement was in line with America's declared intention of 13 January to propose a temporary arrangement for the administration of the West Bank and Gaza Strip, which in essence would translate the five-year review clause of Begin's peace plan into an interim five years in which Israeli military government would end. [11]

Begin's remarks at a dinner on 17 January precipitated the breakdown of the Jerusalem talks, having apparently been provoked by Kāmil's tough reiteration of Egyptian demands on his arrival in Jerusalem. Kāmil's demands for total Israeli withdrawal from all Arab lands and for "self-determination" for the Palestinians had apparently upset Begin who proceeded to sternly lecture Kāmil, whom he called "a young man" who did not know that "self-determination" had been misused in Europe and had contributed to the outbreak of World War II. Begin went on to declare that peace could not be restored if Israel had to go back to the "aggressive-provoking lines" that existed before the 1967 war, or if it had to agree to divide Jerusalem again. [12] US Congressional leaders, who were among the 700 guests present at the dinner, were as shocked by Begin's remarks as Kāmil himself.

The next day, Sādāt surprised Washington, as much as everybody else, by abruptly recalling Kāmil and the Egyptian delegation from the Political Committee's meeting and by announcing that the meeting scheduled for 19 January would not be held (see essay, "The Egyptian-Israeli Negotiations"). The Israeli Cabinet sharply criticized Sādāt's decision as an "extreme" move that proved "that the Egyptian government deceived itself that Israel will submit to demands it has never considered feasible." [13] Dayan warned on 20 January that the peace talks between Israel and Egypt might never resume if Sādāt insisted on an advance Israeli commitment to dismantle its settlements in Sinai. [14] The Arab states opposed to Sādāt's peace initiative (Syria, Iraq, etc) decried Egypt's decision to "suspend" the

Jerusalem talks as a "mere manoeuvre," while Yāsir 'Arafāt declared that force, *not* negotiations, was the way to obtain Palestinian rights; he branded the US as the true enemy of the Arabs. On the other hand, Jordan supported the Egyptian move and blamed the Israelis for the breakdown of the talks because they wanted "only land and not peace." Saudi Arabia also endorsed Sādāt's action. [15]

Pravda expressed the view that Israeli intransigence had caused Sādāt's peace initiative to "fade away like a mirage in the Sinai desert." [16] Soviet satisfaction at the breakdown of the Jerusalem talks was consistent with its general resentment of the leading American role in the peace process, as well as with its frustration over Sādāt's peace initiative—which, for all practical purposes, had buried the Soviet-US joint declaration of October 1977. But no real benefit could accrue to Moscow as a result of the failure of the Jerusalem talks because it was itself caught in the quagmire of disunity among the anti-Sādāt Arab states (see essay, "Inter-Arab Relations").

Despite the deep American disappointment with the breakdown of negotiations, both Carter and Vance maintained an optimistic stance. The President described the suspension of political talks between Egypt and Israel as only a "temporary setback," adding that it "obviously has been and can be a serious situation, but we have hopes that it will all be straightened out and both the political and military talks will reconvene." [17]

In the context of this survey, it seems clear that Egyptian-Israeli differences over the problem of the Palestinians lay at the heart of the breakdown of the Jerusalem talks—as they had of the Ismā'īliyya summit, despite the subsequent contribution of the American formula at Aswān and the notion of an "interim arrangement" for the West Bank. At the time, these American contributions to the peace process could not bridge the deep differences between Egypt and Israel. [18] In a statement made in Sādāt's presence on 20 January, Vance identified the Palestinian problem as the most important reason for the breakdown of the Jerusalem talks. He stated that he did not wish to go into detail, "except to say that there has been one principle which is the most difficult of all, and that is one which deals with the Palestinian problem and . . . in which the differences remain. . . ." [19]

SĀDĀT AND BEGIN VISIT THE US

The fact that the breakdown of the Jerusalem talks took Vance by surprise revealed basic conceptual differences between Washington and Cairo, and between Washington and Jerusalem. However, in an effort to identify the specific issues impeding further direct negotiations, and of reviving the peace process, invitations were issued to Sādāt and Begin to visit the US in February and March respectively. The US wished to persuade Sādāt to discontinue both his "television diplomacy" (in favour of "quiet diplomacy") and his abrupt moves and counter-moves. It also hoped to soften Begin's stand on the problem of Israeli settlements in occupied territories, particularly in Sinai; to persuade him of the ultimate need to withdraw Israeli forces from all the occupied territories, including the West Bank and Gaza Strip; and to reassure him about the historic US commitment to Israel's security. On 28 January, the White House confirmed that Carter had invited Sādāt to visit Washington for "extended talks on 4-5 February on the situation in the ME." Sādāt actually arrived on 3 February and was at once taken to Camp David for quiet talks with Carter. These lasted until 8 February—longer than had been expected.

In Cairo, the visit was thought to offer Sādāt three important opportunities. First, it would allow the Egyptian leader to pursue his public relations campaign, particularly to the American people, but also as part of his effort to rally wider support in North Africa and Western Europe. Second, it would give him a chance to urge Carter to pressure Israel to be more flexible. Third, it would allow him to make a personal plea for American arms.[20] As seen from Israel, two considerations motivated this last request: Egypt wished to counter growing Soviet and radical threats in Africa—on Egypt's flank in Libya and in Ethiopia (the source of the Blue Nile and a neighbour of Egypt's ally, the Sudan); it also desired to neutralize American arms support for Israel by demanding *parity* with Israel.[21] (In order to counter the Egyptian chances of realizing such objectives, as well as to counter the publicity attracted by Sādāt's visit and to impress American opinion with the sincerity of the Israeli desire for peace, Moshe Dayan visited the US immediately after Sādāt's departure.)

The American desire for "quiet diplomacy" was not realized after the secluded Camp David weekend: Sādāt's determination to impress American public opinion and Congress surfaced the moment he arrived in Washington. In his speech to the National Press Club on 6 February and again in his talks with Congressional leaders the following day, he took a tough line against Israel. His speech to the Press Club, reportedly reviewed by Vance himself before delivery, contained a direct appeal to the American people "to exert [their] influence" on Israel to prevent the peace venture from suffocating in "rhetoric and futile argumentation." In a major positive note, he declared that while it was true that he was "rather disappointed," he was "determined to persevere."[22] He also made a strong appeal to Congress for weapons and told American reporters that in addition to American F-5E jet fighters (whose sale to Egypt the Administration was about to ask Congress to authorize), he wanted the most advanced supersonic F-15s and F-16s. Many Congressmen believed that Sādāt made this request largely as a bargaining stance.

The basic American objective in inviting Sādāt was realized when, in a White House statement issued on 8 February, he repeated his promise to persevere in the peace process. The statement also embodied the principles that underlay US participation in the peace process, emphasizing two of them in particular: one stated categorically that the principle of withdrawal (established in Resolution 242) was "applicable to all fronts of the conflict"; the other repeated the Aswān formula that "there must be a resolution of the Palestinian problem in all its aspects; it must recognize the legitimate rights of the Palestinian people and enable the Palestinians to participate in the determination of their own future."[23] On the other hand, emphasizing these two principles did not weaken the "historic [US] commitments to the security of Israel." Although some Israelis feared that the US was "tilting" toward Egypt, James Reston insisted that it was only the rhetoric that had changed; there was no evidence that the Administration was going to move from its "middle position."[24]

When Sādāt left the US, a Gallup poll indicated that he ranked just behind Carter as the man Americans most admired. Without doubt, Sādāt's visit reinforced the American conclusion that for the ME peace process to succeed, Israel would eventually have to dismantle its civilian settlements in Sinai and gradually give up control of the West Bank and Gaza Strip. On a number of occasions after Sādāt's visit, Vance and Carter spelled out the American position on the more crucial West Bank issue. Vance stated on 10 February that the US believed that "there should be a homeland for the Palestinians, and that it should be linked with Jordan."[25] Carter stated in private meetings that he favoured putting the West Bank and Gaza Strip under some kind of international control—either Israeli-Jordanian or UN—for a period of five years, after which time the inhabitants would indicate in a referendum whether they wished to continue the arrangement or link up with Israel or Jordan.[26]

In contrast to Sādāt's visit, that of the Israeli Prime Minister proved disappointing to Washington. Even before Begin's arrival, a number of disagreements between the Administration and Israel contributed to unprecedented tensions. The issue of the Israeli settlements in occupied territories peaked on 7 February, when the State Department issued a chronological survey of the issue. This was in response to the controversial occupation of an archaeological excavation site at Shiloh, on the West Bank, by a group of would-be settlers who declared their intention of converting it into a permanent settlement.[27] In a White House statement issued at the end of Sādāt's visit (8 February), Carter stressed "his conviction that Israeli settlements on occupied territory were contrary to international law and an obstacle to peace." Dayan flatly rejected this assertion on 9 February. But three days later, Vance repeated the view that the Israeli settlements were "contrary to international law and that therefore they should not exist." A State Department official denied that the Administration had ever endorsed Israel's intention to keep its settlements in Sinai after the area was returned to Egyptian sovereignty—an interpretation which the Israelis had attached to Carter's reaction to the peace plan Begin first presented in December 1977. Not only did Dayan cast doubts on America's ability to continue as a "neutral intermediary," but the Israeli government regretted and protested against Vance's statement. This was seen in Washington as "the strongest criticism of US policy" that Begin's government had made since coming to power nearly nine months earlier.

In addition to the settlements issue, American-Israeli differences over US arms sales to Egypt and Saudi Arabia, and over the interpretation of Resolution 242 (regarding Israeli withdrawal from occupied territories), increased tension before Begin's arrival. Moreover, a new disagreement arose over the situation in Lebanon. This followed the Palestinian terrorist attack inside Israel and the subsequent invasion of South Lebanon by Israeli troops on 14 March[28] (which delayed Begin's visit, originally scheduled for 13–16 March). While condemning the Palestinian attack, the Carter Administration declared that the scale of Israeli military retaliation into Lebanon was not justified. US support for Security Council Resolution 425 (19 March) angered the Israelis who resented the Americans' disregard of their own preference for direct Israeli-Lebanese-Syrian contacts without outside help.[29]

The talks between Carter and Begin were expected to be "extremely blunt" and at their conclusion, on 22 March, a joint statement was not even produced. The President commented that their discussions had been "detailed and frank"; he said he had emphasized to Begin the importance of reaffirming that "all principles of Security Council Resolution 242 must apply to all fronts", and that the opportunity for security through a "true and enduring peace" must not be allowed to "slip into the cycle of hatred and violence."[30] Begin did not address himself to these points; he dwelt on the nature of the "decisive problem" of Israeli security; emphasized the Israeli contribution of three documents for peace; and expressed the hope that the spirit of the Jerusalem, Washington, and Ismāʿīlyya meetings would be renewed and that the negotiations would be resumed.

Neither side had expected to close the gap on the issues that divided them, but American officials had hoped that Begin would return to Jerusalem and discuss the disputed points with the "hardliners" in his own government to determine whether some compromise could be found to permit a resumption of the negotiations. However, the Cabinet gave unanimous support to Begin, indicating that the Israeli government had no intention of compromising on the positions outlined by him in Washington.

ARMS FOR PEACE

The fourth major development in the 1978 peace process was the Carter Administration's success in acquiring Congressional approval on 15 May for its controversial "package" arms sale to Egypt, Israel and Saudi Arabia. The Administration's decision to sell 15 F-15 fighter planes and 70 F-16 fighter bombers to Israel, 50 F-5E planes to Egypt, and 60 F-15 planes to Saudi Arabia had been announced three months earlier, on 14 February, and been defended on a number of grounds. For instance, Vance argued before the Senate Foreign Relations Committee that the proposed sale would enhance American-Saudi relations at a time when Riyadh was a "major stabilizing force in international financial matters and in decisions affecting the pricing and supply of oil." The Secretary of Defence, Harold Brown, contended that Saudi Arabia needed the F-15 fighter jets in order to protect its vast territory and oil facilities from Soviet-supported hostile neighbours such as Iraq, South Yemen and Ethiopia. The Arms Control Director, Paul Warnke, viewed the sale of weapons to Saudi Arabia and Egypt as a means of arms control: American sales would pre-empt the purchase of even more sophisticated weapons by these countries from other suppliers and would thereby more effectively maintain a regional military balance. He also argued that other suppliers would be likely to impose far less stringent constraints on any subsequent use or transfer of aircraft than the US. [31]

Opposition in the Senate was led by Jacob Javits, Clifford Case, Daniel Moynihan, Joseph Biden, Richard Stone and Henry Jackson. Javits argued that Carter had set out to "teach the Israelis a lesson" and wondered if the US was going to sap Israel's vitality and morale. He belittled the concern expressed by proponents of the sale over possible adverse Saudi reactions if Congress rejected it, contending that the Saudis "really think this country is the strongest and most dependable country for their investment and for themselves." He added that "the Saudis are not crazy enough to lean on France for their security." [32] Senator Case declared: "It is time that we restored to our thinking the concept that a strong Israel is not just a beneficiary of the US. It is also essential to the security of the US and of all the West." [33] Supporters of the sale included the Senate majority leader, Robert C. Byrd, Abe Ribicoff, John Glenn, and John J. Sparkman, chairman of the Senate Foreign Relations Committee. Their arguments were significantly in line with those of key members of the Administration; they also cited a variety of economic, political, military and strategic considerations.

However, the most influential support for the Administration's policy came from one of Israel's staunchest supporters, Senator Ribicoff. He delineated the economic, strategic and political interests to the US in approving the arms package, and also emphasized the importance of it to the ME peace process. The sale of these military aircraft was an "emotional issue," but also a military, economic and diplomatic one which affected "the vital security of the US." The question that had to be decided, he said, was "what is in our best national interest?" He stressed that Israel had been "the bedrock" of American policy in the ME and that Israel, as the home of persecuted and homeless Jews from all over the world and as "the only democratic country in the ME," could not have existed and "cannot exist without strong US support." A "strong and secure Israel is in our national interest. But a strong US—militarily, economically and diplomatically—is also in the best interest of the State of Israel." [34] He then argued the importance of Saudi Arabia to the US since the "new realities of geo-politics and eco-politics" had combined to make it "a major world power."

The Carter Administration had argued that the sale of aircraft to Egypt would help keep alive the Sādāt peace initiative without weakening Israel's military capability. Since opposition was directed primarily against the sale of F-15s to Saudi Arabia, Senator Ribicoff emphasized how that sale would also help the peace process. "The Saudis," he said, "are central to the search for peace in the ME. They have a moral and economic force in the Islamic Arab world. They can use financial power constructively. They have been close to the US and are not a 'confrontation state.' They have backed moderate Arab regimes. And they have looked to the US as a partner. . . . Our country has always been open to sincere offers of co-operation." [35]

At the end of ten hours of debate, the Senate voted 54 to 44 to approve the "package" sale of aircraft to the three ME countries and, by doing so, presumably avoided dealing a severe blow to the prospects for peace in the ME. Hedrick Smith of the *New York Times* wrote: "The significance of the vote went far beyond the arithmetic of the jet sales to the more delicate issue of just how far America should go in combining its traditional commitment to Israel with new and expanding support for Arab moderates." [36] A *Washington Post* editorial regarded the work in the Senate as due to "much more than the gathering weight of Arab oil and money. At least since 1973, successive Administrations have felt that the best way to launch a process leading toward peace is for the US to make itself equally useful and trusted on both sides." [37] (Also see essay, "Military and Strategic Issues in the ME-Persian Gulf Region in 1978.")

THE LEEDS CASTLE CONFERENCE

The fifth major development in the 1978 peace process was the Foreign Ministers' conference on 18–19 July at Leeds Castle (UK) when the US "intermediary role figured more prominently than before. The most relevant events preceding this development were the Israeli replies to questions posed by the US as early as April, and the Egyptian "peace plan" which was made public in early July. Both these events, as well as the Leeds Castle conference that followed them, occurred largely as the result of American initiatives.

In its continuing efforts to break the deadlock between Israel and Egypt, the State Department presented two major questions to the Israeli government: (1) Would a final settlement of the sovereignty issue in the West Bank and the Gaza Strip be possible after five years of proposed limited self-rule? and (2) How would the Palestinian Arabs achieve a measure of political self-expression at the end of that time? Underlying these questions was the more fundamental problem that divided not only the Arabs and Israelis, but also the Israeli government and Israeli society. That was whether Israel was going to give up its historical claim to the biblical lands of "Judea and Samaria" permanently; if so, when and how much of that land would it relinquish? [38]

The immediate US goal was to obtain an Israeli commitment to discuss the "permanent status" of the occupied territories after the five-year transition period that the Begin plan presumably provided for. But the Israeli replies seemed to sidestep that very issue. The Israeli Cabinet announced on 18 June that it would negotiate "the nature of future relations" after five years of limited Palestinian self-rule. This vaguely-worded statement appeared to leave open the possibility that limited autonomy might continue in the occupied areas indefinitely. The Defence Minister, Ezer Weizman, and four other Cabinet members from the Democratic Movement for Change voted against the Begin reply. Weizman proposed opening negotiations with Egypt during the five-year period, but leaving such crucial points as the settlements and sovereignty open to further talks. Two other plans also surfaced within the Cabinet. One by the Foreign Minister envisaged an active role for Jordan in the autonomy period; a permanent status for the inhabitants of the territories after five years; an Israeli military presence after five years, and the right for Jews to settle there. The other and more conservative plan was proposed by the Minister without Portfolio, Chaim Landau. It avoided any mention of a "final" status for the areas, but proposed that at the end of five years, Israel would make up its mind on the basis of its experience during the trial period. Amid considerable criticism, the Israeli Parliament approved the Begin reply to the US on 19 June. The voting was 59 in favour, 37 against and 10 abstentions.

Although the Carter Administration was disappointed, the President maintained an optimistic stance. Sādāt characterized the Israeli reply as "vague" and "not positive," but he was mild-toned and not pessimistic. Nevertheless, the US was obviously concerned that the Israeli response was probably inadequate to persuade Sādāt to resume direct talks with Israel. Three days of official silence were broken on 21 June when the State Department expressed "regret" that the Israeli reply did not fully respond to American questions. Vance is reported to have told the Congress that because Israel had shown no flexibility in its reply, the best possibility for resuming talks would be for Sādāt to present a counter-proposal. Perhaps the US could then offer a compromise. A more severe criticism of the Israeli reply was voiced by Senator Javits, one of Israel's firmest friends on Capitol Hill. In a speech to the Senate, he said that Israel faced "a real danger" if it failed to produce a more forthcoming statement of its positions; he called on the Begin government to accept Resolution 242 as "the firm basis for negotiations"; criticized Egypt, Saudi Arabia and Jordan for failing to carry forward their part of the peace process; warned that "time is only on the side of those who seek anarchy or war in the ME, not peace"; and called on Sādāt to make a "formal Egyptian counter-proposal" to Begin's plan.[39] Carter himself criticized the Israeli reply on 26 June, stating that Israel's refusal to make commitments about the future of occupied Arab lands was "very disappointing," but he hoped for "real progress" in subsequent weeks. He said that he had learned "not to be surprised by temporary setbacks," and added: "Our commitment to the policy of seeking a comprehensive and effective peace in the ME is constant and very dedicated. We will not back off on this."[40]

Though only made public on 5 July, the Egyptian proposals had been under discussion for weeks and had been submitted to Vice-President Mondale during his visit to Egypt to pass on to the American and Israeli governments. The six-point Egyptian "peace plan," entitled "Proposals Relative to Withdrawal from the West Bank and Gaza and Security Arrangements," called for the following:

(1) "A just solution of the Palestinian question in all its aspects" on the basis of the Palestinians' "legitimate rights" and "the legitimate security concerns" of all the parties.

(2) A transitional period of five years during which the orderly transfer of authority will take place and, at the end of which, "the Palestinian people will be able to determine their own future."

(3) Future talks between Egypt, Jordan, Israel and representatives of the Palestinian people, with UN participation, with a view to agreeing on the details of the transitional regime, on the timetable for the Israeli withdrawal, on mutual security arrangements and on other details.

(4) Withdrawal of Israeli forces and settlements from the West Bank (including Jerusalem) and the Gaza Strip.

(5) Abolition of the Israeli military government at the outset of the transitional period; Egyptian supervision of the administration of the Gaza Strip; Jordanian administration of the West Bank, in co-operation with the representatives of the Palestinian people, who would exercise direct authority

over the administration of these areas, while the UN supervised and facilitated the Israeli withdrawal and restoration of Arab authority.

(6) Egyptian and Jordanian guarantees of the security arrangements to be agreed upon and continued subsequently in the West Bank and Gaza.

Four days after being announced, on 9 July, the Israeli Cabinet described the Egyptian proposals as "completely unacceptable," but nevertheless decided to send Foreign Minister Dayan to the meeting proposed by Washington at Leeds Castle. Although the Israeli government statement did not amount to a "rejection" of the Egyptian proposals, it appeared tougher than other Israeli reaction. For example, in a point-by-point commentary on the Egyptian plan, the *Middle East Intelligence Survey* (Tel Aviv) concluded that "the document does reflect readiness [by Egypt] to accommodate some of the Israeli demands" as pointed out by Dayan on 13 July.[41] A senior American official cited four "similarities" in the Egyptian and Israeli plans, including calls for a five-year transitional period, some form of government in the West Bank and the Gaza Strip, detailed negotiations for security arrangements, and commitments to "true peace" in the ME.[42] Even before the talks in Britain started, hopes for a resumption of direct Egyptian-Israeli talks began to rise. Sādāt held a surprise meeting with Israel's Defence Minister, Ezer Weizman, in Austria on 13 July.[43] The substance of their discussions was not made public, but Egypt reportedly softened its 5 July position in two respects: it was willing to accept the presence of Israeli forces in a limited strategic role on the West Bank after a peace agreement, and conceded that Israel could continue to have some standing in the administration of the West Bank.[44]

The American objective in convening the Leeds Castle conference was to revive direct Egyptian-Israeli negotiations, with the hope that the talks between these two parties could be broadened at a later stage. Before the Leeds Castle conference, as before the Jerusalem talks, the US considered it necessary to formulate a set of principles to govern a "comprehensive plan." Shortly before the conference, Vance repeated at a press conference that Resolution 242 "clearly applied to the West Bank and Gaza," and that the question of East Jerusalem had to be negotiated among the parties. In response to a question as to whether the Secretary of State had "a contingency peace plan formulated," Vance said that the US was prepared to make "suggestions" to break the stalemate.[45]

The Leeds Castle negotiations began on 18 July. Although the substance of these unprecedentedly detailed and direct talks was not made public, it is clear that they were based on three documents: the Egyptian and Israeli plans, and a paper long under discussion for a "declaration of principles which would set a framework for broader negotiations." It also seems clear from press reports that as well as clearly defining the wide gap between Egypt and Israel on a number of basic issues, the Leeds Castle talks revealed some areas of consensus. According to some unidentified participants in the negotiations, Egypt, like Israel, did not envisage a redivision of Jerusalem: it should remain one city, with free and open access and a single set of city services like Washington, DC—where thousands of commuters and tourists travel back and forth daily between the district of Columbia, Maryland and Virginia. Despite the fact that Egypt's insistence that Arab sovereignty be restored to East Jerusalem was rejected by Israel, it seemed that this bedrock problem was now at least negotiable. Other points of consensus seemed to include agreed methods for controlling terrorism on the West Bank and Gaza, and the agreed need for free exchange and travel between those areas and their Arab and Israeli neighbours. But consensus on these items was counterbalanced by severe disagreement on the most basic issue blocking a comprehensive peace settlement:

Israeli withdrawal from the West Bank. With American encouragement, Egypt sought to assure Israel that, in return for an agreement to withdraw, its security would be protected in the arrangements for a transition and with an eventual successor regime in the West Bank and Gaza. Egypt took pains to discuss demilitarized zones, zones of limited armament, early warning stations and the positioning of US or other neutral forces in crucial areas along the Israeli border; and it agreed, although reluctantly, that the Israeli garrisons could remain in the West Bank during the proposed five-year transitional period. After the Leeds talks, however, Dayan repeated that Israel "absolutely rejects" any commitment to the principle of withdrawal until a much later stage." [46]

Perceiving some points of consensus between Egypt and Israel, the US took an optimistic view of the Leeds talks; it considered the "candid and probing" discussions a significant step toward a resumption of the negotiations broken off at Jerusalem; and it expected another joint meeting of the Egyptian and Israeli Foreign Ministers in a couple of weeks. Egypt, however, did not share this American optimism. In the weeks following the Leeds talks, Egypt was not persuaded either by Vance's strong statement in support of the principle of withdrawal, nor by the Israeli Foreign Minister's subtle shift of emphasis on the sovereignty problem. Vance warned on 23 July that the ME negotiations would bog down unless Israel accepted, at least in principle, the withdrawal of its forces from the West Bank. On the next day, 24 July, Dayan told the Knesset that Israel would undertake to discuss the sovereignty of the West Bank and the Gaza Strip in five years, if the Arabs meanwhile accepted the Israeli peace plan granting the inhabitants partial autonomy. This formula fell short of the US request for an Israeli commitment to resolve the issue in five years, but was nevertheless more forthcoming than that adopted by the Israeli Cabinet on 18 June. This slight shift of policy was endorsed by the Knesset on 24 July by a vote of 68 to 37. It was followed by an even softer stand the next day in a closed meeting of the Foreign Ministry when Dayan said that Israel "will find a solution" to the issue of sovereignty in the occupied territories. [47] These slight "concessions" did not persuade Sādāt that further talks would bear fruit. In a very tough statement on 30 July, he said that there would be no more talks until Israel agreed that all occupied territories should be returned to the Arabs and recognized that the land issue was non-negotiable. Neither the American rebuke on 31 July of Sādāt's rejection of further talks, nor the visit of Vance to Egypt, moved Cairo to accept the idea of resuming talks at Foreign Ministers' level. On the other hand, the idea of a meeting between Sādāt, Begin and Carter was seized upon by the Egyptian leader as soon as it was mentioned by Vance.

THE SITUATION BEFORE CAMP DAVID

The crowning achievement of the American role in the 1978 ME peace process was the Camp David summit. The White House announced on 8 August that Begin and Sādāt would join Carter at Camp David on 5 September in an attempt to revive the momentum toward peace in the ME. This decision had been taken a week earlier at Camp David "not because the prospects for peace were so good, but because the risks [of failure] have, in fact, risen." US officials made no attempt to minimize the serious hazards involved in convening a summit meeting with no assurance of success. But without prompt Presidential action, they said, the slowdown in momentum and the intensified polemics threatened a collapse of the peace process "with grave dangers for the ME and serious political and economic consequences for the world at large." [48]

There was no public indication in advance of the summit meeting of any

29

noticeable change in the positions of Israel and Egypt on the core issue of sovereignty in the occupied territories. Any optimism that might have been derived from Begin's 20 August statement about an Israeli plan for a "partial but permanent" agreement with Egypt evaporated by 27 August when he stated flatly that Israel would not present proposals at the Camp David summit which included "foreign sovereignty" for the West Bank and Gaza. A Cabinet statement on the same day simply indicated that the Israeli delegation would seek a peace agreement and a continuation of negotiations beyond the summit meeting. This statement confirmed previous speculation that a "partial but permanent" agreement with Egypt meant only that Israel might offer Egypt half of the Sinai, dividing the peninsula on a line from al-'Arish on the Mediterranean to Sharm al-Shaykh on the Red Sea, in return for whch Egypt would be asked to offer some of the components of "full peace," such as diplomatic relations, trade and tourism. But no *quid pro quo* was intended on the West Bank and Gaza.

The Egyptian officials who, before Carter's call for the summit meeting, had been talking gloomily about the failure of Sādāt's initiative and about Egypt's return to the Arab fold, now found new hope. They also believed that the similarity between the Egyptian and American interpretations of Resolution 242 would make it possible for the two Presidents to persuade Begin to change his position on the central problem of Israeli withdrawal from the occupied territories. In this context, Vance's forceful assertion in Alexandria that the US would accept Sādāt's call to become "a full partner" in negotiations must have appeared encouraging to the Egyptians. In stating that the US would present its own ideas for a compromise if they would help break a deadlock, Vance had in fact intended to discourage any Egyptian expectation of American pressure on Israel at the summit.

The divergent expectations of the ME leaders became clear on their separate arrivals at Andrews Air Force Base on 4 September before they proceeded to Camp David. Sādāt stated: "This is no time for manoeuvres and worn-out ideas. It is a time for magnanimity and reason"; at the same time, he described the summit as "a crucial crossroad" for world peace. He also said that if Carter joined as "a full partner" in the negotiations, "together we shall overcome." Begin, on the other hand, described the goals of the summit conference in much more modest terms, saying that he had come "to reach an agreement so that the peace process can continue and ultimately be crowned with peace treaties." Carter imposed a news blackout on the summit's daily proceedings and said that he would stay at Camp David for as long as necessary. He also stated firmly that compromises would be "mandatory" if there was to be progress. No matter what great ideals and mundane concerns motivated President Carter to place his own personal prestige and political fortunes on the line, this unprecedented intermediary effort by the US was an act of statesmanship which rivalled President Sādāt's historic visit to Jerusalem.

THE CAMP DAVID ACCORDS

Although the long-term consequences of the Camp David summit cannot yet be foreseen, the framework agreements resulting from this extraordinary meeting call for preliminary analysis. Many observers seemed to consider that the Camp David summit produced clear-cut winners and losers. As a consequence, for instance, Sādāt was seen in some quarters (and not only by his opponents) as having "caved in," committed "treachery," and "sold out" his fellow Arabs. Begin was regarded as having struck a "shrewd bargain" and won a great "victory," and as having realized his long-held goal of concluding a "separate peace" with Egypt.

However, the results of the Camp David summit defy any such simplified characterization. Basically, Egypt committed itself to "full peace" with Israel as soon as the first phase of the Israeli withdrawal from Sinai was completed. This was a major concession, given Sādāt's position before April 1977—that normalization of relations with Israel was for a future generation of Egyptians—or even his later softened position of postponing normal relations until five years after the conclusion of a peace treaty. Israel in turn committed itself to the full withdrawal of its forces from 'Sinai, the abandonment of its air bases, and the relinquishment of its settlements.

Israeli concessions over the far more difficult problems of the West Bank and Gaza Strip did not quite match up to those of Egypt but here, too, compromises were reached. Although Egypt obtained no unequivocal Israeli commitment to the establishment of Arab sovereignty in these areas (as previously demanded in its peace plan), Israel did agree to negotiate peace on the basis of Resolution 242 which it accepted would explicitly apply to "all fronts." (In a confrontation with Carter in March 1978, Begin had challenged this interpretation of the Resolution.) Furthermore, Israel agreed: (1) to determine, rather than merely discuss, the "final status" of the West Bank and the Gaza Strip; and (2) to do so together with representatives of the Palestinians, as well as with Egypt and Jordan, no later than the third year after the beginning of the five-year transition period, instead of after the end of that period as Israel had insisted prior to Camp David. Israel did not commit itself to totally withdraw its forces from these areas during the transitional period, but it did consent to grant "full autonomy"; to reduce its forces to about half their present strength (possibly from 11,000 to 6,000); to confine them to "specified security locations"; and to abolish military and civilian government in that period. The questions of sovereignty and the presence of Israeli troops after the five-year period were deliberately left open. On the Palestinian problem, Israel did not explicitly commit itself to the principle of "self-determination," but it did recognize the "legitimate rights of the Palestinian people" and promised Palestinian participation in negotiations on the resolution of the problem "in all its aspects." Significantly, the Camp David accords failed to mention the thorny issues of the status of Jerusalem and Israeli settlements in the West Bank and Gaza. In the exchanged letters and relevant discussions, it was agreed that the city of Jerusalem should remain "undivided," although the Egyptian claim to Arab sovereignty over East Jerusalem was sharply rejected by Israel. It was also apparently agreed that the establishment of new Israeli settlements should be frozen for a time—but for exactly how long was disputed by Israel and the US.

Like the status of Jerusalem and Israeli settlements, the problems of the Golan Heights and the PLO were not mentioned in the accords. However, Israel's acceptance of a number of provisions, including the application of Resolution 242 to "all fronts," seemed to indicate a willingness to make peace with Syria—provided that it was genuinely ready to negotiate. Although Palestinians from outside the West Bank were in effect vetoed (by Israel and others) from participation in the negotiations, Begin seemed to indicate in his October interview with *Newsweek* that PLO members and sympathizers from inside the West Bank and Gaza Strip could not similarly be excluded.

The framework accords prominently reflected a number of ideas carefully promoted by the US since November 1977 to bridge gaps between Egyptian and Israeli positions. These included the applicability of Resolution 242 to "all fronts," the "legitimate rights" of the Palestinians, a five-year "transitional period," the solution of the Palestinian problem in "all its aspects," and the participation of the Palestinians in the determination of the "final status" of the West Bank and Gaza Strip. In fact, the Camp David accords far surpassed their limited and immediate objective of breaking the deadlock that had followed Sādāt's 30 July rejection of further direct negotiations with Israel after the Leeds Castle talks. After 30 years of Arab-Israeli conflict, they prepared the ground for the signing of a peace treaty between Egypt and Israel.

At the same time, this momentous development produced the greatest challenge and opportunity for achieving the fundamental and long-term American goal of a "comprehensive" ME peace settlement. This was not only to sign a separate peace between Israel and Egypt, but to extend such a peace settlement to include Israel and the other Arab states as well. The vehement opposition of the rejectionist Arab states and the ambivalence of Jordan and Saudi Arabia to the peace process underscored the nature of the new challenge to US diplomacy.

The success of American foreign policy toward the Arab-Israeli conflict in the near future will thus largely depend on its ability to deal effectively with three basic questions. First, will the US be able to persuade Israel to understand and accept that, although the signing of a peace treaty with Egypt will dramatically reduce the chances of war (partly because of the short-run change in the military equation in its favour), it will prove illusory in the long run unless it is accompanied by settlements on all other fronts? Second, will the US be able to persuade other Arab parties to join the negotiations, and hence prevent the threat of Egyptian isolation in the Arab world which could adversely affect the stability and survival of the Sādāt regime as well as the future development of its peaceful and normal relations with Israel? Finally, will the US be able imaginatively to involve the Soviet Union in a constructive role in the peace-making process—particularly when Palestinian and Syrian entry into the negotiations becomes crucial; or will it be tempted instead to consolidate short-term strategic gains and entirely exclude the USSR from the ME peace process?

R. K. Ramazani

US ASSISTANCE TO MIDDLE EAST COUNTRIES 1977-79
(thousand US dollars)

	FY 1979 (proposed)		FY 1978 (estimate)		FY 1977 (actual)	
	Economic[1]	Military[2]	Economic[1]	Military[2]	Economic[1]	Military[2]
Afghanistan	24,096	600	26,137	525	21,426	193
Algeria	2,278	—	3,260[4]	—	6,129	—
Bahrain	236[3]	—	551	—	741	—
Egypt	956,667	400	935,585	200	908,208	—
Gaza	1,217[4]	—	1,055	—	1,654	—
Israel	790,400	1,000,000	792,200	1,000,000	746,200	1,000,000
Jordan	101,797	132,500	100,523	132,100	80,385	131,486
Jordan—West Bank	1,397[4]	—	1,735	—	1,511	—
Jordan Valley	50,000	—	—	—	—	
Lebanon	655[4]	25,650	28,583	50,600	8,816	25,036
Morocco	30,553	46,535	30,280	46,300	29,262	30,783
Oman	579[3]	—	492	—	368	—
Sudan	24,178	7,950	21,836	250	6,636[4]	103
Syria	113,924	—	107,224	—	99,846	—
Tunisia	27,043	26,200	31,063	26,125	25,846	24,446
North Yemen	14,576	600	7,853	525	16,639	357

[1] Includes AID, PL 480 food aid, Peace Corps.
[2] Includes grants, training and credit sales.
[3] Peace Corps only.
[4] PL 480 aid only.
FY = Financial Year.
Source: AID Congressional Presentation FY 1979. *The Middle East*, January 1979.

NOTES

1. *Middle East Intelligence Survey (MEIS)*, Tel Aviv; Vol 5, No 16 (16–30 November 1977).
2. Department of State, *The Secretary of State*, 6 December 1977, pp. 2–3.
3. Also see chapters on Jordan and Iran, and essay, "The Negotiating Process: Attitudes of Interested Parties."
4. For text, see *New York Times (NYT)*, 5 January 1978. Emphasis added.
5. For text, see *MECS 1976–77*, p. 29.
6. *NYT*, 5 January 1978.
7. *NYT*, 6 January 1978.
8. See *MECS 1976–77*, pp. 30–31, 141–42.
9. For text, see *NYT*, 18 January 1978.
10. *Washington Post (WP)*, 18 January 1978.
11. *NYT*, 14 January 1978.
12. *Ibid*, and *WP*, 18 January 1978.
13. *NYT*, 19 January 1978.
14. *WP*, 21 January 1978.
15. *NYT*, 22 January, and *WP*, 20 January 1978.
16. *WP*, 25 January 1978.
17. *NYT* and *WP*, 21 January 1978.
18. For further explanations of Sādāt's move, see *NYT*, 19, 20 January 1978 (e.g. "pressure tactics and psychological warfare; simple misunderstanding; personal pique; clash of cultures; collision of conflicting national interests").
19. Department of State, *Bulletin*, Vol 78, No 2011 (February 1978), pp. 33–39.
20. *WP*, 29 January 1978.
21. *MEIS*, Vol 5, No 21 (1–15 February 1978), pp. 161–62.
22. For excerpts of his speech, see *NYT*, 7 February 1978.
23. For text, see *NYT*, 9 February 1978.
24. *NYT*, 10 February 1978.
25. See Department of State, *The Secretary of State*, 10 February 1978, p. 4.
26. *NYT*, 11 February 1978.
27. For text, see *NYT*, 8 February 1978.
28. See chapters on Israel and Lebanon, and two final essays in the section of the Arab-Israeli Conflict, "South Lebanon" and "Armed Operations; Situation along the Borders."
29. *MEIS*, Vol 15, No 24 (16–31 March 1978), pp. 188–89.
30. For the excerpts, see *NYT*, 23 March 1978.
31. See US Congress, Senate, Committee on Foreign Relations, *Middle East Arms Sales Proposals*, 95th Cong, 2nd Sess 1978, pp. 16–45.
32. See US *Congressional Record*, Proceedings and Debates, 95th Cong, 2nd Sess (Vol 124, No 71), p. 57381.
33. *Ibid*, p. 57382.
34. *Ibid*, p. 57398.
35. *Ibid*, p. 57399.
36. *NYT*, 16 May 1978.
37. *WP*, 17 May 1978.
38. See William Claiborne, *WP*, 17 June 1978.
39. *NYT*, 22 June 1978.
40. *NYT*, 27 June 1978.
41. See *MEIS*, Vol 6, No 7, 1–15 July 1978.
42. *NYT*, 16 July 1978.
43. See also essay entitled, "The Negotiating Process: Attitudes of Interested Parties."
44. *WP*, 17 July 1978.
45. See Department of State, *The Secretary of State*, 10 July 1978, p. 6.
46. *WP*, 21 July 1978.
47. *NYT*, 25 July and *WP*, 26 July 1978.
48. *WP*, 9 August 1978.

The Soviet Bloc and the Middle East

To all appearances, 1978 was not "the USSR's year" in the Middle East. It was not "America's year" either to the full extent which it might have been but for certain hard-to-shift ME obduracies. But this thwarting of US achievement was no actual achievement of the USSR itself, for all its anxiety to take a hand in the process.

A central concern of Soviet ME policy since the 1973 war has been to secure a presiding role for the USSR in any ME peace conference or settlement (see *MECS 1976–77*, p. 35). The US-Soviet joint statement of 1 October 1977 was presumably felt by Moscow to be a step towards this goal; but President Sādāt's own astonishing peace initiative of November 1977 seemed to push the co-chairmen of any Geneva peace conference on to the sidelines. In October, Brezhnev had felt able to tell the visiting Indian Premier that, with the "serious efforts made in recent months to move forward to a comprehensive settlement" of the ME conflict, "new opportunities have been opened up," of which the parties involved should "take advantage, with the co-operation of the Geneva conference co-chairmen."[1] A month later, the Soviet media had to draw their own conclusions from the Sādāt-Begin joint communiqué in Jerusalem. Tass's principal indictment of it was that it omitted any mention at all of the Geneva conference (and, also, of the Palestinians). Indeed, Tass noted, the Israeli press was claiming that the face-to-face talks entirely undermined the preparations for a new Geneva conference.[2] On 27 November 1977, in a Moscow television discussion on the Sādāt-Begin talks, the Tass head Zamyatin said that when in New York during the UN General Assembly session he had obtained a document which revealed Israel's aims during the talks with Egypt: the first was to divide the Arabs by holding separate talks; the second was to isolate the PLO; and "the third aim was to remove the Soviet Union from the process of the ME settlement."[3]

Brezhnev, in an end-of-the-year interview for *Pravda* on the USSR's international position, made no bones about the significance of the alteration that had taken place, and about his own view of this. "The affairs of the ME—this is an acute problem. In it there have recently been some changes and, regrettably, changes of a negative order. And they occurred just when it seemed that matters were proceeding in a positive direction, towards the convocation of the Geneva peace conference, and much had already been done for this, including the joint efforts of the USSR and the US as co-chairmen of the conference. The convening of a conference in Geneva and a general settlement in the ME have become a more difficult matter." (The latter observation had earlier been made by Gromyko to the visiting Syrian Foreign Minister 'Abd al-Halīm Khaddām on 28 November.)[4] The USSR, said Brezhnev, wanted a genuinely durable peace "and not a shaky armistice"; so far from leading towards this, "the notorious talks between the Egyptian and Israeli leaders" would destroy any hope of it, create a deep rift in the Arab world, "and above all undermine the Geneva conference before it has started."[5]

The resulting Soviet sense of "outsiderness" was evident in much of Moscow's early comment on the Egyptian-Israeli talks. In a Moscow broadcast in Arabic at the end of January 1978, Pavel Demchenko said that one of the principal "negative points" about the talks was the exclusion of the USSR. But, the commentator insisted, attempts to deprive the USSR of influence in the ME were very shortsighted, since in fact no major international issue could now be settled without Soviet participation.[6]

The hostility of other Arab governments to Sādāt's initiative was of course made much of by the Soviet media; and, from the outset, Moscow could claim a solidarity in sentiment with the "anti-capitulationist front." Here, of course, the main Soviet concern was that this front should reciprocate the USSR's desire for solidarity with it. Thus *Pravda*'s North Africa correspondent, reporting the Tripoli summit conference decisions, was careful to point out that the conference had not only upheld Arab unity against "separatist trends," but had also "given a decisive rebuff to attempts to drive a wedge between the Arab states and the USSR."[7] Indeed, the Arab People's Congress set up by the Tripoli conference sent a delegation to the USSR in January, which had talks with the Soviet Afro-Asian Solidarity Committee and other sub-government organizations; other such delegations visited the USSR later in the year.

The Soviet leaders conferred at an early date with Arab leaders and representatives about the new situation in the Arab world. The Syrian Foreign Minister arrived in Moscow on 28 November 1977; when reminded by Gromyko that Syria was one of the countries with which the USSR had been holding consultations about a conference in Geneva, 'Abd al-Ḥalīm Khaddām replied that the new situation "requires careful analysis." Only after that "shall we be able to say whether the door of the Geneva conference is still open."[8] On 1 December, President Aḥmad al-Bakr of Iraq sent his special envoy, Tāriq 'Azīz, to Moscow with a message for Brezhnev. 'Azīz told Gromyko that his visit was an opportunity for discussing "how to deal with the capitulationist policies of certain well-known Arab parties."[9] President Boumedienne visited Moscow in January; the joint Soviet-Algerian communiqué condemned Sādāt's action.[10]

THE USSR'S ARAB POLICY IN THE THIRD WORLD CONTEXT

With Brezhnev acknowledging that the changes brought about by Sādāt's action represented a setback for Soviet expectations, it is natural that Soviet commentators should have made a point of placing this setback in the wider context of the progress of Soviet influence and authority in the Third World—and, indeed, in the world as a whole. At the end of January, in a *Pravda* article on this theme, M. Tumanov said that in the ME imperialism, the Israeli leaders and "certain Arab regimes" were working in concert to destroy the Arabs' friendship with the USSR and thereby deprive them of "their natural allies" in the struggle for political and economic independence. "There is talk sometimes, in the reactionary press, of the possibility of undermining, or even totally removing, the influence of the Soviet Union in the ME. Only the politically shortsighted can reason in this way. As everyone today knows, the Soviet Union's role in the world is determined by its very existence and by its power; it is a role which no one can undermine, let alone remove, whether in this or any other region of the world." As for the USSR's allies in "the national liberation struggle," there were of course "ebbs as well as flows" in this struggle—but, the Soviet commentator insisted, it was "the general movement forward" that prevailed.[11]

However, that was in January 1978. Later in the year what Brezhnev would no doubt call "positive changes" took place to the advantage of Soviet policy in important areas contiguous to the ME—in the Red Sea and the Horn of Africa, and in Afghanistan. The Afghanistan events seemed to justify, *d'un seul coup*, the USSR's confident reiterations about the "socialist future" for "the liberated states." But, more than this, the revolutionary and Moscow-oriented regime which replaced Daud's rather assertively non-aligned one created new and serious external worries

35

for Afghanistan's neighbour, Iran—whose domestic preoccupations were already quite sufficient in themselves. [12]

As for the Soviet and Cuban military involvement in Ethiopia and in Eritrea, the significance of this new theatre of Soviet strategic intervention for the ME proper was not only a function of its geographical proximity. The USSR's intervention in the Somali-Ethiopian conflict represented a further evolution of the 1970s "Brezhnev doctrine" justifying Soviet Third World intervention. Angola had been the case *par excellence* of the policy enunciated by Brezhnev at the 25th CPSU congress in February 1976: "Our party supports and will continue to support peoples fighting for their freedom. . . . We act as we are bid by our revolutionary conscience, our Communist convictions." [13] But this "internationalist" enthusiasm for intervening on the side of peoples fighting "for their freedom" was carried a stage further when the USSR decided to support one already independent African people, the Ethiopians, against another, the Somalis—having itself already decided which side was in the right and which in the wrong. The "intervention doctrine" was accordingly extended to provide for intervention in support of a people fighting "for the integrity of their frontiers" (for the principle of the sacrosanctness of independence-date frontiers, Moscow claims OAU and also UN authority). With a doctrine so susceptible of convenient extension to cover a particular case, Third World governments might well ask themselves which of their number the Soviet Union would next feel impelled by its "revolutionary conscience" to support militarily against its neighbour.

More than this, however, Arab and Muslim states resented—or at least regretted—the fact that both in the Ogaden and in Eritrea, the Soviet bloc countries were assisting the hated Christian Habash to crush rebellions by his Muslim subjects; moreover, the Eritrean Muslim rebels had long been aided by Arab countries—by Libya, for one, as well as by the Arab Red Sea states.

However, Moscow had made its choice and its calculations. By 1977, the regimes of the Arab Red Sea littoral states were not pro-Soviet, with the exception of the PDRY. Indeed, in April 1977, *Izvestiia*'s seasoned Third World affairs commentator, Kudryavtsev, wrote indignantly of the "fuss about the Red Sea" which he said had been raised by "imperialism and its agents"; nevertheless this concern had been reflected in discussions in the Khartoum and Ta'izz conferences of Sudan, Egypt, the YAR, the PDRY and Somalia in February and March 1977. "Some Arab circles have been putting into circulation, for the Red Sea, the term 'the Arab lake.' This plainly smells of nationalism. . . ." Ethiopia, Kudryavtsev pointed out, had a Red Sea coastline of 625 miles. [14] By 1977, in fact, there was no reason any longer to imagine that Arabism was a political virtue in Soviet eyes.

The intervention doctrine was re-expounded by Brezhnev at the congress of the Soviet youth organization in Moscow in April 1978. Repudiating charges that the USSR "interfered in the affairs of the young states," Brezhnev declared: "The USSR takes its unvarying stand in support of respect for the sovereignty of these—as of all other—states, and of non-interference in their internal affairs, and of the inviolability of their frontiers." [15]

By now, of course, this is not only a Soviet doctrine but, since Cuba's assumption of the role of comrade-in-arms of any suitably "revolutionary young state," also a Soviet-bloc doctrine. If "internationalism" is to be the watchword for the exercise, it is perhaps felt to have a more plausible ring if, say, East Germans or Bulgarians—or Cubans—are the visible "internationalists" engaged.

ISRAEL'S LEBANON INTERVENTION

A month before Brezhnev's speech quoted above, Israel's combined land and air incursion into South Lebanon had taken place. A Tass statement declared that "direct aggression against the sovereign state of Lebanon is manifest."[16] *Pravda*'s Beirut correspondent called it "an unprovoked and criminal aggression against a sovereign state."[17] *Pravda*'s political commentator, Yuriy Zhukov, recalled that on 9 March (before the actual Israeli attack) Brezhnev had received the PLO leader, Yāsir 'Arafāt, and declared the USSR's "unswerving support" for the Palestinian people.[18] The "insolent Israeli aggressors," Zhukov declared, "will not be permitted to practise brigandage in broad daylight in other people's territories." Yet Moscow's official public reaction—apart from its UN Security Council denunciations—was apparently limited to "the media," with Tass stating only that the Israeli government bore "the responsibility for the dangerous consequences of the entire new worsening of the ME situation."

Could Moscow have acted more vigorously, and may it indeed have contemplated doing so? On the face of it, Israel had blatantly disregarded that "sovereignty of states and inviolability of their frontiers" of which the Soviet Union, according to its leaders, was now the proclaimed champion. The answer is perhaps to be found in the very same speech of Brezhnev quoted above. Although not specifically mentioning Lebanon, a little after the passage already quoted concerning Soviet support for the sovereignty of states, he referred to "Israel's insolent activities." Significantly, he stated that "the peoples of the young states will be the more successful in defending and upholding their independence" according as their *solidarity and friendship* with the "socialist countries" is the firmer and stronger. Is it farfetched to interpret this as a reflection of the Soviet reading of the Lebanon situation in March 1978 in terms of what (if any) action should be taken by the USSR following the Israeli intervention? One needs to recall Soviet disillusionment with Syria after its earlier intervention in Lebanon. This perhaps contributed to a feeling in Moscow that the "progressive" Arab countries were not so firmly on the Soviet side as they might be. In addition, openly expressed Soviet doubts about the cohesion of the Palestinians may have reflected misgivings about their real supportworthiness. If the USSR contemplated any actual intervention of its own, all this must have weighed heavily against it; even as regards any show of force, it could see who were the real losers in this situation—the Palestinians. It may have asked itself why had it so warmly espoused their cause in the first place? Because, at that time, it seemed to provide the key to one of the mainsprings of Arab political action. But where was Arab political action—let alone Arab military action—now?

During 1978, PLO delegations which went to Moscow received their meed of Soviet declarations of support for the Palestinian cause against "the capitulationist schemes" of President Sādāt. The Palestinians' need for reassurance of support by the socialist bloc countries—Yāsir 'Arafāt visited Cuba in July—was matched by Soviet appreciation of renewed PLO commitment to "the strengthening of friendship and co-operation with the USSR." In July, an independent Fath delegation visited Moscow and had a meeting with Ponomarev at the CPSU Central Committee. A PFLP delegation previously visited Moscow in June and was also received by Ponomarev. Nā'if Hawātima, leading the latter delegation, used the Moscow platform to "call on the PLO, in our capacity as one of its principal members, for a series of initiatives to mobilize the popular masses behind a plan of action" to oppose "Arab reaction and the defeatists."[19] When Soviet commentators like Kudryavtsev write from time to time about the urgent need for unity in the ranks of "the Palestine resistance," they do so from a first-hand awareness of divided counsels in the movement.

MOSCOW AND THE ARAB "STEADFASTNESS FRONT"

More serious for Moscow's estimate of its own present and future authority among the Arabs have been the disagreements between those Arab governments, of varying political complexion, which share a common public opposition to President Sādāt's peace initiative. The Soviet media applauded the Tripoli summit conference, and the later Baghdad conference, and also that measure of Syrian-Iraqi *rapprochement* which preceded the latter. The Soviet view of the urgency of unity among "the Arab progressive regimes" was reflected in a Moscow broadcast in Arabic in October 1978; with "the future of the Arab nation at stake," the commentator said, "will it fall victim to the strong influence of American imperialism and Zionist Israel . . .?" It was "now more necessary than ever to achieve unity of action among the Arab countries."

With Syria, and notably with President Asad himself, Soviet diplomacy and personal contacts during 1978 achieved a degree of restored cordiality and quasi-unanimity on Arab and ME issues (with mutual reservations about events in the Horn of Africa) such as seemed unlikely a year before. With Baghdad there were serious difficulties resulting from Iraq's internal problems with its Communist party, a partner of the Ba'th party in Iraq's National Progressive Front. As had happened in similar circumstances in previous years, local CP unpopularity tended to affect the USSR's own standing. Moscow Radio denied in June that there had been any disloyalty by the Iraqi CP to its Ba'th allies; *Pravda* reported those articles in the Iraqi CP organ *Tarīq al-Sha'b* which sought to explain the CP's stance. [20]

With Jordan there were encouraging contacts for Moscow, including the visit of the Jordanian Crown Prince to the USSR in October, and also a visit by a delegation of Jordanian shaykhs to Soviet Central Asia.

ARABIAN PENINSULA AND PERSIAN GULF

The PDRY Premier, 'Alī Nāsir Muhammad Husnī, visited Moscow in February and had talks with Kosygin and Gromyko and the USSR Defence Minister, Dmitriy Ustinov. With Brezhnev, he agreed that the armed conflict in the Horn of Africa "played into the hands of the imperialists and reactionary forces." It was of course vital for the USSR, at that critical period, to have the sympathy of the regime which afforded it the best staging-post for its latest African ventures. However, the PDRY Premier also visited Peking in April, perhaps to show that he was not in any particular pocket.

Soviet cordiality was resumed with North Yemen in 1978. The YAR Chief of General Staff visited the USSR in April, and the Foreign Minister arrived in May, when the 50th anniversary of the Soviet-Yemeni treaty was celebrated.

On Bahrain's National Day in August, a Moscow Radio commentary declared the USSR's readiness to establish diplomatic relations with Bahrain if there was a desire on the part of its own government to do so. Similar Soviet avowals of a desire for friendly relations with Saudi Arabia are also put out from time to time by Moscow Radio—although there has not been any noticeable lessening of the anti-Saudi stance in Moscow's general Arab world propaganda.

IRAN

From April 1978, when *Pravda* published its first brief and fairly reticent reports on the anti-government disturbances in Iran, until November when Brezhnev made his own verbal "intervention" on the subject, there was a slow but appreciable crescendo in the sharpness of the Soviet media's treatment of the subject. By the end of this period, Soviet reporting of and comments on the Iranian events, taken all together, amounted to a cautious but quite clear avowal of Soviet sympathy with what was presented as a mass movement of protest against the government in power.

On 19 November 1978, *Pravda* published a statement by Brezhnev in the form of a reply to a *Pravda* correspondent's question about "the possibility of military intervention" by the US or other Western powers. Any such "interference, let alone military intervention, in the affairs of Iran—a state which has a common frontier with the Soviet Union—would be regarded by the USSR as a matter affecting the interests of its own security." This was printed in the centre of the first page of *Pravda*, at the top.

TURKEY AND CYPRUS

The Turkish-Soviet *rapprochement* to which Ecevit's government gave further momentum in 1978 was one that both sides found politically useful. For Turkey, indeed, it was very effective in expediting the settlement of some outstanding issues—concerning frontier demarcation, the continental shelf, etc—which might otherwise have proved more contentious. Premier Ecevit's visit to the USSR in June, the results of which he described as most gratifying, was preceded by the visit of the USSR First Deputy Minister of Defence, Marshal Nikolay Ogarkov, to Turkey in April. One result of this visit was an official protest by Cyprus after reports that the USSR had agreed to supply arms to Turkey; this produced an official Soviet denial.

David Morison

NOTES
1. *Pravda*, 22 October 1977.
2. *Ibid*, 23 November 1977.
3. BBC Summary of World Broadcasts, 27 November 1977.
4. *Pravda*, 29 November 1977.
5. *Ibid*, 24 December 1977.
6. Moscow Radio in Arabic, 26 January 1978.
7. *Pravda*, 10 December 1977.
8. *Ibid*, 29 November 1977.
9. Iraqi News Agency, 2 December 1977.
10. *Pravda*, 15 January 1978.
11. *Ibid*, 28 January 1978.
12. See *USSR & Third World*, No 2-3 (1978), pp 22-24.
13. *Pravda*, 25 February 1976. *USSR & Third World*, No 1 (1976), p. 1.
14. *Isvestiia*, 16 April 1977.
15. *Pravda*, 26 April 1978.
17. *Ibid*, 16 March 1978.
18. *Ibid*.
19. Moscow Radio in Arabic, 4 June 1978.
20. *USSR & Third World*, No 2-3 (1978), p. 40.

Western European and EEC Policies towards Mediterranean and Middle Eastern Countries

PRAGMATIC MEDITERRANEAN POLICY AND THE "GLOBAL APPROACH"

Since its inception, the European Economic Community (EEC) has devoted particular attention to its economic relations with the Mediterranean region. The special status of the regions in North Africa formerly colonized by France and Italy (Tunisia and Libya) was initially recognized by the "Rome Treaties." While still a French territory in 1958, Algeria also came fully under the provisions of EEC Treaty Article 227. The six EEC nations proceeded to develop closer relations with the northern Mediterranean littoral states through Association Agreements with Greece (effective from 1 November 1962) and with Turkey (effective from 1 December 1964). These envisaged a gradual removal of tariffs finally leading to both nations' full membership in the EEC,[1] as well as financial support by the Community. Although these arrangements were principally financial in character, their political overtones were shown by the role played by the US in pressing for the completion of the negotiations and by the general wish to tie the two south-eastern NATO partners more closely to Europe. The hope was for their full participation in the European economic system. During the 1960s and early 1970s, a number of agreements were made containing economic or politico-economic elements, but the Turkish and Greek models were not repeated. Instead, the treaties were largely restricted to the establishment of preferential trade relations, notably those with Israel, Lebanon, Morocco and Tunisia, Malta, Cyprus, Egypt, Spain and Portugal.[2]

The EEC took a pragmatic approach toward these agreements in order to strengthen Mediterranean nations and at the same time contribute to the political stabilization of the whole region. No concept of the form which relations should take with third parties in general, or with the Mediterranean states in particular, had been worked out beforehand. Thus the multiplicity of treaties became confusing and unmanageable—quite apart from the fact that individual agreements with different Mediterranean nations began to produce contradictions in Community policy and led to demands for equal treatment. In early 1972, therefore, the European Council directed the European Commission to make proposals for a "global Mediterranean policy."[3] This it did in July 1972, and in November 1972 (i.e. before the oil crisis of October 1973), the Council established its Mediterranean policy based on them. It declared the Community's willingness to make full treaties with all the Mediterranean littoral states which wanted them, as well as with Jordan. These treaties would include full access to the Community market for industrial goods, preferential access for agricultural produce, economic co-operation and, if the occasion arose, financial and technical assistance by the Community. The nature of each treaty would be determined by the circumstances peculiar to each country.[4]

Nevertheless, the "global policy" did not achieve extensive agreement between the EEC and the Mediterranean countries, which was hardly surprising in view of the multiplicity of competing interests among the Europeans themselves, among the Mediterranean states and in bilateral relations.[5] The guidelines of this policy were not originally intended to apply to relations with Greece and Turkey; priority went instead to Spain, Israel and the Maghrib nations. The first treaty—with Israel—was signed in May 1975, followed in April 1976 by those with Morocco, Algeria and Tunisia. Negotiations with the Mashreq nations of Egypt, Syria and Jordan were completed in January 1977. The agreement with Lebanon was delayed until May 1977 due to that country's internal political crisis.

Thus, by mid-1977, the EEC had established a system of agreements with all of the Mediterranean nations (and Jordan)—except for Libya and Albania. Although restricted to economic relations, the agreements were nevertheless intended to make a long-term contribution to the realization of two foreign policy goals: (1) the economic and social development of the Mediterranean nations through close economic co-operation, in order to encourage economic and political stability in the region; and (2) the establishment of close economic co-operation as a contribution to the foundation and protection of a lasting peace.

"EUROPEAN POLITICAL CO-OPERATION" (EPC)

In spite of these implicit political elements, the Community's treaty policy did not by any means seek to create a comprehensive Mediterranean "policy"; it was simply an expression of the importance the EEC attached to that region. In fact, the EEC had no institution which would have been able to plan or carry out common political action, although steps in this direction were first suggested at the summit conference of member-states in December 1969. These only came to fruition with the agreement on European Political Co-operation (EPC) in 1970 which established the framework (set by the Davignon Report) for political negotiations. It provided for quarterly meetings of the Community's Foreign Ministers, which were quite apart from routine summit meetings and actually outside the institutional framework of the Community. A Political Committee, consisting of the political directors of the Foreign Ministries, prepared the meetings of the Foreign Ministers. An indication of the political importance attached to the Mediterranean region was that the EPC chose the ME and the crisis there as one of its two political priorities; the other was the Conference on Security and Co-operation in Europe (CSCE).

There were various obstacles preventing the six original EEC member-countries from establishing a common stand on the problems of the ME, however. For one thing, the traditions and interests of the Community members bordering on the Mediterranean differed from those bordering on the North Sea, especially on issues touching the Arab world. Moreover, the political-psychological importance of Israel was not the same in all the Community states. As permanent members of the UN Security Council, France and Great Britain had a special position with regard to the ME conflict. Finally, there was insufficient co-ordination of positions among the Western Europeans themselves as well as with the US. These differences were reflected in the reception given to a report of the Political Committee, which had been accepted by the Foreign Ministers in May 1971. Not only did the member-states react differently, some with considerable reservations, but it was openly disapproved of by the US and Israel.

On the other hand, the Six did reach agreement on how to approach the most delicate issues of the ME conflict: the question of Israel's withdrawal from areas occupied in 1967 (with "minor modifications"); the modalities of "recognized and guaranteed borders" (international guarantees, demilitarized and internationally controlled security zones); the demand for an "administrative internationalization" of Jerusalem; the settlement of the question of the Palestinian "refugees"; as well as shipping rights through the Suez Canal and the Gulf of 'Aqaba. The EEC nations gave the impression that they wanted to take their own initiative in ME negotiations and exercise pressure on Israel over the territorial question. However, Israel reacted strongly in denying any authority to the European Community to negotiate in the conflict. In contrast, the EPC report met with a positive response in Arab capitals, while the US and the USSR showed reserve.

Although there was no declared connection between the EEC's "global" approach to its economic and political relations with the Mediterranean nations and the attempt at political agreement within the EPC, the energy crisis which arose from the Arab oil embargo in late 1973 soon showed that the re-ordering of economic relations in terms of partnership and equilibrium would be an important element in overall relations between the two areas.

European engagement in the ME conflict seemed to meet with resistance for two principal reasons. On the one hand, Western Europe seemed to possess insufficient political weight to make an effective contribution to a solution of the conflict; her "interference" thus seemed only to create confusion. On the other hand, Western Europe's dependency on oil occasioned suspicion that, under pressure of the "oil weapon," she might side too strongly with the Arabs and thereby weaken Israel's bargaining position.

THE EURO-ARAB DIALOGUE: PREPARATION AND BASIS

After the American and Russian agreement during the October 1973 crisis to limit attendance at the Geneva conference to themselves and the parties directly engaged in the conflict, the Nine increasingly concentrated on developing European-Arab policy outside the confines of the Arab-Israeli conflict.[6] This idea of a Euro-Arab dialogue, which four Arab ministers had presented in Copenhagen in December 1973 on behalf of the 20 member-nations of the Arab League, corresponded with European notions about a new form of diplomatic and political contact with the Arab region. A "dialogue" would reflect the duality in Western Europe's approach to its economic and political relations with the ME, which was the product of differences between EEC members' individual relations with Israel and the Arab nations, and of US-Israeli mistrust of European political initiatives.

The concept of the Euro-Arab dialogue, which evolved in the first half of 1974, reflected the efforts of the Nine to establish relations with the Arab world on a basis of stable long-term partnership. It was understood from the outset that the dialogue should not impede initiatives on "the politics of oil" on the wider international stage; above all, it should not interfere with attempts at a peace settlement for the ME. What this meant in effect was that the Arab-Israeli conflict should not appear on the agenda of the dialogue. This was made clear by the Federal Republic of Germany's Foreign Minister, Hans-Dietrich Genscher, at a press conference on 11 June 1974, in which he formally confirmed the beginning of the European-Arab dialogue. Institutionally, this was to be conducted separately both from talks about economic relations with the ME nations, which were to be arranged according to the principles of the "global approach," and from those of the EPC.

The Euro-Arab dialogue developed against the following background:

(1) For a long time, a number of Arab states had pressed for Mediterranean security issues to be included on the agenda at the Helsinki CSCE, so that the discussion could be related to both European *and* ME security, stability and peace. These efforts met with only a limited response from those present at Helsinki, where the dominant feeling was that the CSCE should restrict itself to security in Europe and not become embroiled in peripheral problems.

(2) The October 1973 war dramatically brought home the connection between the security of both regions. Not only did the involvement of the two superpowers in the ME conflict immediately affect Europe, but the US actually alerted its nuclear forces and transferred military equipment (stored in West Germany)

to Israel without first consulting its NATO allies—a decision which created difficulties for the Federal Republic both with the Arab states and with the US.

(3) The Arabs' condition for lifting the oil embargo against most of the European nations was that they should make a statement in favour of the Arab position in the conflict with Israel. This pressure underlined the precarious dependence of the Community's economic prosperity on its ability to establish a balanced policy in the ME.

(4) While the ME statement made by the Nine on 6 November 1973 did not presage an active policy in the Arab-Israeli conflict, it did show that Western Europe had adjusted to the changed situation in the ME and was ready to support peace initiatives founded on internationally recognized facts and resolutions. However, the Nine did not allow themselves to be forced into a pro-Arab position; their stand was based on two sets of principles: those set out in the EPC working paper endorsed by the Six in 1971; and the various Security Council Resolutions (especially 242 and 338) together with the principle of respect for the rights of the Palestinians mentioned in the UN General Assembly Resolution of 13 December 1972, which had the support of the Nine.

The guidelines of EEC policy, as laid down by the November 1973 statement, included the following: balanced consideration of Arab and Israeli interests; no annexation of territory by force and consequently an end to the Israeli occupation, exercised since the June war of 1967, following a process of negotiations leading to the recognition of the right of Israel to exist within guaranteed boundaries; and respect for the right of the Palestinian people to self-determination in a national homeland of their own.[7] The Nine also demanded international guarantees, but refrained from making suggestions. Finally, the statement recalled the various ties which have existed between members of the Community and the Mediterranean states. The decision to make balanced "global" agreements on economic relations with all Mediterranean nations was once again mentioned in this context.

In preparatory bilateral talks on the Euro-Arab dialogue, the European statement made it easier to show understanding for justified Arab concerns, while at the same time insisting on parity for Israel.

ELEMENTS OF THE EUROPEAN-ARAB DIALOGUE

The European-Arab dialogue constitutes a framework for negotiations which involves both the EEC and EPC. Whereas the EEC is largely restricted to economic affairs, trade policy and technical co-operation, and the EPC provides an avenue for inter-governmental co-operation parallel to that of the Community but without actual political executive power, the Euro-Arab dialogue is involved in both areas. A European Co-ordinating Group was constituted as the EPC-EEC executive and negotiating body for the dialogue, consisting of special delegates of the nine governments at ambassador level and of representatives of the EEC Commission.

A General Commission was inaugurated on 31 July 1974, consisting of delegates of the 21 members of the Arab League and the nine members of the EEC. Its function was to establish the principles of European-Arab co-operation and to co-ordinate the activities of the various working groups. For some time, the Arab side argued that co-operation must be based on a comprehensive political agreement, and emphasized such sensitive issues as the occupied territories and Palestinian representation. However, the European side insisted that political problems be excluded from the talks. This disagreement delayed the beginning of the dialogue until summer 1975, when it finally met at expert level. The Europeans were firm in stating that, in spite of their respect for the Arab position, they would not allow themselves to be held to ransom politically; nor would they be willing to pre-empt international agreements. The Arabs thus came to accept the special character of the dialogue as a framework for negotiations, dedicated primarily to European-Arab co-operation in certain limited areas. These were defined at the first meeting of experts at Cairo in June 1975, when working groups were constituted for the following: agricultural development; industrialization; projects for infrastructure; development of trade; finance; scientific and technical co-operation; and cultural and social co-operation.

In effect, the dialogue is an attempt at a new form of international diplomacy and structured co-operation between the EEC and the Arab League. On the European side, the Nine participate as a unit, institutionalized in the committees of the EEC and EPC; on the Arab side, the members of the Arab League and its General Secretariat take part. Many reservations have been expressed regarding the multilateral and collective approach of the dialogue, but this can be justified, in particular because it builds upon the sum of bilateral relations. In addition, the dialogue should be "an inter-regional policy of order," working out common long-term goals.

The success of the dialogue cannot yet be measured in concrete results. Without doubt, political agreement and economic co-operation have become closer. In the cultural sphere, too, new contacts could be established. Capital involvement and entrepreneurial co-operation have been encouraged, and the opportunity for permanent dialogue has lessened the chances of short-term, politically motivated actions being undertaken against the interest of any other party. While progress in the seven working and 16 project groups has been small, some has been made in the areas of industrialization (extension of the petrochemical industries), infrastructure (including technical education), agriculture and cultural-scientific co-operation. In other areas, however, the difficulties seem almost insurmountable: the demand that the European market be opened to Arab products is as controversial as a treaty on the protection of capital investment, or parity for Arab *Gastarbeiter* with Europeans. Nevertheless, the progress made by the working groups in late 1975 and early 1976 was sufficient for the General Commission to meet for the first time in May 1976 in Luxembourg. (A Palestinian representative was included in the Arab groups of experts, which acted as unified delegations, and another served on the General Commission.) The programme of Luxembourg aimed at the following: (1) an evaluation of the results of the experts' meetings to date; (2) the establishment of a timetable and the co-ordination of the various working and project groups; and (3) the exchange of political statements.

However, no spectacular results were achieved at the Luxembourg meeting since this, too, was marked by Arab attempts to reach consensus on fundamental political positions on the Arab-Israeli conflict, particularly on the Palestinian question. While the European side had assumed that the members of the Arab League were represented jointly in the delegations at Luxembourg—as had been the case in the groups of experts—the Arabs explained in their introduction that the member-states were represented individually; since the Community accepted this statement silently, a quasi-recognition of the PLO was thereby achieved.

As a result of decisions taken at Luxembourg, the second session of the General Commission in Tunis (10–12 February 1977) was preceded by intensive meetings of all working groups, by flanking sessions of the General Commission, as well as by a political discussion by the Foreign Ministers of the Nine (London statement of 31 January 1977). This drew significantly on the ME statement of 6 November 1973 and once more particularly asserted the rights of the Palestinians. It also announced the readiness of EEC members to take a concrete part in a ME peace settlement and to consider contributing to guarantees for the security of participants. It was emphasized that a settlement would have to include the right of the Palestinian people to express their national identity. This formulation should be interpreted in connection with the statement of the EEC representative at the 31st UN General Assembly (October 1976) that the Palestinian people must be allowed their own territory.[8]

Even though this statement did not fully satisfy the Arab participants, it did create a favourable climate that allowed the General Commission to make progress in such questions as the financing of the dialogue and co-operation in the transfer of technology, agriculture and cultural relations. The only political compromise was the agreement to consider the creation of a political committee for the discussion of political questions in the context of the existing dialogue.

The Euro-Arab dialogue has so far been conducted in a state of tension between the strong desire for closer co-operation on the one hand, and different political attitudes on the other. The third session of the General Commission in October 1977 in Brussels was marked by similar friction. Once again it was preceded by a statement of EEC Heads of Government (published on 29 June 1977); this drew significantly on previous statements, but spoke out more clearly for the creation of a homeland (German = *Heimstatt*, French = *patrie*). In a politically fortunate coincidence, the members of the EEC and of the Arab League voted together in the UN General Assembly on 27 October 1977 against Israel's settlement policy and in favour of a resolution which determined, among other things, "that measures and actions taken by Israel in the Palestinian and other Arab territories occupied since 1967 have no legal validity and constitute a serious obstruction of efforts aimed at achieving a just and lasting peace in the ME."

One notable political result of the third session of the General Commission was the decision to take the proposal to create a joint committee for political consultation (originally made by the Arab side at the second session) a good deal further. In addition, the working groups were able to identify common projects for which feasibility studies could begin. These covered such areas as training for marine transport, the harmonization of harbour statistics in Arab countries, the development of new harbours in Basrah and Tartūs, and a symposium on "new cities." The following decisions were taken concerning agriculture and rural development: a feasibility study for an irrigation system in the Juba Valley in Somalia; a meat-extraction project in Sudan; and a seed-potato project in Iraq. Preparations for a symposium (in Hamburg in 1979) on cultural relations between Western Europe and the Arab world were also to be expedited.

THE STAGNATION OF RELATIONS DURING 1978

Compared with the rapid improvement in Arab-European relations between 1973 and 1977, there was a marked stagnation during 1978. President Sādāt's visit to Jerusalem in November 1977 not only paralysed the Arab League—the European Community's political and economic partner—for long periods; it also once again accentuated a general dilemma facing the EEC in the Arab world. On the one hand, the dominant American role in the ME peace process reduced the political influence of the EEC in the area, at the same time obscuring the image of Western Europe as a possible "third power" alongside the two "super-powers." On the other, the difficulties of agreeing on a common Community position towards political developments in the ME was once again demonstrated. It was particularly difficult for France to express support for Sādāt's initiative in view of the Arab "Rejection Front's" opposition to it. After struggling to find a satisfactory wording, the nine member-states finally issued a diluted statement which expressed the hope that "the unprecedented dialogue begun in Jerusalem will open the way to comprehensive negotiations leading to a just and lasting overall settlement.'' Otherwise, the Heads of Government confined themselves, at their meetings in April and September 1978, to repeating their well known positions (see above). A statement issued by the Council of Ministers in September 1978 on the results of the Camp David conference was cautious, indicating a wait-and-see attitude.

The divisions within the Arab League have to a great extent prevented further progress in the working groups. However, the group for Economic Co-operation was able to produce the outline of an Investment Protection Agreement at its session in February 1978; while that for Scientific and Technological Co-operation passed resolutions in connection with the foundation of an Arab polytechnic and the building of a desalination plant in Kuwait. Under the prevailing circumstances, only limited results could be achieved in the fourth session of the General Commission, held in Damascus from 9–12 December 1978.

The co-operation treaties signed in 1977 with the Mashreq countries (Egypt, Jordan, Lebanon and Syria) and with Israel came into operation on 1 November 1978. In anticipation, the Council of Ministers agreed in October 1978 that the EEC Commission should set up permanent delegations in the treaty countries. This step has been taken in the past when a permanent EEC diplomatic presence in important capitals has been thought useful. (The Community cannot itself set up diplomatic missions. Full diplomatic representation by the Community continues to be carried out by the ambassador of whichever country provides the chairman of the Council of Ministers at any particular time.)

It did not prove possible to improve relations between the EEC and its treaty partner, Turkey, during 1978, which remained at a low ebb. However, leaders of the Republican People's Party, which was returned to power at the beginning of 1978, declared their desire to renegotiate the Ankara protocol to the Association Treaty. The Prime Minister, Bülent Ecevit, explained his government's views during his visit to Brussels in May 1978 (also see chapter on Turkey). However, by late 1978, no significant initiatives were taken to this end. Turkey's wishes are centred on increased openings in the European market for certain industrial goods, more financial aid, the removal of tariffs and other restrictions on Turkish agricultural products, and greater freedom of movement for Turkish workers in the Community. Much more than its predecessor, however, the RPP government lacks the political will to improve relations and has no precise proposals about individual measures. The party's strong Left-wing would, in the long term, prefer to see Turkey develop an independent political and economic framework, rather than integrate into the EEC. In view of these uncertainties, as well as the country's catastrophic economic situation and its unresolved political tensions, Turkey proposed in October 1978 that the co-operation treaty be put on ice for five years, and that Turkey suspend her obligations to further reduce tariffs on EEC products. The Community agreed to consider this proposal.

Udo Steinbach

STRUCTURE OF ARAB LEAGUE EXPORTS TO THE EEC

	1970	1975	1976	70–75 index
Mineral fuels	85.6	93.7	93.9	318
(of which refined petroleum products)	1.0	1.8	2.6	509
Raw materials and chemical products	5.8	3.2	1.3	159
Agricultural products	6.4	2.0	1.7	89
Manufactured products	2.2	1.1	0.5	142
	100%	100%	100%	291

STRUCTURE OF COMMUNITY EXPORTS TO ARAB COUNTRIES

	% 1970	% 1975
Agricultural products	12%	7.2%
Raw materials and chemical products	16%	9.7%
Manufactured products	31%	26.1%
Machinery and transport equipment	41%	52.7%

EEC EXPORTS TO ARAB COUNTRIES

	1970	1971	1972	1973	1974	1975	1976
Total (in million ua)	3,455	3,874	4,486	5,561	10,001	14,320	16,745
Index	100	112	130	161	290	414	484
Change in relation to previous year (%)		+ 12.1	+ 15.8	+ 24.0	+ 79.8	+ 43.2	+ 16.9
Arab countries' share of total EEC exports (%)	6.2	6.2	6.7	7.0	9.2	12.6	13.4

THE TRADE BALANCE BETWEEN THE EEC AND THE ARAB COUNTRIES IN 1976 (million ua)

Surplus countries		Deficit countries	
Saudi Arabia	+ 8,802	Egypt	−835
Libya	+ 1,892	Algeria	−601
United Arab Emirates	+ 1,740	Tunisia	−424
Iraq	+ 1,579	Morocco	−477
Kuwait	+ 1,536	Jordan	−493
Qatar	+ 932	Syria	−381
Oman	+ 79	Bahrain	−218
Mauritania	+ 25	Sudan	−267
		North Yemen	−121
		South Yemen	−61
		Somalia	−35

FINANCIAL AND TECHNICAL CO-OPERATION, 1977–81 (million ua)

	Algeria	Morocco	Tunisia	Egypt	Syria	Jordan	Lebanon
EIB loans	70	56	41	93	34	18	20
Special loans	19	58	39	14	7	4	2
Grants	25	16	15	63	19	18	8
Total	**114**	**130**	**95**	**170**	**60**	**40**	**30**

DIRECTION OF TRADE. 1976

Total EEC imports in 1976 were 159,354 European units of account (EUA). Imports from Arab League countries totalled 31,703 EUA and were comprised as follows: Saudi Arabia 11,878 (37.4%); Libya 4,019 (12.6%); Iraq 3,569 (11.6%); UAE 2,942 (9.9%); Kuwait 2,532 (7.9%); Algeria 2,152 (6.7%); Qatar 1,235; Morocco 839; Egypt 678; Syria 649; Tunisia 411; Oman 370; Sudan 222; Mauritania 136; Bahrain 59; Lebanon 40; Somalia 18; Jordan 13; North Yemen 9, and South Yemen 7.

Saudi Arabia, Algeria and Libya absorbed over 41% of the Community's total sales of 18,947m EUA to Arab countries in 1976. The breakdown was as follows (in million EUA): Saudi Arabia 3,075; Algeria 2,753; Libya 2,127; Iraq 1,991; Egypt 1,513; Morocco 1,316; UAE 1,172; Syria 1,030.

ACTIVITIES INITIATED THROUGH THE EURO-ARAB DIALOGUE, OCTOBER 1977

	Estimated Costs	Estimated contributions ($) Arab	European
A. Symposium on relations between the two civilizations (Hamburg)	250,000	125,000	125,000
B. Basic infrastructure			
1. Study on the needs of Arab countries for training programmes in the field of maritime transport	200,000	160,000	40,000
2. Harmonization of statistics in Arab ports	60,000	48,000	12,000
3. Study for the development of the new port at Basrah (Iraq)	500,000	400,000	100,000
4. Study for the development of the new port Tartūs (Syria)	500,000	400,000	100,000
5. Symposium on the theme of "New Towns"	20,000	10,000	10,000
C. Agriculture and rural development			
1. The Juba Valley, study for irrigation project at Bardera (Somalia)	1,200,000	960,000	240,000
2. Project for meat production in Sudan	50,000	40,000	10,000
2. Project for growing seed potatoes in Iraq	1,800,000	1,440,000	360,000

Source (for preceding statistics and tables): Commission of the European Communities, *Information: The European Community and the Arab World* (Co-operation-Development 169/78).

The value of the ua is based on gold and corresponds to US$1.20635; £0.41666.

The value of the EUA is determined every day in relation to a basket of all Community currencies. On 1 January 1978, the EUA was equivalent to US$1.21; £0.64.

NOTES
1. Cf Theo M. Loch and Hajo Hasenpflug, *Die Assoziierungs- und Präferenzpolitik der EG* (Bonn, 1974). Also Udo Steinbach, "Auf dem Wege nach Europa? Die Beziehungen zwischen der Türkei und der Europäischen Gemeinschaft durchlaufen eine kritische Phase," in *Orient*, 1/1977, pp. 79–101.
2. For more details, see Loch/Hasenpflug, *op. cit.* Also H. Andresen, "Über die Verwirklichung einer gemeinschaftlichen Mittelmeerpolitik," in *Europa und die arabische Welt: Probleme und Perspektiven europäischer Arabienpolitik, Europäische Schriften des Instituts für Europäische Politik*, Vol 41–42 (Bonn, 1975), pp. 293–326. R. Regul, *Die Europäischen Gemeinschaften und die Mittelmeerländer, Schriftenreihe Europäische Wirtschaft*, Vol 75 (Baden-Baden, 1977). Avi Shlaim, "The Community and the Mediterranean Basin," in Kenneth J. Twitchett, *Europe and the World, The External Relations of the Common Market* (London, 1976), pp. 77–120.
3. Three Mediterranean problems were on the agenda of the European Council in 1972: the renegotiation of treaties with Morocco and Tunisia "on an extended basis"; the consequences of opening up the Community to Spanish and Israeli foreign trade; and the applications of Spain, Israel and Turkey for incorporation into the general preference system. Any decisions on these matters would have had consequences 'for existing treaties as well as for those under negotiation.
4. See Andresen, *op. cit.*, pp. 304–6.
5. Cf Loukas Tsoukalis, "The EEC and the Mediterranean: Is 'Global' Policy a Misnomer?'" in *International Affairs* (London, July 1977), pp. 422–38.
6. Cf Günther van Well, "Die Entwicklung einer gemeinsamen Nahost-Politik der Neun," in *Europa-Archiv*, 4/1976, pp. 119–28.
7. For the full text, see *Europa-Archiv*, 2/1974, pp. D29f.
8. Cf Ursula Braun, "Der europäisch-arabische Dialog—Entwicklung und Zwischenbilanz," in *Orient*, 1/1977, pp. 30–56.

China's Middle East Policy

Although China's actual policies towards the Middle East have changed considerably over the years, the underlying perspectives and attitudes have had a certain consistency. Ever since the early 1940s when Mao Tse-tung analysed international affairs from within the Yenan caves in the country's north-west hinterland, the Communist leadership has held two propositions regarding the ME. First, it has maintained that the ME (or as the Chinese have sometimes significantly called it, "West Asia") is of such profound importance in the balance of world forces that whichever external great power dominates the region will thereby be able to exercise considerable leverage over China. In other words, the region has been seen geographically as an important dimension of any attempt by hostile powers to encircle China. Second, and not unrelated to the first proposition, the Chinese have always argued that external intervention by the great powers is the primary cause of the continuation of local conflicts in the area. Indeed, the exploitation of local conflicts has been seen as the principal means by which the great powers have been able to gain deep penetration of the region.

LIMITED ACTIVE INFLUENCE

Despite this geopolitical interest in the region, China's active influence there has been severely limited by the conjunction of its non-interventionist doctrine and its relative economic backwardness. Although in the late 1960s China's leaders regarded liberation movements in Afro-Asia as a main force against imperialism, headed by the US, they felt that such movements had to be basically independent, self-reliant, nationalist and non-sectarian. Even within south-east Asia, where China's access to the revolutionary movements engaged in armed struggle was more direct, Peking forbore from exporting its revolution or from becoming such a major supplier of aid that a dependency situation was established. Thus although China's political support for, and indeed its supply of small arms and training facilities to, Palestinian forces in the 1960s and early 1970s were of some importance, they were never decisive in terms of actually shaping the political orientation of the Palestinian movements—and still less in determining their activities. China's relative economic backwardness also meant that it has simply lacked the capacity to project its forces much beyond its borders. Moreover, in terms of advanced military technology, China is generally regarded as 10–20 years behind the two super-powers and even the West European countries. As a result, China was unable to give more than token support to the Egyptian request for spares and replacements for the advanced Russian weaponry received before the break in Egypt-Soviet relations. In fact, China was only able to help with regard to the obsolescent MiG-17, MiG-19 and the less sophisticated aspects of the MiG-21 aircraft. Indeed, according to the Japanese Self-Defence Agency, it was Egypt which proved helpful to China in this regard by supplying it with a MiG-23 that could be used as a prototype.[1]

THE INTERNATIONAL DIMENSION

China's position in global strategic terms presents something of a paradox.[2] At the level of the central strategic balance between the two super-powers, China is a very important factor indeed. As Dr Schlesinger, the former American Secretary for Defence, once put it, China's shift from being a close ally to a major adversary of the Soviet Union has been the single most important strategic change to the advantage of the US since World War II. As a result, about a quarter of Soviet military might is tied down in the Soviet Far East, and the Soviet leaders' old nightmare of having to prepare for a war on two fronts has long since become a reality. In its own way, of course, China challenges Soviet influence in every part of the globe, while in many respects China and the US have become *de facto* allies. Nevertheless, below the level of super-power relationships, China's capacity to exert influence and shape outcomes is strictly limited. Even at the super-power level, a good deal of China's influence stems from peculiar circumstances. For instance, it is the only country which can credibly claim to be able successfully to withstand a full-scale invasion by either the Russians or Americans. Considerable uncertainty surrounds the effectiveness of China's nuclear force as a second-strike weapon. China would clearly be unable to inflict the kind of devastating destruction on the USSR which could be wreaked upon itself. But it is unknown what kind of limited damage could be inflicted by the Chinese, or whether that would constitute a sufficient deterrent to the Soviet Union. However, the situation is developing—and China's potential is clearly very great. It is in fact the uncertainty of China's current second-strike capability and the certainty of its future potential, combined with the delicate balance between the two super-powers, which combine to give China the degree of leverage which it currently exercises.

At another level of analysis, China is at once an active participant in international affairs and idiosyncratically withdrawn from the rest of the world. Ever since the break with the Soviet Union in the late 1950s, China has been free of external dependencies and has studiously sought not to have other countries dependent upon it. Thus China's political system is perhaps the most autonomous in the world. Likewise, its domestic economy is largely insulated from changes in the international economic system. Alone of Third World countries, China's domestic economy was virtually unaffected, either positively or negatively, by the quadrupling of oil prices following the October War of 1973. Even now that China is actively seeking to quadruple its foreign trade so as to import advanced technology for its ambitious modernization programme, the doctrine of self-reliance is being modified rather than discarded.

Some of the key elements in China's foreign policy stem from considerations of its own experience with the outside world. Thus China's leaders continually urge upon fellow Third World countries the virtues of sovereignty and independence. They never tire of repeating to Third World forums that "political independence means very little without economic independence." A *sine qua non* is a diversified agriculture which is able to meet the minimum food requirements of each nation's population.[3] China's leaders have consistently stressed since 1951 that they share two basic factors in common with all the countries of Asia, Africa and Latin America: first, a history of colonial or semi-colonial intervention and resistance to such controls; and second, a need to modernize economically. The main threat to these countries, and indeed even to the smaller and medium-sized developed countries, comes from attempted expansion by the greater imperial powers. In the 1970s, these have been identified as the US, but principally the USSR.

THE VIEW OF THE MIDDLE EAST

To return from these general considerations to the ME, China's Communist leaders have held for the past four decades that, as elsewhere in the world, external intervention is the main danger and principal cause of the perpetuation and exacerbation of local conflicts. Hence the Chinese are in principle opposed to the view common in the West that lest essentially local conflicts spark off a new world war, they should be settled through the agency of the great powers who alone can effectively guarantee any settlement. As seen from China, it is precisely great power intervention which constitutes the real danger of war. In fact, the Chinese object to an interventionist peacekeeping role—even for the UN. Far from considering the UN as a neutral body standing above the fray, they see it as reflecting the shifting global balance of forces. Thus in the 1950s and early 1960s, the UN was seen essentially as a body which served American interests; still later as serving the collusive aspects of super-power diplomacy. In the 1970s, it has come to be looked upon as the arena of struggle between Third World countries and the two superpowers. The Chinese, however, have not vetoed enabling resolutions in the Security Council for peacekeeping forces in the ME because the sovereign countries concerned have so far indicated a desire for their presence. To veto such resolutions would be to counter an even more cherished Chinese principle, namely the inviolability of sovereignty. (It also happens to be practical politics.) The Chinese have resolved the dilemma by withdrawing altogether from such votes, as abstention might be regarded as endorsement of the process.

In so far as there has been consistency in China's policies towards the ME, it has involved two considerations: first, that the precise dangers posed by particular great powers have always been interpreted according to Chinese leaders' analyses of the overall balance of world forces—especially as to which imperialist power is in the ascendancy; and second, that nationalism is the main positive force in the area. That is why the Chinese have always urged the Arab nations to emphasize unity and why their main support has been directed, not towards the more radical or self-styled Marxist groups in the PLO, but rather towards encouraging unity among the Palestinians. The result is that China's leaders have consistently supported al-Fath and the PLO as a whole.

However, it is the first of these two considerations which has tended to dominate policy. In the early 1950s, China's leaders were less exercised by the influence of Britain and France than by that of the US. The former two were seen as declining imperialist powers whereas the latter was not only regarded as more powerful, but also as engaged upon an expansionist course mainly aimed at controlling what now would be called Third World countries through economic, political and military interventionism. It is worth recalling China's initial suspicion of Nāsir as a leader whose coup had enjoyed American backing[4] (although by the time of the Suez crisis in 1956, China's leaders had changed their view of him). Mao's January 1957 analysis of the significance of the crisis, though dated, is still revealing about underlying Chinese attitudes and the way in which China's leaders, even today, tend to place regional issues within a larger global context:

". . . A man called Nāsir nationalized the canal, another called Eden sent in an invading army, and close on his heels came a third called Eisenhower who decided to drive the British out and have the place all to himself. The British bourgeoisie, past masters of machination and manoeuvre, are a class which knows best when to compromise. But this time they bungled and let the ME fall into the hands of the Americans. What a colossal mistake! Can one find many such mistakes in the history of the British bourgeoisie? How come that this time they lost their heads and made such a mistake? Because the pressure exerted by the US was too much and they lost control of themselves in their anxiety to regain the ME and block the US. Did Britain direct the spearhead chiefly at Egypt? No, Britain's moves were against the US, much as the moves of the US were against Britain.

"From this incident we can pinpoint the focus of struggle in the world today.

The contradiction between the imperialist countries and the socialist countries is certainly most acute. But the imperialist countries are now contending with each other for the control of different areas in the name of opposing Communism. What areas are they contending for? Areas in Asia and Africa inhabited by 1,000m people. At present this contention converges on the ME, an area of great strategic significance, and particularly on Egypt's Suez Canal zone. In the ME, two kinds of contradictions and three kinds of forces are in conflict. The two kinds of contradictions are: first, those between different imperialist powers, that is between the US and Britain and between the US and France; and second, between the imperialist powers and the oppressed nations. The three kinds of forces are: (1) the US, the biggest imperialist power; (2) Britain and France, second-rate imperialist powers; and (3) the oppressed nations. . . ." [5]

More than 20 years later, the Chinese mode of analysis is broadly similar except that as elsewhere in the world, the ME is seen as caught up in the struggle between the Soviet Union as the ascendant imperialist power, and the US as the declining one on the defensive. Those which Mao called "the oppressed nations," now regarded as Third World countries, are seen as the main force resisting super-power encroachment. The "second-rate imperialist powers" of 20 years ago have long been regarded as spent imperialist forces, themselves now possible targets for imperialist domination, by the Soviet Union especially. Hence, the Chinese interest lies with the Third World countries. It will be noted that, unlike their Soviet counterparts, the Chinese have long since stopped dividing Third World governments into progressive or reactionary categories. The prospect of domestic revolutions of a genuine Marxist-Leninist kind, i.e. along Leninist or Maoist lines, is not seen as imminent in Africa or the ME. In any case it is given far less emphasis. The more frequent Chinese refrain is that because of its domestic structures, the Soviet Union is bound to continue its expansionist military policies which will inevitably lead to a major war with the US centred upon Europe. The Chinese argue that the outbreak of this war can be put off only if the countries faced with the Soviet threat demonstrate military preparedness, emphasize their independence and co-operate together within their own regions.

China's leaders have propounded this view in private and in public to every conceivable kind of audience for more than five years—throughout all the leadership changes both before and after the death of Chairman Mao. It is futile to question the sincerity of China's leaders, or to point to the self-serving aspect of the analysis by which China's main enemy is necessarily the main enemy of all other countries. Virtually every aspect of China's foreign policy can be seen to be guided and shaped by these considerations.

RELATIONS WITH THE GULF STATES

The Chinese argue that events of 1978 not only confirm their analysis, but also indicate a further extension of Soviet global designs. Soviet military intervention in Africa—in particular through its Cuban "mercenaries"—has extended from Angola to the Horn of Africa and is linked to Soviet attempts to control the Red Sea and the Gulf through gunboat diplomacy and subversion, which led to the establishment of even more pro-Soviet regimes in Aden and Afghanistan. A recent major editorial in the *People's Daily* depicted all of this as directly linked with the USSR's alleged instigation of Vietnam to clash with China. Events in both areas were part of a grand design for gaining control of the Indian Ocean and the Gulf, as well as for penetrating south-east Asia so as to encircle China and outflank Europe. [6]

Such analyses certainly explain China's active encouragement of a Gulf security community.[7] The idea originated with Kuwait in 1976 as a means of stabilizing and settling border questions, to a large extent because of the Iraqi claim on its territory. Although mutual suspicions prevented discussions among the Gulf countries at the time, the idea has been revived more recently because of increased Soviet pressure in the area as a whole. This was perhaps the most important factor in the opening of diplomatic relations between China and the Sultanate of Oman on 26 May 1978, an event revealingly commemorated in a *People's Daily* editorial:

"Today the Omani government is dedicating its effort to the struggle in defence of national independence and for the development of the economy. Following in foreign affairs the principles of neutrality and non-alignment, Oman advocates unity and co-operation among the countries in the Gulf and the Red Sea area and opposes big power contention there. All this carries the firm support of the Chinese government and people."

With the country's leaders also keen to gain the recognition of Saudi Arabia, the Chinese media have carried favourable references to Saudi policies with increasing frequency. It is presumably only a question of time before the Saudis drop their objection to China as that "godless country." Recognition would have favourable consequences for Peking in that Saudi Arabia is one of the last significant countries to continue to recognize Taiwan as the sole legitimate government of China; it would also help in Peking's relations with Muslim governments in south-east Asia. But there can be little doubt that China's main interest in Riyadh centres upon the Gulf, the Red Sea and the Horn of Africa, where the two countries share common fears of Soviet penetration.

China has gone to some length to cultivate relations in the Gulf. Several senior Chinese officials have visited the area, the most notable of course being Chairman Hua who spent three days in Iran at the end of August. This was the first occasion on which the chairman of the Chinese Communist Party ever visited a non-socialist state. Although the Shah, his family and successive governments have forged excellent relations with China's leaders since Empress Farah Pahlavi paved the way to Peking in 1972, there can be no doubt that from the Chinese perspective, Iran's strategic significance was the main reason for its being selected for this singular honour. Interestingly, Hua Kuo-feng's visit coincided with upheavals in Iran which presented the Chinese leader with a unique opportunity to gain insight into the problems of an autocrat introducing rapid economic development to a traditional Islamic society. Whether the visit heightened Chinese consciousness of the fragility of one of the seemingly most stable regimes in the area cannot be known; but in less than a month of Hua's return, a *People's Daily* editorial (mentioned above) warned more urgently than ever about the danger of Soviet subversion, which it claimed had reached a new stage.

The Chinese have also received proof within the past year that national aspirations of Third World countries for independence are an effective counter-force to Soviet pressures. Thus China drew satisfaction from the execution in Iraq of local pro-Soviet Communists, and lavished much praise upon Somalia for severing relations with Moscow. China's leaders saw Somalia as only the latest of supposedly client-states, after Egypt and the Sudan, to assert national independence in the face of increasing Soviet attempts to deepen its hold and to subordinate the clients' interests to those of its own. China's leaders have not been slow to emphasize this trend, whereby countries which have turned to the Soviet Union inevitably find their own national aspirations frustrated and their sense of independent dignity abused by the Soviet drive for dominance. However, the Chinese do not believe that Soviet dominance can easily be shaken off. Given the fragility of many of the governments concerned, there is also always the danger of subversion, coups or assassinations—as shown by events in the People's Democratic Republic of Yemen and Afghanistan.

THE ARAB-ISRAELI CONFLICT

From a Chinese perspective, the significance of the Arab-Israeli conflict in both regional and global terms has changed in recent years. But at the same time, the peace initiatives and strategy of President Sādāt have raised certain dilemmas for Chinese policy. Since the October War of 1973, the importance of the Soviet Union as a factor in the conflict has progressively declined. Beginning with Egypt, but also including (however reluctantly or timorously) the other front-line states of Syria and Jordan, there has grown the recognition that the key to Israeli withdrawal from the territories occupied in 1967 rests exclusively with Washington. Thus it was under the aegis of Kissinger that initial Israeli withdrawals were effected, first in Sinai and then in the Golan Heights (even though Syria had first rejected the proposed moves out of hand). In 1978 it was under the aegis of President Carter that Premier Begin and President Sādāt eventually agreed on the Camp David accords. Although progress to a settlement of the Palestinian question on the West Bank and to a peace agreement with Syria and Jordan is still fraught with many obstacles, the way to a peace treaty between Egypt and Israel seems clear. But since not a single Arab state has supported this latest Sādāt move—the PLO in particular has been vociferous in its objections—the Chinese face a dilemma in that they have all along supported the Palestinian cause and urged unity among the Arab countries. President Sādāt's initiative in visiting Jerusalem in November 1977 could have been seen as an attempt to solve local problems locally, without reference to the external great powers. That was indeed how the Chinese saw it at the time. They were also pleased by Sādāt's emphatic declaration that a separate peace was ruled out; that peace would require the establishment of Palestinian national rights through self-determination on the West Bank; and finally that peace would require Israeli withdrawal from the territories occupied in 1967.[8] The Chinese subsequently criticized the Begin government for intransigence, but at the same time gave subtle indications that they might be prepared to recognize Israel (presumably once its government had acceded to Sādāt's terms). The Chinese were alarmed by the temporary Israeli incursion into the Lebanon, but after its withdrawal they sought official contact with Israel at the UN—the first time for this to happen since the abortive attempts at recognition in the early 1950s.[9]

China has continued to support Sādāt's peace initiatives,[10] though doubtless would have preferred them not to have involved Washington which has strained its relations with other Arab states and the PLO. As a result, China's support has been only tacit: its news agency has released factual accounts of Sādāt's achievements, while passing over in virtual silence the protests and activities of the rejectionist states. Strangely, it was precisely at this time that diplomatic relations were established with Libya; in Peking, Major Jallūd took the opportunity to lecture his hosts about the necessity of supporting Arab unity and of opposing Sādāt's unilateral moves. Although China has striven hard to maintain and deepen its existing relations with all the Arab states and the PLO, and has repeatedly called for Arab unity, its main concern is with helping to deny the Soviet Union access to the region. Clearly, the Chinese believe that if Sādāt's initiatives end in failure, the Soviet Union will benefit most. That may be the main reason for China's support of Sādāt, despite his current isolation in the Arab world.

The Chinese argue in private, and quite truthfully, that they have never called for the extinction of Israel or for "driving the Jews into the sea"; they insist that their opposition has been to Israeli policies of aggression and the forced occupation of the territories of Arab states. They also claim to have consistently supported the Palestinian cause for the recognition of their national rights—though perhaps not so vigorously as a few years ago. Whatever its attitude to Israel, China's more salient consideration is the role of external powers, specially that of the Soviet Union. Thus the Chinese are likely to continue to support the Sādāt initiative. At the same time they are likely to make every effort to extend their contacts with all the Arab states and the PLO. (Interestingly, the Chinese do not regard Syria as a Soviet dependency despite its exclusive reliance on Moscow for advanced weapons.) China's message to ME countries is likely to continue to emphasize the need for Arab unity and to recognize, in the words of a visiting Chinese leader to President Asad, that "the reason why Israeli Zionism is so stubborn and reactionary is because it enjoys the covert or overt connivance and support of the super-powers which have been bolstering it with manpower and materials. This is the root cause of the prolonged turmoil in the ME and the lack of solution to the problem." [11] The underlying point of this lecture was that the Soviet Union, too, was in fact a supporter and instigator of Israel.

Since China is not a major factor in the ME, either in economic or military terms, its influence is necessarily more nebulous and less effective than that of the other great powers. At the same time, because of its significance in the global strategic configurations of the two super-powers and its importance as an adversary to the Soviet Union, China's influence cannot be dismissed out of hand, nor be said to be the result of its prestige as a Third World power with enormous potential. Likewise, it would be foolish to under-rate the influence of China's appeal to ME (and other) countries in its emphasis on the nationalist virtues of sovereignty, independence and mutual co-operation against external interventionism.

Michael B. Yahuda

NOTES
1. *International Herald Tribune*, Paris; 19 January 1978. It was claimed that China also planned to obtain samples of Soviet surface-to-air missiles, anti-tank missiles and T-62 tanks. In return, China would supply spares for Egypt's MiG-17, -19 and -21 aircraft.
2. For an extensive analysis of this, see Michael B. Yahuda, *China's Role in World Affairs* (Croom Helm, 1978).
3. For a more extended presentation of the Chinese viewpoint, see Vice-Premier Teng Hsiao-ping's speech to the sixth special session of the UN General Assembly on 10 April 1974 in *Peking Review*, Special supplement to No 15 (12 April 1974). See also editorial in *The People's Daily*, 1 November 1977; "Chairman Mao's Theory of the Differentiation of the Three Worlds is a Major Contribution to Marxism-Leninism" in *Peking Review*, No 45 (1977), pp. 10–41.
4. See Yitzhak Shichor, *The Middle East in China's Foreign Policy 1949–74* (London University PhD Thesis, 1976), p. 74.
5. *Selected Works of Mao Tse-tung*, Vol V, pp. 361–62.
6. *People's Daily*, 19 September 1978. An editorial, "A New Development of the Kremlin's Global Strategy," was carried in the daily bulletin of the New China News Agency (NCNA).
7. See *MECS* 1976–77, p. 47.
8. On 27 November, the NCNA carried a brief factual summary of Sādāt's declaration, while totally ignoring the protests of other Arab states and the PLO.
9. See BBC Summary of World Broadcasts SU/5855 for article in *Pravda* of 1 July 1978. This cited Frana Press and the Israeli paper *Yedi'ot Aharonot* as sources for a meeting between Ming Chen-tung (a member of the official Chinese UN mission) and Herzog (the leader of the Israeli mission).
10. *Le Monde*, 22 September 197, quoted Vice-Premier Teng Hsiao-ping as expressing to the Gaullist leader Jacques Chirac his "satisfaction" with the Camp David accords.
11. NCNA, 10 July 1978.

The Regional Politics of the Red Sea, Indian Ocean and Persian Gulf

Uncertainty and flux continued to characterize developments in the Indian Ocean region during 1978, especially in the strategically important north-west quadrant. In the earlier part of the year, instability in and around the Horn of Africa occupied the centre stage. The long-anticipated passing of President Kenyatta raised unsettling questions with regard to the succession, to Kenya's future stability, and to whether the US might in the future be denied the use of Mombasa, the only remaining port facility available to it in southern Africa. Later in the year, the bloody military coup in Afghanistan sent ripples of apprehension far beyond that landlocked nation's mountainous borders. Assassinations in the Yemens rocked the Arabian Peninsula, chilling the atmosphere in nearby monarchical states. And the unrest troubling Iran had repercussions around the world, most especially in the capitals of the major powers.

Two of those powers—the USSR and the US—appeared to be pursuing their established policies towards the area, with relatively few changes. For its part, the USSR continued to inspire and fuel insurgencies around the periphery and steadfastly supported the new Marxist military regime in Ethiopia—despite the damage that alliance caused to Soviet relations with Somalia. Ambivalence seemed to dominate US policies, although by forcing a patent slowdown in the Indian Ocean demilitarization negotiations with the USSR, and by continuing to develop the modest base at Diego Garcia, Washington appeared to be sending out mild signals of disapproval of Soviet actions.

THE CRISIS IN IRAN

While events in the Horn of Africa dominated the scene in the early part of the year, the most critical development in the Indian Ocean in 1978 took place in Iran. In 1963 the Shah, Muḥammad Reza Pahlavi, began a modernization programme which came to be known as the "White Revolution"—or more recently as "The Shah and the People Revolution." This provoked violent rioting by religious elements backed by wealthy landlords, whose power over Iranian society was broken by the Shah. Although the revolt of these elements was quelled in 1963, their opposition continued. Meanwhile, from the early 1970s, the Shah rapidly increased the pace of modernization, using new wealth derived from oil.

The modernization and liberalization programme, so necessary if Iran were to achieve modernity, inevitably began to challenge religious values. The need to bring in large numbers of foreign technicians and experts of various kinds with different religious and social values (e.g. about 40,000 Americans), also caused the nation's religious leaders increasing concern. They saw their own position in society threatened and began to oppose the Shah openly and violently.

On 8 September 1978, massive violence erupted in Tehran and elsewhere in Iran, when thousands rioted and the military forces were ordered to open fire. Several hundred were killed before even a modicum of order could be restored. In these riots, the religious elements were joined in their protests by well-organized radicals of all orientations who did not themselves enjoy widespread support. However, as the religious issue had deep roots and provided a natural rallying point for much of Iranian society, the radicals worked to exploit the issue, even though they had little interest in it.

56

Ironically, the radicals' plans and ideas for modernization and liberalization would almost certainly be more antithetical to religious values than those of the Shah. It was also clear that the opposition elements in Iran—religious and otherwise—were receiving support in the form of training and money from outside sources. One must assume Soviet support in various forms, and strongly suspect financial backing from Libya's leader, Col Qadhdhāfī. It was also reported that some terrorist elements in Iran had been trained in Beirut by George Habash's Palestinian forces.

In addition, the religious elements received active political and other forms of support from Ayatollah Khomeyni. At the peak of the rioting, he was using Iraq as a base but was forced to leave that country because of his open activism. Khomeyni's continued presence in Iraq could have been construed as a violation of a 1975 agreement under which Iraq halted efforts to infiltrate or support subversion in the Persian Gulf region; in return, Iran withdrew its heavy support for the Kurds who were fighting for greater autonomy within Iraq. Nonetheless, in the last days of 1978, there was increasing evidence of very substantial external political and financial support for those opposing the Shah.

The widespread violence, produced by the combination of religious and radical elements, raised serious questions about the future of Iran and, by implication, about the entire Persian Gulf area. All forms of traditional rule in the region would be jeopardized by the overthrow of the monarchy in Iran. There is serious doubt, for instance, as to how long the monarchy could continue in Saudi Arabia.

Western governments and media largely rallied to the Shah's support because it became apparent—even to those who had criticized him in the past—that there was no sensible or safe alternative to his leadership. Opposition elements had no practical plans or ideas about governing the country, and their assumption of power would very likely lead to total chaos, with adverse spillover effects for the entire Persian Gulf region. Strikes in the Iranian oil industry in November 1978 revealed how even a 50% cut in Iranian oil production could affect the industrial nations. For instance, if the cut continued for any length of time, Japan—which receives 43% of Iran's oil—would very soon be in trouble.

There can also be no doubt that turmoil in Iran would offer the USSR its long-awaited opportunity to change the political and military balance in the Persian Gulf to its advantage. Despite the risks involved, the temptation to make a significant move would seem irresistible, because of the heavy dependence of the US and the Western industrialized nations on Persian Gulf oil.

Furthermore, with any perceived change in the inclination and capability of Iran to act as the protector of royal and quasi-royal rule in the Persian Gulf, radical elements in the area would almost certainly attempt coups against the smaller shaykhdoms and emirates such as Oman, the UAE, Kuwait, Bahrain or Qatar. For example, Iraq could revive its claims to Kuwaiti territory. These were first asserted in 1960 and successfully countered by British troop landings; when reasserted in the spring of 1973, they were deterred by Saudi Arabia as well as Iran, which made clear its anxiety over the possibility of Iraq's takeover of the disputed territories. There would certainly be little to prevent the Iraqis from achieving their aims if the Iranian military leadership were in disarray.

Save for Iraq, whose monarchy was overthrown in 1958, the Persian Gulf states are presently headed by pro-West royal or quasi-royal leaders. If they were overthrown and replaced by regimes with close ties with the Soviet Union, the oil sealanes and tanker terminals would become highly vulnerable to harassment.

Finally, the future of Pakistan may also be affected by the crisis in Iran. Pakistan's position *vis-à-vis* its two neighbouring antagonists, India and

Afghanistan, has continued to weaken since the 1971 Indo-Pakistani war. Iran has consistently and publicly taken the position that an attack on Pakistan, or threats to Pakistan's territorial integrity, would be construed as threats to Iran itself, and that Iran would assist Pakistan militarily—as indeed it did in the early 1970s when the Baluchi tribes sought greater autonomy. Afghanistan, too, has asserted claims to Pathan populated territory in Pakistan's North-West Frontier Province (for details, see below). It is always possible that the Pathan and Baluchi questions may be pressed more forcefully than in the past—and with Soviet or other outside support. Any weakening of Iran's ability to employ effective military force or act as a deterrent to threats aimed at Pakistan could therefore have serious repercussions in Pakistan as well as in Iranian Baluchistan, which is located in south-east of the country on the Indian Ocean, contiguous to Pakistan's Baluchistan province. The potential for trouble is obvious if Iran were unable or unwilling to come to Pakistan's aid in this area.

THE HORN OF AFRICA
During the early part of 1978, developments in the vicinity of the Horn of Africa created the greatest single impact. With the infusion of massive Soviet military support and Cuban military forces, Lt-Col Mengistu Haile Mariam's junta turned its attention from recent successes in the Ogaden to the long-lived rebellion in the troubled northern province of Eritrea. By the end of the year, Addis Ababa had made no real progress in restoring its authority in Eritrea.

To the south, Moscow's break with Somalia—effected in the autumn of 1977 when Muhammed Siyad Barreh tore up the Treaty of Friendship and Co-operation and ordered the Russians to leave the country—was accepted relatively quietly. The expeditious withdrawal of Soviet forces and installations from Berbera and Mogadishu suggests that Moscow anticipated from the outset that it would be unable to walk the international tightrope represented by the attempt to back both sides in the bitter, local conflict. In the Kremlin, Ethiopia was clearly viewed all along as a prize far outstripping the possible loss of Somalia.

Moscow's strategic calculations were apparently dominated by Ethiopia's geographic position—abutting Sudan, Kenya, Djibouti and Somalia, but a short distance from Uganda and a highroad to Tanzania and Zaire. Being such an excellent staging base for subversive incursions into Central Africa, an Ethiopia closely aligned with Moscow would offer great scope for promoting Soviet ambitions. Moreover, with Soviet warships operating from Massawa, Russian influence could be extended north to the Suez Canal. The loss of Berbera notwithstanding, facilities in Massawa, coupled with continued access to Aden and use of the anchorages off the South Yemeni-owned island of Suqotra, could give the Soviet navy maritime dominion over the Bāb al-Mandab at the southern end of the Red Sea as well as over the adjacent waters of the Gulf of Aden. While the import of these possible developments could hardly be lost on the nations of East and Central Africa, they created most immediate anxiety throughout the remainder of the northwest quadrant of the Indian Ocean, particularly in Saudi Arabia and Iran.

The conflict between Ethiopia and Somalia had already generated serious concern in Riyadh and Tehran, where it raised numerous security issues. Questions arose about the spillover effects that a successful new radical regime in Ethiopia would produce across the Arabian Peninsula and in the Persian Gulf. Of primary concern, of course, was the sanctity of the oil transit routes. Thus, the political threat posed by an activist Marxist government in Ethiopia, and the economic threat presented by possible Soviet dominance of the Red Sea and the Gulf of Aden, were especially disturbing.

THE RED SEA AND PERSIAN GULF

Iran and Saudi Arabia share important national security interests including the maintenance of the monarchical governments currently in power; the continuation of similar, or at least compatible, governments in nearby countries; unfettered flow of Persian Gulf petroleum to world markets; and freedom from hegemony exercised by external powers—particularly the Soviet Union. The policies of these two governments have therefore understandably been directed at preserving political stability throughout the region and insulating it against encroachment by radical regimes bent on destruction of the existing political order.

For these reasons, both Iran and Saudi Arabia have been active in Indian Ocean and Persian Gulf affairs over the years. However, with the exception of the Arab-Israeli wars of 1967 and 1973, Saudi Arabian activity has been largely confined to economic as opposed to military measures. Iran, on the other hand, has acted in both fields, as evidenced by the seizure of the Tumb Islands and Abu Musa, and intervention in the Kurdish rebellion in Iraq. Iran's most recent military effort came in response to Sultan Qābūs' request for aid in putting down the insurgency in Dhufar, the western-most province of Oman.

Since 1973, the Shah of Iran has provided ground, air and naval support which played a significant role in the successful containment of the South Yemeni-backed Dhufar rebels. While the insurrection appeared to be essentially moribund in 1978, the continued presence of a Marxist government in Aden—and perhaps now with the added support of a newer one in Addis Ababa—mean that the rebellion could be rekindled at any time.

That Saudi Arabia and Iran share interests in the north-west quadrant of the Indian Ocean is of course not a recent development. Riyadh has long sought to entice Islamic Somalia away from its previous Soviet alliance, but with little success. In 1978, however, thanks to Moscow's actions in the Horn, the prospects of accomplishing this aim looked considerably brighter. However, American reluctance to transfer arms to Somalia did little to help Riyadh's cause. (One reason for Washington's attitude was that it did not want to revive Kenyan anxieties about pan-Somali ambitions which the US would appear to be endorsing if it supplied arms to Mogadishu.)

While the assassination of the President of the Yemen Arab Republic, Ahmad Husayn al-Ghashmī, on 24 June 1978 had no wider international implications, the situation was different in the People's Democratic Republic of Yemen. Two days later, on 26 June, President Sālim 'Alī Rubay' was killed and two of his aides executed in a bloody coup. The coup's leader, 'Abd al-Fattāh Ismā'īl, is generally regarded as having strong ties with Moscow. This shift in South Yemen toward the USSR was viewed as a setback for the policies of China which had been working to counter Soviet influence throughout the region. For moderate nations in the area, it was also a sharp blow to attempts to contain the growth of pro-Soviet regimes. The coup led to the cancellation of a US diplomatic mission which was scheduled to depart for Aden on 27 June to open discussions about improving relations between the two countries.

One of the most significant events in 1978 was the dramatic shift in American arms policy toward the moderate Arab states, particularly Saudi Arabia. After long and heated debate, Congress assented to President Carter's proposed sale of 50 F-15 Eagle interceptor aircraft to Riyadh—the first time the US provided an Arab state with one of its most sophisticated fighter aircraft. The Administration's arguments, that the planes could pose no meaningful threat to Israel and were desperately needed by Saudi Arabia to protect its vulnerable oilfields from external attack, ultimately prevailed.

However, this did not constitute the only change in US arms policies with respect to the Indian Ocean and Persian Gulf regions. Despite the ambivalence of its policy toward Somalia, other transfers suggested that the Administration was discovering the necessity of providing military support to some friendly nations, notwithstanding Presidential campaign pledges to bring a complete halt to the international traffic in weapons.

One beneficiary of this altered US position was Pakistan. The arms embargo imposed after the 1971 Indo-Pakistani war was finally lifted and, in September 1978, Pakistan took delivery of two refurbished destroyers which had recently been retired from the US navy.

AFGHANISTAN AND PAKISTAN

A bloody coup in the mountainous state of Afghanistan in the early part of 1978 sent waves of apprehension through the Persian and Oman Gulf littorals. Fighting erupted in Kabul on 27 April and continued for almost four days. The new Afghan Prime Minister and Chairman of the Revolutionary Council was Nūr Muḥammad Taraki, leader of the People's Democratic Party, a group generally regarded as Communist. The country was renamed the Democratic Republic of Afghanistan. The true nature of the new government was further revealed when every member of the Central Committee of Taraki's party was given a Cabinet post, and when the military component of the new government turned out to be either Communist party members or party sympathizers. The events in Afghanistan served to confirm longstanding apprehensions in Iran, Saudi Arabia and the rest of the Persian Gulf states of expanding Soviet influence in the oil-rich region.

The Kabul coup also held implications for Pakistan's current military government in relation to the two fiercely independent tribal groups—the Baluchis and the Pathans. Living on both sides of the border between Afghanistan and Pakistan's North-West Frontier Province, the Pathans constitute one of many tribes which straddle frontiers in the Indian Ocean area. This complex problem dates back to 1893 when, in drawing the Durand line to delineate the boundary between British India and Afghanistan, Britain essentially bisected the Pathans. On the partition of British India, Pakistan inherited the Durand line. However, the Afghan government continues to object to its existence, claiming that it divides a people who wish to be united; that it did their nation a grievous wrong; and that the struggle to right that wrong has not yet ended. One solution often put forward is the formation of a new country—Pakhtunistan.

Although succeeding Afghan governments have supported the establishment of a Pakhtunistan state, its boundaries have never been clearly defined. Islamabad is firmly convinced that most, if not all, of the required territory would be carved out of present-day Pakistan. The fact that the population would be predominantly Pathan also suggests that such a state would—at the very least—be closely allied with Afghanistan. Another possibility is that the existence of rich mineral reserves on both sides of the present frontier could lead Kabul to seek to absorb the Pakistani Pathan area into Afghanistan itself. Understandably bitter over the loss of East Pakistan (now Bangladesh), Islamabad cannot view these recent developments in Kabul except with deep concern.

South of the junction of the Pakistan-Iran-Afghanistan borders is another tribal enclave, this one populated by the Baluchis. Straddling the Iranian-Pakistani frontier, the Baluchis have long presented a separatist threat to both nations. Moreover, the Soviet Union has consistently encouraged them to form still another independent state—Baluchistan—by channelling funds and small arms through Iraq. The fear in Iran and Pakistan is that, after the upheaval in Afghanistan, the historic Baluchi drive for independence will receive new impetus and support from the Soviet Union, this time routed directly through Kabul rather than circuitously via Iraq. Thus, the prospective loss of sizeable portions of their countries to any new state is a prime concern in Islamabad and Tehran. There is also the worry that, with Afghanistan in the Soviet camp and a new state of Baluchistan beholden to the Soviet Union, Moscow would at last possess a direct corridor to the Indian Ocean. One suspects that these and other "beyond the border" ramifications provided the fundamental motivation for the USSR to back the April coup in Kabul.

INDIAN OCEAN NEGOTIATIONS

The USSR and US continued their negotiations to "demilitarize" the Indian Ocean in 1978. The talks originated at a conference of non-aligned nations in Lusaka (Zambia) in 1970 when the notion of an Indian Ocean "zone of peace" free from great power rivalries was put forward. The following year, Sri Lanka introduced a resolution to that effect in the UN. The major maritime powers were generally cool to the idea, and it failed to win universal acceptance. However, in 1975, some members of Congress began to insist that the US evince real interest in the proposal. Senate Resolution 117 required the President to use his best efforts to achieve mutual limitations on US and Soviet forces and facilities in the Indian Ocean area before accepting the need to develop US naval and air facilities on the island of Diego Garcia. A subsequent amendment to the 1976 military construction bill—sponsored by Senator John Culver of Iowa—effectively barred the use of funds for further construction on the island until the President reported on the status of negotiations.

Two factors operated to produce the Congressional stand. First, one segment of the American legislature steadfastly opposed any construction in the Indian Ocean under any circumstances. A second group, essentially economy-minded, refused to support the requisite funding until a clear need for the facilities could be convincingly demonstrated. A more fundamental force was the post-Vietnam mood in the US: Americans seemed to oppose any "new" military undertakings, especially in the absence of existing firm commitments. The thrust of this opposition manifested itself in a host of other American policies and endeavours, including aid to anti-Communist factions in Angola and arms sales to various countries around the world, Iran and Pakistan in particular.

With the impetus provided by the new American President, the talks got under way, despite serious reservations in many quarters. But events in the Horn of Africa in 1977 and 1978 apparently convinced the US Administration that some sort of linkage between Soviet actions abroad and Soviet desires for detente ought to be established. Determined not to let the Strategic Arms Limitation Talks (SALT) become embroiled in such linkage, the President and his advisers apparently turned to other initiatives. It would seem that they focused on the Indian Ocean negotiations, and have thus effected a noticeable reduction in the urgency which they had previously commanded.

As for Diego Garcia, construction is proceeding according to the limited plans approved by Congress. Even when completed, the facility will be modest in nature. Nonetheless, the continuing development of the base, when taken in conjunction with the slowdown in Indian Ocean negotiations, can reasonably be viewed as a mild signal to the USSR that the US is unhappy with its current actions in the region. On the other hand, the American ambivalence demonstrated throughout 1978 can also be considered a signal to friendly nations and potential adversaries alike that the US will not take any stronger action until it clearly perceives that its own immediate vital interests are directly and critically involved.

Professor A. J. Cottrell and Rear-Admiral Robert J. Hanks

Military and Strategic Issues in the Middle East-Persian Gulf Region in 1978

During 1978, five events occurred in the Middle East-Persian Gulf region which helped to shape the emerging military and strategic relationships between the various parties. These were the Camp David accords between Egypt and Israel in August 1978 which raised the chances of a separate peace between the two most important military powers in the region; the PLO attack on Israeli civilians in March 1978 and the subsequent incursion by Israeli military forces into South Lebanon; the continuing controversy over the nature of the Arab-Israeli military balance, and the debate about the Carter Administration's decision to sell the highly sophisticated F-15 *Eagle* air-superiority fighter to Saudi Arabia; the continuing involvement of the Soviet Union and Cuba in the war in Ethiopia against the Eritreans; the domestic crisis and violence in Iran and the awesome possibility that the Shah might be overthrown, with unforeseen and potentially dramatic consequences for the Western world.

THE STRATEGIC IMPLICATIONS OF AN EGYPTIAN-ISRAELI PEACE

By the end of the year, enough groundwork had been established between Israeli and Egyptian peace negotiators for most observers to feel that, for the first time since the creation of the State of Israel in 1948, a separate peace between the two countries was possible. While much remained to be negotiated, speculation arose as to the military and strategic consequences of an Egyptian-Israeli peace. Such a treaty would not result in an immediate relaxation of military vigilance by either Egypt or Israel; indeed, both countries might spend more money in the short run as they re-established new defensive positions. Over time, however, each party would probably feel less threatened by the other and therefore feel less need to deploy large forces earmarked for a Sinai contingency. Of course, this process might be accelerated if joint Egyptian-Israeli ventures for the economic development of the Sinai were undertaken after a settlement.

An Egyptian-Israeli peace treaty would have most profound strategic consequences for the remaining Arab states. The balance of military power in 1978 between the antagonists (including Egypt) still favoured Israel, and this seemed likely to continue. Thus, in practical terms, a peace settlement would rule out a serious Arab war option for many years to come. The removal of the Egyptian military forces in one fell swoop would reduce Arab capabilities by almost two-thirds. While Syria, Jordan, Lebanon and Iraq might contemplate military activity against Israel's other borders, they would undoubtedly run a great risk of overwhelming retaliation. In these circumstances, it is difficult to imagine their current leaders deciding on such a course.

The *de facto* decoupling of the Arab-Israeli equation would have the further effect of theoretically "releasing" Egyptian forces for other military contingencies in Africa and the Arab world. Whether or not the Egyptian leadership would choose to play a more assertive military role in its relations with other states is difficult to tell. However, from the perspective of its Arab neighbours, especially Libya and Sudan, the prospects of armed confrontation with Egypt would now assume new and more serious proportions. The fact is that while Egypt's armed forces have always been compared unfavourably to Israel's in the context of inter-Arab or

African relations, they are a well organized and experienced force, and one of the best equipped. In theory, Egypt would be capable of soundly defeating Libya in the event of another war or skirmish between the two countries. It might also be able to assume a greater role throughout the Red Sea area as a "policeman," which might have special importance for the West if Iran were to abandon this declared role.

CHANGING PERCEPTIONS OF THE ARAB-ISRAELI MILITARY BALANCE

Despite the euphoria in most Western circles over the prospects of an Egyptian-Israeli peace, the possibility of failure was not entirely absent. Thus, concern about the military balance persisted.

The concept of a military balance in its common form of tabulated arsenals and stockpiles is a static picture of the strategic situation, frozen in time. This "static" balance must be contrasted with the "dynamic" balance between opposed military groupings. The former measures current inventories, force levels and overall posture, whereas the latter deals with inventory acquisitions and "lead time," changes in organization and force posturing, and evolution in battle doctrine. Thus a military balance is an attempt both to assess the war-fighting capability of opposing states and also to provide some means for estimating potential military capability over time. Defence policy must therefore be based on the perceived military balance, and especially on the emphasis of its future direction.

In the ME, the Arab-Israeli military balance has altered little since 1977.[1] However, the future military balance became the source of considerable controversy, especially in the context of US foreign and arms sales policy. Some American observers could foresee a deteriorating strategic situation for Israel in the medium term. Based upon gloomy Israeli General Staff scenarios, it was argued that, eventually, Israel could face a force of 14 Syrian, Jordanian and Iraqi divisions on its eastern front, together with an expanding modern Arab air force capable for the first time of serious offensive operations against Israel. The conclusion was that, while Israel would remain stronger than any combination of Arab forces through the next 18 months, its long-term future could be bleak.

An entirely different perception was aired by other commentators. Of particular interest was a controversial article appearing in the October 1977 issue of *Armed Forces Journal International* by Anthony Cordesman, a former US Defence Department official.[2] Based in part on Israeli force goals set forth in a 1974 plan called "Matmon B" (literally, "treasure"), Cordesman's figures raised the spectre of an Israeli "Goliath—a state able to wage aggressive war with minimal risk." Cordesman not only discounted potential Arab force build-ups, but also dismissed the possibility of Israel ever again having to face a united Arab coalition on three fronts: "Israel counts all major Arab forces in asking for aid, and not the major military threat."[3] In contrast, Egypt and Syria were portrayed as static war machines, unable to deploy even their combined strength because of unreadiness and inefficiency.

The impression of an unbridled Israeli war machine was further underscored by a report in the December issue of the same journal entitled, "Israel Asks $15 Billion, 10-year 'Matmon-C' New US Arms Package." In it, Benjamin Schemmer confirmed Cordesman's statistics of the "Matmon-B" request. According to these sources, "Matmon-B" had called for increases of 63% in the number of Israeli armoured divisions, 33% in armoured brigades, 100% in main battle tanks, 200% in armoured personnel carriers, 66% in artillery battalions, 233% in surface-to-surface missile batteries, and 36% in combat aircraft—*all* by 1986. The "Matmon-B" plan was clearly outdated by 1977, however. Schemmer took care to stress that a new "Matmon-C" plan placed far more emphasis on the transfer of technology than on equipment stockpiles. The essential components of the new Israeli aid request were Cobham armour, 12R improved *Maverick*, AIM-9L technology for *Shafrir III*, *Hellfire*, modified FLIR, and a 900% increase in anti-tank guided weapons.

The analysis presented by Cordesman was interesting because it reflected a distinct body of opinion in US defence and foreign policy circles which believes that Israel has exaggerated its defence needs. However, Cordesman and others overlooked two important factors in assessing the Arab-Israeli military balance. First, they focused only on the planned build-up on the side of Israel, ignoring that of its potential enemies. In the three years from 1975 to 1977, Egypt, Iraq, Jordan, Syria and Saudi Arabia—five states within near striking distance of Israel—spent an average of $15,477m a year on military programmes. Israel's annual defence effort averaged $4,011m, or 26%. Although Israel's relative position has indeed improved from 23.8% to 28.8% in three years, one might reason that this is hardly enough to create a "Goliath."

Furthermore, several bilateral Arab arms agreements promise to substantively reward massive government defence efforts. In the early months of 1977, Iraq made a reported $3 bn three-year arms deal with the Soviet Union. In February of 1978, Syria concluded an arms agreement with the USSR which, according to Israeli analysts, was the "largest ever signed by Moscow and an Arab country." [4] In the early summer of 1978, Saudi Arabia finally concluded negotiations for the purchase of substantial numbers of French *Mirage* F.1C, AMX-10 and AMX-30, and the US agreed to sell the F-15 *Eagle*. These were the largest deals; there were many others, covering the entire range of modern weapons and technology including *Mirage V*, *Lynx*, *Lupo* FF, *HOT, Milan, Swingfire, Redeye, HAWK*, and even 2,000 Pinzgauer all-terrain vehicles for the Syrian army. In any raw calculation, the five Arab "confrontation states" can hardly be said to possess "static" military establishments.

The second factor overlooked by Cordesman was the disparity between plans and their realization. Appearing soon after the traumas of the October War, "Matmon-B" represented a plan for drastically improving Israeli security. To this extent, it represented a "best-case" aid package which few Israelis expected to receive.

Irrespective of the merits and flaws of the Cordesman thesis, the article was to some extent a barometer of the perceived Arab-Israeli balance—especially in Washington. The appearance of articles calling, in effect, for a reversal of the traditional US-Israeli relationship of equal allies to one of client status for Israel was seen by some as a signal of a shifting climate of opinion in Washington. By labelling Israel "a militaristic state whose military build-up has gone far beyond the requirements of defence," and by making this pronouncement in a defence journal, Cordesman put in writing what many of his former colleagues had believed for a long time.

ISRAEL'S INTERVENTION IN LEBANON

If, by the beginning of 1978, Israel was viewed by some in Washington as approaching a "militaristic state . . . able to wage aggressive war with minimal risk," then the intervention in Lebanon by major units of the Israeli Defence Force (IDF) could only have added to that impression. (Also see essays, "South Lebanon" and "Armed Operations; The Situation along the Borders," in the section, The Arab-Israeli Conflict.) As an extension of existing policy, however, the military operation was strictly limited, both in scope and objective.

When PLO infiltrators fought a gun battle from a tour bus near Ma'agan Mikha'el on the Haifa–Tel Aviv road on 11 March, 32 Israeli civilians died. Two days later, Menahem Begin vowed that Israel "would cut off the evil arm of al-Fath." On the night of 14–15 March, two to three brigades (10–12,000 men) invaded South Lebanon and, supported by long columns of tanks, assaulted major PLO camps at al-Bass, Burj al-Shimālī and Rashīdiyya. At the same time, *Saar* and *Reshef*-class gunboats shelled Tyre and Saida, and attack aircraft hit both coastal cities and Beirut as well. The Chief of Staff, Lt-Gen Mordecai Gur, announced the creation of a "security belt" in South Lebanon, 10 km deep. The following border strongholds were seized: al-Nāqūra, Bint Jubayl, Mārūn al-Ra's, Yarūn, Alma al-Sha'b, al-Tayba, al-Khiyām, and Ibl al-Sāqī.

On 15 March, the Israeli High Command announced that operations had reached the "mopping-up stage." Gur reported that a night assault had initially been employed, involving mainly infantry forces, with air, naval, armour and engineering corps support. Toward morning, the operation had taken on a more mobile aspect, using combined infantry and armoured forces, again with artillery and air support and with naval forces operating along the coast. It had been a full-scale assault, with Israeli forces (reported at over 20,000) treating the then-estimated 5,000 PLO irregulars as a regular army. Support in the initial infantry assault was provided by a wide range of weapons including 175mm self-propelled artillery.

The Israeli intervention in Lebanon was not described by Israeli leaders as a punitive measure or a permanent occupation: its objective was the elimination of PLO strongholds. However, continued PLO rocket attacks on Israel from farther north prompted an Israeli advance beyond its self-declared "security belt." On 17 March, the stronghold of Tibnīn, 2.5 km north of the zone, fell.

On the same day, the US began to push in the Security Council for a UN peacekeeping force to separate the combatants in South Lebanon. A formal proposal was introduced to that effect on 18 March. Rocket attacks by the PLO across the occupied zone into Israel continued, however, and Gur warned that "we cannot tie ourselves down if they keep up the attacks." By a vote of 12–0, the Security Council decided on 19 March to create a peacekeeping force for Lebanon and called for an Israeli withdrawal (for Resolution, see essay on South Lebanon).

In order to create a buffer zone of sufficient depth to protect northern Israel from rocket attacks before the balance of the UN forces arrived, Israeli armoured columns were sent toward the Lītānī River and all major villages in the central-west section of the front were seized. The only exceptions were those border areas immediately adjacent to the Syrian frontier, and a stretch of the Mediterranean coast encompassing Tyre and the coastal road north to Saida. Israeli units took Bazūriyya, less than 4 km from Tyre, but did not make any move on the port itself.

By the end of 19 March, two of the three bridges across the Lītānī—the Khardalī and Qaqaiyya crossings—were covered by Israeli guns. The third, the Qāsimiyya bridge on the coastal road, was reached but deliberately left open. On 20 March, the Israeli move to the Lītānī was officially announced. On the following day, the Israeli Defence Minister, Ezer Weizman, proclaimed a ceasefire. There was to be a delay in the deployment of the 4,000-man UN peacekeeping force, but Israel began a phased withdrawal on or around 28 March. Although the spectre of a deadlock arose when Israel announced that it would not withdraw all of its troops until the PLO did the same, this was partially resolved by 6 April. A two-stage withdrawal was then agreed upon, to commence on 11 April.

Various questions were raised by the Israeli occupation, the first being whether the operation had achieved its objectives? Some wondered whether or not it had been "flawed" by Israeli inability to "cut off and destroy" PLO forces in South Lebanon.[5] It was assumed that Israeli intelligence was accurate enough to permit the use of airborne units deep in South Lebanon to close the exits to PLO forces in the South without, at the same time, arousing Syrian ire. The failure of Israel to capture, in the first moments of the incursion, the Lītānī bridges, the coastal road, or the mountain defile interdicting the road north to Bint Jubayl to prevent a PLO escape, was also criticized. (Also see discussion on this issue in the essay on South Lebanon.)

A second question was whether the Israeli forces could have caught and destroyed the 8,500–10,000 guerrilla irregulars south of the Lītānī on 14 March. In attempting an answer, several operational factors should be taken into consideration. First, the PLO irregular forces—dug-in and awaiting Israeli attack—fought well. Such groups as the Sā'iqa-Syrian unit of the PLO (by far the most effective combat force opposing the Israeli sweep), were led almost entirely by former non-commissioned officers in the Syrian army. Second, anticipating the defensive nature of PLO dispositions, the Israeli High Command followed a cautious operations plan in order to limit casualties. As it was, only 18 Israeli troops were killed in a week of combat, as opposed to some 250–400 PLO members.

The use of airborne forces to isolate and entrap the balance of PLO guerrillas south of the Lītānī would have demanded very large-scale operations. Only c. 2,000 PLO members were deployed in the initial area of Israeli incursion, whereas c. 7–8,000 were in rear echelon supporting positions farther north. A major airborne lift would have been required to contain these forces on the Lītānī until they could be destroyed.

A third question was whether much higher Israeli losses would have been justified in the destruction of more PLO personnel south of the Lītānī. It is quite possible that, given the shifting climate of opinion in the US toward Israel, a more intensive action would have been considered "extreme" and might have further eroded Israel's support in both the Administration and in Congress. In the Arab world, such an operation would probably have "hardened" the position of Egypt, as well as that of Syria and Jordan. Tenuous Egyptian-Israeli peace negotiations might have collapsed, and Syria would have been hard put to ignore the destruction of the PLO within a stone's throw of its forward occupying units in Lebanon.

It can therefore be argued that Israel's operations in South Lebanon were successful within the limits already imposed by political objectives. Al-Fath was evicted from Lebanon south of the Lītānī River; a buffer zone encompassing that area was created, policed by UN troops; Israeli losses were minimal; and the delicate state of Egyptian peace negotiations was not further jeopardized.

US ARMS SALES AND THE F-15 SALE TO SAUDI ARABIA

During the early months of the Carter Administration, the President decided to reduce the level of US arms sales to less-developed countries. The details of this decision were spelled out in several important policy statements, most notably in May 1977 when new goals and procedures for the transfer of conventional arms to all but the closest allies were set out. As these directives excluded NATO, Japan, Australia and New Zealand from the Administration's restrictive policy, it was assumed that the brunt of the reductions, slowdowns or delays in arms sales would be felt in the ME which, aside from the allied countries, accounted for nearly all major US exports. It was thus something of a surprise when in mid-1978 the Administration came out in favour of a multi-billion dollar arms sales package of modern jet airplanes to Egypt, Israel and Saudi Arabia. The real controversy concerned the proposed Saudi sale. The President had agreed that Saudi Arabia should be allowed to purchase up to 60 F-15 *Eagle* air-superiority fighters. Although Israel had already placed an order for the *Eagle* in 1976, the Saudi sale was seen as a new escalation of the ME arms build-up.

Supporters of the Saudi sale fell into two categories: those who generally approved a more "even-handed" US policy towards the Arabs; and those who, while regretting the need to sell such weapons to Arab states, nevertheless felt that countries like Saudi Arabia were too important to be alienated by a US refusal to sell arms. Critics of the agreement also fell into two general categories: those who were opposed, *a priori*, to arms sales to Arab states (including Israel's staunchest supporters in the US Congress); and those who, while accepting the need to sell arms to the Arabs, felt that the Administration had distorted the arguments in favour of the F-15 sale to Saudi Arabia on the one hand, and had ignored some of the fundamental strategic consequences of the action on the other. (Also see chapter on Saudi Arabia.)

In reality, both sides had plausible cases and both argued on geopolitical, economic and military grounds. Supporters claimed that Saudi Arabia was too important to ignore politically. Irrespective of its oil potential, the Saudi regime was conservative and had thwarted many pro-Soviet actions throughout the ME region. Furthermore, if Saudi Arabia was denied American airplanes, it could get similar—though not so sophisticated—weapons from France, and in the process become less amenable to holding down oil prices and increasing its own oil production. In military terms, the merits for the sale were less compelling but, in view of the troubles in the area, it was reasonable to argue that Saudi Arabia should have some means of protecting itself against potential hostile action from neighbouring radical Arab states, most notably South Yemen and Iraq.

Critics used similar arguments to oppose the sale. At the geopolitical level, while admitting the importance of Saudi Arabia, there was the feeling that US policy should try to minimize dependence on ME oil. Moreover, the US already had great bargaining power with the conservative Arabs, so that, if push came to shove, they would be unlikely to desert the US in reprisal against a delay or refusal of a particular arms sale. However, the most substantive argument of the critics was a military one. There was no doubt that the introduction of the F-15 into the Saudi inventory would make a difference to the overall Arab-Israeli balance—not in the short run because, as supporters correctly pointed out, it would take Saudi Arabia many years to maintain and operate such a sophisticated weapon. But, over time, the Administration's policy set a precedent of selling the most sophisticated weapons in the US inventory to important countries irrespective of their immediate military requirements, their technical competence to operate them, or, in reality, the end use to which the weapons might be put.

Although from the Israeli perspective this precedent was set in the early 1970s when the US agreed to sell Iran similar sorts of equipment, the Saudi F-15s would make a military difference which no Israeli planner could ignore. Furthermore, if the F-15s were taken in conjunction with other advanced weapons programmes that the Arab states had underway, the very favourable military balance currently in Israel's favour would change in the mid-1980s. The critics also pointed out that the Administration's argument that the Saudis had no interest in fighting Israel was not confirmed by the facts. The Saudis had contributed military forces to the Arab-Israeli wars in 1948, 1967 and 1973. Furthermore, they presently based most of their forces in the north, not in the south: with a larger military establishment, modern weapons and a new generation of leaders, it would be facile to say that they would not be prepared to fight against Israel in a future war.

THE SOVIET-CUBAN INVOLVEMENT IN ETHIOPIA
Throughout 1978 there were reports of continued fighting between Eritrean and Ethiopian forces in the Eritrean province. It was also reported that the Somalis,

having been ousted from the Ogaden earlier in the year, were still engaged in a guerrilla campaign against Ethiopian and Cuban forces in that region. It thus seemed that, after some major military successes in Angola and the Ogaden, the Soviet Union and Cuba were tied down in something of a quagmire in Ethiopia. This posed serious dilemmas, especially for the Cubans who in the past had been among the staunchest supporters of the Eritrean Liberation Front. Although details on Cuban casualties were hard to come by, some observers felt that a substantial loss of life might eventually sour the Cuban people to Fidel Castro's African adventures. To this extent, the continued involvement was something of a blessing to those in the Western world who had been pointing up the dangers of Soviet geopolitical gains in the region. A quick success against Eritrea would have paved the way for establishing major Soviet bases on the Red Sea which could have a serious impact on the balance of power in the region. Although most Arab states remained highly supportive of the Eritrean cause, there was evidence of a crack in the Eritreans' military front in November 1978. But it was not immediately possible to say whether this would lead to the Eritreans' military collapse, to a possible political settlement, or simply to a new phase of guerrilla warfare.

THE CRISIS IN IRAN

By far the most ominous event of the year was the crisis in Iran, with the protests and violence that erupted earlier in 1978 climaxing with the departure of Shah Pahlavi for an extended "vacation" in January 1979 and the precarious political environment caused by the impasse between Prime Minister Shahpur Bahktyar and the Muslim leader Ayatollah Khomeyni.

The strategic implications of a collapse in Iran would be of enormous consequence to the Western world. Even if the Shah were to regain control of the country, it is doubtful that Iran could, in the short run, resume its role as policeman of the Gulf. This would leave a vacuum since neither Saudi Arabia nor any of the Arab emirate states would be capable of assuming that task, although they would be able to provide funds for other countries, such as Jordan, to play a more active role. Even more serious, if anarchy or civil war broke out and the armed forces were not united—with some elements supporting revolutionary groups of both Left and Right—the potential for Soviet involvement would increase. In very blunt terms, the loss of Iran into the Soviet orbit would be a major disaster for the Western world. If Iran became a *de facto* Soviet satellite, Moscow would have the capacity to exert great influence over Gulf politics. *In extremis*, the Soviet Union would be able to use its military power to enforce its wishes on Gulf countries and, if necessary, interfere with Western oil supplies. Most observers felt that the Soviet Union would only exercise this option in the event of a major world crisis in which a showdown with the West seemed inevitable. Nevertheless, the chances of a Soviet "grab" for the Gulf were probably greater than an attack on Western Europe. However, the most accepted assumption was that the Soviet Union would use its political power to "Finlandize" the pro-Western Gulf states. Furthermore, it took little imagination to see that countries such as Japan would probably prefer to accommodate Soviet wishes in other areas—such as the Far East—rather than run the risk of having their oil cut off, with the subsequent disaster for the Western economic system. Hence the Soviet Union had everything to gain in the short run by not interfering directly in the Iranian situation.

Aside from Soviet involvement, the Iranian crisis was a major disaster for US foreign and arms sales policy. A neutral Iran, or even a friendly Iran, would probably not be able to afford to pay for all the current arms ordered from the US and Britain, and would almost certainly have to forego the long-term modernization plans envisaged by the Shah. If the relationship between the US and Iran were to deteriorate to the point where American property or civilians were threatened, the US would have to withdraw *all* technical advisers; if necessary, it could shut down the Iranian air force and important elements of the Iranian navy and army by withholding weapons spare parts. If a radical Iranian regime wished to turn to other suppliers such as the Soviet Union, it could do so but would pay a great price in terms of wasted energies and skills. (It should be remembered that the Shah "Americanized" most of the Iranian armed forces to the point where even the mechanics were taught English for their basic work on repairs of modern equipment.) In short, the prospects for Iran becoming a regional "super-power" by the mid-1980s—a projection often made in the mid-1970s—had all but vanished in the early months of 1979.

Another serious problem for the US related to the sensitivity of some of the American equipment Iran had purchased. Were the Soviet Union or its agents to get hold of F-14 aircraft and *Phoenix* missile systems, there would be a serious breach of security which would add to the debate in the US about the wisdom of selling such sophisticated weapons to potentially unstable governments. (See, for instance, the earlier discussion of F-15 sales to Saudi Arabia.) Another security problem for the US would be the denial of access to CIA-manned intelligence facilities, which for years have monitored Soviet military activity in its southern regions by using electronic surveillance devices located in northern Iran. Although none of these security breaches would be decisive in themselves, they would be symptomatic of a further erosion of American power and credibility in the area. The management of the Iranian crisis by the Washington Administration, together with its abrupt cancellation of the defence treaty with Taiwan, raised grave doubts in the minds of many local countries as to the long-term viability of American guarantees. All in all, the Iranian crisis threatened to sour, if not openly wreck, American diplomacy throughout the ME. At the time of writing, Saudi Arabia, Egypt and Israel, for different reasons, were increasingly of the opinion that the US could not be relied on in the future and that other foreign policy options would have to be considered.

Geoffrey Kemp and Michael Vlahos

NOTES
1. For the size and composition of the armed forces of individual states in the ME, see statistics following the Economic Section of each relevant chapter.
2. Anthony Cordesman, "The Arab-Israeli Balance: How Much is Too Much?" in *Armed Forces Journal International*, October 1977.
3. *Ibid.*, p. 36.
4. *The New York Times (NYT)*, 16 March 1978.
5. See, for instance, Drew Middleton, *NYT*, 20 March 1978.

The Middle East and Africa

African/ME relations continued to be dominated by four principal issues in 1978: the Arab-Israeli conflict; Arab and Israeli policies towards African conflicts; Afro-Arab economic co-operation; and, closely linked, the impact of higher oil prices on African economies.

AFRICAN ATTITUDES TO THE ARAB-ISRAELI CONFLICT

President Anwar al-Sādāt's peace initiative in the ME neatly divided the Arab states in Africa: Morocco and Sudan gave strong initial backing to his policy; Libya and Algeria were uncompromisingly hostile; while Tunisia characteristically remained neutral. Black Africa, however, was overwhelmingly in favour of the Egyptian initiative, although enthusiastic endorsement was reflected more in the African media than in public statements by the continent's leaders, most of whom privately supported the move but preferred to avoid unnecessary entanglements in inter-Arab conflicts. The attitude of most black African leaders was reflected by President Julius Nyerere of Tanzania when he said that his country would not resume relations with Israel until the Arab states did so, and "until the Palestinian people regain their rights in their homeland." [1] At the same time he asserted that there was an organic link, as well as mutual security interests, between Arabs and Africans since "what may happen in Africa will definitely have its effect on the Arab states and vice versa." The existence of strong support for Sādāt's initiative was shown by the success of Egyptian missions sent to various black African countries to win endorsement for it. According to Ambassador Ahmad Sidqī, his mission to ten West African states in December 1978/January 1979 had obtained "full support for President Sādāt's peace efforts" from Nigeria, Ghana, Togo, Ivory Coast, Liberia and Sierra Leone. (He did not give the results of his visit to Guinea, Guinea-Bissau, Gambia and Senegal.) [2]

The great majority of African leaders have always supported Israel's sovereignty within its 1967 borders, and few have showed much sympathy for the attitudes of the Arab "confrontation states." Nevertheless, in the absence of any final agreement between Egypt and Israel, and despite the strong private reservations of (arguably) a majority of member-states in the Organization of African Unity (OAU), that organization continued to adopt resolutions committing them to the maximalist position of the Arab states and the PLO as expressed in the three "Nos" of the Khartoum Declaration. It was interesting to reflect, five years later, that the resolution rubber-stamped by the OAU in the frenzied atmosphere following the October 1973 war was drafted by the Egyptians in the language of the PLO at its most obdurate. Although virtually all OAU members formally terminated their diplomatic relations with Israel in October 1973, a few countries (such as Lesotho, Mauritius, Swaziland, Malawi and Botswana) have never formally severed their ties, while others—notably Ivory Coast and Kenya—continue to maintain conspicuous economic and other links. The Presidents of Ivory Coast, Senegal and Zaïre also held private meetings with Israeli leaders in 1977 and 1978. Even the Ethiopian revolutionary regime maintained a military connection with Israel as late as the spring of 1978 (see below).

There was only one significant change in the OAU's position on the ME conflict during 1978. At its meeting in Tripoli from 20–28 February—three months after Sādāt's visit to Jerusalem—the OAU Council of Ministers reaffirmed its previous resolutions on the ME with the following additional clause: "Reaffirms its full backing for the Arab 'confrontation states' and the Palestinian people in their lawful struggle to regain, by every means, their occupied lands and usurped rights." The Egyptian delegation walked out of the Tripoli session on 20 February during an attack by President Qadhdhāfī in which he recalled that the Afro-Arab summit in Cairo in 1977 had agreed to an economic boycott of Israel and South Africa, adding: "Unfortunately, the Egyptian· government had failed to implement the boycott, and Israel thus had access to the Suez Canal."

However, solidarity with the "confrontation states"—in opposition to Egypt's position—found no place in the long resolution adopted by the OAU Council of Ministers five months later (7–18 July), an omission undoubtedly reflecting the influence of Sudan and Egypt on a summit held in Khartoum. The wording of its "Resolution on the Palestinian Issue" (reproduced in full in Appendix 1) is compatible with Security Council Resolutions 242 and 338, as well as with President Sādāt's formula in his negotiations with Israel. Thus, it speaks of the "Palestinian people's legitimate and inalienable right to their homeland, including their rights to self-determination, to sovereignty, and to the establishment of their independent state on their territory." A more ambiguously worded resolution was also agreed at Khartoum in support of UN Resolution 32/4B on the observance of an International Day of Solidarity with the Palestinian people on 29 November of each year. This resolution "invites the peoples of African states and all peace-loving peoples to support the Palestinian people in their just struggle to liberate their land and return to their homeland." After hearing a statement by a PLO representative, the OAU Council of Ministers adopted another resolution requesting the Arab League to grant observer status to African liberation movements (see Appendix II).

Israel's economic and other relations with South Africa—which expanded considerably during the period of Premier Yitzhak Rabin's government and, more so, after the formation of Premier Menahem Begin's coalition—provided effective ammunition for the Palestinians' cause. (Until the Security Council made the arms embargo against SA mandatory in late 1977, Israel had sold it certain types of weapons, although it denied allegations of exchanging nuclear research information.) The fierceness of emotions aroused by Israeli-South African ties was illustrated by a statement made by the Chairman of the OAU for 1978–79, President Numayrī of Sudan, in opening the Council of Ministers meeting on 7 July 1978: "Cohesion between South Africa and Israel, and their efforts to co-ordinate their economy and war policies, makes it incumbent on the thoughtful leaders of our continent to confront the danger by an Afro-Arab response so that our forces will be unified in a degree commensurate with the danger menacing us from the south and the north." [3] The growing Israeli-South African connection was particularly embarrassing to African leaders anxious to play a more positive role in helping to mediate in the ME conflict.

Apart from Israel, the other notable target for OAU attack was Iran which under the Shah had supplied 95% of all South Africa's oil imports. African attitudes showed a considerable hardening towards the Shah's rule during 1978. At the beginning of the year, the OAU sent a mission to all the major oil-producing countries (Venezuela, Ecuador, Indonesia, Malaysia, Abu Dhabi, Kuwait, Saudi Arabia, Qatar and Iraq) to persuade them to support an oil embargo against South Africa and Rhodesia. Only Iran refused to receive the mission. The OAU press spokesman, Dr Peter Onu, said the reason given for Iran's refusal was that it did not consider oil a political weapon. However, the Shah said he was willing to receive the OAU mission delegates as "tourists"—a proposal described by Dr Onu as "a snub" to the OAU. The organization also strongly criticized the Shah's regime for seeking to intervene in African affairs by its proposal that anti-Soviet nations should provide military support for Somalia in its conflict with Ethiopia (see also essay, "Regional Politics in the Red Sea, Indian Ocean and Persian Gulf").

ARAB AND ISRAELI INTERVENTION IN AFRICAN CONFLICTS

The states of the ME played a considerable role in African conflicts during 1978. However, the Arab states took different sides in most cases, their positions not always reflecting the same pattern of alliances as in the ME context. In the Horn of Africa, for example, Egypt, Iraq, Syria and the Gulf states—as well as Iran—supported Somalia and the Eritreans against the Ethiopian military regime; while South Yemen, Libya and the Palestinian organizations sided with the Ethiopians—along with the Israelis, Cubans and Russians (see *Middle East Contemporary Survey [MECS] 1976–77*, pp. 57ff). This curious alignment of forces had its origins in a variety of particularist interests in the Red Sea region going back to the time of Emperor Haile Selassie's reign and the early period of President Nāsir's rule in Egypt.

The late Emperor, with his strong suspicions of Arab ambitions in the Muslim coastal areas of Ethiopia, had established particularly close military ties with Israel. This axis provided a reason, or at least a pretext, for the Arab states to work against the Emperor's rule. Nāsir had been the first to promote the idea of turning the Red Sea into an "Arab lake"—partly as a means of tightening the blockade against Israel. Saudi Arabia, which had always been suspicious of Nāsir's real intentions, saw his policy in the Red Sea as being directed as much against itself as against the Israelis; but with the advent of Sādāt, and especially after the Russians became allied to Somalia, the Saudis began to play a leading role in promoting the idea of an "Arab lake"—a policy it pursued in close accord with Egypt and Sudan.

When the Eritrean liberation struggle was launched in the early 1960s, Nāsir was the first Arab leader to realize that, by supporting it, he could weaken Haile Selassie's rule. On their side, the Eritreans initially considered that the Arabs would be their closest allies; therefore, despite the fact that perhaps fewer than half the Eritreans are Muslim, the Eritrean Liberation Front (ELF) projected its rebellion as a Muslim struggle against "Amhara Christian domination." These tactics won the support of Libya, Syria and Iraq, as well as of Egypt. The Eritreans were also able to attract some support from the Russians and Cubans—to whom they emphasized their opposition to the American and Israeli "puppet," Haile Selassie. This was the background to the incongruous alliances which developed as the conflicts in the Red Sea area intensified. The pattern became even more complex after the Russians and Cubans withdrew their support from Somalia in favour of Ethiopia in 1977. With its Moscow and Havana orientation, South Yemen joined the alliance system with Addis Ababa; Libya did as well, but for a different reason—because it shared the Ethiopian regime's hostility to Sudan and Egypt.

Notwithstanding its growing ties with the Russians and Cubans, the Ethiopian military regime was still anxious to retain Israeli support—both because it did not wish to become altogether dependent on its Communist allies, and because of the Ethiopian army which held the Israelis in high esteem. Israel's interest was to prevent the Arabs from succeeding in gaining complete control over the Red Sea through the secession of Eritrea. Notwithstanding the paradox, Ethiopia's military ruler, Col Mengistu Haile Mariam, found it expedient to maintain close military links with Israel. This continued until February 1978 when that country's Foreign Minister, Moshe Dayan, incautiously spoke in public of Israel's support for Ethiopia. Mengistu then felt that he had no option but to submit to pressure from his allies and end the association. All military contacts between Israel and Ethiopia were effectively cut.

The massive Soviet/Cuban commitment to Ethiopia after 1977 intensified the fears of anti-Communist regional powers—Saudi Arabia, Sudan, Egypt and Iran—causing them to increase their commitments to the Somalis, and the former three to the Eritreans. Iraq and to a lesser extent Syria also maintained their support for the Eritreans and Somalis. In fact, when the Soviets launched their massive airlift of arms to the Ethiopians in late 1977, Ahmad al-Bakr refused to allow them to over-fly Iraq, making his decision public in an interview to a Washington weekly.[4]

This Arab support for the Eritreans and Somalis—at a time when the Somali Republic's army was fighting in the Ogaden in support of the secessionist West Somali Liberation Front—was strongly criticized by a majority of black African countries, led by Kenya and Tanzania. They based their stand on the OAU Charter which categorically rejects violence as a means of changing established borders. In their view, a majority of Arab states were intent on carving up Ethiopia. Thus an influential Nigerian political weekly wrote: "Of all the external intruders in the Ethiopian-Somali conflict, the Arab intervention is the most effective and deadly."[5]

At the time of the Somalis' military (though not yet final political) defeat in the Ogaden in March 1978, the future of Eritrea was still undecided, a situation which produced several particularly sharp contradictions. The Cubans, South Yemenis and Libyans had been unwilling—at least initially—to commit themselves to the kind of military operation just completed in the Ogaden because of the support they had given to the Eritrean struggle in the days of Haile Selassie. Saudi Arabia, while supporting the Eritrean cause, did not wish to see the Eritrean People's Liberation Front (EPLF)—the strongest of the three liberation forces—emerge victorious because of its leaders' support for Marxist-Leninist ideas: a Marxist Eritrea was only slightly less welcome to the Saudis than a Soviet-influenced Ethiopia. The Saudis therefore sought to strengthen the role of the smallest of the three Eritrean movements—the Eritrean Liberation Front-Popular Liberation Forces (ELF-PLP), led by Osman Sabbe. But—and this was another contradiction—Sabbe was also supported by the Syrians and Libyans. The reason for this was that he had been instrumental in nailing the Eritrean flag to the mast of Islam, and had become the principal "treasurer" of the movement in Arab capitals. Osman Sabbe's front gained in strength towards the end of 1978 when the big Ethiopian army push in Eritrea (which began in April), succeeded in seriously weakening the Eritrean Liberation Front (ELF); many ELF cadres chose to join him rather than the EPLF.

Despite the massive input of sophisticated Soviet weapons, the Ethiopian army still failed in its objective of crushing the Eritrean opposition during 1978. The tenacity of the Eritrean resistance—together with the reluctance of the Cubans, South Yemenis and Libyans to take up arms against it—was a major obstacle hindering the consolidation of Mengistu's Marxist-Leninist revolution. The Soviet-Cuban plan for overcoming this difficulty was to persuade the Ethiopian and Eritrean leaderships to agree to a "Marxist-Leninist federation of Ethiopian and Eritrean states," which would give the Eritreans a considerable measure of autonomy but not complete independence.

While the Russians used their influence to weaken the Mengistu regime's opposition to their federal plan, the Cubans, South Yemenis and Palestinians tried to promote the idea with the EPLF and ELF. However, it was unacceptable to both sides—just as in 1976-77 Somalia had rejected a similar plan to establish a federation between itself and the Ethiopians.

Because of the different elements within the PLO, the Palestinians were able to play a number of different roles in the conflict. Initially, the Palestinians and Eritreans were both opposed to Haile Selassie's Ethiopia and to his reliance on

Israel for counter-guerrilla activity in Eritrea. In practical terms, Eritrean guerrillas trained with PLO cadres, while the EPLF and ELF foreign missions shared common experiences with Palestinians in different Arab capitals. The divisions within the Eritrean movement had also resulted in its different factions identifying with particular factions in the PLO. The closest links, though, were with the Popular Democratic Front for the Liberation of Palestine (PDFLP). Its leader, Nā'if Hawātima, was the principal link between the Russians, the EPLF and ELF. The PDFLP had an office in Addis Ababa as well as in Aden; the PLO and the Popular Front for the Liberation of Palestine (PFLP) were also allowed to open offices in the Ethiopian capital in 1977. On at least one occasion in the latter part of 1978, Moscow asked the PLO leader, Yāsir 'Arafāt, to undertake a special mission to Mengistu to try to reach agreement on the federation plan with Eritrea. These moves to reconcile the Eritrean and Ethiopian positions had made no substantial progress by the end of 1978.

The Ethiopian regime's relations with the Palestinians (as well as with the South Yemenis and Libyans) produced yet another contradictory situation, since many of Mengistu's speeches consisted of bitter tirades against "the Arabs' wish to dominate the Red Sea and carve up Ethiopia." However, he began to adopt a more sophisticated line in 1978 by distinguishing between the "reactionary pro-imperialist Arab leaders" and the "progressive" Arab forces. The Palestinians could thus emerge to play a leading role in Addis Ababa as the "progressive Arab vanguard."

The PFLP, led by Dr George Habash, was a member of the preparatory committee which organized the Afro-Arab Solidarity Conference that opened in Addis Ababa on 17 September 1978 with speeches by Fidel Castro and Mengistu Haile Mariam. The resolutions pertaining to the ME conflict reiterated strong support for the PLO as "the genuine representative of the Palestinian Arab people"; condemned the "unilateral attempt made to resolve the conflict between Israel and Arab countries"; and supported the Palestinian Arabs who, "resisting the continuous conspiracy of imperialism, Zionism and reactionary Arabs, struggle for their national rights and self-determination, and to form their own government in their own land." Another resolution strongly criticized China for "supporting aggression against Angola, Ethiopia and Vietnam." The conference noted with "consternation and anger the collaboration of the Chinese leaders with the reactionary imperialist and fascist governments of Chile, the racists of South Africa and Israel. . . . The anti-Soviet stance of the Chinese leaders has become an obstacle for the struggle of national liberation movements."

The coalition of anti-Communist Arab states, which had crystallized around the struggle in the Horn of Africa, was also active in other conflict situations in the continent. Thus, when Zaïre's copper-rich province of Shaba was twice invaded from across the Angolan border by anti-Mobutu elements in 1977 and 1978, Egypt and Sudan both gave active military support to Kinshasa. The principal mover in both those military operations was Morocco, whose policies closely accorded with Egypt's and Saudi Arabia's. The Saudis were also reported to have contributed substantially to a £10m fund for Jonas Savimbi's UNITA forces, the principal antagonists against President Agostinho Neto's MPLA regime in Angola.

King Khālid expressed Saudi Arabia's concern about "the spread of Russian influence in Africa" during visits he made to Washington and Paris in 1978. After his talks with President Giscard d'Estaing in May 1978, there were reports of a three-way link between Saudi Arabia, Morocco and France in resisting Soviet influence, as well as over the conflict in the Western Sahara.[6] Although the Saudis took the side of the Moroccans and Mauritanians, most Arab governments avoided partisanship in the Sahara conflict. The Arab League sought to play a mediatory role, but with conspicuous lack of success. The Arab countries also largely sought to avoid taking sides in the conflict between Libya and Chad, but did give their support to President Numayrī's mediation efforts.

AFRO-ARAB CO-OPERATION AND THE RISE IN OIL PRICES

The Arab oil-producing countries had made grants and loans totalling $3 bn to non-Arab African countries by the beginning of 1978. The Arab Bank for Economic Development in Africa (BADEA), which started operations in 1975, approved just over $261m in soft loans to non-members of the Arab League during the first two years of its operations. The Tunisian president of BADEA, Dr Chedli Ayari, insisted that the Arabs were not helping Africa in order to repay a debt of gratitude for any support received for Arab causes, particularly that of the Palestinians.[7] "The Arabs owe Africa nothing," Dr Ayari said at a press conference in London. "The causes Africans are supporting and upholding are Afro-Arab causes; and the aid we are giving the Africans is part and parcel of a mutual commitment to co-operation and solidarity."

Following the Afro-Arab summit in Cairo in March 1977, a permanent Ministerial Committee for Afro-Arab Co-operation was set up, partly for the purpose of discussing the allocation of the $1,462 bn pledged by the oil-producing ME states. However, only a small part of the funds committed were in fact channelled into the multilateral funds of BADEA, the African Development Bank (ADB) or the OAU. Thus, of the $1 bn pledged by Saudi Arabia, $850m went to the Saudi Development Fund for spending on African projects; $120m was allocated to BADEA, $12m to the ADB, and $2m to the six recognized liberation movements in Southern Africa. Kuwait's commitment of $241m was divided between the Kuwait Fund for Arab Economic Development ($200m) for use in Africa; BADEA ($20m) and ADB ($10m). Another $10m was earmarked for feasibility studies and $2m for the Southern Africa liberation movements. The United Arab Emirates' commitment of $137m was channelled through the Abu Dhabi Fund for Arab Economic Development ($100m), BADEA ($20m), ADB ($10m), feasibility studies ($5m) and the Southern Africa liberation movements (2m). Qatar's pledge of $80m went to the Qatar Development Bank ($50m), BADEA ($20m), ADB ($5m), feasibility studies ($3m) and liberation movements ($2m). Libya made no direct commitment to the Cairo fund, but pledged $2m to the liberation movements, to whom Egypt and Jordan also gave $1m each.

BADEA and the UN Economic Commission for Africa (ECA) reached an agreement in March 1977 to ensure better co-ordination and more efficient implementation of their activities. The BADEA Board of Governors decided in December 1977 to increase the bank's capital by half, but gave no details about how the increase was to be financed other than to announce that some member-states had increased their shareholding by 100%. (For subscriptions and voting powers of BADEA member-states, see Appendix III.) Dr Ayari also announced after the meeting of Governors in December that a decision had been taken to establish a consultancy company to recruit Arab technical personnel for BADEA-financed projects. He added that a marked feature of all Arab institutions was the growing integration of Arab technical experts into African development programmes.

The Permanent Ministerial Committee for Afro-Arab Co-operation (see above) held its first meeting in Yaounde (Cameroon) in May 1977. Dr Sayyid Nawfal, the Arab League's representative, announced that the $11m aid pledged to the African liberation movements would be channelled through the OAU. The Permanent Committee held its second meeting in Cairo at the end of October 1977, when it was agreed to establish four co-operation committees on agriculture, communications and transport, industry, and culture and education.

An Afro-Arab conference of trade union leaders met in Algiers from 16–21 October 1978 to discuss closer co-operation in the field of labour relations. Such a meeting had first been mooted in 1975 by the International Arab Trade Union Confederation (IATUC), but at the time it had been confined to establishing closer ties with francophone African trade unions only. The OAU, however, proposed that the framework should include all African trade unions. The Arab League provided $50,000 to its affiliate Arab Labour Organization (ALO) to convene the conference in association with the IATUC, the OAU and the Algerian General Federation of Workers. One commentator summed up the conference by pointing out that Afro-Arab labour relations, "just like Afro-Arab relations in other fields, are still only tentative, and both sides are trying to probe each other's intentions and goals. For many years the Israeli trade union federation, the Histadrut, was active in Africa, but its role has been strongly challenged since the 1973 Arab-Israeli war." [8]

The main cause of tension between black African states and the Arab world since 1973 has been the quadrupling of oil prices. Although a formula was reached within the framework of Afro-Arab co-operation to provide a measure of compensation for the poorer African countries who suffered the greatest burden from higher oil import costs, the amounts offered were felt to be unsatisfactory by a number of African governments. This cause of friction between Arab oil-producers and African countries was further accentuated by the decision of OPEC countries in late 1978 to raise oil prices again by a further 14–15%.

Colin Legum

NOTES
1. Interview with *al-Ittihād*, Abu Dhabi; quoted by R Abu Dhabi, 11 August 1977.
2. *West Africa,* London; 8 January 1979.
3. R Omdurman, 7 July 1978.
4. *Newsweek,* Washington; 10 July 1978.
5. *Afriscope,* Lagos; September 1977.
6. *The Guardian,* Manchester; 30 May 1978.
7. *Voice,* London; 1 August 1978.
8. *The Middle East,* London; November 1977.

THE MIDDLE EAST AND AFRICA

APPENDIX I: OAU COUNCIL OF MINISTERS RESOLUTION ON THE PALESTINIAN ISSUE (CM/RES. 632/XXXI)

Having studied the OAU Administrative Secretary-General's report on the developments of the Palestinian issue (Doc CM/881(XXXI); having heard the statements made by various delegations and in particular the statement made by the representative of the PLO; recalling the resolutions adopted at previous sessions of the Assembly of Heads of State and Government and the Council of Ministers on the ME and the Palestinian issue; recalling also the report of the *Ad-Hoc* Committee on the exercising by the Palestinian people of their inalienable rights, which reaffirms the Palestinian people's legitimate and inalienable right to their homeland including their rights to return to self-determination, to sovereignty, and to the establishment of their independent state on their territory; guided by the principles and objectives of the OAU and UN Charters, the common destiny of the African and Arab peoples and their continuous joint struggle against Zionism and racism for the sake of freedom, independence and peace; recalling that the Palestinian issue is the core of the ME conflict, and that the PLO is the sole legitimate representative of the Palestinian people; taking cognizance of the statements made on the Palestinian issue and the critical situation currently prevailing as a result of the perpetuation of the Israeli occupation of Palestine and the Arab territories, and of Israel's denial of the legitimate and inalienable rights of the Palestinian people, as well as Israel's refusal to abide by the UN General Assembly resolutions; aware of the fact that the Palestinian issue is an Arab and African one; reaffirming the legitimate character of the struggle being waged by the Palestinian people under the leadership of the PLO, with a view to recovering their national rights; reaffirming as well that it is impossible to achieve a just and durable peace without the withdrawal of Israel from the occupied Arab territories and its recognition of the legitimate rights of the Palestinian people; noting that the alliance between the Zionist regime in Israel and the racist regime in Rhodesia and South Africa aim at the pursuit of a policy of terrorism and liquidation of the Palestinian and Arab peoples in the occupied Arab territories, of the African peoples in South Africa, Namibia and Zimbabwe, and that Israel and the racist regimes resort to the same means; denouncing the repeated Israeli acts of aggression against the Palestinian people, both inside and outside occupied Palestine, as evidenced by the daily acts of repression and terrorism, as well as the establishment of settlements and the alteration of geographical, demographic and cultural features, which constitute an overt and glaring violation of the 14th Geneva Convention on the protection of civilians in times of war. These acts of aggression reached their climax when Israel invaded South Lebanon, thus confirming its aggressive and expansionist nature:

1. Reaffirms all the resolutions previously adopted by the Council, as well as its total and effective support to the Palestinian people under the leadership of the PLO, their sole legitimate representative, as well as their right to return to their homeland, [to] sovereignty, to self-determination and to the establishment of their independent state;

2. Reaffirms its support to the Palestinian people in their legitimate struggle, by all available means, including armed combat, for the sake of recovering their usurped rights;

3. Vigorously denounces the aggressive Israeli schemes and ambitions as well as Israel's policy of expansion aimed at the Palestinian people, which reached its climax in the occupation of South Lebanon last March;

4. Condemns once again the unholy alliance between the Zionist regime in Israel and the racist regimes in South Africa, Zimbabwe and Namibia, and imperialism; urges all member-states to face the dangers of this alliance aimed at the Arab and African peoples, while affirming that the most efficient means of facing racists, Zionists and imperialists is armed struggle;

5. Calls on the international community to further isolate Israel at diplomatic, economic, political and military levels, in implementation of the UN Charter;

6. Requests the states that have as yet not explicitly recognized the rights of the Palestinian people, which have been sanctioned by international charters and resolutions, and in particular the US, to confirm these rights and to recognize the PLO as the sole legitimate representative of the Palestinian people;

7. Concurs with the recommendations of the UN Committee entrusted with the exercising by the Palestinian people of their legitimate and inalienable rights, particularly their right to return to their homeland, to self-determination and to the establishment of their independent state;

8. Requests further that the Security Council reconsiders its attitude as regards the recommendations of that Committee, since they henceforth constitute the will of the international community, as they have been adopted by the UN General Assembly at its 31st session;

9. Requests the Administrative Secretary-General to follow the developments of the Palestinian issue and to report back to the Council of Ministers at its next ordinary session.

APPENDIX II: OAU COUNCIL OF MINISTERS RESOLUTION ON GRANTING OF OBSERVER STATUS TO AFRICAN LIBERATION MOVEMENTS IN THE ARAB LEAGUE (CM/RES.644/XXXI)

Having attentively listened to the statement of the representatives of the PLO; noting the similarity of the struggles of the Palestinian people and the African people against Zionism and colonialism; further noting the need of members of the League of Arab States and the PLO of being appraised on the latest developments in the liberation struggle in the southern part of Africa, and in conformity with the spirit of Afro-Arab co-operation in all fields:

Requests the Administrative Secretary-General to contact his counterpart in the League of Arab States with a view to granting observer status in the League of Arab States to African liberation movements recognized by the QAU [and] Arab League.

STATEMENT OF SUBSCRIPTIONS AND VOTING PGWER OF MEMBER STATES OF BADEA

Members	Subscriptions			Votes attributed	
	Amounts (in US dollars)	Shares	% of total	Number of voices	% of total
Jordan	1,000,000	10	0.43	210	3.56
UA Emirates	20,000,000	200	8.66	400	6.76
Bahrain	1,000,000	10	0.43	210	3.56
Tunisia	5,000,000	50	2.17	250	4.23
Algeria	20,000,000	200	8.66	400	6.76
Saudi Arabia	50,000,000	500	21.65	700	11.84
Sudan	1,000,000	10	0.43	210	3.56
Syria	1,000,000	10	0.43	210	3.56
Iraq	30,000,000	300	12.99	500	8.46
Oman	4,000,000	40	1.73	240	4.06
Qatar	20,000,000	200	8.66	400	6.76
Kuwait	20,000,000	200	8.66	400	6.76
Lebanon	5,000,000	50	2.17	250	4.23
Libya	40,000,000	400	17.32	600	10.15
Egypt	1,000,000	10	0.43	210	3.56
Morocco	10,000,000	100	4.32	300	5.07
Mauritania	1,000,000	10	0.43	210	3.56
Palestine	1,000,000	10	0.43	210	3.56
Total	**231,000,000**	**2,310**	**100.0**	**5,910**	**100.00**

Absolute majority: 2,956 voices.
Source: BADEA Annual Report.

ARAB INSTITUTIONS FOR DEVELOPMENT ASSISTANCE: LENDING THROUGH 1977

	Loan Commitments (millions)	Number of Loans	Number of Recipient Countries
National institutions			
Abu Dhabi Fund	Dh 1,599.0 ($406)	45	24
Kuwait Fund	KD 469.9 ($1,560)	114	40
Saudi Fund	SRIs 5,526.0 ($1,568)	54	29
Regional institutions			
BADEA	$209.6	29	21
Arab Fund	KD 295.3 ($1,018)	48	14
Islamic Bank	ID 61.4 ($74)	12	11

Data: Annual Reports of the institutions.

ARAB INSTITUTIONS FOR DEVELOPMENT ASSISTANCE

Institution and Location	Date of Effective Agreement	Initial Authorized Capital	First Loan Approved	1978 Authorized Capital	Type of Assistance	Scope of Assistance	Loan Commitments in 1977	Loan Commitments in First half of 1978
National institutions								
Abu Dhabi Fund for Arab Economic Development—Abu Dhabi, UAE	July 1971	Dh 500m	1974	Dh 2 bn ($513m)	Soft loans for capital projects; equity participation; technical assistance	African, Asian, and Islamic countries	Dh 539m ($138m)	Dh 100m ($26m)
Kuwait Fund for Arab Economic Development—Kuwait City	Dec 1961	KD 50m	1962	KD 1bn ($3.57bn)	Soft loans for capital projects; technical assistance	All developing countries	KD 132m ($460m)	KD 26m ($94m)
Saudi Development Fund—Riyadh, Saudi Arabia	Sept 1974	SRIs 10bn	March 1975	SRIs 10bn ($2.83 bn)	Project finance	All developing countries	SRIs 3,148m ($893m)	SRIs 1,433m ($412m)
Regional institutions								
Arab Bank for Economic Development in Africa—Khartoum, Sudan	Feb 1974	$231m	Jan 1975	$392m	Concessionary project loans; technical assistance	African countries	$66m	$21m
Arab Fund for Social and Economic Development—Kuwait City	Dec 1971	KD 102m	Feb 1974	KD 400m ($1.43 bn)	Soft loans for capital projects; technical assistance	Arab League members	KD 104m ($363m)	—
Islamic Development Bank—Jidda, Saudi Arabia	April 1975	ID 2 bn	Oct 1976	ID 2bn ($2.43 bn)	Noninterest-bearing project loans; equity participation; foreign trade financing	Islamic countries and communities	ID 55m ($67m)	ID 14m ($18m)

Data: Annual Reports of the institutions; Arab Fund for Social and Economic Development, *Summary of Loans and Technical Assistance Extended to Developing Countries,* First and Second Quarters of 1978.

ARAB INSTITUTIONS FOR DEVELOPMENT ASSISTANCE: LOANS BY SECTOR THROUGH 1977 (%)

	Agriculture	Industry	Infra-structure	Other
National institutions				
Abu Dhabi Fund	3.3	37.1	50.7	8.9
Kuwait Fund	17.5	23.1	54.6	4.7
Saudi Fund	7.6	15.7	72.6	4.1
Regional institutions				
BADEA	5.5	22.0	61.6	10.9
Arab Fund	9.4	22.3	66.3	2.0
Islamic Bank	8.0	—	83.4	8.6

Data: Annual Reports of the institutions; Chase World Information Corporation, *Arab Aid: Who Gets It, For What, and How* (New York, 1978).

ARAB INSTITUTIONS FOR DEVELOPMENT ASSISTANCE: LOANS BY COUNTRY GROUP THROUGH 1977 (%)

	Arab Countries	Non-Arab African Countries	Non-Arab Asian Countries	Other
National institutions				
Abu Dhabi Fund	79.9	4.1	16.0	—
Kuwait Fund	69.1	10.2	20.6	—
Saudi Fund	53.2	9.7	33.6	3.5
Regional institutions				
BADEA	—	100.0	—	—
Arab Fund	100.0	—	—	—
Islamic Bank	63.7	26.4	9.9	—

Data: Annual Reports of the institutions.

Source (of four preceding tables): *IMF Survey*, 5 February 1979.

THE ARAB-ISRAELI CONFLICT

The Egyptian-Israeli Negotiations

From their inception until the conclusion of the Camp David conference, the course of the Egyptian-Israeli negotiations divided into two distinctive phases: from the Dayan-Tuhāmī talks in September 1977 to the collapse of the Political Committee in January 1978; and from Ambassador Atherton's first shuttle later that month until the signature of the Camp David agreements in September 1978. (The ensuing negotiations over the Egyptian-Israeli peace treaty marked a third stage not surveyed in this volume.)

In the preliminary Egyptian-Israeli contacts and during Sādāt's visit to Israel, both Begin and Sādāt were most probably surprised by what the other was ready to concede so as to offer an incentive for a dialogue towards peace and to facilitate its course. This included Begin's willingness to give up the whole of Sinai right away and Sādāt's willingness to sign a full-fledged peace with Israel (which Begin had formerly held that no Arab was willing to do). Although it could be demonstrated that Sādāt's concept of settling the Arab-Israeli conflict was the outcome of a gradual development starting years earlier, his visit to Jerusalem nevertheless constituted a departure, not only from the orthodox Arab approach, but from his own earlier views. Begin too departed radically from concepts and positions he had championed as the Opposition leader. By Sādāt's own testimony, the welcome he received in Israel surprised him, while the intense desire for peace reflected in the demonstrations in Egypt in support of Sādāt's initiative impressed many Israelis.

Soon after their talks in Jerusalem, however, both Sādāt and Begin apparently had second thoughts, to the effect of having unnecessarily given away too much. Such doubts were possibly reinforced by opposition to their moves, the extent of which neither had apparently foreseen: Begin was attacked for his Sinai concessions by members of his own party as well as by Labour, while Sādāt was criticized throughout the Arab world.

On the basis of the initial generosity displayed by both, each had apparently overestimated the other's readiness for further concessions. Begin seemed to believe that Sādāt could be made to sign a separate peace; Sādāt apparently believed that his visit, his implied recognition of Israel and his willingness to sign a peace treaty with her had made his overall view of the settlement—particularly regarding Israel's withdrawal from the West Bank—acceptable to Begin. By the time they met again in Ismāʿīliyya, both had retreated to less forthcoming positions. Sādāt would not move any further towards a peace treaty which in any way resembled a separate deal. He now sought an Israeli renunciation of any territorial or political claim to the West Bank and the Gaza Strip, hoping thereby to facilitate Jordan's joining the negotiations. This was unacceptable to Begin, whose basic objective was to get Egypt to agree to the preservation of Israel's hold over the West Bank and Gaza Strip in exchange for Sinai. This objective was reflected in Begin's Peace Plan of December 1977 which envisaged administrative autonomy for the Arab residents of the West Bank and Gaza Strip. Furthermore, Sādāt apparently retracted his initial acceptance of demilitarization of all of Sinai east of the Mitla and Gidi passes. Begin, for his part, now maintained that his offer to return Sinai to Egypt did not signify the evacuation of the Israeli settlements and airfields. Begin now also yielded to internal pressures and allowed Agriculture Minister Sharon to take action on his settlement projects in Sinai and the West Bank. An atmosphere of mutual distrust, disappointment and bitter recrimination soon prevailed, ending in the collapse of the Political Committee on 18 January 1978. Even American mediation, now invoked by both sides (despite their original attempts to dispense with it), failed to produce an agreed "statement of principles" regarding the Palestinian question phrased so as to enable Jordan to join the negotiations and Egypt to progress towards a Sinai settlement.

The failure affected US participation in the Egyptian-Israeli negotiations: the Administration soon moved from the role of mediator or "honest broker" (which Israel thought it should play) towards that of "active partner."

The Carter Administration's view of a ME settlement had all along been closer to Israel's than to Egypt's with respect to the "nature of peace," yet closer to Egypt's view on the territorial and Palestinian questions. The American and Egyptian positions moved closer still as a result of the Carter-Sādāt talks in January and February 1978. This was followed by intensive American efforts to get Israel to accept the US position that, in terms of Security Council Resolution 242, Israeli withdrawal should apply to the West Bank as well as to other fronts, and that the Palestinians should be enabled to participate in determining their own future. The US also insisted that Israeli settlements in the territories occupied in 1967 were illegal and constituted an obstacle to peace. The Administration's efforts included attempts to expose Begin to criticism on the part of US Jewry and public opinion in Israel. The Saudi-Egyptian-Israeli aircraft package deal (see essay on the US and the ME) underlined America's increasing strategic commitment to Egypt and represented a significant diminution of Israel's preferential status as a recipient of US arms.

In April 1978, the US asked Israel whether it would be willing to negotiate the "permanent status" (i.e. the future sovereignty) of the West Bank and the Gaza Strip after a five-year transitional period. Although Washington expected an affirmative reply, the Israeli Cabinet was divided in its approach to the American and Egyptian positions. Defence Minister Weizman advocated an affirmative response. He had met Sādāt several times since the Jerusalem visit and had consistently emphasized the general strategic significance of peace with Egypt, while playing down the points of controversy. He held that Sādāt was genuinely seeking peace and would be willing to sign an Israeli-Egyptian peace treaty and to negotiate over the West Bank if Israel accepted the applicability of Resolution 242 to all fronts and the Palestinians' right to participate in the determination of their own future. Foreign Minister Dayan, on the other hand, while unwilling to antagonize the US Administration, thought that Israel should not commit itself at that stage to negotiating West Bank sovereignty after five years. The eventual Israeli reply, formulated in an atmosphere of tension in the Cabinet, was in effect negative and was so considered by the US.

A month later, however, Israel reconsidered its position. Following Sādāt's talks with Weizman and with Israel's Labour Party leader Shimon Peres in Austria, and the issuing of the "Vienna Document," Dayan informed the US at the Leeds Castle conference in July that Israel was willing to negotiate the permanent status of the West Bank after the transitional period. Furthermore, Israel was willing to discuss a territorial compromise on the West Bank—an eventuality it had previously excluded. Egypt, for its part, expressed willingness to sign a peace treaty with Israel, provided the latter accepted complete withdrawal from the territories occupied in 1967. This was a change from Egypt's settlement plan submitted in early July which had made no reference to a peace treaty or to other aspects of the "nature of peace." Egypt now also expressed willingness to serve as interlocutor over the West

Bank, although in its own settlement plan it had proposed that during the five-year transitional period West Bank administration be supervised by Jordan, and that of the Gaza Strip by Egypt.

At first it looked like the new positions would create a new momentum, but this did not happen. Begin rejected in public a privately made Egyptian proposal for a unilateral Israeli gesture of goodwill, i.e. turning over parts of Sinai to Egypt before negotiations continued. Following this rejection, Sādāt expelled the Israeli military mission, which had remained in Egypt since December 1977 as a symbol of the continuity of direct contacts; he also called off the Foreign Ministers' conference due to be held in Sinai in August. With Egyptian-Israeli relations at their lowest ebb since the beginning of Sādāt's initiative, President Carter decided to throw his weight into the balance and invited Sādāt and Begin to the tripartite summit at Camp David.

The Camp David agreement consisted of an operational framework for an Egyptian-Israeli peace treaty, and a detailed statement of principles governing the settlement of the West Bank-Gaza Strip-Palestinian question. The latter was formally designated "framework for peace in the Middle East."

The principles embodied in the framework for an Egyptian-Israeli peace treaty had for the most part been agreed upon in earlier stages of the negotiations, with the notable exception of the evacuation of the Israeli Sinai settlements. This was not the case with the "framework for peace in the ME." Though it contained elements from Israel's autonomy plan, Israel now agreed to language it had considered unacceptable at the Ismāʿīliyya meeting. These concessions included the applicability of Resolution 242 to the West Bank; a role for Jordan in the West Bank and in determining the permanent status of the area; the mention of Palestinians' legitimate rights, including the right to participate in the determination of their own future and in the negotiations on the permanent status of the West Bank and Gaza Strip; withdrawal of the Israeli military government; and restrictions in the size and location of the Israeli military presence. In general, this "framework" provided for a greater measure of actual self-rule for the Palestinians in the West Bank and Gaza Strip than had been envisaged by Israel in the original autonomy plan.

The Camp David agreement did not validate the Israeli government's hope that, in exchange for the return of Sinai, Egypt would for all intents and purposes withdraw from further involvement in the Arab-Israeli conflict. On the contrary, the agreements provided for a direct Egyptian role in the settlement in the West Bank and Gaza Strip. Moreover, in the ensuing negotiations, Egypt insisted (with American support) that the peace treaty was part of a comprehensive Arab-Israeli settlement, and that its implementation must be made conditional on progress in the West Bank and Gaza Strip. The significance of this Egyptian position transcended the delay in the conclusion of the treaty. In a sense, the Camp David agreements constituted an agreement to postpone any decision on the most difficult aspects of the West Bank-Gaza Strip-Palestinian problem, such as ultimate sovereignty, the future of East Jerusalem and of Jewish settlement in the West Bank. Israel rejected such a postponement, with the result that the peace treaty was not signed by 17 December 1978, the deadline set at Camp David.

SĀDĀT'S VISIT TO ISRAEL

On assuming office in January 1977, President Carter had set himself the goal of launching negotiations with the participation of all parties involved leading to a comprehensive settlement of the Arab-Israeli conflict before the end of 1977. However, as Carter's first year of office drew to a close, the outlook for convening a Geneva conference did not seem encouraging. Syria and the PLO—having concluded from US policy throughout 1977 that the Administration would go to great lengths, even at the expense of Egypt and Israel, to persuade them to join the conference—had decided to hold out for maximum advance gains. In Israel, Menahem Begin's new government, elected in May 1977, seemed a great deal less amenable to US policies than that of his predecessor, Yitzhak Rabin.

It was against this background of threatening stagnation that, on 9 November 1977, President Anwar al-Sādāt told the Egyptian People's Assembly (PA): "Israel will be astonished when it hears me saying now before you that I am ready to go to their house, to the Knesset itself and to talk to them." [1] Ten days later, on Saturday evening, 19 November 1977, hundreds of millions of television viewers saw Sādāt land at Ben-Gurion Airport for an official visit to Israel, the first ever by an Arab Head of State. A mood of euphoria, awe and hope swept Israel; disbelief—and fury—spread through most parts of the Arab world. (For Arab reactions, see following essay in this section, and essay on Inter-Arab Relations.)

SĀDĀT'S OBJECTIVES

Sādāt's declared objective in visiting Jerusalem was to bring about a new dynamic in the political process. Beyond that, he apparently hoped that his move would create circumstances so novel as to facilitate a rapid conclusion of a peace agreement with Israel. Such an agreement would provide for the return of Sinai, but would also lay down agreed principles for a comprehensive settlement, so that it could not be interpreted as a separate deal.

Sādāt seemed to have felt that Egypt could not extricate itself from the conflict in the foreseeable future if the slow-paced, inconclusive efforts to bring the parties to the Geneva conference were allowed to drag on the way they had. Although he believed that the US held "99% of the cards," its efforts had reached stalemate. During the preparations for Geneva, he said, "it became quite clear that a high wall of doubts, fears and deeply rooted lack of confidence created a state which I defined as a psychological barrier separating us in a manner that caution prevailed in every sentence, stubbornness abolished every step and fear virtually frustrated all efforts." [2]

Sādāt was disappointed by the US Administration on at least two counts: first, by reintroducing the USSR into the peace process by means of the joint US-Soviet declaration of 1 October 1977 (in disregard of Sādāt's unequivocally expressed views); and second, by abandoning focal pro-Arab points included in that document when confronted by public opposition in the US. Sādāt was worried by the US courting of Syria and of the PLO. The US proceeded on the assumption that a settlement acceptable to radical and pro-Soviet Syria would be acceptable to the rest of the Arab states and would therefore eventually be comprehensive and stable. From Sādāt's point of view, the US approach afforded the USSR, Syria and the PLO undue power to influence Egypt's interests in the settlement. Another negative implication was that the restoration of Sinai to Egypt would have to wait until the Palestinian problem was solved, though the former was doubtless much easier to achieve than the latter.

Sādāt's assessment of the prospects for a Geneva conference was not shared by his Foreign Minister, Ismā'īl Fahmī, who was said to have argued that a firm basis for reconvening the conference had already been constructed and that Sādāt's initiative was a mistake. Their differences (which led to Fahmī's resignation two days before the visit) [3] reflected a pattern of divergence between the cautious approach of the professional diplomat on the one hand, and Sādāt's inclination for dramatic short-cuts on the other.

Sādāt was apprehensive that the 1977 stalemate would not only stall the diplomatic process, but might lead to an Egyptian-Israeli military confrontation which, in view of the present military balance, was likely to undo Egypt's gains of 1973. After the Jerusalem visit, he revealed that he had feared a deliberate Israeli attack or, more likely, a war sparked by mutual misreading of intentions, particularly after the election victory of the Likud. [4]

Sādāt's frustration over the diplomatic stalemate reflected his determination to end the Israeli occupation of Sinai without recourse to a new war. The prolonged mobilization of Egypt's armed forces at almost wartime level was adversely affecting various material and spiritual aspects of Egyptian life. It slowed down domestic development and exposed the country to external pressures because of its need for conflict-related financial aid from Arab sources. Furthermore, the October 1973 war had served as a lesson that war was too costly and too risky a method of regaining Sinai. As Sādāt put it: "We have avenged what took place in Dayr Yāsīn and the 1967 defeat. . . . We must seek another method besides war to solve our problems. Otherwise, bloodshed between us will not end." [5] (The death of Arab civilians, including women and children, in the village of Dayr Yāsīn near Jerusalem on 19 April 1948 in an operation by Menahem Begin's *Irgun Zevai Leumi*, is frequently pointed to by Arabs as proof that peaceful Arab-Israeli coexistence is impossible.) The way out of the conflict was first to break down the "psychological barrier" of misunderstanding and mistrust. This was to be done by convincing Israel—its government and its people—that Egypt genuinely accepted Israel within its 4 June 1967 borders and recognized its security needs, while being no less genuinely committed to complete Israeli withdrawal and to a just solution to the Palestinian problem. Once reassured with regard to Egypt's real intentions, Sādāt believed that Israel would be willing to work out with him a set of principles for a comprehensive settlement, which could constitute a basis for negotiations between Israel and each of the Arab parties to the conflict. The dramatic visit to Jerusalem was to give Israel that reassurance.

SETTING THE STAGE

Sādāt's statement on 9 November 1977 startled the Israeli and many other governments. Yet the Israelis were surprised more by the dramatic method with which Sādāt had chosen to start his direct dialogue than by Egypt's willingness to do so: attempts to arrange meetings between Sādāt and Israeli leaders had been under way almost since he took office in 1970. Following Sādāt's announcement on 4 February 1971 of his readiness to consider an interim Sinai settlement, Israel's then Prime Minister, Golda Meir, reportedly attempted to meet with him through American and Romanian mediation. The USSR also tried to promote such a meeting in May 1972 in order to establish a ME "detente" in the context of the global detente which was then emerging. But at that time, Sādāt declined the idea. Similar efforts by Prime Minister Rabin in 1976, conducted this time through Iranian and Moroccan mediation, were no more successful. [6]

Israeli efforts to establish a direct dialogue with Sādāt were resumed by the new Likud government. The subject of a Begin-Sādāt meeting was raised by Premier Begin in his talks in Romania with President Ceauşescu, and by Foreign Minister Dayan in his talks with the Shah in Tehran, both in August 1977. [7] Ceauşescu conveyed to Sādāt his impression that Begin was a strong leader dedicated to peace. At a secret meeting held in Tangier on 20 September 1977 between Sādāt's confidant, Deputy Premier Hasan al-Tuhāmī, and Dayan, the latter proposed a Begin-Sādāt meeting. Egypt replied that such a meeting could take place only after Israel withdrew from Sinai. When this position was rejected, Egypt demanded at least an Israeli undertaking in principle to withdraw from Sinai. In response, Dayan reportedly expressed willingness to recognize Egypt's complete sovereignty over Sinai, though he insisted afterwards that this was not an official government proposal.[8] The communication of vital intelligence material by Israel to Egypt regarding plots to assassinate Sādāt was also said to be helpful in creating a positive atmosphere between the two governments.[9]

Still, despite those contacts, the Israelis remained apprehensive regarding Sādāt's real intentions. This was illustrated in a public warning by the Chief of Staff, General Gur, on the eve of Sādāt's arrival that military movements west of the Suez Canal could mean that the visit was an attempt at military deception similar to that practised in October 1973.

Begin responded to Sādāt's statement of 9 November by broadcasting a speech to the Egyptian people, calling upon them to put an end to the conflict and to co-operate for the sake of peace, and by publicly inviting Sādāt to address the Knesset. An official invitation was then communicated to Sādāt through the US.

SĀDĀT IN JERUSALEM

Sādāt's visit started with a formal and solemn, yet visibly emotional, reception ceremony at Ben-Gurion Airport on Saturday evening, 19 November 1977. On the following day, the official events included prayers at al-Aqsā Mosque and a stop at the adjacent Dome of the Rock, followed by a visit to the nearby Church of the Holy Sepulchre; a visit to Yad va-Shem, the Holocaust memorial; his address to the Knesset; and a meeting with a delegation of West Bank and Gaza Strip personalities. On Monday, 21 November 1977, Sādāt met with representatives of the Knesset factions, paid a visit to President Ephraim Katzir and participated in a joint press conference with Begin. Between official events, Sādāt held private meetings with Israeli leaders, one with Begin alone and two with him and a number of ministers, including Foreign Minister Dayan and Defence Minister Ezer Weizman. A departure ceremony at Ben-Gurion Airport on Monday afternoon concluded the visit.

Sādāt's Knesset address and his political discussions obviously had the most significant bearing on the peace process. Yet, the purely ceremonial occasions also served to convey his message. His airport reception and the visit to President Katzir were interpreted, and were probably meant to be interpreted, as implicit recognition of Israel's sovereignty. His visit to Yad va-Shem could be seen as an acknowledgement of Israel's sensitivity on security matters.[10] His prayers at al-Aqsā Mosque and his meeting with the West Bank-Gaza delegation were symbolic of his commitment to Islamic Jerusalem and to the Palestinian cause. Most clearly, though, Sādāt's message came through in his Knesset address, delivered in Arabic (for its text, see Appendix I).

The most striking aspect of Sādāt's speech was the way it conveyed acceptance of Israel: "In all sincerity, I tell you we welcome you among us, with full security and safety. . . . We really and truly welcome you to live among us in peace and security."[11] Acceptance of Israel, Sādāt explained, constituted one aspect of just and permanent peace. However, it could not be reached before Israel withdrew totally from the territories occupied in 1967, including East Jerusalem. Neither could it be reached without a solution of the Palestinian problem: "The Palestinian problem is the heart and core of the conflict. Peace cannot be achieved without the Palestinians . . . the only way to deal with [the Palestinian problem] in the direction of just and permanent peace is the establishment of a state of the Palestinian people." In return, Israel would obtain all the international security guarantees it deemed necessary. Just, permanent and comprehensive peace would then be established through a peace agreement whose principles should be an end to the state of belligerency; total Israeli withdrawal; Palestinian self-determination, including statehood; and security through international guarantees. Sādāt emphasized that the peace must be comprehensive and that he was not seeking a separate deal, a partial peace, nor an additional disengagement agreement. He called upon the Israeli people to urge their leaders to work for peace. [12]

Sādāt's address thus reiterated his basic view that an Arab-Israeli settlement must be based on Arab acceptance of Israel in return for complete Israeli withdrawal from the territories occupied in 1967 and Palestinian self-determination. The new element in the address was the way Sādāt expressed acceptance of Israel in the area and recognized its security needs; this perhaps implied an acceptance not only of Israel's *de facto* existence (with which he had argued for some time that Arabs ought to come to terms), but also of the legitimacy of that existence. This last point was underlined by the fact that Sādāt refrained from making any mention of the PLO in his address.

In his reply, Begin did not touch upon the questions of territories or the Palestinian problem, focusing instead on the nature of peace (for the text, see Appendix II). Begin called for normal relations between Israel and the Arab states, including diplomatic relations, economic co-operation, and open borders and free movement. He announced that Israel's borders were thenceforth open to Egyptian citizens. He asserted that everything should be negotiable and that no preconditions should be imposed on the talks. Finally, he invited the Heads of State of Syria and Jordan to negotiate peace treaties with him. [13]

Unlike Begin, Shimon Peres, the parliamentary opposition leader, did refer to the questions of the territories and the Palestinians (for the text, see Appendix III). He came out in favour of territorial compromises, recognized the existence not only of a Palestinian refugee problem but also of a "Palestinian identity" rightfully seeking expression, and implied preference for the solution of the latter problem within a Jordanian context. [14]

Although the stated objective of Sādāt's visit was to deliver a message, not to negotiate (and indeed he categorically denied having discussed the specifics of a settlement in Jerusalem), [15] in his private meetings with Begin and his key ministers, substantive issues were raised. However, at their joint press conference on 21 November, Sādāt and Begin disclosed only that they had agreed on two principles: that there should be no more war between the two countries; and that Israel had security problems which should be solved through negotiations. They also agreed to continue the direct dialogue. [16]

At a later date, however, Sādāt said that in Jerusalem, Israel had offered a separate peace treaty, which he rejected. [17] Begin flatly denied having made such an offer. [18] It appears, however, that in their private meeting on 20 November, the two leaders did discuss an offer by Begin to return Sinai to Egypt. Begin told Sādāt that Israel had no claims to Sinai and that in the context of a settlement, the Israeli Defence Forces (IDF) would withdraw to the international border. Begin made no mention of the Israeli settlements and airfields in Sinai at that meeting. This produced a crisis when Weizman, in his talks with Sādāt on the eve of the Ismā'īliyya summit, and Begin himself at the summit, raised the question of the Israeli settlements and airfields in Sinai (see below).

In exchange for the return of Sinai to Egypt, Begin demanded total demilitarization of Sinai east of the Mitla and Gidi passes. Sādāt's response became a controversial issue that marred the subsequent Egyptian-Israeli dialogue. Israel asserted that Sādāt had pledged that his army would not cross the passes eastwards; Egypt denied that Sādāt had promised total demilitarization of Sinai east of the passes. The controversy erupted when the Egyptian-Israeli Military Committee conven:d to discuss security arrangements in Sinai (see below).

Sādāt's visit and statements in Jerusalem introduced new elements to the Arab-Israeli conflict. Despite his later denial,[19] Sādāt's visit did in fact establish Egypt's informal recognition of Israel and appreciation of its security needs. It validated, in principle and practice, the concept of direct Arab-Israeli negotiations as the preferred means to ending the conflict. It also established the validity of starting peace negotiations with Israel prior to its withdrawal from the territories held since 1967. Sādāt's move made it imperative for Israel to come forward with a specific peace proposal. Israel had never previously submitted official proposals regarding the territorial and Palestinian problems, having insisted on Arab recognition as a prerequisite.

THE AMERICAN REACTION

Initial American reactions to Sādāt's announcement of 9 November 1977 were surprise and apprehension. Washington apparently had no advance knowledge of Sādāt's plan, and was apprehensive lest a direct Egyptian-Israeli dialogue produce a separate agreement and thus jeopardize chances for a comprehensive settlement. The Americans were particularly concerned about a possible radicalization in Syria's position and made it unmistakably clear that Sādāt had not acted at their instance. The US Administration noted with relief that both Sādāt and Begin declared in Jerusalem that they were seeking a comprehensive settlement. However, it was only after Egypt made it clear on 26 November that the next step would be a preparatory conference for Geneva (to which all interested parties would be invited), that Carter welcomed Sādāt's visit to Israel. Yet, in line with its comprehensive approach, the Administration remained reluctant to support a process likely to by-pass that very objective. Nevertheless, it could hardly afford to withhold support from an attempt by two of its closest allies in the ME to make peace with each other. US policy towards Sādāt's initiative therefore consisted of supporting Egyptian-Israeli contacts as a step towards a comprehensive settlement. This policy was articulated in mid-December by Carter's National Security Adviser, Zbigniew Brzezinski, who envisaged future negotiations as unfolding in three concentric circles or consecutive stages: the innermost circle or first stage consisted of US-assisted Egyptian-Israeli peace negotiations; the second, of negotiations between Israel and "moderate" Arab parties (i.e Jordan); and the third, of negotiations between Israel and "radical" Arab parties (viz Syria and the PLO), with the participation of the USSR in the framework of the Geneva conference. Geneva was thus relegated to become the final, rather than the initial, station along the road to peace. (See also essay, "The US and the ME: The Peace Process.")

THE IMPACT IN ISRAEL

Addressing the People's Assembly five days after the conclusion of his visit, Sādāt stated: "The first and greatest aim of the peace trip has been achieved—the barriers of doubt, lack of confidence and fear have been destroyed."[20] Sādāt held that his visit had convinced the Israeli government of the sincerity of the Arabs' desire to reach a just peace and had acquainted the Israeli public with the genuine Arab position. "Perhaps the most important point which has become clear to every Israeli," he said, "is the right of the Palestinian people to establish their state on their land and to return home."[21]

Sādāt's appraisal was doubtless influenced by the enthusiastic welcome he had received from the Israeli public, which was elated by the visit and encouraged by various aspects of Sādāt's message, primarily its acceptance of Israel. Indeed, a public opinion poll immediately after the visit showed that 90% of Israelis questioned believed that Egypt did desire peace (as compared to 40–60% previously).[22] Yet Sādāt misinterpreted the Israelis' public display of affection[23] as evidence of their acceptance of *his* concept of the peace settlement. As it turned out, the overwhelming majority of those polled continued to see no contradiction between their own desire for peace and their opposition both to withdrawal to the 1967 borders and to a Palestinian state.[24] As residual distrust of Sādāt's intentions persisted in government and in the public at large, his claim of having destroyed such barriers proved an overstatement.

THE CAIRO CONFERENCE (14–22 DECEMBER 1977)

Reporting on 26 November 1977 to the People's Assembly on his visit to Israel, Sādāt announced a dramatic new move: the assembly in Cairo, as early as 3 December, of all the interested parties to lay the groundwork for reconvening the Geneva conference, "so that we will not go to Geneva to hold discussions lasting for years."[25] By 28 November, formal invitations had been delivered to the US, USSR, Israel, Syria, Jordan, Lebanon, the PLO and the UN.

EGYPT'S OBJECTIVES

Sādāt asserted that his call for a preparatory conference for Geneva was the second step in his plan: "My initiatives are the result of a study I made and a plan I reached. My visit to Jerusalem was the first stage of the plan. The second stage will be the Cairo conference. There will be other initiatives."[26] However, Sādāt's critics maintained that it was an improvised step aimed at keeping alive the psychological effects of his visit, at giving Israel an opportunity to reciprocate to his gesture, and at bolstering his own prestige.[27] Sādāt gave credence to the latter view when he said that he had decided to propose the Cairo conference after his return from Jerusalem when he felt that the Egyptian public was pressing for speedy negotiations.[28] He also observed that the Cairo conference (or a similar step) was necessary for him to keep the initiative in the peace process.[29]

Sādāt explained that his specific objective was to draw up a working paper of guidelines for Geneva which would be essential in order to prevent the collapse of the conference over procedural matters.[30] According to this approach, Geneva would set the seal of international and Arab approval on a settlement whose principles were to be formulated in Cairo. Countering Soviet and Syrian objections that only the co-chairmen of the Geneva conference (i.e. the US and the USSR) were entitled to issue invitations to a preparatory meeting, Egypt described the Cairo conference as "informal" and "unofficial."

Egypt had every reason to expect that Syria (and consequently Lebanon), the USSR and the PLO would refuse to attend the Cairo conference.[31] Sādāt pledged, however, that even if the other Arab parties did not show up, he would still not seek a bilateral agreement with Israel; rather, he would try to reach agreement on the principles of a comprehensive settlement, on the basis of which each Arab country could then negotiate its own peace agreement with Israel. If they declined to do so, he would submit the principles agreed upon to an Arab summit.[32]

Sādāt was aware that if the USSR, Syria and the PLO attended the Cairo conference, that meeting would encounter the same difficulties that had prevented the reconvening of Geneva. Partly in an effort to keep them away, Sādāt vehemently attacked Moscow, Damascus and the PLO before and during the conference, severed diplomatic relations with Syria, and closed Soviet consulates and cultural centres (5 and 7 December respectively; see chapter on Egypt). In addition, Sādāt questioned the PLO's status as the representative of the Palestinians: although he invited the PLO, he argued that "the true Palestinians" whom he had met in

Jerusalem (i.e. the West Bank and Gaza delegation and the crowd that had welcomed him in al-Aqsā Mosque) were welcome at the conference.[33] The implication was that only those Palestinian Arabs actually living under Israeli occupation should be viewed as representing the Palestinian cause, not PLO leaders who did not share this experience. Following the Tripoli conference of Arab governments opposed to Sādāt's initiative, in which the PLO took an active part (see essays on the PLO and on Inter-Arab Relations), Sādāt declared that the PLO had itself thereby annulled the 1974 Rabat resolutions which named it the "sole legitimate representative" of the Palestinians.[34] In order to provide the Cairo meeting with a semblance of Palestinian legitimacy, Sādāt met a delegation of supporters from the Gaza Strip in Cairo on the eve of the conference.

ISRAEL'S VIEW

Israel was apparently not consulted before Sādāt made his call for the Cairo conference. Its precise nature was not clear in advance; neither was there any certainty regarding the parties that would attend. Israel consequently assigned it little substantive significance. In line with Egypt's formal invitation, which significantly asked the Israeli Foreign Minister to send "his representative" to the conference, the Israeli delegation was made up of officials rather than Cabinet ministers. Headed by the Director-General of the Prime Minister's Office, Eliyahu Ben-Elissar, its instructions were to concentrate on presenting Israel's point of view on the nature of peace. Substantive progress was expected to be made elsewhere: at a meeting of the Egyptian and Israeli Foreign Ministers, then scheduled to take place following the Cairo conference (which Israel thought would last no longer than 10 days);[35] at secret meetings of Egyptian and Israeli political leaders, such as that between Dayan and Tuhāmī on 3 December 1977,[36] where issues related to the Sinai and to Israel's plan for West Bank settlement were apparently discussed;[37] and at the Carter-Begin talks in Washington (see below). Significantly, Begin chose the opening day of the conference to announce his forthcoming trip to the US.

THE US VIEW

Once more, Sādāt's initiative caught the US by surprise, and again Washington feared that, in view of the negative Soviet and Syrian attitudes to the conference, it might harm the chances for a comprehensive settlement in Geneva. Jordan, the only Arab country which did not object to the conference in principle, was constrained from attending by the Syrians who rejected it, and by the Saudis, who were at best reserved. US fears of a separate Egyptian-Israeli deal revived, and there was growing anxiety that the USSR and Syria might be antagonized. Following reassurances of Sādāt's commitment to the Geneva conference, the US announced on 29 November that an American representative would be at Cairo. But at the same time, it pressured Sādāt into delaying the conference for two weeks, during which the Administration tried to persuade other parties to attend. First, the US tried to convince the Soviet Union that it was fully committed to Geneva, that the Cairo conference was not an American trick to bypass Geneva and the USSR, and that the latter should moderate its opposition to the conference. This was not made easier by Sādāt's anti-Soviet measures; according to one report, the US barely managed to dissuade Sādāt from severing relations with Moscow altogether.[38] Next, Secretary of State Cyrus Vance toured the ME from 9–15 December in order to express American support both for the Cairo conference and for Geneva, to enlist Arab (mainly Saudi) support, and to persuade at least one additional country (Jordan) to join the conference—or, failing that, to enter the next stage of negotiations, expected to be held at Foreign Minister level. King Ḥusayn's position was that he would attend the conference only if all the other parties did so. The US then reluctantly accepted that only Egypt, Israel, itself and a representative of the UN Secretary-General would be in attendance.

THE CONFERENCE PROCEEDINGS
The actual nature of the Cairo conference—a stopgap or cover for more important contacts—was made obvious at the opening ceremony on 14 December by the Egyptian and Israeli representatives, both of whom merely restated their governments' declared positions. Egypt emphasized the full realization of the legitimate rights of the Palestinian people as the main element in a comprehensive settlement; Israel, by contrast, emphasized the nature of peace. On the question of what should constitute the legal basis for a peace settlement, the Egyptian representative listed Resolution 242, "international law," the UN Charter and "the relevant UN resolutions." (The latter term probably implied General Assembly Resolution 194 of December 1948, which gave Palestinian refugees the option of returning to their homes and property or receiving compensation; and General Assembly Resolution 3236 of November 1974, which reaffirmed the right of the Palestinian people to national independence and self-determination, and their right to return to their homes and property.) The Israeli delegate mentioned only Resolution 242 (which refers to the problem of refugees, but not to the Palestinian problem) as the basis for a settlement.

The dispute over the placing of a PLO name-plate in the conference room and over the raising of a Palestine flag along with those of other invited parties demonstrated that the difficulties stemming from the problem of Palestinian representation were not entirely solved by the PLO's failure to show up. Israel objected to both the name-plate and the flag, and they were removed. More important was the dispute over who would represent the Palestinians at the peace conference: Egypt named the PLO (in spite of Sādāt's statements quoted above), while Israel referred to "an appropriate delegation of Palestinian Arabs." most probably implying West Bank and Gaza Strip mayors who were not PLO members.[39]

It even proved difficult to reach agreement on the conference agenda. Egypt objected to an Israeli-backed American proposal that Resolution 242 constitute the basis for negotiations. The disagreement was overcome when Egypt accepted an interpretation of the Resolution's clause on the refugee problem as referring to the Palestinian problem. Israel proposed that the issue of the nature of peace be the first item on the agenda, while Egypt insisted that withdrawal and the Palestinian issue be discussed first. There was also disagreement over whether the peace talks were aimed at reaching a peace treaty, which Israel demanded, or a peace agreement, which was Egypt's position.[40]

The Cairo conference was suspended on 22 December pending the conclusion of the Sādāt-Begin summit which it had been agreed to hold in Ismā'īliyya. The conference was formally concluded on 26 December 1977.

ISRAEL'S PEACE PLAN
While the Cairo conference was still in progress, Begin paid a visit to the US (see below), taking with him a newly drafted peace plan for the West Bank and Gaza Strip and for Sinai. Some points of the plan became known during Begin's visit to the US. The plan as a whole was officially disclosed for the first time in the Knesset on 28 December 1977 and approved by an overwhelming majority on that day (for the text, see Appendix IV).

The peace plan consisted of two parts: the Administrative Autonomy plan for the

Arab residents of the West Bank and Gaza Strip, and proposals regarding the Sinai front. The main points of the Administrative Autonomy plan were as follows.[41] The administration of the military government in the West Bank and the Gaza Strip will be abolished and an administrative autonomy of, by and for the Palestinian Arab residents of those areas will be established (Articles 1, 2). These residents will elect an Administrative Council to direct all the administrative affairs relating to them. The Council will appoint representatives to the governments of Israel and Jordan (Arts. 3–10, 12, 13, 23). Security and public order will be the responsibility of the Israeli authorities (Art. 11). Residents will be able to choose either Israeli or Jordanian citizenship, and the election laws of the state whose citizenship they choose will apply to them (Arts. 14–18). A committee comprised of representatives of Israel, Jordan and the Administrative Council will study the existing legislation in the West Bank and the Gaza Strip and determine by unanimous vote which laws will remain in force and which abolished (Art. 19). Israeli residents will be entitled to buy land and settle in those areas, and residents of the areas opting for Israeli citizenship will be entitled to buy land in Israel (Art. 20). A committee comprised of representatives of Israel, Jordan and the Administrative Council will determine regulations governing the entry of Arab refugees to the West Bank and Gaza Strip. This will be decided by unanimous vote only (Art. 21). There will be freedom of movement and of economic activity for Israelis in the West Bank and Gaza Strip and for the residents of those areas in Israel (Art. 22). Israel stands by its right to claim sovereignty over these areas; since other claims exist, however, the question of sovereignty there will be left open (Art. 24). Freedom of access to the holy places in Jerusalem will be guaranteed (Art. 25). The plan's principles will be subject to review after five years (Art. 26).

As regards Sinai, Begin's plan called for withdrawal of Israeli forces to a defence line in central Sinai, to be followed after several years by a complete withdrawal to the international border; demilitarization of Sinai east of the line of the Mitla and Gidi passes, and the maintenance of only limited Egyptian forces in the area west of the line; retention of the Israeli settlements in Sinai under Israeli jurisdiction and defended by Israeli units (apparently not the IDF); and freedom of navigation in the Straits of Tiran to be guaranteed either by a UN force or by joint Egyptian-Israeli patrols.

The Israeli peace plan was based on the view that Sādāt urgently needed peace and would be ready to sign a separate treaty with Israel provided he was given back Sinai, and provided Israel displayed a modicum of flexibility regarding the West Bank and Gaza Strip. This view was reflected, for example, by Defence Minister Weizman who was quoted as having told Likud members of the Knesset: "The Egyptians are fed up [with the Arab-Israeli conflict]. They would be willing to go for a separate agreement with Israel, if only a formula was found that would enable them to delay [decision on] the question of the comprehensive settlement to a later date."[42]

The peace plan was founded on the assumption that a satisfactory Egyptian-Israeli agreement over the Sinai (taking Egypt practically out of the Arab-Israeli conflict) was realizable under existing conditions, whereas a West Bank-Gaza Strip settlement which did not give sovereignty to the Arabs was not. Therefore, the plan aimed at dissociating Sinai from West Bank-Gaza Strip issues. This was to be done by keeping the question of sovereignty in the West Bank and Gaza Strip open while administrative autonomy replaced the military government.

Having recognized Egypt's total sovereignty, the rest of the peace plan relevant to Sinai revolved around security matters: the retention of the Israeli settlements (mostly located in the Rafiah salient in the north-east) was designed to maintain a barrier between Egyptian Sinai and the Gaza Strip (and, for that matter, the West Bank).

Begin's proposals for Sinai drew criticism from members of his own Right-wing Herut party, as well as from Labour party spokesmen who described them as "too hasty." Criticism was also voiced by residents of the Israeli settlements in Sinai who were concerned about the implications of being placed under Egyptian sovereignty. This latter criticism apparently led Begin to add the provision that the settlements would not only be maintained and defended by Israeli forces, but also be linked to Israeli administration and jurisdiction. This point was apparently not included in the plan shown by Begin to Carter on 17 December 1977, but was added sometime between that date and the Ismā'īliyya summit a week later (probably following a Cabinet debate on 22 December 1977). The US and Egypt complained about "a discrepancy" on that point between the plan shown to Carter and the one shown to Sādāt.[43]

Unlike Sinai, the West Bank and the Gaza Strip raised not only security but also sovereignty problems. The Likud election platform, approved on 1 March 1977, stated that the Likud government would strive for peace treaties with Egypt and Syria whereby the interests and needs of the parties would be taken into consideration.[44] This was interpreted as readiness for withdrawals on the Sinai and Golan fronts.[45] Regarding the West Bank, however, the same document stated that "the Jewish people's right to Eretz Yisrael [the land of Israel] is eternal, inalienable and interlocked with its right to peace and security." Judea and Samaria "will not be handed over to any foreign rule; between the [Mediterranean] Sea and the Jordan [River], there shall be only Israeli sovereignty."[46] In the same vein, the Likud government's basic policy guidelines, presented to the Knesset on 20 June 1977, asserted that "the Jewish people has an eternal, historic right to Eretz Yisrael, the inalienable heritage of its forefathers." (Nevertheless, the government would not apply Israeli law and jurisdiction to any part of Judea, Samaria and the Gaza District as long as negotiations were conducted for peace between Israel and its neighbours.)[47]

Past Israeli governments had proposed "territorial compromise" as a solution to the West Bank-Gaza problem, i.e. partitioning the areas under dispute between Israeli and Arab (preferably Jordanian) sovereignty. This approach was unacceptable to Begin since it implied ceding sovereignty over part of Eretz Yisrael to the Arabs. It was equally unacceptable to the Arabs: Jordan had reportedly ruled out territorial compromise when secretly approached on the matter by Dayan in October 1977.[48]

Instead, Begin adopted the concept of "functional compromise": rather than partitioning territory, *control* and *administration* would be divided between Israel and the local residents, although Israel's military hold over the territories would continue. The resolution of the problem of sovereignty could thus be postponed. As Begin put it, there was only one way of reaching agreement over the contradictory claims for sovereignty over these areas: "To agree to decide that the question of sovereignty remain open, and to deal with people, with nations [rather than territory]; that is to say, administrative autonomy for the Arabs of Eretz Yisrael, and for the Jews of Eretz Yisrael—genuine security."[49]

The "functional compromise" concept had originally been introduced by Labour governments as an alternative to the territorial compromise concept rejected by Jordan. In the Labour view, however, administrative control of the territories was to be entrusted not to the local residents but to Jordan. Begin would not accept this proposal, fearing that once Amman's formal status in the territories was secured, Jordan would lay claim to a political and eventually to a military presence there.

Begin's approach thus differed from Labour policy over the role envisaged for Jordan. Indeed his plan was criticized by Labour spokesmen for keeping Jordan out of the settlement. It should be noted, however, that the option of a territorial compromise was kept open by Dayan. Having frequently demonstrated a pragmatic approach as compared with Begin's more ideological one, Dayan stated on the eve of the Cairo conference that Israel was willing to discuss a territorial partitioning of the West Bank and Gaza.[50] He pledged that the presence of Israeli settlements there would not hinder agreement over the boundary line or decide where the ultimate boundary should be.[51]

Begin was also criticized for accepting the principle that future arrangements should apply equally to the West Bank and the Gaza Strip. In the past, Israel had drawn a distinction between the two areas, aiming in future negotiations to hold on to the Gaza Strip, while settling for "territorial compromise" in the West Bank.

Spokesmen for various groups also argued that had administrative autonomy along the lines of Begin's plan been the final outcome of the peace negotiations, Israel could perhaps have lived with it. But as a starting position, the plan would inevitably lead to the ultimate emergence of an independent Palestinian state. Former Premier, Yitzhak Rabin, argued that in drafting his plan Begin had accepted the Arab position that none of the territories taken in 1967 could be incorporated into Israel, and in so doing "he will sooner or later bring us back to the lines we had before the Six-Day War."[52] Questions were raised regarding Israel's ability to preserve its Jewish character should Palestinian Arabs exercise their right under the plan and acquire Israeli citizenship *en masse*.

BEGIN'S US VISIT (14-19 DECEMBER 1977)

Begin's decision to go to Washington and submit his peace plan to President Carter was apparently prompted by his talks with Secretary Vance in Jerusalem on the eve of the Cairo conference (12 December 1977). Vance conveyed the Administration's expectations for specific Israeli peace proposals. He also underlined the US intention of maintaining a central role in the evolving negotiations. Begin's visit was in part intended to obtain for Israel the credit for "restating" the US into the negotiations: thus Begin showed Carter his peace plan before he submitted it to Sādāt—even before he tabled it in the Israeli Cabinet. Such deference to Carter's standing would, it was believed in Jerusalem, make it easier to win his approval of the plan. It would also produce the right setting for Begin to introduce it to the American public in general and to US Jewry in particular, which was another objective of his visit. The Administration welcomed Begin's visit, although it took place at very short notice. On the eve of their talks, Carter remarked that the PLO, through its "completely negative" attitude, had removed itself "from any immediate prospect of participation in the peace process."[53]

Begin met Carter and senior Administration officials on 16 and 17 December. During this time, Carter twice phoned Sādāt to inform him of Begin's proposals and to obtain his reaction. Sādāt apparently responded very positively,[54] and at a press conference held following Carter's calls, he expressed great optimism.[55]

After the visit, Begin characterized the official Administration reaction to his plan by saying: "Our plan has won wonderful support from the US, from the President, who stated it would be a fair basis for peace negotiations, from . . . his advisers, the Secretary of State and others."[56]

In this statement, Begin did not seem to draw a distinction between the Administration's encouragement of his willingness to come up with a peace plan on the one hand, and its views on its substance on the other. Carter expressed his appreciation for Begin's "constructive approach" and his conviction that Begin and

Sādāt "together are taking important steps down the road to a just and comprehensive peace"; he also said that "the understanding and statesmanship" demonstrated by Begin "make a notable contribution." [57] Yet Carter's support of the peace plan seems to have been limited to the part which dealt with Sinai. He reportedly told his guest that the proposals regarding the West Bank and Gaza Strip did not allow enough negotiating room to Sādāt; he urged Begin to improve those proposals, both in substance and in the way they were "packaged." [58]

WEIZMAN'S VISIT TO EGYPT (20–21 DECEMBER 1977)

As Egypt and Israel were preparing for the Sādāt-Begin summit in Ismā'īliyya, Israel's Defence Minister met Sādāt and his War Minister, Gen 'Abd al-Ghanī Jamasī, in Egypt. This was the first publicized visit of an Israeli minister to an Arab country, and was also significant because it established a direct and largely discreet avenue for Egyptian-Israeli contacts. The visit was undertaken at Weizman's initiative, though the idea had initially been suggested by Sādāt during their meeting in Jerusalem. Weizman was the only Cabinet minister who had met the Egyptian President in private in Jerusalem. The two were said to have established a good rapport; Sādāt later occasionally depicted Weizman as the Israeli leader with whom he could conclude peace—in contrast with Begin. At their Jerusalem meeting, Sādāt and Weizman had agreed to work to prevent acts of hostility from occurring as a result of misreading the other's moves or intentions. Weizman reverted to that topic in Egypt, discussing with his hosts possible measures to reduce tensions and to limit the risk of an accidental outbreak of violence. He presented a set of proposals to be implemented while the peace talks were still in progress, including immediate mutual withdrawals of some Egyptian and Israeli forces from their front lines; restriction of large-scale military manoeuvres to locations removed from the front; and establishment of a "hot line" between the Egyptian and Israeli commands. The last proposal was subsequently put into effect.

Weizman also discussed military aspects of the Israeli peace plan in Sinai and in the West Bank and Gaza Strip. Sādāt made a point of playing down the Sinai issues, assigning the discussion of details to Jamasī. He himself focused instead on the West Bank and Gaza Strip, demanding that Israel issue a "declaration of intent" whereby it explicitly announced its preparedness to withdraw from all Arab lands. Regarding Sinai, Sādāt and Jamasī stressed that demilitarization must be mutual; that Egypt would not give up sovereignty over any part of the Sinai; and that the Rafiah salient settlements must be dismantled and the area cleared of Israelis. Sādāt told Weizman: "I would like you to tell Begin that I will not allow a settlement on one square centimetre within my international borders, even if that should require that I fight you to the end of the world." [59]

Another controversial point stemmed from contradictory versions of Sādāt's statement on the demilitarization of Sinai during his private talks with Begin in Jerusalem (see above). During his talks with Jamasī, Weizman brought up Israel's demand that Sinai be demilitarized east of the Mitla and Gidi passes. When this was rejected by Jamasī, Weizman referred to Sādāt's acceptance of it when in Jerusalem. According to Weizman, Jamasī replied: "Well, the President is not a military man" [60] (possibly an implied admission of the correctness of the Israeli version). The Egyptian position on this point was that parts of the Egyptian army, though not its bulk, would be stationed east of the passes.

Weizman's visit helped to set the stage for the Ismā'īliyya summit in that it acquainted the Egyptians further with Israel's peace plan, and produced first-hand Egyptian reactions to it. The outlook for the summit was not too promising: reporting to the Cabinet on his visit, Weizman characterized Egypt's position as "tough." [61]

THE ISMĀ'ĪLIYYA SUMMIT (25–26 DECEMBER 1977)

As Weizman's visit had made Egypt and Israel more aware of the gap separating their positions, the first matter to be attended to at the summit was how to ensure the continuation of the negotiations. The summit opened with a private meeting between the two leaders, at which Begin proposed, and Sādāt accepted, that the negotiations should continue at ministerial level in two committees. The first, a Military Committee, comprised of Egyptian and Israeli War and Defence Ministers respectively, would convene in Cairo and discuss all the military issues concerning Sinai. The second, a Political Committee, comprised of the Egyptian and Israeli Foreign Ministers as well as US and UN representatives, would convene in Jerusalem and discuss the Palestinian problem and civilian Israeli settlements in the Sinai. In line with Israeli policy, it was agreed at the summit that the negotiations should lead to a peace treaty rather than a peace settlement. (Israel viewed Egypt's preference for an "agreement" as an attempt to stop short at a status of non-belligerency [in Arabic *ittifāqiyat salām*, the approximate equivalent of "peace agreement"] rather than proceed to a full peace [in Arabic: *muʿāhadat sulḥ*, or "peace treaty"].) It was also agreed that the IDF would withdraw from Sinai and that Israel would not claim sovereignty over any part of it.

The delegations next worked on formulating a joint statement to provide the conceptual framework for peace negotiations. Israel proposed that the two governments express their determination to continue efforts to reach a comprehensive peace settlement by means of negotiated peace treaties based on Resolutions 242 and 338. According to Israel's original peace proposal, the Palestinian Arab residents of Judea, Samaria and the Gaza district would enjoy self-rule.[62]

Egypt's counter-proposal contained two clauses: one stated that Israel would undertake to withdraw from Sinai, Golan, the West Bank and the Gaza Strip; the other called for Israel's acceptance of self-determination for the Palestinian people.[63] Israel rejected both clauses. Finally, according to Begin's account of the summit, the parties agreed on a draft joint statement of principles[64] (for the text, see Appendix V). According to Begin, this was not issued because members of the Egyptian Foreign Ministry objected to it on the grounds that no agreed formula had been reached regarding the Palestinian Arabs.[65] In the event, agreement was not even reached on the terms to be used in reference to that problem: Israel spoke of "the problem of the Arabs of Eretz Yisrael," thereby limiting its scope to the present residents of the West Bank and the Gaza Strip, while Egypt adhered to the term "the Palestinian problem."

It was the Palestinian issue, then, which prevented a joint statement of principles from being published in Ismāʿīliyya. Instead, Sādāt presented the positions of both sides in a concluding statement, documenting the disagreement on the Palestinian problem as follows: "The position of Egypt is that on the West Bank and Gaza Strip a Palestinian state should be established. The position of Israel is that Palestinian Arabs in Judea, Samaria [namely the West Bank of Jordan] and the Gaza Strip should enjoy self-rule." In view of this difference, Sādāt concluded, it was agreed to refer the issue to the Political Committee.[66]

After Ismāʿīliyya, Begin blamed the failure of the summit to produce a joint statement of principles on "those people in the Egyptian Foreign Ministry whose thinking is limited to the routine." Sādāt himself, Begin said, had told him that he regarded Israel's proposals as satisfactory.[67] According to Dayan, Sādāt had been willing to accept a statement of principles which merely affirmed that there should be a just solution to the problem of the Palestinians, but members of his entourage convinced him against it.[68] Foreign Ministry officials reportedly argued that concessions on the Palestinian issue would likely damage Egypt's inter-Arab and international position.[69]

Nevertheless, both Sādāt and Begin were demonstratively pleased with the outcome of their meeting. Sādāt said that he was "completely satisfied with the Ismā'īliyya talks" because "war has become inconceivable. This in itself is a great achievement. . . . After Ismā'īliyya, I can confirm that war has become beyond our thinking."[70] He also expressed satisfaction with the establishment of the two committees; with the fact that, for the first time, Israel had put forward a specific peace plan; and with the extent to which Israel had moderated its positions, thereby saving "another 25 years of talk about the problem."[71] Finally, he complemented Begin for genuinely seeking peace.[72] Begin too stated that the summit had been successful;[73] he "had come to Ismā'īliyya a hopeful Prime Minister and was leaving there a happy man."[74]

This appraisal was not borne out by subsequent developments. Indeed, Dayan sounded a more sober tone immediately on his return from Ismā'īliyya by stating that there were still many difficulties which he was not sure could be resolved. He was uncertain of Egypt's willingness to make concessions and overcome obstacles.[75] Dayan also complained that the Egyptians were closely linking the Palestinian issue with the prospects of peace with Israel,[76] a remark which reflected his disappointment over Egypt's unwillingness to accept the autonomy plan in exchange for Sinai.

Sādāt apparently came away from the Ismā'īliyya meeting convinced that Begin would not accept his view of what constituted an acceptable compromise: peace, recognition and security for Israel in exchange for complete Israeli withdrawal and Palestinian self-determination, possibly leading to the establishment of a Palestinian state. From then on, Sādāt sought ways other than direct talks to get Begin to accept that compromise. One of them was to secure US support for his own positions and to have the US exert pressures on Israel. Within a week of the meeting, in fact, Sādāt declared that he expected the US to apply pressure on Israel in connection with the Palestinian issue.[77]

The US Administration had already been involved in the course of the Ismā'īliyya summit, which was arranged by Secretary Vance probably at Begin's request.[78] When Weizman's talks in Egypt revealed that Cairo's position was likely to create a crisis, Carter contacted Sādāt, asking him to show greater moderation.[79] Carter was said to have tried to persuade Begin to tell Sādāt at Ismā'īliyya that Israel was prepared in principle to withdraw from the West Bank and Gaza Strip. When Begin refused, the US apparently suggested to Sādāt that it would raise no objections if he rejected the Administrative Autonomy plan.[80] Following the summit, the US assumed an increasingly active role in the Egyptian-Israeli negotiations, as indicated by the Carter-Sādāt meeting in Aswān shortly after Ismā'īliyya.

THE CARTER-SĀDĀT TALKS IN ASWĀN (4 JANUARY 1978)

The US position on the Palestinian question was stated by Carter in a television interview on 29 December 1977. He described the Administrative Autonomy plan as a "long step forward," and said that Israel's demand that her troops remain in the West Bank permanently was a realistic negotiating position. While reaffirming his support for a Palestinian "homeland or entity," Carter rejected the idea of an independent state: "My own preference is that they [the Palestinians] not be an independent nation but be tied in some way with the surrounding countries, making a choice, for instance, between Israel and Jordan. . . . Permanent peace can best be maintained if there is not a fairly radical, new independent nation in the heart of the Middle Eastern area."[81]

Carter's statement, which was apparently intended to induce Begin to display further flexibility with regard to the West Bank and Gaza Strip, did not depart from the US preference for a Palestinian "homeland" rather than an independent state. Nevertheless, Sādāt took umbrage at Carter's statement for creating the impression of considerable US support for Begin's approach. He felt that Carter's words might undermine Egypt's contention that a just solution for the Palestinian problem could be reached through the US. Sādāt expressed surprise, embarrassment and disappointment, and charged Carter with making his (own) task of conducting the peace negotiations very difficult. [82]

Carter's statement prompted Egypt to publish its counter-proposals to Begin's plan earlier than expected, on 31 December 1977, instead of at the Political Committee scheduled to meet in mid-January. The proposals, which were communicated to the US, called for Israel's acceptance of the principle of complete withdrawal from the West Bank and the Gaza Strip, and of the inalienable right of the Palestinians to self-determination. These principles, the Egyptian draft declared, were not negotiable. Once they were accepted by Israel, negotiations should focus on security for both parties and on the manner and timetable for Israeli troop withdrawal and self-determination. [83]

Egypt's reaction to Carter's statement in turn prompted the US to clarify its position. Carter stressed that he did not support an Israeli military presence in the West Bank and Gaza Strip after a settlement was implemented, and that his stated opposition to a Palestinian state was "merely an expression of preference." [84] Vance insisted that the Administration did not support Begin's proposals regarding the West Bank and Gaza Strip—though it regarded them as a good "opening position." [85] Finally, it was decided to add a stop-over in Egypt to Carter's tour of six European and Asian capitals in order to allay Sādāt's concern. [86] (Israeli officials informally protested against Carter's omission of a visit to Israel on that occasion.)

In their meeting in Aswān on 4 January 1978, Carter and Sādāt agreed that the peace negotiations must aim at a comprehensive settlement; that the next step in the negotiations should be the formulation of a statement of principles for that comprehensive settlement; and that the US would play an active role in helping the Political Committee formulate such a declaration of principles. [87]

These points of agreement were reflected in Carter's statement following the meeting. He also listed the principles which the US thought should constitute the basis for a comprehensive settlement, thereby in effect proposing an American draft statement of principles:

"First, true peace must be based on normal relations among the parties to the peace. Peace means more than just an end to belligerency. Second, there must be withdrawal by Israel from territories occupied in 1967 and agreement on secure and recognized borders for all parties in the context of normal and peaceful relations in accordance with UN Resolutions 242 and 338. Third, there must be a resolution of the Palestinian problem in all its aspects. [It] must recognize the legitimate rights of the Palestinian people and enable the Palestinians to participate in the determination of their own future." [88]

There were no new elements in the way the statement treated the first two components of the settlement, but there were in relation to the Palestinian issue. Firstly, stating that the Palestinian problem must be resolved "in all its aspects" implied that a settlement needed to address itself to the problems of the Palestinians both inside and outside the West Bank and the Gaza Strip—on the humanitarian level (i.e. the refugee problem) as well as on the political level (namely the Palestinians' national aspirations). This approach differed from Israel's as well as from UN Resolution 242, which made reference only to "refugees." Secondly, the term "legitimate rights of the Palestinian people," frequently employed in Arab statements, had first been used by the US in the joint US-Soviet declaration of 1 October 1977—to Israel's great dismay.[89] Finally, the affirmation that a resolution of the problem required Palestinian participation in the determination of their own future was formally mentioned for the first time. It was very close to, though not quite identical with, Egypt's concept of self-determination and implied that the Administrative Autonomy plan could only be a transitional arrangement. This new American concept was thought to have been drafted by Egypt and communicated to the US on 31 December 1977 along with Egypt's counter-proposals to the Israeli plan.[90]

Beyond these general principles, Carter and Sādāt agreed in Aswān on several more specific issues. Firstly, they agreed that Jordan should play a key role in the solution of the Palestinian problem. This was implied by the term "participation" ("of the Palestinians in the determination of their own future") since Jordan was the most likely partner with whom they would "participate." Ever since the Cairo conference, the US had emphasized Jordan's role in the West Bank and in solving the Palestinian question. Sādāt, too, had made it clear that he would prefer the Palestinians to choose King Husayn rather than the PLO as their representative.[91] The Aswān exchanges were designed, *inter alia*, to make it easier for Jordan to join the negotiations.

Secondly, Carter and Sādāt agreed that the Palestinians' participation in determining their own future would be implemented following an interim period, probably of five years, during which some form of a joint Israeli-Jordanian-Palestinian administration would run West Bank and Gaza Strip affairs. An in-dependent state would probably not be one of the options open to the Palestinians at the end of that period; they would have to choose between various forms of links with Jordan.

Thirdly, Sādāt agreed in Aswān to the principle of minor border corrections. This was the US interpretation of the withdrawal clause in Resolution 242: it was closer to Israel's argument that the resolution referred to "territories," not "the territories," but it rejected Israel's view of the clause as a basis for major territorial changes. Egypt's acceptance of slight border corrections was, however, formally conditioned on their being mutual.[92]

Following Aswān, then, the US was more closely in agreement with Egypt—and in disagreement with Israel—on the crucial territorial and Palestinian issues. The US and Egypt also were agreed that their common positions on these issues should form the basis of the statement of principles to be worked out by the Political Committee.

THE MILITARY AND POLITICAL COMMITTEES
The Political Committee of the Cairo conference convened in Jerusalem on 17 January 1978, but was abruptly and indefinitely suspended by Sādāt a day later. As a result, the negotiating process was considerably slowed down and was not ef-fectively revived until September 1978. This setback must be viewed against the background of the negative atmosphere which prevailed after Ismā'īliyya, major contributing factors being the anti-Begin press campaign in Egypt and Israel's policy regarding settlements in the West Bank and Sinai.

THE ANTI-BEGIN PRESS CAMPAIGN
Following the Ismā'īliyya summit, the Egyptian press reverted to language regarded as offensive to Jews and Israel and to Premier Begin personally—a tenor which had

subsided since November 1977. Articles and anecdotes related in the press and cartoons depicted the Jews as immoral, hypocritical, unreliable, unmanly, intransigent, insecure, greedy, ill-intentioned and chronically suspicious of everyone. Begin was depicted as a latter-day Shylock.[93] Israel's positions in the negotiations were sharply criticized: it was argued that whereas the Israeli people wanted peace, Begin wanted land; consequently the people would be the victims of Begin's policies. Hints were made to the effect that the military option was still open to Egypt.[94] It was noted in Israel that the campaign was conducted by newspapers loyal to Sādāt (those critical of his regime attacked Sādāt's initiative rather than Israel's response). This intensified doubts concerning the sincerity and durability of Sādāt's acceptance of Israel and his determination to pursue a dialogue with it.

ISRAEL'S SETTLEMENTS POLICY AND ITS REPERCUSSIONS

The Egyptian press campaign was largely connected with the Israeli government's own policies with regard to settlements in Sinai. At the time of Sādāt's visit and perhaps before, Israel had made it clear that it recognized Egypt's sovereignty over Sinai. In its peace plan, however, Israel demanded the right to maintain its settlements there, to have them linked to Israeli administration and jurisdiction, and defended by Israeli forces. Egypt rejected that demand as contradictory to Israel's recognition of its sovereignty over Sinai, and demanded that the settlements be evacuated. Israel explained its position by arguing that the continued existence of settlements and the maintenance of a few airfields after withdrawal were the basis of its acceptance of Egypt's sovereignty over Sinai, and that Sādāt had known this all along. Israel maintained that the settlements would be under formal Egyptian sovereignty.

The Sinai settlements being such a sensitive issue, the Israeli government adopted three secret resolutions governing future settlement activity on 3 January 1978. These represented a compromise following submission of a plan for a substantial settlement effort by Agriculture Minister Ariel Sharon in his capacity as Chairman of the Ministerial Committee on Settlements. The resolutions provided for the setting up of three new settlements in the West Bank in three months time; bolstering the settlements in the Rafiah salient by expanding arable land and increasing their population; and breaking ground for six new sites in eastern Sinai, west of the Rafiah salient.[95]

Implementation of those decisions started promptly, with the media in Israel carrying news of a drive to set up 24 new settlements in the Rafiah salient alone before the next round of Egyptian-Israeli talks. Sharp reactions from Cairo and Washington prompted the Israeli government to reconsider. Nevertheless, the decisions were reaffirmed by the Cabinet on 8 January 1978, with the addition only of the word "existing" to one of its phrases, which now read: "Bolstering the existing settlements in the Rafiah salient." Begin also assured Carter and Sādāt that Israel was not establishing new settlements.

Sādāt was said to have invited Israel to "burn down" its settlements (according to the Israeli version of his statement, or to "plough them over," according to the Egyptian version). Begin responded by warning that Israel would withdraw its peace plan and demand territorial changes, as justified under international law, if Egypt insisted on complete Israeli evacuation of the Sinai.[96] Carter reacted by saying that it was inconceivable that Israel would jeopardize the peace talks by an argument over settlements, and that the latter were illegal and in contravention of the Geneva conventions.[97]

THE MILITARY COMMITTEE'S DELIBERATIONS

When the Military Committee convened in Cairo on 11 January 1978, the positions presented by Israel were based on its peace plan, while Egypt submitted her own plan for security arrangements in Sinai. (Cairo had previously argued that, once peace was established, security arrangements would be altogether unnecessary.) At the end of four days of deliberations (which included a meeting between Sādāt and Weizman), the parties were in disagreement over most issues.

As a prerequisite for discussing the specifics of a settlement in Sinai, Israel demanded an Egyptian commitment to stay out of any future Arab-Israeli military confrontation. Egypt wanted the specifics, particularly the issue of the Sinai settlements, to be discussed first. Israel also demanded that the size of the Egyptian armed forces be reduced and that a clause be included to that effect in the peace settlement. Egypt displayed willingness to reduce its armed forces, but only of its own accord and not as a formal component of the settlement. On the Sinai settlements, Israel maintained its position that they should remain under an extra-territorial status, linked to Israeli administration and jurisdiction, and defended by Israeli forces. Egypt demanded total Israeli evacuation of the Sinai, rejecting out of hand proposals to maintain the settlements through leasing, lending or exchanging territories. Israel further demanded a special status for three of its airfields in Sinai after the withdrawal of the IDF. Egypt rejected this, but offered to allow Israeli Air Force training flights over Sinai during and possibly after the withdrawal period. Egypt rejected Israel's demand that free navigation in the Tiran Straits be secured by IDF units which would remain in Sharm al-Shaykh. Instead, Egypt proposed a clause in the peace agreement that would declare the Gulf of 'Aqaba an international waterway open to innocent passage.

Among the agreements reached was that Israel should withdraw its military forces from Sinai in two stages: first to the al-'Arīsh Ra's Muhammad line, then to the international border. Yet there was disagreement over the timetable for this withdrawal: whereas Israel requested 3–5 years to complete it, Egypt would agree to no more than 18 months. As a compromise, Israel proposed that the resumption of Egyptian sovereignty over Sinai be distinct from Israeli withdrawal. Certain token expressions of Egypt's sovereignty would be admitted immediately after the signing of the peace treaty.[98] This was rejected by Egypt.

Egypt did agree in principle to Israel's proposal that, following withdrawal, Sinai should be divided into three zones: a UN-controlled demilitarized area in eastern Sinai, along the international border and the Red Sea coast (in which Israel wanted its settlements to be included); a fully demilitarized area in central Sinai; and a limited-armament area in western Sinai. In public, Egypt insisted that demilitarization be mutual; privately, its delegation hinted at a willingness to drop that demand. Still, there was disagreement over the delimitation of these areas. Israel demanded that the part of Sinai east of the Mitla and Gidi passes, as well as the passes themselves, be fully demilitarized. Egypt was willing to fully demilitarize an area stretching no more than 40 km west of the international borders (whereas the passes were almost 200 km away).

To supervise the implementation of the security arrangements, Israel proposed early warning stations in the Sinai. This was accepted by Egypt, provided that no Israeli presence was admitted.

The Military Committee adjourned on 14 January 1978, pending progress in the Political Committee. The Israeli delegation left for home, leaving behind a small liaison mission to preserve continuity. Following US-mediated contacts it was agreed to reconvene the committee on 19 January but, as a result of the suspension of the Political Committee on 18 January, this was delayed until the 31st.

THE POLITICAL COMMITTEE'S DELIBERATIONS

The convening of the Political Committee was delayed by disagreement over its agenda. Also in dispute was whether the discussions over the agenda should be the first item of the committee's deliberations, as Israel proposed, or should be concluded prior to the committee's opening, as Egypt demanded. Egypt's position eventually prevailed.

Egypt's objective in the Political Committee was to achieve a statement of principles on which the negotiations, and eventually the comprehensive peace settlement, would be based. It insisted that Israel accept two principles before beginning negotiations on specifics: complete Israeli withdrawal, and the Palestinians' right to self-determination. Sādāt held that this would enable King Ḥusayn to join the peace process—a development which he believed was essential to achieve real progress. Hence Egypt's insistence that a statement of principles should be agreed upon prior to the start of the negotiations; hence also Egypt's proposal for the order of items on the agenda: first, complete Israeli withdrawal; then the right of the Palestinians to self-determination; and only lastly the peace arrangements to follow withdrawal (the "nature of peace").

Israel, on the other hand, wanted the nature of peace to be the first item on the agenda, since it would not make commitments regarding the future of the West Bank and the Palestinian issue before being certain of what it would get in return. Israel proposed that the issue of the West Bank and Gaza be referred to as "secure and recognized borders" instead of Egypt's proposed term, "complete Israeli withdrawal"; it suggested that the Palestinian issue be termed "the right of the Palestinian Arabs to self-rule" rather than "the Palestinians' rights to self-determination." An Israeli proposal to add the issue of the Sinai settlements to the agenda was rejected by Egypt on the grounds that it was not a matter for discussion.

The controversy over the agenda was accompanied by Egyptian threats and pessimistic utterances—possibly designed to get the US to apply pressure on Israel. Egypt delayed the departure of its delegation to Jerusalem, and Sādāt threatened that he was ready to declare the failure of his peace efforts because of Israel's attitudes. He also accused Begin of trying to sabotage his initiative, and said that there was no hope for a statement of principles to be achieved in the Political Committee.[99]

Finally, on 15 January 1978, an American compromise formula was accepted, not without US pressure on Israel. It established a three-point agenda: (1) a declaration of principles which would govern the negotiation of a comprehensive peace settlement in the ME; (2) guidelines for negotiations related to the issues of the West Bank and the Gaza Strip; and (3) the elements of peace treaties between Israel and her neighbours in accordance with the principles of Security Council Resolution 242.[100]

What Egypt and Israel proposed to include in the statement of principles reflected disagreement on a number of major points. Regarding the issue of withdrawal, Israel's formula called for withdrawal from territories occupied in 1967 to secure and recognized borders on the basis of Resolutions 242 and 338 (which, in Israel's view, implied territorial changes rather than complete withdrawal). The five-point Egyptian draft statement of principles submitted to the committee called for "Israel's withdrawal from the Sinai, Golan, West Bank and Gaza, in accordance with Resolution 242 and the principle [contained in its preamble] of the inadmissibility of acquisition of territory as a result of war"[101]—in other words, complete Israeli withdrawal.

With regard to the Palestinian problem, Israel reiterated its Administrative Autonomy scheme, whereas the Egyptian draft called for "the achievement of a just settlement covering all aspects of the Palestinian problem on the basis of the right of self-determination, through talks with the participation of Egypt, Jordan, Israel and representatives of the Palestinian people." [102] This wording clearly echoed Carter's Aswān statement.

The Egyptian draft was part of a proposed arrangement whereby Israel would withdraw from the West Bank and Gaza Strip over a five-year transitional period, during which those areas would be run by the UN, while a joint Egyptian-Israeli-Jordanian-Palestinian Committee worked out security arrangements. At the end of that period, the Palestinians in the West Bank and Gaza Strip would exercise their right to self-determination through a referendum. This arrangement was to be conditional upon an unequivocal Israeli pledge accepting Palestinian self-determination. [103]

Following the understanding reached in Aswān, US views of the objectives of the Political Committee were close to Egypt's. Like Egypt, the US thought the Committee should agree on a statement of principles enabling Jordan (and, in the US view, Syria as well) to join the peace process. Like Egypt, the US advocated an interim solution of several years for the West Bank-Gaza and Palestinian problems. The American concept, introduced following Carter's talks with King Husayn (see following essay in this section) and with Sādāt in early January (see above), reflected an attempt to develop autonomy in such a way as to satisfy Jordan. Thus the US seized on Article 26 (providing for revision of the scheme after five years) in order to introduce the principles of Israeli withdrawal and Palestinian self-determination. At the end of that period, the US proposed that the Palestinians would determine their future by means of a referendum, in which they would opt either for the continuation of the joint Israeli-Jordanian-Palestinian interim administration or for a federal or confederal link with Jordan. Military control during the interim period would be exercised jointly by Israel and Jordan. After termination of the interim period, Israel would have to accept Arab sovereignty over the area. [104]

Events in the Political Committee evolved on two separate planes: the committee's talks, both formal and informal; and concurrent developments outside the committee but linked to its deliberations. The outside atmosphere was one of crisis, created by hard-line statements from both sides and by spectacular steps on the part of Sādāt, such as going into seclusion on the eve of the convening of the committee (suggesting that he was about to make a dramatic decision).

The committee's talks, by contrast, were characterized by a businesslike atmosphere, although the Egyptian Foreign Minister, Ibrāhīm Kāmil, made a strongly-worded opening statement. [105] Following the opening speeches on 17 January 1978, the committee went into closed session and Egypt and Israel exchanged their proposals for the statement of principles, as set out above. The meeting was adjourned till the evening of 18 January to enable the delegations to study the drafts. In the interval, the American delegation prepared a compromise proposal and conferred with both sides.

On the afternoon of 18 January, Sādāt instructed his delegation to halt the talks and return home immediately. According to Israeli press reports, his instructions reached Jerusalem just when Egypt and Israel were on the point of agreeing to an American compromise draft on the Palestinian problem, whereby Israel would accept in principle the concept of the Palestinians' participation in the determination of their own future. The Israeli delegation had made its acceptance conditional on the following: that the term "Palestinian" be interpreted to designate West Bank and Gaza Strip residents only; that the words "legitimate rights" and the word "own" be deleted from the phrase "their own future" in the

Palestinian clause; and that that clause would not call for the solution of the Palestinian problem "in all its aspects." [106]

Carter was later reported to have complained to Sādāt that he called off the talks when the parties were nearing an agreement. [107] The US had tried to dissuade Sādāt, but to no avail.

Following the recall of the Egyptian delegation, the Egyptian army was put on alert. Sādāt declared that the resumption of the talks would be conditional on Israel's acceptance of the principle of the inviolability of the territory and sovereignty of others. [108] Israel interpreted this as laying down pre-conditions. It reacted by postponing the resumption of the Military Committee's deliberations, declaring that it would reconvene only when Egypt restrained its press campaign against Israel, the Jews and Begin.

Sādāt's move was apparently not just prompted by the course the Jerusalem talks had taken; but rather because he felt Israeli leaders had misread his situation and motivation. Judging from an analysis published in Cairo which probably reflected official thinking, [109] Egypt had come to feel that Israeli leaders assumed that Sādāt had made his initiative from despair; that the Egyptian people wanted peace at any price, and that Sādāt could therefore be pressed for concessions; that Egypt had dissociated itself from the Arabs to the point of eventually agreeing to a separate peace; and that support for Sādāt by public opinion in the world at large was dwindling—and would diminish further—if the negotiations became bogged down over details. Hence the Israeli assessment that Sādāt would not give the West Bank-Gaza-Palestinian issues priority over Sinai.

Such an evaluation of Israel's approach was clearly reflected in Egyptian statements explaining Sādāt's move. [110] They accused Israel of leading the talks into a vicious circle and of dragging its feet in order to sabotage the peace process and diminish world-wide support for Sādāt's initiative. Sādāt also made a point of refuting (what he described as Israel's view) that his situation was weak and that he would settle for a separate peace. "Egypt does not seek peace at any cost," he declared. "I broke off the negotiations because Israel did not agree to withdraw from the Golan, the West Bank and Gaza before Sinai." [111] Sādāt accused Israel of having escalated the problem of the Sinai settlements on the eve of the Jerusalem talks "to a blatant provocation" in order to poison the atmosphere and to "topple the Egyptian initiative." [112]

The central theme in the reactions of Israeli leaders, particularly of Begin and Dayan, to Sādāt's sudden move and his subsequent statements was that the Egyptian President had backtracked on his former positions. Dayan, for example, argued that Sādāt's demand for the removal of the Israeli settlements in Sinai had never been raised before. [113] He also said that Sādāt was now negotiating over the Golan, West Bank, Gaza Strip and East Jerusalem—which he had not done earlier. [114] Sādāt was criticized for retracting the pledge he had given to Begin in Jerusalem not to let the Egyptian army cross the Mitla and Gidi passes, and for renewing his demand (which he had unofficially agreed to drop) for reciprocal demilitarization.

Sādāt's recall of his delegation from the Political Committee reflected his assessment that in direct talks he would not be able to get Israel to accept what he considered vital for the peace process: complete withdrawal and acceptance of Palestinian self-determination in advance of further negotiations. He therefore opted to call in the third party—the US— whose positions on these points were close to his own, and to persuade it to play a more active role in exerting pressures on Israel. Sādāt indicated that the first US step in this direction should be to provide Egypt with the same amount and quality of weapons which Israel possessed. He argued that Israel's "intransigence" resulted from the unlimited arsenal it received from the US, making the latter responsible for the failure of the peace process thus far.[115] This aspect of Sādāt's explanation of the breakdown of the Political Committee served as a dramatic overture for his new "peace offensive," the central event of which was his visit to Washington (see below).

ATHERTON'S SHUTTLES (22-31 JANUARY 1978)

The US continued its efforts to get the two parties to agree on the statement of principles in order to make it possible for the Political Committee to reconvene, preferably with the participation of Jordan. This was done by the US Assistant Secretary of State, Alfred Atherton, in shuttle trips between Jerusalem and Cairo.

Atherton's revised American proposal for the statement of principles was turned down by both parties, though for different reasons. The major disagreements continued to relate to the Palestinian issue and the problem of withdrawal. The clause on the Palestinians in the US draft was based on Carter's Aswān statement. Israel objected to the Egyptian and American wording, "the Palestinian problem," as referring to Palestinians everywhere, whereas it wanted to limit the issue to the residents of the West Bank and Gaza Strip only. Instead it proposed the term "the Palestinian issue." Israel also objected to the phrase "in all aspects" for the reasons described above.

Egypt insisted that the clause on withdrawal contain an explicit reference to complete Israeli withdrawal from the occupied territories. Cairo made it clear that it would not settle for a vague formula on this issue such as that contained in Resolution 242—which Israel supported.

By the time Atherton left the area on 31 January to attend Sādāt's talks in the US, no agreed statement of principles had been worked out.

THE MILITARY COMMITTEE RECONVENES (31 JANUARY-2 FEBRUARY 1978)

On 29 January, the Israeli government approved the resumption of the Military Committee's deliberations in Cairo. Two days later, the Committee reconvened. At the preceding meetings, Israel had demanded that Egypt submit detailed counter-proposals, particularly to Israel's proposal that the Sinai settlements remain under Israeli security protection, administration and jurisdiction, though under Egyptian sovereignty. When the talks resumed, Egypt submitted a counter-proposal which marked some progress from Israel's point of view.[116] Egypt was now willing to consider leaving the Rafiah salient settlements as part of a UN-controlled buffer zone, provided they were not under Israeli jurisdiction nor defended by Israel, and provided that it was made clear that this arrangement was temporary. Egypt was also willing to allow Israel the use of its Sinai airfields for a few years following the conclusion of the peace settlement.

On the eve of the talks, Begin called upon Sādāt to honour the pledge he had given him in Jerusalem to demilitarize Sinai east of the Mitla and Gidi passes.[117] In its counter-proposal, however, Egypt was willing to accept no more than a 40 km wide fully demilitarized, UN-controlled zone along the international border. Egypt was willing to turn the area stretching thence to the passes into a limited-armament zone, but with the two passes proper excluded from it.

The talks were adjourned on 2 February, pending the Israeli government's examination of Egypt's counter-proposal, and Sādāt's return from his US and European tour. Although the talks were expected to resume in mid-February, Egypt announced on 3 February that the Committee would not reconvene until progress was achieved in the political talks, thereby underlining its contention that it was not seeking a separate agreement.

SĀDĀT'S VISIT TO THE US (3–8 FEBRUARY 1978)

Sādāt's visit to Washington was part of the "peace offensive" which Egypt launched following the collapse of the Political Committee talks. This offensive also took the Vice-President, Ḥusnī Mubārak, to eight Arab states; the Deputy Prime Minister, Ḥasan al-Tuhāmī, to China and North Korea; the State Minister for Foreign Affairs, Butrus Ghālī, to Yugoslavia; and Sādāt himself to Great Britain, West Germany, Austria, Romania, France, Italy and Morocco as well as to the US.

One purpose of these visits was to enlist support for Egypt's positions, particularly on the issues of Israeli withdrawal, Palestinian self-determination and the Israeli settlements. Another purpose was to isolate Begin both internationally and domestically. Sādāt therefore met European leaders he believed capable of influencing Israel, such as British Prime Minister James Callaghan, West German Chancellor Helmut Schmidt, Romanian President Nicolae Ceauşescu and Austrian Chancellor Bruno Kreisky. He also met American Jewish leaders, and the Israeli Labour party leader, Shimon Peres, in Salzburg on 11 February 1978. Sādāt complained to all of them that Begin had failed to respond to his peace initiative and had become an obstacle to peace.

Four months later, Peres disclosed that Sādāt had told him that he understood Israel's needs for border rectifications and for the presence of the Israeli army in strategic locations in the West Bank.[118] Sādāt also submitted to Peres a verbal counter-proposal to the Administrative Autonomy plan. Peres communicated the scheme to Begin, who did not disclose its existence to the public, insisting that Egypt submit it formally in writing. According to Sādāt's counter-proposal, the West Bank should be linked to Jordan, and no Palestinian state should be established. Minor border rectifications could be admissible; an Israeli military presence in strategic locations in the West Bank could be maintained during and after a five-year interim period; and demilitarized zones and other security arrangements should be established. The future of the Israeli settlements would have to be negotiated.[119] Sādāt followed up that meeting by several others with Peres and Weizman in the following months. In these talks, his positions were considerably more flexible than Egypt's official stance.

Sādāt's visit to the US was to a large extent an American initiative. The Egyptian walkout from the Political Committee had taken the US completely by surprise; nor were its reasons for doing so well understood in Washington. Furthermore, Israel was complaining that Sādāt had changed his positions. One of Carter's purposes in inviting Sādāt was therefore to find out first hand exactly where he stood on substantive issues. Another was to persuade him to abandon his dramatic "media" diplomacy in favour of quiet and patient negotiations. Yet media exposure was one of Sādāt's own objectives in the US. Through his public appearances and his talks with Carter, Sādāt sought to achieve a deeper American understanding of, and greater support for, Egypt's positions, particularly on the Israeli settlements, withdrawal and the Palestinian problem; to undercut Israel's preferential status, stemming from the US commitment to its security, by creating a corresponding American commitment to Egypt's security; and finally to bring about a change in the American role from mediator or "honest broker" to "full partner."[120]

Sādāt was helped in the pursuit of his objectives by international developments. Increasing Soviet and Cuban involvement in Africa and the Red Sea region underlined Egypt's status as America's major ally in that part of the world, second only to Saudi Arabia. Similarly, Arab opposition to Sādāt's initiative brought home to the American public the risks he had taken and encouraged the feeling that he was entitled to US support.

The message Sādāt conveyed to the American public through the media and Congressional committee briefings focused on the charge that the Israeli government, and Begin in particular, had deliberately attempted to "erase the impact of the historic initiative and divest it of its driving spirit." [121] Particularly bitter criticism was directed against Israel's policy regarding the settlements. On the Palestinian problem, Sādāt went back to his pre-Aswān position of insisting on Palestinian self-determination. He stressed the need for complete Israeli withdrawal, including from East Jerusalem. He urged the US to assume a more active role in the peace process by using its influence on Israel, and demanded US arms.

In their talks at Camp David, Carter and Sādāt dealt with the framework and procedure of the negotiations, with the US role in their conduct, as well as with the principles of the settlement. Carter urged Sādāt to resume the political negotiations and conduct them without disruption. It was agreed that Atherton would resume his efforts to work out an agreed statement of principles, and that the Military Committee would be reconvened.

Sādāt proposed that, as a "full partner," the US submit its own plan for a settlement. [122] (In view of the similarity between the American and the Egyptian positions on basic issues, it was held in Israel that such an American step would be tantamount to exerting US pressure on Israel to accept Egypt's positions.) Sādāt justified his proposal by arguing that the massive American military and economic aid for, and political support of, Israel made the US a full partner whether it liked it or not; moreover, as long as it clung to a neutral position, the US would not be able to accelerate the peace process. Sādāt's apparent implication was that he might discontinue his peace initiative if the US did not meet his expectations.

After the visit, the US public position continued to be that of "honest broker," and it still refrained from taking sides. Overt pressure on Israel, the Administration implied, could be counter-productive. Yet, in effect, the Administration began to apply increased indirect pressure on Israel by undercutting support for its position among the US public, in Congress and in the American Jewish community (see below). Carter was also making preparations to grant Sādāt's arms requests, at least in part.

The White House issued a six-point statement of principles, as reaffirmed by Carter to Sādāt during their talks, underlining "US participation in the search for peace." [123] On the issue of withdrawal, the statement reaffirmed the US position that the peace settlement must be based on all the principles of Resolution 242, including withdrawal of Israeli armed forces from territories occupied in 1967. This language indicated that the US had not accepted Sādāt's demand for complete withdrawal, and supported instead slight border rectifications. Yet the reference to "all the principles" of Resolution 242 implied US support of Egypt's position that the reference in the Resolution's preamble to the inadmissibility of the acquisition of territory by war should be accepted by Israel as one of the principles of the peace settlement. Moreover, the statement went on to say that "Resolution 242 is applicable to all fronts of the conflict"—thereby rejecting Israel's argument that it did not necessarily apply to the West Bank (see below). On the Palestinian problem, the statement reaffirmed the Aswān formula, thus ignoring Israel's objection to the phrase that the issue be resolved "in all its aspects," as well as its opposition to the mention of the Palestinians' "legitimate rights."

On the question of the Israeli settlements, the White House statement put the US squarely on Egypt's side, reaffirming "the longstanding US view that the settlements were contrary to international law and an obstacle to peace, and that further settlement activity would be inconsistent with the effort to reach a peace settlement." Speaking two days later, Vance repeated that all the Israeli settlements in Sinai were contrary to international law, adding flatly that they should therefore not exist. [124] His statement signalled a further move towards the Egyptian position, since it was an implicit call on Israel to dismantle the settlements, rather than merely pointing to their illegality.

ATHERTON'S SHUTTLE—THE SECOND ROUND (20 FEBRUARY–8 MARCH 1978)

In the period between Sādāt's Washington visit in February and Begin's in March, there were no direct Egyptian-Israeli contacts, although a skeleton staff of the Israeli delegation to the Military Committee stayed on in Egypt. Negotiations were limited to Atherton's renewed attempts to reach an agreed statement of principles with regard to the West Bank-Gaza Strip-Palestinian problem. The renewal of Atherton's mission had been agreed upon by Carter and Sādāt, but was only reluctantly accepted by Israel which would have preferred the renewal of direct talks with Egypt.

Israel wanted the statement of principles to be phrased in general terms which would allow it to sign an agreement with Egypt on Sinai without being obliged to accept the principle of withdrawal on the other fronts before negotiations on the West Bank even started. Egypt and the US, by contrast, held that the statement of principles should contain a clear Israeli acceptance of the principle of withdrawal from the West Bank, which they hoped would draw Jordan into the negotiating process.

Israel's proposal for the statement of principles regarding the West Bank and Gaza Strip stated that on the basis of Resolution 242, there would be a withdrawal of Israeli armed forces from territories occupied in 1967, and that Israel would maintain secure and recognized boundaries. On the Palestinian question, Israel proposed that there should be a just resolution of the problem of the Palestinian Arabs; those in Judea, Samaria and the Gaza Strip would have the right "to participate in the determination of their future" through talks to take place among Egypt, Israel, Jordan and representatives of those Palestinian Arabs. [125]

Egypt's counter-proposals on these two issues were tougher than formerly. Reacting to Israel's position on the applicability of Resolution 242 (see below), Egypt now demanded an explicit Israeli commitment to the principle of withdrawal on all fronts. Egypt also reiterated its insistence on Israel's acceptance of Palestinian self-determination. The latter point was interpreted in Israel as a bid for a US mediation proposal which would feature the Aswān formula as a compromise.

In his talks in Amman, Atherton was told that Jordan would not join the peace process without Syria's approval. [126] However, the Syrian government evaded the suggestion that he add Damascus to his shuttle. Atherton was said to have been told on 4 March 1978 that Jordan would not join the peace process unless Israel first accepted complete withdrawal and guaranteed the Palestinians' national rights, including self-determination. [127] Atherton's mission was suspended on 8 March.

THE DETERIORATION IN US-ISRAELI RELATIONS (FEBRUARY-MARCH 1978)

Sādāt's visit to the US was followed by a deterioration in US-Israeli relations, described by Defence Minister Weizman as an "acute confrontation such as Israel has never experienced before." [128] This was due in part to an Administration policy of pressuring Israel into changing its positions, particularly on the issue of withdrawal and of the Israeli settlements in the West Bank and Sinai, and in part due to Israel's own policy on these issues at the time. Editorials in the US press described Begin as a liability to Israel and to US Jewry; they argued that it was America's task to bring the debate within Israel over his policies to a head. [129] In Israel, the impression gained ground that the US sought to have Begin replaced.

The sharpest controversy was over the settlements issue. It flared up for the second time in late January when a settlement—described by the government as an archaeological excavation site—was set up in Shiloh on the West Bank. This was followed by press reports of preparations to turn three military camps near Nablus into civilian settlements, as the first stage of a plan to establish 40 settlements in the West Bank.

On 27 January, President Carter sent a message to Begin (the third on this issue during the month) expressing regret over the matter, as well as confidence that Begin would honour the commitment personally made to him and would not permit settlement activity to proceed.[130] Carter repeated the reference to that personal commitment in his 30 January press conference. He recalled that when Begin and Dayan had visited him in December 1977, he understood from them that no new settlements would be authorized: the number of settlers would be increased only by expanding the population of existing settlements and would be limited mostly to military installations.[131]

Carter's reference to an Israeli commitment precipitated a bitter controversy between the two governments. Israel emphatically denied having made such a commitment. The dispute was further aggravated by the statements made on the subject by Carter and Vance at the conclusion of Sādāt's visit to the US (see above).[132] Israel responded by describing Vance's statement that the settlements should not exist as contradicting past US policy on that issue; it reasserted its position that the settlements were legal, legitimate and necessary.[133] In response, the White House endorsed Vance's statement as a reiteration of the position the US had held throughout.[134]

Carter subsequently complained to Congress and to Jewish leaders that the Israelis were "less than candid" with him about their intentions regarding the settlements. The Administration also pointed out for the first time that a discrepancy existed with regard to the settlements in Sinai between the peace plan Begin had submitted to Carter and the one later shown to Sādāt in Ismā'īliyya (for both, see above). Israel conceded that the clause providing for the settlements being linked to Israeli administration and jurisdiction did not appear in the text submitted to Carter, having been added as the result of a Cabinet discussion after Begin's return from the US. Israel argued, however, that this made no real difference because what Egypt objected to was the very existence of the settlements, not their being linked to Israel in one form or another.

The settlements controversy became a major impediment for Foreign Minister Dayan, who arrived in the US shortly after Sādāt's visit in an effort to offset the gains made in US public opinion by the Egyptian leader. The main message Dayan tried to convey was that the obstacles to peace were Sādāt's hard-line positions, not the settlements.

The controversy with the US was paralleled by a heated dispute over the issue within the Israeli government. The central figure behind the drive to expand settlement activity in Sinai was Agriculture Minister Sharon; he was most firmly opposed by Defence Minister Weizman. The dispute reached a climax during Weizman's US visit in March. Before leaving for Washington, he ordered a halt to all ground-clearing and expansion of settlements in Sinai. (Like all military government authorities, that in Sinai operates under the Ministry of Defence.) With his departure, however, Sharon and his supporters in the Cabinet pressured Begin to resume the work in Sinai. In a widely publicized trans-Atlantic telephone conversation with Begin, Weizman threatened to resign if the work was allowed to resume. The Cabinet eventually upheld Weizman's instructions.

US-Israeli relations were further strained—and Israel's position in American public opinion weakened—by another controversy: the applicability of Resolution 242 to the West Bank. Eager to get Jordan to join the peace process, Egypt had demanded unequivocal Israeli acceptance of the applicability of Resolution 242 to all fronts. Israel argued that as long as there was no partner with whom to negotiate the future of the West Bank (i.e. unless and until Jordan joined the negotiations), it should not be required to make an advance commitment to withdraw from that area. According to Israel's interpretation, Resolution 242 did not necessarily apply to all fronts; hence the question of withdrawal from the West Bank should be resolved through negotiations, not in advance of them.

This position drew sharp criticism both at home and abroad. Begin's domestic critics reminded him that he himself had resigned from the Cabinet in August 1970 when it had decided to accept Resolution 242 as the basis for a peace treaty—precisely because he thought the decision was tantamount to a commitment to return parts of the West Bank and Gaza Strip to Arab rule. Others warned Begin of the consequences of abandoning a position held by Israeli governments since 1967, and of going back on his own declared willingness (conveyed to the US after taking office) to accept Resolution 242 without reservation.[135]

Carter warned on 2 March that abandonment of the commitment to Resolution 242 as the basis for negotiations and settlement "would put us back many months or years."[136] Israel responded by informing the US, and stating in public, that it accepted Resolution 242 in principle, but regarded it as open to interpretation. This did not satisfy the US. Carter declared on 9 March that the abandonment of Resolution 242 as applicable to the West Bank and other occupied territories would be a very serious blow to the prospects of peace and a complete reversal of the policy of the Israeli government and of other governments in the area.[137]

A further strain in US-Israeli relations developed as a result of a change in the Administration's ME arms sales policy. Following Sādāt's visit, the Administration began to process a proposal to sell 50 F-5E fighters to Egypt, 60 F-15 fighters to Saudi Arabia and 75 F-16 fighter bombers and 15 F-15 fighters to Israel. From Israel's point of view, this was a serious setback. In the first place, the fact that Egypt received lethal arms from the US set a precedent as Washington had formerly only supplied it with non-combat equipment. Secondly, by tying the sales together in a package deal (a measure designed to secure acceptance of the Arab part in Congress), the Administration signalled that Israel no longer enjoyed a preferential status over Arab arms recipients. Finally, the deal itself and in particular its timing were viewed in Israel as a punitive measure for its positions in the peace negotiations. However, Carter denied any connection between the aircraft deal and the controversy with Israel over the settlements.[138]

Israel launched a campaign to convince Congress not to approve the deal—an effort resented by the Administration as unwarranted interference. While Israel argued that Egypt should not be sold US arms before a settlement was achieved, the main thrust of its criticism was directed at the Saudi sale. The Administration maintained that Saudi Arabia was a moderate non-confrontation state which had never been directly involved in aggression against Israel, and that the F-15s would be deployed in a way that would not jeopardize Israel's security. Israel refuted these arguments by pointing to the close military co-operation maintained between Saudi Arabia and the "confrontation states." It warned that if the deal went through, it might have to reconsider its peace plan for Sinai, particularly its position regarding the Sinai airfields. Israel also charged the US with a breach of agreement. It claimed that the F-15 and F-16 sale had been promised to Israel as part of the Sinai agreement of September 1975. By making the sale part of a package deal with Saudi Arabia and Egypt, the Administration was disregarding its predecessor's undertaking.

BEGIN'S VISIT TO THE US (20–23 MARCH 1978)

Begin's visit to Washington was preceded by Defence Minister Weizman (7–11 March 1978). The Administration apparently viewed Weizman as the Israeli minister most capable of exercising a moderating influence on his government's policy. Weizman's dramatic telephone conversation with Begin˙regarding settlement activity in Sinai underlined that point. Consequently, when Weizman was invited for an unscheduled meeting with Carter, observers deduced that the Administration not only wished to strengthen his position, but would have been pleased to see him replace Begin. Nevertheless, Weizman's visit—interrupted as it was by the terrorist attack in Israel on 11 March (see last essay in this section)—could not drastically change the atmosphere of crisis which had developed in US-Israeli relations and which continued to mar the ensuing Begin-Carter talks. Begin's talks with Carter and his appearances before Congressional committees and the general public clarified more than any previous exchanges the issues and depth of Israeli-US disagreements. Although Begin did submit a somewhat revised Israeli proposal for principles to govern the peace settlement, his positions were presented by Carter to Congress in a negative form, namely as a list of Israeli rejections of American positions and proposals. In a pointed indication of the prevailing mood, no agreement was reached on the wording of a concluding statement, and none was issued.

The talks came in the wake of Israel's operation in South Lebanon (see essay below). In order to pre-empt a possible Israeli attempt to use the question of its withdrawal from South Lebanon as a bargaining point in the peace process, the US rapidly helped push through a Security Council resolution calling for Israeli withdrawal from that area. The Carter-Begin talks consequently focused only on the peace process. A further shift in the US role from that of "honest broker" towards "full partnership" was indicated by Washington's submission of its own draft of a declaration of principles to govern the settlement. The part dealing with the West Bank-Gaza-Palestinian problem was presented as a set of reservations and additions to Israel's Administrative Autonomy plan which the US still officially regarded as a fair basis for negotiations. In substance, however, the American proposals were closer to Egypt's positions than to Israel's.

Regarding the West Bank-Gaza issue, Begin proposed a formula according to which the Egyptian and Israeli governments would express their intention to negotiate peace treaties on the basis of Resolution 242 and to implement all its principles. On this basis, Israeli forces would withdraw from occupied territories, and secure and recognized borders would be set up.[139] This formula did not satisfy Carter since it contained no explicit Israeli undertaking to withdraw from the West Bank. He conveyed to Begin his impression—based on his talks with Sādāt and other Arab leaders—that contrary to their public positions, the Arabs would not insist on total Israeli withdrawal and would not object to minor border rectifications.[140] On the strength of this assumption, Carter demanded that Israel accept the applicability of Resolution 242 to all fronts. He proposed that the Israeli withdrawal be carried out during a five-year interim period, following which Israeli forces would be allowed to remain for a limited period in strategic outposts along the Jordan Valley and elsewhere. He also proposed additional security arrangements such as UN buffer zones, demilitarization and American security guarantees. According to Carter's account, Begin was unwilling to accept the applicability of Resolution 242 to all fronts,[141] arguing that the principle of Israeli withdrawal from all fronts was not part of that resolution, but rather a matter to be discussed in the peace negotiations.

Regarding the Palestinians, Israel's proposal stated that a solution should be sought for the problem of the Palestinian Arabs in Judea, Samaria and the Gaza District, and that they would have the right to participate in the determination of their future through talks to be conducted by Egypt, Israel and representatives of the Arab residents of those areas. The US proposal on this issue was a reaffirmation of the relevant clause in Carter's Aswān statement. Carter conveyed to Begin his impression, again based on his contacts with Arab leaders, that no independent Palestinian state would be created as a result of the Palestinians' participation in determining their own future. [142] He proposed that at the end of the five-year interim period, a referendum should be held offering the Palestinians one of the following three choices: continuation of the interim arrangement (namely administrative autonomy); affiliation with Israel; or affiliation with Jordan. Begin rejected the idea on the grounds that it "would unavoidably lead to what even the Americans do not want: the establishment of a Palestinian state." [143]

Carter and Begin also discussed the Israeli settlements. Carter demanded a halt to all settlement activity while the peace process continued. According to Carter's account, Begin was not willing to cease settlement activity in the West Bank during the period of active negotiations or to give up the Sinai settlements. Israeli official sources pointed out, however, that Begin explicitly undertook not to authorize any new settlements in Sinai during negotiations, and implied a willingness to halt further settlement activity in the West Bank for as long as the negotiations with Egypt continued. [144]

Following the talks in Washington, Administration officials indicated that Carter was now convinced that Begin's views, at least on the West Bank, were "an unshakable matter of deep conviction," and that progress was unlikely so long as he remained in power. [145] Carter was reported to have told Congressmen that "Begin had [peace] within his grasp and he let it get away." [146] This statement was denied by Carter. [147]

The peace process had now reached an impasse. Begin's standing in the US continued to decline. In Israel, the "Peace Now" movement came into being, voicing fears that Begin's stand would lead to a new war. Begin's health worsened, and he did not fully recuperate until July. In the interval, Dayan and Weizman took the initiative—each in his own way—in devising means to break the impasse and to take the pressure off Israel.

THE SĀDĀT-WEIZMAN TALKS (30–31 MARCH 1978)

The invitation extended late in March to Defence Minister Weizman to visit Egypt and meet Sādāt was given two contradictory interpretations in Israel which reflected conflicting views about Sādāt's real intentions. Weizman maintained that Sādāt was genuinely seeking peace with Israel and argued that there was a chance of achieving progress through direct talks. He apparently assumed that, following the Carter-Begin meetings, Sādāt had realized that progress towards a comprehensive settlement through American mediation was unlikely in the near future; consequently, he was interested in preserving the momentum of his initiative through unpublicized direct talks. The fact that Egypt invited Israel's Defence Minister to Cairo and made his visit known while the Israeli army was still in South Lebanon was cited as an indication of the importance Egypt attributed to such direct talks.

A different view was put forward by Dayan—generally sceptical regarding Sādāt's intentions—who thought that Sādāt was trying to drive a wedge between the US and Israel by inviting Weizman for direct talks. Dayan maintained that without American mediation, no real progress could be achieved. [148]

Weizman took to Cairo the Israeli proposals for a statement of principles which had been submitted by Begin to Carter a week earlier (see above). Sādāt surprised

Weizman on the first day of their talks (30 March) by presenting new proposals which constituted a considerable departure from Egypt's public positions. Though not fully disclosed until four months later, Sādāt's proposals[149] were similar to those of Carter to Begin and, like them, were based to a large extent on the Administrative Autonomy plan. He told Weizman he would prefer Jordan to join the negotiations, but if Amman did not do so within "several weeks," Egypt would negotiate over the future of the West Bank and the Gaza Strip, and would be willing to sign a separate peace—provided Israel accepted total withdrawal from the West Bank and Palestinian self-determination. He also said that, at the end of the interim period, Palestinian self-determination would not include the option of an independent state. Furthermore, Sādāt reportedly agreed to a limited Israeli military presence in camps during and after the five-year period; the rest of the area would be demilitarized. He also showed willingness to discuss the continued existence of the Israeli settlements even after the interim period, provided they came under the authority of the Administrative Council and did not contain Israeli military forces. Neither did Sādāt deny the right of Israelis to settle in the West Bank provided they used private land purchased from Arab owners. The problem of refugees was to be handled by the Administrative Council; Israel would have a veto over the entry of Palestinian refugees from abroad, and internal security would be handled by local Arab police.[150]

However, Sādāt surprised Weizman again on the second day of the talks (31 March) by withdrawing his new proposals. He expressed interest in continuing the dialogue with Weizman, but made this conditional on Israel's offering new proposals. Weizman subsequently pressed the Cabinet to adopt new decisions, and was even said to have threatened to resign if this was not done.[151] The government's position was that it was Egypt's turn officially to submit counter-proposals to Israel's peace plan, which it had not yet done.

THE AMERICAN "QUESTIONS" TO ISRAEL (MAY-JUNE 1978)

The Carter-Begin talks in March had ended in an impasse with regard to the statement of principles. As noted above, a major difficulty in working out that statement was the controversy over the applicability of Resolution 242 to the West Bank. In view of US pressure on Israel to show flexibility on this issue, the Cabinet reconsidered its position. According to a directive issued by Dayan to Israeli embassies on 16 April 1978, Israel's position was that "Resolution 242 served as the basis for negotiations between Israel and all neighbouring countries—Egypt, Jordan, Syria and Lebanon."[152]

The new element in this formula was the specific mention of Jordan as a negotiating partner, implying Israel's willingness to negotiate with Ḥusayn over the West Bank. However, the US was still not satisfied since the new formula contained no explicit recognition of the principle that Resolution 242 meant Israeli withdrawal from at least parts of the West Bank and Gaza Strip, or that it applied to all fronts. Furthermore, Dayan's directive also stated that the Administrative Autonomy plan was compatible with Resolution 242. (The plan called for withdrawal of the Israeli military administration, but not the IDF, from the autonomous areas.) Finally, on Begin's insistence, the directive contained a rejection of territorial compromise or minor border corrections, as well as of total withdrawal.[153]

When this formula was turned down by the US, Dayan suggested a new approach. During his talks with Vance in the US (26–28 April), he proposed to abandon efforts to work out a statement of principles, arguing that it led nowhere because the parties adhered to positions anchored in ideology. Instead he proposed the creation of a framework for discussing the practical aspects of a settlement for the West Bank and Gaza Strip; this would precede, rather than follow, the formulation of a statement of principles.

The Administration reacted favourably to Dayan's idea, believing that his approach could be used (just as well as the controversy over Resolution 242) to force Israel into taking decisions on the West Bank and Gaza Strip which it considered necessary. The US was therefore willing to abandon the search for a statement of principles for a while; to endorse Israel's rejection of total withdrawal and of a Palestinian state; to put aside its demand for a Palestinian referendum; and to take the Administrative Autonomy plan—the only plan submitted thus far by the parties—as the basis for practical negotiations of the future of the West Bank and Gaza Strip, as Dayan proposed.

There was one basic difference between the American and Israeli views on the Administrative Autonomy plan: whereas the US regarded it as an interim arrangement for a five-year period, at the end of which Arab sovereignty would have to be established there, Israel sought an indefinite continuation of the autonomy arrangement, whereby the question of sovereignty would be left undecided.

The Administration then posed to Dayan, and later to Begin (who again visited the US from 1–8 May, ostensibly to participate in celebrations marking Israel's 30th anniversary), two basic questions. Since the Administrative Autonomy plan lent itself to review after five years, was Israel willing at the end of that period to negotiate over the sovereignty (or, in the American wording, "the permanent status") of those areas? If so, what mechanism could Israel offer as a substitute for the referendum that would give the Palestinians an option other than living under Israeli rule after the five years.

Bearing in mind the ideas which Sādāt had conveyed to Weizman in March, Dayan in turn sought to have Egypt reaffirm to the US its willingness to play a major role in solving the West Bank issue. He consequently asked the US to find out from Egypt whether it was willing to represent the Palestinians in the West Bank and Gaza Strip. He also asked whether Egypt accepted the American interpretation of Resolution 242 (which did not call for a total Israeli withdrawal), as well as Carter's Aswān formula regarding the Palestinians' role in the peace settlement.[154] Observers believed that Dayan submitted his questions in the expectation that Egypt's replies would be negative. This would render the American questions to Israel irrelevant since Israel would then be able to argue that, in the absence of a negotiating partner, there was no point in its making a commitment as to the outcome of the negotiations on the West Bank.

The American questions were put before the Israeli Cabinet, and Dayan's questions were communicated to Egypt. Unable to persuade Jordan to negotiate for the West Bank, and unwilling to commit itself to doing so before being assured of Israel's commitment to withdrawal, Egypt delayed its response. When finally made, the US Administration reportedly considered it too intransigent to be communicated to Israel.[155] In the meantime, Egypt tried to exert psychological pressures on Israel while it was considering how to reply to the American questions. Thus, Sādāt hinted that he had a surprise decision in store which he would disclose on Revolution Day (23 July); that he might not renew the UN Forces' mandate in Sinai, due to expire in October 1978; that he might resign, declare a freeze on the peace process as long as Begin remained in office, call off his initiative, or even go to war.[156] Yet, simultaneously, Egypt intimated in an unofficial response to Israel's questions in mid-May that it might put forward a peace plan calling for an interim period, following which Egypt, Jordan and representatives of the West Bank and Gaza Strip would discuss security arrangements with Israel, and the Palestinians would determine their future.[157] This would have signified somewhat greater flexibility as compared with previous Egyptian positions.

At the same time as posing the questions, the US Administration communicated to Israel its own idea of the reply which it expected. Israel should undertake to resolve the question of the permanent status of the West Bank and Gaza Strip at the end of the five-year period; meanwhile, it should conduct negotiations with that aim in view. To determine the permanent status of those areas, negotiations should be conducted by representatives of Israel, Egypt, Jordan and the Palestinians living there. The outcome of such negotiations would have to be approved by the latter.[158] To press its point, the State Department declared in public that Israeli willingness to discuss withdrawal from the West Bank and Gaza Strip would open the way to a comprehensive settlement, whereas failure to do so would spell the end of the peace efforts and put most vital American interests in the ME in jeopardy.[159]

Within the Cabinet, Begin's position was that Israel should not be drawn beyond the five-year review clause included in the original Administrative Autonomy plan, and should not commit itself to a hypothetical situation five years hence. Weizman proposed that Israel should respond in the affirmative to the first question by expressing its willingness to discuss the permanent status of Judea, Samaria and the Gaza Strip after five years. He deliberately used the term "permanent status"—as it appeared in the American proposal. Begin objected to the term as implying that the Administrative Autonomy plan could not be a permanent arrangement. As to the second question, Weizman proposed that the permanent status of those areas be determined through negotiations between Israel, Egypt, Jordan and representatives of the local population. Dayan, who also objected to the term "permanent status," proposed that Israel respond to the American questions by expressing willingness to discuss "the nature of the future relations" between Israel, Jordan and the West Bank and Gaza Arabs. He apparently hoped to avoid a new collision with the US by including in the reply detailed practical proposals for negotiations on the West Bank and Gaza Strip to take place during the Autonomy period.

On 12 June 1978, Dayan submitted to the Cabinet, as part of Israel's draft reply, a document proposing that "the nature of the future relations between the parties" should be discussed during the five-year period, and suggesting arrangements and issues to be included. These were continued Israeli military presence in strategic locations; the right of Jews to purchase and to settle land; and the barring of any Arab army from entry into those areas. A central theme in Dayan's proposals was a larger role for Jordan in the autonomy. Unlike Weizman, Dayan thought that Jordan, not Egypt, was the main partner for negotiations over the West Bank. He therefore proposed a "functional compromise" whereby Israel would hold the territory, but Jordan would run the administration of the West Bank. Dayan's proposals were opposed by both Begin and Weizman as overcommitting Israel. Begin also argued that an increased Jordanian role might lend substance to Jordan's claim to sovereignty over the West Bank.

The Cabinet debate was conducted against a background of tension, fed by personal clashes and by rumours that each of the three main protagonists had threatened to resign. Finally, despite Weizman's emphatic opposition, the Cabinet adopted a formula which in fact constituted a negative reply to the first question: "The government of Israel agrees that five years after the application of the administrative autonomy . . . the nature of the future relations between the parties will be considered and agreed upon, at the suggestion of any of the parties." In its reply to the second question, the government provided a substitute for the referendum, but it did not clarify who "the parties" to the negotiations would be: "For the purpose of reaching an agreement, the parties will conduct negotiations between them with the participation of representatives of the residents of Judea, Samaria and the Gaza District, as elected in accordance with the administrative autonomy." [160]

The reply was approved by the Knesset on 19 June 1978. The US expressed regret and criticized Israel for failing to respond fully to its questions. Carter stated on 1 July that the US was about to communicate Egypt's peace plan to Israel which, in his view, it was likely to reject; the US would then submit its own compromise proposals. If those were not accepted by the parties, the Geneva conference would have to be reconvened. [161]

MONDALE'S VISITS TO JERUSALEM AND ALEXANDRIA (30 JUNE-3 JULY 1978)

The original objective of Vice-President Walter Mondale's visit to Jerusalem was ceremonial: to participate in the 30th anniversary celebrations. The visit was part of the Administration's efforts to placate Israel's supporters in the US following Congress approval on 15 May 1978 of the aircraft package deal (see above). At Sādāt's insistence, Egypt was added to Mondale's itinerary.

However, the visit assumed more than just ceremonial significance. Its timing was calculated to influence the way Israel would reply to the American questions (not yet delivered when the date of the forthcoming visit was announced). Moreover, in Jerusalem, Mondale presented the US view of what the peace settlement should look like: it should be based on almost total Israeli withdrawal on all fronts and on recognition of Israel's security needs. Mondale maintained that Israel's proposal of almost complete withdrawal from Sinai, supplemented by various security arrangements, should also be applied to the West Bank and Gaza Strip. He said that there should be an almost complete withdrawal from those areas, except for slight border changes for security purposes, negotiated and agreed upon by the parties. Palestinian self-determination should not include the option of a Palestinian state, and the PLO was not to be a partner in the negotiations. The preferred arrangement for the West Bank would be a link with Jordan. [162]

Israeli officials were critical of the parallel Mondale drew between Sinai and the West Bank and Gaza Strip. They argued that whereas there was no dispute over sovereignty in the former area, this was not the case in the latter. Furthermore, the strategic implications to Israel's security of withdrawal from the West Bank would be much more serious than those of withdrawal from the Sinai. [163]

By the end of his tour, Mondale had received agreement from Egypt and Israel to send their Foreign Ministers to a conference with Vance in London. He was also handed Egypt's new peace plan.

THE EGYPTIAN PEACE PLAN AND INFORMAL PROPOSALS

Egypt submitted its formal settlement proposals to the US through Vice-President Mondale on 3 July 1978, and to Israel a day later. The Egyptian plan allowed Begin to substantiate his contention that Egypt's positions were uncompromising, and that its formal proposals were tougher than those put forth informally. Yet by submitting its plan, Egypt opened the way for the US to produce a compromise plan in an attempt to bridge the gap between the Israeli and Egyptian positions. Moreover, by formulating its proposals in a manner that could not be interpreted as setting pre-conditions, Egypt made it possible for the US to convene the Foreign Ministerial conference in London which Begin had only agreed to on the understanding that the Egyptian plan did not contain pre-conditions.

The gist of the Egyptian plan—namely that the West Bank should revert to Jordan and the Gaza Strip to Egypt for the duration of the transition period—had been made public by the Egyptian media soon after Israel replied to the American questions and before the plan was formally passed on to Israel. On 25 June, the Israeli Cabinet decided to reject the suggestion that the West Bank and the Gaza Strip should revert to Jordanian and Egyptian control as an unacceptable pre-condition.[164] President Carter rebuked Israel for rejecting the plan before it had even been submitted.

The full version of the Egyptian plan called for Israel's withdrawal from the West Bank (including the settlements and East Jerusalem) and the Gaza Strip within a transitional five-year period, during which time those areas would be placed under Jordanian and Egyptian administration respectively, with the UN exercising a supervisory function. Negotiations among Egypt, Jordan, Israel, representatives of the Palestinians and the UN would deal with security arrangements, the timetable of Israel's withdrawal and similar issues. After five years, the Palestinian people would be able to determine their own future.[165] (For the text of the plan, see Appendix IX.)

Egypt described the plan as a display of flexibility: it made no reference to a Palestinian state; it accepted the principle of a phased withdrawal; and it ran counter to Arab consensus over the PLO as the sole legitimate representative of the Palestinians. In Israel, however, the plan was seen as less flexible than earlier formal statements of Egypt's positions. Israeli comment singled out the following points. The plan did not address itself to the nature of peace. As its title, "Proposals Relative to Withdrawal from the West Bank and Gaza and Security Arrangements," indicated, it made no reference to peace treaties or other components of peace. Unlike earlier Egyptian documents, such as the draft statement of principles Egypt had submitted in Ismaʻīliyya and in the Political Committee in Jerusalem, the plan did not say that the Israeli withdrawal should be carried out in accordance with Resolution 242. Neither did the Egyptian plan accept the Aswān formula calling for the Palestinians' "participation" in the determination of their own future. Instead, it reiterated the original demand for Palestinian self-determination. Significantly, the plan referred to the "Palestinian people" as a whole, not to the residents of the West Bank and the Gaza Strip only. The specific demand for Israeli withdrawal from East Jerusalem and from the Israeli settlements, and the role assigned to the UN, had also not formed part of earlier Egyptian documents. For these and other reasons, the Israeli Cabinet rejected the plan on 9 July 1978. But in deciding that it contained no pre-conditions, Dayan's participation in the London conference was approved.

As preparations for the conference proceeded, Sādāt met Shimon Peres for a second time. The venue was Vienna under the aegis of the Socialist International. Its Chairman, Willy Brandt, and the Chairman of its ME Committee, Chancellor Kreisky, participated in part of the Sādāt-Peres talks on 10 July. At the meeting, an attempt was made to formulate an agreed statement of principles more forthcoming than Egypt's recent peace plan. This would enable the Israeli parliamentary opposition to make a credible case against the government that its hard line was not warranted by Egypt's "real" positions, as disclosed to Peres. This could force Begin to moderate his positions or risk losing the support of a large and growing segment of public opinion in Israel and among American Jewry.

An agreed statement of principles was indeed formulated in the form of a Socialist International statement on how to achieve peace in the ME. This was issued by Brandt and Kreisky on 10 July. Unofficially it was made known that both Sādāt and Peres had endorsed the statement (though it was actually formulated with the help of Abba Eban, Peres' Labour party colleague).[166] The "Vienna Document" called upon Egypt and Israel to resume direct negotiations leading to peace treaties. Peace, it said, should be based on normal and friendly relations between the ME countries and on close regional co-operation. Secure borders should be set up in accordance with Resolution 242. An Israeli withdrawal to secure borders on all fronts would be agreed upon in negotiations. Demilitarization and security arrangements for Israel should also be provided. In order to achieve peace, the document stated, a solution must be found to the Palestinian problem in all its aspects, including recognition of the Palestinians' right to participate in the determination of their future through contacts in which their elected representatives would participate.[167] The document thus established the principle of secure borders to be reached through negotiations; it contained no recognition of the PLO and no explicit support for a Palestinian state.

As an expression of West European positions endorsed by Sādāt, the "Vienna Document" could be considered a considerable achievement for Israel. Government spokesmen criticized it nonetheless, arguing that in actual fact it implied total withdrawal and the eventual return of the PLO to the political scene.[168] Moreover, Begin resented Peres' meetings with Sādāt. When a subsequent meeting between Peres and King Ḥusayn in London was suggested, he withheld his consent, charging Peres with attempting to compete with the government in conducting peace negotiations of his own.[169]

Shortly after his meeting with Peres and a few days before the convening of the Foreign Ministerial conference in England, Sādāt and his War Minister, Gen Jamasī, conferred in Salzburg with Weizman (13 July). Weizman reportedly later told the Cabinet that at the meeting Sādāt had offered Israel peace "in all its aspects."[170] According to Weizman, Sādāt had accepted in principle minor border changes in the West Bank, and was willing to accept an Israeli military presence in varous locations there even after the five-year period.[171] Sādāt reportedly also proposed that the West Bank be returned to Jordan after the five-year period. Until then Israel, Jordan and West Bank representatives would form a joint transitional committee with its own police force. Israel would be able to retain its settlements, presumably under Jordanian sovereignty.[172]

On the basis of their talks, Weizman told the Israeli Cabinet that he believed it was possible to conclude peace with Sādāt, and recommended the start of practical, discreet negotiations, in which the Egyptian leader would be more flexible than in official negotiations.[173] The Cabinet deferred decision on Weizman's recommendations pending the outcome of the forthcoming Foreign Ministerial conference.

THE LEEDS CASTLE CONFERENCE (18–19 JULY 1978)

The Egyptian-Israeli Foreign Ministerial conference was arranged by the US as a means of reviving the formal direct dialogue suspended since the Political Committee talks were called off in January. In order to remove the conference from the adverse effects of direct contact with the media, it was eventually convened in the relative isolation of Leeds Castle, outside London.

The Israelis probably assessed that if both Egypt and Israel came to the conference with their respective peace plans only, the US would inevitably table its own compromise proposals which would no doubt be closer to Egypt's positions than to Israel's. At any rate, Dayan seems to have been able to convince Begin that since Egypt had renewed direct, formal contacts with Israel, and since a discussion of both countries' peace plans had been started, Israel could now state its willingness to discuss the question of sovereignty over the West Bank and Gaza Strip at the end of a five-year period. Dayan thus informed the conference that Israel had modified the position it had stated only four weeks earlier in reply to the first American question. Dayan further told the conference that Israel would seriously consider a peace settlement based on territorial compromise in the West Bank and Gaza if a proposal to that effect were submitted.[174] These new positions were put to the Knesset on 25 July.

Begin now disclosed that in June, when the Cabinet discussed the questions submitted by the US, he had actually been willing to state Israel's readiness to decide on the question of sovereignty over the West Bank and Gaza Strip after five years, yet had rejected such a formula (as proposed by Weizman) "because I was ill and I did not want there to be a government crisis."[175]

For his part, the Egyptian Foreign Minister said that if Israel accepted complete withdrawal (referring also to East Jerusalem), Egypt was willing to sign a peace treaty with Israel. (This was not stated, it will be recalled, in Egypt's formal plan.) Belatedly responding to Dayan's questions addressed to it in April, Egypt now informed Israel that it did regard itself a partner for negotiations over the West Bank.[176] Egypt's statement of its willingness to sign a peace treaty with Israel was seen by the US as a considerable concession. This view was endorsed by Dayan who said after the conference that he was now convinced that Egypt was genuinely willing to establish peace in the ME.[177] This statement was in turn cited by US officials to back their contention that now that Egypt had made a significant concession, it was Israel's turn to do likewise.[178]

These exchanges apart, the conference ended with both Egypt and Israel standing by their respective peace plans.[179] Nevertheless, both sides declared that the talks had improved their understanding of each other's positions, and that there was room for further dialogue. It was consequently decided to resume the deliberations two weeks later, possibly at the American surveillance station at Umm Khashība in Sinai.

THE CRISIS THAT LED TO CAMP DAVID

In his talks with Weizman in Salzburg, Sādāt had indicated his interest in an Israeli gesture of goodwill. For example, he proposed the immediate and unilateral return of al-'Arīsh and the Mount Sinai area to Egypt. (Al-'Arīsh had been the administrative capital of Sinai; Sādāt had vowed to erect a church, a synagogue and a mosque on Mount Sinai and to conduct tri-denominational prayers for peace.) The gesture was to be presented publicly as an Israeli initiative which Sādāt would be able to use to justify the resumption of direct talks at Foreign Ministerial level. It would also help him escape from the corner into which he had manoeuvred himself when he declared that October 1978 would be a decisive turning point. The idea of the gesture was rejected by both Begin and Dayan. Dayan pointed to the asymmetry between Sādāt's absolute refusal even to discuss the question of the Israeli settlements in Sinai, and his proposal of a one-sided Israeli gesture.[180]

Begin sought to use the Egyptian proposal in a new approach to the peace process. He proposed abandoning attempts to reach a comprehensive peace treaty, suggesting instead special agreements that would gradually create what he termed "peace relations." He stated: "We have to distinguish between peace relations and peace treaties. We want a peace treaty. However, if it transpires that this is difficult and will take a long time . . . it is possible to create peace relations, as was the case in Germany. . . . So we are prepared to draw up bilateral agreements on a permanent basis . . . not interim agreements and not unilateral agreements for Israeli withdrawal, but mutual and permanent [agreements]."[181]

This was the consideration behind the Israeli response to Egypt's initiative regarding the goodwill gesture which Begin made public before it was formally communicated to the Egyptian government. "A unilateral step by any country is inconceivable," Begin declared. "There is no person and there is no country that can receive something for nothing. Egypt will not receive al-'Arīsh and Mount Sinai on a unilateral basis." [182]

Sādāt took offence, not so much perhaps at the substance of the Israeli response as at the manner and tone in which it was announced. Sādāt therefore refused to accept the letter containing Israel's formal response. He also expelled, on 27 July, the Israeli military mission which had been in Egypt since the start of the Military Committee talks, thereby cutting off the direct Egyptian-Israeli communications system it had maintained. This gave symbolic expression to Sādāt's decision to abandon the avenue of direct talks and to conduct any future negotiations through American mediation. Egypt was ready to resume talks, he said, "whenever there is complete agreement upon the fact that there will be no compromise upon land or sovereignty." [183] Sādāt told Alfred Atherton (now undertaking a new shuttle in an attempt to set the stage for the Foreign Ministers' conference agreed upon at Leeds Castle), that he would not resume the talks with Israel in any form unless it announced that it had no territorial claims and no demands for border changes. [184]

The US expressed disappointment at Sādāt's position. [185] Egypt in turn expressed dismay over the American reaction and declared that it would not agree to renew the direct talks unless the US came up with a clear, specific peace plan of its own. At this point Carter, through Secretary Vance, invited Begin and Sādāt to a tripartite summit in Camp David to start on 5 September in order to formulate a framework for peace. Their acceptance was announced on 3 August.

President Carter's move seemed something of a gamble, since it was believed that if the summit ended in failure, the President's personal position would suffer seriously. Carter explained his decision to take the risk by pointing to the major stake the US had in the ME, and particularly to the dangerous implications a new war could have for American national security. According to Carter, the Administration's hopes for success were based on the appraisal that the complete seclusion of Camp David and the President's participation as a full partner rather than a go-between, would enable him to overcome the personal mistrust between the two leaders and cause them to come to terms with one another. [186]

Carter's stated intention to assume the role of an active partner helped Sādāt accept the invitation to Camp David. He had been under Saudi pressure to co-ordinate his policies with the Arab "confrontation states" (see essay on Inter-Arab Relations) and—as noted above—had committed himself not to resume direct talks with Israel until it first renounced all territorial claims and demands for border changes. Now, in view of the new US role, the Camp David talks would no longer be an exclusive, direct Egyptian-Israeli dialogue.

In order to minimize the consequences of failure as well as the psychological pressures, the Administration made a point of lowering expectations: the prospects for complete success, Administration sources indicated, were remote; an agreement in principle on the renewal of direct talks was presented as the best that could be hoped for from the summit. Egypt, on the other hand, implied that for the summit to be successful, it should produce without delay an Israeli acceptance in principle of withdrawal from the West Bank and Gaza Strip. Egypt depicted the summit as "the last chance" for an agreement. Israel rejected this view, however, feeling instead that the pace of the deliberations should be slow and cautious. [187]

Begin again brought up the idea of a permanent partial peace, suggesting that if Egypt and Israel failed to reach agreement on the principles of a comprehensive settlement at Camp David, they could negotiate a "partial agreement of a permanent nature." [188] Egypt rejected the idea, insisting that the summit should be devoted to seeking agreement on the principles of a comprehensive settlement, not to working out separate agreements. [189]

Controversy was also aroused by reports leaked on 13 August to the effect that Israel had decided to set up five new agricultural-military outposts in the Jordan River valley. It turned out that such a decision had indeed been made by the Ministerial Committee on Defence on 28 June, but had been kept secret since then. In the face of criticism at home and abroad, the government resolved on 14 August to freeze that decision until after the Camp David summit.[190]

THE CAMP DAVID SUMMIT
THE DELIBERATIONS
The actual work of the summit[191] started on 6 September, when Israel and Egypt submitted their respective drafts of the framework for a settlement. Israel's draft was based on its peace plan of December 1977; Egypt's on the plan it submitted in July 1978. The latter called, *inter alia*, for complete Israeli withdrawal from Sinai, Golan, the West Bank and Gaza Strip, and East Jerusalem; for the removal of the Israeli settlements from those areas; for reparations by Israel for damages inflicted upon Arab civilians and civilian establishments by its armed forces; and for the setting up, through self-determination, of a Palestinian national entity in the West Bank and Gaza Strip following a five-year transitional period, during which time those areas would be administered by Jordan and Egypt respectively, in cooperation with the representatives of the Palestinian people.[192] After Israel had stated its position regarding each clause in the Egyptian draft, it became obvious that the US would have to submit a compromise draft as the basis for further negotiations. This it did on 10 September.

Carter's original tactic was to chair trilateral sessions with Sādāt and Begin. Since three such sessions (on 6 and 7 September) failed to break the ice between the Egyptian and Israeli leaders, Carter began meeting with each of them separately.

The Israeli delegation voiced sharp objection to the repeated reference in the US draft to the inadmissibility of the acquisition of land by war—a principle cited in the preamble of Resolution 242. Israel argued that this did not apply to land seized in a defensive war. In his meeting with Begin on 12 September, Carter was persuaded to delete this clause from the US draft. He was also prevailed upon to endorse Israel's demand for an open-ended military presence on the West Bank. Begin in turn agreed that the question of sovereignty over the West Bank should be "decided," and not merely "discussed," by the end of the five-year transitional period. The Egyptian delegation, for its part, insisted on the inclusion of the "inadmissibility" clause in the draft compromise. The issue was resolved on 13 September by an agreement to include a general reference to Resolution 242 "in all its parts" in the final texts.

Meanwhile Egyptian and Israeli experts, attempting to work out a final agreed formulation of the US draft, came up on 13 September with two documents separating the framework for a comprehensive settlement (namely the West Bank-Gaza Strip-Palestinian issue) from the framework for the Egyptian-Israeli peace treaty. These two frameworks were henceforth discussed separately. From that point onwards, Carter's bilateral talks with Sādāt and Begin focused on the Sinai framework, while Secretary Vance conducted the drafting group which concentrated on the framework for the comprehensive settlement.

The discussions of the Sinai framework produced a crisis on 14 September over Sādāt's demand for complete evacuation of the Sinai settlements. When this was rejected, Sādāt declared that his patience was at an end and that he was leaving. In an emotional 15-minute meeting on 15 September, Carter changed his mind, reportedly warning that his departure would seriously damage US-Egyptian relations and consequently leave Egypt strategically vulnerable. Sādāt decided to stay and agreed that the Egyptian demand for the evacuation of the Sinai settlements be brought before the Knesset as a condition for the conclusion of a peace treaty. The Knesset would vote on it within two weeks from the conclusion of the summit.

Following his brief talk with Sādāt, Carter set 17 September as the deadline for the termination of the conference. In order to remain within that deadline and yet conclude the conference successfully, it was agreed on 16 September to exclude questions on which agreement could not be reached from the final texts. These would be dealt with in the form of letters, signed jointly by Egypt and Israel, which would set out the two countries' respective positions on those issues as well as their undertaking to discuss them again in the future. However, the wording of the letters soon produced yet another controversy which threatened to wreck the summit only hours before its conclusion.

The sharpest debate erupted over East Jerusalem. The US had earlier demanded that Israel agree to raising an Arab (probably Saudi) flag over the Temple Mount. On 17 September, it submitted a proposed letter on Jerusalem containing the positions of all three parties and describing East Jerusalem as occupied territory. This prompted the Israeli delegation to threaten to leave immediately. The crisis was solved by the substitution for the joint letter of four separate ones, one each from Egypt and Israel to the US and one from the US to each of the other two governments. (According to Egypt's Deputy Prime Minister Ḥasan al-Tuhāmī, who was present at Camp David as one of Sādāt's closest advisers, Dayan was willing to accept the Arab demand for an Arab presence in East Jerusalem, provided that security and peace were safeguarded. Nevertheless, Israel rejected an Egyptian proposal for an Arab force to be formed in East Jerusalem to maintain security there. Egypt, for its part, rejected Israel's proposal of hoisting the flags of Islamic countries over the Islamic holy places in Jerusalem.[193] Dayan described Tuhāmī's remarks as a "fabrication.")[194]

Another highly controversial point was the length of time during which Israel undertook to refrain from establishing new settlements in the West Bank. In order to avoid a deadlock, Begin said on 16 September that Israel would forego further West Bank settlements "during the negotiations." According to Begin, he meant the period of three months during which the Egyptian-Israeli peace treaty was to be negotiated.[195] The US argued, however, that Begin had agreed that the freeze would also apply to the period during which the West Bank-Gaza Strip agreement would be worked out.[196] The delicacy of the controversy which flared up after the conclusion of the framework agreements was underlined by attempts by Gush Emunim members to set up new settlements in the West Bank, beginning on 19 September. Their attempts were forcibly thwarted by the IDF.

THE AGREEMENTS

The framework for a comprehensive settlement and the framework for an Egyptian-Israeli peace treaty were signed by Sādāt and Begin and witnessed by Carter in an emotional ceremony at the White House on 18 September 1978. (For the texts of both framework agreements, see Appendix X.) Most of the letters accompanying the two frameworks (dealing with the Sinai settlements, East Jerusalem, Egypt's role in the West Bank-Gaza settlement, and differences over the terms "Palestinians" and "West Bank") were released by the White House on 22 September. (For their texts, see Appendix XI.) The US Defence Secretary's letter to the Israeli Defence Minister regarding US assistance in the construction of two air bases in the Negev to replace those in Sinai was released by the Pentagon on 29 September. (For the text, see Appendix XII.)

In addition to the publicized texts of the agreements and the accompanying letters, there were apparently written or verbal agreements or understandings which were not made public at the time. For example, it was reported that a secret verbal understanding was reached regarding an increased role for Egypt and Israel in blocking Soviet influence in the ME and north-east Africa. That understanding included, *inter alia*, co-operation between Egypt's and Israel's intelligence services; modernization and streamlining of the Egyptian armed forces with US aid, and increased American economic aid to Egypt.[197]

The signing of the Camp David Framework Agreements was depicted by the Administration and perceived internationally as a genuine breakthrough. It restored much of Carter's diminishing popularity at home, and won Sādāt and Begin the 1978 Nobel Peace Prize. The heightened opposition in the Arab world to the agreements added weight to the view that, following Camp David, Egypt and Israel were closer than ever to solving their differences. Yet the course of the negotiations demonstrated that Sādāt and Begin had failed to reach a compromise on some of their fundamental goals. Whereas Begin was primarily seeking to dissociate Egypt from further involvement in the Arab-Israeli conflict, Egypt was seeking to retrieve Sinai without appearing to relinquish its Arab commitments and without waiving its claim to a central role in determining the Palestinian issue. The question, then, was whether Camp David provided a way out of the deadlock prevailing since January 1978. For all its genuine achievements, the Camp David conference did not provide an altogether affirmative answer to that question. This can be gathered from the contradictions between Sādāt's and Begin's respective interpretations of the relationship between the two framework agreements which differed chiefly on two points: whether the framework for the Egyptian-Israeli peace treaty was meant to serve as the model for future peace settlements with other Arab parties to the conflict; and whether the implementation of the Egyptian-Israeli treaty was conditional on, or otherwise linked to, the future evolution of Israel's relations with other Arab parties, particularly concerning the West Bank-Gaza Strip settlement.

Taking the formal view, Begin was justified in arguing that Israel's point of view had prevailed. The language of the Camp David agreements did not explicitly point to a link between the implementation of the Egyptian-Israeli treaty and the West Bank-Gaza Strip settlement, except for the "understanding" that a comprehensive settlement must be reached.[198] Neither did the timetables included in the agreements substantiate such a linkage. The Egyptian-Israeli framework called for the signing of the treaty within three months, for an interim withdrawal in the Sinai three to nine months after its signature; and for the establishment of normal relations following the interim withdrawal. The establishment of normal relations could therefore take place 6–12 months after the Camp David summit, although the latest date given by the framework for the implementation of the peace treaty was two to three years after its signature. The framework for the West Bank-Gaza Strip settlement, on the other hand, called for a transitional period of five years starting with the establishing of the self-governing authority, and for negotiations to determine the final status of those areas to start no later than the third year of the transitional period. No date was set, however, for setting up the self-governing authority, nor was the time from which the five-year period was to be counted laid down in the accords. (See text, Appendix X.) The Egyptian-Israeli peace treaty could therefore be signed and normal relations between the two countries established before negotiations on the final status of the West Bank and Gaza Strip even started.

Egypt, on the other hand, maintained that the agreement over the Sinai definitely set the model for further peace treaties. According to Sādāt, "the document of the

The Camp David Agreement on Sinai

- – ···–·· International boundary

- ++++ The 1949 Armistice line

- ········ The 1975 Sinai -II - agreement line

- –·–·– The approximate line of the first phase of Israeli withdrawal

- – – – The approximate boundaries of the demilitarized and limited-forces zones after final withdrawal

- [A] The Egyptian limited-forces zone in which only one division would be deployed

- [B] The Egyptian demilitarized zone in which only three border guard battalions and police units would be stationed

- [C] The Egyptian demilitarized zone in which only police would be stationed

- [D] The Israeli limited-forces zone in which only four infantry battalions would be deployed

  Zones C and D would be patrolled by U.N. Forces

- ➔ A highway to connect Egypt with Jordan through Israeli territory

- — Existing road

- ⊁ Airfield

- ◉ Town

- • Village or Bedouin settlement

- ▲ Israeli settlement

- ■ Israeli town under construction

  The number of Israelis residing in Sinai and the Gaza Strip was 3,500 on 31 December 1977

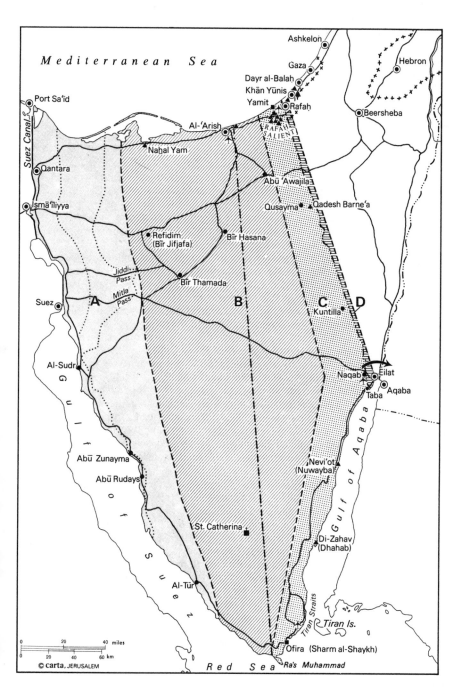

first framework invites all the Arab front-line states—Syria, Jordan and Lebanon—to participate in the negotiations and to conclude peace treaties on the same basis that decided the framework of the negotiations for the just and comprehensive solution in its general guidelines and the peace framework between Egypt and Israel. . . . We agreed to base the negotiations between Egypt and Israel, which will end before three months as regards withdrawal from Sinai, on the same basis as the negotiations that would take place between Syria and Israel as regards withdrawal from the Golan Heights.'' [199]

On his way home from Camp David, Sādāt expressed hope that King Ḥusayn would agree to join the peace process. However, he said that if King Ḥusayn did not participate, "then I will resume the negotiations on the West Bank and Gaza and these negotiations will proceed in parallel with the negotiations on Sinai.'' [200]

The framework for settlement in the West Bank and Gaza Strip definitely provided for future Egyptian involvement. For example, Egypt would be one of the parties to negotiate the final status of those areas (the others being Israel, Jordan and the elected local representatives). Egypt would also be one of the parties to determine the modalities for establishing the elected self-governing authority in the West Bank and Gaza Strip. The resolution of the refugee problem was also to be worked out by Egypt and Israel (see text, Appendix X).

Yet beyond that kind of involvement, the Camp David agreements did not establish a formal link between the implementation of the settlement in the West Bank and Gaza Strip and the future course of Egyptian-Israeli relations. From this point of view at least, the agreements could be viewed as an achievement for Israel. This could not be said, however, of the principles for the West Bank-Gaza settlement outlined in the Camp David framework. According to the agreements, autonomy in the West Bank and Gaza Strip would be a transitional, not a permanent arrangement, with the final status of the West Bank and Gaza Strip being decided following the five-year transitional period in which autonomy would obtain. The Israeli military government, as well as the civilian administration operating under it, would be withdrawn and replaced by the self-governing body whose authority would derive from an Israeli-Jordanian-Egyptian agreement, rather than from the Israeli military government as envisaged by the Administrative Autonomy plan. Israel's military presence would be restricted both in size and location. Security and public order in the West Bank and Gaza Strip (which according to the original plan were to be in Israeli hands) would be the responsibility of a "strong local police force" which could include "Jordanian citizens." (The latter term probably referred to officers of the Jordanian government, since West Bank inhabitants are Jordanian citizens.) Israel implicitly recognized the applicability of Resolution 242 to the West Bank and conceded to Jordan a role in setting up the institutions of the autonomy, in policing those areas during the transitional period, and in negotiating the final status of those areas. Israel consented to the use of the term "Palestinian people" (as opposed to the West Bank-Gaza residents) and recognized that they possessed "legitimate rights," including the right to participate in the determination of their own future. Israel further agreed that the elected representatives of the inhabitants of the West Bank and Gaza Strip would have the right to ratify or reject any agreement on the final status of those areas.

The texts of the Camp David agreements made no mention of the PLO. Soon after the conference, however, when an authoritative US official was questioned on the future role of the PLO, he declared: "Provision is made [in the Camp David agreements] for some Palestinians outside those territories to participate in the initial negotiations as agreed by the negotiating parties to set up the Palestinian self-governing authority. Later on, in the negotiations among the Palestinians themselves for the nature of their government after the transitional period, nothing is stipulated as to how they shall conduct that discussion. And one would assume that they would not talk about a subject as momentous to their future without in some way involving people throughout the [Palestinian] movement. I must also say specifically that no one will be prohibited from participating in the political process in those areas.'' [201]

Similarly, no explicit reference to the creation of a Palestinian national entity was made in the texts of the agreements. Nevertheless, the US view that the framework for the West Bank-Gaza Strip settlement should eventually lead to such an entity was implied by the same official when he tried to explain to "some of our friends in the ME" who were displeased with the agreements that changes in the situation would produce new conditions which would make it possible to resolve issues later that cannot be resolved now. [202]

The Camp David agreements—which were approved by the Knesset on 28 September following a highly emotional two-day long debate—removed the obstackles which had held up a settlement with regard to strictly bilateral Egyptian-Israeli issues. The agreements, however, did not bridge the basic gaps separating Egypt and Israel concerning the former's dissociation from the conflict: they did not constitute a genuine compromise on the West Bank-Gaza-Palestinian issues, nor did they resolve the differences between each side's view of the future of Egyptian-Arab ties. Indeed, in both these respects, they contained the germs of future dispute.

Israel Altman

NOTES
1. R Cairo, 9 November—Daily Report (DR), 9 November 1977.
2. Sādāt's address to the People's Assembly (PA), 26 November 1977; R Cairo, 26 November—DR, 28 November 1977.
3. *Al-Mustaqbal*, Paris; 3 December 1977.
4. Sādāt's interview, *Der Spiegel,* Hamburg; 5 December 1977.
5. Sādāt's interview, *October*, Cairo; 1 January 1978.
6. Shmuel Segev, *Sadat—ha-Derekh la-Shalom* ("Sādāt—The Road to Peace"), Tel Aviv: Massada, 1978 (Hebrew), pp. 41, 42, 67.
7. *Ibid*, pp. 42–43.
8. *Ma'ariv*, Tel Aviv; 30 December 1977, 26 June 1978; Segev, p. 55.
9. *Time*, New York; 6 August 1978.
10. Sādāt's interview, *October*, 1 January 1978.
11. *Jerusalem Post (JP)*, 21 November 1977.
12. *Ibid*.
13. Israel Broadcasting Authority (IBA), 20 November—DR, 21 November 1977.
14. IBA, 20 November—BBC, 22 November 1977.
15. Sādāt's interview, *Der Spiegel*, 5 December 1977.
16. *JP*, 22 November 1977.
17. Sādāt's interview, NBC TV, Middle East News Agency (MENA), Cairo; 27 December—DR, 29 December 1977.
18. *US News and World Report*, 6 February 1978.
19. Sādāt's address to the PA on 26 November, R Cairo, 26 November—DR, 28 November 1977; Sādāt's interview, *Events*, London; 30 December 1977.
20. R Cairo, 26 November—DR, 28 November 1977.
21. *Ibid*.
22. *Ha'aretz*, Tel Aviv; 30 November 1977.
23. Sādāt's Alexandria University speech, R Cairo, 27 July—DR, 28 July 1978.
24. *Ha'aretz*, 30 November 1978.
25. R Cairo, 26 November—DR, 28 November 1977.
26. Sādāt's press conference in Cairo on 10 December 1977, R Cairo, 11 December—DR, 12 December 1977.
27. *Al-Watan al-'Arabī*, Paris; 2 December 1977.

28. Sādāt's interview, *Corriere Della Sera,* Milano; 20 December—DR, 23 December 1977.
29. *October*, 26 December 1977.
30. Sādāt's interview to ABC TV in Cairo, MENA, 28 November—DR, 30 November 1977; Sādāt's interview, Tunisian Radio and TV, quoted by R Cairo, 4 December—DR, 6 December 1977.
31. Sādāt's radio and TV birthday interview, R Cairo, 27 December—DR, 29 December 1977; Sādāt's 21 January speech to the PA, Cairo all Services, 21 January—BBC, 23 January 1978.
32. Sādāt's interview to NBC quoted by MENA, 27 December—DR, 29 December 1977; Sādāt's interview to CBS, MENA, 28 December—DR, 29 December 1977.
33. Sādāt's interview to US television networks, quoted by MENA, 1 December—DR, 2 December 1977.
34. Sādāt's press conference, R Cairo, 11 December—DR, 12 December 1977; Sādāt's press conference, MENA, 17 December—DR, 19 December 1977.
35. Begin's interview to *New York Times (NYT)*, 14 December 1977; Dayan's comment, R Israel Defence Forces (IDF), 12 December—DR, 13 December 1977; *Ha'aretz*, 7 December 1977.
36. *International Herald Tribune (IHT)*, Paris; 10–12 December 1977; *Ha'aretz*, 9 December 1977
37. *Ma'ariv*, 14 December 1977.
38. *Al-Watan al-'Arabī*, 16 December 1977.
39. *Ma'ariv*, 13 December 1977.
40. *Ibid*, 30 December 1977.
41. *JP*, 29 December 1977; Israel TV service, 28 December—BBC, 30 December 1977.
42. *Yedi'ot Aharonot*, Tel Aviv; 28 December 1977.
43. *Ma'ariv*, 9 February, 5 March 1978.
44. The Likud's Ninth Knesset Election Platform in Hebrew (Tel Aviv: The Likud's Information Department, 1977), p. 2.
45. See *MECS 1976–77*, p. 428.
46. See note 44.
47. *Ha'aretz*, 21 June 1977.
48. *Ma'ariv*, 7 April 1978.
49. *JP*, 29 December 1977.
50. *The Times,* London; 13 December 1977.
51. *The Guardian,* London; 13 December 1977.
52. *JP*, 8 January 1978.
53. USIS Official Text, Tel Aviv; 16 December 1977.
54. *Washington Post (WP)*, 18 December 1977.
55. MENA, 17 December—DR, 19 December 1977.
56. Israel Government Press Office, *Daily Press Bulletin (GPO)*, 21 December 1977.
57. White House statement, 17 December 1977, *Department of State Bulletin*, January 1978.
58. *NYT,* 21 December 1977.
59. Sādāt's 21 January speech to the PA, Cairo all services, 21 January—BBC, 23 January 1978.
60. *Ma'ariv*, 25 December 1977.
61. *Ha'aretz*, 23 December 1977.
62. Begin's 23 January Knesset speech, IBA, 23 January—BBC, 25 January 1978.
63. *Ibid*.
64. For the full text of the statement, see Appendix V.
65. *Ibid*.
66. *JP*, 27 December 1977. For full text, see Appendix VI.
67. *Ma'ariv*, 11 August 1978.
68. Dayan's television interview, Israel TV, 4 August—DR, 7 August 1978.
69. *Ma'ariv*, 28 December 1977.
70. Sādāt's interview, Mexican TV, 2 January—DR, 3 January 1978.
71. *Ibid*; Sādāt's interview with US TV networks, MENA, 5 January—DR, 5 January 1978.
72. Sādāt's interview, *October*, 1 January 1978.
73. *GPO*, 26 December 1977.
74. Statements at 26 December press conference, Cairo all services and Israeli radio and TV, 26 December—BBC, 29 December 1977.
75. *Ha'aretz*, 27 December; *The Times*, 28 December 1977.
76. *Yedi'ot Aharonot*, 27 December 1977.
77. Sādāt's interview, Mexican TV, MENA, 2 January—DR, 3 January 1978.
78. Begin's 28 December Knesset address, Israel TV service, 28 December—BBC, 30 December 1977.

79. *Ma'ariv*, 26 December 1977.
80. *Ha'aretz*, 25, 28 December 1977.
81. USIS, News Report, 30 December 1977.
82. Sādāt's interview with CBS, ABC networks, 29 December 1977; R Cairo, 30 December—DR, 31 December 1977.
83. *NYT*, 1 January 1978.
84. *The Guardian*, 31 December 1977.
85. *JP*, 1 January 1977.
86. *The Guardian*, 31 December 1977.
87. Sādāt's interview with US Television networks, 4 January 1978, MENA, 5 January—DR, 5 January 1978.
88. *Department of State Bulletin*, February 1978.
89. See *MECS 1976–77*, pp. 29–31.
90. *Ma'ariv*, 2 January 1978.
91. Sādāt's interview, ABC, 4 January 1978, MENA, 5 January—DR, 5 January 1978.
92. Egypt's Foreign Minister Kāmil, *Der Spiegel*, 9 January—DR, 11 January 1978.
93. E.g. *October*, 25 December; *Al-Ahrām*, Cairo; 31 December 1977.
94. *Al-Akhbār*, Cairo; 28 December 1977.
95. *Ha'aretz*, 24 February 1978.
96. *Ma'ariv*, 9 January 1978.
97. *Department of State Bulletin,* February 1978.
98. Israel TV, 10 January—DR, 11 January 1978.
99. *October*, 15 January 1978.
100. *GPO*, 15 January 1978.
101. MENA, 19 January—DR, 20 January 1978.
102. *Ibid.*
103. Sādāt's interview, *JP*, 13 January 1978; Sādāt's 21 January speech to the PA, R Cairo, 21 January—BBC, 23 January 1978.
104. *WP*, 8 January 1978.
105. *JP*, 18 January 1978. For the texts of the three opening speeches, see Appendix VII.
106. *Ha'aretz*, 20 January; *Davar*, Tel Aviv; 20 January; *Ma'ariv*, 23 January; *NYT*, 23 January 1978.
107. *Ha'aretz*, 2 February 1978.
108. MENA, 20 January—DR, 24 January 1978.
109. *Al-Siyāsa al-Dawliyya*, Cairo; No 52 (April 1978), pp. 22–23.
110. E.g. the Information Ministry's statement of 18 January announcing the recall of the Egyptian delegation from Jerusalem (R Cairo, 18 January—BBC, 20 January 1978). Or Sādāt's 21 January speech to the PA, R Cairo, 21 January—BBC, 23 January 1978.
111. *Ibid.*
112. *Ibid.*
113. *GPO*, 21 January 1978.
114. *Ha'aretz*, 22 January 1978.
115. *Ibid.*
116. *Ha'aretz*, 5 February; *Ma'ariv*, 10 February 1978.
117. *Ha'aretz*, 28 January 1978.
118. *'Al-Hamishmar*, Tel Aviv; 21 June 1978.
119. *Ibid*, 16 July 1978. Cf IBA, 19 June—BBC, 23 June 1978.
120. Sādāt's 6 February news conference, R Cairo, 7 February—DR, 8 February 1978; Sādāt's speech at the National Press Club, MENA, 6 February—DR, 7 February 1978; *October*, 9 April 1978.
121. Sādāt's speech at the National Press Club on 6 February, as above.
122. *Ha'aretz*, 6 February 1978.
123. *Department of State Bulletin*, March 1978. For full text see Appendix VIII.
124. USIS Official Text, 13 February 1978.
125. Begin's 29 March statement to the Knesset, *GPO*, 29 March 1978. March 1978.
126. *Ha'aretz*, 27 February 1978.
127. *Ma'ariv*, 5 March 1978.
128. *Ibid*, 24 March 1978.
129. E.g. *NYT*, 7 March; *WP*, 9 March 1978.
130. *NYT,* 30 January 1978.
131. *Department of State Bulletin*, March 1978.
132. USIS Official Text, 13 February 1978.
133. *GPO*, 12 February 1978.
134. *NYT*, 14 February 1978.

135. *Ma'ariv*, 3 March; *NYT*, 8 March 1978.
136. USIS Official Text, 3 March 1978.
137. *NYT*, 10 March 1978.
138. Carter's news conference, 17 February; USIS Official Text, 21 February 1978.
139. *Ma'ariv*, 28 March 1978.
140. *WP*, 26 March 1978.
141. *Ibid.*
142. *Ibid.*
143. Begin's 29 March Knesset speech, *GPO*, 29 March 1978.
144. *Ha'aretz*, 29 March 1978.
145. *WP*, 26 March 1978.
146. *Chicago Tribune*, 29 March 1978.
147. Carter's news conference in Brasilia, 30 March; *NYT*, 31 March 1978.
148. *Ha'aretz*, 4 April; *Ma'ariv*, 7 April 1978.
149. *Ma'ariv*, 19 May, 11 August 1978.
150. *Ibid.*
151. *JP*, 13 April 1978.
152. *Ha'aretz*, 18 April 1978.
153. *Ibid,* 19 April 1978.
154. *JP,* 21 June 1978.
155. *Ma'ariv*, 23 June 1978.
156. E.g. al-Sādāt's news conferences on 30, 31 May 1978, MENA, 30, 31 May—DR, 1 June 1978.
157. *NYT*, 12 May; Sādāt's interview with *Chicago Tribune*, quoted by MENA, 15 May—DR, 16 May 1978.
158. *Ha'aretz*, 8, 19 June 1978.
159. Statement by Harold H. Saunders, 12 June, International Communication Agency of the US (USICA), Official Text, 13 June 1978; Statement by Alfred L. Atherton Jr, 15 June, USICA Official Text, 16 June 1978.
160. *GPO*, 18 June 1978.
161. *WP*, 2 July 1978.
162. Speech by Vice-President Walter Mondale at the State dinner at the Knesset, 2 July— USICA Official Text, 3 July 1978.
163. *Ma'ariv*, 3 July 1978.
164. *Ibid*, 26 June 1978.
165. *The Times*, 6 July 1978.
166. *Ma'ariv*, 12 July 1978.
167. *Ibid*, 11 July 1978.
168. *Ibid*, 12 July 1978.
169. *Ma'ariv*, 20 July; *Ha'aretz*, 21 July 1978.
170. *Ma'ariv*, 17 July 1978.
171. IBA, 15 July—DR, 17 July 1978.
172. *JP*, 17 July 1978.
173. *Ha'aretz, Ma'ariv*, 16 July 1978.
174. *Ha'aretz*, 28 July 1978.
175. *Ibid*, 27 July 1978.
176. *Ibid*, 19 July 1978.
177. *Ibid*, 20 July 1978.
178. *Ma'ariv*, 23 July 1978.
179. *Ha'aretz*, 20 July 1978.
180. Dayan's interview, IBA, 21 July—DR, 24 July 1978.
181. Begin's interview, Israeli TV, 26 July—DR, 27 July 1978.
182. IDF Radio, 23 July—DR, 24 July 1978.
183. R Cario, 30 July—BBC, 1 August 1978.
184. *JP*, 3 August 1978.
185. E.g. *The Times*, 1 August 1978.
186. *US News and World Report*, 21 August 1978: Carter's remarks on 4 September, USICA Official Text, 5 September 1978.
187. Begin's Address to the Nation, IBA, 2 September—BBC, 4 September 1978; *Economist, Ma'ariv*, 4 September 1978.
188. *Newsweek*, 28 August 1978.
189. *JP,* 21 August 1978.
190. *JP*, 15 August 1978.
191. This account draws mainly on *Ma'ariv*, 22 September, and *Newsweek*, 2 October 1978.

192. The full text in *al-Ahrām*, 19 September 1978.
193. MENA, 27 September—BBC, 29 September 1978.
194. *Yedi'ot Aharonot*, 28 September 1978.
195. Begin's statement to the Knesset, 25 September; *GPO*, 25 September 1978.
196. Carter's 18 September address to Congress, USICA Official Text, 19 September 1978.
197. *Newsweek*, 23 October. See also *The Economist Foreign Report*, London; 20 September 1978.
198. E.g. Begin's interview, Israel TV, 18 September—DR, 19 September 1978.
199. Sādāt's 2 October speech in the PA, R Cairo, 2 October—BBC, 3 October 1978.
200. MENA, 22 September—DR, 25 September 1978.
201. Statement by Assistant Secretary of State, Harold H. Saunders, before the ME Sub-committee of the House International Relations Committee, 23 September, USICA Official Text, 23 September 1978; Harold Saunders VoA interview, 29 September, USICA Official Text, 29 September 1978.
202. *Ibid.*

THE ARAB-ISRAELI CONFLICT

APPENDIX I: SĀDĀT'S SPEECH TO THE KNESSET

(20 November 1977)

In the name of God, Mr Speaker of the Knesset, ladies and gentlemen. Allow me first to thank the Speaker of the Knesset deeply for affording me this opportunity so that I may address you. And as I begin my address, I wish to say peace and the mercy of God Almighty be upon you, and may peace be for us all, God willing. Peace for us all, all the Arab lands and in Israel, as well as in every part of this big world, this world which is so complexed [sic] by its sanguinary conflicts, disturbed by its sharp contradictions, menaced now and then by costly wars launched by man to annihilate his fellow men. Amidst the ruins of what man has built, and the remains of the victims of mankind, there emerges neither victor nor vanquished. The only vanquished remains always a man—man, God's most sublime creation, man whom God has created as Gandhi, the apostle of peace, put it, to forge ahead, to mould a way of life, and to worship God Almighty.

I come to you today on solid ground to shape a new life and prepare a peace. We all on this land, the land of God, we all—Muslims, Christians and Jews—we all worship God and no one but God. God's teaching and commandments are love, sincerity, purity and peace.

I do not blame all those who received my decision when I announced it to the entire world before the Egyptian People's Assembly—I say I do not blame them. I do not blame all those who received my decision with surprise and even with amazement. Some even, struck by violent surprise, believed that my decision was no more than verbal juggling to cater for world public opinion. Others still interpreted it as political tactics to camouflage my intention to launch a new war.

I would go as far as to tell you that one of my aides in the Presidential Office contacted me at the late hour following my return home from the People's Assembly and sounded worried as he asked me: "Mr President, what would be our reaction if Israel should actually extend an invitation to you?" I replied calmly: "I will accept it immediately." I have declared that I would go to the end of the world. I would go to Israel, for I want to put before the people of Israel all the facts.

I can see the point of all those who were astounded by my decision, all those who had any doubts as to the sincerity of the intention behind the declaration of my decision. No one would ever have conceived that the President of the biggest Arab state, which bears the heaviest burden and the main responsibility pertaining to the cause of war and peace in the ME, could declare his readiness to go to the land of the adversary while we were still in a state of war. Rather we all are still bearing the consequences of four fierce wars waged within ten years. All this at a time when the families of the 1973 October War are still suffering the cruel pain of widowhood and bereavement of sons, fathers and brothers.

As I have already declared, I have not consulted, as far as this decision is concerned, with any of my colleagues or brothers, the Arab Heads of State, or the confrontation states. Those of them who contacted me following the declaration of this decision spoke of their objection because the feeling of opposite mission and absolute lack of confidence between Arab states and the Palestinian people on the one hand, and Israel on the other, still surges in us all.

It is sufficient to say that many months within which peace could have been brought about have been wasted over differences and fruitless discussions on the procedure for the convocation of the Geneva conference, all showing utter suspicion and absolute lack of confidence. But, to be absolutely frank with you, I took this decision after long thinking, knowing that it constitutes a grave risk for, if God Almighty has made it my fate to assume the responsibility on behalf of the Egyptian people and to share in the fate-determining responsibility of the Arab nation, the main duty dictated by this responsibility is to exhaust every means in a bid to save my Arab people and the entire Arab nation the horrors of new, shocking and destructive wars, the dimensions of which are foreseen by no other than God Himself.

After long thinking, I was convinced that the obligation of responsibility before God and before the peoples makes it incumbent upon me that I should go to the farthest corners of the world, even to Jerusalem, to address members of the Knesset, the representatives of the people of Israel, and acquaint them with all the facts surging in me. Then I would leave you to decide for yourselves. Following this, may God Almighty determine our fate.

There are moments in the life of nations and peoples when it is incumbent upon those known for their wisdom and clarity of vision to overlook the past with all its complexities and weighing memories in a bold drive towards new horizons. Those who, like us, are shouldering the same responsibilities entrusted to us, are the first who should have the courage to take fate-determining decisions which are in consonance with the circumstances. We must all rise above all forms of fanaticism, above all forms of self-deception and above all forms of obsolete theories of superiority. The most important thing is never to forget that infallibility is the prerogative of God alone.

If I said that I wanted to avert from all the Arab people the horrors of shocking and destructive wars, I must sincerely declare before you that I have the same feelings and bear the same responsibility towards all and every man on earth, and certainly towards the Israeli people.

134

THE EGYPTIAN–ISRAELI NEGOTIATIONS

Any life lost in war is a human life, be it that of an Arab or an Israeli. A wife who becomes a widow is a human being entitled to a happy family life whether she be an Arab or an Israeli. Innocent children who are deprived of the care and compassion of their parents are ours. They are ours, be they living on our lands or Israeli lands. They command our top responsibility, to afford them a comfortable life today and tomorrow. For the sake of them all, for the safeguarding of the lives of all our sons and brothers, for affording our communities the opportunities to work for the progress and happiness of man, feeling secure for the progress and happiness of man and his right to a dignified life, for our responsibilites before the generations to come, for a smile, for a smile on the face of every child born in our land. For all that I have taken my decision to come to you, despite all hazards, to deliver my address.

I have shouldered the prerequisites of the historic responsibility and therefore I declared a few years ago—on 4 February 1971, to be precise—that I was willing to sign a peace agreement with Israel. This was the first declaration made by a responsible Arab official since the outbreak of the Arab-Israeli conflict. Motivated by all these factors dictated by the responsibilities of leadership—on 16 October 1973 before the Egyptian People's Assembly—I called for an international conference to establish permanent peace based on justice. I was not in the position of one who was pleading for peace or asking for a ceasefire.

Motivated by all these factors, dictated by duties of history and leadership, we signed the first disengagement agreement, followed by the second disengagement agreement in Sinai. Then we proceeded, trying both open and closed doors, in a bid to find a certain road leading to a durable and just peace. We opened our hearts to the peoples of the entire world, to make them understand our motivations and objectives and to leave them actually convinced of the fact that we are advocates of justice, and peacemakers. Motivated by all these factors, I also decided to come to you with an open mind and an open heart and with a conscious determination so that we might establish permanent peace based on justice.

It is fated that my trip to you, the trip of peace, should coincide with the Islamic feast, the holy feast of 'Id al-Adhā, the Feast of Sacrifice, when Abraham, peace be upon him, the great-grandfather of the Arabs and Jews, submitted to God. I say when God Almighty ordered him, Abraham went, with dedicated sentiments, not out of weakness but through a giant spiritual force and a free will to sacrifice his very own son, prompted by a firm and unshakeable belief in ideals that lend life a profound significance.

This coincidence may carry a new meaning to us all, which may become a genuine aspiration heralding security and safety and peace.

Let us be frank with each other, using straightforward words and clear conceptions, with no ambiguity. Let us be frank with each other today while the entire world, both East and West, follow these unparalleled moments which could prove to be a radical turning point in the history of this part of the world, if not in the history of the world as a whole. Let us be frank with each other as we answer this important question: how can we achieve permanent peace based on justice?

Well, I have come to you carrying my clear and frank answer to this big question so that the people in Israel, as well as the whole world, might hear it, and so that all those whose devoted prayers ring in my ears, pleading to God Almighty that this historic meeting may eventually lead to the results aspired to by millions, might also hear it. Before I proclaim my answer, I wish to assure you that in my clear and frank answer I am basing myself on a number of facts which no one can deny.

The first fact: no one can build his happiness at the expense of the misery of others. *The second fact*: never have I spoken or will ever speak in two languages. Never have I adopted or will ever adopt two policies. I never deal with anyone except in one language, one policy, and with one face.

The third fact: direct confrontation and a straight line are the nearest and most successful methods to reach a clear objective.

The fourth fact: the call for permanent and just peace, based on respect for the UN resolutions, has now become the call of the whole world. It has become a clear expression of the will of the international community, whether in official capitals, where policies are made and decisions taken, or at the level of world public opinion, which influences policy-making and decision taking.

The fifth fact, and this is probably the clearest and most prominent, is that the Arab nation, in its drive for permanent peace, based on justice, does not proceed from a position of weakness or hesitation, but on the contrary, it has the potential of power and stability which tells of a sincere will for peace. The Arab declared intention stems from an awareness, prompted by a heritage of civilization that, to avoid an inevitable disaster that will befall us, you and the whole world, there is no alternative to the establishment of permanent peace based on justice—peace that is not shaken by storms, swayed by suspicion or jeopardized by ill intentions.

In light of these facts—which I've placed before you the way I see them—I would also wish, in all sincerity, to warn you. I warn you against some thoughts which could cross your minds. Frankness makes it incumbent upon me to tell you the following.

First, I have not come here for a separate agreement between Egypt and Israel. This is not part of the policy of Egypt. The problem is not that of Egypt and Israel. Any separate peace between Egypt and Israel, or between any Arab confrontation states and Israel, will not bring permanent peace, based on justice, in the entire region. Rather, even if peace between all the confrontation states and Israel were achieved, in the absence of a just solution to the Palestinian problem, there would never be the durable and just peace upon which the entire world today insists.

Second, I have not come to you to seek a partial peace—namely, to terminate the state of belligerency at this stage, and put off the entire problem to a subsequent stage. This is not the radical solution that would steer us to permanent peace.

Equally, I have not come to you for a third disengagement agreement in Sinai, or in the Golan and the West Bank, for this would mean that we are merely delaying the ignition of the fuse. Rather, it would also mean that we are lacking the courage to face peace, that we are too weak to shoulder the burdens and responsibilities of a durable peace based on justice. I have come to you so that together we can build a durable peace based on justice, to avoid the shedding of one single drop of blood from either of the two parties.

It is for this reason that I have proclaimed my readiness to go to the farthest corner of the world. Here I would go back to the big question: How can we achieve a durable peace based on justice? In my opinion, and I declare it to the whole world from this forum, the answer is neither difficult, nor is it impossible, despite long years of feuds, vengeance, spite and hatred, and breeding generations on concepts of deep-rooted animosity. The answer is not difficult, nor is it impossible—if we sincerely and faithfully follow a straight line.

You want to live with us, in this part of the world. In all sincerity, I tell you we welcome you among us, with full security and safety. This in itself is a tremendous turning point, one of the landmarks of a decisive historic change.

We used to reject you. We had our reasons and our claims, yes. We refused to meet with you anywhere, yes. We used to brand you as "so-called Israel," yes. We were together in international conferences and organizations and our representatives did not—and still do not—exchange greetings with you, yes. This has happened and is still happening.

It is also true that we used to set, as a pre-condition for any negotiations with you, a mediator who would meet separately with each party. By this procedure the talks for the first and second disengagement agreements took place. Our delegates met in the first Geneva conference without exchanging a direct word, yes. This has happened.

Yet today I tell you, and I declare it to the whole world, that we accept living with you in permanent peace based on justice. We do not want to encircle you, or be encircled ourselves, by destructive missiles ready for launching, nor by the shells of grudges and hatred. I have announced on more than one occasion that Israel has become a *fait accompli*, recognized by the world, and that the two super-powers have undertaken the responsibility of its security and the defence of its existence.

As we really and truly seek peace, we really and truly welcome you to live among us in peace and security. There was a huge wall between us which you tried to build up over a quarter of a century, but it was destroyed in 1973. It was a wall of a continuously inflammable and escalating psychological warfare. It was a wall of fear of the force that could sweep the entire Arab nation. It was a wall of propaganda that we were a nation reduced to a motionless corpse. Some of you had gone as far as to say that even after 50 years the Arabs would not regain their strength. It was a wall that threatened always, with a long arm that could reach and strike anywhere. It was a wall that warned us against extermination and annihilation if we tried to use our legitimate right to liberate the occupied territories. Together we have to admit that that wall fell and collapsed in 1973.

Yet there remains another wall. This wall constitutes a psychological barrier between us. A barrier of suspicion. A barrier of rejection. A barrier of fear of deception. A barrier of hallucinations around any action, deed or decision. A barrier of cautious and erroneous interpretation of all and every event or statement. It is this psychological barrier which I described in official statements as constituting 70% of the whole problem.

Today, through my visit to you, I ask you: why don't we stretch our hands with faith and sincerity so that together we might destroy this barrier? Why shouldn't ours and yours meet with faith and sincerity, so that together we might remove all suspicion of fear, betrayal and ill intentions? Why don't we stand together with the bravery of men and the boldness of heroes who dedicate themselves to a sublime objective? Why don't we stand together with the same courage and boldness to erect a huge edifice of peace?

An edifice that builds and does not destroy, an edifice that is a beacon for generations to come, of the human message for construction, development and the dignity of man. Why should we bequeath to the coming generations the plight of bloodshed, death, orphans, widowhood, family disintegration and the wailing of victims. Why don't we believe in the wisdom of God conveyed to us by the Proverbs of Solomon: "Deceit is in the hearts of them that imagine evil, but to the counsellors of peace is joy. Better is a dry morsel and quietness therewith than a house full of sacrifices with strife."

Why don't we repeat together from the Psalms of David: "Hear the voice of my supplications when I cry unto Thee, when I lift up my hands toward Thy holy oracle. Draw me not away with the wicked and with the workers of iniquity which speak peace to their neighbours but mischief is in their hearts. Give them according to their deeds and according to the wickedness of their endeavours."

Ladies and gentlemen, to tell you the truth, peace cannot be worth its name unless it is based on justice—and not on the occupation of the land of others. It would not be appropriate for you to demand for yourselves what you deny others. With all frankness and with the spirit that has prompted me to come to you today, I tell you: you have to give up, once and for all, the dreams of conquest and give up the belief that force is the best method for dealing with the Arabs. You should clearly understand and assimilate the lesson of confrontation between you and us—expansion does not pay. To speak frankly, our land does not yield itself to bargaining; it is not even open to argument.

To us the national soil is equal to the holy valley where God Almighty spoke to Moses, peace be upon him. None of us accepts ceding one inch of it, or accepts the principle of debating or bargaining over it. I sincerely tell you also that before us today lies the appropriate chance for peace, if we are really serious in our endeavour for peace. It is a chance that time cannot afford again. It is a chance that, if lost or wasted, the plotter against it will bear the curse of humanity and the curse of history.

What is peace for Israel? It means that Israel lives in the region with her Arab neighbours, in security and safety. To such logic, I say yes. It means that Israel lives within her borders, secure against any aggression. To such logic, I say yes. It means that Israel obtains all kinds of guarantees that insure those two factors. To this demand, I say yes. More than that, we declare that we accept all the international guarantees you envisage and accept, we declare that we accept all the guarantees you want from the two super-powers or from either of them, or from the big five, or from some of them.

Once again, I declare clearly and unequivocally that we agree to any guarantees you accept because in return we shall obtain the same guarantees. In short, then, when we ask what is peace for Israel, the answer would be that Israel live within her borders with her Arab neighbours in safety and security, within the framework of all the guarantees she accepts and which are offered to the other party. But how can this be achieved? How can we reach this conclusion, which would lead us to permanent peace based on justice?

There are facts that should be faced with all courage and clarity. There are Arab territories which Israel has occupied and still occupies by armed force. We insist on complete withdrawal from these territories, including Arab Jerusalem.

I have come to Jerusalem, the City of Peace, which will always remain as a living embodiment of coexistence among believers of the three religions. It is inadmissible that anyone should conceive the special status of the City of Jerusalem within the framework of annexation or expansionism. It should be a free and open city for all believers.

Above all, this city should not be severed from those who have made it their abode for centuries. Instead of awakening the prejudices of the Crusades, we should revive the spirit of 'Umar al-Khattāb and Salah e-Din—the spirit of tolerance and respect for rights.

The Holy Shrines of Islam and Christianity are not only places of worship, but a living testimony of our uninterrupted presence here—politically, spiritually and intellectually. Here let us make no mistake about the importance and reverence we Christians and Muslims attach to Jerusalem.

Let me tell you, without the slightest hesitation, that I have not come to you under this roof to request that your troops evacuate the occupied territories. Complete withdrawal from the Arab territories occupied in1967 is a logical and undisputed fact. Nobody should plead for that. Any talk about permanent peace based on justice, and any move to insure your coexistence in peace and security in this part of the world, would become meaningless while you occupy Arab territories by force of arms. For there is no peace that could be in consonance with, or be built on, the occupation of the land of others. Otherwise it would not be a serious peace. Yet this is a foregone conclusion, which is not open to discussion or debate—if intentions are sincere and if endeavours to establish a just and durable peace for ours and the generations to come are genuine.

As for the Palestine cause, nobody could deny that it is the crux of the entire problem. Nobody in the world today could accept slogans propagated here in Israel, ignoring the existence of the Palestinian people and questioning even their whereabouts. The cause of the Palestine people and their legitimate rights are no longer ignored or denied today by anybody. Nobody who has the ability of judgement can deny or ignore it.

It is an acknowledged fact, received by the world community, both in the East and in the West, with support and recognition in international documents and official statements. It is of no use to anybody to turn deaf ears to its resounding voice, which is being heard day and night, or to overlook its historical reality. Even the US, your prime ally—which is absolutely committed to safeguard Israel's security and existence and which offered and still offers Israel every moral, material and military support—I say, even the US has opted to face up to reality and facts and admits that the Palestinian people are entitled to legitimate rights, and that the Palestine problem is the core and essence of the conflict, and that so long as it continues to be unresolved, the conflict will continue to aggravate, reaching new dimensions. In all sincerity, I tell you there can be no peace without the Palestinians. It is a grave error of unpredictable consequences to overlook or brush aside this cause.

I shall not review past events since the Balfour Declaration 60 years ago. You are well acquainted with the relevant facts. If you have found the legal and moral justification to set up a national home on a land that did not all belong to you, it is incumbent upon you to show understanding of the insistence of the people of Palestine in establishing once again a state on their land. When some extremists ask the Palestinians to give up this sublime objective, this in fact means asking them to renounce their identity and every hope for the future.

I hail the Israeli voices that called for the recognition of the Palestinian people's rights to achieve and safeguard peace. Here I tell you, ladies and gentlemen, therefore, that it is no use to refrain from recognizing the Palestinian people and their rights to statehood and their rights of return.

We, the Arabs, have faced this experience before, with you and with the reality of Israeli existence. The struggle took us from war to war, from victims to more victims, until you and we have today reached the edge of a horrifying abyss and a terrifying disaster, unless together we seize this opportunity today of a durable peace based on justice.

You have to face reality bravely, as I have done. There can never be a solution to a problem by evading it or turning a deaf ear to it. Peace cannot last if attempts are made to impose fantasy concepts on which the world has turned its back, and announced its unanimous call for the respect of rights and facts. There's no need to enter a vicious circle on Palestinian rights. It is useless to create obstacles. Otherwise the march of peace will be impeded, or peace will be blown up.

As I have told you, there is no happiness to the detriment of others. Direct confrontation and straight-forwardness are the short cuts, and the most successful way to reach a clear objective. Direct confrontation concerning the Palestinian problem and tackling it in one single language with a view to achieving a durable and just peace lie in the establishment of their state. With all the guarantees you demand, there should be no fear of a newly born state that needs the assistance of all countries of the world. When the bells of peace ring, there will be no hands to beat the drums of war. Even if they existed, they would be soundless.

Conceive with me a peace agreement in Geneva that we would herald to a world thirsty for peace. A peace agreement based on the following points:

1. Ending the Israeli occupation of the Arab territories occupied in 1967.

2. Achievement of the fundamental rights of the Palestinian people and their right to self-determination, including their right to establish their own state.

3. The right of all states in the area to live in peace, within their boundaries, their secure boundaries, which will be secured and guaranteed through procedures to be agreed upon, providing appropriate security for international boundaries, in addition to appropriate international guarantees.

4. Commitment of all states in the region to administer the relations among them in accordance with the objectives and principles of the UN Charter, particularly the principles concerning the non-resort to force and the solutions to differences among them by peaceful means.

5. Ending the state of belligerency in the region.

Peace is not a mere endorsement of written lines. Rather it is a rewriting of history. Peace is not a game of calling for peace to defend certain whims, or hide certain ambitions. Peace, in its essence, is a joint struggle against all and every ambition and whim. Perhaps the examples and experience taken from ancient and modern history teach us all that missiles, warships and nuclear weapons cannot establish security. Rather, they destroy what peace and security build. For the sake of our peoples, and for the sake of the civilization made by man, we have to defend men everywhere against the rule of the force of arms, so that we may endow the rule of humanity with all the power of the values and principles that promote the sublime position of mankind.

Allow me to address my call from this rostrum to the people of Israel. I address myself with true and sincere words to every man, woman and child in Israel. I tell them, from the Egyptian people who bless this sacred mission of peace; I convey to you the message of peace, the message of the Egyptian people, who do not know fanaticism and whose sons—Muslims, Christians and Jews—live together in a state of cordiality, love and tolerance.

This is Egypt, whose people have entrusted me with that sacred message—the message of security, safety and peace. To every man, woman and child in Israel, I say: encourage your leadership to struggle for peace. Let all endeavours be channelled towards building a huge edifice for peace, instead of strongholds and hideouts defended by destructive rockets. Introduce to the entire world the image of the new man in this area, so that we might set an example to the men of our age, the men of peace everywhere.

Be heroes to the sons. Tell them that past wars were the last of wars and the end of sorrows. Tell them that we are in for a new beginning to a new life—a life of love, prosperity, freedom and peace. You, bewailing mother; you, widowed wife; you, the son who lost a brother or a father; you, all victims of wars, fill the earth and space with recitals of peace. Fill bosoms and hearts with the aspirations of peace. Turn the song into a reality that blossoms and lives. Make hope a code of conduct and endeavour. The will of peoples is part of the will of God.

Before I came to this place, with every beat of my heart and with every sentiment, I prayed to God Almighty, while performing the 'Id al-Adhā prayers at the al-Aqsā Mosque and while visiting the Church of the Holy Sepulchre, I asked God Almighty to give me strength, and to confirm my belief that this visit may achieve the objective I look forward to for a happy present and a happier future.

I have chosen to set aside all precedents and traditions known by warring countries, in spite of the fact that occupation of the Arab territories still exists. Rather, the declaration of my readiness to proceed to Israel came as a great surprise that stirred many feelings and astounded many minds. Some even doubted its intent. Despite it all, the decision was inspired by all the clarity and purity of belief and with all the true expression of my people's will and intentions.

And I have chosen this difficult road, which is considered by many and in the opinion of many the most difficult road. I have chosen to come to you with an open heart and an open mind. I have chosen to give the great impetus to all international efforts exerted for peace. I have chosen to present to you and in your own home the realities devoid of any scheme or whim, not to manoeuvre or to win a round, but for us to win together the most dangerous of rounds and battles in modern history—the battle of permanent peace based on justice.

It is not my battle alone, nor is it the battle of the leadership in Israel alone. It is the battle of all and every citizen in all our territories, whose right it is to live in peace. It is the commitment of conscience and responsibility in the hearts of millions.

When I put forward this initiative, many asked, what is it that I conceive as possible to achieve during this visit and what my expectations were. And, as I answered the questioners, I announce before you that I have not thought of carrying out this initiative from the concept of what could be achieved during this visit.

But I have come here to deliver a message. I have delivered the message and may God be my witness.

I repeat with Zachariah, "Love right and justice." From the Holy Koran I quote the following verses: "We believe in God and in what has been revealed to us and in what was revealed to Abraham, Ismael, Isaac, Jacob and the tribes and in the books given to Moses, Jesus and the Prophet from their Lord. We make no distinction between one and another among them, and to God's will we submit."

Peace be upon you.

Source: Jerusalem Post, 21 November 1977.

APPENDIX II: BEGIN'S SPEECH TO THE KNESSET

20 November 1977

Mr Speaker, Mr President of the State of Israel, Mr President of the Arab Republic of Egypt, ladies and gentlemen, members of the Knesset: We send our greetings to the President, to all the people of the Islamic religion in our country, and wherever they may be, on this occasion of the feast of the festival of the sacrifice 'Id al-Adhā. This feast reminds us of the binding of Isaac. This was the way in which the Creator of the World tested our forefather, Abraham, our common forefather, to test his faith, and Abraham passed this test. However, from the moral aspect and the advancement of humanity, it was forbidden to sacrifice human beings. Our two peoples in their ancient traditions know and taught what the Lord, blessed be He, taught while peoples around us still sacrificed human beings to their gods. Thus, we contributed, the people of Israel and the Arab people, to the progress of mankind, and thus we are continuing to contribute to human culture to this day.

I greet and welcome the President of Egypt for coming to our country and on his participating in the Knesset session. The flight time between Cairo and Jerusalem is short, but the distance between Cairo and Jerusalem was until last night almost endless. President al-Sādāt crossed this distance courageously. We, the Jews, know how to appreciate such courage, and we know how to appreciate it in our guest, because it is with courage that we are here, and this is how we continue to exist, and we shall continue to exist.

Mr Speaker, this small nation, the remaining refuge of the Jewish people who returned to their historic homeland, has always wanted peace, and since the dawn of our independence, on 14 May 1948, 5 Iyar Tashah, in the declaration of independence in the founding scroll of our national freedom, David Ben-Gurion said: We extend a hand of peace and neighbourliness to all the neighbouring countries and their peoples. We call upon them to co-operate, to help each other, with the Hebrew people independent in their own country. One year earlier, even from the underground, when we were in the midst of the fateful struggle for the liberation of the country and the redemption of the people, we called in our neighbours in these terms: In this country we will live together and we will advance together and we will live lives of freedom and happiness. Our Arab neighbours, do not reject the hand stretched out to you in peace.

But it is my bounden duty, Mr Speaker, and not only my right, not to pass over the truth that our hand outstretched for peace was not grasped and one day after we had renewed our independence, as was our right, our eternal right, which cannot be disputed, we were attacked on three fronts, and we stood almost without arms, the few against many, the weak against the strong, while an attempt was made, one day after the declaration of independence, to strangle it at birth, to put an end to the last hope of the Jewish people, the yearning renewed after the years of destruction and holocaust. No, we do not believe in might and we have never based our attitude toward the Arab people on might. Quite the contrary, force was used against us. Over all the years of this generation we have never stopped being attacked by might, of the strong arm stretched out to exterminate our people, to destroy our independence, to deny our rights. We defended ourselves, it is true. We defended our rights, our existence, our honour, our women and our children, against these repeated and recurring attempts to crush us through the force of arms, and not only on one front. That, too, is true. With the help of God Almighty, we overcame the forces of aggression, and we have guaranteed existence for our nation. Not only for this generation, but for the coming generations, too. We do not believe in might. We believe in right, only in right. And therefore our aspiration, from the bottom of our hearts, has always been, to this very day, for peace.

THE ARAB-ISRAELI CONFLICT

Mr President, Mr President of Egypt, the commanders of all the underground Hebrew fighting organizations are sitting in this democratic house. They had to conduct a campaign of the few against the many, against a huge, a world power. Here are sitting the veteran commanders and captains who had to go forth into battle because it was forced upon them and forward to victory, which was unavoidable because they were defending their rights. They belong to different parties. They have different views, but I am sure, Mr President, that I am expressing the views of everyone, with no exceptions, that we have one aspiration in our hearts, one desire in our souls, and all of us are united in all these aspirations and desires—to bring peace, peace for our nation, which has not known peace for even one day since we started returning to Zion, and peace for our neighbours, whom we wish all the best, and we believe that if we make peace, real peace, we will be able to help our neighbours, in all walks of life, and a new era will open in the ME, an era of blossoming and growth, development and expansion of the economy, its growth as it was in the past.

Therefore, permit me today to set forth the peace programme as we understand it. We want full, real peace with complete reconciliation between the Jews and the Arab peoples. I do not wish to dwell on the memories of the past, but there have been wars: there has been blood spilt: wonderful young people have been killed on both sides. We will live all our life with the memories of our heroes who gave their lives so this day would arrive, this day, too, would come, and we respect the bravery of a rival, and we honour all the members of the younger generation among the Arab people who also fell.

I do not wish to dwell on memories of the past, although they be bitter memories. We will bury them; we will worry about the future, about our people, our children, our joint and common future. For it is true indeed that we will have to live in this area, all of us together will live here, for generations upon generations: The great Arab people in their various states and countries, and the Jewish people in their country, Eretz Yisrael. Therefore, we must determine what peace means.

Let us conduct negotiations, Mr President, as free negotiating partners for a peace treaty, and, with the aid of the Lord, we fully believe the day will come when we can sign it with mutual respect, and we will then know that the era of wars is over, that hands have been extended between friends, that each has shaken the hand of his brother and the future will be shining for all the peoples of this area. The beginning of wisdom in a peace treaty is the abolition of the state of war. I agree, Mr President, that you did not come here, we did not invite you to our country in order, as has been said in recent days, to divide the Arab peoples. Somebody quoted an ancient Roman, saying: Divide and rule. Israel does not want to rule and therefore does not need to divide. We want peace with all our neighbours: with Egypt, with Jordan, with Syria and with Lebanon. We would like to negotiate peace treaties. . . .

And there is no need to distinguish between a peace treaty and an abolition of the state of war. Quite the contrary, we are not proposing this nor are we asking for it. The first clause of a peace treaty is cessation of the state of war, forever. We want to establish normal relations between us, as they exist between all nations, even after wars. We have learned from history, Mr President, that war is avoidable, peace is unavoidable. Many nations have waged war among themselves, and sometimes they used the tragic term perennial enemy. There are no perennial enemies. And after all the wars, the inevitable comes—peace. And so we want to establish, in a peace treaty, diplomatic relations as is the custom among civilized nations.

Today two flags are flying over Jerusalem: the Egyptian flag and the Israeli flag. And we saw together, Mr President, little children waving both the flags. Let us sign a peace treaty and let us establish this situation forever, both in Jerusalem and in Cairo, and I hope the day will come when the Egyptian children wave the Israeli flag and the Egyptian flag, just as the children of Israel waved both these flags in Jerusalem.

And you, Mr President, will have a loyal ambassador in Jerusalem, and we will have an ambassador in Cairo. And even if differences of opinion arise between us, we will clarify them like civilized peoples through our authorized envoys.

We are proposing economic co-operation for the development of our countries. There are wonderful countries in the ME. The Lord created it thus: oases in the desert, but there are deserts as well and we can make them flourish. Let us co-operate in this field. Let us develop our countries. Let us eliminate poverty, hunger, the lack of shelter. Let us raise our peoples to the level of developed countries and let them not call us "developing countries."

And with all due respect, I am willing to confirm the words of his majesty the King of Morocco, who said—in public too—that if peace arises in the ME, the combination of Arab genius and Jewish genius together can turn this area into a paradise on earth.

Let us open our countries to free traffic. You come to our country and we will visit yours. I am ready to announce, Mr Speaker, this day that our country is open to the citizens of Egypt and I make no conditions on our part. I think it is only proper and just that there should be a joint announcement on this matter. But, just as there are Egyptian flags in our streets, and there is also an honoured delegation from Egypt in our capital and in our country, let the number of visitors increase; our border will be open to you, and also all the other borders.

And as I pointed out, we want this in the south and in the north and in the east. And so I am renewing my invitation to the President of Syria to follow in your footsteps, Mr President, and come to us to open negotiations for achieving peace between Israel and Syria and to sign a peace treaty between us. I am sorry to say but there is no justification for the mourning they have declared beyond our northern border. Quite the contrary, such visits, such links, such clarifications can and must be days of joy, days of lifting spirits for all the peoples. I invite King Ḥusayn to come to us to discuss all the problems which need to be discussed between us. Also genuine representatives of the Arabs of Eretz Yisrael, I invite them to come and hold talks with us to clarify our common future, to guarantee the freedom of man, social justice, peace, mutual respect. And if they invite us to go to their capitals, we will accept their invitations. If they invite us to open negotiations in Damascus, in Amman or in Beirut, we will go to those capitals in order to hold negotiations with them there. We do not want to divide. We want real peace with all our neighbours, to be expressed in peace treaties whose contents I have already made clear.

Mr Speaker, it is my duty today to tell our guest and the peoples watching us and listening to our words about the link between our people and this country. The President recalled the Balfour Declaration. No, sir, we did not take over any strange land; we returned to our homeland. The link between our people and this country is eternal. It arose in the earliest days of the history of humanity and has never been disrupted. In this country we developed our civilization, we had our prophets here, and their sacred words stand to this day. Here the kings of Judah and Israel knelt before their gods. This is where we became a people; here we established our kingdom. And when we were expelled from our land because of force which was used against us, the farther we went from our land, we never forgot this country for even a single day. We prayed for it, we longed for it, we believed in our return to it from the day the words were spoken: "When the Lord restores the fortunes of Zion, we will be like dreamers. Our mouths will be filled with laughter, and our tongues will speak with shouts of joy." These verses apply to all our exiles and all our sufferings, giving the consolation that the return to Zion would come.

This, our right, was recognized. The Balfour Declaration was included in the mandate laid down by the nations of the world, including the US, and the preface to this recognized international document says: [in English] "Whereas recognition has the Bible given to the historical connection of the Jewish people with Palestine and to the grounds for reconstituting their national home in that country," [ends English]—the historic connection between the Jewish people and Palestine [in English]—or, in Hebrew, Eretz Yisrael, was given reconfirmation—reconfirmation—as the national homeland in that country, that is, in Eretz Yisrael.

In 1919 we also won recognition of this right by the spokesman of the Arab people and the agreement of 3 January 1919, which was signed by Emir Faysal and Hayim Weizman. It reads: [in English] Mindful of the racial kinship and ancient bonds existing between the Arabs and the Jewish people, and realizing that the surest means of working out the consummation of the national aspirations in the closest possible collaboration in the development of the Arab state and of Palestine [ends English]. And afterward come all the clauses about co-operation between the Arab state and Eretz Yisrael. This is our right. The existence— truthful existence.

What happened to us when our homeland was taken from us? I accompanied you this morning, Mr President, to Yad Vashem. With your own eyes you saw the fate of our people when this homeland was taken from it. It cannot be told. Both of us agreed, Mr President, that anyone who has not seen with his own eyes everything there is in Yad Vashem cannot understand what happened to this people when it was without a homeland, when its own homeland was taken from it. And both of us read a document dated 30 January 1939, where the word "Vernichtung"—annihilation—appears. If war breaks out, the Jewish race in Europe will be exterminated. Then, too, we were told that we should not pay attention to the racists. The whole world heard. Nobody came to save us. Not during the nine fateful, decisive months after the announcement was made, the like of which had not been seen since the Lord created man and man created the Devil.

And during those six years, too, when millions of our people, among them 1.5m of the little children of Israel who were burned on all the strange beds [sic], nobody came to save them, not from the East nor from the West. And because of this, we took a solemn oath, this entire generation, the generation of extermination and revival, that we would never again put our people in danger, that we would never again put our women and our children, whom it is our duty to defend—if there is a need for this, even at the cost of our lives—in the hell of the exterminating fire of an enemy. Since then, it has been our duty for generations to come to remember that certain things said about our people must be taken with complete seriousness. And we must not, heaven forbid, for the sake of the future of our people, take any advice whatsoever against taking these things seriously.

President al-Sādāt knows, and he knew from us before he came to Jerusalem, that we have a different position from his with regard to the permanent borders between us and our neighbours. However, I say to the President of Egypt and to all our neighbours: Do not say, there is not negotiation, there will not be negotiations about any particular issue. I propose, with the agreement of the decisive majority of this parliament, that everything be open to negotiation. Anyone who says, with reference to relations between the Arab people, or the Arab peoples around us, and the State of Israel, that there are things which should be omitted from negotiations is taking upon himself a grave responsibility. Everything can be negotiated.

No side will say the contrary. No side will present prior conditions. We will conduct the negotiations honourably. If there are differences of opinion between us, this is not unusual. Anyone who has studied the histories of wars and the signing of peace treaties knows that all negotiations over a peace treaty began with differences of opinion between the sides. And in the course of the negotiations they reached an agreement which permitted the signing of peace treaties and agreements. And this is the road which we propose to take.

And we will conduct the negotiations as equals. There are no vanquished and there are no victors. All the peoples of the area are equal and all should treat each other with due respect. In this spirit of openness, of willingness to listen to each other, to hear the facts and the reasoning and the explanations, accepting all the experience of human persuasion, let us conduct the negotiations as I have asked and am proposing, open them and carry them out, carry them on constantly until we reach the longed-for hour of the signing of a peace treaty between us.

We are not only ready to sit with the representatives of Egypt, and also with the representatives of Jordan and Syria and Lebanon. If it is ready, we are ready to sit together at a peace conference in Geneva. We propose that the Geneva conference be renewed, on the basis of the two Security Council Resolutions: 242 and 338. If there are problems between us, by convening the Geneva conference we will be able to clarify them. And if the President of Egypt wants to continue clarifying them in Cairo, I am for it. If in a neutral place, there is no objection. Let us clarify anywhere, even before the Geneva conference convenes, the problem which should be clarified before it is convened. And our eyes will be open and our ears will listen to all proposals.

Permit me to say a word about Jerusalem. Mr President, you prayed today in the house of prayer sacred to the Islamic religion, and from there you went to the Church of the Holy Sepulchre. You realized, as those coming from all over the world have realized, that ever since this city was unified, there has been completely free access, without interference and without any obstacle, for the members of every religion to the places sacred to them. This positive phenomenon did not exist for 19 years. It has existed for about 11 years, and we can promise the Muslim world and Christian world, all the peoples, that there will always be free access to the sacred places of every religion. We will defend this right to free access, for we believe in it. We believe in equal rights for all men and citizens and respect for every faith.

Mr Speaker, this is a special day for our legislative chamber, and certainly this day will be remembered for many years in the history of our nation, and perhaps also in the history of the Egyptian nation, maybe in the history of all nations. And this day, with your agreement, ladies and gentlemen, members of the Knesset, let us pray that the God of our fathers, our common fathers, will give us the wisdom needed to overcome difficulties and obstacles, calumnies and slander, incitement and attacks. And with the help of God, may we arrive at the longed-for day for which all our people pray—peace. For it is indeed true that the sweet singer of Israel [King David] said: "Righteousness and peace will kiss each other," and the Prophet Zachariah said: "Love, truth and peace."

Source: IBA, 20 November—DR, 21 November 1977.

APPENDIX III: EXCERPTS FROM PERES' SPEECH TO THE KNESSET

20 November 1977

Mr Speaker, Mr President of the Egyptian Arab Republic [as heard], Mr President of the State of Israel, members of the Knesset and guests: I am not speaking today in the name of the Opposition but on behalf of what unites our people. Among our people there is no opposition to peace and, even though there are differences about a possible and desirable settlement, there are no differences about the urgent need for a peace settlement. Mr President, as you could feel wherever you went, our people are united in their desire for peace. At last, a full peace, a real peace.

We are also united in welcoming your visit to Jerusalem—the city of faith, peace and unity, a city of hope and prayer. Your coming here is something new, a move by a leader of vision. The leader of Egypt is mapping a path for the Arabs, the representative of a long and illustrious history. Mainly, it is a move that must not be wasted. You have shown courage in taking the risk of abandoning old habits and inflexible ways for a new opening and a new way of approach. In war one also takes risks, but the chances that it provides are always bitter. In wars even the winners pay a high price. If we take a risk to bring about peace, losses are also involved.

Your coming signifies a new beginning. I promise you that all of us will try to free ourselves from preconceptions in order to see things in a new light and against a new background. We shall support any move that the Israeli government adopts for the sake of a peace settlement, and we shall continue to contribute as much as we are able so that your visit here is a real success for all the sake of our peoples and for the sake of peace.

Mr President, I listened very attentively to your remarks. I could not agree with their content, not with regard to peace—we have a different view—and not with regard to a settlement. However, all negotiations begin with disagreement. We shall listen to you and you will listen to us. We can find either compromise or a third path that we have not thought about—neither you nor we. Therefore, this dialogue from this rostrum is very important.

In your standing here on the rostrum of our Knesset, together with the Prime Minister of Israel, before the elected representatives of our people—its Jewish, Muslim, Christian and Druze residents—we can feel that a moment of breathtaking opportunity in the process of history has been created as hundreds of millions of peace-loving people are watching us now and are following every moment of this visit. Millions of viewers and thousands of years of history are directed towards this rostrum—Egyptian history and Jewish history. You and we are the descendants of the oldest histories of mankind—a history that has known conflict and co-operation, a history full of suffering, a history that knows hope. From the heights of the most famous of man's buildings—the Pyramids—from the pages of the oldest of man's writing—the Bible—the piercing question of whether we shall be able to reach the real heights in the goals of life is being posed so that we shall be able to escape the distress of war into the wide open spaces of peace, as we have been released from the burden of slavery to the nadir of liberty.

It is not only a long past that binds us, but also a great future. The eyes of millions of anxious Egyptian, Syrian, Jordanian, Palestinian and Jewish mothers are upon this rostrum in order to see if we can tell them and their children that there will no longer be war, no more threats, no more bereavement, destruction or refugees, and that beginning now, there is a chance for the youth of our peoples to be able to grow up in an atmosphere free from fear, enmity and the threat of catastrophe. All are waiting for the message that wisdom has overcome enmity and that political art has overcome military doctrine. Your coming here is a part of this task. You and we exist and we are talking with each other, without even solving the differences of opinion between us. Your coming has created a possibility that did not exist before—a possibility for which, if we know how to invest even part of the effort in peace that we invested in the army, then your visit will be remembered forever as the beginning for which we waited.

Members of the Knesset, we have waited for this moment—for this visit—for 30 years. We have always believed that a face-to-face meeting between the leaders of the peoples would create the conditions for fruitful dialogue and a momentum that will bring peace. . . .

Ever since 1973 we have found solutions which none of us had expected in advance. Through the mediation of our friends the Americans we agreed to sign—and you mentioned this—an agreement, the interim agreement of 1974, and a settlement on the way to a settlement in 1975. These agreements were criticized at the time. It was claimed that Israel was giving up very concrete things, withdrawing from territories that appeared to be essential to it, while Egypt and Syria agreed to things which were basically political—a promise of calm in the field, renewal of life in the region, a striving towards peace. We should not have been able to do this had we not decided to believe that Egypt, the Egyptian President and the Egyptian people, were facing in the direction of peace. Peace requires that attempts are made to conduct dialogue, and it also calls for patience; we must not deny this. It requires a response to the expectations of many citizens in both countries. You must also take some risks, even at the price of security and the danger of war, for the benefit of man, the improvement of society, the development of agriculture, the expansion of industry, the advance of science and the raising of the standard of living of every citizen. We preferred, as you did, the proposals of the US as they were shuttled back and forth by air rather than having the menacing intervention of the USSR, which could have contributed to peace instead of encouraging war.

Your coming here cuts across precedent and the ways of the past. Your promise that everything is open to discussion gives your visit real, strong and immediate content. The desire to discuss your proposals with good will and to take a proper step forward brings the horizon closer. Everyone, we and you, will express his opinions and we will find the common path.

I am speaking on behalf of the Israeli labour movement—a movement which, from the day of its inception and up to now, has not ceased to believe in peace and good human relations between the workers at home and the peoples abroad. I am convinced that the socialist movements of the world, including the Egyptian socialist movement, are not simply trade union class movements, but people's movements which believe that the worker cannot do well unless his country is doing well. They are not only national movements but also universal ones. They support humane and democratic socialism to liberate man from oppression, exploitation and discrimination, and to liberate peoples from tyranny and enmity. All efforts must be synchronized for this purpose which includes the dignity of man, the justice of this society and world peace. . . .

Each and every people, Mr President, will determine its own identity and will have the ability to manifest its identity, to pray to its God, to educate its children in the spirit of its heritage, to express its own opinion, to move freely, and to be in contact with members of other peoples, respecting the equality between people, honouring the differences between groups of people, and avoiding turning equality into privilege and difference into violence. There is no choice but for peace to be based on mutual compromise as opposed to war, which is built on one-sided decisions.

We shall support an honourable and real compromise and we shall not demand that any of the parties make compromises in one sphere—in its self-defence capability. We have announced that we are willing to make compromises with each of the Arab countries—territorial compromises—so long as this does not endanger our security, just as our neighbours would not want their security to be endangered. What we gain in the sphere of peace we shall be able to save in the sphere of security, but peace will exist between us while security will exist for each of us.

What is important is that we are not seeking the involvement of foreign forces in our region. We have rejected them during periods that were difficult for us and we are not seeking them in a period in which the chances for peace—as I believe—have increased. Peace must create permanent and recognized borders and must provide an answer to the refugee problem. There are refugees on both sides. A third of Israel's residents came from Arab countries. They are not refugees; they are residents in all respects. About half of the Palestinians live between the Jordan River and the sea. Most of them are residents, but some of them are refugees. With joint forces we shall be able to raise them all to a new standard of living, to a new life in which there is no refugee nor outcast, but residents living normally in all respects.

We are prepared to advance towards peace in any settlement that is desirable for all of us—with every country separately, with all countries in parallel. We recognize that Egypt has a senior status, a position of leadership in the Arab world and in the whole region, and in the final analysis peace can be based on a progressive unity between the peoples so that they will not be stuck with a wedge dividing them. We have to replace the unities that created enmity with a new unity that will create peace.

As far as can be seen, Mr President, there is no reason, between us and Egypt, no shadow of a reason, to continue any sort of dispute. We are convinced that we have the strength to straighten out the things in dispute, or apparently in dispute, within the foreseeable future. The enmity between us was an extended mistake, and an arrangement between us is within reach.

There is no reason for a dispute between us and Jordan. We have had a taste of Jordanian shells, but we have also had a taste of the open bridges. We regret the shells, but we are also convinced that over the open bridges can come a real campaign of peace, with no obstacles.

We are prepared to conduct negotiations for a lasting peace with the Syrians. It is possible to reach a speedy peace agreement with Lebanon. And let us not hide it, let us not disregard it, we are aware of the existence of the Palestinian identity. Every people has the right to decide its own identity, and this does not depend on the authorization of another nation. But the granting of expression to the Palestinian identity must be done without endangering Israel's security. I can also say that Jordan—no, that is not my affair. We have already seen how civilized nations found ways and solutions to the problem of different identities on one piece of land near another piece of land without having bitterness dictate the solution, a way of existing side by side in peace, every unit under its own leadership, running its own affairs, within existing political frameworks, which made it possible to live. The holy places, economic needs, the security circumstances demand extra open-heartedness. No border whatsoever must prevent approach to the holy places. The drawing up of a political map should not distort an economic map, and security needs must not interfere with the spiritual legacy of each one of our nations. Negotiations for peace can be held anywhere, any time, in any way. They can be held in Geneva, in Cairo, in Jerusalem. They can be open, they can be secret, they can be direct, they can be intermingled with the participation of countries which will be called to them. They can be intensive, they can be gradual. The only thing which must not happen is that this should fail. . . .

Today you are an honoured and majestic guest on the soil of our country. We very much respect the new renaissance, in fact, the revolution of the great independence which you and your generation have brought to the Egyptian people and to the Arab world. This renaissance and the revival aroused hidden energies which we thought had already been lost and forgotten in the long history. But much energy was also wasted in the tragic conflict between the two peoples. Let us put an end to it. Let us reunite our strengths, while we remain faithful, each of us, to his own way, his own belief, his dream. We should co-operate and together turn the area into the most fruitful area in the world, into the most flourishing society which this area has ever known. In the words of the Prophet Jeremiah, who said 2,500 years ago: "You shall not see the sword, nor shall you have famine, but I will give you assured peace in this place. . . ."

Source: IBA, 20 November—BBC, 22 November 1977.

APPENDIX IV—ISRAEL'S PLAN FOR ADMINISTRATIVE AUTONOMY: "SELF-RULE FOR PALESTINIAN ARABS, RESIDENTS OF JUDAEA, SAMARIA AND THE GAZA DISTRICT, WHICH WILL BE INSTITUTED UPON THE ESTABLISHMENT OF PEACE"

As announced by Mr Begin in the Knesset on 28 December 1977

1. The administration of the Military Government in Judaea, Samaria and the Gaza district will be abolished.

2. In Judaea, Samaria and the Gaza district, administrative autonomy of the residents, by and for them, will be established.

3. The residents of Judaea, Samaria and the Gaza district will elect an Administrative Council composed of 11 members. The Administrative Council will operate in accordance with the principles laid down in this paper.

4. Any resident, 18 years old and above, without distinction of citizenship, or if stateless, will be entitled to vote in the elections to the Administrative Council.

5. Any resident whose name is included in the list of candidates for the Administrative Council and who, on the day the list is submitted, is 25 years old or above, will be entitled to be elected to the Council.

6. The Administrative Council will be elected by general, direct, personal, equal and secret ballot.

7. The period of office of the Administrative Council will be four years from the day of its election.

8. The Administrative Council will sit in Bethlehem.

9. All the administrative affairs relating to the Arab residents of the areas of Judaea, Samaria and the Gaza district will be under the direction and within the competence of the Administrative Council.

10. The Administrative Council will operate the following Departments: education; religious affairs; finance; transportation; construction and housing; industry, commerce and tourism; agriculture; health, labour and social welfare; rehabilitation of refugees; and the administration of justice and the supervision of local police forces; and promulgate regulations relating to the operation of these Departments.

11. Security and public order in the areas of Judaea, Samaria and the Gaza district will be the responsibility of the Israeli authorities.

12. The Administrative Council will elect its own chairman.

13. The first session of the Administrative Council will be convened 30 days after the publication of the election results.

14. Residents of Judaea, Samaria and the Gaza district, without distinction of citizenship, or if stateless, will be granted free choice (option) of either Israeli or Jordanian citizenship.

15. A resident of the areas of Judaea, Samaria and the Gaza district who requests Israeli citizenship will be granted such citizenship in accordance with the citizenship law of the state.

16. Residents of Judaea, Samaria and the Gaza district who, in accordance with the right of free option, choose Israeli citizenship, will be entitled to vote for, and be elected to, the Knesset in accordance with the election law.

17. Residents of Judaea, Samaria and the Gaza district who are citizens of Jordan or who, in accordance with the right of free option will become citizens of Jordan, will elect and be eligible for election to the Parliament of the Hashemite Kingdom of Jordan in accordance with the election law of that country.

18. Questions arising from the vote to the Jordanian Parliament by residents of Judaea, Samaria and the Gaza district will be clarified in negotiations between Israel and Jordan.

19. A committee will be established of representatives of Israel, Jordan and the Administrative Council to examine existing legislation in Judaea, Samaria and the Gaza district, and to determine which legislation will continue in force which will be abolished, and what will be the competence of the Administrative Council to promulgate regulations. The rulings of the committee will be adopted by unanimous decision.

20. Residents of Israel will be entitled to acquire land and settle in the areas of Judaea, Samaria and the Gaza district. Arabs, residents of Judaea, Samaria and the Gaza district who, in accordance with the free option granted them, will become Israeli citizens, will be entitled to acquire land and settle in Israel.

21. A committee will be established of representatives of Israel, Jordan and the Administrative Council to determine norms of immigration to the areas of Judaea, Samaria and the Gaza district. The committee will determine the norms whereby Arab refugees residing outside Judaea, Samaria and the Gaza district will be permitted to immigrate to these areas in reasonable numbers. The rulings of the committee will be adopted by unanimous decision.

22. Residents of Israel and residents of Judaea, Samaria and the Gaza district will be assured freedom of movement and freedom of economic activity in Israel, Judaea, Samaria and the Gaza district.

23. The Administrative Council will appoint one of its members to represent the Council before the Government of Israel for deliberation on matters of common interest, and one of its members to represent the Council before the Government of Jordan for deliberation on matters of common interest.

24. Israel stands by its right and its claim of sovereignty to Judaea, Samaria and the Gaza district. In the knowledge that other claims exist, it proposes, for the sake of the agreement and the peace, that the question of sovereignty in the areas be left open.

25. With regard to the administration of the holy places of the three religions in Jerusalem, a special proposal will be drawn up and submitted that will include the guarantee of freedom of access to members of all the faiths to the shrines holy to them.

26. These principles will be subject to review after a five-year period.

Source: New York Times, 29 December 1977.

THE ARAB-ISRAELI CONFLICT

APPENDIX V: DRAFT JOINT STATEMENT OF PRINCIPLES AGREED TO, BUT NOT ISSUED, BY EGYPT AND ISRAEL IN THE ISMA'ILIYYA SUMMIT

(From Begin's 23 January Knesset Speech)

The Governments of the Arab Republic of Egypt and Israel are determined to continue their efforts to reach a comprehensive peace settlement in the region. Within the framework of such a settlement, they express their willingness to negotiate peace treaties on the basis of the principles envisaged in the Security Council Resolutions 242 and 338. The two sides agree that the establishment of a just and lasting peace requires the fulfilment of the following to act in accordance with Resolution 242: withdrawal of Israeli armed forces from territories occupied in the 1967 conflict; termination of all claims of state of belligerency, and respect for and acknowledgement of the sovereignty and territorial integrity and political independence of every state in the area and their right to live in peace within secure and recognized boundaries free from threats or acts of force; guaranteeing freedom of navigation through international waterways in the area; achieving a just settlement of the refugee problem; guaranteeing the territorial inviolability and political independence of every state in the area through measures including the establishment of demilitarized zones.

Source: IBA, 23 January—BBC, 25 January 1978.

APPENDIX VI: SĀDĀT'S STATEMENT AT THE CONCLUSION OF THE ISMA'ILIYYA SUMMIT CONFERENCE, 26 DECEMBER 1977

In the name of God, let me seize this opportunity to express my gratitude for the efforts you have done to cover the historical moments here in Isma'īliyya. As you know, after my visit to Jerusalem on the 20th of November, a new spirit prevails in the area and we have agreed in Jerusalem and in Isma'īliyya also to continue our efforts towards achieving a comprehensive settlement.

We have agreed upon raising the level of the representation in the Cairo conference to ministerial level and, as you have heard yesterday (Sunday), we have agreed upon two committees—a political committee and a military committee headed by ministers of foreign affairs and ministers of defence. The military committee will convene in Cairo. The political committee will convene in Jerusalem.

Those committees shall work in the context of the Cairo conference, meaning that they will report to the plenary whenever they reach any decision. [On] the question of the withdrawal, we have made progress, but on the Palestinian question, which we consider the core and crux of the problem here in this area, the Egyptian and Israeli delegations here discussed the Palestinian problem.

The position of Egypt is that on the West Bank and the Gaza Strip, a Palestinian state should be established. The position of Israel is that Palestinian Arabs in Judea, Samaria, the West Bank of Jordan and the Gaza Strip should enjoy self-rule.

We have agreed that because we have differed on the issue, the issue will be discussed in the political committee of the Cairo preparatory conference.

I hope I have given you some light upon our work and thank you again.

Source: Jerusalem Post, 27 December 1977.

APPENDIX VII: THE POLITICAL COMMITTEE OPENING SPEECHES, 17 JANUARY 1978

Israeli Foreign Minister, Moshe Dayan

My colleagues, the Foreign Minister of Egypt, the Secretary of State of the US, the Representative of the UN, distinguished delegates and guests to the political committee. I have the honour to open the meeting of the political committee of the peace talks in Jerusalem.

It gives me a great deal of pleasure to welcome you, and to express the hope that Jerusalem, city of eternal peace, sacred to our three faiths, will inspire our talks, and that we be worthy of its grace. I feel sure that we shall all of us do our utmost towards real achievements in the peace-making process.

A particular word of appreciation is due to the Secretary of State, who has come specially from Washington; his efforts in the cause of peace in the ME, and of course those of the President of the US, are a basic and fundamental factor in the joint efforts to this end of the peoples of our region.

Since the establishment of Israel, we have experienced many wars, and following them efforts, from time to time, to reach a settlement. Almost every expression in the dictionary has been used to describe these; ceasefire, armistice agreements, separation of forces, reduction of forces, interim agreements, step-by-step, buffer zones, demilitarized zones, UN emergency forces, UN Truce Supervision Organization, and so on and so on. Only one expression is missing—peace talks. These, in the full meaning of the words, are taking place now for the first time.

Israel has desired it very much through the years, but only now—thanks to President Sādāt's readiness for it—have we reached this stage. We are all, of course, aware of the distance between the beginning of peace talks and concluding a peace treaty. But we are on the right path.

We know that in this committee we are faced with three subjects. First, the principle of the achievement of peace treaties between Israel and its neighbours: Egypt, Jordan, Syria and Lebanon. Secondly, the principles of a just solution of the problem of the Palestinian Arabs residing in Judea, Samaria and the Gaza Strip. Thirdly, an agreement on a peace treaty between Egypt and Israel.

Distinguished delegates, any one of these subjects could well deter any one familiar with the problems of the ME. But it is, however, clear to all that these questions can only be resolved by a peace settlement freely achieved between the parties and not by more wars, not by acts of terrorism, not by economic boycott. No solutions are to be found in these. They can only create more suffering, more destruction, more casualties and more refugees fleeing their homes.

If 30 years of hostility in the ME have any lesson for us, it is only that the longer we delay the peace settlement, the graver and more complex the problems become and all the harder to resolve.

Distinguished delegates, I should like to conclude with an observation addressed to all of us. A peace settlement is the alternative to war, and not a substitute to war. It can only be achieved by concession, compromise and mutual agreement. Any attempt to solve our problems and differences by ultimatums would miss the whole point, destroy the very purpose of peace talks. The only way to make progress in our joint task is to explore the various problems and search for agreed solutions. We may have to adopt unconventional approaches at times; but the problems we face and the situation we find ourselves in, are also not conventional. Thirty years of hostility to Israel, and of refusal to accept her existence, have left their mark; a great deal of goodwill, wisdom and imagination are called for in order to open up a new page and to pave the road to peace.

Egyptian Foreign Minister, Muḥammad Ibrāhīm Kāmil

It is quite inspiring that we are meeting here in the city of peace, which is most sacred to us all. The time has come, after 30 years of bitter and mortal strife between the peoples of this region, when we must resolve to live together in a world of peace and justice, and avoid the hideous tragedy of senseless waste and misery.

It was only appropriate and natural that this process of peace be initiated by President Sādāt, since Egypt, with its cultural heritage, geographical position and human resources, has always for the last 7,000 years, borne a special responsibility in the region. It has always lived up to the challenge of history, and its destiny is to continue to do so as an integral part of the Arab world.

Because we believe in the most sacred fundamental rights of all peoples: because together with all peoples of the UN, we believe that we must save succeeding generations from the scourge of war: because we must endeavour to lay aside the anger and hatred in our hearts by eradicating aggression and injustice: we have come here today to continue the process of peace initiated by President Sādāt on 20 November, which received overwhelming support.

As a manifestation of this support, we appreciate today the active participation of Secretary of State Vance, whose tireless efforts will no doubt contribute to the progress of our work. We also welcome at our meeting the presence of the representative of the Secretary-General of the UN.

We have not come to seek a separate peace, or a temporary peace. We have come to Jerusalem, where from time immemorial human destiny has experienced an encounter with the Divine. We have come to speak of a just and comprehensive peace based on withdrawal from all the Arab territories occupied by Israel since June 1967, including Jerusalem, the holy city of peace. We have come to realize the fundamental rights of the Palestinian people, who have been struggling for decades to end their subjugation and their diaspora, to exercise their national rights in accordance with the most sacred principles of equal rights and self-determination of peoples.

It would be tragic that you should deny the existence of this Palestinian reality, especially when we have declared our readiness to accept you as part of the ME. Would you let the deception of futile argument ruin this unique opportunity, when peace can become a dweller of your fields and homesteads? Can you not see that the Palestinian people are no less entitled than any other people to achieve their legitimate rights? There will be no real peace in Palestine for the House of Israel unless there will be an equal house there for the Palestinian people.

Let us work together, with vision and imagination, with courage and dedication, transcending formalities and polemics, to erect the permanent structure of a comprehensive and lasting peace for all the peoples of the area based on law and justice. Let us work for the day when we can build the city of true virtue (al-madīna al-fadīla) in the land of Palestine.

US Secretary of State, Cyrus Vance

Let me first express to our host my delegation's appreciation for the arrangements that have been made for the meetings that are opening today.

We owe a deep debt of gratitude to President Sādāt and to Prime Minister Begin for their steps toward peace which have brought us to this room. We are here because of the courage and vision of President Sādāt and Prime Minister Begin in sweeping aside the barriers that for so long separated Arabs from Israelis, barriers that have caused so many wars and so much bloodshed. We are here to work to bring to fruition the task begun by President Sādāt and Prime Minister Begin in Jerusalem and in Ismā'īliyya, and in the Cairo conference, of which this committee is an outgrowth.

President Carter has sent me to represent the US at the opening of these talks to demonstrate the importance that we attach to them and to their success. Since the very beginning of the Arab-Israeli conflict, we have played an active role in the search for a settlement. Our friendships with all of the parties are warm and strong. For the meetings that begin this morning, we pledge to support the efforts of the parties to reach agreement.

The common goal of all—Egypt, Israel, the US, and those absent today, but who we hope will soon join in our efforts—is a just, lasting 'and comprehensive peace. If this committee is to succeed in its goal of preparing the way for such a peace, it must come to grips with the difficult problems of substance which continue to separate the parties.

As President Carter has said, we believe there are certain principles which must be observed before a just and comprehensive peace can be achieved. First, true peace must be based on normal relations among the parties to the peace. Peace means more than just the end to belligerency. Second, there must be withdrawal by Israel from territories occupied in 1967 and agreement on secure and recognized borders for all parties, in the context of normal and peaceful relations in accordance with UN Resolutions 242 and 338. And, third, there must be a resolution of the Palestinian problem in all its aspects. The solution must recognize the legitimate rights of the Palestinian people and enable the Palestinians to participate in the determination of their own future.

Those of us here today bear special and very heavy responsibility as representatives of our governments and as individuals. We must deal with and overcome many difficult problems. We will be held accountable, today by world opinion, tomorrow by history. We will not be judged lightly if we fail.

It is entirely fitting that the work be done in Jerusalem—Jerusalem, city of peace, city which has known so much strife and bloodshed, city holy to our three religions. We must carry forward here the work already begun. As President Carter recently suggested, the road to peace can lead through Jerusalem and Cairo ultimately to a comprehensive peace.

It is also fitting that this work should begin as Israel approaches its 30th anniversary. There could be no greater gift, to the people of Israel and the people of the Arab world, than to make this anniversary the birthday of peace.

So, in this place and at this time, let us strive to make a reality of the peace for which the peoples of this area have so long yearned.

Source: Jerusalem Post, 18 January 1978.

APPENDIX VIII: THE PRINCIPLES WHICH UNDERLIE US PARTICIPATION IN THE SEARCH FOR PEACE IN THE MIDDLE EAST

As reaffirmed by President Carter to Sādāt during their talks in February 1978

The US will remain faithful to its historic commitments to the security of Israel and to the right of every state in the area to live in peace within secure and recognized boundaries.

Helping the parties achieve a negotiated comprehensive settlement of the ME conflict remains of highest importance in American policy, and President Carter will spare no effort in seeking ways to move the peace process forward.

A peace settlement must go beyond the mere termination of belligerency. It must provide for the establishment of normal peaceful relations between Israel and its neighbours.

The peace settlement should be comprehensive and should be embodied in peace treaties between Israel and each of its neighbours.

The settlement must be based on all the principles of Security Council Resolution 242, including withdrawal of Israeli armed forces from territories occupied in 1967, and the right of every state in the area to live in peace within secure and recognized boundaries. Resolution 242 is applicable to all fronts of the conflict.

There can be no just and lasting peace without resolution of the Palestinian problem.

The President reaffirmed what he said at his meeting with President Sādāt in Aswān on 4 January. There must be a resolution of the Palestinian problem in all its aspects; it must recognize the legitimate rights of the Palestinian people and enable the Palestinians to participate in the determination of their own future.

President Carter also reaffirmed the longstanding US view that Israeli settlements in occupied territory are contrary to international law and an obstacle to peace and that further settlement activity would be inconsistent with the effort to reach a peace settlement.

Source: Department of State Bulletin, March 1978.

THE EGYPTIAN–ISRAELI NEGOTIATIONS

APPENDIX IX: EGYPT'S PEACE PLAN PUBLISHED BY THE EGYPTIAN FOREIGN MINISTRY UNDER THE HEADING "PROPOSALS RELATIVE TO WITHDRAWAL FROM THE WEST BANK AND GAZA AND SECURITY ARRANGEMENTS," ON 5 JULY 1978

1. The establishment of a just and lasting peace in the ME necessitates a just solution of the Palestinian question in all its aspects on the basis of the legitimate rights of the Palestinian people and taking into consideration the legitimate security concerns of all the parties.

2. In order to ensure a peaceful and orderly transfer of authority there shall be a transitional period not exceeding five years at the end of which the Palestinian people will be able to determine their own future.

3. Talks shall take place between Egypt, Jordan, Israel and representatives of the Palestinian people with the participation of the UN with a view to agreeing upon:

    a. Details of the transitional regime.

    b. Timetable for the Israeli withdrawal.

    c. Mutual security arrangements for all the parties concerned during and following the transitional period.

    d. Modalities for the implementation of relevant UN resolutions on Palestinian refugees.

    e. Other issues considered appropriate by all parties.

4. Israel shall withdraw from the West Bank (including Jerusalem) and the Gaza Strip, occupied since June 1967. The Israeli withdrawal applies to the settlements established in the occupied territories.

5. The Israeli military government in the West Bank and the Gaza Strip shall be abolished at the outset of the transitional period. Supervision over the administration of the West Bank shall become the responsibility of Jordan, and supervision over the administration of the Gaza Strip shall become the responsibility of Egypt. Jordan and Egypt shall carry out their responsibility in co-operation with freely elected representatives of the Palestinian people who shall exercise direct authority over the administration of the West Bank and Gaza. The UN shall supervise and facilitate the Israeli withdrawal and the restoration of Arab authority.

6. Egypt and Jordan shall guarantee that the security arrangements to be agreed upon will continue to be respected in the West Bank and Gaza.

Source: New York Times, 6 July 1978.

APPENDIX X: THE CAMP DAVID AGREEMENTS

Signed at the White House on Sunday, 17 September 1978

A FRAMEWORK FOR PEACE IN THE MIDDLE EAST

Muhammad Anwar al-Sādāt, President of the Arab Republic of Egypt, and Menahem Begin, Prime Minister of Israel, met with Jimmy Carter, President of the United States of America, at Camp David from 5 September–17 September 1978, and have agreed on the following framework for peace in the ME. They invite other parties to the Arab-Israeli conflict to adhere to it.

Preamble

The search for peace in the ME must be guided by the following:

The agreed basis for a peaceful settlement of the conflict between Israel and its neighbours is UN Security Council Resolution 242 in all its parts.

After four wars during 30 years, despite intensive human efforts, the ME, which is the cradle of civilization and the birthplace of three great religions, does not yet enjoy the blessings of peace. The people of the ME yearn for peace, so that the vast human and natural resources of the region can be turned to the pursuits of peace and so that this area can become a model for coexistence and co-operation among nations.

The historic initiative by President Sādāt in visiting Jerusalem and the reception accorded to him by the Parliament, Government and people of Israel, and the reciprocal visit of Prime Minister Begin to Ismā'īliyya, the peace proposals made by both leaders, as well as the warm reception of these missions by the peoples of both countries have created an unprecedented opportunity for peace which must not be lost if this generation and future generations are to be spared the tragedies of war.

The provisions of the Charter of the UN and the other accepted norms of international law and legitimacy now provide accepted standards for the conduct of relations among all states.

To achieve a relationship of peace, in the spirit of Article 2 of the UN Charter, future negotiations between Israel and any neighbour prepared to negotiate peace and security with it, are necessary for the purpose of carrying out all the provisions and principles of Resolutions 242 and 338.

Peace requires respect for the sovereignty, territorial integrity and political independence of every state in the area and their right to live in peace within secure and recognized boundaries free from threats or acts of force. Progress toward that goal can accelerate movement toward a new era of reconciliation in the ME marked by co-operation in promoting economic development, in maintaining stability and in assuring security.

Security is enhanced by a relationship of peace and by co-operation between nations which enjoy normal relations. In addition, under the terms of peace treaties, the parties can, on the basis of reciprocity, agree to special security arrangements such as demilitarized zones, limited armaments areas, early warning stations, the presence of international forces, liaison, agreed measures for monitoring, and other arrangements that they agree are useful.

Framework

Taking these factors into account, the parties are determined to reach a just comprehensive and durable settlement of the ME conflict through the conclusion of peace treaties based on Security Council Resolutions 242 and 338 in all their parts. Their purpose is to achieve peace and good neighbourly relations. They recognize that, for peace to endure, it must involve all those who have been most deeply affected by the conflict. They therefore agree that this framework as appropriate is intended by them to constitute a basis for peace not only between Egypt and Israel, but also between Israel and each of its other neighbours which is prepared to negotiate peace with Israel on this basis. With that objective in mind, they have agreed to proceed as follows:

A. West Bank and Gaza

1. Egypt, Israel, Jordan and the representatives of the Palestinian people should participate in negotiations on the resolution of the Palestinian problem in all its aspects. To achieve that objective, negotiations relating to the West Bank and Gaza should proceed in three stages.

(a) Egypt and Israel agree that, in order to ensure a peaceful and orderly transfer of authority, and taking into account the security concerns of all the parties, there should be transitional arrangements for the West Bank and Gaza for a period not exceeding five years. In order to provide full autonomy to the inhabitants, under these arrangements the Israeli military government and its civilian administration will be withdrawn as soon as a self-governing authority has been freely elected by the inhabitants of these areas to replace the existing military government. To negotiate the details of a transitional arrangement, the government of Jordan will be invited to join the negotiations on the basis of this framework. These new arrangements should give due consideration both to the principle of self-government by the inhabitants of these territories and to the legitimate security concerns of the parties involved.

(b) Egypt, Israel and Jordan will agree on the modalities for establishing the elected self-governing authority in the West Bank and Gaza. The delegations of Egypt and Jordan may include Palestinians from the West Bank and Gaza or other Palestinians as mutually agreed. The parties will negotiate an agreement which will define the powers and responsibilities of the self-governing authority to be exercised in the West Bank and Gaza. A withdrawal of Israeli armed forces will take place and there will be a redeployment of the remaining Israeli forces into specified security locations: The agreement will also include arrangements for assuring internal and external security and public order. A strong local police force will be established, which may include Jordanian citizens. In addition, Israeli and Jordanian forces will participate in joint patrols and in the manning of control posts to assure the security of the borders.

(c) When the self-governing authority (Administrative Council) in the West Bank and Gaza is established and inaugurated, the transitional period of five years will begin. As soon as possible, but not later than the third year after the beginning of the transitional period, negotiations will take place to determine the final status of the West Bank and Gaza and its relationship with its neighbours, and to conclude a peace treaty between Israel and Jordan by the end of the transitional period. These negotiations will be conducted among Egypt, Israel, Jordan and the elected representatives of the inhabitants of the West Bank and Gaza. Two separate but related committees will be convened, one committee, consisting of representatives of the four parties which will negotiate and agree on the final status of the West Bank and Gaza, and its relationship with its neighbours, and the second committee, consisting of representatives of Israel and representatives of Jordan to be joined by the elected representatives of the inhabitants of the West Bank and Gaza, to negotiate the peace treaty between Israel and Jordan, taking into account the agreement reached on the final status of the West Bank and Gaza. The negotiations shall be based on all the provisions and principles of UN Security Council Resolution 242. The negotiations will resolve, among other matters, the location of the boundaries and the nature of the security arrangements. The solution from the negotiations must also recognize the legitimate rights of the Palestinian people and their just requirements. In this way, the Palestinians will participate in the determination of their own future through:

(i) The negotiations among Egypt, Israel, Jordan and the representatives of the inhabitants of the West Bank and Gaza to agree on the final status of the West Bank and Gaza and other outstanding issues by the end of the transitional period.

(ii) Submitting their agreement to a vote by the elected representatives of the inhabitants of the West Bank and Gaza.

150

(iii) Providing for the elected representatives of the inhabitants of the West Bank and Gaza to decide how they shall govern themselves consistent with the provisions of their agreement.

(iv) Participating as stated above in the work of the committee negotiating the peace treaty between Israel and Jordan.

2. All necessary measures will be taken and provisions made to assure the security of Israel and its neighbours during the transitional period and beyond. To assist in providing such security, a strong local police force will be constituted by the self-governing authority. It will be composed of inhabitants of the West Bank and Gaza. The police will maintain continuing liaison on internal security matters with the designated Israeli, Jordanian and Egyptian officers.

3. During the transitional period, representatives of Egypt, Israel, Jordan and the self-governing authority will constitute a continuing committee to decide by agreement on the modalities of admission of persons displaced from the West Bank and Gaza in 1967, together with necessary measures to prevent disruption and disorder. Other matters of common concern may also be dealt with by this committee.

4. Egypt and Israel will work with each other and with other interested parties to establish agreed procedures for a prompt, just and permanent implementation of the resolution of the refugee problem.

B. Egypt—Israel

1. Egypt and Israel undertake not to resort to the threat or the use of force to settle disputes. Any disputes shall be settled by peaceful means in accordance with the provisions of Article 33 of the Charter of the UN.

2. In order to achieve peace between them, the parties agree to negotiate in good faith with a goal of concluding within three months from the signing of this framework a peace treaty between them, while inviting the other parties to the conflict to proceed simultaneously to negotiate and conclude similar peace treaties with a view to achieving a comprehensive peace in the area. The framework for the conclusion of a peace treaty between Egypt and Israel will govern the peace negotiations between them. The parties will agree on the modalities and the timetable for the implementation of their obligations under the treaty.

C. Associated Principles

1. Egypt and Israel state that the principles and provisions described below should apply to peace treaties between Israel and each of its neighbours—Egypt, Jordan, Syria and Lebanon.

2. Signatories shall establish among themselves relationships normal to states at peace with one another. To this end, they should undertake to abide by all the provisions of the Charter of the UN. Steps to be taken in this respect include:

(a) Full recognition.

(b) Abolishing economic boycotts.

(c) Guaranteeing that under their jurisdiction the citizens of the other parties shall enjoy the protection of the due process of law.

3. Signatories should explore possibilities for economic development in the context of final peace treaties, with the objective of contributing to the atmosphere of peace, co-operation, and friendship which is their common goal.

4. Claims commissions may be established for the mutual settlement of all financial claims.

5. The US shall be invited to participate in the talks on matters related to the modalities of the implementation of the agreements and working out the timetable for the carrying out of the obligations of the parties.

6. The UN Security Council shall be requested to endorse the peace treaties and ensure that their provisions shall not be violated. The permanent members of the Security Council shall be requested to underwrite the peace treaties and ensure respect for their provisions. They shall also be requested to conform their policies and actions with the undertakings contained in this framework.

A FRAMEWORK FOR THE CONCLUSION OF A PEACE TREATY BETWEEN EGYPT AND ISRAEL

In order to achieve peace between them, Israel and Egypt agree to negotiate in good faith with a goal of concluding within three months of the signing of this framework a peace treaty between them.

It is agreed that:

The site of the negotiations will be under a UN flag at a location or locations to be mutually agreed.

All of the principles of UN Resolution 242 will apply in this resolution of the dispute between Israel and Egypt.

Unless otherwise mutually agreed, terms of the peace treaty will be implemented between two and three years after the peace treaty is signed.

THE ARAB-ISRAELI CONFLICT

The following matters are agreed between the parties:

(a) The full exercise of Egyptian sovereignty up to the internationally recognized border between Egypt and mandated Palestine;

(b) The withdrawal of Israeli armed forces from the Sinai;

(c) The use of airfields left by the Israelis near al-'Arish, and Sharm al-Shaykh for civilian purposes only, including possible commercial use by all nations;

(d) The right of free passage by ships of Israel through the Gulf of Suez and the Suez Canal on the basis of the Constantinople Convention of 1888 applying to all nations; the Strait of Tiran and the Gulf of 'Aqaba are international waterways to be open to all nations for unimpeded and non-suspendable freedom of navigation and overflight;

(e) The construction of a highway between the Sinai and Jordan near Eilat with guaranteed free and peaceful passage by Egypt and Jordan; and

(f) The stationing of military forces listed below:

Stationing of Forces

(a) No more than one division (mechanized or infantry) of Egyptian armed forces will be stationed within an area lying approximately 50 km (30 miles) east of the Gulf of Suez and the Suez Canal.

(b) Only UN forces and civil police equipped with light weapons to perform normal police functions will be stationed within an area lying west of the international border and the Gulf of 'Aqaba, varying in width from 20 km (12 miles) to 40 km (24 miles).

(c) In the area within 3 km (1.8 miles) east of the international border there will be Israeli limited military forces not to exceed four infantry battalions and UN observers.

(d) Border patrol units, not to exceed three battalions, will supplement the civil police in maintaining order in the area not included above.

The exact demarcation of the above areas will be as decided during the peace negotiations.

Early warning stations may exist to insure compliance with the terms of the agreement.

UN forces will be stationed: (a) in part of the area in the Sinai lying within about 20 km of the Mediterranean Sea and adjacent to the international border, and (b) in the Sharm al-Shaykh area to ensure freedom of passage through the Strait of Tiran; and these forces will not be removed unless such removal is approved by the Security Council of the UN with a unanimous vote of the five permanent members.

After a peace treaty is signed, and after the interim withdrawal is complete, normal relations will be established between Egypt and Israel, including full recognition, including diplomatic, economic and cultural relations; termination of economic boycotts and barriers to the free movement of goods and people; and mutual protection of citizens by the due process of law.

Interim Withdrawal

Between three months and nine months after the signing of the peace treaty, all Israeli forces will withdraw east of a line extending from a point east of al-'Arish to Ras Muḥammad, the exact location of this line to be determined by mutual agreement.

ANNEX

Text of UN Security Council Resolution 242 of 22 November 1967
(adopted unanimously at the 1382nd meeting).

The Security Council, expressing its continuing concern with the grave situation in the ME; emphasizing the inadmissibility of the acquisition of territory by war and the need to work for a just and lasting peace in which every state in the area can live in security: emphasizing further that all member-states in their acceptance of the Charter of the UN have undertaken a commitment to act in accordance with Article 2 of the Charter:

1. Affirms that the fulfilment of Charter principles requires the establishment of a just and lasting peace in the ME which should include the application of both the following principles:

(a) Withdrawal of Israeli armed forces from territories occupied in the recent conflict;

(b) Termination of all claims or states of belligerency and respect for and acknowledgement of the sovereignty, territorial integrity and political independence of every state in the area and their right to live in peace within secure and recognized boundaries free from threats or acts of force;

2. Affirms further the necessity

(a) for guaranteeing freedom of navigation through international waterways in the area;

(b) for achieving a just settlement of the refugee problem;

(c) for guaranteeing the territorial inviolability and political independence of every state in the area, through measures including the establishment of demilitarized zones;

3. Requests the Secretary-General to designate a special representative to proceed to the ME to establish and maintain contacts with the states concerned in order to promote agreement and assist efforts to achieve a peaceful and accepted settlement in accordance with the provisions and principles of this resolution.

4. Requests the Secretary-General to report to the Security Council on the progress of the efforts of the special representative as soon as possible.

152

Text of UN Security Council Resolution 338 (adopted by the Security Council at its 1747th meeting on 21–22 October 1973).

The Security Council:

1. Calls upon all parties to the present fighting to cease all firing and terminate all military activity immediately, no later than 12 hours after the moment of the adoption of this decision, in the positions they now occupy:

2. Calls upon the parties concerned to start immediately after the ceasefire the implementation of Security Council Resolution 242 (1967) in all its parts;

3. Decides that, immediately and concurrently with the ceasefire, negotiations start between the parties concerned under appropriate auspices aimed at establishing a just and durable peace in the ME.

Source: USICA, *Official Text*, 18 September 1978.

APPENDIX XI: TEXT OF THE EXCHANGE OF LETTERS ACCOMPANYING THE CAMP DAVID AGREEMENTS, RELEASED BY THE WHITE HOUSE ON 22 SEPTEMBER 1978

All letters from Mr Carter are dated 22 September 1978; all others are dated 17 September 1978.

To President Carter from Prime Minister Begin:
I have the honour to inform you that during two weeks after my return home, I will submit a motion before Israel's parliament (the Knesset) to decide on the following question:

If during the negotiations to conclude a peace treaty between Israel and Egypt all outstanding issues are agreed upon, "are you in favour of the removal of the Israeli settlers from the northern and southern Sinai areas or are you in favour of keeping the aforementioned settlers in those areas?"

The vote, Mr President, on this issue will be completely free from the usual parliamentary party discipline to the effect that although the coalition is being now supported by 70 members out of 120, every member of the Knesset, as I believe, both of the government and the opposition benches, will be enabled to vote in accordance with his own conscience.

To President Sādāt from President Carter:
I transmit herewith a copy of a letter to me from Prime Minister Begin setting forth how he proposes to present the issue of the Sinai settlements to the Knesset for the latter's decision.

In this connection, I understand from your letter that Knesset approval to withdraw all Israeli settlers from Sinai according to a timetable within the period specified for the implementation of the peace treaty is a prerequisite to any negotiations on a peace treaty between Egypt and Israel.

To President Carter from President Sādāt:
In connection with the "Framework for a Settlement in Sinai" to be signed tonight, I would like to reaffirm the position of the Arab Republic of Egypt with respect to the settlements:

1. All Israeli settlers must be withdrawn from Sinai according to a timetable within the period specified for the implementation of the peace treaty.

2. Agreement by the Israeli Government and its constitutional institutions to this basic principle is therefore a prerequisite to starting peace negotiations for concluding a peace treaty.

3. If Israel fails to meet this commitment, the "framework" shall be void and invalid.

To Prime Minister Begin from President Carter:
I have received your letter of 17 September 1978, describing how you intend to place the question of the future of Israeli settlements in Sinai before the Knesset for its decision.

Enclosed is a copy of President Sadat's letter to me on this subject.

To President Carter from President Sādāt:
I am writing you to reaffirm the position of the Arab Republic of Egypt with respect to Jerusalem.

1. Arab Jerusalem is an integral part of the West Bank. Legal and historical Arab rights in the city must be respected and restored.

2. Arab Jerusalem should be under Arab sovereignty.

3. The Palestinian inhabitants of Arab Jerusalem are entitled to exercise their legitimate national rights, being part of the Palestinian people in the West Bank.

4. Relevant Security Council resolutions, particularly Resolutions 242 and 267, must be applied with regard to Jerusalem. All the measures taken by Israel to alter the status of the city are null and void and should be rescinded.

5. All peoples must have free access to the city and enjoy the free exercise of worship and the right to visit and transit to the holy places without distinction or discrimination.

6. The holy places of each faith may be placed under the administration and control of their representatives.

7. Essential functions in the city should be undivided and a joint municipal council composed of an equal number of Arab and Israeli members can supervise the carrying out of these functions. In this way, the city shall be undivided.

To President Carter from Prime Minister Begin:
I have the honour to inform you, Mr President, that on 28 June 1967—Israel's parliament (the Knesset) promulgated and adopted a law to the effect: "The government is empowered by a decree to apply the law, the jurisdiction and administration of the state to any part of the Eretz Israel (Land of Israel—Palestine), as stated in that decree."

On the basis of this law, the government of Israel decreed in July 1967 that Jerusalem is one city indivisible, the capital of the State of Israel.

To President Sādāt from President Carter:
I have received your letter of 17 September 1978, setting forth the Egyptian position on Jerusalem. I am transmitting a copy of that letter to Prime Minister Begin for his information.

The position of the US on Jerusalem remains as stated by Ambassador Goldberg in the UN General Assembly on 14 July 1967, and subsequently by Ambassador Yost of the UN Security Council on 1 July 1969.

To President Carter from President Sādāt:
In connection with the "Framework for Peace in the Middle East," I am writing you this letter to inform you of the position of the Arab Republic of Egypt, with respect to the implementation of the comprehensive settlement.

To ensure the implementation of the provisions related to the West Bank and Gaza and in order to safeguard the legitimate rights of the Palestinian people, Egypt will be prepared to assume the Arab role emanating from these provisions, following consultations with Jordan and the representatives of the Palestinian people.

To Prime Minister Begin from President Carter:
I hereby acknowledge that you have informed me as follows:

a) In each paragraph of the agreed framework document the expressions "Palestinians" or "Palestinian people" are being and will be construed and understood by you as "Palestinian Arabs."

b) In each paragraph in which the expression "West Bank" appears it is being, and will be, understood by the Government of Israel as Judea and Samaria.

Source: USICA, *Official Text*, 23 September 1978.

APPENDIX XII: TEXT OF US DEFENCE SECRETARY'S LETTER TO ISRAEL'S DEFENCE MINISTER

Released by the Pentagon on 29 September 1978

The US understands that in connection with carrying out the agreements reached at Camp David, Israel intends to build two military bases at appropriate sites in the Negev to replace the air bases at Eytam and Ezion which will be evacuated by Israel in accordance with the peace treaty to be concluded between Egypt and Israel. They also understand the special urgency and priority which Israel attaches to preparing the new bases in light of its conviction that it cannot safely leave the Sinai bases until the new ones are operational.

I suggest that our two governments consult on the scope and cost of the two new air bases, as well as on related forms of assistance which the US might appropriately provide in light of the special problems which might be presented by carrying out such a project on an urgent basis.

The President is prepared to seek the necessary Congressional approval for such assistance as may be agreed upon by the US side as a result of such consultations.

Source: IBA in English, 29 September—BBC, 2 October 1978.

APPENDIX XIII: CHRONOLOGY

20 September 1977	—	The Dayan-Tuhāmī meeting in Tangier
19–21 November 1977	—	Sādāt's visit to Israel
14–22 December 1977	—	The Cairo Conference
14–19 December 1977	—	Begin's US visit
20–21 December 1977	—	Weizman's visit to Egypt
25–26 December 1977	—	The Ismā'īliyya Summit
4 January 1978	—	The Carter-Sādāt talks in Aswān
11–14 January 1978	—	The Military Committee deliberations in Cairo
17–18 January 1978	—	The Political Committee deliberations in Jerusalem
22–31 January 1978	—	Atherton's first shuttle
31 January–2 February 1978	—	The Military Committee—second round

THE EGYPTIAN-ISRAELI NEGOTIATIONS

3–8 February 1978	—	Sādāt's US visit
11 February 1978	—	The Sādāt-Peres meeting in Salzburg
20 February–8 March 1978	—	Atherton's second shuttle
20–23 March	—	Begin's US visit
30–31 March 1978	—	The Sādāt-Weizman talks in Egypt
26–28 April 1978	—	The Vance-Dayan talks; US questions posed to Israel
19 June 1978	—	Israel's reply to US questions
30 June–3 July 1978	—	Mondale's visits to Jerusalem and Alexandria
3 July 1978	—	Submission of Egypt's Peace Plan to the US
10 July 1978	—	The Sādāt-Peres meeting in Vienna; the "Vienna Document"
13 July 1978	—	The Sādāt-Weizman meeting in Salzburg
18–19 July 1978	—	The Leeds Castle Conference
23 July 1978	—	Begin's rejection of the "Goodwill Gesture"
27 July 1978	—	The expulsion of the Israeli Military Mission from Egypt
6–17 September 1978	—	The Camp David Summit
28 September 1978	—	Approval of the Camp David Agreements by the Knesset

The Negotiating Process:
Attitudes of Interested Parties

While Sādāt's initiative promptly involved Israel, the US and Egypt itself in the momentous, complex and tension-fraught political process described in the preceding section, it left ·outside the scope of active participation a number of Middle Eastern and other countries, each of which had a major stake in the course of events. Their attitudes are discussed in this section. From among them, Jordan stood out from the start as a possible candidate for joining the diplomatic process launched by Sādāt—a position which marked it off from all other major Arab countries, which either vehemently criticized the Egyptian President, or dissociated themselves from his initiative in more restrained ways. Three countries—Morocco, Iran and Romania—actually took a hand in preparing the ground for Sādāt's initial steps; the subsequent disclosure of their roles was unprecedented in the history of Arab-Israeli contacts. Most major Arab countries felt the need to rethink or restate their positions on the Arab-Israeli conflict, not only over the immediate situation created by Sādāt's moves, but also towards the fundamentals of the conflict. The USSR and the UN Secretariat were guided in their reactions chiefly by the fact that the by-passing of the Geneva conference deprived them, for the time being at least, of playing a direct role in the ME political process. For two groups—the PLO and the inhabitants of the West Bank and Gaza—reactions to Sādāt's new policies were altogether central to events of the year; they are therefore dealt with in separate essays. The realignment of inter-Arab affiliations and divisions which followed Sādāt's initiative is also described separately in the essay, "Inter-Arab Relations." Brief references in this section to the various stages of the Egyptian-Israeli-US negotiations can be followed up by consulting the detailed account given above.

JORDAN

From the very beginning of his initiative, Sādāt had hoped to draw at least one other Arab side into the negotiating process. In the circumstances, that candidate could only be Jordan. Thus, instead of having to struggle against the American drift towards the PLO,[1] Amman now found itself courted by the participants and supporters of Sādāt's initiative, who tried to persuade King Ḥusayn to join in. Paradoxically, however, this improved position posed a dilemma for Jordan. Since the 1967 war, Jordan had displayed a willingness to conclude peace with Israel in exchange for a complete Israeli withdrawal from the West Bank (including East Jerusalem); King Ḥusayn had also secretly met Israeli officials on various occasions.[2] Unlike other Arab leaders, he did not therefore find Sādāt's initiative objectionable in principle. Furthermore, the initiative implied that both the US and Egypt now accepted Jordan as the main partner to a solution of the Palestinian problem. However, formally bound by the resolutions of the 1974 Rabat summit conference—which had made the PLO the "sole legitimate representative of the Palestinians"—Ḥusayn felt that he could not legitimately claim to negotiate on their behalf. In his view, only a prior commitment by Israel to a complete withdrawal and acceptance of Palestinian self-determination (according to the Jordanian interpretation[3]) could overcome the Rabat obstacle. Since Israel would not make such an advance commitment, and since Sādāt's Arab opponents were applying pressure to prevent Jordan from joining, Ḥusayn concluded that direct participation in the negotiating process would be too onerous. But at the same time, Jordan could not afford completely to disclaim involvement in the moves launched by Sādāt, since this would debar it from sharing in possible future gains and might even jeopardize its entire future standing in the West Bank. Jordan's way out, at least for the time being, was a form of "negotiations by proxy": it left Cairo to continue negotiating over the West Bank and the Palestinian issue until its own requirements could be fully met; then the Kingdom would join the talks. However, this attitude suited neither Egypt, Israel nor the US. Assisted by several other countries, they made a sustained effort to obtain Jordan's agreement to direct participation.

One of the first moves made by the US when it learned of Sādāt's imminent visit to Jerusalem was "to use whatever influence [it] had" to convince Menahem Begin not only to invite the King—which he did—but also to convince Husayn to accept the invitation.[4] However, Husayn recalled that he had visited Cairo only two days before Sādāt's announcement that he would address the Knesset, yet Sādāt had given him no hint of his intentions. As the King felt this signified that Egypt was seeking a separate settlement with Israel, he termed the visit "a negative action."[5] Only when Jordan's initial suspicions of a separate deal subsided did Husayn speak of the visit in more positive terms, as "courageous."[6]

This change of attitude was more propitious to persuading Jordan to join the negotiations, and US efforts in this direction were reinforced by Egypt, Israel and Morocco. Sādāt contacted Husayn during the last days of November 1977, informed him in detail of his talks in Jerusalem,[7] and invited him to participate in the Cairo conference in December. Morocco's Minister of State for Foreign Affairs, Muḥammad Boucetta (Abū Sitta), visited Amman on 1 December, carrying a personal message from King Hasan II to Husayn, presumably with the same purpose. And Israel reiterated its call for Husayn to meet Begin, both through public invitations and through "prominent Arabs from the West Bank."[8] Jordan rejected the invitations, but reserved the option of joining later if its conditions were met. Thus Husayn declared that "although we have been affected by what has happened . . . we will now exert efforts to deal with the facts and responsibilities in a most constructive manner."[9] Although the basic condition for Jordan's participation was that "the knot of the Rabat summit decisions [be] untied—and only Arabs and Palestinians in particular can untie it," he made it clear that in case of "the complete recovery of territories occupied in 1967, including . . . Arab Jerusalem, Jordan would find it impossible to refuse the liberation of Arab land."[10]

On 8 December 1977 (shortly before the Cairo conference convened), Husayn visited Cairo and conferred with Sādāt. Realizing that Jordan would not participate in his initiative, Sādāt was reported to have agreed to negotiate on Jordan's behalf,[11] with the aim of achieving a declaration of principles which could enable Jordan to join in later. The US Secretary of State endorsed the Egyptian-Jordanian understanding during his visit to Amman on 12 December.

The situation again changed when Jordan officially rejected the Israeli plan for autonomy in the West Bank and the Gaza Strip. A Cabinet statement termed the plan a manifestation of Israel's will "to keep all the occupied Palestinian territories . . . and give this a legal character."[12] This unequivocal rejection prompted intense activity to change Jordan's attitude. The Shah invited Husayn to visit Tehran between 30 December 1977 and 3 January 1978 for talks both with himself and with US President Jimmy Carter (then visiting Iran). Both attempted to persuade Husayn to join the Egyptian-Israeli Political Committee. However, the "beneficial and fraternal" talks with the Shah, as well as "the frank and clear" discussions with Carter,[13] did not cause Husayn to change his mind. Carter said in

Tehran that "at the moment," Sādāt was "strongly representing the Arab position"; there was thus "no reason for Jordan to join the talks directly" until "certain principles are enunciated." [14] At about the same time, a "senior Jordanian source" stated that Amman was indeed involved in the negotiations but, for the time being, indirectly. [15] On 7 and 8 January 1978, the British Defence Secretary, Frederick Mulley, visited Amman and (possibly at the request of the US) [16] also argued the case for Jordanian participation in the talks—but with similar results. At the same time, Sādāt invited Husayn to confer with the King of Morocco, the Shah and himself at Aswān on 9 January; Husayn, however, declined. [17]

The recall of the Egyptian delegation from Jerusalem, on 18 January 1978, prompted new activity. Sādāt telephoned Husayn twice, on 20 and 23 January. On 22 January, Husayn received a message from King Hasan. On 28 January, Alfred Atherton Jr, the US ambassador-at-large, conferred with the King; so did the Egyptian Vice-President, Husnī Mubārak, on 31 January. However, as there seemed no prospect for a change of mind in Jordan, such activity subsided. At the end of January, Husayn was still expressing his readiness to join the negotiations if Egypt and Israel agreed on a declaration of principles. [18] In February, by contrast, he stated that "the question now is not one of declaration of principles. [These] have already been unanimously defined and announced in UN Security Council Resolution 242. . . . What is required is . . . a commitment to translate [principles] into facts." [19] During February, too, Israel's Foreign Minister repeatedly stressed that Jordan had become the main obstacle to the peace-making process—simply by not joining it. [20]

Between February and May, only sporadic efforts were made to draw Jordan into the political process. One instance was the visit to Amman of British Foreign Secretary, Dr David Owen, on 25 February. Nevertheless, Jordan continued to be indirectly involved in the negotiations through constant contacts with the US, Egypt and other parties. Thus, Atherton visited Amman between each of his shuttle trips between Cairo and Jerusalem, and Sādāt's suggestion of 10 May—to the effect that the West Bank be placed under Jordanian control during the transitional period—was made only after he had exchanged messages with Husayn. According to Israeli newspapers, whose reports could not be independently verified, there had also been high-level contacts between Israel and Jordan. [21]

Increasingly sceptical about the possible success of Sādāt's initiative, Jordan joined the Saudi efforts at the end of July and early August to "reunite Arab ranks" (see below). Husayn later stated that at that point Sādāt could have returned to the "ranks of confrontation states under the overall leadership of Saudi Arabia . . . without loss of face." [22] Sādāt's subsequent acceptance of the invitation to the Camp David summit elicited contradictory reactions from Amman: it was encouraged by Washington's decision to become a "full partner" in the negotiations, believing that the summit would thus become a "test of strength between the US and Israel." [23] At the same time, it predicted that Israeli intransigence would cause the summit to fail. [24] Husayn himself reiterated that he would "never hesitate in exercising [Jordan's] duties towards the cause of peace . . . [and] the right of our people"; but he added that he required "clear proof that Israel has changed its attitude on the issue of withdrawal, on the cause of the Palestinian people and the requirements for a dignified and just peace." [25]

During the Camp David summit, Husayn was vacationing in London, but he had arranged to meet Sādāt in Rabat during the latter's stopover there on his way back to Cairo. When the texts of the Camp David accords became known, he decided to return to Amman immediately. On arrival (19 September), he presided over a special Cabinet meeting which discussed the agreements and then issued a statement declaring that Jordan was neither "legally nor morally bound" to them. It asserted Jordan's belief in a "just and comprehensive solution," and said that "separate actions by Arab parties away from collective Arab responsibility" were "weakening the Arab position," thereby diminishing "the chances of reaching the aspired just and comprehensive solution." After reiterating Jordan's conditions for such a settlement, the statement concluded by saying: "Jordan, while considering the Palestinian people to be the principal party in the final settlement of the Palestinian problem, will not hesitate to exercise its responsibilities and role towards the cause of peace in the area, and safeguarding and defending the rights of the Palestinian people."[26]

The same points were made to the US Secretary of State when he visited Amman on 20 September in an unsuccessful attempt to persuade Jordan to assume the role reserved for it under the Camp David accords. They were reiterated in several statements and interviews in which Ḥusayn stated that, in order to be acceptable to Jordan, the Camp David agreement on the West Bank and the Gaza Strip would have to be substantially modified.[27] Following Vance's visit, the Jordanian government drafted a list of questions for clarification by the US on the Israeli autonomy plan. Some of these related to the modalities of self-rule during the transition period (in whom would supreme authority be vested during the period, and what would the source of its finances be). Other questions related to the future of the West Bank and Gaza after the transition period (ultimate sovereignty, continued presence of Israeli troops); the status of East Jerusalem; the status of Israeli residents in the West Bank during and, possibly, after the transition period; the future role of the US in solving outstanding problems, and the solution envisaged for the Golan Heights.[28]

SYRIA

Among the "confrontation states," Syria's hostility to Sādāt's initiative was the most vehement and uncompromising. It was matched or surpassed in violence only by the reactions of two states not bordering on Israel: Iraq (see below) and Libya (see essay on Inter-Arab Relations). Syrian President Ḥāfiz al-Asad—Sādāt's ally in the 1973 war—was the only Arab leader whom Sādāt visited in the interval between the announcement of his plans and his arrival in Jerusalem. During their talks in Damascus on 16 and 17 November 1977, Asad sought to dissuade Sādāt from proceeding with the initiative. When he failed, Syria started a forceful campaign against Sādāt. Official statements termed his visit to Israel "treacherous," "capitulationist,"[29] "a painful blow to the Arab nation," "a grave offence to the memory of the martyrs,"[30] and "part of a Zionist-American plot to eliminate the Palestinian problem."[31] Spokesmen of the regime compared Sādāt with Nazi collaborators such as Pétain or Quisling, or men such as Neville Chamberlain and Rudolf Hess.[32]

To understand the vehemence of the Syrian reaction, two sets of considerations must be taken into account. One was that, in one single blow, Sādāt's initiative deprived Syria of most of the benefits of the policy it had followed since the 1973 war—a policy largely determined by its traumatic disappointment with Egypt in that war. Sādāt's new policy undercut Syria's chance to make Israel's eastern front a Syrian area of influence in that it caused Jordan (at least until the Camp David summit) to take up a position differing from, and at times opposed to, that of Syria; it destroyed the improved bargaining position *vis-à-vis* the great powers which Syria had created for itself between 1974 and 1977; and it negated the veto power over the ME peace-making process which Syria had secured in 1977. (For subsequent developments in Syria's global relations, see essays on the US and the Middle East and the USSR and the Middle East, as well as the chapter on Syria. For the earlier Syrian policy of consolidating a regional power base, see *MECS 1976–77*, pp. 151–60.)

The other set of considerations stemmed from the Syrian regime's fundamental view of the nature of the Arab-Israeli conflict. After the 1973 war, Syria had faced the dilemma of reconciling its basically "rejectionist" doctrine with practical necessities: by the fact that it bordered on Israel, had lost territories in 1967, and could not afford to dissociate itself from the process of pragmatic policies initiated by Sādāt after the war. The dilemma had been temporarily resolved by the Syrian Ba'th party's adoption in 1975 of a two-stage strategy.[33] This had enabled Syria to participate in the "political process" (e.g. the 1974 Golan disengagement agreement and the 1977 preparations for resuming the Geneva conference) in pursuit of its *interim* aims, defined as the restoration of the pre-1967 border and the establishment of a Palestinian state, without giving up the *ultimate* goal of the "liberation of *all* of the Palestinian soil." But Sādāt's initiative revived the dilemma. Asad felt he could neither adopt the stand of Sādāt nor that of the out-and-out "rejectionists." Yet Syria could not remain inactive either. To join Cairo would have signified the abandonment of the ultimate goal—an intolerable price; but to adopt a clear-cut "rejectionist" position would have meant risking war with Israel—possibly at a disadvantageous moment and under adverse circumstances. On the other hand, inactivity would lay Syria open to criticism from every conceivable Arab quarter, and perhaps domestically as well.

To meet this challenge, Syria took several steps:

(1) It reinforced its image as Israel's principal challenger by reviving the use in its media of anti-Israeli language which had become infrequent in more recent years. Thus "the Zionist entity" again was commonly used when referring to the State of Israel, and the areas within the pre-1967 borders were again described as "the land occupied in 1948" (as distinct from the territories occupied in 1967). Press comment on the "artificial" and "inherently aggressive character" of Israel proliferated, accompanied at times by predictions of Israel's eventual collapse and disappearance. The practice of printing "Israel" in inverted commas was maintained in most publications.

(2) For the first time since 1976, Damascus again publicly claimed to have a special focal role in the overall conflict. This was so, Asad argued, because Syria was "the symbol of Arab struggle and the pioneer of Arab steadfastness";[34] more importantly, "the Syrian compatriot considers Palestine to be southern Syria [and] the Palestinian compatriot considers Syria to be northern Palestine. Therefore the question of Palestine is strictly a Syrian issue and [only next] an Arab security issue. To us, the struggle to liberate Palestine is [first] a domestic and [then] an Arab national commitment of our [Syrian] people and [the Arab] nation."[35]

(3) Intense efforts were devoted to countering both Sādāt's arguments in support of his initiative and Iraq's against the Syrian line (see below). Syria reasserted the 1975 two-phase programme as the sound alternative to both.

An internal organ of the Ba'th party (circulated mainly among party members, but frequently quoted by the Syrian media and occasionally made available to the public at large) criticized the Iraqi position as "a curtain hiding the painful remoteness from reality, the abstention from [genuine] struggle, and the utter inability to plan this struggle scientifically."[36] The main points made in arguing against Sādāt's initiative were the following. His visit to Jerusalem gave "a kind of legitimacy to the Zionist entity" and implied the "*de facto* recognition of the

[Israeli] annexation of Jerusalem";[37] this was "a mortal sin."[38] Sādāt had erred both in his strategy and in his tactics: he abandoned "the ultimate goal" in order to achieve interim objectives, and he wasted the Arab trump card before bargaining had even begun.[39] Sādāt had transformed "the real struggle" for a comprehensive settlement into a mere "conflict over Sinai."[40] Asad argued that by waiving the military option, and by proclaiming "no more war," Sādāt had given up both the war and the peace options.[41]

Syria's own policy *vis-à-vis* Israel was not put forward in any one major statement or declaration. Pieced together from various passages in official public statements, in media comments and in party publications, the following composite emerged.

The Arab goal of ensuring Palestinian self-determination was often given the widest possible interpretation. An internal Ba'th publication explained that it meant "the liberation of Palestine—i.e. an end to the Zionist existence on Palestinian soil."[42] Liberation required two major obstacles to be overcome. (1) The Palestinian people and the Arab nation must prevail over a new kind of imperialism, "the imperialism of the settler." Unlike other kinds of imperialists, the settler "has no homeland . . . to return to." Consequently, "for 'Israel' . . . the question is, to stay or to perish."[43] (2) Both super-powers want a political settlement. Under these circumstances, the struggle will be protracted and must be planned "scientifically"—i.e. the Arabs must adopt "phases" as the only valid strategy, and the only tactic affording the necessary flexibility. "Real 'rejectionism' expresses itself in perpetual action and in a combined struggle using all means—political as well as military."[44]

In order to emphasize the importance of the "political struggle" (as distinct from Sādāt's "political process" and Iraq's rejection of any form of non-violent struggle), Syrian spokesmen listed the objectives it had been on the point of achieving when Sādāt disrupted Arab efforts: "the isolation of 'Israel' in the international arena; international understanding of the racialist nature of Zionism, and international recognition of the Palestinian people [and] . . . of the PLO as [their] only legitimate representative."[45] However, Syria was not entirely committed to the "political struggle": it was recalled that Damascus had only given qualified acceptance to Security Council Resolution 242.[46]

While displaying tactical flexibility, the strategic principles had to remain firm. The interim goals were worth a price, but under *no* circumstances should this be so heavy as to detract from the following requirements. (1) They must not "harm the historical rights of the Arab nation in Palestine . . . by a reconciliation [*sulḥ*] with and recognition of 'Israel', or by concession of territory."[47] This stand was reflected in public statements rejecting diplomatic relations or any other steps which could imply recognition of Israel.[48] (2) They should gain "substantive achievements for the Palestinian people, which will allow them to preserve their unity, their specific personality and the resources for their struggle, and enable them to defend their national problem and maintain it as a living and dynamic problem, so as to make it possible to concentrate the struggle in the next phase around it [i.e. the Palestinian problem]."[49] The only way to meet these requirements was to establish "an independent and [fully] sovereign Palestinian state" in the West Bank and Gaza, because in "a state without sovereignty annexed to another Arab state [i.e. to Jordan] . . . the Palestinian identity will dissolve" and the problem be reduced to "a mere border conflict between 'Israel' and several Arab states." All these, as well as Israel, were UN members and therefore "protected by the UN Charter, which emphasizes the territorial integrity of all states"[50]—thus impeding the ultimate goal.

The interim nature of the goals of the first phase did not make it necessary to proceed immediately to the final goal. A second interim goal may be interposed as an extension of the first phase; for instance, a restoration of the 1947 partition borders. Although rarely hinted at in public statements,[51] party publications were occasionally more explicit: "The Palestinian Arab people . . . will be able to demand, from the UN rostrum as well as in the battlefield, the Galilee, the 'little triangle'[52] and the Negev, i.e. more than a half of the territory of 'Israel' within the 1967 borders. It could also demand the return of 1m Palestinian refugees to 'Israel', which is more than the number of Zionists on Palestinian soil. This will create the material basis for the Palestinian secular democratic state."[53] In conformity with such thinking, the immediate goal for the Palestinians was often phrased as meaning a Palestinian state "and the right of the Palestinians to return to their homes."

Syria failed, however, in having its policy *vis-à-vis* Israel recognized as distinct from that of Egypt and of Iraq, or in gaining acceptance for it anywhere outside Syria. Some in the Arab world thought of it as unrealistic since neither Syria alone, nor any probable Syrian-led combination of Arab countries, would be strong enough to force it upon Israel. To others it looked like a piece of doctrinal casuistry put forward to enable Syria to benefit whether Sādāt succeeded or failed.

By mid-1978, Syria saw Sādāt's declarations against continued direct contacts with Israel, together with the Saudi intervention to restore a measure of Arab unity, as heralding the imminent end of the Egyptian initiative—at least in its original form. Not surprisingly, Sādāt's subsequent acceptance of the invitation to the Camp David summit was termed by Damascus an even "graver development" than his visit to Jerusalem. Asad made it one of the comparatively rare occasions on which he himself spoke out against Sādāt. The summit, he predicted, might result in "a fragile, separate, partial solution, which in reality would stiffen enmity and result in the region permanently remaining a centre of tension which will threaten to erupt at any time."[54] Alternatively, the US might make a commitment on "some definite points," but this would only "complicate the issue because it is already apparent that with the power of the Zionist influence in the US, these definite points . . . will not be just, and therefore will be unacceptable to us."[55]

The conclusion of the Camp David agreements carried Syrian attacks against Egypt to a peak. The Syrian media called them a mere "bilateral agreement" and "nothing more than a photocopy of the previous Begin plan." The "sole winner" of the summit was Begin, just "as he was the sole winner at all previous meetings"; Sādāt "has lost whatever assets were left to him."[56] Asad declared that "the enemies of the Arabs could not have achieved a greater victory." Not only did Sādāt abandon Jerusalem and the Palestinian issue, he also deserted from "the Arab trench" and "turned his back on the Arabs and on Egypt's Arab history."[57] An editorial in the Ba'th party organ commented that Sādāt had "officially moved Egypt from the Arab fold into the Israeli fold," and had thus added Egypt's manpower and military strength "to the enemy side."[58] Asad went further, stating that he could not now rule out the possibility that "in the near or distant future, Sādāt will participate with Begin in conducting an offensive operation against us."[59]

IRAQ

Having pursued a rigidly intransigent policy against Israel since its establishment and, since the 1967 war, a consistent policy of rejecting any political settlement,[60] Iraq was perhaps the only major Arab state for which Sādāt's initiative did not pose a dilemma. (This is certainly true with respect to Iraq's position in the conflict with *Israel*; if there was a dilemma, it was over whether or not to modify Iraqi policy towards *Syria* in the light of the new situation; see essay on Inter-Arab Relations.) In the context of the conflict, Iraq regarded the entire sequence of events from Sādāt's visit to Jerusalem up to the conclusion of the Camp David summit as proof that Iraqi policy had been correct all along. Sādāt's "treasonable trip" was but the logical "result of a previous approach,"[61] i.e. the "settlement approach." This, the Iraqi Ba'th party held, was characterized by "unlimited readiness to give in stage by stage"; by "successive, most serious concessions" in the form of "settlement formulae"; and by the "erroneous policy which had nullified the gains of the glorious October [1973] war and has weakened the Arab position."[62] Therefore, Iraq regarded all countries which had a part in the "settlement approach" (mainly by accepting Resolution 242) as blameworthy, but it depicted Syria as the worst among those it called the "settlement regimes." However, Iraqi statements did not play down Sādāt's role in carrying the "settlement policy" to its logical conclusion: Sādāt had acted as "a traitor," "an imperialist agent" (in other statements, "a Zionist agent"), and was "an Arab in name only."[63]

The principal Iraqi reaction to Sādāt's initiative was to draft, and eventually publish, a detailed action programme intended as an alternative to Sādāt's initiative—the only clearly delineated alternative policy to be put forward anywhere in the Arab world. The principles of the Iraqi programme were outlined in December 1977 in a statement announcing the walkout of the Iraqi delegation from the Tripoli conference (see essay on Inter-Arab Relations).[64] The programme was set out in full in the texts of the "Draft Charter" for a "Front of Steadfastness and Liberation" and in an appendix originally intended to remain secret (the "Secret Charter"). These were published in Baghdad two months later.[65]

The aim of the Front was "to liberate all the occupied Arab territories and to regain the rights of the Palestinian people to liberate their usurped land and determine their own future" (paras 2 and 6 of the Charter). The "Secret Charter" explained that this meant the "liberation of *all* Palestinian soil [emphasis added] and the setting up of a democratic state in Palestine" (Part I, para 2). The partners to the Front were required to undertake that "under no circumstances . . . [would they] accept or approve . . . resolutions . . . by any international body . . . that harm the essence of Arab sovereignty over its land . . . or the essence of the historical rights of the Palestinian people" (Charter, para 4). The "legal and actual implication" of this clause was "not to accept Resolution[s] 242 . . . [and] . . . 338," and "not to hold negotiations or make a reconciliation [*sulḥ*] with the Zionist enemy, or to recognize it" ("Secret Charter," I, 2, as well as the Tripoli announcement). The last three conditions were identical to the resolutions of the 1967 Arab summit conference at Khartoum.[66] Another commitment required of the participants was that "the decision to wage war or any ceasefire resolution shall be made in agreement with the sides participating in the Front" ("Secret Charter," Part II, clause "F"). This clause, clearly giving Iraq a veto over the initiation of hostilities as well as their termination, was an application of the lessons of the 1973 war, when Egypt had ceased fighting without consulting Syria, and the latter without consulting Iraq, despite the presence of Iraqi forces on the Golan Heights.

Syria argued that the disavowal by Iraq of Resolution 338, which included the acceptance of the 1973 ceasefire, would mean "direct war with the enemy" on the Golan Heights. Baghdad countered by stating that it was "ready to reach an agreement on a formula which would mean the rejection of both resolutions without renouncing the Syrian regime's pledge regarding the ceasefire."[67] Furthermore, the Iraqi President, Aḥmad Ḥasan al-Bakr, expressed his country's readiness for Syria to delay the rejection of the resolutions until after the accomplishment of "total [Syrian-Iraqi] understanding" and "*after* approving the Front's charter, commitments and plan of action." [68]

According to the Iraqi proposals, the Front was to set up a "Supreme Political Command" which would be "the highest authority" and unanimously adopt "the principal decisions in all the domains" (Charter, para 7). The Command was to "plan and approve" all "bilateral contacts between any side of the Front and other Arab and foreign countries" as would bear directly on the aims of the Front ("Secret Charter," Part I, para 7). This clause, too, was intended to give Iraq the power to veto any possible unilateral action on Syria's part. Another clause laid down that the commitments under the Charter were only the minimum required of an Arab state wishing to join the Front. In addition, "the Front's sides must express, through their political means and information media, stronger and more radical attitudes towards the struggle with Imperialism, Zionism and their allies, as well as towards the liberation of all Palestinian soil and the setting up of a democratic state in Palestine" ("Secret Charter," Part I, 2).

Baghdad further demanded that Syria should open its borders "to the Palestinian revolution movement" for operations against Israel (Tripoli announcement), and that a "Northern Military Front," including Syria and Lebanon, should be formed. Each member-state should allot an agreed part of its armed forces to the "Northern Front" ("Secret Charter," Part II, clause "B"). "The expenditures resulting from the formation of the Front" would be covered by a fund, to which every participant was to contribute an agreed sum ("Secret Charter," Part III, clauses "A" and "B"). Under the authority of the Supreme Political Command, a "Supreme Military Command" would supervise the units stationed in the area of the "Northern Front"; its decisions "must be obeyed by all the combatant troops stationed on the front line with the enemy" ("Secret Charter," Part II, clauses "A" and "C"). Significantly, no mention was made of the need for unanimous decisions with respect to the military command as in the case of the political body.

The Iraqi programme elicited a great deal of sympathy on the part of veteran "rejectionist" regimes. Algeria's Foreign Minister, 'Abd al-'Azīz Bouteflika, stated that Algeria, Libya, the PDRY and the PLO "had not a shade of difference" with Iraq. [69] Yet, acting on their assessment of the prospect of making an impact on the situation created by Sādāt, they preferred to side with Syria. Iraq thus found itself removed from the scene of practical political action. Nonetheless, it upheld its image, at home and towards the world, of the only country with a consistent and "principled" stand in the Arab-Israeli conflict, and as the only genuine "rejectionist."

The conclusion of the Camp David summit was seen to confirm the Iraqi view. The Iraqi Revolution Command Council issued a statement in which it attacked "the treasonous and conspiratorial results of Camp David [which] are an important link in the conspiratorial chain against the Arab nation." However, as before, the main thrust of the Iraqi attack was directed at the "settlement approach" *per se* and at *all* the "settlement regimes" (particularly Syria, though it was not named). The statement added: "The puppet Sādāt regime is not the only colluding party. There are still other parties which have not participated directly in the conference. These parties are conserving their efforts for another day and another role when they will benefit from Sādāt's open treason and the roles of the other parties." [70]

SAUDI ARABIA
Saudi Arabia viewed Sādāt's initiative as doubly negative: for being harmful to the country's inter-Arab standing; and for calling into question the traditional Saudi attitude towards Israel. On the first count, Saudi pique was caused by Sādāt's failure to consult it in advance; this was heightened by his concealment during a

visit to Riyadh on 2 and 3 November 1977 of the plan he had already evolved. More seriously, on the second count, Sādāt had upset the delicate balance in Saudi Arabia's policy on the conflict. Saudi leaders have proceeded on the assumption that both a peaceful settlement (by necessity linked with the recognition of Israel and the acceptance of its continued existence) and a full-scale war might unleash forces of radicalism capable of endangering the Kingdom's domestic security or even the very nature of its present regime; on the other hand, a prolonged stalemate might have a similar result. Saudi Arabia therefore endeavoured to promote Arab solidarity so that policy towards Israel would be based on the broadest possible Arab consensus.[71]

Sādāt's unilateral step not only threatened to lead to a separate Egyptian-Israeli settlement, but also caused the kind of friction in the Arab world which brought radicalism to the fore. For these reasons the basic Saudi attitude to Sādāt's initiative was negative, a reaction reinforced by traditional Saudi hostility (coloured by concepts of Wahhābī Islam) towards Israel, Zionism and Jewry. A statement issued by the Royal Court as early as 18 November 1977 (i.e. before Sādāt's arrival in Israel) asserted that because of "attitudes with uncertain results not in harmony with the general Arab situation . . . the Arab cause has in the present time passed through a difficult phase."[72] Crown Prince Fahd told a Lebanese correspondent that Saudi Arabia was "closer to the Syrians and the Palestinian organizations than to Sādāt."[73] Soon afterwards, however, the Saudi leadership stated that "historical responsibility bids us to maintain self-restraint";[74] "matters are judged by their results" and therefore "the Kingdom will await these results before expressing its views."[75] The following considerations were at work to produce these second thoughts: unwillingness to contribute to Sādāt's difficulties, since his overthrow would almost certainly cause a change of policy in Cairo harmful to Riyadh; unwillingness to confront the US over an issue which it soon became clear was of major importance to Washington; a desire to keep its options open so as to be able to make an appropriate response to changing circumstances; and finally (according to some sources) differences of opinion at Court.[76] Despite the pledge not to express premature views, many Saudi statements during the following months, though studiously vague, unmistakably implied opposition to Sādāt's policy.

Several Saudi statements were made regarding the substance of a settlement with Israel and the possibility of Arab recognition of Israel. Thus the Saudi Foreign Minister, Sa'ūd al-Faysal, said that "*Arabs* will accept Israel in their midst once the *Palestinians* accept it."[77] Crown Prince Fahd told an American interviewer that "if *all* the Arab states recognized the existence of Israel, the Kingdom of Saudi Arabia [would act] . . . within the framework of the Arab states."[78] An Arab journalist was told by Fahd that after complete Israeli withdrawal from the occupied territories and the establishment of a Palestinian state, "we will be ready to *weigh the possibility* of recognizing Israel, after *a united Arab stand is decided upon.*"[79] Western observers regarded such statements as evidence of Saudi moderation in that they mentioned the possibility of recognition at all. Arab audiences were doubtless more attentive to the conditions circumscribing this possibility—to the point of virtually excluding it. The Saudis were thus altogether successful in projecting a favourable image to different groups of listeners.

References to the desirability of an ultimate settlement were couched with similar care. The Court stated that a settlement with Israel should match the various "Arab summit resolutions, which not only define the objectives, but also define the means leading to these objectives"[80] (an allusion to the Rabat summit decisions of 1974, and possibly an echo of the 1967 Khartoum summit prescription of "no negotiations, no recognition, no reconciliation"). Other indications were the Saudi insistence on the Palestinians' right to return to their original homes, and the use of the term "solution" in Saudi pronouncement rather than "peace." For instance, in a statement issued at the conclusion of Cyrus Vance's visit to Riyadh on 14 and 15 December 1977, Saʿūd al-Faysal expressed appreciation for US efforts and the "hope that these will result in achieving a just and lasting solution in the area."[81] The state-controlled Saudi media were more explicit: one radio commentator said that the Palestinian people "were expelled by the Israeli invaders from part of their land in 1948 . . . and afterwards from the remaining land in the aggression of 1967. . . . The land must be given back to its lawful owners."[82] When Begin and Sādāt met in Ismāʿīliyya, a Saudi commentary stated that "the liberation of the Holy Land is a sacred goal. If the circumstances [prevent] a certain generation [from achieving it] . . . its duty is to do everything within its power in order to ensure that . . . it remains open . . . for future generations."[83] On the same day, an editorial stated that "the legitimate Arab rights constitute an integrative whole, which cannot be divided, and under no circumstances must one of its sides be ignored."[84]

Under the impact of Sādāt's initiative, the Saudi attitude on the Palestinian issue was articulated more forcefully. Earlier, in 1976 and 1977, there had already been differences of emphasis on this issue—with Saudi Arabia insisting on a fully independent Palestinian state and Egypt suggesting a Palestinian state linked with Jordan (see *MECS 1976-77*, p. 157). In 1978, as Egypt seemed more willing than before to consider flexible language (such as the "Aswān formula," see preceding section), Saudi Arabia emphasized its policy of "complete backing with money, weapons and even blood for the Palestinian people"[85] and expressed renewed insistence on the establishment of a completely independent and fully sovereign Palestinian state. (No mention was made of its borders or territorial limits.) Similarly, as Egypt gradually dissociated itself from the PLO, Saudi Arabia re-emphasized its acceptance of that organization as "the sole legitimate representative" of the Palestinians. When Sādāt proposed a Jordanian interim administration in the West Bank and an Egyptian one in the Gaza Strip, Fahd stated: "I do not believe that any state, whether Arab or otherwise, could compel the Palestinian people to choose a specific course."[86]

Saudi Arabia's disagreement with Sādāt's policy in the conflict was also hinted at by references to other options open to the Arabs. Thus, Fahd spoke of America's "duty" to "convince" Israel to accept a settlement on Arab terms,[87] and referred several times to the war option as an alternative to Sādāt's course.[88]

As Sādāt's initiative seemed to falter, Saudi calls to break it off became more explicit. At the beginning of May 1978, Saʿūd al-Faysal called for a reassessment of the peace efforts.[89] Later, during the Egyptian-Israeli stalemate early in July, when a return to the concept of the Geneva conference was being mooted, King Khālid stated that it would be better for the Arabs to go to Geneva united, implying that the obstacle to a united Arab stand was Sādāt.[90] Regarding the Leeds Castle talks later that month as a failure,[91] and interpreting Sādāt's refusal at the end of July to resume direct talks with Israel as an expression of readiness to end his initiative, the Saudis launched a major effort to "reunite Arab ranks." Fahd visited Cairo on 30 and 31 July, and then proceeded to Damascus, Amman and Baghdad. He urged Sādāt to concede the failure of his initiative and to rejoin Arab ranks.[92] However, in view of the sharp US reaction[93] and in the light of Sādāt's eventual acceptance of the invitation to the Camp David summit, Riyadh changed course and welcomed the Camp David conference. Yet, Saudi leaders made it clear that they regarded the meeting as a last chance: "Either the matter will be decided in favour of peace or this gate will be finally closed."[94] Assuming that the summit was "a failure even before they begin,"[95] Riyadh was reported to have notified the US that it would suspend efforts to reunite Arab ranks until after Camp David, but that it expected the Administration to blame Israel if the conference failed.[96] Failure, Sa'ūd al-Faysal stated, should lead the Arab nation to a "thorough review of the whole situation":[97] an Arab summit would then become an urgent necessity.[98]

Although Riyadh had not anticipated agreement, it was quick to react to the Camp David accords. A Cabinet communiqué, issued on 19 September, expressed appreciation for "the efforts made by US President Jimmy Carter, before and during the course of the conference." But it went on to say that out of a "profound commitment to its authentic Islamic and Arab principles, and in accordance with its commitments to the resolutions of the Arab summit conferences—in particular the [1973] Algiers and [the 1974] Rabat conferences," Saudi Arabia could not consider the agreements "a final acceptable formula for peace." The communiqué listed the following reasons which made the accords unacceptable: (1) they did not "state definitely Israel's intention to withdraw from all occupied Arab territories . . . at the fore of which is Holy Jerusalem"; (2) they did not "stipulate the right of the Palestinian people . . . whom Israel has rendered homeless . . . to self-determination and the establishment of their state on the soil of their country"; and (3) they "ignored the role of the PLO, which the Arab summit conferences considered to be the sole legitimate representative of the Palestinian people." As for Sinai, the communiqué stated that Saudi Arabia did not consider itself entitled "to interfere in the internal affairs of any Arab country, nor to dispute its right to restore its occupied territories by armed struggle or through peaceful efforts, *provided that that does not clash with higher Arab interests*."[99] Once again, Saudi Arabia used language which could be construed as conveying understanding for Egypt's desire to recover Egyptian land, but which could just as easily be interpreted to mean that Egypt had done wrong in putting its own interests above all-Arab considerations.

In the following weeks—despite US, Egyptian and Moroccan efforts—Saudi Arabia did not change it substantive position. When Vance visited Riyadh from 22-24 September, only the desire not to create difficulties in Saudi-US bilateral relations caused the Saudi side to state that the Camp David agreements could be "an initial step towards peace."[100]

MOROCCO

Morocco was the only Arab country which consistently supported Sādāt from the formative stage of his initiative. This support stemmed from Rabat's unique concept of the Arab-Israeli conflict, which was gradually disclosed during 1976 and 1977 but had apparently developed long before. (It was not until the mid-1970s that Morocco began contradicting accepted Arab policy toward Israel.) The most important sources of this concept are probably King Hasan's personality and general outlook, his "constructivist" views, his preoccupation with domestic problems of development and modernization, and his stated preference for solving problems by "dialogue." Another source is the traditionally friendly attitude of the Moroccan dynasty towards the local Jewish community, including the long-established role of the King as its patron. A third factor may be the impression made on Hasan II by Israel's dynamism and the success of Israeli development projects in Third World states.

The main elements of the Moroccan concept can be summarized as follows:

(1) *Arab-Jewish Affinity*. This idea ran through all Moroccan statements regarding the Arab-Israeli conflict in 1976 and 1977. Moroccan leaders described

Judaism as "a Semitic religion," [101] and referred to both Jews and Arabs as "sons of Ibrāhīm [Abraham] and grandsons of Ismāʿīl [Ishmael] and Ishāq [Isaac]." [102] Israel was not only accepted as a *fait accompli*, but as a factor capable of contributing to the development, modernization and stability of the entire ME. King Hasan said: "Just think of what the Arab world's enormous financial and economic resources and Israel's creative genius could do to transform the entire area." [103]

(2) *The Dangers Inherent in Prolonged Conflict.* Hasan repeatedly described the conflict with Israel as a long-term danger to the future of the Arabs. He argued that it diverted indispensable resources from development and modernization, thereby widening the gap between the Arab world and the industrialized countries. Furthermore, preoccupation with the conflict might expose the Arabs to external aggression on the part of those who "have ideological ways of thinking and interests and aspirations in the region." [104]

(3) *Coexistence and Integration.* The settlement Morocco advocated would provide for "the dignity, freedom and sovereignty of all sides to the conflict and the fruitful coexistence of future generations." [105] Israel should return to the 1967 borders and accept an independent Palestinian state in exchange for peace, reconciliation and full integration into the Arab MÉ, including membership in the Arab League. [106]

(4) *The Need for a Dialogue.* Counting himself among "those in Islam who prefer dialogue," [107] Hasan regarded direct negotiations between Israeli and Arab leaders as the only way to achieve a settlement. Especially vital, in his view, was the need for direct dialogue between Israel and the PLO, which was the recognized representative of the Palestinian people and a "most reasonable" factor in the ME conflict. [108]

Since the 1960s, Morocco had maintained "close but secret relations with Israel," [109] and at times had tried to arrange secret meetings between Jewish and Arab leaders. One such attempt was Hasan's suggestion to the President of the World Jewish Congress, Nahum Goldmann, to meet Yāsir ʿArafāt in Algiers during the latter's secret visit to Rabat in June 1970. [110] The dispatch to Syria in March 1973 of a Moroccan contingent of troops, and its subsequent participation in the October War, were not attributed to a change in Morocco's views to the conflict, but rather to domestic reasons: to keep the army occupied and forestall further attempts at military *coups d'état* similar to those made earlier that year and in 1972. [111] After the 1973 war, Morocco supported Egypt in promoting a "political solution" to the conflict. It also undertook a series of initiatives directed at first towards Jewish leaders, and later towards Israelis as well. These moves were initially prompted by Morocco's interest in enlisting support in its dispute over the Western Sahara, [112] but they soon took on a broader import. Numerous statements were made in 1975 and 1976 referring to the antiquity and equality of status of Moroccan Jewry. The Prime Minister, for instance, said that "since ancient times . . . there has been a Jewish diaspora community (*jāliya*) in Morocco, which enjoys all civil rights and lives in security." [113]

During 1976, Rabat gradually made its concepts public. The Moroccan example of Arab-Jewish coexistence was now referred to as a model for Arab-Jewish relations in general. In conjunction with the Egyptian "peace offensive" of 1976-77, [114] Morocco first spoke of peace with Israel, then of recognition, next of coexistence, and finally of co-operation between Israel and the Arab states for their mutual benefit and the development of the entire ME. Also during 1976, Jewish personalities were invited to Morocco and their visits given publicity. Among them were delegations of rabbis from the US; the chairman of the French League Against Racism and Anti-Semitism, Jean Pierre Bloch; and a leader of the American Jewish Committee, Abe Carlekov. In 1977, such visits came to include Zionist leaders, as well as non-official Israeli personalities such as Nahum Goldmann; Amos Kenan, an Israeli writer and journalist; André Chouraqi, a scholar and former deputy mayor of Jerusalem, himself of Algerian origin; and Shaul Ben Simhon, an Israeli trade union leader who was also chairman of the World Union of Moroccan and North African Jews.[115] In contrast, visits by official Israeli personalities to Morocco and by Moroccan officials to Israel were kept secret—but news of these leaked out in any case. Thus, the then Israeli Prime Minister, Yitzhak Rabin, was reported to have made a secret visit to Morocco in October 1976.[116] In May 1977, Israel's Minister of Agriculture, Aharon Uzan, mentioned "an official delegation from an [unidentified] Arab state" which had visited Israel, met immigrants from the delegates' country, and discussed an Israeli offer of agricultural aid.[117] It was generally assumed that that delegation was Moroccan. Morocco was also said to have been instrumental in arranging the meetings between PLO members and Israelis during the second half of 1976 and the first half of 1977.[118]

In taking these steps—and especially the more overt ones—Morocco seemed to be taking upon itself the task of testing the ground for Egypt by being one step ahead of it. The assumption that, during the first stages immediately preceding Sādāt's initiative at least, Morocco and Egypt had co-ordinated their policies would be entirely in keeping with King Ḥasan's attitude of earlier years. According to press reports, partly confirmed at a later date by the Moroccan Prime Minister,[119] the King had played an important role in arranging secret talks between Israel's Foreign Minister and Egyptian officials. These took place in Morocco in the autumn of 1977 before Sādāt announced his initiative.[120] When that announcement came, on 9 November, King Ḥasan immediately declared his full support. On 18 November, Ḥasan telephoned Sādāt and expressed admiration for his decision to go to Jerusalem.[121] After the visit, Rabat rendered Egypt every possible assistance: Ḥasan publicly expressed support for Sādāt, called for peace and coexistence with Israel, and rebutted the charge that Sādāt had violated the 1974 Rabat summit resolutions.[122] There were a number of exchange visits between Moroccan and Egyptian officials, the most prominent of which was Sādāt's 24-hour stopover in Rabat on his way to Washington (2 February 1978), which indicated the extent of co-ordination and co-operation between the two countries. The Egyptian media used these occasions to underline Moroccan support for Sādāt. Further secret meetings between Dayan and the Egyptian Deputy Prime Minister, Ḥasan al-Tuhāmī, also took place on Moroccan territory.[123] These were in preparation for the Ismāʿīliyya summit.

When the Egyptian delegation was recalled from Jerusalem in January 1978, Ḥasan again offered his good services to Sādāt and Begin.[124] Morocco was reported to have made efforts to persuade the US to give Sādāt firmer backing with respect to both his standing in the Arab world and the negotiations with Israel. It also participated in the efforts to draw Jordan into the negotiations (see above), and to convince Saudi Arabia to give public support to Sādāt. This latter point seems to have been first raised during the visit to Morocco of the Saudi Foreign Minister, Saʿūd al-Faysal, on 17 November 1977; later during the "private" visit by the Second Deputy Prime Minister and National Guard Commander, ʿAbdallah Ibn ʿAbd al-ʿAzīz, in February 1978; as well as in subsequent contacts.[125] At the beginning of August, when Saudi Arabia tried to "revive Arab solidarity" (see above), Ḥasan sent his Chief of the Royal Court, Aḥmad Amīn Ben-Souda, to Riyadh,[126] urging the Saudis to suspend or delay their activity. In what seemed to be a reaction to the Saudi statements that the Camp David summit was doomed to failure (see above), the Minister of State for Foreign Affairs. Muhammad Boucetta stated that the conference was "a stage on the way to solve the problem, and history will not stop if it fails." [127] Finally, in the ongoing contacts with Israel, which were subsequently mentioned publicly by Morocco's Prime Minister, [128] Rabat called on Jerusalem to display greater flexibility, especially on the Palestinian issue. [129] On 27 May, Morocco's ambassador to Kuwait, 'Abd al-Hādī al-Subayhī, said that Hasan had sent a message to Begin warning that Morocco would reconsider its support for Sādāt's initiative if no progress were achieved. [130] In mid-June, it was reported that Hasan had suspended his contacts with Israeli government leaders. [131] This decision did not preclude a visit to Morocco in July by Israel's opposition leader, Shimon Peres, following his meeting with Sādāt in Austria. [132]

After the conclusion of the Camp David summit, Sādāt stopped over in Rabat on his way home. Despite the cordial welcome he was given, it became evident that Morocco's attitude had shifted from outright support to some measure of reserve and caution. Rabat refrained from official comment on the summit results. Hasan apparently had doubts of his own as to the value and significance of the agreements: they appeared to constitute a separate peace; they were vague on the Palestinian issue and ignored the PLO; and they failed to offer a solution for Jerusalem. [133] More importantly, Morocco was concerned over the widening rift between Egypt on the one hand, and Saudi Arabia and the countries following its line on the other. At a moment when, in reaction to the Camp David accords, the emergence of an anti-Sādāt camp of conservative and pro-Western Arab states seemed a possibility, Morocco was unwilling to take upon itself the isolation which outspoken support of Sādāt might bring upon it. Boucetta said that Morocco's task at that point was to "maintain Arab unity and to make the contacts necessary to achieve this." [134] Accordingly, Hasan sent his political adviser to participate in a meeting between Tuhāmī and King Khālid in Geneva on 24 September. [135] An Israeli journalist in Cairo cited Egyptian Foreign Ministry sources as saying that secret contacts were taking place in an effort by Morocco to persuade Jordan, as well as Palestinian notables, to participate in future negotiations on the West Bank and Gaza Strip. [136]

IRAN

Iran's longstanding friendly relations with Jordan and its record of unofficial but continuous co-operation with Israel were reinforced after 1970 by the development of closer ties with Egypt and, after 1973, with Syria as well. [137] By 1977, Iran had thus acquired a position of influence with several of the major parties to the Arab-Israeli conflict. This was especially true of Egypt and Israel. The former was the recipient of Iranian investments and financial aid on a fairly large scale; the latter received from Iran most of the oil needed for domestic consumption as well as for the operation of the Eilat-Ashkelon pipeline. Iran gradually tried to exert the influence thus afforded to work for a lowering of regional tensions. Its interest in greater stability in the area stemmed from fear that another Arab-Israeli war would impede the free movement of Iranian oil, fan Arab radicalism, and make possible renewed Soviet penetration into the region. Such developments might harm Iran's economic development schemes and eventually affect its internal security. Beginning in 1975, if not earlier, Tehran thus became involved in the search for a ME settlement. [138] In the course of 1975, it supported the second Sinai Agreement and encouraged Egypt to reopen the Suez Canal. [139] Iran's guarantee to continue oil supplies to Israel and to cover the loss of the Abū Rudays oilfields, when these were handed back to Egypt under the second Sinai Agreement, helped to finalize that accord in September 1975.

When Sādāt announced his initiative, Iran's reaction was at once favourable;[140] in fact, it soon became known that Iran had actually assisted in preparing for it. According to Sādāt, the idea of going to Jerusalem first came to him on his flight from Bucharest to Tehran on 31 October 1977.[141] In his talks with the Shah on 31 October and 1 November—which Sādāt described as having taken place at "a turning point as far as ME events are concerned"[142]—the Arab-Israeli conflict was one of the main topics. Both leaders, Sādāt said, "centred on the fact that peace is indivisible and that the problems of the area and our problems are also the Shah's problems."[143] The Shah apparently briefed Sādāt on his talks with Dayan, who had made a secret visit to Tehran shortly before.[144] The Shah also apparently promised Sādāt to intervene on Cairo's behalf in Washington during his forthcoming visit there,[145] possibly in connection with the imminent announcement by Sādāt of his initiative.

After the announcement was made, Iran called for speedy progress and expressed the fear that any "delay in attaining . . . a speedy and eye-catching victory . . . will result in Sādāt's . . . facing great difficulties in Egypt and the Arab world and . . . [the strengthening] of his extremist competitors."[146] As early as 16 November, at a press conference in Washington, the Shah stated that he "crossed his fingers" sincerely in the hope that Sādāt's "genuine intentions, resolve and actions for peace succeed, because the opposite is rather alarming and dreadful." If successful, the visit would "certainly be one of the greatest events since the Second World War." Its success depended on "realism and greater flexibility on the Israeli part, and full support for President Sādāt on the Arab part."[147] From then on, both in official statements and in media comments, Iran praised Sādāt, attacked his Arab adversaries, blamed Israel for intransigence and called for an adequate Israeli response to the initiative.

At the same time, Iran undertook intensive diplomatic activity in support of the peace negotiations. According to Israeli press reports (which were officially denied by both Iran and Israel), Dayan made a secret visit to Tehran on 27 December 1977 to brief the Shah on the Begin-Sādāt talks at Ismā'īliyya. Dayan was reported to have asked the Shah to use his influence with Ḥusayn in order to convince him to join in the negotiations.[148] During the following weeks, Iranian activity reached its peak. Between 30 December 1977 and 3 January 1978 the Shah was host to President Carter and King Ḥusayn. According to an Iranian source, the Shah recommended that Carter visit Egypt "in order to hearten Sādāt."[149] (Carter did indeed visit Aswān on his way back to the US; see preceding section. But whether this was in response to Iran's prompting is not known.) However, the Shah's efforts to draw Ḥusayn into the peace talks failed (see above). Instead, the Shah endeavoured to aid Jordan by expressing views which he believed Ḥusayn held but was unwilling to express himself. He stated that the Rabat summit decisions regarding the PLO should be modified so as to give Ḥusayn "a role to fulfil," and hinted that the King should be empowered to negotiate on behalf of the Palestinian people. The Shah described Ḥusayn as "a responsible person" who could well represent the West Bank—"a land [which is] part of Jordan." He added: "The better way towards a solution" would be for "the people of Palestine" to decide their own future "and to have a link with Jordan."[150]

The Shah also supported Sādāt's efforts to arrange for King Ḥasan II, King Ḥusayn and himself to meet the Egyptian President at Aswān. The conference was to demonstrate support for Sādāt and to provide yet another occasion to convince Ḥusayn to join the talks. Though he did not obtain the agreement of Ḥusayn and Ḥasan for a quadripartite meeting, he decided to go to Aswān in any case. During this visit, on 9 and 10 January 1978, the Shah expressed his "feelings of deep admiration and friendship" for Sādāt; his belief that Egypt was "following the right path"; and his desire for an agreement to be reached. He stated that "Egypt has opened her hand in a very dignified manner. The ball is now in Israel's court."[151] On 10 January, the Shah went directly from Aswān to Riyadh, where his talks were "characterized by the usual spirit of genuine Islamic fraternity."[152] He tried unsuccessfully to persuade the Saudis to drop their demand for a fully independent Palestinian state and their support for the PLO—two issues which Tehran regarded as providing potential for Soviet penetration in the ME.[153]

During subsequent months, as domestic tension rose (see chapter on Iran), the Shah's involvement in the ME negotiations diminished. However, official Iranian statements continued to express support for Sādāt, to accuse Israel of inflexibility, and to call on the US to exercise greater pressure on Israel. Iran itself gave no sign of wanting to bring pressure to bear on Israel by withholding or threatening to withhold oil supplies, despite occasional rumours to the contrary.[154] On two occasions, the Shah was asked specifically whether he was "prepared to reduce [oil] deliveries to make Israel less intransigent." On the first occasion, in March 1978, the Shah replied that "if there is a general decision by *all, for instance America, to stop delivery of arms*" or to impose an "*embargo on everything* such as had been decided *against Rhodesia and South Africa* . . . by the US and the UN," then "*everything is possible*."[155] On the second occasion, in May, he stated that "if *everybody* ganged up and really imposed [an embargo], it *might* have an effect."[156] Some Western observers interpreted these replies as indicating an anti-Israeli shift in Iran's traditional policy of not using oil supplies for political purposes; others pointed to the many conditions with which the replies were hedged. Recalling the fact that Iran was not complying with the oil embargo against South Africa, the latter group held the replies to be evasive and not indicative of any policy change.

THE USSR

The American-Soviet communiqué of 1 October 1977[157] had seemed to foreshadow the return of the USSR to a prominent role in the ME peace-making process, from which it had been virtually excluded since the Israeli-Syrian disengagement agreement in 1974. However, the improvement the joint statement caused in the US-Soviet atmosphere with respect to the ME turned out to be a mere interlude. The principal parties involved in Sādāt's initiative opposed active Soviet participation in the ME political process. The negative Soviet reaction to Sādāt's moves did not therefore come as a surprise; if anything, the surprise was that the reaction was initially cautious rather than hostile. Moscow's reaction emerged in three stages. At first, the Soviet media refrained from direct comment, simply indicating their attitude by citing unfavourable foreign views.[158] It was only after 22 November (i.e. when reactions in the Arab world had become sufficiently clear) that direct criticism appeared in the Soviet media. The third phase began early in December (at the time of the Tripoli conference; see essay on Inter-Arab Relations): criticism became sharper and was increasingly directed against Sādāt personally. He was accused of "dancing to the tune of imperialist circles"; of betraying the PLO; of abandoning the Palestinians; and of looking for "a group of Palestinian quislings" who. would approve of his concluding a separate deal with Israel.[159] His policy was described as "distortion of the ranks of Arab states," his initiative termed "primitive" and "sensational,"[160] and his trip to Jerusalem "a pilgrimage to Canossa."[161]

The authoritative Soviet view was set forth at the end of 1977 by Leonid Il'ich Brezhnev. He termed Sādāt's initiative "a negative change" which occurred just when "matters were progressing in the right direction [i.e.] towards the reconvening of the Geneva peace conference." Brezhnev reiterated that "the Soviet Union has been and remains a constant supporter of an overall settlement in the Near East, with the participation of all the interested parties, including of course the PLO." He then listed the elements of such a settlement:

(1) "The retreat of Israeli forces from all Arab territories occupied in 1967."

(2) "The realization of the inalienable rights of the Palestinian people, including their right to self-determination [and thereby] to establish a state of their own."

(3) "Securing the rights to independent existence and security for all the states [who are] direct parties to the conflict: the Arab states neighbouring on Israel, as well as the State of Israel."

(4) "Terminating the state of war between the above-mentioned Arab countries and Israel."

Again referring to Sādāt's policy, Brezhnev went on: "We . . . do not think that the path of unilateral concessions to Israel and separate negotiations with it . . . lead to [a comprehensive settlement]. On the contrary, it . . . is creating a deep rift in the Arab world. It is a policy undermining a lasting settlement, and first and foremost the Geneva conference even before its opening. . . . The so-called direct negotiations, namely negotiations between Israel and every one of the states which suffered its attack, are . . . an attempt to deny the Arabs the strength which lies in their unity and in the support by friendly states for their just cause."[162]

Subsequent Soviet official statements and media comment followed Brezhnev's line of argument. Strongly attacking Sādāt's policy, they stressed that only the principles laid down by Moscow were capable of achieving peace in the ME. By contrast, Sādāt's initiative was no more than one of the elements in an American-Israeli scheme to split Arab ranks, evade the Palestinian problem, and strike at progressive and anti-imperialist trends in the Arab world. Every turn in the negotiations was seized upon to prove that, contrary to Sādāt's expectations, he was failing to extract concessions from Israel and instead was falling into an American-Israeli trap from which only further unilateral Egyptian concessions could extricate him. For this reason alone, his initiative was doomed to failure—a point made over and over again in the Soviet media.[163]

Simultaneously, Moscow gave backing to Sādāt's Arab adversaries (all of whom were in varying degrees already Soviet-oriented in their foreign policy) in three ways. It tightened its relations with them, as demonstrated by the frequent visits exchanged between prominent personalities of the USSR and of Algeria, Libya, Syria, the PDRY and the PLO; it increased military assistance and arms supplies to these parties;[164] and it encouraged them to create "a unity of Arab progressive forces [which] is one of the main conditions for a successful struggle to eliminate the consequences of Israel's aggression, to secure the legitimate rights of the Palestinian people and to establish a just and lasting peace in the Near East."[165]

Before and during the Camp David summit, Soviet media repeatedly predicted its inevitable failure, *inter alia* because "influential factors" without whom peace could not be achieved were not represented. Any compromise reached at Camp David could only be the result of further Egyptian concessions at the expense of all-Arab interests. The only way to achieve genuine peace was for the Geneva conference to reconvene and for the acceptance of the Soviet peace plan.[166] The first negative comment on the Camp David accords was made in Radio Moscow's Arabic programme on the very day of their signature, and was soon followed by TASS. On 22 September, in a speech at Baku, Brezhnev warned that "the situation in the Near East remains complex and potentially dangerous," and that the "behind-the-scenes separate deal" concluded at Camp David "can only make the situation in the Near East more explosive." He added that the agreements were a mere "illusion of a settlement" because they ignored "the cardinal pre-conditions of a true settlement," and excluded "some lawful participants whose interests had been sacrificed." The agreements were but a cover for "Egypt's surrender," while enabling Israel to reap "the fruits of [its] aggression." Alluding to the US Secretary of State's ME tour, Brezhnev confidently predicted that American "attempts to compel other participants . . . to succumb to the terms of this deal" would fail.[167] Soviet spokesmen and media echoed his arguments; they also encouraged Syria and other members of the Tripoli bloc (see essay on Inter-Arab Relations) to assemble an all-Arab front against Sādāt and establish a joint Arab policy against the Camp David agreements. While Arab press reports—mostly by newspapers hostile to the Tripoli bloc—speculated on the possibility of a defence pact between the USSR and the Tripoli bloc states, no mention was made of this by Soviet spokesmen or the Soviet media.

ROMANIA

Along with the US and Iran, Romania enjoyed a position of exceptional trust and influence with several parties to the Arab-Israeli conflict. It maintained good diplomatic relations and steadily expanding commercial ties with both Israel and its Arab neighbours,[168] and played an increasingly prominent and independent role in world politics. This allowed Romania to translate into diplomatic action the two-fold interest it had in promoting a ME settlement.

(1) Apart from enhancing Romania's prestige and standing in world politics, a settlement was in keeping with its declared policy of fostering stability, reducing tensions and "solving international problems in a peaceful manner."[169]

(2) More specifically, Bucharest regarded the Arab-Israeli conflict as constituting a threat both to world peace and to Romania's security. Any renewed outbreak of hostilities in the ME carried with it the risk of super-power confrontation, and was therefore a threat to Europe. Because of its geographical proximity to the ME and its membership in the Warsaw Pact, Romania would be especially exposed to danger. This view was expressed by the President of the Republic and Secretary-General of the Romanian Communist Party (RCP), Nicolae Ceauşescu, in December 1977: "Romania believes that there is a close link between European security . . . and security in the Mediterranean area. Proceeding from this consideration, we speak out . . . for intensified efforts aimed at strengthening peace in the entire Mediterranean area."[170]

In the Romanian view, a lasting and just settlement in the ME should include Israeli withdrawal from all the occupied territories; "the solution of the Palestinian people's problems" on the basis of their "right to self-determination and to establish an independent state of their own"; and guarantees for the independence, territorial integrity and security for all the states in the region. Romania also emphasized that a settlement should be reached by direct negotiations between all the parties to the conflict—including the PLO, "the legitimate representative of the Palestinian people"—because only direct negotiations provide "a sure guarantee that the solution that will be agreed upon will be viable and will lead to the establishment of a lasting peace."[171]

From what little evidence is available of Romania's involvement in the peace-making process, it seems that Bucharest preferred to try to bring the parties together rather than mediate between them. Thus as early as May 1972, Ceauşescu had tried to arrange a meeting between President Sādāt and the then Israeli Prime Minister,

Golda Meir.[172] Beginning in 1974, he had repeatedly tried to persuade Israel and the PLO to recognize each other and to start a dialogue.[173] Ceauşescu's assistance in preparing Sādāt's initiative was revealed on 18 November 1977 when Begin expressed his gratitude to Romania.[174] The question of direct Egyptian-Israeli talks had been discussed during Begin's visit to Romania (26–30 August 1977), and several of his proposals, together with Ceauşescu's own impressions and comments, were conveyed to Sādāt during his visit there from 29–31 October 1977.[175]

In keeping with Ceauşescu's policy—and in contrast to the other East European states—Romania welcomed and supported Sādāt's initiative,[176] although it insisted that it should serve as a springboard to reconvene the Geneva conference and to reach a comprehensive settlement.[177] Accordingly, Romania maintained intensive contacts with both Israel and Egypt, who in turn kept Bucharest informed of the progress of the negotiations. At the same time, Romania also continued to maintain contacts and exchange views with Syria and the PLO. Romanian diplomatic activity accelerated after the recall of the Egyptian delegation from Jerusalem in January 1978. Between February and April, Ceauşescu met Sādāt (11–12 February), Peres (14 March), Dayan (2–5 April) and Yāsir 'Arafāt's political adviser, Hānī al-Ḥasan (10–11 April), while Romanian Defence Minister Ion Coman met Sādāt in Cairo (9 March), and Prime Minister Manea Mānescu visited Asad in Damascus (17 March). Arab sources reported that Romania had tried unsuccessfully to arrange direct Israeli-PLO and Israeli-Syrian negotiations, or alternatively a new ME conference as proposed by the UN Secretary-General.[178] At the same time, Romania urged Israel, both publicly and through diplomatic channels, to make an adequate response to Sādāt and to meet Egypt halfway.[179]

Romanian activity reached a peak during Ceauşescu's visit to Washington in mid-April 1978. The Romanian President apparently suggested to the Americans that the Israeli-Egyptian negotiations be directed (a) towards an outline agreement on a declaration of principles, including a commitment by Israel to withdraw from the occupied territories; and (b) towards the convening of a conference—either the Geneva conference or a new framework—which would include Syria, Jordan and "the authentic representative of the Palestinians," i.e. the PLO.[180]

When Romania failed to get US agreement for this course,[181] it restricted the scope of its overt involvement in the ME negotiations, but continued to express regret at the lack of an appropriate Israeli response to Sādāt.[182]

THE EUROPEAN ECONOMIC COMMUNITY

While the overall role of the European Economic Community (EEC) did not change in the period reviewed,[183] Sādāt's initiative brought into sharper focus existing policy differences within the EEC over the ME—especially as between Britain, France and West Germany—which prevented the Community from taking a joint stand. An attempt in November 1977 to have the EEC adopt a joint statement endorsing Sādāt's new policy was vetoed by France.[184] Consequently, although all member-states based their policies on the statement of the EEC heads of government of 29 June 1977[185] (reiterated on 29 October 1977),[186] London, Paris and Bonn in fact pursued independent and, to a certain degree, differing policies towards the peace-making process.

Britain was the most involved and active among the Nine, made possible by its close relations with Egypt, Jordan and Israel, and by its frequent high-level contacts with each of them. Israel for its part not only "accepted positively" the UK's enhanced role,[187] but demonstrated its preference for British involvement, rather than that of other EEC states, by keeping Whitehall informed of all developments connected with Sādāt's initiative and by frequent consultations with London.

Furthermore, of all EEC countries, Britain was closest to the US in its approach to ME affairs.[188] Britain participated in efforts to convince Jordan to join the Egyptian-Israeli negotiations; it followed Washington in December 1977 in its initial favourable reaction to Begin's peace plan; and it came out publicly against the establishment of new Israeli settlements in February 1978. Generally, however, Britain preferred to act through "private representations to both sides," rather than by making "public pronouncements."[189]

Like most EEC states, France maintained good relations with Egypt, but unlike its partners, was also on close terms with the "rejectionist" states. Sādāt, for his part, showed a marked preference for France as compared with the rest of the EEC. During the period under review, he and his Vice-President, Ḥusnī Mubārak, each visited Paris three times. However, French endeavours to play a more prominent role in solving the Arab-Israeli conflict were blocked by Israel because of what Begin described as France's "utterly negative, one-sided and unobjective" policy in the ME.[190] Begin's most demonstrative step in this regard was his rejection, in December 1977, of President Giscard d'Estaing's invitation to meet him in Paris on his way home from Washington. Instead, Begin stopped over in London for talks with James Callaghan. It was there, on 20 December, that he met d'Estaing's envoy, François Ponset.

France then shifted its efforts to other quarters. During November and December 1977, it tried to convince Damascus, if not to join Sādāt's initiative, at least not to oppose it and to tone down Syrian criticism of Sādāt. This was one of the aims of Prime Minister Raymond Barre and Foreign Minister Louis de Guiringaud, who visited Damascus from 26–28 November.[191] Another step in this direction was taken soon after Ponset's meeting with Begin when the French President sent a message to Asad, which included "overall information on Israel's policy" and his own "personal analysis of the situation in the ME."[192] Syria did not respond. Sometime later, France found a new field of activity by means of greater involvement in Lebanon (see below in the section on South Lebanon).

As Egyptian-Israeli contacts proceeded, a gradual shift was noted in the French attitude toward the Arab-Israeli conflict and toward Israel. One view was that "French government statements have reflected a noticeably softer tone on Israel," a "desire to mend fences with Israel," and to restore Israeli confidence in France.[193] At the time of the Camp David summit, Arab sources in Paris attributed to the French government a proposal for a preparatory ME peace conference in Paris if and when the summit meeting failed.[194]

The position of the Federal Republic of Germany (FRG) was a more awkward one. Bonn was at pains to demonstrate support for the US without appearing hostile to the USSR, and to encourage Egypt and Israel in their search for a settlement without placing undue strain on its good relations with Syria, Saudi Arabia, Iraq and other Arab countries. Accordingly, German spokesmen frequently expressed their support for Sādāt's policy of "bringing about and stabilizing peace in the ME," referring to his initiative as "an astonishing development for which one can only have the best wishes." At the same time, Bonn stressed that "peace in the ME is not dependent upon Egypt and Israel alone," and that other Arab representatives as well as the USSR should participate in the negotiations. While affirming that Israel should live within secure borders, Bonn called upon it to make an adequate response to Sādāt's initiative.[195] According to Israeli sources, West Germany tried to persuade its partners in the EEC to issue a joint statement welcoming Sādāt's initiative, but phrased so as to imply the need for greater Israeli concessions.[196]

The difficulties of reconciling the contradictory requirements of Bonn's policy were illustrated by two incidents, both connected with visits there by Arab leaders.

(1) On 23 June 1978, at a joint press conference with visiting Crown Prince Fahd of Saudi Arabia, Chancellor Helmut Schmidt stated that the Palestinians should have "the right of organizing themselves in a state." [197] Israel protested promptly, and in rather strong terms. When visiting Israel a few days later, Foreign Minister Hans-Dietrich Genscher explained that no change had taken place in Bonn's policies. He said that Schmidt's statement did not necessarily mean that Bonn supported the establishment of an independent Palestinian state, nor had Germany deviated from the EEC statement of 29 June 1977. [198]

(2) On 11 September 1978, during an official reception in his honour in Bonn, President Asad made a vehement attack on Sādāt's initiative and on the Camp David summit. President Walter Scheel took what one reporter described as "the unusual step of delivering an impromptu reply" in which he stated that he did not agree with "all [Asad's] evaluations." [199]

After the conclusion of the Camp David summit, the EEC succeeded where it had failed at the time of Sādāt's Jerusalem visit: on 19 September 1978, the EEC Foreign Ministers jointly welcomed the agreements and expressed their common hope that the Camp David accords would constitute "a further major step on the path to a just, comprehensive and lasting peace." [200] This, however, did not quite do away with the differences among the Nine. While Britain unequivocally supported the agreements, [201] France and West Germany were more reserved in their individual reactions, stating that there was still "great uncertainty" and that an overall settlement required "all the interested parties" to be associated with it, "including the representatives of the Palestinian people." [202]

AUSTRIA

Austria was involved in the Arab-Israeli conflict mainly through the activities of its Chancellor, Dr Bruno Kreisky, acting in his capacity as one of the leaders of the Socialist International and the chairman of its fact-finding mission on the ME. Following the 1973 war, Kreisky had visited the ME once each year and had tried to promote an Israeli-Arab and, especially, an Israeli-Palestinian dialogue. Late in 1976, he was instrumental in facilitating meetings between Sādāt and American Jewish leaders. [203] In public statements, Kreisky gave first priority to the Palestinian problem and strongly supported the PLO, emphasizing that the only way to solve the conflict was by direct dialogue between Israel and the PLO.

During 1978, at moments when Egyptian-Israeli contacts were almost deadlocked, Kreisky played a prominent part in arranging two meetings between Peres and Sādāt—on 11 February and again on 9 July. Both took place in Salzburg. Also, together with the chairman of the Socialist International, ex-Chancellor Willy Brandt, he arranged for the discussion which resulted in the publication of the "Vienna document" (see preceding section). The 16 July meeting between Sādāt and Israeli Defence Minister Ezer Weizman—though not arranged by Kreisky—took place on Austrian territory (near Salzburg) by courtesy of the Austrian government.

THE UNITED NATIONS

If the UN had been relegated to a marginal role in the search for peace in the ME for most of 1977, [204] Sādāt's initiative in November tended to eliminate it as an active partner altogether—a situation reflected in the cool, if not hostile, reaction of the UN General Secretariat. When Sādāt declared that the Cairo conference of December 1977 should be regarded as a preparatory step for the Geneva conference, the UN Secretary-General "made it plain [that] he regarded [it] as inadequate . . .

because only Egypt, Israel and the US would be participating [while] Syria, the Soviet Union, Jordan and the PLO have said they would not go to Cairo." Dr Waldheim "seemed to be agitated over the [effective] exclusion of the UN." [205] On 29 November, while accepting the invitation for UN representation at Cairo, he proposed to convene an additional preparatory conference on "neutral ground," under UN auspices and with the participation of all the parties, to follow the Cairo talks. [206] Although this proposal was intended to downgrade the Cairo conference, Egypt welcomed it [207]—expecting Israel to reject it, which it promptly did the same day. [208] Waldheim stated that he did not accept Israel's answer as final, [209] but for all practical purposes he dropped the idea.

Apart from the issue of the UN role, there was another reason for Waldheim's proposal: he was apparently under pressure—behind the scenes—from Sādāt's opponents, mainly the USSR. [210] It was reported that this pressure influenced the Secretary-General's decision to appoint the Chief Co-ordinator of UN Military Forces and Missions in the ME, Gen Ensio Siilasvuo, as delegate to the Cairo conference (rather than an Under Secretary-General for Political Affairs, as Egypt would have preferred), as well as his refusal to allow Siilasvuo to preside at the conference. [211] The same reason was given for Waldheim's absence from the deliberations of the Political Committee in Jerusalem in January 1978. [212]

After an interval of several months, during which the UN did not attempt to influence ME developments other than those in South Lebanon (see appropriate section in this essay), Waldheim stated in an interview in May 1978 that Sādāt's visit to Jerusalem "was not prepared enough, which we now see was a mistake. Sādāt got nothing in return. So I am sceptical about this bilateral approach. The initiative is now petering out. Fresh thinking must be applied and a new approach found. All the parties that were invited to the original Cairo conference . . . including the PLO . . . should now be re-invited to New York. Under the chairmanship of the two [Geneva co-chairmen], the US and the USSR, this conference would be the preparatory phase to Geneva." [213] However, in view of the strong criticism of this statement, a UN spokesman explained that Waldheim's conversation with a *Newsweek* reporter had been "informal"; the fact that it was presented as a formal interview might have put the answers in "a somewhat different perspective." [214] Under the impact of criticism from the US, Egypt and Israel, the Secretary-General did not follow up his own suggestion for several weeks. However, at the beginning of July, Waldheim revived the idea. After consulting American, Soviet and Arab representatives at the UN, [215] he visited the ME, met Sādāt (at Salzburg on 10 July), Asad and 'Arafāt (at Damascus on 17 and 18 July), King Khālid (at Tā'if on 20 July), and sent the UN Under Secretary-General for Political Affairs, Roberto Guyer, to Amman (19 July). Waldheim's proposal went unheeded. Within a month, UN activities were completely overshadowed by events leading to the Camp David summit and the developments set in motion by it.

Moshe Gammer

NOTES
1. See *Middle East Contemporary Survey (MECS) 1976–77*, pp. 90, 93, 95, 130–31, 138, 478–84.
2. *Ibid.* Also *Middle East Record (MER) 1968*, pp. 217–28; *1969–70*, pp. 103–6. A report of a meeting between Husayn and Dayan in October 1977 was carried by *Ma'ariv*, Tel Aviv; 7 April 1978.
3. A third condition—the solution of the refugee problem—was added from time to time, e.g. in *Jordan Times (JT)*, Amman; 13 January 1978.

4. Transcript of Carter's press conference of 28 November, a United States Information Service (USIS) press release, 30 November; *New York Times (NYT)*, 18 November 1977.
5. R Amman, 19 November—US Foreign Broadcast Information Service, Daily Report, Middle East and North Africa (DR), 21 November 1977. Similarly, Husayn's speech of 28 November, Jordan TV, 28 November—DR, 29 November 1977. And his press conference of 1 December, R Amman, 1 December—British Broadcasting Corporation, Summary of World Broadcasts, the Middle East and Africa (BBC), 3 December 1977.
6. The above press conference of 1 December 1977.
7. *Al-Dustūr*, Amman; 30 November 1977.
8. *The Daily Telegraph (DT)*, London; 23 November 1977.
9. Press conference of 1 December; R Amman, 1 December—BBC, 3 December 1977.
10. Interview with *Newsweek*, New York; 12 December 1977.
11. *Yedi'ot Aharonot*, Tel Aviv; 22 December 1977.
12. R Amman, 28 December—DR, 29 December 1977.
13. Husayn's briefing to the Cabinet, R Amman, 4 January—DR, 5 January 1978.
14. *Kayhan International*, Tehran; 2 January 1978. See also the Shah's interview with Barbara Walters (ABC) as reported there, 4 January 1978.
15. Middle East News Agency (MENA), Egypt; 1 January—DR, 3 January 1978.
16. *The Jerusalem Post (JP)*, 4 January 1978.
17. *Kayhan International*, 8 and 9 January; *al-Ahrām*, Cairo; and *al-Dustūr*, Amman; 9 January 1978.
18. Interview with the BBC, 23 January—DR, 24 January, and *Der Spiegel*, Hamburg; 6 February 1978. Also report of Mubārak's visit in *al-Musawwar*, Cairo; 3 February 1978.
19. Interview with Agence France-Presse (AFP), as reported by *JT*, 10 February 1978.
20. E.g. interview with the ABC television network as transcribed by Israel Government Press Office, Daily Press Bulletin (GPO), 9 February; statement at the conclusion of his visit to the US, Israel Broadcasting Authority (IBA), 17 February—DR, 21 February; inteview with IBA, 24 February—DR, 27 February; and speech at the Zionist congress as transcribed by a Zionist congress press release, 27 February 1978.
21. *JP* and *Ha'aretz*, Tel Aviv; 17 May 1978.
22. *Newsweek*, 25 September 1978.
23. *Al-Dustūr*, Amman; 28 August 1978.
24. "One of the King's closest advisers" in an interview with *The Guardian*, London; 21 August 1978.
25. Address to the nation on the occasion of the *'Īd al-Fitr* holiday, R Amman, 2 September—BBC, 4 September; *International Herald Tribune (IHT)*, Paris; 5 September 1978.
26. *JT*, 20 September 1978.
27. E.g. Husayn's press conferences on 23 and 26 September, R Amman, 23 September; *Observer*, London; 24 September; *The Times*, London; 27 September; and interview with *Newsweek*, 2 October 1978.
28. *JT*, 3 October 1978.
29. Joint communiqué by the Syrian Ba'th party and the PLO, R Damascus, 22 November—DR, 23 November 1977.
30. Statement by the National and Regional Commands of the (Syrian) Ba'th party, the Central Command of the Progressive Nationalist Front, and the Syrian government; R Damascus, 17 November—DR, 18 November 1977.
31. Asad's interviews with *al-Ra'y al-'Āmm*, Kuwait; 11 December 1977; and *Newsweek*, 16 January 1978.
32. Foreign Minister 'Abd al-Halīm Khaddām addressing Austrian journalists, R Damascus, 20 December—BBC, 22 December 1977; also his interview with *Der Spiegel*, 19 June 1978.
33. For Syria's policy and strategy, see *MECS 1976–77*, pp. 88–90 and 613–14.
34. Asad's speech on 8 March, when sworn in for his second term as president, *Tishrīn*, Damascus; 9 March 1978.
35. Speech by Sāmī al-'Attārī, member of the National Command of the Ba'th, at a rally of solidarity with the struggle of the Palestinians at Damascus University on 23 May; *Jīl al-Thawra*, Damascus; 30 May 1978.
36. *Al-Munādil*, Damascus; February 1978.
37. Speech by Syrian delegate Muwaffaq 'Allāf at the UN General Assembly, *Tishrīn*, 25 November 1977.
38. Asad's interview with *Kurier*, Vienna; 20 December—DR, 22 December 1977.
39. Deputy Foreign Minister, Dr 'Abdallah al-Khānī, in an interview on 7 January with Dr A. I. Dawisha as reported in *The World Today*, London; May 1978.
40. Khaddām's lecture at Damascus University on 23 January, published as a leaflet in March

1978 by the NC Propaganda, Publications and Information Bureau. The leaflet carried an explanation stating that it was intended to be read out in party meetings.
41. Interview with *Newsweek*, 16 January 1978.
42. *Sawt al-Talī'a*, Damascus; February 1978.
43. *Ibid.*
44. *Al-Munādil*, February 1978.
45. Dr Fādil al-Ansārī, Head of the Information Department of the Ba'th, in an interview with *al-Ba'th*, Damascus; 19 December 1977. And cf Khaddām's interview with *al-Ra'y al 'Amm*, 21 February 1978.
46. Ghālib al-Kiyālī, *Hāfiz al-Asad: Qā'id wa-Risāla [Hāfiz al-Asad: Leader and Mission]*. Damascus, 1978. The reference is to the chapter published in *Tishrīn*, 8 January 1978.
47. *Al-Munādil*, February 1978.
48. *MECS 1976–77*, p. 132; Asad's interview with *Newsweek*, 1 August and with *Der Spiegel*, transmitted by R Damascus, 10 September—DR, 11 September; also Bassām al-'Asalī's article in *Tishrīn*, 18 December 1977.
49. *Al-Munādil*, February 1978.
50. *Sawt al-Talī'a*, February 1978.
51. *MECS 1976–77*, p. 132. Bassām al-'Asalī's article in *Tishrīn*, 13 November 1977.
52. A term used in Arabic and in Hebrew to describe a number of Arab villages c. 30 km north-east of Tel Aviv in pre-1967 Israel, close to the 1949 armistice demarcation line.
53. *Sawt al-Talī'a*, February 1978.
54. Speech at a reception in Bonn on 11 September, Reuter, 12 September 1978.
55. Interview with *Der Spiegel*, transmitted by R Damascus, 10 September—DR, 11 September 1978.
56. R Damascus, 18 September—BBC, 20 September 1978.
57. R Damascus, 20 September—BBC, 22 September 1978.
58. *Al-Ba'th*, 19 September as quoted by R Damascus, 19 September—DR, 19 September 1978.
59. R Damascus, 20 September—BBC, 22 September 1978.
60. For Iraq's attitudes in previous years, see *MECS 1976–77*, pp. 414–15 and *MER 1968*, pp. 228–30; *1969–70*, pp. 107–8. For a comprehensive presentation of the Iraqi position on the eve of Sādāt's initiative, see speech by Foreign Minister Sa'dūn Hammādī at the UN General Assembly on 4 October 1977.
61. Speech at the Tripoli conference by Taha Yāsīn Ramadān, member of the National Command of the Iraqi Ba'th party and the Revolution Command Council; R Baghdad, 2 December—DR, 5 December 1977.
62. Statement by the National Command of the Iraqi Ba'th party, *al-Thawra*, Baghdad; 16 November 1977.
63. From an article by Hasan Muhammad Hasan in *al-Thawra*, 22 November 1977, which contains a lengthy and reasoned critique of Sādāt's policy.
64. *Al-Thawra*, 6 December 1977.
65. Both in *al-Thawra*, 3 February 1978.
66. For the Khartoum summit resolutions, see *MER 1967*, pp. 264–65.
67. *Al-Thawra*, Baghdad; 5 February 1978.
68. Message to the leaders of Algeria, Syria, Libya, the PDRY and the PLO; Iraqi News Agency (INA), 1 February—BBC, 3 February 1978. Emphasis added.
69. Press conference at the conclusion of the Algiers conference; *Algérie Presse Service*, 5 February—DR, 7 February 1978; cf *al-Thawra*, Baghdad; 5 February 1978.
70. INA, 19 September—BBC, 21 September 1978.
71. *MECS 1976–77*, pp. 88 and 580–82.
72. Saudi News Agency (SNA), 18 November—DR, 21 November 1977.
73. *Al-Hawādith*, Beirut; 9 December 1977.
74. SNA, 12 December 1977.
75. SNA, 15 December—DR, 15 December 1977; similarly a Saudi source quoted by *al-Akhbār*, Cairo; 2 February 1978.
76. E.g. *Washington Post (WP)*, 10 January; *Arabia and the Gulf*, London; 16 January 1978.
77. Interview with the Hearst Newspaper Group, *JP*, 25 December 1977.
78. Interview with ABC television network as reported by R Riyadh, 5 January—BBC, 7 January and by *al-Madīna al-Munawwara*, Jidda; 6 January 1978.
79. Interview with *al-Ra'y al-'Amm*, 9 March 1978. Emphasis added in all preceding quotations.
80. SNA, 18 November—DR, 21 November 1977.
81. SNA, 15 December—DR, 15 December 1977.
82. R Riyadh, 8 February—BBC, 10 February 1978; similarly SNA, 11 June 1978.

83. R Riyadh, 25 Decemoer 1977.
84. *Al-Madīna al-Munawwara*, 25 December 1977.
85. R Riyadh, 8 February—BBC, 10 February 1978; similarly SNA, 11 June 1978.
86. Interviews with ABC, as in note 78 above; *Newsweek*, 20 February 1978.
87. Interview with *Newsweek*, 20 February, and conversation with an American businessmen's delegation as reported by SNA, 25 March 1978. Also interview of Information Minister, Muḥammad 'Abduh al-Yamānī, with *al-Bayraq*, Beirut; 13 May 1978.
88. Interviews with *Paris Match*, 21 April; *Al-Bayraq*, 6 May; and *al-Manār*, London; 13 May 1978.
89. *WP*, 3 May 1978.
90. Interview with *al-Siyāsa*, Kuwait; 3 July 1978.
91. Thus editorials in *'Ukāz*, Jidda; 24 July, and in *al-Riyād*, Riyadh; 3 August 1978.
92. *Al-Anwār*, Beirut; 29 July; *NYT*, 3 August; *IHT*, 4 and 5 August 1978.
93. E.g. *The Baltimore Sun*, 3 August; *IHT*, 4 and 5 August; *WP*, 4 August 1978.
94. Fahd's interview with *al-Siyāsa*, 23 August 1978.
95. *'Ukāz*, 26 August 1978.
96. *Al-Nahār al-'Arabī wal-Duwalī (NAD)*, Paris; 26 August 1978.
97. *The Financial Times (FT)*, London; 14 September 1978.
98. Interview with *al-Nadwa*, Mecca; as quoted by SNA, 14 September 1978.
99. SNA, 19 September—BBC, 21 September 1978. Emphasis added.
100. SNA, 24 September; *FT*, 25 September 1978.
101. PM Ahmad 'Uthmān's interview with *al-Dustūr*, Amman; 17 March 1976.
102. Hasan in an interview with R Cairo, 8 July—DR, 11 July 1977.
103. Interview with *Newsweek*, 16 May 1977.
104. Interview with *al-Siyāsa*, 24 June 1978; similarly, interview with *Events*, London; 10 February 1978.
105. Interview as in note 102 above.
106. *Al-Ahrām*, Cairo; 24 December 1977.
107. *Ibid.*
108. Hasan's interview with *France Soir*, Paris; 17 November 1977; and 'Uthmān's interview with *Ma'ariv*, 6 January 1978.
109. *Time*, New York; 14 August 1978.
110. Goldmann's interview with *Yedi'ot Aharonot*, 28 July 1978; also, *Ma'ariv*, 28 July; *Jeune Afrique*, Paris; 3 May 1978. The latter also reports an earlier attempt by the leader of the Leftist Moroccan *Union Socialiste des Forces Populaires*, 'Abd al-Rahīm Bouabid, to arrange a secret meeting between Goldmann and 'Abd al-Nāsir in 1958-59.
111. For the coup attempts, see *Africa Contemporary Record (ACR) 1972-73*, pp. B69–74 and *1973–74*, pp. B75–80. For the contingent in Syria and Morocco's involvement in the October War, see *ACR 1973–74*, p. B84.
112. *Jeune Afrique*, 3 May 1978. For Saharan developments, see *MECS 1976-77*, pp. 170–71, and essay on inter-Arab relations in this volume.
113. 'Uthmān's interview with *al-Dustūr*, Amman; 17 March 1976.
114. For the "peace offensive," see *MECS 1976-77*, pp. 123–24.
115. *Jeune Afrique*, 3 May, and *Ma'ariv*, 28 July 1978; both give additional details.
116. *Le Monde*, Paris; 19 November 1977; *Jeune Afrique*, 3 May; *Ma'ariv*, 28 July; and *Time*, 14 August 1978.
117. IBA, 9 May—BBC, 11 May 1977.
118. *Jeune Afrique*, 3 May 1978. For the meetings, see *MECS 1976-77*, pp. 103 and 190–91.
119. E.g. his interviews with *The Middle East*, London; 4 March and with *al-Anbā'*, Rabat; 7 May 1978.
120. *Newsweek*, 25 September 1977; *Time*, 25 September 1977 and 14 August 1978; *Le Monde*, 19 November 1977; *Ha'aretz*, 1 March 1978; *Ma'ariv*, 7 April, 10 May and 28 July 1978; *Jeune Afrique*, 3 May 1978.
121. R Rabat, 19 November—DR, 21 November 1977.
122. E.g. interviews with *al-Ahrām*, 24 December 1977; *al-Jumhūriyya*, Cairo; 26 January 1978; and *al-Hawādith*, 27 January 1978; also messages to the Secretary-General of the Arab League, reported by MENA, 14 December—DR, 15 December 1977; and to Sādāt, reported by R Rabat, 20 January—DR, 23 January 1978.
123. *Ha'aretz*, 14, 15 December 1977.
124. *Davar*, Tel Aviv; 22 January 1978.
125. R Rabat, 17 November—DR, 18 November 1977; *Arab Report and Record (ARR)*, London; 1-14 February 1978; and Tamar Golan's report from Morocco, *Ma'ariv*, 29 May 1978.
126. SNA, 5 August 1978.

127. MENA, 15 September 1978.
128. Interview with *The Middle East*, 4 March 1978.
129. E.g. report by Tamar Golan about a message from Hasan to Begin after the operation in South Lebanon, *Ma'ariv*, 6 April 1978.
130. *Al-Siyāsa*, 28 May 1978.
131. *Christian Science Monitor (CSM)*, Boston; 16 June 1978.
132. *Ha'aretz* and *Ma'ariv*, 20 July 1978.
133. E.g. Moroccan press review by *Maghreb Arabe Presse*, 19 September—DR, 20 September; and statement by the Moroccan ambassador to the UAE, as reported by the UAE news agency, 26 September 1978.
134. Boucetta's press conference, R Cairo, Voice of the Arabs (VoA; Cairo transmitter to Arab audiences outside Egypt), 25 September; *The Times*, 26 September; also his interview with *al-Siyāsa*, as quoted by MENA, 24 September; cf *FT*, 22 September 1978.
135. MENA, 23 September 1978.
136. *Ma'ariv*, 12 October 1978.
137. In addition to the sources listed below, use has been made in this section of the draft of a hitherto unpublished paper by Yair P. Hirshfeld: "Iran's Policy Towards Israel and the Arab-Israeli Conflict 1948–1978—an Overview." For earlier stages of Iran's relations with ME countries, see *MER 1960*, pp. 216–20; *1967*, pp. 153–55; *1968*, pp. 200–1; *1969–70*, pp. 659–60, 661–62, 663; and *MECS 1976–77*, p. 396.
138. E.g. *al-Nahār*, Beirut; 8 January 1975, commenting on the Shah's visit to Egypt and Jordan at the beginning of 1975.
139. *ARR*, 1975, pp. 331–32.
140. *Echo of Iran; Political Digest*, Tehran; No 157 (4 December 1977), pp. 2–8.
141. Interview with *October*, Cairo; 11 December 1977.
142. Statement to R Cairo, 31 October—DR, 1 November 1977.
143. Interview with Egyptian TV, 4 November—DR, 7 November 1977.
144. *Ma'ariv*, 10 May 1978.
145. Iranian sources stressed that during his visit, the Shah was "expected to discuss ME developments with President Carter," *Kayhan International*, 1 November 1977. Egyptian sources made similar reports.
146. *Political Digest*, No 162 (8 January 1978), p. 5.
147. Pars (Iran's News Agency), 19 November—BBC, 22 November; *Kayhan International*, 19 November; and *Political Digest*, No 157 (4 December 1977), p. 4.
148. *Ma'ariv*, 28 December, and *Ha'aretz*, 29 December 1977.
149. *Political Digest*, No 162 (8 January 1978), p. 4.
150. Interview with ABC television network, as transmitted by R Tehran, 3 January—BBC, 4 January 1978.
151. *Kayhan International*, 10, 11 January 1978.
152. Sa'ūd al-Faysal's statement to R Riyadh, 10 January—DR, 10 January 1978.
153. Deutsche Presse Agentur (DPA), 13 January 1978.
154. E.g. *MECS 1976–77*, p. 140.
155. Interview with *WP*, 6 March 1978. Emphasis added.
156. Interview with *The Chicago Tribune*, 24 May, as reprinted in *Kayhan International*, 25 May 1978. Emphasis added.
157. *MECS 1976–77*, pp. 29–30 and 140–41.
158. For initial Soviet reactions, see Radio Free Europe Research, Background Report No 234 (Eastern Europe), 29 November 1977, and *Middle East Intelligence Survey*, Tel Aviv; 16–30 November 1977.
159. Telegrafnoe Agentstvo Sovetskovo Soiuza (Tass), 5 December—Daily Report: The Soviet Union (DR/SU), 6 December 1977.
160. *Izvestiia*, Moscow; 29 December 1977.
161. *Novoe Vremia*, Moscow; 9 December 1977.
162. Interview with *Pravda*, Moscow; 24 December 1977.
163. E.g. *Izvestiia*, 29 December 1977, 10 June and 22 July 1978; *Sovetskaia Rossiia*, Moscow; 29 December 1977; *Mezhdunarodnaia Zhizn'*, Moscow; April 1978; and A. Kislov in *Aziia i Afrika Sevodnia*, Moscow; June 1978.
164. E.g. *al-Siyāsa*, *al-Mustaqbal* and *NAD*, 31 December 1977; *al-Qabas*, Kuwait; 10 January; *Ha'aretz*, 9 and 12 January; *Ma'ariv*, 13 January; *Akhir Sā'a*, Cairo; 21 June 1978.
165. *Mezhdunarodnaia Zhizn'*, April 1978; see also commentaries on the Tripoli conference by R Moscow in Arabic, 2 December—DR/SU, 5 December 1977; and on the Algiers conference by Tass, 8 February—DR/SU, 9 February 1978.
166. E.g. *Izvestiia*, 7 September 1978.
167. Tass, 22 September 1978.

168. For Romania's refusal in June 1967, alone among all East European states, to sever diplomatic relations with Israel and for its distinctive attitude toward the Arab-Israeli conflict, see *MER 1967*, pp. 38 and 242.

169. Excerpts from speeches by Ceauşescu during a visit to Transylvania, as published in *Lumea*, Bucharest; 23-29 June 1978.

170. Speech at the Communist party conference, R Bucharest, 7 December—Daily Report: Eastern Europe (DR/EE), 8 December 1977.

171. The quotations are respectively from Ceauşescu's speeches in Transylvania (note 169); his interview with the Hearst Newspaper Group, as reported by Agenţia Română de Presă (Agerpres), 9 April—DR/EE, 10 April; his interview with the *Sunday Telegraph*, London; reprinted in *Lumea*, 26 April 1978; and the above speech at the party conference (note 170).

172. Golda Meir, *Hayyay [My Life]* (Tel Aviv: "Sifriyat Ma'ariv," 1975), pp. 290-91.

173. One of these attempts is mentioned by Nahum Goldmann in an interview with *Yedi'ot Aharonot*, 28 July 1978.

174. *NYT*, 19 November, and IBA, 27 November—BBC, 29 November 1977.

175. Begin's disclosures were made in a speech to the Knesset, transcribed by GPO, 28 December 1977. Sādāt's version was given in an interview with *October*, 11 December 1977. See also *DT* and *NYT*, 17 November 1977; *Ma'ariv*, 7 April 1978.

176. Romanian and other East European reactions to Sādāt's trip to Jerusalem were summed up in Radio Free Europe Research, Background Report No 234 (Eastern Europe), 29 November 1977.

177. *Scintea*, Bucharest; 24 November 1977.

178. E.g. *al-Ahrām*, 2 March, 9 April; *Akhir Sā'a*, 19 April; *al-Qabas*, 8 April; *al-Ra'y*, Amman; 11 April; and *NAD*, 13 May 1978.

179. Diplomatic activity reported e.g. in *Ma'ariv*, 9 March, 4, 6, 7, 14 April; *Ha'aretz*, 5 and 6 April 1978; public statements were made in interviews with the Hearst Newspaper Group (note 171) and with the ABC television network as reported by Agerpres, 14 April—DR/EE, 14 April 1978.

180. *NYT*, 18 April. Also *WP*, 13 April 1978 and the above interview with ABC.

181. Failure to agree is implied in the language of the joint communiqué published at the conclusion of Ceauşescu's visit, reported in *The Baltimore Sun, NYT, WP*, 14 April 1978.

182. E.g. Ceauşescu's interviews with *The Guardian* and with the (British) Independent Television Network (ITN), both transcribed in *Lumea*, 16-22 June 1978.

183. *MECS 1976-77*, pp. 51-53.

184. *IHT* and *Frankfurter Algemeine Zeitung (FAZ)*, 21 November 1977.

185. *MECS 1976-77*, pp. 52-53.

186. *Ibid*, p. 53 and *Middle East Economic Digest*, London; 4 November 1977.

187. Dayan's summary of his visit to Britain and the Scandinavian states; GPO, 22 May 1978.

188. Britain's position was set forth in interviews of Foreign Secretary Dr David Owen with *Events*, 16 December 1977, and of the Minister of State for Foreign and Commonwealth Affairs, Frank Judd, with *Events*, 10 March 1978.

189. PM James Callaghan in the House of Commons on 9 February, quoted by *The Times*, 10 February 1978.

190. Interview with R Paris, 11 January—DR, 12 January 1978.

191. R Paris, 25 November and *Le Monde*, 26 November 1977.

192. *Ha'aretz*, 29 December 1977.

193. *IHT*, 12 May 1978.

194. *Al-Anbā'*, Kuwait; 15 September 1978.

195. Statement by Chancellor Helmut Schmidt on 21 November, quoted by *FAZ*, 22 November 1977; also statement by Foreign Minister Hans-Dietrich Genscher on 21 November and by Schmidt in Cairo on 28 December 1977 and following talks with Sādāt in Hamburg on 9 February 1978; *FAZ*, 22 November, 29 December 1977 and 10 February 1978.

196. *Ha'aretz*, 23 January 1978.

197. Reuter, 23 June; *FAZ*, 24 June 1978.

198. *Ha'aretz*, 28, 30 June; *Ma'ariv*, 29 June; *Yedi'ot Aharonot, FAZ*, 30 June 1978.

199. Reuter, 12 September 1978.

200. *The Times*, 20 September 1978.

201. E.g. Foreign Office statement of 18 September, quoted by *The Guardian*, 19 September; Callaghan's letters to Carter, Sādāt and Begin, quoted by *The Times*, 19 September; and Owen's address at the UN General Assembly on 27 September 1978.

202. De Guiringaud's address at the UN General Assembly on 27 September; also Genscher's General Assembly address on 26 September 1978.

203. *MECS 1976–77*, p. 123.
204. *Ibid*, pp. 110–14.
205. *NYT*, 1 December 1977.
206. *The Guardian*, 30 November; *NYT*, 1 December 1977.
207. *Al-Ahrām*, 30 November 1977.
208. GPO, 30 November 1977.
209. *NYT*, 1 December; DPA, 2 December 1977.
210. Waldheim's conversation with the Chairman of the Conference of Presidents of Major (US) Jewish Organizations, Rabbi Alexander Schindler, quoted by *Ha'aretz*, 4 December; also report in *NYT*, 14 December 1977.
211. *NYT*, 14 December 1977.
212. *Ibid*, 12 January and *Ma'ariv*, 13 January 1978.
213. *Newsweek*, 8 May 1978.
214. *JP*, 3 May 1978.
215. *NAD*, 8 July 1978.

The Problem of South Lebanon

The "problem of the South," like several other features of the current Lebanese political scene, preceded the 1975-76 civil war; indeed, it contributed to its outbreak and was transformed by its course and outcome. South Lebanon became a problem area in the early 1970s when, following the Jordanian civil war of 1970, it became the only region of autonomous Palestinian presence and military activity contiguous to Israel. The Lebanese government lost control of that part of the country which became caught up in a vicious spiral of Palestinian anti-Israeli operations, and Israeli retaliatory and preventive actions. A sizeable portion of the largely Shī'ī population left the area and moved to the outskirts of Beirut. These developments contributed to a further disenchantment of the Shī'ī population with the Lebanese political system and to an exacerbation of social and political tensions in Beirut. Both the local population and the Palestinians in the South maintained direct links with Syria.

During the peak of the Lebanese crisis in 1975 and 1976, the Southern part of the country enjoyed a period of unexpected calm and "benign neglect." It was only in the summer of 1976 that fighting began in the South between elements of Lieut Ahmad al-Khatīb's Lebanon's Arab Army (LAA) and embryonic local Christian militias. When the violent phase of the Lebanese civil war was brought to an end by the Riyadh and Cairo Agreements, South Lebanon continued to exist in a political and military vacuum. As such, it both reflected the fragile and incomplete nature of the arrangements worked out in October 1976 and presented them with a severe challenge.

The pattern that was established in South Lebanon in October 1976 persisted through 1977. The Lebanese state, as represented by the Sarkīs Administration as well as the Arab Deterrent Force (ADF), had no authority or presence in the area. Control was divided and disputed between the local Christian militias and a variety of Palestinian and allied groups. As part of its "good fence" policy, Israel openly supported the former. The militias were entrenched in three enclaves near the Israeli border, which the Palestinians sought to erode, and the militias to defend and even to expand. The armed conflict consisted of almost daily exchanges of small weapons' and mortar fire with occasional outbursts of more serious fighting.

The positions of the main actors and parties concerned with the situation in South Lebanon could be summarized as follows.

The Lebanese government sought to reimpose its authority over the areas as part of its normalization and rehabilitation efforts, and considered dispatching Lebanese army units there as the best means of achieving that aim. This also suited the wishes of the Sarkīs Administration's Syrian patrons. Still, the Lebanese authorities recognized the complexities of the situation in the South as well as their own limited capabilities. Hence their ambivalent attitude toward the local militias and their reluctance to denounce the insubordination of the militia commanders and their co-operation with Israel.

These commanders, led by Majors Sa'd Haddād and Sāmī Shidyāq, saw and presented themselves in a dual capacity: as defenders of the local population, and as representatives of the legal authority of the Lebanese army in the South. They claimed that, as the Lebanese state was incapable of defending the legitimate interests of the local population, it fell upon themselves to do so in whatever way possible, including very close co-operation with Israel. Though almost purely

Christian, they claimed to represent the population of the South as a whole.

Syria's outlook on South Lebanon was governed by a number of contradictory considerations. Damascus sought to achieve maximum control of the South commensurate with its position in the rest of the country. Furthermore, control of South Lebanon was seen as a means of increasing its influence over the PLO and its bargaining power *vis-à-vis* Israel. Conversely, though, it could mean renewed friction with the Palestinians and potential armed conflict with Israel. On the whole, Syria's policy was aimed at increasing its influence and presence in the area and eliminating those of Israel, but in a careful and indirect fashion. This meant an effort to have Syrian-controlled Lebanese army units sent to the area as well as support for Palestinian and Muslim units fighting the local militias. However, it was constrained from launching a full-fledged campaign against these militias or their co-operation with Israel.

Israel's position was equally complex. On the one hand, it was genuinely concerned about the area's strategic and tactical importance; it needed to thwart Syrian military entrenchment there and also prevent the area from being used as a base for Palestinian anti-Israeli activity. Coupled with these interests was a commitment to Israel's local Christian allies. Israel sought to retain an open border with South Lebanon in order to preserve its influence there, but also because of the political and symbolic value it attached to the notion of the "good fence." However, other considerations pulled Israel in a different direction. The local militias in South Lebanon had a limited numerical (and therefore military) potential, and their ability to maintain their positions for any long period without direct Israeli participation became increasingly questionable. There were indeed attempts by the militias, as well as by advocates of a far-reaching Israeli commitment to Lebanon, to force the hands of, or at least to prod, the Begin government. Nor could the issue of South Lebanon be divorced from the broader questions of Israel's relationship with Syria and the future of Lebanon as a state. One Israeli school of thought argued that since Israel had already acquiesced to Syria's predominance in Lebanon, it might as well agree to Syrian control in the Southern part of the country. In that case, they explained, Syria would have the responsibility of restraining the PLO, which it would be forced to do because of Israel's ability to deter it in the context of their overall relationship. This line of argument was strongly disputed by those who felt that a Syrian presence along another Israeli border would provide it with major strategic and tactical advantages and would actually diminish Israel's ability to deter Damascus.

Like Syria, the PLO and its constituent organizations were hostile to the local militias and to the notion of an open frontier with Israel. South Lebanon was vital to them as their last autonomous area, and as the base from which a variety of anti-Israeli activities could be launched with relative ease. There was no unified or co-ordinated policy in South Lebanon, but as a rule the Palestinian organizations sought: (a) to combat the local militias; (b) to launch occasional operations against Israel; (c) to conduct both activities with sufficient circumspection so as not to provoke Israel to become massively involved in South Lebanon; and (d) to co-operate with Syria while avoiding Syrian control. Following President Sādāt's visit to Jerusalem and the opening of direct Egyptian-Israeli negotiations, Syrian-Palestinian co-ordination in South Lebanon improved as part of a broader mending of fences.

Among the political forces in Lebanon, the National Movement took a very hostile stand toward the local militias in the South. But it had no military muscle in that area and had to rely on the Palestinians in order to exert military pressure on the militias. The Lebanese Front's position was ambiguous. The militias in the

South were vaguely associated with the major militias in the North and pursued a similar political line. But the militias in the North were hard-pressed for human resources, which they preferred to direct to areas deemed more vital—Beirut and the North. Several Maronite leaders, while not averse to co-operation with Israel as such, chose to avoid the political embarrassment caused by overt and intimate co-operation between Israel and the local militias in the South.

The US viewed the problem of South Lebanon in the context of its more diverse concerns in the Middle East. American policy sought to strengthen President Ilyās Sarkīs and accepted Syrian hegemony in Lebanon. It therefore supported the dispatch of Lebanese army units to the South, and was not at all opposed to an increased Syrian role there. This attitude, together with a willingness to deal with and even formalize the role of the PLO in South Lebanon, resulted in American-Israeli differences which extended to such issues as the interpretation of the Shtūrā Agreement. But Washington was also sympathetic to Israel's strategic and security concerns along the Lebanese border. It did not protest against Israel's support of the local militias, which seemed to reduce the danger of armed conflict in the area, so long as that replaced an actual Israeli presence across the border. However, in September 1977, when Israeli troops became involved in the fighting north of the border in order to save the militias from defeat by superior forces, the US exercised pressure on the Israeli government to bring its involvement to an end.

DEVELOPMENTS IN 1978

The trend of events in South Lebanon during the first few weeks of 1978 seemed by and large to continue the patterns of 1977. The one important change was growing Syrian-Palestinian co-operation, which derived from common opposition to the Egyptian-Israeli negotiations and was reinforced by growing tensions between Syria and the Lebanese Front. This was manifested by the participation of al-Sā'iqa, the Syrian controlled Palestinian organization, in the Palestinian attack on the village of Mārūn al-Ra's on 2 March. The local militias, which had held the village for some months, lost it by 3 March.

The repercussions of the capture of Mārūn al-Ra's seemed to extend beyond the change it brought about in the local military balance. This point was made by Major Haddād, who complained to Israeli reporters that the Israeli government had failed to live up to its statements and to prevent "foreign" (meaning Syrian or Syrian-controlled) troops from operating south of the "red line." A similar position was taken by Mr A. Lin, an activist Likud MK, in a parliamentary question which he presented on 8 March.[1] While Israel reiterated its commitment to the Lebanese Christians and reinforced its military presence and reconnaissance activity along the Lebanese border, the Israeli government indicated that it had no intention of being drawn into a direct military involvement in South Lebanon. Thus, Israel's Deputy-Premier, Yigael Yadin, stated in the Knesset that "Israel will help them [the Christian militias] to resist the barbarous attacks held against them. Still, the government's policy is to maintain calm along our northern border."

THE COAST HIGHWAY ATTACK AND ISRAEL'S LĪTĀNĪ OPERATION

The situation in South Lebanon was radically altered in the second week of March 1978 following the massacre of Israeli bus passengers and other civilians by a Palestinian squad along the Haifa-Tel Aviv highway on 11 March. (For details see essay entitled "Armed Operations; Situation along the Borders," in the section on the Arab-Israeli Conflict.) The attackers, who arrived by boat from Lebanon, came from Damūr, south of Beirut, which had been converted into a Palestinian base. The Israelis deliberated three days (11–14 March) on how to respond to this attack.

The Lītānī Operation turned out to be a massive military offensive which resulted in Israel occupying the whole area south of the Lītānī River, with the exception of the Tyre area. The size of the operation, and the casualties and dislocation that it caused, generated sharp international criticism. Israel's presence in Lebanon lasted three months, the phased withdrawal of Israeli forces being completed only on 13 June. They were replaced by units of UNIFIL, the peacekeeping force created by Security Council Resolutions 425 and 426, passed on 19 March (see below).

The concept of the Lītānī Operation was determined by a complex series of pressures and considerations that the Begin government had to take into account:

(1) The government felt that the severity and central location of the massacre called for a massive retaliation.

(2) Rather than retaliating for the sake of retaliating, it was thought better to solve or at least to alleviate Israel's "problem of South Lebanon" by eliminating the PLO's presence and infrastructure in the area.

(3) It sought to minimize the number of Israeli casualties. The risk of a high casualty rate was considerable due to the nature of the terrain and the complete lack of surprise.

(4) Several political and diplomatic constraints had to be taken into account. The Israeli-Egyptian negotiations were foundering, and Prime Minister Begin was on the eve of a visit to Washington as part of the tripartite American-Egyptian-Israeli negotiations. Thus the impact of a sizeable Israeli operation in Lebanon on the positions of Washington and Cairo had to be weighed carefully. Equally important were the need to prevent a military conflict with Syria and to consider the repercussions of a massive Israeli incursion into South Lebanon on the Lebanese crisis itself.

(5) The Begin government also faced considerable domestic difficulties. These ranged from differences within the Cabinet over its policy in the negotiations with Egypt and the US, to criticisms about the authorities' failure to prevent the massacre in the first place.

Hoping to maximize the projected gains and minimize the risks of its response, the Israeli government finally decided on a major operation. A very large number of troops entered Lebanon with orders to capture a six-mile wide strip along the whole length of the Lebanese-Israeli border. The troops were ordered to proceed cautiously and to cleanse the area of its PLO presence. At the same time, air and naval raids were carried out against Palestinian bases deeper inside Lebanon.

Political and diplomatic activity began almost immediately. The US indicated that it did not oppose the action as such, but insisted on a speedy Israeli withdrawal. Israel stated repeatedly that it intended to withdraw to the international border, but insisted that this be preceded by a solution of the "problem of the South" acceptable to it. Prime Minister Begin expected that the lines of such a settlement would be discussed during his forthcoming visit to Washington, but for reasons that had to do with its general ME policy as well as with its outlook on the Lebanese crisis, Washington refused to wait for such discussions, when it would appear that the future of South Lebanon was being decided between Carter and Begin. Instead, the US pushed for a speedy Security Council resolution dealing specifically with South Lebanon. As Washington saw it, a solution depended first and foremost on a UN peacekeeping force being sent to the area.

This development played an important role in expanding the scope of the Lītānī Operation. As it turned out, the original concept of a six-mile wide *cordon sanitaire* was not viable. Palestinians entrenched in villages north of that line continued to engage the Israeli forces and occasionally launched Katyusha rockets at Israeli

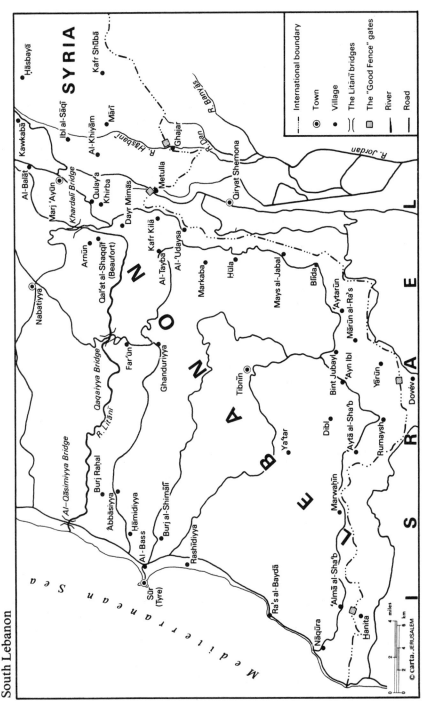

South Lebanon

towns and villages in Galilee. Some villages north of the six-mile line hoisted white flags and seemed to expect an Israeli takeover. But most important was the expected arrival of a UN force.[2] If such a force were to serve as a buffer between the Israelis on the one side, and the Syrians and Palestinians in South Lebanon on the other, then Israel wanted the buffer zone to be broader than six miles. It was therefore decided to seize the whole of South Lebanon up to the Līṭānī River so that the UN force would be stationed on that line. This was achieved within the next few days, the only exception being the town of Tyre and its coastal environs. Since this was a heavily populated area, a military operation there would have been much too costly, both in political terms and in the number of possible casualties.

RESOLUTION 425 AND THE FORMATION OF UNIFIL

It was against this background that the Security Council passed Resolution 425 on 19 March:

The Security Council: taking note of the letters of the permanent representative of Lebanon and the permanent representative of Israel, having heard the statements of permanent representatives of Lebanon and Israel; gravely concerned at the deterioration of the situation in the Middle East, and its consequences to the maintenance of international peace; convinced that the present situation impedes the achievement of a just peace in the Middle East:

1. **Calls** for strict respect for the territorial integrity, sovereignty and political independence of Lebanon within its territorially recognized boundaries;

2. **Calls** upon Israel immediately to cease its military action against Lebanese territorial integrity and withdraw forthwith its forces from all Lebanese territory;

3. **Decides**, in the light of the request of the government of Lebanon, to establish immediately under its authority a United Nations interim force for southern Lebanon for the purpose of confirming the withdrawal of Israeli forces, restoring international peace and security and assisting the government of Lebanon in ensuring the return of its effective authority in the area, the force to be composed of personnel drawn from state members of the United Nations;

4. **Requests** the Secretary-General to report to the Council within 24 hours on the implementation of this resolution.

Two days after the decision was taken to establish UNIFIL, Israel announced a unilateral ceasefire (unilateral so as to avoid the need to deal with the PLO). A Ghanaian General, Emmanuel Erskine, was appointed commander of UNIFIL and, together with other UN officials, set about recruiting neutral troops. The stationing of UN troops already available in the area began on 22 March, and fresh units began to arrive the following day. During the last week of March, 1,000 troops arrived from Iran, France, Sweden and Norway. The arrival of the Iranian and French troops had particularly interesting political overtones. As a Shī‘ī state with regional ambitions, Iran might have been expected to try to use the opportunity to cultivate a political clientele among the Shī‘īs in South Lebanon. It was well known, for instance, that the Shah's government was intensely opposed to the leadership of Imām Mūsā al-Sadr. In the event, though, this did not happen. For its part, France was the former mandatory power in Lebanon, whose troops had been forced to evacuate the area some 30 years earlier. Paris was clearly interested in playing a major role in the Lebanese crisis and viewed the French contingent in UNIFIL as an instrument of that policy. An élite French unit, assigned the difficult task of policing the area of Tyre, soon clashed with Palestinian units there—a conflict which should be seen against a broader political background.

POLITICAL CONSEQUENCES OF OPERATION LĪTĀNĪ

The scale and scope of the Lītānī Operation had important political repercussions—but they were not the ones anticipated in the second week of March. The precautions taken by the planners served to limit the impact of the operation on Israel's relations with the US, Egypt and Syria, as well as on the Lebanese crisis.

As already mentioned, Washington's apprehensions were allayed once it became clear that Israel intended to evacuate South Lebanon and to accept UNIFIL as a buffer between itself and the Palestinians. But in the tense atmosphere produced by the difficult relations between the Carter and Begin Administrations, the Lītānī operation served as yet another source of irritation and friction. On its side, the Israeli Cabinet felt it had been confronted with a *fait accompli* in the Security Council. It was also incensed by the fact that the Carter Administration had chosen to embarrass it and add to its political difficulties by making public a disagreement over the use of concussion bombs in the Tyre area.[3]

Egypt, as it turned out, encountered no serious political problems as a result of the Lītānī Operation. Syria did try to castigate Sādāt by describing the Israeli action as part of a broader strategy of plot and collusion and as designed, among other things, to salvage President Sādāt from his state of isolation in the Arab world.[4] But as long as it felt reassured that Israel was not going to remain in South Lebanon, Egypt was not embarrassed by such insinuations. Thus it did not feel the need to go beyond publishing a Foreign Ministry statement deploring the Israeli action.

The pressure on Syria was heavier. As the foremost military power in Lebanon and as the patron of the Palestinians, Syria could have been expected to intervene on their behalf. Indeed, the Iraqi news agency lost no time in underscoring Syria's failure to do so.[5] Yet Israel had clearly indicated to Syria that it sought to avoid an armed conflict, and had drawn its military plans accordingly. The Asad regime, therefore, formulated a policy which contained the following elements:

(1) Except for some anti-aircraft fire, the Syrian forces in Lebanon took no part in the fighting.

(2) An elaborate explanation was developed and expounded by President Asad and other Syrian spokesmen to account for this conduct. They argued that the Lītānī Operation was in fact a trap laid out for Syria which it had the sense not to walk into. Instead, Syria preferred to support the Palestinians with anti-aircraft artillery, and by allowing free passage through Syrian territory and airspace to all those who wanted to fight on the side of the Palestinians.[6]

(3) Indeed, Syria allowed 600 Iraqi soldiers to cross its territory into South Lebanon.

(4) It also sought to improve its position in South Lebanon by suggesting that Syrian troops, under the banner of the ADF, be given a mandate to police the whole area of Lebanon (including the South, from which they had been barred).[7]

(5) When this failed to materialize, Syria co-operated with UNIFIL and facilitated the forces' installation along the Lītānī. The motive for this co-operation was its desire to expedite Israel's evacuation of the area.

Syria's attitude had a decisive impact on the Palestinians. The PLO was critical of the idea of a UN force stationed along the Lītānī and the cordoning off of an area in which it had been allowed to operate according to the Cairo Agreement of 1969. But this drawback could be offset by a number of actual and potential advantages:

(1) Experience had shown that UN forces and observers could be circumvented with relative ease.

(2) In any case, UNIFIL could also be seen as a buffer limiting Israel's capability to retaliate against Palestinian operations in the future, and it might possibly be another element hostile to the Christian militias.

(3) By accepting the ceasefire and by co-operating with UNIFIL's command and other UN officials, the PLO stood to gain further international recognition and possibly goodwill as well.

Although the more radical elements within the PLO disputed the importance of these considerations, Syria's decision to co-operate with UNIFIL reinforced Yāsir 'Arafāt's position. Failure to co-operate would not just have meant a prolonged Israeli stay, but also friction with Syria. Still, the implementation of the decision did not proceed smoothly. In the confused circumstances of South Lebanon at the end of March, radical Palestinians had ample opportunity to display their opposition, the result being a series of clashes with various UNIFIL units. The clashes with the French paratroopers in Tyre—which led to the wounding of their commander, Colonel Salvan—were particularly severe.

It was characteristic of the situation that the Lebanese government and the chief political forces in the country had no impact on the course of events in the South. President Sarkīs, Prime Minister Salīm al-Ḥuss and spokesmen for both the Lebanese Front and the National Movement published statements which did no more than reflect their well-known positions.

Of greater political significance was the criticism which the Israeli government began to encounter abroad and at home. The pattern was familiar. International public opinion—as represented by the major news media—displayed sympathy to Israel in the wake of the 11 March massacre. However, this sympathy was soon dissipated by the size of Operation Lītānī; as it became known that the operation resulted in a massive flight of civilians and in numerous civilian casualties, reporters and commentators alike became critical of Israel and especially of the Begin government.

This trend had diverse effects on the Israeli domestic scene. As in the past, many Israelis tended to rally in support of the government precisely because of what they perceived as biased external criticism. Other Israelis, though, were reinforced in their opposition to the government and its policies. Criticism was directed at the size of the operation and the very concepts which underlay its planning. The debate soon came to focus on the actual effectiveness of the operation. This hinged to a great extent on the efficiency of UNIFIL which thus became an issue in the domestic Israeli scene.[8] In the event, the resolve displayed by the Force's command and its constituent units served to help the Israeli Cabinet and military authorities by underscoring the success of their strategy, at least in the short run.

PRELUDE TO ISRAEL'S WITHDRAWAL

UNIFIL's deployment along the Lītānī during the last days of March was followed by a ten-week transitional period, which ended with the completion of Israel's withdrawal from South Lebanon on 13 June. This was an eventful and important period. The parties involved in the affairs of South Lebanon realized that the facts and patterns established at that time were likely to have an important impact on the area's future. At the same time, their conduct was moderated by an awareness of the complexity and frailty of the arrangements worked out as a result of the Lītānī Operation.

From the beginning, Israel wanted a strong and effective UNIFIL which would actually seal off South Lebanon and prevent individual members or units of the PLO from returning to the area it was about to evacuate. Such a return would eliminate the achievements of the Līṭānī Operation, present Israel with a renewed challenge in the future, and prove particularly embarrassing for the government. The government set a date for the first phase of Israeli withdrawal, but indicated that UNIFIL's performance—particularly its effectiveness in preventing armed Palestinians from returning to the evacuated areas—would determine its willingness to proceed with the withdrawal plans.[9] In order to underline the seriousness of its intentions, the Israeli government minimized the extent of the first phase of the IDF's withdrawal from South Lebanon. This incensed the Carter Administration, which lost no time in making its displeasure public.

Although UNIFIL at first succeeded in doing what Israel had hoped for, several factors began to militate against its ability to police South Lebanon effectively. One was an obvious reluctance to become actively engaged against determined Palestinians and to suffer casualties as a result. Several countries whose troops participated in UNIFIL indicated that they intended to recall their soldiers if serious incidents continued. These were caused in part by persisting frictions within the PLO. While Yāsir 'Arafāt supported the Syrian line of co-operating with UNIFIL—at least until the completion of Israel's withdrawal—his policy was challenged by radical elements, some from within the ranks of his own organization.[10] It was also difficult to expect the UN Secretariat and some of the countries participating in UNIFIL (like France) to continue to support a policy which was responsive to Israel's demands and in conflict with those of the PLO.

Another difficulty concerned the local militias in South Lebanon. UNIFIL's commanders tended to interpret their mandate as not just to prevent "armed persons" from entering the area, but also to disarm those already in it. This notion was opposed by both Israel and the militias. The militia commanders rejected the very principle that they—as inhabitants of the area—should be put on the same footing as the Palestinians, who were extraneous to it. Furthermore, based on their experience with UN observers in South Lebanon, they suspected the world organization and refused to trust it with their future.[11] In order to bolster their political standing, the militias had in March already begun an attempt to broaden their basis of support and appeal. Accordingly, an effort was made to recruit Shī'īs and to turn the militias into "all Southern" groups. Despite some local and temporary successes, this interesting attempt failed due to two major reasons: first, because of traditional animosities between Shī'īs and Maronites in the South; and second, because of Shī'ī reluctance to become associated with an Israeli-linked group precisely on the eve of Israel's withdrawal from the area.[12]

Israel, in turn, faced a dilemma. It wanted to see a determined and effective UNIFIL, but could hardly afford to support it against the militias, to whom it remained strongly committed. In any case, there seemed to be no point in relinquishing its support for the militias before UNIFIL's effectiveness had been proven. Israel therefore resisted American and Egyptian pressures to disarm the militias,[13] and indicated on a number of occasions that it would scrutinize UNIFIL's conduct before making a final decision and completing its withdrawal from the area.

Developments in April and May did not, in fact, persuade the Israeli government that UNIFIL was likely to live up to its expectations and prevent the return of the PLO to the areas it had evacuated. Yet other considerations had to be taken into account, particularly the need to respond to American and Egyptian demands and expectations that Israel should complete its withdrawal from Lebanese territory. In order to resolve these difficulties, the Israeli government decided on a compromise

Entry into and withdrawal from South Lebanon by the Israel Defence Forces

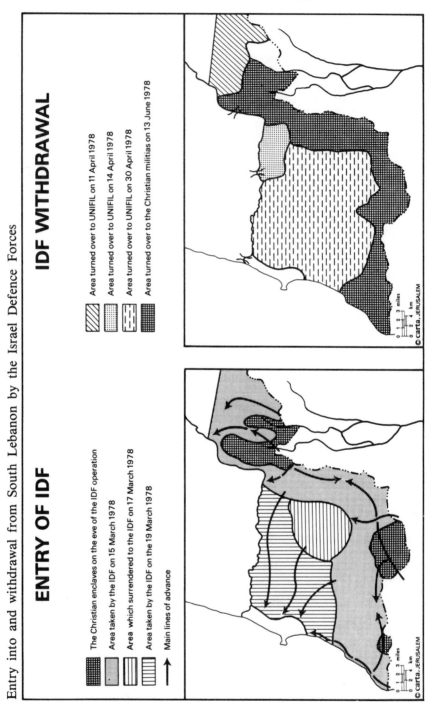

ENTRY OF IDF

The Christian enclaves on the eve of the IDF operation

Area taken by the IDF on 15 March 1978

Area which surrendered to the IDF on 17 March 1978

Area taken by the IDF on the 19 March 1978

Main lines of advance

© Carta, JERUSALEM

IDF WITHDRAWAL

Area turned over to UNIFIL on 11 April 1978

Area turned over to UNIFIL on 14 April 1978

Area turned over to UNIFIL on 30 April 1978

Area turned over to the Christian militias on 13 June 1978

© Carta, JERUSALEM

solution. A date for final withdrawal was set (13 June), but the area adjacent to the Israeli border was not to be handed over to UNIFIL but rather to the local militias. During the weeks preceding its final withdrawal from Lebanon, the Israeli army resupplied and reinforced the militias, preparing them to hold on—not just to their former enclaves—but to a five-mile deep security belt along the Israeli-Lebanese border. [14] This idea bore a striking resemblance to the original concept of Operation Lītānī as envisaged in mid-March, the essential difference being that security in the area was to be guaranteed by proxy.

Surprisingly, this formula received support from two other quarters. One was President Sarkīs' Administration which, having proved incapable of dispatching its own military forces to the area, chose to recognize Majors Haddād and Shidyāq as its representatives in the South. This was a way of reasserting the Lebanese state's authority over the area, but also a symptom of continued estrangement from Syria. [15] Sarkīs' endorsement also made it easier for the US to extend its support to the arrangement thus worked out for the border area. [16] While UNIFIL's command resented the arrangement, it felt compelled to comply and even adopt it formally by designating a "Christian area" on an official map. [17]

SOUTH LEBANON IN THE SECOND HALF OF 1978

Developments in South Lebanon in the latter part of 1978 were shaped by the patterns established on the eve of Israel's withdrawal, as well as by changes during the summer which affected the broader Lebanese crisis.

During the first few weeks following the Israeli withdrawal, UNIFIL gradually established itself as yet another of the forces involved in the struggle to shape the fate of South Lebanon. The hostility between the Force's command and the local militias soon became manifest, and several incidents served to exacerbate relations. UNIFIL and the UN Secretariat viewed the militias as an obstructionist element and as simply a tool of Israeli policies. The militias had a completely different view of the situation: they regarded UNIFIL as a weak and irresolute force serving the purposes of Syria and the PLO. In fact, while UNIFIL proved quite effective in helping to prevent Palestinian operations against Israel from South Lebanon, it had indicated by mid-June that it did not intend to engage in fighting in order to keep all Palestinians out of the area. This touched off an acrimonious debate between the Israeli government and the UN Secretariat which, however, did nothing to change the situation. At the end of June, the following situation prevailed in South Lebanon: UNIFIL, the local militias and a growing number of Palestinians constituted the armed forces directly involved in a struggle for control of all or parts of Lebanon south of the Lītānī; Syria, Israel and the Lebanese government and political forces were involved in an indirect fashion, with the US playing the role of go-between and "crisis manager."

The Syrians made one attempt to change this pattern in late July and early August when they prevailed upon the Sarkīs Administration to dispatch a Lebanese army unit to Tibnīn in South Lebanon. The attempt and its timing were probably influenced by Syria's transition to a more forceful and dynamic policy in Lebanon as manifested by military offensives in the North and in Beirut. But Syria's position in the South was far more complex. The notion of dispatching a Lebanese army unit in order to demonstrate the state's sovereignty and to police a problematic area could hardly be resisted as such. Indeed, it was supported by UNIFIL on precisely those grounds. But Israel and the local militias took an entirely different view of the matter. They argued that the regiment chosen for the task was not a proper Lebanese army unit at all, but one composed of soldiers of "The Vanguards of Lebanon's Army"—a force recruited and trained by the Syrians in the eastern part of Lebanon, which they administered directly. Furthermore, they argued that rather than send the force by a simple route, another through Marj'ayūn and the heart of the Christian enclaves was chosen. Israel and the militias saw this as a clear attempt to challenge the militias as well as the very concepts underlying the "new order" prevailing in the South. As a result, the militias resisted the Lebanese force, which chose to stop rather than fight its way to Tibnīn. At this point it was shelled by Palestinian units—possibly at the instigation of the Syrian authorities who wanted it to advance. Under these counter-pressures, the Lebanese force dissolved and its mission ended in failure.[18]

This episode proved an interesting and important reversal of trends in the inter-related but distinct Lebanese and South Lebanese conflicts. As the failure of the attempt to deploy a Syrian-inspired Lebanese army unit in Tibnīn indicated, a balance of forces had been established in South Lebanon in the aftermath of the Israeli withdrawal and any attempt to upset this balance by one party to the conflict could be thwarted by another. A similar situation had existed during 1977 in the rest of Lebanon following the Cairo and Riyadh Agreements of October 1976. During that period, because of the state of flux in the South, it was the one part of the country where armed conflict continued, while the broader Lebanese conflict was primarily conducted through political channels. But by the summer of 1978, Syria and the Lebanese militias were locked in a military conflict in Beirut and in the North, which culminated in the fierce fighting of September and early October.

This fighting served to overshadow events in the South and to relegate it again to the role of a secondary theatre; but it also had more serious repercussions. For one thing, events in the South continued to be an issue in Lebanon's national politics. Syria and other rivals of the Christian militias used the overt relationship between the local militias and Israel as a convenient pretext for attacking all Christian militias. Also, the shift in the balance which took place in Lebanon in Syria's favour reflected on the situation in the country as a whole. Part of the Phalangist leadership (in contradistinction to the Chamounists and another Phalangist faction) was determined to maintain relations with Syria at almost any price because of the lack of a better alternative. This entailed a change of attitude toward Israel as well as toward the local militias, which occurred in October. Exploiting this change, Syria pressured the Sarkīs Administration to harden its attitude toward the local militia commanders and to issue warrants for their arrest.

As 1978 drew to a close, the "problem of the South" remained in a state of flux, thus reflecting the uncertain trend of developments in the broader issues directly affecting it: the Lebanese crisis, the Arab-Israeli conflict and inter-Arab relations. The limited impact of the events of 1978 on the basic patterns of this problem was demonstrated by the brief renewal of the cycle of violence in the latter part of December when, in retribution for a series of sabotage activities, Israel acted against Palestinian bases near Tyre. The PLO—UNIFIL notwithstanding—responded by launching missiles from South Lebanon against Israeli towns in Galilee.

Itamar Rabinovich

NOTES
1. *Ha'aretz,* Tel Aviv; 7 March; *Ma'ariv,* Tel Aviv, 9 March; *Jerusalem Post (JP),* 10 March 1978.
2. See Zeev Schiff's illuminating commentary in *Ha'aretz,* 31 March 1978, and Chief of Staff Gur's statement quoted in the *Washington Post (WP),* 23 March 1978.
3. See for instance *The New York Times,* 16 March; and *WP,* 18 March 1978.

4. See in particular Foreign Minister Khaddām's statement of 17 March, monitored by British Broadcasting Corporation, Summary of World Broadcasts, the ME and North Africa (BBC), 20 March 1978. This explained that the operation was "part of a general design engineered for the area."
5. Quoted by the BBC, 16 March 1978.
6. President Asad's speech of 19 March, monitored by Daily Report, Middle East and North Africa (DR), 22 March; and *Tishrīn*, Damascus; 27 March 1978.
7. Asad's interview with A. de Borchgrave, *International Herald Tribune*, Paris; 20 March 1978.
8. See Schiff's article mentioned above; Israel's state television interview with Gur on 24 March—DR, 27 March; and *WP*, 22 March 1978.
9. *Daily Telegraph*, London; 12 April; *JP*, 20 April 1978.
10. Statement by Palestinian "rejectionists," quoted by the Iraqi News Agency, 10 April; and *Ma'ariv*, 23 April 1978.
11. *Ha'aretz*, 12 April 1978.
12. *Ma'ariv* and *JP*, 28 March 1978.
13. See the account of Defence Minister Weizman's meeting with Ambassador Lewis in *al-Hamishmar*, Tel Aviv; 11 April—DR, 12 April 1978.
14. *The Times*, London; 13 June 1978.
15. See chapter on Lebanon.
16. *Ma'ariv*, 13 June 1978.
17. *Ibid*, 14 June; *Le Monde*, 18 June 1978.
18. *Ha'aretz*, 6 August 1977. Also see chapter on Lebanon.

Armed Operations; Situation Along the Borders

Except for the Israeli invasion of Lebanon (described above), the incidence of armed clashes along Israel's borders—both the 1967 ceasefire boundaries and the 1974 and 1975 disengagement lines—remained low in 1977–78, as had generally been the case since 1974 (see *MECS 1976–77*, pp. 120–22). By contrast, there was a considerable increase in the number of Palestinian fidā'ī operations in Israel and the West Bank (though not in the Gaza Strip) as compared with 1976–77.

FIDĀ'Ī ACTIVITY

PLO operations against Israeli targets were at a low in 1976. Their increase, beginning in mid-1977,[1] was partly a reassertion of the PLO's fundamental policy of "escalating the armed struggle," and partly attributable to a set of circumstances specific to the period under review:

(1) Morale had been lowered by the PLO's military defeat in the Lebanese civil war and the political discomfiture caused by Sādāt's initiative. By stepping up armed operations, the PLO sought to restore morale among the rank and file and to demonstrate that it was still a factor to be reckoned with.

(2) The improvement of relations with Syria, which had begun gradually after the end of the civil war in October 1976, gathered momentum after Sādāt's initiative. No longer having to maintain a defensive deployment to meet a possible renewal of Syrian military pressure, PLO units reverted to training and carrying out operations against Israeli targets.

(3) Increased aid to the PLO from Arab and non-Arab opponents of Sādāt's new policy accelerated the PLO's recovery and encouraged it to expand operations.

(4) Greater and partially successful efforts were made to recruit members and organize cells in the West Bank and the Gaza Strip, as well as to smuggle in weapons and explosives.

In fact, the number of incidents during the first eight months of 1978 was higher than the total for the whole of 1977 (see Table 1). Yet it still fell far short of the most intensive level of fidā'ī activity between 1968 and 1970,[2] or even of the period immediately preceding the Lebanese civil war (in 1974 and 1975). The fidā'ī effort was directed mainly at targets in territories under Israeli control, i.e. the West Bank, the Gaza Strip and Israel proper. Special efforts were made to increase the number of incidents in Jerusalem.

Israeli and fidā'ī versions of the same incident often differed considerably (see Table 3), with fidā'ī sources as a rule reporting much higher Israeli casualty figures and greater damage. In addition, PLO sources often claimed responsibility for deaths, injuries or damage which according to Israeli spokesmen resulted from accidents or criminal acts. For example, when Defence Minister Ezer Weizman was injured in a car accident near Tel Aviv on 16 November 1977, a fidā'ī report claimed that his car had been attacked near the Lebanese border.[3]

PLO sources frequently issued accounts of fidā'ī operations which were not reported at all by Israeli sources or by foreign correspondents working in Israel. Occasionally, minor incidents were not made public in Israel, or reference to them was censored when they occurred. Some were disclosed later, usually in connection with security investigations or when suspects were arrested or brought to trial. However, the Israeli authorities were not known to have concealed civilian casualty figures or delayed their publication through censorship. Neither was there any record of casualties not originally published by Israeli sources being reported by foreign correspondents under a non-Israeli dateline. PLO reports of incidents involving casualties for which there was no confirmation from Israeli sources must therefore be assumed to fall into one of the following categories:

(1) Reports of operations which in actual fact were foiled but which the PLO described as having been successful. For instance, when explosives were indeed laid, but were discovered and rendered harmless.

(2) Reports issued by PLO spokesmen on the strength of operational instructions which in the event were not carried out.

(3) Reports with no basis in fact, issued for the purpose of raising morale, impressing Arab opinion or scoring in the competition between individual organizations in the PLO.

Examples of all three are included in Tables 3 and 4.

FIDĀ'Ī ACTIVITY IN THE WEST BANK, GAZA AND ISRAEL

In the West Bank and the Gaza Strip, fidā'ī attacks were mainly directed against Military Government installations, Israeli institutions and business firms, Israeli security forces and Israeli and other non-Arab civilians. (For fidā'ī activity against Arab civilians for the purpose of political intimidation, see essay on the West Bank and the Gaza Strip.) In Israel, the purpose was mainly to cause the maximum number of casualties and the greatest possible physical damage. Most fidā'ī operations involved placing explosive charges, especially in crowded places: markets, bus stations, buses and similar locations (see Tables 1 and 2). In more than half the cases, charges were discovered and disarmed, but in some instances heavy casualties resulted.

Most of the incidents in Israel occurred in Jerusalem, for two apparent reasons. First, as the focus of tourism and pilgrimage, incidents in Israel's capital are assured of maximum publicity. Second, the city's large Arab population and its proximity to West Bank population centres facilitate fidā'ī activity. (For the major incidents in Israel, see Table 3.)

The majority of operations described above were carried out by fidā'ī cells in the area of operation, acting on instructions from headquarters in Beirut, Damascus or Baghdad, and using arms and explosives smuggled in from abroad. But a number of operations were carried out directly from bases in Lebanon and other Arab countries, by means of border crossings or of incursions by sea. It was a sea-borne detachment of fidā'iyyūn which was responsible for the most serious incident in Israel since the early 1950s. On the afternoon of 11 March 1978, a group belonging to al-Fath landed near Ma'agan Mikha'el and proceeded on foot to the Haifa-Tel Aviv highway (a distance of 2.5 km) which they reached at a point c. 55 km north of Tel Aviv. There they hijacked a bus, made its passengers hostages and started driving south. On the way, they attacked and stopped another bus and forced its passengers to board theirs. They also fired at passing cars, causing a number of casualties. Police pursued the bus and attempted to stop it at several points *en route*, but succeeded in doing so only at a road block c. 10 km north of Tel Aviv. After an engagement that lasted c. 15 minutes, explosives carried by the fidā'iyyūn blew up in the bus, causing additional casualties. Altogether, 32 Israelis were killed and 82 wounded. Of the 13 fidā'iyyūn in the operation, two were wounded and captured,

199

and nine were killed; two had drowned before reaching the shore.

A curfew was imposed on the entire area because the security forces did not know how many fidā'iyyūn were involved in the operation and could not immediately establish the number of dead bodies in the bus. Large army and police forces carried out extensive searches until the following afternoon when it was finally established that all the fidā'iyyūn were accounted for. Interrogation of the surviving fidā'iyyūn revealed that they had been instructed to attack a major public building in Tel Aviv, but instead of landing close to that city, their boat had drifted north.

Several committees of inquiry, which were set up after the incident, recommended a reorganization of coastal defences and of anti-fidā'ī naval activity. In the following months, a number of reports (mainly from Arab sources), spoke of Israeli patrol boats stopping and searching ships off the Lebanese coast. On 26 August, an Israeli patrol vessel caught a boat carrying two fidā'iyyūn near Ra's al-Nāqūra (Rosh Haniqrah), the point where the Israeli-Lebanese border reaches the sea.

On 30 September, a boat heading for Eilat and carrying *Katyusha* rockets and explosives was intercepted and destroyed by an Israeli naval unit in the Gulf of 'Aqaba, off Dhahab (Di Zahav). Its crew of seven, all members of al-Fatḥ, were captured. Their instructions had been to fire the *Katyusha*s at port installations in Eilat and then to let the boat run aground and blow up in the Eilat resort hotel area, which was expected to be unusually crowded on the eve of the Jewish New Year (falling on 2 October in 1978). The fidā'iyyūn had intended to escape to 'Aqaba in a rubber dinghy. PLO sources claimed that the boat had got through to Eilat and that the attack had been carried out as planned.[4]

OPERATIONS ABROAD

Outside the Middle East, fidā'iyyūn carried out only two operations against Israeli targets. On 20 May 1978, three fidā'iyyūn tried to attack El Al passengers at Orly airport in Paris, but were stopped by Israeli and French security guards. All three fidā'iyyūn and a French policeman were killed and three bystanders wounded. On 21 August, fidā'iyyūn attacked an El Al crew at the entrance to their hotel in London. A stewardess was killed and another wounded; eight other people were injured. One of the fidā'iyyūn was killed as he tried to throw a hand grenade and the other was caught by police.

The sporadic nature of operations against Israeli targets abroad was mainly due to policy decisions on the part of most constituent organizations of the PLO who had come to regard activities outside the ME as politically counter-productive. A contributory reason was that the struggle between al-Fatḥ and the group of Abū Nidāl claimed the attention of their operatives abroad (see essay on the PLO).

ISRAELI COUNTER OPERATIONS

Counter-fidā'ī activities by the Israeli security forces were mainly of a defensive or preventive nature. The IDF concentrated on hindering incursions across the border lines or from the sea, and the police and security service on uncovering fidā'ī cells in the West Bank and the Gaza Strip. Despite a noticeable improvement in the organization of fidā'ī cells and stricter observance of the rules of clandestine operations, many cells were uncovered relatively quickly, a considerable number while still in early preparatory stages of activity. In fact, more cells were uncovered during the period under review than in the preceding year: 78 with an aggregate membership of c. 700 as compared with 57 with c. 400 members (see Table 5).

The IDF attacked fidā'iyyūn targets and concentrations in Lebanon on five occasions. While these attacks were usually carried out in the wake of specific fidā'ī operations, their timing was also influenced by the general situation in the area, especially by developments in Lebanon (see chapter on Lebanon). The operations were as follows. (1) On 9 November 1977, Israeli aircraft attacked fidā'ī targets in Lebanon following *Katyusha* attacks on Nahariya. (2) On 11 November, Israeli aircraft attacked fidā'ī targets (for both operations, see below). (3) On 15 March 1978, following the fidā'ī attack on the Haifa-Tel Aviv highway, the IDF launched a major operation in South Lebanon—"Operation Lītānī." (4) On 9 June, an IDF unit destroyed a naval base of al-Fatḥ at Dahr al-Burj. (5) On 21 August, following the attack on the El Al crew in London, IDF aircraft attacked two fidā'ī bases, at Damūr and at Burj al-Barājina.

THE SITUATION ON THE BORDERS
THE EGYPTIAN-ISRAELI DISENGAGEMENT LINES
This frontier continued to be tranquil. On 21 October 1977, the mandate of the UN Emergency Force was extended for another year by the Security Council with virtually no discussion.[5] In October 1977, however, both armies were put on alert because of tension in connection with the political impasse following the US-Israeli working paper (see *MECS 1976–77,* pp. 141–42). Another contributory reason was the mutual uneasiness created by both armies holding major military exercises simultaneously. As a result, ways and means were devised and agreed upon during and after Sādāt's visit to Jerusalem to preclude either side misinterpreting the other's military moves.

Israel continued to make occasional public complaints of excessive numbers of Egyptian forces being deployed in the Sinai limited forces zone,[6] while Egypt periodically continued to raise the controversial issue of Israel's oil prospecting and exploitation in the Gulf of Suez area.[7] However, both sides and the US sought to play down these issues so as not to make the complex process of the Egyptian-Israeli negotiations even more difficult.

THE ISRAELI-SYRIAN DISENGAGEMENT LINES
Complete calm continued along this frontier—despite reports in December 1977 that, in response to Sādāt's initiative, Syria had decided to permit fidā'ī activity from its territory (see essay on Inter-Arab Relations). The mandate of the UN Disengagement Observation Force was extended, almost as a matter of course, on 30 November 1977 and again on 31 May 1978.[8] The only exception to the general tranquillity was an incident on 1 April 1978 reported by Syria (but denied by Israel) of an explosion of a booby-trapped "nuclear listening device," placed by Israel to tap "the coaxial cable connecting Damascus with Amman." The Syrian report claimed that 11 people had been killed, including high-ranking Syrian officers.[9]

THE ISRAELI-JORDANIAN CEASEFIRE LINE
The only incident reported along this line took place on the night of 11–12 June 1978 when four fidā'iyyūn entered the settlement of Meḥola in the central sector of the Jordan Valley. They were detected by guards who opened fire; one was killed, but the others managed to escape.[10]

Traffic over the "open bridges" across the Jordan River continued (see Table 8). A third bridge was planned to ease traffic over the existing two, but had not been opened by the end of the period reviewed.

THE ISRAELI-LEBANESE FRONTIER
The spate of fighting along Lebanon's southern border in September 1977 was ended by a ceasefire concluded on 25 September (see *MECS 1976–77,* p. 118).

However after a brief lull, incidents resumed. On 6 November, fidā'iyyūn shelled Nahariya with *Katyusha* rockets, killing two persons.[11] Retaliating the same day, IDF artillery heavily shelled fidā'ī positions in Nāqūra.[12] On 8 November, Nahariya was again shelled: two *Katyusha* salvos hit the town and a woman was killed.[13] Israeli artillery returned fire; its shelling of several fidā'ī targets was described as "the heaviest attack in two years."[14] According to PLO statements to Western correspondents, at least six persons were killed and 20 wounded. On the following day, Israeli planes carried out a massive attack on several targets, killing at least 70 persons and wounding over 100, most of them civilian residents of the village of 'Aziyya.[15] Israeli sources later stated that the civilian casualties were caused by the explosion of quantities of ammunition stored in 'Aziyya by the PLO.[16] Israel's Prime Minister expressed his "profound regret at these losses, but . . . not for the action itself. . . . The Israeli Air Force, acting under orders received, sought out as its targets concentrations of terrorists, and stuck to those orders meticulously."[17] On 11 November, a *Katyusha* rocket exploded near Dovév. According to the IDF spokesman, aircraft subsequently sent to patrol the area were fired at south-east of Tyre and attacked the positions from which the fire was directed.[18]

By mid-November 1977, relative calm again returned to this sector. After "Operation Lītānī" in March 1978 (see preceding section), no further incidents were recorded.

"Good fence" activities continued (for background, see *MECS 1976–77*, p. 122). After "Operation Lītānī," the policy was expanded to allow access to inhabitants of Shī'ī villages alongside those of the Christian enclaves. Between June 1976 and September 1978, 5,613 Lebanese visited Israel and 60,870 Lebanese residents received medical treatment. In September 1978, the daily average of Lebanese workers employed in Israel stood at 848. A growing number of villages received Israeli services, including water, fuel and electricity supplies. There were also visits by Israeli agricultural experts and veterinarians. Lebanese villagers bought Israeli goods to the value of £I 33.5m.[19]

Moshe Gammer

TABLE 1: FIDĀʾĪ ACTIVITY IN ISRAEL, THE WEST BANK AND THE GAZA STRIP IN 1977 AND 1978
(According to the Israeli Police Spokesman)

	Total No of Incidents	Incidents involving the placing of explosive charges				Civilian Casualties	
		Total	In the West Bank and the Gaza Strip	In Jerusalem	In other parts of Israel	Killed	Wounded
1977 (January–December)	226	138	—	—	—	6	156
1978 (January–August)	235	136	66	47	20	15	178

Note: The figures given in this table include abortive attacks and attempted acts of sabotage (e.g. explosives placed but dismantled). The total is therefore higher than that given in Table 2 which refers to actual incidents only.

TABLE 2: NUMBER OF INCIDENTS AND CASUALTIES IN ISRAEL, THE WEST BANK AND THE GAZA STRIP, OCTOBER 1977–SEPTEMBER 1978 (According to the IDF Spokesman)

	Number of Incidents and Breakdown by Type of Incident																				Casualties																																
	Small Arms and Grenade attacks				Mining				Sabotage				Clashes with Security Forces				Total				Israeli Security Forces								Israeli Civilians								Fida'iyyun								Civilian Residents of the West Bank and the Gaza Strip							
																					Killed				Wounded				Killed				Wounded				Killed				Wounded				Killed				Wounded			
	I	B	G	T	I	B	G	T	I	B	G	T	I	B	G	T	I	B	G	T	I	B	G	T	I	B	G	T	I	B	G	T	I	B	G	T	I	B	G	T	I	B	G	T	I	B	G	T	I	B	G	T
October 1977	3	2	2	7	—	—	—	—	8	1	—	9	—	1	—	1	11	4	2	17	—	—	—	—	—	—	—	—	—	—	—	—	—	—	—	—	—	—	—	—	—	—	—	—	—	—	—	—	—	—	—	—
November	2	5	3	10	—	—	—	—	7	—	2	9	—	—	—	—	9	5	5	19	—	—	—	—	—	—	—	—	—	—	—	—	1	—	—	1	—	—	—	—	—	—	—	—	—	—	—	—	—	1	—	1
December	—	2	—	2	—	—	—	—	6	2	—	8	—	—	—	·	6	4	—	10	—	—	—	—	—	—	—	—	—	1	—	1	3	—	—	3	—	—	—	—	—	—	—	—	—	—	—	—	—	2	—	2
January 1978	2	—	—	2	—	—	—	—	6	4	—	10	—	—	—	—	8	4	—	12	—	—	—	—	—	—	—	—	1	—	—	1	3	—	—	3	—	—	—	—	—	—	—	—	—	—	—	—	—	—	—	—
February	1	1	—	2	—	1	—	1	10	1	1	12	—	—	—	—	11	3	1	15	—	—	—	—	—	—	—	—	2	—	—	2	38	—	—	38	—	—	—	—	—	—	—	—	—	1	—	1	3	—	—	3
March	1	—	—	1	—	—	—	—	5	8	2	15	1	1	2	4	7	9	4	20	4	—	—	4	8	4	—	12	32	—	—	32	82	—	6	88	11	2	—	13	2	4	3	9	—	—	—	—	3	—	—	3
April	3	2	—	5	—	—	—	—	4	5	1	10	—	—	—	—	7	7	1	15	—	—	—	—	—	—	—	—	—	2	—	2	—	7	—	7	—	—	—	—	3	1	—	4	—	1	—	1	—	—	—	—
May	3	3	—	6	—	—	—	—	1	3	—	4	—	—	—	—	4	6	—	10	—	—	—	—	—	—	—	—	—	—	—	—	—	—	—	—	—	—	—	—	—	—	—	—	—	2	—	2	—	—	—	—
June	1	—	—	1	—	—	—	—	6	5	1	12	—	—	—	—	7	5	1	13	—	—	—	—	—	—	—	—	8	—	—	8	59	—	—	59	—	—	—	—	—	—	—	—	—	—	—	—	—	—	—	—
July	—	2	—	2	—	—	—	—	1	5	1	7	—	—	—	—	1	7	1	9	—	—	—	—	—	—	—	—	—	—	—	—	—	—	—	—	—	—	—	—	—	3	—	3	—	—	—	—	—	—	—	—
August	3	2	—	5	—	1	—	1	15	8	1	24	1	—	—	1	19	11	1	31	—	—	—	—	—	—	—	—	1	—	—	1	50	1	—	51	—	2	—	2	3	5	—	8	1	1	1	3	2	10	8	20
September	—	2	—	2	—	—	—	—	11	9	2	22	1	—	—	1	12	11	2	25	—	—	—	—	—	—	—	—	1	—	—	1	6	1	—	7	—	—	—	—	—	—	—	—	1	—	—	1	3	1	—	4
Total	**19**	**21**	**5**	**45**	**—**	**2**	**—**	**2**	**80**	**51**	**11**	**142**	**3**	**2**	**2**	**7**	**102**	**76**	**18**	**196**	**4**	**—**	**—**	**4**	**8**	**4**	**—**	**12**	**45**	**3**	**—**	**48**	**242**	**9**	**6**	**257**	**11**	**4**	**—**	**15**	**8**	**13**	**3**	**24**	**2**	**5**	**1**	**8**	**13**	**17**	**3**	**33**

Legend for column leadings:
I: Israeli; territory (including East Jerusalem)
B: the West Bank
G: the Gaza Strip
T: Total

Italics = The attack on the Haifa–Tel Aviv highway (see text)
Underscore = German tourists

TABLE 3: MAJOR INCIDENTS IN ISRAEL, THE WEST BANK AND THE GAZA STRIP, OCTOBER 1977–SEPTEMBER 1978; ISRAELI AND FIDĀ'Ī ACCOUNTS

			Israeli Account		Fidā'ī Account	
Date	Place	Type	Target	Casualties	Organization(s) Claiming Responsibility	Casualties
14 October 1977	East Jerusalem	Two explosive charges	Market-place	3 wounded	—	—
13 November	East Jerusalem	Two explosive charges	Residential area	2 killed; 5 wounded	PFLP and PLO	PLO; Several killed and wounded
3 December	East Jerusalem	Explosive charge	Market-place	7 seriously wounded	ALF	10 killed
29 December	Netanya	Explosive charge	Shopping centre	2 killed; 1 wounded	—	—
13 January 1978	Jaffa	Explosive charge	Apartment house	2 killed	—	—
25 January	Jerusalem	Explosive charge	Apartment house	No casualties	PDFLP	5 killed or wounded
14 February	Jerusalem	Explosive charge	Bus	2 killed; 44 wounded	al-Sāʿiqa and PDFLP	—
1 March	Tel Aviv	Explosive charge	Bus	2 killed; 3 wounded	PLO	PDFLP; 10 killed and wounded
16 April	Jerusalem	Molotov cocktail	Military bus	4 soldiers wounded	PDFLP and PLO	PLO; all passengers killed and wounded
26 April	Nablus	Grenade	Bus carrying German tourists	2 killed; 5 wounded	PLO (indirectly)	The bus was carrying 12 Israeli pilots and their wives*
4 May	Acre	Explosive charge	Central bus station	3 slightly wounded	—	—
2 June	Jerusalem	Explosive charge	Bus	6 killed; 20 wounded	al-Fatḥ	—
29 June	Jerusalem	Explosive charge	Market-place	2 killed; 40 wounded	al-Fatḥ	—
15 July	Bethlehem	Explosive charge	Central square	No casualties	PLO	An unknown number of killed and wounded
3 August	Tel Aviv	Explosive charge	Market-place	1 killed; 50 wounded	PLO	—
12 August	Jerusalem	Explosive charge	Observation post for tourists	No casualties	PLO	7 policemen and intelligence personnel killed and wounded
5 September	Jerusalem	Explosive charge	Gas container depot	1 Police Sapper killed	PLO	—

*Al-Dustūr, Amman; 5 May 1978 quoting "sources in the West Bank."

205

TABLE 4: MAJOR INCIDENTS REPORTED BY FIDĀʾĪ SOURCES ONLY; OCTOBER 1977–SEPTEMBER 1978

Date	Place	Type of Incident	Target	Reported by Spokesmen of	Casualties
10 November 1977	Ben-Gurion Airport	Explosive charge	—	PLO	10 killed
13 November	Ashdod	Explosive charge	Bar	PDFLP	25 killed and wounded
16 November	Lebanese border	Clash	The convoy of Israeli Defence Minister	PLO	20 soldiers killed; the Minister wounded*
1 December	Petah Tiqwa	Explosive charges	Factory	PLO	Several wounded
4 December	Haifa	Explosive charges	Park area	PLO	Several killed and wounded
20 February 1978	Beersheba	Explosive charge	Factory	PDFLP	More than 10 killed and wounded
29 April	Tel Aviv	Explosive charge	Intelligence headquarters	PLO	Several killed and wounded
18 May	Tel Aviv	Explosive charge	Factory	PLO	Unspecified
18 May	Eilat	Mining	Highway	PLO	Several killed and wounded
15 June	Jerusalem	Attack	Bus station	PLO	Several soldiers killed and wounded
15 August	Raʾs al-ʿAyn (near Petah Tiqwa)	Explosive charge	Police garage	PLO	Several killed and wounded
26 August	Qiryat Arbaʿ (Hebron)	Rocket attack	Labour exchange	PLO	Heavy losses
30 August	Nablus	Attack	—	PLO	4 watchmen wounded
31 August	Jerusalem	Explosive charges	Water reservoirs	PLO	Water supply of several town-quarters cut off
11 September	Jerusalem	Explosive charges and clash	Intelligence headquarters	PLO	4 badly wounded

*Defence Minister Ezer Weizman was injured in a car accident near Tel Aviv.

TABLE 5: FIDĀ'Ī CELLS UNCOVERED IN THE WEST BANK AND THE GAZA STRIP; OCTOBER 1977–SEPTEMBER 1978
(According to the IDF Spokesman)

Date of Report	No of Cells Uncovered	No of persons Detained	Affiliation of the Cells	Area
10 October 1977	4	55	3 al-Fath; 1 PFLP	Gaza Strip
23 October	2	34	1 PFLP; 1 PDFLP	West Bank
1 November	5	40	PFLP; PDFLP; ALF	West Bank
11 November	2	21	al-Fath	Gaza Strip
15 November	2	37	al-Fath	West Bank
23 November	4	47	3 al-Sā'iqa; 1 ALF	West Bank
26 December	8	66	4 al-Fath; 3 PDFLP; 1 PFLP-GC	West Bank
30 January 1978	10	82	6 al-Fath; 1 PFLP	West Bank
6 February	1	7	Not stated	West Bank
24 March	1	16	al-Fath	West Bank
17 April	1	6	al-Fath	West Bank
4 May	8	66	al-Fath; PFLP; ALF	West Bank
21 May	7	79	1 al-Fath; 1 PFLP-GC	West Bank
28 June	8	64	5 al-Fath; 1 PFLP; 2 PNF	West Bank
5 July	1	7	Not stated	Gaza Strip
29 July	2	8	PFLP	West Bank
28 August	2	—	Not stated	North Sinai and Gaza Strip
1 September	2	11	al-Fath	West Bank
2 September	1	—	Not stated	Gaza Strip
18 September	6	25	Not stated	West Bank
18 September	1	9	al-Fath	Gaza Strip
Total	**78**	**c. 700**	—	—

Note: Reports were usually released a few weeks after the conclusion of the investigation or after the first arrests were made and did not, as a rule, state the precise dates of the investigations themselves. Later arrests connected with the same investigation were not always made public; the number of arrests may therefore be higher than stated for any particular case. The total given is an estimate made with a view to allow for such possible discrepancies.

Not all cells were affiliated with any of the known organizations; these have been disregarded in the column showing affiliations.

The total number of security detainees was 2,800 in June 1978. Of these, 40 were under administrative detention; the rest were prisoners convicted in court or suspects awaiting trial.

TABLE 6: INCIDENTS AND CASUALTIES ON THE ISRAELI-LEBANESE FRONTIER; OCTOBER 1977–SEPTEMBER 1978
(According to the IDF spokesman)

| | Fidāʾī Operations | | | | | | | Casualties | | | | | |
| | Smaller arms and Bazooka fire | Mining | Mortar shelling | Katyusha shelling | Clashes with IDF | IDF operations | Total | Israeli soldiers | | Israeli civilians | | Fidāʾiyyūn | |
								Killed	Wounded	Killed	Wounded	Killed	Wounded
October 1977	—	—	2	—	—	—	2	—	—	—	—	—	—
November	1	—	—	7	1	3	12	3	7	—	—	—	—
December	2	—	1	—	—	—	3	—	—	—	—	—	—
January 1978	1	—	—	—	—	—	1	—	—	—	—	—	—
February	—	—	51	7	—	1*	59	18*	57*	1	3	c. 200*	—
March	—	—	—	2	3	—	5	—	—	—	—	—	—
April	—	—	—	—	1	2‡	3	8	1**	—	—	—	—
May–September	1	1	—	—	—	—	2	3	8	1	3	—	—
Total	**5**	**1**	**54**	**16**	**5**	**6**	**87**	**32**	**73**	**1**	**3**	**c.200**	**—**

The figures given in this table relate to border incidents involving fidāʾiyyūn on one side and Israeli forces or civilians on the other; clashes between fidāʾiyyūn and the South Lebanese militias are not included.

* "Operation Litāni" in South Lebanon.
** Held prisoner by the PFLP-GC.
‡ For an account of both operations, see text.

TABLE 7: UN OBSERVERS AND FORCES ALONG THE ARAB-ISRAELI FRONTIERS IN OCTOBER 1978

Name of Force	Commander	Location of HQ	Composition and Strength	Duties	Legal Basis and Duration
United Nations Truce Supervision Organization in Palestine (UNTSO)	Lt-Gen Ensio Siilasvuo (Finland)*	Jerusalem**	Attached to UNEF 120 Attached to UNDOF 85 Attached to UNIFIL 36 At HQ c. 30**	To man observation posts and check points and to report on observance of the ceasefire. In Sinai and the Golan Heights the observers also carry out periodic checks and patrols on observance of the forces limitation agreements. In South Lebanon they serve also as liaison officers "with the various de facto forces."	Established according to SC Resolution 50 of 29 May 1948 to supervise the (first) truce between the Arab states and Israel; after 1949, supervised the implementation of the armistice agreements; after 1967 supervised the ceasefire on the Egyptian, Syrian and Lebanese sectors.
United Nations Emergency Force (UNEF)	Maj-Gen Rais Abin (Indonesia)	Ismā'īliyya	Maximum strength allowed 4,500 Finnish battalion 637 Ghanaian battalion 595 Indonesian battalion 509 Swedish battalion 634 Canadian logistic unit 840 Polish logistic unit 917 Australian helicopter squadron 46 **Total 4,178**	To man the separation area and the "oil strip" in Sinai, and supervise the observance of the ceasefire and of the military clauses of the (second) Egyptian-Israeli agreement of 1 September 1975.	Established according to SC Resolutions 340 and 341 of 25 and 27 October 1973 respectively, for a period of six months. Mandate extended every six months during the (first) disengagement agreement and every year since 24 October 1975. On 23 October 1978, the mandate was extended for nine months.
United Nations Disengagement Observation Force (UNDOF)	Maj-Gen Hannes Philipp (Austria)	Damascus	Maximum strength allowed 1,250 Austrian battalion 523 Iranian battalion 385 Canadian logistic unit 161 Polish logistic unit 91 **Total 1,160**	To man the separation area on the Golan Heights and to check and supervise the ceasefire and observation of the Syrian–Israeli disengagement agreement.	Established according to SC Resolution 350 of 31 May 1974; mandate extended every six months.
United Nations Interim Force in South Lebanon (UNIFIL)	Maj-Gen Emanuel A. Erskine (Ghana)	Nāqūra	Maximum strength allowed 6,000 Fijian battalion 500 French battalion 644 Iranian battalion 599 Irish battalion 661 Nepali battalion 642 Nigerian battalion 673 Norwegian battalion 706 Senegalese battalion 673 Canadian logistic unit 117 French logistic unit 537 Norwegian logistic unit 218 **Total 5,931**	To man the area from which the IDF had withdrawn, to "confirm Israeli withdrawal, restore international peace and security and assist the government of Lebanon in ensuring the return of its effective authority in the area."	Established according to SC Resolutions 425 and 426 of 19 March 1978 for a period of six months; mandate extended for additional six months on 18 September 1978.

*Serves also as Chief Co-ordinator of UN Peacekeeping Missions in the ME and as Chairman of the Military Committee of the Geneva Peace Conference.
**UNTSO headquarters serves also as HQ of all UN forces and missions in the ME and is manned in rotation by officers detached from them.

THE ARAB-ISRAELI CONFLICT

TABLE 8: TRAFFIC OVER THE "OPEN BRIDGES" IN 1977 (According to an Israeli Government source)

	Visitors			Residents		
	Dāmya Bridge	Allenby Bridge	Total	Dāmya Bridge	Allenby Bridge	Total
Arrivals	52,975	78,408	131,383	149,234	153,104	302,338
Departures	52,115	74,263	126,378	156,642	156,628	313,270

NOTES
1. *Middle East Contemporary Survey* (*MECS*), 1976–77, p. 186.
2. See *Middle East Record 1968*, pp. 271–388, and *1969–70*, pp. 180–237.
3. R Cairo, 17 November 1977.
4. Voice of Palestine (PLO clandestine station transmitting from Lebanon), 1 October—British Broadcasting Corporation, Summary of World Broadcasts, the Middle East and Africa (BBC), 3 October 1978.
5. UN Security Council document S/Res/416.
6. E.g. Israel Broadcasting Authority, 14 November 1977 and 25 July 1978—BBC, 15 November 1977 and 27 July 1978; *Ma'ariv*, Tel Aviv; 14 and 16 November 1977, 18 August 1978; *Ha'aretz*, Tel Aviv; 1 December 1977, 5 January and 26 February 1978.
7. E.g. *Rūz al-Yūsuf*, Cairo; 27 March; Reuter, 13 April; Middle East News Agency, Egypt; 13 and 26 April—BBC, 27 April; *Ākhir Sā'a*, Cairo; 3 May; *al-Ahrām*, Cairo; 13 May; and R Cairo, 4 June—BBC, 5 June 1978. In March, a clash was narrowly averted when oil exploration vessels operating from the Egyptian ports on the western shore of the Gulf of Suez and others operating from the Israeli-held eastern coast approached the same area; Deutsche Presse-Agentur, 12 March 1978.
8. S/Res/420; S/12460.
9. R Damascus, 2 and 12 April—BBC, 4 and 14 April; *Tishrīn*, Damascus; 7 and 13 April; and *al-Qabas*, Kuwait; 25 April 1978. Israel's denial was reported by the Israeli Defence Forces (IDF) Radio, 2 April—BBC, 4 April 1978.
10. Israel Government Press Office, Daily Press Bulletin (GPO), 12 June 1978.
11. GPO, 6 November; *Ha'aretz*, 7 November 1977.
12. *Ma'ariv*, 7 November 1977.
13. GPO, 8 November 1977.
14. *International Herald Tribune* (*IHT*), Paris; 9 November 1977.
15. *The Guardian*, London; *Financial Times*, London; 10 November; *IHT*, 12–13 November 1977.
16. *Ha'aretz*, 13 November 1977.
17. Statement by PM Menahem Begin, quoted in GPO, 10 November 1977.
18. GPO, 11 November 1977.
19. IDF spokesman communiqué, 30 September 1978.

INTER-ARAB AFFAIRS

Inter-Arab Relations

SĀDĀT'S MOVE CAUSES MAJOR REALIGNMENT

Within a single month—from mid-November till mid-December 1977—President Anwar al-Sādāt's peace initiative precipitated a major realignment of blocs and axes in the Arab world. It replaced old divisions and combinations by a new pattern determined by each country's reactions to Sādāt's move. It caused the Egyptian-Syrian-Saudi "core triangle"[1] to fall apart and again, as in 1975, placed Egypt and Syria at opposite ends of the Arab political spectrum; it all but unmade the "special relationship" between Jordan and Syria; severely circumscribed Saudi Arabia's scope for inter-Arab action; forced Syria into an awkward alliance with uncongenial partners; and created a formally constituted but rather uncohesive bloc of "rejectionist states" from which the most "rejectionist" of all—Iraq—stayed aloof. Beyond the concerns of day-to-day politics and polemics, it gave rise to a re-examination of the concept of Arab solidarity such as had previously occurred only in the wake of the major Arab-Israeli *wars*. The new pattern was to last, with only minor changes, during most of the period reviewed. Late in July and at the beginning of August 1978, when Egypt announced the suspension of direct contacts with Israel (see essay on the Arab-Israeli Conflict), indications pointed to an imminent overall change in Arab relations. However, Sādāt's acceptance, on 8 August, of the invitation to the Camp David summit with President Carter and Premier Begin the following month quickly restored the scene to what it had been as regards his radical adversaries, though it produced a certain modification in the attitudes of Saudi Arabia and Jordan.

During the critical four weeks late in 1977, when the new pattern was first established, three camps emerged: a small and dwindling grouping of Arab states who supported Sādāt's policy; a larger one, led by Syria, categorically and vociferously rejecting it; and a third and even larger group, headed by Saudi Arabia, which left little doubt about its reservations, but either muted its criticism, disguising it under such codewords as "restoring solidarity" and "reuniting Arab ranks," or kept silent altogether for long periods. Jordan and Iraq—each for reasons of its own—did not find a place in any of the three groupings.

SĀDĀT'S SUPPORTERS

Initially, four Arab states came out in support of Sādāt: Morocco, Sudan, Oman and Tunisia. From among them, only Morocco remained consistently at Egypt's side. Tunisia soon joined the Saudi camp; Oman (having presumably acted at Iran's prompting in the first place) withdrew completely from the debate after making its initial favourable statement on 19 November 1977; and, from the early spring of 1978 onwards, Sudan very gradually moved away from support for Egypt's stance, eventually falling into line with Saudi Arabia. For a short moment, the Yemeni Arab Republic (YAR; North Yemen) also seemed to range itself alongside Egypt: Foreign Minister 'Abdallah al-Asnaj, for instance, stated on 8 December 1977 that Egypt's professed faithfulness to Arab solidarity must be accepted with "full trust."[2] (Asnaj's personal record has been one of consistent support for Egypt since the mid-sixties at least.) However, Saudi influence soon prevailed and the YAR fell into, and remained in, line with Riyadh.

King Hasan II of Morocco seems to have been the only Arab leader who actively assisted in preparing the ground for Sādāt's initiative, even though he claimed to have had no prior knowledge of the actual shape it assumed. (For details of Moroccan activities in this respect, as well as of Morocco's substantive view of the initiative, see relevant section in the essay on the Arab-Israeli Conflict.) On the eve of President Sādāt's departure for Jerusalem, King Hasan telephoned the President to wish him success in his mission. The two leaders then kept in constant touch at every stage of the negotiating process, often by means of visits to Cairo, roughly once a month, by Muhammad Boucetta (Abū Sitta), the Moroccan Minister of State for Foreign Affairs. Boucetta and other Moroccan envoys also undertook ME tours late in November and during December 1977 to convey Hasan's views to the leaders of Tunisia, Libya, Jordan, Syria, Saudi Arabia, Iraq, the Gulf Emirates and the PLO, as well as Iran. They stressed that, in Morocco's view, Sādāt had not violated Arab summit decisions, nor was he headed for a separate settlement. In messages delivered by the envoys, Hasan appealed for patience and asked the Arab leaders to refrain from criticizing the mission Sādāt had undertaken "in his own name and in the name of the Arab nation." [3] In declining Mu'ammar al-Qadhdhāfī's summit call (see below), King Hasan stated that it was the Arab leaders' responsibility to "go beyond verbal ideological differences and not imprison [themselves] in premature judgements." [4] Later, he appealed to President Asad, King Husayn and PLO leader Yāsir 'Arafāt to meet with Sādāt and resolve their differences. [5]

Egypt's Vice-President, Husnī Mubārak, expressed Cairo's gratitude to Hasan during a visit to Morocco in mid-December 1977. On his way to the US and Western Europe on 2 and 3 February 1978, Sādāt stopped over in Morocco for talks with the King. Mubārak informed Hasan of the outcome of Sādāt's talks during a further visit to Morocco from 21-24 February. An additional visit by Mubārak to Morocco, from 25-28 July, was also undertaken to keep Hasan informed of developments connected with Sādāt's initiative. Hasan not only tried to influence other Arab leaders, but Israel as well: at some time in the spring of 1978, he sent a message (conveyed through the UN) to Prime Minister Begin, apparently urging him to be more responsive to Sādāt's initiative. [6] The consistent nature of Moroccan support for Sādāt again became apparent, in the spring of 1978, when Hasan adopted an attitude toward the Arab League's "Solidarity Committee" (see below) identical with that of Egypt. [7]

Sudan's professions of support for Egypt, though not destined to last, were initially more emphatic than those of any other country in this grouping. On 21 November 1977, the government and the Sudanese Socialist Union (SSU) issued a statement praising Sādāt's Knesset speech and Egypt's "vanguard role in the Arab struggle." [8] The following day, President Ja'far al-Numayrī came to Cairo to greet Sādāt on his return from Jerusalem. He told reporters that "the battle of peace is no less serious than the military battle," and that Sādāt's visit to Jerusalem was another victory, comparable to the battle of October 1973. He hoped Sādāt's critics would eventually applaud what they were now opposing. [9] Numayrī proceeded to try to enlist support for Sādāt. He visited Riyadh for talks with King Khālid (1 December) and sent messages to the leaders of Syria (8 December), Lebanon (12 December) and the YAR (11 January 1978). On 7 and 8 January 1978, Sādāt made a return visit to Khartoum to thank Numayrī for his support. The latter reiterated his previous stand and affirmed that Egypt was not seeking a separate peace (the gravest charge made against Sādāt by his adversaries), but was working for all Arabs according to a comprehensive Arab strategy. Sādāt implicitly downgraded the combined weight of his Arab critics by stressing that Egypt and Sudan alone "constitute two-thirds of the Arab nation." [10] In the following weeks, Numayrī spoke critically of Sādāt's most vocal adversaries.

Numayrī made another visit to Saudi Arabia on 21 and 22 February 1978 for talks which dealt mainly with developments in the Horn of Africa (see later section in this essay). However, these Riyadh meetings also marked the beginning of Sudan's gradual shift from outright support of Sādāt to greater conformity with the Saudi line. This was partly the result of Saudi prompting, partly of domestic developments which lent greater weight to quarters traditionally opposed to Egypt (see chapter on Sudan), and perhaps also to a reassessment of the prospects of Sādāt's initiative after the recall of the Egyptian delegation from Jerusalem in January 1978 (see essay on the Arab-Israeli Conflict). The change in Sudan's attitude became manifest at the beginning of March 1978 when Numayrī called for an Arab summit meeting. Since a summit served as the symbol of Arab solidarity and of a broad consensus (cf *MECS 1976-77*, pp. 175-76), this call was a form of implied criticism—well understood as such by the Arab political public—that Egypt was the one country which had broken ranks. Numayrī himself underscored the shift that had taken place by telling a Saudi correspondent that "the basis of Saudi-Sudanese relations is the Arab solidarity slogan raised by the Saudi kingdom." [11] The second symptom of the new trend was Numayrī's acceptance, later in March, of the chairmanship of the Solidarity Committee set up by the Arab League (the activities of which are detailed later). Again, as with the summit call, the implication was that, in order to allow Arab solidarity to be restored, Egypt would have to modify its current policies. While Numayrī meticulously avoided any expressions which might be interpreted as hostile to Egypt, a statement he made when embarking on the Committee's first mission clearly reflected the distance he had traversed within a few months: "Every Arab," he said, "is entitled to consider [Sādāt's] initiative as wrong or as right. But we are not entitled to tear the Arab front apart." The positive and the negative aspects of the initiative should be explored "in such a way that Arab solidarity will emerge victorious in either case." [12]

THE OPPONENTS: IRAQ AND LIBYA TAKE THE LEAD

The first countries to come out against Sādāt's initiative were Iraq and Libya—the two states which, immediately after the end of the 1973 war, had introduced the term "rejectionist" into Arab political usage to indicate their rejection, not of any particular set of terms for a settlement with Israel, but of a settlement *per se*. In the intervening years, they had on a number of occasions tried to put together a "rejectionist" front or bloc, in particular by appealing to Syria, Algeria and the PLO. All their attempts had failed. In 1976, both had been excluded, or had excluded themselves, from the fairly broad consensus reached at the Riyadh and Cairo conferences (see *MECS 1976-77*, p. 149). Qadhdhāfī had a personal feud with Sādāt ever since the latter came to power (see *MECS 1976-77*, pp. 164-70); Iraq had opposed Egyptian policies in the Arab-Israeli conflict at most times since the 1967 war. [13] Now, with the shock-waves caused by Sādāt's move reverberating throughout the Arab world, both countries felt that the moment had come to make their voices heard.

Even before the date of Sādāt's visit to Jerusalem was set, the Iraqi Ba'th party's highest forum, the National Command (NC), warned on 15 November 1977 that if the visit took place it "would be a national catastrophe." The NC called on "the Arab masses everywhere" and on "all the struggling Arab forces . . . to use all means to prevent [the] implementation" of Sādāt's scheme. [14] Simultaneously, the terms "agent" and "traitor" made their first appearance in the Iraqi media to describe Sādāt. In towns throughout Iraq, "mass demonstrations" called for Sādāt's overthrow. All 'Īd al-Adhạ ceremonies were cancelled "to express the wrath and condemnation of the masses." ('Īd al-Adhạ, the "Feast of Immolation," is a major holiday in the Muslim religious calendar and is celebrated to mark the sacrifices concluding the Mecca pilgrimage. In 1977, it coincided with Sādāt's visit to Jerusalem.)

In Libya, a General People's Congress statement of 18 November 1977 declared that Sādāt was about to commit a "crime against the entire Arab nation" (for GPC, see chapter on Libya). The means of achieving the liberation of Palestine "must be just as honourable" as the "liberation objective" itself. Even if Sādāt were to succeed in making Palestine "free and independent," it would "bring great shame upon us to liberate Palestine in this manner." Palestine should rather remain occupied than for the Arabs "to lick the boots of [its] usurpers." The Arab nation was strong enough to "crush the enemy and achieve liberation" without resorting to "such a humiliating method." The Congress called for the establishment of "an Arab rejectionist front" to continue "the struggle for liberation," pledged to place Libya's resources at the disposal of Syria and the PLO, and threatened sanctions against Egypt should the visit to Israel indeed take place.[15] On 19 November, demonstrators set fire to the Egyptian mission in Tripoli. Four days later, following Sādāt's return from Jerusalem, Libya withdrew its recognition of Cairo; at the same time, it demanded Egypt's expulsion from the Arab League, the transfer of the League's headquarters from Cairo to another Arab capital, and the application of the Arab boycott laws against Egyptians dealing with Israel. Libyan airspace and ports were closed to aircraft and ships belonging to Egypt or bound for, or coming from, that country. At the same time, however, Egyptian workers in Libya were assured of continued "excellent treatment" (see *MECS 1976–77*, p. 167).[16] The Libyan Foreign Secretary, 'Alī 'Abd āl-Salām al-Turaykī, called on all Muslim countries to boycott Egypt for its "betrayal of Islam." He was presumably alluding in particular to Sādāt's participation in the 'Īd al-Adhā prayers at Jerusalem's al-Aqsā Mosque "under Israeli guard"—an accusation which was to be levelled against him time and again.

On 20 November, and again on 27 November, Libya called on all Arab states (except Egypt) to attend an urgent summit conference in Tripoli. The second appeal set the date for 1 December. (In issuing the summit call, Libya based its action on recommendations adopted by the Arab Foreign Ministers at a conference held in Tunis from 12–14 November. Meeting in the interval between Sādāt's announcement of his forthcoming visit to Israel and his actual arrival there, that conference made pronouncements about the "prevailing spirit of Arab solidarity," as if unaware of the drama then unfolding. Among other things, it resolved to prepare for a summit early in 1978 which Libya offered to host.) Anticipating that Saudi Arabia, Jordan and the states which had come out in support of Sādāt would refuse to attend, Libya announced on 27 November that if a plenary summit conference could not convene on 1 December, "a number of heads of the states that bear responsibility for steadfastness and for supporting the Palestine resistance will meet in Tripoli on that date."[17] Syria, Algeria, the Popular Democratic Republic of Yemen (PDRY; South Yemen) and the PLO accepted the invitation. The following day, however, Iraq issued invitations to the same countries for a "rejectionist" conference in Baghdad, asking Libya to postpone its own conference. 'Arafāt immediately went to Baghdad and, following his intercession, Iraq agreed to participate in the Tripoli conference, stating that the Baghdad meeting would take place at a later date.

Syria, meanwhile, had been somewhat slower to react. While Libya's and Iraq's first responses came in the wake of Sādāt's announcement on 9 November of his intention to address the Knesset, Syrian spokesmen and the Syrian media made no reference to the initiative until after the conclusion of Sādāt's visit to Damascus, on

16 and 17 November. Formally, this visit was in response to an invitation issued by President Ḥāfiz al-Asad on 9 November, but before the gist of Sādāt's speech of that date became known in Damascus. (Sādāt had not visited Damascus since May 1975. For the rift later that year, the short-lived Egyptian-Syrian reconciliation of 1976, and the first signs of renewed tension in the autumn of 1977, see *MECS 1976–77*, pp. 147–54.) By what arguments Sādāt hoped to persuade Asad to acquiesce to his initiative is still not known, but it immediately became clear that he had failed completely—as had Asad in dissuading Sādāt. On 17 November, Asad refused to attend a joint press conference with the Egyptian President.

After Sādāt's departure, the first statement on the new situation was issued jointly by the National and Regional commands of the Ba'th party, the National Progressive Front (see *MECS 1976–77*, p. 605) and the Syrian government—an unprecedented combination which lent special weight to its contents. The statement said that Syria had asked Sādāt "to put aside the idea" of going to Israel, and had explained the harm it would cause to "Egyptian-Syrian cohesion," to the Palestine issue, to Egypt itself, and to the pan-Arab struggle. "The decision is a painful blow to the Arab nation. . . . Syria believes that no Arab ruler has the right to take such a step which harms the Arab nation's existence, future and honour. The Arab nation . . . will not forgive any Arab official who takes [such] a step." The signatories called on all Arabs "to take action to foil and contain the expected dangers and to seek formulas that will regain for the Arab nation its strength." In conclusion, they stressed their belief that Sādāt's decision would not "prevent the Egyptian Arab people from facing up to their pan-Arab responsibilities." [18] While thus implicitly appealing to the Egyptian public to oppose their President, the statement did not threaten sanctions against Egypt (as Libya had done).

During the following days, the anti-Sādāt campaign was stepped up. The date of Sādāt's arrival in Israel was proclaimed a day of national mourning. Radio Damascus urged Jerusalem Arabs to stay away from al-Aqsā Mosque during Sādāt's prayer there, called for a strike in the West Bank and the Gaza Strip, and appealed in more explicit terms for the overthrow of Sādāt. "Popular demonstrations" throughout Syria protested against Sādāt's "treason" and the "shame" of his visit. On 22 November, Syria's delegate at the UN General Assembly (then in session) said that Egypt had stabbed the Arabs in the back. The Egyptian delegate walked out.

A joint statement by the Syrian Ba'th party and the PLO was issued in Damascus on 22 November. It condemned Sādāt's move, called on the Egyptian people and army "to confront this treason to pan-Arabism," and appealed to all Arab states to reject Sādāt's policy and to draw up joint plans to foil it. It stressed the special link between Syria and the PLO, which it said the Arabs should now strengthen "militarily, politically and economically in new ways." [19]

It was only during the last days of November that Syria took up contacts with the states preparing for the Tripoli conference. Syria's positive reply to the invitation was made on 30 November. It is noteworthy that Syria's decision was preceded by two moves intended to probe the possibility of alternative approaches. First, Asad attempted to bring Saudi Arabia into a common front meant to deter Sādāt. [20] Then, on 20 November, he sent a message to the Iraqi President, Aḥmad Ḥasan al-Bakr, suggesting that the two countries "set aside" their old quarrel (see *MECS 1976–77*, pp. 160–63) for the sake of "pan-Arab responsibilities." [21] It was only when Asad gathered that Saudi Arabia was unwilling to exert really vigorous pressure against Egypt, and that Iraq was on the point of escalating rather than toning down its dispute with Syria, that he joined the moves which were to lead to the formation of the Tripoli bloc.

THE TRIPOLI BLOC: POLITICAL DEVELOPMENTS

The states which had responded to Libya's second, scaled-down summit call of 27 November (i.e. Syria, Iraq, Algeria and the PDRY, as well as the PLO) met in Tripoli from 2–5 December 1977. Libya, Syria and Algeria were represented by their Heads of State; Iraq by RCC member Taha Yāsīn Ramadān; and the PDRY by 'Abd al-Fattāḥ Ismā'īl, the Secretary-General of UPONF (see chapter on the PDRY). Yāsir 'Arafāt led the PLO delegation in which, however, the "rejectionist" organizations also had considerable representation.

The first phase of the deliberations centred on an attempt by Iraq to have its own action programme accepted by the conference. The programme was a purely "rejectionist" one, with the renunciation of Security Council Resolutions 242 and 338 as its main plank. (Further details are set out below.) Iraq's tactics were to avoid direct contact with the Syrian delegation, while trying to enlist the other participants to bring pressure to bear on Syria to agree to the Iraqi stance. Asad rejected the Iraqi programme and also turned down a modified Iraqi proposal: to form a front of "national progressive" Arab states and the PLO without finalizing its programme. The front's guidelines would then be formulated by a special committee and approved by a second conference of Heads of State, this time in Baghdad.

At this point, the conference seemed to be deadlocked. Libya, the PDRY, the "rejectionist" components of the PLO, and possibly Algeria as well, faced the following dilemma: they could either give rein to their ideological preferences, live up to their past "rejectionist" record and thus side with Iraq at the risk of seeing Syria walk out; or else take Syria's side and resign themselves to Iraq's boycotting their bloc. They chose the latter course, evidently prompted by the consideration that without at least one country bordering on Israel, their grouping would have a rather artificial character which Sādāt could easily ridicule as an alliance of countries remote from the firing-line. A bloc including Syria—"the principal confrontation state," as the Tripoli statement was to call it—was preferable to the ideological purity and consistency attainable by opting for Iraq. When their choice became clear at the last session, Iraq withdrew from the conference. The remaining participants released a statement announcing the formation of a "Front of Steadfastness and Resistance" (jabhat al-sumūd wal-tasaddī), composed of Syria, Algeria, Libya, the PDRY and the PLO, to face "the Zionist enemy and the plots of imperialism." (Iraq had suggested the name "Front of Steadfastness and Liberation." This was more in keeping with the "rejectionist" creed, but was objectionable to Syria, which preferred to hint, however indirectly, at the continued existence of a political option.)

In their concluding statement, the signatories condemned Sādāt's "visit to the Zionist entity, as it constitutes a great betrayal of the sacrifices and struggle of our Arab people in Egypt and her armed forces . . . and [of the] principles of the Arab nation." While acknowledging Egypt's past services to the "all-Arab cause," the statement continued: "Egypt is not the beginning or the end." Its greatness "is only possible within the Arab nation without which she can only diminish in importance." The statement hailed the "national and progressive forces" in Egypt "which reject [Sādāt's] capitulationist policy." The conference further decided to "freeze" political and diplomatic relations with the Egyptian government and to apply Arab boycott regulations to Egyptian individuals and companies dealing with Israel, to stay away from Arab League meetings held in Egypt, "to study" the question of transferring the League's headquarters elsewhere, and to examine Egypt's membership in the League. It called on all Arab states to withhold political and material support from Egypt, and instead provide economic, financial, political and military aid "to the Syrian Arab region now that it has become the principal confrontation state and the base of steadfastness," and "also to the Palestine people represented by the PLO." A further clause reasserted "the legitimacy of PLO representation of the Palestinian people." Finally, "members of the pan-Arab front consider any aggression against any one member as an aggression against all members." [22] The statement contained no condemnation of a political settlement as such.

Compared with earlier statements by the participants, the Tripoli resolutions seemed lukewarm and the Front rather toothless. It even fell short of the measures taken against Egypt by Libya two weeks earlier. What "freezing" relations was to mean in practical terms remained unclear—an uncertainty resolved the following day when Egypt promptly and peremptorily severed relations with the four signatory states and with Iraq. Relocating the League's headquarters or expelling Egypt from it was a mere declarative stance since, under the League's charter, either step required a unanimous vote which the Tripoli bloc knew it could not muster. In a separate statement, Asad and Qadhdhāfī dismissed Sādāt from his position as chairman of the Presidential Council of the Federation of Arab Republics (Egypt, Syria and Libya) for having "violated the Federation's principles and objectives by his visit to the Zionist entity." [23] (The Federation had been formed in 1971, and though its institutions still existed in 1977, it had in fact become defunct in 1973.)

The head of the Iraqi delegation publicly explained his country's walk-out by saying that "the Tripoli summit conference served as an umbrella for Asad to continue his policy which was exactly like Sādāt's." [24] Iraqi spokesmen reiterated their country's intention of forming a Liberation Front, as it originally proposed, and again invited the members of the Tripoli bloc to attend a conference in Baghdad on 15 January 1978. Although no member-state accepted the invitation, Algeria, Libya and the PDRY, as well as some organizations belonging to the PLO, attempted to mediate between Iraq and Syria to pave the way for Iraq's eventual adherence to the Tripoli Front. The principal effort was made by Algerian President Houari Boumedienne, who visited Iraq early in January 1978. A meeting to reconcile Syrian and Iraqi representatives was scheduled to take place in Algiers on 29 January. However, on the previous day an invitation reached Baghdad to attend a second meeting of the Tripoli bloc at Algiers on 2 February. Iraq immediately decided to boycott both the reconciliation meeting and the Algiers summit of the Tripoli Front. President Ahmad Hasan al-Bakr informed Boumedienne that the point of the proposed Syrian-Iraqi meeting had been to make possible Syria's participation at the Baghdad conference. Since that conference was not now going to convene, the reconciliation meeting would serve no purpose. During the remaining days until the opening of the Algiers conference, Iraq made public a personal message sent by Bakr in December to the participants of the Tripoli conference, as well as a draft charter for the alternative Front it had proposed (for details, see below). Both documents had originally been secret. Their release at this time [25] was clearly meant to point up the Algiers proceedings as lacking in resolution and as being only half-heartedly opposed to Sādāt's line, in contrast to Iraq's "principled stand." Their publication was presumably also intended to elicit responses showing that, apart from Syria, the Tripoli bloc was actually in sympathy with Iraq's objectives.

The Algiers conference convened in two sessions: the Foreign Ministers met from 31 January–2 February and discussed a Syrian draft setting forth the Front's principles and defining its institutions. Qadhdhāfī, however, made it known that he would not sign a basic document of this kind as long as Iraq did not join the Front. The Heads of State then met on 3 and 4 February. Qadhdhāfī's objections prevailed; instead of issuing a charter for the Front's institutions, the meeting ended with nothing more than a concluding statement. This followed the general lines of the Tripoli statement of 5 December 1977 and again bore the mark of Syrian policy.

A "just peace" was stated to be the Front's aim. Sādāt was condemned for "working within an Israeli-US plan" intended "to lay down the basis of an Egyptian-Israeli separatist solution"; for undermining the chances for a "just peace"; for isolating Egypt from the non-aligned camp; and for ranging Cairo in opposition to the USSR. Furthermore, Egypt was trying to "draw some Arab countries into this plan" (evidently a reference to Jordan). The conference commended the "Arab people in Egypt and their nationalist and progressive vanguard" for opposing "the imperialist plot that is going on" and for confronting "all attempts aimed at isolating Egypt from the Arab nation." Other clauses reaffirmed the December declaration, reiterated the PLO's status as the "sole legitimate representative of the Palestinians," and denied Sādāt's right to negotiate on their behalf or to "discuss the fate of occupied Syrian Arab territory." The signatories called for further contacts with "Arab countries which have refrained from supporting Sādāt's policy with a view to the establishment of effective Arab solidarity" i.e. of a broader anti-Sādāt bloc. A special resolution endorsed Syria's "special links" with the PLO, as well as its aim of achieving a new "strategic balance" between the Arabs and Israel. Finally, two paragraphs were included in response to special pleading by Algeria and the PDRY respectively: the first expressed "extreme anxiety" over French military intervention in the Western Sahara; the second deplored the "foreign military presence in Oman" (i.e. the presence there of an Iranian contingent engaged against insurgents in Dhufar, the southern region of Oman) and expressed support for the Omani people's "fight for liberation, independence and . . . sovereignty." [26]

Press reports added that Libya had agreed in principle to finance the purchase of additional Soviet arms for Syria and the PLO. [27] To what extent, if at all, Libya honoured this pledge remained unclear. After the entry of Israeli troops into South Lebanon the following month, Qadhdhāfī told the Libyan People's Congress that perhaps "support must be given to Lebanon and not to Syria, especially as Syria has become an onlooker as regards . . . South Lebanon." [28]

While the final statement seemed to suggest Syria's dominant position within the bloc and its ability to determine the language used by it, this impression was largely negated by a remark made by Algeria's Foreign Minister, 'Abd al-'Azīz Bouteflika. Immediately after the conclusion of the conference, he said: "There is not a shade of difference between Iraq's position and that of Algeria, Libya, South Yemen or even the PLO. There are, however, bilateral problems between Syria and Iraq." [29] Syria's Foreign Minister, 'Abd al-Ḥalīm Khaddām, glossed over the failure to have the Syrian draft charter accepted by claiming that the conference's principal achievement had been to "perpetuate the Front" and its "political line." [30]

The Algiers conference turned out to be the last top-level meeting of the Tripoli bloc until after the Camp David summit. The bloc's Foreign and Defence Ministers were called to an emergency meeting in Damascus in the wake of Israel's invasion of South Lebanon on 15 March. However, except for the PDRY, which sent both delegates, only Foreign Ministers attended. Even before the conference opened on 19 March, the tone of its deliberations was set by militant Libyan statements which called on the PLO and "the Lebanese progressive forces" (for the connotation of this term, see chapter on Lebanon) to continue fighting, "without any trusteeship of international [i.e. UN] or isolationist [i.e. Maronite] forces." The Steadfastness Front should "provide all their battle needs," including air cover for camps and towns. [31] In a speech in Tripoli on 19 March, Qadhdhāfī recalled the clause in the Tripoli declaration stipulating that aggression against any member of the bloc was tantamount to aggression against all, adding: "Now that the Palestinian side has been attacked, why is it that Syria has not entered the fighting?" [32] (For Syria's stance on developments in South Lebanon at that stage, as well as for the Security Council resolution of 19 March, see section on South Lebanon in the essay on the Arab-Israeli Conflict.) At the conference itself, Libya and the PDRY criticized Syria for its non-intervention and for its tacit agreement to the deployment of UN forces in South Lebanon. Algeria supported Syria. The PLO (itself divided over this issue, see essay on the PLO) asked for the matter to be submitted to an immediate summit meeting of the bloc, but this request went unheeded. When the conference ended on 21 March, differences were papered over in a joint communiqué which made no mention of the UN role in South Lebanon. It condemned "Israeli aggression" and "Zionist terrorism," demanded complete and unconditional Israeli withdrawal from Lebanese territory, and took the occasion of once again rejecting members' participation in any conference attended by Sādāt. [33]

The Damascus meeting was widely seen as a failure on the part of the bloc to live up to its own principles and implement its own objectives when faced by unforeseen developments—a judgement shared by its members as well as by its opponents. The Egyptian media made the most of what they described as a demonstration of the ineffectiveness of Sādāt's adversaries.

The Information Ministers of the Tripoli bloc met in Algiers in April 1978 to establish guidelines for co-ordinating information work. In a final statement, they reasserted the bloc's policy as set forth on previous occasions and praised those Egyptian journalists and writers who resisted Sādāt's "policy of capitulation." The Ministers recommended a series of steps to promote the bloc's aims by means of the press, news agencies, broadcasts and films in member countries. [14] Arab League meetings held in Cairo in March, July and September were boycotted by the bloc (and by Iraq), as required by the Tripoli decisions.

In a May Day speech, Libya's second most important leader, 'Abd al-Salām Jallūd, offered the following assessment of the bloc's role in inter-Arab affairs: "The Steadfastness and Resistance Front, despite the fact that it has done nothing concrete, and has not taken the offensive and embarked on the action required of it, has played an historic part. It has expressed the will of rejection. . . . The Steadfastness Front will improve and mobilize its potential . . . on the road to a total liberation war. . . . We should work for more dialogue . . . with Iraq, so that Iraq joins the Front. . . . We lack nothing except a political line and a decision." [35]

THE TRIPOLI BLOC: COHESION AND DIVERGENCE

The Tripoli bloc was united in its total rejection of Sādāt's policy on all counts: the treasonous character of direct contacts with Israel; squandering the Arabs' most valuable card by implicitly recognizing Israel (in fact, by addressing the Knesset and visiting East Jerusalem, even recognizing "Israel in its post-1967 form"); betraying the cause of the Palestinians; breaking Arab ranks and disregarding Arab summit resolutions; removing Egypt from among the "confrontation states"; preparing for a separate peace; and exclusively aligning Egypt with the US while alienating the USSR to the detriment of Arab political and military strength. Sādāt's overthrow was thus a common aspiration. However, the bloc was united in little else, and thus incapable of putting forward an alternative policy of its own.

The Tripoli bloc suffered from two main weaknesses: the absence, indeed the hostility, of Iraq; and the divergence of individual views and interests within the bloc. Iraq's adherence to the bloc would have made it a more credible and powerful force for several reasons: its rapidly growing army and speedy access to the Israeli border; the expectation that it would become the first Arab state to possess nuclear arms,[36] its considerable oil wealth and the leverage of OPEC membership, and its long record of extreme militancy towards Israel. In particular, Iraq's adherence would have promoted Syria's aim of "redressing the strategic balance" following Egypt's "defection." It would also have compensated Syria for the diminution, not to say the loss, of its "special relationship" with Jordan (see *MECS 1976–77*, pp. 154–57). Instead, Iraq used every turn of events from November 1977 to the autumn of 1978 to embarrass the rival regime in Damascus, both domestically and in the inter-Arab sphere, escalating a process which had already become conspicuous a year earlier (see *MECS 1976–77*, pp. 160–63).

The divergence of views most harmful to the bloc's cohesion was Syria's isolation within the group, due to its insistence on leaving the door open for the possible resumption of the "political process" at a later stage. Only some quarters within the PLO, particularly those personally loyal to 'Arafāt, sided with Syria on this point. (For details, see essay on the PLO.) The rest teamed up with Syria for their own particularist reasons, which can be summarized as follows:

1. Libya viewed the situation largely as an extension of its feud with Sādāt which, in mid-1977, had led to armed border clashes (see *MECS 1976–77*, pp. 163–70). But as soon as it realized the depth of Asad's bitterness over Sādāt's "betrayal," Libya came to think of Syria as a better partner for joint action against Egypt, even though it was closer to Iraq's distinctively "rejectionist" stance.

2. For Algeria, membership in the bloc was, among other things, a means of enlisting support over the issue of the Western Sahara (see *MECS 1976–77*, pp. 170–71). Libya had moved closer to Algeria on this issue during 1976 and 1977. However, it had not quite given up the idea of becoming something like an arbiter of Saharan affairs and was therefore careful not to identify entirely with Algeria or antagonize Morocco altogether. Thus, for instance, when condemning Sādāt's supporters before his visit to Israel, Libya singled out Sudan and Oman, but made no mention of Morocco.[37] The PDRY had sided with Algeria even before November 1977. Algeria's gain was that Syria moved from a position of neutrality to one of guarded support. However, mention of the Western Sahara in joint statements by the bloc did very little to improve Algeria's standing in this matter and fell far short of Boumedienne's expectations. On other issues, Algeria was usually aligned with Syria and in opposition to Libya and the PDRY. The exception was Algeria's attitude towards Iraq and its frequent efforts to draw the latter into the bloc—even at the expense of diminishing Syria's standing in it.

3. The PDRY was clearly a minor partner in the group or, as the Egyptian media often stated, merely "an ornament" to it. An important consideration in its decision to join was that it expected to find support against Saudi pressures exercised in the context of Peninsular and Red Sea affairs. It received some verbal support for its involvement in the Dhufar rebellion in Oman, but this, too, fell short of effective backing.

4. Notwithstanding the public reconciliation between its feuding components, the PLO remained divided in its expectations. 'Arafāt's first concern in joining the bloc was to compensate the PLO for the loss of Egyptian support and to strengthen the commitment of its member-states to the PLO and to the cause of the Palestinians. In terms of his personal policy, this primarily meant co-operation with Syria. The "rejectionist" PLO groups, on the other hand, sought support from Libya and to some extent from Algeria as well, hoping thus to counteract the preponderance of Syrian influence over the PLO as a whole.

5. For Syria alone, the ostensible objective of the bloc—to defeat Sādāt's initiative—was also the primary motive in joining it.

But for Syria, larger issues were at stake. More than any other Arab state, Syria was aware of the dangers of a separate Egyptian-Israeli deal, particularly to itself. No other Arab country believed as firmly that this was indeed Sādāt's aim and, looking back on the history of Syrian-Egyptian relations between 1973 and 1977, no other country had better reason to believe so. In 1975, for instance, Syria's arguments against the Sinai Agreement had largely centred on this point. In 1978, fear of a unilateral Egyptian-Israeli deal "verged almost on collective paranoia." [38] Yet the question of where to turn for support against Sādāt was not an easy one for Damascus. It was in part influenced by the consideration that a too determined "ganging up" on Egypt would be counter-productive: it might push Egypt into a separate agreement rather than deter it. For a new constellation to be desirable in Syrian eyes, it should not only prevent Syria from relapsing into the isolation characteristic of the years preceding Asad's rise to power, but should also align Syria with allies powerful enough, in military terms, to "redress the strategic balance." It should, if at all possible, harm neither the special relationship with Jordan nor restrict Syrian ascendancy in Lebanon; neither should it prejudice Syria's claim to a dominant voice in any future Palestinian entity (cf *MECS 1976–77*, p. 154).

Yet these aims could not easily be reconciled. As was noted above, Asad's first choice was an anti-Sādāt alignment with Saudi Arabia. Had his *démarche* succeeded, he believed Saudi influence would have kept Jordan at Syria's side. With Syrian and Jordanian armies and the Saudi arsenal to draw on, and with Lebanese territory and the PLO's armed units at its disposal, Syria could then have hoped to reshape the "strategic balance." But Saudi Arabia was as unwilling to put strong pressure on Sādāt as it was to ally itself with radical Arab regimes who might one day turn against conservative ones like itself. Nor was Jordan ready to join Syria in an outright condemnation of Sādāt. (Saudi and Jordanian attitudes are dealt with in greater detail below.) Syria's second consideration was to enlist Iraq particularly, it appears, because of its military strength. Despite the ten-year old bitter rivalry between the regimes, and despite basic differences on the issue of a possible settlement with Israel, Asad appealed to Iraq as early as 20 November 1977—the day of Sādāt's Knesset speech—to let bygones be bygones. As will be seen presently, Iraq gave higher priority to its rivalry with Syria than it did to opposing Sādāt's policy.

The Tripoli bloc, as eventually constituted, was thus clearly a second-best for Syria. It did, and could do, little to help Asad redress the military balance. However, it did formally recognize Syria as the "principal confrontation state" and implicitly acknowledged continued Syrian overlordship in Lebanon. It promised financial aid for Syria's arms needs and also recognized the "special link" between Syria and the PLO. It is extremely doubtful, however, whether any of the member-states, or the PLO, would have endorsed this "link" to the full extent envisaged by Syrian spokesmen in their more revealing and forward-looking statements. On the occasion of a "Palestine Solidarity" rally in Damascus, for instance, Sāmī al-'Attārī, a member of the Ba'th party National Command representing President Asad, stated: "The Syrian citizen considers Palestine as southern Syria and the Palestinian citizen considers Syria as northern Palestine. Both of them believe that Palestine and Syria are part of one homeland. . . . Therefore, the question of Palestine is *strictly a Syrian issue* and an Arab security issue." [39]

If membership in the Tripoli bloc rescued Syria from relapsing into isolation (as appeared possible at the end of November 1977), it did so to a considerable extent at the cost of isolating Syria *within* the bloc it nominally headed. And Syria's insistence, within the bloc, not to close the door entirely to a political solution laid it open to the charge of covertly being in agreement with the Egyptian line and merely keeping a few steps behind for the sake of appearances. This accusation was indeed levelled against Asad by the "rejectionist" groups of the PLO, but most persistently and stridently by Iraq.

THE POSITION OF IRAQ

At the beginning of February 1978, Iraq took the unusual step of making public three secret documents which it had originally submitted to the Tripoli bloc member-states: a letter from President Bakr to the participants of the December 1977 Tripoli summit dated 29 November; an Iraqi draft charter for the establishment of a "Front of Steadfastness and Liberation" (to include the bloc's members and Iraq), which Iraq wanted to be publicly adopted instead of the Tripoli statement; and an appendix to the charter, also to be adopted by the member-states, but to be kept secret.[40] The documents were made public at a time when Iraq no longer hoped to have its own line adopted by the Tripoli bloc; when it had decided not to attend that bloc's second summit meeting at Algiers in February, so as not to find itself once again in a minority of one; and when their impact in depicting the Tripoli group as "lukewarm" would be greatest.

The documents fully reflected Iraq's basic position on the conflict with Israel, centring on the commitment to the "liberation of all Palestinian territory" and the establishment of "a democratic state in·Palestine"; on the agreement "not to hold negotiations or make peace with the Zionist enemy or to recognize it [sic]"; and, consequently, on the need to disavow Security Council Resolutions 242 and 338. Since Resolution 338 had given effect to the 1973 ceasefire, the demand for its revocation by Syria was tantamount to demanding the termination of the ceasefire on the Golan Heights. (A fuller account of these aspects and of the institutional framework Iraq proposed for the implementation of its policy is included in the essay on the Arab-Israeli Conflict.) In the present context, two motifs with a particular bearing on Iraq's inter-Arab (rather than anti-Israeli) stance should be singled out for mention: the attempt to subject the PLO to the exclusive control of the Iraqi-led Front; and the extreme hostility towards Syria running, explicitly or implicitly, through all three documents.

Iraq's position on the future status of the PLO was expressed in a clause in the draft charter which stated: "The PLO, as well as any Palestinian side participating in the Front, is prohibited from receiving any military or financial aid . . . from any Arab or foreign country, except by decision of the [Front's] command." Any "Palestinian side" violating this article would be expelled from the Front. When 'Arafāt expressed reservations concerning an obligation which "could imply some kind of tutelage," the RCC Vice-Chairman, Saddām Ḥusayn, told him that the PLO "would not need aid from any other side"; but he eventually declared Iraq's readiness to revise the paragraph at a later stage.[41] The fact that the bulk of the PLO, including some of its "rejectionist" components, continued to co-operate with the Tripoli bloc rather than rely on Iraq exclusively, together with the bloc's recognition of the PLO's "special links" with Syria, may well have contributed to Iraq's decision later in 1977 to launch a campaign of violence and vituperation against 'Arafāt and al-Fath. (For details, see essay on the PLO and chapter on Iraq.)

The attempt to rein in the PLO should be seen primarily in the context of Iraq's policy to bolster its image as the true champion of the Palestinians and the "cause of liberation.'' Even so, the effort to loosen Syria's hold over the PLO was also implicitly an anti-Syrian move. Similarly, the Iraqi demand that Syria open its border to PLO operations against Israel[42] was a reproach rather than an appeal. Much more explicit were the hostile references to Syria in the three Iraqi documents. Bakr's letter was as critical of Asad as it was of Sādāt. It said that Sādāt's "visit to the occupied territories does not represent the whole illness which has afflicted the Arab nation, or the entire danger facing and surrounding it. . . . The basic problem lies in the policy of settlement . . . and *the brothers in Syria shoulder a basic responsibility for the deterioration of the Arab situation* to this extent [author's emphasis]. After the October [1973] war, they followed the same line as that followed by Sādāt, although they sometimes differed with him on details.'' Iraq's differences with Syria, the letter stated, were thus not "personal or marginal,'' but rather "deep and basic.''

Some of the clauses of the Iraqi draft charter were also clearly directed against Syria. The proposed "Supreme Political Command'' of the Front was intended to circumscribe Syria's freedom of action by assuming responsibility "to take the principal decision in all matters.'' The "secret'' section specified that this included "the decision to wage war, or any ceasefire decision.'' Another of its provisions, laying down that "the decision of the Military Command must be obeyed by all the combatant troops,'' had similar significance. Both reflected the still lingering resentment of Syria's having accepted the ceasefire ending the 1973 war against the wish of the Iraqis, whose troops were then engaged on the Golan Heights, and both were meant to guard against the recurrence of a similar situation. More specifically anti-Syrian were Iraq's demands, also included in the documents, for Syria to terminate its dominant role in Lebanon: "The brother Syrians should express their readiness in principle to withdraw from Lebanon . . . in accordance with a timetable and conditions to be determined by the command of the Front.'' A special command, subordinate to the Front's Supreme Political Command, should co-opt representatives of "the nationalist movement in Lebanon.'' The special command would "formulate the policy, activity and movement in Lebanon,'' thus removing that country's affairs from the control Syria had established over it in 1976 and maintained since then.

A different line of attack centred on inter-party relations between the Iraqi and the Syrian Ba'th. The full story was not disclosed by either side, but press speculation referred to the possibility of a reunification of the two parties (whose split had developed between 1963 and 1968), and to the release of the three leaders ousted and imprisoned by Asad in 1970.[43] They were Nūr al-Dīn al-Atāsī and Salāh Jadīd—President and assistant party Secretary-General respectively from 1966 till 1970; and Yūsuf Zu'ayyin, Prime Minister from 1966 till 1968. Their release after more than seven years in detention would have had a serious destabilizing effect on Asad's regime and did not, in fact, take place. The overall approach of Iraq in the immediate aftermath of Sādāt's visit to Jerusalem was summed up in a Baghdad newspaper editorial which asserted that Iraq had invited Asad to Baghdad (for the rival "steadfastness'' summit), not because the differences between the two countries had been surmounted, but "because we want [his] regime to give up the course it has been pursuing during the past years.''[44]

The Iraqi approach described above was not adopted solely in response to Sādāt's initiative, but must also be seen against the background of the longstanding tension existing between the two Ba'th regimes (see *MECS 1976–77*, pp. 160–63). On the eve of Sādāt's first moves in November 1977, this tension again reached a peak. On 25 October 1977, an attempt was made on the life of Syrian Foreign Minister Khaddām in Abu Dhabi, where he made a stopover during a tour of the Gulf Emirates. The gunman (who missed) was a Palestinian belonging to a pro-Iraqi Palestinian organization. Syria accused Iraq of having given the order. It also blamed Iraq for the assassination on 2 November of a prominent Ba'th member on the teaching staff of Aleppo University. Iraq subsequently blamed Syria for an explosion in Baghdad on 21 October. On 6 November, Baghdad TV broadcast the confession of a woman who admitted carrying explosives from Syria to Iraq for use by saboteurs operating in Baghdad under instructions from the Syrian intelligence service. On 10 November, following a series of bomb incidents in Damascus, Syria closed its border with Iraq. (It was reopened to partial traffic on 15 June 1978.) On 11 November, Damascus announced that it had foiled an Iraqi plot to kill a large number of citizens and tourists and "spread chaos and confusion."[45] On 16 November, Syria banned the transit of cargo, and on 19 November that of passengers, from Turkey to Iraq on the railway passing through Syrian territory.

It was against this unpropitious background that Asad appealed to Iraq to let bygones be bygones, an appeal he backed up by more tangible gestures: the Syrian propaganda campaign against Iraq was halted, and Syria suspended the aid it had until then given to Jalāl Tālabānī's Kurdish faction which had operated against Iraq from Syrian territory (see chapter on Iraq). Iraq did not relent. Speaking more than two months later, Bakr said that Syria would have to accept "the conditions and requirements" of the Iraqi charter; "outside this scope, and for other reasons than these, we see no need at present for holding a [reconciliation] meeting."[46]

With the prospect of reconciliation fading, the mutual propaganda war was stepped up again. The Iraqi media reminded Syria of past sins, such as the retention in 1975 of part of Iraq's share of the waters of the Euphrates; the quarrel in 1976 over transit fees for Iraqi oil piped across Syrian territory to the Mediterranean; and the sanctions against transit trade bound for Iraq across Syrian territory. All these acts were manifestations of "the Syrian regime's attitude towards basic Arab issues, as well as its attitude towards Iraq." The Syrians were further accused of wishing to harm Iraq's economy and of aiding "the sabotage groups of the remnants of the defunct agent pockets" (a reference to Syria's support for Tālabānī's Kurdish faction). Such pressures could not, however, cow Iraq into "bargaining over its national [i.e. all-Arab] responsibilities."[47] At about the same time, the Syrian media resumed the practice of referring to Iraqi Ba'this as "renegades" who had abandoned true Ba'th principles. The main Syrian argument—both with regard to Iraq's attitude to the conflict with Israel and to Iraqi criticism of current Syrian inaction in South Lebanon—was that the Baghdad regime "limited its position to voicing slogans" and to "a propaganda confrontation of radio and TV."[48] In mid-year, the Syrian media concentrated on the "fascist" character of the Iraqi regime and its "campaigns of terror," predicting "an imminent popular explosion" against the regime. Iraq's rulers lived in fear of their own people and therefore resorted to killing. Nor did they hesitate to order the killing of "the sons of the Palestinian people."[49] This was a reference to the campaign of violence by Iraqi-backed Sabrī al-Bannā (alias "Abū Nidāl") against al-Fatḥ, particularly those factions loyal to Syria.

President Asad himself did not appear to have lost all hope of reconciliation. In May 1978, he told interviewers from the Gulf Emirates that in trying to achieve a new "strategic balance with Israel," Syria was trying to "prevent any basic problem between any two Arab countries. Our Iraqi brothers can and must have a more effective role in pooling resources against Israel."[50]

Iraq's uncompromising enmity towards Syria was underlined by a certain ambivalence both in the tenor of Iraqi propaganda and in political action towards Egypt. After the initial blast against Sādāt (see above), the Iraqi media noticeably toned down their condemnation of Egypt. Criticism of Sādāt's policy was combined with expressions of appreciation for, and support of, the Egyptian *people*. A typical comment spoke of the Egyptian people's past "sacrifices for the sake of the Arab cause from a position of leadership in three consecutive wars." The Egyptian people "cannot [now] abandon their position of leadership in the Arab world." [51] Other commentators advocated "solidarity with the Egyptian masses in the face of [Egypt's] tyrant." [52] The frequency of references to Egypt tapered off towards the end of 1977; the Egyptian media reciprocated by concentrating their attacks against the Tripoli bloc, rarely mentioning Iraq's role.

Consular, commercial and cultural relations between Egypt and Iraq were formally re-established on 2 February 1978. An Iraqi Information Ministry statement declared that while the Tripoli bloc summit (then meeting in Algiers, see above) aimed at isolating Egypt, Iraq was opposed to such a policy. [53] In March, Iraq's embassy in Cairo and Egypt's in Baghdad were back in operation, although the ambassadors themselves did not return to their posts. However, the relative normalization of official relations did not prevent Iraq from launching a new programme over Radio Baghdad on 15 February entitled *Sawt Misr al-'Urūba* (literally "The Voice of the Egypt of Arabism"), which was vehemently critical of what it termed Egypt's "ruling clique." It branded the "clique" as "capitulationist," accused it of harassing "revolutionary" Egyptians as well as Palestinians residing in Egypt, blamed it for furthering capitalist tendencies through Egypt's economic "open-door" policy, and charged it with unwarranted intervention in Zaïre to "suppress the revolution" there.

In sum, in the situation created after Sādāt's initiative, Iraq achieved something it had aimed at ever since the end of the 1973 war: it witnessed the destruction of whatever remained of the wartime bond between Egypt and Syria, and watched a bitter feud erupt between the two. However, this did not happen at the instigation of Iraq (as, between 1974 and 1976, it hoped it would); nor did it enable Iraq to force its own line on Syria and place itself at the head of a "rejectionist" front in the Iraqi understanding of that term. Instead, Syria placed itself at the head of a grouping—weak though it was—whose members Iraq regarded as its own potential allies. In the event, despite a measure of ideological sympathy for Iraq, they refused to accept Iraq's programme of action as a prescription for practical politics. Except in the regional context of the Persian Gulf, Iraq's aloofness from the mainstream of inter-Arab affairs became more pronounced during the period reviewed.

THE SAUDI GROUPING

Saudi Arabia and the countries ranging themselves alongside it formed a group only in the loosest possible sense of the term: in contrast to the Tripoli bloc, they held no common meetings, issued no joint statements, and made no attempt to create joint institutions. They did not even define which Arab states belonged with them and which did not. What marked them off from the rest of the Arab world was that they took (and were perceived as taking) their cue from Riyadh over the principal Arab issues raised by Sādāt's initiative. Again in contrast with the Tripoli bloc, their criticism of Sādāt was veiled and intermittent rather than strident and constant. They shared with the Tripoli Front and with Iraq the distaste for Egypt's violation of Arab solidarity and disregard for Arab summit resolutions; they shared the fear that Sādāt's chosen path might lead him into a separate deal with Israel, or suspected him of being prepared to offer Israel a substantive compromise. In Saudi Arabia's case, these suspicions were reinforced by pique at not having been consulted.

However, the Saudis and their supporters did not share the wish to see Sādāt overthrown. On the contrary, Sādāt's fall would be dangerous for Saudi Arabia, as any conceivable successor regime in Egypt would most likely be hostile to it or, worse, harbour ambitions in the direction of the Arabian Peninsula. While the Tripoli bloc and Iraq conceived of the next stage in inter-Arab affairs as one in which a new Egyptian regime would renounce Sādāt and all he stood for, Saudi Arabia and its followers thought of the "restoration of Arab solidarity" (their principal slogan throughout the period under review) as signifying Sādāt's return to the Arab fold. In order to return, he would of course have to give up "unilateral action" and realign Egypt not only with all-Arab aims but with all-Arab tactics. The countries following the Saudi line at most times were Kuwait, the other Gulf Emirates (except for Oman), and the YAR. As noted above, Tunisia joined the Saudi grouping soon after Sādāt's initial moves, and Sudan drew steadily closer to the Saudi position during the spring of 1978. Jordan's policy coincided with that of Saudi Arabia in many respects, but followed a line of its own in others. Its attitudes and activities are described separately.

As with the other Arab states, it was the first Saudi reaction to Sādāt's move which set the tone for the following months. A statement by the Royal Court (a rare occurrence in itself) was issued as soon as the date for Sādāt's visit to Jerusalem was made public. It said that the Kingdom was "surprised" by Sādāt's intention. "On the basis of the Arab summit resolutions, which not only define the objectives, but also . . . the means leading to these objectives, the Kingdom . . . considers the principles of Arab solidarity to be . . . the necessary course for any Arab effort aimed at solving the Arab question. Accordingly, the Kingdom . . . believes that any Arab initiative in this connection should stem from a unified Arab stand." In an implicit warning against a compromise solution, the statement went on to say that Saudi Arabia's position regarding the Arab cause was "based on the resolutions of the Arab summit conferences of Algiers [1973] and Rabat [1974], aimed at achieving withdrawal from all the occupied Arab territories including Jerusalem and the recognition of the Palestinian people's legitimate rights, including the right to return to their homeland and set up an independent state on their territory." It concluded by saying that "King Khālid . . . has sent a message to [Sādāt] explaining the position of the Kingdom . . . in a frank manner that leaves no room for confusion or ambiguity." [54]

A second message, sent after Sādāt's return to Egypt, restated the Saudi attitude. In view of Saudi Arabia's traditionally restrained political style, both statements must be considered forceful demonstrations of displeasure (cf *MECS 1976–77*, p. 159). They marked the first time since 'Abd al-Nāsir's death in 1970 that either King Faysal, or King Khālid after him, had ranged Saudi Arabia against Egypt in inter-Arab affairs.

The basic argument—that "all Arabs should take one common stand in all circumstances" [55]—was sounded again and again in the following months. However, the note of dissatisfaction with Egypt was gradually toned down until revived following the Camp David summit. For one thing, the pro-Western orientation common to the countries of the grouping asserted itself more forcefully during 1978, particularly in the light of their perception of the danger of Soviet penetration into the Red Sea, the Horn of Africa and other parts of Africa. To meet this danger, the co-operation of Egypt was indispensable. So was that of the US, whose antagonism could not be aroused, even though its backing of Sādāt's initiative was often embarrassing. Both reasons, as well as the consideration that Sādāt would eventually have to be received back into the Arab community, made outspoken criticism of Egypt inadvisable. In addition, bilateral Saudi-US relations, particularly at the time of the aircraft deal (see essay on the US and the Middle East), made it imperative for Saudi Arabia to foster in Washington an image of moderation and of its capability to lead a "moderate Arab camp." The attitude which thus crystallized (and which, by and large, was adopted by the other states in the grouping) was articulated in the cautious and ambiguous words of Crown Prince Fahd, who told a Saudi interviewer: "As brothers to fraternal Egypt and to President Sādāt, we shall never cease to maintain contact with Egypt and to give it our views on whatever we think will serve the interest of the [Arab] nation." [56] Yet the wish to avoid any appearance of backing Egypt, however indirectly, was strong enough for King Khālid to turn down two suggestions by Sādāt, in December 1977 and January 1978, to visit Riyadh[57]—a proposal not renewed during the remainder of the period under review. [58] The conflicting attitudes underlying this policy resulted in long periods of official silence on the part of the Saudi camp during the first half of 1978. At the same time, frequent consultations took place between Saudi Arabia and like-minded Arab states. Co-ordination with the Gulf Emirates was particularly close.

An important indication of Saudi Arabia's and the Gulf states' interest in the maintenance of Sādāt's regime was the fact that financial aid to Egypt was neither suspended, nor—as far as is known—cut back. Reports to the contrary were quickly denied by official quarters. [59] Moreover, Saudi and Kuwaiti deposits in Egypt's central bank were not withdrawn as scheduled in order not to aggravate that country's balance-of-payments problems. The Gulf Organization for the Development of Egypt, established in 1976 by Saudi Arabia, Kuwait, Qatar and the UAE, continued to function as before. So did the Arab Military Industries Organization, formed in 1975 by Egypt, Saudi Arabia, Qatar and the UAE. Following a meeting of its Higher Committee in Abu Dhabi on 21 February 1978, the Saudi Defence Minister, Sultān b. 'Abd al-'Azīz, expressly ruled out the possibility that "Arab differences" could affect the Organization's activities. [60]

Between January and August 1978, Saudi policy alternated between attempts to pressure Sādāt into declaring his initiative a failure, or at least discontinuing direct talks with Israel, and efforts, mostly by proxy, to revive Arab solidarity. At times, it combined both aims. The first occasion to apply pressure for the termination of Sādāt's initiative presented itself when the Egyptian delegation was recalled from Jerusalem in January 1978. (For the stages of the Israeli-Egyptian negotiations referred to in this passage, see essay on the Arab-Israeli Conflict.) Comments in the Saudi press and statements by spokesmen of Peninsular states spoke of the momentum of Sādāt's move having been exhausted and argued that, in the absence of Arab solidarity, there was no point in pursuing it in any case. Direct diplomatic steps were also taken, though not publicly acknowledged at the time. Shortly after the break in January, Syrian Foreign Minister Khaddām attested to the shift in Saudi (and Kuwaiti) positions at that juncture. Both countries, he told a Kuwaiti interviewer, had begun "to clarify their attitudes." Their leaders had "assured [Syria] of their rejection of Egypt's present policies." [61] Diplomatic pressure seems to have been applied with various degrees of determination from then on until the Leeds Castle conference in July.

Meanwhile, two attempts were made to bring the Arab countries together again. The first, by the YAR, was apparently tolerated rather than encouraged by Saudi Arabia; the second, by the Arab League, was clearly endorsed by it. In the interval between the conclusion of the Leeds Castle conference on 20 July and Egypt's acceptance of President Carter's invitation to Camp David (8 August), a third attempt was carried out by Saudi Arabia itself, with much greater vigour than the preceding ones—but with just as little success.

The North Yemeni campaign was launched in December 1977 by YAR Foreign

Minister 'Abdallah al-Asnaj (a strong supporter of Egypt ever since he began his career in the mid-sixties). His first round of contacts in December was made within the group of Saudi Arabia's allies: apart from Riyadh, he visited Kuwait, the UAE and Sudan. During the second round (17–25 January 1978), Asnaj conveyed messages from the YAR's Head of State, Aḥmad Ḥusayn al-Ghashmī, to Jordan, Syria and Egypt, as well as to Saudi Arabia. A further round, early in February, included Iraq, Kuwait, Bahrain, Qatar, the UAE, Oman and, once again, Saudi Arabia. His declared aim was to obtain agreement for a conference of the states bordering on Israel with those offering them assistance (the "confrontation states" and the "supporting states") to serve as a stepping-stone towards a comprehensive Arab summit meeting.[62] In March, he conceded failure, blaming "certain Arab states" who refused to participate in a summit attended by Sādāt.[63]

The second attempt was formally launched by the Arab League. Its Council met in Cairo from 27–29 March 1978, with the Israeli incursion into South Lebanon the main point on its agenda. The meeting was boycotted by the Tripoli bloc. Not wishing to be outdone in a demonstration of anti-Sādāt sentiment, Iraq also stayed away, though it had not itself subscribed to the Tripoli decisions. Their absence gave the Saudi grouping an overwhelming majority among those participating. It made use of its dominant position, and of the ostensibly "neutral" subject of Lebanon—"neutral," that is, in terms of the controversy surrounding Sādāt's initiative—to have two resolutions carried which reflected its own approach. The first called for the convention "as soon as possible" of an Arab summit conference "to mobilize all Arab strength and resources to confront the aggressive Israeli defiance" in Lebanon. The stress on the mobilization of resources was intended to make it difficult for the boycotters to reject the summit call. The second resolution was to form a Committee for Arab Solidarity (*lajna lil-tadāmun al-'arabī*) to function "at the highest level, to settle current Arab disputes and create the appropriate atmosphere" for a summit. Probably at Saudi Arabia's prompting, Sudanese President Ja'far al-Numayrī was asked, and agreed, to establish the committee and serve as its chairman.[64] Following a series of soundings by the League's Secretary-General Maḥmūd Riyāḍ (of Egypt), the committee held its first meeting in Khartoum on 22 and 23 April, chaired by Numayrī and attended by the Foreign Ministers of Saudi Arabia, Kuwait, Jordan, the YAR and the UAE—all identified with, or close to, the Saudi line. Maḥmūd Riyāḍ took part as well. The committee approved a working paper dealing with the issue of restoring diplomatic relations between Arab countries which had severed them, the termination of hostile propaganda campaigns, and the full reactivation of the League. In May, Numayrī toured some Arab capitals with a view to having diplomatic relations restored, preparatory to the convention of a summit meeting. In Damascus, he suggested that Egypt suspend the work of the Israeli-Egyptian military committee (then still in Egypt) and continue the negotiations in another forum on neutral ground, away from Egypt and Israel, in return for the resumption of Syrian-Egyptian ties. As a pre-condition, however, Syria insisted on Sādāt's officially renouncing his initiative. Iraq and Algeria gave similar replies. Before returning to Khartoum on 13 May, Numayrī stopped over in Cairo to report to Sādāt. Following another tour of Arab capitals at the beginning of June, Numayrī convened the committee again, on 17 and 18 June. This time, it conceded failure, deciding that each of its members should continue bilateral contacts for the purpose of "paving the way for solidarity." Later in June, Numayrī made one last attempt to infuse life into the committee by calling for a third meeting to be attended by the Heads of State themselves. As Arab attention at that point was riveted on the murder and execution of the Heads of State of the YAR and the PDRY respectively, his call went unheeded. This marked the end of the committee's activities.

In July, the crisis in Egyptian-Israeli relations caused Saudi Arabia to abandon its reserve. The two components of Saudi policy—to urge Sādāt to restrict or terminate his initiative, and to reunite Arab ranks—coalesced as Riyadh perceived a chance to achieve both. Moving onto the centre of the inter-Arab stage, Crown Prince Fahd then launched his own personal venture.

FAHD'S INTERVENTION

Sādāt ordered the Israeli military mission to leave Egypt on 26 July 1978. Four days later, he announced that further direct contacts would depend on Israel's prior agreement not to claim territorial changes. On the same day, Prince Fahd and his Foreign Minister, Sa'ūd al-Faysal, arrived in Alexandria for two days of talks with Sādāt. On 1 August, Fahd and Sa'ūd met King Husayn in Amman and President Asad in Damascus. The following day, they met President Bakr in Baghdad. Their tour thus spanned the entire gamut of Arab politics at that time: Egypt, the Tripoli bloc (via Syria), the Saudi grouping (through the two mediators themselves), and the two Arab "loners," Jordan and Iraq.

No official statements were made at the conclusion of the visits, but Arab press comment left no doubt as to the aim of Fahd and Sa'ūd. The Saudi paper *al-Riyād*, for instance, wrote that after the failure of the Leeds Castle talks, negotiations with Israel should be discontinued and the Arabs turn to the task of closing ranks. A similar line was taken by Jordanian papers. [65] The Syrian *Tishrīn* called on the Arab states directly concerned with the Israeli issue to consult together over their next steps—a guarded appeal to resume contacts with Egypt, the like of which had not been made in the Syrian media since November 1977. Differences between Arab regimes, it said, must not be allowed to blur the fact that the "essential conflict" was with Israel. The same paper claimed two days later that Sādāt had indeed promised "in closed meetings"—presumably in the talks with Fahd and Sa'ūd— that he would "close the door to Tel Aviv" and "open it to the Arab capitals." [66] Similarly, a Jidda daily spoke of the "healthy signs of solidarity and the start of a unified strategy" which had "appeared on the horizon." [67] Fahd reported to the Cabinet that he had come back with "tangible facts," namely Sādāt's "adherence to not signing a separate peace" and "the desire by the other leaders to make the present stage into a situation where the Arab world would be united." [68]

With the announcement by Sādāt on 8 August that he would attend the Camp David summit together with the Israeli Prime Minister, the Saudi effort collapsed. Putting the best face on the matter, Fahd cited King Khālid on 10 August as having expressed "high appreciation for the personal efforts of President Carter and the appreciation of Saudi Arabia for the endeavours of the USA"; it was to be hoped that the Camp David meeting would "achieve a giant step along the road to the desired just peace." However, Fahd expressed his "regret" at the "declared unwillingness of Israel to change her obstinate intentions," and thus serve the cause of justice and help the US efforts for peace. [69]

The Saudi volte-face ended the chances for the restoration of a broad Arab consensus. Not only did the Tripoli bloc and Iraq again step up their attacks against Sādāt, but Syria now also indirectly attacked Saudi Arabia. The Syrian papers referred to Sādāt's consent to go to Camp David as proof of his being an "American agent" who was no longer "worthy of confidence." At that conference, the US-Egyptian-Israeli "tripartite plot" to impose "capitulation and humiliation" on the Arabs would continue as before. As for Fahd's mediation, *Tishrīn* wrote that any further call for Arab reunification, which included Egypt, could "from now on only be seen as *overt collusion with the policy of subservience to the US and capitulation to Israel.''*[70] The Saudi intervention thus had a doubly negative effect on Riyadh's inter-Arab standing: it underlined the diminution of its power to manipulate other Arab countries, and it caused the two main groups who were striving to end Sādāt's initiative in its original form to draw further apart. When Jordan and Kuwait followed Saudi Arabia in making known their attitudes towards the Camp David meeting, the split between the Riyadh camp and Jordan on the one hand, and Syria, its associates and Iraq on the other, assumed a significance it had not possessed before. The split was no longer quite so completely eclipsed by the dispute between Sādāt and his various critics. The effect of the outcome of the Camp David summit on the overall Arab constellation could not accurately be assessed at the time of writing. (See, however, some initial observations in the first essay in this volume, "The Year in Perspective.")

THE POSITION OF JORDAN

More so than for any other Arab country, apart from Egypt itself, the impact of Sādāt's initiative on Jordan derived from the substantive, inherent content of Egypt's new policy, rather than from the change it wrought on the all-Arab scene. Jordan was the only other Arab state which, during the period reviewed, was considered a possible candidate for joining the negotiations. Jordan's assessment of the Arab backing it believed necessary for joining the negotiating process, or of the hostility it might encounter if it were to do so without such backing, certainly played a major part in shaping Jordan's attitude. While the attitude of many Arab countries towards Sādāt was a function of their inter-Arab politics, Jordan's inter-Arab stance in 1977–78 was, by contrast, mostly a function of its perception of the prospects and risks of Sādāt's initiative as such. (Jordan's basic attitude to the initiative is detailed in the essay on the Arab-Israeli Conflict and in the chapter on Jordan.)

In the present context, the first inter-Arab issue that arose in the immediate wake of Sādāt's move was that of Jordanian-Syrian relations. These had been growing steadily closer between 1975 and 1976, but had levelled off in 1977 (see *MECS 1976–77*, pp. 154–57). Jordan's problem was how to dissociate itself sufficiently from the Amman-Damascus axis to ensure Saudi goodwill—now more vital than before—and to create for itself some freedom of manoeuvre with regard to Egypt without openly antagonizing Syria. These considerations governed the language of Jordan's initial reaction to Sādāt's move. The Cabinet statement issued on 19 November 1977 said that "Jordan believes that unilateral behaviour towards the joint question [of the Israeli occupation and of peace] and in the face of Israel is the same as negative action. . . . Unilateral action weakens Arab ranks and negativeness consecrates occupation." Jordan continued to believe that "Arab solidarity and unity of ranks . . . are the best ways to achieve pan-Arab aspirations." Yet the statement went on to urge "the entire Arab nation . . . to be very careful in their reactions towards the Egyptian initiative and the future of Arab relations." The Arabs should avoid falling prey to "internal conflicts and disintegration as a result of emotionalism and hastiness in adopting emotional and negative stands." Jordan urged all Arab countries "to seek to contain differences [and] to take action again to build a unified Arab stand based on positive dialogue and joint efforts."[71]

Jordan's first official and overt inter-Arab contact after Sādāt's return from Israel was the visit of its Prime Minister, Mudar Badrān, to Damascus on 22 and 23 November. On 28 November, Jordan indicated that it would not participate in the Cairo conference to which Sādāt had invited it, nor would it join the Tripoli conference as Syria had urged it to do. The official statement explained that Jordan would only participate in a conference attended by all parties concerned, or in a comprehensive Arab summit.[72] In the following weeks, Jordan largely abstained from officially commenting on Sādāt's activities. Sādāt took pains to keep Jordan informed of developments in the negotiations with Israel and began hinting at the desirability of Jordan's joining them. King Husayn's initial fear of a separate Egyptian-Israeli settlement—already allayed by Sādāt's speech in the Knesset, which Husayn described as "excellent"—thus gradually subsided. In December, Husayn illustrated his "multi-directional" policy of open options by visiting Damascus (7 December), Cairo (8 and 9 December) and Riyadh (18 and 19 December). At that time, no other leader would have thought it feasible to combine a trip to Cairo with one to Damascus. When the Jerusalem talks were broken off by Sādāt in January 1978, a Jordanian statement expressed "full support" for Egypt for insisting on "the basic Arab demands and rights without any relinquishment." The recall of the delegation "should prompt the whole Arab nation . . . fully to support Egypt."[73] This contrasted sharply with the reaction of the Tripoli bloc and Iraq, who termed the suspension of the talks "a farce," and prompted Syrian Foreign Minister Khaddām to describe Jordan's position as "incomprehensible." During the following month, however, the slackening momentum of Sādāt's initiative, the attitude of Saudi Arabia and growing pressure by Syria[74] caused Jordan to exercise greater caution. In February, Husayn told a correspondent that even though Jordanian and Syrian views "sometimes differ," he had "not felt any coolness or tension" between the two countries.[75] Badrān said that Jordanian-Syrian co-ordination continued in various fields.[76] Khaddām reciprocated by saying that Syria had now "ascertained from our brothers in Amman that Jordan will not change its stand."[77]

Husayn seized the opportunity provided by the entry of Israeli troops into South Lebanon in March to call for an urgent all-Arab summit conference to discuss the situation there. At the same time, the summit could act to reconcile Arab differences, adopt a unified Arab policy and pool resources to build up a new "intrinsic" Arab force.[78] Between 19 and 30 March, and again from 9 to 14 April, Jordan contacted Arab capitals to promote the summit scheme; at the same time, it agreed to become a member of the Arab League Solidarity Committee (see above). When both Jordan's summit call and the committee's efforts failed, Jordan resumed its policy of keeping its lines open to all the major Arab countries, without taking a clear-cut stand on the issues under discussion. As part of this policy, Husayn went to Saudi Arabia for talks with Crown Prince Fahd from 20–22 May, and with King Khālid on 22 July. The Egyptian Foreign Minister, Ibrāhīm Kāmil, went to Amman on 26 July, at Sādāt's request, for a meeting with Husayn. The King met Asad in Damascus on 20 July. Their talks resulted in a meeting in Damascus on 2 and 3 August of the Higher Jordanian-Syrian Joint Committee which had last convened in June 1977 (see *MECS 1976–77*, p. 154). Even though its deliberations were apparently of a routine nature, dealing with minor points of economic co-operation, the very fact of the committee's revival bore witness to the desire of both sides to demonstrate at that stage that Syrian-Jordanian relations had not deteriorated beyond repair. The effect of this meeting was, however, largely undone on 13 August by Husayn's favourable reference to the Camp David summit, which again placed Jordan in opposition to Syria.

Throughout the period reviewed, Jordan's inter-Arab policies remained tentative and inconclusive. They were intended to tide the country over a period of uncertainty, of alternating expectations and disappointments, so that it could move unhindered into the appropriate alignment at the right moment—i.e. as soon as the future of the West Bank became clear enough to reveal just which camp that was.

EGYPT'S DEFENCE: DEFIANCE AND JUSTIFICATIONS

The basic tenet of Egypt's defence against its critics, whether those engaging in verbal assault or those keeping a disapproving silence, was the following: Egypt was fully entitled to choose its own political course and rejected any "tutelage" over its conduct by any, or all, of the other Arab states; the path it had chosen, however, was actually in conformity with "all-Arab strategy" (though not all-Arab tactics); Egypt was, at all times and at every turn, faithfully serving the Arab cause. It had not given away any "historic right of the Arab nation," nor had it committed any other Arab state. This line of argument was put forward by Sādāt himself in numerous speeches and countless interviews, and was reiterated by Egyptian spokesmen and the media (with the exception of opposition organs). It remained the constant thread running through Egyptian comment on the Arab scene and underlay Sādāt's reaction to the various efforts (described above) to "restore Arab unity." Egypt was ready to contribute to the closing of Arab ranks, whether by resuming diplomatic relations with the countries with which it had severed them, or even by ultimately attending a summit meeting, but Sādāt insisted that he would not be deflected from his chosen course, abandon the peace initiative, or "allow anyone to interfere with my decision." Arab solidarity had, in any case, not been undermined by Egypt in 1977; rather, it had been undermined by Iraq and Libya in 1973, when they violated the oil embargo, and by Syria in 1974 and 1975, when it attacked Egypt over the first and second Sinai Agreements, and again in 1976, when it fought the PLO in Lebanon.

Within the framework of these principles, Sādāt drew a clear distinction between the Tripoli bloc countries (occasionally including Iraq as well), and the rest of his critics. Differences with the latter were played down; the former, by contrast, were dealt with aggressively, spoken of with contempt and depicted as utterly insignificant. He referred to them collectively as "presumptuous dwarfs" or "pigmies," "mice or monkeys" who "insolently" denied Egypt's sovereign rights and whose "impudence" he would not tolerate. He spoke of Qadhdhāfī as a "spoiled child" and "a mental case," and said he was "deeply sorry" for Boumedienne for having allowed himself to be misled by Libya. The PDRY was merely "grovelling for [Libyan] money." 'Arafāt had let himself become prisoner of Syria and the USSR, evidently—Sādātᶜ implied—against his own better judgement. Under PLO leadership, the Palestinians had become "helpless" and were being "coerced." But Sādāt's greatest bitterness was reserved for Syria. He described Asad as being at the mercy of hide-bound Baʿth party ideologues, and as the hapless executor of designs forced upon him by the USSR. The Baʿth party, governed by its "complexes of impotence, defeatism and opportunism," represented only 2% of the Syrian population, while 98% supported Egypt's line. Referring to the preponderance of members of the minority 'Alawite community in the Syrian leadership, Sādāt asked if it was Asad's intention to turn Syria into an 'Alawite state. Was he out to establish a Greater Syria? Was that why King Husayn had now moved away from Damascus? Having invaded Lebanon and "intimidated" Jordan, Syria imagined itself to be "a great power." In fact, he said, Syria had emerged the main loser, because it had "lost Egypt." [79]

The sanctions imposed on Egypt by the Tripoli bloc elicited vigorous Egyptian counter-measures. (For details, see chapter on Egypt.)

With regard to Saudi Arabia, Sādāt did not deny that there were differences of view, but he dismissed them as "something natural: brothers have differences, but in the final analysis we are brothers." [80] A note of defiance was now entirely lacking in references to Saudi Arabia, however. Referring to Saudi suggestions on the eve of his departure to Jerusalem that the visit be cancelled, Sādāt said that "all the gold in the world cannot possibly buy our dignity or our decisions." [81]

As for Jordan, the burden of Egyptian policy was to draw King Ḥusayn into the negotiating process with Israel, or at least to prepare the ground for his joining at a later stage. The various stages of these attempts (in which Sādāt was aided by the US and by Iran) are described in the second section of the essay on the Arab-Israeli Conflict.

The prolonged polemics brought two conflicting motifs to the fore: the reaffirmation of Egypt's claim to a focal role in Arab affairs, and a stress on Egypt's "otherness" as compared with the rest of the Arab world. The first line of argument centred chiefly on Sādāt's repeated assertion that Egypt was "the key to war and peace" (a claim hotly disputed by Damascus). It found its bluntest expression in Sādāt's words: "I hold the right to decide on war or peace in the area." [82] The other motif was clothed in numerous references to Egypt's long history, ancient culture and present level of civilization which marked it off from other Arab countries. "My people have a certain culture," Sādāt told an American correspondent. "You can't measure us as you measure other Arab countries. . . . We are civilized at heart." [83] Rejection of Arab "tutelage" and pride in Egypt's "Egyptianism" merged in statements like: "I am proud to belong to this people. . . . I am proud of Egyptian man, whom 7,000 years have made into a person of culture"; or "I will bow to nobody except to the people of Egypt." [84] Such thoughts were taken a step further by intellectuals outside the ruling establishment, some of whom called for Egypt's dissociation from its commitments to the all-Arab cause. Most notable in this respect was novelist Tawfīq al-Ḥakīm's proposal that Egypt should proclaim itself neutral "like Switzerland or Austria." [85] This was followed by a lively debate on Egypt's "Arabism" or "Egyptianism." The leadership itself did not share such far-reaching ideas, however. In the face of all Arab claims to the contrary, Sādāt never wavered in his denial that Egypt was heading for a separate deal, or was faltering in its commitment to the Arab cause. As so often before in inter-Arab affairs, ever since the first Arab summit in 1964, the issue of convening a summit conference provided the touchstone (cf *MECS 1976–77*, p. 176). During the first half of 1978, Sādāt rejected the summit calls, since they would result in a conference "without a clear plan . . . and [without] a noble aim." [86] Underlying the rejection was the realization that, under the circumstances, Egypt would find itself on the defensive against a majority of Arab states. But right from the start of his initiative, Sādāt insisted that eventually Egypt itself would call for a summit, present the results of the initiative to it, [87] and emerge fully vindicated and capable of resuming its rightful leading role.

ARAB SOLIDARITY CALLED IN QUESTION

Beyond the issues of the day, the turn in Egyptian policy from November 1977 raised matters of principle as to the meaning of Arab solidarity. At most times, solidarity had been an ideal rather than a guide to action; but at no time had the contradiction between accepted norms of political thought and the actual conduct of political practice been thrown into such sharp focus. The unilateral character of Sādāt's action; his failure to consult other Arab leaders; his flouting of old-established Arab taboos; his disregard for the language of past summit resolutions; his perseverance in the face of Arab pressure; his violation, in the view of some of his critics, of the Arab League charter; the indication of growing "Egyptianist" sentiment in Cairo—all combined to produce profound malaise throughout the Arab world in public discussion of "unified Arab action." Expressions of concern over the future "unity of the Arab cause," over the "blow to national consciousness" and the danger threatening the very "foundations of unity and solidarity" abounded in statements by the Tripoli bloc; they were also to be found in official utterances or in the media of Saudi Arabia, the UAE, Tunisia and others. An editorial in the Syrian *al-Ba'th* went so far as to speak of "the process of Arab collapse." [88]

It is noteworthy that the charge of Egypt's having broken Arab ranks was the one common denominator in the arguments put forward against Sādāt by all his critics. For once, President Asad spoke for them all when he said that Sādāt had "dealt separately and alone with affairs that concern the whole region, which he had no right to do." [89] Other members of the Tripoli bloc, the Saudi grouping, Jordan, Iraq, and eventually Sudan as well, made the same point, although each chose a wording in keeping with its overall policy.

A formal "indictment" of Sādāt was presented on 1 August 1978 at the opening of a public show-trial charging him with "high treason." The charge-sheet had been prepared at the instance of an "Arab People's Congress" (a loose conglomeration of various self-styled "popular organizations") which met in Tripoli immediately after the establishment of the Tripoli bloc in December 1977. The Congress had set up a "Permanent Secretariat" which drew up the indictment, the contents of which were disclosed at a press conference in Damascus on 22 July 1978, timed to coincide with Egypt's Revolution Day. The opening session of the "Arab People's Court" was held nine days later in Baghdad, a rare instance of Syrian-Iraqi co-operation. The court was composed of "judges" described as representing Iraq, Syria, Libya, Algeria, Lebanon, Egypt and Palestine. After a single opening session, it adjourned until November 1978. The trial itself was thus entirely marginal to the events of the year, but is worth mentioning because of the particular stress the indictment placed on Sādāt's "*pan-Arab* crimes," including such offences as "hostility" to the all-Arab national interest, "obstructing Arab action," and the violation of summit resolutions. It also demanded that Sādāt be proclaimed "an enemy of our nation." [90] Underlying such vehement phrases was not only the fear—widespread indeed, as has been shown—of a separate settlement, but the suspicion that in the long run, Egypt might turn its back on the Arab world altogether and disavow the all-Arab mode of nationalism (thus falling prey to "regionalism," as Sādāt's critics would have called it, using the standard Arab pejorative term for defectors from the all-Arab cause). This would not only grievously weaken overall Arab military strength and diplomatic effectiveness, but deal a possibly fatal blow to the pan-Arab creed. It was the latter consideration which prompted most critics of the Egyptian *regime* frequently to express solidarity with, and regard for, the Egyptian *people*.

Despite the almot total consensus about the damage done by Egypt to the cause—even the very concept—of Arab solidarity, opinions differed widely as to the remedy. For Saudi Arabia, this could be achieved primarily by restoring a measure of co-operation between Egypt and Syria, with both looking to Riyadh for guidance, mediation of occasional differences, and money. Such a situation had existed during 1973, and again from the autumn of 1976 till November 1977; Saudi Arabia continued to regard that constellation as the best guarantee both for overall Arab co-ordination and for promoting its own aspirations to what might be called "rule by arbitration." Egypt's own concept of the restoration of solidarity by the resumption of its own central role has already been referred to. Against this view, Syria upheld what a Ba'th party publication called "solidarity against the [Israeli] enemy." [91] Damascus believed that calls for the restoration of solidarity which did not make the "rejection of capitulationist policies" a pre-condition stemmed from weakness and would eventually serve as a cover-up for capitulation. Only after the complete liquidation of the after-effects of Sādāt's initiative could effective solidarity be restored.[92] Syria, the "cradle of Arabism," the guarantor of "vigilance against Zionist-imperialist plots" and the "fountainhead of steadfastness" (all expressions frequently used by Syria's spokesmen and media), thought of itself as the natural leader of such solidarity. In ranging the Arab countries committed to "steadfastness" against those advocating "capitulationist policies," Syria, the other member-states of the Tripoli bloc and Iraq seemed to be harking back to an earlier period—that of the mid-sixties—when the Arab world was divided into "progressive" and "reactionary" regimes, and when the "progressives" deemed only they were capable of promoting unity.

It was the uncertainty surrounding so basic and time-honoured a concept of Arab political thought, combined with the conflicting trends of Realpolitik set out above, which produced two fundamental failures in the system of inter-Arab relations during the period reviewed: the failure to shape an effective Arab coalition against the policy of Egypt which most Arab countries wished to see frustrated; and the failure to put forward a convincing, agreed and feasible alternative policy. This in turn would account for the seeming paradox that in spite of its position of relative isolation, Egypt could continue setting the pace of Middle Eastern events and maintain its own initiative at every critical juncture.

REGIONAL ISSUES

The events described above constituted the central axis on which the emergence or disintegration of Arab alignments revolved after November 1977. There were, however, four spheres of more restricted regional interest which were also dealt with at various levels of inter-Arab contacts: Red Sea and African affairs; Sudan's relations with its neighbours; developments in the Maghrib; and relations among the Arab littorals of the Persian Gulf. While each of these was distinct from the chief Arab preoccupations created by Sādāt's initiative, the first three were not entirely separate from them: those principally involved (Saudi Arabia, Egypt and Sudan in Red Sea and Nile valley affairs; Algeria and Libya in Maghrib developments) were also major parties to the developments surrounding Sādāt's initiative, and a certain nexus can at times be perceived between their conduct in one sphere and the line they followed in the other. Relations within the group of Gulf Emirates, by contrast, increasingly came to take on a life of their own, following their own logic and evolving almost independently of events elsewhere in the Arab world. These are therefore described in the opening section of the chapter on the Gulf states.

RED SEA AND THE HORN OF AFRICA

In reacting to events in the Horn of Africa in 1977 and 1978, the most prominent Arab view, held with increasing forcefulness by the leading states concerned, was that Soviet-Cuban involvement in Ethiopia was part of a larger Soviet scheme for penetration into the Red Sea and for the encirclement of the pro-Western Arab states of the Arabian Peninsula and in Africa. President Ja'far al-Numayrī was the first Arab leader to state that in the long term, Soviet activities in Ethiopia were aimed not only at establishing domination over the Horn of Africa, but at reviving Soviet influence in the Middle East at large by way of the Nile valley. Neighbouring African states were to be "ideologically infiltrated" by an Ethiopia turned Marxist.[93] Sādāt echoed this view when he told a correspondent that "the USSR is after Numayrī in Sudan and after me."[94] Sudan's Vice-President, al-Rashīd al-Tāhir Bakr, took the view that Soviet aims were even more far-reaching: the USSR sought a sphere of influence embracing Iran, the Arabian Peninsula, the Horn of Africa and the Nile valley, creating a Soviet-controlled belt across the oil route from the Persian Gulf to the Mediterranean and straddling the sea lanes of the Indian Ocean and the Red Sea.[95] YAR Foreign Minister, 'Abdallah al-Asnaj, also believed that the war in the Ogaden was primarily being fought in order to threaten the oil states in the Arabian Peninsula.[96] Saudi Arabia held similar views, the close co-operation and frequent consultations between Sudan and Saudi Arabia over Red Sea and African affairs being a conspicuous feature of the entire period. In addition, Sudan made a point of consulting Saudi Arabia on the development of its relations with Libya (see below).

The first occasion to test the impact of these perceptions on the shaping of actual policies came in the summer of 1977, when Somalia sought aid from a number of Arab states in its war with Ethiopia. (For earlier attempts at co-ordination of Arab Red Sea policies, see *MECS 1976-77*, pp. 172-75.) Somali President Muḥammad Siyad Barreh visited Saudi Arabia in July 1977 and obtained promises for financial aid as well as for the supply of military equipment and spare parts, intended to tide Somalia over the interval between the cut-off of Soviet deliveries and the start of supplies from the West.[97] A last and unsuccessful attempt by Barreh to mend fences with the USSR was followed by a visit to Egypt (31 August 1977) and a tour of Saudi Arabia, Syria, Kuwait, Iraq, the UAE and Qatar, as well as another visit to Egypt (13–21 September). His stopover in Iraq was particularly noteworthy: in spite of its close relations with the USSR at the time, Baghdad decided to side with Somalia against Ethiopia, thereby foreshadowing the cooling off of Soviet-Iraqi ties in 1978. Deliveries of Egyptian arms and the dispatch of military advisers to Somalia began in July; Iraqi military aid started to reach the country in August 1977.[98] Although Somalia clearly had the sympathy of a majority of Arab countries (including all the conservative ones, as well as some of the more radical regimes), there was no concerted Arab action or any noticeable degree of policy co-ordination with regard to Somalia in 1977. The cancellation by Somalia of its Treaty of Friendship with the USSR (13 November 1977) reinforced support for Somalia by pro-Western Arab states, but ranged the PDRY against it. Even though the declared policy of the PDRY continued to be one of neutrality in the Somali-Ethiopian conflict, reports from a variety of Western and Arab sources spoke of the presence of a South Yemeni army contingent of 1–2,000 men in Ethiopia at the beginning of 1978 and of its active participation in combat.[99] How long it remained in Ethiopia could not be reliably established. More important than this comparatively minor body of troops, however, was the fact that the PDRY put the port and airfield of Aden at the disposal of the USSR as a refuelling and staging post for the air and sealift of Soviet weapons into Ethiopia, particularly in December 1977 and January 1978.

Libya, which had become a supporter of the Ethiopian regime in 1977 (see *MECS 1976-77*, p. 174), tried to assume a more balanced stance in the beginning of 1978. Notwithstanding its own ties with the USSR, Libya came out against "foreign intervention" in the Horn of Africa and advocated a negotiated Ethiopian-Somali settlement, to be reached through the agency of the OAU. Libya envisaged "the cutting-off of non-African connections . . . [and] bringing back the conflict from its international state to its African state."[100]

Somalia continued its efforts to enlist Arab support, with Barreh himself making further tours of Arab capitals from 27 November–3 December, from 27 December–5 January 1978, and again from 17–24 January. His dissatisfaction with the scope of Arab aid was clearly reflected in the inclusion of Iran in the second of these tours. From then on, Iran rather than Somalia's fellow members in the Arab League became its major supplier of arms and equipment, although Saudi Arabia remained the principal source of financial aid.[101]

A slightly more concerted approach resulted when the Arab League first took up the issue of Somalia early in 1978. In January, Barreh informed the League secretariat that an Ethiopian counter-attack against Somalia was imminent. The League's Secretary-General addressed a note to Arab Heads of State warning that "Soviet, Cuban and Warsaw Pact forces are planning to invade Somalia and occupy it in the near future"; it called on all member-states to foil their plan "for the sake of the interests of the Arab nation" and to take action according to the League Council's resolutions of September 1977.[102] (These had called on foreign states to stay out of the conflict and had advocated a peaceful settlement in co-operation with the OAU, but had avoided any firm Arab commitment to Somalia.) Some Arab states subsequently increased their arms shipments to Somalia, but Arab assistance was not of a kind that could have prevented Somalia's defeat in the Ogaden in the following months.

A second appeal to the League was made by Somalia on 19 February 1978, when it argued that its own territory (rather than the Ogaden) was now threatened by Ethiopian forces. King Khālid responded by a call for immediate and effective aid to Somalia as "a duty dictated by religion and Arab fraternity." He added that Saudi Arabia itself would extend additional material aid and continue to lend moral support.[103] Again, however, practical follow-up fell short of Somali expectations.

During its Council meeting in March (which mainly dealt with the situation in Lebanon), the League took up the Somali issue once again. The Council adopted a resolution calling for humanitarian aid to refugees who had fled from the Ogaden to Somalia and Djibouti, but no practical steps were initiated to implement it. That the general attitude of the Council remained non-committal was all the more noteworthy as the pro-Soviet Arab states, who might have objected to a stronger anti-Ethiopian stance, were absent from the meeting for reasons entirely unconnected with its agenda (see above). Those who participated were generally distrustful of Soviet intentions in the ME and Africa and, though divided on Sādāt's initiative, did not find it difficult to co-operate on the issue at hand. Nevertheless, at a press conference after the conclusion of the meeting, the League's Secretary-General, Maḥmūd Riyāḍ, circumscribed the Council's "assistance to Somalia" by explaining that it was intended to apply only in case of a violation of Somali territory (not in case of operations carried out by Somalia in the Ogaden).[104] It must be assumed that the League's cautious attitude reflected the desire of its African members not to weaken their status in the OAU by pre-judging an issue scheduled to come up in that organization's highest forum in July 1978 (see essay on Africa and the Middle East).

The stabilization of the situation along the Somali-Ethiopian border, following the withdrawal earlier in March of regular Somali troops from Ethiopian territory, was welcomed with evident relief by most League members, whether present at the Council's session or not. Arab states as far apart on most other matters as Libya and Egypt welcomed the Somali decision to evacuate its forces from the Ogaden, regarding it as a step towards an agreed solution to the conflict through the OAU. As the danger of a new flare-up on Somalia's borders receded, Somali contacts with Egypt, Saudi Arabia and the Gulf Emirates continued throughout the summer of 1978 and culminated in a visit to Somalia by the Egyptian War Minister, 'Abd al-Ghanī Jamasī, from 5–8 August. Assisted by a high level military delegation, Jamasī discussed questions relating to military co-operation between the two countries. The results of the talks were not disclosed.

Almost immediately after the conclusion of the Ogaden campaign, the Arab littorals were presented with a new challenge in the Red Sea area, on which they were compelled to take a stand: the Ethiopian army and its foreign auxiliaries moved north in order to subdue the rebellion in Eritrea. (For earlier Arab attitudes towards the Eritrean movements, see *MECS 1976-77*, p. 174.) By 1978, almost all Arab states gave support to the Eritreans in a manner which cut across other divisions. Sudan, most immediately concerned for reasons of geographical proximity, was in the lead. An Egyptian-Eritrean friendship society came into being almost simultaneously with the establishment of an Eritrean information centre in Damascus. Libya, which in 1977 had supported Ethiopia against the Eritrean movement, now declared that it had "always been firm" in "strongly supporting the Eritrean revolution." [105] Libya itself, as well as Syria, made diplomatic efforts to persuade the USSR to take a neutral line between the Ethiopian government and the Eritrean movements, rather than support Col Mengistu's military reconquest of the area. Kuwait and Iraq joined them in these endeavours, Iraq's defence of the Eritreans *vis-à-vis* the USSR being cited as one issue which contributed to a degree of tension between the two in mid-1978. The one Arab country which did not declare support of, or sympathy with, the Eritreans was the PDRY. Its Head of State, Sālim 'Alī Rubay', apparently had doubts about South Yemen supporting Ethiopia against the Eritreans, [106] but after his deposition and execution on 26 June, no further reports were heard of reservations on the part of the PDRY concerning the Soviet line.

Despite the fairly broad Arab consensus favouring the Eritreans, Arab help was not effective. Light arms, medical aid and food were indeed delivered, but Arab aid came nowhere near the level needed to withstand the assault of the Ethiopian army with its newly-delivered Soviet equipment. By September 1978, the Ethiopian army had regained control of most of Eritrea, though it had not stamped out guerrilla activity. One reason contributing to the ineffectiveness of Arab aid was the fragmentation of the Eritrean movement into three "Fronts" which sent separate delegations to Arab capitals. Iraq, Syria and Sudan urged the three "Fronts" to unite, but to no avail. Some Arab states were reported to have made the granting of aid conditional on the establishment of a single Eritrean movement. [107] The group that emerged as dominant was the Eritrean People's Liberation Front (EPLF); some of its leaders were Christians and all were Left-leaning. Saudi Arabia therefore aided only the two others. Iraq and Syria gave their financial support mainly to the weakest of the three groups, the Eritrean Liberation Front–Popular Liberation Forces (ELF–PLF), led by Osman Sabbe. Other Arab states were also doubtful of the desirability of an independent EPLF-led Eritrean state, feeling that it would either complicate Red Sea affairs by bringing another stretch of the Red Sea shore under the domination of Left-wing forces, or else lead to civil war among the three Fronts, with each trying to enlist Arab support for itself. Their declaration in favour of Eritrean self-determination notwithstanding, a majority of Arab states would have been satisfied with some kind of regional autonomy, under which Eritrea would have formed part of a decentralized Ethiopian state. However, the EPLF insisted on complete independence. Before the situation in Eritrea became any clearer, however, it was superseded by events in North and South Yemen as the principal Red Sea issue claiming most Arab attention.

During 1976 and until mid-1977, the PDRY had moved towards greater co-operation with Saudi Arabia, and its integration into the Saudi-led alignment of Peninsular states looked a distinct possibility (see *MECS 1976-77*, p. 173). In the second half of 1977, however, South Yemen reverted to a more markedly radical stance. Its attitude towards the conflict in the Horn of Africa has already been noted. So has its joining the Tripoli bloc. PDRY support for the Omani rebels in Dhufar (near the border with the PDRY) was also stepped up again after an interval of relative inactivity. Relations with Saudi Arabia deteriorated towards the end of

1977. Early in 1978, there were reports of clashes on the border between the two countries, though neither side officially acknowledged that they had occurred. Developments came to a head at the end of June 1978, when YAR President Aḥmad Husayn al-Ghashmī was assassinated and his PDRY counterpart Rubayʻ executed two days later. (For details and background, see chapters on the YAR and the PDRY.) Saudi and Egyptian comment regarded the assassination as yet another link in the chain of Soviet actions in the Red Sea intended to promote Russian penetration.[108] Saudi Arabia issued an official statement saying that Ghashmī had fallen victim to "criminal culprits who sold their religion and their homeland to external forces."[109] The YAR demanded an emergency meeting of the Arab League, which its Secretary-General acceded to at once. The League met on 1 and 2 July. The Tripoli bloc members and Iraq again stayed away. So did Djibouti, which did not wish to be forced into a stand objectionable to either North or South Yemen—neither of which it wanted to antagonize. This conformed with the general policy of Djibouti at the League (of which it had become a member only in September 1977) of not publicly taking sides in disputes of its close neighbours.

At the League meeting, some speakers (not named in press reports) argued that the Soviet, East German and Cuban presence in South Yemen endangered the security of the entire Arab nation.[110] The meeting formally blamed the PDRY for the murder of Ghashmī and resolved to "freeze" diplomatic relations with the PDRY as well as to suspend economic, technical and cultural aid "until its government shows respect for the Arab League's charter."[111] Saudi Arabia and the YAR had moved to expel the PDRY from the League, but the other participants considered this too harsh a reaction. (In the absence of the Tripoli bloc states and of Iraq, the meeting could not, in any case, have met the Charter's requirement for a unanimous vote of all members except the one to be expelled.) As it was, the decision to "freeze" relations and suspend aid constituted the strongest punitive measure ever adopted by the League against a member-state since its establishment in 1945. A Saudi newspaper reported that despite their absence from the meeting, Syria and Iraq had decided to adhere to its decisions. While Syria did not react to the report, an official spokesman said that Iraq saw no reason to reconsider its relations with the PDRY. The League's decision, he said, was "dishonest" and served imperialist and reactionary schemes; North and South Yemen should settle their problem through dialogue. Algeria's Foreign Minister took a similar line.[112] The Central Committee of al-Fatḥ described the resolution as the beginning of a conspiracy against the Steadfastness Front.[113] Most of the Tripoli bloc (and Iraq) thus came to the defence of a fellow member, regardless of the fact that their alignment had come into being in a context completely divorced from Red Sea issues.

In the welter of new developments affecting Somalia, Eritrea and North and South Yemen, the basic issue—that of collective Red Sea security—was well-nigh forgotten. In the first half of 1977, this had been the central concern of inter-Arab contacts on the region's problems (see *MECS 1976–77*, p. 174). But later in the year, only the YAR continued to refer to the needʼto bolster Red Sea security in the face of the "Israeli danger" and the "danger of international disputes."[114] In September 1977, the YAR asked the League to take action to ensure the defence of the straits of Bāb al-Mandab and of the North Yemeni offshore islands against "the increasing Israeli danger." The North Yemeni note to the League complained of the lack of response to the YAR's defence needs on the part of Saudi Arabia, Egypt, Iraq and Libya.[115] However, a subsequent League meeting in November 1977 again ignored the subject. The overthrow of Rubayʻ sharpened the differences of opinion: the PDRY's new leader, ʻAlī Nāsir Muḥammad Ḥusnī, described projects for Red Sea security as "suspect plans" promoted by "reactionary and imperialist forces." The defence of the region should be undertaken by each littoral state "in the framework of [its] territorial borders." [116] Unconfirmed reports spoke of attempts made in behind-the-scene contacts during the OAU summit in Khartoum in July to convene a meeting of the Red Sea Arab littorals. [117] The moment was hardly propitious and nothing came of the attempt.

SUDAN'S RELATIONS WITH ITS NEIGHBOURS

Sudan not only played an active and prominent role in Red Sea affairs, but was also the cornerstone in the inter-relationship within the Egyptian-Libyan-Sudanese triangle (see *MECS 1976-77*, pp. 163–68). In the Sudanese view, relations between these three were not exclusively a facet of inter-Arab politics, but also belonged in the wider context of African affairs. In both spheres, opposition to Soviet penetration was a central tenet in Sudan's policy. Yet, towards the end of 1977 and during the first six months of 1978, a slight shift towards a more non-aligned stance was perceptible in Sudan's regional policies, an adjustment probably partly made in preparation for President Numayrī's assumption of the chairmanship of the OAU in July. Two additional factors had been at work as well, however: Sudan's desire not to be caught between a hostile Ethiopia and an equally hostile Libya; and a turn in Sudanese domestic affairs with the reconciliation between Numayrī and the hitherto oppositional Sudanese National Front (see chapter on Sudan). The Front had relied to a considerable extent on Libyan support and had made an improvement in Sudanese-Libyan relations a condition for co-operating with Numayrī. The Sudanese government announced on 26 October 1977 that it had no objection to resuming diplomatic relations with Libya. (Relations had been severed in July 1976 when Sudan blamed Libya for an attempted coup against Numayrī; see *MECS 1976-77*, p. 165.) During the Arab League meeting at Tunis on 14 November, Sudanese Vice-President, al-Rashīd al-Tāhir Bakr, met with the Foreign Ministers of Libya and Egypt. It was agreed that Sudanese-Libyan relations be resumed and Egyptian-Libyan relations, for long reduced to token representation, be restored to their normal level. Egypt joined the talks primarily in order to avoid the impression that Sudan was not acting in full concert with it.

In the wake of Sādāt's initiative, Libyan-Egyptian relations were severed altogether (see above), yet Sudan went ahead 'as planned and the agreement to resume relations with Libya was finalized in February 1978. Significantly, Sudan chose that moment to declare once again that the Egyptian-Sudanese military pact of 15 July 1976 (see *MECS 1976-77*, p. 165) was defensive in character and not directed against Libya or any other Arab country. [118] The same conciliatory trend was evident in Sudan's agreement to chair a meeting in Libya in March 1978 at which the two countries, as well as Niger, attempted to bring about a reconciliation between the Chad central government and rebel factions in the north. The latter had hitherto been supported by Libya. The prospect of pacification on a long stretch of Sudan's western border was another Sudanese consideration at a time when the situation along its boundaries with Ethiopia, and especially Eritrea, remained tense.

Libya's own interest in the *rapprochement* was that it might contribute towards driving a wedge between Sudan and Egypt—especially since the Mahdist element in the Sudanese National Front was traditionally opposed to close links with Cairo. However, despite Sudan's second thoughts on Sādāt's initiative (see above), Sudanese-Egyptian bilateral relations remained close in 1978, even if Numayrī distanced himself somewhat from Sādāt. Numayrī asserted that Egypt had given its assent to Sudan's normalization of relations with Libya and that these would "never and in no way" develop to the detriment of ties with Egypt. [119] Numayrī himself remained uneasy in his relations with Qadhdhāfī.

In an extension of earlier moves for political and military co-ordination (see *MECS 1976-77*, p. 165), the Sudanese and the Egyptian People's Chambers (Legislatures) held a joint session in Cairo from 24–31 October 1977. Both Numayrī and Sādāt addressed the meeting, the latter describing it as "the united congress of the People's Assembly of the Nile valley, our one country." [120] Egyptian War Minister Jamasī told the meeting that the planning stage for military co-ordination between the two countries had been completed in April 1977. At that time, the two chiefs of staff had held their second meeting in accordance with the provisions of the 1976 defence pact. No further meetings of the chiefs of staff, or of the Joint Defence Council set up under the defence agreement, were reported up to the end of October 1978. Measures to promote military co-operation apparently continued at lower levels. In this and other spheres, the joint meeting of People's Chambers recommended a cautious and gradualist approach. Its final statement said that "any step for integration or unification should be based on the facts of history, common interest and sound scientific planning." [121]

The Higher Ministerial Committee for political and economic integration met twice during the period reviewed: in Cairo from 23–25 January 1978, and in Alexandria from 27–29 June. Joint economic development projects were on the agenda. In the interval, the Sudanese Vice-President, al-Rashīd al-Tāhir Bakr, and the Egyptian Prime Minister, Mamdūh Sālim, met at Abū Simbil (south of Aswān, near the common border) on 27 February. They discussed the establishment of an integrated zone to comprise Egypt's southernmost area, the Governorate of Aswān, and the Northern Province of Sudan. However, just as Saudi influence gradually prevailed over Sudan as regards Sādāt's initiative and as Saudi Arabia became Sudan's senior partner in regional affairs, so did Riyadh assume an important role in the field of economic co-ordination. A Saudi-Sudanese Ministerial Committee, set up in October 1976 for the purpose of economic co-operation, had its first meeting in March 1977 and its second in April 1978. A joint Saudi-Sudanese organization for the exploitation of Red Sea resources, set up in 1975, held a meeting in Khartoum in December 1977. The importance both sides attached to it was demonstrated by the high level of representation: President Numayrī was in the chair and the Saudi delegation was led by its Oil Minister, Ahmad Zakī al-Yamānī.

DEVELOPMENTS IN THE MAGHRIB
In the Maghrib, the issue of the Western Sahara remained the focus of regional activities (see *MECS 1976-77*, pp. 170–71). The main division continued to be that between Morocco and Mauritania (who, having divided the Western Sahara between them in 1976, had become status-quo powers) and Algeria and Libya (who remained unwilling to accept the 1976 settlement as final). Tunisia sided with Morocco and Mauritania, but usually refrained from taking a public stand for fear of antagonizing its two neighbours. Despite their common orientation with regard to the fundamental aspects of the situation, the policies of Algeria and Libya differed markedly. Algeria's primary interest was to prevent the expansion of Moroccan territory and influence; Libya saw the Sahara issue mainly as a lever to promote its vision of a larger Maghrib unity under its own political ascendancy and ideological guidance. Thus, while Algeria had recognized the Saharan Arab Democratic Republic (SADR) as the legitimate claimant to the former Spanish Sahara, Libya refused to follow suit. (The only other Arab country to recognize SADR was the PDRY in February 1978.) Similarly, while Algeria was equally hostile to Morocco and Mauritania (at least until the coup there in July 1978), Libya attempted to foster relations with Mauritania, the weaker partner, and wean it away from Morocco.

During the last quarter of 1977, units of Polisario (the movement which had proclaimed the independence of SADR), escalated their raids into the area of the Western Sahara as well as into Mauritania proper. Reacting to the increased scope and frequency of Polisario operations, King Ḥasan threatened on 6 November 1977 that Moroccan army units (some of which were stationed in Mauritania under a joint defence agreement concluded in May 1977) would exercise the right of pursuit, even if this meant "violating the sovereignty of our [Algerian] neighbours." [122] Algeria retorted that any incursion would be considered aggression against itself. Libya, again not fully backing Algeria, counselled restraint; so did Tunisia. Egyptian Vice-President Ḥusnī Mubārak and Saudi Foreign Minister Sa'ūd al-Faysal both visited Morocco, Mauritania and Algeria in mid-November in a mediation attempt. Morocco welcomed such efforts by Arab states, whereas Algeria suspected Arab mediators of a pro-Moroccan bias [123] and preferred the Sahara issue to be dealt with at the OAU where it hoped for a more sympathetic hearing.

A relative lull ensued in the first half of 1978, during which time military operations were carried out on a more restricted scale, while the propaganda war was stepped up. Libya exploited the quieter interval to pursue its own Maghrib policies. While continuing financial assistance, it terminated military aid to Polisario, thus leaving Algeria to carry a vastly increased burden. Qadhdhāfī then invited Mauritania's President Mokhtar Ould Daddah for an official visit to Libya from 13-15 April 1978, during which he promised financial aid for Mauritania's mining industry, transportation network and fisheries, as well as for uranium ore prospecting. Libya also expressed an interest in Mauritanian labourers coming to work in Libya. Algeria let it be understood that such contacts were tantamount to *de facto* recognition by Libya of the Sahara partition and that Boumedienne deplored this turn in Qadhdhāfī's policies. Neither was Algeria pleased with renewed Libyan efforts to forge closer ties with Tunisia, in continuation of a trend already noticeable in 1977. Libyan-Tunisian relations had had a history of violent ups and downs ever since Qadhdhāfī first mooted a merger of the two states in 1972. At that time, a Supreme Libyan-Tunisian Joint Committee had been set up. It became dormant after 1974, but was revived in October 1977 and in May 1978, met in Tripoli to discuss a wide range of measures for economic co-operation. No operative decisions seem to have been taken, but the meeting served as a weathervane to indicate an improved atmosphere in Libyan-Tunisian relations.

Qadhdhāfī himself next expounded the broader outlines of his concept of the future of the Maghrib during a visit to Algeria (30 May-6 June 1978). In an address to the Algerian National People's Assembly, he spoke of the need for a federal link between Algeria, Tunisia and Libya, which he described as a stepping-stone towards comprehensive Arab union. [124] Morocco and Mauritania, he added, would not be eligible for membership as long as they occupied parts of the Western Sahara. Both Algeria and Tunisia responded coolly however. Tunisia's indirect reply was given in an article in the official organ al-'Amal, which quoted with approval a statement made by the Tunisian President, Habib Bourguiba, as long ago as 1972. Speaking in the presence of Qadhdhāfī, Bourguiba had termed Arab unity a task which would take "decades or centuries" to achieve. [125]

A new series of attempts to mediate in the Sahara issue had meanwhile been undertaken by countries outside the Arab world, notably by France. They led to unpublicized meetings between Algerian and Moroccan representatives in April and May 1978, but produced no change in the attitudes of the protagonists. The mediators were overtaken by events when, on 10 July 1978, Ould Daddah was overthrown and replaced by Lt-Col Mustafā Ould Muḥammad Sālik, hitherto

Mauritania's chief of staff. The new regime was at first expected to adopt policies more radical than those of Daddah. Accordingly, on 12 July, Polisario proclaimed a unilateral ceasefire with respect to operations "inside Mauritania." On 19 July, Boumedienne arranged to meet a Mauritanian delegation in Khartoum, where both sides were attending the OAU summit. When an Algerian attempt to work out a common approach towards Sālik's regime with Libya failed, the latter initiated a series of separate contacts with the new government, both in Mauritania and in Libya. In August, Sālik himself stressed that he "took pride" in the close economic and political co-operation now existing between the two countries. [126] At the OAU meeting, Algeria fared somewhat better: the summit decided to convene a special conference on the Sahara and to form a committee of five Heads of State "to find a solution . . . compatible with the right to self-determination." [127] The indeterminate delay built into this formula was a setback to Algeria, but the mention of self-determination gave cause for satisfaction.

By the same token, Morocco was now concerned about the future of Moroccan-Mauritanian ties. It soon turned out, however, that for all its openness to contacts with Libya and Algeria, Sālik's regime was not so rash as to risk the loss of Moroccan backing. Sālik came out in favour of the continued presence of Moroccan troops (then numbering 9,000) in Mauritania. He also implicitly endorsed the 1977 defence pact by convening the joint defence committee set up under the terms of the agreement; it met in Nouakchott on 5 and 6 August 1978. Sālik also balanced his Libyan contacts by asking Saudi Arabia to resume mediation.

Nevertheless, Morocco plainly felt that it had been put on the defensive by the coup in Mauritania and by the reactions to it by Polisario, Algeria and Libya. The latter two, Hasan believed, were working to draw Mauritania into the radical camp and into opposition to Morocco. Furthermore, an incipient French-Algerian *rapprochement* then in progress was likely, in his view, to be carried forward at the expense of French backing for Morocco. These perceptions found expression in a major speech by King Hasan on 20 August 1978. He promised Mauritania military, diplomatic and financial assistance, as well as aid for its medical and educational services, but at the same time warned Sālik not to compromise over the Western Sahara. Any settlement, he said, "should not transgress upon a single inch of Moroccan territory, and it should not lead to the creation of foreign borders" between the two countries (i.e. it should not unmake the 1976 partition). The "brothers in Mauritania" should beware of the "trap" being laid for them by those "who have recently been killing [them]" and were now "wooing [them]." Algeria and Libya for their part should remember that Morocco kept the peace with those who made peace with it, but fought those who fought it. [128]

At the end of the period reviewed, the Sahara dispute thus remained unresolved. Its impact on the main scene of inter-Arab relations was tangential, but not altogether negligible. Algeria had been influenced in its decision to join the Tripoli bloc partly by the hope of enlisting support there for its Saharan policy, but had reaped no tangible benefits. Egypt and Saudi Arabia had unsuccessfully tried their hands at mediation late in 1977. Egypt had partly been motivated by the desire to repay Morocco for its support of Sādāt's initiative; Saudi Arabia had acted because it felt committed to the role and image of arbiter.

SUMMARY

In 1976–77, a broad overview of inter-Arab relations revealed a rather diffuse picture in which all-Arab questions, regional concerns and strictly bilateral relations each had roughly equal weight, so that no single issue could claim pride of place. In 1978, by contrast, Sādāt's initiative became the one single focus for all major inter-

Arab developments. Bilateral relations, which played so prominent a part in the earlier year, now became mostly subsumed under the larger theme. A case in point was the Libyan-Egyptian quarrel which in 1977 erupted into border fighting, but which in 1978 became just one facet of Arab opposition to Sādāt's policy. Even the Syrian-Iraqi dispute, while retaining its bilateral character, became geared to Sādāt's policy: each side felt that the most damaging charge it could make was that the other was being disingenuous in its opposition to Sādāt. Regional affairs did not suffer a comparable eclipse, but they, too, clearly receded in importance as compared with the basic issues. From among them, Red Sea affairs and the closely related developments in the Horn of Africa were the most important, in which the countries' pro-Soviet or pro-Western affiliations tended to over-ride other considerations. Running counter to the general trend were relations among the Arab littorals of the Persian Gulf which became more self-contained and inward-looking than they had been in the past.

Reactions to Sādāt's move and the ensuing rift between Egypt and its opponents caused a degree of polarization in Arab attitudes which had no precedent in the past decade and which was paralleled only by the deep divisions of the 1950s and 1960s prior to the 1967 war. In the course of the year, however, Egypt's critics themselves became visibly divided: the radicals, such as the members of the Tripoli bloc who wanted Sādāt overthrown, were in sympathy with "rejectionist" thinking and pro-Soviet in their international orientation; while the conservative pro-Western regimes of the grouping led by Saudi Arabia were working to lead Sādāt back into the Arab fold. In November 1977, Egypt had failed dismally to carry the Arab world with it; at the time of the Camp David summit, almost a year later, its leaders might well have noted with some satisfaction that they had once again demonstrated that Arab solidarity could not be made effective *without* Egypt, let alone *against* it.

Daniel Dishon and Varda Ben-Zvi

NOTES
1. For the significance of this term, see *Middle East Contemporary Survey (MECS) 1976–77,* pp. 149–50; for the overall structure of inter-Arab relations on the eve of Sādāt's move, see there pp. 147–78. For the unfolding of Sādāt's initiative in the context of the Arab-Israeli conflict, see essay on that subject in the present volume.
2. Reuter, 8 December 1977.
3. *Al-Ahrām,* Cairo; 24 December 1977.
4. R Rabat, 3 December—monitored by Daily Report, Middle East and North Africa (DR), 5 December 1977.
5. *Events,* London; 10 February 1978.
6. *Ha'aretz, Ma'ariv,* Tel Aviv; 28 May 1978.
7. Hasan's interview with *al-Siyāsa,* Kuwait; 24 June 1978.
8. R Omdurman, 21 November—monitored by British Broadcasting Corporation Summary of World Broadcasts, the Middle East and Africa (BBC), 23 November 1977.
9. R Cairo, 22 November—DR, 22 November 1977.
10. R Cairo, 8 January—DR, 9 January 1978.
11. *Al-Jazīra,* Riyadh; 8 April 1978.
12. *Rūz al-Yūsuf,* Cairo; 8 May 1978.
13. For an example of an earlier rift, in 1970, revealing certain parallels, see D. Dishon (ed), *Middle East Record 1969–1970* (Jerusalem: Israel Universities Press, 1977), pp. 551, 555–57, 569–70, 636.
14. R Baghdad, 15 November—BBC, 17 November 1977.
15. R Tripoli, "Voice of the Arab Homeland" (VoAH; Libyan transmitter beamed to Arab audiences outside Libya), 18 November—BBC, 19 November 1977.
16. R Tripoli, 23 November—DR, 25 November 1977.
17. R Tripoli, VoAH, 27 November—BBC, 29 November 1977.
18. R Damascus, 17 November—DR, 18 November 1977. Similar statements continued well

into 1978: Syrian Information Minister Ahmad Iskandar Ahmad told a correspondent: "Sādāt must fall; we no longer trust him"; *Financial Times (FT)*, 14 April 1978. Syrian Defence Minister Mustafā Talās, addressing a rally: "The Arab people of Egypt are able to expel Sādāt . . . as they expelled King Fārūq"; R Damascus, 17 April—BBC, 19 April 1978.

19. R Damascus, 22 November—BBC, 24 November 1977.
20. Related to the *New York Times (NYT)* by Sādāt, 7 December 1977.
21. Mentioned in a message by Bakr to "rejectionist" leaders dated 29 November 1977 and published on 1 February 1978 by the Iraqi News Agency (INA)—BBC, 3 February 1978.
22. Jamāhīriyya Arab News Agency (JANA), Libya; 5 December—BBC, 6 December 1977.
23. JANA, 5 December—DR, 5 December 1977.
24. R Baghdad, 7 December—DR, 8 December 1977.
25. By INA, 1, 3, 4, 5 February—BBC, 3, 6, 8 February 1978.
26. R Algiers, 4 February—BBC, 6 February 1978.
27. *International Herald Tribune (IHT)*, Paris; 6 February 1978.
28. R Tripoli, 19 March—BBC, 22 March 1978.
29. Algerian Press Service, 5 February 1978.
30. *Al-Ra'y al-'Āmm*, Kuwait; 8 February 1978.
31. JANA, 19 March—DR, 21 March 1978.
32. R Tripoli, 19 March—BBC, 22 March 1978.
33. R Damascus, 21 March—DR, 21 March 1978.
34. R Algiers, 18 April; Algerian Press Service, 19 April—BBC, 20, 21 April 1978.
35. R Tripoli, 1 May—DR, 3 May 1978.
36. See *Washington Post News Service*, 8 August 1978.
37. R Tripoli, 15 December—DR, 16 December 1977.
38. *The Times*, London; 16 May 1978. Explicit references to Egypt's aiming at a separate peace occur in Asad's interview with *Newsweek*, 16 January 1978, and in Foreign Minister 'Abd al-Halīm Khaddām's with *Al-Ra'y al-'Āmm*, 21 February 1978.
39. R Damascus, 24 May—DR, 24 May 1978. Author's emphasis.
40. They were published by INA on 1 and 3 February—BBC, 3, 6 February 1978.
41. INA, 7 February 1978.
42. R Baghdad, 5 December—DR, 6 December 1977.
43. *Al-Akhbār*, Amman; 25 January; *Ha'aretz*, 30 January 1978.
44. *Al-Thawra*, Baghdad; 30 November 1977.
45. *Tishrīn*, Damascus; 11 November 1977.
46. Speech by President Bakr, R Baghdad, 8 February—BBC, 10 February 1978.
47. *Al-Thawra*, Baghdad; 6, 7 February 1978.
48. R Damascus, 3 April, 27 June—BBC, 6 April 1978, DR, 28 June 1978.
49. *Al-Ba'th*, Damascus; 21 June; R Damascus, 27 June—DR, 28 June; *Tishrīn*, 28 July 1978.
50. Interview as rendered by R Damascus, 6 May—DR, 8 May 1978.
51. *Al-Thawra*, Baghdad; 29 November 1977.
52. R Baghdad, Voice of the Palestinian Revolution, Voice of the Central Committee (VoCC; Baghdad broadcast for Palestinian audiences), 20 January—DR, 23 January 1978.
53. Middle East News Agency (MENA), Egypt; 2 February 1978.
54. Saudi News Agency (SNA), 18 November—DR, 21 November; *'Ukāz*, Jidda; 19 November 1977.
55. Crown Prince Fahd's interview with *al-Ra'y al-'Āmm*, 9 March 1978.
56. *Al-Riyād*, Riyadh; 21 December 1977.
57. *Arabia and the Gulf*, London; 9 January 1978.
58. Vice-President Husnī Mubārak did, however, visit Saudi Arabia in January 1978 "to explain recent developments." In May, Mubārak and Foreign Minister Ibrāhīm Kāmil visited Saudi Arabia in order to co-ordinate the two countries' stand on the US-Saudi-Egyptian aircraft sale.
59. Qatari News Agency (QNA), 6 December, R Riyadh, 7 December—DR, 7 December 1977.
60. QNA, 24 February—BBC, 27 February 1978.
61. *Al-Ra'y al-'Āmm*, 21 February 1978.
62. QNA, 9 February—DR, 10 February 1978.
63. *Al-Jumhūr*, Beirut; 16 March 1978.
64. R Cairo, 28 March—BBC, 30 March 1978.
65. *Al-Riyād*, 3 August, similarly 7 August; *Al-Ra'y al-'Āmm*, 7 August 1978.
66. Articles in *Tishrīn* of 7 and 9 August, broadcast by R Damascus, 7 and 9 August 1978.

67. *Al-Bilād*, Jidda; quoted by SNA, 9 August—BBC, 10 August 1978.
68. MENA, 7 August—BBC, 9 August 1978.
69. R Riyadh, 10 August—BBC, 12 August 1978.
70. *Al-Thawra, al-Ba'th, Tishrīn*, all of Damascus, 8 and 9 August 1978. Author's emphasis.
71. R Amman, 19 November—BBC, 21 November 1977.
72. R Amman and Jordanian News Agency (JNA), 28 November—BBC, 30 November 1977.
73. R Amman, 21 January—BBC, 23 January 1978.
74. An explicit example of the Syrian attitude was provided by Bulletin No 44, issued in April 1978 by the Syrian Ba'th Party Information Bureau, which stated that it was Syria's interest to prevent Jordan from joining the negotiations with Israel, so as to increase Sādāt's isolation. *Ākhir Sā'a* (Cairo) reported on 22 February 1978 that Syria had threatened to embarrass Jordan by assisting PLO units to cross into Jordan and carry out raids across the Israeli-Jordanian ceasefire line. A raid of this kind took place on 12 June (see last section of the essay on the Arab-Israeli Conflict).
75. R Amman, 9 February—BBC, 11 February 1978.
76. Interview with al-Ra'y al-'Āmm, 26 February 1978.
77. *Al-Ra'y al-'Āmm*, 21 February 1978.
78. JNA, 6 April—BBC, 8 April 1978.
79. Quotations in this passage are from various speeches and interviews by Sādāt between November 1977 and May 1978.
80. Press conference relayed by R Cairo, 11 December—DR, 12 December 1977.
81. Interview with *NYT* as rendered by MENA, 7 December—DR, 8 December 1977.
82. *Events*, 30 December 1977.
83. Interview with *Newsweek*, 12 December 1977.
84. Cairo TV, 27 December 1977; R Cairo, 8 December—DR, 8 December 1977.
85. *Al-Ahrām*, 3 March 1978.
86. *October*, Cairo; 26 March 1978.
87. *NYT*, 6 December 1977.
88. *Al-Ba'th*, 28 November 1977.
89. Interview with *Newsweek*, 16 January 1978.
90. R Damascus, 22 July—BBC, 25 July; INA, 1 August—BBC, 3 August 1978.
91. *Al-Munādil*, Damascus; February 1978.
92. *Al-Ba'th*, 6 April; R Damascus, 8, 10 April 1978.
93. *Al-Ayyām*, Khartoum; 18 December 1977; Interview with Deutsche Presseagentur (DPA), 12 February—DR, 13 February 1978.
94. Interview with the *Chicago Tribune* quoted by MENA, 15 May—DR, 16 May 1978.
95. *Al-Ayyām*, 28 February 1978.
96. *Al-Jumhūr*, 16 March 1978.
97. *Al-Nahār al-'Arabī wal-Duwalī*, Paris; 6 August 1977.
98. *Al-Yakza*, Kuwait; 5 September 1977.
99. *Arabia and the Gulf*, 19 December 1977; *Al-Sayyād*, Beirut; 2 February; *Al-Watan al-'Arabī*, Paris; 6 May; *Time*, New York; 10 July 1978.
100. R Tripoli, VoAH, 3 March—BBC, 6 March 1978.
101. Estimated $200m by *al-Watan al-'Arabī*, 6 January 1978; and at $300m by *al-Sayyād*, 8 December 1977. Both estimates seem to refer to the total of Saudi grants up to the end of 1977.
102. MENA, 21 January—BBC, 23 January 1978.
103. MENA, 21 February—DR, 22 February 1978.
104. R Cairo, VoA, 29 March—BBC, 31 March; *IHT, Jerusalem Post (JP)*, 30 March 1978.
105. Libyan Foreign Secretary Turaykī in a statement to the Sudanese News Agency (SUNA), 11 July—BBC, 14 July 1978.
106. *Time*, 10 July 1978.
107. *Rūz al-Yūsuf*, 19 September; *al-Mustaqbal*, Paris; 29 October 1977.
108. E.g. *al-Bilād*, Jidda; 27 June, *al-Ahrām*, 30 June 1978.
109. R Riyadh, 24 June—DR, 26 June 1978.
110. *Al-Ahrām*, 2 July 1978.
111. QNA, 2 July—BBC, 4 July 1978.
112. *Al-Riyād*, 5 July; INA, 9 July—BBC, 11 July; R Algiers, 5 July—DR, 6 July 1978.
113. Voice of Palestine (a PLO station broadcasting from Lebanon), 6 July—BBC, 8 July 1978.
114. E.g. Ghashmī's interview over R San'ā, 3 December—DR, 9 December 1977.
115. *Al-Watan*, Kuwait; 1 October; *al-Usbū' al-'Arabī*, Beirut; 24 October 1977.
116. *Al-Nahār*, Beirut; 31 July 1978.
117. *Al-Nahār*, 5 August 1978.

118. Joint communiqué issued at the conclusion of a visit to Libya by Sudan's First Vice-President, Abū al-Qāsim Muḥammad Ibrāhīm; R Tripoli, 8 February—BBC, 10 February 1978.
119. Interview with *al-Sayyād*, reported by R Omdurman, 9 March—DR, 10 March 1978.
120. R Cairo, 24 October—DR, 24 October 1977.
121. R Cairo, 31 October—DR, 1 November 1977.
122. R Rabat, 6 November—DR, 8 November 1977.
123. On 27 May 1978, for instance, an Algiers newspaper, *al-Sha'b*, wrote that Saudi Arabia was supporting Mauritania and Morocco on the Western Sahara issue "in accordance with a colonialist plan that aims at dragging the Algerian revolution into open war."
124. JANA, 4 June—DR, 6 June 1978.
125. *Al-'Amal*, Tunis; 9 June 1978.
126. *Al-Watan al-'Arabī*, 12 August 1978.
127. JANA, 22 July—BBC, 25 July 1978.
128. R Rabat, 20 August—BBC, 22 August 1978.

PALESTINIAN ISSUES

The Palestine Liberation Organization (PLO)

Mainly under the influence of Sādāt's initiative, the status of the PLO declined during the period under review, both in the Arab and international arenas. Sādāt's policy removed the PLO, at least for the time being, from the Middle East peace process; it led to the cessation of US overtures towards the organization, and deepened its dependence on Syria. This dependence was further increased by the Israeli operation in South Lebanon which eroded the PLO's status in Lebanon and brought it under even more direct Syrian military control. Sādāt's initiative and the events in Lebanon markedly intensified existing rivalries within the PLO and produced serious leadership problems for 'Arafāt and al-Fatḥ. Events during late 1977 and 1978 generally tended to underscore the limitations of the PLO in being able to play a decisive role in determining the Palestinians' future, as well as its lack of internal cohesion.

THE PLO IN THE ARAB-ISRAELI CONFLICT
THE PLO ON THE EVE OF SĀDĀT'S INITIATIVE
During the summer of 1977, in the months preceding President Sādāt's visit to Jerusalem, the question of PLO representation at the projected Geneva conference had been perhaps the most serious stumbling block towards its reconvening. US diplomatic activity had been concentrated on efforts to devise a formula which would enlist the PLO to the political process; to that end, the Carter Administration embarked on a series of overtures towards the organization, culminating in the joint US-Soviet communiqué of 1 October 1977. (For a detailed analysis of US policy, see *MECS 1976-77*, pp. 21-31, 199-201.)

Confronted with these US overtures, the PLO displayed an increasingly ambivalent attitude, reflecting the complex set of conflicting considerations and internal rivalries affecting its position. On the one hand, there were 'Arafāt and some of his followers who did not wish to miss the opportunity of joining the political process—the more so as the PLO was reported to be under Egyptian and Saudi pressures to modify its positions. On the other hand, most PLO leaders refused to comply with the US conditions for the PLO's participation in the political process, fearing that the organization would run the risk of serious splits if it were to deviate from the resolutions adopted at the March 1977 meeting of the Palestine National Council (PNC; see *MECS 1976-77*, pp. 203-7). As a result, the PLO did not introduce any change in its official position and failed to respond to US overtures. Unofficially, however, 'Arafāt left some room for speculation about a possible acceptance of an amended version of Resolution 242. Thus, while the PLO avoided a rift within its ranks, its leadership simultaneously left the door open for a further evolution of the US attitude towards the organization, and for its possible inclusion in the political process.

THE IMPACT OF SĀDĀT'S INITIATIVE
President Sādāt's initiative triggered off a wide range of changes in the framework of relations between the PLO and the two major "confrontation states," Egypt and Syria, and ended the period of persistent US overtures towards the organization. (For Sādāt's initiative, see "Egyptian-Israeli Negotiations" in section on Arab-Israeli Conflict.) Perhaps the most important immediate result of Sādāt's initiative was that it removed the PLO from the political process precisely at a point in time

when the organization perceived itself to be closer than ever before to participation in the Geneva conference.[1]

Sādāt's visit to Jerusalem threw the PLO into disarray; its initial reaction was one of disbelief, shock and dismay. Once its appeals to Sādāt to reconsider his decision were rejected, PLO media and spokesmen launched an all-out campaign against the visit, describing it as "high treason" and "betrayal of the most sacred principles of Arab solidarity."[2] PLO spokesmen charged that for all practical purposes Sādāt was ready "to abandon the Palestinian cause," and accused him of contravening the resolutions of the Rabat summit of October 1974.[3] Others emphasized that Sādāt's "treason" endangered not only the Palestinians but "the whole Arab nation" which could, as a result, become "the target of Israeli aggression." Sādāt's declaration that the October War would be the last war led the PLO to assert that his statements reflected "the capitulationist character" of his initiative—for "to adhere to a truce while Arab territories are still occupied by the enemy is nothing less than total surrender."[4] Sādāt's unilateral move was viewed by the PLO as tantamount to recognition of Israel's victory in the historic struggle between the Arab nation and Zionism.[5]

Sādāt's initiative aroused many of the PLO's worst fears, in particular the belief that the initiative might leave it in the most dangerous predicament the Palestinians could confront: a separate Egyptian-Israeli settlement. That Sādāt was ready to defy the major Arab governments and embark on his unilateral move was, in the PLO's view, a clear indication that he was heading towards a separate peace treaty with Israel. PLO leaders were quick to assert that during his visit to Jerusalem, Sādāt surrendered the most important cards possessed by the Arabs. They accused Sādāt of having accepted the Israeli concept of a peace settlement; of granting Arab recognition to Israel; of holding direct negotiations while Arab territories were still occupied; of recognizing Jerusalem as Israel's capital; and, for all practical purposes, of having given up the military option by declaring "no more war." In PLO terminology, such concessions indicated that Sādāt was ready to obtain "a complete Israeli withdrawal from Sinai at the expense of the Palestinian cause."[6] Though counting on Israel's rejection of Egyptian demands as the element that would abort Sādāt's initiative, there was at the same time widespread concern in PLO ranks that Israel might offer Sādāt concessions which, while still excluding the PLO, would tempt the Egyptian president to conclude a separate agreement. The PLO's fear was that a settlement which took Egypt out of the conflict with Israel could spell the end of any PLO role in the final settlement, and remove the organization permanently from the political process. It would also severely undermine the ability of the remaining "confrontation states" to face Israel militarily.

It was also clear to the PLO that Sādāt's initiative jeopardized what had hitherto been accepted as its exclusive right to represent the Palestinian people. While Sādāt addressed himself to the Palestinian problem in his Knesset speech, his failure to make any reference whatsoever to the PLO gave the impression that he was reneging on the Rabat summit resolutions of 1974. These had recognized the PLO as the sole legitimate representative of the Palestinian people. The PLO's anxiety was further substantiated when Sādāt extended invitations to Palestinian notables from the West Bank to come to Cairo for talks "on the question of Palestinian representation at a reconvened Geneva." Indicative of the seriousness with which the PLO viewed the invitations was its communiqué, hurriedly issued on 25 November, denouncing Sādāt's attempt "to divide the Palestinians and to create a new Palestinian leadership which would substitute for the PLO."[7] In addition, the PLO warned West Bank leaders against going to Cairo, impressing upon them the "gravity" of Egypt's invitations and making assassination threats. The PLO's concern mounted in early January 1978 when Sādāt—who described the organization as "irresponsible"—indicated that he would not object if the Palestinians chose King Husayn as their representative. He added that a ME peace settlement would be more easily realized if the Palestinians elected Husayn as their representative. [8] Viewed against the background of the transformation in the PLO's status since the 1974 Rabat summit, the possibility of Husayn representing the Palestinians was tantamount to completely undercutting the internationally-acknowledged gains made by the PLO since the October War.

The PLO was also increasingly apprehensive that Sādāt had abandoned the principles of the Palestinians' right to self-determination and to an independent state. It was alarmed by Sādāt's declared preference for a Palestinian "entity" linked to Jordan, fearing that such an arrangement would render the establishment of an independent West Bank-Gaza Strip state permanently impossible. Such concerns were heightened in early January after the Carter-Sādāt meeting which resulted in the announcement of the "Aswān formula." Read in conjunction with the Israeli autonomy plan published at the end of December (see section on the Arab-Israeli Conflict), the PLO noted that the formula's assertion that "the Palestinians should participate in the determination of their own future" assigned them an extremely limited role in the peace settlement. Instead of granting them the right to self-determination, the formula—as interpreted by the PLO—provided for other forces, presumably Jordan and Israel, to curb that right and limit its implementation. It was from this standpoint that the PLO also rejected Sādāt's proposal, originally put forward in May, that as an interim step Israel could return the West Bank to Jordan and the Gaza Strip to Egypt.

Yet another source of anxiety for the PLO sprang from the new alignment of forces that resulted from Sādāt's initiative. In the past, the PLO had generally preferred to maintain close political co-ordination with Egypt. However, the organization was not only at loggerheads with Egypt, but was allied with Syria—which only shortly before had been conducting a war aimed at breaking the backbone of the PLO as an independent fighting force and bringing it under Syrian tutelage (see *MECS 1976–77*, pp. 192–95). The PLO's alienation from a traditional ally, which forced it into an alignment with its most recent adversary, was regarded by its leadership as extremely detrimental to Palestinian interests. First and foremost, increasing reliance on Syria threatened to deny the PLO any room for manoeuvre between Egypt and Syria, with all the gains that this flexibility had allowed in the past. Furthermore, after its bloody experience at the hands of the Syrians in Lebanon, there could hardly have been a more ominous prospect than a consolidation of Syrian hegemony over the political and military activities of the PLO. Aware of this reality, 'Arafāt was reported to have urged PLO leaders not to burn all their bridges with Egypt "in order not to fall exclusively into Syrian hands." [10]

The PLO sought to devise an inter-Arab policy to cope with the new reality created by Sādāt's initiative. Thus it joined the bloc formed by Arab states opposed to Sādāt's initiative, which convened in Tripoli in early December 1977 and set up the "Steadfastness and Resistance Front"—the Tripoli bloc (see essay on Inter-Arab Relations). Most factions of the PLO were represented at the Tripoli conference, but it did not seem to play a leading role; furthermore, its representatives split in support of different Arab states in line with their respective political outlooks. Thus, 'Arafāt and Zuhayr Muḥsin, head of the PLO's Military Department and Chief of the Syrian-backed al-Sā'iqa, supported Syria's position; others, such as George Ḥabash of the Popular Front for the Liberation of Palestine (PFLP), aligned themselves with Libya and Algeria. The major effort of the PLO as a whole, however, was aimed at reconciling the divergent viewpoints of Syria and Iraq—the latter being absent from the Tripoli conference. By enlisting Iraq to the Tripoli bloc, the PLO sought to obtain two objectives: first, to strengthen the bloc opposed to Sādāt's initiative and increase the pressures applied on Egypt; and second, to maintain unity within PLO ranks by avoiding a split with the pro-Iraqi factions.

Another important task, particularly in 'Arafāt's view, was to keep the PLO's lines of communication with Riyadh open. Prior to the convening of the Tripoli summit, a PLO delegation went to Riyadh to assure the Saudis that the organization's alignment with the Tripoli bloc was merely a temporary expediency imposed on it by Sādāt's initiative. Crown Prince Fahd assured the PLO that the Saudi position regarding "the legitimate rights of the Palestinian people" had not changed. [11] 'Arafāt apparently believed that by maintaining close contact with Saudi Arabia—the central ally of the US in the Arab world—the PLO would retain the option of joining the political process at a later stage.

Deeply concerned as the PLO was over Sādāt's initiative, 'Arafāt and other leaders seemed to share the opinion that it was doomed to failure because of Israel's rejection of the two basic Arab demands: complete withdrawal and Palestinian self-determination. An unidentified PLO leader suggested that as "Mī Begin will give Sādāt nothing in exchange," Sādāt would either have to "rejoin Arab ranks or disappear." [12] It was thus expected that after the initiative reached an impasse, Sādāt would revert to the common positions held by the Arab governments prior to November 1977. Because of such a possibility, 'Arafāt deemed it inadvisable to create too wide a rift with Egypt which would render a future reconciliation impossible. Egypt remained important as a counterweight to Syria and as a means of preserving the option of joining the political process. (For a detailed discussion of PLO-Egyptian relations, see below.)

REJECTION OF ISRAEL'S AUTONOMY PLAN

The PLO sharply criticized the autonomy plan Israel published in late December 1977 for the West Bank and the Gaza Strip (see essay on the Egyptian-Israeli Negotiations). The organization totally rejected the plan, which it maintained could in no way constitute an acceptable solution to the Palestinian problem; it described it as "an attempt to win legitimacy from the Palestinians, Arabs and world opinion for the continuation of Israeli occupation." In its view, the plan not only ignored the Palestinian people and the PLO, but also "obliterated the Palestinian presence through the establishment of self-rule under continued Israeli occupation." Furthermore, it utterly evaded the central issues at stake—"the right of the Palestinians to return to their homes, to self-determination, to a homeland and to an independent state." The PLO concluded that the plan was "a trick aimed at giving the illusion that Israel has given something in return for Sādāt's concessions." [13] Not surprisingly, the PLO denounced the negotiations of the Political Committee held in Jerusalem in January 1978, which were perceived as being conducted on the basis of Israel's plan. [14] (For the PLO's influence on the attitudes in the West Bank and Gaza towards the autonomy plan, see chapter on the West Bank and the Gaza Strip.)

REACTION TO THE CAMP DAVID AGREEMENTS

PLO leaders generally expected the Camp David summit to fail. According to one source, 'Arafāt sought to prepare "an all-Arab safety net" for Sādāt which would enable him to rejoin the Arab ranks once the summit reached an impasse. [15] In an interview with *Le Monde*, 'Arafāt predicted that the summit would produce, at most, "a vague declaration of principles," aimed mainly at "gaining time" and "drawing Husayn" into the negotiation process. [16]

The publication of the Camp David accords shocked the PLO leadership and provoked statements of criticism and condemnation unprecedented in their harshness. 'Arafāt called the agreements "a dirty, mean and rotten deal which smacks of conspiracy." [17] Other PLO leaders accused Sādāt of having abandoned the Palestinian cause altogether in exchange for "a handful of Sinai soil"; they claimed the accords conferred legitimacy on the "continuing occupation of Arab lands." [18] In an official statement issued at the end of the Executive Committee meeting on 19 September, the PLO accused Sādāt of: (1) "complete capitulation to the Zionist enemy"; (2) "complete collusion with Zionist aims to disavow all Palestinian national rights"; (3) "realizing the old objectives of US imperialism"; (4) "realizing the well-known imperialist-Zionist objective of completely isolating Egypt from the Arab national struggle"; and (5) "helping Israel to turn the West Bank and Gaza Strip into a permanent colony." The statement went on to describe the accords as "the most dangerous link in the conspiracy since 1948, as the Zionists obtained from Sādāt what they have been trying to achieve for the past 30 years, namely the liquidation of the Palestinian problem." [19]

Up in arms against the Camp David accords, the PLO continued to align itself with the Tripoli bloc, hoping that pressure and opposition thus generated would prevent Sādāt from implementing the agreements. All PLO spokesmen asserted that the new circumstances demanded a resumption of fidā'ī activity on a large scale. Statements to this effect were made by Zuhayr Muḥsin of al-Sā'iqa, Khālid al-Ḥasan of al-Fatḥ, Nā'if Ḥawātima of the Popular Democratic Front for the Liberation of Palestine (PDFLP) and the PFLP's spokesman, Basām Abū Sharīf. [20] In late October 1978, Salāḥ Khalaf (Abū Iyād) went as far as to threaten that if the Camp David accords were enforced, the Palestinians would be left with no other choice but "to launch a scorched earth policy in the ME." [21]

RELATIONS WITH EGYPT

During 1977–78, four distinct stages could be discerned in the PLO's relations with Egypt: the first lasted from Sādāt's visit to Jerusalem until Yūsuf al-Sibā'ī's assassination in Cyprus in February 1978; the second lasted until early March; the third until the Camp David summit in early September; while the fourth began with the signing of the Camp David accords.

The first period was characterized by a rapid deterioration in relations following Sādāt's visit to Jerusalem. Reacting to PLO condemnation of the visit in late November 1977, Egypt suspended the "Voice of Palestine" radio programme transmitted over Cairo's broadcasting facilities and expelled three PLO officials: Jamāl Sūrānī, the chief PLO representative in Cairo; Harūn Rashīd, his deputy; and Rubhī 'Awād, the al-Fatḥ representative. When PLO criticism persisted, Sādāt retaliated by inviting Palestinian delegations from the West Bank and Gaza to Cairo, thereby signalling to the PLO that he might withdraw his recognition of it as the sole representative of the Palestinians. But simultaneous with such overt confrontation, covert contacts seemed to have continued. Thus, 'Arafāt and Sādāt were reported to have exchanged three messages during December, [22] while Sa'īd Kamāl, the Cairo-based deputy director of the PLO's Political Department, was said to have held a series of meetings with Sayyid Mar'ī, the Speaker of Egypt's parliament and Sādāt's confidant. It is significant that Sādāt's criticism of the PLO usually excluded 'Arafāt who, according to Sādāt, was "under the pressure of other countries." [23]

It is similarly noteworthy that it was not 'Arafāt who signed the Tripoli conference declaration condemning Sādāt on behalf of al-Fath, but his second-in-command in al-Fath, Abū Iyād; the signatures on behalf of all other PLO factions were those of their respective leaders. 'Arafāt also refrained from calling for the overthrow of Sādāt, and usually avoided personal attacks on the Egyptian President. Notwithstanding sharp criticism from within the PLO, 'Arafāt instructed Sa'īd Kamāl to remain in Cairo and to maintain contacts with the Egyptian leadership. It is also significant that Sa'īd Kamāl was not expelled from Egypt when other PLO officials were ordered to leave.

Covert exchanges were revealed on 26 January 1978 when the Egyptian Foreign Minister, Ibrāhīm Kāmil, met Sa'īd Kamāl in Cairo.[24] It then became known that Sa'ī Kamāl would participate in the Arab League meeting due to convene in Cairo in March in violation of the resolutions of the Tripoli conference. (For both the Arab League session and the Tripoli conference decisions, see essay on Inter-Arab Relations.) Subsequently, Rubhī 'Awād (a representative of al-Fath but not of the PLO), who had been expelled in November, was allowed to return to Cairo in early February 1978.[25] A conspicuous attempt was made in Egypt's policy to distinguish between the "official" PLO, whose position was regarded as completely negative, and what Cairo regarded as "the moderate wing of al-Fath." An unidentified Egyptian official conceded that if more than half of al-Fath were to accept Sādāt's *fait accompli*, Egypt would give them full backing. The Cairo correspondent of the *Financial Times* concluded that Egypt was working on a strategy "to split the Fath away from the PLO."[26]

The second stage in Egyptian-PLO relations began when Yūsuf Sibā'ī, chairman of *al-Ahrām* and a close friend of President Sādāt, was assassinated by two Palestinian gunmen in Nicosia on 18 February 1978. Having taken several hostages, including three PLO officials and four Egyptians, the gunmen took off in a Cypriot DC-8. After several countries refused to grant the plane permission to land, it finally returned to Cyprus and landed at Larnaca on 19 February. While negotiations between the gunmen and the Cypriot government were still in progress, an Egyptian commando unit—which in the meantime had landed at Larnaca—attempted to storm the DC-8 and capture the gunmen. In the ensuing battle between the Cypriot National Guard and the commandos, 15 Egyptians were killed, 16 wounded and the remainder surrendered.[27]

The assassination of Sibā'ī, and more so the Larnaca incident, marked a turning point in PLO-Egyptian relations. For almost a month it seemed as if both sides were intent upon a complete breach. Rumours that PLO men had participated in the fighting against the Egyptian commandos, coupled with Sādāt's charges that the PLO was responsible for Sibā'ī's murder, set off a wave of anti-Palestinian sentiment in Egypt—to the point where the prevalent mood could best be expressed by the slogan: "no more Palestine after today." It seemed as if the distinction between the Fath mainstream and the PLO "rejectionists" would be obliterated because of the events at Larnaca. Fearing that Sādāt had orchestrated the upsurge in anti-Palestinian feelings as a pretext for a total break with the PLO, 'Arafāt accused him personally of fomenting anti-Palestinian sentiments and of "injecting the Egyptian people with hatred" to allow them "to escape earlier commitments to the Palestinian cause."[28] Sādāt retaliated swiftly. While *al-Ahrām* hinted that Egypt might withdraw its recognition of 'Arafāt as the PLO leader,[29] the Prime Minister, Mamdūh Sālim, warned that Egypt was about to abolish the special privileges accorded to the 30,000 Palestinians in the country and to equate their status with that of citizens of other Arab countries.[30] The PLO reacted bitterly, accusing Egypt of "mass punishment" of the Palestinians in a move to disengage itself from the Palestinian cause and pave the way for a separate peace treaty with Israel.[31]

At this point, when relations were on the verge of complete breakdown, both sides took steps to forestall further deterioration. 'Arafāt made the first move by instructing several PLO members who lived in Cairo to initiate contacts with the Egyptian authorities. On 5 March, a PLO delegation consisting of Sa'īd Kamāl, Sidqī al-Dajānī and Majdī Abū Ramadān (members of the Executive Committee), and Fārūq al-Husaynī (a member of the Central Council), met Sayyid Mar'ī.[32] This was an obvious violation of the sixth article of the Tripoli resolutions which dictated a political boycott of Egypt. The next day the delegation began a series of meetings with representatives of Egypt's four political parties in order "to explain the PLO's stand on the Larnaca incident."[33] Finally, the delegation held official meetings with the Foreign Minister, Ibrāhīm Kāmil, and the Vice-President, Husnī Mubārak.[34] By the end of March, PLO-Egyptian relations had reverted to the pattern prevailing prior to the events in Cyprus, i.e. opposition to Sādāt's initiative on the one hand, and an effort not to disengage the PLO completely from Egypt on the other.

Following publication of the Camp David accords, however, PLO organs once again embarked on a widespread campaign denouncing the Egyptian move and harshly criticizing Sādāt personally. As after Sādāt's visit to Jerusalem, the terms most frequently used were "capitulation," "surrender," "treason," and "abandonment of the Palestinian cause." This time even 'Arafāt condemned Sādāt personally, describing him as "the agent of Carter and Begin."[35] Despite such an obvious breach, the Acting Egyptian Foreign Minister, Butrus Ghālī, disclosed in mid-October that Egypt continued to be in touch with the PLO through its Cairo office.[36]

RELATIONS WITH JORDAN
The major aims of the Tripoli bloc included the formation of a broad-based Arab front to isolate Sādāt, and to prevent King Husayn from joining his peace initiative. In order to promote these objectives, Syria as well as Algeria exerted increasing pressures on the PLO to mend its relations with Jordan and resume the dialogue with King Husayn[37] (see *MECS 1976-77*, p. 480; and the chapter on Jordan in this volume). President Boumedienne, who visited Amman in January 1978, was reported to have joined Syria in putting pressure on the PLO at the Algiers summit of the Tripoli bloc, which convened on 2 February. He was also said to have been instrumental in arranging the contacts between the PLO and Jordan in early February.[38] The USSR, too, was thought to have impressed upon 'Arafāt the necessity of a PLO-Jordanian *rapprochement*.[39]

'Arafāt and Husayn exchanged letters twice during February 1978: 'Arafāt stressed the importance of setting up a wide Arab front opposed to Sādāt, while Husayn pointed out the necessity of "eliminating the differences between the PLO and Jordan."[40] It is significant, however, that while Husayn reiterated his adherence to the national rights of the Palestinian people, he refrained from making any reference to the Rabat resolutions or to the role of the PLO in future negotiations. Furthermore, he emphasized at great length "the sacred link between the East and West Banks," and said that it was up to the inhabitants of the West Bank and Gaza to decide whether they desired an independent state or "any form of unity" with Jordan. (For Jordan's position on the Palestinian question, see chapter on Jordan.) In early March it was reported that the Jordanian ambassador in Damascus had held talks with PLO officials; that a PLO delegation was about to visit Amman for talks with Husayn; and that Jordan had also released several PLO members held in prison since 1970.[41]

At this point, differences emerged within the PLO as to the merits of opening a dialogue with Jordan (for the nature of this debate, see below). The PLO's principal concern was that a Jordanian-PLO *rapprochement* might produce results totally different from those intended and benefit only Jordan; if Amman's position as the partner for negotiations over the West Bank was enhanced, the PLO would be deprived of its status as the sole representative of the Palestinians. It was also feared that a PLO-Jordanian dialogue would strengthen the pro-Jordanian elements in the West Bank and be interpreted by others as PLO approval of a Jordanian role in the peace process. As a result of deliberations within the PLO, a list of pre-conditions was put forward by the Central Council for resuming the dialogue with Ḥusayn. These were that Jordan should: (1) commit itself fully to the Rabat resolutions; (2) denounce Sādāt's visit to Jerusalem and his entire initiative; and (3) permit the establishment of PLO military bases and political committees in its territory.[42] By imposing such pre-conditions, the PLO sought to attain one of two objectives: if Ḥusayn accepted the pre-conditions, their implementation would considerably strengthen the PLO and improve its dwindling stature following the Lebanese war and Sādāt's initiative; if he rejected them, the onus for frustrating the projected *rapprochement* would be on the King's shoulders, and Syrian-Algerian pressure on the PLO would be eased.

As the PLO probably expected, Ḥusayn refused to comply with its demands and in turn offered what the PLO described as "superficial concessions."[43] Furthermore, there were reports in May that Jordan was about to revive its federation plan (see *MECS 1976–77*, p. 480), thus intensifying distrust in its relations with the PLO.[44]

However, on 22 September in the wake of the Camp David summit, 'Arafāt accompanied Qadhdhāfī on a visit to Mafraq in northern Jordan, where they met Ḥusayn. While the chief aim was to dissuade the King from accepting the Camp David accords, the issue of a fidā'ī return to Jordan was also discussed.[45] Despite Ḥusayn's repeated assurances that "Jordan's stand is firm, straight and clear," PLO spokesmen tended to believe that he was sitting on the fence, ready to join the peace bandwagon once assured of significant gains.[46]

These attempts at reconciliation did not result in any substantial change in the pattern of relations between the PLO and Jordan which had prevailed since the eviction of the fidā'īyyūn from the Kingdom in 1971. Both sides believed their respective positions to be irreconcilable.

PLO-SAUDI RELATIONS

Relations between the PLO and Saudi Arabia in the period under review were largely influenced by Sādāt's initiative and events in Lebanon. In its dealings with the Saudis, the PLO had three major objectives: first, to impress upon Riyadh the necessity of exerting considerable pressure on Sādāt to terminate his initiative;[47] second, to employ Saudi Arabia as a counterweight to Syrian efforts to gain complete control over the PLO whose room for manoeuvre had been curtailed by Sādāt's initiative; and thirdly, to maintain close contacts with the Saudi leadership in order to forestall any diminution in Saudi support of the PLO. 'Arafāt considered the last aim extremely important in view of the likelihood of an unfavourable reaction on the part of the Saudis to the PLO's alignment with countries such as Libya and Algeria and to the growing power of the "Rejection Front" within the organization.[48]

'Arafāt's position towards Riyadh and Saudi policies in general were increasingly criticized not only by the PLO's "Rejection Front," but also by several members of al-Fath. The critics fell into two categories. There were those, like Ḥabash and Hawātima, who rejected in principle "the PLO burgeoisie's" policy of maintaining close relations with Saudi Arabia, as the latter was "an imperialistic element in the area"[49] sharing, *inter alia*, "the aim of imperialism and of Egypt to prevent the establishment of a Palestinian state."[50] This group was supported by Libya, which was reported to have been trying incessantly to persuade 'Arafāt "to disengage the PLO from Saudi Arabia"—but to no avail.[51] On the other hand, there were those such as Salāḥ Khalaf of al-Fatḥ who advocated close relations with the Saudis, but who criticized them for failing to take steps to isolate Sādāt.[52]

PLO-US RELATIONS

PLO-US relations in general were governed primarily by the shift in US policy on the Palestinian issue following Sādāt's initiative. American references to the PLO, which hitherto had been based on a desire for *rapprochement*, as reflected for example in the US-Soviet communiqué of 1 October 1977 (see *MECS 1976-77*, pp. 25-31, 199-201), now became characterized by unqualified condemnation. The PLO reacted with anger, frustration and consistent (though futile) attempts to initiate talks with Washington. Several statements made by PLO spokesmen created the impression that they regretted, *ex post facto*, not having approved the US-Soviet communiqué as a basis for joining the political process prior to Sādāt's visit to Jerusalem. In its statements denouncing the new US policy, the PLO repeatedly demanded that the Carter Administration revert to the commitments it had made in the communiqué with regard to the Palestinian issue. Such a course could serve as a basis for opening a PLO-US dialogue which, in 'Arafāt's words, was "the only road to achieving peace."[53]

The overall reaction of the PLO manifested itself on two levels. On one level, it responded with militancy and aggressiveness, depicting the US positions as aimed at "exterminating the Palestinian presence" or "annihilating the Palestinian identity," isolating the PLO and excluding it from the political process.[54] As a result, the PLO concluded that the only way to combat US policies was to threaten US interests in the region.[55] On the second level, however, the PLO evidently endeavoured—as in the case of its relations with Egypt—to leave the door open for a conceivable *rapprochement* with the US, resulting either from the collapse of Sādāt's initiative or from the revival of the US-Soviet communiqué.[56] The desire to open a dialogue with the US was explicitly and publicly expressed by 'Arafāt on 13 January 1978 when he declared that the PLO was literally "begging" the US to open talks with the organization but to no avail.[57] The PLO unofficially requested Egypt to persuade the US to invite a PLO delegation to Washington to discuss the Palestinian issue.[58] In a personal message to Carter—delivered by Congressman Findley after a seven-hour meeting with 'Arafāt in January 1978 in Damascus— 'Arafāt reiterated his "strong desire" to open a dialogue and requested Carter not to push him "further into a corner" by depicting the PLO as completely negative, since he was operating "under severe internal constraints."[59] PLO spokesmen were at pains to refute the US argument that the projected Palestinian state would turn into a Communist base and a source of radicalism in the region. They argued that on the contrary, it was the lack of a national territorial base and the indifference of the US to the PLO's overtures which had pushed the organization into radicalism and terrorist activities.[60]

The PLO's consistent efforts to project a moderate image in the US reached a peak in early May 1978 when it opened an Information Office in Washington.[61] While evading questions on the PLO's readiness to recognize and conclude peace with Israel, 'Arafāt declared in an interview with the *New York Times* that Israel would have nothing to fear from a new Palestinian state and that the only solution was for the US and the USSR to provide guarantees for both Israel and that Palestinian state. He once again praised the US-Soviet communiqué, describing it as "a fundamental basis for a realistic peace settlement." [62] Following in 'Arafāt's footsteps, the PLO's representative at the UN, Labīb Tarzī, asserted that the establishment of a Palestinian state would bring about a new demarcation of boundaries, whereby the new state might be faced with the necessity of recognizing Israel. [63] But PLO overtures were brought to an abrupt halt in July, following an explosion in Jerusalem which killed two people and for which al-Fath claimed responsibility. (For a description of the incident, see last essay of the section on the Arab-Israeli Conflict.) The US condemned al-Fath as a terrorist organization, adding that the condemnation "applies to its leaders . . . and this includes Mr 'Arafāt." [64] The PLO reacted vehemently, reasserting the necessity "to confront America and its interests through all possible forms of struggle." [65]

The conclusion of the Camp David accords provoked angry reactions from the PLO. These were characterized by recurring threats on US interests in the ME (because of the American-sponsored "conspiracy to liquidate the Palestinian cause"), and by promises that the US and Carter would be duly "punished" by the Arab nation. [66]

PLO-SOVIET RELATIONS

PLO-Soviet relations in the period under review were also governed to a large extent by Sādāt's initiative, which brought about a convergence of interests. On the eve of Sādāt's visit to Jerusalem, the US-Soviet communiqué of 1 October 1977 had assigned an active role to the USSR in the peace-making process; it had also contained the first explicit US recognition of "the legitimate rights of the Palestinian people" which, it was generally believed, aimed at enabling the PLO to join the political process. But Sādāt's initiative excluded both the USSR and the PLO from any role in the peace-making process, at least for the time being. Hence the PLO sought to maintain close political co-ordination with the Soviet Union in order to foil the initiative, while the latter backed the PLO within the framework of its support of the Tripoli bloc. The two most frequent themes in joint PLO-Soviet statements were the depiction of Sādāt's initiative as "gravely detrimental to Arab interests and helping to perpetuate Israeli occupation of Arab lands," and the advocacy of "co-ordination and consolidation of all anti-Sādāt forces." [67] The PLO-USSR co-operation which followed their exclusion from the political process obscured but did not eliminate a basic difference between their respective positions concerning a reconvened Geneva conference. Whereas the USSR demanded that Geneva be reconvened on the basis of Resolution 242, as expressed in the 1 October 1977 communiqué, the PLO continued to refuse to accept participation on such a basis.

During the year, the PLO also attempted to mobilize the USSR as a counter-weight to Syrian attempts to gain complete control over the organization and to put pressure on it in the Lebanese arena throughout 1978 (see below). Following the eruption of hostilities between the mainstream PLO and pro-Iraqi factions, and the subsequent armed conflict between al-Fath and Iraq (see below), the PLO leadership sought Soviet assistance in easing Iraqi pressure as well. To that end, an al-Fath delegation visited Moscow in late July 1978. [68] The aim of the delegation, which comprised members of al-Fath's Left-wing, was to forestall Soviet support for anti-al-Fath forces within the PLO. [69]

THE PLO IN LEBANON

THE PLO'S POSITION IN THE SOUTH

The PLO's freedom of action, both military and political, in the Lebanese arena was reduced by the Lebanese civil war and the Shtūrā Agreement of July 1977 (see

MECS 1976-77, pp. 503-7, 513-22). While it retained its hold over the internal affairs of the refugee camps and managed to maintain its military organization, it was confronted with continued Syrian attempts to dominate it. As the Shtūrā Agreement was generally regarded by the PLO as a setback and as inimical to its interests in Lebanon, its leaders sought to delay the implementation of its third stage which called for the withdrawal of PLO units from the South. The PLO officially informed the Lebanese authorities in early November 1977 that they could not implement the third phase of the Agreement as long as the Christian forces were helping Israel "to extend its control" over the border areas. They emphasized their readiness to pull out of the area "immediately upon the withdrawal of the Christian forces and the entry of the Lebanese army in accordance with the Shtūrā Agreement." [70] Since the Christian forces obviously did not intend to leave the area, the PLO felt under no obligation to comply with the Agreement.

Both the Lebanese authorities and Syria were angered by the PLO rocket attacks on Israeli territory in the first week of November 1977 which provoked Israeli retaliatory air raids. (See essay on the Arab-Israeli Conflict: Armed Operations.) Syria increased its pressure on the PLO to pull out of the border area, and President Asad warned 'Arafāt personally at a meeting on 11 November 1977 that Syria would not let the PLO "give Israel an excuse to create new tension, thereby pulling the Syrians into a war they are not prepared for." [71] Faced with Syrian pressure, the PLO issued an official communiqué bitterly attacking "those Arab countries who have preferred complete silence over the Israeli attacks on Palestinian targets." It reasserted "the right of any Palestinian fighter to stay in South Lebanon while the Zionist enemy and its agents are still occupying parts of the area." [72] To counterbalance Syrian pressure, 'Arafāt left for Egypt and Saudi Arabia in mid-November to seek support for the PLO's position.

It was at this very juncture that Sādāt launched his peace initiative. Syrian officials were reported to have impressed on the PLO the delicate position in which Damascus was now placed. They stressed the need to remove "the problem of South Lebanon as a constant source of tension" which limited Syria's freedom of action in both the inter-Arab arena and in the conflict with Israel. [73] Syrian pressure on the PLO reached a peak at the end of November when it demanded "a total Palestinian withdrawal within a week." The PLO responded that it was operating on the basis of the Cairo and Shtūrā Agreements—to which the Syrians were reported to have replied that "after Sādāt's visit there were no agreements any more." The PLO was now subjected not only to Syrian pressure, but also to persistent demands by certain Lebanese Muslim groups—hitherto its staunch supporters—for withdrawal from the South (for details, see chapter on Lebanon).

When the PLO Executive Committee convened on 24 November 1977, two main positions on the question of withdrawal from the South crystallized: accepting it "in order to deprive Israel of any pretext to invade Lebanon"; or accepting it only on a reciprocal basis, i.e. on condition of a simultaneous withdrawal of the Christian forces. However, the principal concern expressed at the meeting was a byproduct of Sādāt's initiative: some PLO leaders questioned whether the organization could continue to exist. The PLO leadership now considered its presence in South Lebanon as the last and only card at its disposal, which it was reluctant to relinquish unless promised significant concessions in return. Some PLO officials went so far as to express apprehension that a withdrawal from South Lebanon might be followed by demands that the Palestinians return to the refugee camps and give up their arms, thus restoring the situation which had prevailed prior to the emergence of the fidā'ī groups in the 1960s. Yet it was impossible to ignore the Syrian pressure. The official resolution of the Executive Committee therefore emphasized the PLO's acceptance of "the principle of withdrawal" from the South, but made this conditional on the withdrawal of the Christian forces.[74] Thus no actual operational change was introduced in its position.

At this juncture, when it appeared that Syria and the PLO were on a collision course, the Syrians changed their position and began to view the Palestinian military presence in South Lebanon as an asset which improved their bargaining position *vis-à-vis* the Egyptian initiative. PLO-Syrian co-ordination in the political and military fields was now deemed an important weapon in Damascus' effort to demonstrate that "Sādāt had abandoned the Palestinian cause" and that Syria was the Palestinians' real ally. Syria ceased its pressure for PLO withdrawal from South Lebanon, but nevertheless presented the PLO with three conditions: that its units should not launch any military actions against Israel from across the border; that the units should remain in their present positions; and that they should not interfere with the activities of regular Lebanese forces which might be sent into the area.[75]

This new understanding between the PLO and Syria led to significant changes in the situation in South Lebanon, particularly in the nature of the PLO's activities there. Encouraged by Syrian support for their continued presence, PLO units increased their military operations from the end of December 1977 against the Christian enclaves in the Marj 'Ayyūn area.[76] Indicative of PLO intentions was the vast construction of fortifications, roads, arms stores, communication networks and clinics undertaken in the South. In addition, growing amounts of Soviet arms for the PLO arrived in early January 1978 at the Lebanese port of Tyre. Armed clashes with the Christians reached a peak in the second half of January, with both sides exchanging heavy fire along a considerable part of the border area.[77]

At this stage, however, antagonism between the PLO and the civilian population in the South increased to such an extent that the freedom of action of PLO units was threatened. It was not only the Christians who resented the PLO's activities but, more significantly, also the Muslim population which had hitherto been considered behind the PLO. Along the border area, the Shī'īs were reportedly on the verge of announcing a general mobilization against the PLO in January 1978 following several incidents between PLO units and Shī'īs; in Sidon, the Sunnī population declared a general strike in protest against fighting between rival PLO groups in the town and demanded a total withdrawal of all Palestinian units.[78] In view of the rising anti-Palestinian feelings in the South, a PLO delegation and members of the Lebanese Nationalist Movement (see chapter on Lebanon) met on 26 January and decided to form a joint force to supervise security in Sidon. Three days later, PLO units began to withdraw from Sidon, and PLO centres and command offices in the town were closed.[79] On 31 January, an agreement was signed at a meeting between the Central Command Council of the Lebanese Nationalist Movement and senior PLO officials, the main points of which were that: (1) all offices in which arms were held in the towns and villages would be closed, except in areas considered to be points of confrontation with Israel; (2) all positions evacuated by the Palestinians would be handed over to elements of the Nationalist Movement; (3) a joint committee would supervise the implementation of the agreement according to a timetable; and (4) joint committees would crack down on violations of public order by "undisciplined elements." The plan was to be implemented first in the town of Tyre, then in Nabattiyya, and subsequently in all other towns and villages in the South.[80]

THE INITIAL IMPACT OF THE ISRAELI OPERATION IN SOUTH LEBANON

A turning point in the PLO's status in Lebanon in general, and in its position in the South in particular, was reached with the fidā'ī attack in mid-March 1978 on an

Israeli bus on the main Tel Aviv-Haifa highway which provoked the Israeli operation in South Lebanon (see essay on Armed Operations in section on the Arab-Israeli Conflict). The Israeli operation had a fundamentally adverse impact on the organization, although PLO officials expressed satisfaction with their units' performance during the fighting, which they described as "the fifth Arab-Israeli war" and "a war between the Israeli Goliath and the Palestinian David" who had "tarnished the legend of the invincible Israeli army.[81]

The Israeli operation did not destroy the PLO's military power, and its losses in men and equipment were reported to be minimal; nevertheless, in being pushed back from its bases in South Lebanon, the PLO effectively lost access to the border, making it more difficult to stage operations against Israel. The PLO's dependence on Syria increased further, not only in political and military aspects but, most significantly, in a strictly operational context. An illustration of the negative impact of this dependence was provided during the fighting itself when Syria refused to allow Iraqi convoys carrying supplies for the PLO to cross its territory.[82] The growing dependence on Syria, combined with the presence of UN forces and Israeli pressure, deprived the PLO of much of the territorial freedom it had previously enjoyed. Moreover, frictions within PLO ranks were exacerbated by arguments over the organization's attitude towards Syria and the UN presence. (For an analysis of the internal frictions, see below.) The only discernible advantage to the PLO from these developments was its recognition, specifically by the UN authorities, as one of the partners for negotiations over South Lebanon.[83] (See essay on South Lebanon in section on the Arab-Israeli Conflict.)

The ceasefire declared by Israel on 21 March 1978 occurred two days after the passage of Resolution 425 by the Security Council. The initial PLO response to these events, as stated by its spokesman, Maḥmūd Labadī, was that "there could be no truce without an unconditional total withdrawal by Israel."[84] At a meeting convened on 22 March between PLO officials and the leadership of the Lebanese Nationalist Movement, both sides rejected the stationing of UN forces along the Līṭānī River "in a way which would legitimize the Israeli occupation"; they insisted that they should be stationed along the Israeli-Lebanese border.[85]

At this point the Syrians intervened. In a meeting held in Damascus on 24 March, they applied considerable pressure on the PLO leadership to agree to the proposed ceasefire.[86] In a strongly worded statement clearly carrying full Syrian backing, President Sarkīs expressed his government's determination "to check all outside intervention in Lebanon's affairs" and to establish Lebanese sovereignty "on every inch" of Lebanese territory.[87] Also on 24 March, the Lebanese government announced a total ban on the entry of military assistance for the PLO in South Lebanon. The ban applied to both arms and volunteers, the latter being a clear response to reports that c. 400 Iraqi and Libyan troops were on their way to the area.[88]

The PLO was thus caught between its desire to conduct guerrilla warfare against the Israeli forces and reject a ceasefire on the one hand, and Syrian pressure to accept a truce and co-operate with the UN peacekeeping forces on the other. It was not clear to what extent the PLO leadership could in fact enforce a ceasefire on all its factions, even if this were agreed upon. But as the Syrian pressure was too great to ignore, the PLO had no choice but to comply. However, such compliance was not publicly described as acceptance of the ceasefire but as a "readiness to facilitate UN efforts to obtain a total Israeli withdrawal." On 25 March, after talks in Damascus, Fārūq Qaddūmī, head of the PLO Political Department, emphasized "the importance of PLO-Syrian co-operation in supporting the UN mission in South Lebanon."[89] Another reason the PLO adopted this attitude was that it was preferable to keep a low profile for the time being and "to deny Israel a pretext for refusing to withdraw." [90] (For the debate within the PLO on the acceptance of the ceasefire, see below.)

THE PLO'S POSITION IN THE AFTERMATH OF THE ISRAELI OPERATION

In the aftermath of the Israeli operation in South Lebanon and the establishment of a ceasefire, a new situation began to crystallize in Lebanese-PLO relations with regard to the core question—the regulation of the Palestinian presence in Lebanon. Before the ceasefire was fully established, various Lebanese officials indicated that "the circumstances arising from the Israeli invasion" had "rendered the Cairo Agreement of 1969 defunct," and that there had to be a new agreement regulating the Palestinian presence in Lebanon. [91] There were reported to be two main positions in the Lebanese political establishment: one favoured the ending of the Palestinian presence "in all its forms," leaving only the registered refugees; the second agreed to a mere "political presence." The Lebanese parliament was to be convened on 20 April 1978 for "reopening the case of the Palestinian presence in Lebanon." [92]

The PLO was alarmed by the new trend, fearing that the issues of the ceasefire and Resolution 425 would be linked to its military presence in South Lebanon. Various Lebanese groups were poised to exploit the ceasefire issue in order to secure the permanent removal of the Palestinians from South Lebanon. To counter any such move when parliament convened, PLO officials argued that the Palestinian presence in Lebanon had been institutionalized in the Cairo and Shtūrā Agreements, and that they could not be related in any way to the issues of the ceasefire and the Israeli withdrawal. [93] In this spirit, Abū Iyād expressed the PLO's adherence to the Cairo Agreement and its readiness to implement the Shtūrā Agreement. Both 'Arafāt and Abū Iyād were at pains to emphasize that the Palestinian presence in South Lebanon concerned only the PLO and the Lebanese government; no other parties (i.e. Israel or the UN) could be involved in the discussions over that issue. [94] In order to placate the Lebanese authorities, Qaddūmī indicated that although the Cairo Agreement had to remain the framework for discussions, certain changes could be inserted into the agreement with the consent of both parties. [95] In the continuing effort to create a favourable atmosphere prior to the parliamentary session, the PLO Executive Committee met on 13 April and decided to adhere strictly to the ceasefire. [96]

The agreement arrived at by the Lebanese parliament on 23 April contained three articles which dealt directly with the Palestinian issue: (1) implementation of Resolution 425; (2) suspension of armed Palestinian and non-Palestinian action throughout Lebanese territory; and (3) prohibition of any armed presence except that of the legitimate Lebanese forces. [97] Elaborating on the agreement, several Lebanese deputies explained that the formula in the second article constituted a compromise as it had been the initial intention of many deputies to call for the termination of the Palestinian presence altogether and not merely that of an armed presence. The compromise, they explained, aimed at replacing the Cairo Agreement of 1969, creating a new basis for the Palestinian presence which would allow only for Palestinian political activity in Lebanon. [98]

The PLO vehemently attacked the agreement which it described as a formula for leading Lebanon back to civil war and as a breach of the 1969 Cairo Agreement "which could not be revoked unilaterally." [99] On 25 April the Executive Committee reasserted its determination "to defend the armed Palestinian presence in Lebanon." It emphasized that the decision to stop armed Palestinian action could not be taken "except by the Palestine Revolution itself since it is the body which defines the means of its struggle in the Arab territories and in Lebanon in particular." Nevertheless, the PLO once again expressed its readiness to adhere to the Cairo Agreement and "to fully respect the integrity, stability and sovereignty of Lebanon." [100]

The Lebanese-PLO confrontation led to immediate consultations between Syrian, Lebanese and PLO officials in an effort to find a *modus vivendi* between the seemingly irreconcilable positions. These discussions were characterized by the Syrian attempt to impress upon the PLO the need for its policies to conform with those of Damascus. President Asad was quoted as having told 'Arafāt that if the PLO desired his support, it had to co-ordinate its positions with Syrian strategy rather than pursue policies opposed to Syrian interests. [101] Referring specifically to the PLO's military operations in South Lebanon and to the role played there by the PLO's pro-Iraqi factions, Asad was reported to have said that it was not for the Palestinians to decide where and when Syria would go to war. [102]

The pressure exerted on the PLO by Syria resulted in an announcement on 24 May of a PLO-Lebanese agreement, reached by 'Arafāt and Premier Salīm al-Ḥuss, which took the form of official PLO assurances to the Lebanese government. (For the full text of the assurances, see Appendix I.) The three main articles contained the following elements: (1) an assurance by the PLO "to facilitate the mission of the UN forces to bring about the complete Israeli withdrawal"; (2) a condemnation "of all negative practices and excesses in the South," and expression of readiness "to prevent such excesses" (i.e. a commitment to suppress the military activities of the Rejectionist groups); and (3) a promise "to put an end to armed manifestations in the South" (i.e. a commitment to abstain from military operations there). [103] Simultaneous with the publication of the PLO-Lebanese agreement, the Syrian Minister of Information, Aḥmad Iskandar, issued a warning that his government would not tolerate "any attempt by the PLO to provoke the UN forces in South Lebanon." [104]

That the Lebanese and the Palestinians had different objectives in signing the agreement became evident just one day later when conflicting interpretations began to surface. The Lebanese sought to present the agreement as a new and permanent framework for the Palestinian presence in South Lebanon, superseding the 1969 Cairo Agreement. They emphasized that underlying the agreement was the transformation of the Palestinian military presence into one based on political activities. [105] The PLO spokesmen, however, stressed the temporary character of the agreement which originated from, and was directly related to, the continued Israeli occupation of South Lebanon. In their opinion, the major aim of the agreement was "to remove any pretext for delaying the Israeli withdrawal" by "freezing temporarily" the Cairo Agreement; hence their emphasis on terminating "armed manifestations" rather than on the right of an armed presence in the area. They stressed that the agreement "did not touch upon the basis for the Palestinian presence in Lebanon," which continued to be regulated by the 1969 Cairo Agreement. [106]

In accordance with the agreement, a tripartite military committee (consisting of Lebanese, PLO and Syrian representatives) convened on 26 May, after which 'Arafāt ordered a complete ceasefire in South Lebanon. Abū Iyād explained that the order applied to "all operations across the Lebanese border with Israel, including long-range rocket attacks." The military committee also agreed that arms depots should not be established and military vehicles should not appear in residential areas in the South, from the Līṭānī to the Zahrānī Rivers, an area hitherto controlled by the PLO. It also banned the appearance of armed PLO members in public and outlawed shooting during mass rallies, especially in the towns of Sidon, Zahrānī and Nabatiyya—places almost totally controlled by the PLO. [107]

During the June-August 1978 period, the PLO made a conspicuous effort to project a moderate image and maintain a low profile in South Lebanon. Thus, despite the insistence that the 1969 Cairo Agreement was still in effect, it was viewed more as a principle than as a plan requiring immediate implementation. 'Arafāt, however, maintained that the Cairo Agreement entitled the PLO "to return to South Lebanon after Israel's withdrawal." [108]

INTERNAL DEVELOPMENTS

The period under review was characterized by a marked intensification of the rivalries within the PLO.

Under 'Arafāt's leadership, al-Fath continued to dominate the PLO, as it has done for a decade, and managed to achieve considerable co-operation among the various groups under the umbrella organization—in spite of their conflicting ideologies and political loyalties. Nevertheless, 'Arafāt's and al-Fath's authority did not go unchallenged. 'Arafāt's political positions were criticized both outside and inside al-Fath; so was his use of power to preserve his office. The "rejection" elements, outside and inside al-Fath, were strengthened by Sādāt's initiative and reinforced by the PDFLP's move towards the "Rejection Front." Though still in command, 'Arafāt's power and prestige appeared to have diminished somewhat.

THE CHALLENGE TO AL-FATH'S SUPREMACY AND 'ARAFĀT'S LEADERSHIP

Strong differences over the PLO's policy towards South Lebanon in mid-1978 intensified the deep-rooted division of the organization into two main camps (see *MECS 1976-77*, pp. 182–92).

The PLO's official assurances to the Lebanese government promising to "put an end to all armed manifestations in the South" marked a turning point in the relations among its various factions. On the same day, 24 May, the "Rejection Front" and the PDFLP issued a joint communiqué demanding a new command structure which would clip the powers of al-Fath and drastically reduce 'Arafāt's domination over the PLO. They accused al-Fath of autocratic rule which prevented "collective political decisions" and demanded that, regardless of size, each faction be given an equal say in PLO bodies. This could be done by forming a new leadership which would consist of the general secretaries of all factions and "other nationalist elements." As a first step, they demanded that the PNC be reconvened within a month "to enforce" the agreement for Palestinian national unity reached at the Tripoli conference. [109] (See below and Appendix II.)

The statement objected to two main aspects of 'Arafāt's policies which, according to its authors, called for radical changes in the decision-making process within the PLO. First, it charged that 'Arafāt and al-Fath relied on Arab states which "favoured a ME settlement," something that made "independent Palestinian positions" impossible. [110] This was an obvious allusion to al-Fath's relations with Egypt and Saudi Arabia which were anathema to the rejectionists. Second, it condemned the PLO's readiness to stop armed operations in South Lebanon, which reflected "the abandonment of the objectives of the Revolution in the interest of capitulationist policies." It emphasized that such decisions were not binding, and pledged to keep up attacks on the Israeli forces and on anyone who tried to interfere with their actions. [111] 'Arafāt's position was interpreted by his opponents as suicidal, inasmuch as it gave precedence to short-term pressures over long-range aims. Thus they argued that once the PLO was deprived of its military freedom, it was likely to suffer progressively stiffer political constrictions. As for the long-term problem, they felt that 'Arafāt's entire policy was geared towards dragging the PLO into a US-sponsored settlement of the Arab-Israeli conflict. The fact that friction within al-Fath itself, which had come to the forefront several weeks earlier (see below), also centred on these two issues makes it highly probable that the signatories of the joint communiqué sought to exploit the split in al-Fath to further their interests and positions within the PLO.

The 24 May note had criticized the PLO and al-Fath leadership in general, but without referring to 'Arafāt by name; a second statement, issued by the same two groups on 4 June, specifically attacked 'Arafāt for "trying to curb Palestinian activity in South Lebanon" and asserted that he was acting on his own.[112] This charge was immediately interpreted as a major challenge to 'Arafāt and as a motion of no confidence in his leadership. But the groups denied such an assessment, emphasizing that their objection was to the way in which decisions affecting the whole movement seemed to be taken unilaterally by al-Fath.[113] The two groups were joined by Zuhayr Muhsin of al-Sā'iqa who supported their demands for structural changes. He, too, categorically denied that this meant 'Arafāt's replacement.[114]

To counter these charges, al-Fath issued a circular to all its cadres denouncing the "rejectionists' refusal to acknowledge 'Arafāt's leadership." Their reply also sought to ridicule the "rejectionists who have 2.5% of the combat forces and try to teach al-Fath [which had] 95% of the fighters" what armed struggle meant.[115] Nevertheless, since the charges had set off a general debate in the PLO, 'Arafāt was forced to respond to the demand for Palestinian unity; he suggested that all military groups be integrated and unified in one fighting force.[116] This was obviously an attempt to increase al-Fath's control over all military activity since it was by far the largest group. However, to demonstrate his readiness for co-operation with the rejectionists, 'Arafāt appointed a four-man al-Fath committee to enter talks with them.[117]

The proposed dialogue was interrupted by hostilities which began in mid-July between the pro-Iraqi rejectionist groups—the Arab Liberation Front (ALF), the Popular Liberation Front (PLF) and the Popular Struggle Front (PSF)—and units of al-Fath and the Popular Front for the Liberation of Palestine—General Command (PFLP-GC). There were scores of casualties on both sides.[118] The encounters culminated on 13 August in an explosion in the main offices of the PLF in Beirut. The building in which they were housed collapsed with the loss of 200 lives. Despite the PFLP-GC's categorical denial, the PLF held it responsible for the explosion.[119] The military encounters prompted further charges by the Rejection Front that al-Fath was trying to liquidate its opponents, intimidate the PDFLP and "sow fear among all Palestinians."[120] On 5 August, the Rejection Front and the PDFLP jointly denounced the "reactionary conspiracies" and called for the "cessation of the hostilities and the repression."[121]

As the internal strife had assumed dangerous proportions, both sides decided to try and find a *modus vivendi*. A "reconciliation meeting" was held on 16 August among top leaders of al-Fath and the PFLP. A joint statement, issued on 19 August, stressed the only point of agreement: the necessity "to adhere to democratic dialogue" as the only means of solving the contradictions within the PLO (i.e. to stop the armed encounters). The statement also showed a growing awareness among all factions that the internal frictions had caused great damage to the PLO, increased its dependence on various Arab states, and strengthened their ability to exert pressures on it. The statement therefore emphasized that the "present critical stage dictates cohesion and co-ordination among all factions under the aegis of the PLO."[122]

The Central Council, which convened in Damascus on 22 August, had two major proposals for "strengthening national unity" on its agenda. The Rejection Front, though absent from the meeting, insisted that the Executive Committee be composed of one representative from each faction, three from the PLO mass organizations, and only two independents. Al-Fath countered with a demand that the Executive Committee be formed on the basis of equal one-third representation for al-Fath, other factions and the independents. In addition, al-Fath repeated the need to establish a unified military force composed of all Palestinian factions.[123] With such conflicting demands on its agenda, the Central Council was unable to reach any compromise; the final statement confined itself to praising the "positive atmosphere" which had prevailed during the deliberations.[124] However, the Rejection Front re-emphasized its refusal to attend the Executive Committee and the Central Council meetings unless a new programme was adopted and "a new collective leadership" formed.[125]

THE SPLIT IN AL-FATH

In the latter half of 1977 there were reports of growing dissension within al-Fath's leadership, caused mainly by dissatisfaction at the way 'Arafāt handled such sensitive issues as the Shtūrā Agreement, Sādāt's initiative and relations with Syria. The Israeli operation in South Lebanon in mid-March 1978 gave rise to serious friction within al-Fath over the issue of the ceasefire. On 17 April, a group led by al-Fath's Mahmud Da'ūd 'Awda (Abū Da'ūd) decided to defy the PLO decision to adhere to the ceasefire. As this group was about to start operations behind the combat lines, regular al-Fath units—commanded by Khalīl al-Wazīr (Abū Jihād), head of al-Fath's military department and 'Arafāt's confidant—arrested the whole group of 123 and detained them in Beirut. According to several accounts, 96 of the men had come to Lebanon via Iraq and had been taken to South Lebanon by Abū Da'ūd who provided them with false al-Fath membership cards. They were being trained for special operations behind the Israeli lines when arrested at the 'Adlūn camp north of Tyre.[126] A PLO spokesman subsequently asserted that a group of "unruly elements who had come from Iraq to stir up trouble" had been arrested and detained.[127] Abū Da'ūd immediately denied the charges, asserting that his group belonged to al-Fath and had no other objective than "fighting the Zionist enemy."[128] In retaliation for the arrests, a group of Abū Da'ūd's men attacked al-Fath units loyal to Abū Jihād at Ubrā, a refugee camp in Beirut. In a fierce three-hour battle, 16 men were killed and many wounded.[129] As the two sides were massing their forces on 22 April, Abū Jihād's men attacked a camp in Nabatiyya, where one of Abū Da'ūd's groups was reported to be concentrated. Eight of his men were killed in the clash, while several of Abū Jihād's men were wounded.[130] Following the encounters, 'Arafāt was reported to have issued warrants for the arrest of Abū Da'ūd and several of his main supporters. According to one source, Abū Da'ūd was under "virtual arrest" in a Beirut hospital as of 24 April, while other prominent figures in his group were under constant surveillance.[131]

Following this open confrontation and 'Arafāt's pledge to the UN Secretary-General on 17 April to accept a moratorium on PLO military activity in South Lebanon, two main rival factions were reported to have crystallized within al-Fath's leadership. The first consisted of 'Arafāt himself, and included Abū Jihād, Sa'd Sā'il (Abū Walīd) and Hā'il 'Abd al-Hamīd (Abū al-Hawl) of the military command. The second faction included Sālih Nimr (Abū Sālih), Najī 'Alūsh, Mājid Abū Sharāra and Abū Da'ūd—all known for their Leftist inclinations.[132] There were conflicting accounts as to Abū Iyād's position, but it seems that he supported the second faction.[133]

Though the ceasefire issue was the immediate cause of the confrontation, the friction escalated swiftly and assumed proportions of a serious internal power struggle. What worried 'Arafāt, aside from the ceasefire issue, was presumably the evidence that Abū Da'ūd was trying to build his own autonomous organization within al-Fath, and that he was linked with Iraq and perhaps also with the Baghdad-based al-Fath renegade, Sabrī al-Bannā (Abū Nidāl). In 'Arafāt's view, this development represented not only a threat to the integrity of al-Fath, but also a challenge to his own leadership. In view of his pledges to Syria and the UN to observe the ceasefire, any serious violations of his orders—especially if they originated from al-Fath—could damage his position and status as the uncontested leader of the PLO. The opposing faction was concerned that 'Arafāt would seek to exploit the confrontation in order to liquidate the radical wing of al-Fath. Abū Sālih voiced this anxiety by warning that 'Arafāt's conduct heralded "a clamp-down" on all those who, like himself, opposed the PLO association with Egyptian and Saudi policy. [134] In the same spirit, Abū Da'ūd charged that 'Arafāt aimed at "liquidating the democratic forces" in al-Fath in order "to destroy the Palestinian fighting spirit." [135]

At this juncture, 'Arafāt also came under attack from Khālid al-Hasan, a leader of al-Fath's Right-wing, who blamed 'Arafāt for "the profusion of factions and the multiplicity of leaderships." He also attacked the PLO's policy of perpetually asking itself whom it should support, for "this made the Palestinians prisoners of the strategies of others." [136]

An attempt was made on 25 April to heal the rift at an al-Fath Central Committee meeting, after which a statement was issued asserting that "al-Fath's unity is as firm and solid as the mountains of Galilee, Nablus and Hebron." [137] That 'Arafāt managed to overcome the crisis and reassert his leadership was illustrated two days later at a graduation ceremony for 120 Palestinian cadets, which was attended by all major al-Fath leaders. In a statement that sounded not only like a display of unity but also as a warning to the "opposition" leaders present, 'Arafāt stressed that the unity of al-Fath was unshakeable and that "no one will be allowed to touch it." [138]

In order to tighten his control of al-Fath, 'Arafāt began to take steps towards internal reorganization in early May. He was reported to be engaged in centralizing the command of al-Fath's various military and security networks under the organization's military department, headed by Abū Jihād. [139] This alarmed his opponents who accused 'Arafāt of "monopolizing decisions and their execution," and of seeking to entrench his position "by means other than ideological or political inducements"—such as the distribution and flow of funds within al-Fath. [140]

Tension in al-Fath came to the fore again in mid-June when two of Abū Da'ūd's men who had taken part in the 17 April events were convicted by an al-Fath tribunal and executed. [141] Abū Da'ūd immediately issued a statement describing the two as "heroes" and those responsible for their execution as "criminals." He further charged that those in power in al-Fath sought to "terminate the Palestinian armed struggle," which was the only way to "victory of the Arab nation." [142]

The split in al-Fath led 'Arafāt to seek to concentrate even more power in his own hands by tightening his control over the various military networks of al-Fath. His efforts to subdue the Left-wing were generally successful, but at the price of becoming more dependent on Abū Jihād, who headed the security networks of al-Fath.

THE PDFLP'S NEW ALIGNMENT

The positions taken by the PDFLP during the period under review underscored a major change in the configuration of forces within the PLO. Whereas the PDFLP had previously been identified as part of the PLO "mainstream" (consisting also of al-Fath, al-Sā'iqa and the PFLP-GC), it found itself in the same camp as the Rejection Front on most issues that split the PLO in 1978. After Sādāt's visit to

Jerusalem, there were some indications that the PDFLP was moving towards the Rejection Front. 'Arafāt's attempts to maintain contacts with the Egyptian authorities drew sharp criticism from Nā'if Ḥawātima, the head of the PDFLP. Ḥawātima repeatedly declared that al-Fatḥ and 'Arafāt constantly violated the resolutions of the Tripoli conference, and that it was time for the PLO to adopt a rejectionist stand and defeat its Right-wingers who had reached an "impasse." [143] It is similarly noteworthy that the PDFLP joined the Rejection Front's call to reconvene the PNC in order to adopt the Tripoli declaration as the official platform of the PLO (for details see below).

Another object of Ḥawātima's attacks was the special relations between Saudi Arabia and al-Fatḥ in general, and 'Arafāt in particular. He emphasized at great length that rather than strengthening the PLO, relations with the "reactionary Saudi regime" significantly limited its freedom of action and ability to manoeuvre as the Saudis were the allies of the US. [144] The PDFLP also shared the Rejection Front's stand in the Lebanese arena. Thus, it totally rejected the ceasefire and 'Arafāt's acceptance of Resolution 425, expressing determination to continue the "struggle against the Israeli invasion." [145] It accused 'Arafāt of surrendering to the pressure of other "Arab regimes" (i.e. Syria and Saudi Arabia), and explicitly stated that the group would not be bound by "al-Fatḥ's and 'Arafāt's pledges."

The growing mutual understanding between the PFLP and the PDFLP was seen in late March when the two sides opened official talks in order to "co-ordinate policies and devise joint strategies." [146] As a result of the talks, a growing number of joint statements were issued by the Rejection Front and the PDFLP on various issues affecting the Palestinian question. Thus, on 21 April, they issued a joint statement denouncing the eruption of hostilities between two al-Fatḥ groups. [147] Again, on 4 May, both sides jointly rejected 'Arafāt's pledge to co-operate with the UN forces in Lebanon and comply with the ceasefire. [148]

The most dramatic manifestation of the alienation between al-Fatḥ and the PDFLP came on 16 May when Ḥawātima publicly accused al-Fatḥ of "selling out" the Palestinians' right to full independence. He said that the gap was wide "between us and the Palestinian Right [wing] regarding most of the issues related to the Palestinian cause." He added that al-Fatḥ deluded itself in believing that statehood and self-determination could be achieved through "co-operation and alliance with Arab Rightist regimes such as Saudi Arabia and Egypt"; in practice, this meant "the confiscation of Palestine national independence and an end to any struggle for an overall democratic solution." [149]

Co-operation between the two groups reached a peak in late May when the PDFLP joined the Rejection Front in demanding that the PLO's existing leadership be replaced by a collective leadership—a move which would deprive al-Fatḥ of its supremacy and 'Arafāt of his extended power. From then onwards, the Rejection Front and the PDFLP acted jointly in the negotiations with al-Fatḥ in devising a new formula for the composition of the Executive Committee, in the military encounters that erupted in Lebanon, and in rejecting 'Arafāt's positions on the issue of South Lebanon.

The only trace of al-Fatḥ reaction to the PDFLP's new alignment was contained in the circular which al-Fatḥ distributed in response to the Rejection Front's and the PDFLP's note of 24 May regarding structural changes in the PLO. Ridiculing the new partnership, the circular noted that "the Ḥawātimists, whose political programme demands a united Palestinian-Israeli state, met the rejectionists, who turned down everything, and sent a memorandum to al-Fatḥ." [150]

MAJOR ISSUES IN DISPUTE

Internal friction was often triggered by external events which called for a response from the PLO. The magnitude of this internal friction tended to project the organization more than ever before as a precarious coalition of interest groups whose rivalry was further intensified by their varying allegiances to different Arab states which sought to use the PLO as an instrument in the inter-Arab struggle.

Sādāt's Initiative

Sādāt's visit to Jerusalem appeared for a moment to have unified the PLO behind general slogans of condemnation of the Egyptian initiative. It seemed that the division of the PLO into two main camps—the mainstream and the Rejection Front—had become irrelevant, and that a unified PLO was about to emerge. But this façade of reconciliation and unity merely obscured an intensification of internal differences.

The first cause of recrimination was over 'Arafāt's presence at the Egyptian National Assembly when Sādāt made his stunning announcement that he was prepared to visit Israel. Some PLO members went so far as to accuse 'Arafāt of duplicity, specifically charging that he had applauded Sādāt during the speech.[151] 'Arafāt's insistence that he was as shocked as the rest of the PLO hardly convinced the sceptics. More serious points of criticism were 'Arafāt's attempts to refrain from personal attacks against Sādāt and not to sever all ties with Cairo (see above). The Rejection Front claimed that "'Arafāt's policies were one of the factors which made possible Sādāt's visit."[152] Zuhayr Muhsin, leader of al-Sā'iqa—undoubtedly inspired by Syria—criticized 'Arafāt for his attitude towards Sādāt and raised the possibility of "a split in the PLO against the defeatist leadership."[153] Most significantly, several al-Fath members were reported to have opposed 'Arafāt's "lukewarm condemnation" of Sādāt's visit; other reports pointed to a growing "militant unrest" among al-Fath ranks "against 'Arafāt's manoeuvres."[154]

In late November, the PFLP sought to exploit the general "rejectionist" atmosphere, expressing readiness to re-join the Central Council and Executive Committee on the basis of "a new platform, totally rejecting any political settlement, and a return to the original principles of armed struggle."[155] As the proposal failed to elicit any response, the Rejection Front stated on 30 November that it would boycott the Central Council session because of the "capitulationist policies" of the PLO leadership.[156]

The contrast between the outward manifestations of unity and the intensification of internal rivalries persisted in the following months. At the Tripoli conference, convened on 1 December, eight PLO factions issued a joint six-point declaration, thereby seemingly demonstrating an unprecedented level of agreement and unity between the PLO's mainstream and the Rejection Front. (For the full text of the declaration, see Appendix II.) The declaration reasserted the PLO's rejection of Resolutions 242 and 338 and of all conferences based on these resolutions, including Geneva. It re-emphasized the Palestinian people's right to return to their homeland and to self-determination "within the framework of an independent state on any part of Palestine without reconciliation, recognition or negotiation with the enemy, as an interim aim of the Palestine Revolution." Finally, the declaration advocated "a political boycott of the Sādāt regime."[157] It was signed by Abū Iyād for al-Fath, George Habash for the PFLP, Zuhayr Muhsin for al-Sā'iqa, Nā'if Hawātima for the PDFLP, 'Abd al Rahīm Ahmad for the ALF, Samīr Ghawsha for the PSF, Tal'at Tawfīq for the PLF, and Ahmad Jibrīl for the PFLP-GC. There were many other outward manifestations of reconciliation and unity. Thus, on 11 December, 'Arafāt, accompanied by Habash, appeared for the first time in five years at a

PFLP rally marking the 10th anniversary of the founding of the organization. [158] On 1 January 1978—in what was described as "the most dramatic demonstration of Palestinian unity"—10,000 Palestinians from all factions gathered to celebrate the 13th anniversary of al-Fatḥ activity. 'Arafāt appeared as "the uncontested leader of the PLO," with George Ḥabash and Nā'if Ḥawātima beside him in the reviewing stand. [159]

However, this appearance of unity was disrupted almost immediately after the joint declaration was issued. It also soon became known that there had been serious friction during the Tripoli conference not only between 'Arafāt and Ḥabash, but also between 'Arafāt and his second-in-command in al-Fatḥ, Abū Iyād. According to one source, Abū Iyād had supported a proposal made by some "rejectionists" that 'Arafāt resign, whereupon 'Arafāt threatened to boycott the conference and leave Libya. [160] 'Arafāt himself admitted later that while he was addressing the conference, Ḥabash had interrupted him and declared that he was not speaking for "the Palestinian Resistance." [161] 'Arafāt also came under attack from Ḥawātima, his former ally, for failing to adopt a clear-cut stand as to whether he was willing "to line up₊with the Rejectionist Front or follow a pro-Saudi Arabian policy." [162] There were differences, too, over how to interpret the Tripoli joint declaration. While Ḥabash sought to present it as a "rejectionist" document in its essence— which excluded any possibility of PLO participation in the political process— Ḥawātima was still willing to leave the door open for "PLO participation in the Geneva peace talks." [163]

As 'Arafāt continued to pursue his policy of striving to avoid a complete breach with Sādāt, he was attacked with increasing severity from within PLO ranks. Following a statement in mid-December by 'Isām Sartāwī to the effect that Sādāt's visit to Jerusalem was "a step forward" and that there were "no real differences between Sādāt and 'Arafāt," [164] several PLO members accused 'Arafāt of having authorized Sartāwī's statement as well as of having allowed contacts to continue between Sa'īd Kamāl and the Egyptian authorities (see above) in violation of the Tripoli conference declaration. An official PLO communiqué emphasized in reply that only the Executive Committee and the Central Council could "formulate a new policy towards Sādāt," and that transgressors would be considered as "outside the ranks of the organization." [165]

In December 1977, soon after the Tripoli conference, a new element of major strife emerged when members mainly, but not only, of the Rejection Front called for the Palestine National Council (PNC) to be convened to endorse the Tripoli joint declaration as the new platform for the PLO. On 12 December, Ḥabash publicly demanded the convening of the PNC and "the adoption of a new political programme based on the Tripoli declaration, which would explicitly spell out the triple negative: no negotiations, no peace and no recognition." [166] On 30 December, the ALF called for the convening of the PNC for "the translation of the Tripoli declaration into practical policies." [167] Samir Ghawsha of the PSF went so far as to demand that the PNC "remove the defeatist leadership and reorganize the PLO" to enable the organization to execute its "new political programme." [168]

However, the most significant development underscoring the new configuration of forces in the₊PLO was the fact that both Abū Iyād and Ḥawātima supported the move to convene the PNC with a view to incorporating the Tripoli declaration into the PLO's official policy. On 9 February 1978, Abū Iyād declared that unity within the PLO could be easily achieved "on the basis of the Tripoli declaration." [169] Following this line, Ḥawātima stated on 12 February that the PLO must formulate a rejectionist stand by "consolidating the Rejection Front formed in Tripoli and winning over the Right-wing of the PLO." [170] At a PDFLP rally on 26 February,

274

both Abū Iyād and Ḥawātima reiterated their call for "unity in the PLO on the basis of the Tripoli declaration." [171] Whereas Abū Iyād's position tended to substantiate previous rumours of a growing rift between himself and 'Arafāt, Ḥawātima's statements were further indications of the gradual shift of the PDFLP from the PLO's mainstream to the Rejection Front. Despite these mounting internal pressures—even within al-Fatḥ—'Arafāt managed to resist the efforts to convene a special session of the PNC. His reasons seem to be quite clear. First, he was concerned that a new coalition of PNC members, composed of rejectionists and opponents from within al-Fatḥ, might constitute a serious challenge to his leadership. Second, he was apprehensive that a majority of PNC members would vote to incorporate the Tripoli declaration into the PLO's official platform. Furthermore, it seemed obvious that the PNC would have to convene in some place other than Cairo—something 'Arafāt was eager to avoid lest it symbolize a final break with Egypt. 'Arafāt's success in being able to resist the pressures was illustrated by the failure of the Central Council, convened in Damascus in mid-February, to agree on the issue of reconvening the PNC. It merely reiterated its opposition to Sādāt's initiative; its adherence to the resolutions of the Tripoli and Algiers conferences; and its insistence that only the PLO could speak for the Palestinians. [172]

In March, fresh troubles spread within the PLO, this time with regard to Sa'īd Kamāl's participation in the Arab League Council meeting in Cairo. The fact that this action was in clear violation of the Tripoli resolutions and that Kamāl had had several earlier meetings with various Egyptian authorities angered the Rejection Front and a considerable part of al-Fatḥ itself—the more so as Kamāl declared that he had received "clear instructions" from 'Arafāt to attend the League meeting as the official representative of the PLO. [173] Nā'if Ḥawātima was reported to have intervened and forced the PLO to issue a statement asserting that Kamāl was not representing the PLO at the meeting.

Dialogue with Jordan

Following the renewed contacts between the PLO and Jordan in early 1978 (see above), the idea of resuming the dialogue with King Ḥusayn met with mixed feelings within al-Fatḥ and fierce opposition from the rejectionists. Several of 'Arafāt's followers argued that in view of the PLO's declining fortunes, such a dialogue could improve its status and bolster its prestige. They also counselled against ignoring the Syrian and Algerian pressure to enter into talks with Jordan at a time when the PLO could count on hardly any other allies. Among the opponents of a *rapprochement* with Amman were leaders such as Ḥabash who refused, in principle, to have any dealings with Ḥusayn. In Ḥabash's view, Amman "should have nothing to do with the Palestinian problem"—least of all now when its stand was "part of the US attempts to save the Egyptian regime." [174] Mājid Abū Sharāra, the head of al-Fatḥ's Information Department, argued that since Jordan's aim was "to assume the right to represent the Palestinians," the PLO should refuse to resume a dialogue "under such conditions." [175] Abū Iyād suspected that Ḥusayn would seek to exploit a dialogue with the PLO as a means of "extricating himself from political isolation" and so improving Jordan's position in the Arab world. [176] Faced with such strong opposition, the PLO's leadership preferred not to resume negotiations with Amman.

It was therefore no surprise that 'Arafāt's sudden visit to Mafraq in September, as well as his meeting with King Ḥusayn during the Tripoli bloc conference in Damascus, should have aroused sharp criticism within the PLO. Many of its leaders alleged that 'Arafāt had failed to consult the Palestinian delegation before leaving

Damascus, and that he should not have taken such an important step without consulting other PLO leaders.[177] Criticism reportedly abated only after intensive efforts by 'Arafāt to persuade his colleagues that at his meeting with Ḥusayn, he had been firm on "all issues concerning PLO-Jordanian relations."[178]

South Lebanon

As discussed above, Israel's unilateral ceasefire on 21 March and Security Council Resolution 425 set off a fierce debate within the PLO over its decision to comply with the ceasefire—a decision taken under Syrian and reportedly also Saudi Arabian pressures. The initial response of all factions was totally negative; all emphasized their determination to fight "the Israeli occupation of South Lebanon." Abū Iyād explained that a liberation movement could not speak in terms of a ceasefire, but "we might implement it without a declaration."[179] However, George Ḥabash officially announced on 30 March that the Palestinians "cannot know anything called ceasefire," and that his group would not honour "'Arafāt's acceptance of a truce."[180] As late as 4 May, the Rejection Front and the PDFLP issued a joint statement expressing their determination to continue the fight against Israeli forces in South Lebanon, and insisting that 'Arafāt was speaking for himself when he declared a moratorium on PLO activities there.[181]

The confrontation between the two sides over the ceasefire focused as much on ideological as on pragmatic lines. The proponents held that priority had to be given to Israel's withdrawal; any action which might delay it had to be suspended. Second, under the prevailing circumstances in which Syria was the closest equivalent to an ally that the PLO had, it would be impolitic to ignore or resist pressure from Damascus for a ceasefire. Third, 'Arafāt believed that since the PLO had gained international recognition and had "observer" status at the UN, it would be unwise to enter into a confrontation with its peacekeeping forces in South Lebanon. Fourth, 'Arafāt sought to take advantage of the ceasefire period to overcome the deep-seated resentment felt by the South Lebanese who held the PLO at least partly responsible for their long ordeal.

The opponents argued that the PLO had already gone too far in accommodating Arab states, mainly Syria and Saudi Arabia. They claimed that the PLO represented a "revolution" and as such could not be bound by agreements which would make it seem more like a "regime." A ceasefire contradicted the very *raison d'être* of the Palestinian movement and was therefore unacceptable. They emphasized that the net effect of "'Arafāt's conduct" amounted to nothing less than "suspending the fight with the Zionist enemy; leaving the Israelis and the fascist, isolationist, Rightist forces in control of South Lebanon; withdrawing fighters from Lebanese towns and villages, thus restricting the Palestinian military presence; and turning the Palestinian Revolution into a mere information activity." They stressed that all these measures of "'Arafāt and his clique" were being taken at a time when the PLO had never been in a better position to wage a guerrilla campaign.[182]

Despite the considerable pressure of the rejectionists, 'Arafāt managed to impose his authority and avoid a general confrontation with the UN forces or large-scale violations of the ceasefire. In late May it was reported that 'Arafāt was employing a 500-man force in the South, under the command of 'Azmī Saghīr, to assert direct control over Palestinian activities in the area.[183]

THE AL-FATḤ-IRAQ CLASH

Both the PLO's increasing dependence on Syria and Sādāt's initiative led Iraq to increase its efforts to influence the PLO through such rejectionist factions as the ALF, PLF and PSF, as well as by giving more freedom of action to the Baghdad-based al-Fath dissident, Abū Nidāl. Iraqi support of the rejectionist groups was reflected in the Lebanese arena where they entered into direct confrontation with al-Fath. For instance, Iraq encouraged its protégés within the PLO to resist Syrian pressure and defy the ceasefire order in South Lebanon. Consequently, the tension and sporadic clashes between the two sides escalated into serious battles in various parts of Lebanon, claiming the lives of over 100 men. That 'Arafāt managed to impose his will on the PLO constituted a further indication for the Iraqis that their stand and influence within the Palestinian movement were being undermined and that Syria had brought the organization under its own total control. The PLO's position, and particularly 'Arafāt's stand, in the Arab-Israeli conflict was another element in the confrontation between Iraq and al-Fath. Although the PLO rejected a negotiated settlement of the conflict, the Iraqis suspected that 'Arafāt was ready, on certain conditions, to join the US-sponsored political process.

In Iraq's view, the cumulative effect of the new circumstances amounted to a significant decline in its inter-Arab position *vis-à-vis* Syria, coupled with a loss of influence over the Palestinian movement. In order to pre-empt a further deterioration, Iraq launched a world-wide campaign against al-Fath, signalling to 'Arafāt that Iraq could not tolerate being deprived of influence in the PLO. What followed was a period of spiralling terror in the form of attacks and reprisals on Iraqi and PLO targets in various parts of the world. Thus, PLO offices were attacked in London on 4 January, in Kuwiat on 15 June, in Paris on 3 August, and in Islamabad on 5 August. In the course of these attacks, four prominent Palestinian representatives were assassinated: Sa'īd Ḥamāmī in London; 'Iz al-Dīn Qalaq and 'Adnan Ḥamād in Paris; and 'Alī Yāsīn in Kuwait.

'Arafāt attributed these assassinations to Abū Nidāl's group. The PLO stated that it held Iraq and its intelligence network responsible for all Abū Nidāl's actions, arguing that he could not possibly operate out of Baghdad without the active collusion of the Iraqi authorities. Subsequently, 'Arafāt requested that Abū Nidāl's group be handed over for trial by the PLO, but Iraq refused.[184] Retaliating on the Iraqi-sponsored strikes, al-Fath men attacked such targets as the Iraqi embassies in Beirut (22 June and 1 August); in London (28 July); in Paris (31 July) and in Tripoli (19 July and 16 August).

In early August, several mediation efforts were launched by Algeria, Libya and Lebanon, but to no avail. In mid-August, however, the overt confrontation subsided, and by mid-September the verbal recriminations ceased as well. It seems that the convening of the Camp David summit and the subsequent accords were the direct cause for the "truce."

Jacob Goldberg

APPENDIX I: PLO ASSURANCES TO THE LEBANESE GOVERNMENT

(1)   The PLO assured the Prime Minister that it was interested in facilitating the mission of the UN forces to bring about the complete Israeli withdrawal from the South and the restoration of Lebanese sovereignty there.
(2)   The PLO condemned all the negative practices and excesses in the South. It has expressed full readiness to exert every effort to prevent such excesses at the earliest possible time in order to preserve Palestinian-Lebanese relations.
(3)   The PLO has emphasized that it intends to put an end to armed manifestations in the South to help the legitimate authorities carry out their duties and exercise their sovereignty.
(4)   At the request of the Prime Minister, the PLO will seek to ensure the return of the volunteers who came during the Israeli invasion of the South.
(5)   It has been agreed to hold further meetings to regulate Lebanese-Palestinian relations in such a way as to safeguard Lebanese sovereignty and serve the Palestine cause.

Source: R Beirut, 24 May—BBC, 26 May 1978.

APPENDIX II: TRIPOLI CONFERENCE DECLARATION OF PALESTINIAN UNITY

We, the Palestine Liberation Organization (PLO) with all its organizations declare the following:
(1)   Request the establishment of an Arab confrontation and resistance front consisting of Algeria, the Jamāhīriyyah, Iraq, Syria, Democratic Yemen and the Palestine Liberation Organization that will oppose all capitulationist solutions advanced by imperialism, Zionism and their Arab agents.
(2)   Our total condemnation of any Arab party present at the Tripoli summit which refuses the establishment of this front and the announcement of same.
(3)   Ascertain our rejection of the Security Council Resolutions 242 and 338.
(4)   Ascertain our rejection of all international conferences based on these two resolutions, including that of Geneva.
(5)   To work for the fulfilment of the right of the Palestinian people to return to their homeland and the right for self-determination within the framework of an independent Arab Palestinian state on any liberated part of Palestine without reconciliation, recognition or negotiation with the enemy, as an interim aim of the Palestine Revolution.
(6)   Adoption of the political boycott of the Sādāt regime.

Hereby we declare this unity document in the name of all the Palestinian organizations having been signed by the entire leadership of the resistance movement groups. Revolution until victory.

Source: JANA, 4 December—BBC, 6 December 1977.

NOTES
1.   Reuter, 29 December 1977—British Broadcasting Corporation, Summary of World Broadcasts, the ME and Africa (BBC), 2 January 1978.
2.   Voice of Palestine, clandestine (PLO station broadcasting from Lebanon; VoP), 19 November—BBC, 20 November 1977.
3.   *New York Times (NYT)*, 18 November 1977.
4.   VoP, 22 January—BBC, 24 January 1978.
5.   VoP, 20 November—BBC, 22 November 1977.
6.   VoP, 15 December—BBC, 18 December 1977.
7.   *NYT*, 26 November 1977.
8.   Sādāt, in an interview to the American Broadcasting Corporation, 4 January, quoted in the *NYT*, 5 January 1978.
9.   Reuter, 12 May—BBC, 14 May 1978.
10.   *Arabia and the Gulf*, London; 20 January 1978.
11.   *Al-Madīna*, Saudi Arabia; 27 November 1977.
12.   VoP, 19 February—Daily Report (DR), 23 February 1978.
13.   *NYT*, 20 December, VoP, 21 December—BBC, 24 December 1977.
14.   VoP, 14 January—BBC, 16 January 1978.
15.   *Christian Science Monitor (CSM)*, Boston; 22 August 1978.
16.   *Le Monde*, Paris; 2 September 1978.
17.   VoP, 19 September—BBC, 21 September 1978.

18. VoP, 20 September—BBC, 22 September 1978.
19. VoP, 19 September—BBC, 21 September 1978.
20. Syrian Arab News Agency (SANA), 18 September—DR, 20 September; Iraqi News Agency (INA), 19 September—BBC, 21 September 1978.
21. *Financial Times (FT)*, London; 31 October 1978.
22. *Ibid*, 20 December 1977.
23. *Al-Jumhūriyya*, Cairo; 25 December 1977 and 17 February 1978; *Boston Globe*, 25 December 1977.
24. *Al-Jumhūriyya*, 26 January 1978.
25. *Ibid*, 11 February 1978.
26. *FT*, 20 December 1977.
27. *NYT*, 19 and 20 February 1978.
28. Reuter, 24 February—BBC, 25 February 1978.
29. *Al-Ahrām*, Cairo; 25 February 1978.
30. *Washington Post (WP)*, 28 February 1978.
31. *NYT*, 1 March 1978.
32. Middle East News Agency (MENA), Cairo; 5 March—BBC, 7 March 1978.
33. Reuter, 7 March—BBC, 9 March 1978.
34. MENA, 18 March—DR, 20 March 1978.
35. VoP, 19 September—DR, 21 September 1978.
36. Interview to *October*, Cairo; 15 October 1978.
37. Qatari News Agency (QNA), 5 March—DR, 6 March 1978.
38. *Al-Safīr*, Beirut; 5 March 1978.
39. MENA, 11 March—BBC, 13 March 1978.
40. *Al-Nahār*, Beirut; 10 February; QNA, 13 February—BBC, 14 February 1978.
41. *Al-Safīr*, 8 March 1978.
42. QNA, 6 March—DR, 6 March; VoP, 9 March—DR, 10 March 1978.
43. Mājid Abū Sharāra, quoted by QNA, 9 March—DR, 10 March 1978.
44. VoP, 22 May—BBC, 22 May 1978.
45. *Al-Watan*, Kuwait; 23 September 1978.
46. VoP, 23 September—DR, 25 September 1978.
47. See for instance, *CSM*, 22 August 1978.
48. *Arabia and the Gulf*, 28 August 1978.
49. Hawātima's interview to *al-Hurriyya*, Beirut; 6 February 1978.
50. Habash's interview to TASS, 2 June 1978.
51. *Al-Safīr*, 25 September 1978.
52. *Al-Kifāh al-'Arabī*, Beirut; 9 October; *FT*, 31 October 1978.
53. See for example, *NYT*, 17 December 1977 and 2 May 1978.
54. *Neues Deutschland*, 6 April—DR, 8 April 1978.
55. *NYT*, 30 December 1977.
56. See for example, VoP, 9 May—BBC, 11 May 1978.
57. *Daily Telegraph (DT)*, London; 16 January 1978.
58. *FT*, 20 December 1977; *al-Dustūr*, London; 16 January 1978.
59. Reuter, 26 January—BBC, 29 January 1978.
60. 'Arafāt in an interview to the National Broadcasting Corporation, quoted in the *NYT*, 12 April; Abū Iyād in an interview to the *DT*, 16 January 1978.
61. *NYT*, 2 May 1978.
62. 'Arafāt's interview to *NYT*, 2 May 1978.
63. *Ma'ariv*, Tel Aviv; 8 May 1978.
64. *Jerusalem Post*, 2 July 1978.
65. VoP, 1 July—DR, 5 July 1978.
66. 'Arafāt, quoted by VoP, 19 September—BBC, 21 September 1978.
67. A joint Soviet-PLO communiqué issued at the end of 'Arafāt's visit to Moscow; *CSM*, 10 March 1978.
68. QNA, 27 July—DR, 27 July 1978.
69. VoP, 3 August—DR, 4 August; *al-Sayyād*, Beirut; 10 August; *al-Mustaqbal*, Beirut; 16 September 1978.
70. MENA, 16 November—DR, 17 November 1977.
71. *NYT*, 12 November 1977.
72. R Cairo, VoP, 12 November—BBC, 14 November 1977.
73. *Al-Sayyā*d, 1 December 1977.
74. *Ibid; al-Nahār*, 29 November 1977; *Le Monde*, 4 February 1978.
75. *Al-Nahār al-'Arabī wal-Duwalī (NAD)*, Paris; 31 December 1977; *al-'Amal*, Beirut; 3 January 1978.
76. *Ma'ariv*, 18, 20 December 1977; *Ha'aretz*, Tel Aviv; 16, 18 January 1978.

77. *Le Monde*, 1 February 1978.
78. *Ibid.*
79. INA, 27 January—BBC, 30 January; Deutsche Presse Agentur (DPA), 30 January—DR, 1 February 1978.
80. *Al-Nahār*, 3 February; *NYT*, 6 February; MENA, 4 February—BBC, 6 February 1978.
81. 'Arafāt in an interview to *Newsweek*, New York; 3 April 1978.
82. INA, 17 March—BBC, 19 March 1978.
83. MENA, 31 March—DR, 2 April 1978.
84. *The Times*, London; 22 March 1978.
85. *Al-Safīr*, 24 March 1978.
86. *Ibid.*
87. *FT*, 25 March 1978.
88. *NYT*, 25 March 1978.
89. R Damascus, 26 March—BBC, 28 March 1978.
90. Hānī al-Hasan's reported statement to Prime Minister al-Huss; R Beirut, 2 April—DR, 3 April 1978.
91. *FT*, 25 March; MENA, 24 March—DR, 26 March 1978.
92. MENA, 10 April—DR, 11 April 1978.
93. MENA, 7 April—DR, 9 April 1978.
94. Abū Iyād to *al-Nahār*, 2 April; 'Arafāt to *Le Figaro*, Paris; 13 April 1978.
95. *Al-Safīr*, 15 April 1978.
96. *Ibid.*
97. R Beirut, 23 April—BBC, 25 April 1978.
98. MENA, 23 April—DR, 24 April 1978.
99. Reuter, 25 April—DR, 26 April 1978.
100. VoP, 25 April—BBC, 27 April; *NYT*, 26 April 1978.
101. *Al-Manār*, London; 29 April 1978.
102. *Economist*, London; 29 April 1978.
103. R Beirut, 24 May—BBC, 26 May 1978.
104. *The Guardian*, Manchester; 25 May 1978.
105. *FT*, 26 May 1978.
106. VoP, 25 May—BBC, 27 May 1978.
107. *NYT*, 28 May; QNA, 29 May—BBC, 30 May 1978.
108. QNA, 3 June—DR, 5 June 1978.
109. *DT*, 26 May 1978.
110. Reuter, 24 May—BBC, 26 May 1978.
111. *NYT*, 25 May; INA, 29 May—BBC, 31 May 1978.
112. Reuter, 4 June—DR, 6 June 1978.
113. *Events*, London; 16 June 1978.
114. QNA, 28 May—BBC, 30 May; *al-Qabas*, Kuwait; 21 June 1978.
115. *Al-Ra'y al-Āmm*, Kuwait; 15 June 1978.
116. *NAD*, 15 June 1978.
117. *Al-Qabas*, 28 May 1978.
118. *The Times*, 15 July 1978.
119. *WP*, 14 August; *The Guardian*, 15 August 1978.
120. INA, 22 July—DR, 25 July 1978.
121. R Baghdad, 3 August—DR, 4 August 1978.
122. VoP, 19 August—BBC, 21 August 1978.
123. VoP, 22 August—DR, 23 August; *The Guardian*, 21 August; *CSM*, 24 August 1978.
124. VoP, 23 August—DR, 25 August 1978.
125. DPA, 23 August—BBC, 25 August 1978.
126. *Al-Hawādith*, Beirut; 28 April 1978.
127. VoP, 18 April—DR, 20 April 1978.
128. R Baghdad, VoP (BVOP), 20 April—BBC, 24 April 1978.
129. *Al-'Amal*, 21 April 1978.
130. R Beirut, 23 April—DR, 25 April 1978.
131. *Los Angeles Times*, 25 April 1978.
132. MENA, 21 April—BBC, 23 April 1978.
133. *Le Monde*, 19 April; *al-'Amal*, 21 April 1978.
134. *Al-Liwā*, Beirut; 20 April 1978.
135. MENA, 21 April—BBC, 22 April 1978.
136. *Al-Qabas*, 20 April 1978.
137. VoP, 25 May—DR, 27 May 1978.
138. *Ibid*, 27 May—DR, 30 May 1978.
139. *Arabia and the Gulf*, 15 May 1978.

140. *Ibid*, 30 May 1978.
141. VoP, 19 June—DR, 21 June 1978.
142. Reuter, 20 June—DR, 22 June 1978; *al-Dustūr*, 10 July 1978.
143. Interview to *Le Soir*, Brussels; 12 February 1978.
144. *Ibid*.
145. Reuter, 4 May—DR, 6 May 1978.
146. *Al-Manār*, 25 March 1978.
147. BVOP, 21 April—BBC, 23 April 1978.
148. Reuter, 4 May—DR, 6 May 1978.
149. Inter-Press Service, Beirut; 16 May—BBC, 18 May 1978.
150. *Al-Ra'y al-Āmm*, 15 June 1978.
151. *Arabia and the Gulf*, 30 January 1978.
152. Habash's statement to INA, 16 November—DR, 22 November 1977.
153. Interview to *L'Espresso*, Rome; 27 November 1977.
154. *Arabia and the Gulf*, 30 January 1978.
155. INA, 28 November—DR, 29 November 1977.
156. BVOP, 30 November—DR, 2 December 1977.
157. Jamāhīriyya Arab News Agency (JANA), Libya; 4 December—BBC, 6 December 1977.
158. *NYT*, 12 December 1977.
159. *Ibid*, 2 January 1978.
160. BVOP, 3 December—DR, 5 December 1977.
161. *October*, 19 February 1978.
162. Hawātima's interview to Associazione Nazionale Stampa Associatta (ANSA), Rome; 3 December—DR, 6 December 1977.
163. *Ibid*.
164. *Die Presse*, Vienna; 13 December 1977.
165. SANA, 14 December—BBC, 16 December 1977.
166. INA, 12 December—DR, 14 December 1977.
167. *Ibid*, 30 December—DR, 31 December 1977.
168. *Ibid*, 27 January—DR, 1 February 1978.
169. R Algiers, 9 February—DR, 11 February 1978.
170. Interview to *Le Soir*, 12 February 1978.
171. *Al-Nahār*, Beirut; 27 February 1978.
172. VoP, 13 December—DR, 14 December 1977.
173. QNA, 29 March—DR, 30 March; *al-Ahrām*, 13 April 1978.
174. *Al-Safīr*, 9 March 1978.
175. QNA, 5 March—DR, 6 March 1978.
176. *Al-Safīr*, 8 March 1978.
177. *Al-Watan*, 23 September; BVOP, 22 September—DR, 25 September 1978.
178. *Al-Qabas*, 23 September 1978.
179. *NYT*, 30 March 1978.
180. Reuter, 30 March—DR, 2 April 1978.
181. Reuter, 4 May—DR, 6 May 1978.
182. BVOP, 18 April—BBC, 20 April 1978.
183. *The Guardian*, 30 May 1978.
184. *The Observer*, London; 6 August 1978.

The West Bank and the Gaza Strip

The main political developments in the West Bank and the Gaza Strip revolved around President Anwar al-Sādāt's visit to Israel and the chain of events it set in motion—particularly the Israeli proposal for autonomy in the areas and the Camp David accords. Although there were no fundamental changes in the political groupings or trends during the period under review, the previous tendencies were thrown into sharper relief—much more so than under the impact of American initiatives earlier in 1977 (see *MECS 1976–77*, pp. 213–16).

The main groups inevitably found themselves compelled to take a stand on Sādāt's visit and to restate, or redefine, their attitudes at every major turn in the subsequent Egyptian-Israeli-American contacts. On the eve of Sādāt's initiative, the following principal groupings could be discerned:

●PLO supporters, with a number of West Bank mayors such as Karīm Khalaf of Rāmallah in the lead, who argued that as the "sole legitimate representative of the Palestinians," only the PLO leadership was authorized to negotiate on their behalf. Independent spokesmen for the West Bank and Gaza were regarded as an illegitimate "substitute leadership." The mayors belonging to this group held that their 1976 election mandate related to municipal affairs only.

Within this group, some combined adherence to the principle of the PLO's representative status with the conviction that, in terms of practical politics, Jordan was more likely to achieve an Israeli withdrawal from the West Bank and Gaza. The views of the mayor of Hebron, Fahd al-Qawāsimī, were representative of this trend.

●The pro-Hashimites, properly so called, regarded the attainment of Israel's withdrawal from the West Bank and the Gaza Strip as the main goal to be achieved by the "political process" which, to them, primarily meant the Geneva conference. They held that Jordan's political weight was indispensable for this purpose, but also called for the participation of local representatives at Geneva. In their public statements, members of this group frequently affirmed the representative status of the PLO as well. Prominent among them were Anwar al-Khatīb, the former Jordanian governor of Jerusalem, and the Nablus notable, Hikmat al-Masrī.

●A group of notables of the second rank, close to the Hashimite camp but not identical with it, openly criticized the PLO and disqualified it from representing the West Bank and the Gaza Strip at Geneva. One of the main figures in this group was Husayn al-Shuyūkhī. It lacked substantial public support and had failed in attempts to set up a new, potentially representative body in 1977.[1]

●Yet another group, led by the Rāmallah lawyer 'Azīz Shahāda and the East Jerusalem justice Nihād Jārallah, argued that any political settlement should start with the recognition—both by the Palestinians of the West Bank and the Gaza Strip and by Israel—of the other's right to sovereign statehood. They called for a plebiscite in the West Bank and the Gaza Strip, to be conducted during an interim period and under international or inter-Arab supervision. Their ultimate aim was an independent Palestinian state linked with Jordan.[2]

Despite this broad spectrum of opinion, it was obvious that in the period preceding Sādāt's visit, the pro-Hashimites and the PLO supporters were the two dominant local forces. As in the past, they drew their strength from the international and inter-Arab status of Jordan and the PLO respectively, while their local standing varied according to the changing fortunes of these two patrons.

THE IMPACT OF SĀDĀT'S INITIATIVE
INITIAL REACTIONS

President Sādāt's decision to visit Jerusalem came as a complete and bewildering surprise to the inhabitants of the West Bank and Gaza Strip. While popular opinion was as difficult to assess in 1977 as at any time since 1967, it seems likely that reaction at grassroots level was basically one of welcome, but strongly tinged with doubts and suspicions. Many people felt that Sādāt had made the termination of Israeli occupation a real possibility; yet many were fearful that the kind of settlement Sādāt envisaged would not take full account of Palestinian aspirations. The greatest fear was that Sādāt was ready for a separate Egyptian-Israeli agreement.

If popular reaction was confused, local leaders were characteristically divided in their attitudes, the lines of division following the pattern of traditional political affiliations as set out above. PLO supporters, taking their cue from official reactions of the PLO establishment (see essay on the PLO), generally rejected the Egyptian initiative. They suspected that the "political process" as understood by Egypt would bypass the PLO, ignore its political programme, and lead to compromise over the creation of a fully independent Palestinian state. They were critical of Sādāt's having taken unilateral action—thereby splitting Arab ranks— and echoed the "rejectionist" argument that by visiting Jerusalem he had virtually extended unilateral recognition to Israel. In their view, the appropriate way to work out a comprehensive Middle East peace settlement was to reconvene the Geneva conference, with PLO and Soviet participation. Radical PLO supporters therefore did not hesitate to reject Sādāt's policy completely. Prominent among them was the mayor of Rāmallah, Karīm Khalaf, who said: "Sādāt's acceptance of Begin's invitation means ignoring the Palestinian problem, or sweeping it under the carpet. . . . My advice to Begin is to invite 'Arafāt and sit down with him in Geneva." [3] The mayor of Jericho, 'Abd al-'Azīz Suwaytī, who in the past had taken a more moderate line, [4] stated that "Sādāt ignores the origin of the Arab struggle and takes only Egyptian interests into consideration. . . . If he comes to Israel, I will not meet him. . . . After all, he is not coming to solve the Palestinian problem." [5]

Many rank-and-file PLO sympathizers were more ambivalent in their attitudes, however. Being committed to the official PLO position, they were unable to come out openly in favour of the peace initiative, yet they could not ignore the sudden emergence of a possible hope that the Palestinian issue might be solved—even at the exclusion of the PLO. They realized that Sādāt had committed both his personal prestige as the "Hero of the October War" and the prestige of Egypt as the leading Arab country to the achievement of a solution. Egypt had always insisted on its commitment to the Palestinian cause, and there were those among PLO supporters who could not believe that Sādāt would now ignore the basic rights of the Palestinians. Such considerations led some less radical PLO supporters to express the hope that the PLO would eventually join in the peace process. [6] For instance, Hebron mayor Fahd al-Qawāsimī, a known supporter of the PLO, went so far as to welcome the Egyptian initiative publicly by saying: "It will be a good step. It will be an important dialogue. First of all, it will break the traditional enmity which exists between Israel and the Arab states; I also believe this [Begin-Sādāt] meeting will serve the Palestinian problem in particular." [7]

The pro-Hashimites, by contrast, adopted an attitude of cautious support. They were impressed by the fact that the initiative had been taken by the major Arab state and that Sādāt had thrown his country's full political weight into the scales. They were hopeful that the process launched by him would eventually provide a solution for the Palestinians. Moreover, they were less concerned over the issue of PLO participation; on the contrary, they perceived that the new Egyptian policy might enhance their own prospects for taking part in the political process. However, the pro-Hashimites had reservations of their own. Like others in the West Bank and Gaza, they feared that under certain circumstances Sādāt might promote Egyptian interests at the expense of those of the Palestinians. They were particularly affected by King Husayn's delay in formulating his own position towards Sādāt's initiative; as followers of Jordanian policy, they felt unable to take a definite stand so long as there were no clear signals from Amman. Consequently, the pro-Hashimites largely welcomed Sādāt's visit to Jerusalem, but their chief leaders refrained from participating in the receptions held to mark his arrival.

Following Sādāt's Knesset speech on 20 November 1977, the attitude of PLO supporters generally hardened since they were bitterly disappointed by his failure to ascribe any role whatsoever to their organization in finding a solution to the Palestinian question. (For Sādāt's speech and other stages of his initiative, see essay on the Arab-Israeli Conflict.) On the other hand, Sādāt's insistence on total Israeli withdrawal from the West Bank and the Gaza Strip, as well as on self-determination for the Palestinians, further aggravated the dilemma of those PLO sympathizers who had thought that Egypt's new policy might at least serve as a starting point for realizing basic Palestinian aspirations.[8] This made it difficult for pro-PLO leaders to maintain a united anti-Sādāt front, further weakening their already somewhat equivocal local image. Evidence of this trend was their failure, right from the start, to draw the population at large into protest actions against the peace initiative (see below). The pro-Hashimites, for their part, expressed greater support for Sādāt in the wake of his Knesset speech. Its tenor convinced them that he was indeed concerned about finding a solution to their problems. Furthermore, they believed that the speech would help them strengthen their position at a time when the PLO's popularity was relatively low.

NOTABLES MEET SĀDĀT

Against this background, a group of nine West Bank and Gaza Strip notables—most of them prominent pro-Hashimites—met with Sādāt in Jerusalem on 21 November 1977. They were Anwar al-Khatīb, the former governor of Jerusalem; Hikmat al-Masrī, a Nablus notable and former speaker of the Jordanian Chamber of Deputies; Elias Freij, the mayor of Bethlehem; Nihād Jārallah, the President of the West Bank High Court of Appeal; Na'īm 'Abd al-Hādī, a Nablus notable and former Jordanian minister; Mustafā Dūdīn, also a former Jordanian minister; Muhammad Sulaymān al-'Azāyiza, the mayor of Dayr al-Balah in the Gaza Strip; Hājj Furaykh al-Musaddar, a notable from the Gaza Strip, known for his pro-Egyptian orientation; and Ibrāhīm Abū Sitta, a prominent figure in a group of Gazan notables who had been a member of the PLO Executive Committee in 1965 and 1966, but was also known as pro-Egyptian.

The notables were reported to have saluted Sādāt for his peace efforts and for upholding the cause of the Palestinians in his Knesset speech. They told him that every word in his speech was "acceptable to the Palestinian people in the West Bank and the Gaza Strip," and that the majority of the inhabitants supported his peace initiative. "All we wish," they added, "is that the reaction of the Israeli side would be responsive."[9] While reportedly deploring PLO criticism of the peace initiative, they told Sādāt that they regarded the PLO as the legitimate representative of the

Palestinians. However, provided the PLO approved, they did not object to the participation of some Gaza Strip and West Bank representatives in the peace process.[10] But Ibrāhīm Abū Sitta reportedly did voice reservations about Sādāt's attitude towards the PLO and urged the Egyptian President to permit the renewal of "Voice of Palestine" broadcasts from Cairo. (For their discontinuation, see essay on the PLO and chapter on Egypt.) He reminded Sādāt that he had been among the first Arab leaders to support the PLO and asked him to convey the greetings of the Palestinians in the West Bank and the Gaza Strip to Yāsir 'Arafāt.[11]

THE ISSUE OF A WEST BANK DELEGATION TO CAIRO
Reports from Cairo late in November 1977 stated that Egypt's main government party (the Arab Socialist Party of Egypt, headed by Prime Minister Mamdūḥ Sālim) intended to extend invitations to certain leaders in the West Bank and the Gaza Strip to take part in the Cairo conference (see essay on the Arab-Israeli Conflict). This caused great concern within the pro-PLO group. Once again, its leaders were alarmed by the possibility that such participation would eventually lead to the creation of a "substitute leadership" (*qiyāda badīla*) outside the PLO. At a time when its stock in inter-Arab and international affairs was low, the PLO suspected that pro-Hashimites and other anti- or non-PLO elements might find the moment propitious to consider launching an alternative representative body independent of the PLO. There were indications that pro-PLO West Bank leaders consulted PLO personalities abroad and were instructed to initiate various activities to prevent the participation of independent West Bank and Gaza Strip leaders in the Cairo conference. An emergency meeting of PLO supporters, organized by the mayors of Nablus and Rāmallah, was held at the Bīr Zayt College near Rāmallah on 26 November. The participants strongly denounced the proposed participation of any West Bank and Gaza Strip personalities in the Cairo talks, claiming that only the PLO was entitled to represent the Palestinians there. As in the past, they again excluded themselves from serving as possible representatives of the Palestinians in the political process.[12] Karīm Khalaf elaborated on this issue by saying: "The mayors do not represent the PLO; the PLO represents us, and the people elected us to our positions because we are standing behind the PLO."[13]

Khalaf took the occasion to criticize Sādāt once again for visiting Jerusalem and for ignoring the PLO and its political role in his Knesset speech. This position was reiterated by PLO supporters in a statement issued on 29 November on behalf of the Arab Alumni Association in East Jerusalem,[14] as well as in a memorandum published a few days later and distributed to all foreign consulates in East Jerusalem. The memorandum was signed by 16 West Bank mayors, two deputy mayors, several other public figures, and by professional associations. The signatories insisted that they would not attend the Cairo conference as "substitutes" for the PLO and spoke out against anyone planning to set up a new leadership to replace that organization. Yet the signatories had difficulties in defining their views towards Egypt clearly. In the memorandum, for instance, they denounced Sādāt's visit to Jerusalem and his failure to mention the PLO in his speech at the Knesset, yet paid tribute to Egypt's major role in the Arab world and to its past sacrifices for the sake of the Palestinians.[15]

This ambivalence reflected differences of opinion, lack of cohesion and the general weakness felt among PLO supporters and sympathizers at that juncture. Nor was it the only indication of this kind: two pro-PLO leaders, Mayor Fahd Qawasīmī of Hebron and Mayor Ḥilmī Hanūn of Tūlkarm, had stayed away from the Bīr Zayt meeting, apparently because they disagreed with the line adopted by their colleagues.[16] Simultaneously, the difficulties pro-PLO leaders faced in recruiting public support was made evident in Nablus—a PLO stronghold—where they failed in an attempt to collect signatures for an anti-Sādāt petition and turn the event into a mass display of anti-Sādāt sentiment. The petition was to have been submitted by the mayor of Nablus, Bassām al-Shak'a, to the Tripoli conference of "rejectionists" (see essay on Inter-Arab Relations). The differences of approach were compounded when Shak'a himself was later criticized by other· more radical PLO supporters in the West Bank for visiting Jordan in the course of a fund-raising trip.[17]

The pro-Hashimites and the more moderate public figures in the West Bank and Gaza Strip also faced a dilemma, though of a different character. Certain circles within this group were critical of the negative stand of the PLO and its supporters. Their objections resulted from the consideration that, by following the PLO line, the Palestinians risked being left out of the process that was likely to determine their fate. An editorial published on 27 November in the East Jerusalem daily *al-Quds* reflected such views by indirectly criticizing the PLO. It hinted that in rejecting Sādāt's initiative, the PLO tended to ignore the hardships of the Palestinians under Israeli occupation and the dangers of continued Israeli rule. The editorial urged the PLO to be mindful of the wishes of the Palestinians in *all* their territorial concentrations (i.e. those in the West Bank and Gaza Strip, as well as those residing in surrounding Arab countries). It cast doubt on the solutions offered by the PLO and concluded by stating: "Our people have suffered much from rejectionist positions that do not constitute alternative solutions."[18]

While waiting for Jordan to announce its position, prominent pro-Hashimite figures refrained from expressing a clear stand of their own with regard to possible Palestinian participation in the Cairo conference. When King Husayn dissociated himself from Sādāt's policy on 28 November, and when the Egyptians subsequently failed to issue invitations to West Bank and Gaza representatives to come to Cairo, the pro-Hashimites and other moderate leaders abandoned the idea of attending the conference and adopted a wait-and-see policy. Hikmat al-Masrī, a Nablus leader known for his close ties with the Hashimite regime as well as with Egypt, rationalized this attitude by saying that, since the PLO had been officially invited to Cairo to represent the Palestinians, there was no need for others to do so.[19] PLO threats also had an effect: several pro-Hashimite and other moderate leaders were reported to have given up their initial intention to go to Cairo as a result of PLO intimidation.[20]

However, certain notables dissociated themselves from the wait-and-see policy of the more prominent pro-Hashimites. One of the main figures to call for a more active and immediate involvement of West Bankers in the negotiating process was Mustafā Dūdīn of Hebron. He came out strongly against the PLO's claim to "sole representation" of the Palestinians. Furthermore, blaming Israel for having blocked the emergence of a local leadership, he argued that under the new circumstances created by Sādāt's initiative, Israel should openly encourage the formation of such a leadership. Dūdīn expressed his willingness to take part in a representative West Bank delegation to the Cairo conference, provided he received an official invitation. Yet he later declined to join the West Bank delegation which went to Cairo (see below), arguing that this step should have been taken only after consultation and co-ordination with the Jordanian government.[21]

Other attempts to organize delegations of West Bank inhabitants to go to Cairo and become actively involved in the peace-making process were initiated late in November by Burhān Ja'barī of Hebron, Husayn al-Shuyūkhī of Rāmallah and 'Abd al-Ra'ūf al-Fāris of Nablus. The latter, previously a member of the Jordanian Chamber of Deputies, later withdrew from the group, after having consulted

Jordanian and Egyptian officials in Amman. Reports indicated that he cancelled his plans under the influence of threats and pressure from the PLO.[22] Eventually, a West Bank delegation headed by Ja'barī and Shuyūkhī went to Cairo in late December. Though not formally invited to take part in the Cairo conference, they met with government officials and party functionaries and were received by President Sādāt. In all their meetings, they expressed appreciation and support for Sādāt's initiative.[23] They were reported to have criticized the "negative attitudes" adopted by "the Palestinians outside the occupied land" (i.e. the PLO) *vis-à-vis* Sādāt's initiative and to have called on 'Arafāt to join in the peace process.[24] In a memorandum prepared earlier in December, members of the delegation stated that, in their view, the PLO was part of the Palestinian people, but that it represented only the military side of the struggle, while their own delegation represented those Palestinians who had remained on their native soil.[25]

The West Bank delegation to Cairo, as well as the one from Gaza (see below), were viewed with hostility both by PLO supporters and by pro-Hashimites. Pro-PLO circles publicly denounced them as attempting to bypass the Palestinian issue: the delegates could not possibly represent the inhabitants of the West Bank or the Gaza Strip, since "sole representation" had already been vested in the PLO. The position of PLO supporters was articulated at a meeting held at the Arab Alumni Association building in East Jerusalem on 19 December,[26] and in a series of notices published by some of the pro-PLO municipalities.[27] The Palestinian-Egyptian contacts in Cairo augmented earlier fears in pro-PLO quarters of the loss of popular support and the emergence of a "substitute leadership." It was reported that a Nablus PLO supporter, Dr Jamāl al-Khayyāt, was planning to visit Beirut together with some of his colleagues at that time. He hoped to impress upon the PLO leadership there that unless it changed its negative approach towards the peace initiative, the PLO position in the West Bank and the Gaza Strip would be undermined and a new Palestinian leadership would soon emerge.[28]

The pro-Hashimites for their part argued that the visit of the delegations to Cairo was counter-productive, as they were composed of personalities of second rank. Furthermore, their mission was ill-timed because it took place before Jordan had taken a definite stand. Thus, Mayor Freij of Bethlehem stated in mid-December that the time was not yet ripe for such activities and that the members of the delegation were "going to Cairo for a picnic."[29] Freij went on: "To be successful, the Cairo conference must tackle the Palestinian problem in full depth, not just scratch the surface. . . . The opportunity for peace is here. Can Israel afford to block it? There will be no peace without the Palestinians having a right to self-determination. If a vote were held today, the majority of the West Bank population would vote for a confederation with Jordan."[30] The combination of support for, and reservations about, Sādāt; expectation of Israeli concessions; and support for a link with Jordan, such as expressed by Freij, may be taken to reflect views generally held at that juncture by West Bank pro-Hashimites.

LOCAL REACTIONS IN GAZA

In the Gaza Strip, a similar initiative to form a local delegation to visit Cairo was taken in late November 1977 by Shaykh Hāshim Khazindār and Sulaymān al-'Azāyiza. Khazindār was a well-known public figure in the Gaza Strip; he held the position of the local Imām and had previously served several times on the Gaza town council. 'Azāyiza, the mayor of Dayr al-Balaḥ, was generally known for his good standing with the Israeli military authorities and his tense relations with the PLO. A delegation headed by them visited Cairo in mid-December 1977, its other members being mainly people with personal business in Cairo, including some former Egyptian government employees. The delegation was received by Sādāt and by government and party officials. The two leaders expressed support and appreciation for Sādāt's initiative. Shaykh Khazindār told Sādāt that the Gaza delegation was a popular one, "with no political background . . . [and] incapable of representing the Palestinian people. . . . The Palestinian people can only be represented by their legitimate representative, namely the PLO." [31] He called upon Yāsir 'Arafāt to join the Cairo talks. Al-'Azāyiza, on the other hand, took a more hostile attitude towards the PLO, reportedly warning that if it did not attend the Cairo conference, the Palestinians presently in Cairo would assume responsibility for representing their people's cause. Al-'Azāyiza was also said to support the return of the Gaza Strip to Egyptian administration. [32]

Reactions in the Gaza Strip to the issue of local Palestinian participation in the peace process were different in certain aspects from those in the West Bank. The inhabitants of the Gaza Strip, which had been under Egyptian administration from 1948-56 and again from 1957-67, had retained special ties with Egypt. They had family links and trade connections, and still sent their sons there for higher education. Consequently, it was more difficult for them to come out against Sādāt than for the people of the West Bank, who had no similar relationships.

Basically, the Gaza political leadership's stand towards the peace initiative conformed with the traditional affiliations of the two main groups active on the local political scene: the pro-Hashimite group and the pro-PLO/pro-Egyptian group. [33] Rashshād al-Shawā, the mayor of Gaza who headed the pro-Hashimite group but also maintained good relations with the PLO leadership, supported Sādāt's initiative in principle. [34] Lacking a political power base of his own, he was reported to have been willing to visit Amman and Beirut to try to persuade both King Husayn and the PLO leadership to support Sādāt. [35] On the eve of the Cairo conference, it was further reported that Shawā was ready to go to Egypt and negotiate on behalf of the Gaza Strip inhabitants—even without PLO approval—provided he was assured in advance of Israeli concessions on the Palestinian issue. [36] He was also reported to favour Sādāt's suggestion that a future Palestinian state in the West Bank and the Gaza Strip be linked with Jordan. [37] However, King Husayn's absence from the Cairo talks and PLO warnings against Palestinian participation there eventually persuaded Shawā to stay away. He shifted to a wait-and-see policy similar to that of senior pro-Hashimite notables in the West Bank. [38] At the time of the Gaza delegation's visit to Cairo, Shawā was among those who denounced it, asserting that its members represented only themselves. [39]

The local leaders of the group which had hitherto combined PLO sympathies with a pro-Egyptian attitude were faced with the problem of split loyalties: once the PLO turned against Sādāt, they could no longer keep faith with both. All the leading figures in the pro-PLO/pro-Egyptian group deplored the trip of the Gaza delegation to Cairo. But at the beginning of January 1978, some notables within the group—headed by Ibrāhīm Abū Sitta—requested permission from the Israeli authorities to meet in Cairo with Sādāt. [40] Their purpose was to impress upon him the need to make the establishment of a Palestinian state a major goal of the negotiations. At the same time, they wished to meet PLO officials and persuade them to join in the peace process. In fact, the delegation did not leave for Cairo at the time but the projected visit was indicative of differences of opinion among PLO supporters in the Gaza Strip. Some, like Dr Haydar 'Abd al-Shāfī and Zuhayr al-Rayyis, reportedly remained loyal to the PLO line and rejected Sādāt's policies. [41] Others, like Abū Sitta and 'Awnī Abū Ramadān, underlined "the sacred bond which ties our people to mother Egypt"; [42] they reportedly supported Sādāt's initiative in the belief that it might lead to national independence for the

Palestinians, albeit only in parts of Palestine.[43] Abū Sitta was reported to have visited Cairo in the spring and to have met Sādāt. While in Egypt, he hailed the peace initiative and criticized the "rejectionist" Arab states for their constant failure to protect the Palestinian people.[44]

THE AUTONOMY PLAN

The Israeli-Egyptian summit meeting at Ismāʿīliyya on 25 December 1977 aroused renewed hope in the West Bank and the Gaza Strip. Pro-Hashimite leaders and other moderates expected that Israel would now prove more forthcoming in its response, particularly on the Palestinian issue. They believed that Israeli concessions on this point might not only pave the way for Jordan to join the political process, but also for West Bank and Gaza representatives to participate in the talks.[45] Only radical PLO supporters denounced the Ismāʿīliyya summit forum as such, arguing that in the absence of the PLO, it was improper to discuss the Palestinian question there.[46] Some later interpreted the outcome of the meeting as proof of the correctness of their argument that Sādāt's initiative had been a mistake from the start.[47]

The announcement of the Israeli autonomy plan for the West Bank and the Gaza Strip immediately after the Ismāʿīliyya conference caused widespread disappointment in the West Bank and the Gaza Strip, however. The plan was unanimously rejected by the main body of the local leadership—PLO supporters, pro-Hashimites and others—who held that it failed to provide for Palestinian self-determination, for the withdrawal of Israeli troops, and for the cessation of Israeli settlements in these areas. If implemented, it would legitimize and perpetuate Israeli occupation. They also criticized the plan for failing to address itself to the issue of Jerusalem.[48] (For details of the plan, see essay on the Arab-Israeli Conflict.)

This generally negative reaction encompassed differences in argument and emphasis, however. PLO supporters in particular stressed that the plan was unacceptable because it ignored the PLO, disregarded the problem of the 1948 refugees, and precluded the establishment of an independent Palestinian state.[49] Other leaders of various political persuasions pointed out that the idea of self-rule was not new: since 1967, Israel had repeatedly suggested similar ideas which local notables had consistently turned down.[50] Rashshād al-Shawā, for instance, claimed that soon after the 1967 war, he had turned down an Israeli offer to become governor-general of the Gaza Strip; at that time, the possibility of eventual self-government and of a limitation on the Israeli military presence had been held out.[51] Bassām al-Shakʿa asserted that West Bank inhabitants had turned down the concept of self-rule in the 1976 municipal elections, when they chose "their real representatives."[52] (Shakʿa was referring to the electoral victory in 1976 of PLO sympathizers which implied rejection of a self-rule scheme earlier mooted by Israel.)

General disappointment notwithstanding, some local leaders were reported to have been ready to consider the autonomy plan, provided substantial modifications were introduced. Their main demands were for an immediate moratorium on the establishment of new Israeli settlements in the West Bank and the Gaza Strip, assurances of Israeli military withdrawal, and an undertaking that the autonomy plan was a transitional arrangement ultimately leading to Palestinian self-determination.[53] The East Jerusalem daily, *al-Quds*, reflected this approach in a leading article in which it outlined the modifications that would make the autonomy plan acceptable. These were including East Jerusalem in the boundaries of the autonomy; granting every Palestinian the right to return to the West Bank or Gaza Strip if he so wished; transferring title of all (formerly Jordanian) government land and property to the administrative bodies of the autonomy; and granting self-determination to the Palestinians at the end of a five-year period, to be exercised by means of a referendum under international supervision.[54] A similar attempt to modify the plan in some of its essential aspects was made by al-Shawā when he stated early in February 1978 that he welcomed the basic idea of self-rule, but stipulated that it should operate under international supervision and for a transitional period of four to five years. Such a transitional stage was advisable, he said, "to please the Jews and the Israelis and to prove that a small Palestinian state would not be a monster and would not threaten Israel."[55] Similarly, 'Azīz Shahāda proposed UN custodianship for an interim period of one to three years, after which "the opportunity would be given for the Palestinians, both here and abroad, to decide on what they want as their future destiny."[56] Freij followed a similar line: he criticized the Israeli scheme, saying that "autonomy, if it is partial, is not autonomy. . . . To have autonomy with Jewish garrisons all over the country and Jewish settlements . . . and the Israeli army in full charge of internal and external matters, what kind of autonomy is this?" Yet he, too, envisaged an interim period, during which the West Bank could be part of a confederation with Jordan or be administered under the auspices of the UN "until the mood in the ME is ready for independence."[57]

During the year, the military authorities in the West Bank took a number of steps to attract some individuals to the self-rule scheme by offering them positions in the civil administration under the Military Government which carried greater authority than hitherto vested in local appointees. Thus, in February 1978, the post of Director-General of West Bank Health Services was offered to Dr Ḥusayn 'Ubayd, then head of public services in the Military Government civil administration. Similarly, the post of *qāḍī tashrī'*, a legal adviser to the government (vacant since 1967), was offered in May to Khālid al-Bishtāwī, a judge from Rāmallah.[58] The military authorities were reported to have approached other personalities as well, offering them important positions or, in some cases, broadened authority in the exercise of their present duties.[59] Almost all the candidates turned the proposals down, however, generally claiming that the offers contradicted Jordanian law and international rules relating to the administration of occupied territories. Dr 'Ubayd actually resigned temporarily from the position he already held. Those candidates who did not immediately turn down the offers made by the military authorities were said to have made their acceptance conditional on the approval of the Jordanian authorities.[60] On the whole, the attempts to appoint local personalities to key positions in the administration were viewed with suspicion by the local public which regarded them as steps in the creation of an infrastructure for implementing the autonomy plan, regardless of Palestinian attitudes.

The PLO reacted sharply to this move by embarking on a policy of intimidation intended to deter local officials from collaborating with the military authorities in a policy likely to lead to self-rule. In late December 1977 and early February 1978, a PLO squad operating from the village of Silwād (near Rāmallah) assassinated four people in the Rāmallah area, three of whom were known for their close connections with the military authorities. They were: (1) Salīm Jamīl al-Asmar, a Military Government employee at the town planning office, assassinated in Rāmallah on 5 December; (2) Ḥamdī al-Qāḍī, also a Military Government employee who served as deputy to the head of the education office in the Rāmallah district, killed on 26 December on his way to Military Government headquarters near Rāmallah; and (3) the Rāmallah notable 'Abd al-Nūr Khalīl Janḥū (the most prominent figure among the victims), who since 1967 had been known for his close connections with the Military Government through which he had acquired substantial economic and political influence; he was killed on 8 February in the centre of Rāmallah. Three additional assassination attempts were reported to have been made by the PLO in the Rāmallah area against people suspected of collaborating with the military authorities.[61] The intimidation campaign no doubt reinforced to some extent the general unwillingness to co-operate in measures seen as preparatory to the establishment of self-rule.

However, some interest persisted in making the local Palestinian point of view heard at the talks. Thus, in January 1978, at the time of the Israeli-Egyptian Political Committee's Jerusalem meeting, it was reported that several notables from the West Bank and the Gaza Strip tried unsuccessfully to establish contact with the Egyptian delegation.[62]

DISAPPOINTMENT AND SCEPTICISM

A general mood of pessimism spread throughout the West Bank and the Gaza Strip following the collapse of the talks of the Political Committee in mid-January 1978 (for details, see essay on the Arab-Israeli Conflict). Local leaders and public opinion blamed Israel for the failure of the talks. An article by a prominent public figure, published in *al-Quds*, called on people in the West Bank and the Gaza Strip to forget Sādāt's visit to Jerusalem, since it had now become obvious "that President Sādāt offered his peace goods to customers who, from the outset, were unwilling to purchase them."[63] Freij called the breakdown of the Jerusalem talks "a tragedy to the whole region."[64]

The mood of pessimism deepened in the following months, as prospects for a breakthrough were being rated low. The prevailing view was articulated by Zāfir al-Masrī, a Nablus notable and the head of the local Chamber of Commerce: "We so much want relief from the occupation that people hoped that Sādāt's [visit] would bring a settlement; yet as things are, we don't see much progress."[65] PLO supporters now called on Egypt to return to the previous all-Arab strategy and take action to reconvene the Geneva conference.[66] The pro-Hashimites, by contrast, stressed the need for American intervention as a way to break the existing deadlock. Elias Freij, for instance, said: "There is only one way out of the crisis, namely the invitation of President Sādāt and PM Begin for talks with President Carter."[67]

However, continued interest in Sādāt's initiative was expressed in May in a series of leading articles in *al-Quds*, the most widely read paper in the West Bank and the Gaza Strip. Public pessimism notwithstanding, the editorials argued the need for local Palestinians to become actively involved in the peace process, since the solution of their problem was at the centre of any possible settlement. The paper pointed out that in the past the Palestinians had been content to utter empty slogans rather than define their aims more precisely and lay down priorities for themselves. The removal of the Israeli occupation should be "the first and the last goal at this stage."[68] It was time for "the silent majority" in the West Bank and the Gaza Strip to stop being silent.[69]

Despite such appeals, scepticism persisted during the sequence of Egyptian-Israeli exchanges in June and July up to the Leeds Castle conference. Accusations of Israel's lack of responsiveness and inflexibility were accompanied by expressions of growing disappointment with the role of the US, which was regarded as failing to apply appropriate pressures on Israel.[70]

The Egyptian peace plan submitted at the Leeds Castle conference was well received by moderate circles, whose case was articulated by *al-Quds*. It commended Egypt for adherence to the principles of total withdrawal and Palestinian self-determination, adding that Cairo was right to regard "the liberation of the land" as the first priority.[71] The fact that the plan ignored the PLO and its role in the peace process was seen as being of secondary importance: "Even the PLO leaders themselves cannot reject the idea of liberating the land by any available means and in any possible way." [72] Pro-PLO papers, on the other hand, criticized the Egyptian peace proposals for their failure to recognize the "indivisibility of the Palestinian people" (i.e. of the inhabitants of the West Bank and Gaza together with the "Palestinian diaspora"), to acknowledge the role of the PLO, and to provide for a fundamental solution through the creation of an independent Palestinian state. [73]

On the eve of the Camp David conference, the general feeling in the West Bank and Gaza was that the chances for a successful breakthrough were slim. Local leaders believed that success would only be possible if the US decided to play an active role and submit proposals of its own. As long as Israel continued its policy of establishing new settlements and insisted on a military presence in the West Bank and the Gaza Strip, they felt the road to comprehensive peace was blocked. PLO supporters ruled out any chances for success, since they believed it extremely unlikely that the US would exert pressure on Israel. [74] This view was reflected in the words of Karīm Khalaf who said that the American position was "vague and lacked seriousness. . . . Had Washington wanted peace, it would have adopted the means taken by President Eisenhower in 1956." Present American mediation efforts were not likely to produce "any positive results." [75]

All the phases of Sādāt's initiative—from the visit to Jerusalem to the eve of the Camp David summit—highlighted more clearly than any other series of events since 1967 that West Bankers and Gazans did not possess the political leverage, the cohesive local leadership, nor perhaps the determination which might have enabled them to take control of their own affairs. Despite the critical import for themselves of the challenge posed by Sādāt, they were compelled to watch events they could not shape and take note of Arab and international trends they could not influence. They had to suit their actions to signals received from abroad—mainly from Amman and the Beirut offices of the PLO. Nevertheless, many had come to feel that a real possibility for a change in their status had emerged. Even though aware that the PLO and, to some extent, Jordan stood in their way, local leaders perceived more clearly than at any time in the past the vital importance of taking a hand in developments affecting their most immediate and direct concerns.

THE MILITARY GOVERNMENT AND THE POPULATION
PROTEST ACTION AND INTERNAL SECURITY
Relative calm prevailed in the West Bank and the Gaza Strip throughout late 1977 and 1978. While in previous years many Israeli measures—in particular those interpreted by the population as foreshadowing the eventual annexation of the territories—had led to serious riots and demonstrations, [76] similar steps caused only mild protests during the period under review. When the settlement of Shiloh was established near Nablus in February 1978, only small-scale student demonstrations took place in Nablus and Jenin. [77] Similarly, when the Israeli authorities declared certain lands near the towns of Rāmallah and al-Bīra to be "closed areas" in May and July 1978 respectively, local residents from the village of Nābī Sāliḥ and from al-Bīra did not demonstrate, but rather asked the Israeli High Court of Justice for an injunction to stop the takeover of the land and prohibit the establishment of Jewish settlements on it. The Court ruled that work at these sites should cease until legal proceedings were completed. [78] Again in May, when the Military Government suspended the registration of sales or purchases of real estate belonging to West Bankers living abroad—thereby arousing suspicions that Israel was about to seize such property—no violent protest action ensued. (Registration had been suspended because of the use of forged powers-of-attorney in a few cases. It was resumed after stricter measures to authenticate such documents were devised.) [79]

Generally speaking, then, economic or political measures considered objectionable by the local public elicited verbal protests or led to court action rather than to violence. This was true even of the most spectacular such event—the dismissal of the mayor of Bayt Jālā in July 1978 (see below). Moreover, anniversary days "traditionally" marked by mass protests—those of the 1967 war, of the establishment of the State of Israel, and the "Day of the Land" of Israeli Arabs (30 March)—passed without serious incident.[80] Reactions to the Israeli operation in South Lebanon in March (see below) were the exception to this general trend. On this occasion, the military authorities' restraint in handling the demonstrators (mostly high-school students)—by imposing fines rather than dispersing the crowds by force—contributed to continued calm. Subsequently, parents often co-operated with the authorities in attempts to discourage young people from demonstrations likely to turn violent.[81]

This relative tranquillity was primarily due to the impact on local public opinion of the political process described above. Extreme forms of protest came to be seen as unnecessary, possibly even counter-productive, at a time when the end of the Israeli occupation seemed to have become a real possibility. In consequence, as mentioned above, PLO calls for anti-Sādāt rallies, demonstrations or business strikes went largely unheeded.

THE MILITARY GOVERNMENT AND THE MUNICIPALITIES

Another reason for the relative calm in this period was a certain liberalization of Military Government policy, particularly towards the towns headed by the more radical West Bank mayors and towards those mayors themselves. The Military Government's relationship with these municipalities had deteriorated fairly steadily since the 1976 local elections. Some of the mayors had created a situation of continued confrontation between themselves and the Military Government, which reciprocated by using restrictive measures against them—measures intended to limit their ability to exercise their mayoral functions and to reduce their political influence as local leaders.[82]

The first sign of a more liberal policy towards these towns came in October 1977, when the military authorities for the first time allowed West Bank and Gaza Strip mayors to bring in funds collected abroad. (For new fund-raising trips during the period reviewed, see below.) Also in October, 'Atā'allah Rashmāwī, a known PLO supporter and member of the Palestinian National Front (PNF), who had been arrested in 1974, was released from administrative detention. He then joined the municipal council of Bayt Sāhūr to which he had been elected in the 1976 municipal elections.[83] The shift in policy was again demonstrated on 8 February 1978 when the Minister of Defence, Ezer Weizman, responded favourably to a series of requests submitted to him during a visit to Rāmallah by the mayor, Karīm Khalaf. Weizman agreed, among other things, to permit the mayor to go on a fund-raising trip abroad in order to expand the nearby Bīr Zayt college—a stronghold of militant Palestinian nationalism; to widen the municipal boundaries; and to visit local men in jail.[84] Most of these requests had previously been turned down by the military authorities as part of the counter-measures taken against radical West Bank mayors, among whom Khalaf was one of the most active.

On 2 May, the Minister of Defence dismissed Brig-Gen David Hagoel from his post as Military Commander of Judea and Samaria. Hagoel was held responsible for the violation of standing orders forbidding Israeli soldiers to enter the premises and grounds of Arab schools. The orders had been disregarded in an incident in Bayt Jālā on 21 March, when soldiers followed young demonstrators into the Iskandar Khūrī high school and threw teargas grenades into classrooms. Hagoel was charged with covering up the infraction.[85] The removal of Hagoel was received with satisfaction by West Bankers who had come to see him as one of the main figures implementing the hard-line policy towards local mayors.[86]

Hagoel's successor, Brig-Gen Binyamin Ben-Eliezer, gave more demonstrative expression to the new policy of liberalization. In May and June, he visited the West Bank towns headed by pro-PLO mayors, whom the military authorities had previously largely avoided. In his meetings with the municipal councils, the new Military Commander agreed to most of the requests earlier denied and approved most of the municipal development projects previously held up, whether for political reasons or because of red tape. He approved the extension of municipal authority to new areas; expressed readiness to release administrative detainees; promised large-scale financial assistance; and cancelled various restrictions placed on the activities of mayors after 1976. He was also reported to have instructed the local military governors under his authority to apply a more flexible policy in their dealings with the population.[87]

During a visit to Hebron on 31 May 1978, the new Commander approved, among other things, the establishment of a new vocational school, improvements in the municipal water supply system and the building of a new industrial centre. In Rāmallah, on 6 June 1978, he approved most of the town's development projects and agreed in principle to the establishment of a technical college there. In Tūlkarm, the new Commander responded to requests made by the mayor to lift restrictions imposed by the military authorities during the preceding period. Ben-Eliezer agreed to lift the existing ban on area-wide meetings of mayors. In future, one such meeting could be held annually, provided it dealt only with municipal affairs and refrained from discussing political issues. He also withdrew the objection to mayoral visits to prisoners in jail. On 18 June 1978, Ben-Eliezer visited Nablus where relations between the municipality and the military authorities were particularly tense because of the militant attitude of its mayor, Bassām al-Shak'a, and the restrictive measures taken against him in retaliation. Ben-Eliezer promised to take up the problems left unattended since the 1976 elections and generally improve co-operation between the municipality and the Military Government. He approved financial grants from the Military Government to carry out local development projects and authorized the transfer to Nablus of municipal funds hitherto kept in deposits in Amman.[88]

Following these visits by Brig-Gen Ben-Eliezer, Ezer Weizman toured the two main West Bank cities, Nablus and Hebron. In Nablus, Weizman authorized the purchase by the municipality of three generators for the local power station. This longstanding request had previously been denied by the military authorities on the grounds that the extra power could be obtained by linking Nablus to the Israeli national power grid. Weizman also agreed to the resumption of work (suspended in 1976 by the Military Government) for improving the town's water supply and authorized the purchase of equipment required for the development of additional local sources of water.[89] In Hebron, the Defence Minister approved most of the mayor's requests relating to local development projects. In addition, he permitted the return to the city of Dr Ahmad Hamza al-Natsha, a member of the PNF who had been deported to Jordan during the 1976 election campaign in which he had headed a pro-PLO list. Shaykh 'Abd al-Hayy 'Arafa, the Mufti of Hebron who had been deported in 1973 but had received permission to visit the city for a limited period in May 1978, was also now allowed to resume permanent residence there.[90]

Other aspects of the unofficial and undeclared liberalization of Military Government policy during this period were the suspension of the practice of blowing up houses belonging to men caught in terrorist acts or to their families, and of houses used to shelter them; and the discontinuation of administrative arrests and of deportations of public figures suspected of being pro-PLO activists.[91] The improved atmosphere created by these measures appeared to encourage the mayors of the three largest West Bank towns (Shak'a of Nablus, Qawāsimī of Hebron and Khalaf of Rāmallah) to adopt a new policy of closer co-operation with the military authorities. This new approach related solely to economic issues, development projects and administrative affairs, however; it excluded co-operation on political issues or on matters which could be linked, however remotely, with preparations for implementing the autonomy plan (see above).[92]

The new policy did not preclude the Military Government from taking firm action following "serious infractions" of law and order. One such case occurred on 26 April 1978, when a bus carrying West German tourists was attacked in Nablus. (For details, see last section of the essay on the Arab-Israeli Conflict.) Following the attack, the military authorities imposed a six-day curfew on the city, and subsequently barred Nablus residents from travelling to Jordan via the Jordan River bridges—a ban which caused considerable damage to the city's economy. During this period, the military authorities also broke off contacts with the mayor and city council, holding them responsible for the deterioration of security in their area of jurisdiction.[93] Some time earlier, in February, the mayor of Rāmallah had been given a personal warning by the Minister of Defence about the deteriorating security situation in the town where a number of assassinations had recently occurred (see above).[94]

The mayor of Bayt Jālā (Bishāra Dā'ūd) and three councilmen were removed from office by the military authorities on 3 July 1978 after being convicted of a criminal offence, viz attacking policemen on duty in Bayt Jālā on 17 August 1977. The policemen had been engaged in a search for drugs. The Military Government cited Jordanian law according to which a person convicted of an offence of this kind is barred from holding public office. Although the action had legal validity, critics of the Military Government interpreted Dā'ūd's dismissal as a political move made under a legal pretext and intended to remove a prominent PLO supporter from the scene. At the end of October 1978, Dā'ūd was replaced by a moderate pro-Hashimite, Farah al-A'raj, a move which was seen to bear out that interpretation.[95]

Generally, then, the military authorities tended to restrict the scope of possible political action by PLO supporters and indirectly to aid those co-operating with the Military Government, or those considered likely to take part in the autonomy project. Thus, pro-PLO mayors were forbidden to convene for deliberations on political issues.[96] By contrast, Mustafā Dūdīn (for whose views, see above) was permitted to establish an agricultural association, called "The Association of the Hebron District Villages." He also received financial assistance from the Military Government to launch it—possibly in the expectation that his chairmanship of the association would enhance his standing in the local community.[97]

REACTIONS TO THE ISRAELI OPERATION IN SOUTH LEBANON

The entry of Israeli troops into South Lebanon in mid-March elicited strong feelings of solidarity and identification with the Palestinians in South Lebanon. In fact, the Israeli operation precipitated five days of violent student demonstrations in the main West Bank and Gaza towns. Many schools suspended classes; business premises closed, and Arab labourers stayed away from work in Israel. In Nablus, two youngsters were run over and killed after the driver of an Israeli vehicle was stoned by demonstrators and lost control of the wheel.[98] (For details of the Israeli operation, see essay on the Arab-Israeli Conflict.)

This resentment against Israel was accompanied by profound disappointment at the indifference displayed by Arab states towards the plight of the Palestinians in South Lebanon. The local press was united in condemning the passive role of the Arab countries and blamed them for exploiting the Palestinian cause for their own interests. *Al-Sha'b* commented: "All the Arab regimes want to see the Palestinian front weakened to the point of collapse so as to remove obstacles in the way of the proposed settlement" with Israel.[99] The Arab states were criticized for their inability to unite at a time of crisis and to take firm action to protect the Palestinians or to safeguard overall Arab interests.[100]

Disappointment, often bordering on despair, gave rise to an intensified feeling among the West Bank and Gaza population that Palestinians everywhere had been abandoned and become isolated. This in turn created a temporary upswing in public sympathy for the PLO. The resistance of PLO units in South Lebanon (as described by PLO sources) became a source of pride for the local population.[101]

When the fighting died down, emotions gradually subsided, as did criticism of the Arab states. It was now argued that Palestinians in the West Bank and Gaza should refrain from condemning the Arab states at a time when, in the light of the ongoing peace contacts, they needed Arab backing more than ever before.[102] By the end of March 1978, attention was again focused on the issues stemming from Sādāt's initiative.

FUND RAISING IN ARAB COUNTRIES

West Bank and Gaza Strip mayors continued to travel to oil-rich Arab states on fund-raising missions in late 1977 and 1978, in accordance with the aid programme adopted by the Arab League in the spring of 1977.[103] Especially noteworthy were the fund-raising delegations from Nablus and Rāmallah who until then had been denied permission to go abroad (see above). The Nablus delegation left on 30 November 1977 and visited Libya, Kuwait, Saudi Arabia, Tunis and the UAE. It returned late in March 1978, after reportedly collecting $11m, partly from government sources and partly from the local Palestinian communities.[104] Two Rāmallah delegations went to Algeria, the first in October 1977 and the second, headed by Mayor Khalaf, in March 1978. On his return at the beginning of May, Khalaf stated that he had obtained $10m in Algeria, and that Iraq and Libya had jointly pledged an additional $3m to the Rāmallah municipality.[105] As in the past, the PLO extended its patronage to some of the fund-raising activities, hoping thereby to enhance its prestige in the West Bank and the Gaza Strip.[106]

In the course of 1978, however, it became apparent that the Arab aid programme did not meet the municipalities' expectations. Some mayors held that fund-raising activities had not been properly co-ordinated and that exaggerated demands had been put forward in some cases. On the other hand, mayors complained on several occasions that Arab donors had reneged on their promises. Algeria was said to have withheld support from several municipalities because, on second thoughts, it was unwilling to finance development projects meant to be carried out under the Israeli administration. Reports indicated that conservative Arab oil countries also withheld financial assistance from municipalities run by radical mayors or councils.[107] While limited funds did reach several municipalities and public institutions in 1978,[108] it became apparent that expectations for major contributions in response to municipal missions were misplaced. In the upshot, Jordan remained the only Arab country extending regular financial support to the West Bank and the Gaza Strip.

THE WEST BANK AND JORDAN

In 1978, Jordan again increased financial aid to local municipalities and public institutions, thus reversing a policy it had adopted shortly before the 1976 municipal elections of substantially reducing aid. Many mayors and other public figures visited Jordan during the period reviewed in order to obtain funds and, in numerous cases, were successful. Even pro-PLO mayors, who had declined to visit Jordan to solicit funds since 1976, changed their attitude and went to Amman for this purpose. [109] First among them was Bassām al-Shak'a, the mayor of Nablus, who visited Amman at the end of November and the beginning of December 1977, and again in August 1978. During his first visit, he was given a cordial welcome, was received by King Husayn and Crown Prince Hasan, met government officials, and was reportedly promised financial aid. During his second visit, Shak'a obtained commitment for a 300,000 Jordanian dinar loan to finance municipal development projects. [110] Next among the more radical mayors to visit Jordan was Karīm Khalaf of Rāmallah. His first-ever visit to Amman took place in February 1978; a second visit followed in August. He, too, conferred with government officials and discussed local development projects. [111] Mayor Qawāsimī of Hebron, who was also counted among the pro-PLO mayors and had not visited Amman since the summer of 1976, [112] made four visits during the period under review. These were to obtain approval and financial aid for development projects in his city, including the establishment of a cement factory. [113]

The visits of these mayors to Jordan were of special significance in that they revealed a resurgence of political realism on both sides. Pragmatic assessments of day-to-day interests superseded ideological considerations which, in the initial period after the elections, had made these mayors unwilling to seek contacts with Jordan and Jordan unwilling to deal with them. The pro-PLO attitudes of some of them may in any case have had an element of lip-service even in 1976. By 1978, the mayors had come to understand that continued public reservations towards Jordan would slow down municipal development schemes, and Jordan had resumed its policy of using to greatest advantage the political leverage which West Bank dependence on Jordanian finance afforded it.

West Bank economic dependence on Jordan was underlined by the contents of three memoranda drafted by a delegation of the West Bank Chambers of Commerce for submission to the annual congress of the Jordanian Union of Chambers of Commerce in Amman in January 1978. The memoranda included a request for a larger quota for agricultural and industrial exports from the West Bank to Jordan, or via Jordan to neighbouring Arab states, together with a request to raise the salaries of West Bank employees still being paid from Amman. [114]

West Bank interest and involvement in Jordanian political developments were illustrated by reactions to the establishment in April 1978 of the Jordanian National Consultative Council (see chapter on Jordan), which comprised a relatively small number of Palestinian members. The pro-Hashimite daily al-Quds criticized the Jordanian authorities for their failure to give Palestinians adequate representation, and expressed the hope that the composition of the Council was not indicative of a tendency in Jordan to sever its ties with the West Bank. [115]

HIGHER EDUCATION

Matters relating to higher education in the West Bank received special attention during the last quarter of 1977 and in 1978. [116] The political divisions marking off pro-Hashimites from PLO supporters were as noticeable in the ostensibly "neutral" field of education as in most other West Bank affairs. The first noteworthy event was the conversion in October 1977 of the Nablus al-Najāh college into a university, now named al-Najāh National University (jāmi'at al-najāh al-wataniyya). It was intended to attract students from the West Bank and the Gaza Strip who would otherwise have to study in Arab countries. The university's Board of Governors was headed by Ḥikmat al-Masrī, a prominent pro-Hashimite notable. During the latter part of 1977 and in 1978, Masrī was engaged in raising funds from Arab sources for the new university. At its convention in Qatar in December 1977,[117] the Union of Arab Universities recognized al-Najāh's new status.

The second event of note was the establishment late in 1977 of the Council for Higher Education (*majlis al-ta'līm al-'ālī*) by educationalists and professionals from the West Bank and the Gaza Strip, together with some West Bank mayors. This was to function as a national body to plan, co-ordinate and supervise higher education. The founders elected a nine-man Executive Board in December 1977, and in July 1978 set up a special committee to co-ordinate the activities of the three existing universities of Bīr Zayt, Bethlehem and Nablus. The Council was recognized by the Union of Arab Engineers in April 1978, and by a convention of heads of Arab universities meeting in Baghdad in May 1978.[118] As most of the founders of the Council and most of the Council Board and Committee members were known as PLO supporters, it must be assumed that the PLO encouraged or tacitly approved of their activities.

LOCAL GAZAN ISSUES
One of the main sources of income in the Gaza Strip is the export of citrus fruit to Arab countries, to Iran, and (to a lesser extent) to Europe. During 1977 and 1978, Gazan citrus exporters had to contend with a number of problems. For about two months during the 1977–78 exporting season, Iran raised its customs duties on citrus fruit, making it difficult for Gazan exporters to market their products there.[119] When the rate was reduced again in February 1978, Iraq banned the transit through its territory of citrus consignments from Gaza to Iran. Iraq explained that it was acting on instructions from the Arab Boycott Office which suspected that Gaza Strip citrus actually originated in Israel.[120] A delegation of the Gaza Strip Citrus Producers' Union visited Jordan and Iraq in April 1978 in an unsuccessful attempt to have the ban rescinded.[121] In July, a similar delegation attended a meeting in Amman of representatives from Egypt, Jordan, Syria, the PLO and the Arab League. The PLO representative reportedly demanded that citrus shipments from Gaza be co-ordinated in advance with the PLO.[122] This was typical of PLO tactics of using every opportunity to further its aim of gaining influence over, and possibly control of, economic and civic activities in the Gaza Strip. Its effect on the 1978–79 citrus season could not be assessed at the time of writing.

Jordan and Egypt remain the two countries in the Arab world of most immediate concern to the Gaza Strip. Contacts with the former were chiefly economic and generally handled by the Shawā family (headed by Rashshād, the mayor of Gaza), whose members are the main entrepreneurs in Gaza. Ties with Cairo had more strongly political overtones and were maintained by a group of notables known for their pro-Egyptian orientation. (For their activities in the wake of Sādāt's initiative, see above.) Two notables belonging to this group, Fā'iz Abū Raḥma and Sāmī Abū Sha'bān, visited Cairo in October 1977 to arrange for the admission of a larger number of Gaza Strip students to Egyptian universities. They also took up the issue of the payment of salaries by Egypt to Gaza Strip residents previously employed by the Egyptian administration.[123]

Rashshād al-Shawā remained the most prominent political leader in the Gaza Strip. Although he had rivals, there was no indication of any erosion in his position during the period under review.

Dan Avidan and Elie Rekhess

NOTES
1. *Yedi'ot Aharonot*, Tel Aviv; 14 October 1977.
2. For a fuller account of these groupings, their aims and the personalities involved, see *MECS 1976–77*, pp. 209–16.
3. *Ma'ariv*, Tel Aviv; 16 November 1977.
4. See *MECS 1976–77*, p. 210.
5. *Ma'ariv*, 16 November 1977.
6. *The Times*, London; 6 December 1977.
7. *Ma'ariv*, 16 November 1977.
8. Hilmī Hanūn, the mayor of Tūlkarm, praised the speech as a positive one and maintained that in reply, Begin failed to address himself to its most relevant points. *Ma'ariv*, 7 December 1977.
9. R Cairo, 21 November—British Broadcasting Corporation, Summary of World Broadcasts, The ME and Africa (BBC), 23 November 1977.
10. *Ibid*. *Ma'ariv*, 22 November 1977.
11. *Ha'aretz*, Tel Aviv; *JP*, 22 November 1977.
12. See above, as well as *MECS 1976–77*, p. 216.
13. *Al-Sha'b*, East Jerusalem; 27 November 1977.
14. *Ibid*, 30 November 1977.
15. *The Times*, 6 December; *Filastīn al-Muhtalla*, Beirut; 13 December 1977.
16. *Ha'aretz*, 4 December 1977.
17. *Yedi'ot Aharonot*, *Ma'ariv*, 7 December 1977.
18. *Al-Quds*, East Jerusalem; 27 November 1977. ·
19. *Ha'aretz*, 30 November 1977.
20. *Ha'aretz*, 30 November; *Ma'ariv*, 7 December 1977.
21. *Davar*, Tel Aviv; 22 November; *Ha'aretz*, 30 November; *al-Anbā'*, Jerusalem; 1 December; *al-Quds*, 13 December 1977.
22. *Ha'aretz*, 16 December; *Ma'ariv*, 29 December 1977.
23. *Davar*, 22 December; *Ma'ariv*, 23 December 1977.
24. Middle East News Agency (MENA), Egypt, 22 December; *Ma'ariv*, 23 December 1977.
25. *Ha'aretz*, 9 December 1977.
26. *Al-Fajr*, East Jerusalem; 25 December; *al-Quds*, 23 December 1977.
27. See, for instance, notices denouncing the delegations published in *al-Sha'b*, 21, 23 December and in *al-Quds*, 24 December 1977.
28. *Ha'aretz*, 22 December 1977.
29. *JP*, 16 December 1977.
30. *Ibid*.
31. *Ibid*, 13, 28 December 1977.
32. R Cairo, 12 December; MENA, 12 December—Daily Report (DR), 13 December; *JP*, 13, 28 December 1977.
33. For the general background of the main political forces active in the Gaza Strip, see *MECS 1976–77*, pp. 220–21.
34. See statements in *The Times*, 9 December; *Ma'ariv*, 21 December 1977.
35. *Ha'aretz*, 30 November 1977.
36. *JP*, 13 December 1977.
37. *Ma'ariv*, 18 December 1977.
38. *JP*, 28 December 1977.
39. *Davar*, 30 December 1977.
40. *Al-Sha'b*, 3 January 1978.
41. *Al-Fajr*, 2 January; *Davar*, 4 January 1978.
42. *Al-Sha'b*, 7 January 1978.
43. *Davar*, 4 January 1978.
44. Quoted in *Jarīdat Misr*, Cairo; 23 May 1978.
45. See, for instance, statements to this effect made by Elias Freij and Rashshād al-Shawā: *al-Anbā'*, *al-Quds*, 25 December 1977.
46. *Al-Sha'b*, 25 December 1977.
47. E.g. 'Abd al-'Azīz Suwaytī in *Ma'ariv*, 27 December 1977.
48. *Al-Quds*, 30 December; Agence France-Presse (AFP), 19 December—DR, 19 December 1977; *Ha'aretz*, 1 January 1978.
49. *Al-Sha'b*, 21 December 1977.
50. *Al-Sha'b*, 21 December; *al-Quds*, 29 December 1977.
51. *JP*, 18 December 1977.
52. Voice of Palestine (PLO station transmitting from Lebanon), 30 December 1977—DR, 5 January 1978.

53. *Al-Quds*, 29 December 1977; *Ha'aretz*, 9 April, 4 September 1978.
54. *Al-Quds*, 29 December 1977.
55. *JP*, 2 February 1978.
56. *The Middle East*, London; February 1978, p. 39.
57. *Ibid.*
58. *Ha'aretz*, 7 March; *al-Sha'b*, 17 April; *JP*, 18 May; *al-Quds*, 25 May 1978.
59. *Al-Sha'b*, 19 April; *al-Fajr*, 21 May; *al-Quds*, 25 May 1978.
60. *Al-Tali'a*, East Jerusalem; 27 February; *Ha'aretz*, 1 March; *al-Quds*, 5 March; *al-Sha'b*, 19 April, 28 May, 11 June 1978.
61. *Al-Anbā*, 27 December 1977; *Ha'aretz*, 9 February 1978. The PLO squad responsible for this series of assassinations was reportedly captured later in September by the Israeli security forces, *Ma'ariv*, 20 September 1978.
62. *JP*, 11 January; *Ma'ariv*, 16 January; *al-Quds*, 18 January 1978.
63. Article by the judge Taysīr Kan'ān in *al-Quds*, 23 January 1978.
64. *Ma'ariv*, 19 January 1978.
65. *Al-Sha'b*, 15 February 1978.
66. See statement by Ḥilmī Hanūn, *ibid.*
67. *Ma'ariv*, 19 January 1978.
68. *Al-Quds*, 8 May 1978.
69. *Ibid*, 7, 8, 11, 14 May 1978.
70. *Al-Quds*, 12, 20, 21, 22 June, 1, 8, 10 July; *Ha'aretz*, 20 June; *al-Fajr*, 5, 10 July 1978.
71. *Al-Quds*, 6 July 1978.
72. *Ibid.*
73. *Al-Fajr, al-Sha'b*, 6 July 1978.
74. *Al-Quds*, 1 August; *al-Sha'b*, 9 August; *al-Fajr*, 17 August 1978.
75. *Al-Dustūr*, Amman; 8 August 1978, quoted in Reuter, 8 August 1978.
76. See *MECS 1976–77*, pp. 216–17.
77. Israel Defence Forces (IDF) radio, 8 February—DR, 9 February 1978.
78. *JP*, 21, 26 May, 18 September; *al-Quds*, 17 July; *al-Sha'b*, 11 September 1978.
79. *Financial Times (FT)*, London; 23 May; *JP*, 24 May 1978.
80. Israel Broadcast Authority (IBA), 30 March, 5 June—BBC, 1 April, 7 June 1978.
81. In the Gaza Strip, a "Parents' Committee" played a role in preventing demonstrations on the "Day of the Land"; *JP*, 22, 30 March 1978.
82. See *MECS 1976–77*, pp. 216–19.
83. *Al-Fajr*, 1 November 1977. For details on the PNF, see *MECS 1976–77*, p. 223, note 12.
84. *Al-Quds*, 9 February 1978.
85. *JP*, 3 May 1978; *International Herald Tribune (IHT)*, Paris; 4 May 1978.
86. *Al-Quds*, 4 May 1978.
87. *Ibid.*, 7 June 1978.
88. *Al-Fajr*, 22 May; *al-Quds*, 1, 7, 14, 17 June 1978.
89. *Al-Quds*, 21 June 1978.
90. *Al-Fajr*, 18 June; *Al-Quds,* 21 June 1978.
91. *Davar*, 7 July 1978.
92. *JP*, 8 June; *al-Fajr*, 21 June 1978.
93. *Al-Quds*, 30 April, 4 May; *al-Tali'a*, 4 May 1978.
94. *Ha'aretz*, 10 February 1978.
95. IBA, 3 July—BBC, 6 July; *Ma'ariv*, 5 July 1978; *Ha'aretz*, 30 October 1978.
96. *Al-Fajr*, 7 July 1978.
97. *Al-Fajr*, 26 May; IBA, 18 July—DR, 18 July 1978.
98. *Davar*, 19 March; IBA, 19, 20 March—BBC, 20, 22 March; *JP*, 20 March 1978.
99. *Al-Sha'b*, 19 March 1978.
100. *Al-Quds*, 18 March; *al-Sha'b*, 19 March; *al-Fajr*, 20 March 1978.
101. *Davar*, 24 March; *Ha'aretz*, 29 March 1978.
102. *Al-Fajr*, 23 March 1978.
103. See *MECS 1976–77*, pp. 212–13.
104. *Al-Quds*, 29 March 1978.
105. *Al-Sha'b*, 13 October 1977, 7 May 1978; IBA, 7 May—BBC, 9 May 1978.
106. In the UAE, for instance, the local PLO representative assisted the al-Bīra delegation in establishing the necessary contacts; UAE News Agency, 8 July—DR, 12 July 1978.
107. *Al-Quds*, 5 June, 5, 31 August, 3 September 1978.
108. Limited amounts were reportedly brought by the mayors of Bethlehem, Bayt Jālā and al-Bīra; see respectively in *al-Anbā'*, 5 February; *al-Quds*, 4 May; *al-Fajr*, 23 January 1978.
109. See *MECS 1976–77*, pp. 209–10; IBA, 6 November—BBC, 8 November, *al-Fajr*, 9 December 1977; IBA, 12 February—BBC, 14 February; *al-Quds*, 23 January, 7 February, 16 April, 2 May 1978; *The Economist*, London; 2 September 1978.

110. IBA, 1 December—BBC, 3 December; *al-Fajr*, 9 December 1977; *al-Sha'b*, 22 August 1978.
111. IBA, 13 February—BBC, 14 February; *al-Ra'y*, Amman; 7 August—DR, 8 August 1978.
112. See *MECS 1976–77*, p. 209.
113. R Amman, 3 October—DR, 4 October 1977; *Ha'aretz*, 3 November 1977; *al-Quds*, 22 July 1978; *al-Sha'b*, 7 September 1978.
114. *Al-Quds*, 6 January 1978.
115. *Ibid*, 21 April 1978.
116. A general survey of the history of institutions of higher education in the West Bank and the Gaza Strip can be found in *Shu'ūn Filastiniyya*, Beirut; No 79 (June 1978), pp. 158–85.
117. *Al-Anbā'*, 12 October; *al-Quds*, 14 October; *al-Sha'b*, 6 November, 13 December 1977, 3 May 1978.
118. *Al-Quds*, 17 December 1977, 4 May, 2 June, 29 July 1978.
119. *Al-Fajr*, 19 December 1977; *JP*, 9 February 1978.
120. *JP*, 10 April; *al-Fajr*, 24 April 1978.
121. *Al-Fajr*, 24 April, 1 May; *al-Quds*, 3 May 1978.
122. *Al-Quds*, 27 July; IBA, 12 July—DR, 13 July 1978.
123. *Al-Quds*, 5 October 1977.

International Journal of AFRICAN HISTORICAL STUDIES

Published by Africana Publishing Company, this quarterly journal is now in its twelfth year of publication and has become a leading journal of African history. The development of better historiographic tools in the last decade, the high standards of scholarship, and the extraordinary liveliness of African studies as a field are all evident in the pages of the journal. Scholars from diverse disciplinary backgrounds and with diverse intellectual approaches contribute original work ranging in scope from prehistoric archaeology to slave economics and social aspects of the African diaspora.

The diversity of its articles, the willingness to allot space to scholarly controversies, the review essays, and an extensive, up-to-date book-review section make it a thorough and vigorous review of recent literature in African historical writing and essential reading for historians and specialists of Africa.

Recent and Forthcoming Articles:
- Richard Caulk, "Armies as Predators: Ethiopia"
- David Northrup, "Nineteenth-Century Patterns of Slavery and Economic Growth in Southeastern Nigeria"
- Owen J. M. Kalinga, "Trade, the Kyungus, and the Emergence of the Mgonde Kingdom of Malawi"

Review Articles:
- Merrick Posnansky, "Kilwa: An Islamic Trading City on the East African Coast"
- Jeanne Penvenne, "Angola under the Portuguese"

SUBSCRIPTION RATES—Volume 12—1979

Libraries and Institutions	$45.00
Individuals	$30.00

Back-issue rates available on request. Published quarterly.

AFRICANA PUBLISHING COMPANY
a division of Holmes & Meier Publishers, Inc.
30 Irving Place, New York, N.Y. 10003

MIDDLE EAST ECONOMIC ISSUES

Middle East Oil: International and Regional Developments

The oil exporting countries of the Middle East and North Africa maintained their predominant position within the international petroleum market throughout 1977 and 1978. Disagreements over price within OPEC (the Organization of Petroleum Exporting Countries) were aired for the first time in public in December 1976 and led to a temporary breakdown of the common price structure during the first half of 1977. Yet neither the organization's long-range cohesion nor its control of world oil prices seemed to have been seriously impaired by this interlude of dual price structure.

All oil exporting countries continued to increase their imports (of goods and particularly of services) as they worked to transform their oil wealth into economic and social development for the longer term. After the enormous surpluses due to the price jump of 1973, several OPEC countries outside the ME started going into deficit on the current account of their balance of payments—Algeria and Indonesia in 1975, Nigeria in 1976, and Venezuela in 1977. The oil countries of the ME, by contrast, and foremost among them Saudi Arabia, continued to accumulate financial reserves year by year, and their newly acquired economic and financial power was increasingly recognized on the diplomatic scene. The notable exception was Iran, where political unrest first reduced and then halted oil exports toward the end of 1978.

THE RISE OF MIDDLE EAST OIL

Developments of 1977 and 1978 further consolidated the structure imposed on the world oil market since the autumn of 1973. In the quarter century before 1973, oil had replaced coal as the leading energy source for the industrial world; yet among large industrial powers, only in the US and in the USSR is there substantial indigenous production. (The US, once the leading producer, was overtaken by the USSR in 1974 and by Saudi Arabia in 1976, but continues in third place.) Western Europe and Japan have instead relied heavily or exclusively on oil imports. The shift from coal to oil thus meant a growing reliance on imported energy. The volume of petroleum in international trade nearly tripled in each of the decades preceding 1973, from 3.7m barrels a day (b/d) in 1950 to 9m b/d in 1960, to 25.6m b/d in 1970, and to as much as 34.2m b/d in 1973. This expansion in volume was accompanied by a shift to the ME and North Africa as the major producing areas. In 1950, Venezuela produced nearly the same amount of oil as the four countries then in production around the Persian Gulf (Iran, Iraq, Saudi Arabia and Kuwait). Yet by 1973, Venezuelan production had only doubled, whereas that in the ME had increased fourteenfold. In 1978, the ME and North Africa accounted for 41% of world oil production, 69% of world exports, and 63% of proven reserves.

As production shifted, so did patterns of leadership among the oil producing countries. After World War II, Venezuela was the first country to introduce the so-called principle of "50:50" profit-sharing between governments and producing companies. In 1960, OPEC was founded on Venezuela's initiative (the other initial members being the four Persian Gulf countries mentioned earlier). But in OPEC's first major contest with the international oil companies in 1970–71, Libya took the initiative in raising tax rates and prices, and Iran in having the governments of the Gulf negotiate jointly with the score of companies active in producing oil in the region. In the crisis of 1973, and increasingly since, the leading partner in OPEC has been Saudi Arabia.

The 50:50 division of profits, established in the ME in 1951-54, had shifted by 1965 to 65:35 in favour of governments, and by 1972 to 83:17. Until 1971, steady or falling prices in a vastly expanding market had enabled the companies to meet the higher payments to governments while increasing their own net income from petroleum production. By 1972, still higher payments were beginning to eat into the companies' earnings. Meanwhile, the opening up of the US as a major market for ME oil (as a result of the decline of domestic production since 1970 and the lifting of the 14-year old import quotas in the spring of 1973), led to an unprecedented 15% rise in OPEC production, with nearly half of that increase coming from Saudi Arabia.

The companies' inability to absorb further financial demands, and the emergence of Saudi Arabia and the US as the leading exporter and importer respectively, were the three developments that set the stage for the crisis of autumn 1973: the embargo proclaimed by all Arab exporting countries against the US and certain other importers; the cuts in production (amounting to 25% between September and November 1973) enforced by all of them except Iraq; and the two rounds of price increases unilaterally imposed by all 13 OPEC members, Arab and non-Arab alike. As a result, government revenue from each barrel of Saudi Arabian light petroleum (OPEC's "marker crude") rose from $1.77 to $3.05, and to as much as $9.37 by mid-1974; and total oil revenues of Middle Eastern and North African governments from $10.8 bn in 1972 to $17.6 bn in 1973 and $75.7 bn in 1974.[1]

OPEC AND THE OIL COMPANIES

OPEC has maintained its ascendancy in the world market, but not through the time-honoured cartel tactic of limiting total production and allotting shares to its members; several proposals along these lines have been discarded since the early 1960s. The restrictions imposed by Arab governments in the autumn of 1973 have remained the only instance of *co-ordinated* production cuts, and here the immediate motivation was political: pressure on the US and through the US on Israel. Several individual OPEC members have periodically set production ceilings, either to prevent a lowering of the cumulative yield over the entire lifetime of a field, or to prevent too rapid or early an accumulation of foreign exchange. But only in Venezuela and in Kuwait, and occasionally in Libya, have those ceilings seriously cut into production. On the other hand, there have always been other countries willing (and, except in 1973, able) to make up for the deficiency.

The market for petroleum, which OPEC now controls, differs from that of many other mineral raw materials through its strong vertical integration. In the quarter century after World War II, seven major companies dominated all phases of petroleum operations, from exploration and production through transportation and refining to sales to the ultimate consumer: Exxon, BP, Shell, Gulf, Texaco, Standard of California, and Mobil. Thus more than half of world production outside the Soviet bloc, and more than three-quarters of non-Communist trade in petroleum, has consistently been in the hands of these companies. The crisis of 1973 marked a notable shift of control from companies to governments within an unchanged vertically-integrated structure.

The key elements of control are the periodic meetings at which OPEC governments set an agreed price for "marker crude." The earlier more intricate system (of "posted prices," royalties, income taxes, government and company equity shares in production, and company buy-back prices) was greatly simplified in 1975. Since then, the floor and ceiling for the prices that international companies can charge for OPEC oil have been determined by a fixed level of government revenue per barrel and by government official sales prices. Prices for OPEC crudes other than the "marker crude" are expected to be set by individual governments with due allowance for differentials of gravity, sulphur content, and distance from markets. But the system does not work with precision. Tanker rates and demand for different types of crude oil fluctuate, and payment terms range from 30–90 days. Thus there often are slight discounts from, or premiums over, the standard OPEC price.

There has been no challenge to the right asserted by OPEC countries since October 1973 to set prices and, if they choose, production levels—two privileges earlier claimed and zealously defended by the companies. Compared to this loss of control over price and volume, official "nationalization" of former production concessions has usually been of far less importance; indeed, in many countries it amounted to no more than a bookkeeping transaction that further increased the government's revenue from the average barrel of exported petroleum. Of all the ME oil countries, only Iraq has severed its connection with the international oil companies, taking charge of its own production and marketing. A lack of established marketing outlets, along with a desire for a larger market share, presumably explain why Iraq is persistently reported to be offering slight discounts below the officially established OPEC price levels. By 1978, however, there were signs of a beginning *rapprochement* between Iraq and the international companies.

Elsewhere in the ME and North Africa, the multinational companies (despite the total or partial official nationalization of their local affiliates) continue to be in charge of production and contractual bulk purchasing of most of the oil. The companies benefit from the arrangement first of all by having access (in preference to any competitors) to large quantities of crude oil, and secondly by the spread between the set level of government revenue and the government official sales price. After deduction of the physical production cost, this represents a *de facto* discount in their favour—averaging 2.4% for all of OPEC, but ranging from 1.2–4% in the ME and up to 10% in Ecuador and Indonesia.

It should be noted, however, that in the mid-1970s the National Iranian Oil Company was beginning to handle an increasing share of the production and marketing of Iranian oil (by 1978 c. 20%), and that it had entered a variety of partnership arrangements with international companies in overseas ventures, such as the North Sea, in order to gain additional experience. There has been much discussion, both in the ME and among outside observers, of the possibility of a progressive shift by oil exporting countries from the production and export of crude oil to various "downstream" operations such as refining, shipping, overseas marketing, or the establishment of a petrochemical industry.

There are many indications that the main incentives for such "downstream" investments are other than economic. For instance, a modest rise in crude oil prices would yield greater additional revenues than would the value added by refining and transport. Moreover, in the ME, such "downstream" projects would have to compete with many urgent development projects for trained manpower and capital; and in the world at large, ME tankers, refineries and petrochemical factories would face stiff competition from existing facilities (e.g. refineries and chemical factories in Europe) with considerable excess capacity.

OPEC PRICES AND THE OUTSIDE WORLD

OPEC countries produce half the world's oil, and c. 90% of the portion that enters foreign trade. But non-OPEC exporters, whether among developing or industrial countries (Oman, Malaysia, Mexico; Canada, Norway, the Soviet Union) all imitated the fivefold price rise of 1973–74, and have since adjusted their prices upward in line with OPEC's. Within limits set by government price controls, even American domestic oil producers have followed suit. Fuels competing with oil, though not geared directly to OPEC's price, have responded to the same upward pull: the price of coal more than doubled in 1973–75, and that of uranium rose even more steeply. These increases were caused by a series of labour disputes in the US coal industry (which accounts for a quarter of world output) and by the formation of a cartel by uranium producers—both encouraged by the certainty that a quintupled oil price gave coal and uranium customers little choice but to foot the bill. This ability of OPEC to act as price leader not only for the world's petroleum, but even for the entire energy market, has greatly enhanced the economic strength of the organization. It also puts into question the widely held hope that alternative fuels, developed over a decade or more, will eventually set a ceiling to OPEC price increases. The obvious possibility is that by the time such new fuels come to the market, they will have risen near enough to the OPEC price so as not to offer effective competition.

Nor has elasticity of demand—that is, consumer resistance to rising prices—yet acted as more than a mild brake on OPEC. World oil consumption, which had risen rapidly throughout the 1950s, 1960s, and early 1970s, declined by 1.2% in 1974 and 1% in 1975—only to rise again by 6% in 1976, setting record levels in 1976 and 1977. It is generally agreed among experts that these figures reflect a combination of the impact of the price rise of 1973–74 and of the global recession of 1973–75.

Before 1973, every 1% increase in the world's gross product was accompanied by a proportionate or slightly larger increase in its energy consumption. Since 1973, this "GNP/energy coefficient" is estimated to have declined from 1.0 to 0.9 or less. Before 1973 there was, as we saw, a rapid shift from energy sources such as coal into oil. (Between 1966 and 1973, the proportion of petroleum in global energy consumption rose from 38% to 45%.) Since 1973, the share of oil in total energy has remained constant (1973, 45.1%; 1977, 44.4%). And since it is likely to take a decade or more to develop major new alternatives, no sharp decline in the share of oil is likely in the near future.

In short, the world has started economizing with its energy and has stopped shifting from other energy sources toward oil. Yet a stable ratio of oil in the energy total combined with *any* positive GNP/energy coefficient means that oil consumption will rise (though not as fast as before) in times of prosperity, and go down only in times of depression—which is precisely the effect that has obtained since 1973.

OPEC's own market has reflected not only these global economic conditions, but some rather significant shifts in petroleum geography. First, consumer countries have preferred to rely on non-OPEC sources that are beginning to flow into the market. North Sea oil became available in large quantities in 1975; the Soviets saw in high-priced oil a convenient source of much needed hard currency and stepped up their exports to the West; the first oil was produced in Alaska in 1977, and Mexico has tripled its production since 1973. Second, in the US (outside Alaska), production of oil has declined steadily since 1970, and natural gas since 1972. Hence in 1974–75, as oil consumption declined during the recession, oil imports continued at a virtually unchanged rate—as natural gas was replaced by oil, and domestic oil by imports. Then in 1976 and 1977, oil imports rose far more sharply than did overall consumption from 6.0m b/d in 1975 to 8.7m b/d in 1977, declining again to 7.9m b/d in the first half of 1978. While a certain amount of this additional oil was from such sources as Mexico and Norway, OPEC supplied as much as 84% of US imports in 1977; conversely, the rise in US imports in 1975–77 was equivalent to c. 10% of OPEC's production in that earlier year. From 1979 to about 1981, it is likely that US imports will level off or decline further as additional oil becomes available from Alaska, only to rise once again when Alaskan oil has been absorbed by rising consumption and declining oil and gas production in the "lower 48 states."

These contradictory trends of a reduced GNP/energy coefficient, global recovery from the 1972–75 depression, diversification of oil supplies in the international market, and steeply rising US requirements have meant that demand for OPEC oil since 1973 has oscillated far more sharply than global consumption (see Table 1).

Even so, further rises in OPEC price levels in 1975 partly compensated for the temporary decline in demand. Thus the total value of OPEC countries' exports (including a very minor amount of non-oil exports) dropped from $119 bn in 1974 to $110 bn in 1975, to rise once again to $129 bn in 1976 and to $149 bn in 1977. [2]

Prospects were that demand for OPEC oil would decrease somewhat between 1979 and 1981 or 1982, as leading economies went into recession and as oil from the North Sea, Alaska and Mexico makes up for the decline in US production and any added demand corresponding to economic growth. A renewed sharp increase in demand for OPEC oil was foreseen by many observers for the mid- or late-1980s— the exact date depending on whether the world makes a rapid or halting recovery from the recession of the 1970s, and whether leading countries, foremost the US, succeed in adopting effective programmes of conservation and production of energy alternatives. [3] A sharp increase in demand for imported oil suggests, in turn, the possibility of a set of price rises comparable to those of 1973–74. Presumably such considerations were reflected in the statement of Saudi Arabia's Petroleum Minister, Shaykh Aḥmad Zakī al-Yamānī (following the adjournment of the Conference on International Economic Co-operation in 1977) that indexing of the price of oil was not opportune for the next few years and would be made unnecessary by market developments after that.

OPEC'S PRICING POLICY

Ever since mid-1974 there had been recurrent reports of behind-the-scenes disagreements at the OPEC ministerial meetings (usually held twice a year), with Saudi Arabia favouring smaller price increases or none, and others—notably Iran and Algeria—pressing for sizeable increases. The price increases of the mid-1974 to mid-1976 period, averaging at a cumulative rate of 8.3% a year, reflect the resulting compromises. More specifically, a 7.5% increase in the winter of 1974–75 was followed by a 9.2% increase in October 1975, an average increase of 7% in January 1977 (of which more below), and a further average increase of 3% in July 1977. During the world's slow recovery from recession, these rises were thus kept deliberately below the prevailing rate of inflation: the price of OPEC's "marker crude" (i.e. Arabian Light f.o.b. Ra's Tanūrah) rose by 27% from 1974 to 1977, whereas the IMF calculates that world consumer prices in the same period rose by as much as 41% (see Table 1). Prices of imports by OPEC countries presumably rose much more sharply, although no reliable calculations are available.

The pricing preferences of individual OPEC members reflect both economic and ideological factors. Saudi Arabia—with an oil revenue *per capita* of over $4,000 per annum, limited resources of population, agriculture and industry, and rapidly accumulating the world's largest foreign exchange reserves abroad—has a tangible stake in preserving the health of the world economy on which the value of its foreign assets depends. By contrast, Algeria has been running a negative balance of payments on the basis of oil production that is virtually at maximum capacity; hence it stands to lose financially in the long run if the price of oil rises less rapidly than the combined rate of inflation and of nominal returns on investment. Iran, with ample population and non-oil resources, also is interested in maximum short-term returns and, moreover, counts on its ample reserves of natural gas to sustain the economy once its oil runs out. Venezuela and Indonesia, reluctant to invest large sums in exploring entirely new tracts, but with limited present reserves, also have good reason for favouring rising prices.

Economically, the OPEC members thus naturally divide into those with *per capita* incomes from oil below $1,000 (Venezuela, Iraq, Iran, Algeria, Nigeria, Indonesia, Gabon and Ecuador), and those with oil incomes *per capita* above $4,000 (Libya, Saudi Arabia, Kuwait, Qatar and United Arab Emirates). Kuwait and Libya, however, have more commonly sided with the first group, preferring to limit their incomes by cutting production rather than by slowing down price increases. Their foreign exchange accumulations are much smaller in absolute terms than those of Saudi Arabia, so that their effect on the total world economy is not as palpable. Moreover, the more "radical" orientation of their foreign policy implies a relative lack of concern about the general health of the international capitalist economy.

These latent differences surfaced for the first time at the OPEC ministerial meeting in Qatar in December 1976. 11 of the 13 members insisted on a 10% price increase for January 1977, and a further 5% increase for July 1977. But Saudi Arabia, joined by the United Arab Emirates, refused to go beyond an immediate increase of 5%. The result was the first breakdown of OPEC's common price structure. Yet it is important to keep in mind first, that the dispute was not between those who wanted to raise or lower the price, but between those who wanted to raise it by different amounts; second, that no general pattern of competitive price cutting ensued; and third, that the dual price structure persisted for only six months. The overall result seemed to confirm both the basic cohesion of the OPEC cartel (for which there is, after all, a collective reward of c. $100 bn a year), and the dominant position of Saudi Arabia within it.

Not surprisingly, OPEC members such as Algeria, Iran and Indonesia, that have been eager for maximum short-term returns, have already been producing at (or near) full capacity, whereas those favouring lower short-term returns have not. For example, whereas Algeria was producing virtually at full capacity in late 1976, Iran could have expanded production by 15%, and Saudi Arabia by as much as 35%. Saudi Arabia's spare capacity of c. 3m b/d was indeed larger than the total production of any other single OPEC member except Iran. This meant that if the common price broke down and Saudi Arabia and the Emirates went to capacity production, they could take away c. 20% of the business of the other 11 members, converting any 10% price increase into a net loss of c. 10%.

The actual effects of the dual price structure were not as drastic as that. A 35% increase in production, such as Saudi Arabia was theoretically capable of, must be phased in gradually. The international companies which handle distribution cannot shift their sources of supply at will—first, because crude oils of various gravities or sulphur contents are not freely interchangeable at the refinery; second, because the companies can ill afford to break binding contracts or even customary supply relations; and third, because the experience of the embargo and cutbacks of 1973 makes a shift to Arab sources seem particularly risky. The Saudis themselves limited the impact of the dual price structure, since they made their additional oil available only to major companies, rather than on the spot market—and the major companies, in addition to having the widest established distribution networks, have similarly wide networks of supply and thus are the companies· most keenly interested in preserving what they regard as "global market stability."

Still the financial effects of OPEC's temporary dual price structure on individual member countries were clear-cut. Comparing production figures for the first half of 1977 with those of the second half of 1976, we see that the OPEC total declined by 5%—a natural result of the widespread stockpiling in anticipation of the January

1977 price rises. Libya and Nigeria went against this trend, increasing their production by 4% and 5% respectively, despite their 10% price rises. The reason for this was an exceptionally cold winter in the US which, combined with an acute natural gas shortage and environmental regulations, created an exceptional demand for their low sulphur oil. Indonesia, which had voted with the majority but then implemented only a 6% increase, saw production rise by as much as 10%. But in the Persian Gulf, where total production went down by 7%, Saudi Arabia and Abu Dhabi (largest of the Emirates) registered gains of 2% and 3%, whereas the other Gulf producers experienced heavy losses: Iran 12%, Iraq 13%, Qatar 16% and Kuwait as much as 19%. This in turn meant that, whereas Saudi revenues increased by about 7% over the previous six months, Iran's went down by 3% and Kuwait's by as much as 11%.

At the OPEC meeting in Saltsjöbaden (Sweden) from 12–13 July 1977, the Saudi and Emirate delegates agreed to join the others at the price level of 10% above 1976; in return, the other 11 dropped their insistence on a further 5% increase for the remainder of the year. Yamānī referred to the experience as an important lesson for producing and consuming countries. Presumably the lesson to other producers was that they could ill afford to set a price above that sanctioned by the Saudis; and to consumers, that Saudi Arabia was in full earnest in trying to persuade its OPEC partners to slow down oil price increases—as it had been assuring high American officials for two years. Perhaps there was a further intended lesson, already announced by Yamānī in December, that he expected the US to show its "appreciation" for such Saudi moderation by bringing Israel closer to an agreed solution to the conflict between itself and the Arabs.[4] (Also see chapter on Saudi Arabia and essay, "Deficits in Saudi Arabia.")

1979 PRICES AND FUTURE CONCERNS

Having overcome its price split in mid-1977, OPEC reaffirmed its unity at the following meeting at Caraballeda (Venezuela) on 20–21 December 1977. The Iranians this time joined the Saudis in advocating a price freeze—a policy which OPEC maintained for the remainder of 1978. Various proposals for new policy departures remained at the stage of technical study or preliminary discussion. These included Venezuela's proposal of a price increase, the proceeds of which would go into a fund to aid the developing countries; a proposal that the "marker" price be set in terms of a "basket" of currencies or be indexed in some other fashion; and demands that OPEC countries join in concerted "downstream" investments (see above). Saudi Arabia made it clear, however, that no serious thought was being given to abandoning the US dollar as the chief medium of payment. To avoid widespread inventory buying by oil companies in anticipation of annual or semi-annual OPEC price increases, Shaykh Yamānī advocated a scheme by which future price increases would be imposed in small quarterly or monthly steps rather than in major jumps of 7–10%.

A prolonged wave of violent protest against the Shah's regime swept over Iran in the summer and autumn of 1978, and spread to the oilfields in mid-October. Production declined from 6 m b/d for September to 1.1 m b/d in early November, briefly rose to normal, only virtually to cease by late December. The shortfall and interruption of production in Iran were made up mostly by Saudi Arabia, where output rose from 8.4 m b/d in September to over 10 m b/d in November, and even higher in December. The events in Iran constituted a vivid reminder of the instability of the ME political situation, of the vulnerability of the region's petroleum industry, and of the heavy dependence of the non-Communist industrial world on energy supplies from the area. Moreover, the Saudis, with their production at least temporarily near capacity, could exercise less of a restraining influence on OPEC's pricing than previously. The result was the decision at OPEC's ministerial meeting at Abu Dhabi on 17 December to raise its prices for 1979 by an average of 10%. In line with Yamānī's plan, this was to be achieved in quarterly instalments, with the government sales price of "marker crude" going from its $12.70 level of mid-1977 successively to $13.34 on 1 January, $13.84 on 1 April, $14.16 on 1 July and $14.54 on 1 October. The Saudis also defeated attempts to have the US dollar replaced as OPEC's medium of price calculation.

Such increases implied an added strain on the US balance of payments as long as the country's heavy dependence on oil imports continued. They implied less of a hardship for most Western European countries and Japan which, though even more heavily dependent on imports, had earlier benefited from the sharp decline of the dollar and hence of dollar-denominated oil prices. But they only partly compensated OPEC countries for the deterioration that rising global prices and the declining dollar had inflicted on their terms of trade since mid-1977.

EXPORT SURPLUSES AND INVESTMENTS

The vast surpluses that OPEC countries began to amass in 1974 are still growing, though at a slower rate. Merchandise imports, which in 1974 amounted to a little more than one-quarter of the value of exports, have doubled since then. This reflects the vast needs for economic development, including "infrastructure" facilities, as well as for heavy arms purchases by some countries (notably Iran and Saudi Arabia). Net imports of services also loom large and for most countries seem to be on the increase. These reflect both heavy shipping charges due to port congestion and the acute need for foreign expertise. Thus in 1975, the ratio between imports of services to goods was c. 1:4 in Algeria, 1:3 in Iran and Iraq, 1:2 in Libya, and as high as 1:1 in Saudi Arabia.

The 13 OPEC countries together spent less than half of their export earnings in 1974, but nearly three-quarters in 1976. Yet this cumulative figure hides considerable disparities. Algeria has shown a current account deficit since 1975. By contrast, Saudi Arabia's surplus (on its current account of goods, services and transfers) was as high as $23 bn in 1974, and still stood at nearly $14 bn both in 1975 and in 1976, a rate that seemed to be holding up in 1977. This meant that the holdings of foreign currency reserves by the government and the Saudi Monetary Agency have mounted extremely rapidly: at $14.3 bn in 1974, they exceeded those of the US; at $35.4 bn in 1975, they surpassed those of West Germany to become the largest in the world; at $45.8 bn in 1976 and $50.1 bn early in 1977, they exceeded those of West Germany and the US combined.[5] At the end of 1976, Saudi income from this cumulative surplus was conservatively estimated at $3.8 bn a year, or more than their total oil earnings in 1972.

The uses to which OPEC countries have put their growing surpluses, as estimated by the Bank of England, are shown in Table 2. There was a heavy concentration in the Eurocurrency market in 1974, probably a holding action while making longer-range plans. Since 1975, there has been a shift toward dollar investments and holdings of US government securities, reflecting both the major investors' distrust of the economic and political climate in many Western European countries, and the increasingly close relations between Riyadh and Washington. A growing proportion of the total annual surplus (21% in 1974, 29% in 1976) has gone (a) into foreign aid, and (b) into direct investments outside the US and the UK—two categories which the Bank of England unfortunately does not attempt to separate. These figures therefore include the highly publicized direct investments by Iran in Krupp, Kuwait in Daimler-Benz, and Libya in Fiat, as well as Kuwaiti expenditures on economic development in other Arab countries, and sizeable annual subsidies by Saudi Arabia (that have been aimed at strengthening the "moderate front" in inter-Arab politics and reversing the advance of Soviet influence in north-east Africa). The oil countries' contributions to international organizations reached a peak in 1975, and have since declined.

There has been recurrent speculation that the rapidly growing foreign exchange needs of the oil countries, and the beginning of a negative balance on current account in such countries as Algeria and Iran, would threaten the common OPEC price structure and lure member countries into a progressive price war for market gains at each other's expense. Against this it must be considered that, in terms of increased earnings, such gains would of course be illusory; and that the countries with dwindling or negative current accounts have already resorted to several other obvious alternatives (such as borrowing on the international capital market while their credit is good, and pressing for *higher* rather than lower prices within OPEC councils). Above all, it must be realized that the large surplus production capacity of Saudi Arabia works as a price guarantee in both directions. If successive downward turns of a spiralling price war should push everyone toward capacity production, the Algerians would lose money on the very first round—whereas the Saudis could make up for declining unit earnings by increased production until the price had dropped by one-third or more.[6] On the other hand, the Saudi excess capacity, as noted above, was almost fully used during the Iranian troubles in December 1978.

Saudi Arabia's continued dominance in OPEC (and hence OPEC's price moderation) would thus seem to depend crucially on the Saudis' willingness and ability to open up a larger portion of their enormous oil reserves rather rapidly, keeping their productive capacity well ahead of actual production. Earlier plans to increase the capacity from the present 11.8 m b/d to 14 m b/d in 1980 and 16 m b/d in 1982 seem to have been quietly shelved by late 1978. There thus was increasing doubt whether or not OPEC would return to the 1974–78 period of stable or declining oil prices even after the political crisis in Iran had subsided.

Indications toward the end of 1978 were that OPEC should not be seriously threatened for the next several years, either by competition from outside or by fatal internal dissension. The experience of the dual price system early in 1977 indicated that the cartel's existence was so much in the interest of all members that price unity would be reconstituted even after a temporary lapse. Similarly, the rather chaotic situation of early 1979 still left the OPEC "marker" price intact as the floor price. For the next several years, the inflow of new oil from the North Sea, Alaska, Mexico and other sources may possibly meet much of the increasing demand and thus slow down or arrest any momentum toward increases in OPEC's real (or even nominal) price. By the 1980s, demand for OPEC oil may be expected to increase once again—how fast and how sharply depending on the ability and willingness of the US and other importing countries to curtail their consumption of energy and to stimulate its domestic production. A sharp rise in demand, in turn, could be expected to lead to even sharper rises in price.

All this implies a continuing major role for ME oil producing countries in economic, financial and political councils, both of the region and of the world at large.

Dankwart A. Rustow

TABLE 1: OPEC AND WORLD PETROLEUM: VOLUME AND PRICE 1973–78

	1973	1974	1975	1976	1977	1978	% Annual Change					% Change	
							1973–74	1974–75	1975–76	1976–77	1977–78	1973–77	1974–78
World Energy Consumption (mtoe)	6,064	6,115	6,128	6,458	6,687		0.8	0.2	5.4	3.6		10.3	
World Oil Consumption (mt)	2,773	2,730	2,701	2,882	2,972	2,985	–1.6	–1.1	6.7	3.1	0.8	7.2	7.6
Oil as % of World Energy	45.7	44.7	44.1	44.6	44.4								
OPEC Oil Production (mt)	1,543	1,539	1,368	1,544	1,557	1,473	–0.3	–8.9	12.8	0.8	–9.5	0.9	–4.3
Oil Price ("marker crude," $US per barrel)	2.70	9.76	10.72	11.51	12.40	12.70	261.5	9.8	8.4	7.7	2.4	359.3	30.1
World Consumer Prices							15.3	13.6	11.5	11.4	9.8	62.7	54.9

m t = million tons.

mtoe = million tons oil equivalent (1 ton per year = 0.0201 barrels a day for average crude oil).

"marker crude" = Saudi Arabian Light f.o.b. Ra's Tanūrah.

Oil prices are annual averages.

All percentage changes are positive, unless marked (–) as decreases.

Sources: BP Statistical Review of the World Oil Industry 1977 (lines 1–4); IMF, *International Financial Statistics*, December 1978 (lines 5–6); *Oil and Gas Journal*, 25 December 1978 (1978 figures).

TABLE 2: OIL EXPORTING COUNTRIES OF THE MIDDLE EAST AND NORTH AFRICA: PRODUCTION, TRADE AND INTERNATIONAL RESERVES

	Population (m)	Petroleum Production (m b/d)[2]			Petroleum Capacity (m b/d)	Prices[1] (US$/barrel)			Foreign Trade Exports (US$ bn)			Imports (US$ bn)		Exports (US$ per capita)	International Reserves (SDR bn)			
	mid-1978	1976	1977	Jan-Oct 1978	mid-1978	1 Oct 1975	1 Jan 1977	1 July 1977	1976	1977	1978	1976	1977	1978	1974	1975	1976	1977
Algeria	17.6	1.08	1.15	1.23	1.2	13.10	14.30	14.45	5.2	5.2	4.9	5.3	7.2	250	1.4	1.2	1.7	1.6
Iran	35.2	5.92	5.71	5.65	7.0	11.62	12.81	12.81	23.4	24.3	23.5	12.9	13.8	700	6.8	7.6	7.6	10.1
Iraq	12.5	2.28	2.25	2.54	3.2	11.45	12.67	12.65	8.8	9.7	9.9	3.5	4.1	800	2.7	2.3	4.0	5.8
Kuwait[3]	1.2	2.18	1.96	2.03	3.3	11.30	12.37	12.37	9.8	9.8	9.3	3.3	4.8	7,800	1.1	1.4	1.7	2.5
Libya	2.8	1.93	2.08	1.95	2.5	12.49	13.92	14.20	8.4	9.7	9.3	4.7	5.3	3,400	3.0	1.9	2.8	4.0
Oman	0.6	0.37	0.34	0.32		11.63	12.77	12.77	1.6	1.6	1.5	0.7	0.8	2,700				
Qatar	0.2	0.49	0.44	0.48	0.7	11.17	11.84		2.2	2.0	2.1	0.8	1.2	13,000				
Saudi Arabia[3]	7.9	8.76	9.41	7.92	11.8	11.51	12.09	12.70	36.1	40.9	34.8	11.8	17.4	4,400	11.7	19.9	23.3	24.7
UAE[4]	0.7	1.95	2.02	1.83	2.5	11.92	12.50	13.26	8.5	9.5	8.9	3.4	4.5	13,700	0.4	0.8	1.7	0.7
Total 9 countries		24.94	25.35	23.93	32.1				104.0	112.6	104.2	45.9	59.0		27.0	35.1	42.6	56.0
for comparison:																		
13 OPEC countries[5]		30.92	31.53	29.64	39.2				128.7	149.1	136.8	67.7	89.5		38.4	48.5	56.6	62.8
United States[6]		9.73	9.83	10.37					115.0	120.2	136.0	129.6	157.0		13.1	13.1	15.8	16.0
World		59.56	62.16	60.72					903.5	1,025.6	1,070.0	924.4	1,055.7		180.2	194.4	222.3	262.8

[1] Government official sales prices for the most prevalent variety of crude.
[2] 1m b/d of crude petroleum is approximately 49.8m tons per year (based on world average gravity).
[3] Including one-half of Neutral Zone.
[4] The oil producing Emirates are Abu Dhabi, Dubai and Sharjah.
[5] OPEC members are 8 of the 9 above (except Oman), Ecuador, Gabon, Indonesia, Nigeria, and Venezuela.
[6] Includes Alaska; production figures include natural gas liquids.

Sources: BP Statistical Review of the World Oil Industry 1977 (petroleum production, 1975–77); *Petroleum Intelligence Weekly*, 18 December 1978 (petroleum production 1978 and capacity); *Petroleum Economist* October 1978 (petroleum production 1978: US and world); IMF, *International Financial Statistics*, October 1978 (trade and reserves). Parra, Ramos and Parra, *International Crude Oil and Product Prices*, April 1978 (prices).

TABLE 3: OPEC PRICES, REVENUES, AND DEPLOYMENT OF SURPLUSES, 1974–78

	1974	1975	1976	1977	(1st qtr) 1978
		(US dollars per Barrel)			
(1) Petroleum Price	9.76	10.72	11.51	12.40	12.70
		(billion US dollars)			
(2) Government Oil Revenues	89.8	96.8	113.2	129.1	31.9
(3) Exports	118.8	109.8	128.7	149.1	33.9
(4) Imports	33.3	54.5	67.7	89.5	22.7
(5) Balance of Trade	85.5	55.3	61.0	59.6	11.2
(6) Balance of Payments Surplus	57.0	35.7	35.3	33.5	5.4
of which:					
(a) US treasury and banks	9.5	3.1	4.8	3.9	0.7
(b) Dollar investments	2.1	6.9	6.7	5.3	1.1
(c) Eurocurrencies	15.0	4.3	6.4	3.6	1.0
(d) UK treasury and banks	5.3	−0.3	−2.4	0.1	0.2
(e) Sterling investments	0.7	0.3	0.5	0.4	
(f) Other currencies	9.0	5.0	7.0	7.5	1.5
(g) Foreign aid, other investments etc.	11.9	12.4	10.3	12.4	0.9
(h) Contributions to international organizations	3.5	4.0	2.0	0.3	

(1) For "marker crude"; the figures are annual averages.

(2) These reflect payments as made, which lag behind oil exported; see note 2 to text.

(3) The difference between lines 2 and 3 consists of non-oil exports, production costs and company revenue for oil, and late payments (cf line 2).

(5) line 3 minus line 4.

(6) This is the current account balance of goods, services and private transfers. The breakdown given in the source has been simplified; it includes the following entries in the original:

(a) US treasury bonds, notes, and bills; and US bank deposits.

(b) Includes "holdings of equity, property etc."

(c) Foreign currency deposits and foreign currency borrowing in the UK (i.e., only the London part of the Eurocurrency market) and British government foreign currency bonds.

(d) UK government stocks and treasury bills, and sterling deposits in the UK; the minus signs indicate net reduction of holdings.

(e) Includes "holdings of equity, property etc."

(f) Bank deposits outside the US and the UK.

(g) "Special bilateral facilities," including "loans to developing countries"; as well as "other investments," including "holdings of equity, property etc."

Sources: IMF *International Financial Statistics*, October 1978 (lines 1, 3, 4, and 5); Bank of England, *Quarterly Bulletin*, December 1976, September 1978 (lines 2 and 6).

NOTES
1. For the factors leading to OPEC's rise, see D. A. Rustow and J. F. Mugno, *OPEC: Success and Prospects* (New York, 1976). The appendix contains detailed statistical information up to and including 1975.
2. See Table 3, line 3. Export data are for the period of the actual movement of goods: those for government oil revenues (Table 3, line 2) for the period of payment, which by virtue of prevailing terms usually lags two months. Thus, if a $7.5 bn payment due to Saudi Arabia for oil exported in 1974 but made in 1975 is credited to 1974 (cf Rustow and Mugno, p. 131, line 1) the revenue figures, too, show a decline from 1974 to 1975.
3. See Organization for Economic Co-operation and Development, *World Energy Outlook* (Paris, 1977); United States Central Intelligence Agency, *The International Energy Situation: Outlook to 1985* (Washington, 1977); Caroll Wilson et al., *Energy: Global Prospects 1985 to 2000* (New York, 1977); Dankwart A. Rustow, "US-Saudi Relations and the Oil Crises of the 1980s," *Foreign Affairs*, Vol 55, No 3 (July 1976), pp. 494–516.
4. For Yamānī's remarks at a press conference following the Qatar meeting, see *Keesing's Contemporary Archives*, 1977, p. 28320.
5. See International Monetary Fund, *International Financial Statistics*, October 1978, p. 317; note that Table 3 of this essay does not include the Saudi Arabian Monetary Agency (SAMA) holdings. For further details on the surpluses of the under-populated Arab countries, see *IMF Survey*, 24 November 1975 and 24 October 1977.
6. For a fuller discussion see Rustow and Mugno, *OPEC*, p. 101, and Rustow, "US-Saudi Relations," p. 503–5.

Deficits in Saudi Arabia:
Their Meaning and Possible Implications

According to an official announcement made in September 1978, the Saudi Arabian Monetary Agency (the central bank) had transferred 3,200m Saudi rials ($961m) from reserves to supplement the current government budget. In other words, current revenues—largely from oil exports—were insufficient to pay for current expenditures. [1] At about the same time, a publication of the International Monetary Fund (IMF) noted that in the first quarter of 1978 Saudi Arabia had incurred an overall deficit of $1,372m in its international transactions. During the first nine months of 1978 there was a precipitous decline in Saudi international reserves from $30 bn at the end of 1977 to $20 bn at the end of September 1978. [2] These developments were clearly in sharp contrast with what had transpired in previous years when government revenues exceeded, or greatly exceeded, expenditures; when financial surpluses were accumulating in the central bank; when exports were far higher than imports; and when foreign assets, including international reserves, were reaching unprecedented levels.

Three questions immediately come to mind. What are the factors underlying these developments? Do they constitute a temporary digression, or signify a longer-term trend? What are the possible implications for Saudi Arabia, as well as for other countries? The answers to these questions might be obtained from an analysis of economic developments, trends and policies during the 1960s, and especially since 1973–74. Any economic analysis of Saudi Arabia must necessarily begin with oil.

DEVELOPMENTS PRIOR TO THE "OIL CRISIS" OF 1973–74

During the 1960s, Saudi Arabia assumed an increasingly important position in the world oil market. Although the major oil-exporting countries had established OPEC in 1960, oil prices (in terms of current dollars) remained quite stable throughout the decade. Since there was some inflation in the 1960s—especially during the latter part of the decade—this meant that, in real terms (i.e. in constant dollars), oil prices were declining. The result was a distinct trend towards the substitution of oil for other sources of energy. While world energy consumption was rising by c. 5% per annum (pa)—more or less in line with real growth in gross product—world oil consumption was rising more rapidly, by c. 7% pa. Saudi Arabia, with one-quarter or more of total world reserves, was well-placed to take advantage of this trend. The Saudi share of world oil production was rising steadily, reaching 7.4% in 1969. [3] In terms of world oil exports its share was far greater. The US, the world's largest producer of petroleum (until it was overtaken by the Soviet Union in 1975), was becoming increasingly dependent on oil imports: the rate of growth of production was declining, while consumption was continuously rising.

1970 marked a turning point. US production peaked and began to decline—until Alaskan oil started flowing in 1977. The gap between US oil production and consumption began to widen sharply, and since the US alone accounted for over 30% of world oil consumption in 1970, this had a strong impact on the world oil industry. For entirely different reasons, Libyan production was sharply curtailed after 1970 (until 1976); Venezuelan production declined steadily after 1970; Kuwait began to curtail output after 1972; and Iraqi production dropped sharply in 1972 as a consequence of its nationalization of the foreign oil companies. In other words, market forces enabled OPEC to raise prices sharply during the 1971–73 period. Between the beginning of 1971 and 1 October 1973—i.e. *before* the October 1973 war—the so-called posted price of crude oil (i.e. the price used for the purposes of estimating taxes to be paid by the oil companies to the Saudi government) increased by 67%. However, the market price of oil (which was usually far lower than the posted price) rose far more sharply—by 123%—during this period of less than three years.[4] As one researcher succinctly pointed out: "1970 marks the dividing line for the international oil industry when oil prices began to escalate, and a buyers' market was suddenly transformed into a sellers' market. This has certainly strengthened OPEC as an organization, and thus placed within its orbit the setting of oil prices which was previously in the hands of the oil companies."[5]

Saudi Arabia took full advantage of the "sellers' market" to augment its production, and exports rose sharply. During the 1960s Saudi oil production was rising by an annual average rate of 11%, while world oil production was rising by 8% pa. However, in 1970, Saudi oil production increased by 18%, and during each of the following three years, by 26% pa. This includes 1973, despite the embargo declared by Saudi Arabia and other Arab oil exporters following the October war. Between 1970 and 1973, Saudi Arabia virtually doubled its oil production. At least until the outbreak of the October war, there was no suggestion by Saudi leaders that their motivations for this policy were anything but economic. Saudi Arabia's position within the world oil industry and within OPEC had been significantly enhanced, rising from 7% of world oil production in 1969 to 13% in 1973, and from 15% to 25% of OPEC production. In 1969, Venezuela and Iran had been the leading producers in OPEC; by 1973, Saudi Arabia was far ahead of both.

Oil revenues paid to the Saudi government rose from $334m in 1960 to $1,214m in 1970, a rise of almost 14% pa compared with the increase of 11% pa in oil production. This was due to some revisions of the oil agreements in favour of the government.[6] What is noteworthy is that government expenditures, especially towards the end of the decade, were beginning to rise even more rapidly. In fiscal year 1969-70 there was a budgetary *deficit* of c. $89m.[7] Directly related to the rising level of governmental expenditures was the level of imports. The balance on current account (exports of goods and services minus imports of goods and services and transfers), which had been positive during the 1960s until 1967, turned negative in the last two years of the decade. There was a deficit of $92m in 1968 and another deficit of $86m in 1969.[8] While budgetary deficits in other countries are quite commonplace—and are often a matter of deliberate fiscal policy—this was (and is) not the case in Saudi Arabia. It is clear, in retrospect, that the very sharp increases in oil production between 1970 and 1973 were in large measure a reaction to the budgetary and balance of payments deficits of the previous years. The "sellers' market" enabled Saudi Arabia both to increase production at far higher rates than it had previously experienced, and also to take advantage of rising international prices. This policy was clearly designed to enable the authorities to proceed with an even faster pace of economic and social development, with their inevitable effects on imports, without incurring the deficits experienced towards the end of the 1960s. While oil production in 1973 was twice that of 1970, government oil revenues were over three-and-a-half times higher, rising from $1,214m in 1970 to $4,340m in 1973.[9]

The budgetary deficit in 1969-70 apparently had a temporary restraining effect on government expenditures. In fiscal year 1970-71 expenditures increased by less than 4%, while revenues rose by 40%, and a budgetary surplus re-emerged. In 1971-72, revenues again increased by 40%, while expenditures rose 29% (measured in Saudi rials). Measured in US dollars, the increase in revenues was 49%, while the increase in expenditures was 37%.[10] In fiscal year 1972-73 (ending July 1973), revenues increased by 48%, while expenditures increased by 34% (both measured in dollars). [11] The slowdown in expenditures in 1970–71 was very temporary; as soon as revenues began to rise sharply, expenditures followed suit. However, so long as revenues were rising at so rapid a pace (due both to far higher volumes of exports and higher prices), the fiscal cash surplus was growing.

Similar developments can be discerned—as one might expect—from an examination of the balance of payments during this period. The sharp rise in exports in 1970 accounted for a reversal in the balance on current account—from a deficit in the previous two years to a positive balance of $71m in 1970. One of the consequences of the deficits of 1968 and 1969 was a cutback in foreign aid in the following two years. Foreign aid to other Arab countries (mainly Egypt and Jordan), which had reached a peak of $93m in 1969, was reduced to $81m in 1970 and $68m in 1971. The positive balance in the current account was mainly responsible for the rise in Saudi Arabia's international reserves to $662m in 1970—the same as in 1968, though still $100m lower than the peak level reached in 1967. Subsequently, exports rose very sharply, both in terms of volume and of price, while the budgetary restraint in 1970–71 affected imports. In the following years the sharp rise in government expenditures led, both directly and indirectly, to a sharp rise in imports. Between 1969 and 1973 imports rose from $2,013m to $5,593m, an annual average rise of almost 30% measured in current dollars. [12] Measured in constant dollars (i.e. discounting for the rise in prices in goods exported by the industrial countries), the real rate of growth of imports was over 20% pa between 1969 and 1973. Of possibly greater importance was the *acceleration* in the rate of growth of imports. In 1973 imports rose by 73%, measured in current dollars, or by 47% in real terms. [13] However, the rise in export earnings during this period was even more rapid, and international reserves rose from $607m in 1969 to $3,877m in 1973. Foreign assets (international reserves plus other foreign holdings not included in international reserves), rose from $824m in 1969 to $5,082m in 1973. [14]

Since the early 1960s there has been a more systematic attempt by the government of Saudi Arabia to utilize its growing oil revenues to develop the economy. The emphasis was on infrastructure—transportation and communications, electricity and water, as well as education and health. Between 1964–65 and 1969–70, GDP (at factor cost, in constant prices) increased by an annual average rate of 9.2%. However, most of the growth was in the oil sector. The non-oil sector had a growth rate of 6.8% pa during this period. The most rapid areas of growth were transportation and communications, electricity, gas and water. There was very little growth in agriculture, but manufacturing—mainly small-scale light industry—showed a more rapid rate of growth. Other than petroleum refining, the only larger-scale industry was cement. [15] However, even by the end of the 1960s, Saudi Arabia was, by most standards, a most underdeveloped country in terms of educational standards, technical, professional and managerial skills, and the available infrastructure. The production of crude petroleum constituted 47% of GDP and petroleum refining an additional 7% in 1969–70. Agriculture accounted for 6% of GDP, though it employed c. 40% of the labour force. In absolute terms its contribution to GDP was estimated at $219m. Excluding petroleum refining, the manufacturing sector accounted for less than 3% of GDP—the equivalent of $96m. Other than cement, the largest component in this sector was the production of carbonated beverages. Construction had expanded at the relatively slow rate of 5% pa during the 1964–65 to 1969–70 period, accounting for 5% of GDP. The rest of the economy consisted of various services, of which the largest sector was "public administration and defence." In the non-oil sectors of the economy, services accounted for about two-thirds of GDP. [16]

The sharp rise in oil revenues during the first years of the 1970s permitted the authorities to accelerate expenditures both on investment and consumption. Between 1969-70 and 1972-73 (ending July 1973), GDP (at factor cost in constant prices) grew at an average rate of 16.5%. However, the growth was predominantly in the oil sector, which increased by 23% pa. The growth rate of the non-oil sector was 7.6% pa, slightly higher than the 6.8% rate which had prevailed in the previous five years. The highest rates of growth were in construction, transportation and communications, electricity, gas and water.[17] Investment was rising rapidly during this period, but could not match the rapid growth of the oil sector. During the latter half of the 1960s, investment (gross fixed capital formation) constituted 16-17% of GDP, followed by a decline to 14% in 1972-73. However, in absolute terms, there was a rapid increase in investment of c. 19% pa (in constant prices) between 1969-70 and 1972-73.[18] Real private consumption was increasing during the first years of the 1970s, but apparently at a far slower pace than during the latter half of the 1960s. On a per capita basis, the growth in private consumption during the early 1970s may have been in the order of 1% pa or less—if the official figures are reasonably accurate.[19] On the other hand, government consumption was rising far more rapidly, indicating a higher growth rate of public services, education, health etc, as well as of military expenditures.

A study of the Saudi Arabian economy by Prof Donald Wells came to some important conclusions with respect to the 1960-71 period. Briefly summarizing, they were the following: (a) Even during those periods when government revenues rose rapidly, total government appropriations tended to keep pace with revenues. There were years when actual revenues were higher, or far higher, than what had been projected by the Finance Ministry (such as 1970 and 1974 when both oil production and prices rose very rapidly). In those years, appropriations for government expenditures and actual expenditures lagged behind actual revenues, and surpluses were accumulated. However, appropriations were then increased in the following year. (b) Expenditures on public consumption (civilian and military) increased steadily. In these categories, actual expenditures matched appropriations, and often exceeded initial plans. However, expenditures on development (capital formation) often lagged behind appropriations, due to problems of manpower, managerial expertise and bureaucracy. Unspent allocations to development were often transferred to consumption expenditures, including the military forces. Summing up this period, Prof Wells concluded: "The experience of Saudi Arabia during the 1960s suggests that both the desire and the capability for increasing spending rapidly were present. Whenever revenues increased, rises in expenditures followed quickly, almost automatically. It does not follow that Saudi Arabia was always capable of spending its new level of revenues immediately. The experience does demonstrate that expenditures rose rapidly and that the gap between revenues and expenditures closed whenever the Saudis had had time to adjust to the new levels of income and wealth."[20]

It does not follow that spending was necessarily efficient in terms of enhancing the short and long-term welfare of the population. But it provides us with a clue to a better understanding of developments in the post-1973 period. It contradicts the widely-held view that Saudi Arabia is a "low absorber" and would therefore continue to accumulate surpluses in its balance of payments, since it does not "need," or cannot utilize, the huge volume of revenues which were flowing to Saudi Arabia during the 1970s, especially after the major price increases of 1973-74.

THE "OIL CRISIS" OF 1973-74
Shortly after the outbreak of the October 1973 war, the Persian Gulf countries declared a unilateral price increase of 70%. On 17 October 1973, the Arab members

of OPEC announced an embargo, designed to pressure the Western countries, in particular the US, to take a pro-Arab stand in the Arab-Israeli conflict. At the same time the Arab members of OPEC decided upon a monthly reduction in their overall oil production. Three weeks later, on 5 November 1973, the Arab members of OPEC decided to impose much sharper reductions in their oil production and exports, namely a cut of 25% from the "normal" October level of production. The oil embargo was officially ended in mid-March 1974.[21] Saudi oil production and exports in the last quarter of 1973 were 19% below the peak levels attained in the previous quarter. However, as noted earlier, the percentage increase in Saudi oil production in 1973 as a whole (26%) was the same as in the previous two years and, in absolute terms, far higher. No less important—despite the oil embargo (until mid-March 1974, at least officially)—Saudi oil production and exports during the first quarter of 1974 were almost 10% higher than in the previous quarter. They were also c. 10% higher than during the first quarter of 1973.[22]

At its meeting of 23 December 1973, OPEC declared its largest single price increase—from $5.12 per barrel, the price as of 16 October 1973, to $11.65. This was to take effect from 1 January 1974. The oil embargo had already raised prospects of oil shortages, and the far higher oil prices would undoubtedly have a severe impact on the balance of payments of the oil consumers. Moreover, the anticipated huge accumulation of "petrodollars" would, it was believed, create critical problems in international financial markets. This in turn would add to the contractionary effects of the oil price increases and bring about a severe recession in the Western countries. A study by the Organization for Economic Co-operation and Development (OECD) of mid-1974 projected that the cumulative financial surpluses of OPEC would reach $740 bn by 1980.[23] A widely-quoted World Bank study, also of mid-1974, came to similar conclusions. The study projected that the cumulative financial surpluses of OPEC would reach $654m by 1980, and would rise thereafter by c. $100 bn pa to reach $1,200 bn by 1985. The projections were that Saudi Arabia and some of the other so-called "small absorbers" would be the beneficiaries of three-fourths of these surpluses, since they were "unable" to absorb such huge sums and spend them on internal social and economic development. The "high absorbers" (those countries with relatively large populations in relation to their oil production) would succeed in spending all or most of the much larger volume of oil revenues. The World Bank estimates appear to have been accepted by the US government as a basis for determining policies.[24]

It is apparent, in retrospect, that the authors of the above-mentioned studies made some grievous errors. In 1975, a Morgan Guaranty Bank study projected that the OPEC cumulative financial surplus would peak at c. $250 bn in 1978.[25] This was probably the most optimistic forecast, from the oil-consuming countries' point of view made at that time. The well-known firm of oil consultants, headed by Walter Levy, projected in mid-1975 that the cumulative surplus of OPEC would reach $500 bn in 1980.[26] Subsequent studies by various research organizations generally tended to revise their earlier projections of OPEC surpluses, downwards. OPEC surpluses on current account reached a peak of $62 bn in 1974, of which $23 bn was accounted for by Saudi Arabia. In 1976 the OPEC surplus was $42 bn, of which Saudi Arabia's share was $14 bn. Some OPEC countries were already incurring deficits in 1976, despite the far higher oil prices; others, mainly those with smaller populations in relation to their oil revenues, were still benefiting from surpluses. In September 1978 the US Treasury estimated that the OPEC surplus would be $18 bn in 1978, but would decline to $10 bn in 1980.[27] The estimates of Morgan Guaranty were that in 1978 six of the 13 OPEC members would be in deficit (c. $10 bn) with respect to their balance on current account, while the others (mainly the small population countries) would still be in surplus. [28]

However, even the most "optimistic" forecasts turned out to be on the conservative side. OPEC countries were rapidly turning into "high absorbers," including those which were expected to have high and persistent surpluses. Some of the non-governmental researchers were far more perceptive than official bodies. It is interesting to note, in this regard, that even as late as August 1977 a report of a US Senate committee stated: ". . . the smaller Persian Gulf states, Saudi Arabia, Kuwait and the United Arab Emirates . . . have tiny populations and non-industrial economies which can absorb only a small fraction of their annual petrodollar revenues. . . . There is no reason to believe that this pattern of accumulating surpluses for the oil exporters (almost solely by the small-population countries) and chronic deficits for the oil importers will be reversed in the near future. The grim conclusion of the US Treasury (in testimony presented to the committee in March 1977) is that the OPEC countries will continue to pile up excess revenues of over \$40 bn per year, perhaps for the next two decades." [29] As noted above, more recent US Treasury estimates indicate a complete reversal, at least with respect to the short term.

The question that arises is why the initial forecasts of OPEC surpluses were so pessimistic, and why even subsequent projections usually proved to have an upward bias in terms of the size of the surpluses? These projections are usually based on a model which includes the following variables: the expected (real) growth of world gross product; [30] the projected energy coefficient (i.e. the ratio of growth in energy consumption, including all sources of primary energy—petroleum, gas, coal, hydroelectric power, nuclear power, etc—to growth in gross product); projections of growth for non-petroleum energy supplies; the (residual) required demand for petroleum; the projected supply of petroleum from non-OPEC sources; and, as a residual, the required supply of OPEC oil. [31] Having projected the anticipated demand of the oil-consuming countries for OPEC oil, there remained the question of its future price. In many studies it was simply assumed that the real dollar price of oil would remain constant during the period being studied. This would then provide an estimate of future OPEC oil revenues in constant dollars. In addition to oil revenues, some estimates were made for anticipated non-oil revenues, in particular from interest and dividends flowing to the OPEC countries from their investments. The bulk of these investments (by the central banks of the OPEC countries) is in government bonds of the Western countries, some highly secure commercial paper and other securities, and deposits in the major Western commercial banks. There is relatively little direct investment by the central banks of OPEC in industrial firms in the West. In any case, having estimated future exports (of goods and services) of OPEC, the crucial question was at what rate OPEC would increase its imports of goods and services. After making some guesses as to the future level of foreign aid by OPEC (government transfers), the researchers would obtain an estimate of anticipated OPEC surpluses in the balance on current account (the export of goods and services, minus imports of goods and services and of government transfers). While there were many variations in these studies, the above-mentioned variables were the crucial ones for these projections.

In retrospect it is not difficult to explain why the projections of OPEC financial surpluses made in late 1973 and 1974 were so inaccurate. The energy coefficient increase in previous decades had been approximately one, i.e. the consumption of energy rose by c. 1% for every 1% increase in (real) gross product. Moreover, since the real price of oil had been declining for about 25 years, there was a tendency to substitute oil for other energy sources. Hence, until 1973, world energy consumption was rising by c. 5% pa—approximately in line with the growth of gross product—while oil consumption was rising by over 7%.[32] One of the more difficult questions that arose in 1974, apart from the impact of higher oil prices on future economic growth, was that of the future relationship between growth in gross product and energy consumption, in particular oil consumption. While the price elasticity of demand for petroleum is known to be highly inelastic in the short run, economic theory posits that elasticity tends to increase over time.

The studies grossly under-estimated the effect of higher oil prices on the energy coefficient, and on the substitution of other sources of energy for oil. Between 1973 and 1977 world energy consumption grew at an annual average rate of 2.5%, less than half the rate that had prevailed during the 1960s. This was due *both* to the recession in various countries, *and* to the significantly lower energy coefficient. Between 1973 and 1977 world gross product (in real terms) increased by an annual average rate of 3.2%, while energy consumption increased by 2.5% pa. Thus, even in this relatively short period, there was a significant decline in the energy/GDP coefficient from its historical ratio of about one to less than 0.8. Oil consumption increased at a significantly lower rate of 1.8% pa, indicating that the trend of substituting oil for other sources of energy had been reversed.[33] In 1977, gross product in the non-Communist countries increased by almost 5%, while energy consumption increased by about half that rate.[34] The gross product of the US increased by 4.9% in 1977, while energy consumption increased by 2.1%.[35] During the 1973–77 period, gross product in the US increased by an annual average rate of 2.0%, while energy consumption increased by a mere 0.3% pa.[36] Clearly, the effect of the far higher oil prices had a much greater impact on the energy coefficient than had been anticipated. One of the assumptions in the 1974 World Bank study was that the growth of world energy consumption would slow down from 5.5% pa—the rate which prevailed in the 1960s— to 4.7% in the 1970s and 4.2% by 1980.[37] This was clearly way off the mark. The sharp decline in the energy coefficient was a result of both conservation measures (taken as a consequence of the oil price increases and various governmental regulations, such as those in the US mandating a steady increase in automobile fuel efficiency), as well as substitution in consumption (the change in relative prices stimulating consumption of those goods and services which require less energy in their production). Thus the sharp decline in the rate of growth in energy consumption was *both* a function of the slowdown in the rate of growth of the world economy during the 1973–77 period, *and* a significant decline in the energy coefficient.

Another source of error in many studies was the failure to allow for the effect of substitution of other sources of energy for oil—a reversal of the trend prevailing until 1973 when real oil prices were almost steadily declining. The World Bank study of 1974 assumed that the pre-1973 trend would continue, at least until 1980, and that oil would constitute an even higher share of energy consumption.[38] Though this was true of the US during the 1973–77 period—due to policies which stifled the production of natural gas, and other problems—it was not the case for the world as a whole. Between 1965 and 1973 the share of petroleum in world energy consumption rose rapidly from 38.6% to 45.7%, a continuation of earlier trends. In 1977 the trend had been reversed, with oil constituting 44.4% of world energy consumption.[39]

Most studies made in 1974, and many of more recent vintage, seriously underestimated the impact of the far higher oil prices on the pace of exploration, discovery and production of new sources of oil—outside OPEC. A report by an energy economist published in December 1977 included a compilation of various projections made in earlier decades regarding impending oil (and other mineral) shortages. He concluded, on the basis of the historical evidence, that the "experts" have "always been biased in a conservative direction." The studies which projected future shortages failed to consider that "even a hint of scarcity raises prices and stimulates supply. This increase in supply comes about from new finds, as well as new technologies that suddenly transform seemingly uneconomic resources into viable reserves." Although he agreed with President Carter's energy conservation programme, on the grounds of national defence and balance of payments, he argued that it "is based on the unduly pessimistic forecast that the world is fast running out of oil." [40] Even within the relatively short period 1973–77, non-OPEC oil production has risen at a much faster pace than OPEC production: the former was 14% higher in 1977 than in 1973; the latter less than 1%. [41] The recent major discoveries in Mexico and smaller oil discoveries elsewhere probably presage a continuation of this trend.

By far the *most* important source of error in these studies was the gross under-estimation of future spending patterns on the part of OPEC countries, and the impact of these patterns on imports. Though estimates of future OPEC financial surpluses made after 1974 were far more realistic, they most frequently under-estimated what they termed the "absorptive capacity" of the smaller-population Arab oil exporters (i.e. their ability to increase expenditures, and hence imports). The studies of Morgan Guaranty Trust Company have been among the few which, since 1975, concluded that OPEC financial surpluses would be of far smaller magnitude than had been earlier envisaged. However, even these studies tended to under-estimate the future rapid growth in OPEC imports. A Morgan Guaranty publication in mid-1978 reported the following: "The most significant—and the least expected—factor in the decline of the OPEC surplus has been the continued increase in OPEC imports of goods and services. OPEC imports of goods and services will have grown from $29 bn in 1973 to an estimated $142 bn this year (1978), or by more than 37% on average per year during 1974–78. In real terms the average annual increase is estimated to be of the order of 25% during 1974–78— among the highest in the world. Saudi Arabia, a country conventionally described as a 'low absorber,' has experienced an average annual increase in imports of goods and services of over 55% during this period, raising its import level this year to a projected level of $33 bn, the highest level among OPEC members." [42] Iran, the second largest oil exporting country, with a population of c. 35m in 1978, was importing *less* than Saudi Arabia, with a population of 6–7m.

THE SAUDI ROLE IN OPEC AND THE OIL MARKET SINCE 1973

While OPEC as a whole (excluding Saudi Arabia) *reduced* oil production significantly between 1973 and 1977, Saudi production continued to rise by an average annual rate of 5.2%. The only other major OPEC oil exporter which showed a significant increase in production in 1973–77 was Abu Dhabi—another so-called "small absorber." [43] The oil price increases in 1973–74 produced a recession in the major Western countries and a decline in oil consumption for the first time in decades, resulting in an "oil glut" which persisted until the latter part of 1975. While most OPEC countries reduced their production in 1974, Saudi Arabia increased its by 13%. OPEC decided on a 10% price increase as of 1 October 1975 but, because of the oil glut, both official and unofficial discounting was widespread, especially in 1975. According to the Saudi Minister of Petroleum, Iraqi price cuts were at times "almost $1 per barrel." Iraq was the only major oil exporter which succeeded in raising its oil production (by over 14%) in 1975; all the others were forced to cut back. [44] Although the Saudis frequently announced that so-called "production ceilings" were to be imposed on oil companies operating in their country (primarily Aramco), in reality market conditions have been the greater determinant of their production and exports. Both before and since 1973, the Saudi policy seems to have been to increase oil production and acquire a larger share of the OPEC oil market. The thesis which stated that the so-called "low absorbers" (including Saudi Arabia) would willingly reduce oil production in order to prevent surpluses at the existing price, is not supported by the evidence. Within this five-year period, 1973 through 1977, only in 1975 did Saudi Arabia (and to a very minor extent, Abu Dhabi) reduce oil production. The *Washington Post* reported in February 1976 that Shaykh Yamānī "sought to portray the lowered production [in 1975] as a deliberate Saudi policy. But [oil] industry sources said that Saudi Arabia could not find buyers for any more crude oil in the present depressed world market." [45] 1976 was a year of economic recovery in most Western countries, and oil consumption increased by 6.7% following two years of absolute declines. Saudi Arabia took full advantage of the new market situation to raise its oil production by 21.5%. OPEC, excluding Saudi Arabia, increased its production by 12.7%. The other larger producers among OPEC countries with an even higher rate of growth in production in 1976 were Libya and Abu Dhabi—the so-called "small absorbers."

Following the major oil price increase of 1 January 1974, Saudi Arabia was reported to have been the main opponent at OPEC meetings to continued large increases in oil prices. At the OPEC meeting in Qatar in December 1976, Saudi Arabia, joined by the UAE (Abu Dhabi accounts for the bulk of UAE production), split with the other 11 members of OPEC. The latter decided on a 10% price increase as of 1 January 1977, to be followed by an additional 5% increase as of 1 July 1977. Saudi Arabia and Abu Dhabi announced that they would restrict themselves to a 5% price increase as of 1 January. The Saudi spokesmen asserted that their motivation for this relative price moderation (in contrast with the OPEC "hawks") was political, namely: fear that major oil price increases would create more economic difficulties in the West, and so enhance the danger of Communist take-overs in such countries as Spain, Portugal, Italy and others; and expectation that the Western countries would show their appreciation by taking a more pro-Arab stance in the Arab-Israeli conflict and also be more forthcoming in their aid programmes to the poorer Third World countries. [46] While not ruling out political motivations for Saudi actions, it is the thesis of this writer that Saudi economic actions, including oil production and pricing, are determined largely by what it views as its vital economic interests. Following an examination of internal economic developments in Saudi Arabia in the post-1973 period, we shall return to this issue.

It might be noted, at this point, that Saudi Arabian medium and heavy oils—which were far more difficult to sell—were raised in price by 2.8% and 1.2% respectively as of 1 January 1977, while the more marketable varieties (Arabian light and Arabian Berri) were raised by 5%. [47] This widened the price differential between Saudi Arabia and the other members of OPEC (especially Kuwait and Iran) whose production consists mainly of the heavier varieties of oil. Saudi spokesmen stated that they would increase their production sharply, presumably in order to compel the 11 OPEC members to rescind their larger price increases. However, various technical contraints, as well as a fire and a storm at the main oil terminal, precluded this. During the first half of 1977 production was 13.8% above the comparable period in 1976, but a mere 2.5% above the second half of 1976. Oil exports increased at an even lower rate, by 8.3% and 1.6% respectively. [48]

Saudi Arabia (and many others) had clearly over-estimated its strength in OPEC and in the oil market generally. At the OPEC meeting in mid-1977 it was agreed that Saudi Arabia and the UAE would raise their prices by an additional 5% (to conform with the 10% increase of the other OPEC members), and that the rest would forego their announced additional 5% increase as of 1 July 1977. It is noteworthy that even after the agreement, Saudi Arabia did not raise the prices of its medium and heavy varieties by 10% above the level prevailing before 1977. The price of the popular light crude was 10.4% higher, while medium crude was 8.4% higher, and heavy crude 6.9% higher.[49] This reflected market conditions and the Saudi desire to bring production of various grades of crude oil more into line with the respective proportions of their reserves.

Generally speaking, the world oil market was beginning to weaken during the second half of 1977 as Alaskan crude began to flow and production from the North Sea began to rise rapidly. Other non-OPEC producers were also raising their production quickly, especially Mexico and other smaller producers. On the other hand, although gross product was rising in most Western countries, oil consumption was rising at a far lesser rate, for reasons noted earlier. During the latter half of 1977, as well as in 1978, there was widespread price cutting—official and unofficial—by various members of OPEC including both the so-called "low absorbers" (Kuwait and Libya), and such "high absorbers" as Algeria, Iran and Nigeria. Iran entered into barter agreements, which were indirectly based on lower oil prices.[50] The large increase in production, especially from the North Sea, adversely affected the sales of Algeria and Libya, and also those of Saudi light crude which in September 1977 was reportedly being offered at a discount on what is referred to as the spot market.[51]

The OPEC agreement of mid-1977 and discounting by other OPEC countries removed the price advantage of Saudi oil. The result was a 1.6% decline in Saudi oil production in the latter half of 1977 as compared with the first half. For OPEC as a whole (excluding Saudi Arabia), there was an increase of 1.9%. Yamānī again stated in September 1977 that his country intended to impose a "production ceiling" of 8.5m barrels per day in order to put pressure on the US to secure "a total Israeli withdrawal from Arab lands." What he failed to mention, as *The Guardian* noted, was that an oil glut was building up in the world market and that "there were technical problems because of pressure declines in some of [Saudi Arabia's] biggest oil fields. . . . The Saudis announced a slowdown in production so that pressure could build up again [in the oil fields] rather than in order to bring pressure to bear in the ME negotiations.[52] In reality, Saudi production during the second half of 1977 averaged 9.1 million barrels per day (mbd) compared with 9.3 mbd during the first half.[53] Nor was there any cutback in Saudi production following the Yamānī announcement of September 1977. Saudi production during the last quarter of 1977 was slightly *higher* than during the third quarter.

Since many oil importers feared that the OPEC meeting scheduled for the end of 1977 would decide on higher prices, stockpiling was common towards the end of the year.[54] For 1977 as a whole, the Saudis succeeded in raising their oil production by 7.0%, while there was a slight decline in the rest of OPEC. Although world oil consumption was 3.1% higher in 1977 than in 1976, world oil production—excluding OPEC—increased by 5.9%.[55] Nonetheless, in 1977 the Saudis had succeeded in raising their share of world oil production to 15.3%, and of OPEC production to 29.8%—both all-time highs.[56]

At the OPEC meeting in Caracas in December 1977, there were demands to raise the oil price in order to compensate for inflation in the West (which raises the cost of OPEC imports) as well as the decline in the value of the dollar in terms of its exchange rate *vis-à-vis* most other "hard" currencies. (The price of oil is denominated in US dollars.) In effect, by leaving official prices unchanged, the Caracas meeting decided "to agree to disagree." Despite all the political rhetoric, the fundamental determinant was the oil market situation. The *Petroleum Economist* noted that "the price standstill is to be explained in economic rather than political terms. When they met in Caracas, the [OPEC] ministers could not close their eyes to the over-supply situation evident in the markets for months past. As a cartel they had developed no machinery for collectively reducing output in time of slack demand, but had in effect relied upon Saudi Arabia to make the adjustment for them." [57] The Saudis were not accommodating—quite the contrary.

There was a further deterioration in the oil market (as viewed by OPEC) during 1978, and a number of member-countries (including Libya, Algeria and Kuwait)[58] offered further direct or indirect price discounts, such as extended credit terms. The OPEC meeting of mid-1978 left the official prices unchanged. This was again basically a reflection of economic forces, as was noted in the *Petroleum Economist* of October 1978: "The present [oil] surplus cannot be denied. Alaskan oil is backing up on the US west coast and is having to be shipped over 7,000 miles through the Panama Canal to refineries in the Caribbean. Mexican production is having to seek markets as far afield as Eastern Europe. North Sea oil is driving indigenous coal and African oil out of parts of the European market." [59] Data for the first half of 1978 indicate that Saudi Arabia suffered a sharp 17.2% drop in oil production compared with the first half of 1977, and a 15.8% decline compared with the second half of 1976. OPEC as a whole (excluding Saudi Arabia) suffered a much smaller decline—6.1%—as compared with the first half of 1977. On the other hand, production in the non-OPEC countries increased 6.3%. World oil production in the first half of 1978 was 1.8% lower than during the first half of 1977. [60]

The decline in production was not due to supply constraints. On the contrary, OPEC production during the first half of 1978 was far below its level five years earlier, and there was considerable unused capacity. Since demand for OPEC oil is essentially a residual, the rise in production in non-OPEC countries and the apparent slackening in oil consumption were the main determinants. Though the 1.8% overall decline in world oil production may reflect some changes in stockpiles, it seems likely that it was mainly a result of the changing trends in oil consumption. The sharp increase in North Sea and Alaskan production had a particularly adverse effect on producers of light grades of crude oil, including Algeria, Libya and Saudi Arabia. The bulk of Saudi production consisted of Arabian light. The Saudi authorities issued instructions to Aramco in February 1978 that no more than 65% of total production should consist of Arabian light crude. This move apparently stemmed from economic considerations: the weak market situation prevailing for light crudes in the short term; and, in the longer term, the fact that, while most of its oil reserves were of the medium and heavier varieties, three-fourths or more of its production consisted of Arabian light. [61]

It is quite clear that Saudi Arabia, as well as some of the other so-called "small absorbers," have refused to act as the residual suppliers within OPEC; they have not reduced their oil production and exports in order to balance supply and demand at higher OPEC prices, nor permitted other OPEC members to increase their production (or at least not to reduce it). On the contrary, Saudi Arabia and Abu Dhabi have pursued policies which tended to increase their shares of the OPEC market. The "production ceilings" announced periodically by Saudi spokesmen have not been the basic determinants of Saudi oil production; this was evident, for example, from oil developments in the last quarter of 1977 when Saudi production was greatly in excess of its announced "production ceiling." Market conditions permitted a higher level of production and exports, and the Saudis took full advantage of this situation. The decline in Saudi production during most of 1978 again reflected market conditions—including some price cutting by other OPEC countries, as well as the Saudi's longer-term concern with the great imbalance between production and reserves of its various grades of petroleum. Although at the time of writing, no data was available for the last months of 1978, there is little doubt that the reduction in Iranian oil exports caused by political disturbances in the country offered Saudi Arabia and other producers an opportunity to increase their exports which they exploited. The OPEC countries had excess capacity of over 10 mbd. [62] Iranian production averaged 5.6 mbd during the first half of 1978; Saudi production was 7.7 mbd during the same period, while its capacity was 11–12 mbd. [63]

The factors underlying the Saudi policy of maximizing production and oil revenues have not yet been explained. An examination of internal economic policies and developments in Saudi Arabia since 1973 will provide some important clues to a better understanding of its oil policy.

ECONOMIC DEVELOPMENTS IN SAUDI ARABIA SINCE 1973
Budgetary revenues in fiscal year 1973–74 (ending July 1974) were three times those of the previous year. As noted earlier, this was due to the sharp increase in oil prices, to the government "take" per barrel and, to a far lesser extent, to a continued large increase in production. The Saudi authorities accelerated their expenditures, mainly on social and economic development, to twice the level attained in the previous year (both revenues and expenditures measured in current dollars). The fiscal cash surplus rose very sharply from almost $1 bn in 1972–73 to $6.3 bn in 1973–74. The far higher oil prices decreed by OPEC as of 1 January 1974 had an even greater impact on budgetary revenues in the following fiscal year, rising from $11.8 bn in 1973–74 to $28.4 bn in 1974–75. Expenditures were again raised very sharply from $5.2 bn to $10.0 bn, while the cash surplus rose from $6.3 bn to $18.8 bn in 1974–75. [64]

During 1974 and the first half of 1975, the Saudi authorities were working with US consultants on their latest Five-Year Development Plan for the period mid-1975 to mid-1980. The goals of the plan included "a high rate of economic growth by developing economic resources; maximizing earnings from oil over the long term and conserving depletable resources; reducing economic dependence on exports of crude oil; and developing human resources by education, training and raising standards of health." The development strategy consisted of three key elements: "(1) diversification of the economic base through emphasis on increasing agricultural and industrial production; (2) rapid development of the Kingdom's manpower resources; and (3) development of the economic regions of the country by a wide distribution of productive investment and social programmes." According to official estimates, the labour force would reach 2.3m in 1980, with the number of foreign workers reaching 813,000 or 35%. GDP (at factor cost, in constant prices) was expected to increase by an annual average rate of 10.2%, with the non-oil sector growing at an even faster rate of 13.3% pa. The private sector was to be provided with various incentives and aid to stimulate an even more rapid rate of growth. [65]

In the non-oil sectors, the most rapid rates of growth were projected for manufacturing, construction, public utilities, transportation and communications, education and health services, defence, and various public and private services. The agricultural sector was expected to show a much smaller rate of growth of only 4%, slightly higher than during the previous five years. Measured in 1974–75 prices, the Plan envisaged that total government expenditures (current and development) would amount to $141.5 bn, of which defence would account for $22.2 bn, and public administration $10.8 bn. Over one-half of total expenditures was expected to be on major construction programmes, including schools, hospitals, housing, military bases, highways, ports, airports, electricity, water (desalination plants), sewage, various industrial projects, etc. If one adds the smaller projects, construction would account for c. 60% of total expenditures during the Plan period. The planners stated that the major constraint on the growth of imports was the capacity of ports and transportation but that, if these constraints were removed, total imports of goods and services would rise rapidly, to $19.6 bn in 1979-80.[66]

What actually occurred since the adoption of the Plan (mid-1975) was in many important respects far different from what had been envisaged. The planners had anticipated that there would be problems of manpower, administrative delays, and bottlenecks related to inadequate infrastructure, in particular the limited port capacity and other transport facilities necessary for the far larger volume of imports required by the Plan. However, they appear to have grossly under-estimated the magnitude of these problems as well as the inflationary pressures which the execution of the Plan would engender. The planners anticipated, or assumed, a 10% rate of inflation.[67]

Budgetary expenditures—which were rising very rapidly since the beginning of the decade, and even more so after the major oil price increases of 1973-74—continued their rapid climb. In fiscal year 1975-76 (the first year of the Plan), total budgetary revenues were $29.3 bn (cf $28.4 bn in 1974-75). Oil revenues, which constituted 90% of total budgetary revenues in 1975-76, were slightly lower than in 1974-75; but the cumulative surplus of the previous years had increased sharply, and income from investments rose rapidly. (The government's budgetary surpluses are held almost exclusively by the central bank. The oil revenues, paid by Aramco and other foreign companies to the government in dollars, are the main source of foreign assets held by the central bank in various banks and other financial institutions in the West, from which it receives interest and dividends.) In any case, although there was a small increase in governmental revenues in 1975-76, budgetary outlays continued to rise rapidly, reaching $23.2 bn (cf $10.0 bn in 1974-75). The cash surplus, which had been rising rapidly since 1970-71, dropped to $11.1 bn in 1975-76 (cf $18.8 bn in 1974-75). Though Saudi oil production declined in 1975 as a whole, there was a significant rise in production during the latter half of the year and a much sharper increase in 1976. The 10% increase in oil prices decreed by OPEC as of 1 October 1975 also contributed to a significant rise in oil revenues in fiscal year 1976-77. Budgetary revenues rose to $38.5 bn (cf $29.3 bn in 1975-76). However, expenditures rose even more rapidly, and the cash surplus again declined—to $8.9 bn. What is noteworthy is that without the sharp increase in oil exports, the budgetary surplus would have been very small in 1976-77, possibly around $2 bn, even after taking into account the higher oil prices. In other words, the current surplus would have been almost erased in the second year of the Five-Year Plan if it had not been for the sharp rise in the volume of oil exports. This was due to the hectic rise in government expenditures.[68]

The rate of growth of government expenditures between 1972-73 and 1976-77 was 80% pa when measured in current rials or 85% in current dollars. The money supply (M_2) had been rising sharply since the beginning of the decade—from a growth of 26% in 1971-72 and 39% in 1972-73 to 73% in 1975-76 and 62% in 1976-77.[69] Many contracts were signed with foreign companies to implement projects designated in the Plan, particularly in infrastructure—ports, airports, roads, telecommunications, electricity, water, educational and health facilities and housing, as well as various industrial projects. Military expenditures were rising very rapidly. Special banks were established to provide funds to the private sector for housing construction, industry, agriculture, etc. Imports were rising very rapidly, limited only by bottlenecks in the ports and in other transport facilities. However, with the aid of foreign contractors, the severe congestion in the ports was eliminated by early 1977.

The economy as a whole was expanding very fast. According to official statistics, non-oil GDP which had been growing by 7.6% pa (in constant prices) between 1969–70 and 1972–73, expanded at an annual rate of 17.0% between 1972–73 and 1976–77. The governmental non-oil sector was growing even more rapidly as a result of major infrastructural investments and other expenditures. The government's very large infusion of capital into the private non-oil sector stimulated rapid expansion there as well. Aside from the various governmental, business and personal services, construction was by far the most rapidly growing sector, followed by transportation and communications. The public utilities sector expanded at the relatively more moderate pace of 11–12% pa which had been its rate of growth during the three-year period prior to 1972–73. The small manufacturing sector (other than petroleum refining) showed a similar rate of growth both before and after 1972–73. The agricultural sector was also continuing to grow at the 3–4% annual rate which prevailed before 1972–73.[70]

Expenditures on GDP are given only in current market prices, and the rapid inflation during this period makes it more difficult to assess their growth. Nonetheless, some conclusions might be derived from the figures. Using the official cost of living index as the deflator for private consumption, there would appear to have been a growth rate of 7.0% pa during the 1972–73 to 1976–77 period (cf 4.5% pa during the previous three years). In order to assess the real growth in private consumption *per capita*, however, reasonably reliable population figures are necessary. Such figures are notoriously poor in Saudi Arabia.

POPULATION ESTIMATES AND LIVING STANDARDS

According to official data based on a census taken in 1974, the population was 7.0m, of whom 27% were Bedouins. 2.7m lived in cities of 30,000 or more.[71] There was no indication as to whether this included foreigners. Data published by the IMF—based on statistics provided by the Saudi authorities—indicate that the population figure for 1974 was 8.7m.[72] However, unofficial sources are unanimous in their view that even the lower figure is highly exaggerated. An American economist stated that "based on conversations with various [Saudi] officials, our estimate [of the population] in 1974 is 3.75–4.0m."[73] Another report published in 1975 quoted a "government expert" as the source for a population estimate of c. 4m, *including* over 1m foreigners.[74] The influx of foreign workers (in many cases with their families) has accelerated since 1974. The *Arab Economist* of 1978 put the unofficial estimate of foreign workers at 2m.[75] A US Senate Committee report of December 1977 stated that the population "estimates run from 3.5–8m but it is generally agreed that the lower figure is closer to the mark. . . . A far more serious division within the society is emerging with the influx of foreign labour; perhaps 40% of the total population is foreign."[76]

To return to the question of growth in real private consumption per capita, i.e. the rise in living standards. Assuming that the native Saudi population was increasing at a rate of 2.5–3.0% (which is common in the Arab countries), and adding the rate of population growth arising from the large-scale influx of foreigners, especially since 1973, it would appear that the average rise in per capita private consumption was very small.[77] Furthermore, as noted in a British economic journal, "there are doubts about the reliability and comprehensiveness of the [official] cost of living index."[78] Unofficial estimates show that this rose far more rapidly than indicated in the official figures.[79] For instance, one can well understand the Saudi government allocating far larger sums for food and other subsidies in order to prevent or reduce internal discontent. There are also reports that a wealthy class has arisen in the cities, in addition to the Royal Family. If its consumption has risen at a much faster rate than indicated in the "average" figures, others have suffered an even lower rate of improvement in living standards. On the other hand, what may be happening—though there is no statistical evidence to support this—is that the very large number of foreigners (Yemenis and many others from the poor Asian and African countries) are consuming far less than would be indicated in the national averages, and that the native Saudis have improved their living standards at a commensurately faster rate. Furthermore, private consumption does not take into account the major growth in public consumption—expanded free educational, health and other services which have contributed to raising living standards.

The rise in government consumption (i.e. excluding public investment) has been extremely rapid. In 1969-70 public consumption constituted 37% of total consumption; by 1973-74 the ratio had risen to one-half; and in 1976-77 it reached about two-thirds. In other words, in the latter year, government consumption was about double private consumption—a most unusual ratio. Even in Kuwait, which provides a wide range of free public services, the ratio of public to total consumption was 46% (cf 66% in Saudi Arabia in 1976-77).[80] It appears that, in addition to the wide range of public civilian services and an inflated bureaucracy, escalating military expenditures plus allocations to internal security were responsible for the very rapid increase in public consumption in recent years.

MILITARY EXPENDITURES

Other than total planned military expenditures, which are included in the budget, there is little detail available from official Saudi sources. Actual military expenditures, *ex post*, are not revealed; nor is there a breakdown of actual government expenditures in other sections of the budget. It is generally believed that while there has been a shortfall in recent years (until 1976-77) in investment expenditures, this is not true of the military nor of other areas of public consumption.

Budgeted military expenditures have risen very sharply as follows (fiscal years, in million dollars):

1971–72	1972–73	1973–74	1974–75	1975–76	1976–77	1977–78	1978–79
555	903	1,523	2,504	6,721	9,039	9,107	13,815

A large part of this budget is for the construction of military bases. A contract was reportedly signed in 1978 for the construction of a "military city" c. 100 km south-east of Riyadh at a cost of $15 bn.[81] American sources also reported that during the period 1973-77, US sales of military equipment and installations to Saudi Arabia were c. $15 bn.[82] The US Department of Defence notified Congress in September 1978 that it proposed to undertake $7.7 bn in military construction, and to sell $2.3 bn of military equipment to Saudi Arabia. Estimated US sales of arms to Saudi Arabia in 1978 were c. $3.7 bn.[83] It would also appear that the budgetary figures for military spending exclude "expenditures on the police force and internal security services."[84] The construction of "military cities" is probably included in the "projects" budget or in government investment. The rest of the military budget is categorized as government consumption, and probably explains a major part of its unusually rapid increase and very high level.[85]

INVESTMENT, EXPORTS AND IMPORTS

Investment (gross fixed capital formation) has risen rapidly in recent years. The rate of growth (in constant prices) between 1972-73 and 1975-76 was 24% pa (cf 19% in the previous three years).[86] An increasing share of total investment was on construction—86% in 1976-77; the growth rate in this sector probably rose even more rapidly in the latter year.

332

As noted earlier, export revenues rose sharply between 1971 and 1973 because of the very large increases in the volume of oil exports and, to a lesser extent, as a result of the oil price increases during this period. Revenues from oil exports took a quantum leap in 1974, rising to $30.1 bn from $7.5 bn in 1973. While Saudi oil exports continued to rise in 1974, the bulk of the increase was due to the escalation in oil prices. The drop in oil production in 1975 reduced export revenues, despite the increase in oil prices which came into effect on 1 October 1975. Saudi oil production again increased sharply (22%) in 1976, and revenues rose to $35.5 bn. Oil exports in 1977 were $40 bn, both as a result of a 7.9% rise in the volume of exports and a similar (average) increase in prices. Service exports were also rising rapidly. In recent years, with the large accumulation of foreign assets, the bulk of service exports consists of interest and dividends from abroad. Of the $4,642m in service exports in 1976, $611m was from tourism, mainly from the pilgrimage. [87]

Imports of goods and services were rising rapidly during the 1970s, but especially since 1973. Measured in current dollars, imports were rising by 36% pa between 1970 and 1973, reaching $5.6 bn in the latter year. Between 1973 and 1977, imports climbed at an even faster pace—by an annual average rate of 52%, reaching $29.5 bn in the latter year. This development was directly related to the sharp increases in governmental budgetary expenditures, discussed earlier. The major oil price increases, especially of 1973-74, raised export revenues to such levels that, despite the sharp growth in imports, the export surplus (exports of goods and services minus imports) rose to unusually high levels—a peak of $24.0 bn in 1974. Thereafter, the rate of growth of exports was far more modest but, in absolute terms, offset the continued climb in imports until 1977. The export surplus remained at c. $17 bn in each of the years 1975-77. Foreign aid, grants plus loans, rose during this period from $0.5 bn in 1973 to an average annual rate of almost $3.5 bn in 1975-77. There is evidence, however, that a small part of the aid is in the form of grants, and an increasing share in the form of loans.

The current account surplus (the export surplus minus foreign aid) reached a peak of $23.0 bn in 1974, dropped to $13.9 bn in 1975, and to $12.8 bn in 1977. The cumulative current account surpluses raised (net) foreign assets from $5.1 bn in 1973 (of which $3.9 bn were defined as international reserves) to $60.7 bn at the end of 1977 (of which $30.0 bn were defined as international reserves). As noted earlier, there was a very sharp drop in the international reserves—from $29.4 bn at the end of September 1977, and $30.0 bn at the end of 1977, to $20.4 bn at the end of September 1978. [88] This was due to the decline in oil exports and the continued rise in imports. Clearly, there had been a sharp worsening in the balance of payments in 1978 (no figures were available at the time of writing). The rise in oil exports during the last quarter of 1978, mainly as a result of the crisis in Iran, has probably modified the trend, at least temporarily. [89]

PROBLEMS FACING THE SAUDI ARABIAN ECONOMY
MANPOWER PROBLEMS
In this analysis of the economic problems of Saudi Arabia, the listing does not claim to be exhaustive. Clearly, too, the various social, political, cultural and economic problems are in many ways inter-related. By far the most important difficulty is manpower. Social, cultural and religious mores practically exclude the adult female population from the labour force. Both Saudi and foreign female labour is permitted to work only in such occupations as nursing, teaching, etc.—and only where this involves contacts with females. In mid-1978, the government ordered inspections of various firms in order to enforce the rules. [90]

Adult males probably number one-fourth of the total Saudi population of c. 4m.

No official data are available on the size of the armed forces, but foreign reports published in early 1978 gave their number as 103,000. With the massive flow of arms to the country, there is little doubt that their strength must continue to grow.[91] The internal security forces and the bloated bureaucracy engage many other Saudis. Thus the number available for the civilian labour force, aside from the administration, is quite limited. Of possibly greater importance is the quality of the Saudi labour force.

EDUCATION PROBLEMS

The educational levels of the large majority of the population are low, even though the authorities have made a massive effort to expand educational facilities and to enrol a much larger number in schools. Enrolment in elementary school increased by 10% pa between 1970-71 and 1975-76. The growth rate of secondary and higher education has been even more rapid. The teaching staff, especially on the higher educational levels, is largely imported,[92] but there are serious defects in the quality of education. Furthermore, despite the fact that the government pays students for attendance beyond the elementary grades (in addition to all expenses, including clothing, tuition, books and supplies), there is a sharp dropout rate after elementary school. In 1975-76 the number in post-primary schools (seventh to twelfth grades) was 32% of those in elementary schools. The ready availability of well-paying jobs open to Saudis discourages their entering or remaining in secondary education. An even more serious problem is the aversion of the Saudis to technical education. Technical secondary schools were organized many years ago with German aid, but they attract very few students. In 1975-76 the total enrolment in these schools was 4,063.

Higher education has grown rapidly in recent years reaching 26,000 in 1975-76, in addition to c. 4,000 Saudis studying abroad. Here, too, there is a great imbalance between the large numbers in the humanities and arts, and those in sciences and engineering.[93] The Vice-Chancellor of Riyadh University noted in 1978 that only one out of ten engineering students enters the profession after graduation. Within the last ten years, only 530 had graduated from the engineering school.[94] Foreign observers deplored the standards of the universities (with the exception of the University of Petroleum and Mineral Resources). "Elsewhere the graduate standard is reckoned to be on a first-year university level." There is also some indication of a decline in standards.[95]

ATTITUDES TO WORK

Manpower problems are compounded by the mores of the country. The *Arab Economist* noted that "Arabs of the Gulf [Saudi Arabia, Kuwait, etc.] loathe manual labour and look down on alien labourers."[96] There has been little success in persuading Saudis to enter road building, engineering, factory work or any sort of technical apprenticeship.[97] A study of the Saudi economy by an American economist, published in 1974, noted the following: "On the whole, education does not stress the subjects most helpful to create a modern labour force. Science and mathematics as well as vocational training are neglected in the curriculum. . . . It appears that the average Saudi would rather let a foreigner do his work for him than do it himself. The best example one can give is the use of foreign technical advisers. Ideally, he should be hired to do a specific job, do his duties, and encourage his native counterparts to learn from him. Then after a year or two, the advisers should be out of a job because several Saudis are available to take over and carry on themselves. This rarely happens."[98] Thus, there is no evidence that the Saudis are making any significant progress in developing a modern labour force. The *Financial*

Times concluded that "the attitude that manual work is generally beneath acceptable Saudi social status *raises the gravest questions about the Kingdom's stated desire to industrialize."* [99]

FOREIGN LABOUR
The foreign labour force has grown very rapidly, especially with the acceleration of government spending since the early 1970s. The massive outlays under the latest Development Plan require an even greater dependence on foreign labour. As noted earlier, the 1975-80 Development Plan projected that by 1980, foreigners would constitute 35% of the labour force; according to various reports, however, this ratio has long been surpassed. If it were government policy to accord citizenship to many of these foreigners, they might be viewed as a permanent part of the labour force. In fact, Saudi Arabia (like other countries in the Gulf region) rarely grants citizenship to foreigners, including Arabs from other countries. During the period 1970-71 to 1974-75, citizenship was granted to an average of 572 pa, of whom three-fourths were females. [100] Most of the foreigners, especially those from the poorer countries, will probably remain in Saudi Arabia for the indefinite future, but their position creates social, political and economic problems. There are restrictions on foreigners in terms of business ventures, and Saudi citizens are clearly favoured with respect to many occupations and positions, as well as educational opportunities and other benefits bestowed by the state. The Saudis are concerned that the rapid pace of economic development, compounded by a heavy reliance on foreign labour, will undermine or weaken the traditional social and moral values of the country—a concern that must necessarily have economic implications. [101]

A campaign against illegal residents was reported in 1978 with the result that wages for unskilled workers in construction rose precipitously—from $15-22 per day to as high as $45. (Labour accounts for about one-half of total costs in construction.) The Director-General of the Central Labour Office in the Western Province stated in 1978 that the shortage of workers was aggravated by their lack of skills. A survey taken by this office showed that 90% of the foreign workers brought into Saudi Arabia in the previous year were illiterate, and that 50% had neither training nor skills. [102] In 1977 the authorities issued a regulation which would penalize, with fines or imprisonment, those who encouraged the defection of foreign workers from their current jobs to others. [103]

COST OF LIVING
Inflationary pressures were rising rapidly. According to the official cost of living index, prices rose by 17% in 1973; 21% in 1974; 35% in 1975; and 32% in 1976. [104] As noted earlier, foreign observers believe that the official indices seriously understate the extent of inflation. The rapid increase in government expenditures was aggravated by bottlenecks at the ports and other infrastructural impediments. By 1977 these bottlenecks were eliminated or reduced, and the government increased its food and other subsidies significantly. In 1977 the official cost of living index rose 11.3%. [105] However, manpower problems have not been eliminated. In fact, the continued rise in government expenditures, aggravated by the large increase in wage rates, must surely mean that inflationary pressures will persist. While subsidies may diminish the impact of inflation (as reflected in the cost of living index), they do not by any means eliminate overall inflationary pressures. In fact, subsidies usually have the opposite effect, at least in the long run.

RISING CONSTRUCTION COSTS AND INFLATION
About 60% of total expenditures envisaged in the 1975-80 Plan is for con-

struction, and the unusually rapid rise in construction costs has probably been the single most important factor in accelerating government expenditures. For instance, in two separate but similar housing projects (one bid in July 1975 and the other in December 1976), the cost per square foot reportedly rose more than three times.[106] Official statistics show that construction prices rose by 21% in 1973-74; 44% in 1974-75; and 79% in 1975-76—the first year of the Development Plan.[107] However, reports from contractors, as well as various official announcements regarding major projects, indicate that the price rises were far greater and are continuing. The major gas-gathering project, budgeted for $4.5 bn in the Development Plan, had risen to $16 bn by 1976. In the summer of 1978 it was decided to reduce the planned capacity of the programme by 30%, but even at this reduced level, cost estimates had risen to $21 bn.[108] Mistubishi Heavy Industries of Japan decided to "postpone" the construction of an ethylene plant since the cost had risen from $346m to $1,700m.[109]

The problem of inflation, especially in construction, has many important implications. In a study published in 1978, an American scholar, T. H. Moran, estimated the cost of implementing the 1975-80 Development Plan at mid-1977 prices. Utilizing what he regarded as very conservative assumptions, he calculated that the cost of implementing the Plan had risen from $141.5 bn to $296.5 bn. Even so, he cautioned that his figures "far understate what would in fact have to be spent to complete the Plan since it implicitly assumed that everything is accomplished at once with no further diseconomies of scale in implementation. This is plainly unrealistic." He also noted that it was assumed—probably unrealistically—that Saudi inflation rates would be "brought down to OECD rates by 1980. . . . The projection of [inflation] assumed here is widely believed by Saudi officials and expatriate experts to be too low." He also noted that while the Plan had projected that the costs of "administration" during the first year of the plan would be $1.8 bn, they were in fact $5.8 bn. He assumed that the authorities could, and would, reduce this by 25% during the following four years of the Plan period.[110]

Data available since 1977 indicate clearly that Prof Moran's estimates were indeed far too low. His estimate of $296.5 bn for the Plan's implementation included the rise in cost of the gas-gathering project from $4.5 to $16 bn. As noted above, estimates published in mid-1978 showed that costs had risen to $21 bn—even after a 30% reduction in planned capacity. As for a reduction in administrative expenditures which Moran assumed, available data indicate that these have continued to rise sharply. The largest percentage increase in the 1977-78 budget was for "salaries and allowances" in government administration—89% above that for the previous year.[111] The data available since Moran completed his study strongly reinforce his conclusion that "the authorities in Riyadh, like their counterparts elsewhere in OPEC, will have to reconcile themselves to a future in which they will have to spend much more to get much less than their planners had calculated in the euphoria of the 1973-74 petrodollar surplus."[112]

The Saudi Minister of Finance and the Governor of the Central Bank stated in May 1977: "We don't have a [financial] surplus; we have a temporary liquidity." They projected that even with rising oil prices and a greater volume of oil exports, expenditures would catch up with income by the end of the decade (1979-80), and that deficit spending in the 1980s would exhaust the financial reserves by 1990. "Actual revenues are still less than expenditures, but we are talking about the day that the two curves [rapidly rising expenditures, and revenues rising at a far more moderate pace] would meet."[113] It would appear that most foreign observers either ignored or discounted these statements—possibly viewing them as an attempt to reduce external pressures for more Saudi foreign aid. However, in retrospect, it is apparent that even those two officials seriously underestimated the rapidity with which costs and expenditures would rise, nor did they anticipate the decline in oil production and revenues which took place in 1978. Hence the "two curves" met much sooner than they had projected. It was reported that the budget planned for 1978–79 was reduced at the last moment from $42.2 bn to $37.8 bn. In mid-1978, the Ministry of Finance issued instructions to those ministries with "projects budgets" that they were to limit themselves to 70% of the original allocations, unless they received special approval.[114] As noted earlier, it was reported in September 1978 that the Ministry of Finance had drawn almost $1 bn from reserves held by the central bank.

THE PRIVATE SECTOR: MANUFACTURING AND INDUSTRY

The 1975–80 Plan states the following: "Manufacturing is a point of concentration of the Development Plan as a whole, for the Kingdom can reduce its dependence on sales of crude oil only by expanding and diversifying its manufacturing activities." The Plan goes on to list the various products to be produced including petrochemicals, refined oil products, fertilizers, steel, aluminium, food processing, construction materials, automobile assembly and parts production, fabrics, carpets and other consumer and health products.[115] The larger industries were to be established by the government in partnership with the private sector, domestic or foreign.

The Kingdom set up the Saudi Basic Industries Corporation as an instrument to implement the programme, and established the Industrial Development Fund in 1974 to grant interest-free loans to private industries. Various additional incentives were provided to induce Saudi enterpreneurs to overcome their "industrial shyness."[116] However, it seems that the impediments to initiating ventures were of greater magnitude than the incentives. According to an official report published in 1977, total (cumulative) private investment in industry was $570m, of which $340m was by Saudis and $230m by foreign private investment.[117] One of the reasons given for this failure was "that profits obtainable from acting as middlemen, from bribes, from merchanting trade and commissions, have been far too great to attract large numbers of entrepreneurs into Saudi Arabia's embryonic industrial sector." More recently, the government seems to have shelved or sharply curtailed plans to establish steel and aluminium industries.[118]

Many of the small "industrial" enterprises were started by Yemenis and other foreigners, but a ruling issued in 1977 banned non-Saudis from owning such concerns. Various enterprises were initiated for the manufacture of building materials which, in view of the construction boom and the high costs of transporting foreign imports, should have been relatively successful. About 70% of the loans given by the Saudi Industrial Development Fund were for the production of building materials. However, it appears that most of these businesses were "struggling," had not reached projected production or sales, and were experiencing problems both with respect to price and quality.[119]

The obstacles facing the authorities in establishing a strong industrial sector are formidable. They include, as noted earlier, the woeful lack of skills and managerial expertise; the restrictions imposed on foreign labour and its high cost; the aversion of Saudis to manual labour; and construction costs which are multiples of those obtaining elsewhere. This is especially true of heavy industry. The economics of many projects appear dubious, and many are therefore being shelved or abandoned.[120] In mid-1978, the Minister of Industry dismissed as "wicked" those who questioned the official industrialization policy.[121] However, foreign economists concluded in mid-1978 that "many of the [industrial] projects, both small and

337

large, which have sprung up in recent years . . . are not competitive. . . . Many of the companies [the Saudi Industrial Development Fund] has promoted have turned out to be inefficient and more expensive than imports. . . . [In] heavy industry, generally based on petrochemicals, the problems are . . . more acute. . . . Put bluntly, most of the heavy industries now operating have been disastrous, and there is little reason to suppose that the new ones will be different. . . . The implications for the country's future are obviously momentous. . . . [An] American engineering and construction company won a contract to manage the development of two oil refineries, a petroleum product plant, and metal industries [at a cost estimated to be $10 bn, to be established in Yenbo as part of a major industrial complex] . . . but how competitive they will be in world markets, even with cheap fuel and feedstock, must be queried." [122]

Despite the admonition by the Saudi Minister of Industry, the conclusion appears to be that the projected industrial sector will not contribute significantly to either import substitution or exports in the foreseeable future. The authorities have put far less emphasis on the development of modern agriculture, and production has increased slowly—far less than population growth. This leads to the conclusion that the goal of the planners to reduce the Kingdom's "dependence on sales of crude oil . . . by expanding and diversifying its manufacturing activities" will not be realized, at least not to any significant extent, in the foreseeable future.

OPEC AND THE OIL MARKET—FUTURE PROSPECTS

Since the 1973–74 "oil crisis," there has been a proliferation of studies attempting to project future supply and demand for petroleum. Generally speaking, the methodology involves a host of "guesstimates" including the future rate of real economic growth; the energy coefficient; the growth of non-oil energy supplies; the (residual) demand for petroleum; the growth in non-OPEC petroleum production; and, as a residual, the demand for OPEC oil. The usual preliminary assumption is that the real price of oil will remain constant. If the projections indicate that a "shortage" will occur at some future period, the real price of oil would presumably rise to the extent necessary to balance supply and demand. In many respects this parallels the methodology used to forecast future OPEC revenues and, based on assumptions about future OPEC imports (and transfers), projects the volume and growth of OPEC financial surpluses. As noted earlier, most of the errors made by those who projected huge OPEC financial surpluses were due to gross underestimation of future OPEC imports. However, there were also significant errors in calculating the other variables. Both the rate and magnitude of decline in the energy coefficient, and the growth in the non-OPEC oil production, were underestimated. The frequent "pessimistic" projections raised questions as to whether the "low absorbers" in OPEC, in particular Saudi Arabia, would be "willing" to close the gap between demand and supply by increasing production much beyond their revenue "needs." In none of these studies has the author seen a realistic assessment made of the rapid acceleration in the revenue requirements of the "small absorbers," especially of Saudi Arabia. That OPEC producers might apply pressures to increase oil revenues, or that competition might emerge within OPEC and between OPEC and other oil exporters for limited markets were not even considered as possibilities.

The studies projecting future oil supply and demand which have appeared since mid-1977 have been far more optimistic (from the point of view of oil consumers) than those of earlier years. A study prepared by the Petroleum Industry Research Foundation Inc (US) suggested various scenarios for the 1975–90 period. In all the variants, they assumed that net Communist bloc exports would cease by 1985 (an assumption disputed by other researchers). With respect to future (real) economic growth (1975–90), even a "moderate" rate was considered by them to be "optimistic." With respect to the energy coefficient, the ratio used (somewhat less than 0.75) in the low variant was higher than what had obtained in the 1973–77 period in a number of major industrial countries. One of the most dubious assumptions made was that non-OPEC oil production as a whole would not vary. The authors of the study admitted that their decision not to vary non-OPEC oil production to 1990 was "open to some question." In their projections of demand, they assumed that real oil prices will be constant throughout the 1975–90 period. Their "overall findings are that an oil shortage before the late 1980s is unlikely." In considering the 1990–2005 period, the variant they considered most probable was that "no supply constraint is likely . . . and no substantial real price increase would be required to balance supply and demand. A structural decline in the non-Communist world's general economic growth rate, which we consider not at all unlikely, would enhance the probability of this scenario." [123]

Using a somewhat different approach and other assumptions, a mid-1977 study by the US International Trade Commission projected that world oil supplies would be sufficient to the end of 1985 (the period under study), and that real oil prices would remain approximately constant. This study was far more optimistic about Soviet oil production, supporting the view that the USSR's outer continental shelf might have oil and gas reserves equal to those of the ME. Their projection was that demand for OPEC oil would rise from 26.7 mbd in 1975 to 32.1 mbd in 1985. [124] (In their "most probable" variant, the study by the Petroleum Research Foundation had projected that the demand for OPEC oil would be 32.8 mbd in 1985 and would rise to 35.8 mbd in 1990. The implied growth rate of demand for OPEC oil was thus 1.0% pa in 1976–85 and 1.8% pa between 1985 and 1990.) In the study by the US International Trade Commission, the implied growth rate of demand for OPEC oil was 1.9% pa between 1975 and 1985.

A study prepared by British oil consultants for the US Department of Energy used a different set of assumptions and concluded that demand for OPEC oil will be "no more than 36.5 mbd in 1985, and substantially the same in 1990. [125] The implied growth rate of demand for OPEC oil for 1977–85 period was 2.0% pa, and 1.2% pa for the 1977–90 period. US crude oil imports would remain substantially unchanged between 1977 and 1985, but subsequently would decline. US imports of refined oil products were expected to increase until 1980 and then decline. The *Petroleum Economist* noted that this forecast of demand for oil in the non-Communist world in 1985 "is a long way below [the figure] suggested in the much-criticized study by the US Central Intelligence Agency" of April 1977. [126] In the scenario which the Petroleum Research Foundation considered more probable, the forecast demand for oil in the non-Communist world in 1985 was significantly lower than in the British study.

A study of the near-term oil market (until 1982) prepared by a US bank and published in December 1977 concluded that demand for OPEC oil would be declining sharply. OPEC production was 31.5 mbd in 1977, and was expected to decline to 26.0 mbd in 1982. "It's our estimate that the supply of oil from sources other than the OPEC countries is likely to rise at a 9% or 10% annual rate over the next few years. But world demand for oil won't be rising nearly that fast. Instead, it's likely to rise at maybe 3% or 3.5% annual rate. With total demand for oil worldwide growing slowly, and with competing sources for oil increasing rapidly, the OPEC nations are going to be placed in an embarrassing squeeze. . . . Meanwhile, their need to sell oil abroad so that they can buy the imports they need for their ambitious military and development programmes will be growing. It's going to get harder for them to maintain control of the cartel's pricing capabilities in the face of this increasing competition from other sources." [127]

The sharp rise in oil prices in 1973–74 induced a significant downward effect on the growth rate of demand for oil—for all the reasons noted earlier. It also intensified the search for oil in non-OPEC countries. Between January 1974 and January 1978, the world's proven oil reserves *increased* by c. 15 bn barrels. [128] In other words, newly discovered reserves greatly exceeded current oil production. Mexican oil discoveries have been particularly large since 1977, and this has been the case both with respect to oil and gas in a number of other countries. Mexico's proved and probable reserves in 1972 were officially announced at 2.6 bn barrels; in 1977, they were set at 16.8 bn barrels. The *Wall Street Journal* quoted US experts who believed that Mexican potential oil reserves were much larger—"second only to Saudi Arabia." [129] Mexico's President stated in September 1978 that proved and probable reserves had risen to 57 bn barrels, and that "potential reserves" were 200 bn barrels. The original production target of 2.5 mbd for 1982 was expected to be reached by 1980 and would continue to rise in the following years. [130] Mexico's proved and probable reserves of 57 bn barrels were equivalent to two-and-a-half times *world* oil consumption in 1977.

A World Bank study in 1978 noted that the developing countries, excluding OPEC, were currently producing only 6% of world oil production, although they have an estimated 40% of the world's potential oil reserves. The study concluded that 75% of Latin American oil, 80% of African oil, and 95% of Far Eastern oil has yet to be intensively prospected and developed. [131] Experts varied widely in their estimates of the world's potential oil reserves and, as noted earlier, the projections seen in retrospect have usually proved to be very conservative. What is indisputable is that the sharp rise in oil prices decreed by the OPEC cartel in 1973–74 has set into motion powerful economic forces which have intensified the search for non-OPEC oil and gas sources. Research and development expenditures designed to exploit vast reserves of oil shale, tar sands and heavy oils have also accelerated. Specialis.s believe that there are good prospects for "technological breakthroughs" which would make these reserves commercially feasible. In addition, new technology has been developed to increase the recovery rate from conventional oil wells—from the current 25–30% of oil in the ground to 40% or higher. [132] Clearly these developments will take decades before becoming commercially significant. Other sources of energy, such as solar energy, are also receiving increasing attention. A study group set up by the US government concluded that solar energy could produce 20% of the country's energy requirements by the year 2000, whereas the US Department of Energy had previously estimated this share to be 10%. [133] The Arab producers in OPEC with the largest oil reserves occasionally voiced concern about long-term prospects. *Business Week* reported that the "Arab producers are concerned enough about the growing interest in research on alternatives [to oil] that at their Cairo meeting [1977] they set up a special committee to study the problem." [134] Iraq's Vice-President was quoted as stating that his country would not participate in efforts towards the harnessing of solar energy because "this would replace oil." [135] The Saudi Minister of Finance also expressed concern in 1977 about the "development of alternative sources of energy." [136]

All the above relates to the effects of the sharp oil price increases of 1973–74 on the supply side, both short and long-term. On the demand side, we have already noted the significant decline in the energy coefficient and the reversal of the previous trend where, until 1973, oil was steadily replacing other energy sources. The combined effects of both supply and demand forces have fundamentally altered widely believed perceptions of shortages. As the *Petroleum Economist* noted:

"There is, in academic and certain government circles, a growing suspicion about the concept of an impending oil shortage; a feeling that world energy markets may be facing a deluge, not a drought." [137] Prof Paul Samuelson wrote in 1975: "The OPEC monopoly, by its dramatic quadrupling of the price of oil, has set into motion forces making for lessened energy use [and for undermining OPEC's monopoly power]." [138] Clearly, the elasticity of both supply and demand for oil, and in particular OPEC oil, has increased at a much faster pace than was believed possible or probable just a few years ago. However, the least foreseen of the developments of the last few years has been the phenomenal growth in the perceived "needs" of the OPEC countries in terms of consumption, investment and military expenditures, and of the impact of these on imports. While the focus of this study is Saudi Arabia, it appears that events there are in many respects being emulated in other major oil-exporting countries. As the *Petroleum Economist* noted: "Local inflation and construction delays . . . have been responsible for soaring OPEC expenditure levels. The real cost of building an industrial plant or urban complex in the ME has recently been found to be from two to three times as high as for an identical plant built on the US Gulf coast." [139]

THE SAUDI ARABIAN ECONOMY—FUTURE PROSPECTS

We have seen that within a few years following the unprecedented growth in oil revenues in 1973–74, the Saudi authorities had accelerated expenditures to the point where current surpluses were rapidly diminishing and deficits were beginning to emerge in 1978. This is entirely consistent with the conclusions reached by Prof Donald Wells with respect to the 1960s, namely that "the gap between revenues and expenditures closed whenever the Saudis had had time to adjust to the new levels of income and wealth." [140] The gap closed far more rapidly than had been anticipated or planned because of inflation, especially in construction costs. Inflation also compelled the authorities to expend far larger sums on subsidies (direct and in-direct) and on salaries in the public sector, including the military forces. The military budget escalated to levels far higher than had been projected. The con-struction of major military complexes (the military cities), the purchase of sophisticated and expensive weaponry from abroad and the expansion of the armed forces have been very costly. Budgeted military expenditures during the first four years of the 1975–80 Plan were $38.6 bn (cf $5.5 bn in the previous four years). This was already greatly in excess of the $22.2 bn designated in the Plan for the full five-year period. [141] If the military budget for the last year of the Plan (1979–80) remains at the level of 1978–79, total military budgets will have been two-and-one-third times the original planned level. As noted earlier, there are indications that *actual* military outlays have exceeded those designated in the budget. Finally there is no way of measuring the cost escalation due to administrative incompetence and corruption—kickbacks and commissions. [142]

Estimates offered by Saudi officials in mid-1978 were that total expenditures during the Five-Year Plan period will be c. $200 bn—$60 bn above the figure originally designated. [143] However, in real (physical) terms, the implementation of the projects envisaged in the Plan will be far less than anticipated. Reports from Saudi Arabia in mid-1978 indicated that "the major portion of construction under the second Five-Year Plan is yet to begin." [144]

Reference has already been made to Prof Moran's study of the Saudi Develop-ment Plan and what it would cost to implement at mid-1977 prices. He made a number of "conservative" assessments of future price increases and assumed that the Saudis would reduce administrative costs from the high level reached during the first year of the Plan, 1975–76. Given the benefit of more recent data, it is obvious that his assumptions were indeed very conservative, and that the cost escalation has proceeded at a much faster rate than he anticipated. Moran also simulated what he termed an "immediate drastic" cutback in government expenditures for the last three years of the Plan—mid-1977 to mid-1980. This included a 90% cutback in investment in economic resources, i.e. industrial plants, petrochemicals, agriculture; a 75% cutback in military expenditures; a 50–75% cutback in investments in infrastructure, desalination, gas-gathering projects; a 75% reduction in expenditures on health, education, housing; and a 25% cutback on administrative outlays. In effect, this would mean stretching out the implementation of the Plan from the scheduled five years to more than 20 years. Moran concluded that even in this scenario, assuming "constant real oil prices," the implementation of the Plan "will require exports of 8–9 mbd to finance year by year, or 7–8 mbd by the late 1970s if the Saudis are willing to draw down their financial reserves to zero in ten years." [145]

The budget announced for 1977–78 called for total expenditures of $32.1 bn (cf actual expenditures of $30.2 bn in the previous year). The budget for 1978–79 (even after the last-minute cutback) projected that expenditures would rise to $39.4 bn. [146] No data are available, at this writing, for actual expenditures in 1977–78, but there is every reason to assume that they equalled or exceeded planned spending. There is certainly no indication that the Saudis have considered or implemented an "immediate drastic" cutback. At most they may have slowed down the prevailing sharp rate of growth in expenditures. As noted earlier, the Ministry of Finance issued instructions in mid-1978 (the beginning of the fiscal year 1978–79) that those ministries with projects budgets were to limit their expenditures to 70% of allocations, unless special approval was granted. It is not clear whether this included the military budget, but the likelihood is that it did not. However, even assuming that projects in the military budget were included in the cutback instructions, and that the directive was applied completely by the various ministries, this would imply that 1978–79 expenditures would remain at the previous year's level. [147] In fact, reports published in late 1978 showed that some ministries had delayed or scaled down the size of some projects, but that others were simply accumulating debts owed to foreign contractors. Three Italian road contractors reported that they had not been paid since April 1978; payments on the major microwave contract were reported to be months in arrears; and the British Department of Trade stated that some British companies had reported payments problems. [148] In other words, expenditures in terms of obligations were being curtailed far less than the 30% directive of the Finance Ministry; in many cases, actual payments were simply being postponed.

The question that arises is whether the Saudi authorities can really implement a significant reduction in expenditures, let alone the "immediate drastic" cutback envisaged by Moran. It appears highly improbable. Over one-third of the 1978–79 budget is for military expenditures, [149] and it is doubtful that this allocation would be seriously curtailed, if at all. As noted earlier, new contracts for the construction of a "military city" near Riyadh and additional orders for arms and military construction (announced by the US Defence Department in September 1978), do not indicate any slowdown in this large component of the budget—quite the contrary. The perception of the Saudi leaders seems to have been voiced by Yamānī in mid-1978 when he said that never before "has a country had such a valuable resource [oil] and been so ill-equipped to defend it." [150] The problems of internal security, current or future, add to the impetus to increase military spending. [151]

With respect to civilian expenditures, any significant cutback would be difficult or impossible. In many cases contracts have been signed, though actual work may not have commenced in 1978. In other cases work has actually begun, and cutbacks or delays would be even more difficult and costly. Cutbacks in one project could also have adverse effects on others which are dependent on its output.[152] However, of greater importance than the contractual commitments and technical difficulties which major cutbacks or lengthy delays might cause, are the heightened expectations of the Saudi population. In a revealing interview in 1977, a Saudi minister stated the following: "I was born in 1940. My mother died of typhoid because there was no doctor in town. She was only 28. I almost lost my sight because there was no eye doctor. There were scorpions in our house; I was stung more than once. I was lucky to survive. The [infant] mortality rate was 60–70%. A family had six or seven children in order to end up keeping one of them. We had no electricity. . . . Unless you bear in mind this yearning of our people for a better life after 3,000 years of subhuman existence, you will not understand what is going on in Saudi Arabia."[153] Rising expectations engendered by the huge flow of oil revenues will necessarily create serious resistance to any cutbacks which might adversely affect the population. The government has been keenly aware of this problem and has therefore increased subsidies very sharply in recent years on food, health, education, housing, etc. Cutbacks in the huge administrative outlays would mean either dismissals or salary cutbacks, or both—steps which would necessarily be politically hazardous. As Moran phrased it: "The record of survival for regimes that try to stop, or reverse, the process of social mobilization and rising expectations once it is started, should not recommend this as a promising strategy for a monarchy."[154]

In addition to these more general problems, there are particular difficulties which impede budgetary reductions. A severe cutback would delay development along the Western coast of the country for many years and exacerbate internal regional tensions. (Saudi oil is in the Persian Gulf area.) Furthermore, curtailing the "awarding of many new contracts will hit particularly hard the many members of the Saudi hierarchy whose family income depends upon commissions from the successful negotiation of *new* contracts."[155] Some of the civilian projects, including roads and communications, are considered important from a military point of view. Contracts were awarded in early 1978 for the construction of a 48-inch trans-peninsula oil pipeline to the Western coast. The purpose is to promote the development of that part of the country and—equally important—to reduce Saudi dependence on oil exports via the Persian Gulf.[156] The recent distrubances in Iran have undoubtedly enhanced the importance of this project for the Saudis.

All this does not imply that there are no areas of possible cutbacks—but these are necessarily limited, given all the above-mentioned constraints. Projects of the Ministry of Health were being re-evaluated by the government in view of the imbalance between health facilities and available staff.[157] It was reported in late 1978 that the Ministry of Health needed additional medical staff of 6,000 to fill vacancies in existing facilities.[158] The fiscal problems will undoubtedly give additional impetus to re-evaluations of proposed new projects by the Ministry of Health as well as by others.

Reports published in mid-1978 quoting the Saudi Ministry of Planning indicated that a number of major new contracts had been awarded, mainly in transportation and communications, desalination, sewage, housing and other infrastructural investments. All of these projects, as well as earlier ones, have a momentum of their own, and cost estimates are most often on the low side. In addition, the ministry was pressing for the initiation of a number of very costly new projects, including a new international airport near. Riyadh at an estimated cost of $3–4.5 bn. Cost estimates for the Jidda international airport now under construction run as high as

$7 bn. A contract was to be awarded for a new campus for the University of Riyadh at a cost of $3.4 bn. A $545m contract for precast concrete units for this project had been signed in April 1978. The King was reported to be pressing for the initiation of the King Khālid military city to be built near the Kuwaiti border, designed to house 70,000. A special port had already been built purely in order to import materials needed for this project. Additional major projects include the building of Sunrise City in the Eastern Province, which is to be a palace and cabinet complex for the royal family and ministers, and the Olympic Stadium for the Riyadh sports city. The latter project is being sponsored by the son of the Crown Prince.[159]

Given the problems faced by industry, one can surmise that further cuts will be made in the construction of new industries. However, excluding the oil sector, these include only a small fraction of total planned expenditures. The bulk of civilian investments is related to infrastructure. A reduction in civilian current expenditures (as distinct from investment) would be most difficult for all the reasons already noted. Foreign aid is one area which will probably be affected. Aid disbursements—grants and loans—totalled over $3 bn pa in 1975-77. Unofficially it was reported that "many Arab countries complain behind the scenes that they never receive anything like the aid that Saudi Arabia has actually promised—but they are unable to complain about this publicly because of fears that the aid flows will be turned off completely."[160] At a meeting of the Council of State in 1977, the Minister of Finance proposed curtailing foreign aid.[161] In addition to foreign economic aid, there is military aid to some other Arab countries, but this is never officially reported. However, in mid-1977, Sādāt stated that Saudi Arabia had agreed to pay all the costs of developing Egypt's armed forces until 1981.[162] The reference was presumably by Saudi Arabia to Western arms suppliers for shipments to Egypt. In October 1978, Saudi officials were reported to have complained about the high cost ($600m) of the 50 F-5 fighter aircraft it had ordered for delivery to Egypt.[163] Official Egyptian reports indicate that grants received from the Arab oil countries (Saudi Arabia, Kuwait and Abu Dhabi) have declined sharply in recent years, from c. $1 bn in 1974 and 1975 to $623m in 1976, and $384m in 1977.[164] Clearly this was determined, in large measure, by Saudi fiscal problems. (The cutback in 1976 and in 1977 antedated the Sādāt visit to Jerusalem.) Saudi budgetary problems had been clearly responsible for curtailing foreign aid after 1969-70.[165]

Given the magnitude of domestic expenditures—as well as the contractual, technical, political and social constraints which impair the ability of the authorities to curtail spending—a cutback in foreign aid would contribute only marginally to a solution of the country's fiscal problems. Another option is to augment domestic revenues. In mid-1978 the price of gasolene was almost doubled—the first increase in five years.[166] However, the increased revenues from this source are puny in relation to the total Saudi budget. As the export of refined oil products had been declining, the move may have been intended to increase export revenues by restricting domestic consumption.[167] Indirectly, the higher price of gasolene might curb the rising volume of automobile imports. The authorities could also impose or increase customs duties on imports, especially on "luxury" items. Vehicle imports in 1975 were five times their level two years earlier,[168] and there is every reason to believe that they have continued to rise rapidly. However, the prospects of a significant contribution from an increase in domestic revenues (excluding oil revenues and income from foreign investments) are dim. In fiscal year 1976-77, revenues other than oil and investment income were less than $1 bn—2.5% of total revenues. Expenditures in that year were over $30 bn. Oil revenues accounted for 89% of total governmental receipts, and investment income for over 8%.[169]

344

The authorities may decide—or may have no choice—but to draw down the country's financial reserves. Early in 1977 the Deputy Minister of Finance was quoted as stating: "Spending will not increase, but revenue will. All the new revenue will go to investment outside." [170] In other words, the plans at that time were to continue to accumulate financial reserves. The Saudi authorities view these reserves as a "cushion" which would protect them during periods when oil revenues diminish, or when revenues do not increase as rapidly as expenditures. However, in the autumn of 1978, the Minister of Finance stated: "We are not thinking of continuing as investors in the international market; in fact, this is something we wish to avoid. We believe we are only investors in the international market on a temporary basis, as our aim is to invest internally." [171] At about the same time, the director of the foreign investment department of the Saudi Arabian Monetary Agency (the Central Bank) stated that the department was not interested in tying up funds in foreign long-term investments and loans because of the country's need to develop the Saudi economy. [172] Clearly, the anticipation in the autumn of 1978 was that, despite efforts to hold down spending, there would continue to be fiscal deficits and that the country would have to draw on its financial reserves.

The development of manufacturing, and even more so of agriculture, has been encountering great difficulties as already noted. The prospects that these or other sectors of the economy will make a significant contribution either towards exports or import substitution in the foreseeable future are poor. Hence, the country will continue to be heavily, if not almost wholly, dependent on oil income to finance growing internal expenditures and, as a consequence, a rising volume of imports of goods and services.

It has been the thesis of this essay that economic motivations, both long-term and short-term, are the prime determinants of Saudi oil policies. This does not preclude political motivations, so long as they do not come into serious conflict with fundamental economic interests. Some Saudi officials have been rather candid in their more recent remarks. The Minister of Petroleum stated in a speech at the University of Riyadh in mid-1978: "Concerning the effects of the 1973 war on price increases, Arab sources always used to say that if it were not for the Ramadan War (the Arab-Israeli war of October 1973), oil-producing countries wouldn't have been able to raise the price of their oil and wouldn't have accumulated such wealth. But this is not true, since two months before the Ramadan War we had notified the oil companies that we were going to effect big increases in oil prices." [173] This comment may have been meant as a response to Egyptian and other Arab demands and claims for far greater aid from Saudi Arabia and the oil-rich Arab countries. "Egyptians believed that they had fought and lost thousands of their countrymen so that OPEC could quadruple its revenues without lifting a finger." Egyptians were indeed disappointed and bitter that aid from the rich Arab countries was relatively small, and even declining. [174] It is difficult to know what might have been. Clearly, market forces were, and are, basic determinants of oil pricing, and the effectiveness of any cartel—OPEC included—is circumscribed by market forces. As Yamānī stated in his lecture: "The ability of these countries [OPEC] to manipulate prices originates from the law of supply and demand, which says [that] when supply exceeds demand prices fall, and when demand exceeds supply prices rise." [175] The increase in oil prices between the beginning of 1971 and shortly before the war of October 1973 was over 120%; this was after prices (measured in current dollars) were stable during the decade of the 1960s and, as noted earlier, was due to market forces.

It has already been noted that Saudi Arabia "violated" the oil "embargo" declared by the Arab members of OPEC after the last quarter of 1973. Oil production was raised during the first quarter of 1974 despite the embargo which called for monthly reductions in oil production. The *New York Times* reported that it was informed by an Aramco official that the "embargo" came at a propitious time, since a cutback in production was important for technical reasons.[176] Presumably, the technical problems were of relatively short duration, and the Saudis raised production from January 1974 on, despite the official embargo.

Saudi Arabia differs from most other oil-exporting countries in many basic respects. Its possession of about one-fourth of the world's proved and probable oil reserves is unique. Despite the high and growing volume of Saudi production, new discoveries have always exceeded current output. It is therefore impossible to estimate the probable "life span" of Saudi oil. In mid-1978 the head of Petromin (the Saudi national oil company) stated his belief that Saudi oil would last another 80 years.[177] Furthermore, there is a high degree of probability that oil will continue to be of overwhelming importance in terms of export (and government) revenues for the foreseeable future. Therefore, in determining oil pricing policies, the Saudi authorities must necessarily take into serious account the effect of higher (real) prices on the longer-term demand for oil. We have already seen that since the major oil price increases decreed by OPEC in the last months of 1973, there has been a significant change in terms of the energy-GDP coefficient, the substitution of non-oil energy sources, and considerable investment (including research and development) both in terms of energy conservation and in developing commercially feasible alternatives to oil. Following the major oil price increase which came into effect on 1 January 1974, reports always picture Saudi Arabia as the "dove" on pricing in OPEC councils. Its generally "dovish" position stems from its fears that continued (real) price increases will accelerate the above trends and, in the longer run, adversely affect the (real) price of oil—and hence, the country's future prosperity. Saudi officials rarely give voice to this concern, but foreign observers and researchers take note of this constraint with respect to Saudi oil pricing policies.

A study by the International Institute for Strategic Studies noted that the sheer magnitude of Saudi Arabia's oil reserves "places the country in a separate category. She may be able to produce oil well into the twenty-first century, and possibly even into the twenty-second. . . . Any further disruption of the international oil market, therefore, would increase the danger of making the Saudi oil worthless [in the longer run]. For this reason, the country cannot be interested in further disturbances of supplies [restrictions on supplies or an oil embargo] and price increases; a stable relationship with consumer countries would serve her interests best."[178] When Prince Fahd said in January 1978, "I don't see another [oil] embargo under any circumstances,"[179] there is good reason to believe that this accords with his country's most fundamental economic—as well as political—interests. Another more recent study also noted that, among the factors which determine the Saudi policy of not raising real oil prices is "its concern about the impact of a continuing increase in real oil prices on the irreversible development of new energy sources, reflecting Saudi Arabia's unique long-term resource position."[180]

The present size of the Saudi financial reserves, and the fact that so much of it is denominated in dollars, puts an additional constraint on its desire, or acquiescence, to oil price increases. In his lecture at the University of Riyadh in mid-1978, Yamānī said: "Most of our [foreign] investments are in dollars, so that when the dollar value falls, the value of our investments also falls. But this loss is of a temporary nature and it goes up if the dollar returns to its previous levels. We believe that the dollar will return to its rising tendency; therefore, it is in our interest not to take any moves that would lead to a further depreciation of the dollar's [exchange] rate. This explains Saudi Arabia's stand on the dollar, which may conflict with the points of view of many other oil producing countries, but which at the same time is in the interest of Saudi Arabia."[181] The reference is both to large oil price increases or the proposal by many OPEC members to denominate the price of oil in currencies other than the dollar, or to base it on a "basket" of currencies.

The Saudi directive to Aramco in February 1978 that no more than 65% of its crude exports should consist of the Arab light variety is also consistent with its longer-term interests, since most of its oil reserves are of the heavier grades of oil. In this case, it also accorded with its short-run interests, since rising production from the North Sea and Alaska was "flooding" the market with light oil, and discounting was taking place in the oil markets.[182] In 1977, when there was an over-abundance of the heavier oils, the Saudis increased the differential between the prices of its heavier oils and those of the other members of OPEC.

We have seen that, especially after 1969, Saudi policy was to take full advantage of market opportunities to capture a growing share of the world and, in particular, the OPEC market. Its share of the latter rose sharply—from 15.3% in 1969 to 24.5% in 1973. Following the budgetary deficit of 1969-70, it began to accumulate large and growing financial surpluses. However, as these surpluses were accumulating, Saudi views of their perceived "needs" also rose rapidly. The very large oil price increases of 1973-74 and the flood of revenues raised their perception of current and future "needs" to a much higher plane. The Deputy Finance Minister was expressing broadly-held views when he said in 1977: "It is only a pseudo-surplus. When every Saudi has a house and an education, we'll have the luxury of talking about a surplus."[183] Of course, one must add their perception of defence needs and all the other categories of expenditures. After the major oil price increase of January 1974, when the Saudis became increasingly aware of the longer term adverse effects of further real price increases, they attempted to continue to raise the volume of oil exports. Between 1973 and 1977, Saudi oil production increased by an average annual rate of 5.2% as compared with the unusually high rate of 24.1% in the previous four years when market conditions were far more favourable. However, the rest of OPEC was suffering an average annual decline of 1.6% during the 1973-77 period. Thus the Saudi share of OPEC production rose to a peak of 29.8% in 1977.

Another factor which accounts for Saudi Arabia's relative price moderation is its increasing awareness of the fact that, during times of market weakness, other OPEC members offer various discounts (official and unofficial) in order to raise or maintain their share of the oil market. During 1978—until the disturbances in Iran altered the market situation drastically in the last quarter of the year—the Saudis favoured either a price freeze in 1979 or a modest price increase, i.e. a decline in the real price of oil. In early 1978, when market conditions were particularly weak, both Yamānī and Prince Fahd suggested that the price of oil, in current dollars, might be maintained until 1980.[184] In September 1978, the *Petroleum Economist* stated: "It is widely assumed that OPEC will approve a price increase of 5% . . . as long as other OPEC members [other than Saudi Arabia] have spare capacity that they are willing to mobilize at discounted prices. However, the Saudis may look darkly on any new price regime that would operate at further expense to their own treasury."[185] Yamānī expressed this view very clearly in his lecture at the University of Riyadh in mid-1978: "We have fixed production and prices and have subsequently borne the consequences of the fall in production alone. Other countries like Nigeria, Algeria and Libya reduce their prices from one time to the other in order to increase sales. . . . As to the present oil prices, I don't think they may be raised, because they are actually showing a falling tendency due to the existence of surplus oil supplies in the world."[186]

Saudi concern about its rapid decline in oil production was well-founded. During the first nine months of 1978—as compared with the same period in 1977—Saudi oil production declined by 16.4% (cf a 2.1% decline in the rest of OPEC). This was due in large measure to increasing competition from other OPEC members in terms of discounts, as well as continued rising production in non-OPEC countries. World oil production was approximately unchanged, but non-OPEC production increased by 6.8% (at the expense of OPEC); within OPEC, the other members were attempting to increase sales—at the expense of Saudi Arabia. OPEC production as a whole declined by 6.4%, and its share of world oil production fell sharply. The trend away from OPEC oil was continuing at an even more rapid pace. Until 1973, OPEC was providing an increasing share of world oil production, reaching 54.3% in that year. In 1977, OPEC's share fell to 51.2% and, during the first three-quarters of 1978, it was down to 47.6%. Saudi Arabia had succeeded until 1977 in countering the other OPEC countries' downtrend. Its share within OPEC had risen from 24.5% in 1973 to 29.8% in 1977; within world oil production, it had grown from 13.3% to 15.3%. However, during the first nine months of 1978, the Saudi share of OPEC and world oil production fell drastically—to 26.3% and 12.5% respectively. Under the conditions prevailing until October 1978, any price increase would further adversely affect the Saudi position.[187]

The disturbances in Iran towards the end of 1978 altered the current oil market situation drastically. No precise data are available at this writing (December 1978) with respect to oil production during the last quarter of the year; Iranian output during the first nine months of 1978 averaged 5.7 mbd, or 9.3% of world oil production. The subsequent decline in Iranian production was no doubt significant and may have erased the surplus in oil supplies. Moreover, the fears of oil consumers that as of 1 January 1978 OPEC would be in a much stronger position to raise prices contributed to anticipatory buying. There is little doubt that Saudi Arabia and others raised production significantly during the last quarter of 1978 to take full advantage of the new market situation. The deterioration in its financial position, as well as its overall policy of maximizing its share of the market, would impel the Saudis (as well as other producers) to take such action. The OPEC meeting at the end of December 1978 decided on a price increase which would average about 10% for 1979 as a whole. (On a December 1978 to December 1979 basis, the increase is 14%.)

Following the precipitous oil price increase of 1 January 1974, its real price tended to fall, due to all the factors noted earlier. Measured in constant dollars, the price of oil during the last quarter of 1978 was c. 13% lower than in the first quarter of 1974.[188] Assuming that the new OPEC prices prevail in the marketplace in 1979, they will further stimulate inflationary pressures in the industrial countries. If the latters' export prices rise in 1979 at the same annual rate as in the first half of 1978—c. 14% pa—the real price of oil will continue to decline, despite the higher nominal prices decreed by OPEC.

In the short turn, the disturbances in Iran and the decline in its oil production have provided the Saudis with a temporary respite from the financial squeeze which they had been encountering in 1978. This may explain their ready acquiescence in a larger than expected price increase. The same is also true of many other OPEC countries suffering balance of payments problems. Morgan Guaranty Trust projected that six of the 13 OPEC members were having current account deficits in 1978, and that the surpluses of the others were declining rapidly. The bank projected that the OPEC surplus as a whole would also continue to decline rapidly in the coming years.[189] The Bank of England estimated that the current account surplus of OPEC as a whole in the first half of 1978 was $6.4 bn (cf $20.9 bn in the first half of 1977).[190]

No one can predict when and how the current political upheaval in Iran will end. All one can say with reasonable certainty is that, no matter what government emerges, it will press for increased oil production. Those members of OPEC with "radical" regimes—such as Algeria and Iraq—attempt to maximize their oil exports in every way possible, and are often amongst the first to offer discounts when the market situation is weak. Unless similar upheavals take place in other major oil exporting countries, one can project that the fundamental trends in the oil and energy markets will reassert themselves and create increasing problems for the oil-exporting countries. The fact that Saudi Arabia and others have emerged as "high absorbers" can only contribute to a further weakening of the oil market—as viewed by the exporters. There is little doubt that this is of serious concern to Riyadh. Budgetary deficits and drawing down their reserves run counter to basic Saudi policies.

Since January 1974, when the Saudi government increased its participation (ownership) of Aramco to 60%, and agreed in principle to a 100% takeover, there have been negotiations with the company for completion of the nationalization.[191] By the end of 1978, there was no indication of an agreement being reached. It has been reported that one of the Saudi demands is that Aramco should commit itself to a minimal production level of 7–8 mbd, with light crude constituting no more than 65%. The authorities are also demanding penalty clauses if Aramco fails to meet this commitment as a result of changes in prices or market conditions.[192] Saudi oil production (including small amounts from other companies) averaged 7.7 mbd during the first nine months of 1978 (cf 9.2 mbd during the same period in 1977).

The rise in non-OPEC oil production, and especially more recently from Mexico, is particularly worrisome for Saudi Arabia and other OPEC countries. US imports from Mexico were rising sharply. In the third quarter of 1978, they were almost double the level prevailing in the last quarter of 1977. The share of Saudi crude oil as a percentage of US crude oil imports had reached a peak of 23% in 1975, but fell to 16–17% during the first nine months of 1978. Imports from Saudi Arabia were still far higher in absolute terms, but the trend was unmistakable. An announcement by Mexico towards the end of 1978 of yet another major new discovery of oil and natural gas will accelerate this trend in coming years. In addition to non-economic considerations, Mexico's proximity to the US market gives it a decided advantage in terms of transportation costs. The laying of a pipeline for natural gas from Mexico to the US will further tend to reduce US imports of crude oil from more distant sources.[193] With a population of 65m and a per capita GDP of c. $850, Mexico has every reason to expand its oil production and exports to the maximum.

Saudi financial reserves were probably c. $70 bn in 1978—equivalent to about twice the oil revenues received in 1977. Given the constraints preventing a significant cutback in Saudi expenditures—and the difficulties encountered in augmenting oil revenues, at least in real terms—the Saudis will probably have no alternative but to draw upon these reserves. At the same time, they will make every effort to increase their oil exports and revenues. Since this situation appears to prevail in varying degrees in other OPEC countries, the struggle for market shares in the oil market may well increase. This will probably mean a continued decline in the real price of oil. When Prof Samuelson wrote in 1975 that the quadrupling of oil prices by OPEC in 1973–74 would set into motion economic forces which would undermine OPEC's monopoly power, he probably did not visualize the strength of these forces and the rapidity of their operations. Of greatest moment, and unforeseen by so many, are the internal developments in Saudi Arabia (and in other OPEC countries) and their impact on international oil and financial markets.

Eliyahu Kanovsky

TABLE NO 1: WORLD OIL PRODUCTION AND CONSUMPTION

	(Million Metric Tons)				(Average Annual Rate of Growth or Decline in Percentages)		
	1965	1969	1973	1977	1965–69	1969–73	1973–77
A Oil Production							
Saudi Arabia	110	160	378	464	9.7	24.1	5.2
Iran	95	168	293	284	15.3	14.9	-1.0
Abu Dhabi	14	29	63	80	21.0	21.3	6.3
Kuwait	119	140	152	99	4.3	2.0	-10.2
Iraq	64	75	99	110	3.9	7.2	2.8
Libya	59	150	105	100	26.3	-8.5	-1.0
Algeria	27	45	51	54	13.7	3.6	1.1
Soviet Union	243	328	421	540	7.8	6.4	6.4
US	431	515	519	466	4.5	0.2	-2.7
Total World	1,565	2,144	2,844	3,042	8.2	7.3	1.7
Total OPEC	720	1,041	1,543	1,557	9.7	10.3	0.2
OPEC—excluding Saudi Arabia	610	882	1,165	1,092	9.6	7.2	-1.6
World excluding OPEC	845	1,103	1,301	1,485	6.9	4.2	3.4
B Oil and Energy Consumption							
World Oil Consumption	1,592	2,097	2,773	2,972	7.1	7.2	1.8
World Energy Consumption	4,121	5,084	6,064	6,687	5.4	4.5	2.5
World Energy Consumption excluding Oil	2,529	2,987	3,291	3,715	4.3	2.5	3.0
US Oil Consumption	549	668	818	867	5.0	5.2	1.5
US Energy Consumption	1,340	1,633	1,828	1,853	5.1	2.9	0.3
World Energy Consumption excluding US	2,871	1,351	4,237	4,834	5.6	5.3	.3.4
World Oil Consumption excluding US	1,043	1,429	1,955	2,105	8.2	8.1	1.9
C Ratios (Percentages)							
Saudi Oil Production / World Oil Production	7.0	7.4	13.3	15.3			
OPEC (excl. Saudi) Oil Prod. / World Oil Production	39.0	41.1	40.9	35.9			
Saudi Oil Production / OPEC Oil Production	15.3	15.3	24.5	29.8			
OPEC Oil Production / World Oil Production	46.0	48.6	54.3	51.2			
US Oil Consumption / World Oil Consumption	34.5	31.8	29.5	29.2			
US Oil Consumption / US Energy Consumption	41.0	40.9	44.8	46.8			
World Oil Consumption / World Energy Cons.	38.6	41.3	45.7	44.4			
World (excl. US) Oil Cons. / World (excl. US) Energy Cons.	37.5	41.4	46.1	43.5			

Notes:

Prod: Production, Cons: Consumption, excl: excluding.

[1] Energy consumption is in terms of oil equivalent in millions of tons, and includes oil, natural gas, solid fuels, water power and nuclear power.

[2] Saudi and Kuwaiti oil production include half shares of the Neutral Zone.

[3] In order to convert to millions of barrels per day, the above figures would be divided by about 50, e.g. 50m tons of oil production per year is equivalent to approximately 1m barrels per day.

Sources: BP Statistical Review of the World Oil Industry 1977 and earlier issues.

TABLE NO 2: THE SAUDI ARABIAN OIL INDUSTRY

	1969	1970	1971	1972	1973	1974	1975	1976	1977
Crude Oil Production in millions of barrels	1,174	1,387	1,741	2,202	2,273	3,095	2,583	3,139	3,358
Production in millions of barrels per day	3.2	3.8	4.8	6.0	7.6	8.5	7.1	8.6	9.2
Proved Oil Reserves in billions of barrels	86.0	88.1	90.2	93.0	97.0	103.5	107.9	110.2	110.4
Probable Oil Reserves in billions of barrels	120.0	123.9	127.5	156.4	164.5	172.5	175.6	177.5	177.6
Crude Oil Exports in millions of barrels	1,020	1,174	1,528	1,988	2,557	2,888	2,406	2,934	3,136
Exports of Refined Oil Products in millions of barrels	158	208	194	207	212	210	175	206	188
Government Oil Revenues in millions of dollars	949	1,214	1,885	2,745	4,340	22,574	25,676	30,748	36,900

Notes:
[1] Aramco, the Arabian American Oil Company, dominates Saudi oil production, accounting for 96-98% of total production in recent years.
[2] The figures for proved and probable oil reserves are for the Aramco concession area. The figures are for the end of the year.
[3] Despite the rapid increases in oil production, both proved and probable reserves have continued to increase. This has been essentially true since commercial oil production began in Saudi Arabia in the later 1930s.
Source: Saudi Arabian Monetary Agency, *Annual Report 1397 (1977)* and earlier issues.

TABLE NO 3: SAUDI ARABIAN BUDGETS—REVENUES AND EXPENDITURES (million Saudi rials—in parentheses, million dollars)

Fiscal Years	Total Revenues (Actual)	Oil Revenues	Of which from Investments	Total Expend. (Actual)	Surplus (Cash Basis)
1389-90 (12 Sept 1969 to 1 Sept 1970)	5,668 (1,260)	5,119 (1,138)	n.a.	6,079 (1,351)	-400 (-89)
1390-91 (2 Sept 1970 to 21 Aug 1971)	7,954 (1,768)	6,827 (1,517)	n.a.	6,294 (1,399)	1,600 (356)
1391-92 (22 Aug 1971 to 9 Aug 1972)	11,116 (2,628)	9,795 (2,316)	252 (60)	8,130 (1,922)	3,340 (790)
1392-93 (10 Aug 1972 to 29 July 1973)	15,325 (3,899)	13,455 (3,424)	440 (112)	10,159 (2,585)	3,800 (967)
1393-94 (30 July 1973 to 19 July 1974)	41,705 (11,748)	39,267 (11,061)	857 (241)	18,595 (5,238)	22,200 (6,254)
1394-95 (20 July 1974 to 9 July 1975)	100,103 (28,438)	94,190 (26,759)	4,207 (1,195)	35,039 (9,954)	66,200 (18,807)
1395-96 (10 July 1975 to 27 June 1976)	103,384 (29,287)	93,481 (26,482)	7,929 (2,246)	81,784 (23,168)	39,100 (11,076)
1396-97 (28 June 1976 to 16 June 1977)	135,957 (38,515)	121,191 (34,332)	11,418 (3,235)	106,737 (30,237)	31,300 (8,867)
Budgetary Projections					
1397-98 (17 June 1977 to 5 June 1978)	146,493 (42,217)	130,481 (37,603)		111,400 (32,104)	
1398-99 (6 June 1978 to 26 May 1979)	130,000 (39,394)	115,134 (34,889)		130,000 (39,394)	

Notes:
[1] Prior to December 1971, the official exchange rate of the Saudi Rial was 4.50 rials to the US dollar. In December 1971, there was a revaluation of the rial to 4.14 rials to the dollar. Since that time there have been a number of additional revaluations of the rial. The exchange rate during the first half of 1978 averaged 3.45 rials to the dollar.
[2] The figures in parentheses are in millions of dollars. Due to the revaluations of the rial during this period, the figures in dollars give a better indication of changes in revenues and expenditures than do the figures in

rials, especially since oil prices and oil revenues paid to the government by Aramco and the other companies operating in Saudi Arabia are in dollars. However, the data on revenues and expenditures are no indication of constant price changes. Inflation in Saudi Arabia has been quite high in recent years. The rates of inflation are discussed separately.

[3] The dollar figures given for the projected budget for 1978–79 are based on the author's estimate of a further revaluation of the rial, averaging 3.30 to the dollar.

[4] The bulk of revenues is from payments by the oil companies. Income from investment refers to returns on foreign investments. These consist mainly of holdings by the SAMA in the US and in other Western countries. Other revenues not specified in the table consist mainly of customs duties, income tax on foreign companies operating in Saudi Arabia other than the oil companies, and some other taxes, fees and revenues from the sale and rental of property.

[5] Especially during the years following the major oil price increases, revenues projected by the budget were far less than actual revenues. With respect to expenditures, the realized figures were most often far less than those projected in the budget. This was especially true of that part of the budget designated as "projects," i.e. investment expenditures. However, this situation had changed in more recent years as the pace of government spending gathered momentum. In 1396–97 (1976–77), the last year for which actual revenues and expenditures were available at the time of writing, anticipated expenditures were SR 90,574 (designated as SR 110,935 minus expected shortfall in expenditures of SR 20,361), but actual expenditures were SR 106,737. Approximately half (SR 54,652) was for various projects, mainly infrastructural investments.

[6] The last column in the table indicates the surplus in the budget on an actual cash basis. There is a discrepancy between this column and the difference between actual revenues and expenditures given in the table. The surplus, on a cash basis, approximates the changes in government deposits with the banks—in recent years, almost solely with the SAMA, the central bank. The difference between the monetary and fiscal accounts arise from a number of factors. In recent years a number of specialized governmental credit institutions were established including those designed to provide long-term low-interest credits to the private sector for housing, industry, agriculture and others. In the fiscal accounts, a transfer from the budget to these institutions is recorded as an actual expenditure, despite the fact that these institutions had not lent some or most of these funds during that fiscal year. This was especially true during the years 1973–75 when most of these institutions were established. In 1396–97 (1976–77), the gap between transfers to these institutions and actual loans by them was quite narrow.

[7] The budgetary figures (and the national accounts) are in fiscal years based on the Muslim lunar calendar.

Sources: SAMA, *Annual Report 1397 (1977)* and earlier issues; IMF, *IFS,* various issues.

TABLE NO 4A: GROSS DOMESTIC PRODUCT (at factor cost, by economic activity)

Line A in each sector is in current prices in millions of Saudi rials
Line B is in constant prices of 1389–90 (1969–70)
Line C is the implicit price deflator, with 1389–90 (1969–70) designated as 100

		1389–90 (1969–70)	1390–91 (1970–71)	1391–92 (1971–72)	1392–93 (1972–73)	1393–94 (1973–74)	1394–95 (1974–75)	1395–96 (1975–76)	1396–97 (1976–77)
Crude Oil	A	8,106	12,581	16,932	26,284	78,345	104,696	109,560	
and	B	8,106	9,922	12,427	15,556	18,158	17,339	17,510	
Natural Gas	C	100	126.8	136.3	169.0	431.5	603.8	625.7	
Petroleum	A	1,241	1,474	1,442	1,811	4,347	5,766	5,962	
Refining	B	1,241	1,355	1,300	1,378	1,417	1,300	1,352	
	C	100	108.8	110.6	131.4	306.8	443.5	441.0	
Agriculture	A	984	1,016	1,059	1,139	1,242	1,392	1,586	
	B	984	1,010	1,050	1,089	1,130	1,174	1,221	
	C	100	99.8	100.	104.6	109.9	118.6	129.9	
Mining and	A	47	50	51	90	146	248	576	
Quarrying	B	47	49	55	77	96	122	158	
	C	100	102.0	92.7	116.9	152.1	203.3	364.6	
Other	A	431	484	543	617	730	931	1,191	
Manufacturing	B	431	484	543	599	665	740	828	
	C	100	100	100	103.0	109.8	125.8	143.8	
Electricity,	A	273	298	302	319	328	318	342	
Gas and	B	273	298	329	381	417	459	526	
Water	C	100	100	9.18	83.7	78.7	69.3	65.0	
Construction	A	934	1,007	1,174	1,809	2,720	4,949	11,522	
	B	934	957	1,053	1,396	1,737	2,189	2,846	
	C	100	105.2	111.5	129.6	156.6	226.1	404.9	

		1389–90	1390–91	1391–92	1393–94	1394–95	1394–95	1395–96	1396–97
		(1969–70)	(1970–71)	(1971–72)	(1972–73)	(1973–74)	(1974–75)	(1975–76)	(1976–77)
Transport and	A	1,243	1,479	1,567	2,121	2,718	3,946	5,776	
Communications	B	1,243	1,468	1,544	1,849	2,224	2,721	3,370	
	C	100	100.8	101.5	114.7	122.2	145.0	171.4	
Business and	A	2,216	2,387	2,635	3,415	4,773	6,598	9,913	
Personal	B	2,216	2,309	2,482	2,827	3,226	3,706	4,352	
Services	C	100	103.4	106.2	120.8	148.0	178.0	227.8	
Government	A	1,678	1,805	2,145	2,534	3,490	4,990	8,152	
Services	B	1,678	1,722	1,834	1,981	2,177	2,438	2,730	
	C	100	104.8	117.0	127.9	160.3	204.7	295.0	
Total GDP	A	17,153	22,581	27,858	40,139	98,839	133,834	154,583	
(factor cost)	B	17,153	19,582	22,621	27,133	31,247	32,188	34,890	
	C	100	115.3	123.2	147.9	316.3	415.8	443.1	
Total GDP	A	17,399	22,921	28,258	40,603	99,315	134,211	155,053	193,100
(market prices)	B	17,399	19,907	22,963	27,495	31,643	32,372	35,092	40,700
	C	100	115.1	123.1	147.7	313.9	414.6	441.9	474.4

Note: The national accounts are in terms of fiscal years as indicated in Table No 3.
Sources: SAMA, *Annual Report 1397 (1977)*, and earlier issues.

TABLE NO 4B: GROSS DOMESTIC PRODUCT BY BROAD SECTORS—OIL AND NON-OIL SECTORS (at factor cost, millions of Saudi Rials)

		1389–90	1390–91	1391–92	1392–93	1393–94	1394–95	1395–96	1396–97
		(1969–70)	(1970–71)	(1971–72)	(1972–73)	(1973–74)	(1974–75)	(1975–76)	(1976–77)
Oil	A	9,347	14,328	18,673	28,684	83,410	111,206	116,332	140,934
	B	9,347	11,542	14,014	17,413	20,063	19,058	19,191	22,172
	C	100	124.1	133.2	164.7	415.7	583.5	606.2	635.6
Non-Oil Sector	A	7,806	8,235	9,184	11,403	15,430	22,629	38,251	52,128
	B	7,806	8.040	8,607	9,720	11,183	13,127	15,700	18,205
	C	100	102.4	106.7	117.3	138.0	172.4	243.6	286.3
Of which,									
Private	A	5,700	5,841	6,308	7,765	10,133	13,971	20,405	30,782
Non-oil	B	5,700	5,747	6,127	6,926	7,833	9,018	10,525	12,420
	C	100	100.8	103.0	112.1	129.4	154.9	193.9	247.8
Government	A	2,106	2,412	2,876	3,638	5,297	,658	17,846	21,346
Non-Oil	B	2,106	2,293	2,480	2,794	3,350	4,104	5,175	5,785
	C	100	105.2	116.0	130.2	158.1	211.0	344.9	369.0
Total	A	17,153	22,581	27,857	40,087	98,840	133,835	154,583	193,062
GDP	B	17,153	19,582	22,621	27,133	31,246	32,186	34,891	40,376
	C	100	115.3	123.2	147.7	316.3	415.8	443.0	478.2

Notes:
[1] The figures for total GDP for 1389–90 (1969–70) are from official sources. The sectorial breakdown in Table 4B is the author's own estimate (with respect to 1969–70).
[2] There are some minor discrepancies between the data in Table 4A and Table 4B, apparently due to revised estimates in the latter. However, the discrepancies are not significant.
[3] The definition of the oil sector in Table 4B is somewhat broader than that indicated by the first two sectors in Table 4A; however, the differences are not significant.
Source: SAMA, *Annual Report 1397 (1977)*, p. 43.

TABLE NO 4C: AVERAGE ANNUAL REAL RATES OF GROWTH 1389–90 (1969–70) to 1396–97 (1976–77)

Oil Sector	13.1%
Non-oil Sector	12.9%
Of which	
Private non-oil sector	*11.8%*
Government non-oil sector	*15.3%*
Total Gross Domestic Product	**13.0%**

TABLE NO 5: EXPENDITURE ON GROSS DOMESTIC PRODUCT (current market prices, in million Saudi rials; million dollars in parentheses)

	1389-90	1390-91	1391-92	1392-93	1393-94	1394-95	1395-96	1396-97
	1969-70	1970-71	1971-72	1972-73	1973-74	1974-75	1975-76	1976-77
Private Consumption	5,859	6,412	6,914	7,896	9,828	13,828	18,923	25,307
Government Consumption	3,421	3,798	4,285	5,335	9,864	15,911	28,197	50,019
Gross Fixed Capital Formation	2,597	2,832	3,403	5,694	8,400	14,866	33,743	60,860
Changes in Stocks	209	-205	95	-113	835	2,402	2,091	-2,993
Exports (Goods and Services)	10,302	15,189	19,862	30,012	85,682	114,641	120,284	140,321
	(2,289)	(3,375)	(4,696)	(7,637)	(24,135)	(32,568)	(34,358)	(39,751)
Less—Imports (Goods and Services)	4,990	5,205	6,303	8,272	15,293	27,257	48,184	72,763
	(1,109)	(1,157)	(1,499)	(2,105)	(4,308)	(7,743)	(13,650)	(20,613)
Total GDP Market Prices	17,398	22,921	28,257	40,551	99,315	134,210	155,053	200,752
	(3,866)	(5,094)	(6,690)	(10,318)	(27,976)	(38,128)	(43,924)	(56,870)
Gross Domestic Fixed Capital Formation								
By Sector								
Government	1,214	1,204	1,443	1,985	3,416	7,348	23,421	39,987
Non-Oil Private	1,056	1,150	1,289	1,669	2,351	3,859	5,926	17,382
Oil Sector	327	577	671	2,040	2,632	3,659	4,397	4,491
By Type								
Construction	1,968	2,196	2,595	4,706	6,214	11,505	27,060	52,493
Machinery and Equipment	629	736	808	988	2,186	3,361	6,683	8,377

Note: The national accounts are in terms of fiscal years as indicated in Table No 3.
Source: SAMA, Annual Report 1397 (1977); IMF, International Financial Statistics, various issues.

TABLE NO 6: BALANCE OF PAYMENTS AND MONETARY SURVEY—SELECTED DATA (in million dollars—except for price index and money supply which indicate percentage changes from previous year)

	1969	1970	1971	1972	1973	1974	1975	1976	1977
Exports-Goods	1,785	2,089	3,505	4,328	7,531	20,091	27,150	35,467	40,084
Exports-Services	235	283	341	464	764	2,556	3,296	4,647	6,127
Imports-Goods	825	829	866	1,275	2,103	3,713	5,998	10,396	14,355
Imports-services	1,045	1,208	1,795	1,619	3,098	4,394	6,537	11,118	13,674
Private transfers	134	183	208	267	392	518	852	1,473	1,504
Export surplus	7	52	977	1,631	2,702	24,022	17,059	17,127	16,678
Government transfers	93	81	68	157	498	1,015	3,128	3,328	3,887
Current account surplus	-86	71	909	1,474	2,204	23,007	13,931	13,798	12,793
Foreign assets (net)	824	957	1,760	3,154	5,082	20,130	39,323	52,255	60,665
International reserves	607	662	1,444	2,500	3,877	14,285	23,319	27,025	30,034
Consumer Price Index (% change)	3.4	0.2	4.5	4.4	16.6	21.4	34.6	31.6	11.3
Money Supply (% change)	5.7	6.1	14.3	40.7	35.0	45.5	79.2	66.5	50.3

Notes:
[1] Exports and imports of goods are fob figures.
[2] Exports of services are largely from interest and dividends received from foreign investments. Much smaller sums are from the pilgrimage and some other sources.
[3] The import of services includes payments to Aramco and other oil companies operating in the country; freight, insurance and other expenditures related to commodity imports; travel expenditures of Saudis going abroad; and, especially in recent years, large payments by the government for the services of foreign contractors and consultants. It appears that payments related to military imports are also included, at least in part, in the import of services.
[4] The export surplus was calculated after deducting private transfers, mainly remittances by foreign workers, since these also represent the importation of services, i.e. labour services.
[5] The figures for "net foreign assets" are for the central bank plus other banks in the country. In recent years the central bank held about 98% of net foreign assets. International reserves represent that part of foreign assets considered liquid. Of the $30,034m held at the end of 1977, foreign exchange accounted for $27,212m. The balance was in gold and the reserve position in the IMF. The figures for foreign assets and international reserves in the table are end-of-year figures.

SAUDI OIL DEFICITS

[6] The calculation of the export surplus and the surplus on current account may not always tally with the individual items in the balance of payments, due to rounding.

[7] What are termed "government transfers" include both grants and loans. In this item in particular, there have been frequent official major revisions. For example, in the April 1977 issue of the *International Financial Statistics*, the figure given for official transfers in 1975 was $753m; in the August 1977 issue, the figure was raised to $1,588m in 1975; and in the September 1977 issue, the figure was again raised to $3,128m in 1975.

[8] It has already been noted in the text that there are serious doubts with respect to the accuracy of the consumer price index. Most observers believe that it is seriously understated. As for other official price indices, see the implicit deflators in Tables Nos 4A, 4B.

[9] The money supply includes M_1 and M_2 and is in Saudi rials. The calculation was based on end-of-year data.

Source: IMF, *International Financial Statistics*, various issues.

NOTES

1. *Middle East Economic Digest (MEED)*, London; 29 September 1978, p. 36.
2. International Monetary Fund (IMF) *International Financial Statistics (IFS)*, December 1978, p. 319. *IMF Survey*, 4 September 1978, pp. 264–66.
3. See Table No 1.
4. *Institute of Development Studies Bulletin*, Special Issue "Oil and Development," October 1974, p. 29. The reference is to Saudi Arabian light crude oil, often referred to as "marker crude" which serves as a benchmark for pricing the various grades of crude oil.
5. *Ibid*, p. 75.
6. Saudi Arabian Monetary Agency (SAMA) *Annual Report 1392–93*, p. 93.
7. See Table No 3.
8. IMF, *IFS*, May 1978, p. 369.
9. See Table No 2.
10. The Saudi Rial has been revalued a number of times since December 1971. In more recent years it has been pegged to the changes in the value of the Special Drawing Rights (SDRs) of the IMF.
11. See Table No 3.
12. The reference to imports in this context is to goods and services as well as what are referred to in the Saudi balance of payments as "private transfers." These are essentially the remittances of foreign workers in Saudi Arabia. In other words, they constitute a payment for an imported factor of production. Other countries such as Jordan and Egypt, which are the recipients of remittances from their nationals working abroad, include these in the category of exports of services. See IMF, *IFS*, May 1978, pp. 330, 331, 369.
13. *Ibid*, p. 49.
14. See Table No 6.
15. SAMA *Annual Report 1391–92*, p. 107.
16. See Table No 4A and 4B. Also, D. A. Wells, *Saudi Arabian Development Strategy* (Washington, DC: American Enterprise Institute for Public Policy Research, 1976), pp. 18–21.
17. See Table No 4A and 4B.
18. IMF, *IFS*, May 1978, pp. 330–1. The official data on expenditures on GDP are given only in current prices. Since the bulk of investment is on construction (see Table No 5), the implicit price deflator of the construction sector has been used as the deflator for gross fixed capital formation as a whole. See Table No 4A.
19. As noted above, expenditures on GDP are given in current prices only. The official cost of living index has been used to deflate these figures. They indicate a growth rate of real private consumption of 13.0% pa in 1964–65 to 1969–70, and 4.4% pa from 1969–70 to 1972–73. Population figures are notoriously poor in Saudi Arabia. It is known that, in addition to the natural increase, probably of c. 2.5–3% pa, there was considerable migration to Saudi Arabia, rising with the increasing pace of investment. See IMF, *IFS*, May 1978, pp. 330–1; SAMA *Annual Report 1397 (1977)*, p. 142; and Table No 5.
20. Wells, *op. cit.*, pp. 23–24.
21. *Oil and Development*, October 1974, pp. 12–14.
22. SAMA *Annual Report 1395 (1975)*, p. 113; IMF, *IFS*, November 1975, pp. 322–23.
23. *MEED*, 11 October 1974, p. 1187.
24. *Ibid*, 13 April 1975, p. 5. G. B. Ghobrial, "OPEC's Economic Significance," in R. A. Stone, *OPEC and the Middle East* (New York: Praeger), pp. 92–95.
25. *New York Times, (NYT)*, 13 February 1975, p. 1.
26. *NYT*, 14 November 1975, p. 3.
27. IMF, *IFS*, various issues; *MEED*, 15 September 1978, pp. 17–18.
28. Morgan Guaranty Trust Company, *World Financial Markets*, July 1978, p. 3.

29. Subcommittee on Foreign Economic Policy of the Committee on Foreign Relations, US Senate, *International Debt, The Banks and US Foreign Policy* (Washington, DC, August 1977), pp. 33-34.
30. Some studies deal with the non-Communist world, and then make estimates for anticipated net exports or imports from the Communist bloc to the other oil-consuming countries.
31. Often these studies use a number of variants with respect to each of the variables, and then offer alternate projections.
32. See Table No 1.
33. Lawrence Klein, "Oil and the World Economy" in *Economic Impact* No 3 (1978), p. 53; published in Washington, DC. For growth in energy and oil consumption, see Table No 1.
34. *Business Week*, 6 November 1978, pp. 100, 105.
35. IMF, *IFS*, September 1978, p. 398; The British Petroleum Company Ltd, *BP Statistical Review of the World Oil Industry 1977* (London, 1978), p. 25.
36. *Ibid.*
37. *Oil and Development*, October 1974, p. 30.
38. *Ibid.*
39. See Table No 1.
40. *Business Week*, 5 December 1977.
41. See Table No 1.
42. Morgan Guaranty Trust Company, *World Financial Markets*, July 1978, p. 3.
43. See Table No 1.
44. *Washington Post (WP)*, 17 February 1976; *The Middle East*, London; June 1976, p. 47.
45. *WP*, 17 February 1976.
46. *WP*, 18 and 30 December 1976; *Daily Telegraph*, London; 30 December 1976.
47. SAMA *Annual Report 1397 (1977)*, p. 17.
48. *Ibid*, pp. 126, 129.
49. *Ibid*, p. 17.
50. *Business Week*, 30 January 1978, p. 32; 20 February 1978, p. 41-42; *Events*, London; 29 July 1977; Economist Intelligence Unit, *Quarterly Economic Review-Oil in the Middle East*, No 1 (1978), pp. 2-4.
51. *MEED*, 16 September 1977, p. 20.
52. *The Guardian*, 12 September 1977.
53. *Petroleum Economist*, September 1978, p. 399.
54. IMF, *IFS*, October 1978, p. 317.
55. *BP Statistical Review of the World Oil Industry 1977*, pp. 6, 8.
56. See Table No 1.
57. *Petroleum Economist*, January 1978, p. 2.
58. *Events*, 21 April 1978, p. 38; *The Middle East*, August 1978, pp. 73-74.
59. *Petroleum Economist*, October 1978, p. 406.
60. *Ibid*, p. 445.
61. *Petroleum Economist*, August 1978, p. 323; *Arab Economist*, September 1978, p. 36; *MEED*, 27 October 1978, p. 7; Economist Intelligence Unit, *Oil in the Middle East— Quarterly Economic Review*, No 2 (1978), p. 2.
62. *An-Nahar Arab Report and Memo*, 10 April 1978, p. 9.
63. *Petroleum Economist*, September 1978, p. 400.
64. See Table No 3.
65. US-Saudi Arabian Joint Commission on Economic Co-operation, *Summary of Saudi Arabian Five-Year Development Plan (1975-1980)*, (Washington DC, 1975), pp. 1-19. This publication will be referred to subsequently as *The Development Plan*.
66. *Ibid*, pp. 10-53.
67. *Middle East Annual Review 1977*, London; p. 45.
68. See Table No 3.
69. SAMA *Annual Report 1397 (1977)*, p. 22; IMF, *IFS*, October 1978, pp. 316-17.
70. See Tables No 4A and 4B.
71. Kingdom of Saudi Arabia Central Department of Statistics, *The Statistical Indicator 1977*, Tables Nos 2-1, 2-2.
72. IMF, *IFS*, October 1978, p. 316.
73. R. Knauerhase, *The Saudi Arabian Economy* (New York: Praeger, 1975), p. 13.
74. *MEED*, 18 April 1975, p. 39.
75. *Arab Economist*, September 1978, p. 13.
76. US Senate Committee on Energy and Natural Resources, *Access to Oil—The United States Relationships with Saudi Arabia and Iran* (December 1977), p. 37.
77. Assuming that the native Saudi population numbered 4m in 1974, and that the rate of natural increase was 3%, the number of Saudis increased by about 120,000 in that year.

The official figures for the number of foreigners entering the country in 1974 with residence permits was 144,000, plus 15,000 who were given temporary permits. See Kingdom of Saudi Arabia *Statistical Yearbook*, 1395-1975, p. 276. It is well known, and recent actions on the part of Saudi authorities against illegal residents confirm this, that many entered the country illegally. Therefore, an assumed population growth rate of 6-7% pa is probably a conservative figure. Given the official rise of 7.5% pa in private consumption, the per capita increase was probably very small.

78. Economist Intelligence Unit, *Saudi Arabia-Quarterly Economic Review*, 1978, p. 9.
79. Economist Intelligence Unit, *Saudi Arabia-Quarterly Economic Review*, No 4 (1977), p. 8; *Middle East Currency Reports*, February-March 1978, p. 20.
80. IMF, *IFS*, October 1978, p. 224.
81. The military budgets are from SAMA, *Annual Report 1397 (1977)*, p. 123; the latter report is from *MEED*, 15 September 1978, p. 37.
82. Economist Intelligence Unit, *Saudi Arabia-Quarterly Economic Review*, No 2 (1978), p. 5.
83. *MEED*, 15 September 1978, p. 37.
84. US Senate Committee, *Access to Oil: The United States Relationships with Saudi Arabia and Iran,* December 1977, p. 50.
85. See Table No 5.
86. See Table No 5. Expenditures on GDP are given only in current market prices. Since the bulk of investment is on construction, the deflator for construction in Table No 4A has been used as the deflator for gross fixed capital formation.
87. SAMA *Annual Report 1397 (1977)*, pp. 140-41; See Table No 6.
88. As of 1 April 1978, there appears to have been a redefinition of Saudi international reserves, although the available data at this writing do not indicate its nature. However, there was a decline from $30,034m at the end of 1977 to $28,727m at the end of March 1978. As of the end of April 1978, the international reserves were given as $22,630m according to the new definition. How much of the decline during the month of April represents a real decline and how much is due to the redefinition of international reserves is not clear. From the end of April 1978 to the end of September 1978, reserves dropped again to $20,377m. At this writing, data on net foreign assets are available only until March 1978. See IMF, *IFS*, December 1978, pp. 318-19.
89. See Table No 6. The import figures include "private transfers" as they are essentially payments for imported labour services.
90. Economist Intelligence Unit, *Saudi Arabia-Quarterly Economic Review*, No 1 (1978), p. 17; *MEED*, Special Report-Saudi Arabia, August 1978, p. 53.
91. *Financial Times (FT)*, London; 20 March 1978.
92. Kingdom of Saudi Arabia, Central Department of Statistics, *The Statistical Indicator, 1977*, Table 9-1 to -10.
93. *Ibid. FT*, 28 March 1977, p. 16.
94. *MEED*, 14 April 1978, p. 35.
95. *FT*, 17 April 1978, p. 26.
96. *Arab Economist*, September 1978, p. 16.
97. *MEED*, Special Report-Saudi Arabia, August 1978, pp. 53-54.
98. R. Knauerhase, "Saudi Arabia's Economy at the beginning of the 1970s," *Middle East Journal*, Spring 1974, p. 128.
99. *FT*, 28 March 1978, p. 16. Author's emphasis.
100. Kingdom of Saudi Arabia, *Statistical Yearbook* 1395-1975, p. 252.
101. US Senate Committee Report, *Access to Oil—The United States Relationships with Saudi Arabia and Iran*, December 1977, p. 44.
102. *MEED*, 22 September 1978, p. 33.
103. *MEED*, 10 June 1977, p. 38.
104. IMF, *IFS*, October 1978, p. 316.
105. *Ibid.*
106. *MEED*, Special Report—Construction, June 1978, pp. 15-16.
107. See implicit price deflator for construction in Table No 4A.
108. *MEED*, 3 November 1978, p. 36.
109. *MEED*, Special Report—Saudi Arabia, December 1976, p. 11.
110. T. H. Moran, *Oil Prices and the Future of OPEC* (Washington DC: Resources for the Future, 1978), pp. 13-16.
111. SAMA, *Annual Report 1397 (1977)*, p. 11.
112. Moran, *op. cit.,* p. 7.
113. *WP*, 23 May 1977.
114. *Events*, 14 July 1978, pp. 28-29; *MEED*, 17 November 1978, p. 5.
115. *The Development Plan*, p. 47.

116. SAMA, *Annual Report 1397 (1977)*, pp. 65–70.
117. *MEED*, Special Report—Saudi Arabia, August 1978, p. 15.
118. *Middle East Currency Reports*, London; February-March 1978, p. 52.
119. *MEED*, 30 June 1978, pp. 12–14; *FT*, 20 March 1978, p. 23.
120. *FT*, 28 March 1978, p. 14.
121. *MEED*, Special Report—Saudi Arabia, August 1978, p. 79.
122. Economist Intelligence Unit, *Quarterly Economic Review—Saudi Arabia*, No 3 (1978), pp. 11–12.
123. Electric Power Research Institute, *Outlook for World Oil into the 21st Century*. Prepared by the Petroleum Industry Research Foundation in New York, May 1978, Summary and Chapter One.
124. *MEED*, 19 September 1977, p. 19.
125. *Petroleum Economist*, October 1978, pp. 426–28.
126. *Ibid.*
127. Irving Trust Company, *The Economic View from One Wall Street*, December 1977 and April 1978.
128. *Ibid.*
129. *Wall Street Journal*, 5 July 1978, p. 8.
130. *The Economist*, 9 September 1978, p. 89.
131. *Events*, 30 June 1978, p. 60.
132. *Petroleum Economist*, March 1978, pp. 86–87.
133. *Ibid*, September 1978, p. 397.
134. *Business Week*, 30 May 1977, p. 25.
135. *Arab Economist*, June 1978, p. 36.
136. *Ibid*, December 1977, pp. 16–17.
137. *Petroleum Economist*, October 1978, p. 406.
138. *Newsweek*, 24 March 1975, p. 45.
139. *Petroleum Economist*, August 1978, p. 327.
140. Wells, *op. cit.*, pp. 23–24.
141. *The Development Plan*, p. 21.
142. See, for example, the press interview by the Minister of Industry, *NYT*, 10 July 1977, p. 6F.
143. *Arab Economist*, August 1978, p. 12.
144. *MEED*, Special Report—Construction, June 1978, pp. 15–16.
145. Moran, *op. cit.*, pp. 17–19.
146. See Table No 3.
147. 60% of total outlays have been assumed for projects. Measured in current dollars, total expenditures in 1978–79 would remain approximately at the previous year's level. See Table No 3.
148. *MEED*, 1 December 1978, p. 41.
149. *Arab Economist*, August 1978, p. 32–33.
150. *Fortune*, 31 July 1978, p. 113.
151. See, for example, *FT*, 20 March 1978; *NYT*, 25 November 1976, p. 8.
152. *Arab Economist*, September 1978, p. 35.
153. *NYT*, 10 July 1977, p. 6F.
154. Moran, *op. cit.*, p. 28.
155. Moran, *op. cit.*, pp. 20, 24.
156. Economist Intelligence Unit, *Quarterly Economic Review—Saudi Arabia*, No 2 (1978), p. 7.
157. *MEED*, 17 March 1978, p. 35.
158. *MEED*, 3 November 1978, p. 39.
159. *MEED*, Special Report—Saudi Arabia, August 1978, pp. 35–36; *NYT*, 24 April 1978, p. D1, and 5 June 1978, p. D1.
160. *Middle East Currency Reports*, February-March 1978, p. 51.
161. *Ibid*, May 1977, p. 32.
162. *MEED*, 22 July 1977, p. 15.
163. *MEED*, 27 October 1978, p. 41.
164. IMF, *IFS*, October 1978, p. 132.
165. See Table No 6.
166. *MEED*, 9 June 1978, p. 44.
167. IMF, *IFS*, October 1978, p. 316.
168. The calculation is in current dollars. See SAMA *Annual Report 1397 (1977)* p. 137.
169. See Table No 3.
170. *Events*, 25 March 1977, p. 34.
171. *MEED*, 13 October 1978, p. 37.

172. *MEED*, 7 September 1977, p. 24.
173. *Arab Economist*, August 1978, p. 34.
174. Mohammed El Behriry in R. A. Stone, *OPEC and the Middle East* (New York: Praeger, 1977), p. 207-8.
175. *Ibid.*
176. *NYT*, 25 December 1977, p. 16.
177. *MEED*, 28 July 1978, p. 35.
178. H. Maull, *Oil and Influence: The Oil Weapon Examined* (London: The International Institute for Strategic Studies, 1975), pp. 29-30.
179. *MEED*, 13 January 1978, p. 28.
180. Petroleum Industry Research Foundation, *Outlook for World Oil into the 21st Century*, prepared for the Electric Power Research Institute, May 1978, p. 6-15.
181. *Arab Economist*, August 1978, p. 35.
182. Economist Intelligence Unit, *Quarterly Economic Review—Oil in the Middle East*, No 2 (1978), p. 2.
183. *Events*, 25 March 1977, p. 3.
184. Economist Intelligence Unit, *Quarterly Economic Review—Saudi Arabia*, No 1 (1978), p. 5.
185. *Petroleum Economist*, September 1978, p. 400.
186. *Arab Economist*, August 1978, p. 35.
187. *Petroleum Economist*, December 1978, p. 537; Table No 1.
188. For this estimate the IMF index of export prices of the industrial countries has been used—a reasonable basis for estimating the prices of OPEC imports. The price of oil is also from the IMF monthly *International Financial Statistics*. The latest available data for the export price index are for the second quarter of 1978. The indicated decline in the constant dollar price of oil is 8% between the first quarter of 1974 and the second quarter of 1978. Assuming that the export price index rose between the second and fourth quarters of 1978 at the same rate as in the previous two quarters, the constant dollar price of oil was 13% lower in the last quarter of 1978. The price of oil used in this calculation is for prices at Ra's Tannūrah in Saudi Arabia. The prices of service exports rose far more rapidly. This is particularly true of labour, management and transportation services imported by Saudi Arabia and other OPEC countries from the industrial countries.
189. Morgan Guaranty Trust Company, *World Financial Markets*, June 1978, p. 3; July 1978, p. 3.
190. *Petroleum Economist*, October 1978, p. 435.
191. SAMA, *Annual Report 1395 (1975)*, pp. 2-3.
192. *MEED*, Special Report—Saudi Arabia, August 1978, p. 21.
193. *Petroleum Economist*, December 1978, pp. 504, 527-8.

Oil Statistics

CRUDE OIL PRODUCTION IN SELECTED COUNTRIES (thousand b/d)

	1976	1977	% change
Soviet Union	10,443	10,995	+5.0
United States	9,724	9,931	+1.8
Saudi Arabia	8,580	9,203	+7.0
Iran	5,883	5,663	-4.0
Iraq	2,176	2,266	+3.8
Venezuela	2,294	2,235	-2.9
Nigeria	2,067	2,098	+1.2
Libya	1,928	2,078	+7.4
United Arab Emirates	1,905	2,009	+5.1
Kuwait	2,148	1,971	-8.5
World Total	**59,245**	**61,914**	**+4.2**
OAPEC Countries	18,863	19,710	+4.2
OPEC Countries	30,464	31,139	+1.9

Source: *Arab Oil and Gas*, 16 March 1978.

WORLD CRUDE PRODUCTION (million barrels)

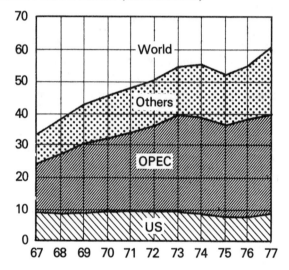

Source: *World Oil*, 15 February 1978.

ANNUAL CRUDE OIL PRODUCTION OF MAJOR MIDDLE EAST OIL PRODUCERS (million barrels)

	1973	1974	1975	1976	1977
Saudi Arabia	2,774	3,096	2,583	3,140	3,356
Iran	2,152	2,211	1,965	2,166	2,080
Iraq	718	681	821	835	827
Libya	796	551	551	700	757
Kuwait	1,103	930	761	787	704
Abu Dhabi	476	516	512	583	608
Qatar	208	189	160	178	161
Dubai	80	88	93	115	116

Source: *Petroleum Economist*, June 1978.

MIDDLE EAST OIL PRODUCTION (million b/d)

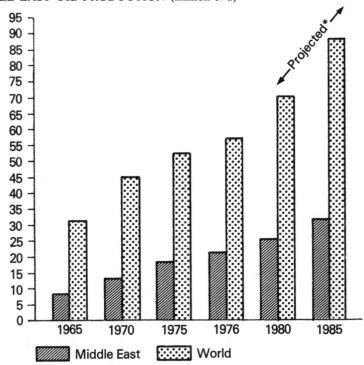

■ Middle East ▒ World

*Oil production required to satisfy world oil demand.

Source: Oil and Gas Journal, August 1977.

OPEC COUNTRIES 1976: OIL AND GAS

	Crude Oil				Natural Gas	
	Production *Million b/d*	*Exports* *Million b/d*	*Consumption* *Million b/d*	*Reserves* *Billion bls*	*Production* *Billion cu m*	*Reserves* *Billion cu m*
Algeria	1.07	.944	.083	6.8	24.4	3,564
Ecuador	0.19	.168	.043	1.7	0.3	340
Gabon	0.22	.196	.006	2.1	1.8	71
Indonesia	1.50	1.227	.280	10.5	8.7	680
Iran	5.88	5.214	.431	63.0	50.3	9,348
Iraq	2.42	2.241	.100	34.0	13.3	764
Kuwait	2.15	1.791	.030	67.4	11.2	898
Libya	1.93	1.847	.054	25.5	17.9	731
Nigeria	2.07	2.013	.110	19.5	22.1	1,246
Qatar	0.50	.487	.006	5.7	4.7	779
Saudi Arabia	8.58	8.032	.160	150.0	47.1	1,785
U.A.E.	1.94	1.933	.012	30.5	15.4	636
Venezuela	2.29	1.370	.231	18.3	37.1	1,190
Total OPEC	**30.74**	**27.463**	**1.501**	**441.3***	**254.3**	**22,174†**
Total World	56.97	32.200	—	652.0	—	63,195

*Including 6.3 for the Neutral Zone.
†Including 142 for Neutral Zone.
Source: December 1977 *OPEC Review* (published by the OPEC Secretariat in Vienna); *Petroleum Economist*, February 1978.

OPEC PRODUCTION COMPARED WITH OTHER MAJOR OIL PRODUCERS (million barrels)

Producer	Production			% of World Total in 1977
	1973	1975	1977	
OPEC	11,299	9,935	11,377	50.3
of which:				
Saudi Arabia	2,774	2,583	3,356	14.8
Iran	2,152	1,965	2,080	9.2
Soviet Union	3,140	3,600	4,013	17.7
United States	3,995	3,648	3,625	16.0
Canada	716	576	539	2.4
World Total	**21,134**	**20,117**	**22,610**	—

Source: Derived from *Petroleum Economist*, June 1978.

HOW MIDDLE EAST OIL RESERVES HAVE GROWN (million barrels)

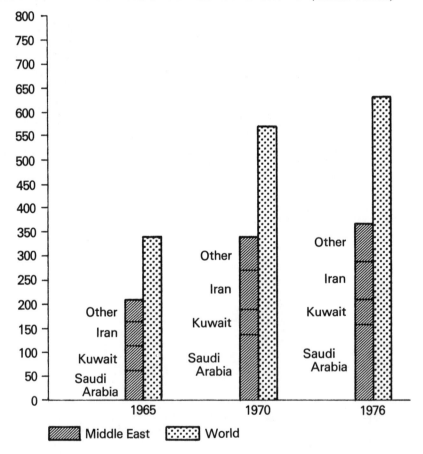

Source: *Oil and Gas Journal*, August 1977.

OIL STATISTICS

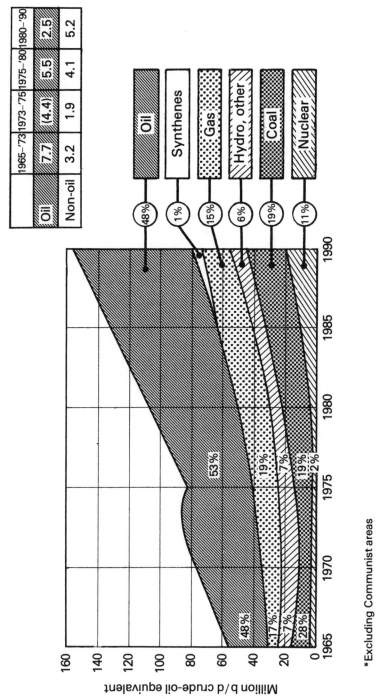

WORLD ENERGY SUPPLY*

Growth rate %/year

	1965–'73	1973–'75	1975–'80	1980–'90
Oil	7.7	(4.4)	5.5	2.5
Non-oil	3.2	1.9	4.1	5.2

Oil — 48%
Synthenes — 1%
Gas — 15%
Hydro, other — 6%
Coal — 19%
Nuclear — 11%

Million b/d crude-oil equivalent

1965 · 1970 · 1975 · 1980 · 1985 · 1990

48% · 17% · 7% · 28%
53% · 19% · 7% · 19% · 2%

*Excluding Communist areas

Source: Oil and Gas Journal, August 1977.

363

MAJOR OAPEC COUNTRIES' OIL REVENUES (million US dollars)

	1973	1974	1975	1976	1977
Saudi Arabia	4,340	22,574	25,676	37,809	42,384
Iraq	1,843	5,700	7,500	8,500	9,631
United Arab Emirates	900	5,536	6,000	7,000	9,030
Kuwait	1,980	8,645	7,706	8,063	8,934
Libya	2,223	5,999	5,101	7,500	8,850
Algeria	988	3,299	3,262	3,699	4,106
Qatar	464	1,802	1,700	2,092	2,071
Total	12,738	53,555	56,945	74,663	85,006

Source: *Arab Oil and Gas*, 16 June 1978.

INDEX OF MAJOR OAPEC COUNTRIES' OIL REVENUES (1972 = 100)

	1973	1974	1975	1976	1977
Saudi Arabia	158	822	935	1,377	1,544
Iraq	320	991	1,304	1,478	1,675
United Arab Emirates	163	1,005	1,089	1,270	1,639
Kuwait	121	529	472	493	547
Libya	142	384	326	480	566
Algeria	161	538	532	603	670
Qatar	182	707	667	820	812
Total	161	675	718	941	1,071

Source: Derived from *Arab Oil and Gas*, 16 June 1978.

NET OIL IMPORTS BY MAJOR OECD COUNTRIES (million tonnes)

	1960	1972	1976	1977[e]
United States	66.3	221.2	350.5	413.6
Japan[1]	29.9	229.0	257.6	268.7
West Germany	27.1	132.5	135.0	132.2
France	25.4	110.9	115.1	107.0
Italy	19.3	88.6	91.8	89.7
United Kingdom	45.3	109.7	79.3	51.2
Spain	4.9	31.7	46.0	45.3
Sweden	13.1	27.2	28.3	26.5
Netherlands	9.1	27.4	26.5	24.9

[e] Estimate.
[1] Based on fiscal year.
N.B. Bunkers are considered as exports.
Source: OECD.

Also see Tables 1 and 2 in the essay, "Deficits in Saudi Arabia: Their Meaning and Possible Implication."

PART II
COUNTRY BY COUNTRY
REVIEW

MIDDLE EAST COUNTRIES
BASIC DATA

Country	Capital	Most Important Natural Resources	Area 1000 Km[2]	Population in million (mid-1976)	GNP per capita (US$ 1975)
Bahrain	Manāma	Crude Oil	0.6	0.27[1]	2,210
Egypt	Cairo	Cotton, Crude oil, Cereals, Rice, Fruits, Vegetables, Iron	1,000	38.07[1]	260
Iran	Tehran	Crude Oil, Natural Gas	1,648	33.40[1]	1,660
Iraq	Baghdad	Crude Oil, Dates, Cement	435	11.51[1]	1,250
Israel	Jerusalem	Citrus Fruits, Potash	20.7	3.46	3,790
Jordan	Amman	Phosphates, Vegetables, Fruits	98	2.78[1]	460
Kuwait	Kuwait	Crude Oil	24	1.03[1]	15,190
Lebanon	Beirut	Fruits, Citrus Fruits, Vegetables, Forests	10.4	2.96[1, 2]	1,070[4]
Libya	Tripoli	Crude Oil, Vegetables, Fruits	1,760	2.44[1, 3]	5,530
Oman	Muscat	Crude Oil	212	0.79[1, 2]	2,300
Qatar	Doha	Crude Oil	20	0.10[1, 2]	10,970
Saudi Arabia	Riyadh	Crude Oil	2,400	9.24[1, 2]	4,010
Sudan	Khartoum	Cotton, Gum, Cereals	2,500	16.13[1]	270
Syria	Damascus	Cotton, Crude Oil, Vegetables, Fruits, Livestock	185	7.60[1]	720
Turkey	Ankara	Cotton, Wool, Tobacco, Chrome, Copper	780	40.16[1]	900
United Arab Emirates	Abu Dhabi	Crude Oil	83	0.23[1, 2]	13,600
Yemen (North)	San'ā	Coffee, Cotton, Maize, Fish	195	6.87[1, 2]	200
Yemen (South)	Aden	Coffee, Fish	288	1.75[1]	250

Sources: UN, *Monthly Bulletin of Statistics* (population) ; World Bank, *Atlas* (GNP).
Notes: [1] "estimates of questionable reliability". [2] estimates computed by UN. [3] 1975. [4] 1974.

CURRENCIES

Country	Currency Unit		Approximate Equivalent in other currencies*				
			US Dollar	Pound Sterling	Deutsche mark	Swiss Franc	French Franc
Bahrain	Bahraini Dinar = 1000 Fils		2.61	1.25	4.51	3.89	10.40
Egypt	Egyptian Pound = 1000 Milliemes	(1)	2.56	1.27	4.62	3.87	10.70
		(2)	1.45	0.722	2.62	2.20	6.06
Iran	Iranian Riyal = 100 Dinars		0.014	0.007	0.025	0.021	0.057
Iraq	Iraqi Dinar = 1000 Fils		3.39	1.63	5.85	5.03	13.50
Israel†	Israeli Pound = 100 Agorot		0.053	0.025	0.091	0.078	0.210
Jordan	Jordanian Dinar = 1000 Fils		3.42	1.67	5.90	5.08	13.62
Kuwait	Kuwaiti Dinar = 1000 Fils		3.77	1.80	6.51	5.60	14.99
Lebanon	Lebanese Pound = 100 Piastres		0.338	0.161	0.585	0.503	1.349
Libya	Libyan Dinar = 1000 Dirhams		3.38	1.61	5.84	5.02	13.47
Oman	Omani Riyal = 1000 Baiza		2.89	1.38	5.00	4.30	11.52
Qatar	Qatar Riyal = 100 Dirhams		0.261	0.124	0.450	0.388	1.038
Saudi Arabia	Saudi Riyal = 100 Halalas		0.309	0.147	0.533	0.459	1.229
Sudan	Sudanese Pound = 1000 Milliemes		2.50	1.19	4.32	3.72	9.97
Syria	Syrian Pound = 100 Piastres		0.255	0.121	0.440	0.389	1.016
Turkey	Turkish Lira = 100 Kurus		0.040	0.020	0.069	0.059	0.159
United Arab Emirates	Dirham = 100 Fils		0.261	0.125	0.451	0.388	1.040
Yemen (North)	Riyal = 100 Fils		0.220	0.105	0.380	0.327	0.876
Yemen (South)	Yemeni Dinar = 1000 Fils		2.93	1.40	5.06	4.36	11.66
US$ rate $1 =				0.4776	1.7275	1.4863	3.9870

*As in London on 30 October 1978. †As in Tel Aviv on 23 November 1978. [1] Official rate. [2] Parallel market rate.
Note: Exchange rates listed are middle rates between buying and selling rates as quoted between banks.

The Arab Republic of Egypt
(Jumhūriyyat Misr al-'Arabiyya)

While Sādāt's peace initiative dominated the scene in foreign affairs, the main feature of Egypt's domestic developments was the fluctuation in the party system, which stemmed from the regime's experimentation with a multi-party system. This political question and the whole range of domestic problems became more urgent as public euphoria subsided in the months following Sādāt's initiative. In particular, Egypt's chronic economic problems remained acute, causing widespread daily hardship.

Despite continuing criticism of the regime and despite the repressive measures taken against its critics, Egyptians continued to see Sādāt as the country's uncontested leader. The highest echelons of the leadership immediately surrounding him remained largely unchanged between the Jerusalem visit and the Camp David agreements, and the army did not try to interfere in politics.

POLITICAL AFFAIRS
SĀDĀT'S LEADERSHIP
SĀDĀT'S POLITICAL POSITION
There was no doubt that Sādāt's dramatic visit to Jerusalem on 19 November 1977 and the Camp David agreements of September 1978 enhanced his popularity and consolidated his control over the domestic situation. This strong position contrasted sharply with events only 11 months before—at the time of the January 1977 food riots, when mass unrest had forced Sādāt to call in the army to control the situation and to impose a complete curfew on Cairo for the first time since 1952 (see *MECS 1976–77*, pp. 288–92). In 1978, Egyptian crowds flocked enthusiastically to greet their leader whenever and wherever he made a public appearance. It became commonplace to see hundreds of thousands of Egyptians lining the streets to watch and participate in huge demonstrations or rallies, many chanting rhythmically: "Our soul, our blood we sacrifice for you, Sādāt!" Sādāt remained the dominant figure and Egypt's ultimate decision-maker.

Nevertheless, there was a great deal of resentment against various aspects of Sādāt's programme. Criticism came from Centrist political forces as well as from the small parliamentary opposition—which became quite vociferous during 1978— and the extraparliamentary radical forces which categorically rejected Sādāt's policies. The criticism was directed mainly against economic hardships, corruption in government, and the negative side-effects of the liberalization process. The beginning of the experiment with the multi-party system created an atmosphere in which not only the government but also Sādāt personally could be exposed to sharp attack.

To ameliorate the economic malaise, the regime had to make a difficult choice between a policy of austerity involving subsidy cuts, and a policy aimed at avoiding social unrest and at preventing a repetition of anything like the 1977 food riots. Towards the end of 1977 and the beginning of 1978, the government tried to cut subsidies on staple foods without making any public announcements. But within a few days, protests about food shortages and soaring prices led the government to restore the subsidies.[1] In spite of this, inflationary pressures caused the prices of basic commodities such as sugar, tea, margarine, soap, matches and cheaper clothing to rise by as much as 50% during the year reviewed, while salaries increased by only 15%, leaving low-income earners in a particularly difficult position.[2]

The issue was exploited by the opposition which summoned the People's Assembly for emergency sessions to discuss these problems.[3] When signs of popular unrest became noticeable in March 1978,[4] Sādāt chose to intervene. In an interview given to *October* magazine, he accused the New Wafd party and the Progressive Unionist Socialist Alignment Party (PUSA) of exploiting the economic grievances and fomenting public unrest. (For the revival of the Wafd, see *MECS 1976-77*, pp. 299-300.) Sādāt called for patience and tolerance and said he was confident that the government would work out solutions to the economic malaise.[5] To counteract criticism, Sādāt decided to raise salaries and to request the resignation of the Deputy Prime Minister for Economic Affairs, 'Abd al-Mun'im al-Qaysūnī.

Sādāt was also obliged to face up to increasing charges of corruption in his government. In his speech on the anniversary of the "corrective revolution" of 15 May 1971, he referred to rumours of cases of corruption involving his name and that of his close associate and former Housing Minister 'Uthmān Ahmad 'Uthmān. Sādāt said he regretted that he was being subjected to "these attempts to cast doubts." He declared: "I have never been [put] in the position of having to defend myself; there is nothing that makes it necessary for me to defend anything."[6] He then passionately defended 'Uthmān, attesting to his honesty, devotion and loyalty to Egypt.

Nevertheless, Sādāt did elaborate on a rumour to the effect that he was holding a sum of £1m in his own name in the Central Bank. He explained that this was a grant by the ruler of Qatar made in 1972 as a down payment for the equipment, engines and transport charges of an aircraft plant he expected to receive from the USSR in May 1972. When the money was not used for nearly two years, 'Abd al-'Azīz Hijāzī (then Prime Minister) told Sādāt that he had used the funds to buy food supplies. Sādāt also dealt with the affair of the pyramid zone tourist project, which had been strongly criticized on two counts: the government's readiness to damage a historical site symbolizing the nation's heritage for the sake of financial gain and allegations that officials dealing with the project had become involved in illegal transactions. Sādāt acknowledged that "such a project might need amendments and adjustments," and added that he had told Prime Minister Mamduh Sālim that if the pyramid area project was wrong, he should examine and correct it; if it could not be corrected, he should cancel it. A few weeks later, the whole project was abandoned.

However, the influence of these criticisms and problems on Sādāt's position of leadership was limited. He continued to enjoy a high degree of popularity, due to his peace initiative and, later, to the Camp David agreements.

THE DOMESTIC INFLUENCE OF THE PEACE INITIATIVE
Sādāt's visit to Jerusalem produced a sense of euphoria in Egypt unknown since the October War in 1973. The gesture was considered an act of supreme heroism and chivalry which, in one fell swoop, elevated Egypt's national pride to a new peak. This appreciation was expressed in the enthusiastic welcome Sādāt received on his return from Jerusalem on 21 November 1977.

Such optimism supported Sādāt's contention that it was possible, and even necessary, to come to terms with Israel in order to free Egypt of its economic burdens and deal with the neglected internal problems aggravated by the military confrontation.[7] Attacks on Sādāt by the media of the "Steadfastness Front" members (see essay on Inter-Arab Relations), accusing him of betraying the Arab world, misjudged the Egyptian domestic situation; in fact, they only intensified the resentment against the Arab states—many of them rich and unaffected by the exigencies of the conflict—who had left Egypt to carry the main burden. Much of the Egyptian resentment was channelled against the Palestinians who were depicted as ungrateful and irresponsible. Anti-Palestinian feelings reached a peak after the assassination, on 18 February 1978, of the chairman of the *al-Ahrām* board of directors, Yūsuf al-Sibāʿī—one of the country's intellectuals who had begun to question Egypt's commitment to the Palestinian cause. [8]

In the initial stage of the peace initiative, criticism of Sādāt's policy was negligible in Egypt compared with the reaction of other Arab countries. The most noteworthy and embarrassing reaction was the resignation of the Foreign Minister, Ismāʿīl Fahmī, and the refusal of his deputy to replace him (see below). However, both lacked public support, and their protest was soon forgotten in the rush of events. The only elements opposing the peace initiative who had some influence over the public were the Leftists (particularly the Soviet-oriented Marxists), some of the Muslim Brethren and other radical Islamic groups siding with the Arab "rejectionists"; but their voices were all but drowned in the tide of general enthusiasm. However, the lack of progress in the negotiations during the first eight months of 1978 had a sobering effect, and the Egyptian public once again became preoccupied with its daily problems. Yet the public disappointment was not translated into criticism of Sādāt but was directed mainly against Israel which was seen as intransigent, unco-operative and clinging to out-dated conceptions (see below: Foreign Affairs).

The Camp David agreements in September 1978 revived popular support for Sādāt's policy. On the eve of the summit, the Egyptian public was sceptical that an agreement could be reached. Even after the accords were published, initial reactions were lukewarm, but public support gradually grew. Although the Fahmī affair repeated itself when his successor as Foreign Minister, Ibrāhīm Kāmil, submitted his resignation—along with other members of the Egyptian delegation—it had even less of an impact. Unlike Fahmī, Kāmil was neither popular nor influential, and from the beginning had been overshadowed by his two principal aides—Butrus Butrus Ghālī and Usāma al-Bāz. Also unlike Fahmī, Kāmil did not leave the foreign service but was retained with the rank of ambassador.

POWER BASES: THE MILITARY
There was no hard evidence during 1978 of criticism against Sādāt in the army. Some rumours of disaffection among the officer corps were reported in Lebanese newspapers and in the media of the "Steadfastness Front" countries, but the Egyptian authorities firmly denied these reports. Sādāt himself ridiculed those who spread such rumours as misguided persons incapable of understanding that the officers in Egypt were professionals who left politics to the politicians. [9] When the former War Minister, Gen ʿAbd al-Ghanī Jamasī, was asked to comment on these reports, he stated flatly that the Egyptian army obeyed the political leadership faithfully and unquestioningly. Jamasī added that since the announcement by Sādāt of his intention to visit Jerusalem, not a single soldier had been arrested (for subversion). [10] The Western press tended to confirm the view that the military resolutely supported Sādāt's initiative. Some Western journalists who were given permission to interview high-ranking Egyptian officers quoted them as expressing their support for Sādāt's peace policy and their wish not to be involved "in another Yemenite war" because of the Palestinians. [11]

It seems that Sādāt's confidence in the army's full support provided him with the freedom of manoeuvre he required to conduct the negotiations. Sādāt felt he could afford to keep an Israeli military delegation in the heart of Cairo (and later at Janaklīs air base) for nearly six months, and to receive the Israeli Defence Minister in Cairo—even at the time of the Israeli invasion of South Lebanon—without having to worry too much about negative reactions from his army. Gen Jamasī himself gradually became involved in the negotiations, and even became a key figure in them for a time. In fact, the greatest problems affecting army morale were apparently low salaries and inflation. This was recognized by the People's Assembly which approved a 15% raise in military pay in late June 1978. [12]

The officer corps—particularly the higher ranks—seemed more preoccupied with the prospects of changes in the top echelons of the armed forces than with politics. For the first time in four years, there were major reshuffles in senior posts. The first did not affect the two most senior generals—the War Minister, Gen (fariq awwal) Jamasī, and the Chief-of-Staff, Lt-Gen (fariq) Muhammad 'Alī Fahmī—but dozens of major-generals (liwā) were replaced or transferred, including two army commanders (those of the Second and Third Army) and the chief of operations. The changes were explained by the need to infuse new blood into the ranks of the Egyptian command which had remained unchanged for almost four years. [13]

As was only to be expected, these changes produced a wave of reports about unrest in the Egyptian army. Some even saw a link between the reshuffle and the sudden resignation of the former Chief-of-Staff, Sa'd al-Dīn al-Shādhilī, from his post as ambassador to Portugal. However, it appears that these rumours were without foundation. The changes had been announced long before; most officers affected were transferred rather than replaced, and some were promoted.

Notwithstanding Sādāt's confidence in the army, he continued to apply traditional control and surveillance measures and constantly to "feel the pulse" of the military. One way of doing this was through visits to different units where, accompanied by Jamasī, the Egyptian President explained his policy and answered questions. [14]

The second and more conspicuous series of changes in the military command took place in the wake of the Camp David agreements. On the morning of the announcement of the composition of the new Cabinet (see below), Sādāt issued a republican decree relieving War Minister Jamasī and Chief-of-Staff Fahmī of their posts, and appointing them as his military advisers. Sādāt appointed his Chief of Intelligence, Kamāl al-Dīn Hasan 'Alī, as the new Defence Minister, and Gen Ahmad Badāwī as Chief-of-Staff. [15] 'Alī was a former member of the National Defence Council and thus had been involved in the major decisions made by Sādāt between 1975 and 1978. Badāwī had been the commander of the Egyptian Third Army in the 1973 war and was acknowledged as one of the "October War heroes." There was no apparent reason for the sudden dismissal of Jamasī and Fahmī, both of whom definitely belonged to the "October generation." Jamasī had been chief of operations during the war, masterminding its planning and execution, and had replaced Shādhilī as Chief-of-Staff when the latter was dismissed by Sādāt at the height of battle. Fahmī had· been commander of Air Defence and had also made a name for himself as a war hero.

According to Western sources in Cairo, [16] the reason for the reshuffle was a sharp conflict that had developed between Jamasī and the Vice-President, Husnī Mubārak. Jamasī had tried to prevent Mubārak from gaining personal influence among the senior officers. The dispute came to a head during the Camp David summit, when Jamasī would not defer to Mubārak, as Sādāt's deputy. (During the October War and until his appointment as Vice-President, Mubārak had ranked lower than Jamasī in army seniority.) Accordingly, Mubārak asked Sādāt to choose between them. Whatever the real reason, Jamasī was deprived of his source of power—the armed forces. Moreover, his appointment as Sādāt's military adviser was apparently only temporary.

The changes also involved the replacement of the Navy commander, thus giving the Egyptian armed forces an almost completely new high command.

Another striking change was the dismissal of the chairman of the Arab Military Industries Organization (AMIO), Ashraf Marwān, who was Sādāt's former Secretary for Arab Affairs. Cairo newspapers described his removal as part of the anti-corruption campaign. However, this particular dismissal was linked to the fact that Marwān's sister-in-law ('Abd al-Nāsir's daughter) Huda, had distributed leaflets against the Camp David agreements in Cairo. [17]

POWER BASE: THE ADMINISTRATION

According to the usual Egyptian pattern, the government continued to function essentially as a form of high-level technocrats assisting the President in his role as principal decision-maker.

A new government was sworn in on 7 May 1978. It was again headed by Mamdūh Sālim and incorporated changes which had occurred following Fahmī's resignation in November 1977. The new government was modelled on the previous one—except that there were 31 ministers (instead of 32), with two (instead of five) serving as Deputy Prime Ministers (see Table, as well as *MECS 1976–77*, pp. 301–4).

The resignation of the Prime Minister, Mamdūh Sālim was reported on 21 August by *al-Aḥrār*, the organ of the Rightist Socialist Liberal Party, which suggested that he had decided to withdraw from political life and would not assume any party or state posts. [18] The next day, Sādāt asked Sālim to "continue to fulfil his duties." The reason for the delay in considering Sālim's resignation was to avoid a disruptive top-level change just before Sādāt's departure for Camp David. Sālim finally left his post on 2 October 1978 and was replaced by Mustafā Khalīl, until then Secretary-General of the Arab Socialist Union (ASU). In fact, rumours that Sālim would resign and that Sādāt would himself take over the premiership had been circulating in Egypt since January 1977. Nevertheless, Sādāt had repeatedly praised Sālim in his speeches and had given him his full backing. Sālim, who was also head of the Misr Party (see below), had first submitted his resignation on 27 July after Sādāt announced his intention to form, and lead, a political party of his own (see below). Sādāt had then asked Sālim to stay on. Sālim again offered to resign in mid-August when 279 of the 286 Misr Party members in the People's Assembly announced that they would join Sādāt's new party.

Despite his uncertain position, Sālim had remained firmly in charge of day-to-day administration. He reacted in the traditional Egyptian way to complaints of increasing economic hardship—mainly by replacing finance ministers and key functionaries, or by reorganizing the economic ministries' offices. Such was the case in October 1977 when he unified technical and financial services, [19] and in mid-1978 when he separated them again. [20] The key ministers were not affected by these changes. More significant was the case of the Deputy Prime Minister for Economic Affairs, 'Abd al-Mun'im al-Qaysūnī, who was forced to resign because of differences of opinion over the implementation of Sādāt's "open-door" economic policy. Qaysūnī had consistently demanded strict economic measures to cure the Egyptian economy and had opposed the government decision to raise salaries (see above). Sālim, on the other hand, was more keenly aware of the political difficulties and social tensions that would result from implementing Qaysūnī's tough policy. When Qaysūnī failed to persuade the Cabinet to adopt his policies, he felt compelled to resign. However, he remained close to the leadership and continued to function as a respected economic expert. Qaysūnī was also appointed by Sādāt as a

SĀLIM'S CABINET
(8 May 1978)

Portfolio	Incumbent
Prime Minister	Mamdūḥ Sālim
Deputy Prime Minister for Financial and Economic Affairs	Gen Muḥammad 'Abd al-Ghanī al-Jamasī
Deputy Prime Minister for Electricity and Energy	Sultān Aḥmad
Minister of State for the People's Assembly Affairs	Aḥmad Fu'ād Muḥi al-Dīn
Industry, Oil and Mineral Resources	Aḥmad 'Izz al-Dīn Hilāl
Education and Minister of State for Scientific Research	Mustafā Kamāl Ḥilmī
Minister of State for Local Government, Youth, Popular and Political Organizations	Muḥammad Ḥāmid Mahmūd
Trade	Zakariya Tawfīq 'Abd al-Fattāḥ
Irrigation and Minister of State for Sudanese Affairs	'Abd al-'Azīm 'Abdallah Abū al-'Ata
Minister of State for Cabinet Affairs, Follow-up and Control	'Īsa 'Abd al-Ḥamīd Shahīn
Economy and Economic Co-operation	Ḥāmid 'Abd al-Latīf Sā'iḥ
Health	Ibrāhīm Jamīl Mustafa Badrān
Finance	Mahmūd Salāḥ al-Dīn Ḥāmid
Land Reclamation	Ibrāhīm Shukrī
Tourism and Civil Aviation	Muḥib Ramzī Stīno
Social Security Affairs	Amāl 'Abd al-Raḥīm 'Uthmān
Interior	Muḥammad Nabawī Ismā'īl
Development and New Organization	Hasab Allah al-Kafrāwī
Foreign Minister	Muḥammad Ibrāhīm Kāmil
Minister of State for Foreign Affairs	Butrus Butrus Ghālī
Transport, Communications and Maritime Transport	Na'īm Abū Tālib
Minister of State for War Production	'Abd al-Sattar Mujāhid
Labour and Professional Training	Sa'd Muḥammad Aḥmad
Minister of State for Administrative Development	'Alī al-Salmī
Planning	'Abd al-Razzāq 'Abd al-Majīd
Justice	Ahmad Muhammad Dā'ūd
Housing	Aḥmad Tal'at Tawfīq
Supply	Nāsif 'Abd al-Maqsūr Tahūn
Waqf and Minister of State for Azhar Affairs	Shaykh Muḥammad Mutawālī al-Sha'rāwī
Information and Culture	'Abd al-Mun'īm al-Sāwī

(For the composition of Sālim's previous Cabinet, formed on 26 October 1977, see *MECS 1976–77*, pp. 302–3.)

member of the ASU Central Committee.[21]

The resignation of Ismā'īl Fahmī as Foreign Minister on 17 November 1977—the eve of Sādāt's visit to Jerusalem—had serious implications. He was opposed to the peace policy and refused to accompany Sādāt on his visit to Syria (see essay on Inter-Arab Relations). His dramatic move was the most serious protest made against the peace initiative. Sādāt accepted the resignation and appointed Fahmī's deputy, Muḥammad Riyād, to replace him; but in a spirit of solidarity, he declined. Sādāt temporized by appointing Butrus Ghālī as acting Foreign Minister and took him along to Jerusalem. The fact that Ghālī was a Copt apparently figured heavily in Sādāt's decision not to appoint him as Foreign Minister. Instead, he chose Egypt's ambassador to the German Federal Republic, Muḥammad Ibrāhīm Kāmil, who was a personal friend (and had been Sādāt's cell-mate in his underground days). Ghālī remained Minister of State for Foreign Affairs. Unlike Qaysūnī, Fahmī disappeared completely from the political scene. On a few occasions he gave interviews to Lebanese papers appearing in Paris and London. No punitive measures were taken against him.

Ten months later, following the Camp David agreements, Kāmil too resigned. Yet, unlike Fahmī's protest, this was not seen as a challenge to Sādāt's position. Kāmil, after all, had accepted Sādāt's policy towards Israel when he agreed to take the post of Foreign Minister. Judging from the fact that Kāmil remained in the foreign service, some observers concluded that he had resigned on purely personal grounds, possibly because he was relegated to a secondary role in the negotiations, where he was overshadowed by Usāma al-Bāz, Butrus Ghālī, Jamasī and even Ḥusnī Mubārak.

Following the Camp David agreements, the long-expected reshuffle of the Egyptian Cabinet finally took place. In his speech on the anniversary of 'Abd al-Nāsir's death (28 September), Sādāt explained that one reason for major changes was the need to hand over the leadership of the country to the "October generation." He said: "You have heard me several times asking that the 'October generation' . . . take its responsibility for leadership in the different fields of revival and awakening. . . . When I say the 'October generation,' I mean those who participated in the military, civilian or popular efforts [for] the victory of October." A second reason was the need to face the challenges of the post-Camp David era, namely the establishment of "democracy, peace and social welfare." According to Sādāt, Egypt had reached a stage which demanded a greater effort from both the leaders and the people. "We are facing a transformation from an economy of war to one of peace," he said.

In order to attain these goals, Sādāt proclaimed a comprehensive reform of domestic policy and to this end outlined the following ten-point programme for the next Cabinet. (1) Reform of bureaucracy and management. (2) Complete integration of planning bodies at various levels and in various fields. (3) Reassessment of the national resources. (4) A firmer control over the income of the citizen. (5) Reassessment of the "open-door" policy. (6) Complete revision of all the institutions linked with foreign aid. (7) Review of prices in order to lighten the burden on the people. (8) Clear planning to solve housing, communications and hospitalization problems. (9) A general plan for the development of Sinai that would include exploitation of its oil and mineral resources, its tourist sites and airports and also land reclamation—to help Egypt become more self-sufficient with regard to its food supply. (10) New research projects on the problems of villagers that would deal with the co-operative system, crop pricing policy, marketing and agricultural credit. [22]

The composition of the new Cabinet, under Mustafā Khalīl, was announced on 4 October[23] (see Table). It included 32 members, 11 ministers from Sālim's Cabinet and 20 new faces—all technocrats (three of whom were former chiefs of regional departments). Unlike former Cabinets, Khalīl's included only one deputy prime minister. To symbolize the transition from war to peace, the title War Minister was changed to Defence Minister.

ARAB REPUBLIC OF EGYPT

KHALĪL'S CABINET
(5 October 1978)

Portfolio	Incumbent
Prime Minister	Mustafā Khalīl
Deputy Prime Minister for	
the People's Assembly Affairs	Fikrī Makram 'Ubayd
Defence and War Production	Kamāl al-Dīn Ḥasan 'Alī
Oil	Aḥmad 'Izz al-Dīn Hilāl
Interior	Muḥammad Nabawī Ismā'īl
Tourism and Civil Aviation	Maḥmūd Amīn 'Abd al-Ḥāfiz
Social Security Affairs	Amāl 'Abd al-Raḥīm 'Uthmān
Planning	'Abd al-Razzāq 'Abd al-Majīd
Building and New Organizations	Ḥasab Allah al-Kafrāwī
Minister of State for	
Foreign Affairs	Butrus Butrus Ghālī
Supply and Interior Trade	Nāsif 'Abd al-Maqsūr Tahūn
Agriculture	Aḥmad Muḥammad Dā'ūd
Education, Culture and Scientific	
Research	Ḥasan Muḥammad Ismā'īl
Justice	Aḥmad 'Alī Mūsā
Minister of State for Follow-up	
and Control	'Alī Muḥammad al-Salīm
Minister of State for Government	
Affairs and Local Government	Sulaymān Mutawālī Sulaymān
Land Reclamation	Tawfīq Ḥāmid Karāra
Irrigation and Minister of State	
for Sudanese Affairs	Muḥammad 'Abd al-Hādī Samāḥa
Minister of State for the	
People's Assembly Affairs	Muḥammad 'Umar 'Abd al-Ākhir
Transport, Communications and	
Maritime Transport	'Alī Fahmī al-Daghastānī
Housing	Mustafā Mutawālī al-Ḥafnawī
Industry and Mineral Resources	Ibrāhīm 'Abd al-Raḥmān 'Atāllah
Electricity and Energy	Mustafa Kamāl Sabrī
Minister of State for	
Economic Co-operation	'Alī Jamāl al-Nāzir
Waqf and Minister of State	
for al-Azhar Affairs	Muḥammad 'Abd al-Raḥmān Bisār
Minister of State for Housing	
Affairs	Ḥusnī Muḥammad al-Sayyīd 'Alī
Minister of State for War	
Production	Kamāl Tawfīq Aḥmad Nassār
Health	Mamdūḥ Kamāl Jabr
Finance	'Alī Lutfī Muḥammad Luftī
Minister of State	Muḥammad Aḥmad al-'Aqīlī
Economy, Foreign Trade and Economic	
Co-operation	Ḥāmid 'Abd al-Latīf al-Sā'iḥ
Labour and Professional Training	Sa'd Muḥammad Aḥmad

The new Cabinet did not include an Information Minister: it was explained that the radio and television authority and the information authority were to become independent. For reasons unknown, the new Cabinet did not include a Foreign Minister; Butrus Ghālī continued as acting Foreign Minister. On 16 October, Sālim was appointed Presidential Assistant; so was the Assembly Speaker, Sayyid Mar'ī, who had resigned from his post.

The post-Camp David era thus marked the end of the career of those who had formed "the old guard of May 1971." Within a year of the beginning of Sādāt's peace initiative, the major political figures had disappeared from the centre of the stage and been relegated to marginal posts. Sālim and Jamasī had both been considered potential successors to Sādāt. With their elimination, Vice-President Mubārak emerged—intentionally or unintentionally—as the sole candidate.

SĀDĀT'S GENERAL PROGRAMME

There was no essential modification in 1978 of the goals which had first been declared in the 1974 "October Paper" (the manifesto published by Sādāt laying down the guiding principles for Egypt's development). Sādāt maintained his adherence to the same tenets: economic and political "openness" (*infitāh*); development based on science and technology; a traditional Islamic outlook; emphasis on the "Egyptian personality"; a pro-Western orientation in global affairs, and an Arab policy on the regional level.

The problem, of course, was how to reconcile and apply so wide a range of principles which were not entirely compatible. Many problems also emanated from the contradictions in the political structure since an active pluralistic party system made the task of applying Sādāt's programme more difficult (see below). Moreover, dealing with fundamental and chronic economic problems was hindered by the exigences of economy measures and shortcomings in the public services. Working under these constraints, Sādāt and Sālim formulated the following goals of their "policy of reconstruction," which was to be attained by the beginning of the 1980s:

a. Minimizing inflation and fighting unemployment.

b. Obtaining foreign aid to implement Egypt's development projects.

c. Achieving self-sufficiency in food resources through the "Green Revolution"—i.e. the accelerated expansion of arable lands.

d. Improving the social services.

e. Building new cities and developing new areas in order to cope with overpopulation.

f. Reconstructing the transport and telecommunications systems.

g. Adapting the government to the multi-party system which Sādāt had promised to develop. [24]

THE IDEOLOGY OF DEMOCRATIC SOCIALISM

Ever since his election to the Presidency in 1970, Sādāt has been aware of the lack of an ideological framework within which his political goals could be presented and which would fill the vacuum created by the decline of Nasserism, crystallize the identity of his own regime and counterbalance radical ideologies of the Left or the Right. His "October Paper" and the programmatic passages in his speeches were never moulded into a systematic doctrine comparable to 'Abd al-Nāsir's National Charter. Sādāt was reluctant to commit himself to a full-fledged official ideology—probably because of his anti-doctrinaire disposition and his apprehensions that such an ideology might alienate the intelligentsia.

Sādāt appears to have had second thoughts in 1978 and opted for more specific ideological formulations. The explanation is to be found in the growing domestic political difficulties his regime had to confront. (For measures against the opposition taken in May, see below.) It seems that Sādāt was disappointed by the weakness of the then ruling Misr Party which had failed to mobilize grassroots support and win wide endorsement for the government's domestic and foreign policies. Moreover, the party had not been able to create a programmatic framework which could withstand opposition attacks, especially from the Left.

Whatever the reasons, Sādāt announced in his 20 June speech to the ASU Central Committee that he intended to present a paper defining "Democratic Socialism" as the path chosen by his regime. The paper was to be prepared by a team of intellectuals from Egyptian universities, headed by the rector of Cairo University, Dr Sūfī Abū Tālib, and would then be debated in public. It was to be accompanied by "a code of ethics for democratic political activity" which would guide democratic life in Egypt.[25] Similar ideas had previously been mooted in mid-1977, but Sādāt's peace initiative had postponed their discussion. At that time, the ideology had been presented as approximating West European social democracy, while at the same time reflecting Egypt's own political culture. These ideas were further developed and, in July 1978, the new version of the paper on "Democratic Socialism" was submitted for public debate. The difference between the two versions lay in the fact that the 1978 draft placed greater emphasis on giving the ideology Egyptian roots and on stressing its authentic Egyptian character.[26]

The "Democratic Socialism" doctrine, in its final form, called for the realization of the "goals of this crucial stage." This required "a strategy for the development of Egypt's civilization through the acceptance of a moral code of conduct."[27] Dr Sūfī Abū Tālib, the architect of the doctrine, explained that it was the culmination of modern Egyptian history which had gone through three main stages: (1) The stage of the national struggle against foreign domination, which had lasted from the early 19th century till the 1952 revolution. (2) The stage of "socialist transformation" which started with the 1952 revolution. (3) The stage of "Democratic Socialism," which began with Sādāt's "corrective revolution" of May 1971 (i.e. with the purge of Nasserite "centres of power" which had challenged Sādāt's authority), whose aims still remained valid: to build a modern state (dawla 'asriyya), to establish social welfare, to liberate the occupied territories and to free Egypt from foreign influences in the political, cultural and economic fields.

According to Abū Tālib, the ideology of "Democratic Socialism" was thus basically identical with that of the May 1971 "corrective revolution." The values and ideas of both were said to stem from three main sources:

1. *The values of Arab civilization:* Egypt is seen as an integral part of the Arab world and as sharing the values of Arab culture. "Democratic Socialism" thus does not draw on "imported" (*mustawrada*) ideologies: it draws its inspiration from Egyptian-Arab concepts of a revived human universal civilization (*hadāra insāniyya mutajaddida*). Arab civilization provides two main values, that of faith (*imān*) and social justice (*'adāla ijtima'iyya*), on the basis of which "Democratic Socialism" will build a "well-balanced society" (*mujtama' mutawāzin*) capable of reconciling the interests of the individual with those of the community.

2. *The lessons of the past:* The history of Egypt up to 1952 provides instructive examples of both good and bad regimes, allowing appropriate lessons to be drawn for the solution of contemporary problems.

3. *Contemporary Democratic Socialism:* According to Abū Tālib, there are today two main socialist schools of thought. One is "scientific socialism" which in fact connotes the Communist way of social transformation; the other is "reformist socialism" (*ishtirākiyya islāhiyya*) which, as its name implies, aims at reforming society by peaceful means. Since the beginning of the present century, the latter has come to be referred to as "Democratic Socialism," indicating that it purports to combine both social justice and political freedom. It does not preach the doctrine of historical determinism and is easily reconciled with religious belief. "Democratic Socialism" rejects the principles of class struggle, revolution through violence (*thawra damawiyya*), and the dictatorship of the proletariat. It is not opposed to private property or private enterprise; indeed, it

allots them a special role in society. Nevertheless, it calls for the intervention of the state through democratic channels in order to achieve reform.[28]

EXPERIMENTING WITH A MULTI-PARTY SYSTEM

Towards the end of 1977, the multi-party system continued to gain momentum (see *MECS 1976-77*, pp. 298-301). At that time, Sādāt did not try to restrain the elements pressing for greater political participation, probably because he felt that he had enough power to control the liberalization process and to guide it according to his own best interests. Political liberalization was in line with social and economic "openness," internal reform and a Western orientation. It also served Sādāt's intention of projecting the image of a benevolent ruler responsive to public opinion. Sādāt was constrained to some extent by the need to act according to the rules of the parliamentary system which he himself had laid down in the Parties Law of 1977.

By the beginning of 1978 there were only four parties, since the Parties Law stipulated that at least 20 Assembly members must support a new party before it could be founded. Since there was no practical possibility for creating additional parties in the existing parliamentary situation, the system seemed fairly stable.

THE RULING PARTY

The Arab Socialist Party of Egypt (ASPE; *hizb misr al-'arabī al-ishtirākī*) or, as it was popularly called, the Misr Party had served as the ruling party since the inception of the party system and had an overwhelming majority in the People's Assembly (286 members out of 360). It was led by the Prime Minister, Mamdūh Sālim, who was assisted by three secretaries: Fu'ād·Muhī al-Dīn, Muhammad Hāmid Mahmūd and Muhammad Abū al-Wāfiyya. Most ministers were party members. The party issued a weekly organ, *Jarīdat Misr*.

Although the ASPE described itself as a Centrist party, in fact it was largely a metamorphosis of the ASU—the single political organization set up in 1962 which eventually became the basis, first for the so-called "platforms" and then for the new parties. Most of its leading members had held high rank in the ASU. Ideologically, the ASPE reflected Sādāt's ideas, but it permitted a measure of freedom of expression so that from time to time party members voiced opinions not completely in agreement with the President's. When Sādāt announced the imminent formation of a party of his own (see below), the ASPE underwent a crisis which was resolved two weeks later, on 13 August 1978, when party members decided to join Sādāt's National Democratic Party (NDP) *en bloc*.[29]

THE PARTY OF THE RIGHT

The Socialist Liberal Party (SLP; *hizb al-ahrār al-ishtirākiyyūn*) developed originally from a "platform" of that name and managed to win 12 seats in the People's Assembly. Sādāt regarded it as a "constructive opposition," and therefore included its leader, Mustafā Kāmil Murād, in his entourage during the visit to Jerusalem in November 1977. The organ of the SLP was called *al-Ahrār*.

The SLP generally endorsed the government's foreign policy but staunchly opposed it on economic and social issues, arguing that Egypt should complete the shift towards a liberal economy. The party suffered two setbacks: first, when some of its members joined the New Wafd party; and, again, when some went over to the new NDP. By August 1978, it was left with only two Assembly members—Murād and Muhammad 'Abd al-Shāfi'ī, a very active politician known for the boldness of his attacks on the government. In particular, he accused the Information Minister, 'Abd al-Mun'im al-Sāwī, of violating the constitution by restricting journalists' freedom of expression.[30]

THE PARTY OF THE LEFT

The Progressive Unionist Socialist Alignment Party (PUSA; *hizb al-tajamu' al-taqaddumī al-wihdāwī*) represented the legal Left in Egypt. It had only two members in the Assembly and, until the desertions from the SLP, it was the PA's smallest party. Its leader was Khālid Muhī al-Dīn, and its organ, *al-Ahālī*.

The party drew its strength from the traditionally Leftist public in Egypt—Nasserite elements, and Leftist students, intellectuals and workers (see below)—and had extra-parliamentary influence out of proportion to its Assembly strength. Some of the PUSA's supporters were members of illegal subversive organizations and had probably been among the fomentors of the 1977 "food riots."

Aware of the potential influence of PUSA on the public—particularly in view of the economic difficulties and growing social pressures—the Egyptian authorities kept the party under close surveillance, occasionally arresting members on charges of subversion and of instigating demonstrations. They also accused PUSA of acting on Moscow's instructions. The government frequently used the party as a scapegoat, accusing it of being responsible for social unrest. On 22 December 1977, *al-Ahrām* reported that five PUSA members had been arrested on a charge of distributing pamphlets calling for the overthrow of the regime and for the rejection of Sādāt's peace initiative.[31] By the end of 1977, 19 PUSA members had been arrested on charges of subversive activity.[32] In February 1978, the Interior Minister prevented PUSA leaders from holding a rally to commemorate the 1977 "food riots" on the grounds that it was intended to incite the masses against the government.[33]

Unlike the other parties, PUSA had a well-defined ideology, upholding many elements of Nasserism and particularly advocating a greater involvement of the state in social and economic affairs. It rejected the regime's liberalization programme and vigorously opposed the economic "open-door" policy, which it claimed had brought back *nouveaux riches* who were once again conspicuously displaying their wealth and power. The PUSA particularly attacked the well-to-do entrepreneurs in Sādāt's entourage, notably his close adviser, the former Housing Minister 'Uthmān Ahmad 'Uthmān.[34] The main tenets of PUSA's foreign policy were a more balanced attitude towards the super-powers (i.e. a *rapprochement* with the USSR); better relations with the "Steadfastness Front" states and the PLO; and a renewed emphasis on Egypt's role in the Arab world and on its commitment to the Arab cause.

THE NEW WAFD PARTY

A group of former leading members of the historical Wafd party combined in mid-1977 to create a new party (see *MECS 1976–77*, pp. 299–300). On 5 January 1978, the group submitted an official request to the ASU Central Committee—the body responsible under the Parties Law for the approval of new political parties—for permission to set up a party to be named the New Wafd (*al-wafd al-jadīd*). The name was chosen advisedly since, according to the Parties Law, the old Wafd—having been part and parcel of the *ancien regime*—could not be re-established as such. On 4 February 1978, the ASU approved the application.[35]

Overnight, the New Wafd became Egypt's second largest party, when 22 Assembly members (many of them "Independents") joined it. Headed by one of the old Wafd leaders, Fu'ād Sarrāj al-Dīn, it soon attracted wide public support—mainly because it appeared as an authentic expression of the quest for parliamentary democracy.

Of the party's 224 founding members, 118 were identified as workers and *fellahs*. (The Parties Law stipulated that one-half of all members of any party should represent workers and *fellahs*, and the other half the remaining sectors.) The New Wafd thus remained within the letter of the Parties Law, but hardly conformed to its spirit. Fu'ād Sarrāj al-Dīn's strong personal leadership made the New Wafd "new" in name only. All major decisions were taken in Sarrāj al-Dīn's house and not in the party institutions. It had offices only in Cairo and Alexandria. Like the old Wafd, it represented the interests of the privileged *petite bourgeoisie* concerned very largely over economic policies, on which they took a conservative line.

The programme as submitted to the authorities revealed serious ideological differences between the New Wafd and the regime. It did not clearly stipulate that the new party had adopted the principles of the 1952 revolution or those of 15 May 1971. It specifically rejected the concept of the "alliance of the people's working forces" (*tahāluf quwa al-sha'b al-'āmila*), one of the basic tenets of the regime. Moreover, the programme declared that the party would strive to "put an end to the exclusive powers of the President of the Republic." [36] In order to meet the demands of the Parties Law, these differences were omitted from the final programme which, as eventually approved, professedly adhered to the regime's concepts (including socialism, agrarian reform and the presidential regime) [37] which were in fact totally unacceptable to the founders of the party. What remained of the original programme was a call to transform the existing presidential regime into a parliamentary system, and to amend the procedure for electing the president so as to make it easier for more than one candidate to run for the office. It also opposed simultaneous membership of the Cabinet and the People's Assembly. [38]

The new party did not, on the whole, oppose Sādāt on foreign policy issues. It favoured a reduction of Egypt's commitment to the Arab world—a point on which it agreed with Sādāt's policy—and thus approved of his peace initiative. However, foreign policy issues were of secondary concern to the New Wafd. In domestic affairs, it demanded greater political freedom and a lessening of state intervention in social and economic activities. In both fields, the New Wafd presented itself as an alternative to Sādāt's regime, but failed to state clearly the nature of its alternative policies.

THE PEOPLE'S ASSEMBLY
The establishment of the multi-party system enlivened parliamentary life, and the People's Assembly enjoyed greater freedom of expression than it had known since the 1952 revolution. The opposition parties criticized many aspects of government policy, and the Assembly became a forum for heated debates, mainly on domestic problems (housing, food shortages, corruption etc). Foreign policy issues were usually raised only by the Leftist opposition. [39] The government became increasingly aware of the seriousness of the challenge from the Assembly and devoted a great deal of time and effort to answering its critics. Parliamentary criticism was usually directed against the Prime Minister, the Cabinet and the ASPE. The very rare occasions on which members attacked Sādāt himself were firmly dealt with: the ruling party invoked its overwhelming majority to censure the transgressor. When, for example, a New Wafd deputy, Shaykh 'Ashūr Nasr, representing a constituency in Alexandria, called for the overthrow of Sādāt, he was first deprived of his parliamentary immunity and later of his Assembly membership. [40]

THE PRESS
Since the 1973 war, freedom of expression in the Egyptian press has gradually increased, and a new dimension was added with the establishment of party organs. There were three party newspapers in 1978 (see above). After the ASPE decided to disband, *Jaridat Misr* suspended publication on 26 September 1978. [41] *Al-Aḥrār*

had ceased publication even earlier, when the SLP started dwindling (see above). The surviving party newspaper, *al-Ahālī*, kept up a constant and unprecedented barrage of criticism against the regime. Among its contributors were prominent journalists such as Muḥammad Ḥasanayn Haykal and Aḥmad Bahā al-Dīn. Since its first issue, *al-Ahālī* had attacked the limitations on democracy, the Press Law, corruption in the ruling élite, and the government's failures to deal with housing, food and public services. The paper was also critical of the government's foreign policy, coming out against Sādāt's Western orientation and his peace initiative. For instance, it criticized Sādāt for receiving the Israeli Defence Minister in Cairo in March 1978 at a time when Israeli troops occupied South Lebanon.[42] The authorities impounded complete issues of *al-Ahālī* on seven different occasions and denounced it for being "anti-Islamic"; its editor-in-chief, Lutfī Shukrī, was interrogated by the police on one occasion following the publication of anti-clerical views.[43]

Unlike the party organs, the old-established and virtually state-controlled press remained cautious towards the multi-party experiment. They all supported the ruling party, but the daily *al-Akhbār* and the weeklies *Ākhir Sā'a* and *al-Musawwar* showed some sympathies with the New Wafd and the SLP; whereas the dailies *al-Ahrām* and *al-Jumhūriyya* and the weeklies *Rūz al-Yūsuf* and *October* identified unreservedly with the ruling party. All these newspapers reflected a common governmental line on all aspects of the Arab-Israeli conflict.

SĀDĀT CURBS THE OPPOSITION

The attacks of opposition parties on the government reached a peak in May 1978. Unable to contain the growing criticism, ASPE demanded a reassessment of the party system. In what amounted to a reversal of his policy of liberalization, Sādāt decided to mount a vigorous campaign against the opposition which he launched in his speech on 14 May 1978 marking the anniversary of the "corrective revolution." Sādāt declared that there had been a steady deviation from the democratic principles he had introduced. Freedom of expression had been exploited to cast doubts on the government's ability to cope with Egypt's problems. The Assembly had shown a lack of responsibility and had made the government's work more difficult. Assembly members compelled ministers to spend their time answering unnecessary questions which only helped to foster rumours hostile to the regime. Sādāt said that the Wafd Party, in particular, had tried to turn back the pages of history to the pre-1952 revolution period, presenting itself as an alternative to his regime. The PUSA, for its part, had misused the freedom of expression granted by the regime in order to sow discord. The PUSA's newspaper, Sādāt said, "is no more than a leaflet of the kind they issued when they operated underground." While the Egyptian press had contributed to the spreading of false rumours against the regime, Egyptian journalists writing in the Arab press outside the country had gone further by directly attacking their government's policy. Therefore, Sādāt declared, he would request the Press Union to take punitive measures against "unpatriotic journalists." He would also ask the secretary of the ASU's Central Committee to investigate whether oppositional activity by the parties conformed to the code laid down by the Parties Law.

The Presidential Office issued a communiqué on 14 May 1978, announcing that it would hold a referendum on proposed guidelines for future democratic practices. The communiqué explained: "Lately, an intention to undermine democracy was uncovered. It was to be carried out by politicians with narrow party and personal interests who had already corrupted political life in the past, before the [1952] revolution and after it, by those who belong to organizations working against national unity and against the existing social order, and by those who intend to misuse the liberties guaranteed by the 15 May revolution. But the worst thing was the harm done to the things we hold sacred and to our religious feelings. . . . Since these things have a direct bearing on the supreme interests of the state, the President of the Republic is obliged to conduct a referendum, according to paragraph 152 of the constitution, particularly since the state is in a critical stage and facing the liberation struggle and the needs of construction and the consolidation of the internal front.''

The President said that he had found it necessary to hold the referendum to gain approval of the following proposed measures:

1. Anyone known to hold principles harmful to the official religion [of the state] will be banned from jobs in the top-level administration of the state or the public sector. Moreover, he will not be allowed to be a candidate for the board of directors of public and labour organizations, nor write for a newspaper, work in the mass media or have any position that could influence public opinion.

2. The following will be prohibited from membership in [any] political party or from engaging in any political activity:

(a) Anyone who was involved in corrupting political life before the [1952] revolution. This clause is aimed at those who filled ministerial functions and were members of the then existing political parties, and those who were part of the leadership of those parties except the National Party and the Socialist (Young Egypt) Party [two radical nationalist opposition parties of the monarchy period].

(b) Anyone who has been tried by the Tribunal of the Revolution on the charge of setting up centres of power, and anyone who has been convicted of crimes connected with the undermining of personal liberties or democracy, either physically or morally.

(c) Anyone known to have engaged in activities whose aim was to corrupt political life in the country, to endanger national unity and social order, either on a private basis or through a political party organization, or subversive organization aimed against the regime and society. This applies also to the publication of articles or false rumours which could harm the national interests of the state and also to the spreading of defeatism or incitement to undermine the social order and the national unity.

''3. The press is the fourth authority and the property of the people, according to Law 156 of 1960. The press must respect the regime of the state which is [based on] social democracy, social welfare, national unity and the socialist achievements of the workers and peasants. The press must also honour the Press Charter.''

The next three clauses called on the People's Assembly to draft bills for the conduct of the proposed referendum and to define penalties for violations of the principles stated above. They made the Attorney-General responsible for prosecuting suspected cases of infraction of any of these laws and for presenting the findings to the Assembly, which was to discuss them and make final decisions.

A week later, on 21 May, the referendum was held. On the next day the Interior Minister, Nabawī Ismā'īl, announced the results: c. 9.5m out of c. 11m eligible voters (85.4%) had participated; of these, 9,202,553 (98.29%) had voted in favour and 159,578 against.[44]

The Assembly acted speedily to pass legislation turning the principles approved in the referendum into law. At the same time, the Prosecutor-General (responsible for handling the prosecution of political crimes) began to investigate charges that

PUSA and politicians identified with it were fomenting unrest. The authorities recalled 34 Egyptian journalists working abroad to be questioned by the Prosecutor-General on their writings. Five other journalists, including the Nasserist Muḥammad Ḥasanayn Haykal, were forbidden to leave Egypt until the investigation was concluded.[45] The press was put under close surveillance. Mustafā Amīn, who had criticized the massive adherence of the ASPE members to Sādāt's party in August, was forbidden to write political articles. According to al-Aḥrār, Jalāl al-Dīn al-Ḥamāmisi from al-Akhbār, Yūsuf Idrīs from al-Ahrām and a group of journalists from Rūz al-Yūsuf were also restricted. (Mustafā Amīn was allowed to resume writing at the end of September.)[46]

Meanwhile, the regime staged a large-scale campaign against the New Wafd and PUSA which it accused of having conspired together in order to overthrow the regime. According to the Interior Minister, Nabawī Ismāʿīl, the two parties cooperated in planning joint action against the government, both inside and outside the Assembly.[47]

On 1 June, the Assembly endorsed the results of the referendum and barred New Wafd politicians, led by Sarrāj al-Dīn, from engaging in political activity. On 2 June the New Wafd announced its voluntary dissolution. Those of its Assembly members who had not been barred from active politics again became Independent deputies.[48] Two days later, on 4 June, PUSA announced the freezing of all its activities in order "to reassess the future of the party in the light of the measures taken by the regime."[49] On 11 June the party announced that it would continue functioning as before.[50]

THE CREATION OF THE NATIONAL DEMOCRATIC PARTY

Faced with a parliamentary crisis which endangered the very foundations of the multi-party system, the authorities became increasingly aware of the weakness of the ruling party and of its inability to dominate political life. At first they considered reorganizing and revitalizing the party by giving it a more democratic character. Later, however, this proposal was abandoned in favour of creating a new ruling party, to be headed by Sādāt himself. On 22 July 1978, in his traditional Revolution Day speech, Sādāt announced his intention of creating a new party and of amending the clause in the Parties Law which made such a move conditional on the support of at least 20 Assembly members. This amendment, he said, was also needed to facilitate the creation of more parties, for he intended to continue his policy of party pluralism.[51] In the same speech, Sādāt also declared that the ASU's Central Committee had been abolished; instead, it would be an advisory assembly (majlis shūra) with no clearly defined function. For all intents and purposes, this measure put an end to the existence of the ASU.

The formation of Sādāt's new National Democratic Party (NDP; al-ḥizb al-watanī al-dimuqrātī) was announced on 6 August. The founding committee was headed by Fikrī Makram 'Ubayd, deputy and former ASPE member.[52] The party was intended to symbolize a revival of the spirit of Egypt's first Nationalist Party (al-ḥizb al-watanī), founded by Mustafā Kāmil in 1907. As was to be expected, its platform reflected the ideology of democratic socialism (see above), as formulated by Dr Sūfī Abū Tālib, who had become the party's ideologue.

Sādāt's announcement created a crisis in the Assembly since it was taken to signify his lack of confidence in the ASPE. No sooner was the founding of the NDP announced than ASPE members began to flock to the new party. The NDP had soon absorbed the ASPE, whose chairman, Mamdūḥ Sālim, resigned on 31 August. Political "reform" thus reverted to the old formula of a ruling party with virtually no legal opposition in the Assembly.

The NDP began organizing itself in August 1978, and its structure was announced in *al-Ahrām* on 24 September. To stress its democratic character, the different bodies constituting the party's hierarchy were presented in ascending order, as follows:

+ The District (or Constituency) Congress (*mu'tamar al-dā'ira*)

Includes members of the district and elects the District Committee.

+ The District Committee (*lajnat al-dā'ira*)

Includes 14 members, including youth and women representatives and the district's deputy in the People's Assembly. They elect the District Authority Bureau.

+ The District Authority Bureau (*hay'at maktab al-dā'ira*)

Consists of a secretary with two assistants (one of whom must be a worker or a peasant) and a treasurer.

+ The Governorate Congress (*mu'tamar al-muḥāfaza*)

Consists of all the District Committees in that governorate and some members of the Department Committee.

+ The Governorate Committee (*lajnat al-muḥāfaza*)

Consists of all the Assembly deputies in the governorate and of two elected members from each district. This Committee elects the Governorate Authority Bureau.

+ The Governorate Authority Bureau (*hay'at maktab al-muḥāfaza*)

Consists of a secretary and two assistants (at least one of whom must be a worker or a peasant) and is responsible for party activities and finance at the governorate level.

+ The Permanent Party Assembly (*al-majlis al-dā'im lil-ḥizb*)

Includes the members of the General Secretariat and the governorate secretaries. Its main task is to implement the decision of the General Congress and to plan party activity at the national level.

+ The General Party Congress (*al-mu'tamar al-'āmm lil-ḥizb*)

Includes the representatives of the electoral constituencies and of the Parliamentary Party Authority and the members of the Permanent Party Assembly; its task is to elect the party chairman and his deputy.

+ The Supreme Party Assembly (*al-majlis al-a'la lil-ḥizb*)

Is responsible for drawing up the policy of the party. The General-Secretariat is elected from among its members.

+ The General Secretariat (*al-amāna al-'āmma lil-ḥizb*)

Composed of a General Secretary and a number of specialized secretaries to supervise day-to-day party work.

+ The Parliamentary Party Authority (*al-hay'a al-barlamāniyya lil-ḥizb*)

Includes all the party's deputies in the People's Assembly, co-ordinates their activity in the People's Assembly and decides on the party's vote.

Following Sādāt's announcement that he would facilitate the establishment of new parties, two new groups emerged in the People's Assembly:

a. A group headed by the former Minister for Land Reclamation, Ibrāhīm Shukrī. His party was to be named the Socialist Labour Party (*ḥizb al-'amal al-ishtirākī*)—an attempt to revive the Young Egypt Party.[53] Sādāt sought to turn this party into a new "constructive opposition" and therefore invited one of the former ASPE Secretaries, Maḥmūd Abū al-Wāfiya, to join it. He also suggested that some members of his own party join the Socialist Labour Party "opposition."

b. A group headed by Maḥmūd al-Kāḍī who sought to found a National Front Party (*ḥizb al-jabha al-wataniyya*) representing a political trend "Left of the Centrist NDP."[54]

EXTRA-PARLIAMENTARY OPPOSITION

There were no significant changes in the size, structure, composition and *modus operandi* of the illegal opposition parties in 1978. As far as is known, this opposition remained limited in scope, with no foothold in the army. Its principal members operated abroad and so did not endanger Sādāt's regime. The Egyptian security services did not ease their efforts to harass and repress clandestine opposition groups whenever they made an appearance. The illegal opposition was therefore unable to effectively exploit the crisis in Egypt's relations with other Arab states or the country's chronic internal problems.

COMMUNISTS

The Communists occupied pride of place among illegal opposition groupings (see *MECS 1976–77*, pp. 292–95). The Egyptian Communist Party and the Egyptian Workers' Rally remained the two most prominent organizations which were seen to be actively working against the regime.[54] Because the authorities attempted to repress all vestiges of Communist activity, many Egyptian Communists went into exile in Arab countries (Lebanon and Iraq) or in Western Europe (France) where they engaged in open activity against Sādāt's regime. Occasionally they published communiqués or open letters in the press in Lebanon and Europe.[55] Nevertheless, the bulk of the Communists remained active in Egypt where they were mainly engaged in attempts to disseminate their views. According to the authorities, PUSA co-operated with them.[56]

Communists were accused of trying to foment strikes, of encouraging acts of sabotage in industry,[57] and of being behind the parliamentary crisis in May 1978. According to the authorities, they exploited freedom of speech and political activity in attempts to undermine Egypt's internal stability. Communists were arrested on a number of occasions while distributing tracts against Sādāt's policies (e.g. the "surrender" to Israel, or the referendum). The Egyptian press reported that 22 Communist cells were uncovered in 1977, and at least 230 supporters arrested during 1978. Most of them had been active in medium-sized towns and belonged to the educated middle classes.

THE NEO-NASSERISTS

Unlike the Communists, the neo-Nasserists did not constitute a well-defined movement but rather belonged to a trend which represented a wide range of political orientations—from the Marxists on the Left to the Qadhdhāfīsts on the Right. Some prominent figures among the neo-Nasserists were active outside Egypt, mainly in Libya and Algeria: 'Abd al-Majīd Farīd, head of the Presidential Office under Nāsir, had served as Boumedienne's adviser until the second half of 1978; and Ḥikmat Abū-Zayd, a woman Minister for Social Affairs under Nāsir, had decided to live in Libya.[58] The most outstanding figure inside Egypt was Haykal, 'Abd al-Nāsir's former confidant, who launched bitter attacks in *al-Ahālī* against Sādāt's policies, particularly on his peace initiative.

The neo-Nasserists came under pressure from the authorities after the May crisis.

The government released facts about the activities of some of them in 1974 when, on Qadhdhāfī's initiative and with the close co-operation of 'Abd al-Majīd Farīd and Ḥikmat Abu-Zayd, a subversive organization called the "Front for the Liberation of Egypt" (*al-jabha li-taḥrīr misr*) was set up to infiltrate the ranks of Egyptian workers in Libya and to carry out sabotage operations in Egypt.[59]

ISLAMIC RADICALISM; COPTIC REACTIONS

In contrast with 1977, the Islamic radical opposition was not particularly active in 1978 (see *MECS 1976–77*, pp. 295–98). The Muslim Brethren, by far the largest Islamic radical group, respected the unwritten truce with the authorities. The latter in turn showed tolerance towards their activities and allowed them to publish their organs, *al-Da'wa* and *al-I'tisām*, although these expressed direct and indirect criticism of Sādāt and his peace initiative.[60]

The other extremist Islamic groups were not visibly active—probably because of the firm measures that had been taken against them. As expected, the trials against members of the *al-takfīr wa-hijra* terrorist organization resulted in death sentences for five of its top leaders, including the "supreme commander," Shukrī Mustafā.[61] Others were given prison terms of varying lengths.[62] (For background on this organization, see *MECS 1976–77*, p. 296.)

The forces of "established" orthodox Islam continued their efforts to strengthen Egypt's Islamic character. The main field of activity was the People's Assembly, where special efforts were made to pass Islamic laws such as the bills decreeing amputation for thieves,[63] imposing the death penalty for apostasy,[64] or prohibiting usury.[65] The Assembly passed a bill authorizing flogging of any Muslim caught drinking or trading in alcoholic beverages.[66]

The authorities were apparently content to let Islamic orthodox forces counterbalance the influence of the Leftists, e.g. in the students' association[67] (see below). The regime often used Islamic themes in its campaign against the Left. For example, the Assembly's Committee for Religious Affairs issued an appeal warning against "the attacks" of Communism against Islam.[68] The Prime Minister, Mamdūḥ Sālim, also met Shaykh al-Azhar at the beginning of the campaign against the Left in May 1978, "in order to find ways of containing the waves of heresy and ideological deviation."[69]

This situation seems to have alarmed the Coptic minority which had already protested against the Islamic bill imposing the death penalty for apostasy (see *MECS 1976–77*, p. 298). The regime sought to allay such fears. The fact that the apostasy law was not brought up again in the Assembly after mid-1977 was possibly due to the government's desire not to antagonize the Copts. Nonetheless, a number of Coptic-Muslim clashes occurred, mainly in Minyā (Upper Egypt). On 20 May 1978, *al-Manār* reported that as a result of such a clash, a Coptic church was set on fire in Minyā. On 1 July, the same paper reported further clashes in which a number of people were killed and several schools destroyed.

A Coptic church group in Australia stated that in August 1978, two Sunday school teachers were murdered in the governorate of Kalyūbiyya. A month later, a Coptic priest in the town of Samalawt was beaten to death at his home; his wife and two sons were seriously injured. Other reports said that Christian students at Asyūt University were attacked and thrown out of the dormitories. A religious procession was attacked in the governorate of Sohāj; so was the monastery of al-Fakhūry.

The situation of the Copts was raised by Pope Shanūda III when he met former Prime Minister Sālim on 9 September 1978. As a result, the death of the priest killed at Samalawt was investigated once more. However, the Copts were not altogether reassured. A group of Copts demonstrated in front of the UN building in New York on 24 October to protest against the treatment of their co-religionists in Egypt.

STUDENTS

Generally speaking, relative calm characterized campus life in Egypt in 1978. However, the process of politicization of the students' organizations continued and the parties, as well as clandestine Communist and Marxist cells, sought to gain greater influence. The principal contenders for student sympathy were the Islamic groups and the radical Left. In the student association elections of December 1977, the Islamic lists succeeded at the expense of their rivals at almost all universities. At the University of Alexandria, for instance, Islamic candidates captured all the seats allotted to the faculties of medicine and engineering; 47 of 48 seats in the faculty of pharmacology; 43 of 60 in the faculty of science; and 44 of 48 in the law faculty. Tension between Islamic-oriented and Leftist students grew, especially in universities previously known as "Leftist bastions" such as Cairo, 'Ayn Shams and Alexandria. On 29 April 1978, 12 Leftist students were arrested at Cairo University for having set fire to an auditorium. In July, Cairo University refused to allow 400 Rightist students to run an Islamic Summer Camp. Student opinion was preoccupied with the rivalry of student groups, and political events at the national level had little impact on campus life. No campus riots were reported in the period under review. This may have been partly the result of the repressive measures in force on campuses since the 1977 "food riots" rather than the indifference of students to events outside the universities.

FOREIGN AFFAIRS

Sādāt initiative *vis-à-vis* Israel was the cornerstone of Egyptian diplomacy in 1978 and left its imprint on Egypt's relations with the Arab world, the super-powers and Africa.

In the Arab world, the initiative was criticized by the great majority of Arab states, even though their opposition took different forms: the rejectionists and the PLO went so far as to accuse Sādāt of betraying the Arab cause and to demand that he be ostracized; most conservative states, notably Saudi Arabia, called for all-Arab reconciliation, but implied that this would only be possible if Sādāt publicly conceded the failure of his initiative (see essay on Inter-Arab Relations). However, in the face of pressures both from within and without, Sādāt demonstrated his overriding determination to persevere. On a number of occasions he declared that his initiative would never fail because "it has become a part of the world's patrimony." (For a detailed account of the Egyptian-Israeli negotiations, see section on the Arab-Israeli Conflict.) Another striking development in 1977–78 was that Egypt began to seek a more realistic understanding of Israel, including its internal political dynamics. Nonetheless, Egypt continued to uphold its political and moral commitment to the Arab world by refusing to accept a visibly separate agreement with Israel.

Egypt's relations with the USSR remained strained as a result of the many specific disputes between them, as well as the differences in their basic attitudes. Relations became even more difficult in the wake of the peace initiative. On the other hand, the year under review was marked by increasing co-operation and close relations with the US. The Carter Administration's decision to supply Egypt with 50 F-5E fighter planes admitted it to the American "lethal weapons market."

Africa continued to constitute an area of interest and a source of apprehension. Although its support for those African regimes which opposed Soviet influence was more declaratory than real, Egypt skilfully presented itself as a bulwark against Soviet penetration in Africa.

EGYPT AND THE SUPER-POWERS
RELATIONS WITH THE USSR
On the eve of Sādāt's initiative, diplomatic and economic relations between Egypt and the USSR had already reached a very low point (see *MECS 1976-77*, pp. 306-8). They deteriorated still further as a result of the Soviet attack on this initiative which elicited a sharp reaction from the Egyptian leader. Stopping just short of a complete severance of diplomatic relations, Sādāt recalled the Egyptian ambassador and military attaché from Moscow[70] and ordered that all cultural centres and consulates of the USSR, Bulgaria, Hungary, Czechoslovakia, Poland and East Germany throughout Egypt be closed except those in Cairo.[71] He also forbade the circulation in Egypt of three Soviet newspapers.[72] In speeches and interviews, Sādāt struck a decidedly anti-Soviet note. He was convinced—or at least gave the impression of being convinced—that the Kremlin leaders had put a price on his head and had decided to conspire to topple his regime. The Soviets were accused of being behind the unrest in Egypt and of providing money, arms and advice for carrying out acts of sabotage inside the country. Moscow was also said to have initiated ties with clandestine extremist Leftist groups in Egypt, as well as the Leftist party in the People's Assembly (see above).

Sādāt often expressed his fears of Soviet designs in Africa, maintaining that one of its main objectives was to install a pro-Soviet regime in the Sudan. Such a regime would then co-operate with pro-Soviet Libya in bringing about the strangulation of Egypt.[73] Sādāt's belief that it was too late to mend relations with the USSR seems to have crystallized early in 1978 when he failed to receive any favourable response from the Soviet Union to his tentative move for *rapprochement*. Sādāt, who on many occasions had praised Brezhnev's political wisdom, stated that only the Soviet leader could improve relations between the two states. Some exploratory contacts then took place between the two countries' UN delegations.[74] The Speaker of the People's Assembly, Sayyid Mar'ī, met a high-ranking Soviet official in early March 1978,[75] but with no apparent results; parallel efforts initiated by Romania's President Ceauşescu and Morocco's King Ḥasan II also came to nothing.[76]

The situation was similar in the economic field. The 1978 commercial protocol with the USSR was not signed so that economic relations were still governed by interim arrangements.[77] Egypt maintained its embargo on cotton shipments to the USSR and continued to freeze payment of its military debts to Moscow. Moreover, as of December 1977, Egypt demanded full payment in advance of dues for Soviet ships passing through the Suez Canal.[78] Finally, following the non-delivery of Soviet spare parts for civilian planes, Egypt failed to renew the contracts of Soviet civilian experts still working in the country.[79]

The USSR, for its part, continued to apply a complete embargo on military hardware and spare parts to Egypt.

RELATIONS WITH THE UNITED STATES
Egypt's relations with the US continued to be determined by its efforts to enlist American support in modifying Israeli negotiating positions it found objectionable; to secure a continuous flow of American economic and financial aid; and to try to break Israel's "monopoly" of American military supplies by demanding an even-handed arms sales policy as between Egypt and Israel. Accordingly, Egypt continued to conduct its relations with the US on two main levels: first, that of the Arab-Israeli conflict; and second, bilaterally.

The Conflict with Israel
Since November 1977, Egypt's view of the US role combined three elements, each of

which came to the fore at various times: disappointment at Carter's inability to put pressure on Israel; reluctant understanding for the American position; and ultimate faith in its even handedness. Since then, Sādāt twice had "misunderstandings" with the US. The first, which arose over Egyptian distrust of the US position on the Palestinian issue, was settled after Sādāt and Carter met at Aswān on 4 January 1978 and released the "Aswān formula"[80] (for its contents, see essay on the Egyptian-Israeli Negotiations). The second seems to have been generated during Sādāt's visit to Austria in July. There were reports that Sādāt had decided to prolong his stay in order to enable him to meet Carter who was due to arrive in Germany in mid-July. The meeting did not take place and, perhaps coincidentally, Egypt announced that it would not participate in further direct talks with Israel. *Al-Ahrām* expressed Egypt's disappointment with the American role in a manner which suggested that Sādāt had deliberately avoided meeting Carter as a gesture of protest.[81]

However, Egypt's hopes were soon raised again by Carter's announcement of his intention to convene the Camp David summit on 5 September 1978 and to play a more active role in the negotiations—i.e. to become a "full partner," as Egypt had urged.[82] Egypt had been trying for some time to induce Washington to present its own position in the form of written "suggestions" so as to bring about a test of strength between the US and Israel. Cairo believed that this would pave the way for an imposed settlement on terms more acceptable to itself than to Israel because of the basic similarity of the Egyptian and American positions (a similarity presumably arrived at during Sādāt's visit to the US in February 1978). The Camp David agreements capped the Egyptian policy towards the US and were taken as proof by Sādāt that he could count on Carter. Nevertheless, Egypt continued to urge the US to maintain its role as a "full partner"—not only until a peace treaty between Egypt and Israel was signed, but in particular during the negotiations on the West Bank issue.

The Bilateral Level

Sādāt was able to point to substantial results in the development of bilateral relations with Washington. Constant efforts to strengthen relations found expression in the flow of American delegations to Egypt, including congressmen, senators, academics and journalists; the heavy exposure of Sādāt on American TV; and the many Egyptian delegations sent to the US. The Assembly Speaker, Sayyid Mar'ī, led an important delegation which toured the country for 30 days from 14 June-15 July.[83]

Egypt continued to receive American economic and financial aid under congressional foreign aid bills. These reached a total of $1,000m a year, a sum representing nearly one-third of Egypt's total non-military aid from foreign sources. The US Ambassador, Herman Eilts, stated that one piece of bread out of three in Egypt came from American aid, as did every bar of soap and every can of preserves.[84]

On the military level, 1978 marked a major breakthrough in Egypt's relations with Washington. For the first time Egypt was given access to the US "lethal weapons" market, after Congress approved the supply of 50 F-5E fighter planes within the framework of the package deal with Saudi Arabia and Israel. The aircraft were to be delivered by 1981.[85] A plant for the assembly of American-made jeeps was scheduled to start operations at the end of 1978.[86]

Egypt's War Minister, Jamasī, visited the US from 6-15 June 1978—the first such visit since 1950. In Egyptian eyes, this development was unique in giving palpable expression to the new state of relations between themselves and the

Americans. Jamasī received a warm welcome; he had discussions with senior officials and two unscheduled meetings with President Carter, during which he presented his views on the conflict with Israel, on African issues and on the future of military relations with the US. Although Jamasī stated that it was too early to present a list of arms needed by Egypt, he did not rule out such a development in the future. Indeed, it was decided that an American military delegation should visit Egypt to study the needs of its army, but no date was set. The only immediate results were agreements on the timetable for delivering the F-5E planes and on the training of Egyptian pilots in the US.

EGYPT AND THE ARAB WORLD
Sādāt's visit to Jerusalem produced one of the most serious crises ever in Egypt's relations with the Arab world, since it violated the Arab taboo against direct negotiations with and recognition of Israel. Sādāt acted from the conviction that it was worth risking temporary damage in Egypt's relations with the Arab world in order to achieve Israel's withdrawal from the Arab lands occupied since 1967. Moreover, Sādāt was confident that even if his Arab counterparts were not sympathetic to his initiative, they would not obstruct it; that they would eventually recognize the wisdom and success of his policy and end up by joining him, even if belatedly.

Nevertheless, Sādāt made a last-minute effort to persuade Syria, if not to back his initiative, at least not to oppose it. But Sādāt's trip to Damascus (16–17 November 1977) did not prevent a rift between the two countries[87] and was one of the first signs of deterioration in Egypt's relations with the Arab radical camp (represented by Syria, Libya, Algeria, the PDRY, Iraq and the PLO). On 6 December 1977, Egypt severed diplomatic relations with these five countries; the PLO representative had already been expelled from Cairo at the end of November. Even though Sādāt expressed his readiness on a number of later occasions to restore relations with the rejectionist countries, he always made this conditional on their acceptance of his policy towards Israel.[88] By stipulating this condition, Sādāt clearly indicated that he had no intention of initiating a reconciliation with his radical rivals—whom he called "midgets" and "mentally feeble creatures," unable to unite and agree among themselves even on minor issues.[89] (For an account of the overall changes in Arab alignments in the wake of Sādāt's initiative, see essay on Inter-Arab Relations.)

RELATIONS WITH THE RADICAL CAMP
Syria
Tension between Egypt and Syria had persisted since the 1973 war, but had eased for about a year because of a reconciliation—more apparent than real—achieved in 1976 (see *MECS 1976-77*, pp. 151–54). Sādāt's peace initiative destroyed whatever remained of their improved relations which, from the end of 1977, became worse than ever before (except for the period immediately after the break-up of the Syrian-Egyptian union in 1961). A ruthless propaganda campaign developed in 1978 in which both sides made scathing personal attacks.

Following the severance of relations, Egypt suspended flights of its civilian airline to Syria on 9 December 1977. (These were not resumed until May 1978.)[90] It also suspended the operation of the shipping line that normally plied between Alexandria and Lādhiqiyya, a measure described as having been taken on purely economic grounds.[91] Later in December, the Cairo authorities expelled Syrian students from Egypt.[92] At the same time, Egypt launched a propaganda campaign against Damascus, accusing it of giving in to Soviet pressures and asserting that

Asad had become a "prisoner" of the Syrian Ba'th party.[93]

Egypt also exploited the Lebanese crisis in March 1978 to attack Syria (see essay on South Lebanon in the Arab-Israeli Conflict). For the first time, the Egyptian media described the Syrian troops in Lebanon as an "occupation force."[94] Egypt claimed that the Syrian presence in Lebanon was intended to draw attention away from the calm prevailing along the Golan front as a result of the commitments Syria had made in its disengagement agreement in May 1974, including the prevention of PLO operations across its border against Israel. Egypt's criticism was especially sharp during the Israeli military campaign in South Lebanon. It accused Syria of being in "collusion" with Israel and of denying the Palestinians any aid while the fighting was at its height.[95]

For the remainder of the period under review, and especially after the Camp David summit, Syria took the lead among Sādāt's most bitter critics.

Algeria

Egypt watched Algeria's drift towards the radical Arab camp with apprehension but was powerless to stop it, particularly since it stemmed from basic geo-political considerations. What was especially disturbing for Egypt was the Algerian-Libyan *rapprochement* (see *MECS 1976-77*, p. 171).

After the severance of diplomatic relations, an Egyptian Interests Section was opened in the Tunisian embassy in Algiers. In December 1977, Cairo considered suspending flights of its national airline to Algiers after its personnel were molested by an angry mob.[96] Sādāt then used *October* as a forum in which to settle the historical account of Egypt's relations with Algeria, accusing Boumedienne of having constantly tried to undercut Egypt's leading position in the Arab world.[97] The Egyptian media called Boumedienne "another Qadhdhāfī" and accused him of anti-Egyptian machinations ever since the 1960s.[98]

Sādāt was reported in January 1978 to have rejected a message from Boumedienne designed to persuade him to abandon his peace initiative.[99] Reports of a meeting between Boumedienne and Sādāt in Khartoum on 19 July 1978 during the OAU conference were denied by both presidents.

Libya

Sādāt's declaration of his intention to visit Jerusalem again unleashed the two regimes' basic enmity (see *MECS 1976-77*, pp. 163-70). Tension along the Egyptian-Libyan border increased at the end of 1977, with both countries concentrating troops there.[100] A senior Libyan official claimed that Egypt had plans to overthrow Qadhdhāfī's regime and to seize the Libyan oilfields.[101] Again, as in 1976 and 1977, the Egyptians discovered and dismantled Libyan-organized terrorist groups,[102] and Tripoli was blamed for many of Egypt's internal troubles. Qadhdhāfī was referred to by Sādāt as a "lunatic" and as the worst of his enemies. Although he called Qadhdhāfī "a lost case," Sādāt did not exclude Libya from the list of Arab adversaries with which he was generally willing to improve relations—on Egypt's terms—as set out above.

The People's Democratic Republic of Yemen

After the rupture of relations, the Egyptian media stressed the PDRY's connection with Arab and other terrorist movements, condemned its participation in the war against Somalia and its aid to the Soviet-oriented Ethiopian regime. Egypt frequently emphasized the PDRY's negative role in the area.[103] The overthrow of Rubay' in Aden, and the PDRY's part in the assassination of North Yemen's President al-Ghashmī in June 1978, sharpened Egypt's awareness that the PDRY's influence needed to be contained. As a result, Egypt encouraged a motion tabled in the Arab League Council at the beginning of July 1978 which called on Arab states to "freeze" their relations with South Yemen (for details, see essay on Inter-Arab Relations). Even so, the Egyptian media deplored the mildness of the motion and declared that it was high time for moderate Arab states to develop a common strategy to remove the presence of the Soviet Union and its satellites from the area.[104]

The PLO

PLO attacks on Sādāt's forthcoming visit to Israel led the Egyptian authorities to close down the "Voice of Palestine" radio station (which transmitted from Cairo) on 18 November 1977—on the eve of the visit.[105] A few days later, on 23 November, Egypt expelled Jamāl Surānī, the permanent PLO delegate in Cairo, and Rubḥī 'Awad, the Fatḥ representative and chairman of the Association of Palestinian Students in Egypt.[106]

Egypt's anger at the PLO's stand was reflected in the fact that, in his speech to the Knesset, Sādāt did not mention the PLO as a partner in the negotiating process. Later, on another occasion, he spoke of the "real Palestinians" living under oc- cupation—as distinct from "the cabaret fighters" in Beirut. Moreover, Sādāt frequently criticized 'Arafāt for allowing himself to be manipulated by Syria and the USSR.[107]

The conflict between Cairo and the PLO was further aggravated after the murder of Yūsuf Sibā'ī, who was chairman of Egypt's Press Association, a prominent writer and a close friend of Sādāt. He was shot in Cyprus on 18 February 1978 by two armed Palestinians. Even worse, Cairo suspected that PLO members had participated alongside the Cypriot forces in the shooting against the Egyptian commando rescue team at Larnaca Airport on 19 February. In a furious outburst, the Egyptian media attacked 'Arafāt and the Palestinians and explicitly called for the abandonment of Egypt's commitment towards the Palestinian cause.[108] Radio Cairo "Voice of the Arabs" began using the term "the so-called PLO,"[109] and Prime Minister Sālim announced that the People's Assembly would "consider" cancelling facilities which were granted to Palestinians living in Egypt.[110] The climax was reached when Sādāt condemned the Fatḥ attack on the Tel Aviv-Haifa highway on 11 March 1978 (see essay on Armed Operations in the Arab-Israeli Conflict), possibly for fear that Israel would take retaliatory action that might have severe repercussions on his peace initiative. Sādāt called the Palestinian action "irresponsible, a tragic and sad incident."[111] Finally, on the eve of the Leeds Castle conference (18–19 July), Anīs Mansūr, editor-in-chief of the weekly *October*, ex- pressed what had already been accepted as Egypt's official but undeclared position: that the PLO should not be involved in any negotiations on the future of the West Bank and the Gaza Strip.[112]

Nevertheless, Egypt continued to maintain contacts with the PLO in order to exercise a certain degree of influence over it, but mainly to try to undermine al- Fatḥ's relations with other PLO factions and with Syria. The contacts were acknowledged in December 1977 by Acting Foreign Minister Ghālī, and later by Foreign Minister Ibrāhīm Kāmil himself.[113] At the beginning of February 1978, the Egyptian authorities permitted the PLO's representatives to return to Cairo.[114] The PLO was even allowed to broadcast a programme over Radio Cairo called "The Palestine Corner," but it was not permitted to operate a station under its own name as had been the case in the past. The new broadcasts were closely supervised by the Egyptian censors. Egypt also continued to support the PLO in international forums.

Relations with Iraq

Egypt's relations with Iraq had been hostile since the end of the 1973 war. However, both accorded their respective relations with Syria a higher priority, and thus found a *modus vivendi* for avoiding mutually damaging acts. When Iraq decided to participate in the Tripoli summit in December 1977, this understanding broke down. Egypt severed relations with all the Tripoli bloc members and with Iraq even though the latter walked out of the summit (see essay on Inter-Arab Relations). Immediately afterwards, Iraqi students as well as the staff of the Iraqi News Agency in Egypt were expelled.[115] At the beginning of May 1978, Egypt disbanded a terrorist group connected with Abū Nidāl who headed an Iraqi-backed Palestinian organization which had split off from al-Fath in the early 1970s (see essay on PLO). This group was reported to have planned to destroy the Mina House Hotel and the Tahara Palace, the residences in which Israeli representatives and negotiators lived during their stay in Egypt.[116] Sādāt publicly accused Iraq of stirring up and financing anti-Egyptian propaganda. He also reminded Baghdad that it had exploited the October War to enrich itself, since it did not adhere to the Arab embargo.[117]

In contrast with the continued tense relations with the Tripoli bloc, Egypt and Iraq gradually initiated a number of measures which eased the tension between them. Cultural centres and chambers of commerce were reopened in Baghdad and Cairo; so were the Iraqi and Egyptian consulates in Basrah and Alexandria. Economic ties between the two countries were maintained.[118] Most significantly, the Egyptian War Minister, Gen Jamasī, disclosed on 17 May that Egypt was continuing to receive spare parts for Soviet weapons from Iraq.[119]

RELATIONS WITH THE CONSERVATIVE CAMP

Saudi Arabia

The main target of Egyptian diplomatic efforts in the Arab world was Saudi Arabia since its backing would secure the support of the entire conservative Arab world, whereas its opposition—or even neutrality—to Sādāt's peace initiative would prove too difficult to surmount.

Although Sādāt did not consult Saudi Arabia in advance of his initiative or prior to each of its main stages, he tried to explain his steps—once taken—through messages or visits by high-ranking Egyptian diplomats. The outstanding example of this policy was Mubārak's visit in mid-May 1978 to Saudi Arabia (and Jordan) to present the Egyptian ideas which had been mooted earlier and were later consolidated under the title: "Egyptian proposals for withdrawal from the West Bank and the Gaza Strip." Egypt hoped to obtain Saudi acquiescence in its plan, and Mubārak returned with the impression that he had at least succeeded in persuading Saudi Arabia not to oppose it. Mubārak's visit was also noteworthy as an indication that Saudi-Egyptian contacts were no longer carried out at the level of heads of state. Since Sādāt did not confer with King Khālid (because the Saudis preferred to avoid a meeting likely to arouse Arab controversies), Vice-President Mubārak became the key figure on the Egyptian side, while the Saudis were represented by Crown Prince Fahd, Prince Turkī al-Faysal, Foreign Minister Sa'ūd al-Faysal and Defence Minister Sultān Ibn 'Abd al-'Azīz.

Despite Saudi Arabia's dispute with Egypt over its policy towards Israel, there was active co-operation between them concerning Soviet penetration into the Horn of Africa and Black Africa. Apparently it was Riyadh that initiated and financed the Egyptian military aid to Somalia and Chad. Both countries held close consultations on the future of Eritrea, on the events in Zaïre, and on the strengthening of the Sudanese regime. They also worked together in considering the political

393

repercussions of developments in South and North Yemen in June 1978.[120]
Saudi economic aid was not used as a lever against Egypt. Nor did political differences affect the situation of Egyptians working in Saudi Arabia who were estimated to number 500,000 in 1978. Egypt opened a special office in Riyadh to look after their interests.[121]

Co-operation continued at the military level as well. Sādāt said on several occasions that Saudi Arabia had committed itself to financing Egypt's five-year military plan.[122] A minor diplomatic incident was created when the Minister of State for Foreign Affairs, Butrus Ghālī, made an ill-advised statement to the Assembly's Foreign Affairs Committee about the possibility of the transfer to Egypt of the F-15s purchased by Saudi Arabia from the US in the event of a war with Israel. But an Egyptian communiqué promptly denied that Ghālī had ever made such a pronouncement.[123]

Jordan
Egypt displayed a certain ambivalence in its relations with Amman. While it frequently expressed eagerness for Jordan's participation in the peace negotiations, Sādāt nonetheless did not consult the Kingdom in making his moves and regarded it with some mistrust which stemmed from Husayn's earlier "Syrian connection" (see *MECS 1976-77*, pp. 154–57). This suspiciousness was shown when Husayn visited Cairo on 7 November 1977, but was not informed of the initiative to be launched only two days later. During Husayn's next visit, in December, Sādāt failed to tell him that he was about to convene the Cairo conference. He apparently assumed that these moves would eventually be accepted by Amman, since the Egyptian position was that Jordan should play an important role in any interim solution of the West Bank issue, and that the territory should become linked to the Hashimite Kingdom.

The underlying distrust was also shown after Mubārak's visit to Amman in May 1978. According to the Lebanese press,[124] Jordan suspected Mubārak of having acted in bad faith by falsely reporting that Saudi Arabia supported Egypt's proposals on the West Bank. A similar misunderstanding occurred after the Camp David summit. Sādāt had arranged to meet Husayn in Rabat on his way home to Cairo, and was apparently convinced that he would agree to enter the negotiations alongside Egypt on the basis of the Camp David framework agreement on the West Bank and the Gaza Strip. However, Husayn refused to meet Sādāt in Morocco, let alone join in the negotiating process.

EGYPT AND THE LEBANESE CRISIS
Egypt kept a low profile and rarely initiated diplomatic moves during the crisis in Lebanon in 1977–78 (see chapter on Lebanon and essay on South Lebanon in the Arab-Israeli Conflict). Egypt denied rumours reported in March 1978 of its intention to participate in the Arab Deterrent Force.[125] The only occasion on which Egypt did offer to mediate was after former President Faranjiyya's son, Tony, was assassinated on 13 June.[126]

Nevertheless, Sādāt twice chose to refer publicly to the Lebanese crisis after the Israeli invasion in March 1978. In the first reference, Sādāt claimed that he had received assurances from Israeli Defence Minister Weizman in their talks on 31 March that his country would not permanently occupy South Lebanon, and that it was only conducting a mopping-up operation.[127] On the second occasion, after the Israeli withdrawal had begun, Sādāt contacted 'Arafāt and asked him to intervene personally to stop PLO operations against Israeli forces. He warned that PLO attacks were giving Israel a pretext for returning to South Lebanon and for turning a temporary presence into a permanent occupation.[128]

Sādāt also regarded the Lebanese crisis as a test of the US attitude towards Israel. He drew attention to the fact that only 24 hours after the US had intervened, Security Council Resolution 425—calling for immediate Israeli withdrawal from South Lebanon and the formation of UNIFIL—had been approved.[129] He added that if Carter had been US President in 1967 and "the Zionist [Arthur] Goldberg" had not been US representative at the UN, things would have been "different today."[130]

THE IMPACT OF THE NEGOTIATING PROCESS
REASSERTION OF "EGYPTIANISM"
Resentment over the dissociation of most Arab countries from Egypt's policy towards Israel, as well as the expectation that a peace settlement would set Egypt free to devote its energies to domestic development and reconstruction, promoted the expression of neutralist ideas among Egyptian intellectuals.

In the beginning of March 1978, the well-known Egyptian writer, Tawfīq al-Ḥakīm, published an essay in *al-Ahrām* on Egyptian neutralism,[131] in which he contended that Egypt would not succeed in rebuilding the country as long as its resources and efforts continued to be devoted to purposes removed from the Egyptian masses; this resulted from its excessive involvement in foreign affairs. Ḥakīm argued that Egypt's future, tranquillity and stability could be secured only by pursuing a neutralist course similar to that of Switzerland or Austria. Egypt's geo-political position, its role in world trade through its control of the Suez Canal, and its place as the cradle of cultures important to the world—all these factors combined to reinforce demands for such neutrality. Being at the fulcrum of the Arab world and freed by a neutralist policy, Egypt could devote its efforts to an Arab cultural renaissance.[132]

Ḥākim's appeal sparked off a public debate in Egypt between supporters of neutralism and their opponents, including intellectuals and journalists of the Egyptian Left such as Yūsuf Idrīs, Aḥmad Bahā al-Dīn and 'Abd al-'Azīz Ramaḍān. This debate raised questions about Egypt's future relations with the Arab world. The ideological premise on which the concept of Arab nationalism rested was called into question, and there were calls for the rejection of the idea of Arab unity.[133] The debate continued until May 1978, when domestic politics again claimed attention (see above).

"PREPARING FOR PEACE"
The impact of Sādāt's initiative could also be discerned in the sudden preoccupation with the implications of peace in socio-economic and cultural fields. One illustration of this was the statement of the Prime Minister, Mamdūḥ Sālim, that "ancient nations which wage war for the sake of principles and to protect human rights do not wait till the end of the war and let themselves be caught by surprise by peace. Those nations begin to prepare to meet all the demands and to solve all the problems that will arise in the transition from war to peace. . . . [indeed,] the problems of peace are more complicated ones, and greater than any of the problems of war."[134]

Egyptian economists cited the following advantages which Egypt could expect to derive from peace:

(1) Providing a safeguard against the devastating effects of a future war.[135]

(2) Concentration on solving the basic problems of the economy and society, and getting Egypt back on the track of economic growth and development.[136]

(3) Creation of an atmosphere favourable to foreign investment. (Some

claimed that peace was a pre-condition for the eventual success of Sādāt's "open-door" policy.)[137]
(4) Gradual reduction of defence expenditure and the size of the army.[138]

Sādāt ordered the National Council (the body responsible for Egypt's long-term planning) to start work on an overall plan for the development of Sinai, and to co-ordinate the partial schemes prepared earlier by various government depart-ments.[139] This initial preoccupation with the contingencies of peace receded when the negotiations became stalled, but was revived with greater vigour after the Camp David agreements.

THE IMAGE OF ISRAEL

From November 1977 onwards, certain changes became apparent in the Egyptian attitude towards Israel. A few days before Sādāt's visit to Jerusalem, attacks on Israel ceased in the media. Israel became a focus of interest and the subject of many reports intended to explain the basic facts about the country. Thus, a gradual process of "humanization" of Israel took place. The media took their cue from Sādāt and began to relate to Israel as one of the states in the ME with which Egypt had to deal. Egyptians were amazed at the warmth of the Israeli public's reaction to Sādāt's visit, and the direct contact with its people and leaders provided many surprises. The reactions of Anīs Mansūr, editor-in-chief of the weekly *October*, were typical. He found that the Foreign Minister, Moshe Dayan, looked "fragile"; Golda Meir was small and had a "waxen complexion"; and neither they nor President Katzir were the awe-inspiring figures he had taken them to be. Most of all, Mansūr could not get accustomed to thinking of Prime Minister Begin, "the former terrorist," as a human being.[140] He acknowledged that "all these pictures we drew were drawn out of hatred and anger, and a desire for revenge."[141] He con-cluded that "our image of the Jews [i.e. the Israelis], as that of the Egyptians in the eye of the Israelis . . . was inherited [from the past] and remained unchanged. . . . Nevertheless," he added, "there will be no peace if this image does not change, our image and theirs; there is no other way to realize this but by getting closer, by sitting together and getting to understand one another."[142] This new approach was ex-pressed by Mansūr in the following terms: "We used to tell about you, the 'so-called Israel.' Books were printed in Egypt which told about the 'so-called Israel.' Sometimes, the words Israel, Zionism, the tripartite aggression, Tel Aviv, Jaffa and the Dead Sea were simply erased from books."[143] Now, he said, it was necessary for Egyptians and Israelis to be re-educated in order to understand each other.

With the emergence of growing difficulties in the peace talks, images again became more negative and the focus shifted to attempts to understand the Israeli political structure and the interplay of political forces in Israel.

THE PERSONAL IMAGE OF BEGIN

In the period between Sādāt's meeting with Begin at Ismā'īliyya and the conclusion of the Camp David summit, much of the resentment displayed by Sādāt and the Egyptian media over Israel's negotiating attitudes focused on the person of Menahem Begin. According to Sādāt, Begin appeared as a leader who lacked vision, who was unable to grasp the real implications of his initiative, and who adopted intransigent attitudes because of domestic problems and issues of party politics. At every difficult turn in the negotiations, Begin was described in the Egyptian media as the main "obstacle to peace." Occasionally he was called a "new Hitler."[144] At such times, Sādāt said he had no common language with the Israeli Prime Minister and felt he was not being understood by him. Sādāt declared that he detected a trait of bitterness in Begin's character which prevented him from establishing friendly relations with people around him.[145] Most of the anti-Semitic allusions in the Egyptian media during the year were also focused on the person of Begin.

PERCEPTIONS OF ISRAELI DOMESTIC POLITICS
The Israeli political structure, and particularly the way it affected the course of the negotiations, became another object of special interest which led to the "discovery" of Israel as a political community. This process was made more acute because of the limited Egyptian understanding of political behaviour in an open society. Egyptians likened developments in Israel following Sādāt's initiative to the after-effects of an earthquake.[146] Egyptian observers apparently expected the Israeli public to translate its feelings into political action in a way which would have a strong influence on the government. Sādāt himself had counted on three factors to modulate Begin's initial stand: the Cabinet, the Knesset, and the extra-parliamentary opposition.

The Egyptians hoped that Begin's influence in the Cabinet would be balanced by that of the Defence Minister, Ezer Weizman. From their first meeting in Jerusalem, Sādāt had taken a liking to Weizman and had been impressed by his pragmatism.[147] When asked in Salzburg in mid-1978 whether he was aware that his remarks about Weizman weakened the Defence Minister's position in the government, Sādāt answered that this was not his intention, but that he could not hide his feelings.[148] Nevertheless, it is instructive to note that in a crisis situation—such as the Israeli operation in South Lebanon—al-Ahrām's editor reverted to the former attitude of calling Weizman "the leader of a barbaric action whose hands are stained with Palestinian and Lebanese blood." However, the overall view taken was one of respect.[149]

Egypt's position towards the parliamentary opposition in Israel was ambivalent. On the one hand, it was seen as committed to the common Zionist approach and thus reflecting current government negotiating positions no less than the coalition parties themselves;[150] yet it was expected to exercise its influence in order to modify those positions. Sādāt fostered personal contacts with the opposition leader, Shimon Peres, whom he met twice during 1978 (in February and in July) in Austria. His intention in doing so was indicated by Anīs Mansūr who remarked that the July meeting in Salzburg had served to strengthen the Knesset opposition.[151] Similarly, 'Alī Hamdī al-Jamāl stressed that Egypt and Israel's principal opposition party, the Alignment, were in agreement on many points of principle raised during the negotiations. However, Sādāt was well aware of the criticism to which Peres was subjected from the coalition parties and declared that it was not his intention to drive a wedge between them. In a different context, when speaking to home audiences, Sādāt cited the conduct of the Israeli opposition as a model of responsibility in that whatever differences might exist between Begin and Peres, they were united over questions of vital interest. This remark was intended as indirect criticism of the "irresponsible" opposition in Egypt.[152]

In trying to assess the strength of extra-parliamentary opposition, Egyptian commentators interpreted peace demonstrations in Israel as a symbol of protest against Begin's policy on the part of the masses who were no longer content to remain silent.[153] Special attention was given to the "Peace Now" (Shalom 'Akhshav) movement. Foreign Minister Kāmil regarded this group as a "healthy phenomenon," while Sādāt referred to them as "wise people."[154]

RELATIONS WITH THE THIRD WORLD
AFRICA

Sādāt's policy towards Africa was based on his above-mentioned assumptions regarding Soviet aims. During the second Shaba (East Zaïre) campaign in May 1978, Egypt dispatched a high-ranking officer to study the situation there. According to Gen Jamasī, Egypt had sent a number of artillery pieces and a group of officers to train the Zaïre army in their use, but it had no intention of sending any troops to fight for Zaïre. [155]

During 1978, Egypt sent ammunition and anti-tank missiles to Somalia. [156] Jamasī visited Somalia, reportedly to study the needs of its army and to make an evaluation of the military situation there. [157]

Egypt also sent military aid to Chad. According to one unconfirmed report, Egyptian soldiers were killed in the fighting there. [158]

Egypt maximized its anxiety over developments in Africa in its contacts with the US and West European states. [159]. To US audiences in particular, Egypt presented itself as playing a leading role in the containment of Soviet influence in Africa and as being exposed, for this reason, to Soviet intrigues. Moreover, it was claimed that by its commitment to Western interests and its ability to protect them, it was Egypt—and not Israel—which was the real bastion of the West in Africa and the ME. [160] The US should therefore provide Egypt with the military means to implement its political commitments. [161] Cairo explained the restricted scope of its current involvement in Africa by stating that it could not send a single soldier to fight outside Egypt so long as the conflict with Israel was not ended. [162]

THE NON-ALIGNED BLOC

The early part of 1978 witnessed a steady revival of Egyptian interest in the non-aligned bloc—probably as a result of the realization that this bloc had become more hostile since coming under the influence of the radical Arab states. The missions of Deputy Foreign Minister Butrus Ghālī—a veteran advocate of Third World policy for Egypt—were symptomatic of efforts to redress the balance. Ghālī was sent to India and Sri Lanka (March 1978), and to the Belgrade meetings (May 1978) convened to prepare for the summit of the non-aligned countries in Havana in 1979.

CHINA

There was a constant improvement in relations between Cairo and Peking, as reflected in the number of visits exchanged. In early February 1978, Deputy Prime Minister Hasan al-Tuhāmī (a close personal associate of Sādāt) was sent to Peking on a special mission whose purpose was kept secret. There was speculation that Sādāt would visit China in late 1978 at the head of a high-ranking economic and military delegation, but the visit did not materialize. [163]

Several economic agreements were signed with China, which continued to supply engines and spare parts for Egypt's MiG-17s and MiG-21s. [164]

ECONOMIC AFFAIRS ($1 = 0.391 Egyptian pounds; £1 = £E 0.728)

Few, if any, of Egypt's serious economic problems were solved in 1977–78. [165] Economic growth, as measured by GDP in current prices, reached 17% in 1977. Per capita growth in *real* terms (which takes inflation into account) was not nearly as high and may easily have been negative, as inflation persisted in making its impact felt.

Besides inflation, the regime was faced with the problem of a large foreign debt, the servicing of which acted as a severe strain on an economy whose health was already tenuous. In the short term, there does not appear to be a practical solution for Egypt's chronic problems. In the longer term, however, Egyptian officials hope that such developments as growing revenues from crude oil production, increased foreign investment—particularly through the "open door," austerity measures to combat inflation, and the 1978–82 development plan will make it possible to transform the economy.

AGRICULTURE

Egypt's agricultural production, which had suffered a decline in the rate of growth since the mid-1960s, was estimated to have climbed 15% in current prices in 1977; in real terms, however, the value of output most probably did not increase.[166]

Production of cotton—Egypt's most important export commodity—was estimated to have risen 7.5% in 1976-77 over the previous year, to 415,000 metric tons. However, Ministry of Agriculture sources indicated that the cotton crop failed to achieve its expected output in 1977-78. A decline in production coupled with a 19% increase in domestic consumption forced the textile industry to purchase some of its raw cotton from Sudan and the US.[167]

Egypt's other principal crops witnessed relatively uneventful, if not disappointing, harvests in 1975-76. Production of maize (+9.6%), sugarcane (+6.9%) and vegetables (+5.3% on average) increased, while output of wheat (-3.7%), rice (-5.1%), millet (-2.1%) and citrus fruits (-12.7% on average) fell. Such lacklustre production figures tend to confirm the thesis that agricultural production will continue to be lethargic so long as the government pursues a policy of paying depressed prices to farmers and until the detrimental side-effects of the Aswān dam (e.g. higher soil salinity and rising water tables) are rectified.[168]

INDUSTRY

According to the Minister of Industry, Oil and Mineral Resources, Aḥmad 'Izz al-Dīn Hilāl, industrial production grossed £E 2,783m (c. $4,032m) in 1977, representing an increase of £E 313m (12.7%) over 1976. Public sector production climbed 15.3% from £E 1,726m in 1976 to £E 1,990m in 1977. At the same time, private sector output rose 7.9% from £E 735m to £E 793m. Hilāl reported that "all sectors have contributed" to the growth in production in 1977, especially the metal industry (+22%), metallurgy (+17%), textiles (+13%), food (+12%) and chemicals (+12%).[169]

The actively employed industrial labour force grew 3.36%, totalling 566,008 in 1977, according to Hilāl. At the same time, total wages rose 13.3% to £E 289m.[170]

Despite both the growth in production in 1977 and the enthusiasm engendered by Sādāt's peace initiative, a number of analysts maintain a markedly pessimistic assessment of the industrial sector.[171]

CONSTRUCTION

The construction sector employed an estimated 4.5% of the active labour force in 1976, accounting for 3.2% of gross fixed investment and contributing 4.6% of GDP. Though these figures represent substantial increases from 1973, Egypt's critical housing shortage remains largely unrelieved.

Because of the 2.3% annual population growth and sizeable rural-urban migration, some areas of Cairo have population densities greater than the high-rise districts in New York and Tokyo. The Ministry of Housing and Reconstruction estimated the housing shortage at 1.1m units. In 1977, the Ministry's target of 100,000 new housing units fell short by 43,000. It is estimated that 110,000 new units per year are needed to cope with the population increase and to replace dilapidated dwellings.[172]

OIL

The growth of the petroleum industry is one of the most promising developments in Egypt's recent economic history. In 1976, the first full year of operations following the return of the Sinai oilfields in 1975, production leaped 55% over the level of 1972, the last complete year of operations preceding the October 1973 war. Production rose a further 25.9% in 1977, reaching a total of 412,400 barrels per day (b/d). Estimates for 1978 predicted an output as high as 600,000 b/d; even so, the oil sector will have to expand much more rapidly if it is to achieve the stated goal of 1m b/d, bringing in $3,500m in annual revenue by 1980.[173]

Other intended sources of oil-derived revenue include the planned indigenous petrochemical industry and the Suez-Mediterranean pipeline (for details, see *MECS 1976-77*, p. 273). Official statistics for 1977 reveal that the Sumed pipeline was running at only one-fourth of its capacity of 1.6m b/d.[174] The profitability of any future petrochemical schemes remains only speculative.

BUDGET

Egypt's budgetary expenditure was estimated to have risen 25.2% in current prices in 1977, reaching a total of £E 3,817m (c. $9,755m). An estimated 63.3% of this total was taken up by current expenditure, with the remainder going to investment spending. One particularly controversial expenditure item, the subsidies programme, was cut as an economy measure but then quickly restored as a result of social and political pressures. (For details of the political aspects of the subsidies, see above.)

Total revenue was estimated to have increased by one-third in 1977 over 1976, reaching £E 2,687m (c. $6,869), but leaving a primary deficit of £E 1,130m. With the addition of the emergency fund's deficit of £E 352m, the overall deficit for 1977 was estimated to have totalled £E 1,481m—a decline of £E 144m compared with 1976. External borrowing was estimated to have fallen an absolute £E 18m to £E 470m, which is equivalent to a relative decline from 36.5% to 31.7%.

BALANCE OF PAYMENTS

Complete data on Egypt's balance-of-payments accounts for 1977 were unavailable at November 1978. Available statistics reveal that the merchandise trade deficit widened a further $141m in 1977. This was partly offset by the growth of the exports of services surplus by $436m. However, the sheer size of the merchandise trade deficit led to a $796m deficit for goods, services and transfers combined. This last figure compares favourably with the corresponding deficits of $807m in 1976 and $1,397m in 1975. (These statistics do not include arms purchases.)

DEVELOPMENT

Rapid economic growth has been called "a matter of life and death for Egypt."[175] The success of Egypt's development programme is indeed vital to the country's economic—and to a large extent, social and political—well-being. That fundamental changes are required was illustrated by the statement of the Deputy Prime Minister responsible for financial and economic affairs, 'Abd al-Mun'im al-Qaysūnī, that the first objective of the 1978-82 Five-Year Development Plan "is represented by the attainment of a structural change in the pattern of government investment, with the goal of strengthening national development . . . so that the public sector may expand construction of the facilities whose condition has deteriorated, and the private sector may bear an increasing burden of productive projects." Priority has thus been given to "infrastructure and housing materials projects, to the solution of the transport and communications crisis, and to alleviation of the severity of the shortage of housing utilities. The plan has also devoted special attention to projects to provide foodstuffs." [176]

However, many have criticized the plan, and others have expressed scepticism as to its practicability. The critics disagree about the order of priorities and the size of allocations; the sceptics' doubts are prompted by the questionable achievements of both earlier attempts at development planning and implementation, and the existing "open door" policy. [177]

Development investment for 1978 was set at £E 1,760m (c. $4,498m). Transport and communications (21%), industry and metallurgy (19.6%), services (9%) and electricity (7%) received the largest allocations.

MONEY AND BANKING

Egypt's holdings of international reserves fluctuated during the second half of 1977 and the early months of 1978. At the end of May 1978, they stood at $398m, the lowest since the end of the first quarter of 1977. The bulk of the changes occurred in foreign exchange, as gold remained steady at c. $100m.

At the end of April 1978, the foreign assets of the Central Bank of Egypt reached $E 366m, the highest level since the second quarter of 1975. At the same time, reserve money of the Central Bank reached a record £E 2,204m, which increased by a further £E 103m in May 1978. [178]

FOREIGN DEBT

Estimates of Egypt's foreign debt vary from source to source, ranging from $7 to $17 bn. These estimates rarely, if ever, include the Egyptian military debt to the Soviet bloc, which has been variously estimated at from $4 to $6 bn. [179]

Egypt's credit remained good during 1978, despite the resignation of 'Abd al-Mun'im al-Qaysūnī who had done much to allay the apprehensions of Egypt's foreign creditors, and despite the considerable size of the foreign debt (which, according to many of the aforementioned estimates, exceeds the national product). For instance, the Consultative Group on Egypt (which includes, among others, the US, the Gulf Organization for the Development of Egypt, the IMF and the World Bank) agreed to grant an additional $2.4 bn in loans beginning in 1978. [180] (For details of Qaysūnī's resignation, see above.)

FOREIGN TRADE

Egypt's exports rose 8.5% in 1976 from 1975 and appeared to be growing at a faster rate in the first half of 1977, at which time the Soviet Union and Italy retained their positions as Egypt's first and second largest markets respectively. During 1976 and the first half of 1977, raw cotton and crude petroleum were the country's foremost exports.

According to Egyptian sources, imports actually fell 3.2% in 1976 from their 1975 level. This appears to have been a short-lived trend, however, as imports picked up again during the first half of 1977. The US, West Germany and Italy, in that order, were Egypt's three largest suppliers in 1976 and in the first half of 1977. During this same 18-month period, wheat, iron and steel products, and chemicals were Egypt's largest imports.

Jacques Reinich
Economic section by **Ira E. Hoffman**

ARAB REPUBLIC OF EGYPT

ARMED FORCES

Total armed forces number 395,000. Defence expenditure during 1978–79 amounted to £E 1.11 bn ($2.81 bn). Military service is compulsory for three years. The Army numbers 350,000, including Air Defence Command, and consists of two armoured divisions (each with one armoured and two mechanized brigades); three mechanized infantry divisions; five infantry divisions (each with two infantry brigades); one Republican Guard Brigade (division); three independent armoured brigades; seven independent infantry brigades; two airmobile brigades; two parachute brigades; six commando groups; six artillery and two heavy mortar brigades; one anti-tank guided weapon brigade; and two surface-to-surface missile regiments (up to 24 *Scud*). It is equipped with 850 T-54/55, 750 T-62 medium, 80 PT-76 light tanks; 300 BRDM-1/-2 scout cars; 200 BMP-76PB mechanized infantry combat vehicles; 2,500 OT-62/-64, BTR-40/-50/-60/-152, *Walid* armoured personnel carriers; 1,300 76mm, 100mm, 122mm, 130mm, 152mm and 180mm guns/howitzers; c. 200 SU-100 and ISU-152 self-propelled guns; 300 120mm, 160mm and 240mm mortars; 300 122mm, 140mm and 240mm rocket launchers; 30 *FROG*-4/-7, 24 *Scud* B, *Samlet* surface-to-surface missiles; 900 57mm, 85mm and 100mm anti-tank guns; 900 82mm and 107mm recoilless rifles; 1,000 *Sagger, Snapper, Swatter, Milan* and *Beeswing* anti-tank guided weapons; 350 ZSU-23-4, ZSU-57-2 self-propelled anti-aircraft guns and SA-7/-9 surface-to-air missiles. (There is a shortage of spares for Soviet equipment. M-113 armoured personnel carriers and *Swingfire* anti-tank guided weapons on order.)

The Air Defence Command numbers 75,000 and has 360 SA-2, 200 SA-3 and 75 SA-6 surface-to-air missiles; 2,500 20mm, 23mm, 37mm, 40mm, 57mm, 85mm and 100mm anti-aircraft guns; missile radars include *Fan Song, Low Blow, Flat Face, Straight Flush* and *Long Track*; gun radars *Fire Can, Fire Wheel* and *Whiff*; early warning radars *Knife Rest* and *Spoon Rest*. (There is a shortage of spares for Soviet equipment; *Crotale* surface-to-air missiles are on order.) There are c. 500,000 reserves.

The 20,000-strong Navy is equipped with 12 submarines (ex-Soviet, six W- and six R-class); five destroyers (four *Skory*-, one ex-British Z-class); two escorts (ex-British); 12 SO-1 submarine chasers (ex-Soviet); 16 guided-missile fast patrol boats (six *Osa*-I-, 10 *Komar*-class with Styx surface-to-surface missiles); 26 motor torpedo boats (six *Shershen*, 20 P-6); three SRN-6 hovercraft; 14 ex-Soviet mine counter-measures (six T-43, four *Yurka*, two T-301, two K-8); three landing craft tanks (*Polnocny*-class), 13 landing craft utility (nine *Vydra*, four SMB-1); six *Sea King* anti-submarine warfare helicopters. (Two *Lupo*-class frigates, six Vosper *Ramadan*-class guided-missile fast patrol boats, three SRN-6 hovercraft, *Otomat* surface-to-surface missiles on order.) Reserves number c. 15,000.

The Air Force numbers 25,000 and has c. 612 combat aircraft (additional Soviet aircraft are grounded for lack of spares); 23 Tu-16D/G medium bombers; five Il-28 light bombers; three fighter bomber regiments with 80 MiG-21F/PFM, 90 MiG-15/-17; five ground-attack fighter/strike regiments with 70 Su-7, 19 Su-20, 21 MiG-23 and 46 *Mirage* VDE/DD; nine interceptor squadrons with 108 MiG-21MF. Transports include three C-130, two EC-130H, 26 Il-14, 19 An-12, one *Falcon*, one Boeing 707 and one Boeing 737. Helicopters include 20 Mi-4, 32 Mi-6, 70 Mi-8, 30 *Commando* and 54 *Gazelle*. Trainers include 150 MiG-15/-21/-23U, Su-7U, L-29, 45 *Gomhouria*. AA-2 *Atoll*, R.530 air-to-air missiles; AS-1 *Kennel*, AS-5 *Kelt* air-to-surface missiles. (42 F-5E, eight F-5F, 14 *Mirage* V fighters, 14 C-130H transports, 50 *Lynx* helicopters are on order.) There are c. 50,000 paramilitary forces which include 6,000 National Guard, 6,000 Frontier Corps, 30,000 Defence and Security and 7,000 Coast Guard.

Source: *The Military Balance 1978–79* (London: International Institute for Strategic Studies).

ARMED FORCES: FORMATIONS/MAJOR SYSTEMS

	1973	1978
Armoured divisions	2	2
Mechanized divisions	3	3
Infantry divisions	5	5
Independent Infantry brigades	4	11
Special forces brigades	9	8
Tanks	2,000	2,000
Armoured personnel carriers	3,000	2,600
Artillery	2,220	2,400
Ground-to-ground *Scud* launchers	9	24
Combat aircraft	653	500
Helicopters	160	150
Ground-to-air missile batteries	146	140
Naval vessels	40	32

Source: *Arab Military Strength* (Jerusalem: Israel Information Centre, June 1978).

BALANCE OF PAYMENTS (million US dollars)

	1975	1976	1977
A. Goods, Services and Transfers	-1,397	-807	-796
Exports of Merchandise, fob	1,567	1,609	1,933
Imports of Merchandise, fob	-3,941	-3,842	-4,307
Exports of Services	1,078	1,975	2,884
Imports of Services	-1,178	-1,260	-1,733
Private Unrequited Transfers, net	90	87	99
Government Unrequited Transfers, net	986	623	328
B. Long-Term Capital, nie	588	541	...
C. Short-Term Capital, nie	-509	-264	...
D. Errors and Omissions	-24	-7	...
E. **Total** (A through D)	**-1,343**	**-537**	...

MONETARY SURVEY (million Egyptian pounds at end of period)

	1976	1977	*(Jan–May)* 1978
Foreign Assets (net)	-1,002.7	-726.7	-762.6
Domestic Credit	4,577.0	5,328.7	5,903.4
Claims on Government (net)	*3,215.0*	*3,586.3*	*4,181.1*
Claims on Private Sector	*1,146.6*	*1,536.7*	*1,474.8*
Claims on Specialized Banks	*179.4*	*205.7*	*247.5*
Money	2,238.9	2,943.0	3,246.1
Quasi-money	974.5	1,315.5	1,440.8
Money, seasonally adjusted	2,230.0	2,929.3	3,226.7

NATIONAL ACCOUNTS (million Egyptian pounds)

	1974	1975	1976	1977
Exports	890	948	1,034	1,470
Government Consumption	1,101	1,213	1,571	1,576
Gross Fixed Capital Formation	640	1,228	1,385	1,769
Increase in Stocks	90	83	195	281
Private Consumption	2,871	3,293	3,863	4,505
Less: Imports	*-1,395*	*-1,920*	*-1,772*	*-2,260*
Gross Domestic Product (GDP)	**4,197**	**4,861**	**6,276**	**7,341**
GDP at 1975 prices*	4,674	4,861	5,405	

*Estimates.
Source (of three preceding tables): IMF, *International Financial Statistics*.

BUDGET SUMMARY (million Egyptian pounds)

	1975	1976	1977*
Total Revenue	1,524	2,015	2,687
Total Expenditure	2,628	3,049	3,817
of which:			
Current Expenditure	1,765	2,069	2,418
Investment Expenditure	863	980	1,399
Emergency Fund Deficit	-284	-303	-352
Overall Deficit	-1,388	-1,337	-1,481
Financing (net)	1,388	1,337	1,481
of which:			
External borrowing (net)	210	488	470
Domestic borrowing (net)	1,178	849	1,011

*Estimate.
Source: Ministry of Finance.

PLANNED INVESTMENT (million Egyptian pounds at 1977 prices)

	1978	1978–82	% of public investment (1978–82)
Public	**1,584.1**	**10,175.4**	**100.0**
Agriculture	65.4	395.7	3.9
Irrigation and Drainage	93.8	483.2	4.7
Industry and Metallurgy	344.1	2,412.6	23.7
Petroleum	75.0	562.4	5.5
Electricity	122.6	924.0	9.1
Construction	32.0	213.8	2.1
Transport and Communications	370.5	2,307.3	22.6
Suez Canal	119.0	474.8	4.7
Commerce and Finance	30.7	225.8	2.2
Housing	85.0	585.0	5.8
Utilities	94.6	622.8	6.1
Services	158.5	978.0	9.6
Private	**176.0**	**1,458.0**	—
Total	**1,760.1**	**11,633.4**	—

Source: Middle East Economic Digest

LOANS FROM FOREIGN SOURCES IN CONVERTIBLE CURRENCIES (million US dollars as of 31 December 1977)

	Including Disbursed	Disbursed Only
Loans (principal)		
United States	2,012	795
Gulf Organization for the Development of Egypt (GODE)	1,725	1,225
International Bank for Reconstruction and Development (IBRD)	635	87
West Germany	509	286
Japan	394	159
International Development Agency (IDA)	335	168
Abu Dhabi	329	280
Iran	300	300
Kuwait	278	212

	Including Disbursed	Disbursed Only
Arab Fund for Economic and Social Development (AFESD)	223	25
Saudi Arabia	214	109
Norway	122	—
Qatar	113	88
Other loans (principal) in convertible currencies	469	171
Soviet Union	1,300	n.a.
Other loans (principal) in clearing currencies	600	n.a.

Sources: Ministry of Economy and Economic Co-operation and *New York Times*.

GDP BY TYPE OF ECONOMIC ACTIVITY
(million Egyptian pounds at current prices)

	1975	1976	1977*
Agriculture	1,406.9	1,553.0	1,787
Industry, Petroleum and Mining	1,013.7	1,302.6	1,581
Electricity	71.9	77.5	83
Construction	230.5	249.0	285
Transportation, Communication and Storage	224.2	355.0	479
Trade and Finance	538.5	680.0	795
Service Sectors	1,143.1	1,237.7	1,473
GDP at Factor Cost	**4,779.0**	**5,455.1**	**6,483**
Net Indirect Taxes	82.0	373.0	626.0
GDP at Market Prices	4,861.0	5,828.1	7,109.0

*Provisional Estimates.

GDP AT CONSTANT PRICES BY TYPE OF ECONOMIC ACTIVITY
(million Egyptian pounds)

	1976	1977	% change
Agriculture	1,491	1,490	-0.1
Industry and Mining	918	1,001	9.0
Petroleum	220	324	42.3
Electricity	78	86	10.3
Construction	244	274	12.3
Transportation and Communications	412	475	15.3
Trade and Finance	662	711	5.9
Housing	136	144	5.9
Other Utilities	22	22	—
Services	1,085	1,188	9.5
GDP at Factor Cost	**5,268**	**5,705**	**8.3**

Source (of two preceding tables): Ministry of Planning.

PRODUCTION OF MAJOR AGRICULTURAL CROPS
(thousand metric tons)

	1973-74	1974-75	1975-76	1976-77
Wheat	1,884	2,033	1,960	1,697[1]
Cotton (lint)	441	382	386	415[2]
Rice (paddy)	2,242	2,423	2,300	...
Maize	2,640	2,781	3,047	...
Millet (sorghum)	824	775	759	
Sugarcane	7,018	7,902	8,446	
Citrus Fruits	963	1,013	889	
Vegetables	6,006	6,520	6,867	

[1] Preliminary Estimate.
[2] Estimate based on information provided by the Ministry of Agriculture.
Source: Ministry of Agriculture.

INDUSTRIAL PRODUCTION (million Egyptian pounds)

	1975[1]	1976[1]	1977[2]
Spinning, Weaving and Clothing	504	563	641
Food	535	596	667
Chemicals	179	182	302
Metallurgical and Mining	321	392	471
Total public sector	1,538*	1,733	1,990
Industrial private sector	599	735	793
Total	**2,137**	**2,469***	**2,783**

*Figures do not add because of rounding.
[1] Top four lines reflect public sector only.
[2] Top four lines reflect public and private sectors.
Sources: National Bank of Egypt and Ministry of Industry, Oil and Mineral Resources.

EXPORTS BY COMMODITY (million Egyptian pounds)

	1974	1975	1976	(first half) 1977
Raw cotton	279.1	201.0	154.8	104.9
Crude petroleum	23.9	23.1	109.8	45.8
Cotton yarn and waste	67.9	67.1	62.3	34.0
Petroleum products	26.5	28.7	39.3	23.0
Rice	39.7	24.1	31.0	10.5
Textile products	23.8	33.4	30.3	10.7
Oranges	11.1	18.5	18.9	19.4
Woven cotton	20.1	16.2	17.4	11.5
Potatoes	5.9	3.2	17.2	12.3
Total (including others)	**593.3**	**547.8**	**595.5**	**341.6**

IMPORTS BY COMMODITY (million Egyptian pounds)

	1974	1975	1976	(first half) 1977
Wheat	232.8	213.0	153.6	43.5
Iron and steel and products	46.9	101.8	75.0	40.8
Chemicals, nie	61.8	99.3	71.6	47.7
Capital motor vehicles	12.6	69.7	65.0	39.5
Paper and paper products	30.9	54.8	56.2	19.5
Animal products	10.9	22.8	49.7	17.5
Textile machinery	11.8	19.3	41.3	18.0
Wood and cork	29.0	49.7	39.2	51.6
Consumer motor vehicles	29.5	30.2	38.2	19.4
Animal fats and vegetable oils	46.3	135.2	37.4	12.2
Total (including others)	**920.1**	**1,539.3**	**1,489.9**	**800.7**

DIRECTION OF TRADE (million Egyptian pounds at official exchange rate)

	1975	1976	(first half) 1977
Exports to:			
Soviet Union	237.2	145.7	71.1
Italy	24.6	50.0	28.9
Greece	2.6	21.0	21.5
Czechoslovakia	40.4	33.1	19.9
East Germany	32.2	30.5	19.3
United Kingdom	8.2	23.5	17.7
France	8.3	21.1	13.7
Japan	4.2	20.2	13.4
West Germany	7.8	11.4	11.6
China, PR	20.5	20.1	10.2
Total (including others)	**548.6**	**595.5**	**341.8**

	1975	1976	(first half) 1977
Imports from:			
United States	296.2	244.2	132.0
West Germany	129.0	172.1	87.6
Italy	91.0	118.7	84.3
United Kingdom	70.0	85.1	49.4
France	165.0	91.2	47.7
Japan	50.9	74.1	42.9
Soviet Union	91.2	74.9	38.7
Netherlands	42.0	37.9	24.4
Yugoslavia	21.1	24.1	20.8
East Germany	39.5	25.6	16.7
Total (including others)	**1,539.3**	**1,489.9**	**800.7**

Source (of three preceding tables): Central Agency for Public Mobilization and Statistics.

NOTES
1. *Al-Ahrām*, Cairo; 14, 30 November 1977.
2. *Al-Akhbār*, Cairo; 29, 30 March; *al-Ahālī*, Cairo; 8 March 1978.
3. *Al-Ahrām*, 19 March 1978.
4. *Al-Akhbār*, 12 April; *al-Ahrām*, 11 April 1978.
5. *October*, Cairo; 24 March 1978.
6. Sādāt's speech, 14 May; *al-Ahrām*, 15 May 1978.
7. *Los Angeles Times* reporting from Cairo, cited by *Ma'ariv*, Tel Aviv; 23 November 1978.
8. *Al-Akhbār*, 19 February 1978.
9. Sādāt's interview to *Akhbār al-Yawm*, Cairo; 10 December 1977.
10. Middle East News Agency (MENA), Cairo; 10 December 1977.
11. See for instance the *Financial Times (FT)*, London; 24 November 1977.
12. *Al-Ahrām*, 26 June 1978.
13. *October*, 21 May 1978.
14. See for instance Sādāt's visit to the Suez Canal area, *al-Ahrām*, 7 June 1978.
15. *Al-Ahrām*, 4 October 1978.
16. *Ha'aretz*, Tel Aviv; 4 October 1978.
17. *Al-Akhbār*, 10 October; *al-Ahrām*, 10 October; *Yedi'ōt Aharonot*, Tel Aviv; 12 October 1978.
18. *Al-Ahrār*, Cairo; 21 August 1978.
19. *Al-Ahrām*, 26 October 1977.
20. *Ibid*, 8 May 1978.
21. *Ibid*, 17 July 1978.
22. Sādāt's speech as reported by *al-Ahrām*, 3 October 1978.
23. *Al-Ahrām*, 4–5 October 1978.
24. *Al-Ahrām*, 15 May; *Jaridat Misr*, Cairo; 9 May; *al-Ahrām*, 6, 29 May 1978.
25. *Al-Ahrām*, 21 June 1978.
26. *Ibid*, 7 July; *al-Iqtisādi*, Cairo; 16 July 1978.
27. *Al-Iqtisādi*, 16 July 1978.
28. Sūfi Abū-Tālib, *Ishtirākiyyatuna al-dimuqrātiyya, Īdiyulūjiyyat Thawrat Māyū sanat 1971, al-Iqtisādi*, 16 July 1978.
29. *Al-Ahrām*, 14 August 1978.
30. *Akhir Sā'a*, 23 August; *al-Ahrār*, 20 August 1978.
31. *Al-Ahrām*, 22 December 1977.
32. *Ibid*, 10 February 1978.
33. *Al-Akhbār*, 6 February 1978.
34. *Al-Ahālī*, 3 May 1978.
35. *Al-Ahrām*, 6 January, 5, 11 February 1978.
36. *Ibid*.
37. *Ibid*.
38. *Ibid*.
39. *Al-Ahālī*, 22 March 1978.
40. *Al-Ahrām*, 29 March 1978.
41. *Al-Jumhūriyya*, Cairo; 26 September; Qatari News Agency (QNA), 8 September 1978.
42. *Al-Ahālī*, 1 February, 22 March, 4, 19 April, 3, 8 May 1978.
43. QNA, 8 September 1978.
44. R Cairo, 22 May 1978.
45. *Al-Ahrām*, 28 May 1978.

46. *Al-Ahrār*, 20 August; *al-Ahrām*, 26 September 1978.
47. *Jaridat Misr*, 3 June; *al-Ahrām*, 21 May 1978.
48. *Al-Jumhūriyya*, 3 June 1978.
49. *Al-Ahrām*, 5 June 1978.
50. *Ibid*, 12 June 1978.
51. *Ibid*, 23 July 1978.
52. *Ibid*, 7 August 1978.
53. *Al-Jumhūriyya*, 6 August 1978.
54. *Al-Akhbār*, 3 August 1978.
55. *Al-Safīr*, Beirut; 2 December 1977; 23 February 1978; *al-Thawra Mustamirra*, Beirut; 4 February 1978; *al-Dustūr*, Beirut; 5 December 1977.
56. *Al-Akhbār*, 7 January, 14 May; *al-Ahrām*, 6, 28 May 1978.
57. *Rūz al-Yūsuf*, Cairo; 10 November 1977; *al-Ahrām*, 28 May 1978.
58. *Al-Dustūr*, 5 June; *Akhbār al-Yawm*, 27 May 1978.
59. *Akhbār al-Yawm*, 27 May 1978.
60. *Al-Da'wa*, Cairo; December 1977.
61. *Al-Jumhūriyya*, 20 March 1978.
62. *Ibid*, 22 January 1978.
63. *Al-Ahrām*, 10 August 1977.
64. *Le Monde*, Paris; 6 September 1977.
65. *Al-Akhbār*, 16 February 1978.
66. *Al-Jumhūriyya*, 10 February 1978.
67. *Ibid*, 27 December 1977.
68. *Al-Akhbār*, 23 August 1978.
69. *Al-Ahrām*, 19 May 1978.
70. United Press International (UPI), 3 December 1977; *al-Nahār al-'Arabī wal-Duwalī (NAD)*, Paris; 10 December 1977.
71. UPI, 8 December 1977.
72. UPI, 11 January 1978.
73. *Al-Akhbār*, 3 December 1977.
74. Sādāt's interview to the BBC, 3 June; *al-Ahrām*, 4 June 1978.
75. *Rūz al-Yūsuf*, 6 March 1978.
76. Agence France-Presse (AFP), 4 April 1978.
77. *Al-Jumhūriyya*, 12 February 1978.
78. UPI, 11 December 1977.
79. *Al-Jumhūriyya*, 23 March 1978.
80. Sādāt's press conference in Cairo, 21 January, *al-Ahrām*, 22 January; Sādāt's interview to International Press Media, 5 April, MENA, 6 April 1978.
81. Sādāt's press conference in Khartoum, 18 July; MENA, 19 July; *al-Ahrām*, 7 August 1978.
82. Sādāt's interview to the *Chicago Tribune*, 15 May 1978; Sādāt's speech to the American National Press Club in Washington, 6 February, MENA, 7 February 1978.
83. *Al-Ahrām*, 14 June 1978.
84. *Ākhir Sā'a*, 11 May 1977.
85. *Al-Ahrām*, 14 June 1978.
86. R Lebanon (Phalangists), 18 June 1978.
87. UPI, 16 November 1977.
88. Sādāt's interview to Japanese television, as reported by MENA, 31 May 1978.
89. Sādāt's speech on 8 December; *al-Ahrām*, 9 December 1977.
90. R Monte Carlo, 1 May 1978.
91. *Al-Akhbār*, 9 December 1977.
92. AFP, 18 December 1977.
93. *October*, 26 February 1978.
94. R Cairo, 16 March 1978.
95. *October*, 25 March 1978.
96. *Al-Akhbār*, 2 December 1977.
97. *October*, 5 March 1978.
98. *Al-Ahrām*, 2 December 1977.
99. *Al-Mustaqbal*, Paris; 28 January 1978.
100. R Monte Carlo, 21 December 1977; R Damascus, 24 January 1978.
101. *Al-Mustaqbal*, 24 January 1978.
102. See *al-Jumhūriyya*, 5 December 1977.
103. *October*, 11 June 1978.
104. AFP, 3 July 1978.
105. UPI, 18 November 1977.

106. Reuter, 23 November 1977.
107. MENA, 30 May 1978.
108. MENA, 25 February; *al-Akhbār*, 27 February 1978.
109. R Cairo, Voice of the Arabs (VoA), 27 February 1978.
110. *October*, 5 March 1978.
111. UPI, 14 March 1978.
112. *October*, 16 July 1978.
113. *Washington Post (WP)*, 4 December 1977; AFP, 27 January 1978.
114. Reuter, Cairo; 5 February 1978.
115. MENA, 6 December; Iraqi News Agency (INA), 8 December 1977.
116. *Al-Ahrām*, 3 May 1978.
117. *October*, 11 March 1978.
118. MENA, 30 January; Reuter, 24 March 1978.
119. UPI, 17 May 1978.
120. UPI, 26 January 1978; MENA, 31 July 1978; *NAD*, 23 July 1978; *WP*, 17 July 1978; *al-Qabas*, Riyadh; 9 June 1978.
121. QNA, 18 August 1978.
122. Sādāt's speech at a military airfield, 16 June; MENA, 8 August 1977.
123. UPI, 16 April; R Cairo, VoA, 16 April 1978.
124. *Al-Safir*, 19 May; *al-Sayyād*, Beirut; 22 June 1978.
125. R Lebanon (Phalangists), 8 March 1978.
126. *October*, 15 June 1978.
127. MENA, citing *October*, 9 April 1978.
128. Reuter, 3 June 1978.
129. Sādāt's speech, 27 July 1978.
130. *Ibid.*
131. *Al-Ahrām*, 3 March 1978.
132. *Al-Ahrām*, 3, 13 March 1978.
133. *Al-Jumhūriyya*, 9 May; 11 September; *al-Ahālī*, 16 April; *al-Ahrām*, 30 April 1978.
134. R Cairo, 20 December 1977.
135. *Al-Ahrām*, 16 December 1977; *al-Iqtisādi*, 1 December 1977.
136. *Al-Musawwar*, Cairo; 2 December 1977.
137. *Al-Ahrām*, 16 December 1977; *October*, 8 January 1978.
138. *Al-Musawwar*, 2 December 1977.
139. *Akhbār al-Yawm*, 31 December 1977.
140. *October*, 27 November 1977.
141. *Ibid.*
142. *Ibid.*
143. *Ibid.*
144. *Al-Akhbār*, 21 March; *Rūz al-Yūsuf*, 20 March 1978.
145. Sādāt's speech, 27 July; *al-Ahrām*, 28 July; *Yedi'ot Aharonot*, 19 March 1978.
146. R Cairo, 4 April 1978.
147. See Sādāt's speech of 27 July above; *October*, 9 July 1978.
148. *Jerusalem Post*, 14 July 1978.
149. *Al-Ahrām*, 21 May; see also *al-Jumhūriyya*, 24 May 1978.
150. *Al-Akhbār*, 18 April; *al-Jumhūriyya*, 19 May 1978.
151. MENA, 23 July 1978.
152. Sādāt's speech, 27 July; *al-Ahrām*, 28 July 1978.
153. *Al-Ahrām*, 2 April 1978.
154. *October*, 5 April 1978.
155. AFP, 7 June; Associated Press (AP), 8 June 1978.
156. AFP, 5 July; *Al-Anba'*, Kuwait; 5 July; Ghālī's interview to MENA, 24 May; UPI, 16 February 1978.
157. R Cairo, 22 June 1978.
158. Reuter, 13 February; AFP, 17 February; *Reuter*, 6 August; Sādāt's declaration in Washington, MENA, 7 February 1978.
159. See *al-Watan al-'Arabī*, Paris; 29 July 1978; Sādāt's press conference in Paris, 13 February, MENA, 14 February 1978.
160. *Rūz al-Yūsuf*, 3 July 1978.
161. UPI, 8 February 1978.
162. MENA, 10 July 1978.
163. R Amman, 7 July 1978.
164. UPI, 25 March; AP, 13 July 1978.
165. For background on Egypt's recent economic developments prior to 1977, see *MECS 1976–77*, pp. 227–34.

166. For background, see Eliyahu Kanovsky, *The Egyptian Economy since the Mid-1960s: The Micro Sectors*, Occasional Paper No 62 (Tel Aviv: The Shiloah Center for Middle Eastern and African Studies, Tel Aviv University, June 1978), pp. 5–20.
167. See Economist Intelligence Unit, *Quarterly Economic Review of Egypt (QER)*, London; Nos 1 and 2, 1978.
168. See, for example, Kanovsky, *op. cit.*, and also his contribution in *MECS 1976–77*, pp. 227–34. See also *Middle East Economic Digest (MEED)*, London; "Special Report: Egypt," May 1978, pp. 45–47.
169. *Al-Ahrām*, 27 January—Joint Publication Research Service (JPRS), 18 February 1978. See also *Egyptian Gazette*, 27 January 1978.
170. *Ibid.*
171. See, *inter alios*, both Kanovsky articles cited above; *The Arab Economist*, Beirut; June and August 1978; *MEED* "Special Report" and *FT*, 31 July 1978.
172. *MEED* "Special Report," pp. 25–26.
173. For background, see Kanovsky, "Micro Sectors," *op. cit.* See also *Middle East Economic Survey (MEES)*, Nicosia; 8 May 1978; and *MEED* "Special Report," pp. 17–18.
174. *Ibid.*
175. *Al-Akhbār*, 4 September 1977—JPRS, 12 October 1977.
176. See *al-Akhbār*, 19 December 1977—JPRS, 14 March 1978.
177. See, for example, the two Kanovsky articles mentioned above and his *Recent Economic Developments in the Middle East*, Occasional Paper No 54 (The Shiloah Center, June 1977), pp. 4–12. See also *MEED* "Special Report"; *FT*, 31 July; *Arabia and the Gulf*, London; 11 September; *MEED*, 18 August; *An-Nahār Arab Report and Memo*, Paris; 19 June; and *al-Ahrām al-Iqtisādī*, Cairo; 15 January—JPRS, 14 April 1978.
178. IMF, *International Financial Statistics*, Washington; August 1978.
179. See *MECS 1976–77*, pp. 232–33. For a variety of estimates, see *New York Times (NYT)*, 14 June; *MEES*, 9 January; *an-Nahār Arab Report and Memo*, 20 February; *Mideast Markets (MM)*, New York; 3 July; and the *Economist*, London; 3 June 1978.
180. See *MM*, 3 July; *NYT*, 17 June; and *Events*, London; 30 June 1978.

The Gulf States

GENERAL ISSUES AND DEVELOPMENT

Efforts to increase co-operation between the littoral Gulf states continued during the period under review, and there were some achievements in the economic and political fields, mainly between the Arab littoral states. Iran was mainly preoccupied with its own internal affairs, especially after January 1978 when the opposition to the Shah's regime gradually began to intensify its activities. There was no progress towards creating a defence alliance between the Gulf states, but co-operation in internal security was tightened. Bilateral relations, especially of a financial, economic and technical nature, were strengthened, but some old disputes erupted again, including two of special importance—the border dispute between Bahrain and Qatar, and that between Oman and Ra's al-Khaymah (UAE).

GULF DEFENCE AND INTERNAL SECURITY

Attempts to establish a defensive alliance between the littoral Gulf states were renewed in 1978, after negotiations in previous years had reached deadlock (see *MECS 1976–77*, pp. 330–31). However, it soon became clear that there was still no possibility of establishing military co-operation, especially among the big powers of the Gulf—Iran, Iraq and Saudi Arabia. Iraq was the chief opponent; nor was Saudi Arabia ready to co-operate with the radical Iraqi Ba'th. Yet pressure for such an alliance continued, in particular from among the principalities, the most active being Oman which was still threatened by the PDRY. Parallel with its attempts to revive the idea of a defensive alliance, Oman tightened its military co-operation with Iran during the Shah's visit to Muscat in December 1977 (see chapter on Iran) and, as a counterbalance to the Soviets, established diplomatic relations with Peking in May 1978 (see section on Oman below). The Omanis chiefly stressed the consolidation of the Soviet role in Ethiopia and in the PDRY (in co-operation with the Cubans), and later, in April, in Afghanistan following a Marxist coup which brought the Afghani Communist Party to power. (Also see essay, "The Regional Politics of the Red Sea, Persian Gulf and Indian Ocean.")

Towards the end of 1977, however, the littoral states of the Gulf had become increasingly concerned with internal security. The immediate reason was the assassination by terrorists of the UAE Minister of State for Foreign Affairs (see *MECS 1976–77*, pp. 362–63), which provoked fears of internal subversion and terrorism, especially against the oil industry and oil transportation. As prospects of a defensive alliance waned, the anti-subversion and strategic components of security received renewed attention, and efforts were gradually concentrated on co-operation in the field of internal security. Co-operation in this field had already been established in 1977, mainly on a bilateral basis, between Saudi Arabia and the principalities (see *MECS 1976–77*, p. 331). In 1978 the trend was towards co-operation between the Gulf states' police, security forces and intelligence services through exchange of information and collective action against subversion.

Concern focused at first on the possibility that terrorist action from the UAE might strike at the Hormuz Straits, through which about 90% of Gulf oil passed. As a result, at the beginning of 1978, Oman and Iran began to conduct joint naval surveillance in the Straits. Although they called on other Arab states to join them, for the time being, co-operation remained on this bilateral basis.

The need for greater co-operation in internal security became more acute in April

411

1978 when the Arab Gulf states began to worry about developments in Afghanistan and the future stability of Iran. Their main concern was the possibility that the Shah's disappearance from the scene could provoke upheavals in Iran which might wash over into the Arab littoral states. Oman again took the lead (perhaps in co-ordination with Iran); at the beginning of May 1978, it circulated a new plan for joint Gulf security, accompanied by a warning of widespread Communist and Leftist trends in the area. Iran, Iraq and Saudi Arabia entered negotiations in May to create some type of security belt for the Gulf. It was reported that they had reached agreement to establish a joint intelligence force to protect oil installations, and that all the other Gulf and Red Sea littoral states except the PDRY had decided to join this network. However, Kuwait denied these reports, maintaining its stand that there was need for co-ordination and co-operation, but not for alliances or mutual networks. The Iranian Prime Minister announced in June 1978 that negotiations between the Gulf states and Iran for a common defence and security alliance had been suspended; he accused Iraq and Saudi Arabia of opposing such an idea. This statement only reaffirmed the difficulties in finding a formula even for joint efforts to defend oil installations against sabotage. The dilemma of the Gulf states was that, while co-operation was an obvious prerequisite for security, none was at all keen that others should become involved in its internal affairs. Above all, the Iraqis and Saudis—and especially the principalities—still feared Iranian intervention under the pretext of aid against internal sabotage.

Despite these suspicions and difficulties, neither Iran nor the other littoral Gulf states abandoned the idea of defence and/or internal security alliances; in fact, they intensified bilateral co-operation and co-ordination in internal security from July to September 1978 as the internal situation in Iran deteriorated and the Arab Gulf states became deeply concerned at the possibility of a radical regime emerging in Tehran. They were convinced that the Soviet Union was active behind the scenes, and several newspapers warned of "the Communist threat" and even of a new Pearl Harbour in the Gulf.[1] The Gulf Arab states' gave unequivocal support to the Shah's regime. Any alternative was seen as likely to lead Iran into chaos, with consequent danger to the stability of the whole Persian Gulf.

The Soviet-Cuban consolidation on both sides of the Bāb al-Mandab—in Ethiopia on the western side, and in the PDRY on the eastern side—caused growing concern among the Persian Gulf littoral states, which saw it as a most dangerous threat to the free flow of Gulf oil. Oman even claimed that, following Ethiopia, the Soviets and Cubans would try to penetrate the Arabian Peninsula through their bridgehead—the PDRY—with Oman as the first target. In view of this threat, the Gulf states succeeded in demonstrating a united stand towards the Soviet-Cuban policy of aid to the Ethiopians against Somalia and the rebellion in Eritrea. The Gulf states maintained close contacts with Somalia, Djibouti and the rebel front in Eritrea, continued to extend aid to Somalia and the Eritreans, and demanded that the Soviets and Cubans prevent an Ethiopian invasion of Somali territory and refrain from participating in the Ethiopian war against the Eritreans. Eritrea was especially important because if the rebels managed to achieve independence, the Soviets would be prevented from establishing themselves on the Eritrean shore opposite the Bāb al-Mandab Straits. Leaders of Somalia, Djibouti and the Eritrean rebels visited the Gulf states several times during the year and were generally successful in receiving financial, political and military support. (Also see chapter on Iraq.)

ECONOMIC, TECHNICAL AND CULTURAL CO-OPERATION

Efforts continued throughout 1977–78 to achieve greater co-operation, co-ordination and integration among the Arab Gulf states at all levels, in the economic, technical, cultural and information fields. This was done mainly through consultation between leaders and at conferences (see *MECS 1976-77*, pp. 331-32). However, obstacles were still encountered and no progress was made on such issues as a common currency, common market, co-ordination in industrial development and the establishment of joint companies and ventures.

The third conference of the Arab Gulf Information Ministers, held in February 1978 in Baghdad, ratified the agreement on the Gulf television system approved at the February 1977 conference (see *MECS 1976-77*, p. 331). The Gulf News Agency was functioning and was to start official transmissions in April, but its efforts to integrate information services met with difficulties; even a proposal to establish an oil information organization to maintain a campaign clarifying the Gulf states' oil policy was referred for further discussion with OAPEC members. A decision accepted in February 1977 to set up a radio and television training centre in Qatar was examined yet again, but the Ministers decided to carry out a further survey of training requirements before implementing the project. On the other hand, the corporation for joint programme production by the Arab Gulf states was enlarged, and the Ministers decided to tighten control over other active corporations in the Gulf.

A conference of the Arab Gulf Ministers of Labour and Social Affairs was held for the first time in Bahrain in February 1978. Among topics discussed were proposals for joint development programmes in the social and economic fields, with the aim of securing calm and stability in the region; planning and co-ordination in developing vocational training and manpower resources; and the whole aspect of welfare and the training of social workers.

The third conference of the Ministers of Agriculture, held in Qatar in March, concentrated mainly on developing animal husbandry and fisheries in the region.

The conference of the Education Ministers of the Arab Gulf states, held in Abu Dhabi in April, concentrated on developing a common approach to education in the region through co-ordination of school curriculae and teacher training.

An important conference of the Gulf Ministers responsible for the environment was held in Kuwait in April to discuss plans to protect the Gulf's marine life from oil spills and industrial waste. The need to protect the environment has become acute because of the rapid industrialization along the Gulf coasts, the growth in shipping and the rapid expansion of the region's population. The conference participants (Bahrain, Iran, Iraq, Kuwait, Oman, Qatar, Saudi Arabia and the UAE) reached an agreement which included two treaties and an action plan. The first treaty pledged to combat pollution caused by intentional or accidental discharges from ships or from the shore; the second called for a joint effort by the littoral states to fight oil spills resulting from tanker collisions, blow-outs in the course of oil drilling or leaks from coastal marine industrial plants. The action plan provided for the establishment of a pollution-monitoring system to assess the origin and magnitude of any pollution. In addition, the conference decided to establish three new bodies: (1) a Marine Emergency Mutual Aid Centre to co-ordinate action against oil spills; (2) a Regional Organization for Protection of the Marine Environment to supervise the action plan, based on Kuwait; (3) a regional trust fund totalling $6.32m to finance anti-pollution activities.[2]

Discussions on a common currency and common market proved fruitless, and no harmonization in economic activities or monetary policies was reached. However, at the quarterly meetings of the governors of the Arab Gulf states' central banks, attempts were made to introduce co-ordination in banking and even monetary policies (e.g. revaluation). The meeting of bank governors in February 1978 in Abu

Dhabi was of special importance, as Saudi Arabia and Oman became full members of the conference for the first time, joining Bahrain, Kuwait, Qatar and the UAE.

A significant breakthrough in the rivalry between the Gulf states in industrial development was reached in December 1977 when, under Saudi persuasion and pressure, Shaykh Rāshid, the Ruler of Dubai, agreed to a merger in the operation of his drydock (still under construction) with that of Bahrain which was financed by OAPEC members and began operation in October 1977 (see *MECS 1976–77*, pp. 336–37). Operative co-ordination has long been seen as the only rational way of avoiding destructive competition.

Another field of potential co-operation was that of nuclear power. For several years Kuwait had been planning to build a nuclear power station for generating electricity in co-operation with other Gulf states, but only Qatar and Saudi Arabia had responded positively to its proposal. In May 1978, the three states signed an agreement to complete construction of a nuclear power station by 1986 with a capacity of 1,200 MW and a daily output of 150,000 gallons of water.[3]

Co-operation in economic, technical and cultural fields on a bilateral basis was bolstered by the signing of agreements between Iran and the UAE (December 1977), and Saudi Arabia and the UAE (June 1978). The latter followed the same pattern as the agreements concluded by Saudi Arabia with Bahrain and Kuwait, and by the continued aid of the rich oil-producing Arab Gulf states (especially Saudi Arabia, Kuwait and Abu Dhabi) to Bahrain and Oman (see *MECS 1976–77*, pp. 335, 352).

BAHRAIN-QATAR BORDER DISPUTE

The border between Qatar and Bahrain (drawn up by the British) passes not far from the Qatari seashore, leaving the islands near Qatar in the hands of Bahrain. The possibility of an oilfield being located in the offshore area motivated Qatar to demand that the frontier be redemarcated and that the ownership over Hawar Island—which is virtually uninhabited—be revised. These demands had been rejected by Bahrain. The dispute was revived in March 1978 when the Bahrainis for the first time held military manoeuvres near the island, which were interpreted by Qatar as a Bahraini demonstration of sovereignty. Qatar reacted by detaining some Bahraini fishermen in the area but, after confirming their identities, released them within a short time. In fact, both sides were eager to freeze the dispute and made every effort to calm tensions. Bahrain denied any intention of escalating the border dispute, and both sides expressed the hope that the problem would be settled as between brothers.[4]

OMAN-UAE DISPUTE OVER RA'S AL-KHAYMAH SEASHORE

The border dispute between Oman and Ra's al-Khaymah over a stretch of coastline 16 km long (between Ra's al-Khaymah and Oman's detached territory on Ra's Musandan) was first raised when Sultan Qābūs of Oman discussed his claim over that area with Shaykh Zāyid, President of the UAE, at the Lahor Islamic summit conference in 1974. Sultan Qābūs accused Saqr b. Muḥammad al-Qāsimī, the ruler of Ra's al-Khaymah, of having begun to encroach on the disputed territory in 1951 when the ruler occupied the village of Rims, now about 16 km inside Ra's al-Khaymah's territory, expelling a number of Omanis from their homes and building a new port and an industrial estate there. Shaykh Saqr claimed that, in fact, the disputed territory was recognized as belonging to Ra's al-Khaymah by his own predecessors and by those of Sultan Qābūs.

Oman brought the dispute into the open in November 1977 when oil deposits were discovered in the offshore zone of the disputed coastline. Oman sent troops to its border with the UAE and a warship to the oil rig in the disputed area, demanding the suspension both of oil exploration and of developments in the Sha'm and Dawrah regions along the disputed shore. The Omanis tried to negotiate with the ruler of Ra's al-Khaymah, but he proved intransigent. The entire affair was therefore taken over by the Federal UAE government, while Ra's al-Khaymah suspended its oil exploration in the disputed area. Negotiations were led by the UAE President, Shaykh Zāyid, and the Omani Foreign Minister, with the mediation of Saudi Arabia and Kuwait. According to the traditional tribal system, secret, long and patient negotiations were pursued, without declarations. The aim of Shaykh Zāyid was to contain the dispute and to strengthen relations with Oman. In spite of much diplomatic journeying between Muscat and Abu Dhabi after January 1978, the problem was not resolved. It was reported in April 1978 that three proposals were put forward to solve the dispute: (1) to hold a referendum among the population of the area to decide between the claims of Ra's al-Khaymah and those of Oman; (2) to establish a joint Omani-Ra's al-Khaymah administration, as in the famous Neutral Zone between Saudi Arabia and Kuwait, with an equal division of expenditures and revenues; (3) to set up a judicial arbitration commission which, in case of a decision in favour of Oman, would decide what part of Ra's al-Khaymah would be given to Oman in exchange for the disputed area if Ra's al-Khaymah remained interested in holding that area; or what compensation Oman would pay to Ra's al-Khaymah if the latter should agree to return the area to Oman.[5]

Reports of a compromise appeared in July 1978 whereby Oman would have the right to establish military observation posts along 10 km of the disputed seashore, enabling it to tighten its control over the Strait of Hormuz.[6] However, these reports were not confirmed, and it would seem that no solution was in fact reached. Neither side was prepared to give up its interests, especially since oil was involved. Furthermore, Ra's al-Khaymah continued its development activities in the disputed area and signed agreements with the Kuwaitis to establish two joint companies, the first for the marketing and distribution of oil products, and the second to build a refinery in the disputed area. Kuwaiti participation would enable Ra's al-Khaymah to overcome financial problems created by Abu Dhabi which, in order to bring pressure to bear on Shaykh Saqr for a compromise with Oman, had stopped its financial aid. It should be noted that the Omanis were openly talking of the whole area of the UAE as an integral part of "Greater Oman," and had not given up their dream of controlling the lower Gulf coast. However, the deteriorating situation in Iran (Oman's ally) and the internal tension in the UAE between the President and his deputy (see below) largely overshadowed the dispute.

Aryeh Shmuelevitz

CURRENCY VALUES*

	$1 =	£1 =	DM1 =	SF1 =	FF1 =
Bahrain Dinar	0.383	0.803	0.222	0.257	0.096
Kuwait Dinar	0.266	0.557	0.154	0.179	0.067
Oman Rial	0.346	0.724	0.200	0.232	0.087
Qatar Rial	3.836	8.040	2.221	2.578˙	0.963
UAE Dirham	3.831	8.030	2.218	2.575	0.962

*Valid as of 30 October 1978.
Source: Middle East Economic Digest, 3 November 1978.

OIL PRODUCTION (million barrels)

	1974	1975	1976	1977	(first half) 1978
Bahrain	24.6	22.3	21.3	21.2	—
Kuwait[2]	930.1	760.9	786.9	720.2	341.0
Oman[2]	106.0	124.2	133.8	124.8	57.7
Qatar[2]	189.2	160.3	178.1	159.2	81.2
UAE[1]	612.4	617.1	700.2	735.4	—
Total	1,862.3	1,684.8	1,820.3	1,760.8	—

Sources: [1] World Oil; [2] Petroleum Economist.

INDEX OF CRUDE PETROLEUM PRODUCTION (1975 = 100)

	1970	1972	1974	1976	(first half) 1978
Bahrain	125.4	114.0	110.3	95.2	89.6
Kuwait	143.4	158.0	122.2	103.2	91.2
Oman	n.a.	82.5	85.0	107.4	91.3
Qatar	82.4	110.1	118.1	113.5	102.1
UAE	45.8	70.9	98.6	114.4	107.4

n.a. not available.
Source: Derived from various issues of IMF, International Financial Statistics.

OIL REVENUES (million US dollars)

	1973	1974	1975	1976	1977
Oman[1]	328	1,136	1,442	1,571	1,571
Bahrain[2]	74	262	280	395	437
Kuwait[2]	1,980	8,645	7.706	8,063	8,934
Qatar[2]	464	1,802	1,700	2,092	2,071
UAE[2]	900	5,536	6,000	7,000	9,030
Total	3,418	16,245	15,686	17,550	20,472

Sources: [1] IMF, International Financial Statistics, September 1978, pp.280–81, line 70aa; [2] Arab Oil and Gas, 16 June 1978.
Note: Revenues for Oman are based on a separate source and thus are not comparable with the rest.

COMPARISON OF INTERNATIONAL RESERVES (million US dollars at end of period)

	1969	1971	1973	1975	1977
Bahrain	68	95	74	296	510
Kuwait	182	288	501	1,655	2,990
Oman	n.a.	158	107	239	427
Qatar	16	22	76	104	162
UAE	n.a.	n.a.	92	989	824

n.a. not available or not applicable.
Source: IMF, International Financial Statistics.

FOREIGN TRADE, 1977 (million US dollars)

	Exports	Imports	Balance
Bahrain	1,822	2,029	−207
Kuwait	9,804	4,796	+5,008
Oman	1,574	874	+700
Qatar	2,047	1,225	+822
UAE	9,502	4,502	+5,000

Source: Derived from IMF, Direction of Trade Annual 1971-77.

NOTES
1. E.g. *al-Siyāsa*, Kuwait; 28 June; Emirate News Agency, 1 July—DR, 3 July 1978.
2. *Kayhan International*, Tehran; 1 May 1978.
3. *Al-Yaqza*, Kuwait; 15 May 1978.
4. Qatari News Agency (QNA), 11 March—BBC, 13 March; *al-Ra'y al-'Āmm*, Kuwait; 24 April 1978.
5. *Al-Ahrām*, Cairo; 27 April 1978.
6. *Al-Mustaqbal*, Paris; 8 July 1978.

Bahrain

Bahrain was mainly preoccupied with economic and social problems in 1977–78. The government continued to develop the country as a financial service centre for the Gulf area, attempted to reduce inflationary pressures and to restrict imported labour.

POLITICAL AFFAIRS

Unrest was reported at the beginning of 1978, especially among expatriate Bahraini students, specifically at the Kuwait University. In late January and February, a wave of arrests was made among young people under a policy of what might be termed "preventive intimidation." The arrests followed a clash on 26 January at Kuwait University between students of the National Bahraini Club, considered to be Rightist and supporting the Bahraini regime, and the Bahraini Students' Union, a Leftist group described by some circles as a "bunch of Communists." This was the culmination of a series of incidents which had started when one faction accused the other of reporting to the Bahraini authorities on its members' activities. Four students were wounded and five were temporarily detained. No further details were available, and no further opposition activities were reported.

By the summer of 1978, the government felt itself strong enough to introduce subsidy cuts and to begin increasing prices. First to be cut was the subsidy on fuel oil (by 20%); oil prices were increased by 33%, the first such rise since 1971. As a result, the government saved about BD 8m over the year.

SOCIAL AFFAIRS: EMPLOYMENT

Social concern focused on the problem of manpower. Although strict laws and regulations were issued in 1976–77 aimed at maintaining employment among Bahraini citizens (see *MECS 1976–77*, p. 335), many companies continued to fill vacancies with imported labour without informing the Ministry of Labour. This was in contravention of the law which required the notification of vacancies within seven days. As a result of the evasion, the number of Bahrainis registering as unemployed increased in the second half of 1977 and the beginning of 1978. The government therefore initiated further measures to enforce the replacement of foreigners (for whose numbers there were no reliable figures) by Bahrainis, especially in key posts.

In February 1978, a new Directorate for Manpower Planning was established in the Ministry of Labour and Social Affairs to replace the Department for National Vocational Training. The aim was to place the whole question of meeting manpower requirements on a much broader basis. The Directorate's first task was to conduct a survey to identify the critical jobs in the economy, and the skills and educational background needed to fill them.

The Ministry of Labour and Social Affairs also issued a directive prohibiting the wives of aliens, except for teachers in private schools, from working in Bahrain. The directive was aimed at new applications for work permits, although the Ministry also had the power to withdraw existing work permits if it considered that suitable Bahrainis were available to replace aliens.

A third measure, taken at the end of March 1978, was a programme prepared by the Ministry to replace foreigners by Bahrainis in nine companies in the private sector: BAPCO; Aluminium Bahrain; Gulf Air; Cable and Wireless; the Arab

Shipbuilding and Repair Yard; the Chartered Bank; the British Bank of the Middle East; the National Bank of Bahrain; and the Bank of Bahrain and Kuwait. The programme was later discussed with representatives of the companies, who were given ample time to implement it. The Director of Labour in the Ministry of Labour explained that pressure was to be exerted on the private sector because the Labour Ministry was responsible for seeing that Bahraini graduates found employment, and government departments could not take on any more.[1]

ECONOMIC AFFAIRS

Along with other Gulf states, Bahrain experienced a mild recession in 1977-78, especially in the private sector. To a certain extent this helped to reduce inflation and to allow a more balanced growth and stable expansion. A joint government-business committee, established to examine the state of the economy, took some measures to curb inflation. These included a decision, for the first time in Bahrain, to issue public bonds ($25m worth for five years at 8% interest) to be bought by corporate institutions on the island, the aim being to absorb excess liquidity and so reduce inflationary pressures, as well as to test a less inflationary way of financing government expenditure than the straight conversion of dollar oil revenues into Bahraini dinars.

However, the most important development was the continuing effort to turn Bahrain into a service centre (see *MECS 1976-77*, p. 336). By the end of 1977, Bahrain appeared to have established itself as the main foreign exchange trading centre in the Gulf. Alan Moore, the Bahrain Monetary Agency's Director-General, suggested that "no other centre in the Gulf can provide a market in international foreign exchange with as much depth as Bahrain." The total assets of the two-year old offshore market reached $15.7 bn at the end of December 1977 compared to $6 bn at the end of 1976; 33 offshore banking units were fully operational at the end of 1977, and a further seven were established in 1978.[2]

Yet another innovation was the establishment in October 1977 of a local insurance and re-insurance broking company—National Insurance Services—which was wholly owned by leading Bahraini merchant houses and private investors, and managed by Sedgwick Forbes Middle East. It was to handle all classes of insurance business, including life, and to act as an underwriting and settling agent. Bahrain already had much to offer insurance companies, being the headquarters of Gulf Air, the Arab Shipbuilding and Repair Yard (now operational) and other successful industries, such as Aluminium Bahrain and the refinery, as well as of the current causeway and bridge construction linking it with Saudi Arabia.

Another step aimed at strengthening and widening the service sector was the new law, published in the Official Gazette of 3 November 1977, permitting foreign companies to set up regional offices without Bahraini partners. Previously, as in the other Gulf states, foreign companies had been obliged to take local partners who were to hold more than 50% of company shares. Under the new law, these companies would have to maintain trading activity, to provide services outside Bahrain for a nominal sum of $6,250 annually, to comply with all Bahraini laws, and to provide their offices with officials and capital of not less than $50,000.

On 15 December 1977, the Ruler of Bahrain officially inaugurated the $340m Arab Shipbuilding and Repair Yard drydock complex, financed by Saudi Arabia, Kuwait, the UAE, Iraq, Qatar, Bahrain and Libya. Its construction had taken two years.

The Ruler approved by decree the country's first two-year budget in January 1978. It amounted to BD 560m ($1,420m) to be apportioned equally over 1978 and 1979. BD 275m (c. $695m) of the budget was to be spent on development projects including electricity (BD 66m = $168m), housing (BD 62m = $158m), sewerage (BD 47m = $120m) and development of Sulman port (BD 19m = $48m).[3] The government had already prepared a Five-Year Development Plan (up to 1982) which was to include 600 projects with an expenditure of c. BD 867m ($2.2 bn). The major source of finance, apart from oil revenues, was to be loans and grants provided by neighbouring oil-producing states. The government also began negotiations to take over the US Bahrain Petroleum Company (BAPCO), and was seeking full control over oil and gas production and local marketing facilities, all held by the US company since 1934. The protracted nature of the talks resulted from the fact that there were more than 50 texts of agreements governing the changing relations between the Bahrain government and BAPCO covering the previous 44 years. With the completion of these negotiations, Bahrain would join its neighbours (excepting Abu Dhabi) in enjoying 100% ownership.

The island continued to make use of its new exhibition site (see MECS 1976–77, p. 336). A solar energy technology fair—"Soltech 78"—was held in April 1978 in which 20 Arab, European and American countries participated, along with Australia, Japan and India.

FOREIGN RELATIONS
Bahrain continued to maintain co-operation with its neighbours in the Persian Gulf, mainly with Saudi Arabia, Kuwait and the UAE (all of which extended financial aid to Bahrain), and with Iran. (For details, see above under the Gulf States.)

SĀDĀT'S INITIATIVE
Bahrain's stand on President Sādāt's peace initiative with Israel was at first somewhat confused, with the government deciding to forbid the television broadcast of Sādāt's visit to Jerusalem. However, it soon followed the policy of Saudi Arabia and other Gulf principalities—a declared neutral stand between Egypt and its Arab opponents, while supporting the demand for self-determination for the Palestinians and the establishment of a Palestinian state.

FRENCH NEWS AGENCY REGIONAL OFFICE
The French News Agency opened its regional office for the Persian Gulf in Manāmah, the capital of Bahrain, in April 1978. The government had granted the agency many attractive facilities because of the prospect that it could serve as a centre for international communications as well as advise the local Gulf News Agency, established in 1977. This was another step in Bahrain's development as a service centre for the Gulf.

US NAVAL BASE RE-LEASED
The rumours of October 1977 that the old agreement governing the Jufair naval and airbase lease to the US was still in force (see MECS 1976–77, p. 336) were indirectly confirmed in June 1978. The pro-Soviet coup in Afghanistan, along with the Soviet/Cuban consolidation in the PDRY and the Horn of Africa, enabled the Bahrainis to renew the base arrangement with the US openly and without the slightest opposition, even from radical Iraq. The Saudi Arabians, with gentle but substantial inducements (including financial aid), helped to persuade the Bahrainis to accept renewal of the Jufair lease.

Aryeh Shmuelevitz

ARMED FORCES

Total armed forces number 2,300. Defence expenditure in 1978 was BD 16.7m ($43m). The Army has one infantry battalion; one armoured car squadron; eight *Saladin* armoured cars; eight *Ferret* scout cars; six 81mm mortars; six 120mm recoilless rifles. The Coastguard has 20 patrol launches and the police, two *Scout* helicopters.

Source: The Military Balance 1978–79 (London: International Institute for Strategic Studies).

MONETARY SURVEY (million Bahrain dinars at end of period)

	1976	1977	(Jan–June) 1978
Foreign Assets (net)	162.0	166.2	213.6
Domestic Credit	154.6	210.6	192.2
Claims on Government (net)	−109.8	−91.0	−111.5
Claims on Private Sector	267.9	310.8	314.7
Money	127.9	152.5	162.7
Quasi-money	175.9	203.0	222.8
Other Items (net)	16.3	30.4	31.3
Money, Seasonally Adjusted	129.4	154.5	155.1

INTERNATIONAL LIQUIDITY (million US dollars at end of period)

	1976	1977	(Jan–June) 1978
International Reserves	442.4	510.2	552.1
Gold	6.0	6.3	6.4
Reserves with IMF	5.5	5.8	5.9
Foreign Exchange	430.9	498.1	539.8
Monetary Agency	336.4	443.0	506.9
Government	94.5	55.1	32.9
Commercial Banks: Assets	479.9	241.9	636.6
Liabilities	389.8	180.9	518.9

Source (of two preceding tables): IMF, *International Financial Statistics.*

COMPOSITION OF NON-OIL EXPORTS (fob; million Bahrain dinars)

	1975	1976	1977
Food and Live Animals	4.9	8.2	8.4
Beverages and Tobacco	1.9	2.6	2.4
Manufactures, classified chiefly by material	47.0	64.0	66.4
Machinery and Transport Equipment	13.1	35.1	44.2
Miscellaneous Manufactured Articles	15.1	22.9	32.1
Other	2.0	3.8	4.1
Total	**84.0**	**136.6**	**157.6**

COMPOSITION OF NON-OIL IMPORTS (cif; million Bahrain dinars)

	1975	1976	1977
Food and Live Animals	24.5	39.1	42.8
Beverages and Tobacco	6.0	8.6	10.2
Chemicals	18.5	22.0	30.9
Manufactures, classified chiefly by material	57.0	96.1	106.3
Machinery and Transport Equipment	86.0	155.6	161.0
Miscellaneous Manufactured Articles	33.0	49.6	76.3
Other	7.8	16.6	17.4
Total	**232.9**	**387.6**	**444.9**

Sources (of two preceding tables): Ministry of Finance and National Economy and Statistical Bureau.

SUMMARY OF GOVERNMENT BUDGET (million Bahrain dinars)

	1976 Actual	1977 Actual*	1978 Budget	1979 Budget
A. **Total Revenues**	**191.1**	**230.1**	**218.8**	**228.9**
Oil revenues	156.4	180.7	161.2	160.2
Non-oil revenues	34.7	49.4	57.6	68.7
B. **Total Expenditures**	**203.2**	**256.2**	**280.0**	**280.0**
Current expenditures	88.3	115.1	135.0	150.0
Capital expenditures	114.9	141.1	145.0	130.0
C. **Balance** (A-B)	**-12.1**	**-26.1**	**-61.2**[1]	**-51.1**[1]

*Provisional.

[1] Ministry includes commensurate sum from financing as part of revenue.

Source: Ministry of Finance and National Economy.

GOVERNMENT EXPENDITURE (million Bahrain dinars)

	1976 Actual	1977* Actual	1978 Budget	1979 Budget
Capital Expenditure				
Electricity and Water	25.6	34.3	39.5	46.0
Dredging	2.2	8.9	17.5	30.9
Housing	27.9	43.6	36.7	10.6
Port and Dry Dock	18.1	16.8	17.4	6.3
Roads	6.2	6.7	3.2	5.0
Health	5.0	9.4	4.5	3.6
Education	0.8	3.9	6.2	3.4
Information	0.8	0.9	2.1	3.0
Airport	4.5	1.2	1.1	1.4
Total (including others)	**114.9**	**141.1**	**145.0**	**130.0**
Current Expenditure				
Head of State	6.0	6.0	6.0	6.0
Public Order and Defence	19.9	26.1	34.3	37.5
Health	8.6	12.5	15.4	17.4
Electricity and Water	8.4	11.4	14.0	15.1
Finance	4.4	5.3'	6.5	7.4
Development	2.7	4.1	5.3	6.2
Municipalities	6.0	6.0	6.0	6.0
Subsidy Programmes	3.7	3.0	4.0	4.0
Transportation	2.7	3.1	3.8	4.0
Education	11.3	17.2	19.4	20.8
Total (including others)	**88.3**	**115.1**	**135.0**	**150.0**

*Provisional.

Source: Ministry of Finance and National Economy.

DIRECTION OF TRADE (million US dollars)

	1975	1976	1977
Exports to:			
Saudi Arabia	80.3	195.9	256.3
Japan	169.9	231.3	253.7
United Arab Emirates	59.4	92.7	170.7
United States	251.7	118.8	139.5
Australia	101.6	113.4	121.1
Singapore	74.0	119.6	106.2
Philippines	40.8	45.8	68.3
New Caledonia	21.0	27.3	51.9
New Zealand	26.7	30.7	37.9
Iran	10.7	13.0	35.4
Total *(including others)*	**1,202.8**	**1,517.4**	**1,821.6**

Imports from:

Saudi Arabia	621.8	703.2	915.6
United Kingdom	108.2	172.8	220.0
Japan	69.2	135.8	174.3
United States	91.8	145.1	134.6
West Germany	29.0	62.8	66.2
China PR	36.5	38.4	62.2
Australia	22.6	45.3	58.1
Italy	29.1	22.3	36.9
India	14.6	33.7	35.0
South Korea	2.2	48.0	31.0
Total (including others)	**1,198.0**	**1,668.1**	**2,029.1**

Source: IMF, *Direction of Trade.*

NOTES
1. *Akhbār al-Khalīj*, Manāmah 31 March 1978.
2. *Financial Times*, London; 11 October 1977, 9 January 1978.
3. *Al-'Urūba*, Qatar; 19 February 1978.

Kuwait

Following the death of the Ruler, Shaykh Sabāḥ al-Sālim al-Sabāḥ, on 31 December 1977, Kuwait was preoccupied for several months with consolidating the new government. Speculation as to its composition and the relations between the two major branches of the ruling family was soon ended when the latter managed to overcome all differences under the direction of the new Ruler, and to choose the new family and government functionaries. Other major issues were the continued modernization of the armed forces according to the three-year plan; the ongoing controversy between the government and the newspapers concerning censorship; and the unrest among immigrant workers.

POLITICAL AFFAIRS
NEW RULER, CROWN PRINCE AND GOVERNMENT

On 31 December 1977, the 12th ruler of the Sabāḥ dynasty (founded in 1756), Sabāḥ Sālim al-Sabāḥ, died of a heart attack at the age of 62 after ruling Kuwait since 1967. His cousin, the Crown Prince and Prime Minister (PM), Jābir al-Aḥmad al-Jābir al-Sabāḥ, was immediately proclaimed the new Ruler by the Council of Ministers, while the Deputy PM and Minister of Information, Jābir al-'Alī al-Sālim al-Sabāḥ, became acting PM.

Throughout recent years, the new Ruler had already been acting as the top decision-maker and manager of Kuwait's day-to-day government affairs because of his predecessor's poor health. Unlike other shaykhs, he seldom had holidays abroad, not even during the sweltering desert heat of the summer seasons, and had the image of an able, shrewd and tough statesman. People could set their watches by his arrivals and departures; each afternoon he took home dozens of files which were returned covered with notes and comments the next morning. It was quite clear that he intended to retain firm control over the administration he had enjoyed as Crown Prince and PM.

A most important event was the election of the new Crown Prince. The two branches of the ruling family—al-Sālim, headed by the late ruler, and al-Jābir, headed by the new ruler—had been in frequent conflict since the beginning of the century. An unofficial formula, by which the two top posts had been held in rotation by Sālim and Jābir, kept the struggle under control over the years, though there were departures from tradition. The latest was the case of the late ruler, who was named Crown Prince by his brother, Shaykh 'Abdalla Sālim al-Sabāḥ, the ruler who won Kuwait's independence in 1961: both were Sālims. The question was whether the new Ruler would follow suit and name his brother, the Foreign Minister, Sabāḥ al-Aḥmad al-Jābir, as his Crown Prince (both were Jābirs), or whether he would choose one of the two candidates of the Sālims: the Deputy PM and Minister of Information, Jābir al-'Alī al-Sālim, or the Interior and Defence Minister, Sa'd al-'Abdalla al-Sālim al-Sabāḥ.

The most powerful among the candidates was the Deputy and now acting PM, Shaykh Jābir al-'Alī, a jovial and earthy man, fond of traditional Bedouin pursuits, with strong support among the tribesmen in the hinterland. However, although accumulating much influence over the years, he had also provoked much antagonism. He had angered the Saudi Arabians because of his policy of importing nomadic tribesmen of his mother's tribe ('Ajmān) from Saudi Arabia and settling them in Kuwait—a policy that tended to upset the delicate tribal balance in Saudi

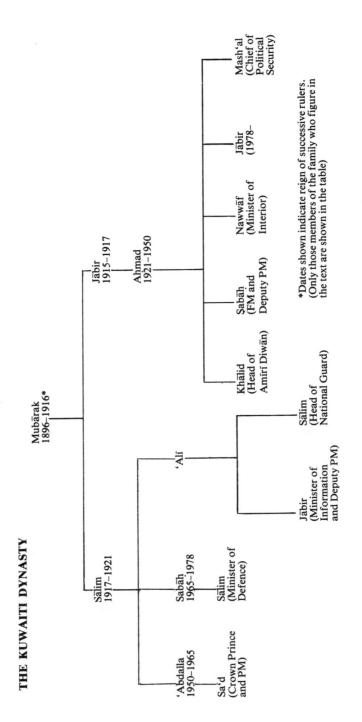

THE KUWAITI DYNASTY

Mubārak
1896–1916*

Sālim
1917–1921

Jābir
1915–1917

Ahmad
1921–1950

'Abdalla
1950–1965

Sabāḥ
1965–1978

'Ali

Khālid
(Head of
Amīrī Dīwān)

Sabāḥ
(FM and
Deputy PM)

Nawwāf
(Minister of
Interior)

Jābir
(1978–

Mash'al
(Chief of
Political
Security)

Sa'd
(Crown Prince
and PM)

Sālim
(Minister of
Defence)

Jābir
(Minister of
Information
and Deputy PM)

Sālim
(Head of
National Guard)

*Dates shown indicate reign of successive rulers.
(Only those members of the family who figure in
the text are shown in the table)

Arabia. He was also reported to have armed his imported relatives and to have used their votes to elect his supporters in the National Assembly. Moreover, he was ten years older than the Ruler, so that the latter could be expected to outlive him. The second candidate, the Minister of Defence and Interior, Shaykh Sa'd al-'Abdalla al-Sālim, was known for his administrative competence, his sturdiness, his popularity among Kuwaiti traditionalists, and his successful negotiations with the Iraqis (see *MECS 1976-77*, pp. 345-46). The third candidate, the brother of the new ruler and Foreign Minister, Shaykh Sabāḥ al-Aḥmad, was considered highly competent and very popular among the populace at large. He served as close adviser to his brother while the latter was PM.

The new Ruler characteristically moved fast to avert any possible dispute. This was also the advice given to him by the Saudis, who are known to believe that such problems should be resolved quickly. The overriding concern was to ensure that the state's stability was carefully maintained. Therefore, no public speculation about the outcome of the reshuffle was permitted, and foreign newspapers referring to the matter were not allowed into the country.

Three weeks after the death of the Ruler, and after intensive discussions within the ruling family and with politicians and other distinguished persons, the government tendered its resignation on 22 January 1978. Thereafter the process of appointments could begin constitutionally. The government was requested to continue in a caretaker capacity until a new one was established.

The next step was surprising in that the new Ruler decided to create a precedent by electing the Crown Prince first, and only afterwards the PM. In this way he hoped to prevent tension and disputes within the family which might cause instability. The ruling family unanimously elected Shaykh Sa'd al-'Abdalla al-Sālim al-Sabāḥ of the Sālim branch, the former Minister of the Interior and Defence, as Crown Prince, a decision which was published officially on 31 January 1978. The election was immediately endorsed by the two other candidates, Jābir al-'Alī al-Sālim and Sabāḥ al-Aḥmad al-Jābir.

The nomination of the PM took another week of consultations. The Ruler had originally opposed the idea of appointing the Crown Prince to the Premiership as well. Now, however, he reconsidered his attitude; this left the way open for the new Crown Prince to assume the Premiership as well. The official appointment of Shaykh Sa'd al-'Abdalla occurred on 8 February 1978 at the end of the 40-day period of mourning. In this decision the new Ruler followed the precedent set by himself in holding both posts, and thus perhaps established a new procedure in the Kuwaiti ruling family. The new government approved by the Ruler on 17 February was almost the same as the previous one, the only changes stemming from the accession of the former PM to the throne and the appointment of the former Interior and Defence Minister as the new PM. Shaykh Jābir al-'Alī remained as Deputy PM and Minister of Information. The other candidate for Crown Prince, the Ruler's brother, Shaykh Sabāḥ al-Aḥmad, also became a Deputy PM, while retaining his Foreign Ministry portfolio. He was also appointed acting Minister of the Interior until 19 March, when he was replaced by Shaykh Nawwāf al-Aḥmad al-Jābir al-Sabāḥ—another brother of the new Ruler. The son of the late Ruler, Sālim Sabāḥ al-Sālim, the former Minister of Labour and Social Affairs, became Minister of Defence, and his portfolio was given to a new figure, 'Abd al-'Azīz Maḥmūd; this was the first time that this important portfolio had been given to a person not belonging to the ruling family. The major change in personnel was the long-expected dismissal of the Minister for Oil, 'Abd al-Muttalib al-Qāzimī, due to dissatisfaction with his handling of the Ministry's affairs. In his place, the PM appointed 'Ali al-Khalīfa al-Adhbi.

THE GULF STATES: KUWAIT

In his address to the nation on 13 February, following the mourning and the nominations, the new Ruler outlined his political programme and stressed that his aims would be as follows: (a) to continue the policies of his predecessor; (b) to entrench genuine democracy by popular participation; (c) to build a modern state capable of applying advanced technology and modern methods; (d) to modernize the general administration and civil service and to improve all public services and utilities; (e) to conserve the natural resources and ensure that present and future requirements of the country could be met; (f) to continue its previous role in developing fraternal co-operation in various fields with the neighbouring Gulf states; (g) to continue to be faithful to the Palestinians represented by the PLO.[1]

The Ruler thus hinted at some of the major problems facing him and the new government, the first being the return to parliamentary life demanded by various circles in the country (see *MECS 1976-77*, pp. 340–41). The new Ruler was considered to be a believer in parliamentary democracy and freedom, but was wary of divisiveness. The government reiterated the need to review the constitution because, as Deputy PM Shaykh Sabāḥ al-Aḥmad said, it was not based on the particular position, traditions and principles of Kuwaiti society, but rather on constitutions effective in developed industrial societies.[2] The new PM promised in May that a special committee to examine the constitution would be set up within a few weeks, but no developments occurred. A second problem involved the shortcomings of the civil service—a dominant theme affecting the economy. According to a survey, c. 28,000 civil servants out of a total of 140,000 were illiterate; a further 26,800 could read and write, but possessed no further qualifications.[3] A third difficulty was the partial economic recession, caused by the shortage of credit available to the private sector, and the slowing down of growth which resulted in bankruptcies, a decline on the stock exchange and a great increase in private sector indebtedness. Fourthly, there was the need to control inflation, reportedly running at between 15% and 20% in the summer of 1977 (see *MECS 1976-77*, p. 347). Although the government called for moderation in consumption, no official action was taken to curb inflation, either through increased taxation or through official intervention to lift the depressed stock market.

THE GOVERNMENT (as at March 1978)

Prime Minister	Sa'd al-'Abdalla al-Sālim
Deputy PM and Minister of Information	Jābir al-'Alī al-Sālim
Deputy PM and Foreign Minister	Sabāḥ al-Aḥmad al-Jābir
Other Ministers:	
Education	Jāsin al-Khālid al-Marzūq
Housing	Hamad Mubārak al-'Ayyār
Public Works	Hamūd Yūsuf al-Nisf
Defence	Sālim Sabāḥ al-Sālim
Interior	Nawwāf al-Aḥmad al-Jābir
Communications	Sulaymān Hamūd al-Zayd
Finance	'Abd al-Raḥman Sālim al-'Atīqī
Public Health	Dr 'Abd al-Raḥman 'Abdalla al-'Awaḍī
Social Affairs and Labour	'Abd al-'Azīz Maḥmūd
Justice	'Abdalla Ibrahīm al-Mufarrij
Electricity and Water	'Abdalla Yūsuf al-Ghānim
Trade and Industry	'Abd al-Wahhāb Yūsuf al-Nifīsī
Oil	'Alī Khalīfa al-Adhbi
Planning	Muḥammad Yūsuf al-'Adsānī
Waqfs and Islamic Affairs	Yūsuf Jāsim al-Ḥajji
Ministers of State:	
Legal and Administrative Affairs	Sulaymān al-Du'ayj al-Salmān
Affairs of the Council of Ministers	'Abd al-'Azīz Ḥusayn

ARMED FORCES

The Ministry of Defence and the Armed Forces continued in 1978 to implement the Defence Development Plan (see *MECS 1976–77*, p. 343). Special attention was paid to the establishment of a Navy, and negotiations were conducted in Western Europe (especially in Britain) for the purchase of missile gunboats and other naval equipment. The British Defence Minister visited Kuwait in March 1978 to discuss arms deals and the problem of manpower. However, the Kuwaiti government was not eager to fill its upper ranks with foreign contract officers. Negotiations were held by the Kuwaiti Chief of Staff while visiting army installations and arms factories in the US during October 1977, and by the Minister of Defence during his visits to Italy and Britain in October-November 1977. When visiting Cairo at the end of September, the Kuwaiti Minister of Defence signed an agreement with Egypt on co-operation in the training sphere. Teams of Egyptian instructors arrived in Kuwait to assist in training Kuwaiti units, especially on Soviet weapons, and Kuwaitis went to Egypt to undergo training there.

Reports continued to circulate in 1978 that the arms deal with the Soviet Union was still in force (see *MECS 1976–77*, pp. 343–44), and that Soviet military experts and Soviet weapons, particularly surface-to-air missiles, were reaching Kuwait. The Kuwaiti Chief of Staff and the Defence Minister both admitted that Kuwait had purchased SAM-6 and SAM-7 missiles, but denied reports that a Soviet military delegation was present in the country to train its army, or that Kuwaiti military personnel had been sent to the Soviet Union to receive training there. However, both again stressed Kuwait's policy of diversification of arms sources and their intention to supply their needs from East and West.[4] (For the composition of Kuwait's armed forces, see below.)

There were two other important developments in 1978, the first being the introduction of pre-military training in all high schools. This was included in the curriculum of the 11th grade as a compulsory course of c. 120 hours, to commence in January 1978. The aim was to turn the youth into a group that could be used for internal civil defence purposes and for extending aid to the armed forces in logistic assignments in the defence and administrative fields. Girls were trained in first aid. The second important development was the decision in March 1978 to start implementing the compulsory conscription law, which had been approved almost two years previously. In mid-April the first groups of recruits were called up for training. The declared purpose was to train a reserve force capable of supplying the needs of the regular army at any time. The Defence Minister promised that no one affected by this law would be exempt from military service.[5] Although Kuwait had become reconciled with its neighbours, it was still alert to the dangers: popular resistance was therefore one of the regime's major concerns.

CENSORSHIP OF THE PRESS

There was strict enforcement in 1978 of the press restrictions imposed in 1976 following the dissolution of the National Assembly (see *MECS 1976–77*, pp. 340, 342). Many newspapers breaking the Press and Publication Law were suspended, the major offences being attacks against Heads of State, especially against President Anwar al-Sādāt, and speculation on the composition of the new government following the death of the Ruler on 31 December 1977 (see above). Few offences were the result of criticism of the regime, although one such related to the weekly magazine *al-Balagh*, published by the Social Reform Society, which printed political articles incompatible with Kuwait's policy. *Al-Ra'y al-'Amm* (14 June 1978) criticized the frequent bans on newspapers and stressed the need for freedom of expression which, it argued, did not always mean chaos and disorderly behaviour. The paper pointed out that the criticism which appeared in the newspapers was mild in comparison with that in democratic countries. It also raised the matter of financial losses caused by the suspensions. But the government, eager to maintain calm and stability and to preserve close relations with Arab and other fraternal states, was determined to continue its restrictive policy. At the same time, it wished to avoid the financial ruin of newspapers. Thus, in December 1977, the Ministry of Information increased its annual financial aid to political and non-political papers and periodicals. The annual aid for a political daily newspaper was raised from 18,000 to 40,000 dinars.[6]

THE PROBLEM OF ALIENS

Two communities of immigrants were active in 1977–78 and both caused problems for the government. The Palestinians demonstrated against supporters of Sādāt's policy, and especially against Egyptian students; they also frequently quarrelled among themselves. Their internal conflicts reached a peak with the assassination of the PLO Branch Head 'Alī Yāsīn in Kuwait in June. The government tried to maintain calm and prevent further clashes with other foreign students and between rival Palestinian factions.

More serious, and even potentially dangerous, were the demonstrations of c. 2,000 Indian workers employed on a $270m housing project by Engineering Projects India, who went on strike at the end of July 1978 demanding higher salaries. The strike soon developed into riots in which the workers wrecked the offices of their employer, and the police had to be called in to quell the disturbances. 403 labourers were detained and c. 200 who were regarded as the main troublemakers were deported.[7] It transpired that they were indeed poorly paid, and could not cover the high cost of living in Kuwait, especially in view of the new rent law which had increased rents by up to 100%. The cost of living was accelerating faster than wages—not only for the Indians but for other Asian workers as well. Dissatisfaction was particularly apparent among those who had worked in Kuwait for many years; they felt they had made a positive contribution to the affluence of the host country, but were getting no reward. The problem could not be solved by police action or deportations, yet the government did not hint at any new policy or labour laws to ensure minimum wage levels or housing conditions. The initiative, it seems, had to come from the Asian countries themselves, since a principality such as Kuwait was in great need of foreign manpower and was consequently susceptible to pressure. Sri Lanka had previously introduced measures to end the exploitation of its nationals in the Gulf area. Its new regulations included a stipulation that recruitment agencies should supply the Sri Lanka Labour Ministry with full details of the terms, conditions and salaries of any recruits going to the Gulf; the agency should pay for the upkeep of a recruit if he had not found employment within three months, and in some cases even return him home at its own expense. However, this was only a partial solution since there were already large numbers of Asian labourers in Kuwait and other Gulf states. In Kuwait alone there were c. 140,000 Indians and Pakistanis.

FOREIGN RELATIONS

Kuwait concentrated on several aspects of its foreign relations during 1978. It helped to strengthen co-operation and co-ordination between the Gulf littoral states in the economic, technical and security fields (for details see The Gulf States, above). It contributed much to the continued improvement in its co-operative relations with Iraq (for details see chapter on Iraq). It was also active with Saudi Arabia in co-ordinating inter-Arab relations, mainly over developments following

President Sādāt's new policy towards Israel (for details see essay on Inter-Arab Relations). Finally, it continued to extend financial aid to various states in the Middle East, Asia, Africa and Latin America (see also *MECS 1976-77*, p. 345) and to expand its economic, technical and trade agreements with various states, including the East European countries and China. Through these wide-ranging activities, it has succeeded in establishing friendly relations with most countries in the world, many of whom are interested in economic co-operation and especially in receiving financial aid.

PRESIDENT SĀDĀT'S POLICY TOWARDS ISRAEL
Kuwait was cautious in its reaction to Sādāt's new policy, mainly because about a quarter of the Kuwaiti population is Palestinian. Although essentially neutral, like Saudi Arabia, in the conflict between Egypt and its Arab "rejectionist" opponents, the Kuwaiti government stressed its insistence on the Rabat summit resolutions, especially those related to the Palestinians' rights, the demand for Israel's complete withdrawal from the occupied Arab territories, and the preservation of the Arab character of Jerusalem. However, Arab unity and solidarity were Kuwait's main interest and, in co-ordination with Saudi Arabia and other Gulf principalities, it made many efforts to heal the rifts by means of a summit conference which all the Arab states would attend. Kuwait tried several times to convene such a summit; until the Baghdad summit conference in November 1978, it refused to participate in any meeting which Egypt did not attend. Co-ordination with the Saudi Arabian position was discussed during several meetings between leaders of both states.

The Kuwaiti newspapers were divided in their attitude towards Sādāt's policy. Some, like *al-Siyāsa*, praised Sādāt and called on the Arab states to join together in his support; others, like *al-Ra'y al-'Āmm*, criticized Sādāt's attempts to reach a peace agreement with Israel. However, papers which raised accusations against Sādāt or his opponents were suspended (see above).

ECONOMIC AFFAIRS ($1 = 0.266 Kuwaiti dinars; £1 = KD 0.557)
Gross domestic product rose 13.8% in 1976-77 compared with 1975-76. With a slight drop in oil production in 1977 and through the first quarter of 1978, it is unlikely that such economic growth, as measured by GDP, will be repeated in 1977-78. But if the noticeable pick-up in crude oil output during the summer months of 1978 continues, there will most likely be a return to growth on the part of the economy as a whole.

Compared to the sharp expansionary trend of the previous three years, monetary developments in Kuwait in 1977 were "relatively moderate." [8] Meanwhile, throughout much of 1977, Kuwait was taking in more and more foreign exchange, and its Central Bank and commercial banks were accumulating foreign assets.

OIL AND GAS
Crude oil production in Kuwait fell 8.5% in 1977 to a level of 720.2m barrels or 1.97m barrels per day (cf 786.9m barrels or 2.16mbd in 1976). In contrast, output rose 7.7% during the first eight months of 1978 compared with the corresponding period in 1977. However, the growth in oil liftings during the summer of 1978 was not large enough to represent a departure from the government's policy of conserving petroleum reserves by limiting output. It is thus premature to suggest that any set pattern of increased production has emerged. [9]

In the latter part of 1977, Kuwaiti officials became concerned about their share of the oil market as exports fell 3.2% in value and 8.7% in volume in 1977 from 1976. In January 1978, the Kuwaitis formally instituted a 10-cent price cut which had been unofficially in force for some months. When the matter was discussed at the 1 February 1978 meeting of the OPEC Ministerial Committee, one reputable source reported that the Kuwaiti delegates "argued strongly that the comparative weakness of their current market position made it essential for them to have the freedom to offer some additional financial incentives to encourage exports; if the requisite endorsement was not forthcoming from the OPEC Committee, they might be obliged to proceed unilaterally." [10]

Ultimately, the OPEC ministers granted Kuwait the opportunity to extend one extra month's credit to its contract customers, which at recent interest rates was estimated to be equivalent to a reduction of 7-8 cents per barrel. In their final communiqué, the OPEC ministers "took note of Kuwait's special circumstances and difficulties and its decision to take required measures to remedy the situation when and if necessary." [11]

In addition to oil, Kuwait's natural gas reserves have been estimated at 892 bn cubic metres. In 1977, natural gas production amounted to 10.3 bn cu m, representing an 8% decline from 1976. [12]

MONEY AND BANKING

Kuwait's international reserves hovered around the $3 bn mark throughout 1977-78. Following a peak of $3,294m in April 1978, reserves dropped below $3 bn briefly at the end of July before climbing back to $3,031m at end-August 1978. In the fourth quarter of 1977, Kuwait's holdings of gold were halved from $244m to $107m, but this was more than offset by the leap in foreign exchange from $1,185m to $2,006m. In 1978, the respective proportions of the components of Kuwait's international reserves underwent little change.

At the end of June 1978, assets of Kuwait's commercial banks reached a new high of $3,275m, while liabilities dropped to $1,410m from their April peak of $1,530m. Net combined foreign assets of the Central Bank plus Kuwait's commercial banks climbed to a record KD 1,415m at the end of the first half of 1978. At the same time, the money supply reached KD 596m, or 32.7% more than at the end of June 1977. During this same 12-month period, the quasi-money supply grew 17.9% to a level of KD 1,128m.

BALANCE OF PAYMENTS

Kuwait's balance of payments surplus reached $4,867m in 1977 (cf $3,212m in 1976) despite a decline of $1,415m in the balance of goods, services and transfers. The growth of the 1977 surplus is most directly attributable to a substantial fall in the long-term capital debit from -$4,084m in 1976 to only -$283m in 1977.

GOVERNMENT FINANCE

According to data published by the International Monetary Fund (IMF), Kuwait's central government revenues fell 17.9% in 1977, from KD 2,839m to KD 2,330m. At the same time, expenditure rose 51.6% from KD 927m to KD 1,406m, resulting in a decline in the revenue-minus-expenditure surplus of 51.7%, from KD 1,911m in 1976 to KD 924m in 1977. [13]

The largest increases in public expenditure in the 1977-78 draft budget were to shares of local companies (+271%), development (+227%) and foreign transfers (+208%). Alternatively, allocations for land purchases were cut 22%. [14]

FOREIGN TRADE AND AID

Kuwait's exports slipped $40m or 0.4% in 1977 from 1976, while imports jumped

44% to $4,796m. As a result, Kuwait's merchandise trade surplus fell from $6,520m in 1976 to $5,008m one year later.

In 1977, Japan retained its position as Kuwait's largest purchaser of exports (23.1%) and supplier of imports (20.8%). Britain (9.6%) and Taiwan (6.1%) were the second and third leading markets for Kuwaiti oil exports, while the US (12.7%) and the UK (9.7%) followed Japan's lead as Kuwait's chief suppliers.

Machinery and transport equipment (41.8%) constituted Kuwait's principal commodity group import for the second straight year in 1976. Manufactured goods (36.5%) and food, beverages and tobacco (13.8%) were second and third respectively. Oil, of course, far outdistanced manufactured goods as Kuwait's leading export. [15]

The Kuwait Fund for Arab Economic Development (KFAED) increased its assistance loans by 60% in 1977, for a total of KD 132m. Recipients of the largest loans were Morocco (KD 10m), Ghana (KD 8.97m) and Afghanistan (KD 8.85m). [16]

Aryeh Shmuelevitz
Economic section by **Ira E. Hoffman**

ARMED FORCES

Total armed forces number 12,000. Defence expenditure in 1977 was KD 93m ($322.2m); military service is compulsory for 18 months. The Army of 10,500 has one armoured brigade; two infantry brigades; 24 *Chieftain*, 50 *Vickers*; 50 *Centurion* medium tanks; 100 *Saladin* armoured, 20 *Ferret* scout cars; 130 *Saracen* armoured personnel carriers; ten 25-pounder guns; 20 AMX 155mm self-propelled howitzers; SS-11, *HOT, TOW, Vigilant, Harpon* anti-tank guided weapons. (129 *Chieftain* medium tanks; Scorpion light tanks; armoured personnel carriers; artillery; SA-7 surface-to-air missiles on order.)

The 500-strong Navy (Coastguard) has five fast patrol boats; 12 inshore patrol craft; 16 patrol launches, and three landing craft.

The Air Force of 1,000 (excluding expatriate personnel) has 49 combat aircraft; two fighter-bomber squadrons (forming) with 20 A-4KU; one interceptor squadron with 20 *Mirage* F-1B/C; one counter-insurgency squadron with nine *Strikemaster* Mk 83; two DC-9, two L-100-20 transports; three helicopter squadrons with 30 *Gazelle*, 12 *Puma*. Trainers include four *Hunter* T67, two TA-4KU. *Red Top, Firestreak,* R.550 *Magic, Sidewinder* air-to-air missiles; *Super* 530 air-to-surface missiles; 50 *Improved HAWK* surface-to-air missiles. (14 A-4KU, four TA-4KU ground-attack fighters on order.)

Source: The Military Balance 1978–79 (London: International Institute for Strategic Studies).

BALANCE OF PAYMENTS (million US dollars)

	1975	1976	1977
A. Goods, Services and Transfers	5,891	6,971	5,456
Exports of Merchandise, fob	8,486	9,679	9,722
Imports of Merchandise, fob	-2,403	-3,301	-3,925
Exports of Services	1,768	2,231	2,577
Imports of Services	-891	-1,100	-1,741
Private Unrequited Transfers, net	-276	-315	-370
Government Unrequited Transfers, net	-793	-223	-807
B. Long-Term Capital, nie	-1,937	-4,084	-283
C. Short-Term Capital, nie	-93	321	-307
D. Errors and Omissions	-1	3	1
Total (A through D)	**3,860**	**3,212**	**4,867**

INTERNATIONAL LIQUIDITY (million US dollars at end of period)

	1976	1977	(Jan–June) 1978
International Reserves	1,928.6	2,989.9	3,285.6
Gold	226.8	106.8	109.0
Reserves with IMF	862.9	877.2	832.4
Foreign Exchange	838.9	2,005.9	2,344.2
Commercial Banks: Assets	2,352.0	2,936.2	3,275.1
Liabilities	1,129.5	1,498.8	1,409.6

MONETARY SURVEY (million Kuwaiti dinars at end of period)

	1976	1977	(Jan–June) 1978
Foreign Assets (net)	898	1,225	1,415
Claims on Private Sector	934	1,237	1,288
Money	394	491	596
Quasi-money	826	1,078	1,128
Government Deposits	342	440	448
Other Items (net)	270	453	532
Money, Seasonally Adjusted	410	511	576

Source (of three preceding tables): IMF, *International Financial Statistics*.

GOVERNMENT EXPENDITURE (million Kuwaiti dinars)

	1973–74[1]	1974–75[1]	1975–76[2]	1976–77[3]	Budget 1977–78[3]
Current Domestic Expenditure	280.9	431.8	658.4	746.0	888.1
Development	70.2	112.9	203.8	353.1	801.1
Land Purchases	19.4	47.7	147.0	108.4	85.0
Local Loans	13.7	14.5	35.7	35.2	—
Contributions to:					
Shares of Local Companies	45.8	5.7	121.5	51.6	140.0
Government Financial Institutions	16.6	226.2	93.5	123.5	—
Foreign Transfers	106.3	324.1	77.5	101.5	211.0
Total	**552.9**	**1,162.9**	**1,337.4**	**1,519.3**	**2,125.2**

[1] Year ending 31 March.
[2] Fifteen months ending 30 June 1976.
[3] Year beginning 1 July, ending 30 June.

GOVERNMENT RECEIPTS (million Kuwaiti dinars)

	1973–74[1]	1974–75[1]	1975–76[2]	1976–77[3]	1977–78[3]
Oil Receipts	584	2,535	2,793	2,598	2,182
Other Receipts	131	215	431	438	391
Total	**715**	**2,750**	**3,224**	**3,036**	**2,573**
Oil Receipts as % of total	82	92	87	86	85

[1] Year ending 31 March.
[2] Fifteen months ending 30 June 1976.
[3] Year beginning 1 July, ending 30 June.
Source (of two preceding tables): Central Bank of Kuwait, *Economic Report for 1977*.

COST OF LIVING INDEX (1972 = 100)

	Relative Weight	1974	1975	1976	1977
Foodstuffs	37.1	135.9	153.7	163.7	175.4
Clothing and Cosmetics	14.5	116.7	124.4	135.6	151.8
Stationery	2.6	124.7	146.5	149.7	157.2
Housing	17.7	102.8	106.0	113.4	124.1
Consumer Durables	14.0	125.1	136.8	138.8	150.9
Transportation and Communication	9.6	121.5	120.8	119.2	130.5
Education, Medical and Recreational Services	4.5	108.0	118.6	128.0	132.1
Total	**100.0**	**122.7**	**133.7**	**141.0**	**152.7**

Source: Ministry of Planning, Central Statistics Office.

GROSS DOMESTIC PRODUCT[1] (million Kuwaiti dinars)

	1972-73	1973-74	1974-75	1975-76	1976-77[2]
Total GDP	**1,521**	**2,157**	**3,511**	**3,226**	**3,672**
% change	15.2	41.8	62.8	-8.1	13.8
GDP, excluding oil exports		497	654	794	982
% Change			39.2	21.4	23.8

[1] Year ending 31 March.
[2] Estimates.
Source: Central Bank of Kuwait.

BALANCE OF TRADE (million Kuwaiti dinars)

	1973	1974	1975	1976	1977
Oil Exports	1,060	3,098	2,493	2,659	2,587
Non-Oil Exports	70	117	170	216	260
Total Exports	**1,130**	**3,215**	**2,663**	**2,874[1]**	**2,847[2]**
Imports	**311**	**455**	**693**	**972**	**1,131[2]**
Balance of Trade:					
With Oil	819	2,760	1,970	1,902	1,716
Without Oil	-241	-338	-523	-766	-871

[1] Figures do not add because of rounding.
[2] Estimates.

COMPOSITION OF EXPORTS (million Kuwaiti dinars)

	1974	1975	1976
Food, Live Animals, Beverages and Tobacco	10.8	9.4	14.5
Manufactured Goods and Miscellaneous Articles	24.3	37.4	82.8
Crude Materials, Mineral Fuels, Lubricants and Related Materials, Animal and Vegetable Oils, Fats, and Chemicals	3,148.0	2,562.5	2,698.3
Machinery and Transport Equipment	31.5	53.5	78.7
Commodities and Transactions not Classified According to Kind	0.1	0.1	0.1
Total	**3,214.7**	**2,662.9**	**2,874.4**

COMPOSITION OF IMPORTS (million Kuwaiti dinars)

	1974	1975	1976
Food, Live Animals, Beverages and Tobacco	78.8	115.1	134.4
Manufactured Goods and Miscellaneous Articles	181.5	215.8	354.8
Crude Materials, Mineral Fuels, Lubricants and Related Materials, Animal and Vegetable Oils, Fats and Chemicals	31.5	41.8	57.1
Machinery and Transport Equipment	156.2	316.2	406.7
Commodities and Transactions not Classified According to Kind	3.5	4.3	19.0
Total	**455.1**	**693.2**	**972.0**

Source (of three preceding tables): Central Bank of Kuwait, *Economic Report for 1977*.

DIRECTION OF TRADE (million US dollars)

	1975	1976	1977*
Exports To:			
Japan	2,342	2,185	2,267
United Kingdom	714	804	941
Taiwan	444	648	599
Italy	298	367	583
South Korea	424	650	568
Netherlands	839	961	561
Saudi Arabia	126	359	546
France	523	416	306
United States	79	74	222
Australia	191	223	186
Total (including others)	**8,644**	**9,844**	**9,804**
Imports from:			
Japan	387	689	998
United States	430	487	610
United Kingdom	244	271	465
West Germany	273	364	442
Italy	108	146	279
South Korea	31	98	222
India	53	130	219
France	79	173	171
China PR	50	75	110
Taiwan	41	72	98
Total (including others)	**2,390**	**3,324**	**4,796**

*Data partly extrapolated and/or derived from partner country.
Source: IMF, *Direction of Trade*.

NOTES
1. R Kuwait, 13 February—BBC, 15 February 1978.
2. *Events*, London; 10 March 1978.
3. *Arabia and the Gulf*, London; 2 January 1978.
4. *Al-Ittiḥād*, Abu Dhabi; 31 March 1978; QNA, 18 April—BBC, 20 April 1978; MENA, 28 August—DR, 29 August 1978.
5. *Al-Ra'y al-'Amm*, Kuwait; 20 January 1978.
6. *Al-Anbā'*, Beirut; 20 November 1978.
7. *Al-Watan*, Kuwait; 27–31 July 1978.
8. Central Bank of Kuwait, *Economic Report for 1977*, p. 5.
9. Figures taken from various issues of *Petroleum Economist,* London.
10. *Middle East Economic Survey*, Nicosia; 6 February 1978.
11. *Ibid.*
12. *Petroleum Economist*, February and November 1978.
13. International Monetary Fund (IMF), *International Financial Statistics*, October 1978.
14. Central Bank of Kuwait, *op. cit.,* p. 38.
15. *Ibid*, pp. 82–91. Also IMF, *Direction of Trade*, various issues.
16. See John Law, *Arab Aid: Who Gets It, For What and How* (New York: Chase World Information Corporation, 1978), pp. 191–98.

Oman

Oman's hold over the Dhufari Province was consolidated in 1977–78 by the transfer of provincial services to civilian control and the continuance of development projects. A band of perhaps 30–50 insurgents still operating in the mountains provoked intermittent incidents. Following developments in the Horn of Africa, fears grew of renewed armed intervention in Oman by the PDRY and Dhufari rebels, aided by Cubans and the Soviets. One of Oman's major steps in the period was the establishment of diplomatic relations with Peking. There was also closer co-operation with France.

POLITICAL AFFAIRS
CABINET RESHUFFLE
A minor Cabinet reshuffle took place on 14 June 1978 after three new ministries were created and one abolished. The Public Works Ministry became a General Directorate; its Minister, Karīm Ahmad al-Haramī, was appointed Minister of Posts, Telegraphs and Telecommunications, one of the three new portfolios. The other two were the Ministry of Civil Aviation, Roads and Ports, under Sālim Nāsir al-Busaydī, and the Ministry of Electricity and Water under Hamūd 'Abdalla al-Hārithī. Busaydī had formerly been Under-Secretary at the Communications Ministry, and Hārithī the legal adviser to the Agriculture, Fisheries, Petroleum and Mineral Ministry. The establishment of the new ministries had long been expected in view of the huge developments carried out in the fields of communications, transportation, electricity and water.

After the reshuffle, the Cabinet comprised 21 ministers and two advisers, in addition to the Prime Minister, Sultan Qābūs.

SEMI-NORMALIZATION IN DHUFAR
Considering that it had suppressed the rebellion in Dhufar (see *MECS 1976–77*, pp. 349–50), the government continued its two-pronged policy of normalization, firstly by returning the region's services to civilian control (for example, the health service was transferred from the armed forces to the Ministry of Health at the end of 1977); and secondly by carrying out its development plan for the region with the aim of diminishing economic and social grievances. Developments covered education, health and communication facilities, the enlargement of Port Raysut, and agricultural projects aimed at building up cattle herds on the mountains and encouraging more intensive cultivation on the coastal plain. Among the most important projects completed were the port of Riswat and the modern hospital in Salalah, the capital of Dhufar, which was also chosen by the Sultan to become the centre of the seventh independence anniversary celebrations in November 1977. Another measure was the decision taken in mid-1978 to establish a council of tribal heads to serve as an advisory body to the local authorities and help them solve local problems and disputes. However, what might be called "local patriotism" among the Dhufaris was far from dead and was exploited by the rebels. In the second half of 1978, simultaneous to reports of an increase in military clashes, Popular Front for the Liberation of Oman (PFLO) agents maintained a propaganda campaign among the Dhufaris against the following; (a) the decision of April 1978 to reverse the plan to build an oil outlet at Port Raysut and to pump oil from Dhufar to an

outlet in Port Muscat; (b) the alleged discrimination in favour of Indian and British workers to the disadvantage of Dhufaris in the province; (c) the fact that the *Ibādiyya* was still the state religion and that the whole judicial system was based on it, whereas the Dhufaris are all Sunnī Muslims.[1]

In fact, the rebellion was not totally suppressed although PFLO military activities were only on a small scale. Periodic clashes were reported, mainly by the rebels' broadcasting service in Aden, and from January 1978 also from Libya. The PFLO continued to maintain close relations with Tripoli, as well as official relations with the Ba'th parties of Iraq and Syria, although both Baghdad and Damascus had recognized the Sultan's regime in Oman and established diplomatic relations with it (see *MECS 1976–77*, p. 351). Libya, on the other hand, with its close ties with the PDRY, remained implacably hostile to Sultan Qābūs' regime and continued to support the PFLO; especially since the Sultan had asked for aid from Iran. Official delegations of the PFLO, led by a member of the Central Executive Committee, visited Iraq and Libya in October 1977 and Syria in April 1978. They also participated in the Algerian summit conference in February 1978.

Although the fighting in Dhufar was effectively over, clashes still occurred in the area of north-west and western Dhufar where, according to a PFLO leader who surrendered in October 1977, c. 30 PFLO members were still operating. He added that c. 200 more were being trained in the PDRY, receiving Cuban aid.[2] According to their own sources, most of the PFLO attacks were aimed against foreigners—the Iranian units and the British instructors and advisers. They included the landmining of an Iranian military vehicle in January1978,[3] and the killing in June of five British technicians from the British-based Airwork Services. Although the two survivors claimed that there were no rebels about and that to their knowledge no war was going on in the area, the killing was considered a sign of the renewal of the insurrection. In fact, there were reports of large-scale infiltrations of rebel forces into Dhufar from the PDRY at the end of May and the beginning of June 1978. A PFLO statement on 9 June—the anniversary of the revolution—claimed that the military setback was only temporary and that the revolution was continuing. Even the PDRY, which generally refrained from officially supporting the rebels, announced in the Prime Minister's anniversary speech its decisive support of the PFLO struggle against Sultan Qābūs, among others.[4]

On the other hand, the continued defection of Dhufari rebels and their surrender to the Sultan's army indicated that some rebels were still interested in taking advantage of the amnesty which has been in force for some years and of the accompanying financial inducements. It was also a sign that morale among the rebels was low. The Sultan's most significant success was the defection of one of the top PFLO leaders and commanders with five other rebels in October 1977. He claimed that he was completely disillusioned with the extreme Communism of the movement. "We were learning all about Marx, but doing very little fighting. For me and many of my colleagues, things were becoming very boring." Nevertheless, he admitted that there were still many who were determined to continue the fight.[5] It seems that a comparatively small number of the Sultan's troops also defected to the PFLO. The defectors of both sides usually joined the army units of their former enemy—the Popular Front Army stationed in the PDRY and the Sultan's Home Guard Force. Known as the Firqa, the latter has c. 3,000 men (of whom about half are defectors), and is trained by British officers of the Special Air Service (SAS).

Despite the strategic importance of Oman as the southern gateway to the Gulf, Britain seemed anxious to end its last direct military commitment and several times during the year held discussions about its final withdrawal (see *MECS 1976–77*, p. 350). Nevertheless, the British government agreed that c. 200 officers and NCOs would remain on loan to the Sultan's armed forces to assist in the army's modernization programme, with a further 465 officers and men serving on a contract basis with the Sultan.

The Jordanian engineers battalion left Oman in December 1977, though a small number of experts remained for advisory purposes.

The small Iranian contingent still in Dhufar (see *MECS 1976–77*, p. 350) was no longer called an expeditionary force designed to help crush the Dhufari rebellion, but a force for the preservation of the security and stability of the Gulf area. Iran thus intended to demonstrate co-operation in the struggle against subversive activities (see above on the Gulf States), and to show that its units were there on a long-term basis. Both aims were reaffirmed by the Sultan's linkage of the Iranian presence to what he saw as the continued danger to Oman from the PDRY and its allies. There was no official confirmation of a report in June 1978 that the Iranian units were to be reinforced in view of the growing activities of the rebels.

NEW DEMOCRATIC OPPOSITION
The Dhufari rebels were not the only active opposition in Oman. In July 1978, there were reports of another movement organized in clandestine cells and including civil servants, merchants and some intellectuals. They supported the Sultan, but opposed his method of governing. Their aim was to introduce reforms and to reverse those "errors" of his which gave fuel to the Leftists' fire. Their complaints included the following: (a) the fact that Oman had become a "police state" as a result of the rebellion in Dhufar; (b) the fact that about 30 families ruled Oman while others, even high officials, had no authority; (c) the existence of a group of court favourites who had become excessively rich; (d) the continuing presence of the British as advisers; (e) inflation; (f) the recognition of China, which they felt could not help Oman against the Soviets, either politically or militarily.[6]

ARMED FORCES
The Omanis continued to expand their armed forces by establishing a small naval force equipped with missile boats to defend their long shoreline of c. 1,700 km.

The Omani army received a transport of new and highly sophisticated *Exhaust* missiles from France in January 1978. (For the composition of the armed forces, see below.)

SOCIAL AFFAIRS
EDUCATION, EMPLOYMENT, WOMEN
The government continued to lay special emphasis on three aspects of its social policy: the development of education; a limitation on imported labour; and the emancipation of women.

In view of the growing need for qualified manpower to carry out its development programme (see *MECS 1976–77*, pp. 351–52) and the increasing threat to native Omanis from imported skilled and semi-skilled labour, the government paid special attention to its campaign to reduce illiteracy and to strengthen the educational system. This was done in close co-operation with Jordan and Egypt. The University of Jordan became the chief adviser to the Omani Ministry of Education and Culture, especially in preparing the syllabus for all levels of the Omani school system. Egypt was also one of the chief suppliers of teachers to Oman, followed by Jordan. According to *al-Jumhūriyya* (30 March 1978), Egypt was asked to increase the number of its teachers in 1979 to 3,000 (sic). In the academic year 1977–78, there were 390 schools with c. 76,000 pupils; c. 600 students were abroad on government scholarships. New school construction also continued.

The question of foreign labour was partially solved by the return of many emigré Omanis from abroad with high qualifications. Nevertheless, it remained true that foreigners, although constituting only 30% of the population, were still running the country. This situation is likely to continue until a new generation of home-educated Omanis has grown up. Meanwhile, restrictions were enacted to prevent an uncontrolled increase in alien workers, and even to encourage a decrease in their number. The Ministry of Labour and Social Affairs published new restrictions in April 1978 aimed at bringing about the "Omanization" of the private sector, which was requested to give maximum employment opportunities to Omani nationals. It became illegal for a non-Omani to be employed in a non-technical job unless it could be proved that there was no Omani national available for it.[7]

Since the coup of Sultan Qābūs in 1970, female education has shown a sharp rise. There were 22,300 girls in 72 schools in the academic year 1977–78 (cf 1,136 in 1970–71) and 52 centres to combat female illiteracy. About 80 girl students were abroad attending higher education courses.

These statistics were presented by Mrs Rājiha 'Abd al-Amīr, the Director of the National Statistical Department, to Oman's first ever women's conference, held from 4–14 March 1978. It discussed such topics as the role of women in Omani society, the situation of women in the rural areas, and women's education. The conference was attended by delegates from women's organizations in Oman, in several other Arab states and in the US. In his opening speech, the Minister of Labour and Social Affairs stressed the need for Omani women to participate in the country's infrastructure.[8]

Another breakthrough in the status of women was the opening in November 1977 of the first college for women teachers in Muscat.

FOREIGN RELATIONS
Oman maintained close relations with its Gulf neighbours, especially Iran, and played a leading role in efforts to create closer co-operation among the Gulf littoral states in defence and internal security. On the other hand, it became involved in a serious border dispute with Ra's al-Khaymah (the UAE) which defied solution, despite intensive negotiations (for details see above, The Gulf States).

Outside the Gulf area, Oman maintained close relations with Egypt, Jordan and Sudan. It developed trade with both the former countries and continued to import manpower from them. However, the most important developments were Oman's firm support of President Sādāt's peace policy and, more significantly, its recognition of China.

SĀDĀT'S PEACE INITIATIVE
Almost immediately before Sādāt's visit to Jerusalem, Sultan Qābūs expressed his support for this "courageous and bold step aimed at driving the wheel of peace forward."[9] Subsequently he was almost the sole Arab ruler to support the Camp David Framework Agreements.

RECOGNITION OF CHINA
Peking's decision to withdraw its support for the Dhufari rebellion was an important factor in opening the way for negotiations between Oman and China on establishing diplomatic relations. The negotiations were carried out in London between the embassies of the two countries, and agreement was reached towards the end of March 1978. However, the Omani government had to delay announcing its recognition because of opposition pressure in the region. Oman forewarned its neighbours—at least Saudi Arabia, the UAE and Iran—of its intention, but (apart

from Iran, which already maintained amicable relations with China), it was very difficult for these regimes to go along with the proposal. Oman's campaign to convince its neighbours of the importance of introducing China to the region as a counterbalance to the Soviet Union and the PDRY was apparently successful in the case of Kuwait, which had already recognized China, and of the UAE, especially in the light of developments in the Horn of Africa. The agreement to establish diplomatic relations at ambassadorial level was officially announced on 26 May 1978. According to the Omani statement, the Government of Oman recognized the Government of the People's Republic of China as "the sole legal government representing the entire Chinese people"; this meant the end of Oman's recognition of Taiwan. The Chinese, for their part, declared their firm support for the Government of the Sultanate of Oman in its "just cause of safeguarding national independence and developing the national economy." The two governments agreed to develop friendly relations and co-operation on the basis of mutual respect for state sovereignty and territorial integrity, mutual non-aggression, non-interference in each other's affairs, equality, mutual benefit and peaceful coexistence.

This was undoubtedly a major revolution in the foreign policy of conservative Oman, whose Sultan was known for his deep animosity to Leftist and, in particular, to Communist ideology and activities. Following the recognition of Peking, Sultan Qābūs and his Minister of State for Foreign Affairs, Qays 'Abd al-Mun'im Zawāwī, intensified their attacks on the USSR, accusing it of maintaining imperialist colonialism in the world and especially in the Arabian Sea area, and calling on all states to resist this new and deadly form of colonialism. They stressed that the PDRY was now a major base for the USSR and that the Soviets were directing their aid to Ethiopia from Aden.

The Omani Foreign Minister began a seven-day official visit to China on 20 June to discuss political and economic co-operation.

ECONOMIC AFFAIRS ($1 = 0.346 Omani rials; £1 = RO 0.724)
Although Oman registered economic growth, as measured by the 4% increase in Gross Domestic Product (GDP) in 1977, the rate of growth was much less than in 1976 (13.6%) or 1975 (30%).[10] The Central Bank of Oman labelled this development a "continuation of the process of consolidation" by which "prudent fiscal management . . . has resulted in placing the economy on a more balanced and sustainable growth path."[11]

Fiscal management may very well have become prudent in 1977, but the slower rate of growth in GDP could easily be attributed to the lack of increase of exports. With oil comprising more than 60% of GDP and 90% of government revenue (excluding grants), the 6.1% fall in oil production in 1977 is revealing in this regard.

CHROME AND OIL
Two mineral discoveries in 1978 were likely to make an important contribution to the country's future economic prosperity. At the beginning of the year, chromite deposits were discovered by Prospection Oman Ltd, which holds Oman's copper and chrome concessions. The deposits were estimated at minimal 2m tons of medium to good quality ore, and marketing possibilities were described as excellent.[12] A no less important discovery was that of a new field of high-quality oil not far from the new oilfields in Dhufar. This will not only provide a welcome economic lift to the province, but also ensure that the country's oil production does not begin to tail off towards the end of this decade, a situation which had been predicted because of the heavy exploitation of the northern oilfields to finance the Dhufari war.

GOVERNMENT FINANCES
For the first time in a number of years, Oman registered a budget surplus in 1977. The estimated budget for 1978, however, indicated that the surplus would be short-lived. The government ran into some difficulties in the first half of 1978 when grants from abroad, which were intended to cover the anticipated budget deficit, failed to arrive in sufficient quantities. As a result, government spending has been held back and business has witnessed a marked slowdown.[13]

MONETARY SURVEY
At the end of May 1978, Oman's international reserves peaked at $449.6m before sliding back to $381.9m at the end of August. This took the form of a fall in holdings of foreign exchange.
The rate of growth of the money supply of c. 9% in 1977 compared with rates exceeding 40% from 1973–76. The quasi-money supply, on the other hand, jumped c. 50% in 1977 over 1976. In neither case was there much change during the first half of 1978.[14]

BALANCE OF PAYMENTS
Provisional statistics from the Central Bank show an improvement in Oman's balance of payments from a deficit of RO 21.7m in 1976 to a surplus of RO 15.1m in 1977. This turnaround is largely the result of an RO 35.4m decrease in the invisibles and private transfers debit side of the payments ledger.[15]

FOREIGN TRADE
According to the IMF, Oman's exports actually fell 1.1% to $1,574m in 1977, reflecting the relative slump in the oil sector. At the same time, imports rose 24% to $873.5m, thereby reducing Oman's trade surplus from $871m to $701m.[16]
In 1977, the UK expanded its lead over the UAE as Oman's leading source of imports, raising its market share to 38% (cf 20% in 1976). Japan, Oman's third largest supplier, came closer to the UAE by increasing its market share from 12.5% in 1976 to 14% in 1978.
In 1977, Japan (51.3%), the US (15.4%) and the Netherlands (9.1%) continued to be the three principal markets for Omani exports, despite the absolute and relative decline in purchases by the latter two.
During the first half of 1977, machinery and transport equipment (41%), manufactured goods (16.6%) and food and live animals (12.7%) all retained their respective positions as Oman's three chief commodity group imports.

Aryeh Shmuelevitz
Economic section by Ira E. Hoffman

ARMED FORCES
Total armed forces number 19,200 (excluding expatriate personnel). Defence expenditure in 1978 was RO 265m ($767m); military service is voluntary. The Army of 16,200 has two brigade headquarters; eight infantry battalions; one Royal Guard regiment; one artillery regiment; one signals regiment; one armoured car squadron; one parachute squadron; one engineer squadron; 36 *Saladin* armoured cars; 36 105mm guns; 81mm, 120mm mortars; *TOW* anti-tank guided weapons.
The Navy of 900 has three patrol vessels (one Royal Yacht, two ex-Dutch mine counter-measures); one training ship (500-ton ex-logistic ship); seven fast patrol

boats (three with *Exocet* surface-to-surface missiles); four coastal patrol craft (under 100 tons), three small landing craft. (One logistic support ship on order.)

The Air Force of 2,100 (including expatriate personnel) has 32 aircraft; one ground-attack fighter/reconnaissance squadron with 12 *Hunter*; one ground-attack fighter squadron with 12 *Jaguar*; one counter-insurgency/training squadron with eight BAC-167; three transport squadrons: one with three BAC-111, two with ten *Defender/Skyvan*; Royal flight with one VC-10, one *Gulfstream*, two AS.202 *Bravo* trainers; one helicopter squadron with 20 AB-205, two AB-206, five AB-214A/B helicopters; two air defence squadrons with 28 *Rapier* surface-to-air missiles. (R. 550 *Magic* air-to-air missiles on order.)

Paramilitary forces include 3,300 tribal Home Guard (Firqa); One *Learjet*, two *Turbo-Porter*, two *Merlin* 1VA, four AB-205, two AB-206 helicopters in the Police Air Wing.

Source: The Military Balance 1978–79 (London: International Institute for Strategic Studies).

BALANCE OF PAYMENTS (million Omani rials)

	1975	*1976*	*1977**
Exports, fob	489.2	545.2	554.5
of which: Oil	*488.1*	*543.8*	*553.0*
Imports, cif	-371.4	-405.5	-392.0
Trade Balance	117.8	139.7	162.5
Services and Private Transfers (net)	-161.4	-161.4	-153.9
Current Account Balance	-43.6	-21.7	8.6
Official Loans and Transfers (net)	124.0	61.0	108.0
Oil Sector Capital (net)	-29.5	30.1	10.7
Errors and Omissions (net)	-52.6	-79.5	-52.3
Overall Balance	**-1.7**	**-10.1**	**75.0**

*Provisional.
Sources: Central Bank of Oman and international agencies.

INTERNATIONAL LIQUIDITY (million US dollars at end of period)

	1976	*1977*	*(Jan–May)* *1978*
International Reserves	308.9	426.7	449.6
Gold	1.9	4.3	7.9
SDRs	0.9	0.9	0.9
Reserves with IMF	29.1	23.6	21.3
Foreign Exchange	277.0	397.9	419.6
Deposit Money Banks: Assets	44.3	96.4	86.9
Liabilities	261.0	94.0	213.0

MONETARY SURVEY (million Omani rials at end of period)

	1976	*1977*	*(Jan–June)* *1978*
Foreign Assets (net)	24.0	`140.8	101.5
Domestic Credit	157.9	115.3	126.0
Claims on Government (net)	37.7	-51.8	-50.2
Claims on Private Sector	120.2	167.1	176.2
Money	102.2	111.3	107.2
Quasi-money	62.4	95.3	102.0
Other Items (net)	17.1	49.6	18.3
Money, Seasonally Adjusted	106.0	115.3	98.3

Source (of two preceding tables): IMF, *International Financial Statistics*.

SUMMARY OF GOVERNMENT FINANCE (billion Omani rials)

	1975 Actual	1976 Actual	1977 Projected
Revenues	459.4	505.4	613
of which:			
Oil Receipts	*373.1*	*454.7*	*480*
Expenditures	495.5	580.7	550
of which:			
Current	*322.5*	*385.6*	*410*
Capital	*173.0*	*195.1*	*140*
Domestic net lending and equity participation	0.9	-1.9	—
Other	-4.3	13.9	—
Surplus or Deficit	**-39.5**	**-63.7**	**63**

GOVERNMENT CAPITAL EXPENDITURES (million Omani rials)

	1975 Actual	1976 Actual	1977 Budget
Roads	39.6	42.8	55.9
Desalination Plant	27.8	29.4	27.9
Utilities	28.9	18.4	25.5
Public Buildings	10.7	20.1	20.8
Education	2.4	3.8	13.6
Harbour and Ports	3.0	7.0	11.2
Dhufar Development	8.3	3.0	10.3
Airport and Aviation	2.2	3.7	9.7
Housing and Urban Development	6.1	10.5	8.1
Health	7.9	8.6	7.4
Total (including others)	**173.0**	**195.1**	**231.0**

Source (of two preceding tables): Central Bank of Oman and Directorate General of Finance.

GOVERNMENT CURRENT EXPENDITURES (million Omani rials)

	1975 Actual	1976 Actual	1977 Budget
Defence and National Security	241.0	271.0	297.0
Recurrent	*67.0*	*104.0*	*136.0*
Capital	*174.0*	*167.0*	*161.0*
Diwan	9.9	23.9	29.4
Transport and Communication	7.9	13.3	26.6
Education	7.2	10.2	14.5
Oil Company Operations	10.3	12.3	13.0
Dhufar Province	4.9	7.5	11.3
Health	6.8	9.0	11.1
Finance and Office of Economic Adviser	12.9	8.3	10.2
Total (including others)	**322.5**	**385.6**	**453.0**

Source: Directorate General of Finance.

NATIONAL ACCOUNTS (million Omani rials)

	1974	1975	1976	1977
Exports	419.1	489.2	545.2	547.2
Government Consumption	197.2	322.5	385.6	...
Gross Capital Formation	174.1	223.1	245.4	235.9
Private Consumption	49.6	78.6	86.6	...
Less: Imports	*-245.6*	*-374.3*	...	...
Gross Domestic Product (GDP)	568.5	738.8	839.2	872.9
Less: Net Factor Payments Abroad	*-122.8*	*-127.8*	*-135.0*	...
Gross National Expenditure = GNP	445.7	611.0	704.2	...
GDP at 1975 prices	568.5	738.8	...	...

Source: IMF, *International Financial Statistics.*

443

ORIGIN OF GROSS DOMESTIC PRODUCT (million Omani rials at current market prices)

	1974	1975	1976*
Construction	58.0	89.2	96.0
Public Administration and Defence	46.4	55.3	61.0
Wholesale and Retail Trade	27.2	48.1	48.0
Transportation and Communication	12.3	23.5	25.0
Agriculture and Fishing	17.4	18.1	21.0
Services	6.7	8.4	15.0
Ownership of Dwellings	4.8	9.3	12.0
Banking	3.5	8.9	10.0
Electricity	1.2	1.8	5.0
Manufacturing	2.0	2.5	3.0
Total Non-Oil GDP	**179.5**	**265.1**	**296.0**
Mining (oil)	389.0	473.7	503.6
Total GDP	**568.5**	**738.8**	**799.6**

*Preliminary.
Sources: Central Bank of Oman and international agencies.

INDICATORS OF INFRASTRUCTURE

	1970	1972	1974	1976*
Cargo handled by ports (thousand tons)	129	331	793	1,440
Total length of roads (km)	1,827	3,258	4,532	9,772
Telephone lines (number)	557	1,208	2,937	6,649
Schools (number)	3	68	176	261
Pupils (thousands)	0.9	24.5	49.2	65.0
Hospital beds (number)	12	526	934	1,252
Electricity (million kwh)	105	130	230	413

*Provisional.
Sources: Central Bank of Oman and Directorate General of National Statistics.

IMPORTS BY COMMODITY GROUP (million Omani rials)

	1975	1976	(first half) 1977
Food and Live Animals	26.8	28.2	18.4
Beverages and Tobacco	3.1	3.9	3.1
Crude Materials	5.6	5.1	3.8
Mineral Fuels, Lubricants, etc.	10.8	16.6	10.8
Animal and Vegetable Oils and Fats	0.9	1.0	1.0
Chemicals	9.0	9.0	6.0
Manufactured Goods	48.5	43.1	24.1
Machinery and Transport Equipment	95.8	91.7	59.6
Miscellaneous Manufactures	18.3	22.5	14.1
Unclassified	12.6	9.3	4.4
Total	**231.4**	**230.5**	**145.3**

Sources: Central Bank of Oman and other Omani agencies.

DIRECTION OF TRADE (million US dollars)

	1975	1976	1977*
Exports to:			
Japan	540.7	680.9	807.1
United States	83.2	248.0	242.0
Netherlands	295.8	229.3	142.9
Trinidad and Tobago	153.7	121.7	142.9
France	99.4	100.6	60.5
Sweden	...	...	52.8
Norway	17.3	7.0	48.9
United Kingdom	95.9	19.9	16.7
West Germany	8.1	18.7	16.7
Italy	6.9	14.0	16.7
Total (including others)	**1,444.9**	**1,575.3**	**1,574.2**
Imports from:			
United Kingdom	131.2	139.8	331.7
United Arab Emirates	120.7	125.7	130.6
Japan	53.0	87.7	123.1
United States	64.6	44.0	62.8
West Germany	68.0	45.7	58.0
Netherlands	35.6	22.3	25.9
France	20.8	20.8	22.6
Singapore	10.1	15.3	20.6
Italy	12.7	9.3	20.2
Australia	13.6	13.9	17.9
Total (including others)	**670.6**	**704.4**	**873.5**

*Data partly extrapolated and/or derived from partner country.
Source: IMF, Direction of Trade.

NOTES
1. Al-Hawādith, Beirut; 21 July 1978.
2. The Times, London; 18 October 1977.
3. Aden Voice of Oman Revolution, 26 February—BBC, 28 February 1978.
4. The Times, 7 June; Aden Radio, 7 June—BBC, 9 June; Aden Voice of Oman Revolution, 9 June—BBC, 12 June 1978.
5. The Times, 18 October 1977.
6. Al-Hawādith, 21 July 1978.
7. Akhbār 'Umān, 13 April 1978.
8. Ibid, 23 March 1978.
9. R Cairo, 19 November—DR, 21 November 1977.
10. For details on Oman's economic performance during 1976, its five-year development plan and foreign aid, see MECS 1976–77, pp. 351–53.
11. Central Bank quotation is reprinted in Grindlays Bank Group, Oman, June 1978.
12. Middle East News (MENA weekly), 5 May 1978. The majority of the world's known deposits of chromite are in Rhodesia.
13. See Economist Intelligence Unit, Quarterly Economic Review of Bahrain, Qatar, Oman, the Yemens, London; No 3 (1978), pp. 16–17.
14. International Monetary Fund (IMF), International Financial Statistics, October 1978, pp. 284–85.
15. See Grindlays Bank Group, op cit.
16. IMF, Direction of Trade Annual, 1971–77.

Qatar

As in previous years, Qatar concentrated in 1977–78 mainly on development, with the aim of securing the stability of the regime and of preparing the country for a future without oil.

POLITICAL AFFAIRS: THE RULER CONSOLIDATING POWER

Following the nomination of the Crown Prince (see *MECS 1976–77*, pp. 354–55), reports continued that Shaykh Suḥaym, the Foreign Minister and brother of the Ruler, was to be compensated by being appointed as Prime Minister or at least as first Deputy Prime Minister. However, no reshuffle occurred. It seems that the Ruler felt confident of his position following the minor crisis of 1977, although no reconciliation was reached with Shaykh Suḥaym, who did not appear to be participating in government meetings.

Another source of anxiety was removed in November 1977 when the deposed Amir, Shaykh Aḥmad bin 'Ali al-Thāni, died in Britain. The Shaykh was deposed in a bloodless coup on 22 February 1972, about a year after Qatar's independence by the present Ruler, Shaykh Khalīfa bin Ḥamad, who was then Crown Prince and Prime Minister. Shaykh Aḥmad, who had been on a hunting trip in southern Iran at the time of the coup, did not return to Qatar but lived in exile in Dubai. As long as he lived, he served as a useful focus for opponents of the regime and even for neighbouring states, who were able to put pressure on the present Ruler; this was done by Saudi Arabia in 1977 (see *MECS 1976–77*, p. 354).

Determined in his policy of granting limited participation in government decisions to Qatari citizens, the Ruler issued a decree on 29 April 1978 extending the term of the Consultative Council for a further four years. The establishment of the Council was one of the first moves of the present Ruler following his coup in 1972. It originally comprised 20 members selected by the Ruler from representatives elected by limited suffrage. The number was raised to 30 in December 1975.

ARMED FORCES

New purchases of weapons were reported in November 1977. These included two squadrons (c. 30 aircraft) of *Mirage* F-1 jet fighters from France, a batch of medium-range ground-to-air missiles from Britain, and an unspecified number of long-range *HAWK* missiles from the US.[1] (For the composition of the armed forces, see below.)

Qatar is an ardent supporter of the Arab military industry. The Minister of Defence, the Crown Prince, called on all Arab states in March 1978 to join together to develop this industry in order to put an end to their dependence on foreign producers.

SOCIAL AFFAIRS: THE QUESTION OF FOREIGN LABOUR (EGYPTIAN AND ASIAN)

The Qatari government paid considerable attention to the question of manpower, and especially to the problem of immigrant workers who comprise about two-thirds of the population. In 1978 the government tried to secure full control over the numbers and source of imported manpower. Qatar continued its traditional policy of recruiting workers in Egypt. The Qatari Minister of Labour and Social Affairs discussed co-operation in this field with the Egyptian Minister of Manpower during his visit to Cairo in November 1977. There were two urgent problems: (a) the competition presented by South Koreans who entered Qatar on a contractual basis; and (b) the Egyptian policy of recalling its experts from Qatar when their contracts ended, even though the Qataris were interested in prolonging them. The Egyptian embassy in Qatar issued a special brochure prepared by its Councillor for Labour Affairs, with information on living conditions in Qatar and some suggestions on how to behave: avoid involvement in politics; refrain from taking part in demonstrations or assemblies; refrain from strikes or work stoppages; and avoid cancelling contracts without a legal reason.

Since the agreement signed by Qatar with Cairo in 1974, the number of Egyptian workers in Qatar employed under special arrangements has steadily increased. The Egyptians work mainly in administration, in technical occupations and in the liberal professions. Most of the physicians and engineers in Qatar are Egyptians. It was suggested that Egyptian workers be trained so as to be able to compete with the South Koreans, and that the Egyptian government consult with its embassy before recalling its workers.[2]

As a measure to diversify its intake of alien workers, the Qataris were active in certain Asian countries. Such workers, including c. 12,000 from Bangladesh, were chiefly concerned with good remuneration over a temporary period before returning home; they were considered highly qualified and not expensive. In February 1978, the Qatari Minister of Labour and Social Affairs visited Dacca to discuss recruiting more workers from that country.

ECONOMIC AFFAIRS

Qatar's chief focus of concern in 1977–78 was the economic field, with the government mainly occupied with its development programme. This reached a turning point in 1978, when the plan for promoting heavy industry reached its final stages (most of the large projects having been launched), and a new plan for promoting light industry was under preparation, to be based on a thorough study of the feasibility of about 20 light industrial projects. The development of both heavy and light industries was accompanied by efforts to develop infrastructure to avoid problems of communication, manpower etc.

The iron and steel complex in Umm Sa'id (40 km south of Doha) was inaugurated by the Ruler on 27 April 1978. It was constructed by the Japanese firm of Kobe Steel and has a capacity of 400,000 tons annually. Other heavy industrial projects include a fertilizer plant, a petrochemical complex with refineries and gas liquifaction units, and an aluminium complex. The 20 light industrial projects under study include paper, paints and plastics, many of them based on crude oil as a raw material. The projects were examined by the Industrial Development Technical Centre in Doha, with the help of the French firm of Serete. In the field of infrastructure, Qatar concentrated mainly on housing and on enlarging the capacity of the ports and Doha International Airport.

The change to light industry also affected the development budget for 1978. Capital expenditure was reduced by c. 20% compared with 1977 (from $1,595m to $1,307m). The major cut was in industrial development—from $440m in 1977 to $390m in 1978. Other allocations in the development budget went mainly towards infrastructure and included $212m for housing; $190m for a power project; $91m for water and sewerage; $62m for transport and communications; $76m for education; and $31m for health. The votes for education and health both showed a considerable reduction compared with 1977 ($206m and $90m respectively), since the infrastructure was already established.[3]

As can be seen, Qatar has chosen a slow and steady pace of economic development and avoided over-ambitious projects. Priority was given to providing solidly-based institutions covering oil, industrial development and finance, and closer attention was paid to those suited to the country's manpower potential and economic resources. Qatar's financial health and political stability, together with its policy of moderate but continued growth, have spurred the government to seek to increase efficiency by bringing new native talent into administration and industry.

FOREIGN RELATIONS

Qatar followed Saudi Arabia's foreign policy in the inter-Arab and international fields. It participated in activities in the Gulf and strengthened its relations with France and Indonesia. For Qatar's co-operation and relations with its neighbours, its border dispute with Bahrain, and its policy on questions of Gulf defence and the Horn of Africa, see above on The Gulf States.

THE SĀDĀT INITIATIVE

Like Saudi Arabia, Qatar refrained from openly supporting Sādāt's initiative and continued to call for Arab solidarity and understanding. Qatari leaders often repeated their call for Arab solidarity and warned that disunity was the greatest threat to the Arab world. They also warned that a surplus in Arab oil production would constitute a weakness in the Arab bargaining position against Israel. Finally, they stressed what they called the sacred Arab commitment to recover all the occupied Arab territories—first and foremost holy Jerusalem—and to secure the Palestinian Arab people's recovery of their legitimate rights, primarily to return to their homeland and to determine their own fate under the leadership of the PLO in its capacity as their sole legitimate representative.

CO-OPERATION WITH FRANCE

During 1977–78, relations between Qatar and France were strengthened, and economic and technical co-operation was intensified. In October 1977, the Ruler of Qatar discussed relations between the two countries in Paris. The French Minister of State for Foreign Affairs visited Qatar at the head of a delegation of French industrialists, chemists and oil experts. He signed a new cultural and technical co-operation agreement between the two countries which provided new possibilities of co-operation in industry, communications and energy.

The French were also involved in the supply of armaments to Qatar, including an order for 30 *Mirage* F-1 jet fighters (see above).

INDONESIA

The President of Indonesia, T. N. J. Suharto, paid an official visit to Qatar in October 1977. The two countries discussed ways of developing closer co-operation and agreed to refer the study of collaborative projects to a joint committee formed specially for the purpose.

Aryeh Shmuelevitz

ARMED FORCES

Total armed forces number 4,000 (all services forming part of the Army). Defence expenditure in 1978 was QR 238m ($61m). The Army of 3,500 has two armoured car regiments; one Guards infantry battalion; one mobile regiment; 12 AMX-30 medium tanks; 30 *Saladin*, 20 EE-9 *Cascavel* armoured, ten *Ferret* scout cars; 12

AMX-10P mechanized infantry combat vehicles; eight *Saracen* armoured personnel carriers; four 25-pounder guns; 81mm mortars. (*HAWK* surface-to-air missiles on order.) The Navy (Coastguard) of 200 has six large Vosper Type patrol craft and 31 small coastal patrol craft. The 300-strong Air Force has four combat aircraft; three *Hunter* ground-attack fighters, one T79; one *Islander* transport; two *Whirlwind*, four *Commando*, two *Gazelle*, three *Lynx* helicopters; *Tigercat* surface-to-air missiles. 30 *Mirage* F-1 fighters and three *Lynx* helicopters on order.

Source: *The Military Balance 1978-79* (London: International Institute for Strategic Studies).

INTERNATIONAL RESERVES (million US dollars at end of period)

	1975	1976	1977	*(Jan–June)* 1978
International Reserves	104.4	137.1	162.2	196.5
Gold	7.7	7.8	7.8	7.9
Reserves with IMF	15.3	18.8	17.6	18.4
Foreign Exchange	81.4	110.5	136.8	170.2
Commercial Banks Assets	278.0	382.0	457.0	489.0

MONETARY SURVEY (million Qatar rials at end of period)

	1975	1976	1977	*(Jan–June)* 1978
Foreign Assets (net)	1,300	1,708	1,973	2,199
Claims on Private Sector	1,126	1,559	2,464	2,403
Money	1,002	1,573	2,087	2,331
Quasi-money	744	1,129	1,579	1,521
Government Deposits	338	266	255	221
Other Items (net)	342	299	516	529
Money, Seasonally Adjusted	1,032	1,620	2,149	2,261

GOVERNMENT FINANCE (million Qatar rials; Lunar years)

	1975	1976	1977
A. Revenue	7,135	8,927	8,146
B. Expenditure	5,302	5,809	7,318
Balance (A–B)*	**1,832**	**3,118**	**837**
Financing:			
Use of cash balances	–1,832	–3,118	–837

*Figures may not add because of rounding.
Source (of three preceding tables): IMF, *International Financial Statistics*.

DEVELOPMENT EXPENDITURE (million Qatar rials)

	1977	1978
Industry	2,780	1,174
Housing	643	920
Power	900	823
Water and Sewage	n.a.	394
Town Planning	n.a.	455
Education	895	331
Transportation and Communications	n.a.	271
Health	391	133
A. **Total** (including others)	**6,300**	**5,165**
B. Current Expenditure	3,107	3,590
Total Expenditure (A + B)	**9,407**	**8,755**

n.a. not available.
Source: *Middle East Economic Digest*, 6 January 1978.

INDEX OF INDUSTRIAL PRODUCTION (1973 = 100)

	1974	1975	1976
Diesel Fuel	224	947	1,491
Low Octane Gasoline	126	656	832
Cement	143	150	173
Kerosene	93	139	170
Flour	172	210	258
Desalinated Water	114	143	146
Electricity	110	149	191
Frozen Shrimp	88	68	n.a.

Source: Derived from Ministry of Agriculture and Industry sources.

COMPOSITION OF IMPORTS (million Qatar rials)

	1973	1974	1975
Foodstuffs, Live Animals, Beverages and Tobacco	148.6	232.6	219.4
Textiles and Clothing	61.4	72.1	103.0
Chemicals and Chemical Products	36.3	53.9	70.6
Transport Equipment	98.5	130.8	263.6
Machinery	273.5	280.3	562.5
Manufactured Goods	98.7	198.0	231.6
Fuels and Crude Materials	19.4	40.7	45.1
Other	42.0	60.5	114.0
Total	**778.4**	**1,068.9**	**1,609.8**

Source: State of Qatar, Customs Department, Yearly Bulletin of Imports, Exports and Transit.

DIRECTION OF TRADE (million US dollars)

	1975	1976	1977
Exports to:*			
France	188.1	296.5	287.2
United States	57.0	120.3	284.6
Thailand	85.1	185.9	220.9
Japan	25.1	27.7	180.8
United Kingdom	314.9	415.5	157.9
Virgin Islands	296.6	254.6	147.9
Belgium	10.9	40.4	140.0
Netherlands	63.9	225.2	95.4
West Germany	112.7	113.2	93.4
Italy	117.1	131.3	93.1
Total (including others)	**1,809.2**	**2,209.4**	**2,046.8**
Imports from:			
Japan	61.7	235.7	305.0
United Kingdom	87.1	138.2	224.0
United States	51.3	65.1	124.4
West Germany	38.4	63.6	99.4
France	14.4	36.3	67.2
United Arab Emirates	12.7	39.7	66.6
Italy	12.1	32.2	46.4
Switzerland	10.7	24.6	24.2
Netherlands	13.4	24.3	23.8
Bahrain	5.1	9.3	12.7
Total (including others)	**412.8**	**·817.0**	**1,225.1**

*Data derived from partner country.
Source: IMF, Direction of Trade.

NOTES
1. R Luxembourg, 9 November—BBC, 10 November 1977; al-Anwār, Beirut; 9 November 1977.
2. Al-Ahrām, Cairo; 19 December 1977.
3. Mideast Market, New York; 16 January 1978.

United Arab Emirates

The campaign between federalists and separatists, especially between the ruling family of Abu Dhabi and those of Dubai and Ra's al-Khaymah, intensified in 1977–78. The differences were not only over the powers of the federal government *vis-à-vis* the local governments of the principalities, but also over the extent of unification between the principalities in various fields. The main issues of contention were the status of immigrant workers; the status of businesses owned by foreigners; the unification of the armed forces; the renewed emphasis on religion and the reintroduction of Islamic laws and practices; the participation of the principalities in the federal budget; federal co-ordination, and even supervision, of development plans in the various principalities; and the slowdown in development, which affected major industrial projects but not the infrastructure.

FEDERAL AFFAIRS
CONFLICT OVER FEDERATION
In its search for an outstanding Arab figure, the Kuwait daily *al-Ra'y al-'Āmm* (30 November 1977) chose Shaykh Zāyid as the sole Arab leader who had managed to conduct a successful experiment in Arab unity, albeit on a small scale. Nevertheless, the struggle between the federalists, headed by Shaykh Zāyid of Abu Dhabi, and the autonomists, headed by Shaykh Rāshid of Dubai, continued to dominate developments in the UAE (see *MECS 1976–77*, pp. 358–59). The struggle reached one of its peaks in May to June 1978 when Dubai, reacting against the further implementation of unity—especially in the armed forces—threatened to secede.

The crisis began early in February following decrees issued by the President, Shaykh Zāyid, appointing his son, Sultān, as Commander-in-Chief of the UAE armed forces and reorganizing the army by cancelling its division into three military regions (see below). Not having been consulted, and fearing Abu Dhabi's intention of gaining full control over the armed forces, Shaykh Rāshid of Dubai and his son, Shaykh Muḥammad, the Federal Defence Minister, seized control of the Dubai army, put it on alert and demanded the cancellation of the decrees. Although reports of a split in the armed forces and government were denied, the plan for reorganizing the army was not implemented, apart from the appointment of the new Commander-in-Chief.

Although the most serious to date, the new crisis was but another in a long series of disputes between the two leaders. Shaykh Rāshid still refused to contribute to the federal budget, although he had agreed to do so at the end of 1976 (see *MECS 1976–77*, p. 359); the Deputy Supreme Commander of the Armed Forces, the Crown Prince of Abu Dhabi, claimed that the lack of contributions was hindering arms procurement.[1]

Another source of dispute was the decision taken in December 1977 cancelling the arrangement for seven-day transit visas (see the Problem of Aliens, below). This caused a considerable reduction in the number of business visitors to the hotels and restaurants of Dubai and in the number of business transactions. Furthermore, the President's intention to revive Islamic laws, including the prohibition of alcohol, was likely to cause even more difficulties to the developing tourism and entertainment services of Dubai.

Despite Shaykh Rāshid's opposition, the President remained determined to proceed with unification. The tension between the two rulers reached such a pitch that regular federal Cabinet sessions were suspended for several weeks as the Prime Minister—another son of Shaykh Rāshid—remained in Dubai. It became clear that the very cohesion of the UAE was in danger, especially since political alternatives to the UAE were being actively discussed for the first time. Among these were a union composed of Dubai, Ra's al-Khaymah (which was already preparing for the moment of disintegration), and Umm al-Qaywayn; and a separate Qawāsim state composed of Ra's al-Khaymah and Sharjah. The Qawāsim tribe, of which the ruling Qāsimī families of Ra's al-Khaymah and Sharjah are members, were the foremost pirates of the lower Gulf until the British intervention at the beginning of the nineteenth century. Relations between the two families, traditionally embittered to the point of attempts to depose one another, were reported to have begun to improve lately.

Abu Dhabi reacted by trying to impose an economic blockade on Dubai's vital trade; it cancelled the transit trade through Dubai and sent a circular to various companies, including oil companies, warning them not to establish their headquarters in Dubai. Several companies transferred their headquarters to Abu Dhabi, while others left the UAE in order to avoid involvement in the dispute. The Ruler of Dubai, though urging that the federal government's powers be restricted *vis-à-vis* the local governments of the principalities, nonetheless stressed that he had no intention of leaving the federation or returning to pre-federation conditions. At the end of May, he sent a letter to Shaykh Zāyid in which he included a six-point plan requesting adherence to the constitution. He asked that the changes introduced in the constitution since its endorsement be reconsidered, especially the methods by which they were being implemented. He also requested reconsideration of the decisions to unify the armed forces and to amalgamate administrations; cancellation of the decree appointing Shaykh Sultān bin Zāyid as Commander-in-Chief of the armed forces, which had not yet been approved by the government and the Supreme Council; a re-examination of all decisions relating to unification; preservation of Abu Dhabi's and Dubai's veto power in the Supreme Council (the constitution provided that Supreme Council decisions be carried by a majority of five members, which must include Abu Dhabi and Dubai); that urgent steps be taken to establish a new capital for the federation outside Abu Dhabi, pointing out that the constitution provided for the establishment of a permanent capital for the federation within a period not exceeding seven years from the date of its establishment.[2]

Shaykh Zāyid refused to comment; but Shaykh Sultān bin Muḥammad al-Qāsimī, the Ruler of Sharjah, said that in spite of some differences in views among Supreme Council members, they firmly believed that the union was necessary and inevitable.[3] Gulf sources did not take Shaykh Rāshid's threats particularly seriously; according to the general opinion, he was raising potentially disturbing possibilities as a means of keeping up pressure on Shaykh Zāyid, trying to strengthen the autonomous power of the principalities at the expense of the federal government as demanded, for instance, in the six-point plan.

No one in the neighbouring countries supported the policy of the Ruler of Dubai. On the contrary, the Saudis demonstrated support for Shaykh Zāyid's proposals to unify the armed forces by sending a cable of congratulation to the new Commander-in-Chief, Brig-Gen Sultān bin Zāyid. The only concession made by the federal government to Dubai was the decision to reinstate the seven-day transit visas for businessmen, foreign experts and state visitors (see the Problem of Aliens, below).

In an effort to solve the conflict with the autonomists, Shaykh Zāyid sent several teams abroad in July 1978 to countries in America, Europe and Asia with experience of federal regimes. One of the teams visited Malaysia which, like the UAE, was established as a federation by several principalities but was redivided into districts for administrative purposes.

THE ARMED FORCES

Towards the end of 1977 and the beginning of 1978, it became clear that efforts to achieve a merger of the armed forces had failed and that the existence of three regional commands would perpetuate the divisions, in particular between Abu Dhabi and Dubai (see *MECS 1976-77*, p. 361). In October 1977, the Deputy Commander-in-Chief, Crown Prince Shaykh Khalīfa bin Zāyid of Abu Dhabi, stated that the armed forces would be reorganized, with the aim of turning them into mobile formations capable of carrying out any mission. He also said that the committee formed by the Supreme Council of Rulers would submit proposals to the Rulers for such a reorganization.[4] However, further activities were postponed, partly because of the official visit to the UAE by the French Defence Minister, Yvon Bourges, at the beginning of December 1977. The visit was a demonstration of the close military co-operation between France and the UAE, and of the satisfactory implementation of their military agreement (see *MECS 1976-77*, p. 361). The French supply of *Mirage* planes, missiles and armoured cars, along with the necessary expertise, training and technical aid (especially to the UAE military college) were highly praised by UAE leaders.[5] Further meetings to strengthen co-operation were held in June 1978, when a French military delegation visited the UAE.

The decisive step in the attempt to finally unify the armed forces was taken by the President, Shaykh Zāyid, as their Supreme Commander, on 31 January 1978, when he issued the two decrees which precipitated the crisis discussed above. The first appointed his son, Sultān bin Zāyid, as Commander in Chief of the armed forces (a post which had so far remained vacant), after promoting him from Colonel to Brigadier-General. The second decree aimed at completing the unification and reorganization of the armed forces by completely merging land and naval forces at all levels and by abolishing the commands in the western, central and northern military regions. The forces in those areas were to be transformed into brigades and regular military formations directly attached to the General Command in accordance with the recommendations of the Supreme Council of Rulers' committee. The President acted in accordance with the constitutional amendment approved by the Supreme Council in 1976, which provided that the state alone has the right to establish land, naval and air forces (see *MECS 1976-77*, p. 359).[6] However, the decrees were issued by the President while on vacation in Pakistan and without consulting the Vice-President or the government, including the Defence Minister. The Vice-President, Shaykh Rāshid bin Saʿīd al-Maktūm, was the acting Head of State at the time, and any such decrees should have come from him. Moreover, the new appointment upset the delicate balance between Shaykh Zāyid and Shaykh Rāshid and once again brought to the surface the controversy between them over the powers of the federal government (see *MECS 1976-77*, pp. 358-59). The immediate reactions of Shaykh Rāshid and his son, Defence Minister Shaykh Muhammad bin Rāshid, are described above. Although Dubai's defence spokesman denied that it had taken such measures as putting its forces on alert, later developments (such as Dubai's order for British Leyland Scorpion tanks in April 1978, and the fact that there was no indication that the decision to cancel military regions and merge units was being carried out) only confirmed that the Dubai units in the central region were not under the complete control of the federal command.

Another opponent of Shaykh Zāyid was the Ruler of Ra's al-Khaymah who, although much less vociferous, also opposed the new decisions. The situation in the northern military region remained unclear as well. Although the Commander-in-Chief's appointment was still a major issue in the dispute between Shaykhs Zāyid and Rāshid, and was not yet approved by the Supreme Council and the government, Sultān bin Zāyid participated in armed forces activities, appearing at the graduation ceremonies of various military schools and courses. These were considered by the army commanders as the most important melting pot of the younger generation and significant contributors to strengthening the federation. Such schools became even more important when, in May 1978, a law providing for compulsory military service of nine years between the ages of 16 and 36 was introduced. Active service would take up 8–16% of this time. [7]

SOCIAL AFFAIRS
RELIGIOUS REVIVAL
Signs of an Islamic revival in the latter part of 1977 became more pronounced in 1978. It seems that Saudi Arabian influence—in part communicated through the UAE's Saudi-born Chief Justice—produced a revival of Islamic practice and a backlash against foreign customs. However, the UAE Minister of Planning, Sa'īd Ghubash, claimed that bringing the Sharī'a back into the nation's daily life was a progressive attempt to combat, with social weapons, the grave social dislocation of the boom years: "Genuine and pressing social problems have sprung from the sudden swamping of the UAE by foreign habits, and the state is trying to minimize disruptive influences." [8]

Stricter censorship was imposed on the mass media in November 1977 in an effort to comply with Islamic teaching and "the public interest." [9] In the same month, for the first time in the UAE, a Sharī'a court sentenced a thief to have his hand cut off. The man was a Pakistani national who had admitted stealing the household effects of a British pilot during his absence abroad. [10]

Muslim Sharī'a laws had been applicable in the UAE in cases of murder, theft and adultery, but they were not strictly applied until the latter half of 1977. The renewal of the Sharī'a penalties was apparently precipitated by the government's intention, hinted at by President Zāyid, that only Sharī'a law should apply to the seven crimes traditionally falling within its jurisdiction (murder, theft, highway robbery, promiscuity, adultery, the use of alcohol and slander)—whether the accused was a Muslim or not. The government also invited Professor Alī Mansūr, the Egyptian Sharī'a expert, to end the duality of legal systems by merging them into one coherent Sharī'a-based law, a task similar to the one he had completed earlier in Libya. Mansūr arrived in December 1977 and headed a special commission to begin preparations for the merger.

Another sign of change was the establishment of a commission on alcoholism, which drafted a prohibition of alcohol bill. However, there was little chance of its being implemented throughout the country. The chief opponent of the bill was the Ruler of Dubai, since one of his most important sources of revenue derived from accommodation and entertainment services. This added yet another grievance to his dispute with President Zāyid (see above).

In an effort to solve the problem of enforcing the tenets of the Sharī'a throughout the country, it was decided to bring all courts in the principalities under the administration of the federal Ministry of Justice, Islamic Affairs and *Waqfs*, and to turn local courts in the capitals into federal courts. But the bill to establish federal courts in June 1978 was only put into effect in the capitals of Abu Dhabi, Sharjah, 'Ajman and Fujayrah. The other principalities—Dubai, Ra's al-Khaymah and

Umm al-Qaywayn—which opposed strengthening the federal government's authority, did not comply with the requirements of the bill.

THE PROBLEM OF ALIENS

The UAE government continued to restrict immigration and to tighten its control over the activities of foreigners in the country (see *MECS 1976-77*, pp. 362-63). Fears of the growing intake of foreign manpower and of hostile immigrant activities against the state, especially following the assassination of the Minister of State for Foreign Affairs, provoked measures aimed at strengthening control over immigrants, with special attention to the Palestinians. The registration of immigrants at the Ministry of Labour and Social Affairs continued without problems according to the new regulations (see *MECS 1976-77*, p. 362). Following registration, the migrant found himself bound to work for one employer or to leave the UAE; this gave the employer a guaranteed stable workforce. Following completion of the registration, the government began to enforce the decree on the importation and employment of alien workers by sending inspection teams composed of representatives of the Labour Ministry, the internal security and the police, to uncover and apprehend violators. Special judges were designated in all UAE courts to devote all their time to considering cases pertaining to managers and senior staff of firms contravening the regulations. Legal steps against workers apprehended as illegal residents and violators of the decree were to be taken directly by the Ministry of Labour and Social Affairs and the Ministry of Interior, without recourse to the courts. In their first tour of duty in Dubai and the northern emirates, the inspection teams found the decree being observed almost without exception. It would seem that most companies had complied and regularized the status of their workers.

Another measure taken by the government in December 1977 was the prohibition of trade in arms and ammunition, and of the possession of firearms. The ban came into force in February 1978. All residents who were not UAE nationals were requested to hand over to the police all arms, ammunition and explosives in their possession, whether licensed or not. UAE nationals were requested to hand over only unlicensed arms and explosives.

This move coincided with spreading rumours in the UAE of a Palestinian group threatening to blow up oil and port installations, unless Palestinians received the same treatment as UAE nationals. The group, calling itself the Leftist wing of the Palestinian resistance movement suicide squad, was responsible for the assassination of the UAE Minister of State for Foreign Affairs. Following his assassination, Palestinians came under strict control. Some leading personalities, like the Ruler of Sharjah, warned that any attempt at sabotage would lead to the deportation of those responsible.[11] It was also reported that the UAE authorities had demanded the transfer of the PLO representative in the UAE who was replaced in February 1978.

Measures were also taken to prevent foreigners, mainly immigrants, from establishing themselves in the UAE. A bill was approved in February prohibiting foreigners from owning real estate or land. Foreigners were given a period of six years to dispose of their property by transferring it to nationals or citizens of the state, although the government was granted the right to dispose of such property within this period. A bill was also pending which would compel all businesses to take in a local partner with a shareholding of not less than 51%, to be acquired within one year of the bill's promulgation; foreign agencies were required to be 100% owned by local citizens. However, this second bill was rejected by the Chambers of Commerce and financial institutes, which claimed that it would cause much harm to development and trade. It was suggested that the move be postponed, at least for several years. The bill's opponents stressed that almost no one among UAE nationals could buy 51% from foreign investors.

One of the major successes of the UAE government was in organizing an extremely strict control over immigration, making it almost impossible to enter the country without a job and virtually impossible to change jobs, once a resident. The measures taken in 1977, in particular the unification of border forces throughout the country under a single administration (see *MECS 1976-77*, pp. 359, 362) and the decree of registration (as above) caused a drop of 65% in illegal infiltration into the country in 1977 from 1976. The number of such infiltrators rose from 1,648 in 1974 to 6,161 in 1975 and reached 7,275 in 1976, but dropped to 2,870 in 1977. The number of launches and boats seized was 13 in 1974, 53 in 1975, 37 in 1976 and 49 in 1977. The increase for 1977, despite the lower number of infiltrators, may be attributed to a switch to smaller vessels to lessen the chances of detection by coastguard patrols.[12]

The government also attempted to tighten control over infiltration through regular sea and air services by abolishing transit visa arrangements, which allowed immigration officers at ports and airports to issue temporary visitors' visas for a maximum of seven days. The cancellation entered into force in December 1977 but was reversed in May 1978 when the former regulations were restored, though only in cases of businessmen, experts and invited guests. This was because UAE business circles, especially in Dubai, claimed that the abolition of the transit visa was detrimental to business.

FOREIGN RELATIONS
The UAE was preoccupied in 1978 with its internal affairs. Nonetheless, it continued to maintain close co-operation with its neighbours in the Gulf in various economic, technical, cultural and security fields, signing co-operative agreements with Iran, Iraq and Saudi Arabia. It also became involved in the border dispute between Ra's al-Khaymah and Oman (see The Gulf States, above).

Special attention was paid to relations, including military collaboration, with the Sudan, whose Defence Minister visited the UAE in March 1978. This was to discuss military co-operation and the need for Sudanese officers in training and command tasks with the UAE armed forces. A Sudanese officers' delegation already serves in the country. Sudanese immigrants to the UAE and economic relations were also of concern.

Relations were also fostered with France, which supplies weapons to the army and air force, as well as technical and training aid (see Armed Forces above). Japan made efforts to maintain its leading trading position as the primary importer of UAE oil and gas, and as the biggest exporter to that country. In January 1978, the Japanese Foreign Minister visited the UAE to discuss strengthening trade and cultural links as well as Japanese participation in UAE development projects. In their joint communiqué, the Japanese praised UAE moderation concerning oil prices and stressed Japan's support for UN Security Council Resolution 242 and the Palestinians' "legitimate rights" to self-determination.[13]

SĀDĀT'S INITIATIVE
Arab solidarity was the UAE's chief concern in its attitude towards Sādāt's peace initiative with Israel. The government expressed anxiety and deep regret at the rift that had occurred in inter-Arab relations, and stressed that the Palestine problem could only be solved within the context of complete Arab solidarity. It tried to maintain an even-handed policy by stressing that Egypt was at the forefront of those Arab states which had made considerable sacrifices for the Arab nation,

particularly the Palestinian cause, and that the confrontation states had the right to take whatever measures they deemed necessary to liberate their territories. However, all this had to be done within the framework of solidarity and in accordance with the principles and resolutions agreed upon by the Arab states.[14] President Shaykh Zāyid at first attempted to reconcile the opposing camps, but after this move failed, the UAE followed Saudi Arabian policy in 1978, while trying from time to time to suggest that the Egyptians had some Arab support in their negotiations with Israel.

ECONOMIC AFFAIRS

THE PRINCIPALITIES

The main domestic concern of the principalities, in particular Dubai, Ra's al-Khaymah and Sharjah, continued to be the development of their infrastructure and industry (see *MECS 1976–77*, pp. 364–65). Ra's al-Khaymah was constructing a cement plant, a lime-brick factory and a large oil refinery in co-operation with Kuwait. Abu Dhabi, on the other hand, continued its slowdown in order to curb continually rising expenditures and thus reduce inflation. It decided to maintain its expenditure level at c. $1.5 bn a year. Therefore no new development projects were planned for 1979, while $75m was to be added for new projects in 1980, and $250m in 1981.

Abu Dhabi's cutback on spending also affected federal expenditures and caused a furious reaction among the autonomist group, mainly Ra's al-Khaymah and Dubai. The former complained that it had to borrow money abroad under harsh financial conditions for its own development, while Abu Dhabi was extending loans on much better terms to countries outside the UAE. Dubai viewed the recession induced by Abu Dhabi and the federal authorities as deliberately engineered against itself, and this only served to worsen the dispute between the two principalities (see above). The financial stringency imposed by Shaykh Zāyid and differences of opinion between the principalities formed a feature of the discussions on the 1978 federal budget.

THE 1978 BUDGET

The federal budget for 1978 was approved in March 1978 at a sum of $2,750m (10,500m dirhams).[15] This compares with $3,330m or 13,150m in 1977 (see *MECS 1976–77*, p. 365). The Federal Council approved the budget with some reservations and with a strongly-worded memorandum to the Supreme Council deploring the continuing economic stagnation and calling for a concerted effort to reflate the economy. On the other hand, members of the Council made it clear that they had been hoping for more expenditure on education, health and other services, as well as for a bigger injection of government cash into the economy. The question of contributions to the federal budget by individual principalities other than Abu Dhabi was raised as in previous years (see *MECS 1976–77*, p. 365). However, the Finance Minister insisted that this was a matter for the Supreme Council alone.

The most important change in the 1978 budget was the omission of any foreign aid allocation. The Finance Minister said that the aid appropriation for 1978— which he did not specify—was so large that it was to be transferred to the Abu Dhabi budget. Foreign aid in recent years had been extended by Abu Dhabi alone, but in the name of the UAE. In face of the internal tension between the federalists and autonomists (see above) and the growing pressure on Abu Dhabi to extend grants and loans to the non-oil producing principalities, it was only natural that

Abu Dhabi decided to handle foreign aid by itself. It could thus put pressure on opponents of the process of unification in the UAE and increase its own prestige abroad.

Aryeh Shmuelevitz

ARMED FORCES
Total armed forces number 25,900. Defence expenditure in 1978–79 was 2.57 bn dirhams ($661m); military service is voluntary. The Army of 23,500 has one Royal Guard 'brigade'; three armoured/armoured car battalions; seven infantry battalions; three artillery battalions; three air defence battalions; 30 *Scorpion* light tanks; 80 *Saladin*, six *Shorland*, Panhard armoured cars; 60 *Ferret* scout cars; AMX VCI, Panhard M-3, 12 *Saracen* armoured personnel carriers; 22 25-pounder, 105mm guns; 16 AMX 155mm self-propelled howitzers; 81mm mortars; 120mm recoilless rifles; *Vigilant* anti-tank guided weapons; *Rapier, Crotale* surface-to-air missiles. (*Scorpion* light tanks on order.) 700 men are deployed in Lebanon in the Arab Peacekeeping Force.

The Navy of 600 has six Vosper Type large patrol craft and nine coastal patrol craft under 100 tons. Four *Jaguar* II fast patrol boats on order.

The Air Force of 1,800 has 46 combat aircraft; two interceptor squadrons with 32 *Mirage* VAD/DAD/RAD; one ground-attack fighter squadron with seven *Hunter* FGA76, two T77; one counter-insurgency squadron with four MB-326KD/LD, one SF-260WD. Transports include two C-130H, one Boeing 720–023B, one G-222, four *Islander*, one *Falcon*, three DHC-4, one DHC-5D, one Cessna 182. Helicopters include eight AB-205, six AB-206, three AB-212, ten *Alouette* III and ten *Puma*. R.550 *Magic* air-to-air missiles; AS.11/12 air-to-surface missiles. (One G-222, three DHC-5D transports, *Lynx* helicopters on order.)

Source: *The Military Balance 1978–79* (London: International Institute for Strategic Studies).

AREA AND POPULATION (in square miles and thousand persons)

	Area	Population, 1975 census*
Abu Dhabi	26,000	235.7
Dubai	1,500	206.9
Sharjah	1,000	88.2
Ra's al-Khaymah	650	57.3
Fujayrah	450	26.5
Ajman	100	21.6
Umm al-Qaywayn	300	16.9

*Census total includes an estimate for nationals abroad.
Source: Grindlay's Bank Group, *UAE* (November 1978).

BALANCE OF PAYMENTS (million US dollars)

	1975	1976	1977
Total Exports, Re-exports, fob	+7,369	+9,053	+10,095
Imports cif	-2,725	-3,389	-4,369
Trade Balance	**+4,644**	**+5,669**	**+5,727**
Other Current Account	-1,732	-2,186	-3,219
Current Account Balance	**+2,913**	**+3,484**	**+2,507**
Capital Account Balance	-1,419	-1,196	-2,238
of which:			
Official Grants, Loans	*-986*	*-1,030*	*-1,047*
Official Direct Investment	*-61*	*-250*	*-103*
Official Direct Participation	*-155*	*-249*	*-593*
Overall Balance*	**+1,493**	**+2,287**	**+378**

*Figures may not add because of rounding.
Source: Financial Times, 26 June 1978.*

INTERNATIONAL LIQUIDITY (million US dollars at end of period)

	1976	1977	(Jan-June) 1978
International Reserves	1,928.6	824.4	779.5
Gold	22.2	24.2	24.7
Reserves with IMF	132.6	117.2	111.9
Foreign Exchange	1,773.9	683.1	643.0
Deposit Money Banks: Assets	2,574.7	2,077.4	2,430.9
Liabilities	892.7	2,262.8	2,512.7

MONETARY SURVEY (million UAE dirhams at end of period)

	1976	1977	(Jan-June) 1978
Foreign Assets (net)	14,866	2,080	2,068
Domestic Credit	2,561	15,594	17,802
Claims on Government (net)	-8,527	-1,136	-811
Claims on Official Entities	399	725	961
Claims on Private Sector	10,688	16,005	17,653
Money	4,725	5,215	5,823
Quasi-money	12,029	10,325	10,604
Other Items (net)	673	2,135	3,443

Source (of two preceding tables): IMF, International Financial Statistics.

FEDERAL EXPENDITURE, 1978 (million UAE dirhams)

	Current	Development	Total*
Council of Ministers	69.0	2.0	71.0
Federal National Council	13.8	2.0	15.8
Ministry of Defence	3,000.0	—	3,000.0
Interior	554.7	107.4	662.1
Justice, Islamic Affairs and Waqfs	104.2	55.5	159.6
Finance and Industry	39.3	1,309.6	1,348.9
Foreign Affairs	127.5	—	127.5
Information and Culture	167.7	58.5	226.2
Education and Youth	914.9	389.4	1,304.4
Health	640.0	136.2	776.2
Electricity and Water	143.6	256.4	400.0
Labour and Social Affairs	287.7	5.2	292.9
Total (including others)*	**7,599.4**	**2,900.6**	**10,500.0**

*Totals may differ from sum of parts because of rounding.

Source: Arab Oil and Gas.

SUMMARY OF FEDERAL BUDGET (million UAE dirhams)

	Provisional 1976	Budget 1977	Budget 1978
A. Revenue	3,114	13,150	10,500
B. Expenditure	2,521	13,050	10,500
of which:			
Current	*1,451*	*9,833*	*6,247*
Development	*748*	*1,403*	*2,901*
C. Balance (A–B)	593	100	0

Sources: Ministry of Finance and Industry and *Arab Oil and Gas.*

EMPLOYMENT BY SECTOR (in percent)

	1968 Census	1973 Estimate
Construction and Manufacturing	25.8	21.9
Government	15.1	20.3
Agriculture and Fishing	17.6	15.0
Trade	10.4	12.9
Transport and Communications	11.1	8.6
Oil	4.0	5.8
Banking	...	1.3
Total (including others)	**100.0**	**100.0**

Sources: UAE Currency Board, *Bulletin*; and Department of Planning, Abu Dhabi.

PRODUCTION OF MANUFACTURING INDUSTRIES
(million UAE dirhams)

	1974	1975	1976	1977
Petrochemicals and Chemicals	60	75	225	1,350
Non-mineral products	100	120	300	450
Food Industries	181	232	288	344
Wood Furniture	70	90	110	150
Mineral Products	70	85	130	150
Engineering	60	80	120	150
Press and Printing	65	90	115	135
Basic Minerals	45	52	65	70
Paper Industries	12	16	20	25
Others	78	100	127	156
Total Value	**741**	**940**	**1,500**	**2,980**
Value Added	310	390	625	1,240

EXPORTS (million US dollars)

	1974	1975	1976	1977
Oil Exports	7,090	6,903	8,413	9,156
of which:				
Abu Dhabi	*6,071*	*5,824*	*6,977*	*7,669*
Dubai	*968*	*1,000*	*1,354*	*1,422*
Sharjah	*51*	*79*	*82*	*65*
Gas Exports	—	—	—	34
Other Exports, Re-exports, fob	441	466	645	906
Total*	**7,530**	**7,369**	**9,053**	**10,095**

*Figures may not add because of rounding.
Source (of two preceding tables): *Financial Times*, 26 June 1978.

COMBINED IMPORTS OF ABU DHABI AND DUBAI, BY COMMODITY
(Million UAE dirhams)

	1975	1976	(first half) 1977
Food and Live Animals	1,092.0	1,250.3	739.1
Beverages and Tobacco	152.1	198.8	86.5
Inedible Crude Materials, Except Fuels	147.8	305.9	200.3
Mineral Fuels, Lubricants, and Related Materials	781.0	930.7	547.5
Animal and Vegetable Oils and Fats	17.9	28.8	15.4
Chemicals	404.5	474.6	313.4
Manufactured Goods, Classified Chiefly by Material	2,834.2	3,351.0	2,219.4
Machinery and Transport Equipment	4,388.2	5,733.6	3,769.6
Miscellaneous Manufactured Items	1,051.7	1,202.9	938.9
Commodities not classified according to kind	112.0	123.9	62.8
Subtotal	10,910.1	13,600.8	8,892.9
Less: Trans-shipments	*274.8*	*409.1*	...
Total Imports, cif	**10,635.3**	**13,191.7**	...

Sources: UAE Currency Board, Abu Dhabi Customs Department and Dubai Statistics Office.

DIRECTION OF TRADE (million US dollars)

	1975	1976	1977*
Exports to:			
Japan	1,613	2,350	2,517
United States	682	1,007	1,645
France	997	1,100	1,082
West Germany	669	380	830
Netherlands Antilles	...	228	456
Netherlands	441	812	435
Virgin Islands	34	...	426
United Kingdom	325	667	413
Spain	...	389	351
Italy	182	267	229
Total (including others)	**6,879**	**8,542**	**9,502**
Imports from:			
Japan	438	596	921
United Kingdom	477	578	777
United States	415	459	529
West Germany	190	256	381
Italy	90	97	186
France	135	133	159
Netherlands	66	98	152
Bahrain	40	21	121
India	86	155	112
Singapore	42	57	84
Total (including others)	**2,669**	**3,327**	**4,502**

*Data partly extrapolated and/or derived from partner country.
Source: IMF, *Direction of Trade*.

NOTES
1. Qatari News Agency (QNA), 12 October—BBC, 13 October 1977.
2. Middle East News Agency (MENA), Cairo; 18 May 1978; *al-Siyāsa*, Kuwait; 6 June—DR, 9 June 1978.
3. QNA, 12 October—BBC, 13 October 1977.
4. QNA, 3 December—BBC, 5 December 1977.
5. QNA, 31 January—BBC, 2 February 1978.
6. Gulf News Agency, 2 May—DR, 3 May 1978;
7. Al-Mustaqbal, Paris; 13 May 1978.
8. *Arab Report and Memo*, 17 April 1978.
9. Reuter, 8 November 1977.
10. QNA, 3 November—BBC, 4 November 1977.
11. *Al-Ahrām*, Cairo; 29 December 1977.
12. *Al-Ittihād*, Abu Dhabi; 12 January 1978.
13. MENA, 17 January 1978.
14. SNA, 19 November—BBC, 21 November 1977; *al-Siyāsa*, 1 December 1977.
15. *Arab Report and Memo*, 13 March 1978.

Iran

1978 was a climactic year in Iran, its eventful and violent course culminating in the fall of the government of Jamshid Amuzegar on 26 August. He was dismissed by the Shah under the pressure of riots very nearly assuming the dimensions of an uprising. The Shah and the new Cabinet under Ja'far Sherif-Emami then introduced major policy changes intended to enable the Shah to weather the storm by means of a combination of conciliatory and repressive measures.

The nature of events in 1978 can best be understood in the light of two separate developments: long-term trends stemming from earlier years in the reign of Muhammad Reza Shah (who ascended the throne in 1941); and a rapid sharpening of opposition sentiments and activity in 1976 and 1977. The first set is best accounted for by reference to the so-called "White [i.e. bloodless] Revolution," also termed the "Revolution of the Shah and the People"—the wide-ranging series of reform measures initiated by the Shah in 1963. At its core was major land reform legislation. Other main fields, either included among the original six principles or in the 13 points added later, were the nationalization of forest and water resources, administrative reform, educational reform and the eradication of illiteracy, and the transformation of industrial workers into shareholders. In all spheres, oil revenue was used to finance development. The reforms, still incomplete 15 years later, were perceived by the Shah as pursuing a threefold aim: turning Iran into a modern state capable of holding its own in the 20th century; preparing an economic infrastructure against the time when oil revenue would run out; and creating a broad power base, firmly anchored in new social, economic and political realities, designed to afford the Shah that measure of stability and domestic security which had eluded him in the 1940s and, especially, in the early 1950s.

The White Revolution drew opposition from three quarters. (1) From those economically damaged by it, in particular the former owners of estates which were split up under the land reform. (2) From religious leaders who viewed the reforms as a process of secularization ultimately incompatible with Islam. (Their opposition was compounded by the fact that many were also affected by the land reform.) (3) From liberals, Leftists and intellectuals, reinforced by the student population, who favoured the reforms as such but resented the paternalistic way in which they were carried out, with the Shah personally directing and supervising the reform schemes down to every detail. Liberals were in time joined by part of the new middle class which owed its very existence to the implementation of the reforms, but felt frustrated at its narrowly circumscribed role in public affairs. Yet, in the period immediately following the launching of the Revolution, the Shah seemed to have overcome all active opposition and to have laid the foundation for a durable domestic stability. From 1963 till 1976, opposition activity remained sporadic. Its most conspicuous manifestations were among Iranian students abroad—an embarrassment, but certainly no danger to the Shah. Student unrest inside Iran, though not infrequent, was firmly suppressed by SAVAK.[1]

The years of ostensible domestic stability also left their mark on foreign policies: the dependence of continued reforms on constant oil revenues made the security of the Persian Gulf and of the oil shipping lanes a primary concern of the conduct of Iranian foreign affairs. This, combined with the increasing sense of confidence created by the Revolution's initial success, led Iran to adopt a more activist policy first in the Gulf area, later in the ME as a whole, in the Horn of Africa, the Indian Ocean and even the Indian sub-continent.

Although the ex-landlords (partly compensated by the absorption of members of their class into the establishment or the rising business community) receded into the background and as a group eventually lost political significance, this was not the case with the other two opposition forces. A deep attachment to the Shī'ī order of Islam remained characteristic of the Iranian population. Secularization remained superficial, eroding the outward signs of orthodox conduct (abstention from alcohol, the observance of the fast and the ban on smoking during the month of Ramadan, the appearance and dress of women in public) without necessarily diminishing the force of religious feelings, the hold of the mosque over the faithful and its ability to reach mass audiences. The Shah consistently stressed his own personal piety and expressed his sense of mission in religious terms, saying: "Perhaps there is a supreme being who is guiding me." [2] Or, again, when launching the White Revolution: "I was convinced that God had ordained me to do certain things for the service of my nation. . . . I consider myself merely as an agent of God." [3] The Revolution, he wrote, was based on the recognition that "our people and our society are devoutly attached to their religion" and think of it as determining "the governing power" and the country's "moral and spiritual order." [4] The religious establishment, however, regarded such statements as mere lip service, totally negated by the process of secularization and modernization presided over by the Shah. This process they perceived as inherently anti-religious. Against it, they upheld the traditional view of the identity of state and religion. Thus, in 1978, Ayatollah Ruhollah Khomeyni (who, though exiled in 1964, continued to exercise great influence over Shī'ī mullahs from abroad) told a Western correspondent: "Our ideal would be the creation of an Islamic state. However, our first concern is the overthrow of the [existing] autocratic regime. . . . Our only frame of reference [for the social order and the political system] is the time of the Prophet and of the Imām 'Alī" (the Prophet's cousin and son-in-law who is second only to the Prophet himself in the Shī'ī faith). [5] If such views were not often stated publicly between 1963 and 1976, it was not because the religious establishment had come to accept the White Revolution, but because they were biding their time. Ironically, their insistence on reactivating the clause of the constitution providing for a board of five religious leaders to review legislation and invalidate laws contradicting Islamic precepts [6] created common ground between them and liberals who also deplored the non-enforcement of the constitution.

Attitudes of liberals towards the Shah's regime and the White Revolution were often ambivalent. Its reformist tendencies conformed with their own inclinations. Resentment of the Shah's autocratic direction of reforms alternated with, or existed alongside, the hope that modernization would inevitably lead to a more liberal way of life and a more democratic political system. The Shah, for his part, took into consideration the strong appeal of the liberal view, as well as his growing reliance on their goodwill and co-operation for the success of the White Revolution. The establishment of stable governing bodies which would be acknowledged as representative by broad sections of the population also seemed linked, in the Shah's view, with the problem of smooth succession and thus with the future of the dynasty. Such institutions, he hoped, might spare his successor the trials he had experienced after his own accession. [7] In 1976, the Shah felt strong enough to initiate some liberalization measures. He also responded to foreign pressures (especially from the Carter Administration) for somewhat greater respect for human rights. Yet at no time did the Shah move beyond cautious, gradual and closely-controlled measures of democratization; nor did he allow them to encroach upon the powers of the throne. For most liberals, thinking in terms of a Western constitutional monarchy, this fell far short of their expectations. For many, the last straw was the establishment in 1975 of *Rastakhiz* ("Resurrection"), the single party organization which replaced the earlier state-controlled multi-party system. Others, who despaired altogether of the possibility of political change under the monarchy, joined Leftist groups working for its overthrow in favour of a Marxist regime.

Developments specific mainly to 1976 and 1977 superimposed themselves on these long-term trends and caused them to accelerate. One powerful catalyst affecting all sectors was the darker side of oil wealth and the forced pace of economic development: rising inflation, rapid urbanization, lack of housing and shortages of consumer goods and even staple commodities, inadequate public services, overcrowded schools, and a ratio of 14 applicants for every admission into the universities. (For details of these developments and their sharpening impact in 1976–77, see *Middle East Contemporary Survey (MECS) 1976–77*, pp. 369–72.) Increasingly the question being asked was whether oil wealth had been put to the best possible use. At the same time, renewed experimentation with more democratic forms of political life was undertaken (see *MECS 1976–77*, pp. 380–81). This raised expectations which, by remaining unfulfilled, added to frustrations in the social and economic field. The Amuzegar government, appointed on 7 August 1977 to deal with the entire complex of domestic malaise, proved powerless to do so in the short time which elapsed until the problems of domestic security claimed its attention entirely.

Gradually during 1976 and 1977, religious, liberal and Marxist opponents found that the disparity of their aims did not prevent their making common cause. Similarly disparate elements had combined in the first stages of every major upheaval in Iran in the present century: at the start of the constitutional revolution (at the beginning of the century); during the rise to power of Muḥammad Musaddiq (in the early 1950s), and during the initial wave of opposition to the White Revolution. To what extent there was actual co-ordination between the major opposition groups until autumn 1978 cannot yet be determined. But whether organized or not, their activities doubtlessly reinforced each other.

Events during the period reviewed fall into three distinct periods: the last quarter of 1977, essentially presenting a continuation of earlier trends, with opposition activities being intensified but still sporadic; from January to August 1978, with religious leaders taking the lead, and with violence increasingly assuming the character of a mass movement; and the initial period of the new government, testing the ground for its first tentative approaches to a new policy.

THE SHAH'S REGIME IN DANGER
THE PRELUDE (SEPTEMBER 1977-JANUARY 1978)

Opposition activity against the Shah's regime, which had come into the open in the spring of 1977 (see *MECS 1976–77,* pp. 379–80), began to gather momentum again when the universities reopened at the end of September. It accelerated slowly but steadily, coming to a peak during the Shah's visit to the US in mid-November. Yet, compared with the events of 1978, developments until January 1978 were but a prelude.

Opposition came from five directions: the universities; Iranian expatriates; professionals and intellectuals; from some quarters within *Rastakhiz* and other parts of the establishment; and from religious leaders.

The Universities

Sporadic student demonstrations and occasional violent clashes between students and police in most cases followed a set pattern: a sudden eruption by a small but well-organized group, creating a disturbance in classrooms, libraries, laboratories and cafeterias and causing damage to property. The ringleaders usually escaped before the police arrived, even though police units were usually stationed on the campus or close by. At times, the government was forced or chose to suspend studies so as to prevent demonstrations, especially on "sensitive" dates (such as the anniversary of the suppression of student riots on 22 January) when students were especially prone to demonstrate. Student activities were particularly in evidence at Tehran University and Aryamehr University (also in Tehran) and at the Tehran Technological Institute.

Student action was usually triggered by marginal academic issues (e.g. the state of the libraries, cafeteria prices, examination dates), but immediately acquired unmistakable political overtones. After the opening of the 1977–78 academic year, demonstrations became more frequent and the number of active participants grew; political, social and economic themes came to the fore; and incidents involving violence escalated in frequency and intensity. The first riots of the academic year occurred at Tehran University on 9 October 1977. Masked students demanded that male and female students be kept apart everywhere except in the classrooms. They caused damage to equipment, burnt students' buses and distributed pamphlets calling on girl students not to frequent the "boys' cafeteria" or ride on "boys' buses." The pamphlet warned the girls: "If you violate these guidelines, your lives will . . . not be safe." The Shah termed the students' approach "black counter-revolutionary reaction and outright treason"; the students, he added, intended to set the country back "to circumstances prevalent 1,500 or 2,000 years ago." [8] By mid-November, student unrest had spread to virtually all the country's universities and colleges.

The stress on demands stemming from a conservatively religious world view may be accounted for by the social background of the student population, many of whom came from lower-class families in provincial towns where they had been inculcated with religious values. However, it is impossible to altogether discount the view that the prime movers of student action were Leftists who used religious slogans as a tactical means to enlist broader support.

Campus agitation came to a peak on the eve of the Shah's visit to the US in November 1977. Students held demonstrations, rallies and political picnics at which the regime and its policies were criticized. On numerous such occasions, the demonstrators clashed with other students supporting the regime, with the university authorities or the police. Violence ensued and damage was caused to buildings and property. Most institutes for higher learning were closed temporarily until order was restored. In some cases, courses were cancelled altogether for the duration of the current term, and students registered in them lost credit points. Foreign correspondents reported that during the November clashes, tens of persons were killed, hundreds injured and many more arrested. Iranian sources mentioned only a few cases of injuries or arrest, but gave no figures. However, arrests were evidently widespread.

In an effort to counter the intensification of student action, the authorities warned that unrest would lead to individual classes or even whole faculties being closed down; students would have to register for such classes the next term or even reapply for admission to the university. They might have to resit the entrance examination (which would give the university authorities an opportunity to sift out unwanted activists). Furthermore, pressure was brought to bear on students' families: parents were invited to meetings on the campuses and were called upon to "guide" their children's behaviour. Finally, police units on the campuses were reinforced. Nonetheless, student ferment continued beyond November into the beginning of 1978. A novel development was that, for the first time, events on the campus were fairly extensively covered by the Iranian press.

Iranians Abroad

Demonstrations against the regime by Iranians abroad, particularly graduate students, had a history of almost two decades. Rallies, hunger strikes and instrusions into Iranian embassies had all been used to draw public attention, especially in the West, to what the demonstrators termed "the Shah's dictatorial regime." [9]

In the last quarter of 1977, opposition activities abroad intensified, stimulated by events in Iran itself. In the US, they reached a peak at the time of the Shah's visit in November. Taking their cue from Carter's Administration, opposition groups mainly stressed the theme of human rights. Pro- and anti-Shah Iranians clashed in the streets of Washington in what was described by the American press as "the fiercest demonstrations Washington has witnessed since the Vietnam war." Iranian sources described the anit-Shah demonstrators as "paid professionals," many of whom were not Iranians. Some Western correspondents spoke of the pro-Shah groups as "rent-a-crowd demonstrators" paid by Iran. Anti-regime demonstrations also took place in Paris during the Shah's stopover there on his way home.

In December, some 25 Iranian students in Los Angeles started a hunger strike to protest against "the mass murder" of "innocent citizens in Iran." They called for a group of journalists, lawyers and human rights supporters to be sent to Iran to investigate violations of human rights. Unusually, the hunger strike was given some coverage in the Iranian press. [10]

On 14 December, students occupied the Iranian embassy in Copenhagen, and on 19 December the embassy in Rome. No violence was reported and the demonstrators vacated the premises after a few hours when they felt that they had scored a propaganda victory.

Student action abroad had little direct influence on the course of events in Iran. A sort of resonance did develop during the period reviewed, however, with reports of campus clashes in Iran stimulating demonstrations abroad and these in turn encouraging students at home—as indeed the students abroad had intended. The fact that the Iranian media mentioned activities abroad (an editorial policy apparently intended to give proof of its recently liberalized approach) helped to establish this echo effect. At the same time, Iranian press comment tended to describe student activism abroad and at home as being directed by the same "foreign anti-Iranian" quarters. [11]

Intellectuals and the Professions

By early 1977, the habit had spread of academics addressing open letters to the Prime Minister or other senior officials to protest against infractions of the constitution, violations of human rights, unjustified limitations of political freedom and infringements of the independence of the judiciary (see *MECS 1976–77*, pp. 379–80). Towards the end of 1977, this trend intensified. Early in October, 54 district court judges sent an open letter to the president of the Supreme Court, Naser Yeganeh, condemning "unconstitutional legislation" and warning of gradual inroads by the executive into the domain of the judiciary. The letter was prompted by legislation aimed at clearing the backlog of court cases (see below). The judges feared that the new law would downgrade the standing of the Supreme Court, and demanded the elimination of "special courts," such as the tax courts operating under the Ministry of Finance. They regarded the existence of such courts as a violation of the principle of the separation of powers. Yeganeh returned the letter with the demand that the judges rephrase it in a manner clearly disavowing any political intent. He also asked them to date it according to the Imperial rather than the Muslim calendar.[12] (For the issue of the calendars, see below.) A few days later, 143 lawyers published a manifesto proclaiming their intention to set up an Association of Iranian Jurists. They, too, criticized the current erosion of judges' independence.

Demands for greater freedom of speech were voiced by poets and writers at a political "happening" held in mid-October at the Tehran Goethe Institute. An audience of thousands attended sessions on four successive nights to listen to unpublished poetry. The readings—which turned into protest meetings—were initiated by the Iranian Writers' Association.[13] Though in existence for nine years, the Association had been prevented from registering legally, in recent years on the pretext that its members refused to join the *Rastakhiz* party. In November, on the eve of the Shah's visit to the US, c. 2,000 people gathered near Aryamehr University in Tehran for a reading from the works of opposition writer, Sa'id Sultanpur.

On 13 November, a group of 56 prominent Iranians distributed a letter printed in the form of a leaflet to residents of Tehran and to foreign correspondents. It called for adherence to the principles of the constitution, for the release of political prisoners, the return of exiles, the abolition of SAVAK, the independence of the judiciary, the abolition of the one-party system, and freedom of association for political, religious and trade union groups. The signatories also demanded new general elections and the acceptance of the UN declaration on human rights. The letter appealed to the people "to raise their voice against absolute rule." Among the signatories were well-known writers, lawyers, university professors, judges and former members of Musaddiq's National Front.[14]

Dissent within the Establishment

The first signs of anti-government attitudes in the Majlis were evident in October 1977 and found expression mainly in critically phrased parliamentary questions—a practice virtually unknown at least since the establishment of the *Rastakhiz* party. Most questions dealt with shortcomings in public services, faulty development plans and other social and economic problems. Although only a few such questions were submitted (mainly by former members of the Pan-Iranist Party),[15] they created a significant outlet for opposition sentiment.

On 23 October, for instance, Aḥmad Bani Aḥmad, a deputy from Tabriz, asked the Minister of Health why he had concealed the outbreak of cholera in contradiction to the government's declared policy of "open information." Moḥsen Pezeshkpur, former leader of the Pan-Iranist Party, submitted a question to the Minister of Agriculture and the head of the Plan and Budget Organization which implicitly condemned land grants made to agro-industrial companies.[16] The critical tenor of such questions was the first overt indication of tensions within the *Rastakhiz* party. These later caused a number of *Rastakhiz* deputies to resign and form new political groupings (see below).

Another form of criticism from within the establishment were complaints by high officials of undue administrative centralization. An outstanding example was that of the mayor of Tabriz who said he was considering taking the government to court for curtailing the authority of the municipalities. The central government, he said, had overstepped the bounds of its authority and had left local government virtually powerless. In Tabriz, for example, government departments were responsible for water and electricity supplies, transportation, drainage, slaughter houses and meat supplies; even the municipal master plan was being drawn up by a government agency rather than the municipality.

The Clerics

Opposition against the regime on the part of the clerics (appealing to popular religious sentiment against what they perceived as the secularization policies of the Shah) was as old as the Pahlavi dynasty. But from mid-1977 onwards, it assumed an overt character it had not possessed before.

During the month of Ramadan (August-September 1977), anti-Shah propaganda motifs were woven into the religious address. Religious leaders reportedly warned their flock to beware of worshipping "two gods . . . one in the heaven and one in the palace." [17] Loyalty to the Shah as against religion was thus equated with the most sinful form of blasphemy known to Islam.

On 7 October, some 100 religious activists tried to incite people near the holy shrine of Rey (south of Tehran) to demand the release of an extremist Shī'ī cleric, Seyyed Mehdi Hashemi, who had been sentenced to death for his part in a number of assassinations at Isfahan. Iranian students in Paris had earlier held a hunger strike to secure his release.

Opposition attitudes were also sounded in sermons. At the end of October, a preacher addressing c. 500 people at al-Reza Mosque in Shiraz criticized restrictions placed on the freedom of the press in Iran and demanded the return of Ayatollah Khomeyni. [18] When the congregation dispersed, some of their number attacked shops in the neighbourhood. [19] Early in November, a preacher at Qom demanded that women should resume wearing the veil, [20] that Iran should break off relations with "certain foreign countries," and that cinemas should be closed down and cultural festivals banned. By contrast, he insisted that youth demonstrations (expected to turn into religious processions) should be permitted. The same preacher called for the return from exile of Khomeyni. [21] Sermons and religious addresses were recorded secretly and the cassettes passed on by hand throughout the country. The thrust of the recorded messages was to denounce the regime's secularization measures and to attack the Shah's autocratic and paternalistic rule. The distribution of such cassettes became an efficient means of mass communication, capable of overcoming both the handicap of illiteracy and the restrictions of press censorship. The press made no mention during this period of any form of religiously motivated opposition to the regime.

Summary of the Prelude (September 1977-January 1978)

Seen in the perspective of later developments in 1978, opposition activity up to January would appear limited, mild and essentially non-violent. Compared with the preceding period, however, the increasing frequency of incidents (some violent), the growing number of people involved in them, and their new-found resourcefulness and daring clearly made these months a formative period for the future rather than a continuation of past trends. One of the signs of new trends being established was the simultaneous increase in assertiveness on the part of opposition elements having no apparent common motivation and no formal links, such as the five groups referred to above. Another was the growing stress on religious motifs even by those not primarily motivated by religious sentiment and even though liberalization and democratization remained the central issues. While the opposition grew more assertive, the government was under pressure, at home and from abroad, to demonstrate a more liberal stance than in the past. In addition, its assessment of the dangers foreshadowed by the events of the last quarter of 1977 was probably inaccurate. It was thus reluctant to deal with the opposition with a heavy hand. It refrained from using more force than (with somewhat inflated self-confidence) it deemed necessary; had security suspects tried in civil courts (rather than in military courts, as had been the usual practice in the past); allowed (selective) coverage of opposition activities by the media; and promised to continue the process of liberalization. Characteristic of such thinking was the appeal made on 13 December by the leader of the progressive wing of the *Rastakhiz* party, 'Abd ul-Majid Majidi, when he called on the government not to over-react to "marginal disturbances," because that was "exactly what the enemies of Iran . . . are looking for." Patience, he said, was the order of the day.

FROM SPORADIC RIOTS TO GENERAL FERMENT
Chronicle of Violence (January-August 1978)
Acts of violence escalated from January 1978, culminating in the burning down of a cinema in Abadan on 19 August, where nearly 400 persons lost their lives.

The groups responsible for the escalation were the same as those listed above, and the main *motifs* of their agitation also remained the same: a return to the values and life style of Islam; respect for the constitution; relief from the economic hardships burdening the lower and lower middle classes; and an end of the "imperialist exploitation" of Iran. The striking difference between this and the earlier period was that the clerics now took the lead and almost immediately became the dominant group among the activists. It was their capacity to appeal to almost all strata of the population which turned the sporadic efforts of 1977 into the mass unrest of 1978. Even so, it remains doubtful whether their appeal to religious beliefs alone would have sufficed to create disturbances on such a vast scale, had it not been for the cumulative effect of social resentment and economic hardship.

The first major incidents bearing the hallmarks of the new period occurred in Qom on 7 and 9 January. On both dates, hundreds of people took to the streets. The second demonstration turned into a violent clash, with official sources reporting six people killed and one person injured by police fire. Dozens of arrests were made. Non-official sources spoke of 70 persons killed and hundreds injured and arrested. Theological students (*tullāb*) were conspicuous among the demonstrators. There were contradictory versions as to what had caused the clash. The religious leadership blamed an article published on 7 January by *Ettela'at* (one of the two most widely read newspapers in Iran) which attacked Khomeyni in unusually sharp terms. The article, signed by Ahmad Rashidi Mutlaq, dealt mainly with the confrontation at the beginning of the 1960s between the religious leadership, then headed by Khomeyni, and the regime over the launching of the White Revolution. It accused Khomeyni of being in the pay of imperialism and of exploiting religion for the promotion of his personal goals, thereby acting contrary to true Islam. It described him as an "adventurer lacking any belief, devoted to imperialism and out for personal gain . . . a man . . . attached to the most reactionary elements . . . [and] looking for an opportunity . . . to involve himself in politics." The article cast doubt on Khomeyni's knowledge of theology and his right to call himself a leader of Islam.

The religious leaders equated a personal attack on Khomeyni with an attack on Islam as such. Moreover, being familiar with the regime's methods of manipulating the press, they concluded that the article had been fed to *Ettela'at* by the authorities. Rumour had it that the Minister of Information, Daryush Humayun (himself a well-known journalist), had written it. (The name used to sign the article was completely unknown to the public and was certain to be a pseudonym.) The religious leadership therefore regarded the publication of the article as heralding a campaign against them by the government. Ayatollah Shari'at Madari said in a press interview that the article had "besmirched our faith" and shocked "all Muslims in Iran." [22]

After the fall of the government in August (see below), when the press enjoyed a spell of unusual freedom, Muhammad Haydari (then on the editorial staff of *Ettela'at*) made disclosures about how the article came to be published. It had been the practice from time to time, Haydari said, to force newspapers to print letters or articles which the authorities wanted published. Such had been the case with the article attacking Khomeyni. *Ettela'at* had tried to postpone publication, or place the article on a back page and use small print. But the Ministry of Information objected and used "the ugliest pressures" to have it published on a main page. The date of publication, he added, turned into a day of mourning for the paper's staff. [23] The official version, by contrast, linked the demonstrations in Qom to the anniversary of the 1935 emancipation of women (7 January) and of the 1962 agrarian reforms (9 January)—two events which had elicited strong religious opposition.

A question which cannot yet be fully answered is why the authorities insisted on having the article published. The government may have wished to demonstrate a hard-line attitude towards Khomeyni and his followers and to discredit them; it may have wanted to stress that reforms, such as emancipation of women and land reform, would continue; it may have reacted to the incipient religious opposition of the preceding months. Whatever the truth, the Qom incidents provided the catalyst for subsequent events and started the cycle of outbreaks every 40 days—each marking the end of the traditional mourning period for the victims of the preceding clash. [24]

In an open letter distributed throughout Iran, Ayatollah Shari'at Madari condemned the firing on the Qom demonstrators as "non-Islamic and inhuman," and called for a return to constitutional rule. He told foreign correspondents that he could have ordered all bazaars and mosques throughout the country to be closed, sending thousands of people into the streets, but that he had turned down such advice so as not to risk further casualties. [25]

On 12 January, shopkeepers in the Tehran bazaar, where religious feeling was traditionally strong, staged a strike to mourn those killed on 9 January in the "barbaric massacre of innocent people." The strike, held in defiance of police threats to revoke shopkeepers' licences, was the first concerted protest action in the bazaar since the summer of 1963. Further riots occurred on 18 and 19 February, when the 40-day mourning period came to an end. The sharpest clashes took place in Tabriz. The cycle continued on 27 and 28 March and on 7 and 8 May. The scale of violence escalated with each successive wave and the clashes spread. The first waves took place mainly in the major provincial towns. In May, the riots spread to Tehran and reached a scale which caused the government to deploy tanks in the streets. At the end of the following 40 days, on 17 and 18 June, religious leaders called for a silent demonstration in order to avoid clashes: they called on the population to keep their businesses closed and to stay at home. In between the cycles of unrest, there were clashes on a smaller scale in many places throughout Iran.

From mid-June onwards, however, the cycle no longer held, as demonstrations and riots became almost continuous. Anniversaries of clashes between police and demonstrators at any time since the rise of the Pahlavi dynasty, dates connected with the White Revolution, any dates of religious significance, and any event interpreted as a sign of secularization (e.g. an art festival in Shiraz in August)—all now provided occasions for further protest action and violence. The beginning of the month of Ramadan (6 August 1978), when religious sentiment usually runs high, saw events carried to a new peak. On 10 and 11 August, major clashes occurred in Isfahan following a gathering at the home of a prominent cleric,

Ayatollah Husayn Khademi, a supporter of Khomeyni who advocated the over-throw of the monarchy and the establishment of an Islamic state. Martial law was then proclaimed in Isfahan (see below). During the following days, clashes and riots took place in many other cities including Tehran. On 19 August, they reached a climax when almost 400 people died in a cinema in Abadan. The Abadan arson became the immediate cause of a change in government policy which later that month led to the dismissal of the government by the Shah (see below).

The dominant role of the religious leader in the events of 1978 was emphasized by the nature of the targets attacked by rioters, many of which had religious significance or stood for secular influence or a Western life-style in the eyes of the demonstrators. Others were chosen because they were seen as symbols of capitalism and social inequality, or of the power of the regime. Many targets fell into more than one of these categories. Recurrent attacks were made on cinemas and theatres, liquor stores, television sale rooms, shops for luxury goods, expensive cars, banks, the headquarters of women's organizations, police stations and offices of the *Rastakhiz* party. A different religious element came to the fore in the attacks on businesses owned or headed by members of the Bahai sect. The Bank Saderat had more branches damaged than any other, presumably because most of its shares belonged to Hojabr Yazdani, a Bahai. Pepsi-Cola distributors were singled out for attacks because its general agent in Iran was also a Bahai. Yet another indication was that riots usually started at centres of religious life (mosques, theological seminars and homes of religious leaders). Sermons and religious lectures were the principal means for spreading opposition propaganda. The anti-regime slogans of the demonstrators never failed to condemn the "dictatorial political system," but also usually placed special emphasis on decrying "anti-religious" policies, on the demand for an Islamic state, and on appeals to permit the return of Khomeyni. At the same time, personal criticism of the Shah and the royal family, and rejection of the monarchy as such, became increasingly direct and more radical.

The simultaneous outbreak of riots in different cities and the similarity in their patterns made it likely that they were well organized in advance. However, simultaneous action in more than one locality and sudden shifts of the centre of gravity of the disorders from one region to another made it difficult for the authorities to suppress riots in their earliest stages, let alone to take pre-emptive action.

Notwithstanding the predominance of the religious leadership and the appeal to religious sentiments, Leftist and nationalist elements usually joined the demon-strators or rioters. It was difficult to assess their contribution to the course of events. Anti-Western and anti-imperialist slogans and demands for political liberalization served the interests of religious, Leftist and nationalist leaders equally well. Whatever the precise share of the latter two, they added their weight to the process of escalation, confident that their primary objective was identical with that of the religious leadership: to overthrow the Shah's regime.

The universities, which had been the focal points of unrest until January 1978, now became sites of secondary activity, but were far from quiet. During the entire period until August, intermittent clashes between students and police occurred on the campuses. There were numerous casualties and considerable damage to property. By and large, campus riots coincided with the general escalation of unrest—a fact to be considered in connection with the unresolved question of the extent of co-ordination among the various opposition groupings. At many universities, studies were suspended for varying periods of time—in some cases because of student strikes, in others at the instance of the university authorities who wished to prevent student gatherings. By mid-May, almost all universities and colleges had closed. *Rastakhiz* wrote that the universities had operated for only one-third of the 1977-78 academic year, and added: "From the educational point of view, it was a year of minimum benefits and . . . its contribution was zero."[26] First-year students, who in the past had not usually been activists, now participated fully in student protests and demonstrations, indicating that they had come under opposition influence while still at secondary school.

Opposition activists abroad now saw their main task as explaining the "real" nature of events in Iran to their foreign audiences. The visit of the Empress to New York in mid-January 1978 was seized upon as a chance to organize protests intended to show Americans that the US was "supporting a dictatorship." The demonstrators carried posters reading: "Down with the fascist Shah." When the Shah arrived in New Delhi, on 2 February, Iranian student demonstrators shouted: "The Shah is a butcher." On 27 February, the Iranian diplomatic mission in East Berlin was temporarily occupied by Iranian students. However, student activities, both in Iran and abroad, remained marginal compared with domestic religious ferment.

The Nature of the Opposition
The overall picture presented by the opposition during the first eight months of 1978 was one of a conglomerate of contradictory forces united only in their rejection of the Shah's regime. As the mullahs were undoubtedly most capable of mobilizing mass support and instigating mass action, other groups—Leftists, liberals or nationalists—were trying to promote their own particular aims while riding the crests of successive waves of religious unrest. The Shah and spokesmen of the regime tried to exploit the disparate nature of the opposition by holding up to ridicule the term "Islamic Marxists" which the Shah claimed they had chosen to call themselves. He implied that Leftists were thereby trying to benefit from the prevalent mood of religious sentiment, regardless of the contradiction in terms. Religious leaders maintained that there was no co-operation, not even at a tactical level, between their supporters and non-religious groups. Khomeyni told an interviewer that the term "Islamic Marxists" is "a false and contradictory concept invented to discredit and eliminate our Muslim people's struggle against the regime. The Islamic idea, based on the oneness of God, is the opposite of materialism. . . . We will not collaborate with the Marxists, not even to overthrow the Shah. . . . We know they want to stab us in the back, and [that] if they achieved power, they would establish a dictatorial regime contrary to the spirit of Islam."[27] Shari'at Madari supported him, saying: "There is no co-ordination between us and the Marxists. . . . Islam and Marxism . . . have nothing in common. . . . We do not agree to be considered as paving the way for atheism. One would not talk of joint positions [or] even about tactical co-operation."[28]

Such reservations notwithstanding, criticism from all opposition quarters touched almost entirely on the same issues. At the same time as demanding an Islamic state, the clerics joined the other groups in insisting on respect for the constitution, in calling for liberalization and democratization, and in criticizing the regime's social and economic policies as well as some aspects of its foreign policy, especially its reliance on the US. Khomeyni described the nature of the Shah's regime in the following terms: "The Shah [is] implementing the imperialists' policy, which strives to keep Iran backward. His regime is dictatorial. Individual freedoms are abolished, and genuine elections, the press and parties are suppressed. The constitution is being violated . . . political and religious associations are prohibited." According to official figures, Khomeyni went on, Iran was importing 93% of the food it consumes. This was the result of "the Shah's so-called agrarian reform.'' He continued: ''Our universities are closed half the time; our students are beaten and imprisoned several times each year. The Shah has . . . squandered the oil revenues . . . on buying [sophisticated] weapons at exorbitant prices. This undermines Iran's independence.'' Turning to foreign relations, Khomeyni said: ''I have several times defined my attitude towards the US and the other big powers who exploit the wealth of poor countries, plant their agents there and support the repression of peoples of the Third World. . . . As long as this is the case, my opposition will remain unchanged.'' [29] He concluded that the monarchy must be overthrown.

Shari'at Madari took a similar line when he told an interviewer: ''The government has taken the human rights of the people and imprisoned them.'' Drinking, gambling and abortion were practised freely. ''The calendar . . . is no longer counted from [the days] of the Holy Prophet.'' [30] In another interview, he complained that the committee of mullahs empowered to review legislation (see above) no longer operated. Again referring to the issue of the Imperial versus the Muslim calendar, he said: ''Over 1,000 years we have oriented ourselves according to the Muslim calendar.'' When it was replaced by the Imperial calendar, neither parliament nor the clerics were consulted. Similarly, the abortion law had been passed without asking the clerics ''as prescribed by the constitution.'' It was things like these which needed changing, he said, and since no changes had occurred, unrest had spread.[31] Intellectuals, liberals, nationalists and Leftists would have omitted the specifically religious points, but would have subscribed to Khomeyni's and Shari'at Madari's arguments on freedom, human rights, the constitution, and social and economic issues. Their criticism of the Shah's subservience to imperialism also followed similar lines.

An instructive statement typical of the moderate intellectual point of view (but which was basically similar to that of other opposition elements) was made to the present writer by a prominent university professor who in recent years had also held important party and government posts. He said that first and foremost intellectuals opposed the patterns of relationship established between the Shah and the people, which he compared to that between God and the farmers: just as the farmer waiting for rain would merely turn his eyes to the sky and pray, so the people of Iran, waiting for reforms, turned their eyes to the palace and waited for the Shah. He alone would decide when to offer which reforms. It was like feeding a child. This made the people passive and kept them from participating in determining fateful issues.

Just as the mullahs attacked the Shah for placing himself above religion, intellectuals attacked him for placing himself above the people. The mullahs held religious law to be the sole source of legislation; intellectuals considered that legislation should ultimately emanate from the people: both denied the Shah the right to legislate.

An opposition grouping more closely organized than the moderate intellectuals was the National Front.[32] Its leader, Karim Sanjabi, described it as composed of ''liberals, traders, intellectuals and students'' who supported ''real independence, democracy and a human form of socialism.'' In Europe, ''we would be described as social democrats.'' He accused the Shah of ''ruining the country and selling its wealth cheaply.'' Agrarian reform had failed. Industrial policy had failed. Non-oil exports were ''laughable.'' Iran had remained under-developed. ''But the biggest disaster is the oil policy. . . . We have found ourselves laden with a mountain of dollars which we are not in a position to invest. This money has ended up in the pockets of speculators, dishonest people and arms traders.'' [33] National Front spokesmen were careful not to comment on religious issues so as not to reveal possible differences of opinion with the clerical group.

Criticism by student circles was much the same as that of intellectuals and National Front leaders as far as general issues were concerned. In commenting on questions of specific concern to themselves, students alleged that the government was interested only in turning out loyal and reliable graduates easy to absorb into the existing system rather than in giving them a decent education. They complained of the lack of freedom at the universities. As already noted, some students stressed Islamic issues as much as the religious leaders; others singled out social problems in their attacks against the regime.

One issue seized upon with equal vehemence by all opposition groups was the replacement of the Islamic calendar, counting from Muhammad's *hijra* ("emigration") in 622, to the Imperial calendar, which begins with the accession of Cyrus the Great. The changeover was ordered quite suddenly by the Shah a few days before the start of the Persian new year in March 1976 which became 2535, instead of 1355. For the clerics, this was a fundamental change and confirmation of the Shah's desire to place himself and the monarchy above religion. Others, especially intellectuals, regarded it as another stage in the Shah's "megalomaniac attempts" to equate himself and the monarchy with the state. Both castigated the step as an attempt "to change history and historiography." The Shah himself said that he had intended to strengthen Iranian nationalism by linking it to the pre-Islamic past and to enhance the institution of monarchy. The change was in keeping with his desire to appear as the direct successor of Cyrus.

Restiveness in the Majlis and Rastakhiz

In modern Iranian history, the Majlis (lower house of parliament) has tended to play an independent role only when the monarchy was weak. During peak periods of the Shah's personal power (1925–41 and 1963–76), it was reduced to being a rubber stamp used to lend legitimacy to the Shah's policies. During the period under review, the gradual weakening of the Shah's power was accompanied by the Majlis assuming a more active role. However, only a few members took an express anti-government line in the Majlis, many of them being ex-members of the Pan-Iranist party. (For its activities before January 1978, see above.)

The most active members were Ahmad Bani Ahmad and Mohsen Pezeshkpur. On 17 March 1978, Bani Ahmad tabled a censure motion asking the government to explain its role in the Tabriz riots the previous month. He rejected the official version which had blamed foreign machinations and "red-black reactionaries." He demanded an explanation of why the Tabriz mosques had been closed in what seemed to him an act of deliberate provocation by local officials, and why tanks and machine-guns rather than water hoses and teargas were used to suppress the riots. Motions of censure were rare occurrences in the Majlis, Bani Ahmad's being the first since the establishment of the *Rastakhiz* party in 1975. The motion was remarkable in that it took the side of the rioters and was an open challenge to the Shah's version of putting the blame on "Islamic Marxists." Bani Ahmad's motion released a string of other anti-government motions and critical parliamentary questions. Vocal interruption of Majlis sessions by government critics became more frequent. The number of deputies manifesting opposition attitudes gradually grew from fewer than 10 (out of 268 deputies) at the beginning of 1978 to c. 30 in August.

A notable instance of parliamentary initiative occurred on 30 May when four deputies (Pezeshkpur, Husayn Tabib, Parviz Zafari and Manuchehr Yazdi) demanded a "meticulously detailed" account of how the government had handled oil revenues since the establishment of OPEC.[34] On 20 June, Pezeshkpur attacked the government for ignoring questions put by deputies. Under the Majlis rules, he said, the government had to make a reply within a week, yet many deputies had not received answers to their questions for several months.[35]

Opposition in the Majlis reached a peak during the debate on a new elections bill, presented on 1 June, which was to govern the elections set for the summer of 1979. Opposition deputies regarded it as a test of the government's readiness to conduct the elections freely. Although the bill was more liberal than the existing one, it did not satisfy the opposition. Many deputies criticized the government for leaving the Majlis only a short time to study its 119 articles.[36] Most active among the critics was Pezeshkpur who claimed that contrary to the spirit of the constitution, the bill would make it possible for the executive to interfere with the elections. He ended his speech by saying: "Gentlemen, why not make it quite clear . . . and say that instead of having elections, the government will send a number of people to the Majlis as members."[37] Bani Ahmad described the bill as "reactionary" and unconstitutional; if passed, it would "put the legislative at the mercy of the executive." Rejecting the accusations, the Minister of Interior, Asadollah Nasr Isfahani, maintained that the bill was constitutional and was intended to prevent "interference or cheating in elections."[38] The bill passed its first reading with 128 affirmative votes, 14 abstentions and seven votes against. By mid-June, more than 200 amendments had been tabled. The Majlis Speaker, 'Abdallah Riyazi, announced on 14 June that since "neither the government nor the Majlis are in any hurry to pass the bill," the debate would be adjourned until October 1978.[39]

Growing criticism in the Majlis led to the reorganization of political groupings, mainly of the Pan-Iranist party. With the resignation of some deputies from the Rastakhiz party (see below) and against the background of events outside the Majlis, the return to a multi-party system now became a distinct prospect. Early in April, Pezeshkpur asked Jamshid Amuzegar (the then Prime Minister and Secretary-General of Rastakhiz) to permit the Pan-Iranist party to resume its activities. When he was not given a positive response by 18 June, he announced that he was leaving Rastakhiz and reviving the Pan-Iranist party. He was followed by three other Majlis members (Parviz Zafari, Manuchehr Yazdi and Husayn Tabib), all of them former Pan-Iranist members. Pezeshkpur accused Rastakhiz of failing to live up to its name: it had not upheld "the principle of 'resurrection'" and did not understand its own "historical roots." He went on: "As true patriots, we believe in the organic unity of the Iranian people. . . . But since the Rastakhiz party has forgotten this sacred principle, I can no longer remain in the party."[40] He added that the Pan-Iranist organ Khak va Khun ("Soil and Blood") would soon resume publication.[41] Later in June, Ahmad Bani Ahmad and two of his followers (Dr Daryush Shirvani and Ashghar Mazhari) resigned from Rastakhiz with the intention of establishing a social democratic party. Both Pezeshkpur and Bani Ahmad emphasized that the constitution allowed the formation of any political party which was not opposed to national independence and religious beliefs. There was thus no need to wait for government permission. On 1 July, however, Bani Ahmad said he and his friends felt that the right atmosphere did not exist for the establishment of a new political organization.[42]

The Shah, the government and Rastakhiz realized that they would have to adjust to the new circumstances, even though they implied that a return to the multi-party system was contrary to their intentions. On 19 June, the Minister of Information, Daryush Humayun, said that the party would not retaliate against those who chose to leave it. Rastakhiz was "the only party with full support, but membership in it was not compulsory."[43] The Shah and the government were obviously becoming resigned to the prospect of an imminent change in the political power structure—the first since the launching of the White Revolution.

The Role of Rastakhiz

The possibility of reviving the multi-party system underlined the failure of *Rastakhiz* to play a significant political role in the tension-laden first eight months of 1978. On the contrary, the party was shaken not only by the resignation of some of its representatives in the Majlis, but also by the emergence of new groups within the party.

Since its inception, *Rastakhiz* had not been regarded as a single party but rather as an umbrella organization capable of accommodating different approaches and views. It had two recognized wings, set up soon after the establishment of the party itself, which were to articulate "differences in views and preferences."[44] They were the so-called "Constructive Wing" (led by Hushang Ansari) and the "Progressive Wing" (under 'Abd ul-Majid Majidi). In fact, their policies were similar and until January 1978, the party as a whole functioned in a routine manner, with little prominence given to the existence of its two wings.

An extraordinary congress of the party was held on 4 January 1978, with the aim of bringing about greater co-ordination between party and government. This was achieved by the unanimous election of Prime Minister Amuzegar as the party's new Secretary-General[45] (replacing Muḥammad Bahri), as well as by an amendment to the party's constitution ensuring that the "co-ordinators" (i.e. leaders) of the wings would be *ex officio* members of the political bureau.[46] The congress gave evidence of being aware of the incipient unrest in the country, but blamed "imperialism and colonialism" (i.e. foreign influence) rather than domestic conditions.[47]

As unrest escalated, the party stressed its support for further liberalization measures, for efforts to ease social tensions and economic hardships, and its devotion to Islam. It organized rallies in support of the regime and its policies. But the scant success of *Rastakhiz* only underscored its lack of real grassroots support and its inability to appeal to a mass public—particularly when compared to the obvious success of the clerics.

In May 1978, three years after its establishment, internal discontent was clearly evident within *Rastakhiz*. The Shah himself admitted that the party's achievements had not risen to his original expectations. The party, he said, had not adjusted to changing circumstances but had continued to act along traditional lines. The process of liberalization had made it possible for the party to take new initiatives and give guidance to the masses, but it had failed to take advantage of the new opportunities. The press criticized the party for failing to serve as a link between the people and the government, and called on it to devise means of involving the people in the political process.[48] The two wings were criticized for their failure "to offer specific platforms and alternative choices," and "to influence party policy."[49] Some commentators attributed the failures of *Rastakhiz*, at least in part, to the fact that former leaders had been government officials concerned with administration. Others, however, complained of a lack of co-ordination with the government during periods when the party leaders were not also holding government posts.

To improve the party's image and performance in the current situation, a new executive board and political bureau were elected. On 20 May, the central council elected an executive board of 55 members, only 12 of whom had belonged to the previous board. Many cabinet ministers did not stand for re-election because of pressure of work in their ministries. On the other hand, parliament was better represented (by 31 Majlis deputies and two senators), and there was at least one member from each province.[50] Following the election of the new board, the co-ordinators of both wings resigned (Ansari on 31 May and Majidi on 4 June). Both said their official duties prevented them from devoting the necessary time to party affairs. On 18 June, Senator Nasrollah Mojdehi was elected co-ordinator of the Progressive Wing. About a month later, he was appointed Minister of Health. On 1 July, Qasem Mo'ini, the Minister of Labour and Social Affairs, was elected co-ordinator of the Constructive Wing. On 11 June, the executive board elected the 15-man political bureau, the party's highest executive organ. Thirteen of the members were also Majlis deputies or senators; only four had belonged to the previous bureau.

These attempts to tighten party organization were undertaken too late: some politicians were already leaving the party; others now challenged the two wings by setting up a third. This initiative came from the Iranian Problems' Study Group, headed by Dr Hushang Nehavandi.[51] The group, which consisted of c. 80 prominent professors and specialists, had been formed by the Shah in 1975 to study the problems arising from the implementation of the White Revolution, and had acquired considerable prestige in the eyes of the public. On 8 June, Nehavandi announced that it was considering forming a third wing, but only if it would be allowed to retain its identity as a group. The Shah encouraged them to enter politics, but at the same time warned that they should not overstep the limits he considered appropriate: "Intellectuals who think constructively . . . should become standard-bearers in the arena of national affairs," he said, but the term "intellectuals" must not be taken to mean "destruction or, God forbid, working against the state." [52] (In the past, the Shah had rejected the proliferation of wings in *Rastakhiz*.) On 21 June, the political bureau accepted the group's request to form a third wing. Within a few days, some 40 Majlis deputies joined the new wing. Its establishment was the first overt attempt by academics and intellectuals to enter politics since 1971, when a university group had formed the Iranian party. This proved short-lived, but many of its founders were now active in Nehavandi's group.

On 22 July, Amuzegar found it necessary to deny rumours that the three wings would transform themselves into separate parties. He stressed that they would continue to operate within the framework of *Rastakhiz*, adding that the wings would not be authorized to nominate their own candidates for the general elections scheduled for 1979. Nevertheless, events within *Rastakhiz* presaged the revival of parties later in the year (see below).

When *Rastakhiz* was set up in 1975, the Shah was at the height of his power. The party was seen as the Shah's creation and identified, with him and through him, with the government. Criticism of *Rastakhiz* in 1978 was therefore tantamount to criticism of the government and the Shah, and thus hardly less a challenge to the Shah's authority than the violence in the streets.

The Government's Response
The outstanding feature of the government from January to August 1978 was the slowness of its reaction to events. It failed to respond at a time when the deterioration of the regime's authority might still possibly have been stopped. The second notable fact was that, for the first time since the launching of the White Revolution in 1963, the Shah lost the initiative. Being on the defensive made the regime appear hesitant, and its formerly marked self-confidence began to crumble.

In dealing with the unrest and violence, the regime clearly distinguished between the religious opposition and other anti-regime groups. While trying to appease the clerics, it did not hesitate to take forceful methods in dealing with the others. Simultaneously, the Shah and his regime attempted to ease pressures by making—or promising—concessions, not only in the field of religious observance, but also regarding liberalization measures and steps to deal with social and economic grievances.

Throughout the first eight months of 1978, the Shah reiterated his belief that he continued to enjoy the confidence of the army and the people at large. In June 1978, he said: "Nobody can overthrow me. I have the support of 700,000 [sic] troops, all the workers and most of the people." It was only out of devotion to the process of liberalization, he said, that "I have not been exercising my strength."[53] It was arguable, however, whether it was the liberalization measures which impaired the Shah's powers to forcibly suppress the opposition. Another approach was to minimize the significance of the opposition groups in the eyes of the public, to ridicule their self-contradictory appellations—such as "Islamic Marxists"—and to cast doubts on their motives. The latter was done by declaring them to be the agents, or victims, of foreign influence. The organ of *Rastakhiz*, for instance, described the opposition as "a group of misguided agents of alien policies and puppets of international imperialism."[54] The Shah, when referring to them as "Islamic Marxists," said that as early as 1963 he had denounced the "unholy alliance between red and black . . . they always go together."[55]

Only after the wave of major riots in May 1978 was there a noticeable change in policy. The government announced that it would no longer "tolerate disorder and rioting." It conceded that its hitherto lenient approach had been misconstrued by the opposition who "thought the government was neglecting its duties or becoming weak"; leniency had been abused "because attacks were made on the people's property . . . [and] public order was disturbed."[56] In reply, opposition leaders warned the Shah that the use of force against demonstrators might well cause the religious leaders to declare "total war" against the regime.[57] Even after a hard-line approach became declared policy, the government still preferred to avoid confrontation with the religious leaders and their followers. It was only on 11 August, after the Isfahan clashes (see above), that the government took the kind of action foreshadowed by its declaration in May: it proclaimed martial law in Isfahan for one month. On the following day, this was extended to three other small towns near Isfahan—Najaf-Abad, Shahreza and Humayunshar. Under the martial law, a curfew was imposed, gatherings of more than three people were banned, and the carrying of arms prohibited. The government also threatened to extend martial law if the unrest continued.

Yet even during the emergency in mid-August, the government and the local military governor, Maj-Gen Reza Naji, tried as far as possible to avoid clashes between troops and the crowds. After a few days, on 16 August, when a modicum of order seemed to have been restored, the military governor ordered the tanks he had brought in to leave Isfahan. It was at this time that the Shah chose to stress once more (as he had done many times during the year) his personal attachment to Islam. On 18 August, he recalled that upon his accession, he had sworn to preserve the Shī'ī religion.[58] The religious leaders were not impressed by this or similar declarations. The Shah's hesitation and his refusal to use force on a larger scale were widely regarded by the religious leaders as a sign of weakness. Some of them cast doubt on the Shah's ability to take more forceful measures—sometimes in a manner calculated to goad the government into action. Shari'at Madari, for instance, said that if the Shah dared to imprison him, "the whole country will blow up." He added: "A word from me and not one shop in Iran is open."[59]

The cautious line adopted towards the religious opposition contrasted with the tough line taken in dealing with student unrest, as had been the case during the last quarter of 1977. Hundreds of students were arrested and charged with disturbing public order, hooliganism, assault of policemen and university staff; and with displaying or shouting slogans against the Shah, the army and the government. A number of universities were seized by security forces, especially in May and subsequent months. Many classes and departments or whole faculties were closed. At Azarbadegan University in Tabriz, all classes were cancelled for the duration of the second term. At Tehran University, dormitories were closed. Students complained that the security forces singled them out for arrest, even in clashes outside campuses. At a trial of 16 students in April, defence lawyers said police had instructions to arrest only students. When "too many" people were arrested, nonstudents were selected for release, but all those possessing student cards were sent to jail.[60] A similarly tough line was taken against Leftist groups and supporters of the National Front (see below).

In mid-April, bombs exploded at the home and offices of two lawyers, Hedayatollah Matin-Daftari and Manuchehr Mas'udi, both of whom were close to opposition groups and known supporters of human rights' causes. Both had defended students arrested in recent riots. At the beginning of April, bombs exploded at the homes of four members of the newly-formed Committee for the Defence of Human Rights and Freedoms. At almost the same time, another member, Habibollah Pejman, was kidnapped and driven to a location outside Tehran and beaten. Several other human rights supporters received threatening calls from "the underground organization for revenge." The callers told them: "You are agents of the US, prepare for death." Another victim, Mahmud Mo'iniyan, one of the leaders of the National Front, said he believed the Shah was intimidating his opponents by such acts because of pressure from President Carter over human rights issues. Without such pressures, opposition figures would simply have been arrested, but under the circumstances it was more difficult than before to detain people who were clearly neither terrorists nor Marxists; this he implied, was why the authorities resorted to intimidation. He added that he had himself been beaten up on 22 November 1977 at a private house in Karaj (near Tehran) by "thugs" who were SAVAK agents and wore armbands of *Rastakhiz*.[61]

Liberalization Measures

According to the Shah's concept, liberalization should indeed be pursued. But it should be gradual and controlled, should take place under his own supervision, and should not be allowed to challenge his prerogatives. Clearly, these two aspects were incompatible. Any attempt to combine liberalization and control in 1978 was no longer practical politics, as the process of gradually reducing control threatened the loss of it altogether.

Demands for greater liberalization related mainly to the following issues: full separation of executive, legislative and judicial powers; genuinely free elections; freedom of speech, press freedom and freedom of political activity; and upholding human rights.

As late as August 1978, the Shah still adhered to his traditional concept, at least in his public statements. In mid-August, he told a correspondent: "It is not that I am obliged, forced or that any condition was imposed upon me. I am not just another dictator; I am a hereditary monarch. I have got to do these things."[62] At a press conference on 18 August, he said he had not realized that the price of liberalization would be so high, but promised that the process would go on all the same.[63] He conceded that in the past, there had been malpractice and disrespect for human rights (as the US Department of State and Amnesty International had pointed out in critical reports).[64] Torture had been practised. But the Shah claimed he had given orders to SAVAK in 1976 that: "Regardless of the case, no torture." Accordingly, he was able to state in 1978 that there was "no torture, for sure. No holding of prisoners without charge."[65]

In December 1977, the government issued a new procedural code enabling civilian lawyers to defend civilians brought to trial in military courts. Foreign observers regarded this as "an important development" and a "significant change." Iranian opposition leaders, however, claimed that the new regulations were so restrictive as to make them irrelevant. They pointed out that civilian lawyers requesting to defend a client before a military court would have to undergo screening before a three-man committee of officials.[66] In June, the Minister of Justice, Gholam Reza Kiyanpur, said that civilian lawyers would in future be allowed to plead before a military court without obtaining special authorization.[67] In the meantime, many cases previously heard by military courts were transferred to ordinary courts. The press was now permitted to report on trials involving offences against internal security, and indeed gave them wide coverage. Another attempt made during the first eight months of 1978 to demonstrate a more liberal approach was the release of hundreds of political prisoners at the orders of the Shah.

In June 1978, the Shah dismissed Ne'matollah Nasiri, who had headed SAVAK since 1965, and replaced him by Naser Muqaddam. Nasiri's deputy, Gen 'Ali Mo'tazed, and a number of senior SAVAK officials were also dismissed. As Nasiri stood for SAVAK's hard line and its disregard for the individual, his dismissal was intended to give SAVAK a less threatening image. However, there were other reasons as well. SAVAK's failure to properly evaluate the threat of internal unrest and to cope with it when it erupted; its failure to predict events in Afghanistan; and the Shah's dissatisfaction with Nasiri's personal performance during the months preceding his removal.

The independence of the judiciary was another major issue in the context of liberalization. This campaign was conducted by the Bar Association and by the Iranian Association of Jurists (IAJ), the latter originally grouped around 64 lawyers who signed a declaration on 12 July 1977 demanding judicial independence (see *MECS 1976–77*, pp. 379–80). Both were particularly active in mid-1978: the Bar Association held elections for its central council on 10 June, and the IAJ held its first general assembly on 8 July. The election campaign for the Bar Association council centred on the issue of judicial independence. The "Progressive Lawyers" list, most of whose candidates were members of IAJ, won the elections. The new chairman was Hasan Nazih, one of the founding members of the IAJ as well as a member of the Committee for the Defence of Human Rights and Freedoms. After taking office, Nazih made a statement underlining the need for the "absolute rule of law" and spoke out for the "unconditional presence of a lawyer to defend any accused, regardless of the charge brought against him."[68] On 18 July, the Minister of Justice promised to consult the Bar Association on the drafting of any future judicial bills.[69] The IAJ general assembly defined its goals as: (1) independence of the judiciary; (2) respect for the constitution on the part of the executive, which should be answerable for its actions; (3) free parliamentary elections; (4) full freedom of expression and assembly; and (5) improvement in the sphere of human rights.[70]

Press freedom was frequently discussed during these months, often by the press itself. During the period of the White Revolution, the press had come to be distrusted as an instrument of the regime. The Minister of Information, Daryush Humayun, himself a prominent journalist, had pointed to the shortcomings of the Iranian press (before joining the government). "Contradictory things are expected from a newspaper," he wrote. "The authorities expect their words and actions to be fully reported . . . only praise pleases them. . . . Readers on the other hand expect newspapers . . . to publish everything that they themselves dare not utter."[71] Over the years, many journalists who objected to official censorship had resigned; others had been pressured into accepting restrictions on press freedom.[72]

In May 1978, the Minister of Information presented an amendment to the press law to the Majlis. Although in some respects more liberal than the existing law, it met with public criticism and the government decided to withdraw the amendment for further consideration.[73]

Attempts to Ease Social and Economic Grievances

During the first eight months of 1978, the government realized the paramount urgency of dealing with social grievances and economic burdens so as to reduce their impact on the growing unrest and ferment, but it found itself hampered by the internal instability already prevalent. Its policies were in line with those first adopted by Amuzegar when he became Prime Minister (see *MECS 1976-77*, pp. 382-86).

Efforts to fight corruption and make the bureaucracy more efficient were reflected in a decree issued in November 1977 which forbade officials to make promises to the public and called on them to restrict public statements solely to matters already implemented.[74] Similarly, government agencies were forbidden to release fraudulent statistics intended to impress the government and public with their achievements.[75] A number of officials (none of them of first rank) were brought to trial on charges of corruption or of being remiss in the discharge of their duties. Examples were the trials of officials of medium rank in the Ministry of Energy held responsible for electricity cuts which had caused public unrest, and of officials at Tehran municipality accused of taking bribes.

In February 1978, the Minister of Justice submitted a bill to parliament—in conformity with the 19th point of the White Revolution (see *MECS 1976-77*, p. 383)—requiring high government officials to list their assets once a year. In May, the Prime Minister appealed to officials in direct contact with the public to act as public servants rather than regard themselves as "masters" as had usually been the case hitherto. In July, the Shah discreetly issued instructions to members of the royal family to refrain from business deals.[76] (Since they were forbidden by law to hold government posts, many had in recent years turned to business activities. Having a member of the royal family in partnership in an enterprise was regarded as an asset certain to increase profits and facilitate dealing with government departments.) However, public opinion demanded much broader and more energetic measures, particularly against persons in top positions whose names had been connected with cases of corruption.

A major source of discontent was the constant rise of housing prices which continued despite the high priority given to this problem by Amuzegar's cabinet. A two-pronged approach was followed to combat real estate speculation: to penalize proprietors for leaving houses or flats empty; and to set official prices for land and prosecute owners trying to sell for higher prices. These steps brought prices down somewhat, but did not solve the housing problem created by the rapid population growth and accelerated pace of urbanization. The problem was particularly acute in Tehran and other big cities.

The functioning of the courts, and in particular the delays of justice, were another source of resentment. The Minister of Justice disclosed in March 1978 that a survey conducted by his ministry showed that 50% of Iranians were dissatisfied with or "hated" the judicial system.

The shortcomings of the educational system, both qualitatively and quantitatively, had been a cause of concern for a decade or more.[77] In 1977-78, high school students seemed to be undergoing a process of politization similar to that of university students, a trend which had not previously been in evidence. Politics apart, the government's failure to meet the growing demand for better education at every level, and for room for more students at the secondary and university level, added to the list of public grievances. Education was not only respected for its own sake, but was regarded by lower and middle-class parents as the one chance for their children to better their station in life. The government was thus faced with a rapidly rising demand for places and was endeavouring to cope without diluting the quality of education. Applications for university admission numbered 48,000 in 1969-70, rose to 295,000 in 1977-78, and reached 335,000 for 1978-79. In 1978-79, the universities had 23,000 places to offer, and the minor colleges a similar number. If allowance is made for those who went to study abroad, over 250,000 young people (and their families) found their hopes shattered.[78]

The independence of the universities from government interference also became an issue—as it had done at other times when the Shah's authority was at a low ebb. In July 1978, c. 200 professors held a seminar at which the following demands were voiced: the establishment of a nationwide association of university faculty members to protect the interests of the teaching staff; greater independence for the universities; and election of chancellors by the teaching staff rather than their appointment by the Ministry of Higher Education.[79]

Most sectors of the economy also gradually began to feel the impact of policies formulated in 1977 (see *MECS 1976-77*, pp. 382-86). Following the uncontrolled boom caused by the rise in oil prices in 1973 and 1974, the government had decided to slow down work on certain development projects. According to the Bank Markazi of Iran, real economic growth was rising at dramatically lower rates in 1977-78 than had been the case in the preceding few years. The downturn was influenced by a decline in the world demand for oil; the lower purchasing power of oil revenues as prices for Western-made industrial products rose; a decrease of agricultural yields as a result of unfavourable weather; and a slowdown in the rate of industrial growth—even beyond the government's declared policy of limiting development. Taken together, these developments resulted in a loss of business confidence which led to a sharp drop in private investment. One of the most telling economic indicators was the lack of activity in the Tehran bazaar—the heart of the country's business life. Despite the changeover to modern marketing methods, the bazaar had maintained its focal place in Iran's business community; it was not only the socio-economic gauge but also the centre of conservatism and religious sentiment. Following years of prosperity and rising expectations, the mood in the bazaar was now one of disenchantment. This made it easier for religious leaders to call for business strikes to which the bazaar—both in Tehran and in provincial cities—responded impressively (see above). Financial support for opposition groups also came in part from the bazaar. (For details on economic development, see Economic section below.)

THE SHERIF-EMAMI CABINET: APPEASEMENT AND REPRESSION
The Formation of the New Cabinet
The Abadan cinema fire became a turning point, forcing the Shah to make new decisions on how to face the mounting opposition. The outrage of nearly 400 people losing their lives in the flames provided justification either for a policy of concessions or for a hard-line. The Shah opted for the former, while simultaneously threatening to adopt the latter should concessions not have the desired effect.

On 26 August, the Shah dismissed Amuzegar's government and appointed Ja'far Sherif-Emami as Prime Minister, charging him with the formation of "a government of national reconciliation." Sherif-Emami was a pragmatic politician and enjoyed wide personal respect.[80] His family background was strongly religious and he had numerous contacts among clerics, yet was personally close to the Shah. He was thought to be capable of once again creating common ground between the Shah, his government and the religious leaders. The composition of the government (see Table), its declared policies and its first practical moves, were proof of the regime's intention to make another attempt at domestic appeasement. This was borne out by the following points made by the Shah in his speech presenting the new government and in Sherif-Emami's initial policy statement: [81]

(1) Sherif-Emami appealed for national reconciliation by calling on "all those interested in the independence of the country and its territorial sovereignty" to rise "to save the country." His main aim, he said, was "a compromise among all strata of society."

(2) The Shah referred to "adherence to Islamic precepts" as the principle which should "enjoy priority." Sherif-Emami said his government was determined to avoid any autocratic tendency "incompatible with Iranian laws." He added: "I will definitely contact and talk with leading religious personages, for whom I have special regard, in order to resolve the differences." (This statement gave rise to rumours that the government might invite Khomeyni to return to Iran; see below).

(3) Both the Shah and the Prime Minister promised democracy modelled on the West: free elections, freedom of the press, of assembly and expression, and an independent judiciary.

(4) Both pledged specific action to ease social grievances and improve economic conditions. Sherif-Emami conceded that "the rapid pace [of development] has unfortunately created some disorders which in many cases have hindered economic progress and disrupted welfare matters." Both spoke of the need to eradicate corruption and improve public services and social welfare. Agriculture and the rural population would receive special attention.

(5) On foreign policy, Sherif-Emami said that its principles had "always been clear. I think they will not change."

The government's programme as presented to the Majlis the following month was along the same lines. [82] The composition of the Cabinet was additional evidence of conciliatory tendencies. It differed from most governments formed after the beginning of the White Revolution in that it was made up largely of politicians rather than technocrats. It was more traditional in character and believed to be less likely to launch experimental or innovative social and economic schemes. The average age of its ministers was 52 (cf under 40 in most governments since 1963). This was an asset in a society in which age still commanded traditional respect, but it was likely to underline the generation gap between the establishment and the non-religious opposition (which was mostly made up of young people).

Among ministerial appointments, the following were noteworthy:

(1) 'Abbas Gharabaghi, an army general and former head of the gendarmerie, became Minister of Interior. This was variously interpreted as pointing to stronger repressive measures against the opposition, or as an implied pledge that the elections in 1979 would be conducted in a manner both firm and fair.

(2) Hushang Nehavandi, formerly Chancellor of Tehran University and a recent sharp critic of the government, was appointed Minister of Higher Education.

(3) Reza Ameli's appointment to the Ministry of Information and Tourism was expected to result in greater press freedom. Ameli, one of the founding members of the Pan-Iranist party, had recently resigned as Deputy Secretary-General of the *Rastakhiz* party.

(4) Amir Husayn Amir Parviz, a well-known agronomist who had played a

major role in implementing the early phases of land reform, became Minister of Agriculture. His appointment was taken as an indication of the high priority given to village affairs.

(5) To appease religious opinion, a new Ministry of Public Endowments (*waqf*) was formed, with 'Ali-Naqi Kani as its head. With the same purpose in mind, the post of Minister of State for Women's Affairs was abolished. It had been the only cabinet post held by a woman.

There were only four ministers to join the Cabinet for the first time: Kazem Vadi'i, Parviz Avini, Jahangir Mahd Mina and Reza Vishka'i, but all had already spent long years working within the establishment. Six ministers retained their posts: Reza 'Azimi, Muhammad Yeganeh, Manuchehr Ganji, Muhammad Reza Amin, Karim Mo'tamedi and Nasrollah Mojdehi. (For their portfolios, see Table.) This was so that some of Amuzegar's technocrats could ensure the smooth working of government departments, particularly those dealing with defence and social affairs.

Conciliatory Measures

The Cabinet's initial steps were taken in a spirit of appeasement towards the opposition, but when this approach was rejected—as evidenced by the riots of 7 September—government policy was reversed and martial law imposed (see below).

During the initial period, the greatest efforts at reconciliation were directed towards the religious opposition. Among the immediate measures taken after the formation of the Cabinet were the following: (1) The Muslim calendar was restored (see above). (2) All gambling houses and casinos were ordered closed. (At least three of the six biggest were owned by the royal family through the Pahlavi Foundation which, until his new appointment, had been headed by Sherif-Emami.) (3) The distribution of publications contrary to "Islamic belief" was banned. This applied to all pornographic matter. (In September, the Ministry of Information confiscated the magazine *Rangin Kaman Now* for expressing anti-religious opinions.) (4) A number of religious leaders in internal exile were released, among them Khomeyni's brother, Seyyed Morteza Pasandideh.

In conformity with his earlier pledges, Sherif-Emami tried to negotiate a "national reconciliation" with religious leaders. On 29 August, the two evening papers, *Kayhan* and *Ettela'at,* published special editions, reporting that the government had invited Khomeyni to return to Iran. For the first time since he was exiled, Khomeyni's photograph was published in the local papers. The government had apparently been ready to send a mission to Najaf (in Iraq) to formally invite Khomeyni to return, but he adhered to his declared attitude of staying abroad so long as the Shah was in power. Sherif-Emami thereupon announced that the government had only contacted those religious leaders residing in Iran.[83] As before, the government took care not to be drawn into needless confrontations with religious leaders. When six (or, according to another source, 14) members of the Committee for the Defence of Human Rights and Freedoms sought refuge in the home of Shari'at Madari, the authorities refrained from arresting them there.[84]

The government initiated a reconciliation with liberal circles by removing most restrictions on the press, which took immediate advantage of the situation. Full coverage was given to· riots and other opposition activities; interviews were published with opposition leaders (including Khomeyni), and editorials appeared criticizing past restrictions on press freedom. (One interesting example was the description in *Ettela'at* of how the paper had been forced to publish an article attacking Khomeyni; see above).

THE AMEZUGAR CABINET

Portfolio	As formed on 7 July 1977	Subsequent Reshuffles	Sherif-Emami's Cabinet as formed on 27 August 1978
Prime Minister	Jamshid Amuzegar		Ja'far Sherif-Emami
Other Ministers:			
Minister of Court	'Abbas Hoveyda		—
Foreign Affairs	'Abbas 'Ali Khal'atbari		Amir Khosrow Afshar
War	Gen Reza 'Azimi		Gen Reza 'Azimi
Interior Affairs	Asadollah Nasr Isfahani		Lt-Gen 'Abbas Gharabaghi
Economic and Financial Affairs	Hushang Ansari	Replaced by Muhammad Yeganeh on 30 November 1977	Muhammad Yeganeh
Industry and Mines	Muhammad Reza Amin		Muhammad Reza Amin
Housing and Town Planning	Firuz Towfiq		Parviz Avini
Commerce	Kazem Khosrowshahi	Replaced by Mehdi Safaviyan on 24 July 1978	Reza Vishka'i
Transport and Roads	Morteza Salehi		Hasan Shalchiyan
Energy	Taqi Tavakkoli		Jahangir Mahd Mina
Agriculture	Ahmad 'Ali Ahmadi		Amir Husayn Amir Parviz
Labour and Social Affairs	Amir Qasem Mo'ini		Kazem Vadi'i
Post, Telegraph and Telephone	Karim Mo'tamedi		Karim Mo'tamedi
Justice	Gholam Reza Kiyanpur	Replaced by Nasrollah Mojdehi on 24 July 1978	Muhammad Baheri
Health	Shoja'al-Din Shaykh ul-Islamzadeh		Nasrollah Mojdehi
Education	Manuchehr Ganji		Manuchehr Ganji
Culture and Arts	Mehrdad Pahlbod		Mohsen Foroughi
Information and Tourism	Daryush Humayun		Reza Ameli
Science and Higher Education	Abul Husayn Sami'i		Hushang Nehavandi

Portfolio	As formed on 7 July 1977	Subsequent Reshuffles	Sherif-Emami's Cabinet as formed on 27 August 1978
Ministers of State			
Parliamentary Affairs	Mahmud Kashefi	Replaced by Hulako Rambod on 3 December 1977	'Ezatollah Yazdanpanah
Executive Affairs	Manuchehr Agah	Replaced by Mahmud Kashefi on 3 December 1977	Manuchehr Azemun
Director of the Plan and Budget Organization	Muhammad Yeganeh	Replaced by Manuchehr Agah[1] on 30 November 1977	Hasan 'Ali Mehran
Director of Public Endowments[2]	'Ali Farschchi	Replaced by Mahmud Kashefi on 3 December 1977	'Ali-Naqi Kani
Women's Affairs	Mrs Mahnaz Afkhami		
Assistant to the Prime Minister and Director of National Mobilization and Civil Defence	Qasem Khaza'i		
Director of SAVAK	Ne'matollah Nasiri	Replaced by Naser Muqaddam on 6 June 1978	
Economic Affairs	Safi Asfiya		
Director of the Iranian Atomic Energy Organization	Akbar E'temad		
Minister of State	Sadeq Kazemi (assistant to the PM)		

[1] Replaced by Morteza Salehi on 24 July 1978, but retained his post as Minister of State.
[2] Became an independent ministry in Sherif-Emami's government.

Within a day of its formation, the government also legalized the formation of political parties. No fewer than 15 parties at once emerged—showing that they had not lost their collective identity during the period of one-party rule. In fact, they had clear links with former political groupings, almost all their leaders being opposition figures well-known from the past, mostly from the 1950s. They had obviously been able to tighten their organization and elaborate their ideologies during the preceding year. The most powerful of these parties was the National Front led by Karim Sanjabi, which had first shown signs of resuming political activity in November 1977. By July 1978, it already felt strong enough to hold a public meeting in Tehran. On 28 August (only two days after the formation of the new government), its provisional executive committee met and formulated 12 demands, including the abolition of SAVAK; an end to the trial of civilians in military courts; guarantees concerning the independence of the judiciary; an amnesty for all political prisoners; the return of all exiles; freedom of speech and assembly, press freedom and freedom of political activity; punishment of those responsible for the recent "mass killings"; and the rehabilitation of those sentenced by military courts.[85] The National Front included the following three main parties: the Iran Party led by Dr Shahpur Bakhtyar; the Party of the Iranian Nation, led by Daryush Foruhar; and the National Iranian Socialist Party, led by Reza Shayan.

Another old party to resume overt activity was the Pan-Iranist Party. Because it had merged with *Rastakhiz* in 1975, it had a number of representatives in the Majlis and 50 became the main opposition group in parliament. Other parties were The Committee for the Defence of Human Rights and Freedoms, led by Eng Mehdi Bazargan (who was also the leader of the Freedom Movement); the Radical Movement, led by Rahmatollah Muqaddam Maraghe'i; the Association for the Protection of the Iranian Constitution, led by Seyyed Mehdi Pirasteh; the Islamic Liberal Party, led by Shaykh al-Din Molavi; the Society of Free Muslims, led by Shaykh Mustafa Rahnema; and the Iranian Party, led by Fazlollah Sadr. At this time Ahmad Bani Ahmad also proceeded to set up the Social Democratic Party he had planned earlier (see above). Some professional associations, such as IAJ, the Teachers' Association (led by Muhammad Derakhshesh) and the Association of Writers all became actively involved in politics. A number of political figures re-appeared on the scene, though they did not form parties of their own. Two of them were 'Ali Amini, Sherif-Emami's predecessor in the premiership in 1961-62;[86] and the Iranian ambassador in Washington, Ardeshir Zahedi, the Shah's former son-in-law, ex-foreign minister and son of Gen Fazlollah Zahedi, who had been involved in the coup that ousted Musaddiq and restored the Shah to power in 1953.

Following the establishment of the new government, the Tudeh (Communist) Party also stepped up its activities, even though it was still illegal. The party had kept up a clandestine existence ever since the mid-1950s, its activities being directed from abroad. At the beginning of September, its central committee issued a statement in Paris inviting "all forces and groups in opposition to the Shah's regime to form a national coalition front on the basis of a national and democratic programme, setting prejudices and quarrels aside, so as not to miss the opportunity which presents itself." The main objective of the front should be "to overthrow the Shah's dictatorial regime" and set up a republic. The central committee went on to demand the release of all political prisoners, the return of all exiles, the dissolution of SAVAK, freedom of the press and assembly, freedom to form parties and trade unions, free elections, the expulsion from Iran of all American military advisers, withdrawal of Iranian forces from Oman, and "breaking off the military treaties which subjugate Iran to the US."[87]

The liberalization of the press was at first maintained, even after the proclamation of martial law (see below). On 12 September, five banned newspapers were permitted to resume publication. The following day, the Ministry of Culture announced that books and films would no longer be censored with respect to social, political or philosophical ideas. On 23 September, the draft of a new press bill was published (before being tabled in parliament) so as "to test public opinion." The bill provided that no publication could be banned without a court order—except for contravening the constitution by publishing matter harmful to Islam, the monarchy or state security. Some press restrictions were gradually re-imposed but, compared with the state of the press prior to the change of government, it still enjoyed relative freedom. Both the press and the state-owned radio and TV network covered Majlis debates, including vigorous anti-government speeches. The Shah remarked on this: "I think the government wanted to show that parliament is the place for debating, not the streets." [88]

The proclamation of martial law notwithstanding, the government reaffirmed its intention of holding free elections in the summer of 1979. The elections and press bills were described as the Majlis' most urgent business when parliament resumed on 6 October 1978.

In an attempt to deal with public grievances, the government declared a crackdown on corruption. Official sources stated that "anybody in any position who has somehow in the past caused discontent through the abuse or irregular conduct of his office" would now be arrested. [89] Among those detained as falling under this definition were a former Health Minister, Shaykh ul-Islamzadeh, and two of his aides who had created discontent by their handling of health insurance matters; a former Minister of Commerce, Fereydun Mahdavi, whose name was connected with a bribery case in 1977 involving two of his deputies; and a former Minister of Agriculture, Mansur Rohani, who had advocated the unpopular policy of setting up agro-industrial complexes to replace traditional small farms. Many other high officials were arrested or confined to their areas of residence until their cases were clarified. Special rules were laid down on 26 September to restrict private business activity by the Shah's relatives.

In many public sector enterprises and in public services, wages and salaries were raised in September and further pay increases were promised. Water, electricity and telephone rates were frozen. The government declared that it would cancel a number of costly development projects and use the money saved for purposes of social improvement. New customs regulations would be worked out to protect local industries, and government agencies were warned to avoid wastefulness: Celebrations to mark the Shah's birthday (26 October) and the anniversary of the coronation of the Crown Prince (31 October) were cancelled and the funds originally allocated for the ceremonies donated to earthquake victims at Tabas. The government also decided to pay compensation for damage caused during the riots earlier in the year.

Also in September, all restrictions on leaving the country, even for those approaching the age of military service, were abolished in order that young people could attend universities abroad. The government promised financial and academic independence for the universities, who would henceforth be authorized to elect their own chancellors, deans and other academic staff. The government also promised that compulsory education would in future be fully implemented; that the anti-illiteracy campaign would be expanded, and that young people from lower-class homes would be given better opportunities to obtain a good education.

Other measures of social policy included proposals to reduce land prices with the aim of lowering housing costs. Low income-earners were promised help in solving their housing problems and in obtaining inexpensive medical care. The Minister of

Health issued instructions not to fine wage-earners for being in arrears in the payment of social insurance fees.

However, popular resentment had developed to a point which made all the above measures appear belated and inadequate.

The Failure of Appeasement; Martial Law

Sherif-Emami's conciliatory policy was not only pursued to allay resentment. It was clear from the selective character of the concessions that they were also intended to split the opposition, and in particular to create discord between the religious and non-religious, and between the more moderate and the radical elements. With regard to the second aspect, the policy failed as all segments of the opposition simply regarded the concessions as signs of weakness. Instead of merely demanding redress for their grievances, the opposition now placed primary emphasis on the overthrow of the Shah himself, as well as on the removal of the dynasty and the termination of the monarchy. Far from splitting, therefore, the opposition rallied around its more radical spokesmen.

As far as can be established, the first to reject the Shah's conciliatory policy was Khomeyni. He was followed on 1 September by Shari'at Madari who refused the offer to negotiate "because there is nothing to negotiate about." He added: "Both our political and religious demands are met by the constitution which must be followed by the government." [90] Soon afterwards, the National Front also rejected any compromise; its spokesmen, Daryush Foruhar, said that those now seeking compromise were "the very same who violated the elementary rights" of the people. What was needed now was a change "in the very foundation of the present political system." Bani Ahmad called on the opposition to boycott negotiations with the government. Muhammad Derakhshesh, the head of the Teachers' Association, said: "We do not consider the Sherif-Emami cabinet a new one. . . . They are the same people who have dragged the country to the brink of bankruptcy and decay." [91]

The immediate result of this attitude of the opposition leaders was a new wave of riots. On 3 September, demonstrations were held in Tehran and many other cities to mark the last day of the month of Ramadan. On 7 September, hundreds of thousands of people defied a government ban on demonstrations (issued only hours earlier) and took to the streets of the capital for a vast but peaceful display of opposition strength, which bore all the signs of having been planned in advance. Most shops and many offices closed in what almost developed into a general strike. A new trend emerged when the marchers threw flowers at military vehicles and appealed to the soldiers to join them. Religious elements predominated. The main call of the marchers was for an "Islamic state" and the return of Khomeyni. But slogans of "Death to the Shah" and appeals to remove the Pahlavi dynasty also appeared. Some banners also condemned the Shah's pro-American attitude, proclaiming: "Americans out of Iran" and "The Shah is Carter's Dog."

The events of 7 September forced the Shah to turn to his one remaining source of strength—the army. On 8 September, martial law was proclaimed for a period of six months in Tehran and another 11 cities (Tabriz, Shiraz, Qom, Mashhad, Abadan, Ahwaz, Qazvin, Zahedan, Kazerun, Karaj and Isfahan. The existing martial law in Isfahan would have expired on 10 September.) A night-time curfew was imposed, gatherings were banned and shops were ordered to re-open. The government declared that it had resorted to martial law because of the mass violation of the ban on demonstrations and as the only means remaining for the government to discharge its responsibilities. [92]

Later the same day, 8 September, violent clashes between troops and demonstrators occurred in Jaleh Square in the south-eastern part of Tehran, resulting in heavy casualties. The conduct of the armed forces was seen as proof of the regime's determination to uphold martial law. The military governor of Tehran, Gen Gholam 'Ali Oveysi (the commander of the ground forces), declared that any violation would be countered according to the powers vested in him under the law. Tanks were deployed in "sensitive areas" of Tehran and other cities. Yet the troops were apparently instructed to use a minimum of force.

On 14 September, when new demonstrations were expected as a mark of mourning for the victims of the preceding week, Khomeyni and Shari'at Madari appealed to people to stay off the streets and thus avoid renewed clashes. The religious leaders did not want to add to the tension between demonstrators and soldiers, since they regarded at least some of the latter as their potential allies. The army for its part also chose to refrain from the use of excessive force. Officers were reported to have called out to crowds demonstrating at Behesht-Zahra cemetery on 14 September: "We are people like you"; "We do not want to kill anyone."

Though observers familiar with the previous bearing of army and police noted a drastic change in this attitude,[93] it did not represent any noticeable shift in the basic loyalty of the army to the Shah. The army was formed and fostered by the house of Pahlavi as a prop for the regime. The loyalty of the senior officer corps stemmed not only from a personal attachment to the dynasty, but also from the social standing, economic rewards and wide scope for professional advancement and promotion which the army offered. The rank and file, in the main conscripted from the lower socio-economic strata of Iranian society, were subjected to conflicting pressures.

After the clashes of 8 September, many opposition leaders were arrested, among them Karim Sanjabi, leader of the National Front; the Front's spokesman, Daryush Foruhar; and Muqaddam Maraghe'i, leader of the Radical Movement. Many others were ordered not to leave their areas of domicile. On 12 September, Ayatollah Shaykh Yahya Nuri, a prominent religious leader from the Jaleh area (see above), was arrested on a charge of instigating riots and inciting people to burn public and private property.[94] The earlier policy of minimizing the gravity of the unrest was now reversed: the consequences of continued ferment were depicted as most dire. Unrest, the Shah and the government argued, would develop into full-fledged civil war which would lead to Iran's eventual dismemberment.

The proclamation of martial law and the decision to involve the army in restoring order were taken because the Shah perceived the riots as assuming the dimensions of a popular uprising directed, more than ever, against himself, the royal house and the very institution of the monarchy. The demonstrators' direct appeal to the soldiers, as well as rumours that Khomeyni had contacted army generals and called on them to withdraw their support from the Shah were additional alarm signals. As the riots continued, particularly in provincial cities in West Iran, it became evident that the period of martial law was but a transition towards a more explicit form of military rule under the Shah. The period under review came to a close when, on 6 November, the Shah dismissed Sherif-Emami and appointed the Chief of Staff, General Gholam Reza Azhari, to head a new Cabinet of generals, including the chiefs of the three branches of the armed forces.

The Shah never regarded military government as a long-term solution and, following the formation of the Azhari government, sought to find a civilian alternative in order to split the opposition and gain time. By the end of 1978, this had proved unsuccessful and the situation continued to steadily deteriorate.

FOREIGN RELATIONS

January 1978 turned out to be a turning point in foreign relations as well as in domestic affairs. Until then, foreign policy focused on the same regions and was dominated by the same issues that had been central during most of the 1970s. The areas of special interest to Iran as well as the intense preoccupation with foreign policy in the final months of 1977 can best be illustrated by a listing of the Shah's major foreign contacts between October 1977 and January 1978.

On 15 October, the Pakistani leader, Gen Ziya ul-Haqq, visited Iran; on 31 October, President Sādāt stopped over in Tehran for a meeting with the Shah on his way home from Bucharest; on 1 November, the President of the UAE, Zāyid Ibn Sultān, visited Tehran; in mid-November, the Shah paid a visit to Washington and on his way back stopped in Paris to meet President Giscard d'Estaing; early in December, the Shah visited Oman. During the last days of the year, President Siyad Barreh of Somalia, King Husayn of Jordan and President Carter all visited Iran. Israeli Foreign Minister Moshe Dayan also reportedly visited Tehran at the end of December. At the beginning of 1978, the Shah left for visits to Egypt and Saudi Arabia.

From then on, as internal unrest escalated, the intensity of foreign contacts decreased sharply. Several times during 1978 the Shah found it advisable to post-pone scheduled visits abroad, e.g. to Bulgaria and Hungary in mid-May, and to Romania and East Germany in September. Retaliatory action was taken by Iran against countries which were considered to have facilitated the activities of ex-patriate Iranian oppositionists. In December 1977, for example, Iran banned the import of goods from Italy and Denmark; in March 1978, it pulled out of an East German trade fair. As far as possible, however, Iran tried not to postpone the visits of foreign leaders—even at peak periods of unrest. Thus, Hua Kuo-feng, the chairman of the People's Republic of China (PRC), visited Tehran late in August, and the Japanese Prime Minister, Takeo Fukuda, came at the beginning of Sep-tember.

CENTRALITY OF THE GULF AREA
Iran's dependence on oil revenues for the implementation of its development plans made the security of the Persian Gulf and the oil shipping lanes a primary concern of its foreign policy. The country took an active hand in efforts to defuse tension in areas close enough to the Gulf to spill òver into it and threaten its stability. Such potential sources of tension were the Arab-Israeli conflict, the disputes in the Horn of Africa, and developments in the Indian Ocean and the Indian sub-continent. Closely related to the attempts to reduce these tensions was Iran's policy of preventing—or containing—Soviet penetration into these areas. Yet, domestic problems markedly restricted Iran's impact on regional affairs. At the outset of the period under review, Iran was perceived by its neighbours not only as stable at home, but as capable of exercising a stabilizing influence in adjacent areas. At the period's end, domestic stability had collapsed, and Iran had itself become a potential threat to the region's tranquillity.

Gulf security remained a major issue (cf *MECS 1976–77*, pp. 330–31 and 392). A series of regional developments including events in the Horn of Africa late in 1977, the coup in Afghanistan in April 1978 and the changes in the YAR and the PDRY in mid-year (see chapters on these two countries) again made the need for a collective Gulf defence agreement keenly felt. However, no progress was made. In November 1977, the Shah told an interviewer: "I do not know what else I can do. I told these people [in the other Gulf states] that I could propose to them either the closest or the loosest pact that they wanted. . . . I do not want to play the role of big brother. . . . I am ready to accept absolute equality. But it seems that it cannot get off the ground." [95] The Shah's words remained descriptive of the situation during

1978 as well. In mid-year, the Shah said that Iran would no longer press for a security pact but was "still ready" to pursue the idea.[96] With no real prospects for collective security in the offing, Iran attempted to bolster Gulf security through a series of bilateral contacts.

Relations with Saudi Arabia
The improvement of Saudi-Iranian relations noted in 1977 (see *MECS 1976–77*, pp. 293–94), continued in 1978. In fact, their basic community of interests in the stability and security of the Gulf, in preventing Soviet penetration and in checking the growth of radical movements asserted itself more strongly. Oil pricing was not a matter of dispute after mid-1977, and other points of disagreement became marginal.

On 11 January 1978, the Shah arrived in Riyadh on his way home from a meeting with President Sādāt in Aswān. The central topics he discussed with King Khālid were Sādāt's peace moves and developments in the Horn of Africa, on which the two parties reported complete agreement. The Shah was reported to have reassured King Khālid that Saudi Arabia had nothing to fear from Iran's arms procurement programme or its purchases of nuclear reactors from the US (see below). These talks were followed up by an exchange of visits and messages. On 15 January, Saudi Foreign Minister Sa'ūd al-Faysal visited Iran and delivered a message from the King. He stated that the Saudis would share in the responsibility of defending Somalia (a fellow Arab League member) if it became the victim of foreign aggression.[97]

On an earlier occasion, during the visit to Iran in November 1977 of the Saudi Minister of the Interior, Nā'if Ibn 'Abd al-'Azīz, matters of internal security had been discussed. Joint measures to combat terrorism were proposed and agreement was reached on the exchange of information relating to subversive and criminal activities.[98]

On a number of occasions, too, the Saudis expressed their concern over the internal situation in Iran and publicly declared their support for the Shah. In August, for example, Crown Prince Fahd praised the progress achieved in Iran under the Shah and accused international Communism and Leftists all over the world of subverting regimes in "these regions." Fahd expressed confidence in the Shah's ability to restore domestic stability. Should he fail, Fahd went on, "the Arab states will have to support Iran and the Shah, because the stability of that country is important to the [entire] region . . . and any radical change will upset its security balance."[99]

Relations with Iraq
Relations with Iraq continued to improve despite a background of tension over a few issues of continuing disagreement (see *MECS 1976–77*, p. 393). This steady improvement was reflected in the series of visits, the most important being those of the Iraqi Vice-President, Taha Muhyī al-Dīn Ma'rūf, accompanied by the Foreign Minister, Sa'dūn Ḥammādī, to Tehran at the beginning of December 1977, and of the Iranian Foreign Minister, 'Abbas 'Ali Kala'tbari to Iraq in February 1978. A number of bilateral agreements covering trade and economic links and cultural cooperation were signed, and technical committees met for detailed discussions on specific issues.

Unresolved differences of opinion related to collective security in the Gulf area, where Iraq opposed Iranian schemes; and to oil price policies. On the latter point, Iran had joined those (notably Saudi Arabia) who advocated a price freeze, while Iraq pressed for price rises. Iran also continued to be concerned about Iraq's massive purchases of heavy arms and the development of its nuclear programmes. On the eve of his visit to the US in November 1977, the Shah told American correspondents: "I wonder how many of your editorial writers and congressmen realize that Iraq has more planes, tanks and guns than we do [even] ground-to-ground *Scud* missiles. . . . We have settled our differences with that country. But any way, in a surprise attack, you never know the consequences of the first strike with weapons that one side has and the other side does not have." [100]

Despite outstanding issues between the two countries, the supportive stand taken by Iraq *vis-à-vis* Iran's internal crisis showed how important it took the need to improve relations. Initially, Iraq had regarded the unrest as being solely a domestic matter and had expressed confidence in the Shah's ability to suppress the opposition. However, when the Shah's regime, and consequently the stability of the region in general, seemed to be in real danger, Iraq became more forthcoming and publicly declared its concern and support for the Shah. The first signs of Iraq's new approach were noticed late in August when it handed over an Iranian citizen who had fled to Iraq after admitting involvement in the burning down of the cinema in Abadan. [101] More significantly, in September, the Iraqi authorities restricted Khomeyni's freedom of action and, in October, got him to leave (after nearly 14 years of exile in Najaf) and take up residence near Paris. In taking these steps against Khomeyni, it remains an open question how far the Iraqi government was motivated by a desire to remove a source of potential friction with Iran, or by its concern that the presence of Khomeyni at one of the centres of Iraq's own Shī'ī community could cause unrest to spill over into their own country.

Relations with other Gulf States

Gulf security and stability were the main topics discussed in early November 1977 during the visit to Tehran of the UAE President and Ruler of Abu Dhabi, Zāyid Ibn Sultān. The promotion of bilateral political, economic and cultural relations was also discussed. A joint communiqué pointed out that "preservation of stability in the region ought to be realized through the co-operation of regional countries without any foreign interference." The two sides were reported to have signed an agreement on the exchange of information regarding subversive groups and Left-wing and Communist activities in the Gulf area. [102]

The Shah paid his first visit to Oman at the beginning of December 1977—after years of close co-operation with and military assistance to the Sultanate. The main issues discussed were the continuation of co-operation in the protection of the Straits of Hormuz, and Iranian technical and economic aid. In his talks and speeches, the Shah reaffirmed the following four positions: (1) Iran would continue to stand by its commitment to render immediate aid to any Gulf state that requested it, and would withdraw its troops just as quickly if asked to do so. (2) Iran continued to stress the need for co-ordination of internal security matters among Gulf states (see also chapter on the Gulf States). (3) Iran upheld the principle of non-interference in Gulf affairs by foreign powers. (4) Iran viewed the situation in the Horn of Africa with increasing seriousness and regarded the security of the Red Sea as an extension of the security of the Persian Gulf. [103]

When the Ruler of Bahrain, Shaykh 'Īsā Ibn Salmān al-Khalīfa, visited Iran at the beginning of June 1978, Gulf security was again the main issue discussed. The two leaders asserted that the preservation of security in the Gulf area was "the responsibility of the littoral states alone." A bilateral agreement was signed to extend scientific and cultural co-operation. [104]

All the littoral states regarded the internal developments in Iran as a potential threat to regional stability and as a danger to themselves. The local press in the Gulf states gave full coverage to the course of events, with comment usually in support of the Shah. Most of the Heads of State publicly expressed their support. For example, Kuwait's Crown Prince and Prime Minister, Shaykh Sa'd al-'Abdallah al Sabāh warned that developments in Iran could affect the security of the Gulf area, and expressed his hope and confidence that the Shah would be able to restore peaceful conditions.[105] In mid-September, the UAE's Foreign Minister was received by the Shah and expressed his government's support for the recent introduction of martial law in Iran.[106]

WIDER REGIONAL POLICIES
Iran's policies towards wider regional problems were similar to those it pursued in the Gulf: it tried to identify potential areas of tension which—directly or in-directly—were likely to affect the stability of the Persian Gulf or endanger its oil routes. It also worked to prevent the spread of Soviet influence into areas adjacent to, or linked with, the Gulf and its shipping lanes.

Iran and the Arab-Israeli Conflict
One such source of potential tension close enough to the Gulf to preoccupy the Iranian government was the Arab-Israeli conflict. Since the 1967 war, Iran had adopted a consistent position, calling for Israel's withdrawal from the occupied territories and for safeguarding the sovereignty of all independent states in the region, including Israel. The constant improvement of Arab-Iranian relations, and especially of Iranian-Egyptian ties since 1970, caused the Shah to move somewhat closer to the Arab position and to demand greater Israeli flexibility. Iran made use of its good relations with both sides to encourage negotiations, but refrained from taking any initiatives of its own. When Sādāt launched his initiative, however, he found immediate encouragement and support from the Shah (for details, see essay on the Arab-Israeli Conflict). The Shah considered a settlement of the conflict, especially one achieved by American mediation, as a development decidedly ad-vantageous to Iran. As early as 16 November 1977, the Shah (then in Washington) praised Sādāt's "genuine intentions, resolve and actions for peace"; he "crossed his fingers" sincerely in the hope that Sādāt's initiative would succeed, adding that this would depend on "realism and greater flexibility on Israel's part." Iranian media coverage of Sādāt's visit to Jerusalem was unprecedented for an event in which Iran was not directly involved.

There was speculation on several occasions in 1978 that Iran was pressuring Israel by threatening to withhold oil supplies. Iranian sources gave no sign of any plan to use oil as a political weapon—a step which would have marked a departure from its traditional policy of keeping oil out of politics. When pressed on this point, the Shah gave only vague answers. For instance, in March 1978, he said: "If there is a general decision by *all, for instance America, to stop delivery of arms"* or impose an *"embargo on everything,* such as had been decided against Rhodesia and South Africa . . . by the US and the UN, then *everything is possible."* On another oc-casion, in May, he replied: "If *everybody* ganged up and really imposed [an em-bargo], it *might* have an effect."[107] The conditions attached to these statements by the Shah made them a mild warning rather than a threat.

Growing unrest in Iran reduced the Shah's involvement in the Arab-Israeli negotiations which followed Sādāt's first moves. In September 1978, Iran welcomed the Camp David agreements as a significant step forward.

Iran's attitude towards the Palestinian issue was ambivalent. In public statements, it remained generally loyal to its traditional policy of calling for the exercise of the "legitimate rights of the Arab-Palestinian people," including the right to self-determination. But Iran did not perceive its interests as being served by the establishment of an independent Palestinian state which would present precisely those dangers Iran was trying to avoid: it was likely to become a focus of instability and a channel for the expansion of Soviet influence. Iran's attempts to encourage King Ḥusayn to join Sādāt's initiative were partly intended to give him—rather than the PLO—a major role in determining the future of the West Bank.

Opposition quarters in Iran had long criticized the Shah for his "relations with Israel and Zionism," his "hostility to the Palestinian revolution," and to the "Arab liberation movements in the Arab Gulf." Now opposition elements also attacked the Shah for his support of Sādāt's initiative. Pro-Palestinian slogans appeared alongside others against the Shah in many protest demonstrations throughout the year. On 16 August, the Iranian Minister of Information accused the PLO of helping to foment unrest in Iran. In pursuing their "very large conspiracy," he said, the rioters were being aided by Palestinian radicals.[108]

Relations with Arab States

While Iran's overall relations with Arab countries (other than the Arab littorals of the Gulf) were in a large measure a function of its attitude towards Sādāt's initiative, bilateral relations tended to develop independently. Thus, while the major theme of Iranian-Egyptian relations was the search for ME peace—the topic of Sādāt's talks with the Shah in Tehran in October 1977 and in Aswān in January 1978—economic co-operation and Iranian financial aid to Egypt continued. In March 1978, an agreement for cultural co-operation was signed. Egyptian media reaction to Iran's mounting domestic troubles was restrained: they were covered, but hardly ever commented upon.

Relations with Jordan were similarly cordial. Those with Syria, which had improved considerably between 1973 and 1977, became strained in 1978 because of Asad's resentment of Iran's positive attitude towards Sādāt's initiative. Syrian media comment also criticized the Shah for his close relations with the US.[109] Libya and the PDRY continued to adopt an attitude of outright hostility towards Iran's regional policies. In frequent and vehement attacks, they denounced the Shah's "dictatorial regime," his "subservience to the US," SAVAK's co-operation with both the CIA and Israeli intelligence against the Arabs, and his "threats to the Arabs of the Gulf." The following Libyan broadcast was typical: "The tyrannical Shah appropriates the wealth of the country while the people are hungry and naked; the fascist Shah arms his soldiers to terrorize the masses and deprive them of their wealth."[110]

The Horn of Africa

In the Horn of Africa conflict, Iran sided with Somalia in an almost instinctive reaction against an Ethiopia which enjoyed Soviet support (see essay on the Red Sea and the Indian Ocean). On 27 December 1977, the eve of President Carter's visit to Iran, Somali President Siyad Barreh visited Tehran. Foreign observers assumed that he asked the Shah to discuss with Carter ways of improving Somali-American relations especially over the ban on the transfer of American arms from Iran to Somalia. The Iranian media pointed out that Iranian military supplies to Somalia had so far been restricted to light arms because existing contracts prevented the country from passing on US-made weapons to third parties.[111] When Carter arrived a few days later, the Shah was reported to have warned him of the dangers inherent in the USSR's increasing penetration into the Horn of Africa and to have stressed his concern over this issue—a concern, he emphasized, which was shared by Saudi Arabia.[112] In January 1978, following reports that Ethiopian aircraft had raided targets in Somalia, the Shah said that Iran could "not remain indifferent" to attacks on Somali territory.[113] Reacting to such pronouncements, the OAU issued a statement on 20 January warning Iran against trying to extend its sphere of influence into Africa: Iran would be well advised not to "preoccupy herself with hypothetical situations which tend to cloud the issue." The statement went on to say that Iran's continued ties with South Africa, which reportedly received 90% of its oil supplies from Iran, did not qualify her to play any role in the African continent.[114]

Relations with India
Iranian-Indian relations have improved in recent years and continued to do so in 1977–78. Iran's basic aims remained to work for overall stability and to counteract Soviet influence in the Indian Ocean region. On 2 February 1978, the Shah visited New Delhi for the first time since 1974 to discuss bilateral, regional and global issues. The major topics were co-operation in safeguarding the stability of the Indian Ocean; contacts for harnessing nuclear energy for peaceful purposes; supplies of Iranian oil to India; and economic co-operation, including the Shah's scheme for an Asian Common Market—a free-trade zone stretching from the Caspian to the South China Sea. The Shah pointed out the importance of making the Indian Ocean "a zone of peace and stability" and stressed that this should be the responsibility of the littoral states alone. Accordingly, he called for the strengthening of the two countries' naval forces in the Indian Ocean.[115]

India's Foreign Minister, Bihari Vajpayee visited Tehran in late May; at the beginning of June, Vajpayee accompanied the Prime Minister, Morarji Desai, on a second visit. These carried forward the discussions on topics dealt with earlier; special attention was also paid to a re-examination of regional issues in light of the coup in Afghanistan.

Relations with Afghanistan
The coup in Afghanistan late in April 1978 presented a twofold danger of the type Iran had been trying to avoid: it created a focus of tension and instability in Iran's immediate geographical proximity, and it paved the way for an intensification of Soviet influence. Viewed from Tehran, the coup appeared as another link in the chain of potentially hostile states encircling Iran. Tehran feared the possible repercussions of the Afghanistan coup on Pakistan, with which it had been trying to improve relations (see below). More specifically, it feared that ideological persuasion or tribal affinity might cause unrest among the Baluchis who straddle the frontiers of Iran, Afghanistan and Pakistan. (See essay on Regional Politics in the Persian Gulf and Indian Ocean.)

Iran's Foreign Minister Khal'atbari said in early May that the new regime in Afghanistan had approached the Iranian government and appealed for the continuation of their previous friendly relations. On 6 May, Iran recognized the new regime. Reports that the new Afghanistan government would not regard bilateral agreements made by the former regime as "automatically valid" were denied in Kabul, while the new Afghani ambassador in Tehran said that his country would strive harder to promote good relations with Iran.[116] At the end of the period reviewed, the new regime's political tendencies were not clearly perceived, and Iran was watching developments in Afghanistan for signs of increased Soviet influence.

Relations with Pakistan
Iran made major efforts to maintain relations with Pakistan at the level of cordiality achieved during the premiership of Zulfiqar 'Ali Bhutto, even after he fell

from power as a result of the military coup of 5 July 1977 (see *MECS 1976-77*, p. 395). On 15 October 1977, Gen Ziya ul-Haqq, the Pakistani Chief Martial Law Administrator, paid a short visit to Tehran to discuss issues of mutual interest and to brief the Shah on the latest internal developments in Pakistan. The Shah encouraged him to improve relations with Afghanistan. At the beginning of February 1978, the Shah visited Pakistan on his way home from New Delhi. The major topic discussed was the Shah's plan for an Asian Common Market (see above), economic co-operation and the need for collective security in the region. The Shah was reported to have agreed to a moratorium on the first repayments due on an Iranian loan to Pakistan of $570m.

During the following months, there were reports of Iranian economic pressure being brought to bear on Pakistan, partly in order to bring it into line with Iran's policy of guarding against Soviet advances, and partly to prevent the execution of Bhutto (who had been sentenced to death under Ziya).[117] The Shah believed that Bhutto's execution would harm Pakistan's stability and thus have repercussions throughout the region. When the Pakistani Supreme Court began hearing Bhutto's appeal on 21 May, the Shah indicated that he would cut off Iran's annual aid to Pakistan if Bhutto were executed. On 9 September 1978, Ziya again visited Tehran and briefed the Shah on the meeting he had held en route with President Taraki of Afghanistan.

RELATIONS WITH THE GREAT POWERS
The US and the West
The entire range of Iranian-US relations was reviewed at the highest level during the Shah's visit to Washington in mid-November 1977 for his first meeting with President Carter. The Shah tried to obtain a firmer US commitment to Iran's security, arguing that America's own security interests were best served by doing so. He pointed to the importance of quiet and stability in the Gulf and Indian Ocean as constituting a common security interest of both countries, and to the tensions in the Horn of Africa, Afghanistan and Pakistan as presenting a danger to both. The Shah also referred to the 1959 Executive Agreement on Defence Co-operation under which the US had promised to provide assistance, including arms procurement aid, to Iran, Pakistan and Turkey. In an interview on the eve of his visit, the Shah said: "It seems to me that most Americans, including congressmen, are not aware that we have a crucial bilateral agreement which stipulates that, after consultation, the US is obliged to come to our assistance if [we are] attacked by a Communist or Communist-inspired country."[118] He warned that Iran would seek arms "elsewhere" if his demands were not met by the US.[119]

The Shah was reported to have asked for 140 F-16A jet fighters (over and above the 160 planes of this type already delivered); up to three additional radar plans of the Airborne Warning and Control System (AWACS) type; and a number of naval patrol craft. He further requested 31 F-4G fighters fitted with electronic warfare equipment. The Shah repeated his request for the F-18L, which at that time was not yet available to the US armed forces. He also asked for technical assistance in operating and maintaining the vast arsenal of US arms already in Iran.

The Shah's demands came as Congressional pressure was building up to block arms sales to Iran; this was seen as a specific application of Carter's policy, announced in May 1977, of curbing overall US arms sales. In order to overcome US reluctance to act contrary to its own declared policy, the Shah promised active help in holding oil prices down to their present level. Prior to the Washington visit he had said that at the forthcoming OPEC meeting at Caracas, the Iranians "will be [passive] spectators";[120] following the talks he said that Iran would try to keep oil prices down in order "to show sympathy and comprehension" of American views. [121] At the conclusion of the talks, it was reported that no definite decision was reached on arms sales because of a Congressional request for further studies on the balance of power in the Persian Gulf region. However, President Carter did publicly stress the importance he attached "to a strong stable and progressive Iran" under the Shah, and that "towards that end . . . it remains the policy of the US to co-operate with Iran in its economic and social development and in continuing to help meet Iran's security needs." [122]

The Iranian media described the talks as a "trade-off" of US arms against Iranian oil policy. They expected a positive US response during Carter's visit to Tehran (31 December-1 January 1978) following the fulfilment of their part of the deal by taking a moderate stand at the Caracas OPEC conference earlier in December. According to American sources, the request for additional F-16A aircraft was not discussed during the Tehran talks. However, agreement was reached in principle on the acceptance of terms for nuclear non-proliferation by Iran; this was intended to pave the way for the sale of six to eight US-made light-water atomic reactors.

In mid-August 1978, the State Department and the Arms Control Agency were reported to have turned down Iran's request for F-4G aircraft with electronic warfare equipment (planes which had not yet been sold to any foreign country). The sale was refused on the grounds that it would introduce a new weapons system into the region and because planes with this kind of equipment were considered offensive rather than defensive. Instead, Iran was offered the less sophisticated F-4E fighter bomber. [123] The refusal was all the more striking against the background of the approval of the F-15 aircraft sale to Saudi Arabia (see chapter on Saudi Arabia). Some Iranian and American commentators felt that the US had come to regard Tehran as less important to its interests than Riyadh. [124] They listed the following possible reasons for such a change: disagreement about the quantity of arms and the standard of weapons technology Iran should have; US doubts about the wisdom of the Shah's ambition to make the Iranian navy and air force dominant in the Persian Gulf and Indian Ocean (the US preferred a joint American-Iranian force which was rejected by the Shah); US suspicions that Iran was seeking to develop a nuclear strike capability; and the greater weight attributed by the US to Saudi (rather than Iranian) influence on future oil prices. In addition, the Shah's view of what the US role in Africa should be was considered seriously as at odds with Carter's non-interventionist approach. In the light of subsequent internal developments, Iran no longer appeared to be a factor for promoting regional stability. In Iran itself, domestic considerations, particularly after the change of government in August, led to a review of the arms purchasing programme in response to public criticism of its "wastefulness" and because of the need to divert funds to ease social and economic grievances.

Carter's insistence on the human rights issue had some influence—though probably only a marginal one—on the onset of domestic unrest. However, when the US Administration began to perceive that the Shah's authority was gravely threatened, Carter gave him his support.

In October 1978, the British Foreign Minister, Dr David Owen, expressed support for the Shah: "It would not be in the interests of this country or the West for the Shah to be toppled." If the Shah were to fall, Owen predicted, it would be effected "initially by a very Right-wing government that would very soon be disrupted by the Left—and the Left is really Communism, the Soviet Union and terrorist-type groupings." Owen's position was subsequently attacked by certain Labour Left-wingers for minimizing violations of human rights in Iran, and by Iranian opposition leaders for supporting the Shah.

The French government, on the other hand, maintained relations with the Shah but at the same time allowed Iranian opposition leaders, particularly Khomeyni, to operate relatively unimpeded on French soil.

The USSR and Eastern Europe

Although Iran officially described its relations with the USSR as "excellent," it was deeply and visibly worried about the expansion of Soviet influence in the region, and by what it regarded as an incipient encirclement by Soviet-backed Leftist regimes. Tehran's concerns embraced the massive purchases of Soviet weapons by Iraq; the coup in Afghanistan; instability in Pakistan; the rising level of political violence in Turkey; the victory of Marxist hard-liners in the coup in the PDRY; the revival, even though on a small scale, of insurgency in southern Oman; events in the Horn of Africa; and Soviet naval activity in the Indian Ocean. All these developments were seen as part of a single picture pointing to Soviet pressures aimed at the Persian Gulf and its approaches. The Soviets, for their part, were gravely concerned over Iran's massive purchases of arms and military equipment. The improvement of relations between Iran and the PRC (see below) gave rise to additional Soviet resentment.

Nonetheless, day-to-day contacts between Tehran and Moscow proceeded smoothly and several agreements were signed during the period reviewed. In November 1977, a cultural agreement was concluded; in December, the permanent commission for economic co-operation submitted a protocol laying down guidelines for future economic co-operation; in April 1978, an agreement was signed on economic and technical co-operation, and another was concluded for the construction of the fourth phase of the second gas trunkline intended to pump Iranian gas to Czechoslovakia, Austria, West Germany and France via Soviet territory. The fourth phase was to connect Qom and Astara, with work scheduled to be completed by September 1980.

The general atmosphere of goodwill was marred by several incidents. In December 1977, Maj-Gen Ahmad Mogharrabi and a civilian, 'Ali-Naqi Rabbani, were sentenced to death in Tehran and executed on a charge of spying for an "alien" power. Late in March 1978, Iranian sources reported that another spy network had been uncovered. Though the "alien power" was not named in either case, the reference was generally understood to be to the USSR. In June, Soviet gunners shot down two Iranian helicopters which had violated Soviet air space. All eight people flying in one of the helicopters were killed; the other was badly damaged. Iranian sources said they had been on an unarmed training flight, had carried no photographic equipment and had violated Soviet air space by mistake. Soviet sources said they had ignored "generally accepted" signals to land.

More significantly, references to "foreign hands" participating in fomenting unrest in Iran were usually interpreted as pointing to the USSR. The actual share of Soviet influence in Iran's domestic troubles cannot yet be assessed, but what can be stated with assurance is that the removal of the Shah could serve Soviet interests. In reporting events in Iran, the Soviet media stressed the economic burdens placed on the "oppressed people" and dwelt on the exploitation of Iran by Western imperialism. They asserted that the oil revenues, rather than being used to improve the situation of the masses, were being spent in a manner bound to widen existing social divisions. Most oil revenues were allocated to finance arms purchases, thus returning petrodollars to Western monopolies and especially to the US. [125]

The Shah attached considerable importance to fostering better relations with East European countries, as witnessed by his visits to Romania and Czechoslovakia in

August 1977, and to Hungary and Bulgaria in May 1978. A visit to Poland and East Germany, scheduled for September, was postponed because of internal unrest. Romania's President Ceauşescu stopped over in Tehran for a short meeting with the Shah on 14 May 1978 on his way to the PRC.

At the beginning of March 1978, Iran broke off trade relations with East Germany, accusing it of allowing persons who had attacked the Iranian embassy there to leave the country without having been brought to trial. In mid-April, the East German Foreign Minister, Oskar Fischer, visited Tehran to convey his government's apologies; economic relations were thereafter resumed.

THE FAR EAST
Relations with China

Iran had sought friendly relations with the PRC ever since the US established contact with Peking in 1971. Iran hoped that China would accept its policies in the Gulf, and believed that Iranian-Chinese diplomatic relations (established in 1971) might contribute to neutralizing the Maoist elements among Iranian Leftists. The prospects of trade were another consideration. The Shah also seems to have believed that good relations with the PRC would strengthen his hand in dealing with the USSR. The latter aspect had come to the fore in recent years when Iran and China found themselves jointly opposing Soviet policies in Africa and sharing concerns over Afghanistan. The steady improvement in bilateral relations culminated in August 1978, when Chairman Hua Kuo-feng arrived in Tehran—the first visit of a PRC Chairman to a non-Communist country. Hua's visit took place after two years of private correspondence between him and the Shah and had been prepared for during earlier visits to Iran by the Chinese Deputy Foreign Minister (in April) and Foreign Minister Huang Hua (in mid-June). Late in July, the PRC Petroleum Minister, Sung Chen-ming, led an economic delegation which met with the Iranian Minister of Industries and Mines and the Minister of Energy, as well as with the chairman of the National Iranian Oil Company. Among the economic issues discussed was the possibility of Iranian participation in developing the Chinese oil industry and oil exports to the PRC.[126]

The major topic of the talks between Chairman Hua and the Shah was Persian Gulf security. Both sides evinced a common interest in preserving tranquillity in the Gulf and in the Indian Ocean, and in limiting Soviet influence there. But the Shah took care not to demonstrate the community of Iranian-Chinese interests to the point of straining Iranian-Soviet relations. In a speech on 29 August, at a banquet in honour of Hua, the Shah avoided controversial issues. The only politically significant passage was a reference to "our mutual understanding" that the security of the Indian Ocean and the Persian Gulf should be a matter for their littoral states.[127] Hua, too, avoided embarrassing his host, his criticism of the USSR being much more restrained than the anti-Soviet statements he had made earlier during the same trip, in Yugoslavia and Romania. He said that China was committed to the struggle against "the policies of aggression and expansionism of the big powers," but he did not name the USSR. No joint communique was issued at the conclusion of the visit, apparently because Iran refused to include any antagonistic references to the Soviet Union. Hua's caution contrasted with the attitude of the Chinese Foreign Minister who, during his visit in June, had told an Iranian correspondent that the Third World should unite with Western nations against the Soviet Union, whom he described as their "common enemy."[128] Soviet reaction at that time was very sharp: "These visits to the Persian Gulf countries had anti-Soviet objectives . . . and [were] to extend Chinese influence . . . to the detriment of the Soviet Union."[129] No similar reaction was reported after Hua's visit.

A cultural agreement was signed during Hua's visit and technical and scientific agreements were drafted.

Relations with Japan
Between 5 and 8 September 1978, at a time when rioting in Iran was at a peak, Japanese Prime Minister Takeo Fukuda visited Iran, accompanied by his Foreign Minister, Sunao Sonoda. Economic topics were the main points on the agenda. Fukuda's visit to Tehran was but one stop on a tour of Japan's oil suppliers in which it hoped to secure guarantees for a stable oil supply and argue the case for oil prices to be set in terms of a basket of foreign currencies rather than in dollars. Iran sought the expansion of its non-oil exports to Japan, as well as a larger percentage share of Japan's overall oil imports. A long-term agreement on the sale to Japan of Iranian natural gas was also discussed, but not concluded. Cultural co-operation was another topic on the agenda and political issues were touched upon. At a Tehran press conference, Fukuda expressed satisfaction that Iran had welcomed the signing of a friendship treaty between Japan and the PRC.[130]

ECONOMIC AFFAIRS ($1 = 70.475 Iranian rials; £1 = Rls 147.66)
The oil sector continued to be the dominant element in Iran's economic make-up in 1977 and 1978, but the rate of increase in revenues from petroleum exports paled in comparison with the growth rates registered in the earlier years of the post-1973 oil boom. Much of Iran's oil revenues has been invested in capital goods in an effort to expand and diversify the country's economic base beyond petroleum-related industries. The extent to which these revenues have been invested wisely is open to question, particularly since Iran's development performance to date has been undermined by instances of either corruption or incompetent planning resulting in artificial shortages, bottlenecks or waste. Such shortcomings notwithstanding, the economy has witnessed considerable growth and modernization during the 1970s.

In Iran, as elsewhere in the ME, the inevitable changes brought about by rapid and large-scale economic growth have contributed to social tension (for details, see above). Disenchantment with the regime has expressed itself in strikes and other disruptions of everyday life which have had negative effects on the overall economy. Both direct foreign investment and locally-funded private investment have declined as a result of the prevailing instability. Rising prices have both been a cause and an effect of some disturbances as inflation has apparently stirred some people to manifest their dissatisfaction with the cost-of-living by public demonstrations, some of which have resulted in property damage and insurance losses; these, in turn, have contributed to yet higher prices being passed on to the consumer.

In less visible, but no less significant, terms, inflation in Iran had an impact on real economic growth which is evident from the fact that while Gross Domestic Product (GDP) in current prices rose 17.1% in 1977, real GDP, as measured in constant 1975 prices, actually fell by more than 2% from the 1976 record high of Rls 3,941 bn.[131]

AGRICULTURE
The agricultural sector suffered in 1977–78, further exacerbating the growing disaffection with the overall performance of the economy. After two consecutive years of real growth in agricultural value added and in production of most principal crops, preliminary figures from Bank Markazi Iran reveal that both value added from arable farming and output of most of the principal crops fell in 1977–78. It appears certain, then, that imports of foodstuffs and agriculture produce, which

amounted to more than $1,500m in 1976–77, rose in 1977–78. If so, Iran's import bill for food could reach $4,000m by 1980, as predicted.[132]

INDUSTRY

Iran's non-oil manufacturing sector has witnessed a period of growth in recent years. In 1976–77, the value of production in nine of the country's ten largest non-oil industries rose above the previous year's levels. Only in the spinning and weaving industries did the value of output fail to increase.[133]

Figures for the first three quarters of fiscal 1977–78 (i.e. 21 March-20 December 1977) show that growth was less widespread than in 1976–77. According to Bank Markazi, overall production rose c. 7.6% during this period. The largest components of this overall growth were chemicals and related products (19.7%) and basic metals (24.2%). In addition, production of non-metal mining products other than coal and oil rose slightly (9.9%). In contrast, though, average output during this nine-month period fell in the following industries: textiles, clothing and leather products (-3.1%); fabricated metal products, machinery and equipment (-2.9%); and food, beverages and tobacco (-1.1%).

OIL AND GAS

Through the first quarter of 1978, Iran retained its position behind Saudi Arabia as OPEC's second largest producer of crude oil, despite a 5.5% drop in output from the first three months of 1977, from 5.8 million barrels per day (mbd) to 5.5 mbd. Preliminary statistics reveal, though, that oil production rose 4.5% during the second quarter of 1978 over the preceding three months.[134]

The share of petroleum in the value of Iran's total merchandise exports reached 97.3% in 1977 and fell only slightly—to 97.0%—during the first half of 1978, when petroleum exports amounted to c. $11.4 bn. Exports of refined petroleum products remained fairly stable through the first half of 1978 at a time when output rose steadily, thus reflecting increased domestic consumption of refined products.

Meanwhile, production of natural gas has risen steadily in recent years as the authorities have tapped more of the country's vast reserves which, at an estimated 400 trillion cubic feet, are second only to the Soviet Union. According to National Iranian Oil Company and Bank Markazi statistics, the value of gas exports jumped 35.7% to c. $246m during 1977, while domestic use rose at an even faster rate— 62.4%. The growing importance of natural gas relative to oil is demonstrated by the change in proportion of Iran's total energy production from 84, 14 and 2% for oil, gas and hydroelectricity respectively in 1976, to 75, 23 and 2% respectively in 1977.[135]

BUDGET

Central government expenditures were budgeted to rise from Rls 2,390 bn to Rls 2,936 bn (c. $41.7 bn) in 1978–79—an increase of 22.8% from 1977–78. At the same time, revenues were expected to grow from Rls 2,267 bn to Rls 2,796 bn (c. $39.7 bn), or 23.3%, resulting in a slight increase in the budget deficit, from Rls 123 bn in 1977–78 to Rls 140 bn in 1978–79.[136]

In his budget speech to the Majlis, Prime Minister Amuzegar asserted his government's intention to discuss the more pressing economic problems, when he declared that "indefatigable efforts will continue to fight inflation, [and] measures will be taken to eliminate the various types of imbalances and bottlenecks as well as to reduce wastage." He went on to include implementation of "the principle of social justice" in his list of budgetary priorities.[137]

In its effort to achieve these objectives, the government has paid considerable attention to the development of the infrastructure. After defence, electricity was given the second largest sectoral allocation (Rls 312.2m in 1978–79 cf Rls 213.5m in 1977–78), and transportation the fourth (Rls 238.5m in 1978–79 cf Rls 129.2m). Other sizeable budgetary increases were allocated to education (+30.4%), social welfare (+88.4%) and health (+29.8%). The only two sectors which suffered real reductions in their 1978–79 allocations were housing (–45.7%) and commercial affairs (–20.3%).[138]

MONEY AND BANKING
International reserves peaked at $13.7 bn in February 1978 before gradually sliding down to $11.9 bn at the end of August.

During the first few months of 1978 the foreign assets of the Central Bank and reserves and foreign assets of the commercial banks also all reached record highs, as did the money supply and quasi-money supply. During March 1978, both the supply of money and quasi-money shot up, averaging an increase of Rls 100 bn each. In the two succeeding months, the supply declined slightly, but quasi-money continued to grow, though at a rate slower than that of March.[139]

BALANCE OF PAYMENTS
Iran registered an overall balance of payments surplus in 1977 of $3,046m, representing a substantial improvement over the 1976 surplus of $440m. This upsurge was largely attributable to a $3,035m improvement in the long-term capital deficit. Otherwise, most of the components of the payments accounts changed little in 1977. The net surplus for goods, services and transfers rose 7.8% for a total of $5,082m; much of this increase was realized by a 25% growth in exports of services.[140]

FOREIGN TRADE
Receipts from oil exports rose only $247m in 1977–78, reflecting the decline in the rate of growth compared with other post-1973 years. Clearly, the glut of oil in the world market has affected Iran's exports.

By contrast, according to preliminary figures from the Bank Markazi, non-oil exports jumped 24% in 1977–78, reversing the decline registered in 1976–77. The bulk of the growth in exports was in fresh and dried fruit sales. Cotton exports fell, however, as they had in 1976–77, thus losing their place as Iran's largest non-fuel source of exports.

Imports rose a further 15.8% in 1977–78, reaching $14,556m. The largest component of this increase was in transport and machinery equipment, demonstrating Iran's efforts to acquire capital.

Japan retained its position as Iran's most lucrative market for exports, though its lead was reduced considerably in 1977, when the US surged past West Germany to become the second leading buyer. In 1977, as in 1975 and 1976, these same three countries remained Iran's largest sources for imports, though in the reverse order from exports (i.e. West Germany first, US second and Japan third).

David Menashri
Economic section by **Ira E. Hoffman**

ARMED FORCES
Total armed forces number 413,000. Defence expenditure in 1978-79 was Rls 700.4 bn ($9.94 bn). Military service is compulsory for two years. The Army numbers 285,000 with the following formations: three armoured divisions; three infantry divisions; four independent brigades (one armoured, one infantry, one airborne, one special force); four surface-to-air missile battalions with HAWK and Army Aviation Command. Equipment consists of 760 *Chieftain*, 400 M-47/-48, 460 M-60A1 medium tanks; 250 *Scorpion* light tanks; *Fox, Ferret* scout cars; c. 325 M-113, 500 BTR-40/-50/-60/-152 armoured personnel carriers; 710 guns and howitzers, including 75mm pack, 85mm, 330 105mm, 130mm, 155mm, 203mm towed, 440 M-109 155mm, 38 M-107 175mm, 14 M-110 203mm self-propelled; 72 BM-21 122mm rocket launchers; 106mm recoilless rifles; *ENTAC*, SS-11, SS-12, *Dragon, TOW* anti-tank guided weapons; 1,800 23mm, 35mm, 40mm, 57mm, 85mm towed, 100 ZSU-23-4, ZSU-57-2 self-propelled anti-aircraft guns; *HAWK* surface-to-air missiles; aircraft including 40 Cessna 185, six Cessna 310, ten Cessna 0-2, two F-27; 202 AH-1J, 210 Bell 214A, 21 *Huskie*, 88 AB-205A, 70 AB-206, 30 CH-47C helicopters. (1,297 *Chieftain/Shir Iran* medium, 110 *Scorpion* light tanks, BMP mechanized infantry combat vehicles, ASU-85 self-propelled anti-tanks, 100 ZSU-23-4 self-propelled anti-aircraft guns, *Rapier, Improved HAWK*, SA-7/-9 surface-to-air missiles; 163 Bell 214A, 350 Bell 214ST helicopters on order). Two companies and one helicopter squadron (400) were deployed in Oman; 385 in Syria (UNDOF); and one battalion (524) in Lebanon (UNIFIL). Reserves number 300,000.

The 28,000-strong Navy is equipped with three destroyers (one ex-British *Battle*-class with *Seacat* surface-to-air missiles, two ex-US *Sumner*-class with one helicopter, all with *Standard* surface-to-surface missiles and surface-to-air missiles); four frigates with MK 2 *Seakiller* surface-to-surface missiles and *Seacat* surface-to-air missiles; four corvettes (ex-US patrol frigates); seven large patrol craft; five *Combattante*-II-class guided-missile fast patrol boats with *Harpoon* surface-to-surface missiles; five minesweepers (three coastal, two inshore); two logistic landing ships; two utility landing craft; two logistic support ships and eight SRN-6, six *Wellington* BH-7 hovercraft. (Three *Tang*-class training, six Type 209 submarines, four *Spruance*-class destroyers, six *Lupo*-class frigates, seven guided-missile fast patrol boats with *Harpoon* surface-to-surface missiles and four logistic support ships are on order). Naval Air formations consist of one maritime reconnaissance squadron with six P-3F *Orion*; one anti-submarine warfare squadron with 12 SH-3D; one transport squadron with six *Shrike Commander*, four F-27. Helicopters include five AB-205A, seven AB-212, six RH-53D and ten SH-3D. There are three Marine battalions. 39 P-3C maritime reconnaissance aircraft and 15 SH-3D helicopters are on order.

The Air Force numbers 100,000 and is equipped with 459 combat aircraft. Formations consist of ten fighter-bomber squadrons with 32 F-4D, 177 F-4E; ten ground-attack fighter squadrons with 12 F-5A, 140 F-5E; three fighter squadrons with 56 F-14A *Tomcat*; one reconnaissance squadron with 16 RF-4E; one tanker squadron with 13 Boeing 707-320L; four medium transport squadrons with 64 C-130E/H, six Boeing 747; four light transport squadrons with 18 F-27, four F-28, three Aero *Commander* 690, four Falcon 20; ten HH-43F, six AB-205, 84 AB-206A, five AB-212, 39 Bell 214C search and rescue, two CH-47C, 16 *Super Frelon*, two S-61A helicopters. Trainers include nine T-33, 28 F-5F, 49 *Bonanza* F33A/C; *Phoenix, Sidewinder, Sparrow* air-to-air missiles; AS.12, *Maverick, Condor* air-to-surface missiles. There are five surface-to-air missile squadrons with *Rapier* and 25 *Tigercat*. (Five RF-4E, 24 F-14, 160F-16A/B fighters; seven E-3A airborne warning and control system aircraft, three F-27 transports; four Boeing 747 transports; 50 CH-47 helicopters and *Blindfire* surface-to-air missile radar are on order.) Paramilitary forces consist of 74,000 Gendarmerie with 0-2 light aircraft and helicopters, and 32 patrol boats.

Source: The Military Balance 1978-79 (London, International Institute for Strategic Studies).

BALANCE OF PAYMENTS (million US dollars)

	1975	1976	1977
A. Goods, Services and Transfers	4,707	4,716	5,082
Exports of Merchandise, fob	20,432	23,959	24,356
Imports of Merchandise, fob	-12,898	-15,435	-15,823
Exports of Services	2,472	2,886	3,629
Imports of Services	-5,280	-6,677	-7,071
Private Unrequited Transfers, net	-1	—	—
Government Unrequited Transfers, net	-17	-17	-8
B. Long-Term Capital, nie	-3,281	-4,609	-1,574
C. Short-Term Capital, nie	-668	-398	-1,016
D. Errors and Omissions	-648	731	931
Total (A through D)	**110**	**440**	**3,406**

INTERNATIONAL LIQUIDITY (million US dollars at end of period)

	1975	1976	1977	*(Jan-Aug)* 1978
International Reserves	**8,897**	**8,833**	**12,266**	**11,949**
Gold	153	152	160	170
SDRs	65	75	85	108
Reserves with IMF	1,122	1,160	1,197	1,111
Foreign Exchange	7,556	7,447	10,824	10,561

MONETARY SURVEY (billion Iranian rials; months ending the 20th)

	1976	1977	1978*
Foreign Assets	601.2	817.2	884.5
Domestic Credit	1,384.5	1,678.7	2,038.9
Claims on Government (net)	*-106.9*	*-25.9*	*234.6*
Claims on Official Entities	*450.5*	*482.1*	*462.3*
Claims on Private Sector	*1,040.9*	*1,222.5*	*1,341.9*
Money	668.0	822.0	934.5
Quasi-Money	842.7	1,082.9	1,272.9
Money, seasonally adjusted	656.9	808.3	957.5

*January-May.

NATIONAL ACCOUNTS (billion Iranian rials; year begins 21 March)

	1975	1976	1977
Exports	1,476.6	1,838.2	1,815.2
Government Consumption	807.4	1,003.6	1,073.8
Gross Fixed Capital Formation	1,065.6	1,477.9	1,831.9
Private Consumption	1,316.0	1,532.5	2,160.8
Less: Imports	*1,104.5*	*1,245.6*	*1,488.4*
Gross Domestic Product (GDP)	**3,561.1**	**4,606.6**	**5,393.3**
Less: Net Factor Payments Abroad	*42.3*	*35.1*	*45.7*
Gross National Expenditure = GNP	3,518.8	4,571.5	5,347.6
GDP at 1975 Prices	3,561.1	3,940.9	3,859.4

Source (of four preceding tables): IMF, *International Financial Statistics.*

EXPENDITURES (billion Iranian rials; year ends 20 March)

	1977–78	1978–79	% Change
Public Affairs	202.1	194.1	–4.0
Defence Affairs	561.1	700.4	24.8
Social Affairs	545.8	689.0	26.2
Economic Affairs	894.3	1,205.9	34.8
Miscellaneous	92.1	76.0	–24.0
Debt Processing	66.3	85.6	29.1
Debt Repayment	58.5	54.9	–6.6
Subtotal I	**2,420.2**	**3,005.9**	**24.2**
Investment and Loans Abroad	80.0	80.0	0
Subtotal II	**2,500.2**	**3,085.9**	**23.4**
Less: Savings	*110.0*	*150.0*	*36.4*
Total	**2,390.2**	**2,935.9**	**22.8**

REVENUES (billion Iranian rials; year ends 20 March)

	1977–78	1978–79	% Change
Taxes	420.8	614.2	46.0
Oil and Gas	1,436.0	1,541.8	7.4
Government Monopolies	30.1	40.8	35.5
Government Services	27.9	34.0	21.9
Miscellaneous	82.2	143.9	75.1
Foreign and Domestic Loans	250.0	400.0	60.0
Interest on loans made abroad	20.3	21.3	4.9
Total	**2,267.3**	**2,796.0**	**23.3**

Source (of two preceding tables): Derived from *Middle East Economic Survey*.

INDEX OF PRICES, WAGES, PRODUCTION (1975 = 100)

	1961	1966	1971	1976	1977	1978*
Wholesale Prices	55	60	67	109	128	142
Home Goods	55	60	68	111	132	147
Consumer Prices	55	59	66	111	142	160
Wages	—	—	35	136	180	255**
Crude Petroleum Production	22	40	85	110	106	104

*First Half.
**First quarter only.
Source: IMF, *International Financial Statistics.*

PRODUCTION OF PRINCIPAL CROPS (thousand tons; year ends 20 March)

	1974–75	1975–76	1976–77	1977–78*
Wheat	4,700	5,500	6,000	5,500
Sugar beets	4,300	4,670	5,200	4,150
Rice	1,313	1,430	1,600	1,400
Barley	863	1,400	1,500	1,230
Cotton (unginned)	715	470	510	535
Green tea	96	80	88	116
Oilseeds	79	100	130	105
Tobacco	14	15	19	15

*Preliminary.
Source: Ministry of Agriculture and Rural Development.

OIL STATISTICS

	1974	1975	1976	1977
Annual Production (million barrels)	2,211	1,965	2,166	2,080
Daily Average (million barrels per day)	6.06	5.38	5.93	5.70
*Receipts from Exports (million US dollars)	17,154	18,871	20,488	20,735

*Year begins 21 March, e.g. 1974 = 21 March 1974–20 March 1975.
Sources: Petroleum Economist and Bank Markazi Iran.

VALUE OF PRODUCTION OF MAJOR NON–OIL INDUSTRIES
(billion Iranian rials at 1969–70 prices; year ends 20 March)

	1974–75	1975–76	1976–77
Automobiles	35.03	44.86	54.69
Spinning and Weaving	27.09	27.78	27.22
Household Appliances	13.47	17.55	22.34
Basic Metals	15.87	19.48	20.09
Tobacco	10.88	11.96	14.17
Sugar	12.87	13.19	13.71
Vegetable Shortening	9.63	10.40	11.27
Radio, Television and Telephone	9.18	9.95	10.03
Cement	6.62	7.86	8.69
Cosmetics and Soap	5.32	5.74	6.66

NON–OIL EXPORTS, BY COMMODITY (million US dollars; year ends 20 March)

	1975–76	1976–77	1977–78*
Fresh and Dried Fruits	74.2	70.2	133.5
Cotton	136.4	122.0	107.5
Carpets	105.3	94.4	90.9
Skins and Leather	28.7	32.2	41.3
Clothes, Knitwear and Textiles	28.7	26.5	31.9
Glycerine and Chemicals	19.1	31.1	29.5
Detergents and Soap	21.5	19.6	18.9
Motor Vehicles	28.7	24.2	17.7
Mineral and Metal Ores	32.3	10.4	57.9
Other	117.3	109.3	140.5
Total	**592.3****	**539.6****	**669.6**

*Preliminary.
**Figures do not add because of rounding.

IMPORTS, BY COMMODITY GROUP (million US dollars; year ends 20 March)

	1975–76	1976–77	1977–78*
Transport and Machinery Equipment	4,973	5,526	6,316
Goods classified by Primary Materials	3,342	4,102	4,251
Food and Live Animals	1,554	1,182	1,572
Chemical Products	835	809	1,033
Raw Materials, excluding fuels	369	365	437
Vegetable and Animal Oils and Fats	291	137	159
Beverages and Tobacco	26	77	131
Minerals, Fuels and Related Products	17	23	28
Miscellaneous	288	346	626
Total	**11,695**	**12,567**	**14,556****

*Preliminary.
**Figures do not add because of rounding.
Source (of three preceding tables): Bank Markazi Iran.

DIRECTION OF TRADE (million US dollars)

	1975*	1976*	1977*
Exports to:			
Japan	4,526	4,046	3,881
United States	1,398	1,483	2,756
West Germany	1,334	1,807	1,696
Netherlands	1,458	1,565	1,454
Italy	1,036	1,155	1,356
United Kingdom	1,412	1,709	1,245
Spain	315	842	1,078
France	1,150	1,309	998
Belgium	434	432	680
Canada	744	677	506
India	461	553	n.a.
Total (including others)	**19,933**	**23,570**	**24,246**

	1975	1976	1977*
Imports from:			
West Germany	1,824	2,304	3,014
United States	2,051	2,033	3,004
Japan	1,662	2,098	2,136
United Kingdom	877	992	1,256
Italy	336	686	996
France	415	630	751
Switzerland	213	434	400
Netherlands	278	394	349
Belgium	251	421	266
Sweden	137	149	218
India	322	394	n.a.
Total (including others)	**10,343**	**12,894**	**13,750**

*Data derived from partner country.
n.a. not available.
Source: IMF, Direction of Trade.

NOTES
1. SAVAK is the State Intelligence and Security Organization, so called after the initials of its name Sazemane Ettela'at va-Amniyate Keshvar.
2. Muhammad Reza Pahlavi, Mission for My Country (London: Transorient, 1960), pp. 54–59. Here he also recalls that, when six or seven years old, figures from the beginning of Islam appeared to him.
3. Muhammad Reza Pahlavi, The White Revolution (Tehran: Kayhan, 1967), p. 16.
4. Ibid, p. 15.
5. Le Monde, Paris; 6 May 1978. The grounding of Khomeyni's attitude in the traditional world view is instructively brought out by comparing his words with the following scholarly description of the medieval concept of the Islamic polity: "Islam is the community of Allah. . . . He is the centre and the goal of its spiritual experience. But he is also the mundane head of the community which he not only rules but governs. He is the reason for the state's existence." Gustav E. von Grunebaum, Medieval Islam (Chicago: 1961), p. 142.
6. The relevant article of the 1907 constitution reads: "It is hereby declared that it is for the learned doctors of theology [the mujtahids] . . . to determine whether such laws as may be proposed are or are not conformable to the rules of Islam, and that it is therefore officially enacted that [for the purpose of such review] there shall at all times exist a committee composed of not less than five mujtahids or other devout theologians." For English text see: Edward G. Broune, A Brief Narrative of Recent Events in Persia (London: 1959), pp. 87–101.
7. R. K. Karanjia, The Mind of A Monarch (London: Allen and Unwin, 1977), p. 51.
8. Ettela'at, Kayhan International (KI), Tehran; 13, 16, 17 October 1977.
9. Official figures for the end of 1977 put the number of Iranian students in the US alone at over 12,000, making them the largest group of foreign students. Another 27,000 had "overstayed" their permits either after graduation or after dropping out, and remained in the US; New York Times (NYT), 14 December 1977.
10. Ettela'at, 6 December 1977.

509

11. *KI*, 16, 17 October 1977.
12. *The Guardian*, London; 7 October 1977.
13. *Ibid*, 26 October 1977.
14. *International Herald Tribune (IHT)*, Paris; and *Financial Times (FT)*, London; 14 November 1977. For details on the National Front, see below.
15. On the Pan-Iranist Party see, Daniel Dishon (ed.) *Middle East Record 1969–1970* (Jerusalem: Israel Universities Press, 1977), pp. 676–77.
16. Echo of Iran, *Political Digest*, 13 October 1977, No 152.
17. *The Guardian*, 17 October 1977.
18. Ayatollah Ruḥollah al-Musavi al-Khomeyni was an influential Shīʻī leader at the religious centre of Qom. He first came to public attention in 1961 after the death of Ayatollah Borujerdi, the recognized spiritual leader of the Iranian Shīʻīs, whom he in fact succeeded. He became politically active in opposing the White Revolution and other aspects of the Shah's policies which he considered as leading to secularization or as contrary to Islam. He owned large estates which were expropriated under the land reform. He was arrested several times but was not brought to trial. After playing a leading role in the riots of 4 June 1963, he was detained again and released only after undertaking to refrain from interference in political affairs. However in October 1964, after opposing the government's plan to obtain $200m for the purchase of American-made military equipment, he was exiled. He chose holy city of Najaf in Iraq as his residence and remained there, together with many followers, until deported by Iraq in October 1978. He then settled near Paris. In October 1977, his son was killed in Iran in circumstances never clarified.
19. *The Guardian,* 29 October 1977.
20. Wearing the traditional veil was forbidden by Reza Shah in 1935, but is still practised by most women. Women appearing unveiled in public were regarded as a symbol of the secularizing policy of the Pahlavi dynasty.
21. *Political Digest*, 13 December 1977, No 158.
22. *Der Spiegel*, Hamburg; 21 August 1978. Shariʻat Madari was regarded as the most influential of the Shīʻī religious leaders residing in Iran prior to Khomeyni's return.
23. *Ettelaʻat*, 30 August 1978.
24. Traditional mourning days for the dead are the fourth, the seventh and the fortieth. The last is the main one.
25. *Washington Post (WP)*, 19 January 1978.
26. *Rastakhiz*, Tehran; 2 May 1978.
27. *Le Monde*, 6 May 1978.
28. *Der Spiegel*, 21 August 1978.
29. *Le Monde*, 6 May 1978.
30. *Philadelphia Inquirer*, 11 June 1978. Similarly in an interview to *FT*, 14 July 1978.
31. *Der Spiegel*, 21 August 1978.
32. The National Front (*Jebheye Melli*) originally came into existence as a coalition of political groupings centred around Musaddiq in the early 1950s, but collapsed at the time of his overthrow. It again became active in the early 1960s. When it renewed activities in 1977, it retained its old ideology as well as many of its old leaders.
33. *Curriere della Sera*, Milan; 21 August—Daily Report, East and North Africa (DR), 25 August 1978.
34. *KI*, 31 May 1978.
35. *Ettelaʻat*, 20 June 1978.
36. *Ibid*, 27 May, 1 June 1978.
37. *Ibid,* 1 June; *KI*, 3 June 1978.
38. *KI*, 5, 6 June 1978.
39. *KI*, 15 June 1978.
40. *Ettelaʻat*, 19 June; *KI*, 20 June 1978.
41. *KI*, 2 July 1978. *Khak va-Khun* had been closed down in 1970.
42. *KI*, 2 July 1978.
43. *KI*, 20, 27 June 1978.
44. *Political Digest*, 30 July 1978, No 190.
45. On 26 December 1977, the Shah said that he no longer held the view that the posts of Prime Minister and Secretary-General could not be held by the same person.
46. Following the dismissal of Hoveyda's government in August 1977, Amuzegar was appointed PM and therefore resigned as Secretary-General. He was succeeded in that post by Muhammad Baheri, former Deputy Minister of the Court. The co-ordinators of the two wings had left the cabinet (Majidi in August 1977 and Ansari in November 1977). As cabinet ministers, they had been *ex officio* members of the party's bureau, but after their resignations they stopped serving it. Co-ordination between party and government had thereby suffered.

47. *Rastakhiz*, 5 January; R Tehran, 4 January—DR, 6 January 1978.
48. *KI*, 3 May 1978.
49. *Kayhan*, Tehran; 8 June; *KI*, 11 June 1978.
50. *Rastakhiz*, 20 May 1978. This was the first time the executive board was elected by the central council. In the past, it had been elected by the founding members.
51. Nehavandi was a former chancellor of Tehran University, an ex-cabinet minister, and recently personal secretary of the Empress.
52. *KI*, 10 June 1978.
53. *IHT*, 20 June 1978.
54. *Rastakhiz*, 24 November 1977.
55. *Chicago Tribune*, 13 January; also *The Sunday Times*, London; 16 April 1978.
56. Government statements on 10 and 15 May—*Ettela'at* 10, 15 May; *KI*, 11, 18 May 1978.
57. *Christian Science Monitor (CSM)*, Boston; 28 May 1978; *Time*, New York; 5 June 1978.
58. R Tehran, 18 August—DR, 24 August 1978.
59. *CSM*, 28 May; *The Times*, London; 5 June; *Philadelphia Inquirer*, 11 June 1978.
60. *Ettela'at*, 4 April 1978.
61. *The Times*, 20 August 1978.
62. *IHT*, 12–13 August 1978.
63. R Tehran, 18 August—DR, 24 August 1978.
64. *Country Reports on Human Rights Practices*, (Report submitted to the US Congress by The Department of State on 3 February 1978), pp. 315–60.
65. *Chicago Tribune*, 13 November 1977; DR, 10 March 1978; *Sunday Times*, 16 April 1978.
66. *The Guardian*, 20 December 1977.
67. *KI*, 7 June 1978.
68. *Ayandegan*, Tehran; 15 July; *KI*, 16 July 1978.
69. *KI*, 20 July 1978.
70. *KI*, 9 July 1978.
71. *Ayandegan*, 17 August 1976—*Political Digest*, 23 July 1978, No 189.
72. This was disclosed by Muhammad Haydari in his article mentioned above; *Ettela'at*, 30 August 1978.
73. The Press Law was originally enacted on 9 March 1908 and amended during Musaddiq's premiership on 4 February 1953.
74. *Kayhan* and *Khwandaniha*, Tehran; 10 November 1977.
75. In November 1977, for example, the Ministry of Agriculture gave a figure of 500,000 tons for cotton production in 1976–77. At a conference on cotton held the same month, it was revealed that the actual crop had been only slightly over 200,000 tons; *Rastakhiz*, 14 November 1977. Many other similar examples had undermined public confidence in government announcements and statistics.
76. *The Times* and *IHT*, 5 July 1978.
77. *Middle East Record 1968*, pp. 491–97.
78. *Ettela'at*, 13 April 1978.
79. *KI*, 27 July 1978.
80. Sherif-Emami had served as Prime Minister between August 1960 and May 1961. He resigned following an outbreak of rioting. Since 1965, he had been president of the Senate.
81. R Tehran 27, 28 August—DR, 28 August 1978; *Ettela'at, KI*, 28, 29, 30, 31 August 1978.
82. *KI*, 11 September 1978.
83. *Ettela'at*, 31 August 1978.
84. *KI* and *Tehran Journal*, Tehran; 19 September 1978.
85. *Ettela'at*, 29 August 1978.
86. In a written statement circulated in Tehran late in July, Amini emphasized the connection between Iran's economic ills and the current riots. He said that Iran needed a government of politicians rather than technocrats to stop the situation from deteriorating: *FT*, 31 July 1978. In mid-September, he said: "I no longer believe that the Shah can be saved, but the regime yes. . . . The Shah must make a sacrifice to save the country and the regime from chaos. He must go, resign, clearly show that he is withdrawing from the scene." *Le Matin*, Paris; 14 September—DR, 20 September 1978.
87. *L'Humanité*, Paris; 6 September—DR, 12 September 1978.
88. *Newsweek*, New York; 25 September 1978.
89. *KI*, 12 September 1978.
90. *KI*, 3 September 1978.
91. *Ettela'at*, 3, 4 September; *Rastakhiz*, 4, 5 September; *KI*, 3, 5, 6 September 1978.
92. *Ettela'at* and *Rastakhiz*, 9 September 1978.
93. E.g. *FT*, 9 September; *Ettela'at*, 16 September 1978.
94. *KI*, 13 September 1978.

95. *Chicago Tribune*, 13 November 1977.
96. *KI*, 11 July 1978.
97. *Rastakhiz*, 15 January; *KI*, 16 January 1978.
98. Qatar News Agency, 8 November 1977.
99. *Al-Siyāsa*, Kuwait; 24 August 1978.
100. *Chicago Tribune*, 13 November; *Newsweek*, 14 November 1977.
101. *Al-Ba'th*, Damascus; 29 August 1978.
102. *Al-Yaqza*, Kuwait; as quoted by DR, 7 November 1977.
103. *Arabia and the Gulf*, London; 12 December; *Rastakhiz*, 16 December 1977.
104. *KI*, 13 June; *Rastakhiz*, 14 June 1978.
105. *Al-Siyāsa*, 30 August; R Kuwait, 15 September—BBC, 18 September 1978.
106. *Tehran Journal*, 18 September 1978.
107. *WP*, 6 March; *Chicago Tribune*, 24 May 1978. Emphasis added in both quotations.
108. *KI*, 17 August 1978.
109. *Al-Ba'th*, 27 August; R Damascus as quoted by DR, 26 August 1978.
110. R Tripoli, the Voice of the Arab Homeland, 14 August—BBC, 16 August 1978. See also: JANA in English, 20, 27 April, 16, 31 May, 31 August—BBC, 24, 29 April, 18 May, 2 June, 2 September 1978.
111. *KI*, 29, 31 December 1977.
112. *Al-Nahār al-'Arabī wal-Duwalī*, Paris; 21 January 1978.
113. *Rastakhiz*, 2 January; *FT*, 3 January 1978.
114. *The Times*, 21 January 1978.
115. *Ettela'at*, 4 February 1978.
116. *KI*, 5 July; R Tehran, 13 July—DR, 14 July 1978.
117. *WP*, 19 May 1978.
118. *Newsweek*, 14 November 1977. In April 1978, US Secretary of the Air Forces, John C. Steson, said the US had "perhaps slightly more than [a] tacit obligation" to help Iran defend itself in the event of a Soviet attack (*KI*, 23 April 1978). Details of his statement and of the 1951 agreement can be found in *Congressional Record, US Senate*, 8 May 1978.
119. *IHT*, 18 November 1977.
120. *Newsweek*, 14 December 1977.
121. *IHT*, 18 November 1977.
122. *Department of State Bulletin*, 26 December 1977, pp. 907-10. Also *NYT*, 16 November and *Washington Star*, 27 November 1977.
123. *IHT*, 17 August 1978.
124. E.g. in *Foreign Report*, 11 January 1978. According to the US Defence Department, Iran was the biggest purchaser of American arms in 1977, buying weapons with $5,800m— more than half of the total of US weapons sold.
125. *Isvestiia*, Moscow; 14 September; *Pravda*, Moscow; 17 September 1978.
126. The PRC imported 300,000 tons of oil from Iran in 1977, for political rather than commercial reasons, as well as to balance mutual trade between the two countries.
127. *Rastakhiz*, 30 August 1978.
128. *Kayhan*, 16 June 1978.
129. R Moscow, 24 June—*Political Digest*, 2 July 1978, No 186.
130. *KI*, 9 September 1978.
131. See International Monetary Fund (IMF), *International Financial Statistics (IFS)*, Washington; October 1978, p. 188.
132. See Echo of Iran, *Iran Economic Service (IES)*, Tehran; No 165 (17 January 1978); and Economist Intelligence Unit, *Quarterly Economic Review of Iran (QER)*, London; No 1 (1978), pp. 13–14.
133. Bank Markazi Iran, *Annual Report and Balance Sheet 2535*, Tehran; June 1977, p. 139.
134. See *Petroleum Economist*, London; June 1978, p. 271; and IMF, *IFS*, October 1978, pp. 186–87.
135. See *Ettela'at*, 27 November 1977—Joint Publication Research Service, Washington; 25 January 1978.
136. *IES*, No 169 (February 1978), pp. 6–8.
137. R Tehran, 5 February—BBC, 7 February 1978.
138. *IES*, No 169, *op. cit.*
139. IMF, *IFS*, October 1978, pp. 186–87.
140. *Ibid*, p. 188.

Iraq

(Al-Jumhūriyya al-'Irāqiyya)

The Ba'thi regime, which has remained in power far longer than any other in the post-1958 period, celebrated its tenth anniversary on 17 July 1978. Apart from its longevity, the regime lists among its most important achievements the completed nationalization of oil; the formation of the Progressive Patriotic and Nationalist Front (PPNF)—a combination under Ba'th control with the Iraqi Communist Party (ICP), with various Kurdish groups and with Nasserite splinters; the liquidation of the Kurdish problem through the autonomy granted to the Kurdish minority (and the collapse of massive Kurdish resistance in the field); and, above all, the stability which, coupled with its huge oil income, has enabled the country to embark on comprehensive development projects in all spheres and areas.

As in every other year since 1975, there were no sensational events or sharp changes of trend in 1978. No evolution could be discerned on the political level: the much-promised democratization of political society never materialized, so that Iraq remained to all intents and purposes a one-party state. Moreover, for all the profession of collective leadership within the party, power has remained in the hands of a nucleus of party members, chief among them President Aḥmad Ḥasan al-Bakr and the Deputy Secretary-General of the Ba'th Party Regional Command, Saddām Ḥusayn—Bakr's kinsman, associate and heir. Indeed, with Bakr's consent, Saddām Ḥusayn assumed even more responsibilities in the period under review.

In order to keep this monopoly of power, the leadership continued to apply often repressive security measures against real or supposed nuclei of subversion. The army remained one such target. Accordingly, the civilian leadership again reverted to purges and executions within the army, though without publicity. Attempts by the ICP to assert itself were treated with a severity unprecedented since 1973, the leadership making it unquestionably clear that it would tolerate the ICP's existence only up to a certain point.

Although the Kurdish problem was less acute than it was before 1975, it still presented difficulties. Judging that the most vulnerable areas were those bordering on Syria, Turkey and Iran—both because of their remoteness and the likelihood of their being turned into bases for Kurdish insurgents from across the border—the regime continued a policy of mass evacuation from those areas (see *MECS 1976–77*, p. 41 f). The ultimate goal was evidently to cut off the Kurdish north from neighbouring countries, so far as possible. Guerrilla acts by Kurdish opposition groups, though forcing the Iraqi army to remain on the alert, neither endangered the regime nor weakened its control of the area. In other respects the "Autonomous Region" remained operational.

Iraq's foreign policy continued to combine radicalism and pragmatism, indicating the regime's wish to reconcile Ba'th ideology with aims and interests ostensibly at variance with those principles. Thus, while it proclaimed an uncompromising position with respect to the Arab-Israeli conflict, Sādāt's initiative and its aftermath, in practice the regime steered away from the anti-Sādāt front because it gave higher priority to its dispute with Syria and wished to avoid a total rupture with Egypt. Furthermore, Iraq's preoccupation with its domestic problems and its determination to become a Gulf power strengthened the need for political

513

pragmatism. Similarly, the Ba'th principle of "Arab unity" had to be adapted to changing trends in the Arab world. The regime continued to regard and to present its Treaty of Friendship with the USSR as a strategic alliance, while it denounced the US as an imperialist and pro-Zionist state with which Iraq would not restore diplomatic relations. However, as in former years, this neither prevented criticism of the USSR nor economic deals with the West (including the US), whenever circumstances seemed to warrant them.

On the whole, the regime's watchword in the period under review was Iraq's independence and self-assertion, hence the still-growing emphasis on the leading role which Iraq must play in the Third World.

PARTY AND GOVERNMENT

The Iraqi-based National (all-Arab) Command, nominally the highest authority in the Ba'th party, held its eleventh congress in early October 1977 after an interval of eight years. The timing of the congress followed earlier developments at the Regional Command level.[1] The congress approved a major political report (the text of which has not yet been published). However, in an interview with *al-Watan al-'Arabī*, President Bakr disclosed some of its main resolutions: (1) persistent efforts are to be made for building a progressive Arab front; (2) the struggle against proposed "capitulationist settlements" [in the Arab-Israeli conflict] is to be strengthened: (3) the fight and effort for unity in all political, economic and cultural areas are to be increased; and (4) Arab popular activity and Arab popular organizations are to be reinforced.[2]

The congress elected a new National Command (see Table I), the changes in its composition undoubtedly being decided by the Iraqi members. Their aim was to remove some non-Iraqis unwilling to follow the Iraqi leadership, while at the same time preserving the image of historical continuity by including such non-Iraqi figures as Michel 'Aflaq, the founder and leader of the party, Munīf al-Razzāz and Shiblī al-'Aysamī. On the other hand, the changes were clearly directed towards the Iraqization of the National Command, thereby securing the local leadership's grip over it. Thus, while only three of the 16 outgoing Command members were Iraqis, the new Command had six Iraqis out of 13. Bakr was elevated to the newly-established post of Deputy Secretary-General, while Saddām Husayn was appointed Assistant Secretary-General, together with two other non-Iraqis. These changes appear to have decreased the power of Shiblī al-'Aysamī, who had been considered the effective Secretary-General.

Table I: The Ba'th National Command as of October 1977

Michel 'Aflaq	Founder leader of the Ba'th; Syrian; re-elected Secretary-General
Ahmad Hasan al-Bakr	The President of Iraq; Deputy Secretary-General
Saddām Husayn +	Deputy Secretary-General of the Iraqi Regional Command; Assistant Secretary-General
Shiblī al-'Aysamī	Syrian; Assistant Secretary-General
Munīf al-Razzāz +	Jordanian; Assistant Secretary-General
'Abd al-Majīd al-Rāfi'ī	Lebanese
'Alī Ghannām	Saudi
Qāsim Salām +	Yemenite
Badr al-Dīn Muddathir +	Sudanese
'Izzat Ibrāhīm (al-Dūrī) +	Iraqi
Taha Yāsīn Ramadān (al-Jazrāwī)	Iraqi
Na'īm Hamīd Haddād +	Iraqi
Tāriq 'Azīz +	Iraqi

+ In the Iraqi-based National Command for the first time.

514

At the end of August 1978, Michel 'Aflaq left Iraq for Yugoslavia after having reportedly objected to Iraqi policy on various issues: the execution of Communists; the handling of the Kurdish affair; and the campaign against PLO leaders (see below).[3] The post of Secretary-General was presumed to have been taken by Bakr in an acting capacity, a difference of only symbolic significance. ('Aflaq was reported back in Baghdad later in 1978.)

Internally, the drive to Ba'thize the country continued unabated. Having succeeded in the past in taking full control of the institutional establishment, the party put even more stress on mass indoctrination. Saddām Ḥusayn, who has also become the leading party ideologist, asserted that lasting allegiance should be based on intellectual rather than on emotional foundations.[4] Other party officials pointed out that the chief aim was to disseminate Ba'th ideology through all educational institutions—from kindergarten to university. At the same time, special party schools continued to recruit and graduate new members, while the "People's Army," a party organization, continued to expand. An (unnamed) Ba'thi official claimed that support for the party had risen from 5,000 members in 1968 to 50-60,000 in 1978.[5] However, it seems that the quick expansion of the party had an adverse effect on its internal discipline and also gave rise to friction between the party leadership and various state organs. Thus, Saddām Ḥusayn repeatedly warned against "manoeuvring" within the party; against the introduction of undemocratic and "incorrect" traditions; against "aloofness" from the people; and against the use of the party membership card for selfish interests. He also admitted that "the main flaw which has been causing us some worry . . . has been the failure to comply strictly with the directions of the Revolution"[6]—a criticism that may hint at difficulties between the party and professional civil servants. More directly, President Bakr stressed the importance of "exercising supervision over the state organs charged with executing the programmes of the party."[7]

It is against this background that the Revolutionary Command Council (RCC)—formally the sovereign body of the Republic—ordered the seizure in February 1978 of the movable and immovable property of 13 prominent Ba'thi lawyers and banned them from practising law. A non-Iraqi source reported that this action was only part of a large-scale purge involving 1,000 officials, many of whom were Ba'thi members.[8] Towards mid-1978, rumours increasingly spoke of a power struggle within the party leadership itself, the main antagonists supposedly being President Bakr and Saddām Ḥusayn. (Reports of rivalry between them are almost as old as the regime itself, but have never been sufficiently corroborated. To all appearances, Ḥusayn is the ailing Bakr's recognized heir.)

During the period under review, the Council of Ministers was reshuffled three times: in October and November 1977, and again in February 1978 (for its composition, see Table II). By far the most important—and, to some, surprising—change was that of October 1977 when Bakr gave up his own post as Defence Minister, which he had held for six years, to Col (*'aqīd*) 'Adnān Khayrallah Talfāḥ. This move was not as sudden as it appeared, however, since Talfāḥ had in practice already replaced him some months earlier. The appointment could be regarded as safe from the regime's viewpoint since Talfāḥ is Bakr's son-in-law and Saddām Ḥusayn's foster brother, brother-in-law and cousin. Furthermore, while Talfāḥ thus became their chief agent in the armed forces, they continued to keep close tabs on it behind the scenes. The November 1977 reshuffle also introduced a new ministry, that of Culture and Arts, and further reduced the influence of Kurds in the Council by relegating the Minister of Transport, 'Azīz Rashīd 'Aqrāwī, to the lower status of Minister of State. The February 1978 reshuffle introduced a leading Ba'thi member, Muḥammad 'Āyish, into the Council in place of an "independent" minister.

515

Table II

The Council of Ministers as of 4 September 1977, and Subsequent Changes (until November 1978)

Portfolio	Incumbent on 4 September 1977	New Incumbent	Date of change	Remarks
Chief of the Executive Authority	Field-Marshal Ahmad Hasan al-Bakr			
Ministers				
Defence	Field-Marshal Ahmad Hasan al-Bakr	Col 'Adnān Khayrallah (Talfāh)	15.10.77	Ba'th; member of the RCC and the Ba'th Regional Command
Interior	'Izzat Ibrāhīm (al-Dūrī)			
Oil	Tāyih 'Abd al-Karīm			
Communication	Sa'dūn Ghaydān			
Foreign Affairs	Sa'dūn Hammādī			
Public Works and Housing	Taha Yāsīn Ramadān (al-Jazrāwī)			
Transport	'Aziz Rashīd 'Aqrāwī	Makram Jamāl (al-Tālabānī)	12.11.77	Kurd; Central Committee member of the ICP
Information	Tāriq 'Azīz	Sa'd Qāsim Hammūdi	15.10.77	Ba'th
Finance	Fawzī 'Abdallah (al-Qaysī)			
Agriculture and Agrarian Reform	Latif Nasif al-Jāsim			
Industry and Minerals	Nājih Muhammad Khalil	Muhammad 'Āyish	18.2.78	Ba'th; member of the RCC and the Ba'th Regional Command
Health	Riyād Ibrāhīm Husayn			
Justice	Mundhir Ibrāhīm (al-Shāwī)			
Labour and Social Affairs	Bakr Mahmūd Rasūl (Bābakr al-Phishdārī)			
Trade	Hasan 'Alī (al-'Āmirī)			
Planning	'Adnān Husayn (al-Hamdānī)			

Portfolio	Incumbent on 4 September 1977	New Incumbent	Date of change	Remarks
Youth	Karīm Maḥmūd Ḥusayn (al-Mullā)			
Higher Education and Scientific Research	Muḥammad Ṣādiq al-Mashshāṭ	ʿAdnān Ḥusayn (al-Ḥamdānī) in an acting capacity	18.2.78	Replaced on 2 April by ʿIsām ʿAbd ʿAlī
Education	Muḥammad Maḥjūb			
Waqfs	Aḥmad ʿAbd al-Sattār al-Jawārī			
Irrigation	Makram Jamāl (al-Ṭālabānī)	ʿAbd al-Wahhāb Maḥmūd ʿAbdallah	12.11.77	
Minister of State for Foreign Affairs	Ḥāmid ʿAlwān (al-Jubūrī)			
Minister of State for Kurdish Affairs	Burhān al-Dīn Muṣṭafā (ʿAbd al-Raḥmān)	Khālid ʿAbd ʿUthmān	18.2.78	Baʿth
Minister of Culture and Arts		Saʿd Qāsim Ḥammūdī in an acting capacity	15.10.77	Replaced on 12 November 1977 by the Baʿthi Karīm Maḥmūd Shintāf
Minister of State	ʿUbaydallah Muṣṭafā al-Barzānī			
Minister of State	ʿĀmir ʿAbdallah	Hāshim Ḥasan [ʿAqrāwī]	12.11.77	Kurd; Secretary of the KDP and member of the autonomous Legislative Council
Minister of State	ʿAzīz Rashīd ʿAqrāwī			
Minister of State	ʿAbdallah Ismāʿīl Aḥmad			

1 The Ministry of Culture and Arts was formed on 15 October 1977.
2 For remarks on the ministers on the Council on 4 September 1977, see MECS 1976–77, pp. 406–7.

517

On the whole, these reshuffles signified the ascendance of younger Ba'thi members. In addition, some ministers were so in name only, with actual authority vesting with certain leading party members. This was particularly true in the Foreign Ministry. Less glaring examples occurred in the Ministries of Interior and Information.

ARMY AND SECURITY

The Ba'th party has consistently attempted to subordinate the army to its own interests and principles. Thus, army "interference" in politics, as understood by the Iraqi Ba'th leaders, has only been allowed insofar as it served the ends of the party. Another prime principle is that no other party may have a foothold in the army: as early as 1971, a law provided the death penalty for political activity within the armed forces outside of the Ba'th party.

Nevertheless, there were a number of indications that, though widely applied, the Ba'thi formula continued to meet with objections and opposition. The recurrent theme in speeches to the armed forces by Bakr, Saddām Husayn and political guidance officers was the need to propagate further the party's principles and concepts among its ranks. In a speech on 6 October 1977 at the Staff College, Saddām Husayn said: "We reject the concept of a professional [i.e. non-political] army as understood and worked for by the Rightists. . . . We reject the slogan of military non-interference in politics, and consider it dangerous and an imperialist-reactionary plot against the nation."[9] At the end of May 1978, two remarkable articles entitled "Political Activity within the Armed Forces" appeared in the Ba'th party organ, al-Thawra. Both emphasized that the army was an exclusive field of the Ba'th party and warned that any other element attempting to break this basic rule would face severe punishment. The armed forces "should abide by the will of the leader party not only because the party is the trustee [literally: owner] of the revolution, but because the armed forces cannot be a field for political competition and rivalries for party gains and blocs and counter-blocs."[10]

At the beginning of June, an Iraqi official disclosed that 21 Communists accused of forming secret cells in the army had been executed (see below). Various sources reported large-scale purges throughout the period under review, the last being the dismissals in mid-1978 of two divisional commanders and the commander of the air force; the execution of nearly 60 army personnel, and the dismissal of c. 300 police officers.[11] Changes in the military office of the Ba'th party were reported in September 1978. (This is the authority which supervises party control over the armed forces.) Among possible causes behind the disaffection of some army personnel were: opposition to the Ba'thization of the army; objection to the policy of diversification of the sources of arms (see below);[12] and bitterness over the promotion of 'Adnān Khayrallah Talfāh as Minister of Defence over the heads of other officers holding higher ranks. Moreover, in April 1978 he was promoted directly from Col ('aqīd) to Gen (farīq awwal)—thus bypassing three grades.

The Iraqi leadership's major preoccupation has been and remains the regime's security and stability. In a significant metaphor, Saddām Husayn likened Iraq to a man with his house in a forest; though possessing a gun, this man should still lock his door: "The public and the party must make certain that they do lock their doors. This must not be taken as a sign of fright."[13] Bakr, for his part, called on Iraqi journalists to shoulder their responsibilities "in safeguarding the citizens from the ideological poisons and the counter-psychological war."[14]

A number of laws and decrees issued in this period reflected the regime's preoccupation with security. On 7 December 1977, the RCC issued a decree pardoning political refugees abroad, including Kurds, provided they returned to Iraq within two months. The decree was extended in March. Though presented as proof of the regime's liberalism, a likely explanation is that it reflected a wish to have political refugees safely at home. A decree issued in May 1978 provided that all residents — Iraqis, non-Iraqi Arabs and foreigners—should fill in a special form giving personal particulars. The evident purpose was to enable internal security services to exercise tighter control. At the beginning of July 1978, the RCC made it a capital crime for retired army and police personnel, as well as former servicemen, to work for party or political organizations other than the Ba'th. On the other hand, on the occasion of the tenth anniversary of the July Celebrations, the RCC granted amnesty to c. 7,000 prisoners (among them 266 politicals).[15] On 13 July 1978, the chief of Iraqi intelligence, Sa'dūn Shākir, disclosed that spy networks had been discovered and that their members had been punished. (The discovery of spy networks—real or imaginary—is a measure of the regime's internal difficulties, or at least a measure of its nervousness, and usually ushers in a wave of reprisals against centres of disaffection.)

It was apparently against this background that the former Premier, 'Abd al-Razzāq al-Nāyif, was assassinated on 9 July in London. While Iraqi news media maintained complete silence on the subject, other sources claimed that Iraqi intelligence was behind the murder. The British authorities certainly acted on this assumption (see below). Nāyif had long been one of the regime's targets. A fortnight after his participation in the 17 July 1968 coup, he was forced out of his post as Prime Minister in yet another coup. In 1971 he was sentenced to death *in absentia* on charges of plotting against the revolution and in 1972 an unsuccessful attempt was made on his life in London. It is difficult to establish whether Nāyif really kept "plotting" against the regime, or whether he was deliberately chosen to serve as a warning. Neither possibility excludes the other. Nāyif's assassination served to focus international attention on the spread of Iraqi intelligence operations. It was also the first link in a chain of terror and counter-terror outside Iraq, which for the first time affected Iraqi officials and property abroad. (For further details see below, and the chapter on the Palestine Liberation Organization.)

At the beginning of September 1978, the Iraqi Ambassador to Sweden, Maj-Gen (*liwā'*) Hasan al-Naqīb, joined the PLO and was appointed a PLO military adviser. He had been retired from the army in 1970 when he was Assistant Chief of Staff. In the same year, as commander of the Iraqi contingent then in Jordan, he had favoured armed intervention on the side of the PLO. Naqīb did not disclose his motives for this latest move, saying only: "Today I see it as my duty to actually participate in the battle."[16] It is likely that strained relations with the Iraqi leadership were behind the move.

THE COMMUNIST PARTY
Ever since 1973, when the ICP joined the Ba'th party in the Progressive Patriotic and Nationalist Front (PPNF), it appears to have followed the Ba'th party in all matters — for the sake of retaining its legal status. Whatever disagreements may have existed did not come to the surface. However, this picture suddenly changed in May 1978 when reports in the Arab and Western press (leaked via Soviet sources),[17] revealed a conflict between the ICP and the Ba'th. The sources disagreed as to the dimensions of the conflict: some reported the execution of 21 Communists; others claimed 40 dead, 1,000 ICP members arrested, as well as Ba'thi demands for a change in the ICP leadership. The official Iraqi account, published at the beginning of June, admitted the execution of 21 Communists on the charge of forming secret cells within the army.

The roots of this particular conflict go back two months when, on 10 March 1978, the ICP Central Committee discussed and approved its political report. Quoting *Tarīq al-Sha'b*, the ICP organ, the Iraqi News Agency claimed that the report praised the revolution's achievements in all spheres, including the PPNF.[18] In mid-April, a conference of Communist parties from different Arab countries was held in Baghdad; again the Iraqi account did not disclose any differences between the regime and the ICP. However, on 4 May, *al-Rāsid*, an Iraqi provincial weekly, published a harsh indictment of the ICP and its political report. It claimed that the report criticized Ba'thi policies on both local and international levels. On the home front, the report accused the regime of persecuting the Communists and of neglecting the Kurdish issue; on the external front it criticized the regime's stand on the Arab-Israeli and the Eritrean-Ethiopian conflicts, and on the question of Soviet-Chinese relations. *Al-Rāsid*, in turn, accused the ICP of attempting to drive a wedge between the Kurdish people and the government, of undermining the PPNF, of blindly following Soviet policy, and of disregarding Iraqi national interests.[19] Then, on 28 and 29 May, came the attack of the Ba'th party organ *al-Thawra* on the other partners of the PPNF, in particular the ICP though it was not mentioned by name. The gist of this attack was as follows: the partners of the PPNF should accept the leading role of the Ba'th; the PPNF formula could not exist within the armed forces; and the partners had accepted these conditions before joining the PPNF. Hence, any attempt to dispute this formula amounted to plotting against the revolution.[20]

Various questions arose as to the whole affair: (1) the discrepancy between the original INA account of the ICP political report and that of *al-Rāsid* almost two months later; (2) the fact that *al-Rāsid*'s charges against the ICP contained no accusation of plotting within the armed forces; and (3) Saddām Husayn's disclosure on 17 July that those executed had been sentenced three years earlier and that the timing of the executions was political. A possible explanation of the conflict may be, firstly, that the differences between the ICP and the Ba'th stem from one fundamental factor, namely the Ba'th aim to turn the country into a one-party state; and secondly, that the regime chose to keep those differences secret so as not to arouse suspicions about its stability. When the news did leak out, official reaction was slow and not greatly publicized, for the same reasons. The causes and timing of the executions may have been determined to serve as a warning or a diversion at that particular stage of the confrontation. Possible factors accounting for this were: disaffection in the army (see above) or in other sectors not necessarily connected with Communist activity; the regime's fear of a pro-Communist coup similar to the one that had taken place in April 1978 in Afghanistan; and, lastly, a signal to Moscow that Iraq would not let its policy be influenced by Soviet susceptibilities (see below).

Following the executions, ICP-Ba'th relations remained ambiguous. Iraqi sources reported that relations had returned to normal, that PPNF meetings were resumed, and that congratulatory cables were exchanged on suitable occasions. However, the pro-Iraqi *al-Dustūr* (published in London), continued to attack the ICP, saying that it had not given up its "old methods of fishing in troubled waters."[21] On the other hand, there were reports suggesting that a section of the ICP had gone underground; that persecuted Communists had fled to the north and were collaborating with Kurdish insurgents; and that three Communists had been assassinated at the beginning of August in Sulaymāniyya. There was no information about the underground ICP-"Central Command" faction which had never abandoned its total hostility to the Ba'th regime.

THE KURDS

As in previous years, the regime continued its policy of placating the Kurdish population on non-vital issues, but of ruthlessly uprooting nuclei of Kurdish disaffection. The principle of "absolute faith in the unity of Iraq" reigned supreme (see below). On the whole, it seems that the Kurds were treated more harshly than in 1976-77, and that attempts at conciliation were given less emphasis.

The second session of the Legislative Council for the Kurdish "Autonomous Region" was opened in October 1977, followed by the formation of the Executive Council. The extent to which these bodies represented the national will of the Kurds may be gathered from the fact that the Legislative Council was appointed by the RCC, while the chairman of the Executive Council, Aḥmad 'Abd al-Qādir [al-Naqshbandī], was appointed by President Bakr. (The Autonomy Law of 1974 stipulated that "the Legislative Council shall be the *elected* legislative authority of the Region.")[22] In November 1977, the RCC decreed that apart from the study of the Arabic language, 40% of all other subjects should be taught in Arabic. Commenting on this decision, *al-Thawra* said it would enable Kurdish students to pursue university level education or to enter government or private employment anywhere in Iraq. It went on to say that the decision was motivated "by an absolute faith in the unity of Iraq."[23] The decision of December 1977 to pardon political refugees (see above) appeared to be motivated by the regime's attempt to curb Kurdish insurgents' activities abroad on the one hand, and to comply with the Iranian demand for the resettling of Kurdish refugees from Iran on the other.

The Iraqi news media widely publicized the development plans initiated in the area and the huge allocations voted for them. In June, Sa'd Qāsim Ḥammūdī, the Information Minister, stated that allocations for development in the Kurdish area had risen from ID 211m in 1977 to ID 690m in 1978.[24] The actual projects referred to in the Iraqi media indicated that a major part of the additional allocation had been used for the construction of more strategic roads and for building a large number of villages for families evacuated from border areas. Later, Saddām Husayn admitted to these population transfers, explaining that they were necessary to provide the villagers with "the requirements of progress and civilization."[25] 28,000 Kurdish villagers were reportedly involved in the resettlement which served to cut off the sources of supply and support from Kurdish insurgents operating across the Syrian, Turkish and Iranian borders. As part of this campaign, the government was reported to have used incendiary bombs to help create a 180-mile buffer-zone along its frontier with Turkey; this followed intense clashes with Kurdish insurgents in June 1978. Apart from these operational objectives, the regime undoubtedly welcomed the introduction of Arabs into the Kurdish region. As Saddām Husayn explained, there was no law preventing Kurds from moving to predominantly Arab areas, or Arabs to predominantly Kurdish areas.[26]

In April 1978, there were reports of large-scale army movements in the north. This coincided with reports of fighting between Iraqi units and Kurdish insurgents, which started in April and grew in intensity in the following months. According to Turkish sources, the fighting resulted in c. 1,000 Kurds and Iraqi soldiers killed; eight Iraqi helicopters shot down; nine Kurdish villages burnt and 26 villages evacuated. Iraqi officials denied the reports, however, claiming that the situation in the north was quiet and stable. Only one case was admitted: the execution of "a few dozen" spies and ten "terrorists" who were said to have carried out bombings and assassinations in Sulaymāniyya in April.[27] Saddām Husayn, while acknowledging that Kurds had infiltrated across the borders, said that such cases "will not disturb Iraq—even if they last for another 20 years."[28]

Developments inside the Kurdish movement showed that certain groups continued to co-operate with the regime, while others relied on the support of neighbouring countries, becoming a pawn in their hands. Thus, when talks of *rapprochement* between Iraq and Syria were underway in December 1977–January 1978 (see essay on Inter-Arab Relations), the Syrian-based Patriotic Union of Kurdistan (PUK) was reported to have been told to stop its activity and to start negotiating with the Iraqi regime. Nothing came immediately of either negotiation: the PUK renewed its activity, and the Syrians were duly denounced by the Iraqi government. Similarly, differences with Turkey over its oil debt to Iraq were reported to have encouraged the former to turn a blind eye to Kurdish activity across the border. Later, however, a security accord between Turkey and Iraq allowed Iraqi aircraft to attack fleeing Kurds inside Turkish territory. Possibly more serious from the Kurdish viewpoint, in mid-1978 much of the fighting was between the PUK, headed by Jalāl Tālabānī, and remnants of the pro-Barzānī Kurdish Democratic Party. The regime's part in this affair is not known.

SHĪ'Ī AND OTHER GROUPS
In contrast with the high "visibility" of the Kurds, the Shī'īs—the other major group which has been the cause of recent troubles—appeared to have been silenced (see *MECS 1976–77*, pp. 405–8). The only residue of those troubles were the visits of officials to the holy shrines, allocations for their maintenance, and the "reproduction" in June of Saddām Husayn's 1977 speech warning against the involvement of religion in politics.

In January 1978, a group of 35 Assyrians (who according to some sources posed as Armenians) fled the country to seek asylum in the US, accusing the Iraqi regime of religious intolerance. One of the refugees complained to the *New York Times*: "We do not feel there [in Iraq] as Christians. We cannot wear the cross. They don't want us to speak Armenian. Most of us were beaten."[29] An Iraqi Foreign Ministry spokesman described this claim as utterly groundless, and Iraqi Christian community leaders were said to have joined the government in condemning the group.

The amnesty granted to prisoners in July (see above) explicitly excluded Bahais and "freemasons." No official explanation was given.

THE ARAB-ISRAELI CONFLICT
The essence of the Iraqi regime's stand on the Arab-Israeli conflict, which it presents as principled and immovable, is the total rejection of any "political" settlement. Ultimately, the solution lies in an all-out military struggle aimed at uprooting Zionism from the area. Furthermore, Iraqi spokesmen claim that the issue is so central to the country that it has become the main criterion for determining Iraq's international relations. This stand has its practical aspects. At home, it is a popular rallying cry and presents the army with an objective and a challenge. On the pan-Arab level, this intransigence—surpassing that of any other Arab country—enhances Iraq's claim to play a leading role in the Arab world. On the international level, the rejection of Israel's right to exist is a means of asserting Iraqi independence from the USSR.

The regime took some spectacular actions, mostly of a propagandist nature, in relation to Sādāt's peace initiative. (For details, see essays on the Arab-Israeli Conflict and Inter-Arab Relations.) Before his visit to Jerusalem, the National Command issued a statement warning Sādāt against such unilateral action which, it said, would be a pan-Arab catastrophe. At the same time, the 'Īd al-Adhā celebrations were cancelled; mass demonstrations were held calling for Sādāt's downfall; and anti-Sādāt propaganda campaigns were launched, ranging from editorial attacks to posters showing Sādāt hanged. Operationally, however, the

Iraqi regime did almost nothing to stop the initiative or to promote its failure. In fact, by boycotting the Tripoli and Algiers conferences, convened in the wake of Sādāt's visit to Jerusalem, it impeded the creation of a viable anti-Sādāt front. Alone among the five "rejectionist" states (Syria, Algeria, Libya and the PDRY), it gradually restored its diplomatic relations with Egypt (soon after they were severed by Sādāt in December 1977) to almost their former level. Only the ambassadors themselves did not return to their posts. This gulf between Iraqi claims and performance was naturally exploited by rivals, and especially by Syria. The Iraqi regime was described as hypocritical and self-interested. It was also accused of collaborating behind the scenes with Sādāt, while using the Palestine cause as a cover for its inter-Arab feuds.

Iraqi officials and news media argued that the Sādāt mission was the result of the "capitulationist" course which had begun with the recognition of Resolutions 242 and 338, and in which several parties participated, chief among them Syria—but never Iraq. Sādāt's course was wrong, but Iraq did not wish to isolate the Egyptian people (hence the resumption of relations). The conferences had been boycotted because they ultimately endorsed a political settlement. Iraq, for its part, remained faithful to the military struggle for which it was ready to involve all its national resources. The best proof, spokesmen maintained, was the detailed programme of action proposed by Iraq to the Tripoli bloc countries which, if accepted, would have activated the struggle against Israel in earnest. (For details of the programme, see essay on the Negotiating Process.) Iraq's much-publicized aid to Lebanon in the wake of Israel's intervention in March 1978 was also depicted as a genuine adherence to the line of all-out struggle. (For details on the intervention, see essay on South Lebanon and chapter on Lebanon.) Above all, it was maintained that Iraq would put all differences aside and come to Syria's rescue if it was attacked by Israel, just as it had done in 1973.

Although it is difficult to predict Iraq's attitude in such an eventuality, one fact is beyond doubt: the Iraqi army is being steadily strengthened, to the extent of an envisaged nuclear capability. It can safely be assumed that one of the targets for this expanded army would be Israel. (For a breakdown of Iraq's armed forces, see end of this chapter.)

As in former years, the Iraqi government continued to back and give sanctuary to the "rejectionists" and anti-'Arafāt splinter groups of the Palestine Liberation Organization (PLO). Chief among these was the "Black June" group of Abū Nidāl (real name: Sabrī al-Banna), whom a PLO court sentenced to death in 1974 for plotting to assassinate Yāsir 'Arafāt. However, the sponsorship given to these factions, over the bitter protests of 'Arafāt and his group, had its non-ideological aspects. The regime was said to have used Abū Nidāl's group for very practical purposes: firstly, to curb the power of the so-called moderate factions within the PLO which, since Sādāt's initiative, had become more dependent upon Syria; and secondly, to strike at Syrian targets.

It is against this background of rivalry, both among the Palestinian organizations themselves and between Iraq and Syria, that signs of deterioration in the relations between Iraq and al-Fath surfaced in April 1978. This deterioration reached its lowest point in July and August 1978 when both parties became engaged in a terror and counter-terror campaign in various countries abroad. (For a detailed account of this, see essay on the PLO.) It is difficult to ascertain which of the parties initiated this campaign or what specific incident provoked it. However, some signposts can be noted. In April 1978, Abū Nidāl announced that 'Arafāt's end was at hand. In May, PLO leaders declared that *all* the Arab countries had abandoned the Palestinians; Iraq protested and cited the help it gave to the Palestinians in

Lebanon. Following the assassination of the PLO representative in Kuwait in June (see essay on the PLO), al-Fath accused the Iraqi government of responsibility and demanded that Abū Nidāl be handed over to it. At the same time an Iraqi Ba'th party plan was reported to have been uncovered by Fath involving the assassination of certain Fath leaders for their collaboration with Syria. [30] Fath reacted by accusing Iraq of attempting to interfere in its affairs by closing its offices in Iraq and withdrawing funds. Fath also claimed that by boycotting the Tripoli and Algiers conferences, Iraq had prevented "the birth of an Arab military strike force which would have frustrated Sādāt's capitulationist course." [31] Fath pamphlets portrayed Saddām Husayn as a professional killer. Iraq's official reaction came only after the first wave of the terrorist campaign at the beginning of August. An official spokesman, while refuting charges of involvement in the conflict, blamed "some reactionary and capitulationist leaders within Fath and the PLO" for engagement in a campaign of "slander against the Iraqi Ba'th party and government." A warning accompanied this reply. [32] In mid-August there were reports of mediation between the two sides. Although the physical attacks seemed to have stopped, verbal assaults continued well into September. (For an Iraqi ex-officer's decision to join the PLO, see above.)

RELATIONS WITH ARAB AND NEIGHBOURING COUNTRIES

As in previous years, and perhaps to a greater extent, the Ba'th party continued to promote its vision of the pan-Arab ideal: the Iraqi Ba'th is a solid base for the movement of the Arab revolution; it cannot limit itself to Iraq alone; the Arab world is ready to accept the leading role of the Ba'th. Michel 'Aflaq declared that "the entire Arab homeland is now ready, although at different levels, to look up to our party as its example," adding that "the party cannot accept limited objectives." [33] Similarly, Taha Yāsīn Ramadān [al-Jazrāwī], a member of both the Regional and National Command of the party, asserted that "the Ba'th party is not only for the Iraqis; it is for all the Arabs." He went on to say that "the present situation, scientifically and practically speaking, is favourable to our expansion." [34] In a speech marking the July anniversary celebrations, President Bakr also declared that "the central objective in which all our potentials and endeavours are pooled" is to make of Iraq "a solid and active base for the movement of the Arab Revolution." [35]

Sādāt's visit to Jerusalem seemed to present the Iraqi regime with an opportunity to assume a leading role in the Arab world, or at least to introduce itself into one of its systems, namely the anti-Sādāt Tripoli bloc. The following moves can be seen as part of Iraq's attempt to seize this opportunity. Iraq was the first Arab country officially to condemn Sādāt's visit—even before it took place—and later prided itself on this achievement. Iraq made repeated attempts to hold the anti-Sādāt front meetings in Baghdad. Subsequently, the regime took pains to point out that it alone had put forward a "programme of action" at the Tripoli bloc meeting. The factors which characterized Iraqi policies at the Tripoli conference in December 1977 may be summarized as follows: (1) a feeling of frustration that the conference was not held in Baghdad; (2) traditional extremism in the Arab-Israeli conflict; (3) bitter rivalry with Syria which Sādāt's visit had not mitigated, and (4) the hope to isolate Syria. (For a detailed account of this conference and the subsequent one in Algiers, as well as for Iraq's stand on the anti-Sādāt front, see essay on Inter-Arab Relations.)

However, by the time of the Algiers conference in February 1978, it became clear that Iraq felt it was more advantageous to leave the Front. Having been thwarted in its second attempt to hold the conference in Baghdad, Iraq boycotted the Algiers conference from the outset. On the other hand, Iraq's radicalism had been thrown into relief by the "capitulatory tendency" manifested by the partners of the Tripoli bloc. The attempts to patch up differences between Iraq and Syria in the interval of the Tripoli and Algiers conferences failed, as did the attempt to isolate Syria. The net result was Iraq's increased isolation from any Arab system. Iraq officials argued, however, that it was not isolated but following an independent path. Moreover, the Arab masses were fully behind the Iraqi stand—and that was what mattered.

In the realm of bilateral relations, Iraqi policy was flexible and far removed from its ideological rhetoric. The resumption of relations with Egypt is one case in point. Leaving aside the official explanation of Iraq's unwillingness to isolate the Egyptian people, as well as the political advantage of playing the Egyptian card against Syria, it is quite clear that an important motive was the desire to expand economic relations with Egypt. Iraqi trade with Egypt is now bigger in volume than with any other Arab country. By the same token differences with Jordan over Iraq's execution of a Jordanian student in September 1977 were quickly smoothed over in view of Iraq's growing transport difficulties through Syria. On the whole, Iraq succeeded in expanding its economic and cultural relations with all the Arab countries up to October 1978, with the exception of Syria. Although relations with Damascus continued to be as bad as ever, diplomatic links were still maintained. (For details, see essay on Inter-Arab Relations. For developments subsequent to the period covered in this chapter, see essay, "The Year in Perspective.")

RELATIONS WITH TURKEY
Three different factors were at play in Iraqi-Turkish relations during the period under review: Iraqi-Syrian relations, the Kurdish issue and oil. Following the ban imposed by Syria in November 1977 on the passage of Iraqi goods from Turkish ports across Syrian territory (see essay on Inter-Arab Relations), the Turkish government took upon itself to transport the majority of these goods through alternative channels. This further accentuated Iraq's dependence on Turkey's Mediterranean outlets and its land routes. Similarly, the curbing of Kurdish activity across the Turkish border (see above) required Ankara's co-operation and goodwill. Although these two factors improved Turkey's bargaining position with regard to its oil debt to Iraq, they did not seem to remove the problem. Iraq stopped its oil supplies to Turkey in November 1977 because of a debt which amounted to $330m by July 1978. However, on 25 August 1978, the Turkish Minister of Energy announced that Iraq had agreed to resume supplies. Turkey was to pay its debt to Iraq in kind (including 400 buses and supplies of wheat), hopefully by 1981. (For the closure of the Turkish Cultural Centre in Kirkūk, see chapter on Turkey.)

THE PERSIAN GULF
The vulnerability of Iraq's north-western flank (no sea outlet, bad relations with Syria) led to a shift of attention to the Persian Gulf in recent years. In the words of one of its leaders: "Iraq is the largest, the strongest Arab country in the whole eastern part of the Arab world. We have a large population, resources, military strength, independence." [36] Largely in consequence, Iraq considers itself a major Gulf power. The "offensive of goodwill" initiated towards the Gulf countries in 1977 deepened further in 1978 (cf *MECS 1976–77*, p. 413). At the same time, Iraq continued to object to any Gulf security pact (see chapter on the Gulf states), though it did call for freedom of navigation, the solution of problems through bilateral agreements, and non-interference by outside powers. To Iraq, the region's stability (including that of the conservative regimes) has become paramount. The

call to preserve the Arab character of the Gulf was maintained but less emphasized in view of improved relations with Iran.

RELATIONS WITH IRAN
The Kurdish Vice-President of Iraq described relations with Iran as "a model of neighbourliness . . . based on mutual respect and non-interference in domestic affairs." [37] On the whole, the period under review was marked by frequent high-level official visits and the signing of various agreements. The visits included that in October 1977 by the Iranian commanders of the air force and the navy; that in November 1977 of the Iraqi Vice-President, Taha Muhyī al-Dīn Ma'rūf, to Tehran; and those in February 1978 of the Iranian Chief of Staff and the Iranian Foreign Minister to Baghdad. The agreements included the regulation of Iranian pilgrimage to the holy shrines in Iraq; the setting up of trade centres; the planning of railway lines; and co-operation in the fields of oil, agriculture and fishing. The common fear in Tehran and Baghdad of a pro-Communist coup, similar to the one which took place in April 1978 in Afghanistan, may be assumed to have given further impetus to these developments.

It is difficult to assess as yet whether Iraq had a role in the Shī'ī disturbances in Iran. (For details of these events, see chapter on Iran and essay on the Red Sea, Persian Gulf and Indian Ocean.) Reports at the end of September 1978 that the Iraqi authorities had put Ayatollah Khomeyni—then in asylum in Iraq—under house arrest showed the regime's interest in maintaining good relations with Iran. If true, the detention may also indicate the regime's fear of the riots spreading to Iraq. Khomeyni was later induced to leave Iraq and go to France. (For the Shī'ī riots in Iraq in 1977, see *MECS 1976–77*, pp. 405, 408.)

RELATIONS WITH KUWAIT
Relations with Kuwait followed the trend established in 1976–77. Official visits were exchanged, resulting in agreements for the construction of a railroad to connect the two countries, and for co-operation in cultural, scientific, information and agricultural fields. The acute problem of the frontier, if discussed, was not mentioned among these agreements (see *MECS 1976–77*, p. 413). The visit of the Kuwaiti Commander of border forces in July 1978 might have been connected with this problem, but again no results were made public.

RELATIONS WITH SAUDI ARABIA
Iraqi-Saudi relations were also marked by visits of high-ranking officials, the most important being that of the Saudi Defence Minister to Iraq in April 1978, when Gulf security was believed to have been the central topic for discussion. It is not known whether any agreement was reached. On the whole, the *rapprochement* between these two regimes appeared to have made progress in 1978.

INTERNATIONAL RELATIONS
THE USSR AND THE EASTERN BLOC
Following the execution of the 21 Iraqi Communists, probably in May (see above), Arab and Western papers reported a crisis in Iraqi-Soviet relations and an imminent abrogation of the 1972 Friendship Treaty. However, this did not materialize. Iraqi officials denied the existence of a crisis between the two countries and asserted that theirs was a strategic alliance. But despite these statements, it seemed that Iraqi policy was in fact gearing for a gradual and cautious cooling in relations.

Though this trend had begun some time earlier (1975), it gathered new impetus in 1978 owing to an accumulation of differences over various issues. To start with, the

Soviet Union supported the rejectionist conferences in Tripoli and Algiers, a stand which Iraq interpreted as pro-Syrian. In April 1978, the Iraqi authorities, suspecting the Soviets of electronic eavesdropping, requested that the Soviet embassy move from its present situation near the Presidential palace—the regime's nerve centre—to a new location. The pro-Soviet coup in Afghanistan in the same month aroused the regime's anxiety and was reported to be one of the causes for the executions of the Iraqi Communists. In an interview to *Newsweek*, Saddām Husayn admitted that the executions had been carried out despite the Soviet ambassador's appeal that the men's lives be spared; moreover, they were intended as a warning to Moscow against meddling in Iraq's internal affairs. In what appeared to be a warning against Soviet activity in the Persian Gulf and the Horn of Africa, he said that the Soviets "won't be satisfied until the whole world becomes Communist." He continued: "By allowing ourselves to be drawn into spheres of influence, we Arabs are ensuring that we will become an East-West battlefield." [38] In fact, the situation in the Horn of Africa further complicated Soviet-Iraqi relations: though tied by a Friendship Treaty, the two countries found themselves supporting opposite sides, Iraq the Eritreans, and the USSR Ethiopia. (For a more detailed discussion of Arab attitudes on the Horn of Africa, see essay on Inter-Arab Relations.)

In May 1978, an Iraqi warning that the Soviet Union should stop supporting Ethiopia against the Eritrean rebels was coupled with a ban on the overflight of a Soviet airlift destined for Ethiopia. [39] At the same time, Iraq's disenchantment with Soviet technology led it to expand its economic relations with the West at the expense of those with the East. Soviet interests were dealt a blow by the Iraqi decision to embark on a diversification of arms sources (see below), which official declarations confirmed was meant to guarantee Iraq's independent path. Although the Iraqi-Soviet Friendship Treaty continued in being, its significance appeared to have declined.

There were no marked changes in Iraq's relations with other East European countries, with the exception of Poland. Following the Polish celebrations on 18 April 1978 of the thirty-fifth anniversary of the Jewish Ghetto uprising, the Iraqi authorities decided to ban the travel of Iraqis to Poland during 1978, allegedly because of maltreatment of some of its citizens. This was followed by an attack on Poland by *al-Jumhūriyya* because of what it described as a "serious change in the government's policy toward the racist Zionist entity." [40] The attack was surprising, less because of its content than because of its timing—coming more than one month after the celebrations—which indicated that it had been politically motivated (perhaps by strains with the USSR). By June, however, there were again exchanges of visits and talks on strengthening relations.

RELATIONS WITH CHINA
Iraq's endeavours to maintain an element of independence in its policy *vis-à-vis* the USSR also caused it to develop relations with China, especially in the economic field. There were various exchanges of visits in 1978, the most important being that of the Chinese Oil Industry Minister in July. He discussed with Saddām Husayn ways to strengthen co-operation between the two countries' oil industries.

RELATIONS WITH WESTERN COUNTRIES
Iraq makes an official distinction between those Western countries which it considers to be "friends" of the Arabs (such as France and Spain), and the "pro-Zionists" and "imperialist" countries (such as the US). Iraqi spokesmen continued to maintain that it was ready to co-operate on all levels with the former group, but only in the economic sphere with the latter. In April 1978, however, the RCC

decided to establish "friendship societies" with ten Western countries, including such "pro-Zionists" as Holland and the US. In any case, the distinction served to leave the door open for taking advantage of superior US technology. According to the London *Observer*, the US had replaced the USSR as early as 1976 as the chief supplier of Iraq's non-military imports.[41]

There was also a marked shift in Iraq's arms purchasing policy in 1978, when almost half its acquisitions were reported to have been made in the West.[42] Military supplies had been almost a Soviet monopoly since 1959. Contracts for purchases included 72 *Alouette* missile-firing helicopters, an unspecified number of *Crotal I* surface-to-air missiles and electronic equipment from France; 500 armoured vehicles and 200 tanks from Brazil; and 50 armoured cars from Spain. Talks were also underway for purchases from West Germany, Belgium and Italy.[43]

Relations with Spain (which in 1976 had refused to establish diplomatic relations with Israel) were given special attention in 1978. This was marked by exchanges of high-level official visits including that of King Juan Carlos in June 1978. Oil and military hardware were the main subjects of negotiation.

Relations with France continued to flourish. Besides further military purchases negotiated during the French Defence Minister's visit in June 1978, France was reported to have supplied Iraq (sometime in 1978) with enriched uranium for its atomic reactor at present under construction. This "bomb-quality" uranium was given despite US protests. At the end of July, relations between France and Iraq became strained for a time when an Iraqi security man killed a French policeman following an attack, probably by al-Fatḥ members, on the Iraqi embassy in Paris (see essay on the LO). However, relations soon returned to normal.

When faced with a similar problem, relations with Britain fared otherwise. In May 1978, diplomatic tension was created following the beating up in Iraq of a British diplomat by Iraqi security officials. Britain made representations at ministerial level. On 26 July 1978, following the assassination of 'Abd al-Razzāq al-Nāyif in London (see above), the British government declared 11 Iraqi officials, among them five diplomats, *personae non gratae*. The official British announcement explained that "the presence in London of known Iraqi intelligence officers has led us to the conclusion that it would be best that they should leave."[44] On the following day, Iraq retaliated by expelling ten British officials, among them eight diplomats. This was coupled with an attack by an official Iraqi Foreign Ministry spokesman on the British authorities "which still maintained an outmoded colonialist mentality towards Iraq." The statement claimed that the "false allegations" and the "uproar" created by the British authorities were baseless, and asserted that Britain would be the loser. Furthermore, an assassination attempt on the Iraqi ambassador on 28 July was described in the statement as the result of the British authorities' neglect of their duty.[45] At the beginning of September 1978, the Iraqi authorities banned Iraqis from travelling to Britain and issued a directive ordering ministries and state organizations not to sign contracts with British companies without the permission of the authorities.

Diplomatic relations with Canada also passed through a crisis. Early in July 1978, the Canadian authorities expelled the Iraqi second secretary who had been caught gathering information on the Kurdish community in Canada. The Iraqi authorities retaliated with the expulsion of the first secretary at the Canadian embassy in Baghdad.

In October 1977, the Iraqi Foreign Minister, Sa'dūn Ḥammādī, was reported to have had secret talks with President Carter (in the US) on the restoration of diplomatic relations. However, nothing materialized. The strain in Iraqi-Soviet relations in May and June 1978 again gave rise to speculation that a restoration of

Iraqi-American relations might be imminent. However, Saddām Husayn made it clear that no change in the American attitude *vis-à-vis* the Arab-Israeli conflict had occurred which could justify such an act. Moreover, he maintained that even if Iraq were "angry" with the Soviet Union, this did not imply friendship with the US. He explained that the "negative" relations with the US were by Iraq's choice.[46]

ECONOMIC AFFAIRS ($1 = 0.295 Iraqi dinars; £1 = ID 0.614)

The Iraqi economy continued to benefit from the appreciable earnings accrued through oil exports in 1977–78. Despite sizeable imports of both capital and consumer goods, the authorities have succeeded in keeping inflation under 10%. Industrial production grew in 1976 and appears to have done so again in 1977. Only agriculture failed to contribute to economic growth. In order to alleviate some of the problems of the agricultural sector, the authorities nearly doubled the ordinary budget of the Ministry of Agriculture and raised development allocations a further 28% in 1978.[47]

AGRICULTURE

Iraq's agricultural sector is characterized by three negative features: (1) it is labour-intensive, engaging c. 52% of the entire work force; (2) it is resource-inefficient, utilizing as little as one-fourth of the country's cultivable land; and (3) it is under-productive, accounting for less than 10% of GDP at factor cost. Insufficient use of both fertilizers and mechanized equipment have combined with inadequate drainage to further hamper agricultural production.

The need for an expanded and better co-ordinated irrigation network has been amply demonstrated by the erratic output levels of agriculture in recent years. During the favourable weather of 1972, 1974 and 1976, harvests were comparatively bountiful; however, in the intervening years (1971, 1973, 1975), output fell considerably because of poor weather. In recognition of this problem, the authorities allocated $3.5 bn from the 1976–80 development budget for irrigation and drainage projects.[48]

INDUSTRY

Industrial production increased in all the major sectors in 1976. According to Central Bank preliminary data, it appears to have risen further during the first nine months of 1977 compared with the corresponding period in 1976.

In 1978, the sectors of industry (ID 801.8m) and transport and communications (ID 432.5m) were allocated a combined 44% of the investment budget of ID 2,800m (c. $9,480m). Even if, as in the past few years, actual expenditures amount only to 50–75% of the original allocations, Iraqi industry and its infrastructure will still be infused with something like ID 616m (c. $2,085m)—a not inconsiderable sum.[49]

OIL

With output of 826.9m barrels in 1977, Iraq ranked after Saudi Arabia and Iran as OPEC's third largest producer, even though the 1977 total represents a slight decrease from the peak of 834.8m barrels in 1976. During the first three months of 1978, production was stepped up 9.2% compared with the corresponding quarter of 1977. This increase is in marked contrast to the rest of OPEC, which cut production 11.5% on aggregate during the first quarter of 1978, compared with the corresponding period of 1977.[50] Production cuts notwithstanding, Iraq's revenue from oil rose 13.3% in 1977, for a total of $9,631m.[51]

In July 1978, the Oil Minister, Tāyih 'Abd al-Karīm, announced the discovery of new oil reserves which exceeded all the reserves found by foreign oil companies operating in Iraq before the 17 July 1968 revolution. The announcement failed to be more specific.[52] Shortly afterwards, a report in the *Washington Post* asserted that recent discoveries had pushed Iraq's total crude oil reserves beyond 100 bn barrels and possibly as high as 130 bn barrels—each estimate being second only to Saudi Arabia's total of 150 bn barrels.[53]

PUBLIC FINANCE

The Iraqi Finance Minister, Fawzī 'Abdallah (al-Qaysī), announced at the end of 1977 that the state budget would be enlarged by 17.6% to ID 7,457m (c. $25.7 bn) in 1978. Ordinary expenditure was to increase by 11.9% to ID 1,850m, and development expenditure by 18.8% to ID 2,800m, with the rest of the budget increase being allocated to the autonomous governmental agencies.[54]

Compared with the 1977 development budget, allocations for agriculture (+28%), transport and communications (+23%), and building, housing and social services (+33%) were all increased in 1978, while that for industry (–17%) was scheduled to decline. It is worth noting, however, that actual development expenditure in 1977 amounted to only 50.7% of the original allocations.

BALANCE OF PAYMENTS

Iraq's balance of payments improved considerably in 1976, largely as a result of a 31% growth in exports of merchandise, compared to a rise of only 8% for merchandise imports. A fall of 22% in imports of services combined with the larger trade surplus to advance Iraq's payments balance from a deficit of SDR 387m (c. $498m) in 1975 to a surplus of SDR 1,669m (c. $1,927m) in 1976.

FOREIGN TRADE

In recent years, foreign trade has been marked by the dominance of oil, which accounts for 98% of total exports and in turn finances imports. Besides crude oil and petroleum products, dates are the only export commodity whose revenue exceeds $10m annually (c. $40m in 1976). For imports, the Iraqis have been spending the largest amounts on machinery and transport equipment (c. $1,888m in 1976).

Preliminary statistics for 1977 revealed that Japan and Western Europe maintained their place as Iraq's chief sources of imports and, together with Brazil and Turkey, the foremost markets for Iraqi crude.

Ofra Bengio and Uriel Dann
Economic Section by **Ira E. Hoffman**

ARMED FORCES

Total armed forces number 212,000. Defence expenditure in 1977–78 was ID 491.5m ($1.66 bn).

Military service is compulsory for two years. The Army numbers 180,000; formations consist of four armoured divisions (each with two armoured, one mechanized brigade); two mechanized divisions; four infantry divisions; one independent armoured brigade; one Republican Guard mechanized brigade; one independent infantry brigade and one special forces brigade. Equipment consists of 1,700 T-54/-55/-62, 100 T-34, AMX-30 medium, 100 PT-76 light tanks; 120 BMP mechanized infantry combat vehicles; c. 1,500 armoured fighting vehicles including BTR-50/-60/-152, OT-62, VCR armoured personnel carriers; 800 75mm, 85mm, 122mm, 130mm, 152mm guns/howitzers; 90 SU-100, 40 ISU-122 self-propelled guns; 120mm, 160mm mortars; BM-21 122mm rocket launchers; 26 *FROG*-7, 12 *Scud* B surface-to-surface missiles; *Sagger*, SS-11 anti-tank guided weapons; 1,200 23mm 37mm, 57mm, 85mm, 100mm towed, ZSU-23-4, ZSU-57-2 self-propelled anti-aircraft guns; SA-7 surface-to-air missiles. (T-62 medium tanks, *Scud* surface-to-surface missiles on order.) Reserves number 250,000.

The 4,000-strong Navy has three SO-1 submarine chasers, six *Osa*-1, eight *Osa*-II guided-missile fast patrol boats with *Styx* surface-to-surface missiles; ten P-6 torpedo boats; two large patrol craft (ex-Soviet *Poluchat*-class); six coastal patrol boats (under 100 tons); five minesweepers (two ex-Soviet T-43, three inshore); three tank landing craft (*Polnocny*-class).

The Air Force of 28,000 (10,000 air defence personnel) has c. 339 combat aircraft; one bomber squadron with 12 Tu-22, one light bomber squadron with ten I1-28; 12 ground-attack fighter squadrons: four with 80 MiG-23B, three with 60 Su-7B, three with 30 Su-20, two with 20 *Hunter* FB59/FR10; five interceptor squadrons with 115 MiG-21; one counter-insurgency squadron with 12 *Jet Provost* T52; two transport squadrons with 10 An-2, eight An-12, eight An-24, two An-26, two Tu-124, 13 I1-14, two *Heron*. Eight helicopter squadrons with 35 Mi-4, 14 Mi-6, 80 Mi-8, 47 *Alouette* III, eight *Super Frelon*, 40 *Gazelle*, three *Puma*. Trainers include MiG-15/21/-23U, Su-7U, *Hunter* T69, ten Yak-11, 12 L-29, eight L-39. AA-2 *Atoll* air-to-air missiles; AS.11/12 air-to-surface missiles (R.550 *Magic* air-to-air missiles, *Exocet* air-to-surface missiles on order). SA-2, SA-3 and 25 SA-6 surface-to-air missiles. (32 *Mirage* F-1C fighters, four *Mirage* F-1B trainers, I1-76 transports on order.) Paramilitary forces include 4,800 security troops, and the 75,000-strong People's Army.

Source: The Military Balance 1978–79 (London: International Institute for Strategic Studies).

ARMED FORCES: Divisions/major systems

	1973	1978
Armoured divisions	2–3	4
Mechanized divisions	—	2
Infantry divisions	4	5
Special forces units	1	3
Tanks	1,200	2,200
Armoured personnel carriers	1,300	2,400
Artillery	1,000	1,500
Ground-to-ground *Scud* launchers	—	9
Combat aircraft	250	450
Helicopters	80	225
Ground-to-air missile batteries	3	50
Missile boats	4	12

Source: Arab Military Strength (Jerusalem: Israel Information Centre, June 1978).

IRAQ

BALANCE OF PAYMENTS (million SDRs)

	1974	1975	1976*
A. Goods, Services and Transfers	1,938	234	2,164
Exports of Merchandise, fob	5,553	5,183	6,812
Imports of Merchandise, fob	-2,349	-3,464	-3,702
Exports of Services	498	449	505
Imports of Services	-1,571	-1,717	-1,336
Transfer Payments (net)	-193	-217	-115
B. Non-monetary Capital (net)	-454	-360	-350
C. Net Errors and Omissions	73	-263	-115
D. Overall Balance	1,557	-387	1,669

*Preliminary.
Sources: IMF, International Financial Statistics and Central Bank of Iraq.

INTERNATIONAL LIQUIDITY (million US dollars)

	1975	1976	1977
International Reserves	2,727.3	4,600.7	6,995.7
of which:			
Gold	168.0	166.7	176.1
SDRs	26.9	32.5	41.5
Reserve Position in IMF	31.9	31.7	33.4
Foreign Exchange	2,500.5	4,369.8	6,744.7
Central Bank Liabilities	43.4	1.4	13.5
Commercial Banks: Assets	269.2	333.9	412.4
Liabilities	42.0	54.5	111.7

MONETARY SURVEY (million Iraqi dinars at end of period)

	1975	1976	(Jan-Nov) 1977
Foreign Assets (net)	860.0	1,438.9	1,944.3
Domestic Credit	107.7	-37.7	-288.4
Claims on Government (net)	-29.9	-201.3	-480.0
Claims on Private Sector	137.6	163.6	191.6
Money	625.6	754.9	838.3
Quasi-Money	257.0	315.0	360.9
Money, Seasonally Adjusted	621.9	748.9	832.5

Source (of two preceding tables): IMF, International Financial Statistics.

CENTRAL GOVERNMENT INVESTMENT ALLOCATIONS AND EXPENDITURES (million Iraqi dinars)

	1976-80 Five-Year Plan				
	1976		1977		1978
	Allocations	Expenditures	Allocations	Expenditures*	Allocations
Agriculture	268.0	190.8	389.9	202.7	499.1
Industry	709.0	515.8	966.0	527.0	801.8
Transport and Communications	242.5	160.5	351.6	193.5	432.5
Building, Housing and Social Services	213.2	118.1	368.0	127.1	489.5
Other	90.8	50.0	281.6	143.8	577.1
Total	1,523.5	1,035.2	2,357.1	1,194.1	2,800.0

*Preliminary.
Source: Ministry of Planning and Ministry of Finance.

IRAQ

BUDGET (million Iraqi dinars)

	1977	1978	% change
Ordinary Revenue	1,653	1,850	+ 11.9
Revenue Allocated for Development Plan	2,357	2,800	+ 18.8
Revenue of Autonomous Government Agencies	1,988	2,519	+ 26.7
Total Revenue	**5,998**	**7,169**	**+ 19.5**
Ordinary Expenditure	1,653	1,850	+ 11.9
Economic Development Plan	2,357	2,800	+ 18.8
Autonomous Government Agencies	2,329	2,807	+ 20.5
Total Expenditure	**6,339**	**7,457**	**+ 17.6**

Source: Middle East Economic Survey.

INDUSTRIAL ORIGIN OF GDP (million Iraqi dinars at current prices)

	1974	1975	1976*
Crude Oil	2,022.7	2,279.0	2,446
Construction	69.1	91.3	355.1
Agriculture, Forestry and Fishing	232.1	297.3	348.7
Manufacturing and Oil Refining	176.1	238.5	324.5
Public Administration and Defence	261.4	372.6	284.9
Transport and Communications	124.1	157.6	217.7
Domestic Trade	168.9	194.9	197.8
Other Services	271.6	312.9	356.5
Other Industry	21.7	26.4	51.6
GDP at Factor Cost	**3,347.7**	**3,970.5**	**4,582.8**

*Preliminary.
Source: Ministry of Planning

AGRICULTURAL PRODUCTION (thousand tonnes)

	1971	1972	1973	1974	1975	1976
Wheat	514	2,465	957	1,339	845	1,312
Barley	509	859	462	533	437	579
Rice	207	315	157	275	240	163
Cotton	13[a]	23	15	15	15	16
Dates	330	450	310	190	...	372

Source: Economist Intelligence Unit, *Quarterly Economic Review.*
[a] Lint only

QUANTUM INDEX OF INDUSTRIAL PRODUCTION (1972 = 100.0)

	Weight	1974	1975	1976
Foodstuffs, Tobacco and Beverages	34.7	128.7	154.8	206.5
Textiles	7.5	106.6	101.6	113.8
Clothing and Shoes	7.9	107.7	111.3	124.3
Petroleum Refining	22.0	110.0	161.6	206.4
Chemical Industries	5.2	115.1	127.2	138.0
Non-Metallic Industries	14.8	98.6	106.2	129.8
Miscellaneous	7.9	149.4	160.0	184.1
General Index	100.0	115.8	137.5	169.7

Source: Central Bank of Iraq.

COMPOSITION OF IMPORTS (million Iraqi dinars)

	1975	1976	(Jan-Sept) 1977
Capital Goods	857.1	698.8	429.0
Food, Drink and Tobacco	207.6	151.7	70.9
Raw Materials	125.4	96.1	64.0
Durable Consumer Goods	60.1	60.8	37.8
Textiles and Clothing	31.4	17.2	21.5
Other Consumer Goods	21.4	17.7	7.6
Miscellaneous	123.9	108.6	54.8
Total	**1,426.9**	**1,150.9**	**685.6**

Source: Ministry of Planning.

DIRECTION OF TRADE (million US dollars)

	1975	1976*	1977*
Exports to			
France	982.6	1,448.9	1,664.7
Italy	1,512.2	1,231.1	1,264.4
Brazil	832.2	1,054.2	1,045.7
Japan	359.5	526.6	673.5
Turkey	458.4	585.8	628.7
United Kingdom	204.6	446.5	527.8
Spain	445.9	352.9	502.1
Netherlands	164.5	176.9	429.8
Yugoslavia	352.4	407.2	429.5
United States	20.7	111.8	382.0
Total (including others)	**8,277.0**	**8,854.0**	**9,664.0**
Imports from:			
Japan	764.6	494.2	794.4
West Germany	754.2	599.3	639.0
France	263.3	262.4	256.6
United Kingdom	238.2	203.3	246.6
Italy	164.4	132.1	199.2
Netherlands	61.0	83.4	155.5
United States	370.3	163.2	154.8
Brazil	200.4	17.5	104.8
Yugoslavia	15.3	56.5	99.0
Sweden	91.9	73.9	99.0
Soviet Union	103.1	119.6	n.a.
Total (including others)	**4,205.0**	**3,469.0**	**4,059.1**

*Data partly extrapolated and/or derived from partner country.
n.a. not available.
Source: IMF, Direction of Trade.

NOTES
1. Al-Watan al-'Arabī, Paris; 28 October 1977.
2. For developments in the Regional Command, see MECS 1976–77, p. 404–5.
3. Al-Hawādith, Beirut; 25 August 1978.
4. Baghdad Observer, 1 December 1977.
5. The Economist, 24–30 June 1978.
6. I.e. R Baghdad, 8 November—monitored by Daily Report, Middle East and North Africa (DR), 9 November 1977; Baghdad Observer, 3 March 1978.
7. Baghdad Observer, 18 April 1978.
8. Al-Nahār al-'Arabī wal-Duwalī (NAD), Paris; 29 April 1978.
9. R Baghdad, 1 November—DR, 3 November 1977.
10. Al-Thawra, Baghdad; 28, 29 May 1978.
11. I.e. Ākhir Sā'a, Cairo; 12 July; al-Safīr, Beirut; 31 July; Events, London; 25 August; Arabia and the Gulf, London; 28 August 1978.
12. Al-Anbā', Kuwait; 8 June 1978.
13. Baghdad Observer, 1 December 1977.

14. *Ibid*, 15 June 1978.
15. Iraqi News Agency (INA), 17 July—DR, 19 July 1978.
16. "Voice of Palestine" (clandestine), 6 September—DR, 7 September 1978.
17. *The Economist*, 24–30 June 1978.
18. INA, 14 March—DR, 17 March 1978.
19. *Al-Rāsid*, 4 May, as quoted by Reuter, 4 May 1978.
20. *Al-Thawra*, 28, 29 May 1978.
21. *Al-Dustūr*, London; 19 June 1978.
22. *Al-Thawra*, 12 March 1974.
23. *Ibid*, 10 November 1977.
24. Reuter, 9 June 1978.
25. Reuter, 21 July; INA, 21 July—DR, 24 July 1978.
26. INA, 21 July—DR, 24 July 1978.
27. *The Middle East*, London; May 1978.
28. Reuter, 21 July 1978.
29. *New York Times*, 4 February 1978.
30. *Ākhir Sā'a*, 21 June 1978.
31. "Voice of Palestine" (clandestine), 16 June, monitored by British Broadcasting Corporation, Summary of World Broadcasts, the Middle East and Africa (BBC), 19 June 1978.
32. Reuter, 6 August 1978.
33. INA, 8 October—BBC, 11 October 1977.
34. *The Middle East*, February 1978.
35. INA, 16 July—BBC, 18 July 1978.
36. Tāriq 'Azīz, member of the National and Regional Command and prominent in the conduct of foreign policy, to the *Middle East*, February 1978.
37. Taha Muhyī al-Dīn Ma'rūf, the Vice-President: INA, 4 December—DR, 5 December 1977.
38. *Newsweek*, 17 July 1978.
39. *Ibid*.
40. *Al-Jumhūriyya*, Baghdad; 23 May 1978.
41. *The Observer*, London; 6 August 1978.
42. *International Herald Tribune*, Paris; 10 August 1978.
43. *Al-Anbā'*, Kuwait; 8 June; Middle East News Agency, Cairo; 22 June; *Newsweek*, 17 July 1978.
44. *The Times*, 27 July 1978.
45. INA, 29 July—BBC, 31 July 1978.
46. INA, 21 July—DR, 24 July 1978.
47. For background details, see *MECS 1976–77*, pp. 417–20.
48. For details, see Economist Intelligence Unit, *Quarterly Economic Review of Iraq (QER)*, London; Annual Supplement 1978, pp. 8–10. Also see *Arab Economist*, Beirut; September 1978, pp. 18–19; and *Baltimore Sun*, 2 August 1978.
49. For details, see *QER*, No 2, 1978, pp. 12–14; *Arab Economist*, August 1978, pp. 20–21; and *al-Thawra*, 22 December 1977.
50. See *Petroleum Economist*, London; June 1978, p. 271. Also see *QER*, op. cit., p. 10. A conflicting report, alleging that Iraqi production increased in 1977 appears in *Middle East Economic Digest*, London; 1 September 1978, p. 21.
51. See *Arab Oil and Gas*, Paris; 16 June 1978, p. 32.
52. INA, 13 July—DR, 14 July 1978.
53. *Washington Post*, 7 August 1978.
54. R Baghdad, 29 December 1977—Joint Publications Research Service (JPRS), Arlington (US); 30 January 1978.

Israel

(Medinat Yisrael)

To a degree exceptional even by Israeli standards, 1978 was a unique, eventful and possibly momentous year, largely because of the convergence of four main factors. First, the commemoration of 30 years of statehood would, under any circumstances, have tended to focus discussion upon the broader topic of national goals and priorities, upon the direction in which the Jewish state and society were going or ought to go. Second, in this first full year of a Likud government led by Menahem Begin, political parties, institutions as well as the public were still in the process of adjusting to the transition of power after 29 years of uninterrupted Labour rule. Third, repercussions from the traumatic Yom Kippur War of five years earlier still affected the national debate and tended to determine the limits of what was possible in both domestic and foreign affairs. But above all, the year was dominated by controversy arising from the participation of Israel in serious and sustained negotiations aimed at a settlement of the Arab-Israeli conflict. This unanticipated turn of events followed the historic visit to Jerusalem by President Sādāt of Egypt in the previous November. (See also "The Egyptian-Israeli Negotiations.")

Beginning with the Sādāt initiative, major diplomatic, economic, social and political developments took place in rapid succession. These called for important policy decisions which, whether taken or deferred, challenged previous political equations and longstanding conventions. In the course of a single year, traditional assumptions were repudiated, political groupings realigned and perplexing questions raised as to the price Israel should or might have to pay for peace with its Arab neighbours. Thus even the spectre of rampant inflation at the rate of nearly 50% pa, or of organized crime taking root, became subordinated to the fundamental aspects of the quest for peace: the relevance of territory for security, contradictory assessments of true Arab intentions, the status of the Palestinians, the "special relationship" with the US, and, ultimately, Israel's place within a Middle East regional configuration.

Perhaps for the first time, Israelis were seeking to come to grips throughout 1978 with sensitive problems and controversial questions long left unasked as well as unanswered. This combination of singularly meaningful events, governmental responses and historical processes had a definite and cumulative effect. The national consensus was strained, while an air of great uncertainty, of profound change and of public anxiety as to Israel's future carried over into 1979.

Five sets of issues clearly predominated national affairs during 1978. The first set, relating to domestic politics, affected the Likud government and its effectiveness as a governing body in general, as well as the actual performance of Menahem Begin in his multiple capacity as Prime Minister, head of the largest group in the coalition and leader of his party. The second set of issues was diplomatic, centring on Israel's peace strategy both *vis-à-vis* Egypt and the US, and on the implications this would have for settlement policy in the administered territories of Judea, Samaria and the Gaza district.

A third set of controversial issues fell within the economic domain. These related to disagreements over the government's New Economic Policy (NEP), the means used for coping with inflation and the strained relations prevailing in the labour sector. The fourth set of issues pertained to the conduct of regularized foreign policy, especially with the US. The fifth set of issues concerned military affairs. Considerable attention was given to the role of the Israel Defence Forces in a situation of peace; their redeployment and equipment needs for the 1980s; and, most immediately, the wisdom of their direct, large-scale intervention in South Lebanon.

POLITICAL AFFAIRS
THE LIKUD GOVERNMENT
Although in presenting his new government to the Knesset on 20 June 1977, the Prime Minister had asked for a year's grace to correct "longstanding distortions in the economic, social and political fields," the Sādāt initiative forced a reordering of priorities. Foreign policy became the overwhelming preoccupation of the Cabinet throughout most of 1978, and hence the main standard for evaluating its performance. Indeed, one of the hallmarks of the government was its inability to make significant inroads into the many other social problems afflicting Israel in areas unrelated to security such as the housing shortage, pooling medical and hospital facilities, or the widening social gap between the middle and upper classes and the disadvantaged who comprise the "second Israel."

In terms of the ability of the Likud coalition to govern under stressful conditions, the results were at best mixed. Considering the ideological and often emotional nature of the issues upon which it was compelled to adopt a clear stand, the Cabinet held up remarkably well. In the face of combined pressure from world opinion and a vocal peace movement at home, the coalition government of four disparate parties and 19 ministers generally tended to take refuge, at least on the surface, in group solidarity. Despite several Cabinet crises and threats of defection, only two members of the Cabinet actually resigned. The Minister of Transport and Communications, Meir Amit, relinquished his portfolio in September following an internal split within his own Democratic Movement for Change. After retracting his earlier resignation in July in opposition to the supplementary budget, Yigal Hurvitz finally yielded his post as Minister of Industry, Commerce and Tourism on 28 September in protest against the decision to remove Israeli settlements from Sinai as part of a peace agreement with Egypt. Otherwise, the coalition held together.

This tendency to close ranks and to accept a minimal consensus was demonstrated on a number of occasions when tensions mounted to the point where a final split seemed near. Two instances are particularly worthy of note. A storm arose over remarks allegedly made by a senior American official following Begin's visit to the US in March 1978 suggesting that if peace was to be achieved, he would have to be replaced. The Cabinet stood firmly behind the Prime Minister and, on 26 March, unanimously approved the peace proposals which he had advocated in Washington. The second instance took place on 24 September 1978 when the Cabinet decided by 11 votes to two, with three abstentions, to approve the Camp David accords signed by the Premier.

As this vote suggests, however, support for the Prime Minister by no means implied unanimity within the government. Cabinet sessions were often stormy, with reports of sharp dissent frequently reaching the local press. Major differences surfaced on matters of substance, of procedure and timing, as well as of broad policy guidelines and specific technical details. At times, these differences suggested strong personal conviction on matters of principle; at others, clashes of personality or of bureaucratic rivalry among ministries. Never far beneath the surface, such divisive tendencies were most pronounced in Cabinet discussions when the agenda included such items as instructions for Israeli negotiators both before and after Camp David; authorization of new settlements or the expansion of existing ones; wage policy; and alternative national service for girls exempt from military duty on grounds of religious conviction.

As might be expected, Israel's official position on the elements of peace was the single most controversial issue and contained the greatest potential for polarizing the Cabinet. As the year progressed, it became possible to discern two main schools of thought. The government was united in wishing to pursue the opening to peace offered by Sādāt in order to finally achieve a resolution of the Arab-Israeli conflict. Nevertheless, they were divided into "enthusiasts" more prepared to take risks, and "reservationists" who were cautious and less willing to compromise on what they felt to be vital interests affecting national security. Among the latter were the Minister without Portfolio, Haim Landau; the Minister of Energy and Infrastructure, Yitzhak Mod'ai; the Minister of Agriculture, Ariel Sharon; Yigal Hurvitz (until his resignation); and the Minister of Education and Culture, Zevulun Hammer. Among the enthusiasts were reported to be the Deputy Premier, Yigael Yadin; the Minister of Finance, Simha Ehrlich; the Minister of Interior, Yosef Burg; Meir Amit (until his resignation); and the Minister of Defence, Ezer Weizman. Often crucial in breaking the deadlock were the Foreign Minister, Moshe Dayan, and the Prime Minister himself. By committing the prestige of their offices, these two served to bridge the gap by suggesting acceptable compromise formulas. Time and again, their pragmatic arguments and appeal to realism were seen as decisive in tilting the Cabinet in favour of making the necessary adjustments which enabled the negotiating process to continue.

Yet often the inescapable impression was of a government whose members appeared to be working at cross-purposes rather than pulling together behind an agreed plan of action. Thus, in January 1978, apparently after much disagreement, the Cabinet decided that no new settlements would be set up in Sinai pending further peace negotiations, but that existing ones would be "strengthened." It subsequently became clear that this was being interpreted by the Ministerial Settlements Committee, headed by Ariel Sharon, as permitting the establishment of new "footholds." Four days after the Cabinet decision of 8 January, Reuter reported that bulldozers were seen clearing new sites in the desert c. 20 miles south of existing settlements. The Defence Minister informed the Cabinet that he had conducted his own investigation into the "earthworks" in northern Sinai and had discovered that 22 "strongholds" approved by the government for 14 established settlements were in fact disguising new settlements. At his insistence, land preparation in Sinai was halted on 31 January.

In January, too, members of the extreme nationalist movement, Gush Emunim, were permitted to move to Shilo, c. 30 km north of Jerusalem, for the purpose of setting up an archaeological site. Reporting the laying of a cornerstone at the camp on 23 January, Israel television revealed that while there was no approval for a permanent settlement, more than IL 250,000 had already been invested in Shilo and that to all intents and purposes a settlement existed there. Abandoning all such pretences, a member of Gush Emunim was quoted as saying that the city would eventually have 40,000 inhabitants. Yet, in response to President Carter's expression of regret at this effort to establish what the US viewed as another illegal settlement on the West Bank, the Deputy Defence Minister, Mordechai Zippori, said on 31 January that his ministry had authorized the preparation of ground at Shilo for archaeological excavation and that there was no intention "at this stage" of setting up a permanent settlement.

Considering that the occurrences took place at a sensitive stage in talks with

Egypt, observers were left puzzled by their timing and judiciousness. Such steps were due either to a lack of co-ordination or were carefully calculated. Both explanations had equally grave implications: the former suggested that Begin was no longer in control of his own Cabinet; the latter, that the government lacked credibility.

In the face of criticism, Begin admitted on 7 March that his government had "got into a mess." Despite assurances that everything would be set right, inconsistencies and internal friction continued. In November, for instance, the Prime Minister apparently decided on his own, without consulting the Finance Minister, to propose that American financial assistance in the transition to peace be largely in the form of a loan rather than an outright grant. On the other hand, while Begin was absent on a visit to Canada, government members felt freer to criticize the Israeli delegation to the Blair House negotiations in Washington and to reserve final consent to the text of a treaty with Egypt. (See also "The Egyptian-Israeli Negotiations.") Also in November, the media speculated about the highly questionable timing of an announcement, attributed to the Minister of Agriculture, of plans for an urban centre in the Gaza district. In an editorial on 13 November, *Ma'ariv* stated: "A new element was introduced into the negotiations crisis which can be an efficient tool in the hands of Egyptian propaganda while it contributes nothing to Israel's security or standing. . . . It is not the first time that such a 'bomb' has been thrown into the negotiating arena."

The Cabinet also came in for serious criticism over its pronounced tendency to sit as the Ministerial Committee on Security. By doing so, it reserved the right according to law to impose censorship on matters relating to national security. The result was to bring down a veil of secrecy, not only on what was discussed at these meetings and on the decisions taken, but also on procedure and voting. The nation's press took sharp exception to such practices, claiming that they curtailed the freedom of the press and unnecessarily limited the public's right to know. In an editorial on 27 October, the influential *Ha'aretz* protested: "The attempt to hide political information on the pretext of security secrets has not succeeded in the past, and therefore it is not clear why the government stubbornly insists on continuing this hypocrisy, unless the core of the stubbornness lies in its attempt to conceal internal rifts and disagreements. . . ." Nevertheless, the Cabinet persisted in meeting as the Ministerial Committee on Security.

The Cabinet's inability to function smoothly as a team arose in part from the presence in it of strong personalities. Five members—Amit, Dayan, Sharon, Weizman and Yadin—were former generals. Past military and political disagreements, combined with different temperaments and assessments of the emerging political situation, inevitably produced sharp clashes of will and opinion. These differences were thought to have prompted a decision in January against Sharon's joining the Political Committee talks with Egypt, and in August against including Yadin as a member of the Camp David delegation. During the successive stages of the peace negotiations, the five former generals were often on opposite sides, while the discussions on settlement policy invariably found Sharon and Weizman at loggerheads.

Preventing deep Cabinet rifts from tearing the government apart therefore required a good deal of Menahem Begin's time and energy. In the case of Ezer Weizman, for example, he preferred to overlook or dismiss a number of instances when the strong-willed Defence Minister impulsively took issue in public with official government positions. Before leaving for the US on 5 March, Weizman had ordered a halt in preparations for two civilian Jewish settlements in the West Bank only to learn upon arrival in New York of plans to call a Cabinet meeting to discuss a complaint by Sharon that Weizman was blocking approved settlement projects. The *New York Times* quoted Weizman's aides in reporting a trans-Atlantic telephone conversation in which the Defence Minister threatened to cut short his American visit, return home and resign if work on the settlements was resumed in defiance of his orders.

In March 1978, Weizman also proposed the formation of a "national peace government," which was interpreted as undermining the position of the Prime Minister. Begin caustically replied: "We *are* the peace government." In June, Weizman was alleged to have warned that the government was leading the country to war. When, in yet another episode in July, Weizman apparently tore up a government peace poster, Begin's only response was to caution his ministers against tantrums. Such demonstrations of patience assured Israel of as impressive a negotiating team *vis-à-vis* the Egyptians and the Americans as political analysts thought it possible to assemble. Whatever their individual and personal differences, Begin, Dayan and Weizman continued to present Israel's minimum demands with full force throughout the year on the basis of a purely functional working relationship. This achievement stood in sharp contrast with the disharmony among the three officials most directly responsible for foreign and defence policy in the previous Rabin government.

The ability of the government to hold together against centrifugal tendencies and under considerable stress owed much to the personal influence and efforts of the Prime Minister. Israeli politics at the national level have always been highly personalized; nevertheless, the strong convictions of Menahem Begin, his personality and state of health dominated the political scene during 1978 to a degree unprecedented since Mrs Golda Meir and the era of David Ben-Gurion. If peace was the central issue of the year, Begin was beyond doubt the main subject of controversy and the principal political actor. For one thing, the Prime Minister was personally and intimately involved in all matters pertaining to the trilateral negotiations between Jerusalem, Cairo and Washington. He orchestrated the overall diplomatic campaign, drafted Israel's 26-point peace plan in December 1977, and flew to Washington to present it personally to the Carter Administration. It was Begin who led the delegation to the Ismā'īliyya talks and, again, to the Camp David summit. Moreover, he led the fight at home for public acceptance of the framework of peace and asserted his authority in insisting upon strict Cabinet and party discipline. Finally, he shared the international spotlight with President Sādāt as co-recipient of the Nobel Peace Price for 1978.

Even on many domestic matters unrelated to the diplomatic effort, it was common knowledge that ministers preferred to reserve judgement or to hold decisions in abeyance pending Begin's final approval. The single outstanding exception was the Finance Minister, Simha Ehrlich, who enjoyed Begin's confidence and to whom authority was delegated for managing the country's troubled economy. Otherwise, governmental authority under the Likud was very much centralized. Contrary to earlier expectations and promises, the Deputy Prime Minister, Yigael Yadin, did not have direct responsibility for social policy, with the result that decisions in many critical areas either required the Prime Minister's consent or else were simply not taken because of his preoccupation with the peace process.

The scene at Ben-Gurion Airport on 22 September perhaps best captures Menahem Begin's personal prominence. Returning from Camp David, he was greeted by thousands of enthusiastic supporters as well as by former bitter critics; as he walked among the crowds, there were repeated shouts of "Begin . . . Begin!" Israelis, especially his former comrades in the independence struggle, were confounded by events in 1978 and by the rather abrupt shift of position on the future of the administered territories. It was Begin's own confidence and self-assurance which served to assuage their fears and to retain their support for the Likud government.

Considering his dominant position in Israeli politics since the Likud election victory in May 1977, it was natural that considerable concern should have been occasioned by conflicting reports about Begin's health. Preceding the Sādāt initiative, the 65-year old Prime Minister had been twice hospitalized for cardiac disorders and exhaustion. Thereafter, his intensive involvement with foreign affairs, along with the more routine business of government and party, could not but raise questions about his capacity to endure such physical and mental strain and still direct policy effectively. This concern was increased by the discordant reports emanating from Cabinet meetings. According to Cabinet and Knesset sources, quoted by the *Jerusalem Post* on 1 August, the Premier admitted that because he was sick and not ready for a confrontation with proponents of a more hawkish view, he had endorsed the reply to the US government on the future of the territories against his own better judgement. Rumours about his health persisted throughout the first half of 1978. It was alleged, for example, that Begin was under heavy medication which might be adversely affecting his faculties. These rumours reached a peak at the end of June with reports in the American press that Begin was gravely ill. In an attempt to dispel such doubts, Professor Mervyn Gottesman, head of the Hadassah Hospital cardiac department, declared on 26 June that the Premier's health was good. This was subsequently confirmed by his many public appearances during visits to the US and Canada, in television and newspaper interviews, and at the rostrum of the Knesset. Still, the issue of succession to the leadership and of possible contenders for the office of Premier remained a topic of considerable speculation.

Meanwhile, Menahem Begin and his Likud government seemed to enjoy wide popular support in contrast to the reservations and even ridicule heard in more select, especially academic, circles. A Dahaf poll, published in the *Jerusalem Post* on 25 December 1977, showed that 82% of those questioned favoured the Prime Minister; only 7.8% declared themselves dissatisfied. As the peace momentum slowed down in the following months, the Premier came under heavy criticism from dovish elements which weakened his claim to represent the entire country. However, the surprise developments at Camp David increased support for him across an even wider spectrum of the public, who came to admire his statesmanlike stand. The results of a further opinion survey conducted by the Institute for Applied Social Research and the Communications Institute of the Hebrew University were released on 10 November. In response to the question, "How do you feel about the way the government is carrying out the peace negotiations?" 22% were dissatisfied, as against 78% who replied either "good" or "very good." To a second question, "How is the government performing under the leadership of Menahem Begin?" 72% expressed satisfaction.

The Prime Minister was able to rely to a considerable extent upon his personal aides during the most difficult periods of the year. Dr Eliahu Ben-Elissar, Director of the Prime Minister's Office and well known for his unswerving loyalty to Begin, was chosen for the sensitive task of leading the Israeli delegation to the Cairo conference (14–22 December 1977). Yehiel Kadishai, a long-time confidant of Begin, wielded considerable influence as adviser and appointments secretary. Another influential appointee was Arye Naor who, as Cabinet Secretary, was responsible for curbing leaks to the press and for issuing carefully-worded statements following Cabinet deliberations. Shlomo Nakdimon, co-opted from the daily newspaper *Yedi'ot Aharonot*, acted as press spokesman, while Harry Hurewitz, author of a laudatory biography of Begin, was brought from South Africa to replace Shmuel Katz as information adviser.

THE LIKUD COALITION

Menahem Begin's ability as a leader was severely tested not only at the national level, but also as manager of a broad, multiparty coalition. By the end of 1977, he had succeeded in forming a Likud (unity) government which enjoyed a majority of 76 seats in the 120-member Knesset. As is customary in the Israeli political system, this was accomplished only through concessions to several smaller parties. Begin's own Likud Party, which held 45 seats, was joined in the coalition by three other party lists:

The National Religious Party (NRP—"Mafdal")	12 seats
The Democratic Movement for Change (DMC)	15 seats
The Agudat Israel	4 seats

Upon accepting his appointment as Foreign Minister, Moshe Dayan withdrew from the Alignment Party, but retained his Knesset seat as an independent. It had taken five months of hard bargaining before a coalition agreement could be hammered out. Nevertheless, the events of 1978 produced more than one coalition crisis which Begin was able to resolve only with great difficulty. In February the coalition was strained by a dispute over a bill concerning the exemption of Orthodox Jewish girls from military service. Although part of the coalition, the DMC actually sided with the opposition Alignment, citing a clause in the coalition agreement which allowed members to vote according to their conscience on religious issues. The DMC supported a private member's bill submitted by Chaika Grossman of the Alignment which would have required girls excused from military service to perform alternative national service on a compulsory basis, and not only as volunteers. The bill was narrowly passed in its first reading and represented an embarrassing defeat for the government. Begin rejected a proposal by the coalition whip, Haim Corfu, which would have required the DMC to vote with the government to defeat all opposition proposals; nevertheless, he said that ways would have to be found to prevent similar parliamentary mishaps. Behind the scenes consultations were held to devise a formula for appeasing the religious parties, which objected to compulsory service of any kind for girls wishing to be exempted because of religious conviction or upbringing. After a bitter and prolonged debate, the Knesset voted on 20 July by 54 to 45 to adopt legislation making it easier for women to avoid conscription into the defence forces by citing religious objections, thereby averting a threatened split in the coalition.

Religion was only one source of friction within the coalition. Its partners also diverged on the future of Jewish settlements and on Israel's peace proposals. These provided the background for repeated threats by the DMC to consider leaving the government. In April, the DMC central committee rejected Begin's attempt to interpret Resolution 242 in such a way as to sanction Israel's permanent presence on the West Bank. The committee also demanded a halt to settlements in the territories for the duration of the negotiations with Egypt. Both these attitudes ran counter to the policies of the Likud and the NRP which favoured increased development of Judea and Samaria.

In June, the DMC continued its pressure from within by threatening to quit if Israel did not reply positively to America's questions about the future of the territories after the five-year autonomy period. While the statement by the government, as finally worded, did win a majority in the Knesset (59 to 37), nine of the ten abstentions came from DMC members. Yadin, the party's founder and leader, found himself increasingly under attack, first because of his inability to encourage the government to show greater flexibility in its negotiating stance, and second because of his failure to obtain a greater role for the DMC in policy-making. Finally, in the weeks just before Camp David, a showdown took place. The resulting split within the DMC left the coalition's strength reduced by eight seats, but still assured of a parliamentary majority.

The need to conciliate religious fundamentalists and secularists, moderates and hard-liners, Leftists, Centrists and Rightists—all within a single coalition—imposed a considerable strain on the Prime Minister's energy and time. While he succeeded for the most part, the contradictions within the coalition nevertheless persisted and appear likely to continue—with or without Begin.

THE LIKUD PARTY

Challenges to his authority from within the Likud Party in general, but especially inside his own Herut faction, were particularly distressing to the Prime Minister. Holding 45 seats in the Knesset, the Likud is itself a coalition of five groupings:

The Herut (Freedom) Movement, its largest component, is headed by Begin and has been his undisputed party base throughout most of his political career.

The Liberal Party, led by Simha Ehrlich, joined Herut in 1965 to form Gahal (*Gush Herut Liberalim*). This became the Likud in 1973.

La'am, consisting of parts of the Free Centre Party, the State List and the Greater Land of Israel Movement, is headed by Yigal Hurvitz.

Shlomzion, the movement of Reserve General Ariel Sharon, ran an independent list in the May 1977 elections, but became a full member of the Likud shortly afterwards.

Ahdut (Unity), a splinter of the independent Liberal Party, joined the Likud in the spring of 1977.

The adjustments in Israeli foreign policy necessitated by the peace effort had a definite upsetting effect upon the Likud's internal party politics. Indeed, some of the most outspoken critics of Begin's peace plan came from within the Likud. Old-time loyalists like Geula Cohen, Moshe Shamir, Yigal Hurvitz, Shmuel Katz and Moshe Arens made blistering attacks against the new policy. An admirer of Begin from the time when he was commander of the clandestine anti-British resistance IZL (*Irgun Zevai Le'umi*), Geula Cohen now bitterly denounced the Camp David agreements. She publicly warned against the fantasy of a false peace, accusing the Premier of deceiving the nation and of abandoning his own principles. Together with Shamir, a noted author and spokesman for the Greater Land of Israel Movement, she repeatedly castigated Begin from the rostrum of the Knesset and was instrumental in organizing a "loyalist circle" as an internal opposition faction within the Herut. During the heated marathon Knesset debate on 28 September, Shamir began by saying: "Mr Prime Minister, I have no confidence in the path you are treading. I have no confidence in your policy. I have no confidence in you." Shamir was also prominent in attempts at forming a broad national anti-peace pact movement.

The disaffection of Shmuel Katz and his break with Begin was notable for several reasons. First, he and Begin had been close comrades-in-arms for many years, sharing similar ideological and political views by virtue of their both having been disciples of Ze'ev Jabotinsky, founder of the pre-state Revisionist movement. Second, Katz consented to serve in the new Likud government as Begin's special adviser on information. Indeed, it was Katz who was sent on an important mission to the US just after the surprise Likud victory with the sole purpose of improving Begin's image as a responsible leader and to explain his policy intentions. Third, Katz was really the first to apparently grasp the changes taking place in Begin's thinking after Sādāt's visit to Jerusalem. As early as 5 January 1978, Katz felt compelled to resign his post out of sharp disagreement with the government's peace plan. Fourth, whereas the criticisms of Cohen and Shamir were inclined to be emotional and often full of invective, those of Katz were more reasoned and intellectual. Rather than retiring quietly, Katz sought to expose in a series of newspaper articles what he saw as the grave flaws in Israel's bargaining position. Because of their likely harmful implications for Israel's future security, he relentlessly charged the Prime Minister with irresponsibility and capitulation, comparing Camp David to the 1938 Munich pact. Such criticism from a former staunch supporter must have been especially telling to a political leader like Begin, for so long accustomed to the deep loyalty of most of his followers.

Other signs of hesitation and dissent were also harmful to Likud's cohesion and to Begin's personal leadership. For example, in the historic Knesset vote on 28 September, 16 Likud members either abstained or voted against the Camp David agreements—despite warnings by the Prime Minister that he would treat the vote as one of personal confidence. Symptomatic of the painful divisions produced by the debate was the position taken by the Speaker of the Knesset, Yitzhak Shamir—another of Begin's oldest associates and hand-picked by him for this post—who registered his apprehensions by abstaining rather than supporting Begin outright.

During the months of controversy, Begin derived support from other sources inside the Likud. Still recalling his leadership of the underground movement and of the party during 29 years in the political wilderness, the rank-and-file membership of Herut continued to give their loyalty to Begin. A second important pillar of support was Simha Ehrlich and his Liberal Party, who consistently voted with Begin in party caucuses and in the Knesset. Ezer Weizman, the number-two man in Herut, also helped to shoulder some of the burden in defending government policy despite other differences with Begin, who in the past had felt Weizman to be challenging his leadership. (According to an opinion poll held on 5 February, 71.6% were satisfied with Weizman's performance, compared with 68.4% with Begin's.) Weizman was influential in encouraging the Prime Minister to accept the political price of the peace initiative, to recognize the sincerity of Sādāt's wish for an end to hostilities, and therefore to persist along the course adopted at the time of the Egyptian leader's visit to Jerusalem.

PARTY POLITICS

The Likud was by no means the only political party to be deeply troubled by developments during 1978. Despite traces of factionalism, bitterness and disillusionment, the Likud in some ways weathered the storm more successfully than the other three major parties: the Alignment, the Democratic Movement for Change and the National Religious Party.

The Alignment (Ma'arach), with 32 Knesset seats, remained a potent political force, although the transition from government to opposition was not easy—either for the party or for its leader, Shimon Peres. After 29 years in power, the 1977 election defeat, in which the Alignment lost 19 seats, had left many members dispirited and without a sense of direction. There was an immediate need to preserve the delicate balance among several ideological factions and groupings retained from the electoral alliance formed in 1969 by Mapam (the United Workers' Party) and the larger Israel Labour Party. The latter was itself created only in 1968 by the union of three earlier parties: Mapai, established in 1930; *Ahdut Ha'avoda-*

Po'alei-Zion, established in 1944; and Rafi (the Israel Labour List), established as a breakaway faction by David Ben-Gurion in 1965. Past memories and rancour still figured in intra-party politics; the fact that Peres had joined Ben-Gurion in leaving Mapai did not help him in asserting his personal leadership over the Alignment. Nor did ideological dogmatism. The position of Mapam on labour policy and union activism represented a constraint against greater flexibility by the party in seeking to appeal for popular support as the only viable alternative to the Likud. Moreover, personal animosities from the close bitter contest for party leadership between the former Premier, Yitzhak Rabin, and his Defence Minister, Shimon Peres, were by no means healed and compounded the difficulties the latter faced in revitalizing the party.

The Alignment suffered, above all, from the lack of a clear-cut political issue. By compromising on points previously thought to be inviolate in the Likud platform— such as surrendering extensive territorial holdings—Begin pre-empted the Alignment and came to dominate the political centre in Israel. One of the great ironies of the political scene in 1978 were the charges levelled against Begin by Alignment spokesmen that, in his eagerness for a peace settlement with Egypt, he was guilty of two sins: stealing the ideas of the Alignment, and offering terms even more generous than those which they had been prepared to concede to the Arabs since 1973. There was considerable truth, therefore, to political analyses which concluded that Begin was freer to act out of expediency—if only because he had no Begin to contend with in the opposition.

So long as peace remained *the* single issue, the three tasks of maintaining a united front, recapturing public attention, and yet acting as a responsible opposition continued to trouble Alignment strategists. Consequently, in the course of the year-long debate in the country and in the Knesset, party leaders were presented with only two real options: either to oppose the government, and thus incur the charge of being an obstacle to peace; or to endorse the overall peace effort, thereby strengthening the Likud and denying itself a basis for contesting power. Not surprisingly, Alignment spokesmen tended to vacillate between the two positions.

In the Alignment's first reaction to the Begin peace plan on 19 December 1977, Shimon Peres criticized it for opening the way to an eventual Palestinian state and for unnecessarily conceding too much—and too soon—in Sinai. In January 1978, Begin was charged by Peres, by former Foreign Minister Yigal Allon and others with responsibility for the breakdown in the Israel-Egypt Political Committee talks in Jerusalem because of the poor timing in authorizing new construction work to begin in the Sinai. In the following months, Peres and his colleagues concentrated on criticizing specific government actions and on making proposals of their own— such as insisting upon a territorial compromise instead of an autonomy scheme.

Yet at decisive moments, the Alignment adopted the second option—that of going along with the government for the sake of peace and national unity. Prior to Begin's departure for Camp David, he and Peres met and agreed upon central points: the right of Jewish settlement, no Palestinian state, and Jerusalem as the undivided capital of Israel. This understanding enabled Begin to negotiate on behalf of the overwhelming majority of Israelis. Afterwards, in the decisive Knesset debate in September, Yigal Allon summed up Labour's ambivalence. In the decade since 1967, the previous government had encouraged the establishment and development of the string of settlements in the Rafiah salient in the Sinai which Israel was now being asked to give up as a pre-condition for peace. The Camp David agreements, Allon therefore said, "put before us a choice between giving a chance to peace with Egypt . . . and complete chaos." Under the circumstances—as hard and as distasteful as the decision was—he and his colleagues were left to conclude only that "despite its shortcomings, the accord must be approved." While Allon himself chose to abstain, 24 Alignment members voted in favour of the government motion. Subsequently, at a meeting of the Socialist International in Paris, Peres described the vote as reflecting a national will and as an historic decision in favour of peace; he also termed "most positive" the role which the Prime Minister had played.

This unique and uncomfortable bipartisan position of the Alignment was perhaps one reason for an earlier unpleasant scene between the two leaders which occurred on 19 July. With Begin's prior consent, Peres had held a three-hour talk with Sādāt in Vienna on 9 July. At the time, the Egyptian ruler approved a "Vienna formula"—suggested by Austrian President Bruno Kreisky, but actually drafted by Peres and Abba Eban—as the basis for an Israel-Egypt declaration of principles. In the Knesset, however, the Prime Minister denied the opposition's right to negotiate and charged it with undermining government efforts. During the debate, which was frequently interrupted by shouts from Likud and Alignment members, Begin divulged for the first time that he had actually forbidden Peres from accepting a discreet invitation to meet King Husayn of Jordan in Europe. This was greeted by calls from the Alignment benches that the Premier was sick, irresponsible and unfit to continue the delicate negotiations with the Arabs.

Such episodes aside, the Alignment continued to give Begin the backing he needed in dealing with Cairo and Washington, while still watching for an opportunity to oust the Likud from power. Towards the end of 1978, Peres seemed to have consolidated his position as party chairman and also to have added to his stature as a world statesman by visits abroad. Steering something of a middle course, he also managed to hold the Alignment together. The alarming economic situation in November finally provided him and other party leaders (such as Gad Yaakobi and Haim Bar-Lev) with a domestic issue on which to launch an attack on the Likud at one of its most vulnerable points.

The Democratic Movement for Change, on the other hand, ended the year as the biggest political loser among Israel's many parties. Founded in 1976, the DMC entered 1978 as an important political factor. It held 15 seats in the Knesset and constituted a main component of the Likud coalition, with aspirations for a central role in national and local political life. By the end of the year, however, the DMC controlled only seven seats, while seemingly being reduced to the status of a junior partner in the government. That it had lost its appeal and viability as a political organization could be seen from its failure in November to contest or to field candidates in the municipal elections.

Two central factors in the DMC's decline were the issue of peace terms and Begin's manner of conducting government business. In fact, however, this weakening of its position could be traced back to the formation of the party and its decision to join the government. When originally founded, the DMC incorporated elements of *Shinui* (Change), a protest movement which had arisen in the wake of the Yom Kippur War and attracted a group of intellectuals and university professors, and of the Democratic Movement, which called for basic social and political reforms. Having done well at the May 1977 polls, the party's leadership debated for months whether or not to join the government before finally agreeing to do so in October. Divergences within the DMC on this issue were revealed in an interview by one unnamed MK: "We lack a common political philosophy. Before the elections, it didn't matter because we planned to work with a weakened Alignment. Now with Likud, we're slipping apart." [1]

If the election returns upset the DMC calculations, so did the Sādāt initiative and Begin's subsequent response, developments which exposed and accentuated the serious internal weaknesses within the party. Members continued to express dissatisfaction with their treatment by the other coalition partners, pointing to their exclusion from key decisions by the Prime Minister and instances where DMC ministers were neither consulted sufficiently nor in time. Resisting demands that the movement leave the coalition, Yadin argued that more was to be gained from seeking to influence policy from within the government than from being relegated to the opposition—particularly when Israel's international position remained so critical.

Nevertheless, opinion polls showed a dramatic decline in DMC support. According to a Reuter report on 16 June, only 22% of those who had voted for *Dash* in the 1977 elections would do so again. In the summer, Yadin came under renewed fire from critics within the party for his continued co-operation with the government. For weeks speculation was rife that a split was inevitable. In the middle of August, the Deputy Prime Minister lost a first test of strength when 59 members of the DMC directorate outvoted his supporters and decided, against his wishes, to postpone internal elections until after a thorough ideological debate. The real issue, however, was seen as whether or not to stay in the government on the eve of the Camp David summit, when Begin was still pictured as intransigent.

The split, which finally came on 23 August, resulted in the 15 seats of the original DMC being divided as follows: seven seats for the Democratic Movement led by Yadin which remained in the coalition; seven seats for *Shai* (the Movement for Change and Initiative) led by Meir Amit and Amnon Rubenstein; and one seat for former DMC member Assaf Yaguri who stood as an independent. This split cast doubts on the survival of a movement which had once appeared a potent political force.

Although the National Religious Party, with 12 seats, was also shaken by events, it managed to bear the strains better than the DMC. Having become disenchanted with the Labour Party, its traditional partner in previous coalitions, the NRP had welcomed the Likud victory, seeing Menahem Begin and Herut as natural allies in pressing Israel's claim to the biblical lands of the patriarchs on the West Bank of the Jordan River. Led by Zevulun Hammer and Dr Yehudah Ben-Meir, members of the NRP youth faction maintained close ties with the Gush Emunim movement and identified with its goal of enlarging the Jewish presence in Judea and Samaria. In recent years they had come to assume key positions within the party, pushing a more hawkish and nationalistic programme.

Like the other parties, the NRP was forced to rethink its position in the first half of 1978; it, too, found itself internally divided. One faction, led by MK's David Glass and Avraham Melamed, favoured a policy of taking risks and making whatever concessions might be found necessary in the sacred cause of peace. Rabbi Haim Druckman, on the other hand, voiced the feelings of a second group which adhered to the original party platform and cited religious injunctions against yielding up any part of the Holy Land. The September debate in the Knesset represented something of a moment of truth for the NRP, as it had for other parties. Five of its 12 MKs, including the NRP's three ministers (Abuhatzera, Hammer and the party's leader, Dr Yosef Burg) voted with the government. Druckman and two others flatly rejected the Camp David accords; the remaining four MKs abstained. Expressing the latter's political and moral predicament, Ben-Meir said that were he to raise his hand in support of the agreements, he would be unable to look Rafiah settlers in the eye; but if Menahem Begin finally presented the Camp David accords as the best agreement Israel was able to make, he could not vote against it. Walking this tightrope between religious beliefs and political commitments, Ben-Meir, Burg and Hammer nevertheless managed to keep the NRP together and safely within the coalition.

ELECTION OF THE PRESIDENT

Israel's complex system of multiple parties, coalition-building and parliamentary government was made even more unpredictable in 1978 by the crossing of existing party lines and the blurring of traditional positions. Although Menahem Begin had quit the National Unity Government in 1970 out of opposition to the very thought of withdrawal, the most recent political controversy found him pressing for territorial concessions, including all of Sinai, Gaza and Sharm al-Shaykh. Herut, swept into office on a hard-line policy, had become a party of peace, acknowledging the rights of the Palestinians. Moreover, the Labour Party, constantly criticized by Begin in the past for its soft approach, now attacked him for yielding too much to Sādāt. A Premier who had celebrated his election victory by pledging that there would be "many more Kaddums" (pioneering settlements), and the NRP, closely identified with Gush Emunim activists, found themselves in a position of having to forcibly remove would-be settlers from unauthorized sites. Uncompromising Herut hardliners like Geula Cohen and Moshe Shamir aligned themselves in opposition to government policy with 'peaceniks' and Communists such as Meir Wilner; while Arye Eliav and Meir Pa'il of the Shelli Party, usually two of Begin's most consistent critics in the Knesset, ended up defending the Premier from detractors within the Likud and the coalition.

Among the many such strange alliances which developed in the new situation, one episode in particular stands out—precisely because it had nothing to do with the dominant and disruptive peace issue. On 28 May, Yitzhak Navon became the fifth President of the State of Israel, succeeding Prof Ephraim Katzir who had decided not to stand for a second term. According to accepted practice, the candidate favoured by the party in power is assured of filling the largely ceremonial office, but in a year of uncertainty and surprises, not even this went according to plan. Begin's initial candidate was Prof Yitzhak Shaveh, a little known physicist chosen for his apolitical background and Sephardi (Oriental Jewish) origins. However, it soon became apparent that none of the coalition partners (aside from Herut) would vote for him. Elimelech Rimalt, a former leader of the Liberal Party, submitted his candidacy on 22 March. But it did not enjoy Begin's favour, and he withdrew his name six days later. On 29 March, Yitzhak Navon allowed himself to be nominated and was elected unopposed on 19 April with 86 votes—the highest number received by any presidential candidate other than Israel's first President, Hayim Weizman.

The new President had a strong political background, having served as personal political secretary to Ben-Gurion from 1951–63. At the time of his selection, he was a leading member of the Alignment; indeed, during the fierce 1977 election campaign it was Navon who appeared almost nightly on television to caution voters about what it would be like to have a government headed by Menahem Begin. Nor was this the only irony. Navon had sought and been denied his own party's endorsement for President in 1973. Now, five years later, he was installed in this office by his political opponents.

While Israelis could but wonder at the strange fortunes of politics, the choice of Navon was greeted with almost universal approval. As Hanna Zemer, editor of *Davar*, wrote on the eve of the Jewish new year, the assumption of the office of President by Navon was "one of the grand gifts of the year that has passed." After his election, Navon sought to exploit the limited authority of his office to symbolize national unity and win the confidence of the public at large.

THE KNESSET

The deliberations of the ninth Knesset were memorable on two particular occasions: on 28 December 1977 when the government won support for its peace proposals;

and on 28 September 1978 when the Knesset endorsed the Camp David framework for a ME peace settlement. Veteran parliamentary observers found it difficult to recall when—since the three-day argument in January 1952 over German reparations—the Knesset had served as the focus for such earnest debate and for decisions of such historic consequence.

The 26-point peace plan was approved in December 1977 by 64 votes to eight, with 40 abstentions (mainly by the Alignment). In the following September the Camp David accords were approved by a margin of 84 to 19, with 17 abstentions. However, these figures do not reflect the intensity of the debate, the range of opinions expressed, or the emotionally charged atmosphere. In his speech to the Knesset, Sādāt had cautioned Israel's leaders and people about the "courage" that would be needed to take "fate-determining decisions" in the coming months. In his opening statement, the Prime Minister admitted that, "for the sake of peace, we have assumed a grave responsibility and considerable risks." He went on: "We have no alternative. . . . One has to accept responsibility with the degree of civic courage without which political decisions are impossible. I have no doubt that the government's way is the only way which will make negotiations and a peace agreement possible." The sharp dichotomy of views at that early stage of contacts with Egypt was reflected by Moshe Shamir. He told parliament: "Ask me what is *my* Eretz Yisrael (land of Israel)! I will tell you: it is the Golan, Galilee, the valleys of this great land, Judea and Samaria, the Jordan Rift, Gaza and—yes—Sinai. They are ours, not as spoils of war but a legacy of the Jewish people." Such sharp attitudes notwithstanding, the government passed its first crucial test in the Knesset after a session of over 11 hours.

The scene was repeated in the following September when the Prime Minister returned from Washington to set before parliament the terms he had agreed at Camp David. The ensuing debate lasted nearly 18 hours, during which a procession of c. 80 speakers put their views on record. What gave this and the preceding debate particular importance was the fact that they were given full live coverage by Israeli television and radio. Work virtually came to a halt as tens of thousands of anxious citizens followed the arguments. Many viewers and listeners stayed up until the close of the session at 3.30 a.m. to learn how individual members actually voted, as much as to see the final outcome. This indicated the educational impact television was beginning to have on Israel's parliamentary life, as well as the degree of public interest aroused by the quest for peace.

Less dramatic perhaps but no less important than the plenary debates was the work of the Knesset's various standing committees, and especially the Foreign Affairs and Security Committee whose members were already concerned with developments in 1978 relating to South Lebanon. Its chairman, Prof Moshe Arens, was a foremost advocate of adopting a clear stand both in protecting the Lebanese Christian community and in dissuading Syria from attempting a complete military and political takeover in Lebanon. Although a member of the Likud, Arens also used his position to urge greater caution upon the government in its policy towards Egypt and the US. On the key issue of the Camp David agreements, he actually voted against the proposals yet retained his chairmanship.

The Committee also maintained a running battle with key ministers and top officials who showed some reluctance to appear before it or to report on sensitive matters of foreign and security policy. While Deputy Premier Yadin tended to be co-operative, the Foreign and Defence Ministers on several occasions rejected invitations to report on the grounds that the Committee, composed of representatives of the larger parties, invariably leaked classified information to the press. In one such confrontation in November 1978, the Chief of Staff, Maj-Gen Rafael Eitan, refused to answer questions and bluntly suggested that the Committee might wish to fire him. Within a matter of hours this, too, was fully reported by the media. Nevertheless, the Committee appeared intent upon maintaining its independent watchdog role. In an unusual resolution on 6 November, the Committee unanimously passed a motion to inform Begin and the delegation in Washington of reservations and general disapproval of the loan requested from the American government. Seven members also protested in a letter against the Cabinet's attitude towards the Committee, and hence to the Knesset as a whole.

LOCAL GOVERNMENT

There could be no mistaking the general thrust of Israeli politics during 1978; the focus was clearly on the larger political and economic issues of peace and inflation. This was one of the impressions confirmed by the results of local elections held on 7 November when, for the first time, balloting for city and town councils took place separately from Knesset elections.

Although the actual pattern of voting lacked clear definition, several tentative conclusions were possible. For one thing, the separation of national from municipal elections made it possible for voters to focus attention on issues of local concern such as education, development plans, property taxes and the quality of life in general. For another, the procedural step of casting two separate ballots—one for party council members, a second for the mayoral candidate—turned the election into a contest of personalities as much as of parties. The Alignment victory in Jerusalem, for example, was attributed to Mayor Teddy Kollek, who won 62,276 votes, 62.4% of the total and c. 15,000 more than were cast for his council list. Similarly in Tel Aviv, where the Likud won 15 of the 31 council seats, credit for this slender victory went to incumbent Mayor Shlomo Lahat. He obtained 58% of the poll, 15% more than the Likud party list.

A third and more disturbing conclusion was the low voter turnout in a country where participation and voting have always been high. In the 1977 Knesset elections, no less than 79.2% of eligible voters cast ballots compared with less than 50% in these first direct municipal elections. This poor result was obtained despite the questionable decision by the government to make election day an official holiday, and despite large campaign expenditure on publicity and advertising. Post-election analysts expressed concern at what was seen as a general lack of enthusiasm verging on apathy. A fourth conclusion was that even though each of the parties claimed victory and improvements upon their 1977 positions, the results were inconclusive in that they did not point to any greater national trend—unless it was that the electorate would in future insist on closer accountability. In Rehovot, outgoing Mayor Shmuel Rechtman faced bribery charges, while mere reports of administrative irregularities were enough in Ramat Hasharon to remove Pesach Belkin from office. Television's official pollster, Hanoch Smith, projected that if a Knesset election were to be held, a resurgent Alignment would make major gains, topping the list with 48 seats to 46 for the Likud; but a poll conducted by Dr Nina Zemach of Tel Aviv University showed the opposite: 54 seats for the Likud and 36 for the Alignment.

THE SETTLEMENTS ISSUE

The question of immediate and future settlement policy remained a foremost subject of governmental and public concern in 1978. It had far-reaching implications not only for the prospects of peace, but for the nature of Israeli society as Jewish pioneering and settlement have always been central to Zionist thought and practice. Moreover, in the decade since the Six-Day War, Israel held *de facto* possession of lands to which it had always maintained a legal-historical claim and which it saw fit both to administer and develop so long as the Arab states refused to negotiate a territorial compromise. On the other hand, however, these areas had a non-Jewish population of over 1m whose incorporation into Israel would imply domination over a sizeable Arab minority which had one of the world's highest rates of population increase. Projections to the year 2000 by Dr Moshe Hartman of the Strategic Studies Centre at Tel Aviv Univeristy suggested that Israel would require 25,000 immigrants annually in order to maintain a Jewish majority; otherwise, in two decades, the Jewish percentage would decline to less than half of the total population.[2]

The problem of policy towards the territories was made acute during 1978 by the Sādāt initiative since peace was being extended as the *quid pro quo* for Israel's relinquishing its control over the West Bank, Gaza and perhaps eventually the Golan Heights. Furthermore, the Egyptian position remained firm in dismissing suggestions of exchange of territory, as in the southern Negev, and in insisting that there could be no Israeli presence whatsoever in the Sinai; existing settlements would have to be dismantled. In addition, the US held steadfast to the argument that the Israeli settlements had no legal basis. The problem was exacerbated by the inability of the Begin government to decide upon and articulate a clear stand on the issue.

Subjected to contradictory and countervailing domestic and external pressures, the government sought to steer a middle course, but without success. Trying to reassure Israeli settlers and nationalists yet without prejudicing the peace talks, the government gave the impression of equivocation, indecision, subterfuge and, in the end, of yielding to superior pressure. Thus, at a press conference in October 1977, the Deputy Defence Minister explained that settlement policy would be based on the military criterion of securing "strategic axes and key points." Accordingly, between 10-14 new settlements were to be established within the next 12 months, and the government approved a special budget of $5.7m for this purpose. But this was before the Sādāt visit.

Even afterwards, however, government support was pledged for continued settlement on all three fronts: Sinai, the Golan and the West Bank. In January 1978, Begin assured settlers in Sinai that they would be protected by "an Israeli force." and administered by Israel. On 1 January, Moshe Dayan and Ariel Sharon flew to the new town of Yamit to allay fears of the settlers there that the entire Sinai would be returned to Egypt. Five days later, a spokesman announced that the Prime Minister and his wife had joined the Ne'ot Sinai settlement to which they hoped to retire upon his departure from office. A few days later on 8 January, the government clarified its policy: there would be no new settlements in Sinai, but it would "extend agricultural lands and encourage additional settlers to move to existing Israeli communities" in the Rafiah salient; existing settlements would stay where they were. These assurances resulted in a property boom in Yamit. In the north, inhabitants of the Golan Heights (comprising the mayors of five Druze villages and representatives of the 25 Jewish settlements established there since 1967) called on the government on 11 January 1978 to annex the Heights to Israel. A committee was also formed to supervise development in the area. On the West Bank, the Knesset Foreign Affairs and Security Committee on 10 January approved the setting up of four new settlements, initially in army camps. These were to supplement the existing 39 settlements and outposts in Judea and Samaria, 23 of them located for security reasons in the Jordan Valley.

Thereafter, however, foreign and domestic criticism resulted in a freeze upon new projects. On 8 May, Israel Radio broadcast a report that the allocation for new

Israeli Settlements in the West Bank

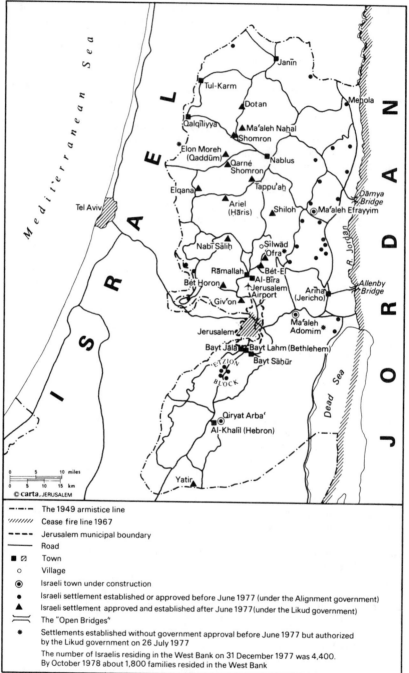

The 1949 armistice line
Cease fire line 1967
Jerusalem municipal boundary
Road
Town
Village
Israeli town under construction
Israeli settlement established or approved before June 1977 (under the Alignment government)
Israeli settlement approved and established after June 1977 (under the Likud government)
The "Open Bridges"
Settlements established without government approval before June 1977 but authorized by the Likud government on 26 July 1977

The number of Israelis residing in the West Bank on 31 December 1977 was 4,400.
By October 1978 about 1,800 families resided in the West Bank

settlements in the 1978 budget was the lowest for three years—only $15m. Whereas the budget for 1977 had provided for 25 new settlements, the provision for 1978 was for only nine. However, work did progress on two projects: constructing a network of roads linking Jewish settlements on the West Bank to the national transportation grid; and "fleshing out" Jerusalem in its south-eastern environs at Gi'von,Efrat and Ma'ale Adomin. In June, Ariel Sharon, the minister responsible for settlement policy, announced that the government would concentrate on strengthening existing points. In August, the Cabinet decided to halt a move to establish five new military settlement outposts in the Jordan Valley. Further discussion of the settlement question was to be deferred until after the Camp David summit.

The agreements in Washington initiated a third phase in the controversy which, on 21 September, had already led to a direct confrontation between the government and the Gush Emunim settlers. On 19 September, the Cabinet had decided at a special meeting and in the Premier's absence to forcibly remove a group of several hundred illegal Gush Emunim squatters on the West Bank and to prevent any further such settlements. Two days later unarmed soldiers evicted the settlers from their site near Nablus—in some cases by carrying them bodily. Subsequent attempts by settlers were similarly foiled by the army. On 24 September, the Cabinet took a major decision, by 11 votes to 2, to remove all settlements from the Sinai peninsula in return for a peace treaty with Egypt. As a result of this decision and despite protests from Yamit residents, financial allocations were halted for economic plans or new investment in construction and agriculture in the Sinai area.

Still, the issue persisted. Differences of interpretation between Begin and Carter surfaced over exactly what had been agreed upon at Camp David: whether Israel had pledged to halt further settlement merely for the three-month negotiating period with Egypt, or indefinitely and until autonomy could be implemented. Here again, questionable aspects of style and timing proved unfortunate. In October 1978, the Cabinet decided to expand or "thicken" West Bank and Gaza settlements while peace talks were continuing in Washington. In November, an occasion was found to announce plans for an urban centre in Gaza. Indicative of the sensitivity and suspicion engendered by the settlement issue was the misunderstanding in April 1978 over the unauthorized presence of the American Vice-Consul in Jerusalem, Edmund Hull, at the West Bank settlement of Haris, 32 km east of Tel Aviv, from which he was ordered out on suspicion of gathering intelligence.

Besides its implications for the peace initiative and Israel's foreign relations, the settlement controversy also had an impact upon public opinion at home. It was instrumental, for instance, in the formation and mobilization of new interest groups. It also ran counter to impressions of general public apathy, because of the direct concern and involvement of large numbers of citizens in these groupings. A *Dahaf* poll of 600 adults in four cities in December 1977 showed that 41.4% were willing to give up Judea and Samaria in return for true peace and appropriate security guarantees, while 21.8% were unwilling to do so. This poll, taken in the wake of Sādāt's dramatic visit,[3] was in strong contrast with an identical one in January 1977 which found 65% of those questioned completely unwilling to consider yielding the West Bank. In January 1978, two surveys by the Israel Institute of Applied Social Research indicated that a majority of Israelis endorsed autonomy for the entire West Bank.[4] These statistics did not reflect the intensity of feelings stirred by the issue.

If President Sādāt had been motivated even in part by a desire to divide Israeli society and to encourage the "peace camp," his stratagem seemed to be working. This was apparent from the emergence of the "Peace Now" movement which attracted a great deal of attention. Many Israelis blamed their own government for the slowing down of the peace momentum in the spring of 1978, and began to express their criticism openly. What quickly developed into a large movement actually began on 7 March when c. 300 army reservists, including officers, addressed a letter to the Prime Minister, asking him to choose peace rather than claims to territories. Replying the next day, the Premier assured them that he was doing everything possible to prevent war and to attain peace. In the meantime, he counselled: "Let the elected government conduct the negotiations for peace, and good citizens would do well not to hamper its fulfilment."

Instead, the reservists initiated a voluntary protest movement which attracted thousands of supporters to a rally on 1 April 1978 in Tel Aviv. Continuing to criticize Begin for his hard-line stance, "Peace Now" stepped up its activity. On 24 April, a spokesman for over 350 Israeli university lecturers submitted their manifesto supporting the movement and urging further concessions for peace. In a message also published in the New York Times, a group of 37 prominent American Jewish leaders and intellectuals greeted "with delight and relief" this emergence of a peace movement in Israel. On 26 April, c. 4,000 "Peace Now" supporters assumed positions for 20 km along the main highway into Jerusalem and waved placards bearing such messages as: "Better a land of peace than a piece of land." For a time in June public attention focused on the hunger strike by peace campaigner Abie Natan against Jewish settlement in the administered territories. His fast ended after 45 days in response to an emotional appeal by the government and the entire Knesset. Yet even supporters of "Peace Now" were shocked at just how far civil disobedience could go when on 22 August, on the eve of the Camp David summit, 100 reservists announced that, if ordered to defend or guard settlements in the territories, they would refuse to do so. While vowing to serve in the Israeli Defence Forces "for the defence of the well-being, security and sovereignty of the State of Israel," they said that they had not committed themselves "to spill blood for the sake of a vision of a 'Greater Israel'." Any further challenge to authority was averted by the Israeli reversal of position at Camp David. Enthusiastically greeting this change, "Peace Now" joined in the large welcome for Begin, finding in the government's policy a clear vindication of the movement and of its tactics. But as a result, it also lost much of its appeal and urgency.

The Camp David agreements had the opposite effect upon a second rival protest group known as the "Secure Peace" movement. For its members, as well as for Gush Emunim, the Sādāt diplomatic offensive represented a direct threat to settlement achievements and plans as well as for the security and future of the state. Thus, in response to the "Peace Now" activities on 15 April, an estimated 35,000 Israelis demonstrated in Tel Aviv in support of the government's tough stand. "Secure Peace" spokesmen questioned Sādāt's sincerity less than his ability to honour and enforce a peace treaty. They also saw Carter as making Israel "the same promises Kissinger made to the Vietnamese."

The dangers of a threat to established authority thus also came from the political Right. Having greeted Begin's election with undiluted enthusiasm, the leaders of Gush Emunim soon found themselves in opposition to government policy. As early as 22 December 1977, their reading of the Israeli peace proposals prompted a demonstration outside the office of the Prime Minister. Begin was described as a "broken idol" and accused of reneging on his election promise to allow settlements throughout the biblical land of Palestine. While Arabs of the territories were seeking—and finding—legal redress in appeals to the Israeli courts against development work near their villages, Gush Emunim continued to demand a more energetic settlement policy, including expropriation of Arab lands where necessary to make room for Jews to settle. They went further by seeking to "create facts" through unauthorized settlement. On 6 July, Gush leaders independently announced their own ambitious master plan aimed at forcing the government's consent to settle 100,000 Jews in the territories within a decade. Subsequent polls indicated that Gush Emunim and the "Greater Land of Israel" movement did not enjoy mass support. In a survey conducted on 31 October,[5] 65% answered in the negative when asked whether Israel ought to continue settlement of the territories while negotiations with Egypt were in progress. Yet the fact that 35% favoured immediate settlement, despite American and Egyptian objections, also suggested how powerful these movements were, and how confused and deeply divided Israelis continued to be over the future of Jewish settlement.

ECONOMIC AFFAIRS
THE NEW ECONOMIC POLICY AND INFLATION
The biggest question on the economic front was how far the government had been successful in regaining control over the economy through the reforms introduced at the end of 1977. The New Economic Policy (NEP) provided for the liberalization of foreign currency control, unification of exchange rates, and the floating of the Israeli pound. The criteria for its success were clearly outlined in a statement by the Bank of Israel: "Attainment of the economic targets, namely the resumption of growth together with a further bolstering of the balance of payments and the slowing of inflation, thus depends first and foremost on a fiscal policy that will lead to the reduction of the public sector's demand and an income policy that will prevent unnecessary cost-push on prices."[6]

By the end of 1978, however, it was painfully clear that the government had failed to set the nation on a course of renewed economic growth and stability. The high rate of inflation evident since the end of 1973 continued unabated. This was brought home in full force by a report in November 1978 showing that the consumer price index had shot up 5.7% in October, the highest monthly increase in 1978. Since January the index went up by 34.8%, so that the total increase for the year was likely to exceed the 42% registered in 1977. As most households could attest, Israel's inflation was running at 50%, despite official disclaimers and the juggling of statistics. Not only was the NEP not reducing inflation, in some ways it appeared to be fuelling it. Most forecasters were agreed that if this situation continued, grave consequences would ensue for the country—and also for a government having to deal simultaneously with the transition to peace and with real economic discontent.

The causes of inflation were fairly clear-cut: it originated in the heavy defence spending after the Yom Kippur War (from IL 5.8 bn in 1972 to IL 15.3 bn in 1973 and IL 41.6 bn in 1977),[7] and was sustained by the sharp rise in the price of oil and other imported primary commodities and by a consequent worsening of its terms of trade. The problem was made more acute by rising expectations at home; uncurbed private consumption which continued at a rate of 3.5%; a surplus of imports over exports; the upward spiralling of wages, prices and the exchange rate of the Israeli pound. While there was general agreement as to the basic causes and characteristics of economic disequilibrium, no consensus developed as to how it might be coped with. The gulf between economic theory and reality was reflected in the experience of the NEP, particularly when it depended upon the government's resolve to take the political risks necessary to enforce reforms.

Treasury officials endeavoured to put the policy in a positive light, defending the NEP as boosting exports and increasing foreign currency reserves. Yet these gains were essentially nullified because of adverse developments in at least five crucial areas: budget expenditure, prices, wages, labour relations and trade.

The Budget

The government introduced a IL 182 bn budget for the 1978 financial year on 9 January. Savings were to be effected in three ways: reduction of arms imports from abroad by $340m, cutting of subsidies, and abolition of export premiums. Estimates included a 4% increase in GNP, 12% in exports, and a ceiling of 30% on inflation. Presented in March 1978 for its second and third readings, the budget was trimmed by IL 3.8 bn to c. IL 179 bn through further cuts in defence and other ministries. But in July, a supplementary budget was requested of IL 28 bn—to a yearly total of IL 206 bn—because of wage rises, inflation, price freezes and the continued effective devaluation of the pound. Instead of the IL 6 bn deficit foreseen in January, IL 12.5 bn was now expected. Whereas the Treasury estimated a 35% rise in prices for the year, the Bank of Israel predicted a 40% increase. Despite the resignation for a brief period of the Minister of Industry, Commerce and Tourism in protest against the proposed increase, the extra sums were approved on 1 August. However, the only way this could be done was by printing additional currency—in itself a prime inflationary step.

Prices

The advance of domestic prices continued unabated because of extra import costs and the government's reluctance—due to its support for a free market system—to regulate consumer prices. The paring of subsidies and removal of price controls were felt in basic commodities such as clothing, electricity and foodstuffs, but most dramatically in real estate and housing. In some sections of the country, such as Jerusalem and along the coastal plain, accommodation was scarce; when the Housing Ministry offered 200 flats at reduced prices in May, hundreds of Jerusalemites queued to apply. The lack of rental housing plus the high price of apartments and of land (up 150% between December 1977 and September 1978 in Tel Aviv; 80–170% in its suburbs[8]) affected young couples especially. In general, those hardest hit by the rampant inflation were the poorer classes, pensioners and larger families. In June, government sources admitted that in a single year alone—from May 1977 to May 1978—prices had risen on an average of 54%.

Knowledge of this fact and of the prospect of further rises in prices had the opposite and undesired effect of stimulating increased purchases, as well as such other disturbing economic behaviour as hoarding, artificial shortages created by wholesalers, and speculative transactions on the Israeli stock exchange. Nor did the increase of Value Added Tax on all purchases from 8–12% act as a credible deterrent. Also meant to bring in additional revenue, the system of VAT was weakened by the government's inability to devise effective methods of collection. Unreported income meant a loss of substantial taxes and aggravated inflation still further because of the circulation of "black money."

Wages

As Finance Minister Simha Ehrlich admitted, the success of NEP depended largely upon holding the line on wages. While promising to make efforts to prevent any decline in real wages, he asked workers to be patient and not to press demands for increases. Yet spiralling prices prompted a subsequent round of wage demands. Apart from consenting to cost-of-living increments, the government sought to take a firm stand, warning that wage hikes must be limited to no more than 15%. This brought it into collision with the powerful Israel Labour Federation, the Histadrut, which pledged to fight against a decline in purchasing power. Under the threat of widespread strikes, the Cabinet tended to reflect a pattern of stubborn resistance followed by concessions—albeit through less obvious means such as retroactive adjustments or exemptions from the 15% wage limit. Not surprisingly, an opinion poll conducted by the PORI Institute for *Ha'aretz* revealed in November 1978 that 49% of those interviewed did not think the government would be able to control the wave of strikes and would be forced to give in to wage demands.

Labour Relations
The government's credibility in economic affairs—in November 1977, Ehrlich had predicted an inflation rate of only 26–28%—suffered further from the deterioration of labour relations. The existence of a Likud coalition and a Labour-dominated Histadrut (its Secretary-General, Yeruham Meshel, was also an Alignment member of the Knesset) would have portended an uneasy relationship at the best of times; rampant inflation guaranteed a clash. Their co-operation was limited to an agreement in April 1978 for a six-month anti-inflation package which placed restraints upon civil service wages. Otherwise, however, they conflicted on most issues, including a government plan in December 1977 to sell 50 public companies in order to encourage capital investment, decentralize authority and strengthen the stock exchange by selling shares to the public.

Conflict with the Histadrut parent organization and with individual unions concentrated on wage demands. Statistics revealed that, apart from sanctions or go-slow strikes, 126 full strikes had resulted in the loss of 416,526 working days in 1977.[9] Announcement of the NEP prompted a wave of protests and strikes at the end of 1977 which set the pattern for the new year as well. A merchant seamen's strike, which began in January 1978 and became the longest running strike in Israel's history of troubled relations, ended on 7 April when the seamen agreed to submit their demand for a 70% wage increase to arbitration. Even as one strike was resolved, other unions began agitating in support of their respective claims. Thus, in one month alone, a strike by press, television and radio journalists prevented the printing of news from 1–3 April, and of broadcasting until 12 April. On 4 April, disruptions by unions forced El Al, Israel's national airlines, to suspend its services until 24 April. On 6 April, 60,000 teachers went on a 24-hour strike in support of their pay claim.

From the standpoint of the economy, matters were made worse by the absence of compulsory arbitration. Labour tensions also exposed the weakness of the Histadrut, whose inability either to satisfy or control individual member unions was revealed by unauthorized wildcat strikes, such as that of communications and postal workers in March. The government was equally vulnerable since, despite threats of resorting to "unconventional measures" or of invoking emergency orders, it preferred to let each strike run its course. Nor did such statements as that of Simha Ehrlich in March that he intended "to break the seamen's strike and remove parasitic workers from El Al" contribute to improving the atmosphere—certainly not when the government's commitment to prevent unemployment in fact perpetuated the longstanding situation of disguised unemployment. Finally, both the government and the Histadrut had less than impressive records in dealing with such economic issues as Arab labour from the administered territories, or the employment by co-operative settlements of minors from the Gaza Strip as underpaid farm hands.

Foreign Trade
Another problem area in which the government's NEP had yet to prove itself was in foreign trade. Exports did register impressive gains, with an increase of c. 28% in the first half of 1978 over 1977 ($1.836 bn as compared to $1.428 bn). Nevertheless, this was not enough, since the trade gap amounted to c. $200m. The precariousness

of Israel's position was demonstrated by events in two specific areas: citrus exports and air transportation.

On 1 February 1978, the first reports appeared of the discovery of mercury in Israeli oranges, which led to a scare throughout Europe. Palestinian groups claimed responsibility at first, explaining that the poisoning of orange consumers was an attempt to sabotage the Zionist state's economy. Israel promptly cut back its export of oranges by c. 40%, shipping only 1.5m crates a week instead of the planned 2.5m. Sales abroad dropped by as much as 30%; the loss in sales for the season was estimated at between $20–30m. In the field of international air travel, El Al sought to remain competitive, negotiating landing rights in Los Angeles, Chicago, Boston and Miami; reducing air fares; and agreeing to charter flights. But the disruption of flights whether due to strikes by union employees or to those at Ben-Gurion Airport, were harmful to tourism and also costly. The airline may have lost as much as $8m as a result of the three-week strike.

The net effect of these economic developments was to aggravate rather than ease Israel's balance of payments difficulties. One of the government's priorities continued to be the search for outside support, including that of world Jewry. Israel also succeeded in acquiring a $90m loan from the International Monetary Fund after a visit by the Fund's delegation in August 1978. It received an estimated $1.8 bn in aid from the US government and sought to increase its aid from South Africa to c. $80m.

In late November 1978, a further budget amounting to IL 300 bn was tabled, one-third of it earmarked for defence needs and another one-third for debt repayment. The Finance Ministry's figures allowed for a 37% rate of inflation. But its call for budget cuts in educational and social services was strenuously resisted by the affected ministries. Thus few economists were convinced that inflation could be held to under 50%. In fact, most speculated about the likelihood of a rise to 60% during the next fiscal year.

ECONOMIC PROSPECTS FOLLOWING PEACE

As much of Israel's economic plight stemmed from its unremitting state of belligerency with neighbouring Arab countries, the year-long negotiations permitted time for contemplating the economic realities and costs of a possible peace. On the one hand, Treasury and inter-ministerial special committees competed in drafting proposals for joint projects with Egypt in the event of peace, open borders, an end to the Arab economic boycott and the free flow of goods, services and people. Serious discussions began about possible collaboration in such areas as tourism, development of the Sinai and scientific enterprises. But more immediately, policy-makers also became aware of new economic problems which were almost certain to arise. Foremost among these was the likely inflationary effect of expenses incurred in such tasks as constructing a wholly new defence system along the border with Egypt. According to one figure, the completion of two modern airfields in the Negev alone would amount to $2 bn.[10]

A second economic concern arising from peace would be the need for new external oil supplies to replace those from Sinai. In March, the Energy Minister indicated that oil pumped from the Sinai fields of At-tur and Alma would be capable of satisfying one-third of Israel's needs within a year. As the negotiations over a treaty progressed, this concern over oil prompted Ehrlich to participate in talks in Washington in an unsuccessful attempt to obtain written Egyptian assurances of favourable terms for the sale of oil from these fields or, alternatively, of American guarantees of an uninterrupted supply, particularly in the light of disturbing developments in Iran, the largest seller of oil to Israel. Another problem identified by economic policy-makers should peace be achieved was the likely increase in Israel's economic dependence upon the US. This would have direct consequences for Israel's sovereignty and also highlights a major problem of Israeli foreign policy. (Also see "Economic Affairs—Supplement" and tables at the end of this chapter.)

FOREIGN RELATIONS
In foreign policy, Prime Minister Begin and the Likud government found themselves faced with difficult, even fateful choices and with few options. Despite the drama of the Sādāt initiative, the conduct of external affairs did not differ fundamentally in 1978 from previous years. Diplomacy remained in the hands of a small political élite rather than of professionals in the Foreign Ministry, who were restricted to performing mostly technical functions. Statecraft, as always, emphasized the primacy of national security. Foreign policy overwhelmingly concentrated upon—and in the public's view was synonymous with—preserving close ties with the US, Israel's principal and almost only major ally. As in the past, international relations were conducted under a cloud of isolation, unfavourable world opinion and a mostly hostile environment. Indeed, the chief distinction of 1978 was the prospect of finally improving Israel's international position by reaching an agreement with Egypt, even if not a comprehensive settlement with the collective Arab states. Consequently, the emphasis was almost exclusively on two target states: Egypt and the US—not so much in a bilateral sense as through a complicated triangular relationship in which Israeli-American relations became inextricably bound up and entangled with those toward Cairo, and vice versa. Indeed, a new word, "linkage," entered the Hebrew vocabulary. Though referring specifically to ties with Egypt hinging upon the pace of autonomy in the administered territories, in a sense it could also be seen as applying to American financial and military assistance being a function of progress in the negotiations. This could be determined by greater flexibility and concessions on Israel's part.

Whatever the wisdom of the government's core peace strategy—and here there were critics on every side—it had at least four primary objectives:

(1) To seek a durable peace and avoid another war by arriving at a separate treaty with Egypt.

(2) Optimally, to assure the friendship and support of the US.

(3) Minimally, to prevent a Washington-Cairo axis to the exclusion of Israel.

(4) To achieve these goals without sacrificing fundamental foreign policy and security tenets, which were: (a) not forfeiting the claim to ultimate sovereignty over Judea and Samaria; (b) a continued presence along the Jordan River; (c) freedom of movement on the West Bank and the right of Jews to settle there; (d) precluding the creation of a Palestinian state under the PLO to the west of the Jordan. In order to ensure these strategic goals, Israeli policy-makers, led by Begin, Dayan and Weizman, showed a willingness to compromise on tactics or secondary issues, such as by consenting to America's pivotal role as a "full partner" in the negotiating process; by agreeing to dismantle settlements; and by accelerating the timetable for an autonomy scheme for the West Bank.

RELATIONS WITH THE UNITED STATES
The centrality of bilateral relations with Washington could be seen in a number of areas and was reflected in the six trips by Premier Begin to the US since taking office: in July and December 1977; and in March, April, September and November 1978. (Also see essay, "The United States and the Middle East: The Peace

Process.'') It was reflected in such public declarations as that by President Carter on 1 May 1978 that the US would "never waver in our absolute commitment to Israel's security. I can say without reservation we will continue to do so, not for 30 years but forever." Whether or not one could justifiably speak of a "special relationship," statistics confirmed the success of Israeli diplomacy in translating a moral commitment into something more concrete. In 1977, the US accounted for 18.9% ($581m) of Israel's total export market, and in turn was the source of 22% of its non-military imports ($956m). [11] The US was also the main supplier of Israel's military requirements, including sophisticated missiles, fighter planes and electronic equipment, as well as financial assistance to prop up a weak, wartime economy. On 1 September 1978, Israel submitted a $2.4 bn aid request to the US for the fiscal year 1979, of which $1.5 bn would take the form of military assistance. After Camp David, an additional special request for a cash grant of $3.37 bn was presented to cover the redeployment of military forces and the building of air bases, as well as for resettling evacuees from Yamit and the agricultural settlements in Sinai. [12] The considerable time and attention which Carter and his advisers devoted to the ME and Israel in particular was yet another measure of the American commitment.

Nevertheless, Israel's American connection came under severe strain during 1978, and suffered more than one setback. Along the route from Jerusalem, Ismā'īliyya, Aswān, Salzburg and Leeds Castle to Camp David and Blair House, serious differences between the Carter Administration and the Begin government surfaced and were given wide publicity. Some of the positions reflected continuity from the time of the Johnson Administration and the Rogers Plan. For instance, the US considered all Jewish settlements across the 1967 "green line" to be illegal; refused to acknowledge either Israeli authority over East Jerusalem, or the western part of the city as the capital of the State; and rejected Israel's interpretation of Resolution 242 as excluding withdrawal from the West Bank. Moreover, Washington pressed upon Israel the need for an early withdrawal from South Lebanon, for acknowledging the "legitimate rights" of the Palestinians to a "homeland," and for proceeding with administrative "autonomy" on the West Bank which would be of limited, not indefinite, duration.

The divergence of interests and of views between the two countries was highlighted by the controversy over the American decision to supply fighter planes to Egypt and Saudi Arabia as well as Israel as a $4.8 bn package deal—notwithstanding protests by the Begin government that such a transaction constituted a "grave danger to the peace-making process and to Israel's security." Senate approval of the sales also represented a defeat for the pro-Israel US lobby. Later in the year, American replies to Jordanian queries as to the future of the occupied territories and the mission of Harold Saunders to Jerusalem (including his talks with West Bank leaders) led to yet another in a series of acrimonious public exchanges. There were hints that the US-Israeli relationship was threatening to become more troubled than special. Once again, Israel was confronted by the cold realities involved in any patron-client situation.

RELATIONS WITH OTHER COUNTRIES

As part of the constant effort at normalizing its international relations, Israel maintained ties with 71 other countries through c. 80 overseas missions. These relations took on extra importance after the Sādāt initiative since Israel was naturally keen to present its policy abroad. Here, too, the balance sheet for the year showed both gains and reverses. On the plus side, there were discreet contacts with Morocco. King Hassan expressed greater understanding for Israel's right to exist in the ME and also supported Sādāt in his diplomatic attempt to resolve the Arab-

Israeli conflict. Similarly, relations were maintained with Romania, the only Communist bloc country which had not severed ties with Israel. In the Western hemisphere, relations were improved with Mexico; on 3 March 1978, an agreement was signed by which Israel committed itself to supply to Mexico 100,000 tons of phosphate a year, while Mexico agreed to increase oil sales to Israel from 20,000 to 30,000 barrels a day. Relations with South Africa were also notable. During a visit to the Republic in February 1978, the Israeli Finance Minister signed a three-part economic agreement on investments, bonds and commercial relations. In addition, Jerusalem made conciliatory gestures towards the Papacy, releasing and expelling Archbishop Hilarion Capucci, who had been convicted of aiding terrorists, and sending congratulatory messages to Pope John Paul I and, following his death, to Pope John Paul II on their respective elections.

Among Israel's traditional friends in Western Europe, Begin paid close personal attention to Britain, holding consultations with Prime Minister Callaghan *en route* to and from the US. Foreign Minister Dayan was particularly active on the European front, paying visits to West Germany, Italy, Switzerland, Romania and Scandinavia. In a multilateral context, ties were strengthened with the European Economic Community. (See essay, "Western European and EEC Policies towards Mediterranean and ME Countries.") Dayan asked the EEC not to meddle in the politics of the ME, although differences of approach did not prejudice the signing of a protocol on economic co-operation in Brussels in December 1977. As part of its effort to gain entry into the EEC, Spain was considering the establishment of relations with Israel at the end of 1978.

Other diplomatic ties either remained broken or were weakened. In the former category, China, the Soviet Union and the Eastern European countries were circumspect towards the Sādāt initiative and made no significant effort at maintaining relations with Israel. Of the Third World countries which had severed ties with Israel in the early 1970s—especially those of black Africa—there were indications of a willingness to restore relations after a peace treaty with Egypt had been signed. With the onset of religious unrest in Iran and interruptions in its oil production, many Israeli nationals working on projects for the Shah's regime were called home. But the two most serious instances of deterioration in diplomatic relations were with Ethiopia and Austria.

Israel had been closely concerned with the developing crisis in the Red Sea area since the fall of Emperor Haile Selassie in 1973 and had succeeded in maintaining close links with Col Mengistu Haile Mariam's military regime, despite its reliance on the Soviet bloc, Cuba and Libya. (See "The Middle East and the Horn of Africa: International Politics in the Red Sea Area," in *MECS 1976-77*, and "The Politics of the Red Sea, Indian Ocean and Persian Gulf Regions" in this volume.) In a still unexplained episode on 6 February 1978, Moshe Dayan unexpectedly confirmed publicly that Israel was selling arms to Addis Ababa for use against Eritrean insurgents and the Somali invading forces in Ethiopia's Ogaden region. Ethiopia reacted promptly by severing trade relations and expelling all Israelis serving in the country. (Diplomatic relations had been severed in late 1973.) In Israel, Dayan was accused of causing "grave and irreparable" damage by his disclosure of Israel's relations with Ethiopia. This same penchant for "open-mouth" diplomacy led to a major rift in relations between Israel and Austria in September 1978 because of references allegedly made by Chancellor Bruno Kreisky in a Dutch newspaper interview. Himself a Jew, Kreisky was quoted as referring to Israel as a police state, as a country with too many generals in government, and whose Premier was a "political grocer."

As always, maintaining close ties with world Jewry and with individual Diaspora communities was an important dimension to Israeli external relations. The Prime Minister himself undertook special missions to Switzerland, the US and Canada to explain Israel's position at various stages in the peace negotiations, and also to enlist Jewish financial support for such projects as relieving poverty for 45,000 families through better housing.

The struggle on behalf of Soviet Jewry and for those Jews still in Syria was maintained. The right of Soviet Jews to emigrate was dramatized during 1978 by international demonstrations aimed at securing the release of the Russian dissident, Anatoly Scharansky. There were emotional scenes when contacts were re-established with the Jews of Egypt following the admission of Israeli negotiators and journalists into that country in early 1978.

MILITARY AFFAIRS

The opening of direct talks with Egypt in no way diminished the central role traditionally played by the Israeli Defence Forces (IDF; *Tsahal*). Pending final peace, the military was called upon to fulfil three customary tasks: defending Israeli citizens and territory from outside attack; enforcing law and order in the administered areas; and coping with terrorism at home and abroad. If anything, the IDF were saddled with additional duties such as enforcing government directives on settlement policy; representing Israel's security interests in the prolonged negotiations with Egypt; preparing for the withdrawal and redeployment of Israeli troops from Sinai in the event of a treaty with Egypt, and making contingency plans for the possible replacement of military rule on the West Bank and in Gaza. These six functions, and especially the methods of implementing them, kept the military in the public eye and invited some criticism.

The single most controversial issue in the field was "Operation Lītānī" conducted in force by *Tsahal* inside South Lebanon between 15 March and 13 June 1978. (See also "South Lebanon.") Defence Minister Weizman and Chief of Staff, Mordecai Gur, justified the deep penetration by c. 20,000 troops as legitimate self-defence. The aim of the operation was not retaliation but the defence of the State and the prevention of attacks by the PLO and al-Fath through continuous deterrent action on the northern border. Other considerations, more obvious than articulated, were generally viewed as, first, to encourage the Christian minority in the Lebanese civil war and, second, to deter Syrian attempts at moving southward towards Israel. These complex ends stimulated debate in Israel, as did the means used for achieving them.

While Israelis understood and even applauded a strong answer to recent attacks from Lebanon, there was some questioning of the magnitude of the response and whether substantial ground action was necessary. Concern was variously voiced about the likely consequences of tension in the north on the peace efforts; about American reaction, and the possibility of military clashes with the Syrians and a sudden escalation in regional violence. Questions were also raised as to the propriety of direct intervention in Lebanon's domestic problems. Both at the time of "Operation Lītānī" and subsequently, doubts were expressed about the success, let alone the wisdom, of this intervention. Most of the Fath personnel had been able to elude the Israeli forces; the position of the Christians worsened after the Israeli withdrawal; and the Syrians appeared to be entrenched in Lebanon. International criticism was strongly voiced, and Security Council Resolution 425 of 19 March called upon Israel to cease its military action and to "withdraw forthwith." American protests were also registered against Israel's use of F-15 jet fighters and especially of US-made cluster bombs in contravention of a 1976 agreement limiting them to self-defence purposes only. (For the task of the armed forces and police in waging an anti-terrorist campaign, for the situation along Israel's borders, for specific terrorist actions and the full dimensions of the security problem, see essay, "Armed Operations; Situation along the Borders," in the section Arab-Israeli Conflict.)

As the peace process intensified, the military was also called upon to enforce the ban on unauthorized settlement by Gush Emunim supporters. This created some unpleasant situations between soldiers and fellow citizens. Nevertheless, the Defence Minister was determined that the settlements' issue should not stand in the way of negotiations with Egypt. Weizman himself personified the central role of the Defence Ministry and of *Tsahal* in the peace process by his series of meetings with President Sādāt and his Egyptian counterpart, Gen Jamasī. Gen Avraham Tamir headed policy-planning teams and participated in the negotiations, including those at Camp David. Until it was ordered out by the Egyptian government on 27 July 1978, the Israeli military delegation served as an important link between the two countries.

Following the Camp David accords and basic agreement in Washington concerning Israel's phased withdrawal from Sinai, the General Staff and Defence Ministry personnel undertook a detailed examination of the military implications of these understandings, particularly of logistics. After demolishing military camps and facilities in Sinai, Israel would still have to be on the alert for possible future eventualities on other fronts; planners were also required to prepare alternative infrastructures to absorb and redeploy the men and equipment coming out of Sinai.[13] Two specific problems were those of conducting training flights in a narrow air corridor within the pre-1967 borders; and measures against possible air attacks from Saudi Arabia flying American-supplied jets from air bases at present under construction. As part of its future planning, the Defence Ministry continued to negotiate Israel's military needs for the 1980s with Washington through "Matmon 'C' "—a ten-year schedule of arms purchases amounting to $1 bn in order to maintain the ratio of 1:2.7 between itself and the Arab confrontation states. (See essay, "Military and Strategic Issues in the ME-Persian Gulf Region in 1978.")

Soon after Lt-Gen Rafael Eitan succeeded Mordecai Gur as Chief of Staff on 16 April 1978, he found himself at the centre of controversy. Despite a reputation for taciturnity, Eitan declared in a television interview on 11 May that the IDF would not be able to defend the country and maintain its independence without the Golan Heights and the West Bank. Criticized for making a political statement, he was nevertheless supported by the Cabinet which, on 14 May, voted by 14 to 3 for a statement to the effect that he had not deviated from the principle of military subordination to the government.

For the first time in Israel, Eitan had to face a discipline problem in the armed forces—a development of considerable concern for a citizen army consisting of 164,000 conscripts and c. 400,000 reservists.[14] One symptom of the loosening of discipline came from reports of disobedience by troops during "Operation Līṭānī." At a press conference on 31 March 1978, General Gur confirmed that 51 IDF soldiers had been prosecuted for looting. Following the death of three soldiers in an ambush in an unauthorized zone on 11 April, Gur ordered an investigation. Another symptom was the dismissal of Tat-Aluf David Hagoel from his post as Military Governor of the West Bank on 2 May 1978 as the result of an incident inside a school in Bayt Jālā on 21 March. (For details, see essay, "The West Bank and the Gaza Strip.") A third symptom was the announcement on 19 May that brutality had driven a religious soldier to commit suicide. Reports of discrimination by officers and NCOs against Orthodox recruits were admitted by the army Ombudsman, Gen Haim Laskov. Apart from the campaign to allow girls to claim exemption from military service on religious grounds (see above), 100 reservists published a letter in August saying that they would disobey orders to guard any Gush Emunim settlement. Moreover, the "war of the generals" over responsibility for shortcomings before and during the Yom Kippur War continued. Collectively these symptoms suggested that one of the main challenges facing the IDF was maintenance of both discipline and high morale, as well as a state of alert in the uncertain transition from 30 years of conflict to a state of uneasy peace.

SOCIAL AFFAIRS

One effect of the salience given to political, economic, diplomatic and military issues was the relative neglect of social problems, which were neither debated seriously nor tackled in earnest by the government. In such an eventful year, attention was deflected from the deeper undercurrents of social change. Yet there were developments which made 1978 something of a transition between past and future. Israel's thirtieth anniversary celebrations tended to be subdued for the most part, with not a little trace of nostalgia for the pre-1948 period of idealism. Two controversial television programmes, *Hirbit Hiza* and "The Holocaust," opened old wounds in recalling unpleasant memories of the 1948 War of Independence and the agonies of the Nazi era for European Jewry. On the other hand, thousands of Israelis and visitors flocked to the newly opened Beit Hatfutsot Museum in Tel Aviv for an encounter with the Jewish cultural legacy.

At the same time there were indications of new social ills, some of which were reflected statistically. Israel's population stood at 3,677,000, of whom 581,000 were Arabs (not including the territories). Since 1948 the population had increased 3.6 times, with 53% of the Jews born in Israel. But there was a serious drop in the Jewish birthrate: 2.5% growth in the years 1972–77 as compared with 4.1% for the non-Jewish community.[15] This demographic problem was made even more acute by the decline in immigration to Israel and by the figures for *yerida* or emigration from the country. The dropout rate of Soviet Jews electing not to come to Israel from Vienna, for example, was given at 50–60%. In general, Central Bureau of Statistics data indicated that 22,500 new immigrants arrived in 1977, while 17,500 Israelis had left, bringing the estimated number of Israelis living abroad to over 300,000.

Perhaps one major explanation was dissatisfaction with the quality of life as reflected in such things as housing (whereas in 1972 it took c. 17 months for an apartment to be built, construction in 1977 averaged two full years) or traffic fatalities (627 people killed in car accidents in 1977 alone). A report on the status of women disclosed that more than half of Israeli women had not completed elementary school, and that 20% of the girls reporting for compulsory military service were rejected as unfit. Although the Cabinet unanimously approved a provision for free high school tuition on 13 March 1978, the need for budgetary constraints at the end of the year threatened these plans. In May, the outgoing Chief of Staff was criticized for remarking that Israel's Oriental Jews would need years to catch up with Western standards, mentally and technologically. Especially alarming were charges of the existence of organized criminal activity which received official confirmation in mid-February following release of the Shimron Report.[16] Evidence of organized crime in such areas as narcotics, agricultural and airport thefts, smuggling, the wholesale agricultural market, burglary and terror among inmates in Israel's prisons illustrated the bitter consequences of three decades of neglect, as well as the immensity of Israel's social problems.

CONCLUSION

Nevertheless, these social issues paled before the immediacy of the major political, economic and peace issues. In attempting to review 1978, one realizes that the year was devoted to absorbing the after-effects of the three consecutive *mahapachim* or upheavals: political (ascendancy to power of the Likud), economic (NEP) and diplomatic (the Sādāt initiative). At the end of the year, little remained of the euphoria of the Sādāt visit and the psychological breakthrough. Peace was proving to be a lengthy, complex process. Moreover, it gave every indication of being a mixed blessing, adding to the already staggering economic problems by stimulating inflation, complicating American-Israeli relations, requiring a return, in effect, to the 1949 armistice lines—and without necessarily easing Israel's military burdens or answering its social problems. There was thus every indication that the threshold of the 1980s and the beginning of Israel's fourth decade would continue the pattern of uncertainty and challenge which had reached a peak in 1978.

THE ARABS IN ISRAEL

When President Sādāt's dramatic visit to Israel in November 1977 launched the process of Egyptian-Israeli negotiations, reactions among the Arab population in Israel quickly crystallized into three main trends: those who believed that Israeli Arabs would now, at long last, be able to serve as a "bridge" linking the Jewish population with the Arab world; those who rejected Sādāt's policy, adhering instead to the concept of the Geneva conference in the form it had assumed earlier during 1977; and those who later came to identify with the "rejectionist" attitudes of the PLO and the Arab world at large.

The emergence of such divergent and contradictory trends can partly be explained by the political, social and economic changes which the local Arabs experienced following their assumption of Israeli citizenship in 1948 and all that this implied. A major factor in the process of change was demographic growth. With an annual growth rate of nearly 4%, a community which had numbered c. 150,000 in the early 1950s had grown fourfold to c. 600,000 in 1978. Exposed to the influences of the surrounding Jewish society, the traditional and conservative Arab population was subjected to an intensified process of modernization and Westernization. Development projects introduced by the Israel government in almost all aspects of life resulted in a social and economic transformation. Traditional agriculture was replaced by modernized and mechanized methods of cultivation. Manpower thus released was absorbed in industry, construction and services, mainly in Jewish towns. Arab villages were provided with an infrastructure of roads, electricity, schools and clinics. Piped water replaced wells. Local government was introduced for the first time in many of these villages. The various aspects of modernization eventually changed the stratification of traditional society. It weakened the clan (or extended family) structure, and paved the way for the rise of a new intelligentsia which gradually strengthened its influence both politically and socially.

All these developments led to a substantial rise in the standard of living accompanied by a rise in the level of expectations, especially among the younger generation brought up and educated in Israel. In recent years, growing feelings of frustration developed among Arabs over such issues as inadequate industrialization in the Arab villages and lack of job opportunities for university graduates. Protests over social and economic issues were intensified by political radicalization which spread following the June 1967 war.

After 19 years of physical detachment from the Arab world, the Israeli Arabs were reunified with the Palestinian community in the West Bank and Gaza in 1967. This encounter marked the opening of a new era characterized by a change of concept of their national identity. Their "Palestinian personality" began to be gradually reconstructed. This was followed by a reassessment of the *status quo* situation which had characterized their relations with the Israeli authorities until then. The October 1973 war further accelerated the process of "Palestinianization." Israel's weakened image, as perceived by the Arabs, and the growing prestige of the PLO in the international and inter-Arab arenas strongly affected the political orientation of many Israeli Arabs. Open sympathy for the PLO and identification with its political aspirations spread, especially among the intelligentsia. The PLO leadership demonstrated a stronger interest in, and concern for, the Israeli Arabs, and sought to incorporate them into the overall national Palestinian struggle.

The socio-economic changes, coupled with political radicalization, laid the ground for a basic change in the pattern of political activity. Generally speaking, protest did not take the form of clandestine organization or terrorist activity. Only a marginal number of Israeli Arabs engaged in sabotage operations carried out either by PLO cadres from across the borders or in the West Bank and the Gaza Strip. The radicals took the view that more effective results could be achieved through the optimal exploitation of the legitimate patterns of political activity offered by Israeli democracy—without overstepping the bounds of law. Elections offered one major avenue to advance this policy. The results of the 1969, 1973 and 1977 Knesset elections clearly reflect a constant rise in the power of the Communist vote within the radicalized camp, together with a gradual decline in support for the Alignment and its affiliated more moderate Arab lists. In 1969, 30% of the Arab vote was cast for Rakah (the Hebrew-language acrostic of New Communist List); in 1973, this had risen to 37%; and in 1977 over 50% of the vote went to a Rakah-dominated list. The overwhelming majority obtained by the Rakah Front in the 1975 Nazareth municipal election further illustrates this tendency.

Parallelling this expression of protest at the ballot box was a new form of political activity introduced in the mid-1970s with the establishment of country-wide action committees. Three influential bodies emerged in 1974–75: the Union of Arab University Students; the Chairmen of the Arab Municipal Councils Committee; and the Defence of the Lands Committee. These organizations were established to promote the specific interests of various pressure groups, institutionally independent of established political entities. Rakah nevertheless played an instrumental role in the establishment and direction of their activities. Following the traditional Communist pattern, the leadership of these bodies was left to non-party figures in an effort to emphasize the representative character of these "front organizations." Their spokesmen declared that they were set up to solve the civil problems of the Arab population, yet they openly demonstrated a deep involvement in purely political issues such as Israeli policy in the West Bank and the right of Palestinians to self-determination. The thin line separating civil, sectional or local issues from national ones was frequently indistinct and blurred.

This was clearly illustrated by the campaign organized in 1976 by the Committee for the Defence of the Lands against the government's decision to expropriate 20,000 dunams in Galilee for development purposes. Of this area, 6,000 dunams belonged to Arab landowners who were to be compensated. The campaign over the civil aspect of the problem gradually turned into a protest against what was defined as "malicious intentions to deprive the Arab population of the last vestiges of its land." Strongly motivated by a sense of self-confidence and power, the Committee opted for open confrontation with the authorities, and called the Arab public to join in a general strike, designated as "Land Day." Violent clashes erupted between demonstrators and security forces on the day of the strike, 30 March 1976. Six Arabs lost their lives and dozens of Arabs, police and soldiers were wounded.

The more moderate political circles among Israeli Arabs expressed similar opposition to the land expropriation, but argued that efforts should concentrate on negotiating with the authorities rather than confronting them. This approach stemmed from their basic view that, given the unique circumstances of living as an Arab minority in the midst of a Jewish majority, the Israeli Arabs should adapt themselves to reality by achieving a *modus vivendi* with the government. Accepting the concept of integration in Israeli society, they tried to implement this aim by co-operating with the authorities and by political activity in Zionist parties, mainly the Labour Party and Mapam. However, the 1976 land crisis and the growing influence of Rakah, as reflected in the 1977 elections, showed that the moderate group was unable to control the course of events or to prevent increasing radicalization.

The political processes of a decade and the polarization of opinion provided the background to the varied reactions to the Israeli-Egyptian peace negotiations in late 1977. These were warmly welcomed by moderate circles whose hopes were raised that, with prospects for peace, they would finally be able to serve as a "bridge" between Jews and Arabs. Analysing the possible impact of a peace agreement on the Israeli Arabs, Mahmūd Abbāsī, a noted Arab writer and member of the Labour Party, suggested that it could lead to the final removal of the psychological and security barriers which had prevented the full integration of the Arab population in Israel.[17] Similarly favourable reactions were voiced in late September 1978 following the Camp David accords. A Haifa advocate, Jamīl Shalhūb, said he believed in the sincerity of Begin and Sādāt, and hoped that despite the "stubbornness of the Arab rejectionist front . . . it would be possible to bring all the parties to the negotiating table. Israel exists and must be recognized by the Arab world. There is genuine joy among Israeli Arabs,"[18] he concluded.

This optimistic view was not shared by the more radical circles. The Communists, committed to Soviet policy, denounced Sādāt's initiative and labelled it a "tragic stage-show."[19] They insisted that no progress could be achieved so long as both Israel and Egypt continued to bypass the PLO and the "legitimate rights of the Palestinians." They strongly advocated the reconvening of the Geneva conference under the chairmanship of the US and the USSR, with the participation of all parties involved including the PLO. Communist leaders rejected Begin's Autonomy Plan. Tawfīq Tūbī, MK, stated that Begin's plan meant giving up the rights of the Arab Palestinian people, the perpetuation of the Israeli occupation "not only for five years but forever," and the recognition of Israel's right to establish settlements.[20]

Paradoxically, Rakah found itself on the defensive, not just from moderate circles, but particularly from extremist elements grouped around the Jerusalem Arab Students' Committee and around the "Sons of the Village" group. The latter, set up in 1973, was reported to be in favour of the establishment of a democratic secular state on the entire territory of Palestine, thus identifying with the "rejectionist front." During the Knesset election campaign of May 1977, it had called on the Arab public to boycott elections to the "Zionist parliament." This group attacked Rakah for being too minimalist in its approach, e.g. by supporting Resolutions 242 and 338. In a political programme published in late 1977, Arab students totally rejected Sādāt's initiative as well as Resolutions 242 and 338 and the proposal to reconvene the Geneva conference. They contended that the PLO should be regarded as the "unifying framework of all the units of the Palestinian revolution, including the rejectionist front."[21] They also claimed the right to self-determination, not only for the Palestinians in the West Bank and Gaza, but also for the Arab "masses in Galilee and the little Triangle."[22] Similar views were expressed in February in a memorandum published by 56 members of the Arab intelligentsia who stated that "any solution to the Palestinian problem must contain an official recognition and international guarantees for the national identity of the Palestinian residents of Israel and of their rights to remain in their homeland." [23]

In spite of the opposition it encountered from the extremist groups and its unfavourable attitude towards the peace negotiations, Rakah's prestige and influence over the Arab public did not diminish. Throughout 1978, the patterns of political activity adopted by the party proved efficient, as was illustrated by the campaign over the land question and in the results of the municipal elections held in November.

Rakah's land campaign was conducted through the Committee for the Defence of the Lands against the demolition of illegally built houses. As a result of demographic growth, a rise in the standard of living, lack of state land released for private building and delays in implementing rural master plans in Arab villages, a growing number of non-licensed houses had been erected in recent years. In 1977, a governmental committee recommended the *post-factum* approval of c. 3,000 illegal constructions and the demolition of 267 others which stood in the way of planned roads and development projects. Attempts to effect these recommendations met with fierce opposition. Violent riots broke out in Majd al-Kurūm (on the Acre-Safed road) in November 1977 when an illegally built house was destroyed. In the course of the clashes, one resident of the village was killed. Under the auspices of the Committee, a widespread protest campaign was organized. In February, as the second anniversary of "Land Day" approached, the Committee accepted Rakah's policy of adopting a low-keyed commemoration and avoiding confrontation with the authorities. The Committee voted down demands by the "Sons of the Village" to declare a general strike and repeat the events of 1976. Spokesmen of the Committee argued that it was more important to further the "organized struggle" and to strengthen the "unity of the ranks"; this was bound to achieve better results than the provocative line suggested by the extremists. The anniversary passed quietly, with public rallies held in major Arab villages, the main one in Sakhnīn, the home of three of the six Arabs who had lost their lives in the 1976 riots. Summing up the experience of the land campaign, Communist MK, Tawfīq Tūbī, strongly attacked the groups which had opposed Rakah's policy. He criticized them for hiding behind "revolutionary words and nationalistic slogans" and for following a path which could lead to "political suicide" for the Arabs in Israel. He concluded: "The Arab masses . . . stress their full unity behind their experienced national leadership, behind the Communists along with the representatives of the national loyal forces working in the country-wide Committee for the Defence of the Lands . . . and in the Democratic Fronts." [24]

It was indeed through these "Democratic Fronts" that the Communists succeeded in strengthening their grip over the Arab population during 1978. Following the Rakah-led Democratic Front victory in the 1975 municipal election in Nazareth, similar fronts (which included representatives of various sectors) were established in almost every Arab village. The results of the municipal elections in November 1978 proved the effectiveness of this tactic: 19 Democratic Front candidates were elected to the chairmanships of local councils compared with only nine previously. The Communist Mayor of Nazareth, Tawfīq Zayyād (MK), was re-elected with a 62% vote defeating the Alignment candidate, Sayf al-Dīn al-Zu'bī (MK), who received only 29% of the vote.

The appointment in September 1977 of a new Adviser to the Prime Minister on Arab Affairs, Dr Moshe Sharon, brought no immediate change in the Likud government's policy in the Arab sector. Interviewed in March 1978, Dr Sharon stated that the two main worries he had encountered were the low priority assigned by the political establishment to the problems of the Arab population, and the absence of a master plan to serve as a policy guideline.[25] In September he announced that he had proposed to the Prime Minister a preliminary liberal master plan which included recommendations in 13 areas such as education, rural planning, industrialization, Jewish-Arab relations, and the possibility of establishing a voluntary national service for Arabs. Dr Sharon also proposed the abolition of his own office, and its replacement by either a ministry or a statutory body with authority to co-ordinate all activities in the Arab sector.[26]

Among the issues which received special consideration by the Prime Minister's office during 1978 were the question of vocational education, industrialization of rural areas, housing for young couples, land settlement and religious affairs. Regarding the land problem, Dr Sharon declared in September that there was a "covert contest" underway between Jews and Arabs for supremacy in "settling the land of Israel."[27] Referring to the Galilee area, he said the Arabs were winning the race with illegal building due, in part, to the absence of approved outline plans and to the shortage of large-scale housing projects. He added that, in order to avoid "points of tension," he opposed the expropriation of Arab lands for Jewish settlements.[28] Earlier, Sharon remarked that the Prime Minister had instructed the Israel Lands Administration to avoid courts and to try and solve land disputes between the government and the Arab sector on the following settlement basis: 50% of the land under dispute should be granted to the citizen who claimed ownership; the rest would remain under state ownership but would be allocated for the public needs of the Arab community.

The government also tried to settle the land problem of the Bedouin in the Negev, which arose from their customary grazing and building rights on lands not registered in their names and therefore formally classified as state lands. Bedouin spokesmen argued in late March 1978 that they were forced to squat illegally because the government had reached no decision over their claim to c. 400,000 dunams. In April, c. 400 Bedouin demonstrated opposite the Knesset against the expropriation of 26,000 dunams in the Dimona area and the activities of a special patrol set up to combat illegal grazing. The reply of the Israel Lands Administration was that Bedouin had claims to only 5,300 dunams of this area and that these were being examined. In late May, a settlement was reached between the Ministry of Agriculture and the Bedouin shaykhs. The Ministry agreed to allow a representative of the Bedouin to accompany the patrols during their activities in Bedouin areas. The Ministry also agreed to provide grazing land for c. 100,000 sheep and goats registered with the Natural Reserves Authority as demanded by regulations, and to deal with questions of land, urbanization and water raised by the Bedouin.

For the Muslim community in Israel, 1978 marked the first year that they were allowed to participate in the Ḥajj—the pilgrimage to Mecca. In late October, more than 2,600 Israeli Muslims crossed the Allenby Bridge to Jordan on their way to Saudi Arabia. Commenting on the event, Dr Sharon said that for the first time since 1948 the government had succeeded in influencing Jordan and Saudi Arabia to permit Israeli Muslims to enter their countries for religious purposes. He added: "By granting the pilgrims a travel document [as demanded by the Jordanians and the Saudis] and not an Israeli passport, the government expressed its goodwill to the Muslims, enabling them to fulfil their religious obligation."[29]

ECONOMIC AFFAIRS—SUPPLEMENT ($1 = 18.98 Israeli pounds; £1 = IL 38.53)

As Israel's economy is for the most part closely intertwined with politics, much of the description and analysis of the country's recent economic performance has been included above. What follows is a brief survey of some of the more technical developments in the agricultural, industrial, monetary and foreign trade sectors.[30]

AGRICULTURE

Agricultural output increased 3.8% in 1976–77 as against a 5.4% rise in 1975–76. This lower rate of increase was attributed to a slowdown in the growth of poultry and dairy farming combined with a decrease in livestock.[31] With the exception of citrus fruits, which were hit by frost and the mercury scare, agricultural exports leaped a further 21% in 1976–77 following the 24% jump in 1975–76. Including citrus, the growth in total agricultural exports amounted to a less spectacular but still impressive 9.4% in 1976–77. (For details of the "mercury scare," see above.) During the first half of 1978, the value of agricultural exports including citrus grew by 21% compared with the first six months of 1977.

INDUSTRY

According to the index calculated by the Central Bureau of Statistics, overall industrial production was 2.9% higher in June 1978 than it had been a year earlier.[32] In percentage terms, the largest increases in output were registered by paper and paper products (+22.9%), mining and quarrying (+22.4%) electrical and electronic equipment (+15.9%) and textiles (+10.7%). The industries of diamonds (-37.4%), leather and leather products (-12.1%), chemical and oil products (-11.4%) and machinery (-1.1%), on the other hand, all witnessed lower production in June 1978 than during June 1977.

The industrial sector as a whole has been undergoing a significant change in its capital structure, the result of which is the growing concentration of productive capacity in export-oriented operations. In contrast to previous periods of export expansion, though, there has been no parallel increase of production for the domestic market—a development which has caused some concern.[33]

MONETARY DEVELOPMENTS

At first glance, one outcome of the New Economic Policy (NEP) has been an increase in the rate of growth of international reserves—11.4% during the first six months of 1978 (cf 4.7% during the first half of 1977). After gaining in each succeeding month following the introduction of NEP, Israel's international reserves reached a record $1,781m at the end of July 1978.[34]

At the end of June 1978, the money supply amounted to IL 23,373m (cf IL 16,144m at the same point in 1977). As much as any other indicator, this rapid increase in the money supply was clear evidence of the extent of monetary expansion following the introduction of NEP.

Another development which became more pronounced after the advent of NEP was the tendency for people to divert savings from conventional accounts either to foreign currency deposit accounts (which jumped nearly 130% between 1 October 1977 and 1 July 1978) or to Israeli currency savings plans (which increased 92%). The latter were linked either to the cost of living or to foreign currency, or to a combination of the two.[35]

FOREIGN TRADE

Exports rose c. 28% during the first half of 1978 compared with the corresponding period in 1977, most of this gain being registered by the industrial sector. Both industrial exports (other than diamonds) and agricultural exports were 10–12% higher for the second quarter of 1978 than for the same period in 1977. For the entire year of 1977, manufactured goods classified chiefly by materials (i.e. including diamonds) again ranked as Israel's foremost commodity group of exports,

making up 50.5% of the total. Food and live animals (14.2%), chemicals (10.6%), and machinery and transport equipment (10.0%) followed as the other leading export groups.
Imports for calendar 1977 rose by 17%. Manufactures classified by material (35.4%), machinery and transport equipment (20.7%) and fuels (15.2%) were once again the three principal commodity groups of imports.[36]
In 1977, as in 1976, the US (18.7%), West Germany (8.9%) and the UK (7.4%) were the three leading markets for Israeli exports. The US (16.4%) ranked as the chief supplier of Israeli imports, followed by the UK (11.3%) and West Germany (7.7%).[37]

Aaron S. Klieman
Section on "The Arabs in Israel" by **Elie Rekhess**
"Economic Affairs—Supplement" by **Ira E. Hoffman**

ARMED FORCES
Total armed forces number 164,000 (123,000 conscripts); mobilization to 400,000 in about 24 hours. Military service is 36 months for men and 24 months for women (Jews and Druzes only: Muslims and Christians may volunteer). Annual training for reservists thereafter up to age 54 for men, up to 25 for women. Defence expenditure in 1978–79 was IL 54.4 bn ($3.31 bn).
The Army numbers 138,000 (120,000 conscripts, male and female), with 375,000 on mobilization. It has 20 armoured brigades, nine mechanized brigades, nine infantry brigades and five parachute brigades. 11 brigades (five armoured, four infantry, two parachute) are normally kept near full strength; six (one armoured, four mechanized, one parachute) between 50% and full strength; the rest at cadre strength. Equipment consists of 3,000 medium tanks, including 1,000 *Centurion*, 650 M-48, 810 M-60, 400 T-54/-55, 150 T-62, 40 *Merkava*; 65 PT-76 light tanks; c. 4,000 armoured fighting vehicles, including AML-60, 15 AML-90 armoured cars; RBY *Ramta*, BRDM reconnaissance vehicles; M-2/-3/-113, BTR-40/-50P(OT-62)/-60P/-152 armoured personnel carriers; 500 105mm howitzers; 450 122mm, 130mm and 155mm guns and howitzers; 24 M-109 155mm, L-33 155mm, 60 M-107 175mm, M-110 203mm self-propelled guns and howitzers; 900 81mm, 120mm and 160mm mortars (some self-propelled); 122mm, 135mm, 240mm rocket launchers; *Lance, Ze'ev (Wolf)* surface-to-surface missiles; 106mm recoilless rifles; *TOW, Cobra, Dragon*, SS-11, *Sagger* anti-tank guided weapons; c. 900 *Vulcan/Chaparral* 20mm missile gun systems, 30mm and 40mm anti-aircraft guns; *Redeye* surface-to-air missiles. (125 M-60 medium tanks, 700 M-113 armoured personnel carriers, 94 155mm howitzers, 175mm guns, *Lance* surface-to-surface missiles, *TOW* anti-tank guided weapons are on order).
The Navy numbers 5,000 (1,000 conscripts), 8,000 on mobilization, and has three Type 206 submarines; six *Reshef*-class guided-missile fast patrol boats, with *Gabriel* surface-to-surface missiles; 12 *Saar*-class guided-missile fast patrol boats, with *Gabriel* surface-to-surface missiles, c. 40 small patrol boats (under 100 tons); three medium landing ships; six tank landing craft; three *Westwind* 1124N maritime reconnaissance aircraft; Naval commando: 300. (Four *Reshef*-class guided missile fast patrol boats, two Qu-9-35 Type corvettes with *Gabriel* surface-to-surface missiles, two *Flagstaff*-class hydrofoils, three *Westwind* maritime reconnaissance aircraft are on order.)
The Air Force has 21,000 (2,000 conscripts, air defence only), 25,000 on mobilization, and 543 combat aircraft; 11 ground-attack fighters and interceptor squadrons: one with 25 F/TF-15, five with 170 F-4E, three with 30 *Mirage*

IIICJ/BJ, two with 50 *Kfir/Kfir* C2; six ground-attack fighter squadrons with 250 A-4E/H/M/N *Skyhawk*; one reconnaissance squadron with 12 RF-4E, 20 V-1, £ E-2C airborne early warning aircraft. Transports include 10 Boeing 707, 24 C-130E/H, six C-97, 18 C-47, two KC-130H. Liaison aircraft include 14 *Arava*, eight *Islander*, 23 Do-27, nine Do-28, 25 Cessna U206, one *Westwind*, 16 *Queen Air*. Trainers include 24 TA-4E/H, 70 *Magister*, 30 *Super Cub*. Helicopters include eight *Super Frelon*, 28 CH-53G, six AH-1G, 40 *Bell*-205A, 20 *Bell*-206, 12 *Bell*-212, 25 UH-1D, 30 *Alouette* II/III; *Sidewinder*, AIM-7E/F *Sparrow*, *Shafir* air-to-air missiles; *Maverick*, *Shrike*, *Walleye*, *Bullpup* air-to-surface missiles; 15 surface-to-air missile batteries with 90 *HAWK*. (15 F-15, 75 F-16 fighters, 30 Hughes 500 helicopter gunships are on order). Reserves (all services) number 460,000; paramilitary forces include 4,500 Border Guards and 5,000 *Nahal* Militia.

Source: The Military Balance 1978-79 (London: The International Institute for Strategic Studies)

BALANCE OF PAYMENTS (million US dollars)

	1975	1976	1977
A. Goods, Services and Transfers	-2,281	-1,088	-559
Exports of Merchandise, fob	2,180	2,671	3,389
Imports of Merchandise, fob	-5,650	-5,320	-5,424
Exports of Services	1,587	1,758	2,167
Imports of Services	-2,168	-2,422	-2,696
Private Unrequited Transfers, net	1,128	1,103	1,083
Government Unrequited Transfers, net	642	1,122	922
B. Long-Term Capital, nie	1,567	878	598
C. Short-Term Capital, nie	459	182	-22
D. Errors and Omissions	106	62	240
Total (A through D)	**-148**	**34**	**257**

INTERNATIONAL LIQUIDITY (million US dollars at end of period)

	1976	1977	Jan–June 1978
International Reserves	1,373.1	1,571.0	1,749.6
Gold	*44.8*	*49.4*	*50.7*
SDRs	*10.1*	*27.0*	*34.2*
Foreign Exchange	*1,318.3*	*1,494.6*	*1,664.7*
Bank of Israel Other Assets	232.9	211.9	90.6
Bank of Israel Liabilities	550.3	570.8	596.4
Deposit Money Banks: Assets	1,986.2	1,875.8*	...
Liabilities	2,914.2	2,798.7*	...

*Up to September 1977 only.

MONETARY SURVEY (million Israeli pounds at end of period)

	1975	1976	1977*
Foreign Assets (net)	821	1,131	1,526
Domestic Credit	41,790	58,457	79,308
Claims on Government (net)	*12,039*	*16,009*	*22,270*
Claims on Private Sector	*29,751*	*42,448*	*57,038*
Money	10,614	13,486	17,633
Quasi-Money	30,791	46,875	62,352
Other Items (net)	1,208	-774	850
Money, Seasonally Adjusted	10,488	13,339	17,739

*Up to September 1977 only.

NATIONAL ACCOUNTS (billion Israeli pounds)

	1975	1976	1977	Jan–March 1978
Exports	25.15	37.44	62.08	24.86
Government Consumption	33.94	41.14	51.98	20.58
Private Consumption	46.68	62.88	88.15	28.28
Less: Imports	*-52.52*	*-68.25*	*-93.62*	*-40.40*
Gross Domestic Product (GDP)	78.02	100.25	143.06	44.33
Less: Net Factor Payments Abroad	*-2.75*	*-3.35*	*-4.14*	*-1.25*
Gross National Expenditure = GNP	**75.27**	**96.90**	**138.92**	**43.08**
National Income at Market Prices	66.00	...	...	...
GDP at 1975 Prices	78.02	79.22	79.67	19.45

Source (of four preceding tables): IMF, *International Financial Statistics.*

SUMMARY OF GOVERNMENT ACCOUNTS (billion Israeli pounds)

	Actual 1975–76	Actual 1976–77	Budget 1977–78	Budget 1978–79
A. Revenue	73.03	97.21	137.55	202.07
of which:				
Income Tax	12.34	17.56	27.93	38.70
Value Added Tax	—	4.90	9.93	17.70
B. Expenditure	73.03	97.21	137.55	202.07
of which:				
Ordinary Budget	49.72	69.40	96.56	135.30
Development Budget	7.26	8.17	11.62	16.70
Debt Repayment	5.48	9.16	15.78	30.00
C. Balance (A–B)	—	—	—	—

ORDINARY GOVERNMENT EXPENDITURE (million Israeli pounds)

	Actual 1975–76	Actual 1976–77	Budget 1977–78	Budget 1978–79
Prime Minister's Office	216	249	271	568
Defence	25,623	35,288	40,775	55,300
Education and Culture	3,681	4,689	6,868	11,535
Health	1,320	1,528	1,647	3,470
Labour and Social Welfare	2,936	1,410	1,121	786
Police	754	1,055	1,349	2,284
Finance	321	431	595	1,082
National Insurance Institute	1,850	2,691	4,101	5,756
Local Authorities	2,334	3,083	4,227	5,575
Interest	5,209	9,145	14,750	21,500
Total (including others)	**49,719**	**69,400**	**96,560**	**135,300**

PRODUCTION OF MAIN AGRICULTURAL PRODUCTS (thousand tonnes)

	1974–75	1975–76	1976–77
Citrus	1,506	1,531	1,528
Vegetables	609	581	582
Sugarbeet	259	324	320
Wheat	243	206	220
Potatoes	163	175	214
Poultry (for meat)	173	188	192
Pome Fruit	124	124	140
Melons and Pumpkins	135	135	132
Cotton, Fibre	49	54	64
Bananas	52	57	62
Livestock Index*	**148**	**161**	**164**
Crop Index*	**150**	**155**	**164**

*1968 = 100.

INDEX OF INDUSTRIAL PRODUCTION (1968 = 100).

	1970	1975	1976	1977
Mining and quarrying	125	157	124	126
Food, beverages and tobacco	114	157	169	181
Textiles	116	148	151	165
Clothing and made-up textiles	126	180	187	202
Leather and its products	113	113	118	127
Wood and its products	114	126	133	132
Rubber and plastic products	138	185	193	209
Chemical and oil products	129	196	211	231
Non-metallic mineral products	126	161	166	154
Metal products	139	196	200	203
Machinery	127	161	154	175
Electrical and electronic equipment	159	277	298	305
Diamonds	102	163	196	206
Total (including others)	**127**	**177**	**185**	**197**

COMPOSITION OF EXPORTS (million US dollars)

	1970	1975	1976	1977
Food and live animals	160.4	323.9	378.6	436.5
Beverages and tobacco	1.7	3.8	3.8	5.2
Crude materials, inedible	37.9	95.1	126.1	154.1
Mineral fuels, lubricants and related materials	...	...	...	...
Animal and vegetable oils and fats	4.7	11.0	9.0	8.8
Chemicals	68.2	242.5	261.2	325.6
Manufactured goods classified chiefly by materials	367.1	874.7	1,124.6	1,556.4
Machinery and transport equipment	38.1	179.1	273.3	307.9
Miscellaneous manufactured articles	79.8	174.9	207.4	259.9
Others	20.8	35.7	30.5	28.8
Total	**778.7**	**1,940.7**	**2,414.5**	**3,083.2**

COMPOSITION OF IMPORTS (million US dollars)

	1970	1975	1976	1977
Food and live animals	161.2	499.3	434.8	460.9
Beverages and tobacco	6.3	14.6	20.7	24.1
Crude materials, inedible	113.2	272.4	296.9	342.4
Mineral fuels, lubricants and related materials	70.9	638.5	681.8	738.8
Animal and vegetable oils and fats	10.3	21.2	15.5	12.9
Chemicals	99.9	276.9	290.9	337.9
Manufactured goods classified chiefly by materials	479.4	1,298.7	1,324.4	1,716.3
Machinery and transport equipment	439.4	977.4	888.3	1,002.1
Miscellaneous manufactured articles	69.8	154.9	170.8	186.6
Others	11.6	18.7	16.3	23.1
Total	**1,462.0**	**4,172.6**	**4,140.4**	**4,845.2**

Source (of six preceding tables): Central Bureau of Statistics, *Statistical Abstract of Israel, 1978.*

ISRAEL

DIRECTION OF TRADE (million US dollars)

	1975	1976	1977
Exports to:			
United States	307.5	437.4	577.4
West Germany	160.5	199.3	275.6
United Kingdom	171.5	180.0	229.7
Netherlands	129.3	159.5	181.0
Hong Kong	113.2	140.0	174.1
France	112.1	136.2	161.4
Belgium	80.2	102.1	159.2
Switzerland	81.4	94.6	115.9
Iran	120.0	120.6	95.8
Japan	99.4	72.8	93.1
Countries not specified	31.3	168.0	330.9
Total (including others)	**1,941.1**	**2,415.2**	**3,083.5**
Imports from:			
United States	998.9	888.2	946.9
United Kingdom	577.9	608.9	653.7
West Germany	435.9	416.6	442.8
Netherlands	181.6	241.8	413.8
Switzerland	125.8	183.6	241.5
Belgium	158.9	126.6	207.4
Italy	206.1	171.5	194.0
France	154.7	150.5	188.4
Japan	88.8	106.9	88.0
Countries not specified	693.4	742.0	720.6
Special categories	1,826.1	1,534.3	1,063.9
Total (including others)	**5,997.4**	**5,667.4**	**5,788.0**

Source: IMF, Direction of Trade.

NOTES
1. Jerusalem Post (JP), 12 January 1978.
2. Ibid, 3 March 1978.
3. Dahaf poll, reported in JP, 25 December 1977.
4. Louis Guttman, "The Israeli Public, Peace and Territory: The Impact of the Sādāt Initiative" (Jerusalem Institute for Federal Studies, January 1978), Part IV, pp. 3–4.
5. Yedi'ot Aharonot, Tel Aviv; 10 November 1978.
6. Bank of Israel, Annual Report 1977.
7. The Military Balance 1976–77 (London: International Institute for Strategic Studies). Israeli Finance Ministry, Budget in Brief, 1976 and 1977.
8. Ma'ariv, Tel Aviv; 13 November 1978.
9. JP, 16 February 1978.
10. Arye Shalev, "Security Arrangements in Sinai in a Peace Treaty with Egypt," Tel Aviv University Center for Strategic Studies, Occasional Paper No 3, October 1978.
11. Ministry of Industry, Commerce and Tourism; also The Israel Economist, April 1978.
12. Ha'aretz, Tel Aviv; 15 November 1978.
13. Interview with Deputy Defence Minister Mordechai Zippori, Ma'ariv, 17 November 1978.
14. The Military Balance 1976–77; also Paul Rivlin, "The Burden of Israel's Defence," Survival (July/August 1978), pp. 146–54.
15. Central Bureau of Statistics, Statistical Abstract of Israel, 1978; Yedi'ot Aharonot, 6 November 1978; Ma'ariv, 13 November 1978.
16. Excerpts from the Shimron Report in JP, 20, 21 February 1978.
17. Uligvan, Tel Aviv; May 1978.
18. JP, 29 November 1978.
19. al-Ittihād, Haifa; 15 November 1977.
20. Ibid, 29 September 1978.
21. Memorandum published in December 1977.
22. Area heavily populated by Arabs in the central region of Israel.
23. Al-Fajr, East Jerusalem; 23 February 1978.
24. Al-Ittihād, 28 April 1978.
25. JP, 31 March 1978.
26. Ibid, 29 September 1978.
27. Ibid.

28. *Ibid.*
29. *Ibid*, 25 October 1978.
30. For background on Israel's economy, see *MECS 1976–77*, pp. 466–73.
31. Bank of Israel, *Annual Report 1977*, p. 323. Other data are taken from the *Statistical Abstract of Israel, 1978* and various issues of the *Monthly Bulletin of Statistics*, both published by the Central Bureau of Statistics.
32. The figures in this paragraph are taken from the *Monthly Bulletin of Statistics*, No 9, 1978.
33. For details, see Bank of Israel, *Annual Report 1977*, pp. 339–45.
34. International Monetary Fund (IMF), *International Financial Statistics*, October 1978.
35. *Monthly Bulletin of Statistics,* September 1978.
36. *Statistical Abstract of Israel, 1978.*
37. IMF, *Direction of Trade Annual, 1971–77.*

Jordan

(Al-Mamlaka al-Urdunniyya al-Hāshimiyya)

The stability that has characterized Jordan since the final eviction of the fidā'iyyūn in 1971 continued to prevail during 1977–78. Though internal quiet was temporarily upset by disturbances in March 1978, the opposition did not prove to possess an autonomous power base that could have enabled it to compete at all seriously with King Husayn's regime. The King was able to rely on the loyalty of the army and the internal security forces, who remain the foundation of Jordan's traditional power structure. Real political power continued to be wielded by the King himself, by his close associates in the Royal family, and by those members of the Trans-Jordanian élite who constitute the prime decision-making group. Although the political élite was not monolithic, the fundamental desire to preserve the State in its traditional form produced a situation in which Husayn's authority was not questioned, and the Royal family and the political élite in general were able to preserve their internal cohesion.

The commemoration of Husayn's Silver Jubilee in August 1977 (see *MECS 1976–77*, p. 474) was followed in June 1978 by Husayn's decision to lay down the line of succession for the more distant future—events which symbolized the regime's staying power and self-confidence.

POLITICAL AFFAIRS
THE ROYAL HOUSE
On 15 June 1978, King Husayn married his fourth wife, Elizabeth Halaby, an American citizen born in Washington and daughter of an American businessman originating from Aleppo (Syria). She converted to Islam and was given the title of Queen Nūr al-Husayn.

Shortly before his marriage, on 7 June, Husayn named his infant son 'Alī successor to the throne, to follow Crown Prince Hasan, Husayn's brother and the present heir apparent. 'Alī is the son of Queen 'Alyā (killed in an air crash in February 1977),[1] and Husayn's only son whose mother was both of Arab descent and born a Muslim. The nomination was intended to clarify in advance that any sons born from his new marriage would not be eligible for the succession. This was also the case with Husayn's two other sons, 'Abdallah and Faysal, born of Husayn's marriage to his second wife, Princess Mūnā (see Table 1); she, too, was not originally a Muslim nor an Arab, but of British origin. Husayn may possibly have been prompted to take this action to forestall criticism both that his marriage was to a foreigner and that it was not long after the death of Queen 'Alyā, who had been a particularly popular figure in Jordan.

As Crown Prince Hasan has no sons of his own (see Table 1), the appointment of 'Alī was no apparent cause for friction between Husayn and Hasan, at least not for the time being. There was no reason to believe that Husayn intended to undermine Hasan's position in any way. Although they are reputed to have differences of opinion, Husayn's authority in all political affairs remains unchallenged, while Hasan continues to deal with the country's economy. The mutual respect, trust and loyalty between the two brothers appears as strong as it has always been.

577

TABLE 1.
THE HASHIMITE DYNASTY

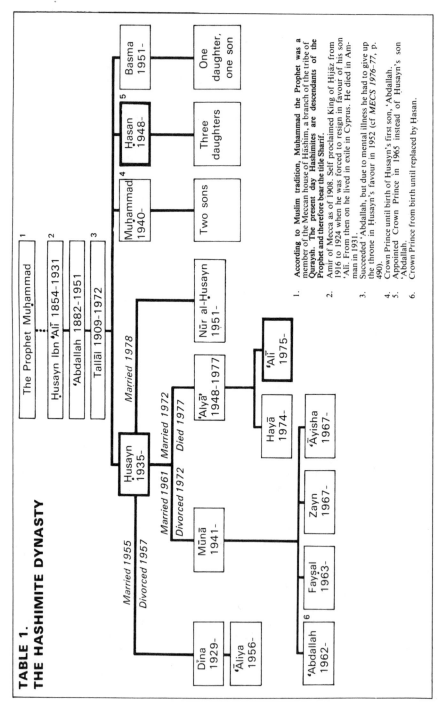

According to Muslim tradition, Muḥammad the Prophet was a member of the Meccan house of Hāshim, a branch of the tribe of Quraysh. The present day Hashimites are descendants of the Prophet and therefore bear the title Sharīf.

1.

2. Amir of Mecca as of 1908. Self proclaimed King of Hijāz from 1916 to 1924 when he was forced to resign in favour of his son 'Ali. From then on he lived in exile in Cyprus. He died in Amman in 1931.

3. Succeeded 'Abdallah, but due to mental illness he had to give up the throne in Husayn's favour in 1952 (cf *MECS 1976-77*, p. 490).

4. Crown Prince until birth of Husayn's first son, 'Abdallah.

5. Appointed Crown Prince in 1965 instead of Husayn's son 'Abdallah.

6. Crown Prince from birth until replaced by Hasan.

THE GOVERNMENT AND THE ECONOMY

Since its formation in July 1976, Mudar Badrān's government has concentrated on internal affairs, particularly on problems related to the economy and the rising cost of living.[2] Addressing the newly formed National Consultative Council on 19 June 1978, Badrān outlined the objectives of his domestic policy, maintaining that "any government in power must aim at ensuring the prosperity and well-being of its citizens" and at providing them "with an atmosphere of security and stability so they can produce and build."[3] It was quite clear that the government regarded controlling the cost of living as important for the preservation of internal political stability.

Measures taken by the government to counter inflation included expanded storage facilities throughout the country for meat, rice, sugar, tea, flour and cooking fat. This in effect turned the Ministry of Supply into the country's wholesaler for these essential commodities, with authority to control prices to protect those with fixed incomes. Flour and sugar were subsidized by the government, and a particular effort was made by the Ministry of Supply to ensure the production of cheap bread. Hundreds of merchants were also punished for profiteering. The chain of special supermarkets established in early 1977 for civil servants[4] was expanded, and the minimum wage of government employees raised in April 1978. The social security law that King Husayn had called for in April 1977[5] was approved by the National Consultative Council in August 1978.

An acute housing shortage, caused in part by the influx of Lebanese, sent land prices and rents soaring to the point where it was difficult for Jordanians to meet the cost, especially out of government salaries. This reportedly aroused some social discontent, particularly amongst professionals and the lower middle class.

Wages increased substantially however; Jordanian sources noted that since 1976, wages and the cost of agricultural produce were among the main contributing factors to inflation.[6] It was reported that wages had overtaken prices during 1977–78, largely as a result of the demand for labour in the Gulf (see below). A consultative committee of representatives of various government agencies started work on the outline of a general wage policy for the country on 15 August. Its recommendations were to be referred to the Prime Minister.

Badrān said in June 1978 that during the first quarter of the year, the average rate of inflation had dropped from 14.7% to 7.3%. This appraisal seemed low and although inflation did appear to be slowing down, others claimed the figure was still at c. 15%.

Another serious problem facing the Jordanian economy was the labour shortage, caused by the increased demand for labour in the Gulf since 1973, as well as by increased local demand resulting from the implementation of the country's own development plans. Approximately 150–200,000 Jordanian labourers worked abroad. While wages had risen sufficiently to attract c. 40,000 foreign labourers (Syrians, Egyptians and Pakistanis), this rise was not enough to encourage labourers in the Gulf to return, or for that matter to satisfy Jordan's own trade unions; they were critical of the employment of foreigners which was helping to keep wages down. It was not part of government policy to stop the export of labour however, since remittances from abroad were an important source of foreign currency. Furthermore, labourers worked mainly in countries that gave Jordan economic assistance, and Jordan could not afford—politically or economically—to take administrative action that could upset their economies. Meanwhile, the government began to attempt to control the drain of labour and reduce its impact on Jordanian economic development.

Although a central objective of the 1976–80 Five-Year Plan (see *MECS 1976–77*,

TABLE 2. THE BADRĀN CABINET

Portfolio	As formed on 27 November 1976	Following Reshuffle of 19 August 1978
Prime Minister, Foreign and Defence Minister	Mudar Badrān	Mudar Badrān
Development and Reconstruction	Ḥasan Ibrāhīm(P)	Ḥasan Ibrāhīm(P)
Minister of State for Foreign Affairs }		
Information	'Adnān Abū 'Awda(P)	'Adnān Abū 'Awda(P)
Culture and Youth	Sharīf Fawwāz Sharaf	Sharīf Fawwāz Sharaf
Education	'Abd al-Salām al-Majālī	'Abd al-Salām al-Majālī
Minister of State for Premiership Affairs }		
Finance	Muhammad al-Dabbās	Muhammad al-Dabbās
Tourism and Antiquities	Ghālib Barakāt(P)	Ghālib Barakāt((P)
Public Works	Sa'īd Bīnū	Sa'īd Bīnū
Agriculture	Salāḥ Jum'a[1]	Ḥikmat al-Sākit[+]
Supplies	Marwān al-Qāsim	Marwān al-Qāsim
Awqāf, Islamic Affairs and Holy Places	Kāmil al-Sharīf	Kāmil al-Sharīf
Transport	'Alī al-Suhaymāt	'Alī al-Suhaymāt
Interior	Sulaymān 'Arār	Sulaymān 'Arār
Justice	Ahmad 'Abd al-Karīm al-Tarāwina	Ahmad 'Abd al-Karīm al-Tarāwina
Health	Muhammad al-Bashīr[2]	'Abd al-Ra'ūf al-Rawābida
Communications	'Abd al-Ra'ūf al-Rawābida[3]	Sa'īd al-Tall[+]
Trade and Industry	Najm al-Dīn al-Dajānī(P)	Najm al-Dīn al-Dajānī(P)
Labour	'Iṣām al-'Ajlūnī	'Iṣām al-'Ajlūnī
Municipal and Rural Affairs	Ibrāhīm Ayyūb	Ibrāhīm Ayyūb

(P) Of Palestinian origin.

[1] On 17 July 1978, Salāḥ Jum'a tendered his resignation, effective as of 1 August. He had accepted a post in the UN Food and Agriculture Organization.

[2] Muhammad al-Bashīr was killed in the helicopter crash with Queen 'Alyā on 9 February 1977 (see *MECS 1976–77*, p. 476). No replacement was made until the reshuffle in August 1978.

[3] Following the death of Muhammad al-Bashīr, al-Rawābida also served as acting Minister of Health.

[+] Newly appointed in August 1978.

pp. 241–42) was to decentralize the Jordanian economy, an appeal by Crown Prince Hasan in March 1978 to stop migration to the cities indicated that this objective was not being achieved. More than half of Jordan's population now live in greater Amman. However, efforts continued to decentralize public services and to give provincial governors greater authority to improve rural services.

THE OPPOSITION

The regime continued to refuse to tolerate any real opposition. Political parties in Jordan have been illegal since they were banned in 1957.

Most prominent and best organized of the illegal parties is the Jordanian Communist Party (JCP), which continues to function underground and publish its own organ al-Jamāhīr. Since the late 1960s and early 1970s, the JCP has established increasingly close ties with the PLO and apparently co-operates with PLO supporters in Jordan. In October 1977, it was reported that the JCP had secretly held its third congress at which resolutions were passed supporting the formation of a "national liberated regime" in Jordan, the establishment of an independent Palestinian state, and close ties between the Jordanian and Palestinian peoples.

Other opposition bodies were affiliated to various factions within the PLO. Supporters in Jordan of the Popular Democratic Front for the Liberation of Palestine (PDFLP) published an underground organ, Tarīq al-Sha'b, and a party called the Jordanian Revolutionary People's Party (ḥizb al-sha'b al-thawrī al-urdunnī) was reportedly affiliated with the Popular Front for the Liberation of Palestine (PFLP). Though not organized as an opposition, the various professional associations also included numerous PLO sympathizers who evidently identified mainly with al-Fath.[7] The Jordanian Bar Association, for example, was headed by Ibrāhīm Bakr, formerly spokesman for the PLO Central Committee, while the head of the Doctors' Union, Ḥasan Khurays, was a known sympathizer of the PLO.

Two Jordanian lawyers, Irshūd al-Hawārī and Milḥam al-Tall, were reported to be planning the formation of a Constitutional Front (jabha dustūriyya) in late September 1977. Later, Milḥam al-Tall was in fact described as spokesman of the "Jordanian Constitutional Front."[8] It was not known what kind of following this Front or other opposition groups attract, but they did not appear to pose any serious threat to the regime in 1978. Overt opposition was usually sporadic and short-lived, seemingly incapable of effective or persistent organization.

President Sādāt's visit to Jerusalem provoked PLO sympathizers to take action. On 19 November 1977, a meeting held at the premises of the Jordanian Bar Association was attended by representatives of professional associations and other voluntary societies. In a statement published in the local press, they denounced "the tragic attitude" adopted by Sādāt; expressed their belief that the "Arab masses . . . foremost the Arab people in Egypt, will foil every treachery, deviation and capitulation"; and called for the formation of a strong front of Arab states that rejected Sādāt's policies, and for the strengthening of ties between the Arabs and the friendly powers "headed by the Soviet Union."[9] The statement, well in line with the policy of the "rejectionist front," was signed by numerous well-known PLO sympathizers, Communists and other veteran members of the opposition in Jordan. They included Ibrāhīm Bakr, Bahjat Abū Gharbiyya and Yāsir 'Amr, all members of the PLO's Palestinian National Council; Shafīq Rashīdāt, Najīb Rashīdāt, 'Abd al-Ḥamīd al-Sā'iḥ, Rūḥī al-Khaṭīb and Sulaymān al-Ḥadīdī, all previously associated with the defunct National Gathering; and JCP members Fā'iq Warrād (Secretary-General of the Party), Ya'qūb Ziyā' al-Dīn and Rushdī Shāhīn; and Rif'at 'Awda.[10]

Some of those who signed the statement had also subscribed to a similar declaration, made in June 1976, which condemned Syria for invading Lebanon and expressed support for the PLO. At that time, *al-Ra'y*, the paper that published the statement, was temporarily shut down by the authorities, and most or possibly all of those who had signed it were imprisoned for about three weeks. No such action was taken on this occasion. The explanation was that the June 1976 statement contradicted the government's policy of outright support for Syria's action in Lebanon, whereas the November 1977 statement did not altogether run counter to official policy, which was itself somewhat critical of Sādāt. Furthermore, such condemnation coming out of Jordan may even have served the regime's purposes at the time, in that it partly obscured and compensated for its own restrained response.

From then on, however, criticism of Sādāt by the opposition was published elsewhere, but not in the Jordanian media.[11] In addition, 14 people who had intended to participate in the Tripoli "rejectionist" conference in December 1977 (see essay on Inter-Arab Relations) were reported to have had their passports confiscated. They were said to include Bahjat Abū Gharbiyya, Rūhī al-Khatīb and Mahmūd al-Mu'ayta (formerly a Commander of al-Sā'iqa—see essay on PLO).

The most salient and serious opposition activity since the expulsion of the fidā'iyyūn from Jordan in 1970–71 occurred in March 1978 in the wake of the Israeli operation against the fidā'iyyūn in South Lebanon (see third essay in section on the Arab-Israeli Conflict). The operation aroused open support for the PLO, particularly among many of the Palestinians in Amman. On 15 March, the Jordanian press published a statement by professional associations condemning the "barbaric Zionist aggression" against Lebanon which they said was designed to strike at the "Palestinian resistance movement, which represents the vanguard of the Arab struggle against the Zionist occupation." They also called on Arab states to take measures to counter the Israeli action.[12]

On 18 March, c. 150 people, representing various shades of the opposition, met at the professional associations' complex in Amman. They elected a permanent secretariat which drew up a statement; the authorities did not allow this to appear in the local press, however. Published instead by "WAFA" (*wikālat anbā' filastīniyya*, the Palestinian News Agency run by the PLO in Beirut) and later in *Hurriyya* (Beirut), the statement protested against "the Arab official silence" in the face of the Israeli operation, called people to strike at US interests in the Arab world, and thanked the USSR for its support. Of more direct relevance to Jordanian internal policies was the support expressed in the statement for the PLO as the sole legitimate representative of the Palestinians, coupled with criticism of Arab regimes (no doubt including Jordan) that denied their own peoples political freedom, but still hoped "to solve the conflict with the enemy through negotiation and coexistence."[13] The usually quiescent faculty of the University of Jordan issued an almost identical statement, which also was not published in the local press. On 19 March, a delegation of the newly-elected professionals' permanent secretariat met with King Husayn and reportedly raised the questions of democratic freedoms and the release of political detainees.[14]

In the first few days after the beginning of the Israeli operation, the two universities[15] and some schools went on strike. Some demonstrations were also held in Amman and elsewhere. On 20 March, police in the capital clashed with demonstrators protesting against the Israeli operation and in support of the PLO. Several people were injured and six men, including two policemen, were taken to hospital. On the same day, the Ministry of Interior issued a communiqué which praised the "noble feelings" that had been expressed in the previous four days, through blood donations and the formation of committees to collect contributions and enlist volunteers to "join their steadfast brothers now bravely resisting the aggression.'' The statement added, however, that the ministry "felt that a small number of people were attempting to manipulate these spontaneous feelings . . . towards suspicious ends which would take a mobbish trend." Therefore in order "to preserve the interests of the citizens and security, strict instructions have been issued [to the security forces] to prevent with utmost severity any demonstration whatever its size may be." [16]

On 21 March, armed security forces were used to break up demonstrations in Amman which not only protested against the Israeli operation, but also shouted slogans against King Husayn. Troops used teargas and fired into the air to disperse the demonstrators. An unknown number of people were injured. Later reports maintained that 300 people had been arrested and three people killed during the March disturbances.

Although critics had shown some muscle in March, they did not have the power to sustain overt opposition. A leaflet of the PDFLP in Jordan and an article in *Tarīq al-Sha'b* later called upon those who had participated in the 18 March meeting to stay together and continue their activity[17]—indications that they had not done so.

As long as the armed forces remained loyal to the King, and without the kind of autonomous power base that the fidā'ī presence had provided until mid-1971, the opposition was no match for the regime. It was therefore not surprising that PLO demands to re-establish its "military and political presence" in Jordan continued to be adamantly rejected by Husayn (see below). Husayn himself also made it quite clear that PLO-oriented opposition would not be tolerated. In an address at the University of Jordan on 20 June, he explained that "Jordan's strength lies in the unity of its people and the cohesion of its sons. . . . We do not want separatist fanaticisms . . . to spread or advocate division." [18]

THE FORMATION OF THE NATIONAL CONSULTATIVE COUNCIL

On 13 April, King Husayn instructed the Cabinet to draw up a provisional law[19] establishing the National Consultative Council (NCC; *al-majlis al-watanī al-istishārī*), whose task would be to "give opinions and advice, as well as to discuss general policy and examine all legislation and laws enacted by the government." Husayn explained that it was necessary to have an "institution where the legitimate expression of the opinions, interests and feelings of the citizens" could take place "in freedom and responsibility." [20]

Ever since the dissolution of the Council of Deputies (lower house of parliament) in November 1974 (in the wake of the Rabat resolutions), the regime had sought some sort of replacement which could fulfil the same role; namely, provide some semblance of democracy, but without impinging upon the regime's power in any substantial way.[21] It would seem likely that the March disturbances and the demands for greater political freedom also influenced the timing of Husayn's decision to form the NCC.

A provisional law, ratified by Royal Decree on 17 April, provided for the establishment of the 60-member NCC. The president and all Council members were to be appointed by the King. While the NCC was to serve a two-year term, the King had the right to dissolve it at any time and to dismiss any member or to accept his resignation. On matters of legislation and policy, the NCC's functions were to be strictly advisory and its recommendations not binding upon the government. It would not enjoy any of the constitutional prerogatives of parliament, have no right to vote on confidence motions and no legislative role. All legislation would remain provisional until the dissolved parliament was eventually reconvened to authorize it.

A Royal Decree was issued on 19 April appointing the 60 members of the NCC,

13 of whom were of Palestinian origin. As in the Cabinet since November 1974, Husayn thus kept Palestinian representation to about one-fifth. This was well below the 50% ratio Palestinians enjoyed in both parliament and the Cabinet prior to the Rabat resolutions, and was intended to preclude accusations that these were being undermined by Jordan. From the outset, Husayn emphasized that the NCC was not intended as a substitute for Jordan's dissolved parliament, in which both the East and West Banks had been equally represented. The NCC's first President, Ahmad al-Lawzī,[22] stressed that the formation of the Council was a temporary measure until full parliamentary life could be restored. The regime clearly did not want to hold elections on the East Bank alone, a step which would signify its formal detachment from the West Bank. Options with regard to the West Bank were thus deliberately left open, with the NCC also serving as a symbol of the regime's obvious hope that the Jordanian parliament—representing both the East and the West Banks—would be reconvened some time in the future. Or, as al-Lawzī put it: "We believe in the unity of the East and West Banks. The people here do not differentiate between East and West Bankers. . . . If the occupation ends, then there will be general elections for parliament again [which] will be formed of an equal number of representatives from both banks."[23]

Opening the first session of the NCC on 24 April, the King called for "fruitful dialogue and sincere co-operation among the various state institutions."[24] In his reply the following day, Ahmad al-Lawzī said the NCC shared Husayn's conviction that the "unity of the two banks [had been] realized by the free will of the people" and "merely underlined an already existing reality, the organic unity of the people in the melting pot of history."[25] Until 21 August, when the NCC adjourned, the Council held weekly sessions in which the foreign and domestic policies of the government were discussed, as were a number of new laws. Two sessions on Jordan's foreign policy were held *in camera* on 8 and 15 May.

'Abdallah al-Rīmāwī[26] proposed on 29 May that the government submit an account of its domestic policy to the NCC. On 12 June, the Council adopted a resolution in this vein and a week later Premier Badrān addressed the Council. He concentrated on his government's economic policy (see above), but also referred to the question of "public liberties" or political freedom. He said that the government regarded the citizens as "the main partner in guiding the homeland's progress," and that it was their "right and duty to be concerned with the homeland's domestic and national issues and to express their opinion on them." However, this applied only so long as opinions stemmed from "their conscience," were aimed at "serving the interests of the homeland" and were "within legitimate boundaries."[27]

These boundaries were not defined however, and in July a number of sessions were devoted to the question of political freedom. Speakers focused mainly on freedom of the press and of political association. They called on the government to relax controls over the press, exercised in the framework of the Press and Publications Law, and to allow the formation of political parties. When Badrān replied on 24 July, he did not accept these complaints. He intimated that the occasional temporary suspension of newspapers or the withdrawal of a newspaper's licence, which had happened only once during his government's term of office,[28] were designed to protect the country's "stability and security."[29] Badrān also made it quite clear that in his view, the time had not yet come for the formation of political parties.

JORDAN, THE PALESTINIANS AND THE ME CONFLICT

Jordan's vital interest in the ME conflict has always been to play a decisive role in determining the political fate of the Palestinians. The regime has constantly sought to obtain inter-Arab and Palestinian backing for such a role, while at the same time seeking to neutralize the PLO.[30] Like the rest of the Arab world, Jordan was taken by surprise by Sādāt's decision to visit Jerusalem. (For details of the visit and its consequences, see essays on the Arab-Israeli Conflict and Inter-Arab Relations.) Unlike the "rejectionist" countries, Jordan did not object to the visit in principle; the main question for Ḥusayn was whether Sādāt's policy would bring Jordan any closer to securing its vital interests in a solution of the Palestinian question.

One facet of Jordan's reaction to the visit—criticism of Sādāt's "unilateral behaviour"[31]—emphasized its preference for "solidarity among the front-line countries and a unified policy," which Ḥusayn maintained were the "only means to achieve any sound and just peace settlement."[32] This criticism reflected Jordan's uneasiness over having to take sides in a divided Arab world at a time when broad-based Arab legitimacy was a primary goal of Jordanian policy on the Palestinian issue. Furthermore, Ḥusayn was embittered by Sādāt's taking such a fateful step without any previous consultation.[33]

Nevertheless, Ḥusayn called on Arab states to restrain their criticisms of Sādāt and not to allow reservations concerning Egypt's policy to be "transformed into a wall of alienation between the Arab states."[34] This was not only a reflection of the basic Jordanian interest in reducing the impact of inter-Arab friction, for the reasons previously mentioned; it also stemmed from Jordan's fears that lasting alienation between Sādāt and the rest of the Arab world might drive Sādāt to seek a separate settlement which would irreparably weaken Jordan's negotiating position with Israel. Another reason for this call for restraint was that a heightened atmosphere of rejection and hostility to Sādāt and his political objectives in the Arab world would make it even more difficult for Jordan to capitalize on any gains that might accrue to it from the initiative.

Although the Jordanians remained critical of the way Sādāt had acted, they took a positive attitude towards the positions that Cairo put forward. They were relieved by Egypt's rejection of a separate settlement and encouraged by Sādāt's emphasis on the necessity of finding a solution to the Palestinian problem—while pushing the PLO to the sidelines of the political process. This inevitably meant the promotion of Jordan's role in the solution of the Palestinian question.

For Jordan, this was a crucially important and positive development and an opening for future possible gains which it did not want to forego. Ḥusayn therefore sought to defend Sādāt, maintaining that the Arabs had to "understand that real peace, by definition, will entail normal relations between Israel and its Arab neighbours."[35] Ḥusayn also maintained that, as far as he was concerned, Sādāt's speech in the Knesset "was excellent."[36] Following the cessation of the Political Committee talks in January 1978, the Jordanian government expressed its "full support" for Egypt's policy, "which upholds the comprehensive settlement and the achievement of the basic Arab demands and rights," and should therefore enjoy the support of the entire Arab world.[37] Egypt's plan for withdrawal submitted to Israel in July—which proposed Jordanian control of the West Bank during a transitional period—was well received in Jordan where Information Minister 'Adnān Abū 'Awda praised the plan for what he maintained was its realistic approach, particularly to the Palestinian question.[38]

The new situation created by Egypt's policy was favourable to Jordan not only in the sense that it reaffirmed US and Egyptian recognition of Jordan's special relationship with the West Bank, but also in that both those countries were now focusing their efforts on the incorporation of Jordan in the negotiating process, rather than the PLO, as had been the case throughout most of 1977.

The Jordanians were keen to preserve their recognized status in regard to the

West Bank and were quick to refute Israeli claims that Jordan had no legal right to sovereignty over the area. In January 1978, following a statement to this effect by Prime Minister Begin, Husayn repeatedly contended that Jordan had such a right, pointing to his country's admission to the UN "as a state of two united banks." [39] An Amman Radio commentary added that Jordan was "internationally empowered by Resolution 242 with the right to regain the occupied Palestinian territory." [40] Whatever the legal validity of these claims, they no doubt revealed Jordanian aspirations. But Husayn believed it was too soon to join the negotiations: he did not expect to win Arab support for a move that would not only strengthen Sādāt, but also be a flagrant violation of the Rabat summit resolutions.

Husayn himself explained that displacing the PLO was "not a decision that can be made by one or two countries, however powerful. Unless the knot of the Rabat summit decisions is untied—and only Arabs and Palestinians in particular can untie it"—Jordan was "not prepared to do anything on [the Palestinians'] behalf." [41] Despite occasional Jordanian references to the PLO's representative status as recognized at the Rabat summit, it was precisely because Jordan sought to undermine and effectively neutralize the role of the PLO, that it genuinely sought Palestinian representation of some sort in the peace process. In fact, Husayn frequently indicated that a distinction had to be made between the PLO and the "Palestinian people as such"; it was the latter who should be involved in any process leading to a solution of the Palestinian problem. [42] Without Palestinian participation, the Jordanians were reluctant to become involved in negotiations (unless they had a clear-cut Arab and Palestinian mandate to do so), fearing that they would be accused of "usurping the rights" of the Palestinians and imposing themselves against the will of the people. The Chief of the Royal Court, 'Abd al-Hamīd Sharaf, explained that Jordan's role "should proceed alongside the Palestinian people and should not be at their expense." He added that Jordan had no intention "to replace the Palestinians" [43] or to play a decisive role in determining the future of the Palestinians unless the people of the West Bank and Gaza were "explicitly ready to ask for it." [44]

Jordan was clearly apprehensive of taking action which it suspected would be counter-productive and self-defeating to its long-term policy of obtaining broad-based inter-Arab legitimacy for a dominant role in settling the Palestinian question. This apprehension was heightened following the Sādāt visit, as the Jordanians did not expect to make the kind of gains that the Arab world would consider justified their joining the negotiations. From the outset, Husayn was sceptical about the territorial gain that he could hope to make in the West Bank; as time elapsed and the Egyptian-Israeli negotiations appeared to be making little headway, the Jordanians became more pessimistic. They therefore remained unwilling to join the negotiations, an act which they felt could incur Syria's wrath, upset the Palestinians on the East Bank and precipitate a barrage of Arab accusations of "betrayal of the Palestine cause," without any real gain to counterbalance the probable damage to their own interests. In late July and early August 1978, the Jordanians came to the conclusion that the Sādāt initiative was petering out, so rather than consider joining it, they began to encourage Sādāt to discontinue the dialogue with Israel and "return to the Arab fold." [45]

Jordan's fear of Arab censure and doubts about the gains to be made led Husayn to seek advance guarantees that it would be worth his while to participate in the negotiations. He maintained that if he "could see the light at the end of the tunnel," he "would not hesitate one second to negotiate," Husayn claimed at first that a set of principles could "provide that light"; [46] but by February, he considered a declaration of principles to be insufficient. He asserted that the "question now is not one of a declaration of principles," as these had already been "unanimously defined and announced in UN Security Council Resolution number 242"; what was required was "tangible proof of Israel's commitment" to accept and implement these principles.[47] This Jordanian position was again reaffirmed on the eve of the Camp David tripartite summit, when Jordan expressed hope that the US role could bring Israel to "respond to the requirements of peace as outlined in Security Council Resolution 242."[48] As for the principles themselves, these had to include complete Israeli withdrawal to the pre-June 1967 frontiers, including withdrawal from East Jerusalem; self-determination for the Palestinian people under international supervision "in complete freedom"; ensuring the right of refugees to return or to receive compensation; and ensuring security for the countries in the area.[49]

Not prepared for any kind of territorial compromise, Husayn maintained that he could not "enter into bargaining about Palestinian territories or Palestinian rights."[50] The King was reported by diplomatic sources to have said that border changes would have to be made with the approval of the Palestinians (the criticism levelled against his grandfather, King 'Abdallah, for making territorial concessions to Israel in the 1949 armistice apparently still fresh in his mind).[51] The Jordanians were only prepared to accept "minor mutual" border rectifications. Arab sovereignty over East Jerusalem had to be restored, although Husayn said that he envisaged Jerusalem as an "open city of peace."[52] He did not accept the idea of Israeli settlements remaining in the West Bank as part of a peace settlement. While Husayn acknowledged that the Israeli withdrawal "couldn't happen overnight," he insisted that it would have to be in "the shortest possible time."[53] According to an Israeli source, Husayn told President Carter during their talks in Tehran (at the beginning of January 1978) that he would be able to accept a temporary arrangement provided it led to full withdrawal within a few years.[54]

A lasting peace, in Husayn's view, should ensure the right of all peoples and states to exist within secure and guaranteed borders.[55] Thus all security arrangements should be on the basis of reciprocity: US guarantees for Israel ought to be given to Jordan as well.[56] Husayn found an Israeli military presence in the West Bank unacceptable unless "some Arab presence were acceptable to the Israelis on their territories."[57]

The Israeli plan for autonomy in the West Bank and the Gaza Strip was also rejected by the Jordanian government. As it failed to commit Israel to total withdrawal, Jordan felt it was designed "to consolidate [the Israeli] occupation and to give this a legal character."[58]

The Jordanians envisaged that the principle of self-determination for the Palestinians would be fulfilled through a referendum to be held after an interim period under UN or other international supervision. The Egyptian proposal for Jordanian supervision in the transition period no doubt fitted in very well with Jordanian thinking and aspirations, as it would allow it greater influence over the outcome of any such referendum.

Jordan was not keen to see Sādāt fail—not only because his policy included various positive factors as far as Jordan was concerned, but also because of fears that failure could "lead to a great disaster" and "total catastrophe."[59] While such statements were undoubtedly meant to encourage the US to bring pressure to bear on Israel to make far-reaching territorial concessions, they also reflected a genuine Jordanian fear of war and of Israel's military potential.[60] Husayn apparently harboured a real suspicion that in the event of war, Israel would seek "to change the status quo of the East Bank" in order "to realize the idea of an alternative homeland for the Palestinians."[61] He was also evidently worried that a failure of the peace process could lead to a wave of militant radicalism in the Arab world and arouse "disillusionment with . . . the kind of leadership that exists in the entire area." [62] The King also predicted that if the talks failed, the validity of Resolution 242 as the basis for a ME settlement would be undermined. [63] This would be undesirable for Jordan as the resolution provides a framework for negotiation acceptable to the Arab world; at the same time—being rejected by the PLO—it served as an obstacle to the latter's involvement in the political process.

With these considerations in mind, the Jordanians did not lend their support to the "rejectionists," but negotiated "by proxy" through Egypt, the US and Iran in an effort to create conditions which would enable them to become more directly involved.

Husayn did not conceal the fact that he still believed his federation plan of 1972 to be the most desirable and realistic framework for a settlement and for future Jordanian-Palestinian relations. [64] He also maintained that if a referendum were to be held in the West Bank, the majority of the population would probably "vote for a large degree of autonomy, coupled with strong confederal links with Jordan." [65] Husayn stressed that due to the strong ties and mutual interests binding the Jordanians and the Palestinians, he could "not imagine that these two peoples . . . could abandon each other." [66] Jordan's ambassador to the US, 'Abdallah Salāḥ—himself of Palestinian origin—insisted that the "massive familial relationships between the people on both sides of the River Jordan render it inconceivable that the government of Jordan, the PLO and the masses of the Jordanian and Palestinian people would countenance suicidal separation." [67]

With both Jordan and the PLO striving to play the dominant role in determining the political fate of the Palestinians, relations between the two continued to be governed by profound mutual suspicion and mistrust. Top level talks between the PLO and Jordan in early 1977 [68] were not resumed until September 1978. Both Husayn and Badrān had previously mentioned that occasional contacts were being made with the PLO. In February 1978, there were reports that Husayn and 'Arafāt had exchanged messages and that the Jordanian-PLO dialogue was about to resume. A PLO source revealed later that such a dialogue had been suggested at the Tripoli bloc conference (for details, see essay on Inter-Arab Relations) in order to "prevent Jordan's drifting behind Sādāt." [69] The PLO therefore demanded that Jordan confirm its adherence to the Rabat resolutions, its refusal to enter the negotiations, and its condemnation of Sādāt. The PLO also reiterated its longstanding demand for the restoration of a military and political presence in Jordan. Against this background it was difficult to detect any basis for genuine reconciliation, particularly when leading figures in the PLO such as Fārūq Qaddūmī and Salāḥ Khalaf expressed the suspicion that Jordan would use improved relations with the PLO as a means of legitimizing its own involvement in the peace process. As Qaddūmī put it, the PLO did not want to be "used as a cover-up for any Jordanian participation" in the negotiations. [70]

However, in September, Yāsir 'Arafāt accompanied Libya's President Qadhdhāfī on a brief visit to Mafraq in northern Jordan where they both met with Husayn. The visit was one of the preliminary signs of a larger realignment in the Arab world which culminated in the Baghdad summit in November 1978 (for details, see essay, "The ME in Perspective").

Whereas Jordan had little chance or desire to establish favourable relations with the PLO, it did seek to cultivate close relations with the West Bank population—as a means of undermining the PLO's influence in determining the future of the area. In fact, Jordan still had substantial influence and room for manoeuvre in the West Bank. Its single most important asset was that it continued to be a central factor in the determination of the West Bank's political destiny.

West Bankers recognized that Sādāt's visit to Jerusalem, and the Egyptian policy that emerged thereafter, had pushed the PLO to the sidelines of the political process and elevated Jordan's role. Though strongly opposed by the PLO, Sādāt's visit was well received by many in the West Bank—much to the distress of PLO supporters in the area. Jordan's position in the West Bank was therefore enhanced by the visit, if only because it helped to demonstrate a weakening of the PLO's hold over the population. Though West Bankers differed in their attitudes to the future of the area, their most profound wish was for an Israeli withdrawal. This factor gave Husayn an extremely important advantage over the PLO since it promoted a tendency amongst West Bankers to accept solutions that, though not ideal, would put an end to Israeli rule.

Egypt's proposals for Israeli withdrawal, which provided for Jordanian supervision over the West Bank during the interim period, were not surprisingly rejected by hard-core PLO supporters in the West Bank. Their opinion, as expressed in the dailies *al-Fajr* and *al-Sha'b*, was that only the Palestinian people had the "absolute right to exist and determine their fate on their land without any interference . . . or trusteeship from anyone." [71] They criticized Egypt's proposals which they said would prevent the establishment of an independent Palestinian state and ignore the PLO. [72] However, *al-Quds*, representing a different but substantial segment of West Bank opinion, stressed what it portrayed as positive elements of the Egyptian proposals, namely the call for complete withdrawal and support for the principle of self-determination. [73] As for Egypt's ignoring the PLO, *al-Quds* explained that Israeli withdrawal was the first priority, and therefore it did not believe that "even the leaders of the [PLO] themselves could oppose the idea of liberation by whatever means or whichever way." [74]

The growing realization in the West Bank that Jordan would be involved in any political solution was fertile ground for Husayn's policy of portraying Jordan as the protector of the Palestinians' right to self-determination. Radio Amman's message was that Jordan adheres "more than ever before to the Palestinian people's right to determine their own destiny by themselves, and to choose the relations they want with their neighbours in absolute freedom and without pressure or compulsion by any other party in the world"—no doubt including the PLO. [75] Husayn also personally assured West Bank leaders that he would accept any results of a referendum in the West Bank. [76] His confidence that these would not be unfavourable for Jordan rested on the assumption that, if successful in neutralizing the PLO, the interest of the West Bank population in preserving their family and economic ties with the East Bank would induce them to accept some type of federal solution.

The West Bank's financial and economic dependence on the East Bank continued undiminished in 1978, despite PLO-inspired efforts to end the West Bank municipalities' financial dependence on Jordan. [77] Even the two staunchest pro-PLO mayors, Bassām Shak'a of Nablus and Karīm Khalaf of Rām'allah (who had previously declined to go to Jordan) made several visits in late 1977 and during 1978 for the purpose of collecting funds deposited in Amman for their municipal projects. Jordan also financed various charitable institutions in the West Bank, and regular trade connections and movement of people across the "open bridges" continued. These direct links gave Jordan a number of avenues of influence over the daily lives of the West Bank population, which served to encourage the notion that "any feasible solution must not separate the two banks." [78]

JORDAN AND THE ARAB WORLD
IN QUEST OF ARAB CO-ORDINATION AND CONSENSUS
Sādāt's visit to Jerusalem caught Husayn in the midst of intensive preparations for

participating in a unified Arab delegation to attend a Geneva conference. During October 1977, Jordanian emissaries had visited Damascus, Cairo and Riyadh; Husayn himself held talks with President Asad, King Khālid and President Sādāt in early November.

Sādāt's initiative forced Husayn to contend with an entirely new situation for which he was totally unprepared, even though he had held talks with Sādāt only days before the latter announced his intention to visit Jerusalem. The newly created rift in the Arab world was particularly inconvenient for Jordan since it coincided with a period of negotiations on the future of the Palestinians, in which Arab agreement for a Jordanian role was of fundamental importance (see above). Husayn spent much of December visiting Syria, Egypt, Saudi Arabia and the Gulf states, trying to reduce the impact of inter-Arab dissension and hostility. His early fears of the possible consequences of Sādāt's initiative faltering (see above) motivated him to try to achieve an Arab consensus and co-ordinated policy. This was intended to prevent undue turmoil in the event of the negotiations failing, as well as to prepare a co-ordinated front for the event of war and develop an "Arab force . . . in the shortest time possible so that Israel will be reduced to its true size." [79]

Husayn's efforts in the Arab arena early in 1978 did not prove to be particularly successful, although the Israeli operation in South Lebanon in mid-March gave them added impetus and a sense of urgency, arousing Husayn's deepest fears that "Israel's target tomorrow will be Jordan." [80] Thus, shortly after the beginning of the Israeli operation in Lebanon, on 17 March, Husayn called for a summit conference to decide on an all-Arab policy. He reiterated his belief that if the Arabs wanted to "reduce the enemy to its proper size and force it to be governed by the logic of international norms and the concept of a just peace, [they] must build sufficient Arab strength which will be capable of changing the present power formula and [of] imposing a fundamental change on the thinking of the Israeli leadership and the international powers standing beside it." [81] A few days later, Jordanian envoys were dispatched throughout the Arab world to discuss the proposed summit. Amman also drew up a working paper which included detailed proposals for the regulation of Arab relations and means "to build the intrinsic power." [82] In the first half of April, envoys were once again dispatched throughout the Arab world to promote Jordan's plan of action.

These efforts were not crowned with success. The pre-condition of the "rejectionists"—that Sādāt announce the failure of his policy—put an end to any serious effort to convene a summit. Nevertheless, Jordan continued to call for the "removal of differences and the quick return of Arab solidarity before the nation is shaken by a new catastrophe that cannot be confronted in the absence of unity and intrinsic power." [83]

JORDAN'S POSITION BETWEEN SYRIA AND EGYPT

Evidence that the special Syrian-Jordanian relationship was cooling, mainly because of fundamentally different attitudes to the Arab-Israeli conflict, was already apparent during much of 1977. [84] However, Sādāt's visit to Jerusalem set the two countries clearly apart, with Syria playing a leading role in the "rejectionist front," and Jordan drifting closer towards Egypt, in the hope of making gains at the PLO's expense. One indication of Syrian displeasure with Jordan was the joint statement issued on 4 December 1977 by the Jordanian and Syrian Communist parties condemning Sādāt and praising the stands of both Syria and the PLO. The statement, published by the official Syrian Arab News Agency, was a pointed act of co-operation between the Syrian regime (where the Syrian Communist Party is represented in the Cabinet) and the best organized opposition in Jordan—a far cry from the statements of political co-ordination issued by Ḥusayn and Asad in 1975 and 1976.

Ḥusayn suggested that Syria's position toward Sādāt may have been "ill-thought through over-reaction." [85] He indicated that Jordan would not follow the Syrian line because his country's policy could not be "prescribed by others." [86] Nevertheless Jordan was clearly reluctant to quarrel openly with Syria; only advance assurances of major gains in negotiations with Israel would have been worth such a rupture. The cost of a breach with Syria was made clear in June 1978 when, without previous co-ordination, Damascus allowed fidā'iyyūn to infiltrate into Jordan with the purpose of carrying out operations against Israeli targets. PLO infiltration was not only a potential source of trouble for Jordan on its frontier with Israel, but could also be used to ferment internal instability.

The risks of a breach with Syria, coupled with pessimism about the consequences of a possible breakthrough in the Egyptian-Israeli negotiations, led Jordan to seek an improvement in its relations with Syria. Ḥusayn met with Asad in July; at the beginning of August, the first meeting since July 1977 of the Higher Jordanian-Syrian Joint Committee was held in Damascus to discuss the furthering of economic co-ordination between the two countries. The shift back to Damascus was accompanied by consistent support in the Jordanian media for Syria's moves in Lebanon, and by a more critical attitude towards Egypt for introducing policies which divided the Arab world. However, in late August, as the tripartite summit at Camp David approached, the divergent attitudes of Syria and Jordan once again became more pronounced. While Syria vehemently attacked Sādāt, Jordan reverted to its more positive wait-and-see position.

RELATIONS WITH OTHER ARAB STATES

Relations with **Saudi Arabia** in 1977–78 continued to revolve around political co-ordination and consultation on general ME issues, as well as Saudi economic aid to Jordan. The cooling of relations with Syria removed a potential source of tension in the relationship with Saudi Arabia, and no pressing problems surfaced on the bilateral level. Frequent high-level contacts were held, with Ḥusayn himself visiting Saudi Arabia four times between November 1977 and July 1978 for talks relating to the Arab-Israel conflict, particularly the co-ordination of policy in the wake of Sādāt's visit to Jerusalem. The Saudis' ambivalent attitude towards Egypt's policy was a central factor in contributing to Jordan's reluctance to join the negotiations.

Relations with **Kuwait** and the **Gulf States** remained favourable during 1977–78. They continued to focus on economic aid to Jordan and Jordanian military assistance to most of the Gulf states.

The Jordanian army's battalion of engineers, stationed in Oman since 1974, returned to Jordan on 22 December 1977. However, some Jordanian officers remained in Oman for training purposes.

A Jordanian military training mission left for Kuwait in June 1978, and in August police cadets from the UAE and Qatar were reported to be receiving training at the Jordanian police college.

Relations with **Iraq** remained stable, with the two countries continuing to develop trade relations. An important element of these was the Iraqi use of 'Aqaba as a means to overcome congestion in its own ports. Jordan did not allow sporadic incidents to upset their basically positive relations. In November 1976, Jordan had accused Iraq of compliance in the fidā'ī attack on a hotel in Amman (see *MECS 1976-77*, p. 487), and in October 1977, it condemned Baghdad for executing a Jordanian student for alleged espionage—a charge the Jordanians naturally denied.

However, after a short interlude of mutual recriminations, relations resumed their normal course.

A marked improvement in Jordan's relations with **Libya** occurred following the restoration of diplomatic relations in April 1976; these were severed by Libya in September 1970 in protest against Jordan's crackdown on the fidā'iyyūn at that time. Libya's new ambassador to Jordan, Sālih Sannūsī, took up his post in September 1977. Premier Badrān paid an official visit to Libya in April 1978 during which agreements on cultural and economic co-operation were signed. In May, Jordan's Finance Minister, Muḥammad Dabbās, visited Tripoli where he concluded agreements for Libyan development loans totalling $70m. However, Libya did not renew its annual grant of $30m, which it had agreed to pay Jordan in accordance with the resolutions of the Khartoum summit of 1967.

JORDAN'S RELATIONS WITH THE MAJOR POWERS
RELATIONS WITH THE US
Jordan's history of close relations with the US continued to be vital for the Kingdom's survival. The US remained Jordan's major supplier of military hardware and one of its main providers of economic assistance. There was no repetition during 1978 of Ḥusayn's concern and even anxiety over a less favourable US attitude which had surfaced in 1977 in the wake of revelations about CIA payments to Ḥusayn and of President Carter's policy on the Palestinian issue (see *MECS 1976–77*, pp. 487–88). In the aftermath of Sādāt's visit to Jerusalem, US statements to the effect that the PLO had removed itself from the peace process, accompanied by continuous efforts to include Jordan in the negotiations, were far more favourable than the American efforts of August-September 1977 to incorporate the PLO in the ME talks. The stress placed by the US on its opposition to an independent Palestinian state and its preference for close federal ties between Jordan and any Palestinian homeland or entity, were also very much in line with Ḥusayn's federation plan,[87] as well as with the Jordanian vision of the solution to the Palestinian question (see above). This evident agreement was reinforced by frequent contacts between the US and Jordan during the year to discuss Jordanian participation in the peace process, including talks between President Carter and King Ḥusayn in Tehran in January and a number of visits to Amman by US Secretary of State, Cyrus Vance (in December 1977), and by the US ambassador-at-large, Alfred Atherton (in January, March, July and August).

However, throughout 1978, the Jordanian media often expressed disappointment with the US role in the peace negotiations, maintaining that Washington was not exerting enough pressure on Israel. Ḥusayn himself said that the US "must pressure Israel to make her contribution to peace." [88] On the eve of the tripartite summit at Camp David, Radio Amman stated that it was not enough for the US "to give advice or undertake consultations." It had "to become a third partner" and "prove the capability of the strongest and richest country in the world to contribute to spreading peace, security and stability in the ME." [89]

US economic aid to Jordan remained at much the same level as in the past. In February 1978, the US State Department requested Congressional approval for $113m worth of economic aid and $85m credits for the purchase of military equipment for fiscal year 1979 (cf *MECS 1976–77*, p. 487). At the end of January 1978, Crown Prince Ḥasan visited the US for talks relating mainly to economic and technical assistance.

RELATIONS WITH THE SOVIET BLOC
Jordan's relations with the USSR have improved substantially in recent years,[90] the

Soviet interest in reconvening the Geneva conference prompting frequent visits to Jordan beginning late in 1975. The head of the Near Eastern Department of the Soviet Foreign Ministry visited Amman at the beginning of November 1977 and again in mid-September 1978. Two Soviet military delegations visited Jordan in late 1977, a tourism delegation early in 1978, and a trade union delegation in May. Amman approved agreements for Soviet assistance for a Jordanian electricity project (December 1977) and cultural and scientific co-operation (May 1978). Jordan's Minister of Information, 'Adnān Abū 'Awda, visited the USSR in mid-1978 to promote co-operation in the field of information.

In a message to the Soviet Foreign Minister on 21 August 1978 (the 15th anniversary of the establishment of diplomatic relations) Premier Badrān expressed Jordan's "great satisfaction" with the state of relations between the two countries.[91]

Improved relations with the USSR were accompanied by expanding ties with other East European countries.[92] Delegations visited Jordan from the foreign ministries of Poland (November 1977) and Czechoslovakia (December 1977 and May 1978). Following the conclusion of a trade agreement in October 1977, Crown Prince Ḥasan visited Poland in May for talks on economic and technical co-operation. A trade agreement was also signed with Czechoslovakia (June 1978), and agreements for cultural and scientific co-operation concluded with Poland (November 1977), Hungary (February 1978), and Czechoslovakia (May 1978).

RELATIONS WITH CHINA
Following the establishment of diplomatic relations with Peking in April 1977 (see *MECS 1976-77*, p. 489), talks on the development of trade were held in Amman in December 1977 between the PRC's newly accredited ambassador and Jordan's Minister of Trade and Industry. A visit to Jordan between 27 June and 1 July 1978 by the PRC's Deputy Minister of Foreign Affairs was followed later in July by a PRC trade delegation. A trade agreement initialled on 22 July was approved by the government on 2 August 1978.

ECONOMIC AFFAIRS ($1 = 0.313 Jordanian dinars; £1 = JD 0.570)
By most indicators, the Jordanian economy witnessed a year of growth in 1977.[93] According to some reports, gross domestic product (GDP) grew 17.9%, from JD 335.8m in 1976 to JD 395.9m (c. $1,257m) in 1977; other sources reported a similar growth rate, but at the higher output levels of JD 400.4m for 1976 and JD 470.9m (c. $1,495m) for 1977.[94] Despite problematic inflation, Jordan's real economic growth rate, as measured by the change in GDP at constant prices, was estimated at the impressive level of 10.4%.[95]

Other indicators of the relatively healthy performance of the Jordanian economy in 1977 include increases in production in the agricultural and industrial sectors; an improvement in the balance of payments; a turn-around in the budget from a deficit to surplus; and greater holdings of international reserves and foreign assets. Two factors whose persistence continued to hamper Jordan's economy, however, were inflation and the widening negative trade gap.

AGRICULTURE
Since the record harvests of 1974, adverse weather conditions have restricted Jordan's agricultural output. In 1977, the third successive year of scant rainfall, production of rainfed staples such as wheat and barley remained at less than one-third of 1974 levels.

In contrast, fruits and vegetables (grown in irrigated as well as in rainfed regions) were produced in greater quantities in 1977 than in 1976. However, the inadequacy of Jordan's irrigation network can be shown by the fact that although fruit and vegetable output rose an average of 24.1% and 1.3% respectively in 1977, their corresponding totals of 103.5m tons and 204.4m tons were still below 1974 levels. In an effort to double the area under irrigation, the government has allocated JD 97.4m (12.7%) to water and irrigation under the 1976–80 Five-Year Plan.[96]

INDUSTRY
Of Jordan's 16 principal industries (as defined by statisticians of the Central Bank of Jordan), 10 enjoyed increased production in 1977 compared with 1976. Foremost among these were producers of sole leather and wool (+ 112.9%), iron (+ 82.8%), pharmaceutical ointments, tablets and kindred products (+ 37.9%), and electricity and fodder (+ 24.0% each). Of the six principal industries which suffered lower production in 1977, the most pronounced declines were in spirits and alcoholic drinks (–12.5%), cement (–8.3%), and textiles (–5.0%).

Compared with the corresponding period in 1977, production in the first half of 1978 climbed in the important industries of phosphates (+ 34.7%), petroleum products (+ 34.2%) and textiles (+ 7.1%). But cement production fell 11.9% during this period.

CONSTRUCTION
Construction activity, as measured by the number of permits issued per annum, fell c. 14% in 1977 from the peak year of 1976. Permits for solely residential construction in both Amman and Zarqā declined an average 14.7% for a total of 2,826, corresponding to 569,400 sq metres. During the same period, the total number of permits issued for both residential and other construction in Amman and Zarqā fell 13.4%. In this case, fewer permits were approved, though for a larger total area of 137,400 sq metres. (For details on rents and the housing market, see above.)

From these data and other sources, it appears that the housing boom in Amman has abated, while the construction of fewer but larger units has marked the non-residential building sector.[97]

LABOUR
Authoritatively reliable statistics on employment are unobtainable. Nevertheless, both official sources and other reports emphasize the imbalance in the labour market created by the emigration of managerial and skilled technical workers.[98]

Of a total population estimated at 2.1m in 1976, 51% were under the age of 15; 3% were either elderly or handicapped, and a further 7% were engaged in full-time studies. Of the remaining 39%, slightly more than one-half (or 21% of the total population) were gainfully employed. The labour force is thus composed of c. 440,000 Jordanians. But this statistic is misleading because a sizeable proportion of this number—estimates range from a minimum of 30% or 130,000, to a maximum of nearly 60% or 250,000—was working abroad in 1976, mostly in Persian Gulf states. At the same time, the local labour market was bolstered by a growing influx of unskilled foreign workers, mainly from Egypt, Syria and Pakistan. The number of these non-Jordanians, who were employed primarily in the construction and agricultural sectors, was estimated variously between 40–60,000 in 1976.[99] (For details of the social problems arising from the influx of foreign workers, see above.)

BUDGET
Preliminary data published by the Central Bank of Jordan reveal that government revenues leaped 73.6% in 1977 over 1976 for a total of JD 322.8m (c. $1,025m).

The bulk of this increase was made up of foreign grants and foreign borrowing, each of which multiplied to levels of JD 120.5m and JD 45.4m respectively. Of this foreign-origin budget support, the US share fell from JD 21.8m to JD 14.3m, while that from Arab states ballooned from JD 19.3m to JD 106.2m. At the same time, revenue from domestic sources rose from JD 110.5m to JD 145.4m.

Total expenditures grew at the slower rate of 41.7% in 1977, for a total of JD 315.9m (c. $1,003m). The larger proportion of this increase was devoted to capital expenditure (55.4%), with the remainder going to recurrent outlays (44.6%). The largest expenditure increases, in absolute terms, were allocated to economic development services (JD 42.7m), finance administration (JD 22.9m), and the recurring defence budget (JD 13.8m).

As a result of the overwhelming increase in grants from the Arab world, Jordan's budget account reverted from a deficit of JD 37.0m in 1976 to a surplus of JD 6.9m in 1977.

DEVELOPMENT
One of the more noteworthy features of the 1976–80 Five-Year Plan is the proportion of private sector financing—slightly more than 50%—of the total budget of JD 765m (c. $2,311m). By contrast, foreign loans constitute the largest component of the public sector's share of the financing (JD 382m).

The largest sums allocated on the expenditure account (in million Jordanian dinars) were to industry and mining 229.1; transport 119.9; water and irrigation 97.4 and housing and government building 86.0. Lesser, yet still sizeable, allocations include electric power, JD 42.8m; agriculture, 40.0m; and education, 34.6m. [100]

As with many other developing countries, however, these initial sums appeared overly ambitious. In the first year of the Plan, for example, actual total expenditure amounted to only 54.7% of that planned, a shortcoming attributed partly to the relative shortage of foreign assistance in 1976. [101] It will be easier to judge the Plan's practicability when the data are published for actual outlays in 1977, when foreign loans were much more readily available.

WAGES AND PRICES
In a study by the International Monetary Fund (IMF), inflation was described as the Kingdom's "most pressing problem" in the short run. In an article on the IMF survey, the *Jordan Times* reported that the government had decided to give "the anti-inflation effort . . . the highest priority." [102] (For details on the political and social problems arising from inflation, see above.)

Estimates of Jordan's inflation rate vary. Until 1978, there was no single cost-of-living index whose accuracy had widespread acceptance. In an effort to rectify this problem, the government introduced a new "Modified Cost-of-Living Index." According to this, Jordan's average rate of inflation for 1977 was 14.5%, while prices for food and housing were said to have risen 14.3% and 7.4% respectively. However, these latter two statistics call into question the reliability of the index as a whole.

IMF officials attribute much of the cause of inflation to "cost push." [103] Wages in Jordan increased 24.4% in the 12 month period ending August 1976, and were thought to have risen over 20% again during the succeeding 12 month period.

BALANCE OF PAYMENTS
Despite a $224.3m growth in the merchandise trade deficit, Jordan's overall balance of payments surplus improved $157.8m to reach a level of $190.9m in 1977.

Increases in exports of services ($123.2m), net government unrequited transfers ($90.7m), and long-term capital (from -$27.4m in 1976 to +$170.8m in 1977) more than compensated for the higher merchandise and services combined deficit ($149.7m), as well as the rise of payments outflows caused by the inversion of credit to debit in the cases of net private unrequited transfers and short-term capital.

Jordan's balance of payments posture is not quite as healthy as its surplus suggests, however. The fact that the two largest components of the surplus are exports of services and net government unrequited transfers constitutes an anomaly which is not necessarily auspicious.

MONETARY DEVELOPMENTS

Jordan's holdings of international reserves jumped 37.9% in 1977 and a further 13.4% during the first quarter of 1978, at which time they reached a level of $768.6m. With its holdings of gold remaining fairly constant, Jordan's additional reserves consisted almost exclusively of accumulated foreign exchange.

Reserves and foreign assets of both commercial banks and the Central Bank of Jordan also rose in 1977; so did the money and quasi-money supplies. Although growth for the latter two was significant in 1977, their rates were divergent: the money supply grew at 19.4%—the slowest rate of growth since 1972; in contrast, the quasi-money supply jumped 30.3% in 1977 and a further 48.7% during the first four months of 1978.

FOREIGN TRADE

In 1977 as in 1976, imports exceeded exports by a wide margin—JD 394.2m in 1977. The rate of increase for imports (33.8%) also surpassed that of exports (21.6%). The scale of the value of Jordan's imports is indicated by the fact that, in 1976, their value (JD 339.5m) was greater than the total GDP at factor cost (JD 335.8m).

Of the 1977 total value of imports of JD 454.4m, the largest components were machinery and transport equipment (34.5%), manufactured goods (22.5%) and food (16.7%). The largest components of the 1977 export total of JD 60.3m were food and live animals (34.3%), inedible crude materials other than fuels, i.e. chiefly phosphates (31.3%) and manufactured goods (15.7%).

Saudi Arabia (25.1%), Syria (12.5%) and Iraq (7.2%) were Jordan's main markets for exports in 1977, while the US (14.8%), West Germany (14.0%) and Saudi Arabia (8.2%) were the Kingdom's chief suppliers of imports.

Asher Susser
Economic Section by **Ira E. Hoffman**

ARMED FORCES

Total armed forces number 67,850. Defence expenditure in 1978 was JD 95.3m ($304m). Military service is compulsory for 24 months. The Army numbers 61,000 and consists of two armoured divisions, two mechanized divisions, three special forces battalions and two anti-aircraft brigades including six battalions with *Improved HAWK* surface-to-air missiles. Equipment includes 320 M-47/-48/-60, 180 *Centurion* medium tanks; 140 *Ferret* scout cars; 600 M-113 and 120 *Saracen* armoured personnel carriers; 110 25-pdr, 90 105mm, 16 155mm, 203mm howitzers; 35 M-52 105mm, 20 M-44 155mm self-propelled howitzers; 81mm, 107mm, 120mm mortars; 106mm, 120mm recoilless rifles; *TOW, Dragon* anti-tank guided weapons; *Vulcan* 20mm, 200 M-42 40mm self-propelled anti-aircraft guns; *Redeye* surface-to-air missiles, *Improved HA WK* surface-to-air missiles. (100 M-113 armoured personnel carriers, M-110 203mm self-propelled howitzers, 100 M-163 *Vulcan* 20mm anti-aircraft guns, *Improved HA WK* surface-to-air missiles on order.) The Navy numbers 200 and has ten small patrol craft. The 6,650-strong Air Force has 76 combat aircraft; one ground-attack fighter squadron, one operational conversion unit with eight F-5A/B, 24 F-5E/F; two interceptor squadrons with 20 F-104A/B, 24 F-5E/F; four C-130B, one *Boeing* 727, one *Falcon* 20, four CASA C-212A *Aviocar* transports; 14 *Alouette* III, two S-76 helicopters; eight T-37C, 12 *Bulldog*, one *Dove* trainers; *Sidewinder* air-to-air missiles. (One C-130H transport, ten AH-1H and four S-76 helicopters on order.) Reserves number 30,000. There are 10,000 paramilitary forces, 3,000 in the Mobile Police Force and 7,000 in the Civil Militia.

Source: The Military Balance 1978-79 (London: International Institute for Strategic Studies).

ARMED FORCES: DIVISIONS/MAJOR SYSTEMS

	1973	1978	
Armoured divisions	2	2	
Mechanized divisions	1	2	
Infantry divisions	2	—	
Special forces brigades	1	1	
Tanks	480	700	
Armoured personnel carriers	606	1,300	
Artillery	320	4500	
Combat aircraft	55	100	
Helicopters	6	15	
Ground-to-air missile batteries	—	14	(being received)

Source: Arab Military Strength (Jerusalem: Israel Information Centre, June 1978).

BALANCE OF PAYMENTS (million US dollars)

	1975	1976	1977
A. Goods, Services and Transfers	67.3	82.3	8.6
Exports of Merchandise, fob	152.9	207.0	253.9
Imports of Merchandise, fob	-649.0	-907.6	-1,178.8
Exports of Services	426.2	793.7	916.9
Imports of Services	-303.4	-391.9	-440.5
Private Unrequited Transfers, net	5.8	11.3	-3.4
Government Unrequited Transfers, net	434.8	369.8	460.5
B. Long-Term Capital, nie	140.6	-27.4	170.8
C. Short-Term Capital, nie	17.1	22.9	-1.4
D. Errors and Omissions	-44.8	-44.8	12.9
Total (A through D)	180.2	33.1	190.9

Source: IMF, International Financial Statistics.

BUDGET SUMMARY (million Jordanian dinars)

	1975*	1976*	1977*	(first qtr) 1978*
A. Total Revenue	193.2	185.9**	322.8	40.0
Of which: Domestic	84.2	110.5	145.4	30.1
Foreign Grants	90.0	41.1	120.5	9.4
Foreign Borrowing	19.0	17.7	45.4	—
Other	—	16.5	11.5	0..5
B. Total Expenditure	209.4**	222.9	315.9	48.9
Of which: Recurring	136.3	144.5	186.0	40.7
Capital	73.2	78.4	129.9	8.2
Surplus or Deficit (A-B)	-16.2	-37.0	6.9	-8.8**

*Preliminary.   **Figures do not add because of rounding.

CENTRAL GOVERNMENT EXPENDITURES (million Jordanian dinars)

	1975*	1976*	1977*	(first qtr) 1978*
General Administration	1.0	1.2	1.3	0.5
Defence	55.3	55.6	69.4	20.7
Internal Order and Security	8.6	11.7	14.4	2.5
International Affairs	2.4	2.4	3.5	0.7
Finance Administration	58.1	54.3	77.2	7.6
Economic Development Services	50.5	45.6	88.2	7.8
Social, Cultural and Information Services	27.7	34.9	43.2	7.8
Communication and Transportation Services	5.8	17.3	18.7	1.2
Total	**209.4**	**222.9****	**315.9**	**48.9****

*Preliminary.   **Figures do not add because of rounding.

SECTORAL DISTRIBUTION OF OUTSTANDING BANK CREDIT (thousand Jordanian dinars, at end of period)

	1975	1976	1977	(first half) 1978
Municipalities and Public Corporations	7,180	8,092	6,916	20,783
Agriculture	3,608	5,162	8,311	10,567
Industry	14,831	21,808	26,599	32,073
General Commerce and Trade	51,372	81,614	81,427	92,304
Construction and Purchase of Land and Buildings	26,280	33,826	29,907	82,888
Transportation	3,691	7,779	11,083	8,111
Tourism, Hotels and Restaurants	1,783	2,518	3,422	4,825
Professional and Private Individuals	7,402	11,365	13,075	16,848
Total (including others)	**121,432**	**183,738**	**201,094**	**289,379**

Source (of three preceding tables): Central Bank of Jordan, *Monthly Statistical Bulletin.*

GROWTH RATES BY SECTOR 1975-77 (million Jordanian dinars)

	GDP			Growth rates (%)		
				Actual		Expected
Sector	1975	1976	1977	1976	1977	annual average
Agriculture	26.0	37.3	41.7	43.5	11.8	7.0
Mining and manufacturing	48.8	61.0	70.0	25.0	14.7	26.2
Construction	16.1	23.3	27.0	44.7	15.9	4.1
Electricity and water supply	3.1	3.6	4.1	16.1	13.9	17.1
Transport and communications	24.9	33.6	42.0	34.9	25.0	10.6
Trade (wholesale and retail)	43.9	50.5	63.1	15.0	25.0	7.2
Financial institutions	4.3	5.2	7.0	20.9	34.6	17.1
Ownership of dwellings	15.7	17.3	23.0	10.2	33.0	12.0
Public administration and defence	56.1	67.3	73.0	20.0	8.5	7.0
Other services	30.1	36.7	45.0	22.0	22.6	8.5
GDP at factor cost	**269.0**	**335.8**	**395.9**	**24.8**	**17.9**	**11.9**
Indirect taxes	37.0	68.4	75.0	84.7	9.6	9.5
Net factor income from abroad	62.0	140.0	143.0	125.8	2.1	10.6
GNP at market prices	**368.0**	**544.2**	**613.9**	**47.9**	**12.8**	**11.5**

Source: *The Middle East*, September 1978.

AGRICULTURAL PRODUCTION, EAST BANK ONLY (thousand tons)

	1975	1976	1977
Field Crops	**74.1**	**100.7**	**93.8**
of which:			
Wheat	50.0	66.6	62.5
Barley	11.8	13.2	12.0
Vegetables	**262.3**	**201.8**	**204.4**
of which:			
Tomatoes	145.1	87.9	85.7
Eggplant	39.6	41.9	24.6
Fruits	**91.7**	**83.4**	**103.5**
of which:			
Citrus	12.8	16.5	36.5
Melons	50.3	23.1	28.1
Grapes	11.1	13.7	22.3

PRODUCTION OF PRINCIPAL INDUSTRIES

	Unit	1975	1976	1977	*(first half)* 1978
Phosphate (dry)	'000 tons	1,352.5	1,701.8	1,769.3	1,105.5
Cement	'000 tons	598.2	586.4	537.6	241.2
Petroleum Products	'000 tons	828.2	1,145.5	1,145.3	689.1
Upper Leather	'000 sq ft	2,230.7	2,910.1	2,873.9	1,409.4
Detergents	tons	4,203.0	5,027.0	6,026.7	2,620.2
Cigarettes	tons	1,998.0	2,407.0	2,700.0	1,303.8
Electricity	m kwh	256.7	323.7	401.3	232.5
Iron	'000 tons	31,304	42,449	77,605	32,019
Textiles	'000 yds	953.0	915.8	869.8	528.8

FOREIGN TRADE BY COMMODITY, ACCORDING TO SITC
(thousand Jordanian dinars)

	Imports		Exports	
	1976	1977	1976	1977
Food and Live Animals	81,378	75,921	16,379	20,643
Beverages and Tobacco	2,104	3,009	1,204	1,265
Crude Materials, Inedible, except Fuels	10,182	11,080	20,078	18,880
Mineral Fuels, Lubricants and Related Minerals	37,171	43,057	639	7
Animal and Vegetable Oils and Fats	3,108	3,066	709	362
Chemicals	16,343	23,192	3,544	5,221
Manufactured Goods classified by Material	65,889	102,318	3,920	9,484
Machinery and Transport Equipment	101,439	156,843	722	778
Miscellaneous Manufactured Articles	20,101	33,329	2,352	3,610
Commodities and Transactions, nes	1,824	2,602	5	3
Total	**339,539**	**454,417**	**49,552**	**60,253**

ACTIVITY IN 'AQABA PORT (thousand tons)

	1975	1976	1977	*(first qtr)* 1978
Number of Vessels	516	1,064	94·	286
Exports *of which:*	870.7	1,631.9	1,722.3	365.6
Phosphates	*856.3*	*1,626.9*	*1,705.4*	*362.8*
Imports	682.6	1,368.6	1,389.1	259.1
Total (of Imports and Exports)	**1,553.3**	**3,000.5**	**3,111.4**	**642.7**

DIRECTION OF TRADE (million Jordanian dinars)

	1975	1976	1977
Exports to:			
Saudi Arabia	4.76	7.47	15.10
Syria	3.58	6.39	7.54
Iraq	2.40	2.33	4.31
India	1.97	1.71	3.89
Japan	1.91	1.92	2.63
Lebanon	2.02	1.66	2.92
Kuwait	2.40	3.28	2.80
Egypt	0.92	1.19	1.07
Total (including others)	**40.08**	**49.55**	**60.25**
Imports from			
United States	24.2	31.0	67.4
West Germany	24.9	51.9	63.6
Saudi Arabia	22.9	34.5	37.1
United Kingdom	21.9	23.7	33.0
Japan	17.1	21.5	28.7
Italy	11.1	19.5	26.0
Romania	8.8	9.5	20.3
France	7.6	10.5	13.4
Lebanon	9.2	7.3	11.7
Syria	6.3	7.5	11.1
Total (including others)	**234.0**	**339.5**	**454.4**

Source: (of five preceding tables): Central Bank of Jordan, *Monthly Statistical Bulletin*

NOTES
1. See *Middle East Contemporary Survey (MECS)* 1976–77, p. 474.
2. Cf *MECS 1976–77*, pp. 474–75.
3. R Amman, 19 June—Daily Report (DR), 20 June 1978.
4. See *MECS 1976–77*, p. 475.
5. *Ibid.*
6. *Jordan Times (JT)*, 4, 6–7 August 1978.
7. During 1970–71, when the PLO still possessed an armed presence in Jordan, professionals supporting the organization were grouped in the "Professionals' Gathering" (*al-tajammu' al-mihnī*), which was affiliated with the opposition "National Gathering" (*al-tajammu' al-watanī*).
8. *Al-Mustaqbal*, Paris; 10 December 1977.
9. *JT, al-Akhbār*, Amman; 20 November 1977.
10. Rif'at 'Awda was imprisoned for conspiring to overthrow the monarchy in 1959. He was later pardoned.
11. See, for example, *al-Mustaqbal*, 10 December 1977, and *al-Watan al-'Arabī*, Paris; 27 January 1978.
12. *Al-Ra'y*, Amman; 16 March 1978.
13. *Al-Hurriyya*, Beirut; 17 April 1978; *Shu'ūn Filastīniyya*, Beirut; May 1978, p. 192.
14. *Ibid.* Also *al-Hurriyya*, 3 April 1978.
15. Jordan has two universities, one in Amman and the other in Irbid.
16. *JT*, 21 March 1978.
17. Leaflet of the PDFLP dated 15 April 1978, in Shiloah Center Archives; *Al-Hurriyya*, 12 June 1978.
18. R Amman, 20 June—DR, 23 June 1978.
19. When parliament was not in session, the Cabinet was empowered by the constitution to promulgate provisional laws. These would later be referred for approval to parliament when it reconvened. For details on the parliamentary situation in Jordan, see *MECS 1976–77*, p. 475.
20. R Amman, 13 April—DR, 14 April 1978.
21. Cf *MECS 1976–77*, pp. 475, 477.
22. A former Prime Minister (from November 1971 to May 1973).
23. *JT*, 3 August 1978.
24. *JT*, 25 April 1978.
25. *JT*, 26 April 1978.
26. One of the founders of the Ba'th party in Jordan and Minister of State for Foreign Affairs in Sulaymān al-Nābulsī's Cabinet, between October 1956 and April 1957. This was

the only Cabinet in Jordan's history dominated by figures usually associated with the opposition. After its fall in April 1957, al-Rīmāwī lived in exile until July 1970, when he returned to Jordan.

27. R Amman, 19 June—DR, 20 June 1978.
28. The licence of *al-Sha'b* was withdrawn by the Cabinet in September 1977 after it had published rumours on the Premier's whereabouts. These were used by the PLO to claim that Badrān had been meeting with Israeli Foreign Minister Dayan.
29. *Al-Ra'y, al-Akhbār*, Amman; 25 July 1978.
30. Cf *MECS 1976–77*, pp. 478–84.
31. R Amman, 19 November—British Broadcasting Corporation, Summary of World Broadcasts, the Middle East and Africa (BBC), 21 November 1977.
32. Husayn in speech to the nation, Jordan Television, 28 November—BBC, 30 November 1977.
33. *Newsweek*, New York; 12 December 1977.
34. Husayn's speech to the nation, Jordan Television, 28 November—BBC, 30 November 1977.
35. *Newsweek*, 12 December 1977.
36. Interview to NBC, reproduced in *JT*, 8 December 1977.
37. R Amman, 21 January—BBC, 23 January 1978.
38. *JT*, 9–10 July 1978.
39. *JT*, 13 January 1978; R Amman, 17 January—BBC, 19 January 1978.
40. R Amman, 18 January—DR, 19 January 1978.
41. *Newsweek*, 12 December 1977.
42. Husayn in interview to NBC, reproduced in *JT*, 8 December 1977.
43. Jordan Television, 27 January—DR, 31 January 1978.
44. *New York Times (NYT)*, 21 June 1978.
45. *Al-Ra'y*, 4 August 1978.
46. *Time*, New York; 30 January 1978.
47. Husayn in interviews to Agence France-Presse (AFP) on 9 February and Austrian newsmen on 7 March; R Amman, 9 February, 7 March—DR, 10 February, 8 March 1978.
48. R Amman, 13 August—DR, 15 August 1978.
49. R Amman, 9 February—DR, 10 February 1978.
50. R Amman, 17 January—BBC, 19 January 1978.
51. *Ma'ariv*, Tel Aviv; 7 March 1978.
52. *Newsweek*, 12 December 1977.
53. *NYT*, 2 January 1978.
54. *Ma'ariv*, 20 January 1978.
55. R Amman, 11 March—DR, 13 March 1978.
56. *NYT*, 8 March 1978.
57. BBC Television, 16 May—DR, 18 May 1978.
58. R Amman, 28 December—BBC, 30 December 1977.
59. R Amman, 12 December—BBC, 14 December 1977; *Der Spiegel*, Hamburg; 6 February 1978.
60. *Al-Nahār*, Beirut; 25 April 1978.
61. Husayn in speeches to the army, reported in *JT*, 26 April 1978; R Amman, 8 May—DR, 9 May 1978.
62. Interview on BBC Television, 16 May—DR, 18 May 1978.
63. *Time*, 30 January 1978.
64. *Der Spiegel*, 6 February 1978.
65. *Newsweek*, 12 December 1977; *Der Spiegel*, 6 February 1978.
66. R Amman, 17 January—BBC, 19 January 1978.
67. *NYT*, 20 June 1978.
68. See *MECS 1976–77*, p. 480.
69. Voice of Palestine (clandestine broadcast from Lebanon), 9 March—DR, 10 March 1978.
70. Voice of Palestine (clandestine), 7 March—DR, 9 March 1978.
71. *Al-Fajr*, East Jerusalem; 25 June 1978.
72. *Al-Fajr, al-Sha'b*, East Jerusalem; 6 July 1978.
73. *Al-Quds*, published in East Jerusalem, is the most widely circulated newspaper in the West Bank.
74. *Al-Quds*, 6 July 1978.
75. R Amman, 18 January—DR, 19 January 1978.
76. *Al-Mustaqbal*, 11 February 1978.
77. See *MECS 1976–77*, pp. 212–13, 483 and essay on the West Bank and Gaza Strip.
78. *Al-Quds*, 21 April 1978.

JORDAN

79. Husayn in interview to AFP, R Amman, 9 February—DR, 10 February 1978.
80. Husayn in interview to NBC, *JT*, 19 March 1978; *al-Nahār*, 25 April 1978.
81. R Amman, 17 March—BBC, 20 March 1978.
82. R Amman, 3 April—DR, 4 April 1978.
83. R Amman, 26 July—DR, 26 July 1978.
84. See *MECS 1976-77*, pp. 484-85.
85. *Newsweek*, 12 December 1977.
86. *Der Spiegel*, 6 February 1978.
87. For details of the plan, see *MECS 1976-77*, p. 480.
88. *NYT*, 8 March 1978.
89. R Amman, 12 August—DR, 15 August 1978.
90. See *MECS 1976-77*, pp. 488-89.
91. *JT,* 22 August 1978.
92. Cf *MECS 1976-77*, p. 489.
93. For a detailed examination of the major developments in Jordan's economy prior to 1977, see *MECS 1976-77*, pp. 239-43.
94. *JT*, 2 August 1978; and International Monetary Fund (IMF), *International Financial Statistics,* Washington; June 1978.
95. *JT*, 2 August 1978.
96. Data derived from Central Bank of Jordan, *Monthly Statistical Bulletin*, Vol 14, No 6 (June 1978), and Economist Intelligence Unit, *Quarterly Economic Review of Saudi Arabia, Jordan (QER)*, Annual Supplement 1977. Also see *al-Dustūr*, Amman; 10 November 1977—Joint Publication Research Service (JPRS), 4 January 1978.
97. See Central Bank of Jordan, *Monthly Statistical Bulletin, op. cit.*, and *JT*, 13 and 15 June 1978.
98. See, for example, the article by the Jordanian Under-Secretary of Labour, Jawād al-'Anānī, in *An-Nahar Arab Report and Memo*, Zurich; 3 October 1977. Also see *al-Dustūr*, 28 October 1977—JPRS, 16 December 1977; and *al-Rā'y*, 18 December 1977—JPRS, 24 February 1978.
99. *An-Nahar Arab Report and Memo, op. cit.* Also see *Financial Times (FT)*, London; 25 May 1978.
100. See *FT, op. cit.*, and *QER, op. cit.*, pp. 30-31.
101. See *al-Ra'y*, 30 October—JPRS, 16 December 1977.
102. *JT*, 4, 6-7 August 1978.
103. *JT*, 4 August 1978.

Lebanon

(Al-Jumhūriyya al-Lubnāniyya)

In the short history of the current Lebanese crisis, the events of 1978 mark the end of the stalemate created by the Riyadh Agreements of October 1976. These had produced a situation characterized by the following inter-related elements.

(1) Continuation of the political conflict between the rival Lebanese coalitions and lack of progress in the efforts to solve the underlying problems that had led to the outbreak of the 1975–76 civil war. Chief among these had been the Muslim demands to restructure Lebanon's political institutions and the need to regulate the Palestinians' presence and activity in the country. Tensions and conflicts also existed within the respective Lebanese coalitions, with several factions and politicians switching alliances or reorienting their policies.

(2) Syria further consolidated its pre-eminence in and hegemony over Lebanon. But this position had yet to be formalized and accepted by Syria's opponents both inside and outside Lebanon.

(3) Continued impotence and frailty of the Lebanese state and its political institutions.

(4) A close interplay between Lebanon's domestic crisis and such regional issues as the Arab-Israeli conflict, Syrian foreign policy and inter-Arab relations. This concerned Lebanon as a whole and South Lebanon as a particular problem area (see essay on South. Lebanon in the section, "The Arab-Israeli Conflict").

During 1977 a delicate balance was kept in Lebanon. Despite occasional outbursts, fighting was not renewed, but no progress was made towards a resolution of the Lebanese crisis. This situation remained unchanged in 1978, as evinced by the failure to form a "political cabinet" or to hold parliamentary elections. But other important changes did occur—primarily Syria's decision to exercise its power in Lebanon much more forcefully. The ensuing conflict with the Christian militias resulted in a resumption of fighting on a large scale in Beirut in September and October—thus again underscoring the regional repercussions of any serious deterioration in Lebanon. These changes should be seen against the background of developments which concerned Syrian policy and the Lebanese Front.

CHANGES IN SYRIAN POLICY

At the end of 1977, the Syrian Ba'th regime found itself in a peculiar position in Lebanon. It had originally intervened in order to promote its own interests as well as to resolve, or at least to contain, the Lebanese crisis. It still sought to enforce a "Syrian peace" which would achieve both: a settlement of the crisis that would also endow it with undisputed and formally recognized control. In a stabilized Lebanon, such control could be exercised indirectly and without the costly and controversial presence of over 30,000 Syrian troops.

In pursuing this policy, Syria could rely on several important assets and advantages. The Arab Deterrent Force (ADF)—commissioned and in part financed by the Arab League—was in fact mostly composed of and controlled by Syrian units. It was the most powerful military force in Lebanon. Syria itself controlled and administered the eastern part of the country. It also exercised direct influence over the administration of President Sarkīs, whom it had brought to power and whose incipient army and security services were trained and controlled by Syrian officers. Syria had several allies among Muslim and Christian politicians, and even its opponents refrained from demanding a Syrian withdrawal. Not only would this be clearly unrealistic, but they also felt that in the absence of a political settlement of the Lebanese crisis, a Syrian withdrawal would be bound to result in a renewal of the civil war. This attitude was reinforced by virtual regional and international acquiescence in Syria's hegemony in Lebanon—at least for the time being.

These assets were balanced by several serious problems. Syria seemed incapable of imposing a political solution acceptable both to itself and to the major political forces in the country. Nor was it able to bring the Lebanese to sign a defence pact or any similar document that would formalize and legitimize Syria's position in Lebanon. The Sarkīs Administration met with great difficulties in trying to build and extend its authority and proved to be far less co-operative than the Syrians had expected.

One of the most agonizing questions for Syria was its relations with the two foremost military forces in Lebanon: the Lebanese Front and the PLO. Syria's early alliance with the Christian militias, the core of the Lebanese Front, was wholly incompatible. It was ideologically and politically awkward for the Syrians, who realized that most Maronite leaders were opposed to their ultimate goals in Lebanon. Syria had come to terms with the PLO, the other major military force in Lebanon, in October 1976, but the impact of their military and ideological conflict had not yet been removed.

Consequently, Syria faced a dilemma during most of 1977: it could not impose its full authority in Lebanon without disarming or subduing the Christian militias and the PLO, yet it was unwilling and unable to pay the political and military price required by an attempt to subdue either of these forces. With their power intact, both could obstruct the efforts of President Sarkīs to develop his authority and build a new Lebanese army. Sarkīs in turn argued that without some display of independence from Syrian control, his regime would never acquire legitimacy and strike roots. In the absence of any progress towards a settlement, Syria had to maintain a large army in Lebanon.

In the long term, the Asad regime seemed to possess an answer to this dilemma, based on a two-pronged strategy:

(1) Avoiding an all-out confrontation and conflict with either the Christian militias or the PLO. However, this was bound to entail a military, economic and political price which Damascus was unwilling to pay.
(2) The gradual and patient extension of Syrian control, the cultivation of its supporters and erosion of its opponents' support and bases of power.

In the short term, however, the Baʻth regime was still faced with many problems. The maintenance of a large Syrian army in Lebanon was an economic burden; according to the Foreign Minister, 'Abd al-Halīm Khaddām, it cost Syria $70m a month, only $5m of which was paid by the Arab League.[1] Syrian public opinion was also critical of the country's protracted and apparently unsuccessful involvement in Lebanon, and the regime itself felt hampered in the conduct of its regional policies.

ARMED CLASHES; SYRIAN POLITICAL PRESSURES

The process of change, which began late in 1977, resulted in several confrontations in 1978 between Syria and the Christian militias on a scale that the Syrians had previously sought to avoid. Several factors accounted for this change. Latent tensions, which had traditionally existed between Syria and parts of the Lebanese Front, were exacerbated by the opening of the Egyptian-Israeli negotiations and the resulting *rapprochement* between Syria and the PLO. Maronite leaders such as Camille Chamoun and, to a somewhat lesser extent, Pierre Jumayyil felt that they had to adopt a firmer stance *vis-à-vis* Syrian pressure which was having a corrosive effect on their positions. They felt the need to resist Syrian encroachment on minor as well as on major issues. Furthermore, it is quite likely that some Maronite leaders who saw a confrontation as inevitable sought to bring it about earlier than planned by the Syrians and under circumstances less advantageous to them. There were also Israelis who felt that an attempt should be made to force the hand of the Likud government and induce it to play a greater and more direct role in Lebanon.

This pattern began to take shape in December 1977 when the Phalanges clashed with units of the ADF in Beirut. The conflict followed a series of strikes and demonstrations which the Lebanese Front had organized as a protest against the three-day suspension of the newspaper, *Le Reveil*. The paper (apparently edited by Amīn Jumayyil) was suspended for publishing an article that incensed the Syrian government. According to one source, it had urged Sarkīs to resign for "having placed the army under Syrian occupation." [2]

THE FAYĀDDIYYA INCIDENT

The December clash was a comparatively minor event that foreshadowed the far more serious conflicts of 1978. The immediate cause was Syria's efforts, during the first weeks of the new year, to conclude a defence treaty with Lebanon. Renewing the ADF's mandate had become entangled and uncertain, and a defence treaty seemed to offer a much better way of formalizing and perpetuating Syria's military presence in Lebanon. But there was opposition to the idea of such a treaty in Lebanon, and several sympathetic Lebanese politicians were invited to Damascus for "working visits" in an attempt to elicit their support. Sarkīs was quoted as saying that "Asad strongly insisted on a defence treaty." [3]

It was against this background that Syrian units of the ADF clashed in East Beirut with "elements of the Lebanese army" headed by Col (*'aqīd*) Antoine Barakāt, commander of the Fayāddiyya barracks. Barakāt had fought on the side of the Lebanese Front in the civil war and was considered to be close to Camille Chamoun's National Liberal Party (NLP). The incident quickly developed into what was described as the most serious armed conflict since the end of the civil war. The Syrian army brought in reinforcements from the Biqā' and engaged the Fayāddiyya troops and the NLP's militia. In the course of the fighting, the ADF shelled the Christian quarter of Ashrafiyya and stormed the headquarters of the NLP. By the time a ceasefire was negotiated on 11 February, dozens had died. The Syrian Foreign Minister and Deputy Defence Minister, Nājī Jamīl, were sent to Beirut, and a joint Syro-Lebanese committee was formed to investigate the incident (Sarkīs was reported to have threatened to resign.) While Leftist opponents of the Lebanese Front accused it of instigating the fighting, the commission of inquiry concluded that it had been primarily caused by contradictory orders issued by the ADF's commanding officers.

The Fayāddiyya incident did not result in immediate overt acrimony between Syria and the Lebanese Front. Pierre Jumayyil emphasized, as he had done in the past, that the incidents revealed the dangers to which both Syria and Lebanon were subject. An NLP delegation visited Damascus soon after the clashes; its public message was one of understanding and co-operation. Syria, in turn, refrained from criticism of the Lebanese Front, but emphasized the two countries' common security concerns. The Syrians demanded that the Lebanese officers responsible for the incident be extradited to Damascus, but had to agree instead to the formation of a joint Syrian-Lebanese military court. Col Barakāt was retired from the Lebanese army at Syria's insistence.

In retrospect, despite the initial calm aftermath, it became evident that the Fayāddiyya incident marked the beginning of a serious rift between Syria and the Lebanese Front, as well as Sulaymān Faranjiyya's estrangement from the Front.

THE 'AYN RUMĀNA AND AL-SHIYĀH CLASHES AND THEIR REPERCUSSIONS
These developments were given further impetus by the fighting which took place in Beirut between 9–14 April 1978. The incidents began as exchanges of fire and shelling between the Christian quarter of 'Ayn Rumāna and the Muslim quarter of al-Shiyāh, along the line separating East and West Beirut. The ADF interfered at a later stage. While it claimed to have done so in order to effect a ceasefire, it was accused by the Christian side of engaging in a massive shelling of 'Ayn Rumāna. An attempt to replace the Syrian units with Saudi and Sudanese soldiers, who would occupy the line separating East and West Beirut, was only partly carried out.

The role of the Palestinians in these incidents became the subject of acrimonious accusations by the Lebanese Front. Spokesmen for the Front accused the Palestinians and the Communists of provoking the incidents. They charged that the PLO had sought to divert attention from the issue of the Palestinian presence in the South (which was about to be evacuated by Israel) and to undermine the Front's relations with Syria.[4] However, a spokesman for the PLO formally denied that Palestinian units had taken part in the fighting in Beirut.

The fighting in 'Ayn Rumāna had several far-reaching repercussions:

(1) It intensified the debate on the role and status of the ADF in Lebanon. The Syrian argument, voiced then and on later occasions, was that the ADF had been placed under the authority of the Lebanese President to help him restore peace. But the number of dissenting voices in Lebanon increased. Camille Chamoun criticized the ADF,[5] though Pierre Jumayyil advocated further co-operation with it. More significantly, the Foreign Minister, Fu'ād Butrus, began to express dissatisfaction with the ADF's activity. This resulted in growing tension between Butrus on the one side, and Syria and the Prime Minister, Salīm al-Huss, on the other.

(2) The tension between Syria and the Lebanese Front became more manifest. While the Front focused its attacks on the Palestinians, the Syrians felt that they were being challenged as well and in turn sought to moderate Chamoun's behaviour (by dispatching a message to him from President Asad), and to weaken the Front by luring Faranjiyya away and cultivating differences between Chamoun and Jumayyil. The Syrian government denounced "the attempt to explode the situation in Lebanon under the slogan of defending it" and threatened to come out against "the forces of dissension."[6]

(3) Tensions within the Huss government finally resulted in its resignation (see below).

DETERIORATION DURING THE SUMMER MONTHS (JUNE–AUGUST 1978)
The killing of Tony Faranjiyya early in June (see below) contributed to a rapid deterioration of Syria's relations with the Lebanese Front. Syrian units, headed by Rif'at al-Asad, entered North Lebanon and units of the ADF, which had chased Faranjiyya's killers, surrounded and shelled the town of Dayr al-Ahmar in the Biqā'. Later in the month, 26 bodies were discovered in the Biqā'. Despite Syrian denials, it was widely believed that Rif'at al-Asad and the units under his command

were responsible. Syria intensified its criticism of the Lebanese Front, though in June these attacks were still only indirect.

Early in July, Syria began an all-out military and political offensive against the Lebanese Front. The purpose was now clearly to break the power of both the National Liberals and the Phalanges through massive shelling of Christian areas of Beirut. The British journalist, Patrick Seale, author of a major sympathetic study of the Syrian Ba'th, defined the offensive as "a determined Syrian attempt to destroy the Maronite community as an autonomous military and political force." [7]

The fighting in Beirut lasted from 1-6 July and resulted in hundreds of casualties. (The Lebanese Front claimed that 460 were killed and 2,000 wounded; the Syrian figures were 40 dead and 180 wounded.) Extensive physical damage was caused in Beirut, and large numbers of Christians left the city for the mountains or went abroad. Fighting was renewed on 22 July, and the shelling of Christian areas by reinforced Syrian units continued intermittently until 11 August.

Syria now explicitly denounced "the bands of the Phalangists and the Chamounists." Its media accused them of "conspiring to replace the legitimate authorities in Lebanon," of being "tied to the traitor Sa'd Haddad," and of co-operating with Israel.[8] Syria buttressed its traditional line with new arguments: the Phalanges and the Liberals are only a minority among the Christians, and at any rate "the conflict in Lebanon is not between Muslims and Christians but between the legitimate authority and those who wield arms against it."[9] A few weeks later, President Asad himself went further: "The Lebanese people are Muslim and Christian—and the majority is Muslim."[10]

While the Phalanges still tried to maintain a working relationship with Syria, Chamoun and other constituent members of the Lebanese Front increased their attacks on Damascus, accusing it of perpetrating genocide in Lebanon.

These developments also affected Syria's relations with the Sarkīs Administration. Damascus increased its pressure on the Lebanese President to implement the decisions agreed at the Asad-Sarkīs meeting in Lādhiqiyya, *inter alia*, to build the Lebanese army on a "patriotic basis"; but Sarkīs chose to tender his resignation (see below).

The clashes in Beirut also generated overt Israeli intervention. Prime Minister Begin and other spokesmen announced an Israeli commitment to the Lebanese Christians—to apply to the country as a whole, not just to the South. Israeli jets flying over Beirut, reinforced by American pressure on Syria, contributed to a temporary ceasefire early in July.

SYRIAN INITIATIVES IN NORTH LEBANON AND RENEWED DETERIORATION IN BEIRUT (AUGUST-SEPTEMBER 1978)

At the end of August, Syria shifted the focus of its offensive on the Lebanese Front to North Lebanon. No direct attack was attempted on the main stronghold of Jūniya, but its position was significantly affected by the Syrian capture of the areas of Batrūn and Bisharī. During their offensive, the Syrian forces shelled the Lebanese army camp at al-Arz and occupied the military airfield of Qulay'āt.

There were a number of reasons for the Syrian drive in the North. One was the desire to cut off the Lebanese Front and its forces in Beirut from their hinterland. This could facilitate a Syrian attack on (as distinct from shelling of) Christian positions in Beirut. The show of strength was also probably calculated to soften the position of the Sarkīs Administration in the negotiations on the renewal of the ADF's mandate.

Camille Chamoun accused Syria of trying to obstruct the Camp David talks and

Lebanon and Beirut

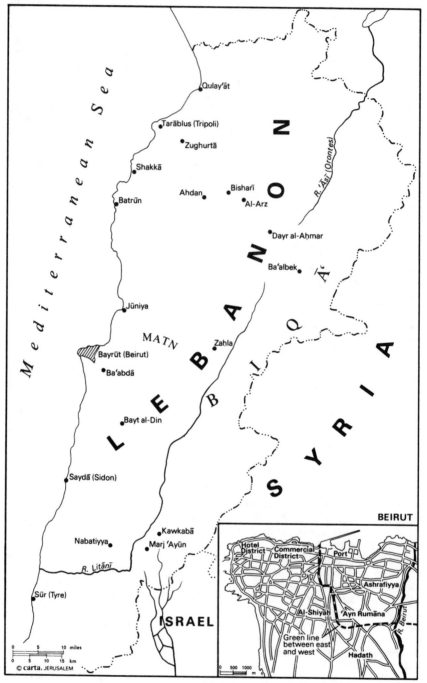

608

of seeking to gain complete control over Lebanon.[11] While still maintaining a more careful stance, Pierre Jumayyil warned of a "popular [anti-Syrian] rising." He demanded that "the positions of the ADF be clearly defined so that they do not serve as a source of threat and fright for the citizens," and insisted that Saudi and Sudanese troops replace Syrian units of the ADF in several places.[12]

Early in September, Syria renewed its shelling of Christian neighbourhoods in Beirut. Ba'abdā, seat of the Lebanese presidential palace, was hit while Sarkīs was in Rome to congratulate Pope John Paul I on his election and to seek the Vatican's intervention to help stabilize the situation in Lebanon.

SYRIA AND THE SARKĪS ADMINISTRATION

During 1978, Syria's relations with Sarkīs gradually turned sour as the Lebanese President sought to retain at least a measure of independence from Syrian control. His positions on several issues—such as support for decentralization and rejection of a defence treaty with Syria—were close to those of the Lebanese Front. The Syrian authorities, who had secured Sarkīs' election in 1976, expected him to be more co-operative. Pressure was exerted on him at several meetings with Syrian officials, the most important of which took place at Lādhiqiyya from 31 May–1 June 1978. His talks with Asad resulted in agreement on a number of issues, such as restoring the Lebanese army and dispatching Lebanese army units to the South. During the following weeks, however, the Syrians complained of "feet dragging" by Sarkīs. Syrian emissaries were reported to have told him that they resented having to carry the burden of "the Lebanese Administration's hesitant policies."[13]

The one member of the Administration particularly close to the President and to his views seems to have been Fu'ād Butrus, the Minister of Defence and Foreign Affairs. Butrus had shown in September 1977 that he held independent views on such questions as the status of the Palestinian organizations in Lebanon. A visit of his to Syria, scheduled for April 1978, was cancelled; according to "informed sources," the authorities refused to have Butrus in Damascus.[14] Following this rebuff and a bomb explosion near his home, Butrus gradually returned to the fold and began to voice views more in line with those of Syria, though his public statements seemed to lack conviction.

The estrangement of Ilyās Sarkīs and Fu'ād Butrus from Syria was counter-balanced by growing co-operation between Damascus and Lebanon's Prime Minister, Salīm al-Huss. He expressed opinions close to those of Syria and began to visit Damascus more frequently. In September 1978, when the extension of the ADF's mandate became a bone of contention between Syrian and Lebanese authorities, it was Huss who negotiated its renewal.

Outside the formal framework of the Lebanese government, Syria cultivated its alliance with Sulaymān Faranjiyya. This rested on a traditional friendship between the Asad and Faranjiyya families as well as on a community of political interests. The final rift between Faranjiyya and the Lebanese Front—the killing of his son and Syria's disaffection with Sarkīs—turned Faranjiyya into the Maronite politician closest to Damascus. Following Sarkīs' short-lived resignation, there was speculation that the Syrians would actually like to see Faranjiyya return to the Presidency. Such speculation was reinforced by his quasi-official three-day visit to Syria in August. During this visit, Faranjiyya and Asad discussed "political and security aspects" of the situation in Lebanon. Asad publicly praised Faranjiyya whom he described (in apparent contrast to Chamoun and Jumayyil) as a leader "who sacrificed for Lebanon and the Arabs and remained free of foreign dependence and co-operation with the enemy." Faranjiyya responded by endorsing Syria's shelling of Eastern Beirut, which he described as a Syrian offensive against a small minority rather than the Christian community in its entirety. [15]

SARKĪS RESIGNS AND RETRACTS HIS RESIGNATION

Some of the issues involved in Syria's relations with the Lebanese government were brought into stark relief by President Sarkīs' short-lived resignation, which he announced on 5 July 1978. Several reasons were given by Sarkīs and others for this step, [16] but the most important seems to have been the ADF's shelling of East Beirut. Sarkīs had only nominal authority over the ADF, and although he had previously recognized his lack of real control, he did not want to be associated with the ADF's attack on Christian neighbourhoods in Beirut. Sarkīs presented the Syrians with a list of conditions for agreeing to retract his resignation: real authority over the ADF, disarmament of all parties to the conflict, implementation of the agreements with the Palestinians, and a free hand in leading the country towards national reconciliation.

Syria reacted with apparent calm. Asad was quoted as having said: "Let him resign; we can always find another Lebanese President." [17] Their natural alternative candidate was Sulaymān Faranjiyya to whom Asad dispatched Muhammad al-Khūlī, one of his confidants, presumably to negotiate the matter. For the time being, however, Syria clearly preferred to have Sarkīs continue in office and so avoid a variety of constitutional and political complications. Accordingly, several pro-Syrian Lebanese politicians were invited to Damascus for consultations. Kāmil al-Asʿad, the Speaker of the Lebanese Chamber of Deputies (CD), who acted as a mediator, brought back alternative Syrian proposals for security arrangements in Beirut. Syria's efforts to reinstate Sarkīs were supported by a number of Lebanese religious and political leaders who feared a return to chaos. Ironically, the strongest pressures were applied by the Lebanese Front whose leaders hoped to see a redefinition of Sarkīs' powers and wanted to pre-empt the possibility of Faranjiyya returning to the Presidency through Syria's intervention. An open letter from Camille Chamoun to Ilyās Sarkīs stated, among other things, that "it is your duty to tell the Syrian deterrent forces that they—not you—ought to go." [18]

The US and several Arab states (including Saudi Arabia and Kuwait) joined the effort to persuade Sarkīs to retract his resignation. He finally did so on 15 July. His speech, detailing the reasons for his resignation and its retraction as well as his plans for Lebanon's future, was as follows:

SPEECH BY ILYĀS SARKĪS

On the retraction of his resignation as President of Lebanon
15 July 1978

"Lebanese people: In these delicate times when the eyes of the world are focused on us and worried about our fate, I approach you to review with you, frankly and simply, the realities of the serious crisis from which Lebanon is suffering. I will also discuss what we must do to get out of the crisis so that you may be aware of the facts and assume your historic responsibilities as citizens.

"When I took over the reins of power at a fateful period, there was unanimous agreement to swiftly quell the fires raging in various parts of the country and rebuild the state, the structure of which had been shaken. At the constitutional oath-taking ceremony, I explained the basis of the policy I was to adopt to achieve this objective. This policy received unanimous support. I then worked out a plan of action later adopted by the Riyadh and Cairo summits. The plan provided for a ceasefire and ending the in-fighting in Lebanon. It also provided for reinforcing the Arab security forces which were present on Lebanese territory at the time so that they would become a deterrent force that could impose adherence to the ceasefire, separate the warring forces, insure implementation of the Cairo Agreement, maintain internal security and supervise the withdrawal of the armed men and the collection of weapons.

"The Arab Deterrent Forces (ADF) continued to carry out their task in anticipation of the re-building of the army. It was natural for these forces to enjoy the same legitimate character, sanctity and immunity as those enjoyed by the regular Lebanese forces and to have the same rights and responsibilities. There can be no state where legitimacy lacks actual forces, and there can be no state where actual forces lack legitimacy. The atmosphere of mutual confidence and understanding that prevailed in the relations between the ADF and the Lebanese played a big role in halting the battles that were taking place at the time.

"However, the conflicts in the area and Arab differences had an impact on the Lebanese arena and prevented the continued implementation of the resolutions of the Riyadh and Cairo conferences. This created an atmosphere of doubt fraught with all kinds of surprises and susceptible to explosion. Obstacles then began mounting daily in the face of the state's attempts to progress, to the extent that all roads appeared to be blocked.

"We tried again to open the way on the basis of a plan of action which was prepared at Shtūrā and which aimed at persuading the PLO to voluntarily implement the Cairo Agreement. Here, again, this effort did not realize our aims. However, I always had hope that the circumstances would change, and we spared no effort to change conditions to facilitate the implementation of the Cairo Agreement and overcome the various difficulties, especially since the in-fighting which had exhausted the country had stopped and the state was in a position to direct some of its efforts toward development, in addition to security affairs. But the atmosphere became clouded again. The Israeli aggression against South Lebanon took place. Successive clashes followed, becoming bigger and more serious. When bloody events take place and the state becomes engaged in dealing with destruction instead of continuing the repairs and reconstruction it had started; when it becomes difficult to complete the establishment of institutions in various fields; when the task of organizing the army clashes daily with all kinds of obstacles; when the resolutions which the state adopts to serve the public interest are challenged in various ways; when the state receives only promises from the sides which can help; when provocations continue and reactions become more violent and when innocent victims fall while the state, deeply pained, is unable to put an end to this deterioration—when all this happens, the mind and conscience of the ruler compel him to give up power. This is how the idea of resignation emerged after long contemplation and careful study of the events and the situation.

"Today, after a chain of persistent contacts with requests for abandoning the resignation idea, and in view of highly respected international, Arab and Lebanese wishes, and after the positive willingness I sensed on all sides, I cannot but reconsider the question of resignation and acquiesce in these noble contacts and wishes. I will try once again to undertake matters and problems in a manner harmonious with the basic rules of exercising authority.

"Lebanese people, today I address you with the same frankness I have always used with you, to explain the bases on which it will be possible to continue to rule and deal with the fateful situation in the country. My giving up the idea of resigning does not mean agreeing to a return to the situations which were the reasons behind my intention to resign. Governing is a responsibility and for this responsibility to be shouldered, certain prerequisites must be fulfilled.

"Violence will continue to threaten security and to threaten the state and legitimacy and the lives of innocent people as long as people continue to possess hundreds or thousands of arms and as long as there are tens of thousands of fighters, and as long as the international conflicts in the area and Arab differences and their reflection on the Lebanese arena prevent the collection of arms from the Palestinian organizations and the elimination of the armed occurrences. The question of collecting arms from the Lebanese will remain a thorny issue which cannot be solved immediately.

"Rule will remain unstable as long as we cannot eliminate the illegitimate armed or unarmed manifestations which some parties and organizations practise. The presence of such manifestations and conditions conflicts with the role of the state and its legal institutions. The state must, therefore, use all its means to undertake these matters and speed up the completion of the preparation of the army and supply it with equipment and implement the compulsory conscription law in order that the army, even though in the stage of growth, may be able to carry out its required role.

"In this framework and in response to the UN resolutions, which provide for putting an end to Israel's aggression, withdrawing of its forces and establishing Lebanese sovereignty over Lebanese soil and the subsequent dispatch of UN forces to South Lebanon, it is natural that the army should enter the South to carry out its national role there. Anyhow, amity and confidence must characterize the atmosphere of the relations between the Lebanese and the ADF, particularly the Syrian forces, in a matter which will reflect the atmosphere of the existing fraternal relations between the Lebanese and Syrian peoples. We must consider these forces as legitimate Lebanese forces which are temporarily replacing our armed forces. They must be treated on this basis and they themselves must act on this basis.

"Syria—acting under the directions of brother President Ḥāfiz al-Asad—shares our heavy burden with us. No temporary conditions must disturb the clarity of these relations.

"O Lebanese: The results of the potential and capacities which the state can mobilize will fall short of the aspired aim if all efforts are not concentrated on the establishment of a solid national unity. The measures and solutions will not bear full fruit if there is no national detente.

"O Lebanese: All the foregoing represents the most important basic prerequisites which must be realized to exercise rule, especially under the delicate conditions through which Lebanon is passing. The Lebanese people must agree on this basis by actually strengthening their state in the difficult path which the state and they are following. Unless this is done the danger of chaos will remain, threatening the interests of individuals and groups and their rights and dignity. The government would then clash with obstacles which would make the management of the rule difficult. Let us derive from the fatal dangers surrounding us absolute determination to save the unity of the homeland, its safety and permanence in response to the will of the Lebanese and in loyalty to the constitutional oath.

"Cutting the state down to size would mean cutting Lebanon itself down to size. This shall not happen in Lebanon with God's will, the vigilance of the Lebanese, their collaboration and fraternity. Long live Lebanon!"

Source: R Beirut, 15 July—DR, 17 July 1978.

If Ilyās Sarkīs had hoped that his resignation would change either his own or the general political situation in Lebanon, he was bound to be disappointed. The leaders of the Lebanese Front were also disconcerted that Sarkīs had returned to office without having won any significant Syrian concessions.[19] The Syrians, in turn, displayed an indifferent attitude towards Sarkīs, who had obviously lost much of his usefulness to them. The Syrians' self-confidence was shown by Asad's assertion that "the Deterrence Force has the right to defend the regime of the [country's] security in any way that Syria sees fit in order to strengthen legitimacy in Lebanon." [20]

THE CONTINUING LEBANESE CONFLICT
THE CENTRAL GOVERNMENT AND THE CD
It was a measure of the continued political crisis in Lebanon that none of the three central political institutions in the country functioned in a satisfactory fashion. As described above, the President's efforts to endow his office with real authority failed. Earlier in the year, against the background of the 'Ayn Rumāna clashes, the Prime Minister, Salīm al-Ḥuss, had tendered his resignation (19 April 1978). It was suggested at the time that personal and political differences between Ḥuss and Fu'ād Butrus constituted an important reason for this step. [21] However, Ḥuss denied that any such differences existed and attributed his decision to an attempt to extricate Lebanon from a position of stalemate.

The President accepted Ḥuss' resignation but charged him with forming a "national unity cabinet" representing the whole political spectrum in Lebanon. This he tried to do for almost a month, but failed. One reason often cited for his failure was Chamoun's insistence on his own inclusion in the Cabinet as Minister of Defence, and Ḥuss' refusal to have "Lebanon's princes" in its ranks. [22] But the real reasons went deeper than that. A "national unity cabinet" would have represented the restoration of a national consensus in Lebanon and, as such, would have signified a virtual end to the domestic political crisis. This was obviously not the case. On 15 May, Ḥuss withdrew his resignation, explaining that this was "the only initiative possible due to the politicians' failure to reach an agreement on a national unity cabinet." [23]

For similar reasons it proved impossible to hold parliamentary elections in Lebanon and replace the 1972 CD. Parliamentary elections had been due in 1976, but in February 1976, at the height of the civil war, the CD's term of office was extended by two years. Another extension was granted in January 1978.

The CD and its committees continued to meet occasionally during 1978, but CD members understood that their discussions were to little practical purpose. Power and authority were vested in Syria and in extra-parliamentary military and political bodies, while the Lebanese CD simply represented an adherence to formal continuity.

The Speaker, Kāmil al-As'ad, began to play a more prominent role in Lebanese politics. However, this derived less from his parliamentary position than from his leadership of the Shī'ī community and his ties with Syria.

ABORTIVE ATTEMPTS AT NATIONAL RECONCILIATION
The Lebanese CD was an active partner in President Sarkīs' unsuccessful effort to arrive at a formula of national reconciliation that would bring an end to the Lebanese conflict. In October 1977, a "parliamentary drafting committee" was formed under the Speaker, Kāmil al-As'ad. During the next few months, As'ad and other parliamentary leaders sought to arrive at a solution of two inter-related and fundamental problems: how to implement the Shtūrā Agreement (regulating the activity of the Palestinian organizations), and how to devise a formula for the reform of Lebanon's political system that would be acceptable to all the major political groupings. The Syrian-inspired Reform Agreement of February 1976 served as the basis for these efforts.

The stormy developments which took place in the winter of 1978 at once underscored the need to arrive at new compromise arrangements and interfered with the efforts to do so. Thus the clashes in Fayāddiyya delayed the efforts to formulate a political compromise, while the massive Israeli incursion into South Lebanon demonstrated the futility of any solution to the Lebanese conflict that did not repudiate the status of the Palestinians in the country.

The most serious—and apparently promising effort—was invested by a committee set up in April. By 23 April, it had reached the following formula:

Out of firm belief in the need to preserve Lebanon's unity, sovereignty and security, the security of its territory and its democratic parliamentary system; in keeping with the positions to which Lebanon has adhered in supporting Arab causes, particularly the Palestinian people's cause and their right to recover their land and exercise all their national and political rights on this land, on the basis of the resolutions passed by the Riyadh and Cairo summit conferences on the collection of weapons, and since all Lebanese in all walks of life have agreed to preserve Lebanon's unity, independence, sovereignty and the security of its territory; since the preservation of these self-evident issues dictates that only constitutional authority should exist in Lebanon; since the representatives of the Palestinian people announced in the statement issued by the six-nation summit conference held in Riyadh and in the resolution passed by the extraordinary session of the Arab summit conference held in Cairo their approval of the supervision of all heavy arms and the elimination of armed manifestations; and since Security Council Resolution 425—to the provisions of which all sides have committed themselves—calls for the stationing of UN forces in the area of southern Lebanon to ensure the withdrawal of the Israeli forces, consolidate international peace and security and assist the Lebanese government in securing the restoration of its authority in the area; and since Resolution 425—which all sides have accepted—dictates the consolidation of international peace and security in addition to its stipulation that it is imperative that Lebanese authority be restored in the area of southern Lebanon; and since the primary task of the Arab security [deterrent] force is to back the Lebanese authorities in order to impose security and guarantee the security of all residents on Lebanese territory, we therefore announce the following:
    (1) UN Security Council Resolution 425 must be implemented. This calls for:
        (a) scrupulous respect for the security of Lebanon's territory and its sovereignty and political independence within Lebanon's internationally recognized borders:
        (b) immediate withdrawal of the Israeli forces from the whole of Lebanese territory;
        (c) restoration of the state's effective authority in the area of southern Lebanon.
    (2) All Palestinian and non-Palestinian armed action throughout Lebanese territory must be halted.
    (3) Any armed presence except that of the forces of the legitimate Lebanese authority must be prevented and Lebanese laws and norms must be applied to all the Lebanese and to all those present on Lebanese territory without exception.
    (4) The Lebanese army must be built on a sound and correct national basis to enable this army to assume its responsibilities and discharge the tasks assigned to it.
    (5) An economic development policy within the framework of the free economic system in its modern concept must be pursued. This policy will be based on exploiting all the country's natural resources. This will help to provide all citizens with equal opportunities and to create sound social justice in all Lebanese areas and among all factions of the people.
    (6) In expressing the will of the people, those taking part in the conference request the legitimate authority to implement it.[24]

This formula was unanimously adopted by the CD in its 27 April session, but it failed to serve as the basis for a real national reconciliation. For one thing, it addressed itself to the pressing problems of the moment rather than to the underlying causes of the Lebanese crisis. Critics of the formula thought that it was merely "a temporary palliative which will please everyone and, equally, give everyone the chance of not putting it into effect."[25] Furthermore, the Syrian authorities resented the formula because of its timing, the approach it reflected with regard to the Palestinian organizations, and the fact that it was not initiated by themselves.

It was hardly surprising, under these circumstances, that the compromise formula remained a dead letter and that the effort to form a "national unity cabinet" in May also failed. During the summer of 1978, as the conflict between Syria and the Lebanese Front escalated, national reconciliation seemed further away than ever, although talk of finding such a compromise continued in Lebanon. In September, in a more realistic vein, Camille Chamoun and other Lebanese Front spokesmen advocated "the rejection of any political solution before the foreign military forces—Syrian or others—leave Lebanon."[26]

ATTEMPTED ECONOMIC RECONSTRUCTION

The Huss government started on the long and arduous road of economic reconstruction by drawing on its emergency legislative powers (see *MECS 1976-77*, p. 507). Some progress had been made in 1977 and early in 1978, but the pace was very slow as financial support from Arab oil producers and Western powers remained meagre. Nor were Lebanese expectations of Arab investments in the country met. What little progress had been made was undone by the events of 1978. First, renewed clashes in Beirut in February frightened foreign investors and diverted additional Lebanese capital out of the country. The heavy shelling of Beirut's Christian neighbourhoods during the summer months caused extensive damage, reversed trends of normalization and led to further emigration from the city and the country. Second, Israel's massive incursion into South Lebanon in the spring resulted in a large influx of temporary refugees converging on Beirut. Their later resettlement in the South put additional strain on the country's resources.

ATTEMPTS AT ARMY RECONSTRUCTION

Even more than economic recovery, the issues involved in reconstructing the Lebanese army could not be divorced from the broader political issues which beset the country in 1978. Among the problems which hampered this process were the army's composition, the allocation of authority over it, the attempt to dispatch it to the South, and the Sarkīs Administration's security plan. (For the disintegration of the Lebanese army during the civil war, see *MECS 1976-77*, pp. 507-9.)

THE COMPOSITION OF THE LEBANESE ARMY

In theory, the issue of the composition of the army was to be regulated by law. During the civil war in December 1975, the Karāmī government had presented the relevant parliamentary committees with a draft of "The Army and National Defence Law." Its purpose was to partially satisfy the demand of Lebanese Muslims that the army—which they regarded as essentially Christian-dominated—should be more representative of the country's population. The law was never passed. Throughout 1977, the Sarkīs Administration tried to build a new Lebanese army that would ensure it of a measure of actual power.

A fresh attempt to redefine the legal basis of the Lebanese army was started after the Fayāddiyya incidents. It was largely inspired by Fu'ād Laḥūd, chairman of the CD's Defence Committee, a former army officer and a respected independent Deputy. The new draft[27] called for a reorganization of the army's General Command, the formation of a Supreme Defence Council (headed by the President), and the expansion of the authority vested in the Minister of Defence at the expense of the Chief of Staff. The use of the army for domestic security was to be determined by the Minister of Defence. The army was to comprise c. 40,000 men, 60% of them career soldiers and the others drafted.

The draft law took account of political realities in the country by affirming that "it is necessary to build a strong army after the determination of Lebanon's identity and the arrival at an agreement on her defence policy which derives from that identity." Although the draft law was discussed and partly amended by CD committees it was not presented for discussion on the floor of the Chamber.

At the same time, an active struggle continued for control of what still remained of the army. The Fayāddiyya incidents showed the Syrians that their efforts to dominate the Lebanese army since 1976 had been far from successful. As Khaddām put it: "These events exposed numerous loopholes in the sensitive problem of the Lebanese army's reconstruction."[28] Syria now increased its pressure on the Sarkīs Administration to purge the army of officers close to the Lebanese Front; it also endorsed the demands of the National Movement to establish a "balanced" or "national" (rather than a "sectarian") army in Lebanon.[29]

PROBLEMS OF RESIGNATION AND RETIREMENT

One obvious procedure for transforming the composition and orientation of the Lebanese army was forced resignations and early retirements. In November 1977, the government accepted the resignation of 31 officers who had taken part in the civil war. The deadline for tendering such resignations, which was due to expire in December, was then extended until June 1978. By that date, another 46 officers had resigned. Nevertheless, the status of the Lebanese army's most controversial officers—Majors (*rā'id*) Sa'd Haddād and Sāmī Shidyāq and Lieut (*mulāzim awwal*) Ahmad al-Khatīb—had yet to be defined.

Majors Haddād and Shidyāq, commanders of the Christian militias in South Lebanon, continued to act as officers in the Lebanese army and as such made no secret of their close co-operation with Israel. Bolstered by Israel's (temporary) occupation of South Lebanon, Major Haddād announced the formation in March of "South Lebanon's Army." When Israel withdrew in June and entrusted the positions it had held to Haddād and Shidyāq, the political problems involved in their status and activity became still more acute.

The Syrians, who for lack of a better alternative had previously chosen to ignore these two officers, now accused them of treason and demanded that they be brought to trial. As its relations with the Lebanese Front deteriorated in July, Syria began to mention the names of Chamoun and Jumayyil together with Haddād and Shidyāq, charging that they sought to dominate all of Lebanon.

In line with their broader orientations, Huss demanded that Haddād and Shidyāq be removed from the Lebanese army while Butrus—apparently supported by Sarkīs—resisted this demand. Haddād and Shidyāq remained in South Lebanon, continuing to view and present themselves as legal representatives of the Lebanese army in that part of the country.

Another officer whose resignation was sought by the Prime Minister was Lieut Ahmad al-Khatīb, commander of the practically defunct Lebanon's Arab Army (see *MECS 1976-77*, p. 508). He spent most of the period reviewed under house arrest in Damascus, while the remnants of his movement continued a marginal operation in co-operation with the National Movement and the Palestinian organizations. In August 1978, as Syria drew closer to the National Movement, he was released and began to reorganize his supporters in South Lebanon. It is quite likely that he was dispatched to that area in order to counterbalance the activity of the Christian militias.

DISPATCHING THE ARMY TO SOUTH LEBANON

Closely related to these issues were the recurrent attempts by Syria to have units of the Lebanese army sent to the South in order to assert the authority of the central government, to challenge that of the local militias, and perhaps even to police the area. One major Syrian effort in this direction (in October–December 1977) was strongly resisted by the Lebanese Front, which was opposed to what it saw as an attempt to dispatch Syrian-controlled units to a very sensitive area. The effort was again renewed in April 1978 after the Israeli incursion into South Lebanon. This time it was the National Movement that chiefly opposed the Syrian drive. Its spokesmen claimed that the Lebanese army was still sectarian, and that it was better to have UNIFIL police the South until the Lebanese army was properly reorganized. The National Front's opposition was translated into action on 19 April: when a 30-man force of the Lebanese army approached the Nabatiyya camp, it was attacked

615

by a unit of Lebanon's Arab Army, commanded by Major Muḥammad Salīm.[30] The local Christian militia and Lebanon's Arab Army switched roles again in the summer, following Israel's evacuation of South Lebanon. During the Asad-Sarkīs meeting (referred to above) and in several other ways, Syria exerted pressure on the Lebanese government to dispatch an army unit to the South. When it was finally agreed to send a force commanded by Lt-Col (*muqaddam*) Adīb Sa'd, several difficulties were encountered: opposition by the local militias; demands by the National Movement to have a more balanced Lebanese army; and insistence by the Lebanese Front that the Palestinians evacuate the South.

More concrete steps were taken after the President withdrew his resignation in July. By that time, the Lebanese Front had dropped its opposition,[31] and a reinforced infantry batallion commanded by Lt-Col Adīb Sa'd began moving south from the Western Biqā'. Not much was accomplished by this battalion, however. It was fired upon by the local militias and—when trying to retreat—by Syrian units. Israel supported the militias in their refusal to let the battalion cross militia-held territory and indicated its determination to keep the "good fence" open. Part of Lt-Col Sa'd's battalion remained in place and part left; the whole issue was forgotten after a time as public attention shifted to other matters.

THE SECURITY PLAN
An attempt was made by Sarkīs in June 1978 to introduce at least a semblance of order into the conflict of military powers and jurisdictions. His statement announcing this new initiative contained an implicit criticism of Syria: "Seeking the help of the ADF is not always possible, nor is it always the ideal situation. Therefore we have sought . . . to handle matters by other means, with the co-operation of the citizens' wisdom, awareness and their sense of responsibility." [32]

Against an immediate background of the clashes in North Lebanon, the President formulated a "Security Plan" which focused on that area. The plan divided Lebanon into three categories: (1) areas for which security was to be the exclusive responsibility of the Lebanese army; (2) areas placed under both the army and the ADF; and (3) areas placed under the ADF and Lebanese internal security forces.

Implementation of this plan was begun in the Matn area late in June, and in Beirut early in July, but it soon came to a grinding halt. There were differences of opinion within the Sarkīs Administration as the Prime Minister wanted to deploy Lebanese army units in the South, while the Minister of Defence preferred to use such units in Beirut. Disagreement on this issue reflected the broader divergence in their political orientations. Thus Ḥuss was supported in his position by Syria which opposed the "Security Plan" and effectively neutralized it. The Syrians seem to have resented the fact that the plan conceived of and presented the ADF simply as an auxiliary force which would only become active when called upon and would have no role to play in certain areas.

TECHNICAL ASPECTS OF MILITARY RECONSTRUCTION
The process of reconstructing the Lebanese army became so heavily politicized that even its technical aspects were encumbered by political difficulties.

When presented to the CD, the "Army's Law" estimated that c. 1 bn Lebanese pounds (£L) were needed to finance both recruitment and training and initial procurement. Financing was expected to be provided by Arab oil-producing states, but as aid from those quarters was slow in coming, the US emerged as the major source of military and financial support.[33] In April 1978, an American military mission visited Lebanon to study the needs of the Lebanese army, and in July a Lebanese delegation went to Washington to discuss military procurement. But

Leftist groups soon began to complain that most of the American arms reaching Lebanon were ending up in the hands of officers active in the Lebanese Front or even in the arsenals of the Christian militias. When he visited London in June 1978, Walīd Junblāt asked Britain to refrain from providing arms to the Lebanese army "since that army was not neutral, but was controlled by the Right-wing parties." [34]

In January 1978, Lebanon's new army had 5,000 men. [35] In an effort to increase this number, the army's command announced "volunteering campaigns" (the latest in August 1978) and called upon Lebanese officers abroad to return and join the army. However, political problems prevented the implementation of the draft law. Its passage was considered a victory for the Muslims who had traditionally viewed the draft as the only effective way of transforming the Lebanese army. But opponents of this change—primarily the Lebanese Front—were still sufficiently well entrenched to prevent the law from coming into force.

THE CONTINUING POLITICAL CONFLICT IN LEBANON

The protagonists in the Lebanese crisis—and the issues which separated them—have undergone several significant changes since 1976. While the underlying differences and controversies concerning Lebanon's identity and future have remained as intense as ever, their importance has come to be overshadowed by other issues, particularly by the attitude of the various Lebanese political groups to Syria's position and role in Lebanon. In the process, secessions and new alignments have changed the composition of the three broad coalitions of 1976—the Lebanese Front, the National Front and the loose Central Camp (for background, see *MECS 1976–77*, pp. 495–504, 509–11).

THE LEBANESE FRONT

During the civil war, a relatively high degree of cohesion was an important determinant of the Lebanese Front's effectiveness. But as the acute phase of the crisis came to an end, traditional rivalries among the three major components of the Front returned to the fore. This process was expedited by genuine differences of opinion with regard to Syria. Sulaymān Faranjiyya and his family were particularly close to Damascus and the Asad regime. The Phalangists and the National Liberals remained ardent supporters of the idea of a distinct Christian entity in Lebanon, but differed on the strategy most suitable to preserve this. The Phalanges generally took the view that in the circumstances prevailing in 1977 and 1978, a confrontation with Syria was untenable; they accordingly sought an accommodation, even at the price of considerable concessions. Camille Chamoun and his supporters advocated a much more militant approach.

These differences were hardly apparent during the first weeks of 1978. Between 21 and 23 January, the leaders of the Front met at the home of Sulaymān Faranjiyya in Zughartā and approved the text of a covenant and a detailed public statement. The latter explained that the Front's criterion for evaluating political developments and structures would be the "preservation of Lebanon's special values." The Front insisted on Lebanon's sovereignty, the maintenance of its "particular entity," and the formation of essential institutions—in particular "the institution of the army." In the future, Lebanon's political structure would be based on "Lebanon's pluralistic society . . . so that every cultural group would look after its own affairs." This in turn would be based on "absolute loyalty to Lebanon and the prevention of any conflict among the Lebanese." An important role was assigned to the Lebanese diaspora and approval was given to establish a "Lebanese institution" for that purpose. [36] In February, Camille Chamoun was elected President of the Lebanese Front for three years; Edward Ḥunayn was chosen as the Front's Secretary-General.

By this time, however, Sulaymān Faranjiyya was already drawing closer to Syria and away from the Front, a trend given further impetus by the Fayāddiyya incident, and even more by the clashes in 'Ayn Rumāna. In April, Faranjiyya became conspicuous by his absence from the Front's meetings. Late in that month his son, Tony, "boycotted" the parliamentary meeting in which the platform for national reconciliation was approved. Faranjiyya was critical of Chamoun and Jumayyil's demand to put an end to Palestinian activity in Lebanon. In May, following his reconciliation with Rashīd Karāmī (see below), Faranjiyya withdrew from the Front altogether.

These developments led to a full-fledged confrontation between Faranjiyya and the Phalanges. Without common membership in the Front to moderate their differences, the struggle for influence and domination in Christian North Lebanon soon became violent. Faranjiyya's supporters physically resisted Phalange attempts to extend their influence into the Zughartā-Shakkā area, which they regarded as their traditional stronghold. Following clashes in which several men were killed, Bashīr Jumayyil announced that "no one could prevent the Phalangist expansion in the North," and that "it was time to put an end to feudalism" there.[37]

After a Phalangist representative was killed in Shakkā, a Phalangist squad laid siege to a home belonging to Sulaymān Faranjiyya in the village of Ahdan, and then shelled it. Sulaymān's son, Tony, his wife and daughter were killed. The Phalanges expressed sorrow at Tony's death; they explained that their men were chasing a group of assassins and did not realize that members of the Faranjiyya family were inside the house in which they claimed the assassins had found asylum.

Whatever the truth of this explanation, the consequences of Tony Faranjiyya's death were far-reaching. The incident placed Sulaymān Faranjiyya squarely in a pro-Syrian and anti-Phalangist posture, deepened the rift between Syria and the Lebanese Front, and contributed to increased violence and suffering in North Lebanon and in other parts of the country. Tony's brother, Robert, became the Faranjiyya heir apparent.

As a result of the developing conflict between the Lebanese Front and Syria, differences surfaced within the Front itself over its proper response to Syria's increasing pressure. A marked difference was evident in the spring between Chamoun's hard line and Jumayyil's efforts to come to terms with Syria. Early in May, after returning from a trip to Damascus, Jumayyil publicly stated the need "to prevent efforts at souring relations between the Lebanese Front and Syria."[38] After making this statement, a joint Syrian-Phalangist committee was formed. These developments led Leftist sources to speculate that, "after having succeeded in fomenting a dispute between Faranjiyya and the Lebanese Front," Syria was trying to sow discord between the Phalanges and the Liberals.[39] But clashes between Phalangists and the National Liberals at that time turned out to be of a limited and personal nature and were swiftly brought to an end.

Despite Syrian denunciations of both the Phalanges and the Liberals, Pierre Jumayyil continued his moderate line towards Syria throughout the violent conflicts of the summer. It was only in September that Jumayyil became publicly critical of Syria, in this respect drawing closer not only to Camille and Dori Chamoun, but also to his own son, Bashīr.[40]

The deterioration of their relations with Syria prompted the Lebanese Front leaders to increase their political and diplomatic activity abroad. Their efforts to draw support from Western governments met with very limited success, but the attempt to mobilize the Lebanese diaspora, particularly in the US, achieved more impressive results. Also of interest were changes in the Front's attitude to Israel. There was considerable speculation in the press about the extent of the Front's co-operation with Israel, including reports of Israeli arms deliveries and meetings between Israeli and Front leaders. Although these were denied by both sides, statements by Camille Chamoun and (in a more reserved fashion) by Pierre Jumayyil implied a willingness to receive Israeli support and a growing readiness to admit it. Thus, Chamoun declared: "We are a minority here, and if we can have friendly relations with another strong minority in the Middle East, then we'll do it. I have no objection to that."[41] Pierre Jumayyil's formulation was: "We have no interest in being a foreign body in the Arab world, but in case of accident we are holding out our hand to the devil. In the South, it is the Palestinians and the Left who have pushed us to the other side of the border."[42]

THE NATIONAL MOVEMENT

In marked contrast to its recent past, the National Movement (divided as it was into a pro-Syrian "National Movement of National and Progressive Forces" and a pro-Iraqi "Front of National and Patriotic Forces and Parties") displayed a surprising degree of cohesion and unity. However, it was unable to make any significant impact on Lebanon's politics in 1978 both because of the growing importance Syria attached to such traditional politicians as Sulaymān Faranjiyya and Rashīd Karāmī, and because of Kamāl Junblāt's absence from the scene.

The traditional positions of the National Movement remained essentially unchanged. It continued to stand for a unified, non-sectarian Arab Lebanon; pressed for the formation of a "national" army; and called for the implementation of agreements reached with the Palestinian organizations. It was vehemently opposed to Israel's presence and activity in the South, and urged the Lebanese "to confront the Zionist danger."[43]

The National Movement generally supported Syrian policy in Lebanon despite the opposition of such pro-Iraqi elements as 'Abd al-Majīd al-Rāfi'ī, the leader of the pro-Iraqi faction of the Lebanese Ba'th.[44] The attitude towards Syria of Walīd Junblāt, heir to the Movement's leadership, underwent a gradual change. While bound by his commitment to the pro-Iraqi components of the National Movement, Junblāt recognized Syria's growing power and importance in Lebanon. He also had to take into account the *rapprochement* between Syria and the Lebanese Communists, another constituent element of his Movement. In pursuing a policy of co-operation with Syria, Junblāt had to reckon with a previously unfamiliar factor—that he and his Movement were assigned only a secondary role in Syria's plans for Lebanon.

FORCES OF THE CENTRE

In promoting its interests and politics in Lebanon, Syria assigned a primary role to those factions and politicians who had not joined, or had chosen to leave, the two major coalitions of the 1975–76 civil war. Three (loose) groupings were most prominent in this central bloc in 1978:

(1) A group of Shī'ī CD members, headed by the Speaker (Kāmil al-As'ad), formed "The National Parliamentary Bloc" in March 1978. Against the background of Israel's "Lītānī Operation," these Shī'ī deputies rallied in support of the South and its mostly Shī'ī population.[45] In doing so, they had to overcome a long tradition of political and personal animosities.[46] The Bloc dealt primarily with problems of the South, including moves to regulate the status and activity of the Palestinian organizations. Its formation and activities also served

to enhance the political standing of Kāmil al-Asʿad, who became one of Syria's important allies in Lebanon. Asʿad's rise was closely linked to the decline in the political 'stature of Imām Mūsā al-Sadr, the spiritual leader of the Shīʿī community and head of "The Movement of the Deprived." Sadr himself disappeared in mysterious circumstances in August on his way from Libya to Italy.

(2) A group of independent Maronite deputies coalesced into "The Maronite Parliamentary Bloc" in February 1978. The Bloc supported the policies of President Sarkīs. As Sulaymān Faranjiyya drew away from the Lebanese Front, he began to support the Bloc so as "to show that the Lebanese Front did not represent all Christians." [47] A plan to co-ordinate the activities of the Shīʿī and Maronite parliamentary blocs did not materialize.

(3) "The Muslim Alignment" was a loose group of moderate Muslim politicians, like Rashīd Karāmī and ʿAbdallah al-Yāfī. The Alignment co-operated closely with "The Front for the Defence of the South"—a group primarily composed of Deputies from South Lebanon.

Like the politicians and factions of the Centre, Raymond Eddé was critical of both the Lebanese Front and the National Movement. But unlike them, he remained a staunch opponent of Syria's policy in Lebanon. From Paris he continued his strong criticism of Syria's conduct and advocated the dispatch of an international peace force to Lebanon. [48]

SYRIA'S QUEST FOR A "BROAD NATIONAL FRONT"
In the summer and autumn of 1977, Syria still sought to organize a "broad national front" in support of President Sarkīs and his policies. The Front was intended to replace the National Movement and, in that way, to ensure the effectiveness of Syrian policy in Lebanon, as well as endow it with an ideological stamp of approval.

The original intention was to base the Front on ʿIsām Qansūh and his pro-Syrian Lebanese Baʿth Party, and on Walīd Junblāt and his Socialist Progressive Party. The principles of the new Front were determined in consultation with Syria and included "loyalty to a free and independent Arab Lebanon which rises above all sectarian fanaticism; . . . strengthening of the legal authority for rebuilding the state and its institutions; . . . the building of a national army; . . . amendment of the electoral. law; . . . political, military and economic co-ordination between Lebanon and Syria . . . and underlining the Lebanese-Palestinian brotherhood and commitment to implement Lebanon's agreements with the PLO." [49]

Syria's efforts continued in November and December, but encountered a number of obstacles. Walīd Junblāt had to take into account the opposition of the pro-Iraqi elements within the National Movement, several members of which were not willing to forsake their independent existence. There was also rivalry between Junblāt and Qansūh over the leadership of the proposed new Front.

These and other difficulties led Syria in January 1978 to abandon the idea of a supportive Front based on Junblāt, Qansūh and their parties. Instead, the notion of a working relationship between Sulaymān Faranjiyya and Rashīd Karāmī, and between them and Syria, emerged as a more practical approach. A number of obstacles had to be surmounted—not least the traditional rivalry between the two leaders from North Lebanon. This was done in stages during 1978, so that by the end of August the ground was prepared for a tripartite meeting of Faranjiyya, Karāmī and Walīd Junblāt.

That meeting did not result in the formation of a "broad national front," but a sufficient degree of understanding was reached to enable the three to formulate a joint communiqué. This listed a series of common aims and principles such as the preservation of Lebanon's unity; support of the legal authority and of Syria's policy in Lebanon; and endorsement of the ADF's presence and activity in Lebanon.[50]

THE PALESTINIAN PROBLEM IN LEBANON

The year which followed Sādāt's visit to Jerusalem was marked by a thorough discussion of the underlying issues of the Arab-Israeli conflict. But in Lebanon, preoccupied as it was with other problems, the Palestinian issue was seen primarily in the context of the practical questions raised by the PLO's presence and activity in the southern part of the state (see essay on the PLO). These questions were treated in four phases:

(a) An attempt to implement the third stage of the Shtūrā Agreement (September–December 1977).

(b) The National Movement's attempt to come to a (limited) arrangement with the Palestinians in the South.

(c) Discussion of the "Palestinian portfolio" in the CD in April.

(d) Agreement between the Prime Minister and the Palestinians in May 1978 on the resurrection of Lebanon's sovereignty in the South.

APPLICATION OF THE THIRD STAGE OF THE SHTŪRĀ AGREEMENT

Several difficulties prevented the third stage of the Shtūrā Agreement from being implemented (for background, see *MECS 1976–77*, pp. 512–13, 517–22). Leaders and spokesmen of the Palestinian organizations stated several times that they were willing to evacuate positions in the South only if the Lebanese army came to the area. But in the absence of a reconstituted Lebanese army, that condition could not of course be met. Furthermore, the Lebanese Front doubted the Palestinians' willingness to implement the Shtūrā Agreement and demanded a Palestinian withdrawal as a pre-condition to sending in Lebanese army units. For their part, the local militias demanded that any Lebanese army units sent to the area be placed under the authority of Major Saʿd Ḥaddād.

As the party most interested in implementing the Shtūrā Agreement, Syria exerted pressures on both the Lebanese government and the Palestinians to proceed with it. Its motive was simple: with loyal Lebanese army units stationed in the South, it could extend its influence to an area which the ADF had not entered. This was precisely the reason which led Israel to resist the move, despite American pressure to comply with it.

Technical preparations were made in October 1977 to implement the agreement, but on the two dates set (late in October and early in November) no actual steps were taken. Syria's *rapprochement* with the PLO in the wake of Sādāt's visit to Jerusalem and the outbreak of renewed fighting in the South led to the shelving of the issue.

THE NATIONAL MOVEMENT'S EFFORTS TO COME TO AN AGREEMENT WITH THE PALESTINIANS

The National Movement sought to devise a working formula to reduce intra-Palestinian conflicts and clashes between Palestinians and the local population in the Tyre-Sayda-Nabatiyya area. A meeting of National Movement and PLO representatives decided at the end of January 1978 to form a joint force to supervise public security in Sayda, to close Palestinian offices there, and to arrange for the departure of armed Palestinian units.[51] Other sources reported a much broader agreement to achieve the following objectives: "The removal of armed offices in the South and handing over the positions which will be vacated to elements of the National Movement; evacuation of all public utilities and seaports and handing over their administration to the authorities; and formation of security committees to apprehend anarchist elements."[52]

However, the agreement was not carried out, and continued contacts between the PLO and the National Movement during the next few months were to no avail.

THE "PALESTINIAN PORTFOLIO" IN THE CD

In the spring of 1978, discussion was renewed on some broader aspects of the Palestinian presence and activity in Lebanon. This followed Israel's "Lītānī Operation," Security Council Resolution 425 and the formation of UNIFIL (for details, see essay on South Lebanon in the section on the Arab-Israeli Conflict). In Lebanese political parlance, this discussion was termed "a reopening of the Palestinian portfolio." It was launched by the Lebanese Front, whose spokesmen claimed that Resolution 425 and the availability of UNIFIL actually cancelled the 1969 Cairo Agreement. They demanded that only the 150,000 Palestinian refugees registered with UNRWA should remain in Lebanon.

While not going that far, the Minister of Defence and Foreign Affairs, Fu'ād Butrus, supported the Front's demand that new agreements be negotiated with the PLO. However, the National Movement was opposed to any far-reaching reviews and revisions, claiming that "it was a manoeuvre designed to divert the attention of the Lebanese from the central problem of Israel's occupation of our land."[53] A middle-of-the-road position was taken by the Southern deputies under Kāmil al-As'ad's leadership. They agreed to discuss the Palestinian presence in Lebanon in the CD, but specified that they had a very definite aim: to seek to end the Palestinians' military presence and to divert it to an essentially political role.

The PLO was obviously opposed to reviewing or revising its position in Lebanon. Its spokesmen repeated the organization's willingness to abide by its agreements with the Lebanese government and to refrain from interfering in the country's domestic affairs. They maintained that "there was no substitute for the Cairo Agreement."[54] This position had Syria's support and easily carried the day.

Another bid at regulating the Palestinians in Lebanon was made in April 1978 by the parliamentary committee which sought to formulate a platform for national reconciliation. The text drafted by the committee was unanimously adopted by 74 deputies on 27 April and included extensive references to the Palestine issue (the text is reproduced above). It demanded the termination of all armed activity—Palestinian and other—in Lebanon's territory, and "the prevention of all armed presence except that of the legal authorities." Curiously, members of Junblāt's parliamentary caucus voted for this text. Walīd Junblāt explained that this did not indicate any change of position, since the Riyadh and Cairo resolutions (of 1976) and the Cairo Agreement (of 1969) were part of the parliamentary agreement. A similar statement was made by Kāmil al-As'ad. In the event, though, the parliamentary agreement remained a dead letter and had no effect on the PLO's position and status.

Of equally limited impact was an understanding reached between the Prime Minister and Yāsir 'Arafāt on 24 May 1978—as Israel was about to complete its withdrawal from South Lebanon. This was not a new agreement but a strictly tactical accord "aimed at providing the circumstances for Israel's withdrawal from Lebanon."[55] 'Arafāt agreed to facilitate UNIFIL's mission so as not to delay Israel's withdrawal, to help restore the state's sovereignty and to put an end to "armed manifestations" in the South.[56] Accordingly, a tripartite committee (composed of representatives of the Lebanese government, the PLO and the ADF) was formed to discuss the means of re-establishing the authority of the Lebanese state in the South. Once again, however, no concrete results were achieved.

ECONOMIC AFFAIRS ($1 = 2.955 Lebanese pounds; £1 = £L 6.203)

Since the onset of the civil war in 1975, the Lebanese economy has been disrupted so often and damaged so severely that it has been impossible to resume anything which even remotely resembles normal activity. During 1977 and 1978, efforts at reconstruction were initiated a number of times, but eventually always became a casualty to the fighting. (For more details of attempts at reconstruction, see above.)

The crippling of the port of Beirut, the exodus of capital and the evaporation of tourism have hit especially hard. The country's statistics-compiling agencies have also suffered, so that it is impossible to draw an accurate picture of Lebanon's economic life. The paucity of reliable statistics notwithstanding, two economic repercussions of the fighting very much in evidence have been war damage and rising prices. In the case of the latter, the *Confedération Général des Travailleurs du Liban* recently estimated (somewhat conservatively, it would appear) that inflation since late 1977 alone has been in the region of 17–20%. In the former case, the Ministry of Finance estimated that, through mid-1978, direct losses resulting from the civil war amounted to £L 7,500m, of which £L 6,200m was inflicted on the private sector and £L 1,300m on the public sector.[57]

MONEY AND BANKING

Lebanon's international reserves amounted to $2,210.1m at the end of June 1978—an increase of $585.5m during the preceding 12 months. During the same 12-month period (i.e. June 1977–June 1978), holdings of gold rose 6.4% to reach $399.9m, while the accumulation of foreign exchange grew 45.1% to a total of $1,807.4m.

The Bank of Lebanon's foreign assets rose 18.5% in 1977, reaching £L 5,873m—a figure nearly triple that of end-1972. During the same period, reserve money also nearly tripled to reach a level of £L 4,751m. The Bank of Lebanon's claims on the government have multiplied even faster during this period, jumping from £L 13m at end-1972 to £L 891m at end-1977.

Both demand deposits (+27.5%) and time and foreign currency deposits (+47.8%) grew significantly during 1977, either indicating confidence in Lebanon's commercial banks or else reflecting the lack of investment opportunities to which some of these funds would otherwise be channelled. This 'over-liquidity' has worried Lebanese bankers.[58]

In 1977, the money supply grew less rapidly than in 1976 (3.2% cf 27.9%), whereas the quasi-money supply jumped by 47.7% in 1977 (cf a 7.6% decline in 1976).[59]

FOREIGN AID

Early in 1978, a consortium of banks operating in Lebanon agreed to loan the Lebanese government £L 150m to help finance projects approved by the Reconstruction and Development Council (RDC). During the first half of the year, the US Agency for International Development supplied Lebanon with $43m, of which $20m was a grant and the remainder in the form of loans. In June 1978, France provided the RDC with a $51.4m loan to finance contracts awarded to French companies. During the same month, the RDC was the recipient of a $150m seven-year loan signed by a consortium of local and foreign-based banks operating in Lebanon.[60] Significant amounts of foreign aid from other Arab states did not appear to have been received during the period under review, however.

FOREIGN TRADE

Despite registering an increase of more than 33%, Lebanon's total exports of $631.8m in 1977 failed to return to even one-half of the 1974 total of $1,454.5m.

Meanwhile, imports more than doubled in 1977, reaching $1,631m, which led to a growth in the trade deficit from $263.3m in 1976 to nearly $1 bn in 1977. Neither exports nor imports returned to their pre-civil war levels and, with the disruptions caused by fighting during much of 1978, they are unlikely to achieve such levels for at least another year.

According to statistics derived from partner countries, Italy surged past at least six other nations to become Lebanon's foremost source of imports (13.4%) in 1977. France (11.4%) and the US (8.3%) followed in second and third positions.

The primacy of the Arab world as Lebanon's leading market was reaffirmed in 1977, according to estimates of the International Monetary Fund, when Saudi Arabia (30.1%), Libya (21.3%), and Syria (8.8%) were listed as the three most active buyers of Lebanese exports. As with other Lebanese economic statistics, however, these figures should be viewed with caution. [61]

BUDGET

Public expenditure is due to rise 34.7% in 1979 compared with the original 1978 allocations. The Defence Ministry (26.3%) was given the largest single allocation, followed by education (19.1%) and public works and transport (16%), and the Ministry of the Interior (10.4%). Loan repayments and debt servicing constitute 6.4% of the total. Labour and social affairs (–29.2%) and agriculture (–2%) were two ministries whose budgets were reduced for 1979. The percentage of allocations which will actually be spent will depend, to a large extent, on political developments.

Itamar Rabinovich and Hanna Zamir
Economic section by **Ira E. Hoffman**

MONETARY SURVEY (million Lebanese pounds at end of period)

	1975	1976	1977
Foreign Assets (net)	6,108	6,617	9,021
Domestic Credit	5,752	6,195	7,097
Claims on Government (net)	–1,148	–1,097	–967
Claims on Private Sector	6,900	7,292	8,064
Money	3,836	4,906	5,062
Quasi-Money	6,817	6,302	9,311
Other Items (net)	1,207	1,605	1,745
Money, seasonally adjusted	3,724	4,754	4,900

Source: IMF, *International Financial Statistics.*

GENERAL REVENUES* (million Lebanese pounds)

	1973	1974	1976	1977
Direct Taxes	286	324	466.6	299.3
Indirect Taxes	408	485.8	960.3	538.3
Income from Government Properties	30	31.2	43.35	17.5
Others	150.9	169.8	224.5	229
Extraordinary Revenues	—	213.5	291.8	—
Total	**874.9**	**1,225.2**	**1,716.5**	**1,084**

*1975 Unavailable.
Source: Al-Ḥurriya, 9 October 1978.

PUBLIC EXPENDITURE (million Lebanese pounds)

	1977	1978	1979*
Presidency	2.1	2.1	2.2
Chamber of Deputies	6.2	7.0	10.3
Prime Minister's Office	27.7	59.2	64.6
Defence	255.1	490.5	738.1
Education	288.3	367.1	536.6
Public Works and Transport	309.8	398.7	450.3
Interior	149.4	145.3	209.9
Public Health	70.0	65.9	91.2
Labour and Social Affairs	50.6	89.3	63.2
Finance	46.4	43.1	50.0
Agriculture	33.7	44.6	43.7
Loan Repayments and Debt Servicing	69.7	n.a.	178.3
Total (including others)	**1,661.5**	**2,083.0**	**2,806.0**

*Proposed.
Sources: *Arab Economist* and *Al-Nahār*, reprinted in *Middle East Economic Digest*.

1979 BUDGET (million Lebanese pounds)

Total Revenues	3,103.9
of which:	
Ordinary Revenues	*1,812.0*
*Other Revenues**	*297.9*
Extraordinary Revenues	*994.0*
Total Expenditures	3,103.9
of which:	
Government Administration	*2,806.0*
PTT	*188.9*
National Lottery	*65.5*
OCBS	*43.5*

*Posts, Telegraphs and Telephones (PTT), National Lottery, and Office des Céréales et de la Betterave Sucrière (OCBS).
Source: *Middle East Economic Digest*.

INDEX OF FOREIGN TRADE (1973 = 100)

	1972	1973	1974	1975	1976	1977
Exports	62	100	238	186	77	103
Imports	72	100	186	161	54	126

SUMMARY OF FOREIGN TRADE (million US dollars)

	1972	1973	1974	1975	1976	1977
A. Exports	377.4	612.3	1,454.5	1,136.4	472.7	631.8
B. Imports	924.0	1,290.0	2,397.0	2,074.0	691.0	1,631.0
C. **Balance (A-B)**	**−546.6**	**−677.7**	**−942.5**	**−937.6**	**−263.3**	**−999.2**

Source: Derived from IMF, *Direction of Trade*.

LEBANON

DIRECTION OF TRADE (million US dollars)

	1975[1]	1976[2]	1977[2]
Exports to:			
Saudi Arabia	397.2	190.4	190.4
Libya	79.3	134.4	134.4
Syria	61.1	41.6	55.8
United States	32.8	4.9	40.0
Jordan	26.0	20.1	32.3
Egypt	76.3	27.2	27.2
Kuwait	46.8	24.1	23.2
United Arab Emirates	43.1	21.4	21.4
United Kingdom	17.6	10.4	13.3
Iraq	44.2	11.7	11.8
Total (including others)	**1,136.4**	**472.7**	**631.8**
Imports from:			
Italy	204.4	35.7	218.8
France	179.5	56.3	186.6
United States	405.3	53.6	136.0
West Germany	178.0	38.2	127.0
United Kingdom	173.0	20.1	93.9
Iraq	58.3	70.0	81.6
Romania	85.0	75.9	66.8
Japan	92.4	3.2	62.7
Belgium	55.2	9.9	62.5
Czechoslovakia	44.7	49.1	53.6
Total (including others)	**2,074.0**	**691.0**	**1,631.0**

[1] 1975 data derived from partner country.
[2] 1976 and 1977 data partly extrapolated and/or derived from partner country.
*Data partly extrapolated and/or derived from partner country.
Source: IMF, Direction of Trade.

NOTES
1. *Al-Hawādith*, Beirut; 4 August 1978. This figure is probably an exaggeration.
2. *Al-Dustūr*, London; 26 December 1977.
3. *Ibid*, 6 February 1978.
4. Voice of Lebanon (VoL; radio station operated by the Lebanese Phalanges), 11 April 1978.
5. *Al-Nahār*, Beirut; 14 April 1978.
6. R Kuwait, 18 April; *al-Ba'th*, Damascus; 24 April 1978.
7. *The Observer*, London; 30 July 1978.
8. R Damascus, 7, 10, 17 July 1978.
9. Syrian News Agency (SANA), 8 August 1978.
10. Asad in an interview to *Der Spiegel*, Hamburg; quoted by R Damascus, 10 September 1978.
11. VoL, 28 August 1978.
12. VoL, 31 August 1978.
13. *Al-Nahār*, 2 July 1978.
14. Middle East News Agency (MENA), Cairo; 14 April 1978.
15. R Damascus, 17, 19 August 1978.
16. VoL, 6 July; MENA, 12 July 1978.
17. *The Economist*, London; 15 July 1978.
18. VoL, 12 July 1978.
19. For reactions of Camille Chamoun and Bashīr Jumayyil, see VoL, 16 July, and *The Times*, London; 17 July 1978.
20. MENA, 18 July 1978.
21. Cf *Arabia and the Gulf*, London; 13 March 1978.
22. Iraqi News Agency (INA), 30 April 1978.
23. *Al-Safīr*, Beirut; 24 May 1978.
24. MENA, 24 April; Qatar News Agency (QNA), 24 April, British Broadcasting Corporation, Summary of World Broadcasts, The Middle East and Africa (BBC), 24 April 1978.

25. *Arabia and the Gulf*, 1 May 1978.
26. MENA, 7 September 1978.
27. For the complete text, see *al-Anwār*, Beirut; and *al-Nahār*, 29 July 1978.
28. *Al-Ra'y al-'Āmm*, Kuwait; 29 March 1978.
29. *Al-Dustūr*, 10 July 1978.
30. *Al-Watan al-'Arabī*, Paris; 30 April; *al-Jarīda*, Beirut; 22 April 1978.
31. VoL, 30 July 1978.
32. R Beirut, 22 June 1978.
33. *Al-Nahār*, 18 December 1977.
34. MENA, 15 June 1978.
35. *Al-Nahār*, 1 January 1978.
36. *Al-'Amal*, Beirut; 24 January 1978.
37. *Al-Safīr*, MENA, 8 June 1978.
38. VoL, 1 May 1978.
39. *Al-Dustūr*, 15 May 1978.
40. BBC, 9 July; VoL, 10 September 1978.
41. *Newsweek*, New York; 4 September 1978.
42. *Le Monde*, Paris; 12 July—Daily Report (DR), 14 July 1978.
43. INA, 25 April 1978.
44. For public statements by Rāfi'ī, see INA, 23 February, and *al-Dustūr*, 15 May 1978.
45. *Al-Nahār*, 24 March; R Beirut, 4 April 1978.
46. *Al-Nahār al-'Arabī wal-Duwalī*, Paris; 8 April 1978.
47. *Al-Mustaqbal*, Paris; 11 March 1978.
48. For Eddé's views, see his open letter to the US in *International Herald Tribune (IHT)*, Paris; 27 July 1978.
49. MENA, 12 September 1977.
50. *Al-Anwār*, 1 September 1978.
51. VoL, 20 January 1978.
52. *Al-Nahār*, 3 February 1978.
53. R Beirut, 11 April 1978.
54. *Al-Mustaqbal*, 22 April 1978.
55. *Economist*, 3–9 June 1978.
56. R Beirut, 24 May 1978.
57. The inflation statistic is taken from *Middle East Economic Digest (MEED)*, London; 24 November 1978, p. 38. The war losses figures are from Economist Intelligence Unit, *Quarterly Economic Review of Lebanon (QER)*, London; No 3 (1978), p. 9.
58. *QER*, No 2 (1978), p. 11.
59. See International Monetary Fund (IMF), *International Financial Statistics*, Washington; October 1978, pp. 226–27.
60. See, among others, Bureau of Lebanese and Arab Documentation, *Argus: Economic Review of the Arab World*, Beirut; No 1 (1978), p. 45; *Syrie et Monde Arabe*, Damascus; No 293 (June 1978), pp. 58–60; *QER*, No 3 (1978), p. 10; and *MEED* various issues in June 1978.
61. See IMF, *Direction of Trade Annual, 1971-77*.

Libya

(Al-Jamāhīriyya al-'Arabiyya al-Lībiyya al-Sha'biyya al-Ishtirākiyya)

After nine years in power, there was no visible threat to Col Mu'ammar al-Qadhdhāfī's regime in Libya. It seemed fairly well established, enjoyed increased oil revenues, and continued to carry out its economic development plan. Economic prosperity appeared to minimize, if not cancel, the initial effects of the "socialist" steps taken by the regime after the publication of the second part of Qadhdhāfī's *Green Book* in February 1978. The beginning of the implementation of "socialist" principles and a partial overhaul of the system of "People's Power" were the two most significant political developments in Libya during the year under review.

Aware of the growing political potential of parochial influences in the Basic People's Congresses, the regime held new "selections" to their leadership posts during February 1978. These selections were controlled by Revolutionary Committees comprised of proven supporters of the regime. This was an open departure from the system of "direct democracy" established in March 1977, and an indication of the regime's distrust of the way the system was working.

The first of the new "socialist" principles to be promulgated, in May 1978, was a property law which limited each Libyan to the ownership of one house, the remainder to be distributed among those not owning homes. On 1 September 1978, Qadhdhāfī implemented the second principle by urging workers to take over the management of the establishments in which they were employed, having previously declared in the *Green Book* that workers should be partners, not wage-earners. The scope of both measures is as yet unclear.

Compulsory military service was introduced for the first time in May 1978. This was made necessary by the accelerated build-up of Libya's armed forces—clearly a lesson of the July 1977 hostilities with Egypt (see *MECS 1976–77*, pp. 169–70 and 536–38).

No organized opposition made itself felt inside Libya, but there was growing resentment both among the small mainly urban propertied class and among part of the religious establishment linked to it by kinship or common interest. However, this resentment has had no perceptible impact on the regime.

In its foreign policy, strongly marked by Qadhdhāfī's sense of Islamic mission, Libya seemed to be more aware of its limitations and vulnerabilities as shown, for instance, by its emphasis on the "long-range" capabilities of its arsenal. The Sādāt initiative scotched any prospect of reconciliation with Egypt and led Libya to emphasize its role among Arab "rejectionists." Increasing French military intervention in Africa, especially near its southern border in Chad, not only poisoned Libya's relations with Paris but, more importantly, reduced the chances for a political settlement in Chad favourable to its interests. The US demonstrated its hostility to the regime by tightening the embargo on military equipment and commercial aircraft. Libya found itself increasingly in agreement with the USSR in Arab and African affairs, strengthened its political co-operation with Moscow and increased the long-range involvement of the Soviet bloc in its development plans. Libyan co-operation with Algeria grew closer; relations with Tunisia improved; and the strategic aspects of relations with Malta were given greater emphasis.

LIBYA

POLITICAL AFFAIRS

THE WORKINGS OF "PEOPLE'S POWER"

The system of government called "People's Power," established in Libya during 1976–77 by Qadhdhāfī, Secretary-General of the General People's Congress (see *MECS 1976–77*, pp. 526–33), operated routinely in 1977. After a month-long discussion by the Basic People's Congresses (BPC) of the agenda for its impending annual session—submitted by the General Secretariat (GS)—more than 1,000 delegates assembled in Tripoli from 12–17 November 1977 for the General People's Congresses (GPC). After discussion and some criticism of the way previous decisions had been implemented, Congress approved the ordinary ("administrative") and development ("transformation") budgets. The latter included additions to and increases in the Five-Year Transformation Plan. Local public works and development schemes were made the responsibility of local People's Committees (PComs). However, to prevent possible waste and obviate subsequent criticism, the GPC adopted the proviso that projects should be carried out only after the necessary studies had been made, the financial resources provided and the executive authority given.[1] Among other matters, the continuing lack of manpower for development was discussed, with Qadhdhāfī and his second in command, GS member 'Abd al-Salām Jallūd, both speaking about the need for a massive transfer of workers—perhaps 50–65,000—from unproductive employment (mainly as low-grade government employees) to the productive sector. No concrete decision appears to have been taken on this issue. In foreign affairs, the GPC ratified international agreements and approved loans and grants to a number of unspecified states, international funds and "liberation movements." The GPC also formally invested the GS with some of the powers previously exercised by the Revolutionary Command Council (which was transformed in March 1977 to the GS); namely, the appointment of ambassadors, Supreme Court judges, governors of the Central Bank etc, and the acceptance of the credentials of foreign envoys. Typically, this "non-event" was described by the regime as "decisions aimed at enhancing . . . the pivotal role of the congresses in the conduct of affairs."[2]

Although Jallūd considered the GPC as having made "tangible progress along the road to direct popular democratic action,"[3] the session demonstrated the difficulties and limitations of "People's Power." "Direct democracy" in Libya faced bureaucratic abuse, negligence and contradictions in local interests, which the delegates faithfully reflected. Thus, the visible and active participation of Qadhdhāfī and Jallūd in the whole proceedings (which, as usual, were dominated by the former) seemed to be as indispensable as their presence appeared to observers to be essential "to preserve the momentum of the Libyan revolution."[4] Indeed, Qadhdhāfī was obviously well aware of contradictions of local interests as well as of the personal shortcomings of some GPC delegates. During the session, he criticized BPCs for inefficiency and lack of initiative. Previously, in October 1977, he had urged educated people to participate in the deliberations of the BPCs, "in order to enlighten citizens about the issues on the agenda."[5] The necessary overhaul of the system was announced by Qadhdhāfī on 7 February 1978: new leadership committees of the BPCs (and later of the Municipal People's Congresses; MPCs) were to be selected and some membership rules amended.

First, Qadhdhāfī firmly established that no one could be a member of more than one BPC. To join more than one BPC, "just to increase members in a Congress, amounts to sabotaging the experiment by one's tribal or localized behaviour."[6] People should not move from place to place to participate in selections. Not only was such action a "rebellion against the will of the people," but also ineffective: selection of a kinsman to a [leadership] committee was of no use whatsoever,

629

because decisions were made by the membership of the BPC as a whole. Family and tribal relations were fine for social purposes, Qadhdhāfī added, but not in BPCs and politics. In order to prevent such malpractice, distinctively coloured cards would be issued to members of the various BPCs. Second, the composition and size of the leadership committees were regulated. Nobody from outside the BPC could be selected, although if a neighbourhood (*mahalla*, small locality, or quarter) decided it had no suitable candidate for the leadership among its own people, it could select a person of another neighbourhood. The participation of women in leadership committees was also encouraged by Qadhdhāfī. The size of committees should be at least five. BPCs which included many neighbourhoods would have bigger committees, with each neighbourhood represented by at least two members. Leadership committees were required to meet at least once monthly. However, the number of their functionaries was reduced by a ruling that each BPC secretary would have only one assistant instead of two (cf *MECS 1976–77*, p. 527). Third, no one could simultaneously be a member of a BPC leadership committee and of a PCom (the local administration); nor could a secretary of a BPC be chairman or member of a PCom, so that "administration was to be independent of the popular watchdog."[7] There was to be one exception, however. At the lowest or neighbourhood level, the chairman and members of the PCom could be in the leadership of the neighbourhood BPC, because it "is only a nucleus and not a PCom for a certain craft or municipality."[8] Fourth, the leadership of the MPCs ("municipality" here being roughly equivalent to sub-district) was to consist of the secretaries of the BPCs of the municipality, who would select a municipal secretary and one assistant.

These new rules revealed a shrewd adaptability of the traditional local leadership (which reflected historical, tribal and social divisions) to the circumstances of "People's Power." This adaptability posed at least a potential threat to the total political control and manipulation of the country by the regime. Qadhdhāfī was quick to detect some undertones of political opposition in the "tribalized or localized" conduct of some, who "think that by selecting a certain leadership they can oppose the idea that 'a house belongs to its occupants'"[9] (one of the new "socialist" slogans of the regime). That the regime's main motive in overhauling the system was political was affirmed in an authoritative article in a Libyan political weekly: "The people . . . should be able to produce committees capable of silencing the doubt-casters and those acting under the pretext of religion on the ground that they own the dinar [the Libyan currency], as if religion and money are . . . two faces of the same coin. . . . Consequently, it is necessary to produce new leaderships and new People's Committees, that will *act in solidarity* to tell the people that . . . whoever owns the dinar does not necessarily have religion. . . ."[10]

The selection of the new BPC leaders began on 9 February 1978 and was completed by the end of the month. Almost immediately, on 19 March 1978, Qadhdhāfī presented them with an agenda for discussion—the proposed property law, compulsory military service and aid to Syria (for all these, see below). He also insisted that they discuss and decide on local issues. The system thus continued to operate along the basic lines originally laid down.

THE REVOLUTIONARY COMMITTEES

As mentioned above, even before the mid-November 1977 session of the GPC, Qadhdhāfī spoke of the need for what he called in his 7 February 1978 speech "the upgrading" of the BPC's leadership, in order to counteract the political potential of local factors. Qadhdhāfī regarded this as sufficiently serious to initiate a deviation from "People's Power" by establishing "Revolutionary Committees" (RComs) outside the system. These committees were first set up at the beginning of November 1977 in Tripoli, some nearby towns, and at Benghazi. Their official standing was demonstrated by their taking over public buildings as offices. Careful not to discredit "People's Power," RComs were said not to be a substitute for the authority of the people nor a departure from an experiment they had agreed to . . . but *organized* revolutionary activity."[11] The committees assumed the following tasks: activating BPCs; guidance of BPC leadership committees and PComs; exercising "revolutionary supervision"; protecting the Revolution and propagating its principles.[12]

No more was heard of the RComs in the interval between the November session of the GPC and Qadhdhāfī's announcement of the "selection" of new BPC leaders on 7 February 1978. During the selection, however, an important role was allotted to the RComs, which he described as "the safety-valve and sieve" of "People's Power."[13] RComs were to control and supervise selections, to ensure their being "democratic, healthy, free of tribalism, fanaticism and shortsightedness." RComs were to prevent the selection of "unworthy" persons, who were still selected because of tribalism or "the legacy of sick people."[14] After the selections, RComs were to assist and guide BPC leaderships and PComs in carrying out their respective tasks. RComs were to have no administrative or judicial powers. They could not dissolve, abolish or replace BPC leaders and PComs, nor reprimand, punish or dismiss their members. However, they had "the power of absolute revolutionary supervision" and could arrest people sabotaging selections on the spot. Being "an instrument guided by the leaders of the Revolution," final authority for their actions was held by the GS.[15]

No information was published about the number of RComs (which apparently were organized throughout Libya), the identity or social background of their members. They were described as a "cross-section of people who joined the revolution from the start, a group of dedicated adherents,"[16] a "progressive vanguard."[17]

The establishment of RComs seemed to have caused friction with the people they were to assist and guide. In his speech of 7 February 1978, Qadhdhāfī repeatedly urged the leadership of BPCs and PComs to harbour no "ill-feeling" against the RComs, describing anybody who did as "not being with us" and as having to "reshape himself" and "join us next year or after ten years." Although Qadhdhāfī did not cast doubt on the patriotism of other leaderships, it was the RComs that were "to be the ones to carry arms against any *coup d'état* or foreign aggression,"[18] since they had declared their readiness to defend and propagate the revolution and to die for it.

The establishment of RComs could be seen as a move by the regime in preparation for the "socialist" legislation which was to follow publication of the second part of the *Green Book*, and a counter to those who had hoped "to destroy the goals of the . . . Revolution and distort" it[19] (also see below). It is reasonable to assume that, contrary to its public attitude, the organization of RComs demonstrated some basic mistrust on the part of the regime towards the potential of "People's Power," as well as a continuing belief in strict guidance from the top.[20]

IMPLEMENTING SOCIALISM

The long-awaited second part of Qadhdhāfī's *Green Book* was published in Tripoli on 1 February 1978, entitled *The Solution of the Economic Problem—Socialism.*[21] The main thesis was that power, wealth and arms—the factors which determine the freedom of man—must be in the hands of the people. Power having been dealt with in the first part, the second part considered wealth. Qadhdhāfī argued that no man could be free unless his essential needs were provided for and owned by him. These included food, clothing, housing and transport. Thus, a house should belong to its occupant, and no landlord should be able to exploit tenants. Wage-earning workers were slaves; to be free they should be partners. Land belonged to no one, but everyone should have the right to put it to agricultural use (including pasture) to the limit of their individual capabilities and without exploiting others. Thus, exploitation was disapproved of, as was excessive private profit. A loophole for personal incentive was left by the provision that differences in individual wealth were permissible, but only for those who rendered a public service.

The publication of these dicta evidently aroused some hostile reaction from the propertied class and part of the religious establishment (see below). This was obvious from Qadhdhāfī's 7 February 1978 speech announcing the new selections for the BPC leaderships, in which he warned that any objection to the implementation of the new "socialist principles" would be an act against the regime ("the Revolution"), and would be treated as such. In a speech 12 days later, he emphasized the Islamic roots of his ideas which, he said, were but interpretations of Qur'ānic "orders and prohibitions." [22] Talking to students at a Benghazi secondary school, he stressed another aspect: by increasing social mobility and ameliorating the prospects of coming generations, socialism meant a better future. Thus, opposition to it was "uneducated and stupid, because we aim at the liberation of men." [23] As on previous occasions when announcing new formulations of his ideas, Qadhdhāfī underlined the universal appeal of his "solution of the economic problem." (Both the "Third International Theory" proclaimed in the autumn of 1972, and the first part of the Green Book published in early 1976, were explicitly addressed to all mankind.) They were not only part of his messianic convictions, but also a means of making Libyans proud of their "mission": "This book is for Muslims, Christians, and even for worshippers of the cow." [24] On May Day 1978, Qadhdhāfī told Libyan workers that if, by popular revolution, they completely took over the management of the establishments they worked in, workers in Arab countries and indeed all over the world would follow their example. [25] Addressing the faculty of the Tripoli University's School of Law, he claimed that new sciences of economy and law could emerge from the ideas expressed in his book. [26]

The first new "socialist" principle was embodied in the new Property Law, promulgated by the GS on 6 May 1978. [27] Its first two paragraphs read as follow: (1) "Every citizen has the right to possess a dwelling suitable for occupation or a piece of land on which he can build a house if he does not already own [one]. This house is a sacred possession. . . . (2) Every citizen possessing . . . more than one house or more than one piece of land has the right to choose from them the permitted house or piece of land. . . ." Nobody could own more than one house except temporarily, although each of one's adult sons was allowed to possess a house of his own. The ownership of residential buildings in excess of the above was to revert to the state, for which compensation would be paid. Buildings used for professional, vocational and industrial purposes were exempted from the provisions of this law. So was landed property owned by corporate persons and by embassies. Nobody, except corporate persons, was permitted to lease property.

The implementation of the new law was detailed in an executive statute issued on 13 May 1978. People coming under the provision of the law were to submit to the General People's Committee (GPCom, i.e. the government) a declaration of their property, family members and preferred dwelling-place. In each municipality, two committees were to be set up: a land census committee to check the declarations and to list the property reverting to the state; and a "conveyance of property" committee, which was to take possession of the properties and transfer ownership to those entitled to it. These had to be Libyan citizens who were forbidden to carry out changes to their new property which might reduce its value without governmental permission. People whose place of work was too far from their normal residence to allow daily travel (a rather frequent occurrence in the Libyan hinterland) were permitted two residences. Compensation was to be supervised by a higher committee and be paid in a lump sum to low-income earners who relied for their living on income from their property; others were to be paid 10,000 dinars in cash and the rest in government bonds—with up to 10,000 dinars maturing annually.[28]

The extent to which this law has actually been implemented was not made public during the period under review. However, it is reasonable to assume that considerable administrative problems were encountered in a country already heavily burdened with a cumbersome bureaucracy. One of the reactions of the propertied classes was to marry off their children as fast as possible, in order that the family might retain a maximum number of houses.

The second "socialist" principle to be implemented was the transformation of workers from wage-earners into partners. Because of the economic complexities involved (obviously the regime wanted no slow-down in development schemes), this was to be a more gradual move. In his May Day speech, Qadhdhāfī told Libyan workers to "prepare themselves *in an organized and thoughtful way,*" so that when the takeover of the means of production was completed, "production will increase and self-sufficiency be achieved."[29] The signal for starting the takeover was given by Qadhdhāfī only on 1 September 1978.

QADHDHĀFĪ'S CONCEPT OF ISLAM

As already stated briefly, the resentment among the propertied class against the ideas expressed in the second part of the *Green Book* was shared by some of the urban religious establishment, members of which belonged to that class or had ties of kinship with it. Some of these *'ulamā* immediately voiced disapproval in their Friday sermons in the mosques of Tripoli. It seems that the *'ulamā*—who had initially supported Qadhdhāfī following the deposition of the Sanussi monarch in 1969 (whose type of Islam they despised)—had grown critical of him, possibly since the execution of some conspiring officers in early 1977 (cf *MECS 1976-77*, p. 533). Qadhdhāfī was thus driven to defend his thinking in terms of religion. He did so in an important speech at the Mūlāy Muhammad Mosque in Tripoli on 19 February 1978 on the occasion of the Prophet's birthday.[30] Not only did he warn the *'ulamā* not to interfere with the "socialist" policy of the regime, but also exposed their close relationship with the propertied class, accusing them of defending its interests against religion. He said that those who distorted the *Green Book* by calling it atheist were those who opposed freedom and justice among men, even though freedom and justice were ordered by God. His ideas were "neither communism nor capitalism, neither atheism nor rebellion against Islam," but "the course of Islam. . . . The first chapter of [the *Green Book*] is meant as an interpretation of a single phrase in the Qur'ān. . . . The second chapter is also a true interpretation of orders and prohibitions by God."

Qadhdhāfī elaborated his views on Islamic doctrine. Having long urged a return to pristine Islam, he emphasized the primacy of the Qur'ān as the sole valid authority for Muslims, an authority which could be understood by every Arab: "Religion is no longer a mystery." He then proceeded to denounce the whole structure of Sunnī legal tradition: one should not follow the "yellowing books" written and circulated by jurists who were "atheists and infidels." These books were the results of bitter political quarrels between Islamic factions in the first centuries of Islam. The four schools of doctrine of Sunnī Islam were superfluous.

The Prophet, who ordered believers to abide by the Qur'ān, never told them to follow the interpretations of Holy Law by the heads of the four schools, nor the books of well-known Islamic thinkers. Furthermore, to hold (as Sunnī orthodoxy prescribes) that "we should follow the sayings (ḥadīth) of the Prophet and hold them sacred like the Qur'ān, is blasphemy." The Prophet's way of life was embodied in his deeds, not in his reported sayings—some of which were false. Only the Qur'ān, containing divine commands and prohibitions, was to be followed. As it was written in "lucid" Arabic, every Arab could understand and apply it himself, "without the help of an Imām or Shaykh."

Having thus disposed of the 'ulamā and of established Sunnī orthodoxy, Qadhdhāfī proceeded to denounce the veneration of saints, a practice very common in Libya as throughout all North Africa, because it could lead to atheism. He included the patron saint of his own tribe, Sīdī Qadhdhāf al-Damm, in his denunciation.

This speech was notable for its rejection of most of Sunnī orthodoxy and its emphasis on ijtihād (the exercise of independent reasoning in interpreting Islamic law) as a right of every Muslim Arab—although he did not use the term itself. Ijtihād is considered forbidden by most orthodox Muslims. To assess these statements, it must be kept in mind that Islam is the most important normative factor shaping Libyan society. It is central to the regime and a cornerstone for Qadhdhāfī's social, political and economic thought. Furthermore, during the nine years of his rule, Islam has served Qadhdhāfī as a powerful legitimizing force. Islam is conceived by him as dynamic, evolving and capable of coping with new realities. There is "nothing in real or invisible life for which the principles are not laid down in Islam."

Qadhdhāfī obviously articulated Islamic ideas current in Libya. Not only can one trace in them various accepted elements of Reformist Islam, but also a clear affinity with the doctrine of the Sanussi fraternity, with which Qadhdhāfī's tribe has been affiliated. Thus Qadhdhāfī seems to have come full circle: having deposed and expelled the Sanussi rulers, he adopted some of their principles, although in a depersonalized version—namely the return to pristine Islam; ijtihād; the propagation of Islam and unification of all Muslims; and holy war (jihād). "Our revolution is correcting [i.e. reforming] Islam, is trying to build it up among 600m Muslims and to spread it throughout the globe." The implications of these views on Libyan foreign policy are obvious (see below).

This speech did nothing to diminish the hostility of orthodox 'ulamā, some of whom denounced Qadhdhāfī in their sermons as a heretic. He reportedly reacted by replacing some of them by faithfuls of the RComs. However, there was no widespread protest against Qadhdhāfī's "heresies" in Libya.

OPPOSITION ACTIVITY

Although no organized opposition manifested itself in Libyan politics during 1977–78, rumours of resistance to the regime repeatedly found their way into foreign news media—probably through Egyptian sources. One report spoke of an attempted coup in October 1977 by a group of officers who supported 'Umar al-Muhayshī, a former member of the Revolutionary Council (cf MECS 1976–77, p. 533); another concerned the arrest in January 1978 of the former Chief of Libyan Military Intelligence. The latter had allegedly tried to assassinate Qadhdhāfī and was denounced as a CIA agent. Rumour also attributed the helicopter crash on 6 March 1978—in which a Libyan Minister of State and two high-ranking East German visitors lost their lives—to an abortive attempt on Qadhdhāfī's life.

More significant, perhaps, was the growing but rather unorganized exasperation among the small, mainly urban, propertied class, caused by the regime's implementation of "socialist" policies. The protests by a section of the religious establishment gave some ideological justification for this sentiment. These groups not only resented the loss of some of their privileges and property (including the takeover of privately-owned manufacturing firms after September 1978), but also the conscription of their sons, most of whom had received higher education. In his 11 June 1978 speech, Qadhdhāfī denounced those who had enriched themselves and had recently started to "smuggle" their children abroad, to western Europe and the US.[31] A by-product of this resentment was a growing hoarding of gold and the emergence of a black market in foreign currency inside Libya, combined with rumour-mongering and hostile information leaked to the Arabic press in London and Paris. However, this disaffection was probably restricted to a rather limited circle of people, while the majority remained either apathetic or not displeased with measures aimed at greater egalitarianism.

Despite the system of "People's Power," Qadhdhāfī continued to exercise his one-man rule, tolerating no dissent. Opposition efforts, including those inspired by Egypt, did not appear to present a serious threat. In fact, the regime seemed firmly based on three factors: (1) tight military and police control (allocations for the security services in the 1976–80 Transformation Plan were almost doubled in November 1977 from 35m dinars to 60m, and the annual allocation for 1978 increased by 20% from 11m in 1977 to 13.5m); (2) the maturing development projects and the continuing prosperity most Libyans were enjoying; and (3) the identification of the leadership with the basic values of Libyan society. But, above all, the continued stability of the regime depended on Qadhdhāfī's leadership, of which a diplomat serving in Libya was recently quoted as saying: "Qadhdhāfī is a good strategist. He knows his country. He has far-out ideas, but his programme is moving along."[32]

MILITARY BUILD-UP AND THE INTRODUCTION OF COMPULSORY MILITARY SERVICE

The noticeable public emphasis on the build-up of the Libyan armed forces, and especially on increasing their long-range capabilities, was probably one of the consequences of the Four-Day War with Egypt in July 1977. This publicity indicated the regime's awareness of the enormous distances involved in defending the country, and of the strategic as well as political need to demonstrate the possession of a long-range offensive (or at least deterrent or retaliatory) capability. Thus a naval exercise of missile boats and submarines near Tobruk on 28 March 1978 got media coverage. The firing-in-training of "long-range missiles" was announced on 30 April 1978. When Qadhdhāfī inaugurated an airbase at Qardābiyya[33] on 11 June 1978 (the anniversary of the evacuation of US bases from Libya), he stressed that Libya possessed more than 1,000 aircraft, "including planes which the USSR and Libya possessed—long-range strategic bombers."[34] On 20 June 1978, the formation of a "Higher Authority" for military industries was announced. With a reported initial budget of 150m Libyan dinars (LD), its mission was to establish the infrastructure of a modern armaments industry.

An indication of the accelerated Libyan military build-up was the increase in annual budgetary allocations for the armed forces (which obviously covered only a part of total military expenditure): from LD 72m in 1976 to 80m in 1977 and 130m in 1978.

However, as with many other Libyan projects, the main constraint on the military effort was the scarcity of available manpower. To this objective aspect, a subjective one was added: many Libyans, and especially better-off and educated ones (essential for operating the new sophisticated equipment Libya received), felt no incentive to enlist. Qadhdhāfī confirmed this situation when he stated on 11 June 1978 that the Air Force Academy wanted students, and that hundreds of aircraft were without pilots.[35]

The lack of military manpower forced Qadhdhāfī to change his mind about compulsory military service, which he had repeatedly called fit "only for slaves."[36] The introduction of conscription had already been decided upon by the GPC in November 1977; but Qadhdhāfī again submitted it for approval by the BPCs in March 1978, arguing that "we cannot leave the country vulnerable," and that the required number of recruits could be attained only by this measure.[37] The compulsory military service law was promulgated on 6 May 1978. Its first paragraph said that "the law shall apply until the people attain their ultimate aim of assuming the task of defending themselves."[38] The law applied to men aged 18-35. University students could obtain deferments until the age of 28, and students of secondary, technical and religious schools until the age of 24. Similar to the Soviet system, the duration of service varied—three years in the ground forces but four years in the air force, navy and air defence. The regime took pains to emphasize that conscription was "a temporary measure to meet a transitional period and specific circumstances."[39] The recurring need to justify this deviation from a previously established principle seemed to point to the measure's unpopularity.

(For an indication of the strength and composition of Libya's armed forces, see statistics at the end of this chapter.)

THE CABINET (unchanged from 3 March 1977)

General-Secretary of GPC	Col Mu'ammar al-Qadhdhāfī
Chairman, GPC	'Abd al-'Atī al-'Ubaydī
Secretaries	
Interior	Yūnis Abū al-Kāsim
Foreign Affairs	'Alī 'Abd al-Salām al-Tūraykī
Planning	Mūsā Aḥmad Abū Fraywa
Justice	Muhammad 'Alī al-Jaddī
Health	Muftāh al-Ustā 'Umar
Labour and Civil Service	Muḥammad al-Tāhir al-Muhjūb
Petroleum	'Izz al-Dīn al-Mabrūk
Agriculture and Agrarian Reform	Muḥammad 'Alī al-Tabbū
Housing	Muḥammad Aḥmad al-Manqūsh
Communications	Nūrī al-Faytūrī 'Umar al-Madanī
Trade	Abū Bakr 'Alī al-Sharīf
Industry and Mineral Wealth	Jādallā 'Azūz al-Talhī
Treasury	Muḥammad al-Zarūq Rajab
Education	Muḥammad Aḥmad al-Sharīf
Social Affairs and Social Security	Muḥammad 'Abd al-Salām al-Faytūrī
Municipalities	Abū Zayd 'Umar Dūrda
Maritime Transport	Mansūr Muḥammad Badr
Electricity	Jum'a Sālim al-Arbash
Youth	Muftāh Muḥammad Ku'ayba
Dams and Water Resources	'Umar Sulaymān Ḥamūda
GPC Affairs	Mīlād 'Abd al-Salām Shumayla
Information and Culture	Muḥammad Abū al-Kāsim al-Zuway
Land Reclamation and Development	'Abd al-Majīd al-Qa'ūd
Nutrition and Marine Wealth	'Amrū Aḥmad al-Muqasabi

FOREIGN RELATIONS

Imbued with a messianic sense of Islamic mission ("Libya . . . is leading a new civilization heralded by the *Green Book*"),[40] backed up by a secure economic base and a satisfactory domestic situation, Qadhdhāfī continued to be involved in many foreign ventures. However, it appears that during 1977-78 he became more keenly aware of Libya's inability "to back up words with muscle,"[41] and of the realities of international power politics. Thus he told the Algerian National Assembly on 3 June 1978: "Whatever magnificent experiments our countries make domestically, and whatever radical transformations they achieve in the political and social fields . . . all these . . . will remain at the mercy of the winds if they are not part of a strong entity which takes its place among the giants of the world. There is no Arab unity but . . . a vacuum in the Arab world. . . . In Africa there is a vacuum."[42] This attitude could be attributed to the lessons learned from the hostilities with Egypt in the summer of 1977, to subsequent developments in the Arab world, and possibly also to Libya's strained relations with the US and, more recently, with France. This way of thinking could also serve to explain growing Libyan ties with the Soviet bloc, apparently developing into long-range and many-sided co-operation.

Together with "revolutionary" (Arab, Islamic and "Liberationist") and economic considerations, strategic interests seemed to play a bigger role in Libyan foreign policy during 1977–78. Libya's strategic position was repeatedly mentioned by Qadhdhāfī (e.g. "Libya, which occupies a strategic position in Africa, is the big gate of Africa to the north").[43] One may surmise that Qadhdhāfī perceives Libyan security through the concept of security belts—a northern one in the Mediterranean and a southern one in Chad and Niger—reinforced by friendship with Algeria and by Soviet support, leaving only the east, i.e. Egypt, as a problem area.[44] The continuous Libyan military build-up, including long-range weapons systems, is another indication of this Libyan view of the world (see above).

RELATIONS WITH THE ARAB EAST (MASHREQ)

Any possibility of normalizing relations between Libya and Egypt was ruled out after Anwar al-Sādāt's visit to Jerusalem. Persistent hostility notwithstanding, the year passed with little of the military tension characteristic of previous years.

Sādāt's announcement of his intention to go to Jerusalem caused Qadhdhāfī to convene the GPC (then in its ordinary annual session) to a special meeting on 17 November 1977 to discuss this "crime against the Arab nation." The resolution adopted expressed in clear terms the Libyan attitude towards both Sādāt and the Arab-Israeli conflict: "Even if through his visit Sādāt were to succeed in making Palestine free and independent, and that is impossible, it would bring great shame upon us to liberate Palestine in this manner. We would rather Palestine remained under occupation forever than we should be smeared with this disgrace."[45]

Like other members of what was to become the Tripoli bloc (see essay on Inter-Arab Relations), Libya not only froze relations with Egypt, but also stepped up the activities of anti-Sādāt Egyptian expatriate groups which had been formed earlier in Libya (cf MECS 1976-77, p. 536). A "Front for the Liberation of Egypt," including former prominent functionaries of the Nāsir regime, organized subversive operations in Egypt through a "military branch." An "Egyptian Revolutionary Committee" was set up in Tripoli and on 21 November 1977 occupied the offices of the Egyptian diplomatic representative. Simultaneously, Radio Tripoli called for a "revolution of revenge and liberation" against Sādāt.

A later and symbolic expression of the Libyan attitude was the change of the Libyan national flag, which had been identical to Egypt's. As "the former flag was defiled when raised in Jerusalem,"[46] Libya now adopted a green flag, the traditional Muslim colour.

Tension between the two countries increased for a short while during January 1978 when unfounded rumours of Egyptian military concentrations and an impending attack made Libya apprehensive.

Qadhdhāfī continued to taunt Sādāt with offers of substantial military assistance, provided that he renounce his initiative. For example, on 19 January 1978, he offered to transfer to Egypt hundreds of tanks if Sādāt decided to embark on a war of liberation. In a speech at Tobruk on 28 March 1978, Qadhdhāfī called for an "immediate unity of armies against the common enemy . . . despite the blood revenge between us and the Egyptian army." [47] Qadhdhāfī later disclosed that these offers, and his proposal that the two commanders-in-chief meet to discuss them, were never answered by Egypt.

Following the Four-Day War between Libya and Egypt in July 1977, and again after the severance of relations in December, many Egyptians employed in Libya returned home, reducing by half the original number of 250,000. But as early as November 1977, the Libyans again began admitting Egyptians with contracts of employment. In April 1978, Egypt acceded to a Libyan request for teachers. Thus, despite the political rupture, a considerable number of Egyptians have continued to work in Libya—an arrangement which is mutually beneficial (cf *MECS 1976-77*, pp. 537-38).

The special session of the GPC called to discuss the Sādāt initiative resolved to put "all Libyan resources at the disposal of Syria." [48] However, when Syria held back in March 1978 during the Israeli occupation of South Lebanon (see section on the Arab-Israeli Conflict), Qadhdhāfī expressed his displeasure by referring the issue of aid to Syria to the BPCs: "Syria deserves support lest it fall as Egypt had. . . . How much to pay? . . . If yes, annually or in one sum, and for how long? How does Syria's [role of onlooker] in Lebanon influence this? It is a new issue." [49] In April it seemed that further aid was decided upon, but made conditional on Syria's adopting more radical stands on the conflict with Israel, on Lebanon, and against the stationing of UN forces there.

Libya continued to support the "Lebanese National Movement" headed by Junblāt. The departure of 200 volunteers for Lebanon was announced on 21 March 1978. Libya also stated its opposition to the stationing of UN forces in Lebanon.

One direct result of Sādāt's initiative was an improvement in relations between Libya and Jordan, with Qadhdhāfī publicly expressing appreciation of King Ḥusayn's refusal to join Sādāt. The Jordanian Prime Minister visited Libya from 4-6 April 1978 and agreed "to expand further the scope of co-operation" between the two countries. [50] Two agreements were signed—one on economic co-operation and the other on scientific and cultural co-operation and exchanges. The supply of Jordanian manpower was also discussed, including the assignment of a number of officers to train the Libyan army. A protocol on economic co-operation signed in Tripoli on 22 May 1978 provided for Libyan investment (amounting to 5% of the capital) in the Jordan Potash Corporation and in a chemical fertilizer plant, and for loans—$50m to the former and $20m to the latter.

Libya resumed relations with Sudan in February 1978; these had been broken off in July 1976, when Ja'far al-Numayrī (and Sādāt) accused Qadhdhāfī of being the main force behind the attempted coup in Khartoum (cf *MECS 1976-77*, p. 535). The reconciliation between Numayrī and his Libyan-backed opponent, al-Sādiq al-Mahdī (see chapter on Sudan), enabled Qadhdhāfī to try and use the latter to wean Numayrī away from full support of Egypt. Early in 1978, Sudan agreed to participate in the Libyan effort to mediate in the Chad civil war (see below). With the resumption of relations, Libya proposed to revive the planning of joint projects in the Darfur (West Sudan)—Kufra (East Libya) regions, including the building of a road.

RELATIONS WITH THE PLO; ATTITUDE ON TERRORISM
No change occurred during 1978 in the radical attitude of Libya in its support of the most extreme tendencies among the Palestinians (cf *MECS 1976–77*, p. 538). The Libyan government decided on 20 July 1978 to amalgamate the various existing offices of Palestinian organizations in the country into one, to be called the PLO office. This was in effect an anti-Fatḥ step, taken after an attack by the latter group on its splinter-rival, the Fatḥ Revolutionary Council (see essay on the PLO). Some Fatḥ members were arrested.

Libya consistently denied assertions during 1978—made by the US State Department among others—that it was engaged in supporting international terrorism. Qadhdhāfī insisted that there was no proof of these allegations, which he claimed stemmed from Libya's support of Palestinian armed groups who were considered terrorists. He stated his position succinctly to a group of European journalists: "The real terrorism is the repression of small states by colonialist states. We support popular revolution everywhere and the principle that the people will try and overthrow their aggressors everywhere." [51]

RELATIONS WITH THE MAGHRIB
Relations with its North African neighbours continued to occupy an important place in Libya's foreign policy during 1978. The solution proposed by Qadhdhāfī for the various conflicts and problems of the region was the cautious, possibly gradual, establishment of a federation. He told the Algerian National Assembly on 3 June 1978: "The idea of a federation between Libya, Algeria and Tunisia . . . deserves all attention and support. . . . The presentation of the idea of federal unity in this form is very reasonable. It could have included all of the Maghrib." [52] The latter allusion was to Morocco, from which Libya remained estranged. Previously, in November 1977, Jallūd had urged a confederal union between the states involved as the only solution of the West Sahara problem. [53]

Although Libya avoided formal recognition of the Sahara Arab Democratic Republic, it continued its close support of the Polisario Front. Libya had been among the very first patrons of Polisario, an attitude which could be attributed at least in part to the West Saharan origin (whether real or legendary) of some Libyan tribes, including Qadhdhāfī's own. Increasing French military intervention in West Sahara stiffened Qadhdhāfī's attitude towards that conflict (see also below). In January 1978, Polisario leaders visiting Libya were promised assistance against French air attacks. Qadhdhāfī supported self-determination for the West Saharans on the ground that they wanted to be neither Moroccans nor Mauritanians, as he told the Algerian National Assembly: "Morocco and Mauritania are involved in a dangerous problem. If the Sahara is Moroccan, why are tens of thousands of Moroccan soldiers fighting there? This means that the Sahara is not theirs. . . . We are against Mauritania getting involved in . . . West Sahara." [54]

Despite the Saharan issue, Qadhdhāfī continued to promote good relations with Mauritania, aiming to disengage it from its Moroccan connections. Ould Daddah (then still President of Mauritania) visited Libya in April 1978 and signed an agreement on co-operation in various economic domains, including the possible use by Libya of Mauritanian labour. Only 13 days after the military coup in Mauritania (on 10 July), the new ruler, Lt-Col Mustafā Ould Muḥammad Sālik, made his first foreign visit to Tripoli (where he had been preceded by a few days by the Secretary-General of Polisario). Libyan proposals for a peaceful solution of the West Saharan problem were discussed, as were means to reduce Mauritania's need for continuing the French military presence.

Libya continued to enjoy close relations with Algeria. Various projects of economic co-operation were evolved, including joint exploitation of oil in border regions. Qadhdhāfī visited Algeria from 30 May-6 June 1978. A joint statement issued at the conclusion of the visit reflected an identity of views on political problems, although Algeria was reported to be less conciliatory than Libya toward Mauritania. Qadhdhāfī told European journalists on 19 June 1978: "We are natural allies of Algeria and will defend one another to the end." [55]

Relations with Tunisia were more complex. On 27 February 1978, the two countries ratified an agreement on the continental shelf, whereby both undertook to abide by the arbitration of the International Court of Justice. Thus a potential conflict between them was removed. Economic co-operation and the planning of joint projects, especially in extending communications, continued. But after the half-yearly meeting of the joint commission, held in Tripoli on 12-13 May 1978 and in which the Tunisian Prime Minister took part, Tunis voiced some disappointment. Co-operation in various spheres was again agreed upon, as was the avoidance of double taxation and the increase of trade. But the Libyans postponed discussions on executing several mutual projects (on which studies had been completed) to the next meeting, set for December 1978. Tunisia therefore had to be content with ongoing economic co-operation.

Although Libya officially refrained from taking sides in Tunisia's serious domestic quarrels, the Libyan Federation of Trade Unions did voice its support for the arrested trade union leader, Habib 'Achour. This carried with it implicit Libyan criticism of the Tunisian government. After his Maghrib federation speech in Algiers on 3 June 1978, Qadhdhāfī sent his close associate and member of the GS, Khuwaylidī al-Ḥamīdī, to acquaint the Tunisians with his ideas on this subject. These were considered unrealistic by the Tunisian government which believed that close co-operation should precede any discussions about unification.

Qadhdhāfī's policies in the Maghrib—a strong alignment with Algeria, improved relations with Tunisia, preserved ties with the new Mauritanian regime, and continued but informal support of the Saharans—all point to attempts to safeguard Libya's extended western and south-western border against any potentially hostile grouping.

POLICY TOWARDS ISLAMIC COUNTRIES AND "LIBERATION MOVEMENTS"
There was no change during 1978 in Libya's activist policy of supporting Islamic causes all over the world; this was tempered only by other more essential interests—such as the security of the country in face of "imperialism" (cf *MECS 1976-77*, p. 540). The officially sponsored "Association for the Propagation of Islam" (*jam'iyyat al-da'wa al-islāmiyya*; literally, Association of the Call of Islam), initiated by Qadhdhāfī in 1970, continued to spread Islam and promote the study of Arabic all over the world. This was done through missionaries (c. 350 of whom were employed by Libya in the autumn of 1977, only two of them Libyan nationals), publications and financial support. The effort was directed mainly at African countries.[56] Qadhdhāfī also urged Europeans and Americans to adopt Islam, stressing that they would have done so of their own accord had they known more about it.[57] During his July 1978 visit to India (devoted mainly to obtaining Indian technical assistance for Libya's development), Jallūd took time to tell a gathering in a Hyderabad mosque that Libya stood by the Muslims of India and the whole world. After the breakdown of the truce between the Philippine government and the Muslim Moro Liberation Front, arranged through Libyan mediation, Tripoli resumed its aid to the Moros, for which it was publicly thanked by their leader during a visit to Tripoli in April 1978.

Libya continued its support for the military regime in Ethiopia, but this was modified over Eritrea. The Libyans considered the Somali withdrawal from the Ogaden a result of their influence on President Siyad Barreh, exerted during his visit to Libya in March 1978. Earlier, in November 1977, Jallūd had warned "progressive forces" in Eritrea that Libya was not their "guardian and cannot accept a reactionary-racialist-American policy."[58] In a succinct statement of his view on the problem, Qadhdhāfī said that Ethiopia and Libya both found themselves to be a "progressive force" and "a common target" of imperialism. "Therefore it is in Libya's interest for Ethiopia not to fall." He added: "60% of Ethiopia's citizens are Muslims, and it is our religious duty not to abandon them. They have been liberated under the new regime." However, there was a significant nuance: Libya did not deny the Eritreans' right to self-determination and disapproved of the use of violence against them.[59] Questioned by European journalists on this issue in June, Qadhdhāfī said that while he was not sure whether Cuba had intervened in Eritrea, Libya had advised both sides to negotiate. He added: "It is up to the Eritreans to demand independence, or not to demand it. Likewise, it is up to Ethiopia to accept such a demand or to dismiss and combat it."[60]

Libya's longstanding hostility towards the Shah of Iran (rooted in his pro-Western policy, his attitude on oil prices and his intervention in Oman) continued in 1978. "After the disappearance of the Shah there will be no problem with Iran," Qadhdhāfī said in an interview.[61] Tripoli regularly broadcast its own anti-Iranian propaganda, as well as messages on behalf of the "Popular Front for the Liberation of Oman." Qadhdhāfī also admitted his support for the "Arabistan Liberation Movement."

Libya strengthened its relations with Turkey, with which it has a record of friendly ties, both under the monarchy and under Qadhdhāfī (based on the alliance against the Italians since the beginning of the century). During 1978, agreements on economic co-operation were signed; credits (including a 20% credit on all oil supplies) and loans were extended to Turkey; joint projects agreed upon and Turkish exports (mainly foodstuffs) increased. Turkey also agreed to supply much-needed manpower, including technicians and instructors; in mid-1977, 10,000 Turks were working in Libya. Although presented as a policy of friendship with a fellow-Muslim country, Libya had obvious economic and strategic reasons for cultivating the relationship (see policy in the Mediterranean).

RELATIONS WITH CHAD

Libya has long had "historical, geographical and spiritual relations"[62] with Chad where, according to Qadhdhāfī, one-fifth of the Libyan population was living.[63] Since the time of the monarchy, Libya had supported the revolt of the mainly Muslim *Front de Libération Nationale* (Frolinat) against the central Chad government. Frolinat's gradual occupation of North Chad led President Felix Malloum not only to denounce Libyan aid to the rebels, but also to depend increasingly on French military support. At the end of 1977, Libya seemed to have decided to work for an African political solution to the Chad civil war, probably because of its growing apprehension of French military involvement and the good chance that in any settlement, Frolinat would be given a share of power in Chad. Urged by Qadhdhāfī, the government of Niger tried to mediate but failed. Chad broke off relations with Libya on 6 February 1978. Enlisting the influence of the OAU Council of Ministers' annual meeting, Qadhdhāfī got Chad to resume relations and to agree to a "four power" summit at Sabhā including Chad, Libya, Sudan and Niger. The meeting, held on 24 February 1978, agreed to a further session with the participation of Frolinat. At this second summit at Sabhā, which continued at Benghazi from 21-27 March 1978, the Chad government "recognized" Frolinat and a truce was agreed upon, to be supervised by a Niger-Libyan military committee. However, the truce broke down within a few weeks and Frolinat resumed its advance into Central Chad, only to be checked by French combat troops who had been flown there in April 1978.

Qadhdhāfī not only denounced French intervention, but also the policy of Malloum. He claimed that although Ndjamena, the capital of Chad, is "100% Muslim, no Muslim has the right to share in the government. They even have no right to use transport facilities and live miserably, poor . . . and naked." [64] Although he denied supporting Frolinat on the scale alleged by Chad, Qadhdhāfī considered it "inevitable that some assistance will be given to this Front by other countries." [65] A further attempt at reconciliation was made in Tripoli from 3–6 July 1978, but it also failed, mainly because of the effects of French military involvement. A formal indication of the failure of Libyan (as well as Nigerien and Sudanese) mediation was the appointment by President Malloum of Hissene Habre, a former rebel leader hostile to Libya, as Prime Minister of Chad on 29 August 1978.

Thus Libyan efforts to increase its influence in Chad through a political settlement of the civil war, by which a government sympathetic to it would come to power and the French military presence be terminated, remained unsuccessful during the period under review.

REPERCUSSIONS ON RELATIONS WITH FRANCE
Since the end of 1969, Libya enjoyed close relations with France, which became an important source of supplies, including advanced military hardware. However, beginning in 1977, the more activist support extended by President Giscard d'Estaing to pro-Western African regimes increased Libyan apprehension and disappointment with France. These were voiced by the Secretary for Foreign Relations of the GS of the GPC in a speech in Paris on 15 January 1978. Not only did he denounce French intervention in Chad, Mauritania and Zaïre, but said that French military concentrations near Libya's borders were evidence of aggressive intentions and were part of an imperialist plot to encircle Libya. [66] Referring to dozens of military and economic agreements which exist between Libya and France, he warned that France's present policy, which in his view was instigated by "US imperialism," would endanger relations between the two countries and presumably jeopardize those agreements. [67]

At the OAU meeting held in Tripoli during February 1978, Qadhdhāfī adopted a violently anti-French attitude and at one point demanded that the "racialists" be "kicked out" from the island of Reunion. [68] Libyan leaders repeatedly warned France of the dire consequences of its actions. "French policies in Africa will lead to the destruction of French interests in Africa," said Qadhdhāfī. [69] He termed French operations as anti-Muslim, thus denigrating France in the eyes of the whole Muslim world and implicitly legitimizing his own support of Polisario and Frolinat. "French planes are, and will be, annihilating the Muslims [in the Sahara] and burning their farms and cattle, as well as burning the farms and cattle of the Muslims in Northern Chad because they are Muslims. . . . Is there any oppression of any Jew? Never. . . . French planes chase the Chad revolutionaries because they are Muslim." [70]

Qadhdhāfī went on to demand, at the 30th session of the OAU Liberation Committee, the establishment of liberation movements not only in Reunion, but also in Portuguese Madeira, the British Admiralty Islands and the Spanish Canary Islands: "These islands . . . like Madagascar must be liberated to complete the liberation of African soil." [71]

Notwithstanding its sharp reaction to a French policy it considers hostile, Libya has tried to retain its "special relationship" with France through continued diplomatic efforts—especially through visits by Jallūd to Paris.

MEDITERRANEAN POLICY

The continued closeness of relations between Libya and Malta (cf *MECS 1976–77*, p. 540) was highlighted by Qadhdhāfī's visit to the island from 1–3 July 1978. A joint statement expressed mutual satisfaction with economic co-operation in such fields as oil (which Libya was supplying Malta below world prices), education and health. Libya also promised political, military and economic aid to Malta, thus obviating the need for foreign bases on the island after the British relinquish their naval base in March 1979. The Maltese seemed mainly interested in assurances of economic aid for the period following March 1979, whereas the foremost Libyan concern was strategic. Thus Qadhdhāfī told a Maltese audience: "The security of Libya is tied to the security of Malta and vice versa. . . . We do not want to set up bases in Malta. . . . We are ready to defend . . . your gains. It is our duty to co-operate with you and to help you until your economy and territory are liberated." [72] It is also possible that some military agreement was concluded during the visit.

During the Libyan leader's visit and after it, Malta's historical ties with the Arab world and Islamic culture were repeatedly emphasized. Qadhdhāfī laid the cornerstone of a mosque and an Islamic centre at Corradino, "to serve the ever-increasing Muslim community in Malta." [73] The Libyan cultural centre in Valetta reported that 10,000 Maltese students were studying Arabic under 51 teachers. After the visit, more joint Libyan-Maltese ventures were agreed upon, including a fishing company, maintenance of light civilian aircraft, and the setting up of a technical agricultural services company.

Qadhdhāfī's eagerness "to become Malta's new military protector" [74] fitted into his wider interest of establishing a zone of Libyan influence in the Mediterranean. In Italy, for instance, the National Oil Company (ENI) received a loan of $250m in May 1978. At the same time, a Libyan-Cretan friendship society was formed to deepen "the historical relations between the two friendly people." [75] There is an historical background to Qadhdhāfī's demand for the "liberation" of Madeira and the Canary Islands, [76] as well as to his allusions to the Arab past of Andalusia. However, the main thrust of his effort was clearly strategic—to safeguard Libya's long and vulnerable maritime frontier, not only by military means (including the build-up of a navy), but also by creating a zone of influence. As in some other areas of importance to Libya, these interests coincided with those of the USSR.

RELATIONS WITH THE SOVIET BLOC

During 1978, relations between Libya and the Soviet bloc continued to grow closer (cf *MECS 1976–77*, pp. 540–41). Despite ideological differences, Libyan and Soviet interests increasingly coincided: to dislodge Western influence from Africa and the ME. "Relations between Libya and the USSR are good, because both countries have the same point of view towards the progress of exploited people and opposition towards colonialism. The USSR supports Libya's positive non-alignment, the liberation of people and emancipation from exploitation," Qadhdhāfī explained. [77] The closer relationship brought increasing Soviet involvement in long-range Libyan development plans and projects.

During the year there was a steady exchange of visits between Libya and the USSR, two of which deserve special mention: from 19–22 December 1977, the Chief of the Soviet General Staff, Marshal Nikolai Ogarkov, visited Libya accompanied by a high-level delegation, and toured air, air defence and naval installations; and from 19–22 February 1978, Jallūd visited the USSR. He acquainted Soviet President Leonid Brezhnev with the decisions of the Algiers summit of the "Front of Steadfastness" (see essay on Inter-Arab Relations), and was reported to have arranged to pay for a Syrian-Soviet arms deal, negotiated by President Ḥāfiz al-Asad who was visiting Moscow at the same time. An agreement was also signed to increase co-operation in the fields of industry, energy, minerals and agriculture. The Soviets described the visit as having established a "tradition of high-level Soviet-Libyan consultation." [78] The joint statement issued on 20 February 1978 stressed the identity or closeness of views on international issues, including the Horn of Africa ("just peace in the Horn"). The Soviets reaffirmed their "continuing many-sided support to strengthen [Libyan] national independence, development and progress." [79] Libya was reported to have signed a contract with the USSR in December 1977 for a 440,000 kilowatt nuclear power plant (with Finnish participation). This will be Libya's second reactor but first nuclear power plant.

Relations between Libya and Eastern Europe broadened during the year as the latter became increasingly involved in the former's development projects. A pointer to these closer relations was the establishment of friendship societies with various Communist countries (on the model of the Soviet-Libya Friendship Society): with the GDR (4 October 1977), Bulgaria (16 April 1978), and Poland (1 June 1978). The high point was Qadhdhāfī's East European tour in June 1978, which was preceded by visits of high-level East bloc officials to Libya. Qadhdhāfī's tour began in Bulgaria (17–20 June 1978), where he signed an agreement of co-operation covering 1978–85. The Bulgarians had previously agreed to double their labour force in Libya and increase meat exports. Czechoslovakia was the next stop (20–23 June 1978), followed by Hungary (24–26 June), the GDR (26–28 June), and Poland (29–30 June).

Of these countries, Libya's most extensive previous relations had been with the GDR. For instance, in October 1977, a joint statement issued at the conclusion of a visit by the Secretary of the Central Committee of the GDR Communist Party had "reaffirmed the importance of co-operation and co-ordination and the maintenance of contacts at various levels to increase co-operation" between the two countries. [80] A special envoy of the GDR Head of State and a frequent visitor to Libya was killed there on 6 March in a helicopter crash. (For the assumption that this was actually an attempt on Qadhdhāfī's life, see above.) While in East Berlin, Qadhdhāfī publicly thanked the GDR for its (unspecified) help during the Four-Day War against Egypt in July 1977. He also signed a ten-year agreement on political, economic and scientific co-operation and was promised medical teams.

On his return (3 July 1978), Qadhdhāfī stated that his visit had "eliminated all contradictions" between Libya and "the progressive world." He claimed that the countries he had visited supported Libyan policy and held identical views about the "imperialist offensive" in Africa. He also announced that he had laid cornerstones of Islamic centres (containing a mosque, a library and a school) in Bulgaria, Hungary, the GDR and Poland. [81] This may reflect the extent to which the East European countries deferred to Qadhdhāfī's views. The more concrete results of the visit were discussed at a publicized joint meeting of the GS of the GPC and the GPCom. The "socialist countries" were to carry out a large part of the Transformation Plan: railways, 4,000 kilometres of roads, a shipyard and a maritime academy, various agricultural projects and waterworks, manufacturing of building material and consumer goods, mineral prospecting and medical aid. Trade between Libya and these countries was to increase; it also seems possible that Libya agreed to sell oil to at least Poland and Czechoslovakia.

An indication of the improving relationship between Libya and the Soviet bloc was provided by two conferences held in Tripoli, the first an International Conference on Development and Co-operation from 8–13 April 1978, the closing session of which was chaired by the head of the World Peace Council. In his opening speech, Jallūd condemned President Carter and said that "given the choice, the peoples of the Third World will choose the socialist system." In its resolutions, the conference denounced the US and thanked the USSR.[82] The second gathering, a "Conference of Solidarity with the People of Chile," took place in Benghazi from 17–19 April 1978.

RELATIONS WITH CUBA

Libyan relations with Cuba seemed to develop mainly in the economic sphere. On 4 January 1978, agreements on economic and cultural co-operation were signed. The Cuban Minister for Economic Co-operation visited Libya in March, and in June Libya agreed to import Cuban sugar. In July, Cuba agreed to send 650 medical personnel to Libya.

RELATIONS WITH YUGOSLAVIA

The conspicuous aspect of Libya's relations with Yugoslavia is military. The Commander-in-Chief of the Libyan armed forces, Brig Abū Bakr Yūnis Jābir, visited Yugoslavia twice (from 16–19 January 1978 and from 10–13 July 1978), while the Yugoslav Minister of Defence, Gen Nikola Ljubičić, visited Libya from 29–31 March 1978. The Yugoslav Minister stated that relations between the two countries in the military domain were "progressing significantly."[83] The Yugoslavs were reported to be establishing ammunition and armament spare-parts factories in Libya.

RELATIONS WITH CHINA

At the conclusion of a visit by Jallūd to Peking on 4 August 1978, the establishment of diplomatic relations between Libya and the People's Republic of China was announced.[84]

RELATIONS WITH THE UNITED STATES

As relations with the Soviet bloc grew closer in 1978, so relations with the US deteriorated steadily (see *MECS 1976-77*, pp. 541–42). On 16 November 1977, Qadhdhāfī attributed US hostility to Libya's stand on oil prices: "The US is leading the battle against oil-producing countries . . . against increasing oil prices." He also stated that "the majority of oil-producing countries . . . are agents of the US, and their rulers are slaves of the US."[85] In fact, however, the US ban on the sale of $400m worth of equipment to Libya, announced on 21 February 1978, was intended to reflect American concern about Libya's support for international terrorism, and its attempts to undermine governments of neighbouring countries friendly to the US. The equipment held up included spare parts for military transport aircraft, two *Boeing* 737 airliners, 400 heavy-duty trucks capable of transporting tanks, and the possible sale of three *Boeing* 747 airliners.[86] The Libyans were angry but nevertheless conceded the logic of the US argument. Thus, an official statement complained that "US policy has lost its self-respect," that US policy was "a product of a community of capitalist exploitation . . . of slaves and of Jewish hatred of semitism [sic], Islam and the Arabs. The American ruling group has allied itself with Judaism against Islam." The Libyans were confident that this decision did not reflect the opinion of American citizens. "We regret a policy so childish. . . . The step taken cannot make us cease supporting the struggle of the

Palestinians. . . . Indeed, Libya will support this struggle against Zionism and the enemies of Semitism and Islam.''[87]

Appeals by American corporations involved in Libya and by the US Department of Commerce (worried about the increasing US trade deficit with Libya—which grew from $814m in 1975 to c. $3,490 in 1977) were of no avail.[88] Qadhdhāfī's characteristic riposte was to describe the US as "the state of world terrorism."[89] Nevertheless, most Libyan commercial contacts with the US proceeded: c. 1,000 US citizens continued to operate the Libyan oil industry, and hundreds of Libyan students remained in America (some in federal schools), including c. 200 in nuclear science faculties.

ECONOMIC AFFAIRS ($1 = 0.296 Libyan Dinars; £1 = LD 0.539)
Throughout 1977 and into 1978, virtually every sector of the Libyan economy continued to derive considerable benefit from the country's abundance of oil. Gross domestic product (GDP), total exports and government revenues—all largely composed from oil sales—rose 13.8%, 19.0% and 31.1% respectively in 1977 over 1976.[90] Other key indicators of Libya's further heightened prosperity in 1977 included increased holdings of international reserves and a greater balance-of-payments surplus.

HYDROCARBONS AND GAS
Production of crude oil rose 6.5% in 1977, for a total of 753.4m barrels or an average of 2.06m barrels per day (mbd)—the highest level of output since 1973. Peak daily production for 1977 (2.12mbd) was achieved during the second quarter of the year. In the third quarter, however, oil liftings dropped below 2.0mbd and plummeted further to an average of 1.86mbd, or 260,000 fewer barrels per day, for the first six months of 1978.

The Libyan government attempted to stem this slide by instituting a series of price cuts in order to stimulate greater demand. Since early 1977, though, a combination of factors has resulted in a serious, albeit not irreversible, decline in demand for Libyan oil. Prominent among them has been the inertia prevalent in the stagnant economies of the industrialized countries. A second factor has been the deterioration of Libya's geographical advantage—being on the "right" side of Suez—following increasingly heavy use of the Canal since its reopening in 1975. A third factor contributing to the decline in demand for Libyan crude has been the growing competition from North Sea oil which has the attributes, relative to Libyan oil, of (a) comparability in lightness and low sulphur content; (b) convenience in its proximity to markets; and (c) stability as a source not prone to the vicissitudes of Libyan foreign policy.

Further development in Libya's oil industry in 1977 included the opening of a natural gas refinery and expansion into the production of other hydrocarbons and related chemicals, such as ammonia, methanol and uric acid.

AGRICULTURE
The perennial problems of unconducive climate and terrain and insufficient manpower continued to plague Libyan agriculture in 1977. Scant rainfall, inadequate underground water resources, lack of cultivable land (less than 2% of the country's total area), the migration of thousands of would-be farmers to the cities or to the oil sector, and the tendency of those who remain to cling to traditional methods of farming have all contributed to the poor response to the regime's attempts to achieve self-sufficiency in foodstuffs.

Compared with the record harvests of 1976, below average rainfall in 1977 led to a decline in the yield of virtually every principal crop. Wheat production is estimated to have fallen by one-half in 1977, barley by one-third. The 1977 yields for legumes and oilseed, vegetables, olives and fruits are estimated to have fallen too, though not as drastically. In contrast, agricultural products from livestock and poultry are estimated to have increased slightly in 1977.

In order to stimulate the agricultural sector, the government has allocated c. 16% of the 1976–80 Five-Year Transformation Plan's expenditure to agriculture and land reclamation. Financial incentives to farmers, including encouragement of the adoption of mechanized equipment and modern fertilizers, are a key component of agricultural policy.[91]

MANUFACTURING

Infused with oil money—an allocation of LD 1.12 bn in the 1976–80 Five-Year Plan—Libya's manufacturing sector grew apace in 1977. Industrial production was reported to have climbed from c. LD 53.1m (c. $179m) to c. LD 72.0m (c. $243m) in 1977—an increase of 35.7%.[92]

Since the 1969 Revolution, the regime has embarked on a policy aimed at diversifying the country's sources of income, particularly through rapid industrialization. As of October 1977, 56 industrial plants were reported to have begun production; 21 were under construction; and a further 22 factories were in advanced stages of planning. Of the total of 77 plants either under construction or already operational, 26 are for foodstuffs, 18 for cement and other construction materials, and 12 for mineral and engineering industries. In addition, factories for spinning and textiles, chemicals, and timber have either begun production or are scheduled to do so shortly.[93]

CONSTRUCTION

Construction, particularly of housing, has been given high priority in the Five-Year Plan. More than LD 1 bn have been allocated for the building of 150,000 housing units. The public sector, through the Housing Corporation, aims to construct at least 80,000 new dwellings between 1976 and 1980; the private sector is scheduled to build the rest. However, the introduction in May 1978 of a new law (which prohibits property owners from retaining more than one housing unit) is likely to discourage private contractors from building as many units as are called for in the government's plans. (For a detailed examination of the political aspects of the housing policy, see above.) In the meantime, however, the authorities began a concerted effort both to sell more new dwellings to low-income Libyans and to rent them to foreign workers.

Other construction projects, such as factories, offices, and transportation and communications facilities, are proceeding at a hectic rate, constrained only by supply bottlenecks and the shortage of skilled labour.

LABOUR

Out of a total population of under 3m in mid-1977, Libya's native labour force was estimated at 499,700, of which 92% were males.[94] The scale of Libya's development programme and the pace of its economic growth have required the hiring of hundreds of thousands of non-Libyans; one source estimated that there were 310,000 foreign labourers working in Libya in mid-1978.[95] (For details of the employment of Egyptians, see above.)

An indication of the problem of giving priority in employment to native Libyans was depicted in a report in the semi-official Tripoli daily, *al-Fajr al-Jadīd*:

"Illiterates and those with less than an elementary certificate constitute the frightening percentage of 70.1% of the labour force."[96]

GOVERNMENT BUDGET

According to preliminary figures for 1977, revenue from oil rose 29% to a level of LD 2,702m. By contrast, non-oil revenues were budgeted to fall 27.6% to a level of LD 355m for the same period.

The increase in the 1978 budget for administrative expenditure was set at 19.2%, for a total outlay of LD 695m; for development expenditures, the increase was set at 17.4%, amounting to a total outlay of LD 1,785m. In 1978, as in 1977, the Libyan government is most certain to enjoy a sizeable budgetary surplus.

DEVELOPMENT

In January 1978, allocations for Libya's 1976–80 "Plan of Economic and Social Transformation" were increased 22.9%, for a total budget of LD 9.25 bn (c. $31.9 bn). The largest portion of the revised budget (13%) was allocated to the industry and mining sectors—illustrating the government's urgency to diversify income-producing sectors. The second largest allocation was for housing (12.2%), and the third for land reclamation (10.6%). In contrast, the combined allocations for education (5.6%), the health sector (3.0%) and social services (1.0%) amount to only 9.6% of the total. (For a fuller description of the Five-Year Plan, see *MECS 1976–77*, p. 543.)

BALANCE OF PAYMENTS

At the end of 1977, Libya's overall balance-of-payments surplus improved a further $1,490m, primarily as a result of a $2,905m net surplus in the exchange of goods, services and transfers. Exports of merchandise and services (almost exclusively oil) rose 31.8% in 1977, while imports of merchandise and services together increased 35.2%. In absolute terms, however, the rise in combined exports exceeded that of combined imports by $580m.

MONETARY DEVELOPMENTS

Libya's holdings of international reserves jumped 56.6% for a total of $4,834m in the 12-month period through the first quarter of 1978. With the country's gold holdings remaining relatively constant, this increase is due almost exclusively to the accumulation of foreign exchange.

Libya's net foreign assets reached a record LD 1,460m through the third quarter of 1977, amounting to a 31.3% growth since the beginning of the year. The money supply also expanded at the exceedingly rapid rate of 27.7%, reaching LD 1,455m at the end of September 1977. Moreover, the amount of quasi-money reached a record high of LD 644m at the same time—though its rate of growth, 15.9%, was less than half the corresponding rate for the money supply.

That these developments are worrisome to Libya's authorities was indicated by the deputy governor of the Bank of Libya in the authoritative Tripoli weekly, *al-Usbū' al-Siyāsī*. In an article entitled "Weapons of Counter-Revolution on the Economic Front Include 650m Dinars Under [floor] Tiles," he denounced "counter-revolutionaries" for their part in raising the volume of currency in circulation outside the Bank in the month of February alone by LD 53m (c. $179m). The clear purpose of the article was to encourage Libyans to make greater use of the banking system instead of holding cash.[97] (For details of the subversive nature of this hoarding, see above.)

FOREIGN TRADE

Oil exports, made up of crude oil, refined oil products and liquefied gas, are estimated to have climbed 19% to more than $10 bn in 1977. Non-oil exports—livestock, groundnuts and some citrus fruits—amounted to less than 1% of Libya's exports sales. The principal customers for Libyan oil in 1976 were the US (26.6%), West Germany (23.2%) and Italy (18.2%).

Libya's main imports in the first six months of 1977 were machinery and transport equipment (c. $808m), manufactured goods (c. $454m), and foodstuffs (c. $340m). During this period, total imports rose c. 21.9% compared with the first half of 1976. Italy (23.0%), West Germany (12.1%) and France (8.1%) were Libya's chief suppliers in calendar 1976, when the nine EEC countries combined to provide 54.7% of Libya's total imports.

Gideon Gera

Economic Section by Ira E. Hoffman

ARMED FORCES

Total armed forces number 37,000. Defence expenditure in 1978 was LD 130m ($448m). The Army numbers 30,000 and consists of one armoured brigade; two mechanized infantry brigades; one National Guard brigade; one special forces brigade; three artillery and two anti-aircraft battalions. Equipment consists of 2,000 T-54/-55/-62 medium tanks (many in storage); 100 *Saladin*, Panhard, 200 EE-9 *Cascavel* armoured cars; 140 *Ferret* scout cars; BMP mechanized infantry combat vehicles; 400 BTR-40/-50/-60, 140 OT-62/-64, 70 *Saracen*, 100 M-113A1 armoured personnel carriers; 40 105mm, 80 130mm howitzers; M-109 155mm self-propelled howitzers; 300 *Vigilant*, SS-11, *Sagger* anti-tank guided weapons; 25 *Scud* B surface-to-surface missiles; 180 23mm, L/70 40mm, 57mm, ZSU-23-4 self-propelled anti-aircraft guns; SA-7 surface-to-air missiles; six AB-47, five AB-206, four Alouette III helicopters; some Cessna 0-1 light aircraft. (16 CH-47C helicopters on order.)

The Navy of 3,000 has three F-class submarines; one frigate (with *Seacat* surface-to-air missiles); two corvettes (one with *Otomat* surface-to-surface missiles), eight guided-missile fast patrol boats: three *Susa* class with SS-12M surface-to-surface missiles, five *Osa*-II-class with *Styx* surface-to-surface missiles; 14 patrol craft; two logistic support ships, two tank landing ships (one *Bidassoa*-, one *Polnocny*-class). Three F-class submarines, three corvettes with *Otomat* surface-to-surface missiles, ten guided missile fast-patrol boats. 80 *Otomat* surface-to-surface missiles on order.

The 4,000-strong Air Force has 178 combat aircraft (some may be in storage); one bomber squadron with 12 Tu-22 *Blinder*; two interceptor squadrons (one operational conversion unit) with 24 MiG-23 *Flogger*; four ground-attack fighter squadrons and operational conversion units with 90 *Mirage* VD/DE, ten VDR, ten VDD; two counter-insurgency squadrons with 32 *Galeb*; two transport squadrons with eight C-130H, one Boeing 707, nine C-47, two *Falcon*, one *Jetstar*. Trainers include two *Mystère* 20, five MiG-23U, 12 *Magister*, *Falcon* ST 2, 20 SF-260, 17 *Galeb*. Four helicopter squadrons with 13 *Alouette* II/III, six AB-47, nine *Super Frelon*, ten CH-47C; AA-2 *Atoll*, R.550 *Magic* air-to-air missiles; three surface-to-air missile regiments with 60 *Crotale* and nine batteries with 60 SA-2, SA-3 and SA-6 surface-to-air missiles. 32 *Mirage* F-1AD/ED fighters; six *Mirage* F-1BD, 150 SF-260 trainers; 20 CH-47C, one AS-61A helicopters on order.

Source: *The Military Balance 1978-79* (London: International Institute for Strategic Studies).

ARMED FORCES: DIVISIONS/MAJOR SYSTEMS

	1973	1978
Armoured brigades	1	1-2
Mechanized brigades	2	3
Special forces	1 regiment	1 brigade
Tanks	250	1,900
Armoured personnel carriers	about 450	1,000
Artillery	150	600
Ground-to-ground missiles	—	27
Combat aircraft	72	150
Helicopters	25	50
Ground-to-air missile batteries	3	40
Combat naval vessels	1	10

Source: *Arab Military Strength* (Jerusalem: Israel Information Centre, June 1978).

BALANCE OF PAYMENTS (million US dollars)

	1975	1976	1977
A. Goods, Services and Transfers	-68	2,334	2,905
Exports of Merchandise, fob	6,240	8,605	11,386
Imports of Merchandise, fob	-4,424	-4,277	-5,214
Exports of Services	375	349	416
Imports of Services	-2,063	-2,160	-3,491
Private Unrequited Transfers, net	-32	-37	-40
Government Unrequited Transfers, net	-164	-144	-152
B. Long-Term Capital, nie	-1,524	-1,407	-1,303
C. Short-Term Capital, nie	304	285	123
D. Errors and Omissions	-262	-163	-235
Total (A through D)	**-1,550**	**1,049**	**1,490**
Reserves and Related Items	1,550	-1,049	-1,490

INTERNATIONAL LIQUIDITY (million US dollars, at end of period)

	1975	1976	1977	*(first qtr)* 1978
International Reserves	2,195	3,206	4,891	4,834
of which: Gold	100	99	104	106
Foreign Exchange	2,088	3,099	4,779	4,720
Other	7	7	7	7

MONETARY SURVEY (million Libyan dinars, at end of period)

	1974	1975	1976	*(Jan–Nov only)* 1977
Foreign Assets (net)	1,281.6	772.3	1,111.7	1,514.2
Claims on Private Sector	451.9	645.3	765.0	876.1
Money	753.9	867.5	1,139.4	1,406.4
Quasi-Money	580.4	492.9	555.5	662.3
Government Deposits (net)	153.6	-256.3	-271.8	-130.0
Money, Seasonally Adjusted	755.4	869.2	1,139.4	1,388.4

Source (of three preceding tables): IMF, *International Financial Statistics.*

GOVERNMENT FINANCE (million Libyan dinars)

	Actual 1975	Provisional 1976	Budget 1977	Budget 1978
Revenue	**1,741.2**	**2,583.6**	...	...
Oil	1,443.2	2,093.6	...	...
Non-oil	298.0	490.0	355.0	443.5
Expenditure				
1. Administrative	460.1	564.0	583.0	695.0
of which:				
Central Government	*377.8*	*480.2*	*493.4*	*601.4*
Transfers to Public Sector	*47.8*	*34.4*	*34.0*	*34.5*
Transfers to Municipalities	*20.0*	*23.5*	*31.5*	*31.5*
Other	*14.5*	*25.9*	*24.1*	*27.6*
2. Development	941.0	1,190.0	1,520.0	1,785.0
3. Special				
of which:				
Foreign grants, loans, etc.	*120.3*	*90.9*	...	...
Commodity subsidies	*94.0*	*76.0*	...	...

Sources: Secretariats of Oil, Planning and the Treasury.

DEVELOPMENT EXPENDITURE (million Libyan dinars)

	1973–75 Plan	1976–80 Plan		
	Actual	Initial	Second Revision	% of second revision
Agriculture	246.8	445.3	498.0	5.4
Land Reclamation	316.7	781.3	977.7	10.6
Industry and Mining	291.7	1,089.8	1,205.0	13.0
Oil and Gas	132.5	648.2	670.0	7.2
Electricity	217.8	543.6	896.8	9.7
Housing	340.7	794.2	1,131.0	12.2
Municipal Projects	177.4	552.6	755.7	8.2
Transport and Communication	177.7	632.1	929.8	10.1
Maritime Transport	59.7	373.5	373.5	4.0
Education	168.4	470.4	521.8	5.6
Health	47.0	171.4	276.3	3.0
Social Services	16.4	43.1	95.8	1.0
Other	46.9	624.5	918.6	9.9
Total	**2,239.7**	**7,170.0**	**9,250**	**100.0***

*Total greater than sum of parts because of rounding.
Source: Secretariat of Planning and Central Bank of Libya.

GDP AT FACTOR COST IN CONSTANT PRICES (million 1975 Libyan dinars)

	1975	1976*	1977*	% of 1977 total
Oil Sector	1,941.4	2,534.0	2,780.0	54.7
Agriculture, Forestry and Fishing	114.3	130.5	124.0	2.4
Mining and Quarrying	18.5	21.5	24.5	0.5
Manufacturing	91.6	108.0	132.0	2.6
Construction	439.3	505.0	568.0	11.2
Transportation and Communication	253.9	269.0	286.0	5.6
Wholesale and Retail Trade	246.2	262.0	279.0	5.5
Public Services	255.7	300.0	343.0	6.7
Banking and Insurance	86.8	100.0	112.0	2.2
Electricity, Gas and Water	17.7	22.5	29.5	0.6
Other Services	319.6	365.0	405	8.0
Total GDP	**3,785.0**	**4,617.5**	**5,083.0**	**100.0**

*Preliminary.

AGRICULTURAL PRODUCTION (thousand tonnes)

	1974	1975	Preliminary 1976	Estimate 1977
Vegetables	460	517	652	640
Olives	23	95	156	140
Fruit	111	124	136	121
Barley	144	192	196	120
Milk	69	81	85	89
Wheat	38	111	130	60
Meat	33	46	50	54
Olive Oil	6	23	25	28
Legumes and Oilseed	18	19	24	22
Eggs	8	3	4	4

Source (of two preceding tables): Secretariat of Planning.

PRODUCTION OF SELECTED INDUSTRIES

	Unit	1974	1975	1976
Grain Mill Products	('000 tonnes)	167.9	183.9	174.6
Macaroni	('000 tonnes)	43.3	45.1	49.0
Tomato Paste	('000 tonnes)	12.6	10.3	12.8
Paper Products	('000 tonnes)	3.6	3.9	4.2
Soap and Detergents	('000 tonnes)	10.2	11.1	12.8
Cigarettes	(billions)	2.7	2.8	2.3
Cement	('000 tonnes)	500	600	700

Source: Department of Census and Statistics, Quarterly Bulletin of Statistics.

DIRECTION OF TRADE (million US dollars)

	1974	1975*	1976*	% of 1976 total
Exports to:				
United States	7.1	1,190.3	2,187.5	26.6
West Germany	1,817.2	1,327.7	1,911.9	23.2
Italy	2,760.2	1,303.2	1,494.9	18.2
Spain	302.5	311.1	467.3	5.7
France	486.1	179.5	291.5	3.5
United Kingdom	1,032.2	238.6	270.0	3.3
Turkey	0.6	92.8	212.4	2.6
Virgin Islands	...	180.1	204.8	2.5
Japan	424.3	263.0	187.8	2.3
Brazil	354.3	169.1	141.1	1.7
Total (including others)	**8,260.8**	**5,866.1**	**8,232.3**	
Imports from:				
Italy	685.8	1,024.0	1,096.7	23.0
West Germany	317.3	540.3	575.7	12.1
France	286.0	380.2	384.7	8.1
Japan	193.1	281.3	359.8	7.5
United States	107.1	174.5	304.4	6.4
United Kingdom	137.3	240.4	265.8	5.6
Lebanon	100.8	136.6	163.9	3.4
Belgium	69.1	81.9	155.5	3.3
Greece	97.6	155.4	153.2	3.2
Spain	78.4	99.7	142.5	3.0
Total (including others)	**2,762.8**	**4,035.3**	**4,774.9**	

*Data partly extrapolated and/or derived from partner country.
Source: IMF, Direction of Trade.

LIBYA

NOTES
1. R Tripoli, 17 November—Daily Report (DR), 18 November 1977.
2. *Arab Dawn*, London; November 1977.
3. R Tripoli, 17 November—DR, 18 November 1977.
4. *Le Monde*, Paris; 15 November 1977.
5. Jamāhiriyya News Agency (JANA), 22 October—DR, 25 October 1977.
6. *Al-Fajr al-Jadīd*, Tripoli; 8 February 1978.
7. *Ibid.*
8. *Ibid.*
9. *Ibid.*
10. *Al-Usbū' al-Siyāsī*, Tripoli; 10 February 1978. Emphasis added.
11. *Al-Jihād*, Tripoli; 8 November 1977. Emphasis added.
12. *Ibid.*
13. *Al-Fajr al-Jadīd*, 8 February 1978.
14. *Ibid.*
15. *Ibid.*
16. *Jamāhiriyya Mail*, Valetta; 4 March 1978.
17. *Al-Jihād*, 10 November 1977.
18. *Al-Fajr al-Jadīd*, 8 February 1978.
19. *Al-Usbū' al-Siyāsī*, 10 February 1978.
20. There is an historical precedent for such action by Qadhdhāfī. In September 1974, he empowered cadres of the previously derided Libyan "Arab Socialist Union" to guide elections of Popular Committees in the framework of the "Popular Revolution." Cf *MECS 1976-77*, p. 527.
21. Mu'ammar al-Qadhdhāfī, *Al-Kitāb al-Akhdar*, al-Fasl al-Thānī, *Hall al-Mushkil al-iqtisādī—al-Ishtirākiyya* (Tripoli, 1978). For Part One, cf *MECS 1976-77*, p. 547 n. 6.
22. *Al-Fajr al-Jadīd*, 21 February 1978.
23. *Ibid*, 4 April 1978.
24. *Ibid*, 20 February 1978.
25. R Tripoli, 1 May—DR, 3 May 1978.
26. JANA, 24 May—Summary of World Broadcasts: The Middle East and Africa (BBC), 25 May 1978.
27. R Tripoli, 6 May—BBC, 9 May 1978, from where the following quotations were taken.
28. R Tripoli, 14 May—BBC, 17 May 1978.
29. R Tripoli, 1 May—DR, 3 May 1978. Emphasis added.
30. For the full text, from which the following quotes were taken, see *al-Fajr al-Jadīd*, 20, 21 February 1978.
31. R Tripoli, 11 June—BBC, 13 June 1978.
32. *International Herald Tribune (IHT)*, Paris; 12–13 August 1978.
33. Qardābiyya, in Sirte, is near Qadhdhāfī's birthplace and was the field of a victorious battle against the Italians in 1915, in which his father was wounded.
34. R Tripoli, 11 June—BBC, 13 June 1978.
35. *Ibid.*
36. JANA, 20 March 1978; cf *MECS 1976-77*, p. 532, and Qadhdhāfī's speech on 29 December—BBC, 31 December 1977.
37. JANA, 20 March 1978.
38. R Tripoli, 6 May—BBC, 9 May 1978.
39. Jallūd interview, JANA, 28 June—DR, 30 June 1978.
40. Qadhdhāfī speaking to an audience in Niger, JANA, 23 January—DR, 23 January 1978.
41. *The Guardian*, London; 8 May 1978.
42. Jallūd interview, JANA, 4 June—BBC, 6 June 1978.
43. JANA, 23 January—DR, 23 January 1978.
44. The concept of security belts was previously articulated in a very similar manner by a Libyan weekly in late 1975, in the context of the large arms deals with the USSR. *Al-Fātih*, Tripoli; 13 September 1975.
45. R Tripoli, 18 November—BBC, 19 November 1977.
46. JANA, 19 June—DR, 22 June 1978.
47. R Tripoli, 28 March—BBC, 30 March 1978.
48. R Tripoli, 17 November—BBC, 19 November 1977.
49. R Tripoli, 19 March—DR, 20 March 1978.
50. JANA, 6 April—BBC, 8 April 1978.
51. R Tripoli, 19 June—BBC, 20 June 1978; cf *Guardian* 8 May 1978; *MECS 1976-77*, p. 539.
52. JANA, 4 June—BBC, 6 June 1978.
53. *Al-Watan al-'Arabī*, Paris; 4 November 1977; cf *MECS 1976-77*, pp. 539–40.
54. JANA, 4 June—BBC, 6 June 1978.

55. R Tripoli, 19 June—DR, 20 June 1978.
56. *Al-Fajr al-Jadīd*, 19 October 1977.
57. JANA, 20 June 1978.
58. *Al-Watan al-'Arabī*, 4 November 1977.
59. *Al-Rā'y al-'Amm,* Kuwait; 30 March 1978. Leaders of the Eritrean Liberation Front—
    Popular Liberation Forces told the press in early May 1978 that Qadhdhāfī had told the
    Cubans that he would not stand idly by if they helped Ethiopia in Eritrea, but there was no
    Libyan confirmation of this.
60. R Tripoli, 19 June—DR, 20 June 1978.
61. *Der Spiegel*, Hamburg; 20 February—DR, 22 February 1978.
62. Libyan Foreign Secretary, 'Abd al-Salām Tūraykī, quoted by JANA, 25 January—DR, 26
    January 1978; cf *MECS 1976–77*, p. 540.
63. R Tripoli, 19 June—DR, 20 June 1978.
64. JANA, 4 June—BBC, 6 June 1978.
65. R Tripoli, 19 June—DR, 20 June 1978.
66. *Le Monde,* Paris; 17 January 1978. Historically, European encroachment on Libya began
    with the destruction of Sanussi strongholds in North Chad by the advancing French at the
    turn of the century. However, the animosity the French felt towards the Sanussis—who
    were of Algerian origin—dated from the 1830s.
67. *Al-Mustaqbal*, Paris; 21 January 1978.
68. R Tripoli, 13 February—BBC, 15 February 1978.
69. R Tripoli, 19 June—DR, 20 June 1978.
70. JANA, 4 June—BBC, 6 June 1978.
71. R Tripoli, 13 February—BBC, 15 February 1978.
72. R Tripoli, 2 July—DR, 3 July 1978.
73. Reuter dispatch from Valetta, 2 July 1978.
74. *The Economist*, London; 5 July 1978.
75. JANA, 14 May—BBC, 16 May 1978.
76. In a speech to the 30th OAU Ministerial Council, 20 February 1978. R Tripoli, 20
    February—BBC, 22 February 1978.
77. Italian TV, 12 April—DR, 14 April 1978.
78. TASS, 13 February 1978.
79. R Moscow, 20 February 1978.
80. R Tripoli, 4 October—DR, 5 October 1977.
81. R Tripoli, 3 June—DR, 5 June 1978.
82. R Tripoli, 9 April—DR, 12 April 1978; JANA, 14 April—BBC, 18 April 1978.
83. JANA, 31 March—DR, 3 April 1978.
84. Qadhdhāfī had announced Libyan recognition of the People's Republic as early as 11 June
    1971.
85. *Al-Fajr al-Jadīd*, 17 November—DR, 30 November 1977.
86. *IHT*, 6 April 1978; *New York Times*, 24 June 1978.
87. R Tripoli, 4 March—DR, 6 March 1978.
88. However, it was argued in the US that if, as a result of Congressional legislation restricting
    trade with countries encouraging terrorism, Libya lost its oil exports to the US (a third of
    its crude production), this would be a serious blow to her. See *IHT*, 8 August 1978.
89. R Tripoli, 19 June—DR, 20 June 1978.
90. For background, see *MECS 1976–77*, pp. 542–47.
91. See *al-Fajr al-Jadīd*, 28 July, 23 October 1977—US Joint Publication Research Service,
    Near East and North Africa (JPRS), Arlington; 13 September 1977, 4 January 1978.
92. *Al-Fajr al-Jadīd*, 15 March 1978.
93. See, for example, *al-Fajr al-Jadīd*, 17 October 1977—JPRS, 22 November 1977; *al-Jihād*,
    1 September 1977—JPRS, 27 October 1977; *The Guardian*, 1 September 1978.
94. *Al-Fajr al-Jadīd*, 23 October 1977—JPRS, 3 January 1978.
95. *Middle East Economic Digest*, London; 1 September 1978. Also see *MECS 1976–77*, pp.
    537–38, 543.
96. *Al-Fajr al-Jadīd*, 23 October 1977—JPRS, 3 January 1978.
97. *Al-Usbū' al-Siyāsī*, 24 March 1978—JPRS, 10 May 1978.

The People's Democratic Republic of Yemen

(Jumhūriyyat al-Yaman al-Sha'biyya al-Dīmuqrātiyya)

The summary execution of the Chairman of the Presidential Council and the UPONF Central Committee Assistant Secretary-General, Sālim 'Alī Rubay', on 26 June 1978 was an important landmark in the continuing struggle for power within the ruling party, the Unified Political Organization—The National Front (UPONF). This struggle, which has characterized South Yemeni politics since the ascendancy to power of the radical wing of the National Front (NF) on 22 June 1969, was mainly between two rival wings, the first led by Rubay' and the second by UPONF Central Committee Secretary-General, 'Abd al-Fattāh Ismā'īl al-Jawfī.

The struggle focused on the character of the South Yemeni revolution, the best way to implement it in the stage following the "liberation from the colonial yoke," and the orientation of the country's foreign policy. While Rubay'—who counted on his loyal supporters in the government, administration and the military—believed in a pragmatic and gradual application of the principles of the revolution and in a more flexible foreign policy, 'Abd al-Fattāh Ismā'īl's approach was more rigid and doctrinaire, demanding not only strict adherence to revolutionary principles, but also the deepening of ideological attitudes at all levels of society, including the less developed tribal elements in the hinterland. In order to propagate these ideas and build up his own support, 'Abd al-Fattāh Ismā'īl began in the last third of 1977 to reorganize the party and to set up the "New Vanguard Party." Realizing that he would need massive support to challenge Rubay' successfully, 'Abd al-Fattāh Ismā'īl started to organize party cells in the six governorates in order to mobilize tribal support. During the first months of 1978, while Rubay' was in relative isolation—particularly since the promised Saudi support failed to materialize—'Abd al-Fattāh Ismā'īl's position was reinforced by the flow of aid from Communist countries. By mid-year, the intense struggle between the two rival wings of UPONF escalated to an open clash in which 'Abd al-Fattāh Ismā'īl's wing, supported by Cuban-trained "popular militia" units, gained the upper hand and took over the government.

The victory of 'Abd al-Fattāh Ismā'īl decided the struggle over the PDRY's foreign orientation in favour of the USSR, which had been vying with Saudi Arabia for preponderance throughout 1976–77. With the downfall of Rubay', any hopes for a *rapprochement* with Riyadh received a major setback. This had an adverse affect on relations with the US (which were about to be formally resumed) and paved the way for closer co-operation with the USSR and other Communist states, thus further strengthening 'Abd al-Fattāh Ismā'īl's position as leader of the ideologically strong Communist wing of the UPONF. For the Soviet Union, this development was also of particular importance because of Aden's strategic location.

Thus, by the end of 1977–78 it seemed that both domestically and in its foreign policy, the PDRY was not only a bastion of radicalism in the ME, but also a potentially important base for pro-Communist revolutionary operations.

POLITICAL AFFAIRS
POWER STRUGGLE CONTINUED
In the last quarter of 1977 and the beginning of 1978, the power struggle deepened between the doctrinaire Marxist-Leninist ideologue, 'Abd al-Fattāh Ismā'īl, and the

more moderate PC chairman, Sālim 'Ali Rubay'. (For its background and earlier development, see *Middle East Contemporary Survey (MECS) 1976–77*, pp. 549–51.) The struggle spread into the government, the party's political bureau, its central committee and its cells in the governorates. While Rubay' attempted to consolidate power mainly in Aden (among government members, militia forces and central party organs), 'Abd al-Fattāḥ Ismā'īl sought to use his influence within the party machinery to gain support, especially in the tribal hinterland. For Rubay' the slow progress being made towards the improvement of relations with Saudi Arabia was a particular source of dissatisfaction. At the same time, he was strongly opposed to the USSR acquiring naval facilities at Aden to replace those lost in Somalia, and to giving support to Ethiopia (see below). On both these issues, he was in direct conflict with 'Abd al-Fattāḥ Ismā'īl.

Rubay''s visit to Saudi Arabia at the end of July 1977—the first by a South Yemeni head of state since independence in 1967—worsened relations between the two factions. Having secured Saudi promises for assistance, Rubay' returned home at the beginning of August hoping that relations between the two countries had been consolidated.[1] Arab press reports at that time spoke of Rubay''s growing ascendancy over his opponents as a result of Saudi backing.[2]

'Abd al-Fattāḥ Ismā'īl, on the other hand, could count on the assistance of those Eastern bloc states (particularly the USSR and East Germany) involved in training the South Yemeni armed forces who had become increasingly apprehensive about the possibility of losing their foothold at the southern entrance to the Red Sea.

GOVERNMENT RESHUFFLE

In a continuing effort to consolidate his power, Rubay' reshuffled the Cabinet and carried out a minor ministerial reorganization on 24 October 1977. Several new ministers were appointed, the most important being Lt-Col (*muqaddam*) 'Ali Ahmad Nāsir 'Antar as Defence Minister, a portfolio previously held by the Prime Minister, 'Ali Nāsir Muhammad Husnī. Rubay' also abolished the Ministry of Housing, assigning its tasks and powers elsewhere. He created two new ministries, Fishery Resources and Installations.

THE CABINET (Formed on 24 October 1977)

Prime Minister	'Ali Nāsir Muhammad Husnī
Defence	'Ali Ahmad Nāsir 'Antar*
Foreign Affairs	Muhammad Sālih Mutī'
Interior	Qāsim Sālih Muslih
Minister of State for Security	Muhammad Sa'īd 'Abdallah
Industry and Acting Minister of Planning	'Abd al-'Azīz 'Abd al-Walī
Local Administration	'Ali Sālim al-Bayd
Information	Ahmad Sālim 'Ubayd*
Communications	Mahmūd 'Abdallah 'Ushaysh*
Installations[0]	Haydar Abū Bākir al-'Attās
Fishery Resources[0]	Muhammad Sālim 'Akūsh*
Agriculture and Agricultural Reform	Muhammad Sulaymān Nāsir
Education	Sa'īd 'Abd al-Khayr al-Nūbān
Culture and Tourism	'Ali 'Abd al-Razzāq Bādhīb
Health	'Abdallah Ahmad Bukīr*
Finance	Fadl Muhsin 'Abdallah
Trade and Supply	Mahmūd Sa'īd Madhī
Justice	'Abdallah Ahmad Ghānim
Labour and Civil Service	'Ali As'ad Muthannā
Secretary of the Presidential Council	'Ali Sālim La'war
Cabinet Affairs Secretary	Nasr Nāsir 'Ali

---

*New Minister   [0] New Portfolio
Housing Minister Nāsir Muhammad Yasīn was appointed the Public Prosecutor, and the Ministry was abolished.[3]

THE PEOPLE'S DEMOCRATIC REPUBLIC OF YEMEN

'ABD AL-FATTĀH ISMĀ'ĪL'S ACTIVITY WITHIN THE UPONF: LOCAL ELECTIONS TO THE VANGUARD PARTY

In order to face the danger inherent in Rubay''s willingness to adopt a conciliatory approach towards the Saudis and possibly also towards the tribal "reactionary elements" in the interior, 'Abd al-Fattāh Ismā'īl took two important measures to strengthen his hand. First, he initiated elections of representatives to the local People's Councils in the First, Second, Third, Fourth and Sixth Governorates. These were held in mid-November 1977 in accordance with a model adopted after the elections held earlier in the Fifth Governorate, Hadramawt. Women voted for the first time.[4] (See *MECS 1976-77*, pp. 552-53.) Although the idea and the impetus for holding the elections were 'Abd al-Fattāh Ismā'īl's, Rubay' tried to turn them to his own account since he appreciated the political importance of securing the backing of the hinterland.[5]

The second and more important measure was the organization of a new style Vanguard Party (*hizb talī'ī min tirāz jadīd*) which had been one of Ismā'īl's major political aims since October 1975. At that time, the NF decided to absorb the two smaller Leftist organizations—the People's Vanguard (which had connections with the Ba'th Party) and the People's Democratic Union (South Yemen's Communist party)—and form the UPONF. Although the NF leadership was predominant, the leaders of the smaller groups—especially the devout Communist, Anīs Hasan Yahyā—had a disproportionately great influence in formulating UPONF policy.[6]

In October 1977, while preparations were underway for the elections to the local People's Councils, 'Abd al-Fattāh Ismā'īl declared that "despite difficulties, negative aspects and mistakes," the UPONF had reached the "objective conditions which are accelerating its shift to [a] vanguard party." He added that after studying class, ideological and organizational questions of the party, the UPONF Central Committee would make a comprehensive assessment of its structure. The new party's basic political document was approved in December 1977, but it was decided to postpone the formal announcement of the new party until sometime in October 1978.[7]

In the six months that followed, 'Abd al-Fattāh Ismā'īl launched an intensive campaign in all the governorates to explain how "to develop our UPONF into a new model Vanguard Party." The PDRY press, especially *Fourteenth October* and the party organ *al-Thawrī*, gave extensive coverage to 'Abd al-Fattāh Ismā'īl's meetings with local party members as well as with representatives of the armed forces, students and workers' unions throughout the country. To all of them he spoke of "deepening the working class socialist ideology," expanding "scientific socialism" and increasing "political awareness." He defined three stages for the achievements of these goals. (1) Re-evaluation of all the class and organizational activities within the party such as "the practice of centralized democracy, collective leadership, criticism and self-criticism." (2) A purge of all "ailments and imperfections in the movement," and of all the "bad blood that has been found inside it." The imperfections were caused by the "bourgeois class . . . remnants of the old authority that has been transmitted from the age of colonialism and has not been able to develop or stay in step with revolution." Another cause of imperfection was the "personal, Bedouin and tribal relations" which impeded social mobilization. (3) Turning the "productive forces" into a "foundation for the new class structure." These forces were the workers in the agricultural and fishery co-operatives (which were established in 1970-71); the soldiers who defended the revolution; and the "enlightened revolutionaries." All these were considered to be "new blood."[8]

ESCALATION OF STRUGGLE BETWEEN RUBAYʿ AND ʿABD AL-FATTĀH ISMĀʿĪL

Rubayʿ was of course well aware of the real intentions concealed behind the ideological rhetoric which his rival used in campaigning for a reorganization of the UPONF. He therefore continued his efforts to secure his power base by making further personnel and administrative changes in government. In January 1978, he cancelled the appointments made in his reshuffle of October 1977 and abolished the post of Minister of Local Administration, the Secretariats for Cabinet Affairs and the Presidential Council, and the Supreme Council for Trade and Supply.[9]

On 7 March 1978, Rubayʿ appointed Nāsir ʿAlī as Labour and Civil Service Minister, replacing ʿAlī Asʿad Muthannā. In addition, the two secretariats he had abolished two months earlier were reinstated, with Muthannā as Secretary for Cabinet Affairs and ʿAlī Sālim Laʿwar as Secretary for the Presidential Council.[10]

In February and March, Arab sources said that the internal dispute within the higher echelons of the UPONF reflected a wider struggle between the Soviets, who were in charge of training the armed forces, the East Germans, who were responsible for organizing the Internal Security units, and the Cubans who trained the Popular Militia.[11] Moreover, al-Siyāsa observed in April that the Soviet Union had supported ʿAbd al-Fattāh Ismāʿīl in his efforts to establish the Vanguard Party in order to strengthen his influence within the UPONF itself.[12]

Having secured the backing of the Political Bureau and Central Committee, as well as of Defence Minister ʿAlī Ahmad Nāsir ʿAntar, ʿAbd al-Fattāh Ismāʿīl ordered the arrest in May of 150 officers loyal to Rubayʿ on charges of having opposed the projected Vanguard Party.[13] Probably in reaction to this move, Rubayʿ attempted to strengthen his own position in the armed forces, visiting units in the Second Governorate at the end of May 1978.[14] He also appointed new commissioners to the various provinces of the Fifth Governorate.[15] On 27 June, the Lebanese al-Safīr reported that Rubayʿ had tried to turn the Internal Security forces into a loyal power base. His followers in the Internal Security were reported to have attempted to create a network by which secret contacts with the Saudis could be arranged. The members of this network, which included army and police officers, were arrested on ʿAbd al-Fattāh Ismāʿīl's orders.

When Rubayʿ—as chairman of the important Armed Forces Organizational Committee (in charge of political indoctrination in the army)—refused to hand over a report on the Committee's activities to the UPONF Political Bureau, he was replaced as committee chairman by Husayn Qamāta, the Commander of the Popular Militia and a Central Committee member.[16] Although his dismissal from the Committee chairmanship was obviously a setback, Rubayʿ nonetheless continued to resist his rival's efforts to undermine his position.

EVENTS LEADING TO RUBAYʿ'S EXECUTION, 24-26 JUNE 1978

On 24 June 1978, al-Anbā reported that Rubayʿ was under house arrest, stripped of his authority though still titular chairman of the Presidential Council. There was no other confirmation of this report.[17] On the evening of 25 June, the UPONF Central Committee held an extraordinary meeting, ostensibly to discuss developments in North Yemen following the assassination on 24 June of Ahmad Husayn al-Ghashmī (see chapter on North Yemen). According to R Aden (probably reflecting the views of ʿAbd al-Fattāh Ismāʿīl), Rubayʿ had refused to attend the meeting "despite all the efforts exerted by the [UPONF] Political Bureau to persuade him to do so." The report went on to say that he would only be willing "to send his resignation to the Central Committee when he felt that it would take him to task for his individual practices and behaviour, which under no circumstances reflect the policy and principles of the UPONF or the revolutionary government and its stands."[18] However, according to al-Nahār, Rubay' did participate in that meeting which lasted until late in the night of 25 June.

The meeting approved two resolutions by 121 votes to 4 (including Rubay"s). The first suspended Rubay' for his involvement in Ghashmī's assassination; the second called for a committee composed of Central Committee members to investigate Rubay"s actions. According to the al-Nahār report, the ongoing dispute between Rubay' and 'Abd al-Fattāh Ismā'īl came to a head at this turbulent meeting. Apparently having decided to resist to the end, Rubay' shortly afterwards deployed military units loyal to him near the Presidential Council Palace and other government buildings. The Central Committee members, headed by 'Abd al-Fattāh Ismā'īl, interpreted these acts as a coup d'état. They reconvened, this time without Rubay', and decided to take firm action. A statement was issued accepting Rubay"s resignation, but it made no mention of the resolutions adopted by the first meeting.[19]

On 26 June, the Iraqi News Agency's correspondent in Aden broke the news that fighting had begun early that morning between armed units loyal to Rubay' and Popular Militia units loyal to 'Abd al-Fattāh Ismā'īl in the Tawāhī quarter and in the Aden airport area.[20] Both sides used artillery and machine-guns. R Aden broadcast Qur'ān recitations at 06.30 instead of its usual programme; communications with the outside world were cut, and the Aden airport was closed. Units loyal to Rubay', including those from the nearby Salāh al-Dīn military camp, began to shell the Central Committee building, the Prime Minister's office, the Defence Ministry and the State Security Ministry—all located in Tawāhī. At the same time, other units from Bāb al-Mandab, the Second and the Third Governorates—all loyal to Rubay'—began to move towards Aden. In the clashes which followed, it soon became clear that the units loyal to 'Abd al-Fattāh Ismā'īl had the upper hand, probably due to the support of the Air Force. By 09.00 the Popular Militia had gained control of at least half of Aden. They blocked and controlled the main roads and a curfew was imposed. Towards noon, when Rubay' and his followers continued to resist, the Air Force bombed the Presidential Council Palace. At 12.00, R Aden resumed its regular broadcasts but made no mention of that morning's events.[21]

According to several reports, 'Abd al-Fattāh Ismā'īl was actively assisted by Soviet and Cuban forces, including 500 Cuban soldiers brought from Ethiopia to help him. There were also rumours that it was Cuban pilots who had bombed the Presidential Palace, and that key installations in Aden were under the control of heavily armed Cuban-trained militia soldiers.[22]

The Central Committee issued a statement at 14.55 accusing Rubay' of staging a coup d'état in violation of all "the principles of organized legitimacy, collective leadership, and the principles and objectives of our revolution and our political organization." It also thanked the armed forces, the Popular Militia and the police "for their vigilant stands protecting the organizational legitimacy represented in the collective command and its commitment and firm implementation of the decisions of the Central Committee and the Political Bureau."[23]

Two hours later, 'Alī Nāsir Muhammad Husnī was appointed chairman of the Presidential Council[24] while retaining his post as Prime Minister. On the evening of the same day, Rubay' surrendered.[25] Shortly afterwards R Aden announced that "after inflicting heavy losses" on the people, Rubay' was executed—together with the Presidential Council and Central Committee member, 'Alī Sālim La'war, and Political Bureau member, Jāsim Sālih.[26] Another report added that the execution was held in Husnī's house.[27] Meanwhile, cables supporting the Central Committee were being received from the armed forces and the unions of students and workers.[28] On 27 June, an "uneasy calm prevailed";[29] only sporadic shooting in Aden was reported[30] and communications were restored.[31]

There were conflicting reports about the injuries supposedly sustained by 'Abd al-Fattāḥ Ismā'īl: one claimed that he had been rushed to Moscow for medical treatment;[32] another that he had been killed.[33] During the following days, however, 'Abd al-Fattāḥ Ismā'īl issued statements accusing "the deviationist" Rubay' of having attempted to destroy the legitimate authority; of having embroiled the country "in a bloodbath"; opposed the projected new Vanguard Party; committed economic crimes; co-operated with "reactionary and imperialist circles"; and attempted to prevent unity with North Yemen.[34]

There were a number of different commentaries on the June events. Some saw it as strictly an internal affair: (1) as an outright power struggle between the two leaders; (2) as a power struggle but one which stemmed basically from disagreements over ideology and policy matters; or (3) as a political dispute over the creation of the Vanguard Party.[35] Others emphasized the regional and even global implications, either as a severe internal struggle centring on foreign policy orientation (i.e. pro-Soviet or pro-Saudi); or as a direct conflict between the Soviet Union and the Saudi Arabians over influence in the PDRY in particular and in the Arabian Peninsula in general.[35] A third group interpreted the events as part of the conflict between North and South Yemen, with the assassination of Ghashmī (Chairman of the North Yemeni Presidential Council) providing the occasion for mutual accusations between Rubay' and 'Abd al-Fattāḥ Ismā'īl that the other was responsible.[37]

The dearth of first-hand information made it impossible to evaluate the relative weight of each of these explanations, but it seems probable that all reflected a basic truth—the continuing and fluctuating power struggle at the very top of the PDRY's leadership.

NEW PRESIDENTIAL COUNCIL AND ITS POLICIES
On 1 July 1978, a new Presidential Council was elected: 'Alī Nāsir Muḥammad Husnī as Chairman, and 'Abd al-Fattāḥ Ismā'īl, Minister of Defence 'Antar, Foreign Minister Mutī' and Culture and Tourism Minister Bādhīb as members.[38] The last three were new to the Council which was enlarged from three to five members. (This had been its original size following the removal of Qaḥtān al-Sha'bī from the Presidency in June 1969. In December 1969, the Presidential Council was reduced from five to three members.)

In several statements which followed, Husnī declared that neither the internal nor the external policies of the PDRY would change. Furthermore, there would be no substantial alteration in the functioning of the governmental institutions nor in the role of the UPONF leadership. He also declared that South Yemen was not interested in hostility with any Arab country and was ready to begin talks with North Yemen and Saudi Arabia "without setting prior conditions."[39]

At the end of July 1978, it was announced that general elections for a new Supreme People's Council would take place in November 1978 to replace the 101-man council appointed by the National Front in 1971.[40]

PURGES, APPOINTMENTS AND PROMOTIONS
Immediately after Rubay''s execution and during the following two months, the regime undertook large-scale purges within the armed forces, the Popular Militia and the various cells and committees of the party, and in the agriculture, fisheries and women's unions. Those regarded as supporters of Rubay' were arrested and

many executed.[41] During this period, there were sporadic clashes between government forces and rebels loyal to Rubay'. This occurred mainly in the Second, Third and Fourth Governorates where tribesmen and army units opposed to the regime co-operated with subversive organizations which operated across the Saudi Arabian and North Yemeni borders. (For further details about the subversive organizations, see *Middle East Record, 1969–70*, pp. 703–7 and *MECS 1976–77*, p. 554.) This led to a further deterioration in relations with North Yemen and Saudi Arabia. Some army officers were also reported to have defected to the YAR and to Oman.[42]

At the same time, there were extensive promotions and appointments, especially in the supreme command of the armed forces, in the Popular Militia and in the Internal Security and Defence ministries. In early July, Defence Minister 'Antar and Interior Minister Muslih were promoted to the rank of Colonel. New deputy chiefs-of-staff were appointed, as well as new commanders for the Air Force and the Popular Militia.[43] Other appointments carried out in July and August included deputy ministers, governors, commissioners and secretaries of the UPONF cells in the hinterland. A new Public Prosecutor was also appointed.[44]

OPPOSITION TO THE REGIME
Opposition to the regime in the period under review emanated mainly from the expelled South Yemeni leaders, the most active of whom were the former FLOSY Secretary-General, 'Abd al-Qawwī Makkāwī, and the former Prime Minister, Muhammad 'Alī Haytham (see *MECS 1976–77*, p. 554). Both were backed, politically and financially, by Saudi Arabia, North Yemen and Egypt.

Makkāwī headed the "United National Front of South Yemen" (*al-jabha al-wataniyya al-muttahida li-janūb al-yaman*), which was set up in Cairo some time in early 1978. He denounced South Yemen's full alignment with the Soviet Union, came out against Communist infiltration into the Arabian Peninsula and the Horn of Africa, condemned the Aden regime for providing the Soviets with naval bases, and accused East Germans and Cuban experts of torturing "thousands of detainees." Makkāwī called for the Arab world's "immediate intervention" to save the people of South Yemen from the "new Soviet imperialism."[45] He also accused the South Yemeni leaders of participating in international terrorist acts, such as the assassination of the Egyptian journalist and author Yūsuf al-Sibā'ī (see chapter on Egypt).[46]

The United National Front was reorganized at the beginning of June 1978. Makkāwī was re-elected its leader; Haytham became his deputy; and the eldest son of the former South Yemeni President, Qahtān al-Sha'bī, was made Secretary-General. Cairo was chosen as the headquarters of the Front, which planned to open branches in some Arab and other Islamic capitals. It was also reported that the Front intended to organize a military wing which would include South Yemeni military expatriates living in several Arab countries.[47] In July 1978, after the leaders of both the Yemen's had been killed, Makkāwī claimed that large numbers of Soviet, Cuban and South Yemeni troops were concentrated on the borders between the two Yemens and Saudi Arabia, as well as close to the Bāb al-Mandab straits.[48]

Various underground and subversive organizations continued to operate in the period under review, mainly with the Saudi and North Yemeni forces (see below). At the beginning of July 1978, an opposition radio station began broadcasting under the name "Radio of Freedom from Inside South Yemen."[49]

FOREIGN AFFAIRS
RELATIONS WITH SAUDI ARABIA
Diplomatic relations between the PDRY and Saudi Arabia were suspended in

November 1977, having only been established in March 1976 (see *MECS 1976–77*, p. 556). The rupture highlighted the deterioration in their relations, particularly from October 1977. The main reason for this was Aden's increasingly important role as supporter of the Ethiopian military regime in the Horn of Africa conflict. The Saudis accused the PDRY of allowing itself to be turned into a staging post for Soviet and other aid to Ethiopia. The strengthening of ties between the PDRY and the Communist bloc—which was also reflected in the growing weight of the anti-Saudi group within the UPONF—further aggravated the situation. The failure of Riyadh's efforts at softening the rigid pro-Communist orientation of the South Yemeni regime exacerbated an already inflamed situation. In the beginning of 1978, Saudi Arabia was reported to have taken the following measures against the PDRY. Firstly, all economic aid was withdrawn.[50] Secondly, an attempt was made to consolidate a unified front (consisting of the Gulf states) against the PDRY's policy in the Horn of Africa.[51] Thirdly, the exiled South Yemeni tribal and military forces opposed to the regime were remobilized. These forces—almost completely inactive since the Saudi-South Yemeni reconciliation in March 1976—were now massed in the Wadī'a area close to the North Yemeni-South Yemeni-Saudi Arabian border. During the first three months of 1978 there were reports of military clashes in the region.[52]

At the end of March 1978, the PDRY Prime Minister visited Kuwait, which from time to time had offered its good offices to reduce the tension between South Yemen and Saudi Arabia. Ḥusnī was urged by the Kuwaitis to try to improve relations with Riyadh.[53] Consequently, the PDRY sent its Interior Minister, Qāsim Ṣāliḥ Musliḥ to Saudi Arabia on 8 April 1978 to meet with King Khālid Ibn 'Abd al-'Azīz and with the Saudi Minister of Interior, Nā'if Ibn 'Abd al-'Azīz. All that was publicly revealed about the talks was that they covered co-operation in security and police affairs.[54] However, relations between the two countries continued to be very strained, a situation which was reflected in Saudi Arabia's refusal to implement the agreement to refine Saudi oil in Aden; this had been signed in May 1977 during the short period of relatively improved relations.[55]

The Saudis regarded the victory of 'Abd al-Fattāḥ Ismā'īl not merely as a personal or domestic change—but as a threat to the traditional system of the whole of the Arabian Peninsula.[56] At the beginning of July, the PDRY Foreign Minister, Muḥammad Mutī', accused the Saudis of reinforcing their troops along their border with South Yemen,[57] and of instigating and supporting the North Yemeni forces against PDRY.[58] He stated: "All that is being broadcast and published about relations between us will not affect our desire to establish a normal relationship. . . . We will . . . continue to ask them to listen to us so that we may explain our policy . . . which is firm and which has remained unchanged following the recent events."[59] However, relations between the states continued strained in the following several months.

RELATIONS WITH NORTH YEMEN

With the assassination of North Yemen's ruler Ibrāhīm al-Ḥamdī in October 1977, the YAR's policy of seeking a *rapprochement* with South Yemen while retaining a clear pro-Saudi orientation came to an end (for both, see chapter on North Yemen). His successor, Ḥusayn al-Ghashmī, adopted an absolute pro-Saudi line, which ensured tension between the two Yemens. In December 1977, the South Yemeni Prime Minister described relations between the two states as "good and developing"; he dismissed reports of military clashes between them as "rumours aimed at creating confusion."[60] In the period that followed, however, relations between the Yemens oscillated between two extremes, statements about friendship and calls for unity alternating with expressions of hostility accompanied by outbreaks of border clashes. (For proposals to unite both Yemens as a constant backdrop to relations, see *MECS 1976-77*, p. 660.) The assassination of Ghashmī and subsequent events in Aden in June 1978 led to a sharp rise in tension between the two states. The North Yemenis severed relations with the PDRY on 24 June 1978, accusing the "criminal clique" of 'Abd al-Fattāḥ Ismā'īl of planning and committing the assassination.[61] The Adeni authorities strongly denied any involvement and condemned the "treacherous methods" which had been used.[62] The Arab League, which convened on 2 July 1978 in Cairo in compliance with a North Yemeni request, held the PDRY responsible for Ghashmī's assassination and decided to freeze political relations with it and suspend economic aid[63] (see essay on Inter-Arab Relations).

The assassination of Ghashmī and the subsequent purges in South Yemen led to a renewal of the border fighting at the end of June and beginning of July. While North Yemen accused the South of amassing troops on the common border, the latter counter-charged that the YAR was mobilizing subversive Adeni organizations. In early July, South Yemen recaptured two border villages in the Bayḥān area in the Fourth Governorate which it claimed had previously been occupied by North Yemeni troops.[64] The North announced that 700 South Yemeni military men from the 'Abbās brigade deployed in Bayḥān, as well as three South Yemeni pilots, had defected to the North (probably as a consequence of the fighting as well as the purges by 'Abd al-Fattāḥ Ismā'īl).[65] This was later denied by Muṭī'.[66]

In an effort to avoid being isolated, the PDRY persisted in its attempts to reach a reconciliation with North Yemen. Thus, the Adeni authorities made great efforts to convince the YAR that it was only Rubay' who had been involved in the assassination plot against Ghashmī.[67] North Yemen's reaction was that reconciliation with the Marxist regime of the PDRY would be possible only if "foreign intervention is eradicated in South Yemen."[68] On 11 July 1978, the South Yemeni Foreign Minister declared that "we have extended our hands and they remain extended to our brothers in San'ā for dialogue on our various problems and their peaceful solution."[69] Several days later the South Yemeni Presidential Council stated that such a dialogue should be based on the following principles:

(1) "The halting of propaganda campaigns and their replacement by responsible information."

(2) "The withdrawal of the troops massed on borders between the two parts [i.e. the two Yemens] wherever they are, the removal of sabotage camps, and the halting of provocations, in order to preserve our people from a destructive war."

(3) "The opening of borders and the resumption of land, air and sea communications and the restoration of life."

(4) "The resumption of economic activity and trade exchanges between the two parts of Yemen."[70]

South Yemen also informed the Arab League of its willingness to receive any Arab mission sent to investigate the situation on its border with North Yemen, on condition that the Arab League reconsider its "boycott decisions" against PDRY.[71] High-ranking South Yemeni officials also declared their willingness to settle disputes peacefully in order not to heighten tension. They accused the "warmongers" of being "enthusiastic about fighting among Yemenis . . . only the enemies of the Yemeni people are pushing for it."[72] In mid-August 1978, the PDRY denied a North Yemeni accusation that several of its naval units had violated YAR territorial waters on 14 August.[73] At the beginning of September 1978, North and

South again began accusing each other of massing troops. The new Chairman of the North Yemeni Presidential Council, 'Alī 'Abdallah Sālih, declared that the PDRY was "hindering union" between the two states, and that "the cruel and conspiring group ruling Aden" was trying "to impose a foreign and abnormal ideology on the Muslim people of Yemen." [74]

RELATIONS WITH OMAN

One of the controversial issues within the UPONF was its attitude towards continuing support for the rebels in Dhufar (see *MECS 1976-77*, p. 557). While Rubay' favoured the reduction of public support for the Popular Front for the Liberation of Oman (PFLO), as part of his efforts to improve relations with the other Peninsula states, 'Abd al-Fattāh Ismā'īl advocated continued aid to the rebels. Since the latter prevailed, South Yemen support continued and relations with Oman suffered accordingly.

In 1976-77, Saudi Arabia—apprehensive that renewed fighting in Dhufar might increase Oman's dependence on Iran—as well as Kuwait had tried to arrange for reconciliation between Oman and PDRY, but with little effect. [75] Oman's ruler, Sultān Qābūs, said in November 1977 that relations would only improve when South Yemen's leaders "cease their attempts to interfere in the internal affairs of Oman, and decide that their duty to the Arab family to which they belong transcends their obedience to the foreign influences to which they have delivered up their country." [76]

Following several mediation attempts by the Kuwaitis, the South Yemeni Prime Minister said in December 1977 that "before thinking of mediation between Oman and PDRY, there should be complete withdrawal of the Iranian forces and of foreign bases in general from Oman." He added: "We in the PDRY are not the only target, because the presence of such bases threatens the safety and security of all the people in the area." [77]

In February and again in May 1978, 'Abd al-Fattāh Ismā'īl accused Iran and "imperialism" (i.e. the US and Saudi Arabia) of trying to control the Gulf and the Arabian Peninsula "by direct invasion" in Oman against the will of the Omani people. [78] Although Ismā'īl was expected to continue support for the Dhufar rebels after assuming power, it was reported that as of August 1978, the PDRY had suspended "the transmission of programmes hostile" to Oman. This measure was interpreted as part of PDRY's continuing desire to break out of its isolation in the Arabian Peninsula. [79] However, there were reports from sources sympathetic to the PFLO which claimed that aid had not been suspended (see chapter on the Gulf principalities).

RELATIONS WITH OTHER ARAB COUNTRIES

President Sādāt's visit to Jerusalem and the subsequent Egyptian-Israeli negotiations led to a sharp rise in the already prevailing tension between Egypt and South Yemen (see essay on Inter-Arab Relations). "Sādāt's apostasy" was strongly condemned as a "Zionist-American" solution which ignores the "progressive front" of the PLO. [80] Consequently, on 7 December 1977, the PDRY severed diplomatic relations with Cairo, claiming that several hundred South Yemeni students had been imprisoned, tortured, subjected to "inhuman treatment" and expelled from Egypt. [81] Throughout the following months South Yemen was an active participant in the Tripoli bloc (see essay on Inter-Arab Relations) and continued to maintain close relations with its members. It stressed the need of joint Arab action which should be preceded by the "closing of the road opened between Cairo and Jerusalem and the unequivocal proclamation of the renunciation of the policy of capitulation followed by Sādāt." [82]

The PDRY announced in December 1977 that it had decided to withdraw its 700-man contingent from the Arab Deterrent Force in Lebanon.[83] A Lebanese attempt to convince PDRY to postpone this action failed, and in mid-January 1978 the South Yemeni force returned to Aden.[84] Gulf sources alleged that the contingent was sent directly to Ethiopia—without even passing through Aden; other sources claimed that the PDRY units had been pulled out from Lebanon because of South Yemen's domestic problems.[85]

RELATIONS WITH SOVIET UNION
The struggle for influence in South Yemen between Saudi Arabia and the Soviet Union continued during the second half of 1977 and the first half of 1978, with the Soviets making a special effort to strengthen their relations with the anti-Saudi faction in the leadership, headed by 'Abd al-Fattāḥ Ismā'īl. One way of doing this was to support the ailing South Yemeni economy. For instance, the Soviet Union continued to refine 400,000 barrels a year in the Aden refinery as a contribution to keeping it in operation. But according to the Soviet ambassador to Kuwait, Moscow had no intention of increasing this quantity because it had many oil commitments and because "no profit was gained from this operation."[86] The Soviet decision to patronize the South Yemeni oil refinery probably contributed to the Saudis' subsequent decisions not to refine its oil in Aden as agreed in May 1977.

In November 1977, the USSR was reported to be exerting pressure in an attempt to gain the right to use the Aden port facilities for military purposes. The pressure was said to have increased following the cancellation by Somalia of her friendship treaty with the Soviet Union in November 1977. The Soviets were also alleged to have asked for full use of the Khormaksar Airport in Aden for military and civilian purposes, and for the right to set up communication centres on PDRY territory. In return, South Yemen was to receive financial aid and more sophisticated military equipment. In December 1977, a massive Soviet arms shipment began to arrive in Aden for aerial transport to Ethiopia. (For Saudi apprehension over these developments, see chapter on Saudi Arabia.)[87] At the same time, rumours which had been circulating for some time that the islands of Perim and Suqotra had become Soviet bases intensified.[88]

At the beginning of February 1978, Prime Minister Ḥusnī visited Moscow, where he signed an economic and technical co-operation agreement.[89] Arab sources commented that Soviet economic aid, which had been reduced in 1976 when the PDRY established relations with Saudi Arabia, had since increased. There were unconfirmed reports that the USSR would boost its aid by 400% by 1980. The increase in Soviet aid was particularly important because of Saudi Arabia's withdrawal of its financial aid (see above), and Kuwait's failure to stand by earlier promises of financial and economic aid on the grounds that the PDRY had not "modified her militant and pro-Soviet foreign policy."[90]

Throughout the period under review, co-operation between the UPONF and the Communist Party of the Soviet Union (CPSU), continued. In March 1978, a protocol on co-operation in 1978–79 was signed in Aden covering the exchange of information on methods of party organization and the training of party cadres.[91] In April 1978, the number of Soviet advisers in PDRY was estimated at 1,100 and increasing.[92] Later, in June 1978, their number was estimated at c. 2,500, mainly engaged in a major build-up of the South Yemeni armed forces.[93]

The Soviet Admiral of the Fleet, Sergei Gorshkov, arrived in Aden on 18 May 1978.[94] According to several sources, a secret 15-year military co-operation agreement was signed, providing for the construction of a naval base which would offer the Soviet fleet facilities for repairs, storage, communications and monitoring. According to several sources, the Soviets had also undertaken to construct an airforce base for the South Yemenis, which would also offer facilities for the Soviet airforce. The Soviets agreed to supply the PDRY with 30 MiG aircraft of an unspecified type, five coastal patrol boats and a major radar network to cover parts of the Gulf and southern Saudi Arabia. The agreement also reportedly stipulated that the Soviet Union would come to the aid of PDRY in the event of foreign aggression. Another provision of the agreement was the construction of a large medical complex in Aden since its medical facilities "proved inadequate to the needs of the Cuban and Soviet wounded in African wars." [95] Soviet and Cuban aid, especially in the form of air support, was considered to have been a determining factor in 'Abd al-Fattāḥ Ismā'īl's victory over Rubay' at the end of June (see above).

At the end of July, Ḥusnī affirmed that the Soviet Union was granting economic assistance to his country and was strengthening its defence ability. He rejected the "fabrications alleging that the PDRY is in turn granting certain naval advantages" to the Soviet Union, and denied that the islands of Perim and Suqotra had become Soviet bases. [96] The good relations between the PDRY and the Soviet Union also extended to Eastern bloc countries. This was reflected in the presence of c. 500 East Germans who were responsible for organizing the police and security departments, [97] and of 80 Bulgarian experts who reportedly were helping to reorganize the party. [98]

RELATIONS WITH CUBA
Cuba was considered to have played an active role in the internal political struggle within the UPONF which ended in the victory of 'Abd al-Fattāḥ Ismā'īl's group (see above). [99] Reports that 500–600 Cuban soldiers had arrived in Aden from Ethiopia to strengthen the Popular Militia units loyal to 'Abd al-Fattāḥ Ismā'īl were denied as "baseless" by the South Yemeni embassy in Kuwait, [100] which added that the PDRY was "perfectly capable of ensuring the protection of its revolution by itself." [101] In mid-1978, the estimated number of Cubans in the country ranged between 700 and 1,200. [102] In July, Ḥusnī said that a small number of Cuban experts were in the Popular Militia, but that they were about to finish their task. [103] On 20 August 1978, R Aden announced that a Cuban party delegation had arrived in Aden. [104] According to Arab sources in Cairo, units of the Soviet fleet which arrived in Aden Port on 18 August landed a Cuban force estimated at 500 fully-equipped soldiers. The Cubans—who arrived "to keep the situation in South Yemen under control"—left for the North Yemeni border where they took up positions. [105]

INVOLVEMENT IN THE HORN OF AFRICA
South Yemen's continued involvement in the Horn of Africa led to a further deterioration in its relations with Saudi Arabia (see *MECS 1976–77*, p. 560, and above). Several hundred South Yemenis together with Cuban military experts were reported to be operating Soviet weapons and providing logistic support to the Ethiopians fighting in Eritrea and the Ogaden. [106] In March 1978, Prime Minister Ḥusnī denied that the PDRY had sent troops to fight on the Ethiopian side, stating that his government called for a peaceful settlement between Ethiopia and Somalia. He also rejected as "completely unfounded" the allegation that South Yemeni pilots had flown jets for the Ethiopian air force. [107]

The Chairman of the Ethiopian Provisional Government, Lt-Col Mengistu Haile Mariam, visited the PDRY in April for talks on the situation in the Horn of Africa. [108] Also in April it was reported that the Eritrean Liberation Front had captured a South Yemeni pilot who was flying for the Ethiopian air force against

Eritrea. The pilot was interrogated and then handed over to the UAE authorities who were asked to return him to Aden.[109]

At the beginning of June 1978, shortly before Rubay' was executed, South Yemen was reported to have withdrawn its forces from Ethiopia.[110]

RELATIONS WITH THE US

The contacts between South Yemen and the US towards restoring diplomatic relations continued throughout 1977 and in the first half of 1978. These had been severed in 1969 (see *MECS 1976–77*, p. 560). In January 1978, *al-Qabas* reported that Rubay' had sent an unofficial request to the US seeking the resumption of diplomatic relations.[111] A four-man US delegation was expected to arrive in Aden at the end of June 1978 to discuss the resumption of diplomatic relations and presumably to suggest that the US could reduce South Yemen's complete dependence on Moscow.[112] But with the execution of Rubay', who was the main supporter of the resumption of relations, the planned visit was cancelled. Observers commenting on the June events in Aden said that the Soviets now had a "free hand"[113] and that the US had suffered a setback in its attempt to reduce Soviet influence[114] in this strategic area which was vital to its security interests.[115]

The South Yemeni Foreign Minister said on 10 July 1978 that his country was prepared to start a dialogue with the US.[116] In August, the Carter Administration was disturbed by prospects of further radicalization in the PDRY as a result of 'Abd al-Fattāh Ismā'īl's seizure of power; it was reported to have concluded that there was no point in trying to pursue the renewal of diplomatic relations with PDRY in the present circumstances.[117]

ECONOMIC AFFAIRS ($1 = 0.342 Yemeni Dinars; £1 = YD 0.716)

The PDRY's economic performance appears to have improved in 1977.[118] Fragmentary evidence for 1978 reveals, however, that the relative success may have been only transitory. For a country not endowed with vast amounts of any valuable natural resources, government policy is a major determinant of economic performance. By acting against the improvement of relations with Saudi Arabia, the Aden authorities witnessed the suspension of much-needed aid. When, for political reasons, the Arab League undertook a boycott of the PDRY, the South Yemeni finance minister tried to minimize its potentially adverse effects by claiming that remittances from Yemenis working abroad—an important component of the balance of payments—would continue and that the Soviet Union, with whom Aden had signed an economic agreement in the first half of 1978, would compensate for much of the Arab aid which was subject to suspension. (For details of the political aspects of these developments, see above and the essay on "Inter-Arab Relations"). Similar scepticism of the impact of the boycott was expressed by some reputable foreign sources.[119]

One area of economic activity which has benefited the PDRY economy since independence and whose contribution did not appear to suffer in 1978 was the port of Aden.[120]

AGRICULTURE

Agricultural production registered mixed results in 1976–77, according to Ministry of Agriculture and Agrarian Reform data. Output of some major crops, such as cotton (–39.6%) and sorghum and millet (–18.1%), fell considerably, while that of others, such as wheat (+23.6%) and vegetables (+19.6%), gained impressively from 1975–76. Most other crops registered little change, with the result that, on overall average, agricultural output failed to increase in calendar 1977, while food production, as measured by the FAO, fell 1% during the year.[121] In addition, fish production failed to register an increase in 1977.[122]

INDUSTRY

South Yemen's industrial sector is small scale, but growing. Production in almost all industries rose in 1977: in percentage terms, output of machinery spare parts (246%), salt (176%), and dairy products (31%) increased dramatically from 1976. It should be noted, however, that given the relatively small base upon which these percentages are computed, actual growth is less spectacular than it may appear.

MONETARY DEVELOPMENTS

Aden's holdings of international reserves increased during each of the first seven months of 1978, reaching $163.5m at the end of July. Composed almost exclusively of foreign exchange, these international reserves registered a 63% total gain during the course of the January-July 1978 period.

At the end of May 1978, Aden's net foreign assets amounted to a record YD 48.8m, or nearly double the end-December 1977 total of YD 24.8m. Almost all of this increase in foreign assets was accumulated by the Central Bank.

Domestic credit, both in the form of net claims on the government and claims on the private sector, expanded only marginally during the first five months of 1978. At the same time, the money supply grew 11%. More than one-third of the money supply growth was registered in the month of January alone, as the rate of increase showed afterwards.[123]

BALANCE OF PAYMENTS

Aden's balance of payments moved from a deficit to a surplus in 1977, according to preliminary data from the Bank of Yemen. The major reasons for this improvement are the growth in remittances from Yemenis working abroad and the increase in grants and loans received by the government.

The growing trade deficit, as evidenced by the fact that imports reached a level more than seven-fold that of exports in 1977 (cf a factor of 6.4 in 1976) bodes poorly for South Yemen in the near future. Moreover, the government's disputes with its neighbours have resulted in a suspension of aid which, despite assertions to the contrary, will most likely have a negative impact on the payments position in the short run, if not longer.[124]

FOREIGN TRADE

According to data compiled by the International Monetary Fund on the basis of extrapolated or derived accounts, Aden's foreign trade picture worsened considerably in 1977, as imports jumped 74% while exports plummeted to less than one-third of their 1976 total. Virtually all of the lost export trade was with Canada, though there do not appear to be any published explanations for this curious development. Trade with Canada aside, Aden's three leading markets for exports in 1977 were North Yemen (21.6%), Japan (15.1%), and the United Arab Emirates (11.6%).

On the import side, Japan (17.8%) passed Kuwait (13.3%) to become the PDRY's principal source of imports in 1977, while the UK (8.9%) remained third.[125]

Machinery and transport equipment overtook food and live animals to become the leading commodity group of imports during the first half of 1977. At the same time, petroleum products from the Aden refinery and fish were the country's largest exports.

Haim Shaked and Tamar Yegnes
Economic section by **Ira E. Hoffman**

THE PEOPLE'S DEMOCRATIC REPUBLIC OF YEMEN

ARMED FORCES
Total armed forces number 20,900. Defence expenditure in 1978 was 19m South
Yemeni dinars ($56m). Military service is compulsory for 18 months. The 19,000-
strong Army consists of ten infantry brigades, each of three battalions; two armoured battalions; five artillery battalions; ones signals unit and one training
battalion. Equipment consists of 260 T-34, T-54 medium tanks; ten *Saladin* armoured cars; ten *Ferret* scout cars; BTR-40-152 armoured personnel carriers; 25
pounder, 105mm pack, 122mm, 130mm howitzers; 120mm mortars; 122mm
recoilless rifles; 37mm, 57mm, 85mm ZSU-23-4 self-propelled anti-aircraft guns;
SA-7 surface-to-air missiles. The Navy, which is subordinate to the Army, numbers
600 and is equipped with three large patrol craft (ex-Soviet, two SO-1, one
Poluchat); two motor torpedo boats (ex-Soviet P-6 class); three minesweepers (ex-
British *Ham*-class); four small patrol craft (under 100 tons), and two landing craft,
tank (ex-Soviet *Polnocny*-class). The Air Force numbers 1,300 and is equipped with
34 combat aircraft (some believed to be in storage). Formations consist of one light
bomber squadron with seven 11-28; one interceptor squadron with 12 MiG-21F,
one fighter ground-attack squadron with 15 MiG-17; one transport squadron with
four 11-14, three An-24; AA-2 *Atoll* air-to-air missiles; one helicopter squadron
with eight Mi-8, some Mi-4 and three MiG-15UTI trainers. Paramilitary forces
consist of the Popular Militia and the 15,000 Public Security Force.

Source: *The Military Balance 1978-79* (London: International Institute for Strategic Studies).

BALANCE OF PAYMENTS (million SDRs)

	1975	1976	Preliminary 1977
A. Goods, Services and Private Transfers	−71.5	−83.5	−98.0
Exports, fob	16.2	38.4	43.6
Imports, cif	−150.2	−247.8	−314.9
Services, (net)	16.5	26.1	19.8
Private Transfers	46.0	99.8	153.5
B. Grants and Loans Received by Government	34.0	90.2	125.9
C. Miscellaneous Capital	9.1	—	—
D. Net Errors and Omissions	9.1	−17.4	−3.7
Overall Balance (A through D)	**−19.3**	**−10.7**	**31.6**

Source: Bank of Yemen.

INTERNATIONAL LIQUIDITY (million US dollars at end of period)

	1976	1977	(Jan–June) 1978
International Reserves	82.22	100.56	150.59
Gold	0.69	1.24	1.26
SDRs	3.53	4.32	4.40
Foreign Exchange	78.00	95.00	144.93
Commercial Banks: Assets	29.76	68.56	72.03*
Liabilities	51.30	48.73	23.31*

*end of May.

MONETARY SURVEY (million Yemen dinars at end of period)

	1976	1977	(Jan–May) 1978
Foreign Assets (net)	7.24	24.84	48.79
Domestic Credit	88.64	119.58	121.46
Claims on Government (net)	60.14	72.51	73.33
Claims on Private Sector	28.50	47.07	48.13
Money	81.51	115.24	128.19
Quasi-money	21.33	35.48	33.35
Other Items (net)	–6.94	–6.29	8.71
Money, Seasonally Adjusted	82.84	117.23	128.19

GOVERNMENT FINANCE (million Yemen dinars; year beginning 1 April)

	1974–75	1975–76	1976–77
A. Revenue	18.13	13.86	24.76
B. Expenditure	27.45	25.55	39.15
Balance (A–B)	**–9.32**	**–11.69**	**–14.39**
Financing			
Net Borrowing	9.32	11.69	14.39

Source (of three preceding tables): IMF, *International Financial Statistics*.

CENTRAL GOVERNMENT EXPENDITURES (thousand Yemeni dinars)

	Actual 1976	*Provisional* 1977
General administration	9,701	10,909
Defence and security	17,134	18,928
Education and guidance	6,332	8,257
Health	2,244	2,445
Social services	460	441
Community services	642	1,220
Economic services	2,317	1,694
Public works and communications	*1,464*	*772*
Agriculture	*853*	*992*
Debt service	324	597
Total	**39,154**	**44,491**

Source: Ministry of Finance.

GROSS DOMESTIC PRODUCT AT CURRENT MARKET PRICES (million Yemeni dinars)

	1974	1975	1976
Agriculture and fisheries	17.16	17.72	24.53
Manufacturing, mining and quarrying*	13.86	6.78	9.34
Electricity and water	1.02	1.93	2.00
Construction	5.64	8.68	10.37
Trade, hotels and restaurants	17.67	19.24	22.95
Transport, storage and communications	8.26	9.55	13.48
Finance, insurance and real estate	3.55	3.01	3.87
Business and personal services	3.44	4.02	4.21
Government services	16.54	18.27	21.47
GDP at factor cost**	**87.15**	**89.19**	**112.33**
Plus: Indirect taxes	*12.77*	*12.98*	*19.04*
Less: Subsidies	*–2.37*	*–2.28*	*–1.63*
GDP at market prices**	**97.55**	**99.90**	**129.74**

*Includes petroleum refining.
**Totals may differ from sum of parts because of rounding.
Source: Central Statistical Organization.

AGRICULTURAL PRODUCTION (production in thousand tons; area in thousand acres)

	1974-75	1975-76	1976-77
Cotton			
production	10.8	8.1	4.9
area	28.0	22.1	13.1
Wheat			
production	20.8	23.3	28.8*
area	28.8	31.6	36.0
Sorghum and millet			
production	72.0	73.3	60.0*
area	114.0	115.0	90.0*
Vegetables			
production	48.5	56.7	67.8
Area	9.5	10.3	11.3
Fodder			
production	275.0	325.0	364.0
area	18.3	19.4	20.1

*Preliminary.
Source: Ministry of Agriculture and Agrarian Reform.

INDEX OF PRODUCTION OF MAJOR INDUSTRIES (1973 = 100)

	1974	1975	1976	1977
Machinery spare parts	130	132	141	488
Salt	80	16	85	235
Water	88	98	93	98
Soft drinks	120	127	160	173
Shirts	113	144	169	249
Dairy products	120	452	692	906
Electric power (Aden)	99	104	113	...
Paints	174	201	222	297
Vegetable oils	75	52	63	...
Aluminium utensils	109	197	294	313
Cotton linters	84	93	68	42

Source: Derived from Central Statistical Organization sources.

COMPOSITION OF EXPORTS (thousand Yemeni dinars)

	1975	1976	Jan-June 1977
Petroleum products	24	5,262	4,273
Fresh fish	1,472	3,907	1,646
Cotton linters and seeds	472	3,565	1,117
Coffee	669	1,170	588
Salt	52	99	120
Hides and skins	226	222	93
Dried fish	182	123	23
Other food and live animals	269	440	1,378
Total (including others)	**3,906**	**15,496**	**9,565**

COMPOSITION OF IMPORTS (thousand Yemeni dinars)

	1975	1976	Jan–June 1977
Food and live animals	21,940	22,235	13,601
Beverages and tobacco	955	1,242	454
Crude materials, inedible, except fuels	1,970	2,531	1,270
Petroleum products	11,641	21,189	11,330
Animal and vegetable oils	683	730	2,634
Chemicals	2,875	3,221	1,766
Manufactured goods classified chiefly by materials	10,602	11,368	5,562
Machinery and transport equipment	10,316	20,103	17,987
Miscellaneous manufactured articles	1,198	2,393	1,148
Unclassified items	54	95	—
Total	**62,114**	**85,107**	**55,752**

Source (of two preceding tables): Central Statistical Organization.

DIRECTION OF TRADE (million US dollars)

	1975	1976	1977
Exports to:*			
North Yemen (YAR)	15.22	11.04	23.72
Japan	7.03	24.92	16.56
United Arab Emirates	9.13	0.09	12.71
China PR	6.57	7.23	7.88
Saudi Arabia	0.58	3.34	6.10
Canada	229.71	244.67	5.57
France	0.05	0.12	4.09
Sri Lanka	2.93	3.22	3.52
Zaïre	2.71	2.98	3.25
Italy	0.48	3.30	3.00
Total (including others)	**333.89**	**333.37**	**109.78**
Imports from:*			
Japan	23.05	42.16	86.86
Kuwait	41.43	55.92	64.81
United Kingdom	20.52	24.23	43.38
United States	3.08	5.50	34.10
Australia	2.68	6.96	25.09
Netherlands	6.24	13.55	24.48
Italy	4.57	12.84	20.34
West Germany	2.52	8.42	18.83
Saudi Arabia	0.02	7.95	15.87
France	2.90	11.62	13.74
Total (including others)	**180.32**	**280.57**	**488.79**

*Data partly extrapolated and/or derived from partner country.
Source: IMF, Direction of Trade.

NOTES
1. R Aden, 2 August—British Broadcasting Corporation, Summary of World Broadcasts (BBC), 4 August 1977.
2. Al-Sayyād, Beirut; 15 September 1977.
3. Middle East News Agency (MENA), Cairo; 24 October—BBC, 26 October 1977.
4. R Aden, 16 November—BBC, 18 November 1977.
5. Fourteenth October, Aden; 18 November 1977.
6. Arabia and the Gulf, London; 15 May; Fourteenth October, 28 May 1978.
7. R Aden, 13 October, 28 December—Daily Report (DR), 14 October; BBC, 30 December 1977.
8. Fourteenth October, 28 February, 17, 24 May; Al-Thawrī, Aden; 15, 22 April 1978.
9. R Aden, 4 January—BBC, 8 January 1978.

10. R Aden, 7 March—BBC, 9 March 1978.
11. *Al-Ahrām*, Cairo; 9 March 1978.
12. *Al-Siyāsa*, Kuwait; 26 April 1978.
13. *October*, Cairo; 7 May; *al-Siyāsa*, 25 May 1978.
14. *Fourteenth October*, 30 May 1978.
15. R Aden, 7 June—DR, 8 June 1978.
16. *Al-Safīr*, Beirut; 27 June 1978.
17. *Al-Anbā*, Kuwait; 24 June 1978.
18. R Aden, 26 June—BBC, 28 June 1978.
19. *Al-Nahār*, Beirut; 27 June 1978.
20. Iraqi News Agency (INA), 26 June—BBC, 28 June 1978.
21. *Ibid.*
22. Qatari News Agency (QNA), 27 June, 6 July—BBC, 29 June, 8 July; *al-Liwā'*, Beirut; 28 June; *al-Anbā*, 28 June; *International Herald Tribune (IHT)*, Paris; 27 June 1978.
23. R Aden, 26 June—BBC, 28 June 1978.
24. R Aden, 26 June—DR, 27 June 1978.
25. Agence France Presse (AFP), 26 June—DR, 27 June 1978.
26. R Aden, 26 June—DR, 27 June 1978.
27. *Ākhir Sā'a*, Cairo; 5 July 1978.
28. R Aden, 26 June—BBC, 28 June 1978.
29. QNA, 27 June—BBC, 29 June 1978.
30. *Financial Times (FT)*, London; 28 June 1978.
31. INA, 27 June—BBC, 28 June 1978.
32. QNA, 27 June—BBC, 29 June; *FT*, 29 June 1978.
33. *Al-Ra'y al-'Amm*, Kuwait; 28 June 1978.
34. R Aden, 28, 29 June—DR, 29, 30 June 1978.
35. *FT*, 28 June; *Arabia and the Gulf*, 17 July 1978.
36. *The Times*, London; 27 June; *IHT*, 28 June; *al-Ittihād*, Abu Dhabi; 29 June; *Arabia and the Gulf*, 17 July 1978.
37. MENA, 26 June; *The Times*, 27 June 1978.
38. R Aden, 1 July—DR, 3 July 1978.
39. AFP, 7 July—DR, 10 July; R Aden, 11 July—DR, 12 July 1978.
40. R Aden, 14 June—BBC, 16 June; R Aden, 30 July 1978.
41. *Al-Ittihād*, 29 June; *FT*, 29 June; *The Guardian*, London; 30 June; *al-Qabas*, Kuwait; 10 July; *al-Nahār*, 29 July 1978.
42. R Cairo, 1 July—BBC, 3 July; QNA, 6 July—BBC, 8 July; Saudi News Agency (SNA), 2 July; *Akhir Sā'a*, 5 July, 23 August 1978.
43. R Aden, 6 July—DR, 7 July 1978.
44. R Aden, 28 June, 4, 7, 9, 31 July, 1, 10, 19 August—DR, 29 June, 5, 10 July; BBC, 10 July, 2, 3, 12, 22 August 1978.
45. MENA, 12 February; *October*, 5, 19, 26 March 1978.
46. *Al-Ahrām*, 21 March 1978.
47. *Al-Anbā*, 3 June 1978.
48. MENA, 12 July—DR, 13 July 1978.
49. SNA, 2 July—BBC, 4 July 1978. For more details concerning clandestine radio stations, see *Middle East Record 1969–70*, p. 1066.
50. *Arabia and the Gulf*, 30 January; *FT*, 27 June 1978.
51. *Al-Manār*, London; 28 January 1978.
52. *Arabia and the Gulf*, 30 January, 6 February, 6 March 1978.
53. *Al-Manār*, 8 April 1978.
54. SNA, 9 April—BBC, 11 April 1978.
55. *Al-Nahār al-'Arabī wal-Duwalī (NAD)*, Paris; 20 May 1978.
56. *Ibid*, 1 July 1978.
57. Reuter, 6 July 1978.
58. *Al-Safīr*, 8 July 1978.
59. QNA, 10 July—BBC, 12 July 1978.
60. *Al-Siyāsa*, 6 December 1977.
61. INA, 24 June; R San'ā, 25 June—BBC, 27 June 1978.
62. R Aden, 25 June—BBC, 26 June 1978.
63. QNA, 2 July—BBC, 4 July 1978.
64. Reuter, 2 July; AFP, 3 July—DR, 5 July; *IHT*, 4 July; MENA, 5 July—DR, 6 July; R San'ā, 10 July—DR, 11 July 1978.
65. Deutsche Presse Agentur (DPA), 30 June; R Riyadh, 2 July; INA, 1 July—BBC, 3 July 1978.
66. QNA, 10 July—BBC, 12 July 1978.

67. Reuter, 4 July 1978.
68. INA, 30 June; *IHT*, 4 July 1978.
69. R Aden, 11 July—DR, 12 July 1978.
70. R Aden, 14 July—BBC, 17 July 1978.
71. INA, 16 July—DR, 17 July 1978.
72. R Aden, 24, 27 July—DR, 25, 28 July; *FT*, 31 July 1978.
73. R San'ā, 15 August—DR, 16 August; R Aden, 18 August—DR, 21 August 1978.
74. Reuter, 3 September 1978.
75. *Arabia and the Gulf*, 24 October 1977.
76. *Ibid*, 7 November 1977.
77. *Al-Siyāsa*, 6 December 1977.
78. R Aden, 5 February—BBC, 7 February; Reuter, 1 May 1978.
79. Gulf News Agency, 14 August 1978.
80. R Aden, 12, 16, 29 December—DR, 13, 20 December 1977, 11 January 1978.
81. R Aden, 10, 14 December—DR, 12 December, BBC, 16 December 1977; *al-Safīr*, 15 January 1978.
82. Algeria Presse Service (APS), 11 April—BBC, 13 April 1978.
83. *Al-Safīr*, 18 December; *The Observer*, London; 18 December 1977.
84. *'Ukāz*, Jidda; 3 January; MENA, 16 January 1978.
85. *Arabia and the Gulf*, 30 January 1978.
86. *Al-Watan*, Kuwait; 29 October 1977.
87. *Arabia and the Gulf*, 28 November, 5 December 1977; *FT*, 17 January 1978.
88. *NAD*, 26 November 1977.
89. R Aden, 5 February—DR, 7 February 1978.
90. *Arabia and the Gulf*, 10 April 1978.
91. R Aden, 15 March—BBC, 17 March 1978.
92. *Arabia and the Gulf*, 10 April 1978.
93. *Akhbār al-Yawm*, Cairo; 17 June 1978.
94. R Aden, 18 May—DR, 19 May 1978.
95. *NAD*, 10 June; *Arabia and the Gulf*, 19 June; MENA, 8 July—BBC, 10 July 1978.
96. *Al-Thawra*, Damascus; 22 July; *Al-Nahār*, 31 July 1978.
97. *Akhbār al-Yawm*, 17 June 1978.
98. SNA, 2 July—DR, 6 July 1978.
99. QNA, 6 July—DR, 7 July 1978.
100. MENA, 28 June—DR, 28 June 1978.
101. AFP, 29 June—DR, 29 June 1978.
102. *Arabia and the Gulf*, 10 April; *Akhbār al-Yawm*, 17 June 1978.
103. *Al-Qabas*, 17 July 1978.
104. R Aden, 20 August—DR, 22 August 1978.
105. *Al-Ra'y*, Amman; 20 August 1978.
106. Reuter, 27 January; *al-Nahār*, 29 April; *Daily Telegraph*, 8 June 1978.
107. *Al-Wathba*, Abu Dhabi; 27 March 1978.
108. INA, 6 April—DR, 7 April 1978.
109. *Arabia and the Gulf*, 10 April 1978.
110. *Ibid*, 12 June; *al-Anbā*, Kuwait, 18 July 1978.
111. *Al-Qabas*, 19 January 1978.
112. *Washington Post*, 3, 28 June; *Al-Manār*, 10 June 1978.
113. *Al-Ahrām*, 27 June 1978.
114. *Christian Science Monitor*, Boston; 28 June 1978.
115. *WP*, 7 July 1978.
116. QNA, 10 July—DR, 10 July 1978.
117. *IHT*, 7 August 1978.
118. For background on South Yemen's economy, see *MECS 1976-77*, pp. 560-63.
119. See *Middle East Economic Digest (MEED)*, London; 14 July 1978; and Economist Intelligence Unit, *Quarterly Economic Review of Bahrain, Qatar, Oman, the Yemens*, No 3, 1978.
120. *The Middle East*, London; September 1978.
121. See *MEED*, 20 October 1978.
122. *The Middle East*, September 1978.
123. International Monetary Fund (IMF), *International Financial Statistics*, October 1978.
124. See *MEED*, 14 July 1978.
125. IMF, *Direction of Trade Annual 1971-1977*.

The Saudi Arabian Kingdom

(Al-Mamlaka al-'Arabiyya al-Sa'ūdiyya)

Two issues dominated the Kingdom's domestic affairs in 1978. One was a carefully concealed power struggle within the Royal Family revolving around the issue of the succession or, more precisely, the issue of who would become Crown Prince after Prince Fahd's eventual accession to the throne. In a characteristically Saudi fashion, it was not only—perhaps not even primarily—a personal rivalry between two or three contenders, but also a struggle over the relative power and standing of two different branches of the Royal Family, each related by kinship through the mothers of the princes, to different tribes. The other problem, which preoccupied spiritual as well as political leaders, was how to prevent the value system of Islam from being eroded by the growing number of aliens whose presence was indispensable to the running of the economy, let alone its expansion. The resulting anxieties led to even stricter insistence on uncompromising observance of the traditional law, both by Saudis and by aliens.

In foreign affairs, Sādāt's initiative and the ensuing political process turned into a challenge to the regime by calling into question basic guidelines which for years had governed the conduct of Saudi Arabia's inter-Arab policies and shaped its attitudes on the Arab-Israeli conflict. Its position as arbiter of Arab affairs, predicated in the first instance on its ability to hold the balance between Egypt and Syria, became untenable as the gulf between them widened. Much against its desire and against the tradition of almost a decade, Saudi Arabia was gradually forced into taking sides in a major inter-Arab dispute. Its negative reaction to the Camp David agreements, with their clear anti-Egyptian implication, ended a period in Saudi inter-Arab policies which had begun after 'Abd al-Nāsir's death in 1970.

Farther afield, events in the Horn of Africa revived fears of Soviet penetration in the Red Sea area which the Saudis felt was likely to spread to the Persian Gulf as well. Saudi Arabia was active in both areas to forestall such developments. However, Saudi-South Yemeni relations, which had seemed well on the way towards significant improvement in 1976, reverted to their earlier state of tension.

All the above themes made themselves felt in Saudi attitudes towards the US: they shaped Saudi expectations of what American policy towards Israel should be, and they made it more urgent than ever to impress on Washington that Saudi Arabia rather than Egypt was able to marshal Arab forces for or against any specific solution to regional problems, and that oil and petrodollars enabled the Kingdom to lend force to its arguments. Finally, they increased Saudi reliance on the US to block Soviet moves in and around the region. In 1978, all these strands merged in the issue of the sale to Riyadh of US F-15 fighter aircraft. The Saudis perceived this as a test of strength between their leverage on Washington and the power of the "Zionist lobby."

POLITICAL AFFAIRS
THE PROBLEM OF THE SUCCESSION
The King's ill health, which became more evident after he underwent two operations in the winter of 1977-78, accentuated one of the major issues in Saudi Arabia—and one least spoken of in public—namely, the question of Royal succession. While a

veil of secrecy prevented any meaningful information from reaching those not immediately involved, it was evident that the issue loomed large and dictated various moves by key figures. The point in question was not who would follow King Khālid Ibn 'Abd al-'Azīz should he die or abdicate: the undisputed successor was the present Crown Prince and First Deputy Prime Minister, Fahd Ibn 'Abd al-'Azīz. Rather, it was the issue of who would become Crown Prince on Fahd's accession. There were contradictory reports on this point. Some claimed that the obvious candidate was Prince 'Abdallah Ibn 'Abd al-'Azīz, Second Deputy Prime Minister and Head of the National Guard. He was reported to be backed by King Khālid and by Prince Muḥammad (the eldest living son of the late King 'Abd al-'Azīz Ibn Sa'ūd and the one held in greatest respect). All three belong to the powerful Jilwā branch of the north-eastern Shammar tribes and were half-brothers of Fahd. Furthermore, 'Abdallah was probably supported by part of the *'ulamā* (the religious notables). According to other reports, Fahd had his own designs, preferring one of his six full brothers from the Sudayrī branch of the family: either Sultān Ibn 'Abd al-'Azīz, Minister of Defence and Aviation and Inspector General of the Army; or the Governor of Riyadh, Salmān Ibn 'Abd al-'Azīz. Both enjoyed the support of several powerful sons of the late King Faysal Ibn 'Abd al-'Azīz, of some younger ministers in the government, and presumably also of part of the *'ulamā*. However, it was assumed that if Fahd had his way, his probable successor would be Sultān.

Despite Fahd's gradual emergence since King Faysal's assassination in March 1975 as the strong man of Saudi Arabia, his ability to impose his will in a question as momentous as that of the succession was affected by two major factors. First, although originally regarded as weak and expected to play only a formal role in the affairs of state, King Khālid proved to be politically more active—at least in domestic affairs—than had been foreseen. Despite ill health, he continued to cultivate connections with tribal chiefs in the traditional royal manner. This probably meant that, if required, he could mobilize their support on behalf of 'Abdallah. Secondly, Fahd was considered by part of the *'ulamā* as too "modernist" and "progressive" and thus dangerous in terms of their traditional Islamic perception of the Saudi Arabian state and society. 'Abdallah, by contrast, was regarded as less inclined towards visions of modernization. Furthermore, some members of the *'ulamā*, as well as some of the princes, feared that if both the King and the Crown Prince were Sudayrī full brothers, altogether too much power would rest with the Sudayrī branch of the Royal Family, to the detriment of the other branches.

In August 1977, it was reported that a Royal Family gathering had decided that King Khālid would go into semi-retirement, retaining the royal title but leaving real power in the hands of Crown Prince Fahd. After Fahd's eventual accession, 'Abdallah was to become Crown Prince. In return for their recognition of 'Abdallah's right to the succession, Fahd and Sultān were said to have demanded that 'Abdallah give up the command of the National Guard then and there. The Guard would then be integrated into the regular armed forces under the command of Sultān. 'Abdallah, who had faced similar demands in the past,[1] opposed this condition since it meant "throwing away his power base now in return for a future promise."[2] Consequently, the proposed arrangement fell through and the succession problem remained unresolved. There were indications that the two contending parties maintained, and even accelerated, their activities to consolidate and broaden their power base. 'Abdallah continued his efforts to expand and modernize the National Guard, procuring more modern weapons and equipment for it, improving training methods and modernizing its infrastructure. In short, he attempted to raise the National Guard to the level of development already achieved by the armed forces under Sultān's command.[3]

The King's continued ill health and the Royal Family preoccupation with his succession kept speculation alive throughout the year. Thus, at the beginning of April 1978, unfounded rumours spread in Arab circles in London that King Khālid had arrived there for medical treatment.[4] Later, in June 1978, his imminent abdication was reported.[5] The King's hospitalization in Ohio for open-heart surgery in October 1978 gave rise to the feeling that, before long, the issue of the succession would become a matter for decision rather than continued speculation.

THE CHALLENGE OF ALIEN RESIDENTS

One major problem confronting Saudi Arabia's rulers and religious notables alike was how to maintain the accelerated pace of economic and technological development which the process of rapid modernization required, while minimizing its harmful effects on traditional Islamic and social values. These conflicting aspirations were in evidence in day-to-day affairs. Many thousands of aliens, of many nationalities and a variety of religious and social patterns, have for several years inundated the sparsely-inhabited country. In addition to the many unskilled labourers, a vast increase has occurred in the number of foreign professionals and other white-collar workers entering the country.[6] Because of the slowness of the training process, it will be many years before these people can be replaced by local staff.

This massive influx of aliens has created growing concern about their cumulative impact on the local population. The Saudi Arabian leadership was worried that such contacts, particularly with Westerners, would not be limited to acquiring modern economic and technological skills, but would extend to the adoption of Western ideas and norms. While this posed a constant major problem to 'ulamā and rulers alike, the latter were also apprehensive that different concepts of government might breed political and social restiveness and undermine their regime.

As regards the political system, the main fear was that, having been exposed to Western influence, educated persons either inside or outside the Royal Family would begin to demand democratic institutions. An abundance of articles published in the Saudi press, written by princes or religious leaders, stressed that the basic values of democracy—equality before the law and social responsibility—were inherent in the sharī'a (the traditional Islamic law). There was no need, they argued, to seek these values through political systems "artificially borrowed" from the West. Another recurrent theme was that the first to suffer from any upheaval in the existing system would be the native Saudis themselves.

As far as traditional social values and norms of behaviour were concerned, the religious leaders were especially apprehensive of "imported ideas" which might lead to "anarchical thinking." They emphasized that Islamic values, traditions and customs must be strictly adhered to as the only "efficient tool" for defending local society against alien influences. These anxieties were defined by an article in the Financial Times on the dilemma of Saudi Arabia's dependence on immigrant labour:

Saudis are uneasily aware that foreign workers probably outnumber the Saudi workforce, which certainly does not exceed 1.5m and is probably less. In the last few months, it has clearly emerged that the establishment feels that foreign labour, male and female, is placing unnecessary strain on the social and moral fabric of the state and, inevitably, in the heart of Islam, on Islam itself. Diplomats argue that though the establishment may not yet know in what direction it wants Saudi society to develop, it has at least made up its mind about what it does not want: ragged Afghans thronging the streets, African prostitutes in the Bāb al-Sharīf district of Jidda, Muslims drunk in public on liquor originating in Western compounds and a general upsurge in crime.[7]

In its attempt to combat infringements of Islamic law and local custom, the regime adopted a number of measures including the prohibition of foreign-type entertainment and the establishment of special neighbourhoods for foreign workers. In 1977–78, there were also indications that the regime had adopted a stricter attitude towards violations of religious law and custom, whether by its own citizens or by aliens.

In January 1978, wide and vivid coverage was given to the story of the public execution in the market place of Jidda of a young Saudi princess, granddaughter of the highly respected Prince Muḥammad Ibn 'Abd al-'Azīz. According to reports, she was shot (or beheaded) in front of her lover. Others claimed they had just been married. The man, a cousin of the Saudi ambassador in Beirut, 'Alī al-Shā'ir, was then beheaded. The Saudi press did not report the event. While some Western sources asserted that the execution should be interpreted as a warning to other young princesses not to marry outside the Royal Family, sources close to the Saudis said that the princess was sentenced to death for adultery by a *sharī'a* court, in accordance with the laws of Islam. The princess, these sources said, had been married before and had not obtained a divorce when she met Shā'ir. Her execution should therefore be regarded as exemplifying the Royal Family's desire for a strict and unrelenting attitude towards those disobeying the law of Islam.[8] (For British involvement in this issue, see below.)

A statement by religious notables was broadcast in January 1978 calling on all citizens to refrain from acts forbidden by Islam or likely to corrupt morals such as concerts of songs, mixed gatherings of men and women, or the use of loudspeakers tuned to drown out the call to morning prayers. The statement also requested people not to be lavish in their preparations for wedding ceremonies and receptions, since ostentatious spending was contrary to the teachings of the Qur'ān and the Prophet.[9]

The authorities also enacted strict laws and regulations aimed primarily at alien residents—whether legal or illegal. Examples of such government action were the public execution, again in Jidda square, in April 1978, of two Pakistani immigrants found guilty of axeing to death a man and his wife—both also of Pakistani origin,[10] In June 1978, two British subjects were arrested by the Religious Police and deported for being found in the company of a Muslim airline hostess (from Egypt) with no one else present.[11]

A particular concern of the Saudi authorities were labourers who remained in the country illegally after performing the pilgrimage. In mid-January 1978, the Interior Ministry warned Saudi citizens not to employ or work with aliens who did not have legal permission to stay in the country.[12] As of April 1978, the Interior Ministry began a campaign against illegal immigrants.[13] In May, the Interior Minister announced that two months would be allowed "to correct the conditions of the people who came to the country but failed to leave." He added that offices were to be opened in all regions of the country "to remedy the conditions of these residents." At the end of the two-month grace period, the Ministry would take the necessary action, including imprisonment, deportation (at the expense of the illegal resident), and imprisonment or fines for those who gave shelter to illegal immigrants or provided them with transportation from one town to another.[14]

At the end of May, the Interior Minister reiterated his call to public and private establishments and individuals to warn all foreign employees to carry documents proving their lawful residence in the country. He also called on Saudi citizens to carry identification documents at all times.[15] In July 1978, a nation-wide campaign was launched "to apprehend every alien contravening the Kingdom's residence laws" or working for someone other than the person who had stood guarantee for his entry into the country.[16] On 1 August 1978, the Saudi Manpower Commission published regulations concerning the licensing of employment agencies for foreign workers. Among other things, each agency was required to "acquaint would-be employees with . . . the expected code of behaviour and employment regulations of the Kingdom."[17]

CLANDESTINE OPPOSITION

As in recent years, there was no indication of serious domestic opposition in 1977–78, except for one uncorroborated report in October 1977 of the court-martialling of officers accused of an attempted coup.[18] Most criticism of the Saudi regime emanated either from radical Palestinian organizations or from an opposition group based in Baghdad. These termed the Saudi Royal Family "reactionary" and described the regime as a "capitalist tool." Significantly, in 1977–78 Baghdad seemed to have replaced Damascus and Aden which, until 1971–72 and 1976 respectively, were the foci of external opposition to the Saudi regime.

A long statement prepared by the "Saudi Council for Solidarity and Peace" (an opposition group connected with radical Palestinian organizations) was published in the Iraqi Communist paper *Tarīq al-Sha'b* on 26 September 1977. It contained a number of points typical of the criticism levelled against the Saudi regime by Leftist opposition groupings. It pointed out, for instance, that Fahd had failed to keep his promise, made after King Faysal's assassination in 1975, to set up a Consultative Council (*majlis shūrā*). Some political prisoners had been released in 1975; political refugees had been permitted to return; and attempts had been made to win some of them over with monetary grants—otherwise "nothing [had] changed. On the contrary, a new campaign of arrests and liquidation [had] been waged against military personnel." The statement further asserted that it had become "a major crime—tantamount to treason" to demand the promulgation of a constitution, the establishment of parliamentary institutions, political organizations, trade unions, social and cultural societies, or to claim equal rights for women. The government had the power to withdraw the licence of any newspaper and appoint and dismiss editors. Saudi newspapers were thus prevented from discussing major issues of financial, military and foreign policy. Furthermore, Saudi oil policy was determined for it by the needs of Western markets. Oil revenues were used to finance "the organs of [domestic] suppression and reactionary plans" in the region. Oil prices were set so as to serve "US imperialist interests," even if Saudi oil policy thereby threatened to undermine OPEC's unity. The principle of "participation" had become a substitute for nationalization which other OPEC countries (Iraq, Algeria and Libya) had carried out. By dropping nationalization, the Saudi regime prevented people from exercising control over their oil wealth.

The statement went on to say that the Saudi economy was run "entirely to favour the interests of the ruling clique, for it enabled it to acquire wealth, control commerce and exploit the country's resources." Foreign capital was given all possible facilities. Surplus income from oil enriched US banks. The Five-Year Plan (announced in May 1975)[19] was no more than an "imaginary legal excuse to squander by various means" funds accumulating from oil revenues and "to enable foreign monopolies to profit from massive contracts . . . to take the oil money back to their countries." Another point made in the statement was that an advanced Saudi military force was being built up with the US as a "joint military activity" to oppose the "liberation" of the Arabian Peninsula, the Persian Gulf and Africa. Lastly, Saudi foreign policy was said to be subservient to US policy. Its main characteristics were "the launching of crusades against Arab and international liberation movements under the pretext of combating communism"; dragging Arab countries, particularly hesitant ones, into line with imperialist policy, either by giving grants and loans, or by threats of aggression; plotting against the liberated Arab countries by encouraging other states to provoke them; prompting the Arab countries whose territories were occupied by the Zionist enemy to accept solutions proposed by the US; giving aid to pro-Western countries and forces to ensure their continued allegiance; allowing "political and financial interference to support the Rightist, reactionary and fascist forces in Europe; and financing the military operations of countries which have sent their armies to fight against liberation movements as has happened in Africa." [20]

FOREIGN AFFAIRS
THE INITIAL IMPACT OF SĀDĀT'S NEW POLICY
President Anwar al-Sādāt's trip to Jerusalem in November 1977 created a problem of special gravity for the traditional conduct of Saudi Arabia's inter-Arab policy. For the first time in this decade, the country was forced to take sides in an Arab rift. Since 'Abd al-Nāsir's death in 1970, the Saudi leadership had succeeded in avoiding any clear-cut public identification or alignment with any single Arab country, bloc or camp. The careful implementation of this policy of "non-alignment" within the Arab world had not previously been hampered by Saudi considerations concerning the Arab-Israeli conflict. For instance, at the time of widespread Arab criticism of the second Sinai Agreement in September 1975, the Saudi leadership managed to maintain a policy of non-identification with either Egypt or its critics through adherence to vague formulae which supporters and opponents of the agreement alike were able to regard as representative of what still remained of a comprehensive Arab consensus. Sādāt's trip and its aftermath (see essay on Inter-Arab Relations) endangered this highly successful Saudi policy. The rift now ran too deep for Saudi Arabia to pose as a symbol of residual consensus, as it were. More than that: Sādāt's unilateral action threatened Saudi Arabia's ambition to act as arbiter of the Arab world—an ambition it had been realizing in steadily increasing measure, particularly since the 1973 war.

The dilemma which the Saudi leadership now faced was this: it could endorse Sādāt's new policy and thereby unmake its relatively good relations with the more radical states which had been so carefully cultivated in recent years; or it could condemn Sādāt's moves and so lose the moderate image it had created with a great deal of sophistication, especially in the US. Provoking a dispute with Syria and the various Palestinian organizations, such as had existed in the late 1960s, could once again stimulate domestic subversion on the part of groups taking their cue from either party. But disavowing Egypt and losing the image of moderation would be no less harmful: it would range Saudi Arabia against the most important single Arab state, and would largely deprive it of the benefits of its close links with the US, in particular of being the Arab country best placed to influence US Middle Eastern policy and most able to rely on the US taking action against Soviet penetration. Typically, the Saudi solution was to adhere to traditional ambiguity, to avoid public identification with either side, and to prevent a situation in which any Arab state could blame Saudi Arabia of having taken sides with its adversary. However, as the situation evolved from November 1977, it was not allowed to do so as convincingly as before.

In their comments on Sādāt's dialogue with Israel, the Saudis repeatedly complained of the lack of advance co-ordination between Cairo and Riyadh. On every occasion they reiterated their basic demands: (1) complete Israeli withdrawal from all the territories occupied in the 1967 war; (2) the return of the Holy Places in Jerusalem to Muslim sovereignty; and (3) the restoration of the legitimate rights of the Palestinians. It is significant that until the beginning of 1977, special stress was usually put on the second demand, but in 1977–78 the emphasis gradually shifted to the third. In an earlier shift, already noticeable during 1977, the abstract formulation of "Palestinians' rights" had been replaced by more concrete references to the urgent need for the creation of a Palestinian state. The Saudis had apparently concluded that a Palestinian state (which they expected to be dependent on Saudi financial aid) would be less dangerous to Riyadh than an embittered Palestinian "diaspora" exposed to manipulation by revolutionary Arab states, inclined towards radicalism, and likely to serve as a tool for political upheavals. While thus adhering to their traditional political tactics, the Saudis gave more weight to the issue of the Palestinian problem. This met three requirements: it maintained Saudi involvement in a major Arab issue; it did not clash too badly with their image as constructive moderates; and it would neither make Saudi Arabia appear to have cast in its lot with the Syrian-led camp, nor in any way be construed as an endorsement of Sādāt's policy. In particular, it would prevent potential critics—such as Syria or the more radical groups in the PLO—from charging that Riyadh had weakened in its stand on the Palestinian issue or on Jerusalem. From the Saudi point of view, such an attitude did not imply the absence of a clear stand on crucial matters; rather, it signified the retention of a maximum degree of manoeuvrability in a volatile Arab world.

RELATIONS WITH EGYPT

All the above considerations formed the main issues on which Saudi-Egyptian relations evolved during the period under review. Saudi Arabia's first statement, made on 18 November 1977—just before Sādāt's arrival in Jerusalem—reflected the basic guidelines of its inter-Arab policy and set the pattern for many subsequent statements. It reiterated the basic Saudi demands for solving the Arab-Israeli conflict (see above), and stressed the Palestinians' right to "return to their homeland and set up an independent state on their territory." Noting that the Arab cause was "at the present moment passing through a difficult phase," it asserted Saudi Arabia's belief in Arab solidarity as "the sound basis and the necessary course for any Arab effort aimed at solving the Arab question. Any Arab initiative should stem from a unified Arab position." [21] An Egyptian and Western attempt to interpret a message from King Khālid to Sādāt (just before his Jerusalem visit) as an expression of support[22] was, immediately rejected. Riyadh declared that its statement of 18 November was the only accurate expression of the country's unalterable stand.[23]

Through the following months, the Saudis tried to satisfy both the Egyptians and the "rejectionist" states, to maintain their role of mediator, and to work for "healing Arab rights." They asserted that Saudi Arabia continued to uphold fraternal relations with Egypt, and denied as groundless a report in December 1977 that the Kingdom was reconsidering its pledges to finance Egyptian arms purchases during the next five years.[24] Simultaneously, in order to satisfy Sādāt's opponents, they emphasized their continuing assistance to the PLO. Thus, when Fahd received a Palestinian delegation at the end of November 1977, he reiterated Saudi Arabia's "firm commitment" to the Palestinian cause which, he said, meant "the fulfilment of their aspirations to their own homeland, like the rest of the states of the region." He added that Saudi Arabia wished "to eliminate [Arab] differences through sincere and constructive dialogue, to try to avoid everything likely to split our nation, or provide an occasion for our enemies to derive satisfaction from our problems." He told the delegates that the position of the Kingdom on the Palestinian issue "has not changed and will never change." [25] During a visit to Riyadh in January 1978, the PLO leader, Yāsir 'Arafāt, was reportedly promised that Saudi Arabia would not agree to any settlement unacceptable to the Palestinians. [26] The visits to Riyadh by the US Secretary of State and President Carter, in December 1977 and January 1978 respectively, were presented as an American attempt to gain Saudi support for Sādāt; [27] nevertheless, they failed to produce a clear Saudi declaration favouring Sādāt's initiative.

Saudi Arabia stated that it would not recognize Israel "even if there was peace in the Middle East" since it had not recognized the People's Republic of China or the USSR (sic). [28] Fahd spoke of the recognition of Israel as an issue which could possibly be discussed "within the framework of a unified Arab stand" provided a comprehensive agreement had first been reached. He added that he could not visualize the Arab states making war with Israel without Egypt, nor Egypt concluding a peace treaty with Israel without the agreement of all the Arab states. [29]

RELATIONS WITH SYRIA

The malaise which characterized Saudi-Syrian relations during the first half of 1977 was relieved somewhat as the year drew to a close, when Jordan began to shift away from the Syrians. The earlier difficulties were mainly due to Saudi distrust of the close relations between Damascus and Amman, and of the Syrian vision of a Syrian-led bloc which would include Jordan, Lebanon and a future Palestinian state. The visit of the Head of the National Guard, Prince 'Abdallah Ibn 'Abd al-'Azīz, to Syria in mid-October 1977 was apparently part of a general Saudi endeavour to maintain good relations with the "progressive-revolutionary" states—relations which it had built up gradually since 1971. However, some observers linked the visit to a Saudi attempt to launch a new round of inter-Arab consultations towards reconvening the Geneva conference.

President Ḥāfiz al-Asad arrived in Riyadh on 7 December 1977 "to explain the great damages which are emerging in the Arab area as a result of the Egyptian President's visit to occupied Palestine." [30] This trip marked a further cautious and gradual improvement of relations between the two states. In April 1978, Saudi Arabia promised aid for several industrial projects in Syria. [31] A month later, American sources revealed that Saudi Arabia was negotiating the possibility of a merger of its radar system with that of Syria and Jordan. [32] In July 1978, the Saudi and Syrian Ministers of Interior concluded talks on co-operation in matters affecting internal security. [33]

RELATIONS WITH JORDAN

Saudi-Jordanian relations focused mainly on the issue of Sādāt's visit to Jerusalem and the ensuing negotiations. Jordan's attitude towards this issue, though not completely identical with that of Saudi Arabia, was compatible with it. King Ḥusayn's two visits to Riyadh—in December 1977 and in July 1978—demonstrated the similarity in outlook of the two Kingdoms. A Jordanian source described the December visit as reflecting a "keen desire to rebuild Arab solidarity, support Arab joint action and guarantee the nationalist rights of the Palestinian people." [34] As in the case of Syria, bilateral relations extended to the field of internal security. [35]

RELATIONS WITH LEBANON

Saudi Arabia's main objectives in Lebanon continued to be to reduce friction between the rival factions there and to maintain active Arab co-ordination. This was to ensure that the Lebanese crisis neither became an exclusively Syrian affair, nor was removed from the Arab domain by becoming an international issue.

Prince Fahd summarized the principles guiding Saudi policy towards Lebanon as follows: (1) Saudi Arabia was against any form of partition in Lebanon; (2) safeguarding the security of Lebanon was of concern to the Kingdom and formed part of its Arab and international policies; (3) Saudi Arabia fully supported Lebanon's own government and institutions and, in particular, the reconstruction of the Lebanese army; and (4) Israel was the sole beneficiary of the dispute in Lebanon.[36]

Despite rumours at the beginning of the year that Saudi Arabia would withdraw its units from the Arab Deterrent Force (see chapter on Lebanon), it paid a sum of $9m on 23 February 1978 as the second instalment of its contribution to the maintenance of the force.[37] The Israeli incursion into South Lebanon in mid-March (see section on the Arab-Israeli Conflict) was strongly and repeatedly denounced as "Zionist aggression," and provided the Saudis with yet another opportunity to demonstrate their support of the Palestinians. King Khālid appealed to President Carter to intervene to end the fighting,[38] while the Saudi Information Minister stressed the need for Arab solidarity to stop the Israeli move which, he said, had "no justification save the desire for more occupation."[39] The fact that Riyadh abstained from expressing a clear attitude towards the Syrian attacks on the Christian quarters of Beirut in mid-1978 probably signalled its acceptance—however reluctant—of Syrian ascendancy in Lebanon.

THE PERSIAN GULF AND THE RED SEA

Saudi fears that Leftist revolutionary elements, operating with Soviet support and backed by a Communist presence on the fringes of the Middle East, might harm the regime did not abate during 1977–78. On the contrary, events in the Horn of Africa, in the south-western corner of the Arabian Peninsula and in Iran fed such anxieties and added to Saudi Arabia's motivation actively to oppose pro-Communist activities in its geographical vicinity. (Also see essay, "The Regional Politics of the Red Sea, Indian Ocean and Persian Gulf.")

Saudi Arabia's longstanding concept of defence and security co-operation among the Gulf states to guard against upheavals and subversion did not produce any more concrete results in 1978 than in preceding years. The Saudis were concerned about reports that "international terrorism," encouraged by the Soviet and Cuban presence in and around the Horn of Africa, might hit the oilfields or the petroleum supply routes. This led to a Saudi effort to establish a "security belt" intended to embrace itself, the Gulf states, Iran and eventually even Iraq.[40]

The visits of Prince Sultān in April 1978 to Iran and Iraq probably dealt with common security arrangements and with a Saudi attempt to draw Iraq into a more comprehensive scheme for Gulf security.[41] Commenting on this possibility, *Arabia and the Gulf* said that, for the Riyadh government, Gulf security was not a question of "neutralizing the area from foreign interference, but of ensuring that the stability of local regimes was not threatened by subversion."[42]

In May 1978, the Saudi Information Minister described the possibility of a terrorist threat to the oil industry as being very remote. He said that there were no dangers threatening the Gulf or the oil there. "What was being repeated from time to time about those dangers were the dreams of those who want harm to come to the Gulf region." Saudi Arabia was establishing "co-operation with the Arab countries in the Gulf in cultural, economic, information and other spheres." The Saudi Kingdom and the Gulf countries were ready "to repel any aggression that might occur, and to stop anyone who thought of harming the security and the stability of the Gulf." [43]

A month later, the *New York Times* (relying on senior French officials and on intelligence sources from other countries) reported that Saudi Arabia, Iran and Iraq were discussing a Gulf security arrangement that could create "a major shift in the strategic balance of the oil-producing area." It was not made clear whether they were seeking a collective security pact or some looser form of defence co-operation. [44] In July 1978, the Saudi Interior Minister again raised the idea of Gulf co-operation, both for the defence of the oilfields and for removing the Gulf from the influence of international conflicts. [45]

Another thrust of Saudi policy in the Gulf area was to ensure greater co-operation among the Gulf states' police and internal security forces, and to improve communications, information exchanges and border control. This was pursued by mutual visits of Interior Ministers and high-ranking security officials. [46]

Relations with Iran continued to be characterized by an element of ambiguity: alongside unadmitted mutual competition, fed by suspicion and deeply-rooted fear, there existed day-to-day co-operation in bilateral relations and in jointly "combating the Communist threat." According to one source, a "growing identity of strategic views" among the US, Saudi Arabia and Iran led to regional co-operation both in the Gulf area and the Horn of Africa. [47] At the same time, however, there were reports from sources hostile to the Saudi regime of hidden tensions in Saudi-Iranian relations; these sources claimed that it was only the internal problems of Iran which prompted the Shah to co-operate with the Saudis. [48]

The Saudis were displeased with Iran's continued presence in Oman (see appropriate section in chapter on the Gulf states), as well as with its reported intention—at the beginning of 1978—to intervene in favour of Somalia against Ethiopia. [49]

While threats to Saudi Arabia from the direction of the Persian Gulf were potential or hypothetical, the danger of a communist takeover in the Horn of Africa and South Yemen was very real and tangible—particularly during the height of the Ethiopian-Somali military confrontation at the end of 1977. In February, Radio Riyadh commented: "By their open interference in the Ethiopian-Somali war, the USSR and its kind are working [according] to a long-term plan aimed at the rapid internationalization of the conflict in the Horn of Africa and the disruption of peace and security throughout Africa. These are sufficient reasons for all African and Western countries to declare their condemnation and to foil their plans. It has been proved beyond all doubt in various parts of the world that once it penetrates any country, communism leaves its evil imprint and spreads its subversive principles which destroy all values and civilizations." [50]

In September 1977 and again in February 1978, the Saudis denied as baseless, false and untrue Ethiopian and Soviet claims to the effect that they had sent forces to the Ogaden region to help the Somali army. [51] However, there were reports during the year that Saudi Arabia would replace the USSR as the direct supplier of economic and military aid to Somalia. [52]

Saudi-Sudanese relations, which had improved in the wake of the abortive coup against Numayrī in the summer of 1976, remained amicable. The two countries co-operated in Red Sea affairs. For instance, a sum of $16m was reported to have been allocated by Riyadh for the 1978 budget of the Saudi-Sudanese joint organization for the exploitation of Red Sea resources. [53]

RELATIONS WITH THE US
Although the Carter Administration had been seriously considering the sale of 60 of

its most advanced fighters—the F-15—to Saudi Arabia since the middle of 1977,[54] negotiations over the $1,500m deal turned into a critical test case for Saudi-US relations in the second half of 1978. Coming at a crucial juncture in the build-up of American influence in the ME, and at a time of great sensitivity owing to the vicissitudes and complications of the Egyptian-Israeli dialogue, the issue came to occupy a very special place in Saudi eyes. On the one hand, the Saudis were keenly aware of the difficulties which would be encountered in absorbing these sophisticated planes, to be delivered in 1983. Yet, out of a sense of urgency dictated by various strategic, inter-Arab and other considerations, they exerted intensive pressure on the Carter Administration and on American public opinion to win Congressional approval for the deal. The Saudis considered that the withholding of what they regarded as a relatively small number of planes—said to have been promised to them by the previous American Administration—would gravely harm the credibility of the US as a reliable ally. This view was shared by senior American officials who advocated strict adherence to the "special relationship" developed between the US and Saudi Arabia. Several sources reported that following the visit by Cyrus Vance to Riyadh in mid-December 1977, the Carter Administration increasingly relied on Saudi goodwill for the success of its ME policy. Indeed, it seemed at times that the struggle over the aircraft sale—which reached a climax in the spring of 1978—was but one manifestation of the rapidly changing US perception of Saudi power, of its influence on the overall state of affairs in the ME, as well as of its ability to bolster, or undermine, the stability of the American dollar.

Saudi statements and actions throughout the period under review indicated that the Saudis were well aware of their enhanced status—especially during a period in which the Americans' ability to direct ME developments seemed more than once to have come to a dead end. At such moments, the danger of a new Israeli-Arab war, and its implications for oil supplies and petrodollar investments, loomed large in American thinking.

The Saudis skilfully exploited their status to promote their own interests. Two Saudi arguments turned into recurrent themes in the campaign to convince Congress to approve the aircraft sale: (1) The US was committed to protect the Kingdom from any potential threat. Preventing or postponing the sale would be a mistake, because it would encourage the Soviet Union—already more active than ever in the Horn of Africa—to stage a comeback in the Arab world. (2) Approval of the sale would cause Saudi Arabia to sponsor a peace settlement more forcefully.

Though not themselves participating in the ME negotiations, the Saudis made it clear that they regarded the US as the major party to any ME settlement, and hinted that their co-operation in influencing actual or potential Arab participants could be crucial in the search for such a settlement. At critical moments during the negotiations for the aircraft sale, the Saudis let it be understood that their continued "moderation"—and even their overall foreign policy orientation towards the US—were at stake. The approval of the deal, they hinted guardedly, could also provide them with the useful additional prestige of having defeated the "Israeli-Zionist lobby." More than that: the Saudis subtly established an interconnection in American thinking between the issue of oil production and oil price policy, and the sale of the F-15s. The supply by Saudi Arabia of 25% of US oil imports, and the huge number of Saudi petrodollars invested or deposited in the US over the previous four years, gave them "enough leverage to affect US interest rates and to strengthen the dollar on foreign exchange markets in the unlikely event they chose to do so." Saudi holdings constituted a potential "money weapon" which could be used to undermine the economy of the industrialized world.

As diplomatic activity to ensure the aircraft sale intensified, various Saudi sources repeatedly mentioned, directly or indirectly, that despite their concern for the stability of Western economies, and despite the purely economic considerations governing their oil policy, they might make use of both oil production rates and the placement of their investments in order to gain political-strategic aims.[55]

When President Carter paid his brief visit to Saudi Arabia at the beginning of January 1978, the key issues reportedly discussed were those of oil, the status of the dollar, the sale of sophisticated arms to Saudi Arabia and "the restoration of the legitimate rights of the Palestinians."[56] There were contradictory reports as to the results of the talks. Some portrayed the prevailing atmosphere as optimistic and emphasized the existence of a broad common denominator between Saudi and American interests in general, and on the Palestinian issue in particular.[57] Other reports spoke of "difficult talks" and of serious differences of opinion.[58] Official Saudi sources said that in restating Riyadh's views on the ME problem, the Saudi Foreign Minister, Sa'ūd a-Faysal, had underlined that the US should play an active and positive role in achieving "a just and lasting comprehensive solution to the ME problem," based on the Saudi demands for the withdrawal of Israel from all the Arab territories occupied in 1967 and the fulfilment of the legitimate rights of the Palestinians.[59]

It was after Carter's visit that the Administration and Congress started discussing the F-15 sale. A State Department official said that the F-15 had been Saudi Arabia's choice and that there was a "longstanding" US commitment "to help Saudi Arabia in its legitimate defence needs."[60]

The US Energy Secretary, James Schlesinger, arrived in Saudi Arabia on 11 January 1978. On the same day, a Saudi Oil Ministry spokesman announced that the Kingdom favoured fixing oil prices in accordance with a basket of currencies rather than in US dollars only. According to one report, Schlesinger proposed an oil deal covering two points. The first provided for the indexation of oil prices for the next decade. Prices were to be frozen during 1978 and 1979, and would then rise in proportion to the rate of inflation, the price of manufactured goods, and changes in the value of the dollar. The second point provided for the purchase by the US of 2.5m barrels per day of Saudi oil at a stable price for three years. In return, the report claimed, the Saudis requested that the purchase of the F-15 planes should be "promoted."[61] On 15 January, the Saudi Finance and National Economy Minister, Muhammad Abā al-Khayl, announced that the Kingdom had no intention of accepting any currency other than the dollar for its oil exports.[62]

Israel's strong objection to the sale of the F-15s, as well as the opposition of many US Senators who attempted to rally support to stop the deal, only deepened Saudi perceptions of it as an acid test of US-Saudi relations. Prince Fahd warned that failure to approve the sale would cause his country to "reassess its friendship" with the US.[63]

However, on 14 February 1978, President Carter announced that the sale of 60 F-15s to Saudi Arabia would form part of a package deal which included the sale of F-5Es to Egypt and F-16s to Israel. In justification of this decision, Secretary Vance said that Saudi Arabia was of "immense importance in promoting a course of moderation in the ME, with respect to peace-making and other regional initiatives and more broadly in world affairs, as in petroleum and financial policy. The Saudi government has a legitimate requirement to modernize its very limited air defence. . . . Their request is reasonable and in our interest to fulfil."[64]

Since the deal had yet to be finalized by Congressional approval, the Saudis were less than fully pleased with the Administration's decision.[65] Strongly lobbying for approval of the sale, high-ranking Saudi officials explained that the aircraft would contribute to the stability of the region and to the defence of Saudi Arabia's oilfields and oil installations. They argued that Communist influence in those parts of Africa closest to the Arabian Peninsula had made the US aware of the importance of the Saudi role in global strategy. "In selling these aircraft to Saudi Arabia, the US would thus be serving its own interests as well." [66] Simultaneously, there were reports that the Saudi Supreme Petroleum Council had decided that negotiations for the supply of Saudi crude for the strategic US oil stockpile would depend on the approval of the F-15 deal by the US Congress. [67]

The US Ambassador to Saudi Arabia, John West, was reported to have told the US Senate Foreign Relations Committee that he believed that Saudi Arabia, the chief proponent of a moderate oil pricing policy, would not hold the line against other members of OPEC if the F-15 sale was rejected or delayed by Congress. [68] Commenting indirectly on Ambassador West's statement, the Saudi Minister of Defence, Prince Sultān Ibn 'Abd al-'Azīz, said that Saudi Arabia rejected bargaining on oil prices because of its commitment to OPEC. His country believed in the principle of "a quiet policy" regarding the measures it adopted *vis-à-vis* its foes and friends alike. [69]

In mid-March, the Saudi Ambassador to the US, 'Abdallah 'Alī Ridā, addressed a letter to all members of the US Congress in which he stated that a postponement of the decision on the F-15 sale "would be extremely harmful because it would be taken as a sign by Communists and radicals that the US was reconsidering its support for Saudi Arabia." On 14 March 1978, the US Deputy Assistant Secretary of State, Brian Atwood, said that the Saudis had stated "categorically" through diplomatic channels that "a delay is just as bad as a rejection" and would cause them to buy their warplanes elsewhere [70] (probably in France, see below). In a further statement, Prince Sultān said that Zionist attempts inside and outside the US would not succeed in aborting the aircraft deal. [71] Official diplomatic pressure exerted on the US Administration was constantly backed up by the Saudi media. Thus *al-Jazīra* wrote that the F-15 deal put US-Saudi relations to the test. The paper added that Saudi efforts to convince the US Congress revolved around hints that a rejection of the deal could upset the ME peace negotiations and make the Saudis less willing to increase oil production to meet Western needs. [72]

Saudi activities were not limited to lobbying in Congress, but were also aimed at influencing American public opinion at large. [73] At the end of March 1978, Saudi Arabia retained a "politically experienced" US public relations firm to lobby Congress for the approval of the F-15 deal, and also to prepare a long-range programme aimed at "enhancing the Saudi image" in the US. The project involved an outlay of $65,000 for the initial six-to-seven week programme and $100,000 for the longer-range plan. [74]

The Saudis intensified their efforts throughout April and May 1978. For instance, Saudi sources hinted that the forthcoming OPEC conference in Tā'if (on 6 May 1978) would have an important role in influencing the US Congress. [75] One typical example of how security matters and oil policy were being linked by high-ranking Saudi officials was the statement of the Oil Minister, Ahmad Zakī al-Yamānī, that "we place great importance and significance on this transaction. We feel we badly need it. It's our security. If we don't get it, then we will have a feeling you are not concerned with our security and you don't appreciate our friendship." He went on to assert that Saudi oil production and dollar policies were primarily based on economic considerations, but added that failure to supply the airplanes would certainly diminish Saudi "enthusiasm to help the West and co-operate with the US." [76] Sounding a rather more threatening note, the Minister of Defence, Prince Sultān, declared that "the losers will be the ones who will not sell. We want to buy arms for our defence and we shall find them." [77] Speaking more diplomatically, but no less ominously, the Saudi Foreign Minister—echoing an earlier statement by Crown Prince Fahd—said that the rejection of the sale by Congress would lead to a reassessment of Saudi-US relations.[78] Simultaneously, other high-ranking officials tried to play down the gravity of these statements. For instance, the Information Minister denied any linkage between oil policy and the aircraft sale, saying that "Saudi policy on the price of oil and the dollar was based on economic foundations and that any change in the Kingdom's policy on these issues would depend on a change of these foundations."[79] The Second Deputy Prime Minister and Head of the National Guard, Prince 'Abdallah Ibn 'Abd al-'Azīz, said that the request for the F-15s was based on a "deep study of defensive needs and not on testing the intentions of friends. . . . Even if the request was not approved—and the world arms market was very wide—the Saudi policy on oil prices and production would not be the subject of change because of emergency factors."[80]

As the debate in Washington neared a climax on the eve of the crucial vote in Congress, Saudi pressures increased. Prince 'Abdallah was quoted as saying that: "As a result of the mistakes of our friends, the Soviet Union might stage a comeback in the Arab world."[81] The Saudi press published articles stressing that Saudi-US relations had not been subject to a similar test since they were first forged at the end of World War II, and that the arms sale would be the last opportunity to rescue US foreign policy from manipulation by world Zionism.[82]

As part of an intensive effort by the US Administration to have the package deal approved by Congress, the US Defence Secretary, Harold Brown, sent a seven-page letter to the Senate Foreign Relations Committee on 10 May. Described by the *New York Times* as "unusual," the letter sought to assure the Committee that the F-15s would not be used offensively against Israel, and that the Saudi government had given assurances that it would not transfer the aircraft to any third country or permit the nationals of any such country to train on the aircraft without US authorization.[83] The Saudi response to Secretary Brown's letter was quick and unequivocal. Its ambassador to Cairo, 'Abd al-Rahmān Abā al-Khayl, said "My country will not accept any conditions being attached to the sale of US war planes . . . conditions that may hurt Saudi Arabian and Arab dignity." The Saudi Foreign Minister added that limitations would be accepted only if similar conditions were imposed on Israel. In a public letter to President Carter, King Khālid wrote that the need for the planes had become a matter of "pressing urgency" because of increasing Communist activity in the region.[84]

When the package deal was eventually approved on 15 May 1978, it was hailed by Saudi officials and the media as an historic decision and a great triumph for Saudi influence in the US; a setback for Zionist influence there, and the beginning of a new era in US-Saudi relations.[85] The Saudi Information Minister spoke of the "psychological significance" of Congressional approval of the deal, although he added that the 60 F-15 aircraft were "hardly enough" to defend the Kingdom.[86]

RELATIONS WITH BRITAIN

The Saudi Minister of Interior, Nā'if Ibn 'Abd al-'Azīz, visited London in October 1977 for talks concentrating particularly on co-operation in the fields of security and police.[87] At the end of May 1978, a British firm was awarded a contract to expand and modernize the telecommunications network of the National Guard. It also provided for the training of National Guard signals staff.[88] The UK-Saudi Joint (Economic) Commission, established in October 1975, held its third session in London in March 1978 to review the progress achieved in trade and economic co-operation and to consider further measures.[89]

Another aspect of Saudi-British relations which attracted wider public attention related to British reactions to Saudi Arabia's treatment of its own nationals and of British subjects working there. The execution of a Saudi princess and her lover in Jidda (see above) gave rise to considerable criticism; in January 1978, the British Foreign Office issued a statement deploring the "tragedy." The Saudi government responded by declaring that the sentence had been passed by an Islamic court and was in accordance with Islamic law, implying that Britain was guilty of unwarranted interference in the due process of law in a foreign country. The British Foreign Secretary, David Owen, immediately apologized to the Saudi government, expressing regret that the Foreign Office statement had caused offence. Thereupon a number of Labour MPs protested against what they called Owen's "grovelling" and shameful apology. They said it was "incomprehensible and totally incompatible with [Owen's] declared defence of human rights that the Foreign Secretary should consider such executions barbaric if the two persons were married, but civilized if they were not." [90]

Two British engineers, who had been arrested in December 1977 for breaking the Muslim ban against the possession of alcoholic beverages, were publicly flogged and then deported in June 1978. Seven other British subjects suspected of brewing beer in their homes were reported to be in jail. Some Labour MPs called the caning "barbaric," but the Foreign Secretary replied that Britain could not intervene since "people must observe the laws of the country in which they were living." [91] A British pilot working for Saudi Arabian airlines was also arrested and accused of illicit manufacture of alcohol. [92] In July, the number of British subjects in custody was put at 32; most were charged with selling or consuming alcohol. [93]

RELATIONS WITH FRANCE

Negotiations for the signing of a "most important arms deal" between France and Saudi Arabia, which had proceeded intermittently since mid-1975, continued at the beginning of 1978. However, it was decided to postpone the conclusion of the negotiations until after the general elections, as the Saudis were reported to be anxious that the Communists might come to power in France following a Leftist victory. [94] In April, after the electoral success of the Right and Centre parties, a $3,500m arms deal was reported to have been finalized, including advanced missiles and other equipment. A consortium of French firms would supply complete military and civilian radar cover for the Arabian Peninsula, including telecommunications and tracking systems, which was expected to extend to Somalia and Sudan as well. It was also reported that arrangements had been made for Saudi down payments to the Dassault industries for the delivery of *Mirage* 2000 aircraft and for work to begin on producing the *Mirage* 4000 model. [95]

King Khālid made a two-day visit to Paris at the end of May 1978 for talks centring on increased economic and military co-operation, as well as on the Soviet-Cuban presence in Africa. [96] The Saudi Foreign and Defence Ministers, who accompanied Khālid on his visit, denied that an agreement had been reached for the supply of *Mirage* aircraft. The Saudi Information Minister said that "the recently raised issue of aircraft was not discussed at all." The Saudi Foreign Minister further denied that there had been any discussion of Saudi financial backing for a joint African security force. [97] In the joint communiqué issued at the end of the visit, the two leaders reviewed the current situation in various parts of Africa, expressed their concern at attempts to cause divisions and instability there, and stressed that, in order to preserve peace and security, the continent should be free from foreign intervention. They expressed the hope that the forthcoming OAU meeting in Khartoum would lead to positive results ensuring each African state prospects for development, respect for its sovereignty, and freedom to achieve its national interests on political and economic levels.

The two leaders devoted special attention to the situation in the ME. They stressed the dangers inherent in the situation, and their bearing on the security and stability of the region and on world peace. The French side restated its policy that a comprehensive solution of the ME problem should be based on Israel's withdrawal from the territories occupied in 1967; on the recognition of the right of the Palestinian people—like other people—to a homeland of their own; and on the right of all states in the region to live in peace and within secure, recognized and guaranteed borders. The French side also reaffirmed the urgent necessity for overcoming all the obstacles obstructing the search for a permanent solution on the basis of Security Council Resolutions 242 and 338, with the aim of starting negotiations between all the parties concerned, including the representatives of the Palestinian people. The Saudi side explained that the Palestine question was the core of the ME conflict. A just peace in the region could not be achieved except by the withdrawal of Israeli forces from all the occupied Arab territories (including Jerusalem), and by the recognition of the legitimate rights of the Palestinian people (including their right to self-determination and to their own state). A comprehensive solution to the ME problem must tackle the Palestinian question in all its aspects in the presence of all sides, including the PLO—the sole legitimate representative of the Palestinian people.

France once again expressed its appreciation of Saudi Arabia's moderate policy on oil prices. The two sides reviewed the possibilities of expanding and diversifying economic co-operation including planning, engineering, geophysical surveying, development of minerals and other sources of natural wealth, infrastructure, public works and other industrial and agricultural development, water resources, energy problems (including the development of new sources of energy), technology, transportation, communications and television. The establishment of an atomic research centre for peaceful purposes was to be considered. The two leaders noted with satisfaction the development of cultural, scientific and technical co-operation between France and Saudi Arabia, and expressed their interest in strengthening this, particularly at the level of universities and the exchange of scholarships between the two countries. They stressed the importance they attached to establishing an "Arab World Institute" in Paris as a means for promoting understanding between the French and Arab cultures.[98]

On 12 June, the French Ministry of Defence denied a report published by the Egyptian weekly *October* that during Khālid's visit, the two countries had signed a $24,000m arms deal for the supply in 1980 of tanks, helicopters and a radar network capable of covering the whole Red Sea.[99]

An agreement to set up electronics industries in Saudi Arabia was signed in July 1978 between France and the Arab Military Industries Organization (also see essay on Inter-Arab Relations).[100]

RELATIONS WITH OTHER WEST EUROPEAN COUNTRIES

West Germany was reported in November 1977 to be engaged in the early stages of negotiations on the possible sale of *Leopard* tanks to Saudi Arabia.[101] In June 1978, Fahd arrived in Bonn to discuss German assistance to the Saudi military industry, economic co-operation, and the political situation in the ME and Africa. Fahd reportedly demanded that West Germany should recognize the PLO and allow it to open an office in Bonn.[102]

King Juan Carlos of Spain visited Saudi Arabia in October 1977.[103] In March 1978, a Saudi military delegation arrived in Madrid to enquire into the possibility of purchasing Spanish-made arms.[104]

King Khālid visited Belgium from 8–11 May 1978. In a joint communiqué issued at the conclusion of the visit, both sides condemned all forms of aggression and called for the immediate implementation in Lebanon of Security Council Resolution 425 (see essay, "The Problem of South Lebanon"). The Belgium side stated that a solution to the ME problem should be based on Resolution 242, while the Saudi side said that there could be no peace in the region without total Israeli withdrawal from occupied Arab territories, and without granting the Palestinians the right to self-determination and a return to their homeland. Both sides expressed anxiety about foreign intervention in Africa, but hoped that the continent's problems could be solved by the OAU. A bilateral agreement on economic and technical co-operation was also signed, and the communiqué noted that talks on an aviation agreement had started earlier that year.[105] Khālid inaugurated an Islamic centre and mosque in Brussels, part of which he had financed himself. Another Islamic centre and mosque was inaugurated by King Khālid in Geneva at the beginning of June 1978.[106]

ECONOMIC AFFAIRS

For a comprehensive examination of the Saudi economy and tables, see essay entitled, "Deficits in Saudi Arabia: Their Meaning and Possible Implication."

Haim Shaked and Tamar Yegnes

ARMED FORCES

Total armed forces number 58,500. Defence expenditure in 1978–79 was 33.30 bn Saudi rials ($9.63 bn). Military service is voluntary. The Army numbers 45,000 and consists of two armoured brigades; four infantry brigades; two parachute battalions; one Royal Guard battalion; three artillery battalions; six anti-aircraft batteries; ten surface-to-air missile batteries with *HAWK*. Equipment consists of 250 AMX-30, 75 M-60 medium tanks; 200 AML-60/-90 armoured, *Ferret*, 50 *Fox* scout cars; 300 AMX-10P mechanized infantry combat vehicles; M-113, Panhard M-3, armoured personnel carriers; 105mm pack howitzers, 105mm and 155mm self-propelled howitzers; 75mm recoilless rifles; *TOW* anti-tank guided weapons; M-42 40mm self-propelled, AMX-30 self-propelled anti-aircraft guns; *HAWK* surface-to-air missiles. (175 M-60 medium tanks; 50 *Fox* scout cars; 200 AMX-10P mechanized infantry combat vehicles; *Dragon* anti-tank guided weapons; M-163 *Vulcan* 20mm self-propelled anti-aircraft guns; *Redeye*, *Shahine* (*Crotale*) and six batteries *Improved HAWK* surface-to-air missiles on order). 700 men are deployed in Lebanon in the Arab Peacekeeping Force.

The 1,500-strong Navy is equipped with three fast patrol boats (*Jaguar*-class); one large patrol craft (ex-US coastguard cutter); four coastal minesweepers; two utility landing craft. (Six corvettes with *Harpoon* surface-to-surface missiles, four fast patrol boats, guided-missile, four gunboats and four landing craft on order.)

The Air Force numbers 12,000 and is equipped with 171 combat aircraft. Formations consist of three fighter bomber squadrons with 60 F-5E; two counter-insurgency/training squadrons with 35 BAC-167; one interceptor squadron with 16 *Lightning* F-53, two T55; three operational conversion units with 24 F-5F, 16 F-5B, 16 *Lightning* F53, two T55; two transport squadrons with 35 C-130E/H. Two helicopter squadrons with 16 AB-206 and 24 AB-205; other aircraft include four KC-130 tankers, one Boeing 707, two *Falcon* 20, two Jetstar transports; 22 *Alouette* III, one AB-206, one Bell-212, two AS-61A helicopters. Trainers include 12 T-41A. *Red Top*, *Firestreak*, *Sidewinder*, R.530, R.550 *Magic* air-to-air missiles; *Maverick* air-to-surface missiles. (45 F-15 fighters; 15 TF-15 trainers; one Boeing 747, four KC-130H transport aircraft; six KV-107 helicopters on order.) Paramilitary Forces: 35,000 National Guard in 20 regular and semi-regular battalions with 150 V-150 *Commando* armoured personnel carriers. 6,500 Frontier Force and Coastguard with 50 small patrol boats and eight SRN-6 hovercraft.

Source: *The Military Balance 1978–79* (London: International Institute for Strategic Studies).

ARMED FORCES: DIVISIONS/MAJOR SYSTEMS

	1973	1978
Armoured brigades	—	1
Mechanized brigades	—	1
Infantry brigades	4	2*
Special forces regiments	—	3
Tanks	120	350
Armoured personnel carriers	200	500
Artillery	90	300
Combat aircraft	70	130
Helicopters	40	60
Ground-to-air missile batteries	11	11
Naval vessels	—	several dozen coastal patrol boats

*Are being converted to mechanized brigades.
Source: *Arab Military Strength* (Jerusalem: Israel Information Centre, June 1978).

NOTES
1. See *Middle East Contemporary Survey (MECS) 1976–77*, p. 567.
2. *Arabia and the Gulf*, London; 2 January 1978. *US News and World Report*, Washington; 20 March 1978.
3. *'Ukāz*, Jidda; 15 December 1977; *al-Yamāma*, Riyadh; 3 March 1978.
4. *Al-Sharq al-Jadīd*, London; 1 April 1978.
5. *Ha'aretz*, Tel Aviv; 8 June 1978.
6. For details regarding the nationalities and numbers of foreign manpower, see *MECS 1976–77*, p. 569.
7. *Financial Times (FT)*, London; 25 July 1978.
8. *The Observer*, London; 22 January 1978; *The Times*, London; 26 January 1978; *Jerusalem Post (JP)*, 29 January 1978; *International Herald Tribune (IHT)*, Paris; 2 February 1978.
9. R Riyadh, 8 January 1978.
10. R Riyadh, 3 April—British Broadcasting Corporation Summary of World Broadcasts, the ME and Africa (BBC), 5 April 1978.
11. *IHT*, 25 June 1978.
12. *'Ukāz*, 19 January 1978.
13. *Ibid*, 23 April 1978.
14. R Riyadh, 16 May, 10 July—Daily Report (DR), 18 May, 11 July 1978.
15. Saudi News Agency (SNA), 31 May—BBC, 2 June 1978.
16. SNA, 7 June—BBC, 9 June; R Riyadh, 6 July—DR, 7 July; SNA, 10 July—BBC, 12 July 1978.
17. SNA, 1 August—BBC, 3 August 1978.
18. *Afro-Asian Affairs*, London; 9 November 1977.
19. See *MECS 1976–77*, p. 569.
20. *Tarīq al-Sha'b*, Baghdad; 26 September—DR, 4 October 1977.
21. E.g. SNA, 18 November—BBC, 21 November 1977.
22. *Al-Ahrām*, Cairo; 24 November; *Washington Post (WP)*, 24 November; *The Guardian*, London; *IHT*, 25 November 1977.
23. R Riyadh, 24 November—DR, 25 November 1977.
24. *Al-Safīr*, Beirut; 7 December; *'Ukāz*, 8 December 1977.
25. R Riyadh, 30 November—DR, 1 December 1977.
26. Qatar News Agency (QNA), 23 January—BBC, 24 January 1978.
27. *The Times*, 15 December 1977.
28. *Al-Hawādith*, Beirut; 9 December 1977.

29. *Al-Madīna*, 6 January; *al-Ra'y al-'Āmm*, Kuwait; 9 March 1978. For Saudi statements before and after Camp David, see essays on Inter-Arab Relations and the Arab-Israeli Conflict.
30. R Damascus, 12 December—BBC, 13 December 1977.
31. *The Middle East*, London; May 1978.
32. *Newsweek*, New York; 28 May 1978.
33. *Al-Bilād*, Jidda; 2 July; The Middle East News Agency (MENA), Cairo; 2 July 1978.
34. R Amman, 18 December—BBC, 20 December 1977.
35. MENA, 27 October 1977; R Riyadh, 14 May 1978.
36. *Al-Nahār*, Beirut; 14 February 1978.
37. *Al-Hawādith*, 6 January; SNA, 24 February—BBC, 25 February 1978.
38. R Riyadh, 15 March; *IHT*, 16 March 1978.
39. R Riyadh, 20 March—BBC, 21 March 1978.
40. *Al-Nahār al-'Arabī wal-Duwalī (NAD)*, Paris; 25 March; *Defense and Foreign Affairs, Weekly Report on Strategic ME Affairs*, Washington; 26 April; *al-Watan al-'Arabī*, Paris; 29 April; *al-Manār*, London; 6 May 1978.
41. R Riyadh, 11 April—DR, 12 April; R Baghdad, 17 April—DR, 18 April; *al-Siyāsa*, Kuwait; 19 April 1978.
42. *Arabia and the Gulf*, 8 May 1978.
43. SNA, 13 May—BBC, 15 May 1978.
44. *The New York Times (NYT)*, 18 June 1978.
45. *Al-Siyāsa*, 18 July 1978.
46. *Al-Yaqẓa*, Kuwait; 20 February; SNA, 9 April—DR, 10 April; SNA, 1 May—BBC, 3 May; *al-Madīna*, 14 May 1978.
47. *Arabia and the Gulf*, 5 December 1977.
48. *Al-Thawra Mustamirra* (organ of the PFLP; formerly published in Beirut; present place of publication not stated), 14 January, 18 February 1978.
49. *NAD*, 29 April 1978.
50. R Riyadh, 6 February—BBC, 8 February 1978.
51. SNA, 18 September—BBC, 20 September 1977; R Moscow, 7 February; SNA, 8 February—DR, 9 February 1978.
52. *Al-Anbā'*, Kuwait; 25 November 1977.
53. R Omdurman, 10 December 1977.
54. See *MECS 1976–77*, p. 579.
55. *NYT*, 1 November 1977; *WP*, 20, 22 December 1977; 3 January 1978; MENA, 1 January—DR, 3 January 1978; *IHT*, 27 December 1977, 4 January 1978; *The Times*, 4 January 1978.
56. MENA, 1 January—DR, 3 January; *WP*, 3 January 1978.
57. *The Times*, 4 January 1978.
58. *The Beirut Daily Middle East Reporter*, January 1978.
59. R Riyadh, 4 January—BBC, 5 January 1978.
60. MENA, 6 January; *The Guardian*, 6 January 1978.
61. *Al-Siyāsa*, 14 January 1978.
62. SNA, 15 January—BBC, 17 January 1978.
63. *WP*, *NYT*, 24 January; *FT*, 25 January; *Arabia and the Gulf*, 6 February 1978.
64. *NYT*, 15 February 1978.
65. *FT*, 17 February 1978.
66. *Al-Qabas*, Kuwait; 1 March 1978.
67. Arab Press Service, Beirut; 1 March 1978.
68. *Daily Telegraph (DT)*, London; 11 March 1978.
69. *Al-Jazīra*, Riyadh; 13 March 1978.
70. *IHT*, 16 March 1978.
71. R Riyadh, 15 March 1978.
72. *Al-Jazīra*, 21 March 1978.
73. *NYT*, 23 March 1978.
74. *IHT*, 30 March; *NYT*, 31 March 1978.
75. *Al-Madīna*, 29 April 1978.
76. *IHT*, 3 May 1978.
77. *Al-Siyāsa*, 3 May 1978.
78. *WP*, 4 May 1978.
79. R Riyadh, 3 May—BBC, 25 May 1978.
80. *The Times*, 8 May 1978.
81. *The Guardian*, 11 May 1978.
82. *Al-Bilād*, *al-Riyadh*, *'Ukāz*, *al-Madīna*, 13 May 1978.
83. *NYT*, 11 May 1978.

84. Reuter, 11, 13, 14 May 1978.
85. R Riyadh, 17, 19 May; *al-Madīna*, 20 May 1978.
86. Reuter, 17 May 1978.
87. SNA, 16 October—BBC, 17 October 1978.
88. R Riyadh, 29 May—BBC, 31 May 1978.
89. *FT*, 2 March 1978.
90. *The Times, IHT, JP,* 2 February 1978.
91. *The Times, The Guardian, NYT,* 15 June; *The Times, IHT,* 16 June 1978.
92. *IHT,* 19 June 1978.
93. *The Times,* 10 July 1978.
94. *NAD,* 21 January; *Akhbār al-Usbūʻ,* Amman; 2 February 1978.
95. MENA, 10 February; *Middle East Economic Digest (MEED),* London; 21 April; *Arabia and the Gulf,* 10 April, 15 May 1978.
96. *Al-Nahār,* 29 May; *The Guardian, Le Monde,* Paris; 30 May 1978.
97. SNA, 30 May—BBC, 1 June; *The Times,* 31 May; Reuter, 31 May 1978.
98. SNA, 31 May—BBC, 2 June 1978.
99. *October,* Cairo; 12 June; R Paris, 12 June—BBC, 14 June 1978.
100. R Riyadh, 22 July—DR, 26 July 1978.
101. *IHT,* 8 November 1977.
102. SNA, 24 June; *al-Watan al-ʻArabī,* 1 July; *al-Anbāʼ,* Beirut; 1 July 1978.
103. R Riyadh, 26 October—BBC, 1 November 1977.
104. R Madrid, 17 March—BBC, 20 March 1978.
105. SNA, 11 May—BBC, 13 May 1978.
106. *Maʻariv,* Tel Aviv; 2 June 1978.

The Democratic Republic of Sudan

(Jumhūriyyat al-Sūdān al-Dimuqrātiyya)

The domestic and external policies of the Sudan during the period under review (September 1977–September 1978) represented a continuous evolution of trends that had become evident the year before. Two major issues dominated the regime in the domestic sphere: achieving a reconciliation with the National Front (NF) and coping with the rapidly deteriorating economy. Both developments seemed to reach a peak during 1978—the former positively, the latter in a decidedly negative way.

The NF leaders had made reconciliation contingent upon the regime's acceptance of certain demands including the curbing of the security apparatus, freedom of the press, safeguarding of civil liberties and fair elections to all key posts in the state. President Ja'far al-Numayrī was thus faced with a serious dilemma: if he acceded to these demands, the means of maintaining his political authority and power would be considerably eroded; if he did not, the security and stability of the regime would remain in jeopardy. By the end of 1977, it was already clear that the regime was determined to meet this challenge, as reflected in its serious efforts to integrate returning NF members into the political system. By contrast, in December–January 1978, the moves towards reconciliation faced some significant obstacles. Numayrī's support of Sādāt's visit to Jerusalem aggravated the difficulties which were already inherent in the process of reconciliation by causing new tensions between Numayrī and the two major leaders of the NF, al-Sādiq al-Mahdī and al-Sharīf al-Hindī. However, while they were united in criticizing Numayrī on the one hand, a deeply-embedded power struggle within the top NF leadership surfaced on the other. Both these developments impeded reconciliation. Nevertheless, the results of the February 1978 elections to the People's National Assembly (PNA) and to the [Southern] People's Regional Assembly (PRA) enabled Numayrī to make further moves towards promoting reconciliation. In March, following significant NF gains in the elections to the PNA and the victory of old-guard Southern politicians over the Alier government in PRA elections, Numayrī announced the appointment of NF and new Southern political figures to top positions in the Sudanese Socialist Union (SSU).

The regime's wish to accelerate reconciliation was also reflected in its April negotiations with al-Hindī who, at that stage, still appeared to have a measure of control over the NF (partly military) camps abroad. The period of intensive negotiations was concluded with an agreement with al-Hindī, which in practical terms meant the dissolution of the NF—a move which was not fulfilled in 1978. While these negotiations were under way, widespread strikes broke out, motivated by a combination of political and economic factors. The Communists hoped to exploit this restiveness to impede the reconciliation with the NF, or at least to find a place for themselves within it—hopes which were only partially fulfilled in 1978. The serious economic hardships which the Sudanese suffered were an important factor in these developments. By mid-1978, when the economic problems had worsened significantly (particularly after the decision to devalue the currency on 10 June), resentment and bitterness increased over the acute lack of basic commodities, the high price increases and the loss of spending-power. Despite intensive measures to reduce these economic hardships—including a Cabinet reshuffle at the end of July—they continued to be a major challenge to the regime.

695

Both the economic crisis and the reconciliation process closely affected Sudan's foreign policies. Because of its dire need for foreign capital, it became more necessary to synchronize its Arab policy with that of Saudi Arabia which, with the smaller Gulf states, are Sudan's main bankers. Numayrī, who had initially supported Sādāt's visit to Jerusalem, changed direction to support a non-committal inter-Arab policy, while still maintaining a special relationship with Egypt. This was also in keeping with the NF's demand for neutrality in Sudan's foreign relations; namely, improving relations with Libya and Ethiopia and cooling those with Egypt. Indeed, in 1978 Sudan did restore relations (albeit uneasily) with both Libya and Ethiopia, while at the same time maintaining a certain aloofness towards Egypt. The increasing Soviet role in Africa, particularly in Ethiopia, worried Sudan and was one of the major reasons why Numayrī played the role of mediator in the African continent. The OAU summit, which met in Khartoum in July, discussed at length the issue of foreign intervention in Africa; leaders were divided over proposals to condemn the Russians and Cubans. Sudan's relations with the Soviets remained strained despite a slight improvement in May. Simultaneously, relations with the US and the West were deepened, mainly in the economic and military aid spheres.

POLITICAL AFFAIRS
THE PROCESS OF NATIONAL RECONCILIATION
Al-Sādiq al-Mahdī's return to the Sudan on 27 September 1977 signified a major step in implementing the policy of reconciliation which had formally begun in mid-1977. While reflecting a measure of understanding and agreement reached between the Sudanese government and its traditional opposition, this development also accentuated and brought to the fore a number of issues affecting the immediate and long-term future of the Sudanese political system (see *MECS 1976–77*, pp. 594–95). In his address welcoming al-Mahdī home, Numayrī thanked him for his response to the invitation to return in order to "strengthen our national and comprehensive unity." [1] In reply, al-Mahdī praised Numayrī's "historic initiative" which called for the consolidation of unity by "a genuine and unified stance towards democratic practices, basic human rights, Islamic legislation and real participation by all the Sudanese people at all levels in the task of national reconstruction." [2]

At about the same time, a "big committee"—as Numayrī called it—was set up under the chairmanship of Vice-President Abū al-Qāsim Muhammad Ibrāhīm containing representatives of the regime and the NF. Its task was to facilitate the integration of NF members returning from exile into the social, economic and political fabric of the Sudan. For about a month, this attempt at integration continued. On 28 November, 'Abd al-Rahman Idrīs—who had been actively involved in the 1975 coup attempt and was among the first group of exiles to return under the terms of the Numayrī Amnesty Law of August 1977—was appointed to the post of Joint Secretary-General of the sole political organization permitted in Sudan, the Sudanese Socialist Union (SSU; *al-ittihād al-ishtirākī al-sūdānī*). On 8 December, he was reported to have been appointed to the SSU Central Committee (CC) as well. Wishing to pave the way for the candidacy of NF activists in the forthcoming elections to the People's National Assembly (PNA; *majlis al-sha'b al-qawmī*), the Sudanese Bar Association began to lobby at the end of November for the abrogation of amendments to the Constitution enacted following the attempted coups of 1975 and 1976; these barred anyone convicted of crimes against the state from running for the PNA. They also demanded the amendment of certain laws. [3] The lawyers' initiative followed a petition submitted a month before by 80 PNA members.

While Numayrī continued to reiterate the eagerness of the Sudanese people to achieve national reconciliation, not all political circles endorsed this policy. Apprehensions were expressed, in public and in private, about the effect reconciliation might have on Sudan's public life. An editorial published in October in the official *Sudanow* by the Southerner and then Minister of Information and Culture, Bona Malwal, reflected typical concern about the role that traditional Islam and its adherents might assume through the reconciliation process: "It would be tragic if the Committee [which was set up in August 1977 to examine the laws of the Sudan and to revise them in conformity with the *sharī'a* (Islamic religious law)] produces results which will divide national opinion." Malwal expressed the hope that this Committee would ensure the application of the principle, "religion to the individual and the country to all." [4] Such anxieties were by no means limited to Southern Christians or animists, but were widely held in secular and Leftist circles. Signs of dissatisfaction and resentment also appeared among military and security circles which apparently feared that the regime might accept NF demands to curb the size of the security forces as part of the reconciliation process. Abū al-Qāsim Muḥammad Ibrāhīm's statement, issued in mid-November, that "no reduction in any of the security apparatus would be made," [5] was probably aimed at reducing these fears.

From its inception, the NF was a coalition of separate, and even rival, political forces, characterized by their traditional, Islamic orientation. The common denominator was their opposition to the regime. The first element to split away from the opposition front was the Islamic Charter Front—a Muslim Brethren organization led by Dr Ḥasan 'Abdallah al-Turābī, who is al-Ṣādiq al-Mahdī's brother-in-law. There is considerable doubt about the political relationship between the two. Al-Mahdī, though insisting strongly on the importance of the religious and cultural aspects of Islam, believes—unlike al-Turābī—that it should be kept out of political life. Released from prison and granted an amnesty under the 7 August 1977 law, al-Turābī has since been co-operating closely with the regime, for example, by serving on official committees to consider legal reform. By September it was unclear whether or not the other parts of the NF were still united. When al-Mahdī returned to the Sudan from exile in London, al-Sharīf al-Hindī—the second senior leader in the NF—remained in exile in Libya, ostensibly for reasons of ill health. Although al-Hindī joined al-Mahdī in praising Numayrī's "historic initiative," saying that "we had responded," [6] it soon became clear that these two leading NF figures did not in fact see eye to eye on the terms of reconciliation. The fact that al-Hindī remained abroad may have signified a growing rift between the two.

Before long, an issue arose which adversely affected the process of reconciliation and further indicated that all was not well between al-Mahdī and al-Hindī, or between them and Numayrī. The issue was provoked by the President's strong support for Sādāt's visit to Jerusalem in November 1977—all the more significant in light of the highly-charged negative atmosphere then prevailing in the Arab world. Neither al-Hindī nor al-Mahdī approved of Sādāt's initiative and so criticized Numayrī's support for it. At the same time, it brought to the surface a power struggle within the NF top leadership which had been latent for some time. The two leaders disagreed about the extent to which Numayrī's statement should be allowed to influence the course of their negotiations for reconciliation. Taking his cue from Libya, al-Hindī declared it a "serious setback for the talks now going on"; [7] al-Mahdī, on the other hand, saw it as "an obstacle" but not severe enough to seriously disturb the negotiations. [8]

Apart from this difference with al-Hindī, al-Mahdī had to cope with other challenges to his leadership: within the Mahdī family, the old rivalry between nephew and uncle (Aḥmad al-Mahdī) still persisted; this also influenced the attitudes of some senior Ansārī followers of the Mahdī family, traditional supporters of the Umma Party as well as other NF elements. The latter were particularly concerned about the secrecy with which Numayrī and al-Mahdī were conducting their negotiations. In fact, it was this very issue which prompted 'Uthmān Khālid Madawī, former Secretary-General of the NF, to leave Sudan in protest in December 1977. And this was only one major expression of such resentment. Rumours that al-Sādiq al-Mahdī had reaped excessive financial benefits (£200,000) "in compensation for the use of his property while he had been in exile"[9] were undoubtedly designed to damage his position. Even more serious allegations were made against al-Hindī, who has a considerable reputation as a business entrepreneur and for combining widespread financial interests with exile politics.

By late 1977, it began to look as if al-Hindī was improving his bargaining strength by continuing negotiations from abroad. Frustrated by his own slow progress, al-Mahdī took a number of steps to restore his authority within the NF as well as his negotiating position with Numayrī. At one level he continued to praise Numayrī's policy of reconciliation. Thus, in an interview in December 1977, he described the President "as a more realistic and a more conciliatory man [in comparison with the period before reconciliation contacts had begun]."[10] Numayrī, for his part, emphasized that the two men were not suspicious of each other, despite existing differences of opinion.[11] When rumours began to spread in January 1978 that the reconciliation efforts had collapsed—in particular because of differences over Numayrī's support of Sādāt's policy—al-Mahdī immediately denied them. But he admitted that Numayrī's move had been "a test case for the reconciliation process, which survived the test."[12]

On a second level, al-Mahdī was concerned with the closure of the NF military camps in Libya and Ethiopia, which contained about 6,000 fighters.[13] Their closure was not only a high-priority issue for Numayrī, but also a key element in the power struggle between al-Mahdī and al-Hindī, since both were aware that whoever controlled the men in the camps would be in a stronger position with regard to the NF as well as the Numayrī regime. Al-Mahdī claimed that his departure from Sudan at the end of 1977 was connected with efforts towards national reconciliation.[14] Numayrī, for his part, confirmed in his monthly TV programme of January 1978, that "brother al-Mahdī had travelled outside Sudan within the framework of our joint efforts to consolidate national unity."[15] At first it appeared that al-Mahdī was not successful in closing camps in Libya and Ethiopia. Some reports suggested that the Libyans were opposed to this course; others that the majority of those in the camps owed their loyalty to al-Hindī rather than to al-Mahdī.

The facts, as subsequently revealed, put a different complexion on the situation. The Sudanese in the camps did not want to return in "defeat," with no status and no place in their society at home. Therefore arrangements had to be made to secure land or other employment for them so that they could rejoin their families with every sign of being both respected and welcome—matters which are extremely important in Sudanese society. Between them, al-Mahdī and Numayrī made the necessary arrangements, but these took time. Meanwhile, relations deteriorated between al-Mahdī and al-Hindī, who made his return conditional on a number of major changes in Numayrī's policies: ending the joint defence pact with Egypt, lifting the security laws, and changing the orientation of the regime's foreign and economic policies.

The strains in the NF leadership came to a head in January 1978 when al-Mahdī dismissed al-Hindī and another senior member, Ahmad Zayn al-'Ābidīn,[16] from the NF Political Bureau.[17] Al-Mahdī explained that this move was "not a question of dismissal" but "a decision that henceforth we will never co-operate with them, now or in the future."[18] Al-Hindī stayed on in Libya, pursuing his exile politics as well as his business interests which range from Saudi Arabia to South America. Al-Mahdī's position was undoubtedly stronger in the NF than al-Hindī's, but their split left open the question of who would speak for the Khatimiyya sect supporters of the old National Union Party in the absence of al-Hindī.

ABORTIVE COUPS REPORTED; RESENTMENT AND ARRESTS IN THE ARMY

Towards the end of January 1978, it was reported that the Sudanese authorities had thwarted an attempted coup on 29 December 1977, and that a number of people had been arrested while trying to subvert members of the army by distributing "money and political tracts against Numayrī's regime."[19] According to a foreign source, a bitter confrontation developed between Numayrī and some of his top officers at the end of January, indicating that some of the regime's policies were resented and strongly criticized even at high army command levels. The "meeting of the [armed forces] high command" (mu'tamar al-qiyādāt)—a body which had been set up by Numayrī but had not been invested with any formal powers[20]—was convened between 30 January and 2 February 1978. Unlike previous meetings, Numayrī and the Defence Minister and Commander-in-Chief of the Sudanese Army, Gen (farīq awwal) Bashīr Muhammad 'Alī, were not invited. But they attended in any case and were confronted with considerable criticism regarding domestic and foreign policy.[21] The Sudanese media did not intimate that any friction existed, reporting only that "the meeting of the high command" had taken place.

Foreign sources reported that at the end of February, about three weeks after "the meeting of the high command," 17 officers were arrested in the wake of an abortive military coup.[22] The most important among those detained were: Gen 'Abdallah Muhammad 'Uthmān, Commander of the 2,500-strong Border Guards and Secretary of the Free Officers' Association; Gen Khālid al-Amīn al-Hājj, Inspector-General of the Armed Forces; Brig ('amīd) Sādiq, in charge of the armed forces personnel and reported to be very close to Numayrī; Col ('aqīd) Fathī Abū Zayd, uncle of Major (rā'id) Ma'mūn 'Awad Abū Zayd, one of the original RCC members; and Col Khālid Hasan 'Abbās, who played a leading role in the 1969 coup which brought the Numayrī regime to power.[23]

ELECTIONS TO THE PEOPLE'S NATIONAL ASSEMBLY (PNA)
AND TO THE SOUTHERN PEOPLE'S REGIONAL ASSEMBLY (PRA)

Preparations for elections to the third People's National Assembly and to the Southern People's Regional Assembly began on 26 September 1977 when Numayrī announced that membership in the third PNA would be increased from 250 to 304 (for the allocation of seats, see Table 1). Two official explanations were offered for this move: first, the larger number of geographical constituencies effected by the 1976 revision of provincial boundaries; and second, the growth of the Sudanese population since the previous elections in November 1973. On 31 October 1977, Numayrī issued a decree forming a committee to supervise the elections, scheduled for the first two weeks of February 1978, and on 14 December he formally dissolved the second PNA.

The results of the February elections clearly reflected the strong popular support enjoyed by the NF and provided a further stimulant to the regime's wish to accelerate the process of reconciliation. Out of the 274 "free" PNA seats (30 others were set aside for Numayrī's appointments), c. 140 were won by opposition candidates. Al-Mahdī's supporters of the Umma Party won some 30 seats, and approximately the same number went to candidates affiliated with the former National Unionist Party. The Islamic Charter Front took c. 20 seats, and between

40 and 60 were won by independent local dignitaries.[24] The first session of the third PNA was held on 13 March during which it elected Abū al-Qāsim Muḥammad Ibrāhīm (the First Vice-President and General-Secretary of the SSU) as its Speaker; Mahdī Mustafā al-Hādī as its superviser; and Muzamil Sulaymān Ghandūr and Otu Andauk as deputy-Speakers. Badr al-Dīn Muḥammad Aḥmad Sulaymān was appointed by Numayrī as leader (rā'id).

TABLE 1: ALLOCATION OF SEATS IN THE THIRD PEOPLE'S NATIONAL ASSEMBLY

Union of the Allied Working Forces: 48	People's Assembly 304 members		Nomination by the President: 30 seats		Administrative Units based on People's Local Councils. Every province elects two: 36 seats
Farmers 5					
Workers 5					
National capitalists 4	Geographical constituencies: 136 seats	Red Sea 5	Northern Darfur 7	Southern Kordofan 8	Northern Kordofan 10	Popular Organizations' Constituencies (Youth, Women, Village Development Committees) Each province elects one from each organization: 54 seats
The People's Armed Forces 4		White Nile 9	East Equatoria 5	Southern Darfur 9	West Equatoria 5	
	Northern 5	Lakes 5	Bahr el Ghazal 7	Khartoum 10	Gezira 17	
Intellectuals and professionals 30	Blue Nile 9	Upper Nile 5	Nile 5	Jonglei 5	Kassala 10	

Source: Sudanow, February 1978.

CHANGE OF LEADERSHIP IN THE SOUTH
In the South, elections to the 110-member second People's Regional Assembly (majlis al-sha'b al-iqlīmī) were held between 2 and 11 February 1978.[25] Their results reflected the strong opposition that had developed to the Southern regional government (officially known as the Higher Executive Council; HEC),[26] headed by Abel Alier, Vice-President of the Republic and until February 1978 also President of the HEC. Growing opposition to the existing regional government—in power since the Addis Ababa Agreement and the cessation of the civil war in the South at the end of 1972—was nourished by a number of factors. Some of these were connected with basic and characteristic Southern sensitivities; others arose in the course of the Alier government's tenure in office. The peace prevailing since the 1972 agreement obliterated secessionist elements in the South, but did not erase religious sensitivities, political apprehensions and economic anxieties. Of these factors, the difficult economic situation was the most vexatious. Although this problem was serious long before the Alier government came to power, it provided ammunition for opposition both to the rapprochement with the North and to Alier himself. Even many of those who remained strong supporters of the agreement with Khartoum had come to resent the slow rate of development in the South and criticized the Alier government for its failure to obtain a larger share of central government investments. The cumulative effects of real economic hardship, feelings of deprivation and disappointment, and local animosities were turned against the Alier government—which was represented as being too compliant with the wishes of the Numayrī regime.

A more immediate rallying point for opponents to the Alier government was the relatively new process of reconciliation with the NF, which was regarded in some Southern circles with resentment and suspicion. There were complaints about Numayrī's failure to consult the Alier government about this process. Some prominent Southerners, such as Bona Malwal, the Information and Culture Minister in the central government, were known to have criticized the reconciliation as premature.[27] This complaint hinged partly on the anxieties among the Christian and animist Southerners about the growth of a militant Islamic influence on the central government through the NF, especially through al-Turābī's Muslim Brethren. This fear was forcefully expressed by the man who defeated Alier—Maj-Gen (liwā') Joseph Lagu, the former leader of the Anya-nya and, until February 1978, commander of the First Division[28]—who said that the adaptation of Sudan's laws to the sharī'a was viewed with great concern in the South.[29]

Two additional causes for the downfall of the Alier government were allegations of a growing prevalence of corruption, and the reappearance—under the 1977 amnesty law—of old-guard politicians from the Sudan African National Union (SANU)[30] who were known for their opposition to Alier's government. Since seven out of 15 of his ministers were defeated, Alier resigned as HEC President (though he retained his position as a Vice-President of the Republic).

Maj-Gen (liwā') Joseph Lagu was unanimously elected by the second People's Regional Assembly on 28 February as its candidate for the position of President of the HEC. Numayrī formally confirmed this appointment early in March. Lagu was also promoted to the rank of Lieutenant-General (farīq). Maj-Gen Yūsuf Ahmad Yūsuf, formerly garrison commander in Malakāl, replaced Lagu as Commander of the First Division.

The new members of the HEC included Joseph Udoho, one of the original SANU founders; Lawrence Wol Wol; Benjamin Bol Akok, who had fled to Ethiopia from where he was believed to have participated in the Juba affair of February 1977 (see MECS 1976–77, pp. 589–90); Samuel Aru Bol, a member of the original 1972 Regional Government who was replaced in 1974 for alleged "tribalist" activities; and Ezekiel Macuei Kodi, a SANU member. Clement Mboro, the founder of the Southern Front[31] and a former Minister of Interior in the government of al-Sādiq al-Mahdī, was appointed Speaker of the People's Regional Assembly.

THE HIGHER EXECUTIVE COUNCIL, as at March 1978

President	Lt-Gen Joseph Lagu
Administration, Police and Prisons	Samuel Aru Bol
Agriculture, Forestry, Animal Resources and Fisheries	Benjamin Bol Akok
Finance and Economic Planning	Lawrence Wol Wol
Commerce, Industry and Supply	Ezekiel Macuei Kodi
Wildlife and Tourism	Samuel Gaitut
Information and Culture	Simon Mori
Rural Development and Co-operatives	Joseph Udoho
Communications, Roads and Transport	Joseph James Toumbra
Health and Social Welfare	Pacifico Lolik
Youth and Sports	Daniel Kout Mathews
Education	Matthew Ubur Anyang
Public Service and Administrative Reform	Akuot Atem
Housing and Public Utilities	Barnaba Dumo
Council's Affairs	Rev-Fr Ireneo Lope
Legal Affairs	Samuel Lupai

Joseph Lagu summed up the results of the elections as "a change in personnel—not a change of system." [32] Yet it was clear that the downfall of Alier's government reflected a deep desire for substantial change in the South. The re-entry of old-guard politicians—legally and by the will of the people—into the Southern political system was an indication of the desire for tougher leaders, some of whom had been detained because of complicity in the abortive coup of July 1976 and the Juba affair of 1977. Nevertheless, Lagu had himself always remained loyal to Numayrī. It was clear that the new government in the South would have to fulfil at least some of the high expectations they had themselves aroused, especially in economic improvement.

APPOINTMENT OF NF AND SOUTHERN LEADERS TO SSU CENTRAL COMMITTEE AND THE POLITICAL BUREAU

With the success of the NF in the PNA elections and the dramatic change in the South, new political conditions prevailed in the Sudan. Indeed, on 10 March, Numayrī announced the appointment of 51 new members to the Central Committee (CC) of the SSU to reflect these changes. The list of new members included a number of prominent NF figures such as al-Sādiq al-Mahdī; Dr 'Abd al-Ḥāmid Ṣāliḥ and Dr Nūr al-Dīn al-Dā'im—two leading figures in the former Umma Party who had been sentenced in absentia to 10 years' imprisonment because of alleged complicity in the abortive coup of July 1976; Muhammad Sharīf al-Tuhāmī, known for his close relations with al-Mahdī; Ḥasan 'Abdallah al-Turābī, former Secretary-General of the Islamic Charter Front; 'Ābidīn Ismā'īl, a politican with known Communist tendencies; and Ahmad 'Alī al-Mirghanī, leader of the Khatimiyya sect, a sūfī tarīka (order), traditionally in competition with the Ansār. The list also included Southern political figures who had won the election, such as Clement Mboro, Benjamin Bol Akok, and Joseph Udoho.

Opening the CC meeting on 15 March, Numayrī stressed the central importance of national unity. "National unity," he said, "is the basis of our independence and the axis of our struggle for progress." [33] On the same day, he appointed the following six new members to the SSU Political Bureau, who officially rank third in position after the President: al-Sādiq al-Mahdī, Ahmad 'Alī al-Mirghanī, Ḥasan 'Abdallah al-Turābī, Clement Mboro, Samuel Aru Bol, and Badr al-Dīn Sulaymān. (Known as a Leftist, Sulaymān was Ombudsman from October 1972 to January 1975, and then Minister of Industry till February 1977. From February 1974 until February 1977, he was also a member of the Political Bureau.) Thus the Southerners got two of the six new positions, the NF two, and the Muslim Brethren one.

Although al-Mahdī's appointment had been officially published, he declined to accept the position, explaining: "It would be premature for me to get involved in the actual structure of an organization [SSU] which I disapprove of." [34] Yet he also insisted that his decision "had nothing to do with any reservation concerning the reconciliation." [35] Another NF leader, al-Mirghanī, also refused to accept the appointment to the CC and the Political Bureau, explaining that family tradition would not permit him to be involved in the political system. [36] It thus became apparent that both leaders refused to accept Numayrī's appointment because they wished to avoid doing anything that might lend legitimacy to Numayrī's political system as long as the NF's important demands—such as curtailing the security apparatus, the abolition of the security laws, and the ending of the 1976 Joint Defence Agreement with Egypt—had not been met.

CABINET RESHUFFLE

Apart from its engagement in the reconciliation process, the regime also had to deal with the serious deteriorating economic situation which became critical in 1978.

Sudan's big balance of payments deficit, its high inflation rate and mounting backlog of unpaid debts (so serious that it experienced difficulties obtaining vital imports such as fuel and pesticides) were grim writings on the wall. It was against this background that Numayrī carried out changes in his Cabinet on 22 March. Dr 'Uthmān Hāshim 'Abd al-Salām, who had been responsible for the Ministry of Finance and National Economy as Minister of State during the six months since the September 1977 Cabinet reshuffle (see government list, below), was named full Minister, taking over from Numayrī. Fārūq Ibrāhīm al-Maqbūl, the Ministry's Under-Secretary, was promoted to Minister of State for Finance and National Economy. The third change was the appointment of Abū Bakr 'Uthmān Muḥammad Sāliḥ as Minister of State for the Presidency at the Council of Ministers.

Numayrī also appointed Dr Mansūr Khālid—who was dismissed in the September 1977 reshuffle as Foreign Minister—as chairman of the publishing house of *al-Sahāfa*, thus filling the vacancy created by the death of Mūsā Mubārak in February 1978. Khālid was also appointed as SSU Assistant Secretary-General for Ideology and Orientation. His appointment to these positions indicated the importance the regime attached to information—particularly at a difficult time when reconciliation was making slow progress and when public resentment about economic hardships was running high.

INDUSTRIAL TROUBLES

Despite unpopular measures taken by the regime to combat the deteriorating economic situation, prices continued to rise drastically. A report prepared in early 1977 by the economic committee of the Sudanese General Federation of Trade Unions estimated that prices had increased 98% since 1974. According to this report, the maximum increase in wages was 17%, which meant a considerable decrease in workers' actual income.[37] Even if these figures were slanted in favour of the workers, they reflected the acute problem of a rapidly rising cost of living, which was further aggravated in 1978 despite measures taken by the regime. By the spring of 1978, various Leftist elements and Communists promoted a series of strikes, partly to gain political dividends and partly to draw attention to themselves while the regime was still engaged in the reconciliation negotiations from which they were excluded. Economic discontent gave the Communists an opportunity to utilize their traditionally strong position in the trade unions.

One Sudanese newspaper summed up the position as follows: "Strike was the word that dominated the first two weeks of April 1978."[38] Indeed, no less than 21 trade union branches (including doctors, teachers, pharmacists and taxi drivers) stopped work.[39] Of these strikes, three drew special attention: the railway workers, the technicians and the medical doctors. In the important railroad junction of 'Atbara (212 miles north-east of Khartoum), 1,200 railway workshop workers began a strike on 3 April, demanding a pay rise and a status similar to that of drivers. When the strike became violent, police intervened and 50 of the strikers were arrested. Their release was ordered by the first Vice-President, Abū al-Qāsim Muḥammad Ibrāhīm, who was able to restore peace and initiate negotiations.

Technicians went on strike on 4 April, demanding an increase in salaries as well as an improvement in their status and working conditions. Two days later, an agreement was concluded which virtually met their demands. There were two apparent reasons for this concession. Firstly, the key position held by the technicians would have enabled them to cause severe dislocation and economic damage, thus adding to existing public bitterness. Secondly, the regime wished to rectify the acute lack of skilled manpower in the country, which was due to the failure to develop an adequate training programme as well as to the exodus of skilled labour to the oil-rich countries. This could only be done by offering increased salaries and improved conditions.

The events in 'Atbara and the short-lived technicians' protest were soon over-shadowed by the doctors' strike in support of wage increases of up to 50%. The regime strongly condemned this action, refused to accede to the doctors' demands, and alleged that they were politically rather than economically motivated. The regime's case was based on a memorandum sent by the Medical Union to Numayrī in January praising the national reconciliation process and requesting that it be extended to include the Communists.[40] Numayrī declared that those behind the strike were "receiving their instructions from Moscow,"[41] and warned the strikers that "the Soviet bear is working among you."[42]

An outcome of these labour troubles was that, in April, Numayrī extended the reconciliation process to include both the Communists on the Left and al-Hindī on the Right.

RECONCILIATION AGREEMENT WITH AL-HINDĪ

After al-Mahdī's failure to close down the NF camps in Libya and Ethiopia (see above), the regime realized that significant progress in reconciliation could only be reached by drawing al-Hindī into the agreement. Such tactics might also prod al-Mahdī to join the political system publicly, before agreement between Numayrī and al-Hindī further eroded his weakened political position.

Numayrī's eagerness to accelerate the process of reconciliation was not motivated solely by domestic considerations, but was also connected with Sudan's foreign policy. The fact that Numayrī had become the chairman of the Arab Solidarity Committee in April (see section on Foreign Affairs below) meant, among other things, that he would have to devote a great deal of effort to the foreign sphere. Furthermore, his scheduled hosting of the Organization of African Unity (OAU) summit in July 1978 provided an additional spur: success for his reconciliation efforts would enable him to point to Sudan as a model for the solution of countries' internal disputes.

After seven days of intensive secret negotiations, a reconciliation agreement was reached in London on 12 April 1978 between al-Hindī and the regime's representatives, headed by the First Vice-President, Abū al-Qāsim Muḥammad Ibrāhīm. The Agreement's main points were as follows:[43]

1. "The permanent [1973] constitution of Sudan was the basic law of government in Sudan and its third section guaranteed the citizens' basic rights and freedoms, including the freedoms of movement, of privacy, of communications, and of housing; the right of citizens to participate in public life and to nominate themselves for public posts and positions; the freedom of belief and worship and engaging in religious ceremonies; the freedom of the Press in serving the ends of the people and the right of peaceful assembly and holding processions." It was recognized that some exceptional circumstances made it necessary to restrict some of these freedoms under exceptional provisions of certain laws, but these provisions must cease with the termination of the circumstances which necessitated them.

2. "The sovereignty of the rule of law, as stipulated in the fourth section of the permanent constitution, and the independence of the judiciary, as stipulated in its eighth section, were to be the bases of government and of justice in the country."

3. "The SSU was the acceptable framework for patriotic work." Both sides

"reaffirmed the building of its organizations through democratic participation and the opening of its ranks to all citizens of Sudan. Positions at all levels, from bottom to top, would be filled by election, so as to achieve comprehensive national unity—the goal of the initiative of the President. The National Congress of the SSU—the highest popular authority in the country—had the right to adopt whatever decisions it saw fit in the realization of the public interest."·

4. "The resolution of the problem of the South, which had exhausted the financial and human resources of the country for 17 years, was a major revolutionary and patriotic action" which received the support of both sides.

5. "The programme for political action and the economic integration was the basis for comprehensive Arab integration."

6. "Sudan's foreign policy was based on the principles of positive neutrality in the Arab field at that critical stage in particular. Sudan, in accordance with its historic leadership role, had the task of supporting and consolidating Arab ranks, purifying its climate of anything which could weaken Arab unity, and mobilizing its combat and political capabilities to meet the challenges of imperialism, racism and Zionism for the sake of regaining the occupied territories, giving the Palestinian people their legitimate and national rights, and establishing an independent state on their territory under the leadership of the Palestine Liberation Organization as the sole legitimate representative of the Palestinian people."

7. It was also agreed to "dissolve the National Front, to return all its members, . . . to eliminate all its camps [abroad], to hand over all weapons and equipment inside and outside the country to the people's armed forces, . . . and to call for the absorption of the returnees, in accordance with their qualifications and skills, into the development projects and other aspects of economic, social and political activity." It was also decided to form joint committees to supervise the implementation of this agreement.

Public references to the agreement by both parties were expressed in glowing terms. While the Sudanese authorities described it as an "historical agreement,"[44] al-Hindī said that he hoped that a new dawn had come.[45] On closer analysis, however, the agreement was seen to represent a considerable lowering of the conditions originally posed by al-Hindī, whose side clearly made the more significant concessions. While the two first points of the agreement were designed to meet al-Hindī's demands that the security laws (enforced in the wake of the abortive coups of 1975 and 1976) be abolished, the other items generally served the interests of the regime. For instance, al-Hindī's readiness to dismantle the NF camps and hand over its weapons to the regime was a serious risk. Moreover, agreeing to the legitimization of the SSU was contrary to his previous insistence that additional political parties be permitted in Sudan and that the SSU's special status be abolished. The fact that the agreement made no mention of a reduction in the strength of the internal security apparatus—which al-Hindī had demanded before April—was another important concession. The agreement's stipulation that Sudan pursue a foreign policy of positive neutrality was aimed to meet al-Hindī's demands for a more non-aligned stance. Yet, it did not go so far as to abrogate the Sudanese-Egyptian Defence Agreement of 1976, which he had wished.

While this agreement was an important step forward, it quite clearly did not solve all the basic differences between al-Hindī and Numayrī. The President stated frankly that "the reconciliation is an admission of existing differences of views . . . and it is an invitation for dealing with them. . . . It is true that reconciliation is not the solution, but it is the means for the solution."[46]

While negotiations between Numayrī and al-Hindī were in progress, three-way talks were being held in London between representatives of Numayrī, al-Hindī and the Sudanese Communist Party (CP). Numayrī's statement at the beginning of May that he was not against the Left in Sudan, and that the majority of the Sudanese Left was "taking part now in the building of Sudan," [47] was one indication of his conciliatory stand vis-à-vis the Communists. On 15 May, 29 Communist detainees were released, including 10 members of the CP's Central Committee.

RECONCILIATION SLOWED DOWN; DEVALUATION OF SUDANESE CURRENCY
Towards the end of May, it seemed that progress in the reconciliation with al-Hindī, al-Mahdī and the Communists alike slowed down for a number of reasons. Al-Hindī was still waiting in Libya for some concrete moves that Numayrī was supposed to take as a condition for his return (such as the cancellation of the security measures), while al-Mahdī and the President were still having differences of opinion. Numayrī, for his part, did not accelerate attempts for further progress because of foreign and domestic preoccupations. During the months of May and June, he was intensely involved with his mission to achieve Arab solidarity (see Foreign Affairs section), and in July, his full attention was devoted to the OAU summit in Khartoum.

Domestically, the steady deterioration of the economic situation, as well as severe difficulties in the supply of basic needs (such as food, water and fuel), required intensive efforts by the regime. Against this bleak background, the information released in May that Sudan had discovered important oilfields appeared as a ray of light. [48] Sudanese hopes reached such a high degree that a foreign source later described the reaction as "an orgy of expectations." [49] An official statement by Numayrī that the existence of oil in Sudan was "no longer open to question" [50] seemed less accurate than another which said that "the results of the search for oil, so far, have been no more than promising." [51] Even if oil did exist there was no indication of its quantity or whether it could be exploited commercially. In any event, the positive effect of oil discoveries on the Sudanese economy would not be felt for some time to come. Indeed, following prolonged pressure from the IMF and a cut-back in government spending, Sudan devalued its currency on 10 June by an effective 20% against the US dollar. This was in order to reduce its foreign exchange deficit, caused by the importing of fuel as well as spare parts. Afterwards, in anticipation of July government salary increases, a number of directives were issued aimed at forestalling runaway inflation.

Meanwhile, it was clear that the regime's negotiations with the Communists had failed, probably over the issue of the country's future political system. While Numayrī insisted upon retaining the SSU as the sole legitimate political party, the Communists argued that it should be replaced by a wide front of various political forces. On 16 July, a foreign source reported that the Sudanese authorities had recently disclosed a new attempt against Numayrī's life. [52] The report added that they had seized all the documents prepared by the dissolved Communist commands in Sudan, who acted in co-operation with the ruling military regime in Ethiopia. [53] Numayrī made a statement at the end of July, claiming that "the people of Sudan have rejected Communism more than once, and they will always reject it." [54] This was seen to indicate that nothing had really changed in the relations between the regime and the Communists.

RECONCILIATION WITH AL-MAHDĪ
In contrast with this lack of progress towards reconciliation with the Communists, agreement was reached in July with al-Sādiq al-Mahdī. His oath on 3 August, on

becoming a member of the SSU Political Bureau, symbolized this accomplishment. At the beginning of July, Philip 'Abbās Ghabbūsh, who headed an opposition organization (see *MECS 1976–77*, p. 589), also announced that he had become reconciled with the regime, declaring: "Our doubts about President Numayrī's government no longer exist." [55] Al-Hindī, still in exile in August, stated: "Numayrī is serious and honest in wanting to implement reconciliation with us . . . but a lot of issues still need to be ironed out." [56] Bābikr Qarār, a leader of national progressive elements in the NF, was expected to return to Sudan. [57] On the other hand, 'Uthmān Khālid Madawī was reported "to have given up and now works as a businessman in Warsaw." [58]

Thus by the end of August, the regime still needed to make progress with the al-Hindī faction which, apart from the outlawed Communist Party, remained the only significant opposition force still not integrated into the Sudanese political system.

CABINET RESHUFFLE AND ADMINISTRATIVE CHANGES

Towards the end of July, following the conclusion of the OAU summit, domestic affairs again became a focal issue. This was reflected by parallel action taken on three levels: political, administrative-governmental, and economic. A Cabinet reshuffle, as well as other changes in the administration, were announced on 29 July (see Table 2). Politically, the most significant change was the removal of Gen (*farīq awwal*) Bashīr Muhammad 'Alī, since 1976 the Defence Minister and Commander-in-Chief of the Sudanese Armed Forces. Numayrī himself took over the Defence portfolio. On the same day the Chief of Staff, Gen Muhammad 'Uthmān Hāshim, was dismissed. His deputy, Maj-Gen (*liwā'*) 'Abd al-Majīd Hāmid Khalīl, was appointed in his place and promoted to the rank of Lt-Gen (*farīq*). Khalīl is known as politically independent. According to one interpretation, the dismissals were based on the generals' pro-Egyptian stance and on their contribution to the shaping of the Sudanese-Egyptian Defence agreement of 1976. The move was considered an indication of Numayrī's intention to follow a more non-aligned foreign policy— meaning an additional moving away from Egypt. As such, the dismissals could also be regarded as a gesture to the leaders of the NF, who oppose close relations with Cairo.

Another move with political and economic implications, which could also be seen as a gesture to the NF, was the appointment of Sharīf al-Tuhāmī, a former NF member and follower of al-Mahdī, to the post of Energy and Mining. He replaced Major (*rā'id*) Ma'mūn 'Awad Abū Zayd, who was appointed to another post in the SSU (see below). Numayrī also dismissed the Minister of Transport, 'Abd al-Rahmān 'Abdallah, appointing in his place Mustafā 'Uthmān Hasan, a former officer who earlier in the year, as chairman of the Seaports Corporation, had succeeded in cutting down the waiting time for vessels at Port Sudan. The dismissal of the two ministers closely connected with fuel and transport indicated the regime's intention to concentrate on solving the economic problems connected with the poor distribution of such basic commodities as fuel, food and water. Mahdī Mustafā al-Hādī's appointment as Commissioner of Khartoum was also seen as an attempt to solve the problems of shortages and rising prices in the capital.

Dr Mansūr Khālid was finally phased out of the political scene by being relieved of all his official duties, both as SSU Assistant Secretary-General for Ideology and Orientation and as chairman of the publishing house of *al-Sahāfa*. Numayrī was quoted as saying that Khālid's "outlook was not close to the people," [59] possibly implying that he was hostile to the reconciliation. [60] Additional changes, this time in the SSU, were carried out by Numayrī on the same day. These included the

TABLE 2: COMPOSITION OF SUDANESE CABINETS

Portfolio	10 September 1977	22 March 1978	29 July 1978
	Cabinet Ministers		
Prime Minister	Ja'far al-Numayrī	Ja'far al-Numayrī	Ja'far al-Numayrī
Foreign Minister	Al-Rashīd al-Ṭāhir Bakr	Al-Rashīd al-Ṭāhir Bakr	Al-Rashīd al-Ṭāhir Bakr
Defence and Commander-in-Chief of Armed Forces	Gen Bashīr Muḥammad 'Alī	Gen Bashīr Muḥammad 'Alī	Ja'far al-Numayrī
Interior and Head of Public Security	'Abd al-Wahhāb Ibrāhīm	'Abd al-Wahhāb Ibrāhīm	'Abd al-Wahhāb Ibrāhīm
Finance, National Economy	Ja'far al-Numayrī	'Uthmān Hāshim 'Abd al-Salām	'Uthmān Hāshim 'Abd al-Salām
Education	Daf'allah al-Ḥājj Yūsuf	Daf'allah al-Ḥājj Yūsuf	Daf'allah al-Ḥājj Yūsuf
Culture and Information	Bona Malwal	Bona Malwal	Bona Malwal[1]
Health	Khālid Ḥasan 'Abbās	Khālid Ḥasan 'Abbās	Khālid Ḥasan 'Abbās
Trade and Supply	Hārūn al-'Awad	Hārūn al-'Awad	Hārūn al-'Awad
Industry	Bashīr 'Abbādī	Bashīr 'Abbādī	Bashīr 'Abbādī
Energy and Mining	Maj Ma'mūn 'Awad Abū Zayd	Maj Ma'mūn 'Awad Abū Zayd	Sharif al-Tuhāmī[+]
Agriculture, Food and National Resources	'Abdallah Aḥmad 'Abdallah	'Abdallah Aḥmad 'Abdallah	'Abdallah Aḥmad 'Abdallah
Transport and Communications	'Abd al-Raḥmān 'Abdallah	'Abd al-Raḥmān 'Abdallah	Mustafā 'Uthmān Ḥasan[+] / Aḥmad 'Abd al-Karīm[+]
Public Services and Administration Reform	Karamallah al-'Awad	Karamallah al-'Awad	Karamallah al-'Awad
Construction and Public Works	Mu'āwiya Abū Bakr	Mu'āwiya Abū Bakr	Mu'āwiya Abū Bakr[2]
Youth and Sports	Maj Zayn al-'Abidin Muḥammad Aḥmad	Maj Zayn al-'Abidin Muḥammad Aḥmad	Maj Zayn al-'Abidin Muḥammad Aḥmad
Social Affairs	Fāṭima 'Abd al-Maḥmūd	Fāṭima 'Abd al-Maḥmūd	Fāṭima 'Abd al-Maḥmūd
Waqfs and Religious Affairs	'Awn al-Sharīf Qāsim	'Awn al-Sharīf Qāsim	'Awn al-Sharīf Qāsim
Irrigation and Hydroelectric Power	Yaḥyā 'Abd al-Majid	Yaḥyā 'Abd al-Majid	Yaḥyā 'Abd al-Majid
Co-operation	Muḥammad Hāshim 'Awad	Muḥammad Hāshim 'Awad	Muḥammad Hāshim 'Awad
Attorney-General	Ḥasan 'Umar	Ḥasan 'Umar	Mahdi al-Faḥl[+]

Portfolio	10 September 1977	22 March 1978	29 July 1978
		Ministers of State	
Presidency	'Izz al-Dīn Ḥāmid	'Izz al-Dīn Ḥāmid Abū Bakr 'Uthmān Muhammad Sālih [+3]	'Izz al-Dīn Ḥāmid Abū Bakr 'Uthmān Muhammad Sālih Yūsuf Mīkhā'īl Najīb [4] Muhammad Mahjūb [5] al-Shīkh Bashīr al-Shīkh [6]
Prime Minister's Office	Khālid al-Khayr 'Umar	Khālid al-Khayr 'Umar	Khālid al-Khayr 'Umar
Finance, National Economy	'Uthmān Hāshim 'Abd al-Salām	Fārūq Ibrāhīm Maqbūl [+]	Fārūq Ibrāhīm Maqbūl
Education	Hasan Ahmad Yūsuf	Hasan Ahmad Yūsuf	Hasan Ahmad Yūsuf
Culture and Information	Ismā'īl al-Ḥājj Mūsā	Ismā'īl al-Ḥājj Mūsā	Ismā'īl al-Ḥājj Mūsā
Planning	*	*	*
Foreign Affairs	Francis Deng	Francis Deng	Francis Deng
Agricultural, Food and National Resources	*	*	Yāsin Ḥākim [+]
Youth and Sports	'Ali Shummū	'Ali Shummū	'Ali Shummū [1]
Communications	Ahmad 'Abd al-Karīm Badrī	*	*

+ Newly appointed.
* No details available.
[1] On 17 September, Bona Malwal was relieved from his post and 'Ali Shummū was appointed instead.
[2] Muhammad Sayyid Ahmad Abdallah appointed on 3 August 1978, as Construction Minister instead of Abū Bakr who died.
[3] Minister for the Presidency at the Council of Ministers, a newly-revived post.
[4] Legal adviser.
[5] Press adviser.
[6] Adviser for the national and local government.

appointment of Hasan 'Abdallah al-Turābī, the Secretary-General of the Islamic Charter Front, as Secretary for Information and Foreign Affairs; the appointment of the former Minister for Energy and Mining, Maj Ma'mūn Abū Zayd, as the SSU Assistant Secretary-General for Ideology and Orientation; and the dismissal of the first Vice-President, Abū al-Qāsim Muḥammad Ibrāhīm, from his post as SSU Assistant Secretary-General for branch organizations. Numayrī also issued a decree for the formation of the Southern Regional Secretariat of the SSU, composed of six Regional HEC members. [61]

While each of these changes had specific causes and implications, it was also possible that Numayrī—who has conducted periodic Cabinet and administrative reshuffles as a means of securing a balance of power within his regime—wished to reduce the threat of a concentration of power in certain hands which might challenge his own position (see *MECS 1976–77*, pp. 588–89).

In August 1978, foreign sources provided information about the escalation of rivalry between political power-groups. According to one report, there was a struggle for power between Vice-President Abū al-Qāsim Muḥammad Ibrāhīm and the Interior Minister and head of the General Security Administration (*jihāz al-amn al-ʿāmm*), 'Abd al-Wahhāb Ibrāhīm, on the one hand; and Maj-Gen 'Umar Muḥammad al-Tayyib, a confidant of Numayrī and head of the National Security Administration (*jihāz al-amn al-qawmī*), on the other. [62] It seemed that Abū al-Qāsim's position within the political system was steadily strengthening and that this led Numayrī to curtail his authority—if only symbolically—by dismissing him from the post of the SSU Assistant Secretary-General for branch organizations. On the other hand, Numayrī's appointment on 12 August of al-Tayyib as chairman of the newly-formed State Security Department (with the rank of Minister) was aimed at strengthening the latter's position. The appointment was made in the framework of a provisional order called the State Security Law of 1978, issued by Numayrī on the same day. This incorporated the National Security Administration and the General Security Department into a unified department called the State Security Department, which was entrusted with the task of safeguarding the country's internal as well as external security.

Also on 12 August, Numayrī issued decrees bringing Sudan Airways and the Public Electricity and Water Corporation—two of Sudan's most ailing state-run organizations—under his direct control. Sudan's electricity and water supplies had become increasingly unreliable, causing widespread resentment. The services of Sudan Airways had deteriorated steadily since late 1976 when the then chairman abruptly terminated the contracts of most of the expatriate staff. Inefficient air services contributed to the shortage of supplies in Sudan, especially in provincial areas—a problem which was further aggravated by the heavy rains and floods of July and August. In addition to its practical implications, Numayrī's move to centralize economic authority also had some psychological impact, emphasizing the realization and readiness at a high level to deal with the poor service infrastructure which had caused strong criticism of the regime.

Numayrī announced his acceptance of the resignation of the Information and Culture Minister, Bona Malwal, explaining that he had wanted to continue his university studies for one year in the UK. [63] In fact, Numayrī had taken strong efforts to dissuade Malwal from this move, but it would appear that as one of the strongest figures among the Southern politicians, he wished to distance himself for a time from the regime. 'Alī Shummū, the Youth and Sport Minister of State, was appointed in his place.

Numayrī's public endorsement of the Camp David accords elicited strong criticism from al-Mahdī who resigned from his posts in the SSU at the beginning of

October and travelled to the US and Britain. He saw Numayrī's support for Sādāt as a violation of their five-point agreement which stipulated that Sudan would follow an independent foreign policy. Thus, by the end of 1978, it was clear that although intermittent progress had been made, the reconciliation process was experiencing difficulties: al-Hindī remained abroad; the April agreement signed by al-Hindī and Numayrī had not yet been implemented; and the Communists remained outside the framework of negotiations.

FOREIGN AFFAIRS
RELATIONS WITH THE SUPER-POWERS
Sudan's relations with the super-powers remained basically unchanged during the period under review, a slight improvement in Sudanese-Soviet relations not impairing those between Sudan and the US. Two factors which were decisive in shaping Sudan's relations with the West, particularly with the US (and with the main conservative Arab states), were its military and foreign capital needs. The volatile situation in the Horn of Africa and Sudan's fears of Soviet expansion in the Red Sea and adjacent regions prompted Numayrī to intensify his efforts to acquire sophisticated weapons. These had begun in 1977 when he approached Britain, France, West Germany—and especially the US—for "defensive" arms.

Acting on the recommendations of a US military delegation, which visited Sudan from 3–17 August 1977, Washington agreed in December 1977 to sell the Numayrī regime a squadron of 12 F-5 fighter planes. In addition, six C-130 *Hercules* planes were delivered by June 1978 in fulfilment of an agreement signed in 1977. The American decision was significant because it marked the first time that the US had agreed to sell combat aircraft to Sudan. At the end of April 1978, it was also reported that the US intended to supply Sudan with air-defence radar systems.[64]

The severe economic crisis prompted Numayrī to seek American private and governmental investments as well. A Joint Sudanese-American Council, set up to encourage US capital into Sudan, held its first meeting in Khartoum from 20–22 February 1978. The idea of this Council grew out of Numayrī's visit to the US in June 1976, and was described by him as "a turning point in the technical, commercial and financial relations with the US."[65] The Sudanese side of the Council consisted of 70 member-companies, two-thirds from the private sector and one-third from the public sector. It was announced in May that the US Congress had agreed to provide all the finance for Sudanese-American projects in Sudan—a move described as "unique in US relations with all other states."[66]

Sudan's severe economic problems and the urgent need for foreign capital were the leitmotif of Numayrī's official visits to the US, Belgium, West Germany and Spain from 19 September to 15 October 1978.

In the beginning of 1978, Sudanese-Soviet relations continued to be strained and even hostile (see *MECS 1976-77*, pp. 595-96). In January, Numayrī asserted that "a big power [USSR] is still continuing its conspiracy against Sudan, desiring to make Sudan its point of entry for a fresh return to the positions it has lost in the African and Arab world."[67] Calling upon the Soviets to leave Africa to the Africans, he said: "We say it loudly to the Soviet Union and its allies: take your hands off Africa and stem the flood of Soviet weapons flowing into it."[68] In April, Sudan accused the Soviets of complicity in the wave of strikes that hit the country at that time (see above). Yet in May, Numayrī announced that in accordance with a "recent request by Moscow,"[69] Sudan and the USSR would restore bilateral relations. A slight improvement in relations was reflected in the return of the Soviet ambassador to Khartoum after his recall a year before (see *MECS 1976-77*, p. 596). Sudan's willingness to resume relations with the USSR was officially attributed to the "removal of the threat of the Soviet and Ethiopian-backed invasion of Sudan, because of the improvement of relations with Ethiopia."[70] Numayrī's *rapprochement* with Moscow was facilitated by the support of former NF leaders like al-Mahdī, al Hindī and al-Turābī for improved relations. Al-Mahdī took the view that the USSR was a part of the elementary balance of international politics and as such could not be ignored;[71] al-Hindī declared that the escalation of hostility in relations between Sudan and the USSR did not serve the interest of either state and that relations should be restored.[72] Improving relations with the USSR was also a way of further consolidating Sudan's relations with Libya and Ethiopia.

SUDAN'S REGIONAL POLICIES
At the end of 1977, Sudan's regional policies had already shifted slightly towards a more non-aligned attitude, expressed mainly in Sudan's willingness to improve relations with Libya and Ethiopia. This attitude reflected foreign interests and also served Numayrī in his role as chairman of the OAU for 1978–79. Domestically, the moves towards reconciliation with the NF made it both possible and necessary to improve the climate of hostility between Sudan and these two neighbours.

Sudan-Libya
Diplomatic links with Libya had been severed by Sudan because of Tripoli's backing of the abortive coup of July 1976 (see *MECS 1976–77*, p. 597). However, during the meeting of the Arab League Ministerial Council, held in Tunis from 12–14 November 1977, Sudan and Libya decided to resume diplomatic relations. Sudan's support for Sādāt's peace initiative later in November delayed the resumption of relations, but these were formally re-established in 8 February 1978. In a communiqué issued in Tripoli on the same day, both sides agreed "to pursue a joint policy based on the principles of Arabism, Islam, African fraternity, socialism, unity, the liberation of Palestine, combating colonialism and racism, and the rejection of the policy of subservience in the Arab region and Africa."[73] Both sides stressed the need to solve "the problems of the region within a purely African framework and without any foreign interference." This last point reflected both sides' concern with the increased foreign involvement in the respective neighbouring regions—the Sudanese concern over the Russians in the Horn of Africa, and Libyan concern over increased French involvement in Chad (see chapter on Libya). In the same communiqué, Sudan explained that the 1976 Joint Defence Agreement between itself and Egypt was of a defensive nature and not directed against Libya. At the same time, Numayrī declared that "this normalization of relations with Libya would never come at the expense of Egypt."[74]

Both sides gave their blessings to the reconciliation efforts between the Chad government and the rebels there. Joint efforts were made to accelerate this reconciliation, but without too much success (see the Libyan chapter). Instability in Chad was felt to be a danger to the security of Sudan in that it could facilitate the entry of hostile elements into the country. Although the two neighbours continued to co-operate over Chad throughout 1978, Numayrī was by no means reassured about the role or intentions of Qadhdhāfī in this conflict.

Sudan-Ethiopia
In October 1977, Numayrī declared that he was engaged in diplomatic efforts with the Ethiopians in the hope of finding a political solution to the Eritrean problem.[75] This was the first sign of an improvement in Sudanese-Ethiopian relations which had deteriorated alarmingly since 1976 (see *MECS 1976–77*, pp. 597–98). The circumstances which produced the improved atmosphere were similar to those in the

Sudanese-Libyan situation, but the difficulties in actually normalizing relations—one of the NF's conditions for reconciliation with Numayrī—were much more complex, partly because of NF military camps in Ethiopia and the effect of their closure on the domestic Sudanese scene.

According to Khartoum, the tension along the border with Ethiopia was a result of Addis Ababa's annoyance over "Sudan's support and backing for the just Eritrean cause." [76] The Sudanese proposed to solve the Eritrean problem by giving the province some kind of regional autonomy—a plan naturally opposed by Ethiopia. The other stumbling block to improved relations was the growing Soviet and Cuban role in Ethiopia, and the "very real danger that this involvement posed to Sudan's independence and to the Horn of Africa." [77]

Nevertheless under the sponsorship of the OAU, Sudan and Ethiopia agreed to resume normal relations on 21 December 1977. The agreement signed between them on that day provided for a Joint Ministerial Committee to deal with all problems affecting bilateral relations. The agreement also called for the suspension of hostile press campaigns and the resumption of air services between the two countries. These were restored on 15 January 1978. Numayrī hailed the agreement as "a new victory—the consolidation of African unity." [78] His optimistic statement was premature, however. In April, Sudanese-Ethiopian relations were still strained; by the end of that month, tension was apparently aggravated after Sudan alleged that Ethiopia had concentrated troops on its border. [79] In mid-May, the Sudanese army was in turn instructed to reinforce its forces on the Ethiopian border. [80]

There was considerable secret diplomacy to arrange for the Ethiopian leader, Mengistu Haile Mariam, to attend the July summit of the OAU in Khartoum, with Sierra Leone's President Siaka Stevens acting as mediator. Mengistu insisted on a meeting with Numayrī on neutral ground to discuss his terms for coming, but the Sudanese leader said it was physically impossible for him to travel to such a meeting. Mengistu did not attend the summit.

Numayrī blamed the Ethiopians for continuing bad relations. He told a press conference on 23 July (on the occasion of the OAU meeting in Khartoum) that the Eritrean problem "can be solved politically, but Ethiopia insisted that it is part of Ethiopia and that other states should not interfere because it is an internal problem." [81] He argued that contrary to Ethiopia's claim, the future of Eritrea was not merely a domestic issue; for example, there were over 300,000 Eritrean refugees in Sudan. [82] Thus, the unsolved Eritrean problem remained a serious stumbling block in improving the two countries' relations.

Sudan-Egypt

The major single factor determining Sudanese-Egyptian relations in 1978 was Sādāt's trip to Jerusalem and the ensuing dialogue with Israel. In October 1977, before Sādāt's visit, Sudan's relations with Egypt not only continued to be very close, but reached a new peak. This was reflected in the joint session of the two countries' National Assemblies, held from 24–31 October 1977 in Cairo. Numayrī used the occasion to applaud both countries' efforts to strengthen integration, but he did not imply that political unity should be immediately established. (Egypt and Sudan are already linked by the 1974 programme for political and economic integration, and by the 1976 Joint Defence Agreement: see *MECS 1976–77*, p. 597.) This spirit of advanced co-operation and integration produced an immediate and positive Sudanese reaction to Sādāt's trip to Israel, which was defined by Numayrī as "a big victory" [83] and as "the bravest mission . . . in our modern history." [84] Sādāt and Numayrī also exchanged visits (see essay on Inter-Arab Relations). Before long, however, when Sudan realized that it was almost alone among the

Arab states to support Egypt, Numayrī declared that steps ought to be taken in order to clarify to the Arab Heads of State the importance of Sādāt's policy, as well as the necessity of achieving Arab solidarity.[85] While this statement could be considered as supporting Egypt, it was also indicative of Numayrī's evolving non-aligned policy. Furthermore, Sudan had to devise a tactic which would enable it to manoeuvre between three conflicting interests: improving relations with Libya (which was vigorously opposed to Sādāt's policy); maintaining the support of Saudi Arabia (Sudan's main "banker," which did not support the Egyptian move); and maintaining close relations with Egypt. Furthermore, Numayrī had to take into consideration the NF's strong criticism of Sudan's initial positive response to Sādāt's policy (see above). The only way out of this complicated dilemma was to pursue a cautious, mainly declarative and symbolic, integration with Egypt, and to combine it with efforts to achieve Arab solidarity.

After a meeting of the Joint Higher Committee for Integration, held in Cairo on 26 February 1978, a joint statement noted the importance of setting up an "integrated zone"—consisting of the Aswān region in Egypt and the Northern Province of Sudan—as an example of economic, social and cultural integration. Another integrative move was a decision allowing citizens to travel freely across the Egyptian-Sudanese border with only identity cards (and not passports), and permitting them to transfer all the currency they needed at current exchange rates set by the central banks of both countries.

Also in keeping with Sudan's policy, Numayrī accepted the position of chairman of a Committee for Arab Solidarity, set up during the Arab League Council meeting in Cairo from 27–29 March. This made it possible for him to manoeuvre among the conflicting political forces and states in the Arab world. But although he had made a series of contacts with Arab Heads of State by mid-1978, nothing substantive resulted from his mediation efforts. Numayrī continued to express favourable views about Egypt's important role in the area; nevertheless, Egyptians began to voice anxieties in private about what they perceived as an effort by Numayrī to abandon his committed position towards Cairo.

SUDAN'S AFRICAN POLICY

The two major issues shaping Sudan's African policy were the increased involvement of the USSR in Africa and the wish to lower the tension among and within African countries. With the approach of the 15th OAU summit meeting in Khartoum (15–22 July), Numayrī made special efforts to strengthen Sudan's image as a champion of African unity. Early in July, he declared: "Africa is one big family. Within this family, we should contain our views and work with each other as equals without permitting foreign labels to divide us."[86] Numayrī attempted to assume the role of mediator in inter-African conflicts on a number of occasions. In January 1978, he proposed a peace plan for both Ethiopia and Somalia. Simultaneously, efforts were made to unify the Eritrean factions. Sudan also cooperated with Libya during 1978 in an attempt to solve the dispute in Chad (see chapter on Libya). As expected, Numayrī was elected chairman of the OAU for 1978–79.

Khartoum-Rabat relations were strengthened by Sudan's support for Morocco on the Western Sahara issue, their mutual support of Sādāt, as well as their joint interest in restraining Soviet penetration of Africa. In April 1977, both countries provided Zaïre with military support in order to repel an armed attack by the National Front for the Liberation of the Congo (FNLC) from across the Angolan border. Bilateral relations were reinforced during the visit to Khartoum of Morocco's Minister for Foreign Affairs and Co-operation, Muḥammad Boucetta, from 21-25 June, when three agreements on trade, aviation and culture were signed.

ECONOMIC AFFAIRS ($1 = 0.411 Sudanese pounds; £1 = £Sd 0.747)

Sudan's economy has witnessed a period of growth in the past few years, though at a markedly uneven pace. Gross Domestic Product (GDP) rose at a rate exceeding 20% during the mid-1970s (the last years for which reliable data are available). During 1975-77, exports grew much faster than imports, even though at the end of the period a considerable trade gap remained. In 1976-77, industrial production increased in most industries; but some, like cement, failed to match output levels surpassed only three years earlier. Agricultural production, on the other hand, grew only slightly in 1976-77. However, output of ginned cotton and groundnuts—the country's most important crops—declined in that period.

Two of the most noteworthy developments in Sudan's economy in recent years have been its growing accumulation of foreign debt and the size and scope of its development programme. The latter is so large that it is simply beyond the means of the country to finance; hence, the government has to rely almost completely on foreign sources. The Sudanese authorities were forced to comply with various demands of the International Monetary Fund, including a devaluation of the currency by an effective rate of 20% in June 1978. A series of expenditure cuts were also announced, including one from the Development Budget.

Sudan continued to be beset by economic problems in 1977-78. The most politically-charged of these were labour unrest, the high cost of living, and disruption in the supply of basic services and commodities (for details, see above). In the longer run, however, the authorities hope that the worst of these problems will subside once the benefits from the development programme are reaped. In the long term, too, Sudan's leaders hope that oil prospecting in the Blue Nile and Darfur provinces will yield substantial quantities, turning Sudan from an oil importer into at least a self-sufficient producer and possibly an oil exporter.[87]

AGRICULTURE

As Sudan's dominant economic sector, agriculture employs an estimated two-thirds or more of the labour force and provides nearly all of the country's exports. Yet, with only c. 15m acres (out of a total in excess of 200m cultivable acres) actually producing, Sudan is still very far from realizing its potential as the "bread basket" of the Arab world.[88]

With such vast areas of cultivable land and plentiful water from the Nile, Sudan's limited agricultural production can be attributed to shortages of modern farming methods and equipment, technical expertise, and the funds necessary to acquire them. In efforts to remedy these problems, Sudan benefits from aid programmes funded, among others, by Kuwait, Saudi Arabia, the World Bank, the US Agency for International Development and the Abu Dhabi Fund for Arab Economic Development. Two major schemes already under way are the $320m Rahd irrigation projects, and a massive 25-year master plan (1976-2000) which has initial capital of $500m and will incorporate 100 integrated projects costing more than $6,500m up to 1985.[89]

Production of Sudan's most important export commodities, medium and longer staples cotton, rose 25.9% and 40.5% respectively in 1976-77 over the preceding year. Preliminary estimates by the Ministry of Agriculture for 1977-78 indicate further increases of 85.6% for medium and 9.7% for longer staples, reaching levels of 334,000 and 609,000 bales respectively.

Other major crops which were estimated to have higher outputs in 1977-78 include sorghum (+ 12.9%), groundnuts (+ 39.7%) and sesame (+ 40.4%). However, wheat production was estimated to have fallen slightly (–1.4%).

INDUSTRY

Industrial production generally rose during 1976–77. Output of sugar, another major commodity, jumped 21.8% to 138,700 tonnes. Textile production likewise increased by more than 20% to reach 140m yards. Soap output gained impressively—up 17.6% for a total of 50,700 tonnes. Lesser, but still significant, increases were achieved in production of flour (+12.4%) and cement (+7.3%). Among new industries, manufacturing dry cell batteries and rolled steel bars expanded their outputs by 43.5% and 78.6% respectively—even though 1976–77 was only their second full year of operation.

In contrast, production of canned fruits and vegetables (–34.4%), cigarettes (–18.6%), shoes (–13.9%), wine (–10.9%) and beer (–7.3%) all declined in 1976–77 from the previous year's levels.

BUDGET

Sudan's total public sector deficit grew 25.3% to a level of £Sd 208.5m in 1976–77, from the prevous year's deficit of £Sd 166.4m. This increase was directly attributable to the much more rapid rise in government expenditure (£Sd 143.9m) compared to the increase in revenue (£Sd 62.4m). However, the total public sector deficit grew at a slower rate than the central government deficit because of a decrease in the actual deficit incurred by other operations and non-financial public enterprises.

The share of the public sector deficit financed by external loans fell from 22.4% (£Sd 37.2m) in 1975–76 to only 10.6% (£Sd 22.1m) in 1976–77. Alternatively, the domestic bank borrowing share of deficit financing rose from 77.6% in 1975–76 to 89.4% one year later.

Sudan's initial 1977–78 budget called for a 9.5% increase in current expenditure and a 92.5% leap in development expenditure, resulting in a total expenditure growth of 33.3%. This was to be partly offset by a budgeted rise in revenue of 40.0%. However, the subsequent devaluation and cutbacks in spending reduced the accuracy of these figures.[90]

MONETARY DEVELOPMENTS

The Sudanese pound was devalued by an effective rate of 20% from $2.50 to $2.00 in June 1978. The devaluation will most likely compound Sudan's short-term balance of payments difficulties and certainly contribute to inflation by raising the prices of imports by commensurate amounts.

Despite such short-term complications, the devaluation was a necessary condition for the approval of additional IMF credit. So long as Sudan refused to devalue and take accompanying measures, such as expenditure cuts, the IMF refused to reschedule debts. Sudan's other principal sources of budget support, particularly Saudi Arabia and the Abu Dhabi-based Arab Monetary Fund, followed the IMF's example.[91]

At the end of June 1978, before the full effects of the devaluation could be felt, Sudan's exchange holdings dropped to $20.2m—the lowest level since before independence in 1956. Net foreign assets stood at £Sd 204.0m at the end of the first quarter of 1978, representing a slight improvement compared with both the preceding three months and the corresponding quarter in 1977. The money supply grew considerably in the first quarter of 1978, however, reaching £Sd 452.2m. It jumped a further £Sd 17.5m in the month of April 1978 alone. Expansion of the quasi-money supply paralleled that of the liquid money supply, reaching £Sd 103.4m at the end of April 1978.[92]

DEVELOPMENT

Despite the reduction of the development budget for 1978–79 to £Sd 202.8m (c. $580m) from the 1977–78 expenditure of £Sd 307m (c. $880m), Sudan's development programme remains a highly significant element in the overall economy and the key to the future.[93] The balance of payments deficit and shortage of foreign exchange have forced the government to curtail some ongoing development projects and to postpone others. Short-term financial difficulties notwithstanding, Sudan's development potential is so attractive that financial assistance from the Arab world, which is already myriad, is most likely to grow rather than contract.

Besides the massive agricultural schemes (see above), other major development projects include the oil pipeline from Port Sudan to Khartoum, the proposed airport at Port Sudan, and large-scale transportation and infrastructure improvement and expansion programmes.[94]

FOREIGN TRADE

According to preliminary data published by the IMF, exports rose 19.3% to $661m in 1977, while imports increased 8.1% to $1,059m. Italy remained Sudan's prime market for exports (10.9%), followed by West Germany (8.1%) and Japan (7.8%). It should be noted, though, that the IMF statistics are not up-to-date on sales to China and the Soviet Union, which have been major purchasers of Sudanese goods in recent years. Meanwhile, the UK maintained its place as Sudan's chief supplier, totalling 15.9% in 1977; Japan (12.0%) and West Germany (11.5%) followed.

Cotton exports continued to be Sudan's major earner of foreign exchange, with sales of £Sd 68.4m in the second half of 1977. During the same period, exports of groundnuts (9.6%) and sesame (6.7%) were the second and third largest exports respectively, contributing to total sales of £Sd 107.2m.

Sudan's three largest groupings of imports for 1977 were, in order: machinery and transport equipment (43.9%); raw materials, including petroleum products (12.1%); and foodstuffs and tobacco (11.1%).

Haim Shaked and Yehudit Ronen
Economic section by **Ira E. Hoffman**

ARMED FORCES

Total armed forces number 52,100. Defence expenditure in 1977–78 was £Sd 82.6m ($237m). Conscription has been introduced. The Army numbers 50,000 and has two armoured brigades; seven infantry brigades; one parachute brigade; three artillery regiments; three air defence artillery regiments and one engineer regiment. Equipment consists of 70 T-54 and 60 T-55 medium tanks; 30 T-62 light tanks (Chinese); 50 *Saladin* armoured cars; 60 *Ferret* scout cars; 100 BTR-40/-50/-152, 60 OT-64, 49 *Saracen* and 45 *Commando* armoured personnel carriers; 55 25-pounder, 40 100mm, 20 105mm and 18 122mm guns and howitzers; 30 120mm mortars; 30 85mm anti-tank guns; 80 40mm, 80 37mm, 85mm anti-aircraft guns. (50 AMX-10 armoured personnel carriers on order.) 1,000 men are deployed in Lebanon in the Arab Peacekeeping Force. The 600-strong Navy is equipped with six large patrol craft (two ex-Yugoslav *Kraljevica*-class); three patrol craft (ex-Iranian) under 100 tons; six fast patrol boats (ex-Yugoslav '101'-class); two tank landing craft and one utility landing craft. The Air Force numbers 1,500 and is equipped with 22 combat aircraft. Formations consist of one interceptor squadron with ten MiG-21MF; one ground-attack fighter squadron with 12 MiG-17 (ex-Chinese); five BAC-145 and six *Jet Provost* Mk 55; one transport squadron with six C-130-H, six An-12, five An-24, four F-27, one DHC-6, two DHC-5D, eight *Turbo Porter*; one helicopter squadron with ten Mi-8, ten BO-105; AA-2 *Atoll* air-to-air missiles. (Ten F-5E, two F-5B, 24 *Mirage* 50 fighters; six EMB-111P2, two DHC-5D transports and ten *Puma* helicopters on order.) Paramilitary forces number 3,500: 500 in the National Guard; 500 in the Republican Guard and 2,500 Border Guard.

Source: *The Military Balance 1978-79* (London: International Institute for Strategic Studies).

BALANCE OF PAYMENTS (million US dollars)

	1975	1976	1977
A. Goods, Services and Transfers	-430.2	-165.0	-73.1
Exports of Merchandise, fob	411.8	588.8	646.2
Imports of Merchandise, fob	-743.2	-625.7	-643.9
Exports of Services	98.6	119.8	166.0
Imports of Services	-243.0	-268.3	-262.1
Private Unrequited Transfers, net	-0.4	-0.1	—
Government Unrequited Transfers, net	45.9	20.4	20.7
B. Long-Term Capital, nie	33.0	44.4	32.4
C. Short-Term Capital, nie	271.7	76.4	94.0
D. Errors and Omissions	2.4	2.4	-1.6
E. **Total** (A through D)	**-123.0**	**-41.8**	**51.7**

MONETARY SURVEY (million Sudanese pounds at end of period)

	1976	1977	*(first qtr)* 1978
Foreign Assets (net)	-210.1	-210.2	-206.5
Domestic Credit	682.4	882.6	934.4
Claims on Government (net)	431.5	595.0	616.5
Claims on Private Sector	250.9	287.6	317.9
Money	306.7	423.8	452.2
Quasi-Money	61.8	91.7	95.3
Money, Seasonally Adjusted	303.9	420.0	440.7

Source (of two preceding tables): IMF, *International Financial Statistics*.

GOVERNMENT FINANCE (million Sudanese pounds)

	Actual 1975-76	Actual 1976-77	Budget 1977-78
Total Revenue	**332.4**	**394.8**	**552.9**
Total Expenditure	**-412.1**	**-556.0**	**-741.1**
of which:			
Current Expenditure	-294.9	-396.6	-434.2
Development Expenditure	-117.2	-159.4	-306.9
Other operations including public enterprises (net)	-86.7	-47.3	—
Total Public Sector surplus (+) or deficit (-)	**-166.4**	**-208.5**	**-188.2**
Financing:			
External loans (net)	37.2	22.1	
Domestic bank borrowing	129.2	186.4	

Source: Bank of Sudan.

NATIONAL ACCOUNTS (million Sudanese pounds; year ending 30 June)

	1973	1974	1975
Exports	151.3	167.1	183.5
Government Consumption	165.5	180.5	207.8
Gross Fixed Capital Formation	95.2	140.2	214.4
Increase in Stocks	10.0	89.1	50.6
Private Consumption	611.0	846.0	1,170.7
Less: Imports	*-136.2*	*-176.7*	*-316.2*
Gross Domestic Product	**896.8**	**1,246.2**	**1,510.8**

Source: IMF, *International Financial Statistics.*

LONG-TERM LIABILITIES OF GENERAL GOVERNMENT (million SDRs)

	Drawings on loans received		Loan repayments	
	1975	1976	1975	1976
Arab Fund	9.7	6.7		
West Germany	11.8	7.0	-3.3	-2.5
IBRD and IDA	19.9	8.4	-6.6	-7.9
Iran	10.4	—		
Iraq	19.4	20.0		
Kuwait	19.4	33.2	-6.4	-23.5
United Arab Emirates	—	13.0		
United States			-16.6	-12.4
Other lenders	22.9	9.8	-45.9	-29.3
Total	**113.5**	**108.1**	**-78.8**	**-75.6**

Source: IMF, *Balance of Payments Yearbook.*

INDEX OF INDUSTRIAL PRODUCTION (1972–73 = 100.0)

	1972–73	1973–74	1974–75	1975–76	1976–77
Beer and Wine	100.0	119.1	123.5	123.5	113.0
Canned Fruit and Vegetables	100.0	89.6	67.0	86.3	56.6
Cement	100.0	115.4	107.2	82.0	88.0
Cigarettes	100.0	132.0	130.5	227.0	184.7
Flour	100.0	98.5	114.5	123.0	138.2
Shoes	100.0	93.7	93.0	100.7	86.7
Soap	100.0	116.8	125.3	145.1	170.7
Sugar	100.0	107.1	114.3	101.2	123.2
Textiles	100.0	101.8	103.1	123.1	148.6
Vegetable oils	100.0	113.1	103.7	126.2	137.3

Source: Derived from Ministry of Industry and Mining data.

COMPOSITION OF EXPORTS (million Sudanese pounds)

	1975–76	1976–77	July–Dec 1977–78
Ginned Cotton	104.6	99.5	68.4
Groundnuts	40.2	36.0	10.3
Sesame	11.5	21.6	7.2
Gum Arabic	10.7	11.9	6.4
Dura (millet)	1.8	4.5	2.3
Hides and Skins	3.5	4.2	1.9
Cake and Meal	5.6	9.1	1.5
Total (including others)	**191.7**	**206.8**	**107.2**

IMPORTS BY CATEGORY (million Sudanese pounds)

	1975	1976	1977
Machinery and Transport Equipment	123.6	153.6	165.3
Raw Materials, including petroleum products	28.2	31.9	45.6
Foodstuffs and Tobacco	64.7	50.5	41.8
Chemicals	40.2	33.4	32.7
Textiles	43.0	21.9	28.2
Other Manufactured Goods	60.2	50.0	62.9
Total	**359.9**	**341.4**	**376.5**

Source (of two preceding tables): Bank of Sudan.

DIRECTION OF TRADE (million US dollars)

	1975	1976	1977*	% of 1977 total
Exports to:				
Italy	57.6	109.0	71.9	10.9
West Germany	27.0	36.5	53.8	8.1
Japan	18.7	41.5	51.6	7.8
France	55.3	36.8	46.0	7.0
Yugoslavia	20.2	30.1	32.5	4.9
United Kingdom	15.9	15.8	23.7	3.6
Greece	2.9	8.3	20.4	3.1
United States	9.6	21.7	18.8	2.8
Portugal	3.8	9.6	14.0	2.1
Hong Kong	10.8	13.8	13.1	2.0
Total (including others)	**437.8**	**554.2**	**661.0**	
Imports from:				
United Kingdom	158.1	199.5	167.9	15.9
Japan	104.8	64.1	126.8	12.0
West Germany	87.8	82.9	121.5	11.5
France	24.3	36.2	104.9	9.9
United States	88.2	92.1	104.7	9.9
Italy	67.3	75.9	74.0	7.0
Netherlands	21.2	19.9	46.6	4.4
Belgium	22.6	32.2	36.1	3.4
Austria	6.0	16.8	26.4	2.5
South Korea	26.6	1.1	22.7	2.1
Total (including others)	**1,033.1**	**980.0**	**1,059.1**	

*Data partly extrapolated and/or derived from partner country.
Source: IMF, Direction of Trade.

NOTES
1. Al-Ayyām, Khartoum; 28 September 1977.
2. Ibid.
3. For the text of the amendments which were demanded by the Bar, see al-Saḥāfa, Khartoum; 29 November 1977.
4. Sudanow, Khartoum; October 1977.
5. Al-Saḥāfa, 16 November 1977.
6. Al-Ayyām, 28 September 1977.
7. Jamāhīriyya Arab News Agency (JANA), Libya; 27 November—Daily Report (DR), 29 November 1977.
8. Al-Nahār al-'Arabī wal-Duwalī (NAD), Paris; 21 January 1978.
9. Arabia and the Gulf, London; 30 January 1978; al-Dustūr, London; 9–15 January 1978.
10. The Middle East, London; December 1977; interview with al-Mahdī.
11. Ibid; interview with Numayrī.
12. NAD, 21 January 1978.
13. NAD, 1 October 1977.
14. NAD, 21 January 1978.
15. R Omdurman, 17 January—DR, 18 January 1978.

16. Minister of Health in the Cabinet before Numayrī's regime. Returned from exile in September 1977.
17. *NAD*, 21 January 1978.
18. *Ibid.*
19. *Al-Nahar Arab Report and Memo*, Beirut; 23 January 1978.
20. *Arabia and the Gulf*, 13 March 1978.
21. *Al-Manār*, London; 11 March 1978.
22. *Arabia and the Gulf*, 13 March 1978.
23. *Ibid*, 27 March 1978.
24. *Washington Post*, 11 April 1978.
25. The legislative body for the Southern region. The first one was set up on 15 December 1973, according to the Addis Ababa Agreement.
26. The HEC supervises the administration and runs public affairs in the South.
27. *Arabia and the Gulf*, 19 December 1977.
28. The first division, which was posted in the South, was established in accordance with the Addis Ababa Agreement. From its inception in 1972 it was headed by Joseph Lagu.
29. *The Middle East*, December 1977; interview with Lagu.
30. SANU was founded in 1962 by Southern exiles who wanted a loose federal system with the North.
31. The ultimate objective of the Southern Front, established in 1964, was regional autonomy for the South within a united Sudan.
32. *Sudanow*, April 1978; interview with Lagu.
33. *Al-Sahāfa*, 16 March 1978.
34. *Africa*, London; May 1978. Interview with Lagu.
35. *Ibid.*
36. *Al-Dustūr*, 10–16 April 1978.
37. *African Contemporary Record 1977–78*, p. 124.
38. *Sudanow*, May 1978.
39. *Arabia and the Gulf*, 17 April 1978.
40. *Sudanow*, May 1978.
41. Agence France-Press (AFP), 9 April—DR, 12 April 1978.
42. Sudan News Agency (SUNA), 9 April—DR, 10 April 1978.
43. For the text of the agreement, see *al-Sahāfa*, 13 April 1978.
44. *Al-Ayyām*, 13 April 1978.
45. Reuter, 12 April 1978.
46. *Rūz al-Yūsuf*, Cairo; 8 May 1978.
47. *Ibid.*
48. *Al-Ayyām*, 9 May 1978.
49. *Arab Report and Record (ARR)*, London; 16–30 June 1978.
50. *Al-Ayyām*, 13 June 1978.
51. *Sudanow*, June 1978.
52. *Al-Anbā'*, Kuwait; 16 July 1978.
53. *Ibid.*
54. *Al-Sahāfa*, 1 August 1978.
55. *The Times*, London; 6 July 1978.
56. *The Middle East*, August 1978. Interview with al-Hindī.
57. *Sudanow*, May 1978.
58. *Ibid.*
59. *Al-Sayyād*, Beirut; 5 October 1977.
60. *Arabia and the Gulf*, 1 May 1978.
61. For the list of names, see R Omdurman, 29 July—BBC, 31 July 1978.
62. *Al-Dustūr*, 14–20 August 1978.
63. *Al-Ayyām*, 18 September 1978.
64. *Middle East Economic Digest (MEED)*, London; 5 May 1978.
65. *Al-Sahāfa*, 22 February 1978.
66. *Al-Ayyām*, 19 May 1978.
67. R Omdurman, 3 January—BBC, 5 January 1978; *al-Sahāfa*, 15 February 1978.
68. R Omdurman, 17 October—BBC, 19 October 1977.
69. *Rūz al-Yūsuf*, 8 May 1978.
70. *Sudanow*, June 1978.
71. *Al-Mustaqbal*, Paris; 17 September 1978.
72. *Al-Watan al-'Arabī*, Paris; 10–16 June 1978.
73. For text of the agreement, see R Tripoli, 8 February—DR, 9 February 1978.
74. *Akhir Sa'ā*, Cairo; 15 March 1978.
75. R Cairo, 25 October—BBC, 27 October 1977.

76. R Omdurman, 26 October—BBC, 28 October 1977.
77. *Sudanow*, February 1978.
78. *Al-Sahāfa*, 5 February 1978.
79. R Omdurman, 29 April—BBC, 2 May 1978.
80. *Al-Sayyād*, 18 May 1978.
81. R Omdurman, 23 July—DR, 24 July 1978.
82. SUNA, 21 July—BBC, 24 July 1978.
83. R Cairo, 22 November—BBC, 24 November 1977.
84. R Omdurman, 23 November—BBC, 24 November 1977.
85. *Al-Ayyām*, 7 December 1977.
86. *Africa*, July 1978.
87. See *ARR*, 16–30 June 1978.
88. See, for example, *The Arab Economist*, Beirut; February 1978, p. 20; and *October*, Cairo; 22 January—Joint Publication Research Service (JPRS), 23 March 1978.
89. See World Bank, *Annual Report 1977*, p. 66; *Arab Economist*, pp. 20–21; and *MEED*, "Special Report: Sudan," 26 August 1977.
90. *MEED*, 9 June 1978.
91. See *Financial Times (FT)*, London; 13 July; *MEED*, 9 June, 29 September; and *Sudanow*, July 1978.
92. International Monetary Fund, *International Financial Statistics*, Washington; July 1978.
93. For background on the development budget, see *MECS 1976–77*, pp. 599, 602.
94. For additional details, see for example, *New African*, London; January 1978; *MEED*, 29 September 1978; and *FT*, 16 February and 13 July 1978.

Syria

(Al-Jumhūriyya al-'Arabiyya al-Sūriyya)

The election in February 1978 of Ḥāfiz al-Asad to a second presidential term symbolized a continuity of power and a stability unprecedented in Syria's post-independence history. Yet the events of the year proved that in some respects stability was more apparent than real. Domestic discontent made itself felt more sharply in 1978, and the cohesiveness of the inner ruling group was breached in one significant instance, the dismissal of Nājī Jamīl. This was the first rift to occur in Asad's immediate entourage since he took power in 1970—or, more precisely, the first to become public knowledge.

Syria's involvement in Lebanon in 1978 became more of a liability in military, political and economic terms, as well as in its repercussions on domestic morale, than at any time before. The immediate burdens were certainly felt more keenly than any potential strategic, regional or international advantages. What was especially detrimental was the fact that developments in Lebanon claimed the attention of Asad and his closest aides to such an extent that the leadership as a whole was impeded in dealing with domestic affairs and with the challenges posed by Sādāt's initiative.

Sādāt's new policy had a serious negative impact both on Syria's standing as a major party to the Arab-Israeli conflict and on its standing in inter-Arab affairs—an impact all the more strongly marked when compared with the great strides Syria had made in both spheres since 1973. Syria interpreted Sādāt's policy as being aimed at a separate settlement with Israel. Accordingly, it felt exposed to a potential threat from the Israeli army, which would now be able to concentrate its full strength in the north, and believed its chances of recovering the Golan Heights to have been reduced, if not eliminated. The validity of the "two-stage strategy," under which Syria had hoped to participate in the political process without prejudicing the attainment of its ultimate goal of "the liberation of all of Palestine," now seemed called into question. On the inter-Arab scene, the survival of Syria's special ties with Jordan was cast into doubt when their respective policies diverged in reaction to Sādāt's moves. Combined with events in Lebanon, this put an end to Syria's efforts to achieve a position of regional ascendancy, at least for the time being.

Relations with Iraq presented a particular problem. In the wake of Sādāt's initiative, Syria desired Iraq's military co-operation against Israel and its political backing against Egypt. Yet Iraq had been, and continued to be, the main source of inspiration for domestic opposition. More than that: by claiming to be the true successor of the original undivided Ba'th party, the Iraqi Ba'th denied the genuineness of the Syrian Ba'th and thereby threatened to undercut the very legitimacy of the Syrian regime.

POLITICAL AFFAIRS
ASAD'S RE-ELECTION

President Ḥāfiz al-Asad's election for a second seven-year term in a referendum on 8 February 1978, and the fifteenth anniversary of the rise to power of the Ba'th regime in Syria a month later, both signified the attainment of an unprecedented measure of stability in a country which had previously been notorious for political vicissitudes.

While Asad's overwhelming electoral victory (99.6% according to official figures)[1] was predictable, the high voter turnout was certainly not assured in advance. Only in August 1977, the majority of the electorate had failed to participate in parliamentary elections as a manifestation of discontent with the regime.[2] An intensive propaganda campaign thus preceded the referendum, concentrating on the challenge posed by developments in the Arab-Israeli conflict, in the inter-Arab situation and in Syria's role in both fields. These were thought to be much more instrumental in enlisting support than any domestic issue. "We have observed," a Syrian journalist stated on the day of the referendum, "that the general feeling among the Syrian people as they vote 'yes' . . . is that they are voting particularly for steadfastness"[3] (a term commonly used in 1978 to connote opposition to Egypt's policy vis-à-vis Israel).

During the course of the election campaign, the party apparatus and the so-called popular organizations played a conspicuous role. (The latter, consisting of trade unions, professional associations and other special-interest groups, were affiliated with and directed by the Ba'th party, though larger than it in membership terms.)[4] Immediately following the approval of Asad's nomination in the People's Council on 22 January 1978, the party apparatus and the popular organizations began operating as channels for mobilizing public support for the regime in general and Asad's re-election in particular. They put to work their highly ramified hierarchy, with functionaries at higher levels passing guidelines on to their subordinates, and officials at lower levels meeting with rank-and-file members of the party and popular organizations throughout the country. Both the party and popular organizations played an important part in organizing mass demonstrations in support of Asad in all Syrian cities.

Another aspect of the campaign was a series of measures taken in the month preceding the referendum intended to gratify particular social groups: (1) servicemen, civil servants and "public sector" (i.e. state enterprise) employees were given salary increases of 10-20%; (2) teachers were given bonuses of 25%; (3) students receiving scholarships in Syria or abroad were given increased grants; and (4) citizens living in Saudi Arabia or the Gulf states were given the opportunity of exemption from military service by making a fixed payment instead.[5] Whether owing to these steps, to the more energetic measures taken to bring voters to the polls, or to the greater significance attached by the public to presidential rather than parliamentary elections, the turnout for the referendum was 97%.

Perhaps as a demonstration of the regime's sense of stability and self-assurance, several measures were relaxed in the wake of the referendum. The sentences of most criminal convicts were reduced by half[6] and, on the occasion of his swearing-in on 8 March, Asad instructed that in cases not affecting the security of the state, orders issued under the provisions of martial law be annulled.[7] More significantly, Asad pledged in his swearing-in address to work in future towards achieving "a new developed formula for our national front in order to involve the greatest number of the masses." Though Asad himself did not elaborate, the "new formula" was interpreted by a Ba'th Regional Command (RC) member, 'Abdallah al-Ahmad, as alluding to a plan to incorporate into the National Progressive Front (NPF) "a large number of independents and people who had left their parties . . . regardless of their former party affiliations."[8] (For the place of the NPF and other public institutions in the structure of the Ba'th regime, see *Middle East Contemporary Survey (MECS) 1976-77*, p. 605.) A non-Syrian Arab source predicted that Asad's pledge would usher in negotiations on the formation of a national (*qawmī*) government, to include the former Ba'th leader, Salāḥ al-Dīn al-Bīṭār, last in office in 1966; Ma'rūf al-Dawālībī, a politician of the pre-Ba'th *ancien régime*; and the Muslim Brethren leader, 'Isām al-'Aṭṭār.[9] Such expectations were apparently prompted by the return of Bīṭār several months earlier from 11 years in exile,[10] and perhaps by the addition of "conservative politicians . . . and scions of prominent Damascus families" to the People's Council in August 1977.[11] As it turned out, apart from the replacement of several Ba'thi representatives in its central leadership[12] (for reasons not connected with the Front's "future formula"), no changes were in fact introduced into the make-up or functions of the NPF. It seems that changes had indeed been planned but were aborted by the resumption of terrorist activity and the imminent upheaval in the regime's upper echelons (see below).

THE REPLACEMENT OF KHULAYFĀWĪ'S CABINET
On 30 March 1978, Asad dismissed the Cabinet of 'Abd al-Raḥmān Khulayfāwī and appointed Muḥammad 'Alī al-Ḥalabī to succeed him as Prime Minister. Ḥalabī, a Sunnī, was a member of the Ba'th RC but reportedly possessed "next to nothing by the way of political following."[13] He had been Chairman of the People's Council for the preceding two years and was replaced in that post by Maḥmūd Ḥadīd, a Ba'th RC member and trade union leader. There were no other significant changes in the composition of the Cabinet: the key Ministers of Defence, Foreign Affairs and Information retained their posts; only three members of second rank were replaced (see Table). The balance of party affiliations remained unchanged: 18 Ba'this, ten members of other parties belonging to the NPF, and eight independents.

The change of government conformed with Syria's Permanent Constitution which calls for the appointment of a new Cabinet at the beginning of each new presidential term.[14] More probably, however, the reshuffle had been planned before Asad's re-election and was delayed so as to appear a routine constitutional measure and avoid two Cabinet changes within a short time. The reason for the change was the need to replace the Prime Minister. Khulayfāwī apparently offered or was asked to resign because of ill health and because of his failure to achieve the goals Asad had set for him in 1976: to cleanse the bureaucracy of inefficiency and corruption, improve the economy and foster greater public confidence in the government. Khulayfāwī's government had not tackled the basic ailments of the Syrian economy; it had not even succeeded in alleviating their effects such as the high cost of living, the consumer goods shortage and the poor performance in essential public services. Its failure to gain public confidence had been conspicuously demonstrated in August 1977 by the low turnout in the parliamentary elections. In fighting corruption, Khulayfāwī was particularly frustrated by the ineffective operation of the Committee for the Investigation of Illicit Profits, established in August 1977, as well as by the failure of his personal efforts to make it progress satisfactorily. He may have also clashed with powerful vested interests in the upper echelons of the regime during attempts to pressure the Committee to pursue its investigation more vigorously.

About a month after its establishment, the Committee issued instructions for the arrest of 28 people, among them directors and general managers of public sector institutions and import agents. (Representation of foreign companies on the basis of commissions for sales was officially forbidden by a law of 1965.) Among the detainees identified by outside sources were 'Uthmān 'Ā'idī, chairman and managing director of the Damascus Méridien Hotel and local agent for several French companies; and Sā'ib Naḥḥās, vice-president of the Damascus Chamber of Commerce and local agent for Peugeot and Volkswagen.[15] However, from the beginning of October onwards, there were frequent indications of difficulties facing the work of the Committee. On 1 October, explosions occurred at the premises of Syria's leading papers—*al-Thawra*, *al-Ba'th*, and *Tishrīn*—and in the government printing press, presumably in response to their active participation in the anti-corruption campaign.[16] Immediately afterwards, *al-Ba'th* pointed to attempts by several "groups" (*fi'āt*) to undermine confidence in the Committee's work by claiming that Syrian society as a whole was corrupt and that the Committee was going to deal only with the small fry. Some of these "groups" argued that in view of the widespread involvement of high-ranking officials, uprooting corruption would weaken the whole structure of the regime.[17] Asad found it advisable to assure the business community, both at a meeting with the Damascus Chamber of Commerce[18] and in a major interview,[19] that the anti-corruption campaign did not mark any change in the regime's economic policy. Finally, a legislative decree of 5 October granting the Committee additional powers[20] also implied that it had hitherto met with difficulties and possibly with intentional obstruction.

Several prominent businessmen previously arrested for investigation by the Committee were released on 25 October after having been cleared of charges of corruption. Among those acquitted were 'Ā'idī and Nahḥās.[21] Subsequently, the Committee was referred to by Asad only on one single occasion (in his 8 March swearing-in address), and no trials or convictions resulting from its work were reported during the remainder of the period reviewed. Even the sentencing in June 1978 of several employees of the Syrian National Oil Company to various prison terms (on charges of accepting $4.7m in bribes from foreign companies) followed action reportedly begun two years earlier.[22] In fact, it was assumed that the Committee's work was allowed to peter out after it had met with opposition from businessmen whose goodwill was indispensable to the functioning of the economy and from members of the ruling élite itself, the most prominent among whom was Asad's brother Rif'at.[23] Thus, a clash of interests with Rif'at Asad apparently featured both in the replacement of Khulayfāwī as Prime Minister and in the more significant dismissal of Nājī Jamīl as Air Force Commander and Chief of the National Security Bureau, which took place at the same time (see below).

THE RULING GROUP: NĀJĪ JAMĪL'S REMOVAL AND ITS AFTERMATH

An almost unprecedented rift within the Ba'thi ruling group occurred at the end of March 1978 when Maj-Gen (*liwā*) Nājī Jamīl was relieved of his duties as Deputy Defence Minister and Commander of the Air Force (functions allowing direct contact with the military) and as Head of the National Security Bureau in the President's Office in charge of co-ordinating the work of the various security services. The only function he retained was as a National Command (NC) member "so that he could devote himself to political activities within the Ba'th party."[24] Apart from the replacement, at an unknown date, of 'Abd al-Ghanī Ibrāhīm as head of the "political department"[25] (the body responsible for indoctrination in the armed forces), this was the first dismissal among the President's coterie, all of whose members had been close associates of Asad since he assumed power in 1970 and had since then held key posts in the regime. By virtue of the combination of posts he filled, Jamīl had perhaps been the most prominent among them. He had also been considered a possible successor to the Premiership during the months preceding his dismissal.[26]

Sources outside Syria (possibly taking their cue from reports intentionally leaked by Damascus[27]) suggested that, as co-ordinator of the security services, Jamīl was held responsible for the failure to uncover and foil terrorist activities which had been harassing the regime for the last two years (see *MECS 1976–77*, pp. 609–10).

TABLE 1. THE CABINET

Portfolio	Khulayfāwī's Cabinet, 7 August 1976	Ḥalabī's Cabinet, 30 March 1978
Prime Minister	Maj-Gen 'Abd al-Raḥmān al-Khulayfāwī (B) (Sun)	Muḥammad 'Alī al-Ḥalabī (B) (Sun)
Deputy PM and Foreign Minister	'Abd al-Ḥalīm Khaddām (B) (Sun)	'Abd al-Ḥalīm Khaddām
Deputy PM for Economic Affairs	Jamīl Shayā (B) (Dr)	Jamīl Shayā
Deputy PM for Public Services	Fahmī al-Yūsufī (B) (Sun)	Fahmī al-Yūsufī
Ministers:		
Defence	Maj-Gen Mustafā Talās (B) (Sun)	Mustafā Talās
Information	Aḥmad Iskandar Aḥmad (B) (Al)	Aḥmad Iskandar Aḥmad
Interior	Brig 'Adnān Dabbāgh (B) (Sun)	'Adnān Dabbāgh
Local Administration	Taha al-Khayrāt (B) (Sun)	Taha al-Khayrāt
Economy and Foreign Trade	Muḥammad al-'Imādī (In) (Al)	Muḥammad al-'Imādī
Agriculture and Agrarian Reform	Aḥmad Qablān (B) (Dr)	Aḥmad Qablān
Industry	Shatyawī Sayfū (B) (Is)	Shatyawī Sayfū
Supply and Internal Trade	Muḥammad Ghubāsh (B) (Sun)	Muḥammad Ghubāsh
Oil and Mineral Resources	'Isā Darwīsh (B) (Ch?)	'Isā Darwīsh
Public Works and Water Resources	Nāzim Qaddūr (AS) (n.a.)	Nāzim Qaddūr
Euphrates Dam	Subḥī Kahhāla (SCP) (Sun)	Subḥī Kahhāla
Communications	'Umar al-Sibā'ī (SCP) (Sun)	'Umar al-Sibā'ī
Power	Aḥmad 'Umar Yūsuf (In) (Sun)	Aḥmad 'Umar Yūsuf
Transport	Nu'mān al-Zayn (In) (Ch?)	Dr Salīm Yāsīn (n.a.) (Dr)
Finance	Sādiq al-Ayyūbī (In) (Sun; K)	Sādiq al-Ayyūbī
Housing and Utilities	Muḥarram Tayyāra (B) (Sun)	Muḥarram Tayyāra
Tourism	Ghassān Shalhūb (B) (Ch)	Ghassān Shalhūb
Justice	Adīb al-Nahāwī (ASU) (n.a.)	Adīb al-Nahāwī
Education	Shākir al-Fahhām (B) (Sun)	Zuhayr Mashāriqa (n.a.) (Sun)
Higher Education	Dr Muḥammad 'Alī Hāshim (former SU) (n.a.)	Shākir al-Fahhām (B) (Sun)
Culture and National Guidance	Najāḥ 'Attār (In) (n.a.)	Najāḥ 'Attār
Social Affairs and Labour	Anwar Ḥamāda (ASU) (n.a.)	Yūsuf Ja'īdānī (ASU) (n.a.)
Health	Madanī al-Khiyamī (In) (n.a.)	Madanī al-Khiyamī
Waqf	'Abd al-Sattār al-Sayyid (In) (Sun)	'Abd al-Sattār al-Sayyid
Ministers of State:		
Presidential Affairs	Adīb Milhim (B) (Sun)	Adīb Milhim
Cabinet Affairs	Ḥusayn Aḥmad Kuwaydir (B) (n.a.)	Anwar Ḥamāda (ASU) (n.a.)
Planning Affairs	George Ḥūrāniyya (n.a.) (n.a.)	George Ḥūrāniyya
Other	Yūsuf Ja'īdānī (ASU) (n.a.)	Safwān Qudsī (ASU) (n.a.)
	Sharīf Kūsh (former SU) (n.a.)	Sharīf Kūsh
	Diyā Mallūḥī (former SU) (n.a.)	Diyā Mallūḥī
	Zuhayr 'Abd al-Samad (SCP) (n.a.)	Zuhayr 'Abd al-Samad

Parties: *(B)* Bath *(ASU)* Arab Socialist Union *(SCP)* Syrian Communist Party *(SU)* Socialist Unionists, formally merged with the Ba'th in 1975
(AS) Arab Socialists *(In)* Independent
Communities: *(Sun)* Sunni *(Al)* 'Alawi *(Dr)* Druze *(Is)* Ismā'īlī *(Ch)* Christian *(K)* Kurd
(n.a.) information not available

The terror victims had been mainly 'Alawīs and—in two of the recent incidents—relatives of President Asad (see below).[28] Being a Sunnī, Jamīl may have been considered unsuitable to head the campaign against terrorists assumed to be Sunnīs opposed to 'Alawī domination.

However, this issue may simply have been used as a pretext by Jamīl's rivals in the ruling group, or even by Asad himself, while their real concern was the apparent accumulation of too much power in his hands. In particular, there had been talk for several years of personal rivalry between Jamīl and Asad's brother Rif'at.[29] Another version attributed this rivalry to Rif'at Asad's enjoying Soviet support, while Jamīl was held to be a protégé of Saudi Arabia and less inclined than other Syrian leaders towards a predominantly pro-Soviet orientation in foreign policy.[30] However, neither the view that Asad's inner circle was divided into a strongly pro-Soviet grouping and one more reserved towards the USSR, nor the assumption of a clear-cut communal ('Alawī-Sunnī) division, was entirely convincing. In all probability, the rivalry between Jamīl and Rif'at Asad was primarily the result of a personal struggle for positions of power, rather than of differences in political or communal orientation. Although removed from all positions of real power, Jamīl was not disgraced—as shown by his retention of NC membership. He was subsequently promoted to the rank of lieutenant-general ('imād), although without being given any specific military appointment.[31]

Jamīl was succeeded as Head of the National Security Bureau by the former Head of Air Force Intelligence, Brig ('amīd) Muḥammad Khūlī, an 'Alawī.[32] Sunnī membership in the ruling group was thus diminished; the most prominent Sunnī now remaining was the Foreign Minister, 'Abd al-Ḥalīm Khaddām. In addition to Khaddām and Khūlī, Rif'at Asad also profited from Jamīl's removal—whether or not he had been personally instrumental in bringing it about. For years, Rif'at's main power base had been the Defence Detachments, an independent armoured unit variously estimated at 9,000–20,000 men, stationed near the capital and entrusted with protecting the regime. His position as commander of the detachments made him indispensable to the President, who was thus compelled to ignore Rif'at's notorious corruption and his reputation for ruthlessness, and to resign himself to the fact that Rif'at had made personal enemies among the higher echelons of the armed forces.[33] A series of transfers of senior officers in the forces in July 1978 was described as an attempt by Rif'at Asad to place his own supporters in positions likely to be useful in the event of an intensified power struggle.[34] (For statistics indicating the strength and composition of Syria's armed forces, see below.)

Under such circumstances, reports (first appearing in mid-1978) that Asad was suffering from a fatal illness acquired political significance.[35] Such rumours were in themselves enough to intensify the ongoing rivalry within the ruling group, or even precipitate a struggle for the succession. The stability of the regime depended in considerable measure on Asad's personal authority, on his ability to keep the balance between contending groups and personalities, and on the personal loyalty to him on the part of members of the ruling group, regardless of their affiliations. The weight of Asad's personality and his political skill had to a great extent preserved the unity of the ruling group and, more importantly, the delicate overall communal equilibrium. Reports of Asad's illness have not been substantiated, however. If anything, they were belied by his intensive activities, including official visits to both West and East Germany and to the USSR.

CRITICISM OF THE REGIME

For several years, in particular since Syria's invasion of Lebanon in 1976, criticism of government policies had been growing, both among the establishment and at grassroots level. In response, an attempt was made to use the Press as a safety valve by allowing it to express restrained criticism on limited subjects. Criticism of economic failures, of inefficiency in the bureaucracy and the public sector, and of the failure to encourage potential investors was thus tolerated by the regime, which itself actually joined the critics—most conspicuously by declaring the anti-corruption campaign of 1977. However, toleration did not extend to the following: (1) expressions of discontent on the part of troops stationed in Lebanon, some of whom felt that casualties were unacceptably high and that the fighting could drag on interminably; (2) criticism among the military establishment of a lowering of army morale and the diminution of Syria's defence capability caused by the military presence in Lebanon (for more details, see below); and (3) opposition of hardliners within the party to what they considered a too far-reaching economic liberalization; to Syria's participation since 1974 in the ME "political process"; and to its failure to intervene on behalf of the Palestinians during Israel's invasion of South Lebanon.

If there was any domestic criticism of Syria's attitude towards Sādāt's initiative, either from more moderate or more radical quarters, almost no indication of it was allowed to surface. The claim that Syria was disingenuous in opposing the initiative, and was in fact an accomplice to it, was only made outside Syria by those who took their cue from Iraqi propaganda (see below). On the other hand, an inquiry on behalf of *Tishrīn* immediately after Sādāt's visit to Jerusalem brought to light carefully veiled hints that the Syrian public did not fully endorse the complete rejection of the initiative. Several of those questioned admitted to having acquaintances who supported the initiative, but were quick to add: "We succeeded in making them see the correctness of our view." [36]

A novel phenomenon in 1978 occurred in newspapers overstepping the limits of permitted criticism, resulting in the replacement of the chief editors of all major Syrian papers (see Table 2), as well as dismissals of lower-ranking media personnel. For instance, the journalist Amīn al-Nafūrī "disappeared" from *al-Thawra* immediately after publishing an article on 30 March in which he argued that, whatever the international circumstances, Syrian intervention against an invasion of Lebanon was imperative and should not necessarily be regarded as an act of rashness or irresponsibility. [37] By making this point, Nafūrī was plainly contradicting the explanation given by Asad for Syria's non-intervention against Israel in South Lebanon (see below).

TABLE 2   RESHUFFLE OF CHIEF EDITORS (February–June 1978)

Paper	Old Incumbent	New Incumbent
Tishrīn	Ghassān al-Rifā'ī	'Amīd Khūlī
Al-Ba'th (official Party organ)	'Adnān Baghajātī	Yāsir al-Farrā
Al-Thawra	'Alī Sulaymān	Ahmad al-Hajj 'Alī*

*Hitherto the editor of *Jaysh al-Sha'b*, organ of the army.

TERRORIST ACTIVITIES

The two-year old terrorist activities in Syria continued to harass, though not to threaten, the regime. Their most prominent victims—and the only assassinations officially admitted to—were 'Alī Ibn 'Abid al-'Alī, an 'Alawī professor at Aleppo University and Ba'thi leader from Jabla, near Lādhiqiyya (Lataqia), killed in November 1977; and Ibrāhīm Na'āma, the 'Alawī doyen of Syrian dentists and deputy chairman of the Syrian-Soviet Friendship Society, killed in March 1978. Both were reported by foreign sources to have been relatives of the President. [38]

Foreign sources also reported the assassination of two more 'Alawī personalities: Dr Yūsuf 'Īd (in March) and Col Ahmad Khalīl, police personnel chief in the Interior Ministry (in August).[39]

The fact that there was a pause in terrorist activities between November 1977 and February 1978 would seem to bear out the regime's claim that Iraq was responsible for these acts: at that time, mediation attempts were being undertaken to achieve Syrian-Iraqi co-operation in an anti-Sādāt front. Their failure at the end of January 1978 was quickly followed by the resumption of anti-Syrian propaganda from Iraq, which had been toned down during the interval. (For details, see below, as well as essay on Inter-Arab Relations.)

In view of their sustained character, however, the terrorist activities were unlikely to have been the work of "foreign agents" alone; more probably, they involved elements from among the majority Sunnī community. These were possibly organized in underground cells belonging to the Muslim Brethren or groups affiliated with them, such as one called "Muhammad's Youth" (*Shabāb Muhammad*).[40] Radical quarters among the Sunnī community had long been hostile both to the socialist and secularist stance of the Ba'th party (the cause of violent Sunnī protest action in 1973), and to the predominance in the regime of members of the 'Alawī minority, a predominance maintained mainly through their control of the armed forces and internal security services. The high number of 'Alawī victims supports the assumption that sectarian tension and Sunnī radicalism were at the back of the terrorist threat. Further evidence was provided by the fact that over half of a group of terrorists whose names were made public in September were from Hamāt,[41] a traditional Sunnī stronghold and the centre of anti-Ba'th riots in 1964 and 1973.

Nājī Jamīl's dismissal as head of the National Security Bureau (see above) underlined the failure of the regime's anti-terrorist efforts. These included such emergency measures as: (1) an amendment to the penal code in March 1978 broadening the definition of terrorist acts, introducing stiffer penalties for them and promising clemency to those who handed their weapons over to the authorities;[42] and (2) regulations issued by the Ministry of the Interior (in June) prohibiting the use of motorcycles in the major cities except by police, army and security services, or specially authorized civilians.[43] In September 1978, however, the authorities announced the exposure of a "sabotage and murder group instructed and financed by . . . Baghdad." The statement said that some of its members had been arrested; others were identified by their names, personal details and photographs so that the public could "help . . . in detecting them."[44]

Opposition groupings in other segments of the political spectrum (such as Nasserite and Marxist elements, or supporters of Asad's predecessor in power, Salāh Jadīd)[45] did not leave a mark on Syrian politics. The exception was the pro-Iraqi Ba'thīs, but neither they nor the other opposition elements had as much potential support as the radical Muslim groups. None of them had any foothold whatsoever in the armed forces, traditionally a pre-condition for posing a political threat.

FOREIGN AFFAIRS
SYRIA'S POLICY IN LEBANON
Syria's military presence in Lebanon became an increasingly heavy burden, both in strategic terms and for the morale and vigour of the domestic front. This was especially so after the beginning of the armed conflict with the so-called Lebanese Front in February 1978 and Israel's invasion of South Lebanon in March. (For the involvement of Syrian troops in Lebanon and the composition and activity of the

Lebanese Front, see chapter on Lebanon; for developments in South Lebanon, see appropriate section in the essay on the Arab-Israeli Conflict; for Syrian-PLO relations in Lebanon, see essay on the PLO.)

With Syrian forces on the Golan Heights depleted[46] and at least 30,000 troops (a high proportion of the country's combat units) stationed in Lebanon, Syria's military capability in facing Israel was somewhat impaired. The units in Lebanon had interrupted their training and engaged in missions which did not provide the kind of combat experience useful in warfare against Israel. The cost of maintaining the contingent in Lebanon, generally estimated at $3m per day,[47] constituted a severe financial strain on the Syrian economy. The Lebanese situation was also a burden in that it continuously preoccupied the upper echelons of the army and the regime in general, most of all the President himself, preventing them from dealing adequately with domestic problems and with the overall ME situation. Among the general public, resentment was aroused by the increasing number of casualties, particularly in the fighting during the summer months of 1978. Inconsistent policies, such as fighting on the side of the Christians in 1976 but turning against them in 1978, and—more importantly—the scanty aid given to the Palestinians in South Lebanon, proved difficult to explain. A domestic security problem was created in March by the necessity of letting an Iraqi unit despatched to aid the PLO cross Syrian territory[48] at a time when terrorist activities, possibly instigated by Iraq, were being resumed (see above).

Being in Lebanon also had a markedly negative influence on the troops of the expeditionary force themselves. Lebanon's anarchic atmosphere was harmful to military discipline and encouraged theft and lootings. Looted goods smuggled in from Lebanon turned up on the Damascus black market. Furthermore, Beirut's cosmopolitan atmosphere was seen as threatening the "ideological integrity" of Syrian troops; this was presumably countered by subjecting men serving in Lebanon to especially strict discipline and by intensifying political indoctrination.[49]

The cumulative effect of the various aspects of involvement in Lebanon was well reflected in the reported statement of a high-ranking Syrian official that Syria's role in Lebanon was "a thankless, difficult, lonely task."[50]

Nevertheless, Syria remained determined: (1) to maintain and expand its military presence to include all of Lebanon down to the Lītānī River and, by proxy, south of the river as well; (2) to make the Lebanese administration subservient to its will; (3) to destroy the capability of any group in Lebanon (in 1978 specifically the Lebanese Front and the Christian militias affiliated with it) to offer resistance or act independently; and (4) to remake Lebanon, as far as possible, in its own image as a state strictly controlled from the top, its political pluralism circumscribed by strict rules, and its Press subject to censorship on the Syrian model. In short, Syria aimed at gaining full, though not necessarily direct, control over Lebanon.

This policy was intended to achieve a series of positive advantages for Syria, but was also devised to avoid negative developments likely to block Syria's advance to regional ascendancy (see *MECS 1976–77*, pp. 613-14) or even endanger the very existence of Asad's regime. On the positive side, Syria regarded Lebanon as one of the "building blocs" for the establishment of its regional predominance. Furthermore, Syria believed that it could turn Lebanon into a full-fledged "confrontation state," to be integrated into an eventual combined north-eastern front and subject to guidance from Damascus on all issues connected with the Arab-Israeli conflict. In Syria's view, this assumed particular importance following Egypt's "defection from the Arab struggle" as a result of Sādāt's initiative. This in turn made it imperative to establish a "new strategic balance" *vis-à-vis* Israel with Syria at its centre (for details, see below). Lebanon would also constitute a source of political leverage for Syria. By controlling the only territory adjacent to Israel from which the Palestinian organizations were still able to operate, Syria would be in a position to dictate to the PLO when to take action and when not to. Thus, in case comprehensive ME negotiations were resumed, Syria would be able to participate from a position of greatly enhanced strength. In addition, Syria could—and indeed did—force the PLO into taking an unequivocal stand against Sādāt. (The PLO leadership had previously attempted to avoid identification with any one side in inter-Arab disputes.) Lastly, Syria would be in a position to threaten an escalation of hostilities in Lebanon at a moment convenient to its own designs, such as in order to torpedo Egyptian-Israeli negotiations.

The primary consideration on the negative side was that Syria's military presence in Lebanon would make it impossible for Israel to attack Syria's southern flank by moving through Lebanese territory. Syrian leaders and spokesmen declared repeatedly that "Lebanon's security is the security of Syria." [51] More specifically, Syrian representatives stated in discussions with President Sarkīs that "the Biqā' [i.e. the eastern part of Lebanon] is considered . . . [Syria's] forward defence line." [52] A Lebanese source also predicted that part of the new Soviet-built air defence system for Damascus would have to be installed in southern and south-eastern Lebanon "if it is to work efficiently." [53] Another cause of Syrian apprehension was that an unchecked escalation in Lebanon might lead to Israeli intervention on a scale bound to draw Syria into a war at the wrong time. When such a danger threatened at the time of Israel's invasion of South Lebanon in March, Asad declared that "Israel's plan would not draw us into positions of adventurism." [54] Other considerations were that Syria should at all times be able to prevent the establishment in Beirut of an anti-Syrian government or of one inclined to co-operate with Israel, as well as to impede the partition of Lebanon and the concomitant creation of a separate Christian entity allied with Israel. An important reason for rejecting partition was that a new entity accommodating a religious minority would by inference bestow a degree of legitimacy on Israel. [55] The danger of renewed inter-communal fighting in Lebanon if Syria withdrew was another cause of anxiety for Damascus; such warfare could have a contagious effect on Syrian society itself, where existing sectarian tensions had, on the whole, been held in check. Lastly, Syria fully realized that to pull out of Lebanon without finding a solution to its problems would be interpreted as a grave defeat for Asad's policies— grave enough to jolt his regime seriously.

The advantages mentioned above had been sought by Syria since 1975 when it began to assume the role of a regional power in its own right, capable of initiating and pursuing policies of its own choosing. However, during the period reviewed, the need to react to foreign initiatives gradually took precedence over Syria's own plans. Damascus felt threatened both by Sādāt's initiative and by the Israeli invasion of South Lebanon, which increased its anxieties about a possible Israeli attack. By and large, the elements in Syrian policy in Lebanon intended to win tangible gains receded, while those aimed at forestalling potential dangers came to the fore.

THE REJECTION OF SĀDĀT'S INITIATIVE

President Sādāt's visit to Jerusalem was preceded on 16 November 1977 by a meeting with Asad in Damascus where the latter failed to dissuade the former from undertaking his initiative. Immediately after Sādāt's departure, a statement by both Commands of the Ba'th party, the government and the NPF central leadership declared Syria's rejection of the initiative, called upon all Arabs "to confront the dangers which will result from the visit," and urged the Egyptian people in particular "to face up to their pan-Arab responsibilities." [56] On the day of Sādāt's arrival in Jerusalem, an official day of mourning was declared throughout Syria; the media attacked Sādāt as a "traitor" and "trader in blood"; and huge anti-Sādāt demonstrations were staged in Syrian cities, setting a precedent for later occasions, particularly 19 January, the anniversary of the 1977 food riots in Cairo (see *MECS 1976-77*, pp. 289-90). As Egyptian-Israeli negotiations proceeded, Syrian leaders insisted that any reconciliation with Egypt was conditional on Sādāt's total and public renunciation of his initiative and the termination of all contacts with Israel. [57] There were also frequent statements to the effect that under no circumstances whatsoever could there be any reconciliation with Sādāt personally and that he should resign. Failing that, the hope was expressed that he would be overthrown. [58]

Considerations relating to the Arab-Israeli Conflict

Since the aftermath of the 1973 war, Syria had been associated with Egypt in the "political process" (see *MECS 1976-77*, p. 613). Yet its rejection of Sādāt's initiative was largely due to different interpretations of the nature of the conflict, and particularly to different conclusions each drew as a result. Syria's attitude was based on the perception of Zionism as an inherently aggressive and expansionist force, which had usurped Arab Palestine in 1948, was alien to the area and could not form a permanent part of it. [59] The implications of this concept were discussed openly by the Ba'th party's internal monthly organ, *al-Munādil*. It considered the historic struggle between the Arabs and Zionism as one which could not possibly be settled by co-existence, but would necessarily be "finally decided in favour of one party or the other." It added that the Arabs' ultimate goal was "the liberation . . . of all Palestinian soil." Turning to the "strategy of phases" (a formula which had been approved by the party's National Congress of 1975), *al-Munādil* pointed to the super-powers' interest in a political settlement, and implied that such a settlement should be accepted, provided that it enabled the Palestinian people to maintain their "struggling potential" and "keep alive" their national cause, and provided that it did not prejudice Arab rights in Palestine by either "reconciliation (*sulḥ*), recognition [of Israel] or the concession of territory." [60] The "strategy of phases" had served to legitimize Syria's participation in the political process (which in the wake of the 1973 war was considered the only means to regain lost territories), but at the same time was being used to set limits on this participation. These excluded any interim arrangement which might impede future struggle for the ultimate goal.

Such doctrines accounted for the extreme gravity with which Syria viewed Sādāt's acts and statements which could be interpreted as Egyptian recognition of Israel. In Syria's view, the question of recognition should not be considered at all: "It has nothing to do with peace but [is a matter of] sovereignty." [61] Peace needed no accompanying positive elements or ingredients of "normalization." As Asad himself put it: "Either [there is] peace or war; when war ends, there will be peace." [62] The desire not to prejudice the ultimate goal had allowed for no more than qualified acceptance of the political process in general, of Resolution 242 or of the Geneva conference. These reservations alone would have dictated the rejection of Sādāt's initiative. Syria's past participation in the political process was now presented by its Foreign Minister as having simply been a means of exposing Israel's intransigence before the international community. [63] Syrian leaders recalled that in 1975 Damascus had rejected a settlement on the Golan Heights because "we cannot possibly accept the Golan as the price of [abandoning] the Palestine problem." [64] The Palestinian state envisaged by Syria (in contrast to the view it attributed to

Egypt) required that Israel not only evacuate the occupied territories, but also return them to "our dispersed Palestinian brothers." Syria rejected the possibility of resettling Palestinians in Arab host countries because this would affect the struggle towards the ultimate goal.[65] Political action to attain interim targets was not considered to exclude simultaneous resort to the military option. A Syrian journalist suggested that pending the achievement of the ultimate goal, attempts might be made to seize Galilee or part of Israel's coastal plain.[66]

Syria's refusal to envisage Israel as a permanent part of the ME and its insistence on the ideological formula of the "strategy of phases" were given special emphasis by the regime because it was apprehensive of potential opposition from radicals within its own ranks who might take their cue from "rejectionist" policies and the propaganda of Iraq (see essay on the Arab-Israeli Conflict).

The Syrians argued that recognition of Israel and renunciation of the military option were not only unacceptable because they obstructed the attainment of the "ultimate goal," but would also be taken by Israel as a sign of Arab weakness. Recognition of Israel would also make it difficult to get foreign countries to boycott Israel or withhold aid from it;[67] waiving the military option would disrupt the ME balance of power. The perception of the need for a new strategic balance had to some extent evolved since 1973—against the background of Syria's mistrust of Egypt and in relation to its attempt to become an autonomous regional power. A Syrian journalist, writing shortly before Sādāt's trip to Israel, argued that ever since 1973 it had become apparent that in the next war Israel's first strike would be directed against the north-eastern front, the strength of which would thus be decisive.[68] Syria's Foreign Minister claimed that the old strategic balance had been disrupted in 1973 by Egypt itself, when it deviated from the operational plans laid down jointly with Syria and unilaterally accepted a ceasefire.[69] The concept of the new balance was elaborated and emphasized following Sādāt's Jerusalem visit, and was presented to the members of the Tripoli bloc, the Soviet Union and presumably also to Saudi Arabia as the basis for Syrian demands for military aid (see essay on Inter-Arab Relations). Syria argued that, by pledging not to resort to war anymore, Sādāt had removed Egypt from the group of "confrontation states" and had thus destroyed the 30-year old ME strategic balance. Now Syria alone (or assisted by a few like-minded Arab states) would have to constitute the Arab side of the equation.[70] The strategic balance was usually presented in terms of military strength. However, Asad said in an interview that he was "concerned not about the military balance of power but about the political balance."[71]

Perhaps the most decisive consideration for Syria was the fear of a separate Egyptian-Israeli settlement. Its mistrust of Egypt, engendered at the end of the 1973 war, had grown in the course of negotiations for the ensuing Sinai agreements. In September 1977, Syria rejected an Egyptian-American-Israeli proposal to organize the Geneva conference in bilateral working groups, for fear that Egypt might exploit the arrangement to arrive at a separate settlement with Israel. Against this background, Syria naturally feared that Sādāt's initiative was aimed at a separate agreement which would vastly diminish the prospects for the return of the Golan Heights and the establishment of a Palestinian state; would leave Syria alone to cope with Palestinian frustration; and would expose it, together with the PLO, to a possible Israeli attack when the country was freed from the need to protect its southern front. Suspicion of a separate settlement created a political dilemma for Syria: it lent added acerbity to the rejection of Egypt's new policy, but it also made Syria's leaders aware that by publicly proclaiming Egypt as being beyond the Arab pale, they might well be pushing Sādāt into, rather than deterring him from, a separate deal.

Inter-Arab Considerations

Following Sādāt's initiative, Syria joined most other Arab countries in accusing Egypt of having damaged Arab solidarity, deviated from all-Arab strategies, violated summit resolutions, and "disregarded the all-Arab character of the Palestinian problem." But Syria harboured additional suspicions and anxieties which related more directly to its own inter-Arab policies. Sādāt's initiative posed three challenges to Syria's attempt, pursued continuously since 1973, to place itself at the centre of a regional bloc capable of acting independently from Egypt on the inter-Arab scene.

(1) If Sādāt were to succeed in drawing Jordan into negotiations with Israel, the previously developed special relationship between Amman and Damascus would collapse altogether (see *MECS 1976–77*, pp. 154–57).

(2) A successful initiative would likely affect the international leverage Syria had gained by participating in the political process and developing relations with the US to the point where Washington (especially under the Carter Administration) had come to consider Syria as a vital partner in this process.

(3) A successful initiative would likely result in the adoption of a formula for the "rights of the Palestinian people" which would preclude Syria from establishing a special relationship with, or extending its patronage over, a future Palestinian state. It is in this context that *Tishrīn* felt the need to reaffirm that "Syria . . . is . . . the lung with which the Palestinian resistance is breathing," [72] and that NC member Sāmī al-'Attārī declared: "Palestine and Syria are part of one homeland. The false borders established by the [1916] Sykes-Picot agreement . . . are no longer acceptable. Therefore the question of Palestine is strictly a Syrian issue and [only next] an Arab security issue." [73]

In the context of broader Syrian-Egyptian competition, which became pivotal after 1973, Damascus rejected Cairo's claim to a central role in inter-Arab affairs. This claim was implicit in the very nature of Sādāt's initiative—a unilateral act meant to redirect Arab policies in their entirety. It was made explicit in the argument, repeatedly put forward by Sādāt and other Egyptian leaders—and emphatically contradicted by Syrian spokesmen—that Egypt held "the key to war and peace" in the ME. Syria's Foreign Minister attributed Sādāt's pretence to all-Arab leadership to his "'Abd al-Nāsir complex." [74] Syria, by contrast, frequently described itself as the true "cradle of Arab nationalism," the stronghold of "steadfastness," and the "major ally of the Palestinian resistance." Following Egypt's "defection," Syria described itself as the "principal Arab confrontation state." [75]

The International Aspect

Yet another reason for Syria's rejection of the initiative was that it excluded the USSR from the peace process—only a matter of weeks after the joint American-Soviet communiqué of 1 October 1977 (see *MECS 1976–77*, pp. 140–41). The communiqué had been hailed by Radio Damascus as having put an end to the US "monopoly over the efforts towards a settlement of the ME problem." [76]

COPING WITH THE INITIATIVE: SYRIA AND THE TRIPOLI BLOC

From the Syrian point of view, rejection of Sādāt's initiative would ideally have taken the form of an Arab bloc or alliance, with itself acting as acknowledged leader, which would be firm in its opposition to Egypt, and at the same time compensate Damascus for the damage caused by Sādāt to its stature on the inter-Arab scene and the international arena, and to its stance *vis-à-vis* Israel. Such an alliance should have made it possible for Syria to continue to pursue a comprehensive political settlement under the combined aegis of the two super-powers or of the UN, as well as to work for a new strategic balance centring on Damascus and restoring to it a credible military option against Israel independently of Egypt.

The attitude of other major Arab states, notably Saudi Arabia and Jordan, made it impossible for Asad to create such an Arab alliance. Syria's search for a combination of anti-Sādāt forces answering its needs and expectations eventually led to the formation of the Tripoli bloc, made up of Syria, Algeria, Libya, the PDRY and the PLO. (For the developments preceding its formation, its constitution at the Tripoli conference of December 1977, its activities, as well as an analysis of its shortcomings as seen from Damascus, see essay on Inter-Arab Relations.) Of special importance to Syria in this context was the question of co-operation with Iraq. As early as 20 November 1977, while Sādāt was still in Israel, Syria asked Libya's Prime Minister, 'Abd al-Salām Jallūd, to take a message to Iraq's President, Aḥmad Ḥasan al-Bakr, urging him "in view of the gravity of the situation, to let bygones be bygones." [77] This Syrian gesture was made despite the ten-year old history of Syrian-Iraqi quarrels and despite the complete failure of a series of earlier mediation attempts. Reconciliation with Iraq would be of major significance for several reasons: first, because of the strength of the Iraqi armed forces (12 divisions as compared to Syria's five) and their easy and quick access to the battlefront (particularly since the settlement with the Kurds in 1975 had eliminated the need to keep strong forces close to the Kurdish areas); and second, because Iraq was capable of causing grave domestic problems if, despite the common challenge posed by Sādāt, it continued an anti-Syrian stance. Indeed as long as this stance persisted, the presence of Iraqi troops in Syria was more of a danger than a benefit.

However, it was precisely the issue of relations with Iraq which turned out to be the most problematic for Syria during the period under review. Iraq's criticism of Syria was voiced, and its demands laid down, in a letter from Bakr dated 29 November 1977 and in an Iraqi draft charter for a "Front of Steadfastness and Liberation." (For the circumstances of their publication and summary of their contents, see section on Iraq in the essay on the Arab-Israeli Conflict, as well as the essay on Inter-Arab Relations.) In his letter, Bakr blamed "the brothers in the Syrian government" for shouldering a "basic responsibility for the deterioration of the Arab situation" leading to Sādāt's initiative in that, after the 1973 war, they "followed the same line as that followed by Sādāt, although they sometimes differed from him on details." To be eligible to join the Front, he stipulated, Syria must adopt a policy of "radical and comprehensive rejection of the course leading to a settlement" and disavow Resolutions 242 and 338. Furthermore, Bakr demanded that Syria withdraw from Lebanon in accordance with a timetable and conditions to be determined by the Front. [78] The demand that Syria reject the two resolutions was delivered as an ultimatum by the Iraqi delegation to the Tripoli conference. According to an Iraqi account, Syria replied that it had no need to reject Resolution 242, since it had never genuinely accepted it in the first place. [79] However, it could not possibly agree to reject Resolution 338 (one clause of which had instituted the 1973 Golan ceasefire); to do so, the Syrians held, would be tantamount to a declaration of war on Israel. The Syrian reply caused Iraq to walk out of the conference. [80]

In the course of further mediation attempts in December 1977 and January 1978, Syria was reported to have suspended the subversive activities previously carried out in Iraq by a Kurdish faction based in Syria and led by Jalāl Tālabānī, and to have made a conciliatory gesture by allowing the return from exile of Salāḥ al-Dīn al-

Bītār,[81] an ex-PM and former associate of Ba'th figures now serving as members of the Iraqi NC. A Jordanian paper also anticipated the unification of the National Commands of the Syrian and Iraqi parties, and the release from detention of Salāḥ Jadīd, Yūsuf Zu'ayyin and Nūr al-Dīn al-Atāsī, the leaders ousted by Asad when he assumed power in 1970.[82] However, recognition of the present Iraqi National Command (some of whose members had belonged to the original Syrian NC ousted in 1966) and the release of Asad's predecessors in power would have called into question the very legitimacy of Asad's regime, and the reappearance of the latter on the Syrian political scene would probably have revived opposition elements presently almost dormant. Both measures were thus unacceptable to Syria.

At the end of January 1978, it was again Syria's refusal to reject the two Security Council resolutions which caused the collapse of the mediation attempt, even though a meeting in Algiers of Syrian and Iraqi representatives had already been set up.[83] Iraqi-Syrian propaganda warfare immediately erupted anew[84] and was followed, coincidentally or otherwise, by a revival of sabotage activity in Syria (see above). There was no more talk of Syrian-Iraqi reconciliation in the following months. Instead, mutual accusations revolved around three issues: stationing Iraqi troops in Syria; Syria's attitude towards an eventual negotiated settlement; and the argument over who had helped, or failed to help, the PLO in South Lebanon.[85] Under the impact of the Camp David agreements, Syria and Iraq effected a reconciliation which was embodied in a "Charter for National Action," signed on 26 October 1978. Tension abated, but major policy differences were not resolved. The impact, let alone the durability of the *rapprochement*, could not be evaluated at the end of the period under review.

Co-operation with the other members of the Tripoli bloc was not without problems either. Syria's positions were only reluctantly accepted, especially by Libya. Following Iraq's example, Qadhdhāfī reportedly demanded at the Algiers summit in February 1978 that Syria revoke its acceptance of the two Security Council resolutions and deny its readiness to participate in a reconvened Geneva conference. Asad rejected Libya's approach, claiming that the two resolutions, being the results of the 1967 and 1973 wars, might in any event be invalidated by a new war. He also maintained that the Tripoli bloc need not necessarily obtain "congruence" of views: having a "clear programme" would suffice.[86] Syria's success in having a reference to the pursuit of a "just . . . lasting peace" incorporated into the concluding statement of the Algiers conference in February 1978 stemmed from the desire of its partners to have at least one "confrontation state" as a bloc member, rather than from a genuine acceptance of this attitude. Another issue over which Syria succeeded in enlisting only reluctant and tacit support was the deployment of UN forces in South Lebanon following Israel's invasion.[87] This was initially opposed by Libya and the PLO. Syria reportedly had to give way on one point at the Tripoli conference: it agreed in principle to permit fidā'ī operations across the Golan ceasefire line, in contrast with its practice in recent years.[88] The reports were not borne out by subsequent events on the Golan, however. (For a more detailed account of Syria's relations with the PLO, see essay on the PLO.)

Although the concluding statements of the Tripoli and Algiers conferences recognized Syria as the "principal confrontation state" and referred to the pursuit of a "just . . . peace," this did not signify that Damascus had become the undisputed leader of the bloc, as it had hoped. Moreover, the bloc's effectiveness as an instrument for opposing Sādāt, strengthening Syria's "steadfastness," and contributing to the achievement of a new "strategic balance" was in any case limited. A number of factors contributed to restricting the bloc's cohesiveness and its capacity for action: differences of views among members; the delay in setting up joint institutions for the Front, pending Iraq's adherence to it;[89] the concern of several participants with peripheral matters (for details, see essay on Inter-Arab Relations); and the remoteness of Libya and Algeria from the battlefield. The PLO's exclusive siding with Syria—in contrast with its past practice not to identify with any one Arab country—was helpful in obstructing Egyptian-Israeli negotiations; but from other points of view, the PLO was of little use in promoting Syria's objectives.

The extent to which membership in the Tripoli bloc enhanced Syria's military strength was difficult to assess. Qadhdhāfī was reported to have pledged $1,000m for the purchase of Soviet arms for Syria, while the presence of Jallūd in Moscow during Asad's visit there in February 1978 was seen to indicate a discussion of Libyan-financed arms purchases.[90] (For reports on Soviet arms deliveries to Syria at that time, see below.) However, later reports spoke of Libya's contribution as a promise yet to be fulfilled. According to reports in September 1978, the Libyan grant had not yet been ratified.[91] Disillusionment with the aid from Tripoli bloc members was occasionally evident in the Syrian media. Al-Thawra, for example, asserted that if Arab support was not forthcoming—a possibility "which seems probable and is being taken into account"—Syria would wage "the battle of liberation" alone.[92]

Co-operation with Saudi Arabia and Jordan, rather than with the Tripoli bloc, would have suited Syria better in some respects: Jordan could have supplied valuable military assistance, and Saudi Arabia financial aid more reliable than that offered by Libya. In addition, ties with both would have made it easier for Syria to retain a political option of sorts, and to keep a line open to the US beyond the restricted direct contacts it maintained itself. On the other hand, close co-operation with Jordan and Saudi Arabia would have been counter-productive in terms of Syrian-Soviet relations. In any case, soon after Sādāt's trip to Jerusalem, it became clear that neither Jordan nor Saudi Arabia was ready to join an Arab combination firm enough in its anti-Sādāt stance to satisfy Syria. The lack of a formal commitment notwithstanding, Syria kept Saudi Arabia continuously informed of its moves. Asad visited Riyadh and the Gulf states in December 1977, immediately following the Tripoli summit conference; Khaddām made a similar visit in February 1978, following the Algiers conference; and the presidential adviser, Adīb Da'ūdī, made a third visit to Saudi Arabia and the Gulf states immediately following Asad's return from the USSR at the end of February (see below). The contacts with Saudi Arabia were not always satisfying to the Syrian side, however. Saudi attitudes towards Sādāt's initiative were presented in Syria as more emphatically negative than was warranted by Saudi Arabia's own statements.[93] Occasional hints were made by Syrian spokesmen and in the media that assistance received from oil-rich countries was inadequate. Allusions to the ties linking these countries to American interests, and thus indirectly to Israel, were intended to display disappointment both with the scope of the aid received from them and with their lukewarm attitude towards Sādāt's initiative.[94]

Jordan posed a special problem for Syria. On the one hand, Damascus was anxious to dissuade Husayn from joining the Egyptian-Israeli negotiations; on the other hand, it was particularly important not entirely to write off the special relationship it had developed with Jordan since 1975. At times, Syria resorted to open criticism of Jordan: Khaddām, for instance, described Jordan's support of Egypt after the suspension of the Jerusalem talks in January 1978 as "incomprehensible."[95] In June, Syria was reported to have taken an active anti-Jordanian step by encouraging the infiltration of fidā'iyyūn into Jordanian territory in order to carry out operations against Israel.[96] Such incursions could pose serious domestic problems for Jordan (see chapter on Jordan). In July, however, Husayn visited Damascus. Early in August, the Higher Jordanian-Syrian Joint Committee, made up of the two countries' Prime Ministers, met in Damascus for the first time since July 1977. The Committee's deliberations were not as meaningful as in previous years, since the thrust toward Syrian-Jordanian integration had already levelled out in 1977 (see *MECS 1976-77*, pp. 154-57). Rather, the meeting was a demonstration that bilateral relations had not been ruptured altogether following Sādāt's initiative.

RELATIONS WITH THE USSR

Following Sādāt's initiative, Soviet military and political backing became more vital to Syria than at any time since the 1973 war. Growing dependence on Soviet goodwill resulted from a combination of factors: Syria's fears of an Israeli attack and its efforts to "redress the strategic balance" (see above); Syria's exclusion from the ME political process at this stage; and the cooling-off in Syrian-US relations.

The USSR, for its part, had been seeking a formal treaty with Syria as compensation for the abrogation of its Treaty of Friendship and Co-operation with Egypt. If the end of the Egyptian-Soviet treaty relationship in 1976 had made Syria a more valuable ally, Sādāt's initiative in 1977—with the harm it did to the USSR's overall standing in ME affairs—redoubled that effect. Moreover, among Sādāt's militant opponents in the Arab world, Syria was closest to the Soviet Union in its views on the nature of a possible regional settlement and the potential role of the Geneva conference in promoting its attainment. Syria's importance to Moscow was further enhanced in mid-1978 when a degree of tension developed in Soviet-Iraqi relations (see chapter on Iraq).

In the course of a series of visits to Moscow by Syria's Foreign Minister (at the end of November 1977), Syria's Chief of Staff, Hikmat Shihābī (in December 1977 and February 1978), and President Asad (in February 1978), various sources reported a resumption of Soviet arms deliveries to Syria. These had been suspended in 1976 to mark Soviet displeasure with Syria's invasion of Lebanon. In January 1978, the actual or imminent delivery of MiG-23 aircraft, T-62 tanks and an advanced version of SAM-6 missiles was reported.[97] The shipments were believed to have been financed by Libya (see above). Asad's visit to the USSR in February 1978 was said to have resulted in agreement on an expanded procurement programme to be implemented in stages: the establishment of an air defence system was to be followed by the delivery of MiG-23 aircraft and T-62 tanks; finally, in the event of hostilities, an air bridge was to supply Syria's additional wartime requirements.[98] Another sign that Soviet criticism of Syria's policy in Lebanon no longer seriously affected bilateral relations was the docking of three Soviet warships at Lādhiqiyya port in June 1978.[99] (Syria had stopped Soviet naval visits in 1976 because of the differences over Lebanon.) Later in the summer, the USSR was said to have assured Syria (and simultaneously warned the US) that it would intervene directly in the event of an Israeli attack on Syria or Lebanon.[100] However, even at this stage, the USSR did not fully back Syria's policy and conduct in Lebanon: on 6 October 1978, the USSR voted at the Security Council for a resolution calling for a ceasefire in Lebanon to facilitate the restoration of internal peace and national reconciliation "based on the preservation of Lebanon's unity, territorial integrity, independence and national sovereignty." The vote was distinctly embarrassing to Syria. On the same date, a Soviet-Syrian joint communiqué, concluding yet another visit to Moscow by Asad, failed to make a positive reference to Syria's role in Lebanon and called instead for the normalization of the situation there, along the lines of the Security Council resolution.[101]

Just as Syria's increased importance to the USSR did not lead to complete Soviet backing, so too did Syria avoid exclusive alignment with Soviet policy on all points. In February, for instance, a call for reconvening the Geneva conference was omitted from the joint communiqué concluding Asad's visit to Moscow because of Syrian reservations.[102] Despite Syria's continued acceptance of the Geneva framework as a matter of principle, its mention at that particular juncture would have been inconvenient in the inter-Arab context, and the Syrians succeeded in making their view prevail. Damascus also disagreed with Moscow over the issue of Eritrea: while the USSR supported the Ethiopian government and rendered it military assistance in its campaign to regain control of Eritrea, Syria declared its continued support for the Eritrean Liberation Front and reasserted that "no foreign force is supposed to have military bases on the Red Sea. . . . All foreign forces must go."[103] However, unlike Iraq, Syria stopped short of taking steps in connection with the situation in the Horn of Africa which could have created real tension in Syrian-Soviet relations.

Syria thus maintained a policy of close co-operation with the USSR, while avoiding excessive dependence on it. This was most significantly manifested in Syria's refusal to conclude a formal treaty with the Soviet Union[104] and in its insistence on maintaining its lines of communications with Washington.

RELATIONS WITH THE US
Relations with the US in late 1977 and 1978 were characterized by mounting Syrian disappointment and suspicion, which gave rise to open and sharp criticism of the US role in the ME. The US gradually realized, and eventually accepted, that if Syria was persuaded to join the process launched by Sādāt's initiative, this could only be at a later stage.[105] At the same time, Washington continued to declare its belief in Syria's major role in overall ME affairs and in its relatively moderate positions on the Arab-Israeli conflict. It also reiterated its commitment to a comprehensive settlement in which Syria would be a full partner.

The increasing US involvement in Egyptian-Israeli negotiations in 1978 made Syria more distrustful of the American role. This process had started in connection with the dispute over PLO representation in Geneva and was emphatically reinforced by the US-Israeli working paper of 5 October 1977 (see *MECS 1976-77*, pp. 141–42). By early 1978, Syria no longer expected the US to apply pressure on Israel in order to produce concessions. Rather, Syria reverted to an earlier view of the US as a full-fledged ally of Israel acting under the *diktat* of pro-Zionist domestic opinion.[106] The US was suspected of encouraging, or even of having planned, a separate Egyptian-Israeli agreement, the conclusion of which would make it easier to force other Arab states to "submit" to imperialist designs.[107] In fierce verbal attacks by leading personalities as well as in the media, the US was once again described as the "imperialist villain" manoeuvring local allies—both Israel and Egypt—in order to subject the area to its domination, expel the USSR, control regional oil resources, strike at Arab "progressive forces," and extend its control to Africa as well.[108]

On the diplomatic level, displeasure with the US role was manifested in the formal and cool manner in which Cyrus Vance was received in Damascus in December 1977,[109] and in the rejection of a proposal for Asad to meet Carter in Tehran in January 1978—by arguing that Syria "has nothing to say" to the US. Moreover, in February Damascus refused to invite Carter's roving ambassador, Alfred Atherton, to Damascus, stating that his ME tour did "not serve the cause of a just and lasting peace."[110] In all these instances, however, Syria stopped short of entirely breaking off contacts with the US—a step fraught with undesirable risks.

At the beginning of August 1978, the US House of Representatives voted 280 against 103 to cut off $90m in economic aid to Syria for the coming fiscal year in protest against its attacks on Christian civilians in Lebanon. Syria's Foreign Minister retorted: "We take our steps . . . whether others like it or not." The US Administration, for its part, declared that, out of its belief in the importance of Syria's ME role and of US-Syrian relations, it would seek to have the funding restored. Eventually, the Congress refrained from earmarking the sum specifically for Syria, but included it in the total development aid appropriations, thus leaving the Administration free to make the grant to Syria at its discretion.[111]

ECONOMIC AFFAIRS ($1 = 3.950 Syrian pounds; £1 = £S 7.179)
Despite the dislocations caused by the Yom Kippur War, the Syrian economy—buttressed by increasing oil revenues—continued to grow in the post-1973 period.[112] However, more recent events, such as a levelling in the oil market, combined with reduced aid from the Arab world following Syria's large-scale intervention in Lebanon in 1976, have caused considerable problems for President Asad's economic managers. Since 1976, economic growth has slowed down; oil exports have dropped; the trade gap has widened; corruption has persisted, and the impact of the black market has increased with the influx of Lebanese goods. Yet, despite these difficulties, the Syrian economy has shown itself to be reasonably resilient and, according to foreign reports, "business is booming."[113]

AGRICULTURE
As in much of the ME, cultivable land in Syria is largely rain-fed. With the opening of the Tabqa dam on the Euphrates River in March 1978, however, major irrigation and land reclamation schemes have become possible. By the year 2000, Syrian planners hope to double the area of land at present under irrigation.[114]

According to the Central Bureau of Statistics, agricultural production grew by an average of 36.8% in 1976. Among the country's major crops, the following experienced sizeable increases in output in that year: wheat (+ 15.5% for a total of 1.79m tonnes), barley (+77.4% for a total of 1.06m tonnes), tomatoes (+ 37.6% for a total of 516,000 tonnes) and grapes (+ 13.5% for a total of 319,000 tonnes). Cotton production, on the other hand, fell slightly in 1976 and was forecast to decrease again in 1977. This was partly due to government policy which is aimed at reducing the land area allocated to cotton (in favour of sugar beet), but which the authorities hoped would be compensated for by higher yields. Cotton remains Syria's most important cash crop and, until 1974, was the country's most important earner of foreign exchange.[115] In 1976–77, Syria was the world's tenth largest producer and fourth largest exporter of cotton.

INDUSTRY
Industrial production rose by an average of 8.6% in 1976. The most impressive gains in the manufacturing sector were in food, beverages and tobacco (+ 22.2%); paper printing and binding (+ 21.6%); and weaving, spinning, ginning and leather (+ 18.0%). Of the remaining categories, electricity and water combined for an average 10.0% increase in output in 1976, while the extractive industries suffered a 19.7% fall in production from their peak in 1975.[116]

An examination of industrial output in 1976 according to product reveals that production of such major goods as cement (+ 11.7% for a total of 1.1m tonnes), sugar (+ 7.7% for a total of 126,100 tonnes) and crude oil (+ 4.9% for a total of 10.0m tonnes) picked up, while that of phosphates (-40.4% for a total of 511,000 tonnes) and woollen fabrics (-4.4% for a total of 1,441 tonnes) lagged.[117] The uneven performance of Syria's industrial sector led the authorities to pursue a development plan aimed at large-scale expansion of local resource-based industries (e.g. textiles and fertilizers) and import substitution in consumer goods. According to the Minister of Industry, Shatyawī Sayfū, projects scheduled to begin operations include an £S 800m phosphate fertilizer project in Homs; a £S 325m cement plant (location not specified); a £S 203m cotton spinning project in Jabla; a £S 180m sugar plant at Tal Salḥab; a £S 118m copper and aluminium cable project in Aleppo; and glass factories costing £S 180m and £S 158m in Damascus and Aleppo respectively.[118]

BUDGET

One of the more noteworthy features of the 1978 budget was the 10% increase in defence spending compared with a 4.7% rise in overall expenditure. From a total of £S 18,202m (c. $4,608m), development expenditure was set at £S 10,646m—an increase of only 1.9% over 1977. Current expenditure in 1978 was scheduled to grow 7.2% for a total of £S 3,233m, while military spending was allocated £S 4,323m (i.e. 23.8% of the overall budget).

A second noteworthy feature was that credit facilities, loans and grants were expected to finance 61% of the 1978 budget. Taxes (16.8%) and public sector profits (17.1%) were the other main sources of revenue.[119]

The Prime Minister emphasized that, with an allocation of £S 10,646m, 1978 would represent the "zenith year" in the implementation of the 1976-80 Five-Year Plan.[120] (For details of the development budget, see *MECS 1976-77*, p. 621.)

MONETARY DEVELOPMENTS

At the end of the third quarter of 1977, Syria's holdings of international reserves amounted to $717m—the highest total since the end of 1975. The overwhelming portion in both cases was in the form of foreign exchange.

At the same time, foreign assets (£S 2,978m) of the Central Bank of Syria exceeded foreign liabilities (£S 1,350m) by a healthy margin. Reserve money amounted to £S 7,228m at this time.

The money supply had grown 23.9% from September 1976 to September 1977, for a total of £S 10,166m. During the same period, the quasi-money supply jumped 38.4%, reaching £S 1,064m at the end of the third quarter of 1977.[121]

BALANCE OF PAYMENTS

With the resumption of large-scale government unrequited transfers from Arab sources, the balance of payments picture improved considerably in 1977. Exports of merchandise and services actually fell $31m. The trade gap grew by only $230m, however, as imports of services fell $260m, while imports of merchandise increased $490m.

A curious fact revealed by IMF statistics was that errors and omissions in Syria's balance of payments accounts reached the considerable sum of $95m.[122]

FOREIGN TRADE

According to IMF data, Syria's exports declined in value by $2m in 1977 from 1976. Italy (13.2%), West Germany (7.9%) and France (7.2%) were Syria's foremost Western markets. The Soviet bloc, Cuba and China purchased an estimated 20.5% of Syria's total exports of $1,063m in 1977. West Germany (14.0%), the Soviet bloc, Cuba and China (10.4%), Saudi Arabia (10.3%), and Romania (8.8%) were Syria's principal suppliers in 1977.[123]

According to data published by the Central Bank of Syria, the three leading exports in 1976 were crude oil (£S 2,585.7m), raw cotton (£S 637.7m) and textiles

(£S 260.8m). They again retained their leading positions in the first half of 1977. As in 1976, Syria's major imports for the first six months of 1977 were machinery and equipment (£S 1,307m), metal and metal products (£S 691.5m), transport equipment (£S 409.7m) and fuels (£S 894.0m).[124]

Dina Kehat
Economic Section by **Ira E. Hoffman**

ARMED FORCES
Total armed forces number 227,500. Defence expenditure for 1978 was £S 4.4 bn ($1.12 bn). Military service is compulsory for 30 months. The Army numbers 200,000, including 15,000 in the Air Defence Command, and consists of two armoured divisions (each with two armoured and one mechanized brigades); three mechanized divisions (each with one armoured and two mechanized brigades); three armoured brigades; one mechanized brigade; three infantry brigades; two artillery brigades; six commando and four parachute battalions; one surface-to-surface missile battalion with *Scud* and two batteries with *FROG*, and 48 surface-to-air missile batteries with SA-2/-3/-6. Equipment consists of 200 T-34, 1,500 T-54/-55, 800 T-62 medium and 100 PT-76 light tanks; BRDM reconnaissance vehicles; BMP mechanized infantry combat vehicles; 1,600 BTR-40/-50/-60/-152, OT-64 armoured personnel carriers; 800 122mm, 130mm, 152mm and 180mm guns/howitzers; ISU-122/-152, 75 SU-100 self-propelled guns, 122mm, 140mm and 240mm rocket launchers; 30 *FROG*-7 and 36 *Scud* surface-to-surface missiles; 82mm, 120mm, 160mm mortars; 57mm, 85mm, 100mm anti-tank guns; *Snapper, Sagger, Swatter* anti-tank guided weapons; 23mm, 37mm, 57mm, 85mm, 100mm towed, ZSU-23-4, ZSU-57-2 self-propelled anti-aircraft guns and SA-7/-9 surface-to-air missiles; 25 *Gazelle* helicopters. (60 T-62 tanks, *Milan, HOT* anti-tank guided weapons, SA-6/-8/-9 surface-air-missiles; 24 *Gazelle* helicopters on order.) 30,000 men are deployed in the Arab Peacekeeping Force in the Lebanon, and there are 100,000 reserves. The Air Defence Command, which is under Army Command with Army and Air Force manpower, consists of 24 surface-to-air missile batteries with SA-2/-3, 14 with SA-6; anti-aircraft artillery; interceptor aircraft and radar.

The 2,500-strong Navy is equipped with two *Petya*-1-class frigates; six *Komar* and six Osa-1-class guided-missile fast patrol boats with *Styx* surface-to-surface missiles; one T-43-class and two coastal minesweepers; one large patrol craft (ex-French CH Type) and eight motor torpedo boats (ex-Soviet P-4). There are 2,500 reserves.

The Air Force numbers 25,000 and is equipped with c. 392 combat aircraft, some believed to be in storage. It is equipped with six ground-attack fighter squadrons, three with 50 MiG-17 and three with 60 Su-7; three fighter squadrons with 50 MiG-23, 12 MiG-27; 12 interceptor squadrons with 220 MiG-21PF/MF. Transports include eight Il-14, six An-12, two An-24, four An-26. Trainers include Yak-11-18, 23 L-29, MiG-15UTI 32 MBB 223 *Flamingo*. Helicopters include four Mi-2, eight Mi-4, ten Mi-6, 50 Mi-8, nine Ka-25 anti-submarine warfare, 15 *Super Frelon*, six CH-47C; AA-2 *Atoll* air-to-air missiles. (12 MiG-23 fighters, 18 AB-212, 21 *Super Frelon* helicopters on order.) Paramilitary forces number 9,500 and consist of 8,000 Gendarmerie and 1,500 Desert Guard (Frontier Force).

Source: The Military Balance 1978–79 (London: International Institute for Strategic Studies).

FORMATIONS/MAJOR SYSTEMS

	1973	1978
Armoured divisions	2	2
Mechanized divisions	3	3–4*
Infantry divisions	—	—
Independent brigades	—	4
Special forces regiments	7	10
Tanks	2,000	2,500
Armoured personnel carriers	1,100	1,200
Artillery	1,200	2,000
Combat aircraft	388	450
Ground-to-ground *Scud* launchers	—	9–12
Helicopters	58	100
Ground-to-air missile batteries	34	70
Naval vessels	12	14

*Including Rif'at al-Asad's forces.
Source: *Arab Military Strength* (Jerusalem: Israel Information Centre, 1978).

BALANCE OF PAYMENTS (million US dollars)

	1975	1976	1977
A. Goods, Services and Transfers	93	−722	−299
Exports of Merchandise, fob	930	1,066	1,064
Imports of Merchandise, fob	−1,425	−2,102	−2,592
Exports of Services	385	314	285
Imports of Services	−503	−505	−245
Private Unrequited Transfers, net	52	53	54
Government Unrequited Transfers, net	654	402	1,136
B. Long-Term Capital, nie	−10	270	287
C. Short-Term Capital, nie	158	135	113
D. Errors and Omissions	−6	13	−95
E. **Total** (A through D)	**236**	**−354**	7

MONETARY SURVEY (million Syrian pounds at end of period)

	1975	1976	(Jan–Sept) 1977
Foreign Assets (net)	1,918	15	819
Domestic Credit	7,537	12,518	13,152
Money	6,965	8,599	10,166
Quasi-Money	919	806	1,064
Import Deposits	444	1,104	1,134
Other Items (net)	1,428	2,025	1,607
Money, seasonally adjusted	6,951	8,590	10,055

NATIONAL ACCOUNTS (million Syrian pounds)

	1974	1975	1976
Exports	4,253	4,861	5,365
Government Consumption	2,707	4,144	4,703
Gross Capital Formation	3,166	5,514	8,097
Private Consumption	10,485	11,901	13,802
Less: Imports	*−5,742*	*−7,605*	*−9,010*
Gross Domestic Product (GDP)	**14,870**	**18,815**	**22,957**
GDP at 1975 prices	16,660	18,815	20,389

Source (of three preceding tables): IMF, *International Financial Statistics.*

BUDGET (million Syrian pounds)

	1976	1977	1978
Total Revenue	**16,564**	**17,391**	**18,202**
of which:			
Current Revenue	9,131	6,947	7,556
Other	7,433	10,444	10,646
Total Expenditure	**15,564**	**17,391**	**18,202**
of which:			
Current Expenditure	2,380	3,017	3,233
National Security	3,691	3,930	4,323
Investment	10,493	10,444	10,646

Source: *Arab Economist*, Beirut; March 1978.

INDICES OF AGRICULTURAL PRODUCTION (1970 = 100)

	1973	1974	1975	1976
A. Vegetable Production	101	209	196	245
Cereals	80	268	248	338
Dry Legumes	111	256	150	279
Vegetables	126	252	288	294
Industrial Crops	110	107	117	119
Fruits	97	187	173	221
B. Animal Production	108	99	187	301
Milk	64	75	126	143
Livestock	139	108	228	454
Eggs	159	174	281	300

INDEX OF INDUSTRIAL PRODUCTION (1970 = 100)

	1973	1974	1975	1976
A. Extractive Industries	186	294	413	345
B. Manufacturing Industries	120	132	143	168
Food, Beverages and Tobacco	126	133	144	176
Weaving, Spinning, Ginning and Leather	113	123	128	151
Wood and Furniture	115	123	130	141
Paper, Printing and Binding	130	144	167	203
Chemicals	120	124	145	157
Non-metal Products (except coal and petroleum)	100	112	118	131
Basic Metal Industries	125	169	285	327
Equipment and Metal Products	141	212	246	288
C. Electricity and Water Industries	121	138	169	186

PRINCIPAL EXPORTS (million Syrian pounds)

	1974	1975	1976	(Jan–June) 1977
Crude Oil	1,607.5	2,376.6	2,585.7	—
Raw Cotton (fibre)	715.0	439.4	637.7	617.2
Textiles	182.8	202.8	260.8	91.3
Tobacco	67.0	81.5	93.2	7.8
Lentils	10.9	18.3	43.2	51.7
Phosphate	81.9	55.8	42.5	28.6
Fresh and Prepared Fruits and Vegetables	38.9	37.1	37.8	18.4
Wool	57.0	29.7	34.5	12.6
Raw Hides and Leather (excluding furskins)	19.3	23.4	28.5	17.0

PRINCIPAL IMPORTS (million Syrian pounds)

	1974	1975	1976	(Jan–June) 1977
Machinery and Equipment	601.7	929.5	1,561.8	1,307.9
Metal and Metal Products	858.1	888.8	1,256.4	691.5
Transport Equipment	263.2	825.8	1,011.0	409.7
Fuels	275.4	396.8	725.4	894.0
Foodstuffs (not including meat, sugar or fruits and vegetables)	581.3	520.3	559.7	420.1
Textiles and Textile Articles	310.9	359.8	441.3	302.0
Chemicals and Chemical Products	333.2	644.1	404.6	285.3
Sugar (raw and refined)	360.7	427.1	315.2	85.7
Resins, Artificial Rubber and products thereof	111.1	197.7	265.4	146.4
Fruits and Vegetables	122.8	124.4	196.8	138.6

Source (of four preceding tables): Central Bank of Syria, *Quarterly Bulletin.*

DIRECTION OF TRADE (million US dollars)

	1975	1976*	1977*	% of 1977 total
Exports to:				
Italy	168.0	200.0	140.6	13.2
West Germany	94.1	109.2	84.1	7.9
France	4.1	75.2	76.3	7.2
Netherlands	1.6	49.8	74.5	7.0
Belgium	98.4	81.2	67.3	6.3
Saudi Arabia	23.3	45.1	58.2	5.5
United Kingdom	74.8	52.3	53.5	5.0
Greece	53.6	17.8	41.9	3.9
United States	6.0	10.3	40.0	3.8
Soviet bloc, Cuba and China	135.9	166.4	218.0	20.5
Total (including others)	**929.9**	**1,065.0**	**1,063.0**	—
Imports from:				
West Germany	215.0	318.5	374.3	14.0
Saudi Arabia	2.7	78.4	275.4	10.3
Romania	73.4	52.7	235.6	8.8
France	125.9	178.8	206.4	7.7
Italy	153.6	202.1	179.0	6.7
Japan	77.4	160.4	160.2	6.0
United States	109.3	129.8	115.2	4.3
United Kingdom	70.7	86.9	107.2	4.0
Belgium	34.0	77.1	87.3	3.3
Soviet bloc, Cuba and China	209.0	238.4	277.6	10.4
Total (including others)	**1,685.4**	**2,365.2**	**2,672.0**	—

*Data partly extrapolated and/or derived from partner country.
Source: IMF, Direction of Trade.

NOTES

1. Official statement on the result of the referendum; R Damascus, 9 February—monitored by British Broadcasting Corporation Summary of World Broadcasts, the Middle East and Africa (BBC), 11 February 1978.
2. See *Middle East Contemporary Survey (MECS) 1976–77*, p. 610.
3. R Damascus, 8 February—monitored by Daily Report, Middle East and North Africa (DR), 9 February 1978.
4. The membership of some such organizations at the end of 1976 was given by *al-Ba'th,* Damascus; 28 October 1977 and *al-Thawra,* Damascus; 15 February 1978, as follows: 259,000 in the General Federation of Workers' Unions, 282,000 in the General Federation of Peasants, 536,000 youth, 55,000 women, 31,000 students, as well as 456,000 children under the age of 14.

5. *Al-Ba'th*, 16 January; *al-Thawra*, 10, 17 January; R Damascus, 15 January—BBC, 17 January 1978 respectively.
6. R Damascus, 13 March—DR, 14 March 1978.
7. Asad's swearing-in address, quoted by R Damascus, 8 March—DR, 9 March 1978.
8. Interview with *al-Qabas*, Kuwait; 17 April 1978.
9. *Al-Sharq al-Jadīd*, London; 15 May 1978.
10. *Al-Sayyād*, Beirut; 5 January 1978.
11. *Arabia and the Gulf*, London; 2 January 1978.
12. *Al-Jarīda al-Rasmiyya* (Official Gazette), Damascus; 19 April 1978, p. 955; cf *Middle East News Agency* (MENA), Egypt; 23 April 1972—DR, 24 April 1972.
13. *Arabia and the Gulf*, 3 April 1978.
14. Text of Syrian Permanent Constitution Article 122, in *al-Thawra*, 1 February 1973.
15. R Damascus, 2 September—DR, 3 September; *Financial Times* (*FT*), London; 3 September; *Arabia and the Gulf*, 12 September; *al-Thawra*, 24 September; *al-Nahar Arab Report and Memo*, Paris; 7 November 1977.
16. United Press International (UPI) reporting from Beirut, quoted in *The Jerusalem Post* (*JP*), 5 October 1977.
17. *Al-Ba'th*, 3 October 1977.
18. Syrian Arab News Agency (SANA), 29 September—BBC, 1 October 1977.
19. Interview with *al-Nahār al-'Arabī wal-Duwalī* (*NAD*), Paris, and *Tishrīn*, Damascus (joint edition); 8 October 1977.
20. R Damascus, 5 October—BBC, 7 October 1977.
21. *Le Monde*, Paris; 3 November; *al-Nahar Arab Report and Memo*, 7 November 1977.
22. *Al-Ba'th*, 12 June; the *New York Times* (*NYT*), 13 June 1978.
23. *Arabia and the Gulf*, 2 January, 6 February; *US News and World Report*, Washington; 16 January; *Ma'ariv*, Tel Aviv; 24 January; *FT*, 21 June 1978.
24. *Le Monde*, 29 March, quoting an official announcement which was not published in Syria, and 1 April; *Arabia and the Gulf*, 3 April 1978.
25. Instead he was appointed Head of the RC Professional Associations' Bureau; see *Tishrīn*, 25 October 1977.
26. *Al-Ra'y*, Amman; 21 March; *NAD*, 1 April; *Arabia and the Gulf*, 3 April 1978.
27. As claimed by *al-Dustūr*, London; 10 April 1978. The paper is hostile to the Syrian regime.
28. *Le Monde*, 1 April; *Ma'ariv*, 10 April; *The Economist*, London; 22 April 1978.
29. Reported e.g. by *al-Nahar Arab Report*, Beirut; 19 July 1971, 5, 12 June 1972.
30. *Al-Dustūr*, 26 December 1977, 10, 24 April 1978; *al-Siyāsa*, Kuwait; 1 April; *Foreign Report*, London; 19 July; *Arabia and the Gulf*, 7 August 1978.
31. *Foreign Report*, 19 July; *Arabia and the Gulf*, 7 August 1978.
32. Voice of Lebanon (VoL), clandestine; 28 March; *Arabia and the Gulf*, 3 April; *al-Dustūr*, 24 April 1978.
33. *Al-Dustūr*, 5 December 1977, 24 April 1978; *US News and World Report*, 16 January; *The Guardian*, London; 12 April; *Foreign Report*, 19 July; *Time*, New York; 7 August 1978.
34. *Foreign Report*, 19 July; Iraqi News Agency (INA), 27 July, 24 August—BBC, 29 July, 26 August; *al-Dustūr*, 14 August; *Ha'aretz*, Tel Aviv; 23 August 1978.
35. *Foreign Report*, 19 July; *Ha'aretz*, 23 August; *Akhir Sā'a*, Cairo; 6 September 1978.
36. *Tishrīn*, 12 December 1977.
37. *Al-Thawra*, 30 March 1978. Nafūrī, a senior military analyst, had been a high-ranking officer and a Cabinet Minister in the pre-Ba'th era.
38. *Le Monde*, 21 March, 1 April; *Washington Post* (WP), 7 April 1978.
39. *Sunday Times*, London; 16 April; *The Guardian*, 5 September; *Jeune Afrique*, Paris; 13 September 1978.
40. *Le Monde*, 1 April; *Jeune Afrique*, 13 September 1978.
41. *Tishrīn*, 18 September 1978.
42. *Al-Jarīda al-Rasmiyya*, 5 April 1978, p. 833.
43. *Al-Thawra*, 2 June 1978.
44. *Tishrīn*, 18 September 1978.
45. *Le Monde*, 11–12 June 1978, published an anonymous letter from Syria giving details of these elements.
46. *Time*, 7 August 1978.
47. E.g. *FT*, 9 June; *Time*, 7 August 1978.
48. *The Guardian*, 21 March, and *NYT*, 25 March, reported their passage.
49. These problems were reported e.g. by *FT*, 14 June; in an article by Patrick Seale reprinted in *JP*, 4 August; and in *Baltimore Sun*, 1 September 1978.

50. Quoted by *Time*, 7 August 1978.
51. E.g. Talās quoted by R Damascus, 17 April—DR, 18 April; Asad quoted by R Damascus, 31 May—DR, 1 June 1978.
52. Reported by *al-Siyāsa*, 22 February 1978.
53. *Al-Nahar Arab Report and Memo*, 20 February 1978.
54. Asad's interview with *International Herald Tribune* (*IHT*), Paris; 20 March 1978.
55. Asad had elaborated this point in a lengthy and revealing speech on 20 July 1976. It came to the fore again in 1978, e.g. in a commentary over R Damascus, 29 July—DR, 31 July 1978: "The armed Phalangist and Chamounist gangs . . . are serving the long-term objectives of Zionism, which wants a justification for its racist religious entity."
56. R Damascus, 17 November—DR, 18 November 1977.
57. E.g. Ahmad Iskandar Ahmad's interview with *NAD*, 29 April; Asad's statement to *al-Wathba*, Abu Dhabi; quoted by R Damascus, 6 May—DR, 8 May 1978; *al-Mustaqbal*, Paris; 20 May; Khaddām's interview with *Der Spiegel*, Hamburg; 19 June—DR, 20 June 1978.
58. E.g. Khaddām's interview with *al-Hawādith*, Beirut; 27 January; NC member Fādil al-Ansārī's statement to *al-Sharq*, Beirut; quoted by MENA, 7 March 1978; Talās' address on the thirty-second anniversary of the French evacuation, quoted by R Damascus, 17 April—DR, 18 April 1978.
59. Asad said in a public address quoted by R Damascus, 18 March—DR, 20 March 1978: "Look at the Crusader invasion and how it receded, the Tartar invasion . . . and other invasions to which we were exposed. . . . We are completely convinced that Israel is nothing but a distorted and defaced form of those invasions to which our people and nation have been exposed throughout our long history. The fate of this invasion will not be any better than that of the previous ones." Similar views can be found in a public address by Talās on the anniversary of the October War, quoted by R Damascus, 6 October—DR, 7 October 1977; in Ansārī's interview with *al-Qabas*, published in *al-Ba'th*, 19 December 1977; in a report on an anthropological study, *al-Ba'th*, 12 March 1978; and in RC member 'Abdallah Ahmad's interview with *al-Qabas*, 17 April 1978.
60. *Al-Munādil*, Damascus; February 1978, pp. 12–13.
61. Khaddām's interview with an unspecified paper quoted by SANA, 4 February—DR, 6 February 1978. Similarly, 'Abdallah Ahmad's interview with *al-Qabas*, 17 April 1978.
62. Interview with *Der Spiegel*, quoted by R Damascus, 10 September—DR, 11 September 1978.
63. Statement to Austrian journalists, quoted by R Damascus, 20 December—DR, 21 December 1977.
64. Khaddām's interview with *al-Ra'y al-'Amm*, Kuwait; 21 February 1978.
65. Khaddām in a lecture at Damascus University on 23 January 1978, published in March as a leaflet by the NC Propaganda, Publication and Information Bureau. The leaflet carried an explanation stating that it was intended to be read out at party meetings.
66. Bassām al-'Asalī, *Tishrīn*, 13 November 1977.
67. E.G. *al-Ba'th*, 22 November; commentary in R Damascus, 22 November—DR, 22 November; Ahmad Iskandar Ahmad in a press conference in Damascus, reported by R Damascus, 26 November—BBC, 28 November 1977.
68. 'Abd al-Rahmān Ghunaym in *al-Ba'th*, 18 October 1977.
69. Interview with *al-Hawādith*, 27 January 1978.
70. E.G. Asad's interview with a Spanish correspondent, quoted by R Damascus, 10 January—DR, 11 January; Ahmad Iskandar Ahmad's interview with *al-Ra'y al-'Amm*, 14 February; NC statement on the anniversary of the coup of 8 March 1963, quoted in R Damascus, 7 March—DR, 8 March 1978.
71. *NYT*, 14 March 1978.
72. *Tishrīn*, quoted by R Damascus, 8 January—DR, 10 January 1978.
73. 'Attārī in a public address, quoted by R Damascus, 24 May—DR, 24 May 1978.
74. Interview with *al-Hawādith*, 27 January 1978.
75. E.G. Asad in an interview with *Newsweek*, New York; 16 January 1978: "You should not forget that Syria is the cradle of Arab nationalism. We have never capitulated from the days of the Crusaders to modern Zionist expansionism."
76. R. Damascus, 2 October 1977.
77. *The Guardian*, 25 November 1977.
78. Text of documents published by INA, 1, 3 February—BBC, 3, 6 February 1978.
79. Interview of Iraqi RCC member Taha Yāsīn Ramadān over Baghdad TV, quoted by INA, 8 December 1977.
80. INA, 6 December 1977.
81. *Al-Sayyād*, 5 January; *Arabia and the Gulf*, 9 January; *FT*, 11 January 1978.

82. *Al-Akhbār*, Amman; 22 January 1978.
83. Khaddām's interview with *al-Usbū' al-'Arabī*, Beirut; 30 January; *FT*, 31 January 1978.
84. E.g. an anti-Syrian statement by a so-called "Provisional Syrian RC," quoted by INA, 4 February—DR, 7 February 1978.
85. E.g. Iraqi Information Minister Sa'd Qāsim Ḥammūdī's interview with Deutsche Presse-Agentur (DPA), Cairo; 16 February—DR, 17 February; Aḥmad Iskandar Aḥmad's interview with *Monday Morning*, Beirut; 20 February; Talās' address on the thirty-second anniversary of the French evacuation, quoted by R Damascus, 17 April—DR, 18 April 1978.
86. *Al-Safīr*, Beirut; 4 February; *NAD*, 11 February 1978.
87. *The Times*, London; 21 March; *FT*, 22 March; *WP*, 23 March 1978.
88. Aḥmad Jibrīl in a statement to *al-Kifāḥ al-'Arabī*, Beirut; quoted by *Daily Telegraph*, London; 23 December 1977; Reuter, 1 February 1978; *al-Siyāsa*, 27 March 1978.
89. *NAD*, 11 February 1978.
90. *IHT*, 25 January; Reuter, Moscow; 22 February; *FT*, 25 February 1978.
91. *Arabia and the Gulf*, 4 September 1978.
92. *Al-Thawra*, 25 April 1978.
93. Khaddām, for instance, told Kuwaiti correspondents that "our [Saudi] brothers have assured [us of] their rejection of Sādāt's initiative"; *al-Ra'y al-'Amm*, 21 February 1978.
94. E.g. 'Abdallah al-Aḥmad's interview with *Tishrīn*, 16 November; *al-Thawra*, 15 December 1977; *al-Ba'th*, 2 March; *Nidāl al-Fallāhīn*, Damascus; 15 March; Asad's interview with *al-Wathba*, quoted by R Damascus, 6 May—DR, 8 May 1978.
95. Interview with *al-Ḥawādith*, 27 January 1978.
96. Israeli TV, 19 June—DR, 20 June 1978.
97. *JP*, 4, 9 January; *al-Safīr*, 22 January; *IHT*, 25 January; *al-Ḥawādith*, 3 February 1978.
98. *NAD*, 4 March; *JP*, *Ha'aretz*, 5 March 1978.
99. *Tass*, 19 June 1978.
100. *Arabia and the Gulf*, 7 August; *al-Siyāsa*, 31 August 1978.
101. Text in R Damascus, 6 October—monitored by BBC Summary of World Broadcasts, the USSR (BBC/SU), 9 October 1978.
102. Text in R Moscow in Arabic, 23 February—BBC/SU, 25 February 1978.
103. Khaddām's interview with *Der Spiegel*, 19 June—DR, 20 June 1978.
104. Arab evaluations that Syria was unlikely to conclude a treaty with the USSR are given in *NAD*, 9 September and *al-Anbā*, Kuwait; quoted by Qatar News Agency (QNA), 27 September—DR, 27 September 1978.
105. Such realization may be traced in a statement by State Department spokesman Hodding Carter quoted by Reuter, 28 February 1978, that the US was still "seeking . . . a comprehensive ME settlement" and continued to "hope that *in the future* Syria's leaders will decide it is in their interest to rejoin the overall peace process" (emphasis added).
106. The effectiveness of pro-Zionist domestic pressures was mentioned by Asad himself in interviews with a Spanish correspondent and with *Der Spiegel*, quoted by R Damascus, 10 January, 10 September—DR, 11 January, 11 September 1978 respectively.
107. Such suspicions were expressed e.g. during Secretary of State Vance's visit to Damascus in December by *al-Ba'th*, 13 December and *Tishrīn*, 14 December 1977.
108. E.g. Khaddām's interviews with *al-Ḥawādith*, 27 January and *al-Usbū' al-'Arabī*, 30 January, and statement to participants in a students' symposium in Damascus, quoted by R Damascus, 24 May—DR, 24 May; Talās in an article in *Tishrīn*, 6 February; Aḥmad Iskandar Aḥmad's interview with *al-Ra'y al-'Amm*, 14 February 1978.
109. *The Guardian*, 14 December 1977. *Tishrīn* warned Vance on 13 December, the day of his arrival, against "carrying an olive branch in one hand and [a knife for] backstabbing in the other."
110. *Tishrīn*, 27 February; *NYT*, 28 February 1978.
111. For the House vote see *Congressional Record*, 2 August; for the Administration statement, Reuter, 3 August; for Khaddām's response, R Damascus, 4 August—DR, 8 August for the eventual Congressional resolution, *Congressional Quarterly Weekly Report*, 21 October 1978.
112. For a concise analysis of the Syrian economy up to 1976, see *MECS 1976–77*, pp. 235–39.
113. See Economist Intelligence Unit, *Quarterly Economic Review (QER)*, London; Annual Supplement 1977 and Nos 1 and 2, 1978. See also *FT*, 21 June 1978; and *Arabia and the Gulf*, 26 December 1977.
114. See *QER*, No 2, 1978; and *al-Thawra*, 24 November 1977—Joint Publication Research Service (JPRS), Washington; 28 February 1978.
115. For details, see Robert E. Evans, *Cotton in Syria* (Washington: Foreign Agricultural

Service, US Department of Agriculture, April 1978), pp. 1–7.
116. Data derived from Central Bank of Syria, *Quarterly Bulletin*, Nos 1 and 2, 1977, pp. 52–53.
117. *Ibid.*
118. See *Tishrīn*, 31 December 1977.
119. See *Arab Economist*, Beirut; March 1978; and *FT*, 13 January 1978.
120. R Damascus, 11 January—BBC, 13 January 1978.
121. International Monetary Fund (IMF), *International Financial Statistics*, August 1978.
122. *Ibid.*
123. IMF, *Direction of Trade*, July 1978.
124. Central Bank of Syria, *op. cit.*

Turkey
Türkiye Cumhuriyeti

POLITICAL AFFAIRS
Two major issues continued to dominate Turkish internal affairs in 1977–78: political violence and the economic crisis. The success of the Republican People's Party (RPP) and the Nationalist Action Party (NAP) in the local elections, and the disputes within the Justice Party (JP)—which caused the defection of 11 deputies— both occurred in December 1977. These developments brought about the fall of Demirel's National Front government and the establishment of a new coalition headed by Bülent Ecevit and based on an alliance of the RPP, the Democratic Party (DP), the Republican Reliance Party (RRP) and defectors from the JP. The new government assumed office amidst great expectation that it would be strong enough to curb political violence and lead the country out of its economic crisis. However, violence was intensified both by the extreme Left and the extreme Right, with the aim of weakening the coalition and eventually bringing it down. The new government, which inherited a seriously weakened economy, introduced severe measures and sought financial aid from the West, the Eastern bloc and Middle Eastern countries, but could not achieve substantial results in a short time.

THE SECOND NATIONAL FRONT CABINET
The general election in June 1977 had been expected to lead to the formation of a strong government capable of effectively tackling the country's many grave problems. Instead, it restored to office a weak coalition of the parties forming the National Front (*Milliyetçi Cephe*; NF) led by Süleyman Demirel (see *MECS 1976–77*, pp. 626, 629–30, 632–35). The coalition consisted of Demirel's own party, the Justice Party (*Adalet Partisi*), Necmettin Erbakan's National Salvation Party (*Milli Selâmet Partisi*; NSP), and the Nationalist Action Party (*Milliyetçi Hareket Partisi*) headed by Alparslan Türkeş.

The rivalry among the three, in particular between JP and NSP, continued unabated and made it impossible for the work of ministries headed by members of different parties to be co-ordinated effectively.[1] One example of the effect of coalition tensions was the NSP's demand to be consulted by the Foreign Ministry (which was headed by a JP member) on ambassadorial appointments. Another was its insistence on having NSP men put in charge of the State Planning Organization (SPO). Both demands were resolutely opposed by the other two parties. The NSP also refused to approve proposed changes in the management board of the Turkish Radio and Television Corporation (TRT). As a result, some controversial appointments were delayed by three months, until November 1977. Even then no fewer than 17 ambassadorial posts were left vacant until April 1978, after a new government had come to power (see below). Yet another example of the inability of the coalition partners to work together was the controversy between the JP and NSP concerning the election of the Speaker of the National Assembly (see also *MECS 1976–77*, pp. 623, 634). The deadlock did not end until 15 Novembr 1977, when the NAP agreed—over NSP protests—to support the RPP candidate, provided he was "a moderate and an anti-Communist." Two days later an RPP deputy, Cahit Karakaş, was elected Speaker.

Another controversy stemming from party rivalry within the government came to a head in the last quarter of 1977; this concerned the choice of a foreign manufacturer to license the production in Turkey of military aircraft, and of the site for the aircraft plant. The Industry Ministry (held by the NSP) chose a site near Konya,[2] but the Defence Ministry (held by the JP) and the SPO had decided that the plant should be located near Ankara. Furthermore, the Industry Ministry had picked the Italian-made MB-339 aircraft as the model to be built in Turkey—but without consulting the Ministry of Defence or the General Staff. The latter strongly opposed the choice on the grounds that the MB-339 was still undergoing tests and was in any case unsuited to Turkey's requirements. The signing of the contract, set for 26 October 1977, was cancelled at the last minute through the Prime Minister's personal intervention. Vehement exchanges ensued among the coalition parties, with the JP and the NSP taking turns in threatening to walk out and thus bring down the coalition. It was only at the insistence of the General Staff that the NSP finally consented that future decisions pertaining to Turkey's aircraft industry be taken in co-ordination with the armed forces and the SPO.[3]

Not surprisingly such internal divisions rendered the coalition incapable of dealing effectively with Turkey's two major problems: political violence and the economic crisis.

POLITICAL VIOLENCE

Armed clashes between Left- and Right-wing factions claimed 130 lives during the government's tenure from October to December. Initially, the number of violent incidents decreased as compared with the period immediately preceding the formation of the government.[4] However, they intensified again as the local elections, scheduled for December, drew near—and even more so afterwards when it became apparent that the government was likely to fall soon. The Minister of the Interior, Korkut Özal (NSP), was firmer than his predecessor in handling acts of violence. In an attempt to dispel the previously prevalent impression that the police had encouraged Right-wing elements in attacking Left-wingers, some 300 policemen were dismissed. Left-wing opposition quarters nevertheless continued to accuse the police of maltreating their sympathizers, and alleged that the policemen whom Özal removed from the force had in fact been dismissed for holding Leftist views rather than for their encouragement of Right-wingers. To prevent student violence, which had seriously disrupted studies during most of 1977, Özal ordered police protection for a number of universities and some high schools. On 5 October 1977, the Minister of Education, Nahit Menteşe (JP), announced that any headmaster or teacher failing to take action against disturbances in his school would be dismissed; students involved in rioting would be expelled, and those old enough would be drafted into the armed forces; scholarships, dormitory privileges and other facilities would be denied to student activists. Despite these steps, however, the most serious cases of violence continued to occur at educational establishments, the majority of casualties being students.

Ankara's ME Technical University (METU) reopened on 7 November after having been closed for eight months. In spite of strict security measures, two explosions occurred on the campus the very day classes resumed. On 2 December, clashes between Leftist students and janitors forced the METU authorities to suspend most of the latter who were discovered to belong to a Right-wing organization. They had been engaged by the former rector, Hasan Tan, who was known to be an NAP sympathizer (see *MECS 1976-77*, p. 625). On 28 December, the executive council of the Hacettepe University in Ankara decided to close the university for a year after the head of the Physics Department, Prof Yalçın Sanalan (known to be a social democrat), was shot and severely wounded. The incident led President Fahri Korutürk to intervene personally in an unprecedented manner: he addressed a sharply-worded message to the Prime Minister demanding "most effective measures to be taken by the government in order to prevent the ugly attacks against members of the university." [5]

The government and the opposition blamed each other for the eruptions of violence. The opposition, as well as some local and foreign newspapermen, held the NAP responsible for instigating acts of violence by means of the youth organization, the "Idealist Club Association" (*Ülkü Ocakları Birliği*), which it sponsored. The "Idealists" had a military arm of their own, the so-called "commandos" or "Grey Wolves" (*Bozkurtlar*).[6] The strength of the "Idealists" (established in 1969) had steadily increased during the 1970s and was aided by two developments:

(1) The intervention of the armed forces in domestic affairs in 1971–72 had virtually eliminated overt Left-wing groups of a radical nature, while Right-wing organizations were not affected by it.

(2) Since the NAP began to share power in 1975, it had gained additional support not only by its propaganda, which presented a mixture of nationalist and socialist slogans, but also by systematically appointing NAP supporters to official positions. In view of the high rate of unemployment (see below), such political patronage was a highly efficient means of attracting support.

In 1977–78, the "Idealists" succeeded in taking control of various student organizations at most teacher training colleges and in the smaller colleges in provincial towns. They were also increasingly successful in removing Left-wing teachers from primary and secondary schools. By and large, most incidents of violence seemed the result of Right-wing activity.

Though sharing responsibility for acts of violence, the extreme Left had not fully recovered from the blow it suffered in 1971–72. Unlike the extreme Right, it had no common coherent ideology, but was split into many groups, each with a different doctrine, which were often as preoccupied with fighting each other as with fighting Right-wingers. In addition, the radical Left lacked the patronage of well-established parties, let alone those with a share in power. The coalition parties nevertheless accused the Republican People's Party (*Cumhuriyet Halk Partisi*; RPP) of acting as patron for radical Left-wingers. In view of RPP leader Ecevit's criticism of the extreme Left and even more in light of his attempts to eliminate radical Leftists from among RPP candidates for the general[7] and local elections (see below), such charges seemed groundless.

Özal's own assessment was that violence was being stimulated by a variety of social tensions. He told an interviewer: "Freedoms and expectations are expanding faster than the development of the country, creating a lot of frustrations." These frustrations caused political polarization among students, and many joined extremist groups because "action attracts young people." [8]

THE ECONOMIC CRISIS

The decline of the Turkish economy (see *MECS 1976–77*, p. 624) became more marked in the last quarter of 1977. The trade deficit increased further, and gold and foreign currency reserves fell to a point lower than at any time during the preceding six years. The shortage of foreign exchange during 1977 slowed down the import of raw materials and of consumer goods. Towards the end of the year, shortages of such staples as coffee, salt and margarine occurred in the larger towns. Output declined in industries using imported raw materials or foreign-made components, and unemployment increased. At the end of 1977, nearly 20% of the labour force was out of work, and inflation had reached an annual rate of 35%. (For further details, see economic section below; for austerity measures taken in September 1977 to remedy the situation, see *MECS 1976-77*, p. 646.)

Another difficulty was the acute energy shortage, resulting in power cuts of a few hours a day becoming commonplace in urban areas. On 24 September 1977, the Minister of Energy and Natural Resources, Kâmran İnan, admitted the existence of a grave energy crisis; on 2 October, he announced the adoption of power-saving measures including a ban on the use of electricity for heating; days of rest in industry staggered throughout the week; and an increase in automobile taxes.[9] However, these measures failed to reduce energy consumption.

Turkish economists and businessmen, as well as some local and foreign press commentators, claimed that the presence of the NSP in government was exacerbating the economic crisis.[10] Erbakan, who had campaigned in the general elections on a platform of accelerated economic development, later proposed an unrealistic industrialization programme. Even the severe constraints on the country's economic progress did not deflect him from his declared objective of rapidly transforming Turkey into one of the world's leading industrial powers.[11] Erbakan's policies contradicted the recommendations of the International Monetary Fund (IMF), with which the government had been negotiating a new loan agreement since September 1977 (see *MECS 1976-77*, p. 646). Its conclusion would have restored the confidence of foreign banks in Turkey's economy and would have made it possible to obtain badly needed foreign currency. The IMF had been pressing for a further devaluation of the Turkish lira by at least 20% (to supplement the 10% devaluation of September 1977). It had also recommended shelving the development programme for heavy industry, and had advocated a cutback in growth and further austerity measures (cf *MECS 1976-77*, p. 646). The inability of the coalition to agree on the IMF's recommendations, despite growing pressure from industrial and banking circles, was largely attributed to Erbakan's stand. The JP, which traditionally represented private business interests, appeared ready to follow the IMF guidelines. The Finance Minister, Cihat Bilgehan (JP), stated on 7 November that the government was willing "to make certain sacrifices to facilitate an agreement with the IMF."[12] However, the NSP remained adamantly opposed to the IMF's proposals. Erbakan's position stemmed not only from his intense distrust of the West and from his realization that compliance with the IMF's demands would curtail his industrial programme, but also from his conviction that his own political future was at stake over this issue. He announced categorically that there would be no further devaluation, and described the IMF's demands as "foreign intervention in Turkey's economic affairs"—an argument which appealed to major sectors of the public.[13]

The IMF negotiators left Turkey on 20 December without having reached agreement. The deadlock was reported to have been due both to the government crisis and to the inability of the coalition to agree on further devaluation.[14]

POLITICAL OPPOSITION

The parliamentary opposition included the RPP, the largest party in the National Assembly (NA), and two right-of-centre liberal parties: the Republican Reliance Party (*Cumhuriyetçi Güven Partisi*; RRP), headed by Turhan Feyzioğlu, with two seats, and the Democratic Party (*Demokratik Parti*: DP) with one member, Faruk Sükan.[15] Both parties were splinter groups from the RPP and JP respectively.

The extra-parliamentary opposition included six minor Left-wing parties, the most influential among them being the pro-Marxist Labour Party of Turkey

(*Türkiye İşçi Partisi*; LPT) headed by Behice Boran, and the two major trade union confederations: *Türk-İş (Türkiye İşçi Sendikaları Konfederasyonu)*, which followed a non-partisan policy; and the radical DISK (*Devrimci İşçi Sendikaları Konfederasyonu:* Revolutionary Trade Union Confederation).[16] However, the most serious opposition was that of dissident groups within the JP, which eventually precipitated the government's downfall.

Relations between the government and the trade unions, which had been strained during the first NF government's tenure, further deteriorated after the NF regained power. Both labour confederations claimed that the austerity measures of September 1977 had brought hardship upon the working class but without requiring any sacrifices from the upper classes. Strikes and lockouts—mainly over labour demands for wage increases to keep up with inflation—were widespread, crippling many factories. The administrative council of *Türk-İş* submitted a memorandum on 5 October 1977 to President Fahri Korutürk, to the Senate, the National Assembly and to individual political leaders both of the coalition and opposition. The memorandum demanded a price freeze; measures to ease the economic burdens borne by labour; a review of minimum wages and an increase in the minimum cost-of-living allowance. It also called for the maintenance of public order and for freedom in education, and concluded by saying that "unless the nation's problems are solved within a reasonable time," *Türk-İş* would call for a general strike.[17]

During September and October 1977, the President of DISK, Kemal Türkler, attempted to establish a National Democratic front capable of a concerted effort to unseat the government. The front was to include the two labour confederations and the RPP. However, there was much disagreement within DISK about the proposed platform of the front and even about the advisability of forming one at all. Türkler's plan failed when in addition to internal disagreements, it became clear that, despite some verbal support, the RPP would not participate actively.[18] Argument about the front nearly caused a split within DISK, and further moves were postponed until the confederation's national convention on 22 December. By then, the NF Cabinet was already visibly nearing its fall, and the issue was no longer relevant. However, Türkler was replaced as President of DISK by the former RPP deputy, Abdullah Baştürk.

Criticism of the government within the ranks of the JP started almost as soon as the second NF Cabinet was formed (see *MECS 1976–77*, pp. 632–33). Pressure within the party gradually mounted until it became a major cause for the break-up of the coalition. JP criticism centred on the following points:

(1) Ministerial and governmental appointments were being made in a manner disproportionately favouring the two smaller coalition parties at the expense of what the JP considered its own fair share.

(2) Control by the NSP and NAP of key economic ministries had deprived the JP of its traditional sources of patronage.

(3) The NSP and NAP were staffing "their" ministries with their supporters and dismissing others, including JP men.

(4) The lack of common ground between the coalition partners and the difficulties of working with Erbakan rendered the government incapable of formulating policies. As a result, foreign issues remained stagnant, the economy deteriorated, and internal security remained shaky.

(5) Continued co-operation with the NSP and NAP was discrediting JP among its constituents. The NSP's policies were felt to conflict with the interests of JP voters. For example, the industrial projects promoted by it competed with the private sector for scarce foreign currency. Furthermore, it was the NSP's

intransigence which had blocked agreement with the IMF. As for the NAP, association with it laid the JP open to the charge of supporting fascism. This turned many centre-of-the-road voters away from the JP and simultaneously enabled the NAP to attract to its own ranks the more Rightist elements from among the JP's supporters.

(6) There was personal criticism of Demirel for surrounding himself with a clique who enjoyed the spoils of office without regard for the interests of the party and the nation.

Opposition within the JP consisted of two major groups. The first advocated that the JP resign from office, feeling that a period in opposition could help rejuvenate the party. This group included the veteran democrats, headed by Zeyyat Mandalıncı,[19] and a faction headed by the Minister of Energy, Kâmran İnan. The second group believed that the only solution to the country's problems lay in forming a grand coalition comprising both the JP and the RPP. This group included the deputies Orhan Alp and Oğuz Aygun, and was particularly opposed to Demirel's continuing as party leader. A grand coalition was also advocated by the armed forces, the business community and the President—all of whom were keen to see Erbakan removed from office.[20]

The Minister of Defence, Sadettin Bilgiç, and the Minister of Youth and Sports, Önal Şakar, resigned on 14 October, ostensibly because they preferred to retain their seats on the party's Executive Board. (The JP's charter limits to seven the number of Executive Board members who may simultaneously serve as ministers.) The opposition press, however, attributed their resignations to discontent within the JP. They asserted that Demirel intended to pacify party dissident groups by appointing their members to the vacant ministries.[21] In fact, the new Minister of Youth and Sports, Ali Şevki Erek, was generally regarded as an NAP sympathizer.

The head of the JP's İzmir branch, Kemel Serdaroğlu, who had earlier called for the dissolution of the coalition, resigned on 31 October at the request of the party's central body. On 15 October, Orhan Alp (JP-Ankara), who had absented himself from the vote of confidence (see *MECS 1976-77*, pp. 632-33) resigned from the party and became an independent deputy.

Despite growing pressure within the party as indicated by these resignations, the JP's Executive Board issued a statement on 15 October strongly rejecting a coalition with the RPP. Addressing a JP National Assembly faction meeting on 18 November, Demirel insisted that it was imperative to keep the present coalition in existence. Despite criticism from a number of deputies, he emphasized that a coalition with the RPP would be tantamount to bringing the Left to power. The JP's mission, he said, was to oppose the RPP.

Though critical of the government, the RPP was meanwhile trying to create for itself an image of moderation. One of its aims in doing so was to convince moderates within the JP that the RPP was not, as Demirel had said, "a threat" to Turkish democracy. Ecevit's policy of stressing moderation was severely criticized by the RPP's Leftist factions headed by Deniz Baykal and Süleyman Genç. The latter demanded a tougher opposition line. Ecevit's policy, however, proved justified when a number of JP deputies resigned after the local elections.

LOCAL ELECTIONS

Elections for provincial, district and municipal councils and for the posts of mayor were held on 11 December 1977. During the election campaign, it became clear that the results would be treated as a referendum for or against the NF and that they could determine the future of the Cabinet. It became evident, however, that in the event of a JP defeat, opposition within the party would increase to the point of precipitating a split which would bring the government down. The RPP's campaign slogan was: "The 11 December referendum—No to the Second NF." [22] It directed its campaign against the government and fought on national rather than local issues. It especially attacked the Prime Minister, calling on JP members to come out against Demirel and thus save the country. RPP speakers accused the NAP of being responsible for the violence and resulting anarchy. The coalition partners also based their campaigns primarily on national issues, stressing that the fall of the government would precipitate a crisis and enable the Communists to gain power. The JP's main theme was: "No power on earth can prevent the JP's caravan from moving on. The government is strong on its feet." [23]

Polling day witnessed a wave of violence in both urban and rural areas in which 15 people were killed.

TABLE I: VIOLENCE IN TURKEY*

	1975	1976	1977	
Dead	34	90	215	(262)
Wounded	694	1,555	2,936	(2,746)
Clashes	159	503	1,321	(1,212)
Bank Robberies	10	39	77	(80)
Explosions	9	170	732	(758)
Demonstrations	139	201	296	

*The Middle East, February 1978. Based on data provided by the Ministry of the Interior under Ecevit's government. Different figures, in parenthesis, were given for 1977 by the Minister of the Interior under Demirel's government. [24]

Electoral participation was low: only 56.7% of those eligible cast their votes. Major gains were made by the RPP and NAP; the NSP managed to retain its strength. So did the JP in terms of the total number of votes cast, but in the elections for mayors of provincial capitals, it suffered a serious setback. The shift away from the JP was especially significant in Aydın, Edirne and Sakarya—all of them traditional strongholds, first of the DP and later of the JP. Türkeş and the NAP's Secretary-General, Necatı Gültekin, claimed in post-election statements that the NAP had been "eating away at the electoral base of the RPP." [25] This was not borne out by the election results: out of five provincial capitals gained by the NAP, three had previously been held by the JP and only two (Bingöl and Yozgat) by the RPP. Moreover, the RPP increased its overall strength in the provincial capitals. It was true, though, that the RPP lost votes to the NAP rather than to the JP, even though local elections usually favour the big parties. In the mid-eastern provinces of Anatolia, where the NAP had been successful in the general elections of June 1977, it continued to make rapid progress, mainly at the expense of the JP.

TABLE II: LOCAL ELECTION RESULTS

Party	Mayors of Provincial Capitals	Mayors of İlçe Capitals (Administrative District)	Mayors of Towns	Total	% of Votes Cast
RPP	42	247	426	715	42.8
JP	15	226	468	709	37.0
NAP	5	17	35	57	6.6
NSP	3	6	37	46	6.7
DP		2	2	4	1.0
RRP		1	6	7	0.5
TUP			1	1	0.2
TLP					0.5
TSWR					0.2
Independents	2	57	111	170	4.5

757

THE FALL OF DEMIREL'S CABINET

The onset of a political crisis was felt as soon as the returns started to come in on election day. JP opponents of Demirel and of the NF coalition began to leave the party. The resignation of three JP deputies—Oğuz Atalay (Konya), Mustafa Kılıç (Ankara) and Şerafettin Elçi (Mardin)—reduced the number of JP seats in the National Assembly to 185, leaving the coalition with 225 seats—one short of an absolute majority. In their letters of resignation, Atalay and Elçi explained that, although they had done everything within their power to help the government function and to serve the nation, they had come to realize that the present structure of the coalition was disastrous for the country as well as for the JP. In his letter, Atalay vowed that as long as the JP was under its present leadership, he would never return to the party. [26]

The resignations of Dr Mete Tan and Güneş Öngüt (both deputies of Afyon), Cemalettin İnkaya (Balıkesir), Hilmi İşgüzar (Sinop) and Tuncay Mataracı (Rize) followed on 14, 15 and 16 December respectively, further reducing the number of JP seats to 180. Following meetings with Ecevit, the eight defectors—acting as a group for the first time—issued a joint declaration on 18 December. This was also signed by Orhan Alp, who had resigned earlier, and by Ali Riza Septioğlu (Independent—Elâzığ). They declared that since the government had failed to follow Atatürk's principles, they had decided to work for its removal from office. They further stated their "determination to continue our legislative duties henceforth as an independent group in order to help those who will form a coalition government capable of protecting the national interest." They called for the formation of a grand coalition between the JP and RPP "in order to solve the country's extremely serious problems." [27]

On 20 December, Enver Akova (JP—Sivas) and Ahmet Karaaslan (JP—Malatya) expressed complete accord with the above declaration and also resigned. Theirs were the last resignations, but criticism within the JP continued. JP Deputies Kâmran İnan and İsmet Sezgin urged the party to leave the coalition, while others, such as İnan Gaydalı, called for the formation of a grand coalition, [28] a recommendation also supported by members of the business community and several newspapers. However, as long as Demirel was in office, this was not a practical proposition. [29] Meanwhile, Demirel accused Ecevit of "playing secret and dark games" in order to take over power. [30] JP members accused the defectors of having received financial inducements from the opposition. In the National Assembly, Mustafa Kılıç was roughed up by JP deputies; the Assembly President, Cahit Karakaş, claimed that some defectors from the JP had been "subject to threats and pressure both outside and inside the National Assembly." [31]

The initial NAP and NSP reaction to the wave of resignations from the JP was to insist that they were internal party affairs. However, as the situation worsened, they blamed external forces: the NSP pointed an accusing finger at the US; the Rightwing publication *Diplomat*, by contrast, accused the USSR. [32]

After establishing contacts with the newly independent group as well as with RRP and DP leaders, Ecevit let it be understood on 20 December that he might form a new government. The following day, the JP general administrative council decided not to ask the Assembly for a vote of confidence, but rather to allow the RPP to unseat the government by means of a censure motion which was tabled that same evening. The opposition accused the government of economic irresponsibility and of allowing the national debt to reach a level that "casts a shadow over the country's independence." The motion also accused the coalition, and in particular "one party" (i.e. NAP), of responsibility for the continuing political violence. [33] Demirel rejected all the accusations, and in turn charged Ecevit with promising ministerial seats to those who would help him topple the government. He added: "I expect that those who have been daring enough to mix intrigue into the government change [sic] in Turkey will receive the requisite answer from the public." [34]

The new group of independents began negotiating with Ecevit almost immediately after their resignation; according to press reports, this included bargaining over ministerial posts. Orhan Alp expressed the group's conviction that as long as the present JP leadership was in office, there was no prospect for the formation of the grand coalition which they advocated. They were therefore prepared to form a government with the RPP alone. Only Cemalettin Inkaya continued to favour a grand coalition as the only way of tackling the country's problems; he refused to support the coalition of Independents with the RPP.

In the meantime violence continued to spread, reaching the highest level of 1977. As the government crisis continued, pressures for an early end to the political uncertainty mounted. The foreign press speculated that, if the situation deteriorated further, the army might intervene.

The RPP's censure motion was debated in the National Assembly on 29 December. NAP and NSP spokesmen warned that its acceptance would throw the country into an endless governmental crisis. JP spokesman Talat Asal claimed that the nation had rejected the RPP's censure motion by its vote in the local elections when the coalition parties together obtained 50% support. "The source of the ruling power," he added, "was the nation only." [35] Demirel warned that the overthrow of his government would only produce a prolonged political crisis. Directly addressing Ecevit, he said: "You will not be able to form a new government . . . [and] even if you do, you will not be able to survive." [36]

On 31 December, the NF government was brought down on a confidence motion by a vote of 228 against 218. The RPP, DP, RRP and 11 Independents voted against the government. Two Independent deputies, Abdülkerin Zilan and Cemalettin İnkaya, were absent. On the following day, Demirel submitted his resignation and the President immediately asked Ecevit, in his capacity as chairman of the largest party in the National Assembly, to form a new government.

THE ECEVIT GOVERNMENT

On 5 January, following intensive contacts with the group of 11 Independents, the RRP and the DP, Ecevit named his Cabinet. In order to accommodate the interests of these deputies (excluding Oğuz Atalay, who declined a ministerial post but agreed to support the government), Ecevit increased the number of Cabinet seats from 29 to 35. Two new ministries were established, the Local Administration Ministry (to deal with the municipalities), and the Ministry of State Enterprises (to control state economic enterprises); and the number of Ministers without Portfolio was increased. By including 13 non-RPP members, Ecevit attempted to minimize the risk of any defections which might endanger the slim three-seat majority he held in the Assembly. [37] Ecevit also took steps to ensure "domestic peace" within his own party by reshuffling its central administration to facilitate the representation of all party factions. [38] He announced that party officials would have to give up their party posts if they became ministers; he also persuaded the RPP's Secretary-General, Orhan Eyüboğlu, and his deputies, Ali Topuz and Hasan Esat Işık, to accept ministerial posts. To avoid the expected opposition from the party's Left-wing faction to the RPP's alliance with Right-wing deputies—especially Feyzioğlu, a staunch opponent of Communism—Ecevit included its leader, Deniz Baykal, in the government as Minister of Energy and Natural Resources. Another Left faction, headed by Süleyman Genç, refused both ministerial portfolios and party posts, but assured Ecevit of its full support.

Immediately after its formation, the government declared that it would bring "peace and academic freedom" to Turkey and ensure freedom and security of life. It also pledged itself "to pursue secular principles and not [to] permit exploitation of religious sentiments for political ends."[39] Ecevit outlined the government's programme to the Assembly on 12 January. He promised "an harmonious and coherent government," the main priorities of which would be to restore law and order and to rehabilitate the ailing economy. He committed himself to a wide range of future projects, including land reform, prison reform, a campaign against corruption within the bureaucracy, and an energy conservation plan. He said that the crisis "which [had] held sway in the country [had] ceased to be a mere domestic issue and affected international relations and the honour of the State." He promised to try to restore Turkey's image. He also pledged himself to follow a "dynamic foreign policy" and to formulate a new "national defence concept," claiming that the old one had been conditioned for too long to meet the so-called "threat from the north" (the USSR).[40] In an obvious reference to the US arms embargo, he said: "Turkey, which has been making contributions far above its economic possibilities to the joint defence system [NATO], has recently been put in a position in which it could not buy defence equipment from its allies and with its own money." This "bitter experience" had revealed the drawbacks of relying on other states, particularly on a single state, and he therefore promised to promote a defence industry as soon as economic conditions permitted. He called for the expansion of the country's links "outside the alliances [NATO, CENTO] and communities [the EEC] . . . with all her neighbours, regardless of ideology." The programme was unusually specific on relations with the EEC: ". . . My government will be determined . . . that our relations with the EEC be reorganized . . . in the interests of our country and economy."

In his government's programme, Ecevit also reiterated earlier promises[41] that a "speedy solution of the Cyprus problem" and negotiations over other disputes with Greece would be one of his priorities.[42] His emphasis on the solution of foreign policy problems, primarily Cyprus, was indicated by the large part devoted to them in the government's programme and by Ecevit's determination to play a prominent personal role in foreign affairs. His appointee as Foreign Minister, Gündüz Ökçün, was a professor of international law who had been a leading negotiator in the 1974 Cyprus talks and was therefore well acquainted with the problem without being too established a politician to find difficulty in following Ecevit's lead.

On 17 January the government won its vote of confidence on a straight party-line vote of 229 to 218. NSP deputy Muhyettin Mutlu (Bitlis) was absent. Of the four Independents not in the government, Oğuz Atalay (Konya), Nurettin Yılmaz (Mardin) and Abdülkerim Zilan (Siirt) voted for the government; only Cemalettin İnkaya (Balıkesir) voted against.

The new government was received with mixed feelings by the public; there was little of the celebration which had greeted Ecevit after his general election victory. The structure of the government and its slender majority gave cause for concern that it might face difficulties similar to those of previous governments. In structure, the government represented ideological trends ranging from the Left within the RPP to Ecevit's own social democratic position, to the centre and moderate Right-wing of the DP and RRP. Nevertheless, the public consensus, as reflected in the press, was that nothing could have been worse than the NF government; and there were hopes, particularly among the business community, that free of NSP pressures, Ecevit could solve the country's problems without repeating Demirel's mistakes.[43]

One welcome appointment was that of Ziya Müezzinoğlu as Minister of Finance.

A former Secretary-General of the Treasury, he had almost 20 years experience at various levels in the Ministry of Finance and was a former ambassador to West Germany.[44] Choosing İrfan Özaydınlı[45] as Minister of the Interior and Necdet Uğur as Minister of Education were regarded as positive steps towards the restoration of law and order. The former was a retired general in the Turkish Air Force, with a reputation as a martinet, and the latter was a former police chief.

TABLE III: THE GOVERNMENT, OCTOBER 1977-SEPTEMBER 1978

	The NF Government 21 July 1977	Ecevit's Government 5 January 1978
Prime Minister	Süleyman Demirel (JP)	Bülent Ecevit (RPP)
Deputy Prime Minister	Necmettin Erbakan (NSP)	Orhan Eyüboğlu (RPP)
	Alpaslan Türkeş (NAP)	Faruk Sükan (DP)
		Turhan Feyzioğlu (RRP)[5]
Ministers of State	Seyfi Öztürk (JP)	Ali Riza Septioğlu (Ind)
	Süleyman Arif Emre (NSP)	Mustafa Kılıç (Ind)
	Sadi Samuncuoğlu (NAP)	Lütfü Doğan (RPP)
	Ali Şevki Erek (JP)[1]	Ahmet Şener (RPP)
		Enver Akova (Ind)
		Salih Yıldız (RRP)
Justice	Necmettin Cevheri (JP)	Mehmet Can (RPP)
National Defence	Sadettin Bilgiç (JP)[2]	Hasan Esat Işık (RPP)
Interior	Korkut Özal (NSP)	Irfan Özaydınlı (RPP)
Foreign Affairs	Ihsan Sabri Çağlayangil (JP)	Gündüz Ökçün (RPP)
Finance	Cihat Bilgehan (JP)	Ziya Müezzinoğlu (RPP)
National Education	Nahit Menteşe (JP)	Necdet Uğur (RPP)
Public Works	Selahâttin Kilic (JP)	Şerafettin Elçi (Ind)
Commerce	Ağah Oktay Güner (NAP)	Teoman Köprülüler (RPP)
Health and Social Welfare	Cengiz Gökçek (NAP)	Mete Tan (Ind)
Customs and Monopolies	Gün Sazak (NAP)	Tuncay Mataracı (Ind)
Food, Agriculture and Husbandry	Fehim Adak (NSP)	Mehmet Yüceler (RPP)
Communications	Yılmaz Ergenekon (JP)	Güneş Öngüt (Ind)
Labour	Fehmi Cumalioğlu (NSP)	Bahir Ersoy (RPP)
Industry and Technology	Oğuzhan Asiltürk (NSP)	Orhan Alp (Ind)
Energy and National Resources	Kâmran İnan (JP)	Deniz Baykal (RPP)
Tourism and Information	İskender Cenap Ege (JP)	Alev Coşkun (RPP)
Housing and Reconstruction	Recai Kutan (NSP)	Ahmet Karaaslan (Ind)
Rural Affairs and Co-operatives	Turgut Yücel (JP)	Ali Topuz (RPP)
Forestry	Sabahattin Savci (NSP)	Vecdi İlhan (RPP)
Youth and Sport	Önal Şakar (JP)[3]	Yüksel Çakmur (RPP)
Culture	Avni Akyol (JP)	Ahmet Tener Kışlalı (RPP)
Social Security	Turhan Kapanlı (JP)[4]	Hilmi İşgüzar (Ind)
State Enterprises		Kenan Bulutoğlu (RPP)
Local Administration		Mahmut Özdemir (RPP)

[1] On 11 November, Ekrem Ceyhu (JP) was appointed Minister of State.
[2] On 14 October, Bilgiç resigned. On 28 October, Minister of Social Security Turham Kapanlı was appointed Defence Minister.
[3] On 14 October, Şakar resigned. On 28 October, Minister of State Ali Şevki Erek was appointed Minister of Youth and Sports.
[4] On 11 November, Ilhami Erdem (JP) was appointed Minister of Social Security.
[5] Resigned on 18 September 1978.

Ecevit's return to power was generally welcomed in the West.[46] He was considered more Westernized than his predecessor and was described as possessing "a statesmanlike quality which . . . Demirel never displayed."[47] But because, while in opposition, Ecevit had frequently sounded more hawkish than Demirel on issues relating to Cyprus and oil prospecting, his new Cabinet was watched with some apprehension by both NATO and the EEC which feared that he might loosen

Turkey's links with its Western allies.[48] At the same time Ecevit was regarded in the West as the one politician who could bring about a Cyprus settlement, improve relations with Greece and restore NATO's fragmented south-eastern flank. As the leader who had launched the Cyprus invasion, he was considered to possess the moral authority necessary to make the concessions required for a Cyprus settlement and, unlike Demirel, he did not have to appease a coalition partner like Erbakan.[49] Furthermore, in the exigencies of office, the smaller coalition partners were expected to exercise a moderating influence.[50]

POLITICAL OPPOSITION
The opposition parties, principally the JP, criticized the government from the outset. Demirel launched a vociferous and relentless campaign against it, also maintaining personal attacks on Ecevit. He stated that "the RPP chairman, who for months has been burning with desire [to be in power] at any cost, is staging the biggest intrigue in Turkish political history. He is forming the government with every guile, plot and dark intrigue. . . . This form of government, which does not derive its strength from the national will, this government, to be formed on the basis of ministerial seats and not the national will . . . is a stillborn monster. This is a terrible mode of government."[51]

Shortly after the government's accession, the NAP began a major campaign against it, probably in direct reaction to being ousted from several ministries previously under its control. Included in the purge were NAP sympathizers who had been appointed during the NF's tenure—many of whom (according to government circles) during its final days.[52] On 3 July it was reported that 30 civil servants had been detained for investigation on charges of holding a meeting with Türkeş with the aim of unseating the government[53]

During Ecevit's first three months, the NSP not only refrained from attacking the government but, after a meeting between Ecevit and Erbakan on 20 January, announced its willingness to co-operate with it.[54] The NSP stance was reported to be the result of the Chief Public Prosecutor's demand, on 17 January, that Erbakan be expelled from the party ·on the grounds that he had violated the principle of secularism during the election campaign in December.[55] Consequently, Erbakan needed RPP support in the Assembly to pass an amendment to the Political Parties Act, which aimed at depriving the Prosecutor of the power to expel a member of a political party without first obtaining a court order. In this case, Erbakan could not be proceeded against, since he enjoyed parliamentary immunity. The amendment was passed in the Assembly but was vetoed by President Korutürk on 26 February on the grounds that it would make an unfair distinction between a party leader who was an MP and one who was not (e.g., Ferruh Bozbeyli, the DP leader). The bill was passed again on 14 March, but was ultimately revoked by the Constitutional Court following an application by the President on 27 May.[56] On 30 March, following staff replacements within the Ministry of Industry, which was previously controlled by the NSP, Erbakan initiated a major attack on the government.[57] Attempts to disrupt its work failed, and claims of imminent defections, resignations and reshuffles proved unfounded, at least until September when the RRP decided to leave the coalition and its leader, Turhan Feyzioğlu, resigned as Deputy Prime Minister. Salih Yıldız, the other RRP representative, decided to remain in the coalition as Minister of State and left the party. (The controversy arose over Feyzioğlu's displeasure with the government's dismissal of the Governor of the Central Bank of Turkey. However, he promised continued support for some government policies.)[58] Although Feyzioğlu's resignation was a blow, the government still controlled 229 out of 450 Assembly seats. Despite the difficulties it was facing and reports of internal tension, the coalition in fact appeared, in the period reviewed, to be the most cohesive government Turkey has known since the 1971 military intervention. Even so, its success hinged on its ability to restore law and order and to heal the economic malaise.

Ecevit's promise to abolish Articles 141 and 142 of the Penal Code, which banned extreme Leftist activities, now appeared hasty, and despite pressure from various directions, including politicians and trade unionists, he did no more than discuss the possibility. Although the articles remained in force, they did not prevent the establishment of a new, pro-Chinese Marxist-Leninist party—the Turkish Workers' and Peasants' Party (Türk İşçi ve Köylü Partisi)—which registered at the Ministry of the Interior at the end of January 1978. Led by Doğu Perinçek, a known pro-Peking Communist, the party represented an additional split in Turkey's Left and might be considered a new challenge to the pro-Moscow Communist Party of Turkey, headed by İsmail Bilen. The new party declared its aims to be the establishment of a classless society based on socialism, the restoration of security of life, and the unification of the nation against threats to its integrity from the two imperialist super-powers—the US and the USSR—which it considered to be the greatest exploiters of all time.

POLITICAL VIOLENCE
Confirming his promise to curb political violence within a short time, Ecevit and his Cabinet established an "internal security co-ordination council" on 5 January 1978. Headed by the Deputy Prime Minister, Orhan Eyüboğlu, it included the Ministers of Justice, Interior, Education, and Youth and Sports. The government moved quickly to purge its departments, educational institutions and the police force, apparently to enable a more impartial and thereby more effective administration to help restore law and order.[59] Sweeping and seemingly inevitable changes were made in the Ministry of the Interior. In order to facilitate more efficient working relations between the central and local administrations, new governors were appointed in 63 out of 67 provinces. Those replaced had been appointed by the previous government, and in times of trouble had controlled the local police, the riot police and the gendarmerie. 53 security directors in the provinces were also replaced, and it was announced that any administrator found guilty of neglecting his duty concerning law and order would be dismissed.[60]

The Minister of Youth and Sports appointed a new Director General of the Student Hostels, which had become hotbeds of extremist elements and hiding places for arms and ammunition. A police sub-station was proposed for each hostel. The Minister announced that "the status of students who had been studying for a number of academic years and had lived continuously in student hostels would be reviewed."[61] This was thought to be aimed at activists who were more interested in political activities than in scholarship.

In January and February 1978, there was a purge of allegedly Right-wing militants from the Education Ministry as well as from certain educational institutions, particularly teachers' training colleges which were reported to be under NAP control.[62] On 29 January, the Minister of Education blocked the admission of students to the teachers' colleges on the grounds that they had been infiltrated by Right-wing militants; this had been done through oral examinations, since revoked by the Administrative Court.[63] About 53 associations were closed during the first two months of the government's tenure, 20 of which were reportedly Rightist and 33 Leftist, including a youth organization in Ankara affiliated to the RPP which was charged with distributing pamphlets calling for violence on the part of party militants.[64]

Despite such measures, however, the government failed to curb the violence which actually escalated after it assumed power. There were armed clashes between rival groups; assassinations of prominent figures in politics, the universities, the army and police; and explosions and bank robberies. The official death toll by the end of August 1978 stood at 345. This rise in violence was attributed by government officials and the press to Rightist attempts to discredit the new government following the sizeable purge of Right-wing elements from its various departments.[65]

Responsibility for the violence apparently rested not only with the Right but also with the Left, which intensified its militancy for several reasons. It was eager to demonstrate its power, since it believed that a government headed by the RPP would be preferable and more likely to retaliate against the Right, under whose heavy-handed policies it had previously suffered. It also seemed that the extreme Left aimed to discredit any ruling government in order to disrupt the status quo and prepare the groundwork for revolution. Since it was more embarrassing to oppose a moderate Left-of-Centre government, the Leftists might have hoped that, by provoking it to use force against themselves, it would be open to charges of fascism.[66]

Violence reached new dimensions when the clashes spread from the universities and urban centres to the small towns and rural areas of the economically backward eastern provinces which already suffered from smouldering tribal, ethnic and religious rivalries. The antagonism between the Shi'ite Turks (known as Alevis) and the Sunnīs, as well as the hostility between Kurds and Turks, had been fuelled by and contributed to the spread of political factionalism in the region. The Alevis were largely influenced by the extreme Left organizations, although their votes in the election went mainly to the RPP, in which Alevi politicians formed a key element on the party's far Left. The Sunnī Turks, as opposed to the Alevi Left, gravitated towards the Right, mainly the NAP. The Kurds, who were mostly Sunnīs, voted along tribal lines; and their Ağas embraced all shades of political opinion, at least in the Kurdish heartlands of Hakkâri and Siirt. In the more accessible areas of Turkish Kurdistan, however, the old tribal structures were breaking down and radical separatist Kurdish movements linked to clandestine extreme-Left Turkish organizations like TIKKO (The Liberation Army of the Workers-Peasants of Turkey; *Türkiye İşçi-Köylü Kurtuluş Ordusu*) were active. Yet in places like Elâzığ, Erzutum, Malatya and Gaziantep—where there were both Kurds and Alevis—some Kurds identified more closely with the NAP in reaction to the growing influence of the pro-RPP Alevis.[67]

Under these circumstances, the parcel-bomb murder on 17 April of the Mayor of Malatya, Hamit Fendoğlu, a Right-wing Kurd, caused understandable concern in Turkish political circles which feared that it might provoke religious and ethnic feuds all over the east.[68] Supporters of the murdered mayor from outlying districts, many of them Kurds, poured into the city, where they were joined by Rightist demonstrators. Estimated at 10,000, the rioters stoned and set fire to government and RPP buildings and to shops known to be owned by RPP sympathizers. Gendarmes and paratroops imposed a curfew, but incidents continued for two more days; nine people were killed and 668 buildings damaged.[69] After order had been restored in Malatya, incidents spread to other areas in the east—from Iğdır and Kars in the north-east near the Soviet border, to Elâzığ and Gaziantep in the south.

The opposition accused the government of dealing ineffectively with the troubles, which Demirel claimed were the outcome of "Communism, divisiveness and subversion."[70] Özaydınlı and Ecevit insisted that Fendoğlu's murder and the subsequent riots were part of a Rightist plot designed to "cause disturbances that would inflame the society [in the east]."[71] The Interior Minister further stated that the police had uncovered evidence linking the incidents with two underground Rightist groups calling themselves the "Turkish Lightning Commandos" (*Türk Yıldırım Komandoları*) and the "Army for the Liberation of Ethnic Turks" (*Etnik Türkleri Kurtarma Ordusu*). The NAP deputy-leader, Sadi Somuncuoğlu, claimed that Özaydınlı's statements were aimed at covering up the incidents and diverting the investigation: "Instead of capturing the anarchists . . . the Minister is employing acts aimed against the domestic order of the state and its integrity for partisan aims."[72] The situation in the eastern provinces was further complicated in May and June 1978 by the spread of the struggle between the Kurdish Barzānīs and the Talabānīs to Hakkâri and Siirt, and by the violation of Turkish frontiers by Iraqi forces operating against the Kurdish rebels.[73]

To help prevent further disturbances, the Interior Minister announced on 24 May that public order units (derived from military units) were to be set up in eight of the eastern provinces to deal with "anarchist and communal disturbances."[74] In a further attempt to ease the situation, Ecevit visited Hakkâri in mid-June, ostensibly to launch a road-building programme. Following a National Security Council (NSC) meeting on 26 June, a major operation was launched against Kurdish Iraqi rebels in Siirt province. Nevertheless, disturbances in the east continued throughout the period under review.

In the meantime, violence reached a new peak in the western provinces when rival groups led a campaign of reciprocal assassination. Teachers' training colleges became the scene of considerable violence, largely as a result of the Education Minister's attempts to rectify the political imbalance in these institutions. On 31 May the director, six teachers and two employees of the Bursa Teachers' Training Institute were beaten with sticks and chains, and on the same day shots were fired at a group of students in the Atatürk Teachers' Training Institute in Ankara. On 5 July, the deputy director of the Atatürk Teachers' Training College in Istanbul was murdered. On 11 July, Prof Bedrettin Cömert of the Hacettepe University was also murdered when shots were fired at his car. On 10 August four cafés, whose clientele was known to be predominantly Left-wing, were sprayed with gunfire from passing cars; four people were killed and 11 wounded.[75] The extreme Left launched a series of attacks on security officers, mainly those who had been involved in operations against underground Leftist movements in 1971–72. The list of victims included two military judges, Col Uğur Gür (killed in March) and Maj Yaşar Değerli (seriously wounded on 7 June), both of whom had served as prosecutors during 1971–72. Two retired officers, Commander Cihangır Erdeniz and Maj Yaşar Çakmak—alleged to have been responsible for the deaths of two Left-wing leaders—were assassinated on 23 and 25 June respectively.[76]

The sharp escalation in violence became the major target of the opposition. Demirel and Türkeş both claimed it was the result of an incorrect diagnosis by the RPP (which believed that the Right was responsible) and laid the blame firmly on the "Communists." They accused the government of failure to establish an impartial administration and claimed that Rightists were tortured by the police.[77] Two attempts to topple the government by censure motions against the Minister of the Interior, on 29 March and 15 June, failed.

Meanwhile, the DP, the RRP and the group of Independents demanded stricter measures against both Left and Right and called on the RPP to sever its ties with radical organizations like DISK. Their principal contention was that the Minister of the Interior, as well as Ecevit, had underestimated the danger from the extreme Left by concentrating too heavily on the Rightist threat. At the same time, the extreme Left within the RPP demanded that similarly harsh measures be taken against the extreme Right.[78] Türk-İş, and even the pro-RPP press like *Milliyet*, called on the government to act more strictly against the anarchists.[79] On 20 March, in protest against the 6 March murder of six Istanbul University students—presumably by Right-wing activists—DISK called a two-hour strike which brought the country to a virtual standstill. Ecevit denounced the strike as unconstitutional, and 750 members were arrested on charges of illegal suspension of work.[80]

Faced with growing terrorism and opposition, the government introduced new measures to combat violence. On 21 July, Ecevit announced that the police were to be reinforced by 20,000 troops and that Turkish policemen would be sent abroad for training.[81] On 29 July, gendarmerie commando units began to serve permanently in sensitive areas of Ankara and Istanbul, although they usually undertook police duties in rural areas.[82] By the end of August it was reported that a team from Britain's Scotland Yard had arrived to assist the local police in an advisory capacity.[83] Sweeping changes were also made in the Turkish Intelligence Service (*Milli Istikbarat Teşkilatı*; MIT) following the appointment of retired Army General Adnan Ersöz as its chief on 29 June (see *MECS 1976–77*, p. 636). The Director General of Police and the Governor of Istanbul were both replaced.[84]

ECONOMIC MEASURES

The new government took radical action during February and March 1978 to remedy the growing economic and financial crisis. The new measures included restrictions on holidays abroad; the raising of the exchange rate guarantee on convertible Turkish deposit accounts; devaluation of the Turkish lira by 30%; a significant increase in the bank rate; and a cutback of one-third in the overseas posts of government departments and public enterprises (for details, see below). The Prime Minister and Finance Minister stressed that the government had inherited an economy in ruins and that a period of austerity lay ahead; but they promised that with the revival of production and acceleration of exports, the economy would be stabilized. The Finance Minister claimed that the economy was experiencing the most severe foreign currency crisis in Turkey's history, and that foreign banks were hesitant to honour the payment orders of the Central Bank of Turkey on the grounds that the country had no foreign currency.[85] Opposition parties, particularly the JP, launched a vociferous attack on Ecevit's policy, arguing that his government had capitulated to the IMF demands at the expense of the Turkish people—mainly the low-income groups whom Ecevit claimed to represent. The government replied that as a member of the IMF, Turkey could not ignore it and that, in contrast to NF government policy, talks with the IMF were to begin after an economic programme had been prepared.

The government also took certain measures to ease the economic burden, especially on the poorer section, and gave incentives to businessmen and industrialists to encourage increased production and exports. The RPP, in particular, was well aware of the need to secure the support of these two sectors, especially in the big cities. Among the measures taken in March to June were the following:

(a) The establishment of an Interministerial Price Control Board on 8 March. Headed by the Deputy Prime Minister, Faruk Sükan, it included the Ministers of the Interior, Industry, Commerce and Local Administration. The Board established committees under the governor of each province to supervise prices and enforce its decisions.

(b) A statement by the Minister of Commerce on 9 March to subsidize all basic foodstuffs, such as meat, milk and eggs.

(c) A bill passed in June provided an increase in orphans', widows' and war veterans' pensions.

(d) A new draft bill submitted to the Assembly in April introduced major changes in state taxes, including a tax-free allowance up to TL 2,850 per month instead of TL 150; increases in corporation tax from 25% to 30%, and on corporation dividends from 20% to 30%; an increase in taxes on real estate; a fourfold increase on stamp duty; a new service tax on advertising and an agricultural income tax on a sliding scale. The aim was to increase government revenues by TL 40 bn annually, of which TL 30 bn would be redistributed to low-income groups, and TL 5 bn to municipalities.

(e) The establishment of an Export Promotion Fund of $20m to encourage industrial exports, and an Export Council to help reduce bureaucracy.

(f) A government decision in May to allocate 50% of the income from exports to exporting industrialists—a move which caused such satisfaction among them, including the business tycoon Vehibi Koç, that they decided to promote exports even at a loss.

(g) A government decision in July to increase the tax rebate on exports from 20-25% to 30-35%, and to accord exporters an exchange rate guarantee in cases where there was a difference in the exchange rate between the time a product was shipped and the time of payment.

Although there was some satisfaction among the business community and especially among industrialists, there was also criticism, in particular of the new draft tax bill, which businessmen and economists claimed would offer merely temporary relief to low-income groups, who would eventually suffer because it contained no anti-inflationary measures. They further claimed that the increase in corporation tax might discourage company formation and capital accumulation.[86]

The trade union confederations did not come out against the new measures as they had in September when the NF government introduced its austerity programme, but expressed the hope that the government would compensate low-income groups. The new leadership of DISK was largely pro-RPP; Abdullah Baştürk, its leader, was an ex-RPP deputy. Hâlil Tunç, leader of Türk-İş, gave his support to the government from the outset. However, on 10 May, when Ecevit gave a firm indication that he was contemplating wage restraint, both Türk-İş and DISK voiced strong opposition. In an attempt to improve relations with both labour confederations, Ecevit held a series of meetings with their leaders during May and June, after which conciliatory statements were issued.[87]

On 21 July, following two weeks of intensive negotiations, the government signed a "social contract" with Türk-İş aimed at eliminating the wage-price spiral within the framework of the government's anti-inflationary plan. DISK, however, rejected the agreement, preferring continued class struggle to what it termed "class reconciliation."[88]

The measures taken by the government to set the economy right were favourably received abroad, particularly by the IMF. The long-expected agreement with the Fund on a two-year programme was reached on 14 March and included $450m of IMF credits. On 24 March, Finance Minister Müezzinoğlu signed the letter of intent, which was approved and ratified by the IMF board exactly a month later. While the opposition emphasized that under the agreement the IMF could have complete control over Turkey's economy,[89] Ecevit and Müezzinoğlu pointed out that the letter of intent had been drawn up within the framework of the government's economic programme.[90] It was further reported that the IMF had not insisted on a wage and price policy, partly because of the social and political implications that might have arisen as a result. Ecevit stated on 9 April that to have cut the growth rate would have increased unemployment and precipitated social upheaval. By the beginning of May, Turkey received the first part of the IMF loan totalling $150m, and on 9 May import transfers were resumed after an interruption of 14 months. However, efforts to obtain further loans from banks and organizations abroad to help overcome the acute foreign currency shortage failed; as a result, the government again suspended import transfers on 18 June. A second part of the IMF loan, totalling $45m, which was due by the end of August, did not arrive because the IMF was allegedly dissatisfied with the government's record in curbing inflation and promoting exports.[91] It was reported that the government had refused to introduce further austerity measures demanded by the IMF delegation during its visit to Turkey in July and August.[92]

THE ARMED FORCES

In view of the intensified violence, there was speculation that the armed forces would intervene, but the General Staff was reluctant to interfere in policies and, in fact, made statements warning against attempts to involve the army. The new Chief of the General Staff, Gen Kenan Evren (see *MECS 1976–77*, p. 625)—who replaced Gen Semih Sancar on 6 March, after the latter's term in office expired—continued his predecessor's policy of keeping the army out of politics.

However, the forces were called to join in efforts to rescue the economy. The Prime Minister revealed on 5 August that the armed forces' contribution included the use of the defence infrastructure for economic ends—such as help on road projects linking remote villages to cities in eastern Anatolia. The JP criticized the government, claiming that such a step was dangerous and that the armed forces should not be given other than their constitutional and legal duties. RPP officials rejected this criticism as improper and unjust. There was no reaction from the army.[93]

In February 1978 the Supreme Military Administrative Tribunal cancelled the decision taken the previous June to remove the Ground Forces' Commander, Gen Namık Kemal Ersun, from office through retirement (see *MECS 1976–77*, p. 636). The ruling was unanimous. However, it was impossible to enforce the verdict because the post was legally occupied and the Tribunal had not cancelled the new appointment. Nevertheless, the verdict was considered a warning to the Turkish government to avoid making political appointments in the armed forces.

(For the strength and composition of Turkey's armed forces, see statistics following Economic section, below.)

FOREIGN RELATIONS

The Cyprus question continued to dominate Turkey's foreign relations during 1977–78. The establishment of the RPP government in January 1978 contributed to the renewal of negotiations over Cyprus. Even though not successfully completed, the renewal was one of the reasons for the lifting of the US embargo on arms supplies and financial aid to Turkey. Another reason, no less important, was the new government's decision to further strengthen its relations with Communist countries, which culminated in the signing of a "political document" of mutual friendship with the USSR. There were efforts to improve relations with Western European countries, especially those governed by social-democratic parties with which Ecevit had established close relations in recent years. The new government further developed relations with Turkey's two Arab oil suppliers—Libya and Iraq. It succeeded in solving longstanding problems in its relations with Baghdad in order to regain oil supplies, and to foster special relations with Tripoli with a view to obtaining financial aid and oil supplies.

Prime Minister Ecevit gave Turkish foreign policy new dimensions by making it more dynamic and giving it a "personal touch." He undertook a series of visits to the US and Europe, as well as to countries of the Soviet bloc, establishing personal relations with political leaders in those states.

GREECE AND CYPRUS

Negotiations with Greece over the disputed Aegean continental shelf and airspace, as well as over the Cyprus problem, had been deadlocked since June 1977 (see *MECS 1976-77*, pp. 638-41). Demirel's government ruled out any progress on the Cyprus issue before the Greek elections of November 1977 and the Cypriot elections of February 1978, hoping that it would then be easier to convene four-party talks (the Greek and Turkish communities on Cyprus, Greece and Turkey) on the Cyprus issue and to revive the stalled Aegean talks.[94]

Ecevit resumed office with a burden of Greek mistrust: not only had he launched the Turkish invasion of Cyprus, but on his last days in office in 1977 he had opened Maraş (Verosha) to Turkish settlement (see *MECS 1976-77*, p. 639). While in opposition, he also had a reputation as a hawk on Cyprus and the Aegean. After the fall of his government in July, however, Ecevit committed himself to try to improve relations with Greece and seek a settlement in Cyprus.[95]

THE CYPRUS PROBLEM

Negotiations between the two Cypriot communities in 1977 foundered on two central questions: how much territory should be returned to the Greek community, and how much political autonomy should be granted to the Turkish minority. The Greeks claimed that the Turkish side failed to come up with meaningful proposals on these questions (see *MECS 1976-77*, pp. 639-41).

The visit of the UN Secretary-General, Dr Kurt Waldheim, to Turkey from 8-10 January 1978 (as part of a tour which also included Greece and Cyprus and aimed at reactivating the deadlocked Cyprus talks) appeared to force Ecevit to come to grips with the problem without waiting for a vote of confidence. Ecevit promised Waldheim that he would submit "concrete proposals" on the territorial aspect, as well as new proposals on the constitutional aspect of the problem; these would be drafted by the Turkish-Cypriot government with the assistance of the Turkish government. On 17 January, Waldheim said that as a result of Ecevit's contribution the road to a settlement had reached a "turning point"—apparently because the previous government had never clearly committed itself to present concrete proposals on the territorial issue. All sides agreed that the Turkish proposals would be submitted first to Waldheim, who would decide whether they were substantive enough to warrant resumption of inter-communal talks.[96] This procedure was welcomed by Ecevit since a settlement worked out by the two communities with the UN—rather than with the US acting as peace-broker—was likely to absolve him of charges of a sell-out of Cyprus or of submission to American pressure.

The President of the Turkish Federated State of Cyprus (TFSC), Rauf Denktaş, and his Prime Minister, Nejat Konuk, arrived in Ankara on 18 January for discussions on the Turkish proposals to Waldheim. In an apparent gesture to improve the atmosphere, Turkey withdrew 500 troops from Cyprus on 24 January.[97] Ecevit's appointment on 8 February of a Left-wing academic, Prof Mümtaz Soysal (an expert on constitutional law), to advise the Turkish-Cypriot government on the draft constitutional proposals was probably welcomed by Greece.[98] Soysal, who was the vice-president of Amnesty International, had used his column in *Milliyet* to assail Demirel's government for its refusal to make concessions on Cyprus and thereby contribute to a settlement. On 13 April, the proposals were presented to Waldheim by Necate Munir Ecegen, legal adviser to the TFSC, and Mümtaz Soysal.

The proposals were divided into three sections:

(1) The Constitution of the "independent, sovereign non-aligned bi-communal and bi-zonal federal republic" provided for limited power to the central government, and was designed to guarantee complete political equality between the two communities. It recommended separate ethnic assemblies, plus a federal assembly, composed of ten delegates from each community, which would convene only in the event of a constitutional crisis and then only with strictly limited powers. The federal government would be responsible for foreign policy, defence, information and a federal budget. Nevertheless, each community was to retain the right to sign separate treaties with any outside country, "particularly their respective motherlands, including the accordance of the most-favoured nation treatment to the said motherland." The two communities were to have their own central banks, but co-ordinated by a federal reserve board. They were also to have separate security forces, the joint command being only for purposes of co-ordination. The two commanders of the respective armies were to work together "as they deem necessary." Persons holding federal office were to be elected by their own communities. The federal executive was to be headed jointly by the presidents of the two federated states, alternating every two years as the "President of the Federal Republic."

Freedom of movement and residence—essential to the Greek Cypriot refugees anxious to return to their former homes in the Turkish–controlled areas—was proclaimed in principle. However, due to security problems, its implementation was to be limited to "selected areas" and subject to "legislation or administrative acts" of the two communities.

(2) With regard to the territories of the federated states, the Turks were ready to relinquish territory in six areas along the ceasefire line as well as the "no-man's land" to be under Greek-Cypriot control. Kokkina, a Turkish stronghold in the north-west, and the Laurijina area in the centre were offered to the Greeks. This section also included a proposal for a joint undersea pipeline to bring water from Turkey, presumably to help the Greeks raise productivity in less fertile areas and as compensation for the loss of land.

(3) Maraş (Varosha), the tourist centre of Cyprus, was included in a separate section in view of its economic importance and its settlement potential. This section stipulated that Greek-Cypriots who return to Maraş would be subject to the laws of the TFSC, and would not be allowed to resettle in too close proximity to the Turkish-populated old city near the port, controlled by the Turkish navy.[99]

Waldheim was reported to have taken the view that the Turkish proposals were "concrete and substantive," but he refused to say whether he would recommend them as a basis for resuming inter-communal talks. On 19 April, he presented the proposals to the Greek-Cypriot President, Spyros Kyprianou, who described them as "a bad joke" and said that to accept them would be a decision "to commit suicide." He claimed that it was not just the content of the proposals but the whole "philosophy behind them that is entirely unacceptable." They amounted to the creation not of a federation or confederation, but rather of two separate states. Commenting on the territorial section, he said that the Turks were ready "to give" the "no-man's land" which they did not control anyway, plus territory at six other points totalling little more than 1%. Thereby, the Turks who constituted 20% of the island's population, were to control 35% of its territory and nearly one-half of its economic resources. He described the Turkish plan for Varosha as merely designed to use the Greek hoteliers to develop tourism, after which they would be expelled from the district.[100] Nevertheless, Kyprianou did not reject further negotiations point blank. He expressed willingness to consider the proposals if Waldheim regarded them as a basis for negotiations, in this way relegating much of the responsibility for future moves to the UN Secretary-General.[101]

Denktaş's reaction to the Greek position was that the Greek-Cypriots were bound to reject any proposals short of restoring the pre-war status quo and that his proposals were merely a "negotiating position." Ecevit hinted that there would be more concessions on the negotiating table,[102] and further stated that, with trust, more powers would be given to the central government, and the crucial rights of freedom of movement and settlement would be activated.[103]

In the meantime, prospects for a resumption of the talks on Cyprus seemed slim: the Turks refused at this stage to consider modifications, and Waldheim's efforts to persuade the Greeks to accept the Turkish proposals proved fruitless. On 2 May, a UN spokesman announced that the Secretary-General had been obliged to postpone the call for a resumption of the inter-communal talks, but that he would continue his consultations with both sides in order "to find a mutually acceptable formula."[104] On 9 May, the Turkish government rejected Waldheim's suggestion of a preliminary meeting to prepare for the full resumption of talks.

However, on 20 July, as the US Congressional debate over the embargo approached a climax, Denktaş made a conciliatory gesture—approved by the Turkish government—by offering a limited UN role in Maraş (Varosha). The proposals, which were reportedly drafted with the help of US officials, included an interim administration to be formed in Maraş under the aegis of the UN simultaneously with the resumption of inter-communal talks. The resettlement by stages of 35,000 Greek Cypriots would begin shortly after the peace talks started. Denktaş claimed that this offer was designed to revive the talks, but Greek-Cypriots and Greek lobbyists in the US charged that the proposal was made only in order to create a favourable impression before the Senate vote on the arms embargo (see below). The Greek-Cypriot government also protested against what it described as "inadmissible" US interference in Cypriot affairs, asserting that the Turkish proposal was inspired by US officials. Nevertheless, on 24 July, probably with an eye to the Senate vote on the embargo, the Greek-Cypriot government submitted an official proposal to Waldheim on the question of Famagusta to "facilitate the resumption of talks." These could only be resumed after Famagusta had been "freed and put under . . . the control of the UN, and the lawful inhabitants of Famagusta are able to return to their homes."[105] Kyprianou further insisted that the talks be held on the basis of an open agenda and in keeping with "the UN resolutions, declarations and conventions on human rights."[106] This was in conflict with Turkey's position that the negotiations must be conducted within the framework of the principles agreed upon with Makarios in February 1977, and on the basis of its own April proposals. Denktaş rejected Kyprianou's proposal on 27 July, claiming that, in effect, it was "rejecting our proposals in an underhand way."[107] Despite expectations that Waldheim would submit a compromise formula on Varosha, no further progress was made during the period reviewed.

RELATIONS WITH GREECE

Responding on 22 January to a congratulatory message from the Greek Prime Minister, Constantine Karamanlis, on his own confirmation as Prime Minister, Ecevit called for the commencement of a "constructive dialogue."[108] His basic approach was that there was no fundamental conflict between the interests of the two countries and that, although the problems were serious, they were largely psychological and by no means insoluble.[109] Ecevit took the view that if the two Prime Ministers met and demonstrated their determination to reach an agreement, this would facilitate talks on a technical level. [110]

Although Karamanlis had accepted Ecevit's proposal for a summit in principle, he felt that substantive preparatory work by the two Foreign Ministers was necessary beforehand. [111] He was also reported to have discouraged a proposal of Ecevit's to fly to Athens to meet him in the manner of Sādāt's trip to Israel. [112] In view of the Greek stance, Ecevit explained that his intention was to initiate talks without any rigid agenda. [113] On 8 February, Karamanlis agreed to meet Ecevit, and the two-day summit was fixed for 10 March in Montreux.

The Greeks' initial reserve could be attributed to fundamental distrust of Turkish motives. They appeared to suspect a deliberate display of Turkish moderation for the benefit of the US, and probably wanted to wait for Ankara's promised proposals on Cyprus. Their change of attitude was probably due not only to Ecevit's further appeal on 6 February, but also to American and German pressure, [114] and to a reluctance to appear intransigent.

No tangible agreement was reached at Montreux, but the two leaders were able to declare that a climate for positive negotiations at a lower level had been created. The next summit was tentatively scheduled for the NATO meeting in May 1978. [115]

The Montreux summit was generally regarded in Turkey as a positive move, even though major disagreements persisted. [116] However, the JP severely criticized the summit, claiming that Ecevit had achieved "a big zero." [117] Expectations of a new era in Turkish-Greek relations were deflated on 11 April when Greece unilaterally announced that talks between the secretary-generals of the Greek and Turkish Foreign Ministries (scheduled for 14 April) had been postponed "due to technical reasons." [118] Greece's move apparently followed President Carter's decision to ask Congress to lift the embargo against Turkey (see below), which the Greeks feared would simply harden Turkey's position. The Greek-Cypriot rejection of the Turkish proposals on Cyprus further strained relations between Ankara and Athens.

Ecevit expressed disappointment over Greece's attitude, claiming that he had been given to understand that their bilateral differences would not be connected with either the arms embargo or the Cyprus problem. [119] Relations deteriorated even further when, on 24 April, Turkey announced that it would not recognize the jurisdiction of the International Court of Justice over its dispute with Greece concerning the continental shelf. [120] Greece appealed to the Court in 1976 (see *MECS 1976–77*, pp. 640–41). Greek misgivings over Turkey's intentions in the Aegean were reported to be due to a reference in a Turkish letter to the Court which was interpreted as questioning Greek sovereignty over the Aegean islands. Ecevit promised that it did not indicate any change of attitude towards the islands' political status.

Relations improved somewhat when, at Karamanlis' request, the two Prime Ministers held a second meeting on 29 May during the NATO summit in Washington. A joint statement "reaffirmed their mutual desire to find peaceful solutions to their bilateral problems," and agreed that the postponed talks between their secretary-generals would be held in Ankara in July without any agenda. [121]

In a move probably intended to ensure Turkey's peaceful intentions, Karamanlis proposed a non-aggression pact on 3 June. Ecevit accepted the proposal, but pointed out that it was something of an anomaly since they were already allies. The pact was apparently not discussed at the meeting between Şükrü Elekdağ, the Secretary-General of the Turkish Foreign Ministry, and his Greek counterpart, Byron Theodoropoulos, in Ankara from 4–5 July, although it was reported to have been raised by the Greek delegation. The two-day meeting concluded with a resolution whereby the secretary-generals agreed: (1) to continue the dialogue in September in Athens; (2) to make mutual efforts before the second meeting to reconvene the committees dealing with the Aegean continental shelf and air space issues; and (3) to prepare a document for their Prime Ministers which would cover all aspects of bilateral relations, with the aim of regulating and improving them. Future negotiations would determine whether the document would finally take the form of a declaration, protocol or treaty.[122]

Negotiations at the technical level on the Aegean air space dispute were held from 31 July to 3 August in Ankara, and continued in Athens from 28 August to 3 September. The second meeting between Elekdağ and Theodoropoulos (in Athens on 18 and 19 September) dealt mainly with the air space issue. The Turkish daily, *Milliyet*, described the meeting as unsuccessful. However, it was agreed to continue exchanges in January 1979.[123] The parties also agreed that talks on the Aegean continental shelf, stalled since February, "should be resumed at the appropriate level on or about 1 December 1978."[124]

THE US AND NATO

The US arms embargo imposed on Turkey following its invasion of Cyprus in July 1974 not only harmed relations with the US, but weakened the south-east flank of NATO and cast a shadow over the credibility of the alliance in Turkey (see *MECS 1976–77*, pp. 641–42).

Both Ecevit and Demirel supported the continuation of Turkey's alignment with the West, but both made it clear that US policies might cause a drift away from their Western orientation. Demirel, whose party had staked its political future on the Western alliances, was apparently forced to take this line under pressure from his two extreme-nationalist coalition partners. Ecevit, on the other hand, believed that Turkey's international relations should be based on its economic and security needs, and on good relations with all its neighbours. Turkey should remain within NATO because the alliance contributed to world peace, and thereby to Turkey's national security. But since membership had failed to meet the country's defence requirements in recent years, a new defence policy was needed; Turkey's relations with NATO would have to be revised in terms of that organization's contribution to Turkey's national defence. Ecevit stressed that this new defence concept would not conflict with Turkey's membership in the alliance but would "close the gaps created by its insufficiency."[125]

On the level of bilateral relations, Ecevit suggested that the US should not become "over involved" in relations between Greece and Turkey but maintain a neutral position. He claimed that the US embargo had not only soured relations, but had induced Greece to take an uncompromising stance which had made it more difficult to solve the problems between the two countries.[126] In accordance with his promise to improve relations with the US, Ecevit invited the US Secretary of State, Cyrus Vance, to Turkey on 20–21 January to discuss a range of issues including the Cyprus problem and Turkey's military relationship with the US. Vance was reported to have promised that he would press for the ratification of the Defence Co-operation Agreement (DCA) signed between the two countries in 1976 (see *MECS 1976–77*, p. 641). However, Ecevit wanted a revision of the DCA since Turkey's defence needs had changed in the intervening period.[127] Following Vance's visit, a US delegation arrived in Ankara on 22–23 February to discuss bilateral relations in military, economic and political fields.[128]

These two visits prompted expectations of an early end to the embargo and a major improvement in Turkish-US relations.[129] But instead, a crisis developed following a statement by Vance to the Congressional Appropriations Committee on 9 March (on the eve of the Montreux summit), announcing that the Administration would wait for the conclusion of the Montreux meeting and the Turkish proposals

773

on Cyprus before presenting the DCA to Congress for ratification. [130] Ecevit saw the statement as encouraging the Greek lobby's attempts to put pressure on Turkey and as likely to encourage Greek-Cypriot intransigence. Consequently he threatened to revise many of his policies as well as Turkey's ties with the Western defence system. Ecevit pointed out that Turkey was not without alternatives as far as its national defence was concerned. He charged that the Carter Administration, while blaming the Congress, was responsible for holding up military aid to Turkey. He also hinted that a "linkage" between a Cyprus settlement and the embargo could work in reverse[131]—a position which contradicted his earlier statements that, since a Cyprus settlement was vital to Turkey's national interest, he would seek it without pre-conditions, including the lifting of the arms embargo. [132]

The US Administration tried to end the rift by offering clarifying statements to the Turkish ambassador in Washington, Melih Esenbel, and through Robert Spiers, the American ambassador in Ankara. Senator Jacob Javits visited Turkey from 24–25 March for talks on Turkish-American relations; he was followed on 28 March by a high-level State Department delegation. The Americans claimed that Vance's statement had been misinterpreted and assured Turkey that the Administration would seek an early end to the embargo. [133] Testifying before the House International Relations Committee on 6 April, Vance made a strong appeal for the embargo to be lifted irrespective of Turkish concessions over Cyprus. This move was apparently made out of concern that Turkey would otherwise reduce its ties with the Western alliance, and out of conviction that, as in the past, the embargo would not succeed in inducing Turkey to make concessions. [134] To facilitate the repeal of the embargo, Carter decided not to ask Congress to approve the DCA; instead, he sought a revision of the accord which dealt with US bases in Turkey and put the aid issue on a year-by-year basis. The Administration proposed to provide Turkey with a military sales loan guarantee of $175m—the same as the previous year—and a $50m loan to help it overcome economic difficulties. This move was welcomed by Turkey, but strongly criticized by Greece and the Greek lobby in the US. [135]

On 3 May, the House International Relations Committee voted by 18 to 17 to lift the arms embargo. [136] Because of this narrow margin, Ecevit refused to comment on the vote; nor did Foreign Ministry officials regard the development as a "bright result." [137] On 11 May, the US Administration's efforts to end the embargo suffered a major setback when the Senate Foreign Relations Committee voted 10 to 8 to maintain it. [138] Senior NATO officials were said to be seriously concerned about the possible consequences to the alliance of the Senate's vote. [139] On 22 May, a NATO Defence Ministers' meeting in Brussels called on the US to repeal the embargo swiftly, and on 29 May Chancellor Helmut Schmidt criticized the Senate decision. [140] In a letter to Carter dated 16 May, Ecevit implied that Turkey would substantially reduce its NATO defence role if the embargo was not lifted. He was reported to have warned that, in the absence of clear-cut guarantees about future US military assistance, Turkey could not make any commitments that might be regarded as provocative by the Soviet Union. [141]

On 30 May, during the NATO summit in Washington, Ecevit pointed out that Turkey's economic situation would not permit it to participate in NATO's long-term defence programme. [142] However, after a meeting with Carter on 31 May, Ecevit said he was encouraged by the President's attitude towards Turkey's economic and defence requirements, and by his promise to persist in efforts to persuade Congress to repeal the embargo. [143] In the next two months the White House stepped up its pressure on Congress, and on 25 July the US Senate voted 57 to 42 to repeal the embargo. [144] However, future US military aid to Turkey, Greece and Cyprus was to depend on efforts made by these countries to solve the Cyprus problem.[145] This decision met with protests in Greece and mixed feelings in Turkey.[146] Ecevit said that "there are positive and negative aspects of the decision"; it showed that the US considered its relations with Turkey and the embargo to be extremely important and, by naming Greece as a party to the Cyprus affair, there was also the likelihood that Athens could be pushed into playing a more active role in solving the problem. This was in line with Turkey's attitude that Greece should share responsibility for a Cyprus settlement. At the same time, Ecevit said that as the Senate decision still maintained the linkage between Cyprus and military aid, it might delay a solution to the Cyprus issue because of the tendency of the Greek lobby to evaluate developments subjectively. He added that it might affect Turkish-Greek and Turkish-American relations adversely.[147] In the view of the JP, however, the Senate decision implied that the embargo was still in force.

On 1 August, in a close vote of 208 to 205, the US House of Representatives followed the Senate in supporting an end to the embargo on condition that Carter report to Congress every two months on satisfactory progress in the Cyprus peace talks.[148] Ecevit's reaction to this resolution was guarded. While he welcomed the repeal, he felt that the conditions attached to it were unrealistic and might make a Cyprus settlement more difficult as well as hinder the development of normal Turkish-American relations.[149]

On 15 August, a US Joint Congressional Committee, responsible for reconciling the separate drafts adopted by the Senate and the House, approved an end to the embargo if Carter certified that Turkey was making an effort in "good faith" to negotiate a solution to the Cyprus problem.[150] The Turkish Foreign Ministry's reaction was that while the new formula offset the drawbacks of earlier legislation, it still contained contradictions.[151] The opposition claimed that the Committee's decision was against Turkey, which as a result would be subjected to American pressure.[152]

Carter formally ended the three-and-a-half-year old embargo on 26 September, by making a formal statement that Turkey "is acting in good faith to achieve a just and peaceful settlement of the Cyprus problem." This coincided with an announcement that Carter had signed into law a $2.8 bn foreign military aid authorization act that empowered him to lift the embargo. Ecevit expressed the hope that this move would open "a new and positive era" in Turkish-US relations.[153] On 3 October, Ecevit announced that some US joint defence installations on Turkish soil (closed after the US had imposed the embargo) would be reopened on 9 October; one would be turned over to the Turkish armed forces, and two would function under a provisional status for a year pending the finalization of a new DCA.[154]

RELATIONS WITH THE EUROPEAN ECONOMIC COMMUNITY (EEC)

Most of the difficulties between Turkey and the EEC—especially those concerning the Additional Protocol of the Association Agreement—remained unsolved during 1977–78 (see *MECS 1976–77*, p. 643). Ecevit nevertheless succeeded in breaking the deadlock that had plagued EEC-Turkish relations during the NF tenure. It was his government's policy that part of the EEC agreement had to be revised as it raised obstacles to the country's economic development.[155] But he admitted in a statement on 20 January 1978 that Turkey would have to undertake "certain structural changes" in its economy to "ensure that our future complete [EEC] membership is possible."[156] In the meantime, the government decided on 30 January to postpone the 10% tariff reduction on EEC exports to Turkey, due under the Additional Protocol on 1 January 1978.[157]

A survey entitled "What can be done within the EEC's Additional Protocol?," prepared on 3 February by the Turkish Businessmen's and Industrialists' Association (TUSIAD), found that although the economy had suffered in its relations with the EEC, this was due only in small measure to deficiencies of the Additional Protocol. According to the survey, most of the loss stemmed from the government's mistaken policies, but for political reasons the blame was put on the Additional Protocol.[158] In a poll conducted by TUSIAD, 65% of the Turkish private sector favoured full membership of the EEC.[159]

The first high-level contact between Turkey and the EEC Commission for 20 months was made in Brussels on 25 May when Ecevit presented the President of the EEC Commission, Roy Jenkins, with an outline plan for a revised agreement. He reportedly asked for deferment of some of Turkey's obligations to lower tariffs on exports, and for compensation for the EEC's failure to allow freedom of movement for Turkish workers by helping it to build up its own industries. He also insisted that, as an associate member, Turkey should benefit from the greater concessions granted to non-associate countries. The value of preferential treatment enjoyed by Turkish agricultural exports to the EEC had been diluted because of similar concessions granted to rival Mediterranean countries (see *MECS 1976–77*, p. 643). Ecevit and Jenkins agreed that Turkish and EEC delegations would meet within two months to decide how the Association Agreement could be made more flexible.[160] After the meeting Ecevit called on the European countries for support in putting together an aid package for Turkey's economy, as well as substantial credit to promote its industrial investment. Ecevit also called on the European members of NATO to fill the gap in its defence capacity left by the US arms embargo.[161]

EEC foreign ministers expressed concern on 21 May that Greece's impending membership should not be allowed to further alienate the already uneasy Turks (see *MECS 1976–77*, p. 643). Britain's Foreign Secretary, David Owen, suggested that Turkey could be drawn into the EEC's political co-operation network when questions involving the eastern Mediterranean were discussed; but some of the other members feared this would dilute the community's principles. It was finally decided that Turkey should share in a special exchange of information on questions of political co-operation affecting the eastern Mediterranean.[162]

From 17–20 July, an EEC technical delegation held preparatory discussions for high-level talks scheduled for the end of September in Brussels.[163] The head of the delegation, Charles Caporale, promised to support Turkey's request to postpone its commitments to the EEC for four or five years, since the difficulties it faced justified such a move.[164]

While in opposition, Ecevit had established close personal relations with social democratic leaders in Western Europe. On 29 January 1978, the Norwegian Foreign Minister, Knut Frydenlund, called on all European social democratic parties to assist Ecevit's government in solving Turkey's economic and international problems. Frydenlund paid an official visit to Turkey from 8–10 February, during which the two countries signed an economic and technical co-operation agreement.[165] Another agreement signed on 28 June provided for the deferment of $90m of Turkey's commercial debt to Norway, cancellation of credit loan rates and a $150m loan, $36m of which was for the construction of a dam and power station.[166] In May, Ecevit visited Germany, Britain and Austria as part of his efforts to secure economic and defence aid. As early as June 1975, after the US imposed its arms embargo, Ecevit had hinted that Germany should replace the US in granting economic and defence aid.[167] During his visit to Bonn from 10–13 May, Chancellor Helmut Schmidt promised more military and economic aid and said that he would urge further such assistance from other countries. The promised aid included an immediate credit of $100m as well as DM 130m capital aid to help finance certain projects which was granted on 8 May.[168] Ecevit's visit to Austria resulted in the deferment of Turkey's debts and in a new $70m loan.

However, Ecevit received no serious response in the period reviewed to his call for the West to extricate Turkey from its economic difficulties, and in effect no fresh loans were received from Western countries. On 16 August, he charged that the US and "some European allies" were partly responsible for Turkey's acute economic crisis, adding: "Whether we want it or not, the support they give us . . . will be the principal factor in shaping the nature of our future relations with them." [169]

RELATIONS WITH THE MIDDLE EAST AND THE ISLAMIC WORLD

The divisions in the Arab world following the Israeli-Egyptian *rapprochement* in November 1977 placed Turkey in an embarrassing situation. In recent years, it had fostered special links with its major oil suppliers, Libya and Iraq (see *MECS 1976–77*, pp. 637, 644–45), while its relations with Egypt were relatively cool due to Cairo's support for the Greeks in the Cyprus dispute. At the same time, while proclaiming a pro-Arab line in the ME conflict, it was reluctant to sever relations with Israel (despite pressure from the Arab countries) and claimed to hold a neutral stance (see *MECS 1976–77*, pp. 644–45). This ambiguous policy was reflected in the government's official reaction to Sādāt's initiative, which was favourable but at the same time reserved and cautious—reflecting an obvious wish not to anger Iraq and Libya.

The JP Foreign Minister, İhsan Çağlayangil, described Sādāt's visit to Jerusalem as "a positive step in the right direction," providing that Israel would "relinquish all the occupied territories . . . and recognize the Palestinians' legitimate rights," including the right to found a state.[170] The reaction of the JP's organ Son Havadıs, as well as most of the Turkish press, was highly optimistic and praised Sādāt's move, describing it as "courageous" and "realistic." They claimed that Sādāt had offered the Palestinians an historical chance, and described as groundless the rejectionists' claim that Sādāt had betrayed the Palestinians.[171] However, the far Left and far Right columnists, like Ali Sirmen and Ilhan Selçuk in *Cumhuriyet* and Ergun Göze in *Tercüman*, were hostile to Sādāt's move, adopting the Libyan-Iraqi line.[172]

Following the Iraqi decision on 20 November to stop oil supplies to Turkey because of its unpaid debts,[173] Deputy Prime Minister Erbakan went to Iraq (26–28 November) to discuss the problem. In addition, between 27 November and 1 December, Deputy Prime Minister Türkeş visited Libya as a special guest of Qadhdhāfī, apparently in the hope of securing loans, credit for a $150m oil debt, and agreement on joint investment projects.[174] Between 30 November and 4 December, during the inter-Arab split and while Turkey was facing oil supply difficulties from Iraq and reportedly from Libya, Çağlayangil paid an official visit to Egypt, during which a five-year economic and technical co-operation agreement was signed.[175]

Both Türkeş and Erbakan claimed that the Foreign Minister's visit to Egypt had been inopportune and had damaged their efforts to improve relations with Iraq and Libya. They called on Çağlayangil to resign.[176] Ecevit and the Minister of Labour, Fehmi Cumalıoğlu (NSP), suggested that the visit had been made under US pressure.[177] In reply, Çağlayangil pointed out that his visit had been fixed before Sādāt's trip to Jerusalem and that its cancellation would have been against Turkey's "traditional policy of not taking sides in conflicts among Arab states." [178] There were no official comments on Çağlayangil's visit from either Libya or Iraq, and the controversy in Turkey was soon overshadowed by the government crisis and the fall of the NF.

The new government's programme made a clear commitment to improving relations with ME and Muslim countries. Ecevit reiterated support for the Palestinians' struggle. At the Ninth Islamic Conference (held in Dakar from 24–28 April), Turkey voted for resolutions calling for withdrawal of all Israeli forces from occupied Arab territory; the Arabs responded by adopting a resolution which supported the Turkish proposals on Cyprus, including the principle of total equality for the two communities. [179]

Turkey's improved relations with Iraq suffered a setback following the Turkish failure to pay off its $330m debt for oil supplies. Although shipments from Libya and Iran continued, Iraq's decision in December 1977 to cut off further supplies seriously affected Turkish industry, as well as fuel and petrol stocks in the cities (Iraq provided two-thirds of its oil supplies). [180] Several other factors were also involved in Baghdad's move. Iraq complained to Turkey in December 1977 that Kurdish nationalists, headed by the pro-Soviet leader Jalāl Tālabānī, were moving between headquarters in northern Syria and Iraqi Kurdistan via Turkey, with the tacit consent of the Ankara authorities. [181] Iraq was reported to suspect that the USSR was exerting considerable economic pressure on Turkey not to interfere too much with Tālabānī activities. [182] Iraqi violations of the Turkish frontier in pursuit of Kurdish rebels were politely condemned but, in view of the sensitive oil situation, the government wished to avoid any worsening of relations. [183]A Turkish operation against the Kurds in Siirt Province on 22 June 1978 was apparently aimed at pleasing Baghdad.

On 10 July, an Iraqi delegation began talks in Ankara on the expansion of economic and trade relations. Despite a Turkish request, the Iraqi delegation refused to discuss postponement of the oil debt, insisting that it be discussed separately and at high-level political talks. [184] On 14 July, an agreement was reached in principle on several industrial and agricultural products to be exported to Iraq. The agreement, which included terms for renewing oil supplies to Turkey, was due to be signed on 22 July in Baghdad by the Minister of Energy, Deniz Baykal. However, his visit was postponed at the last minute because the Iraqis were apparently hurt by Ecevit's failure to visit Baghdad while on a tour of several other countries. They had also expected Ecevit, rather than Baykal, to discuss the oil problems. Disagreement also emerged over Turkish wheat supplies; Iraq had pressed for 400,000 tons, while Turkey could guarantee only 130,000. [185]

Another point of contention was Turkey's intention to divert the course of the Euphrates in order to complete the construction of its Karakaya dam. Iraq insisted on an agreement that would guarantee a regular water flow from the Euphrates before discussing the oil debt with Turkey. The two countries apparently bridged their differences after Turkey had pledged to maintain the flow of water in exchange for oil. [186] Consequently, on 22 August, the Iraqi Minister of Planning, 'Adnān Ḥusayn al-Hamdānī, arrived unexpectedly in Ankara for talks with Minister of State Hikmet Çetin and Baykal. On 25 August an agreement was signed for the resumption of oil supplies, under which Turkey was to repay its debts in kind, primarily with 400,000 tons of wheat by the end of 1979, and 300,000 tons in both 1980 and 1981. Turkey was to obtain 1.2m tons of crude oil from Iraq during the remainder of 1978, and 5m tons in 1979. Iraq was to pay transit fees to Turkey for the passage of 15m tons of crude oil through the Kirkūk-Yumurtalık pipeline each year regardless of whether this amount was actually pumped. Although there was no reference in the agreement to the water issue, Baykal announced that a joint commission would be set up to study Iraq's water rights and requirements. [187] There was speculation that the oil deal also contained some agreement on a common approach to the Kurds. [188]

TURKEY

Turkey's relations with Iran were also affected by oil and the Kurdish question, but to a lesser extent. Although both countries were CENTO members, co-operation between them in recent years had not been good. However, relations improved in the first months of 1978 as Iran began supplying Turkey with oil to make up for the loss of Iraqi shipments.[189] By March, the two countries were negotiating to promote their trade relations, including an agreement on future oil supplies to Turkey. On 12 June, shortly before Hikmet Çetin was due to leave for Iran to sign the agreement, the daily *Hürriyet* accused the Iranian secret police, SAVAK, of fomenting trouble among the Kurdish population of eastern Turkey (see above). *Hürriyet* claimed that the Shah wanted to distract attention in Iran from domestic troubles by creating a crisis with its CENTO ally. It was further claimed that although the two countries were allies, there was a deep mutual distrust between them; Iran feared that Turkey might incite the large Azerbayjani (Turkish) population, while Turkey suspected that Iran might incite not only the Kurds but the Shī'īs (Alevis) in eastern Turkey.[190] This provoked a wave of attacks on Iran in the Turkish press. The Foreign Minister went out of his way to deny the press reports, emphasizing the good state of Turco-Iranian relations. On 4 July, the two countries signed an agreement providing Turkey with 1m tons of crude oil and 500,000 tons of fuel oil, to be paid for by a loan of $150m granted by Iran on 20 July.[191]

Turkey's close links with Libya continued under Ecevit's premiership. When in office in 1974, Ecevit had struck up remarkably cordial relations with Qadhdhāfī, which apparently accounted for Libya being the only Arab country to support the Turkish invasion of Cyprus. On 22 February, the Libyan Prime Minister, 'Abd al-Salām Jallūd, arrived in Turkey for official talks with Ecevit, Baykal[192] and Müezziuoğlu. The joint communiqué issued on 24 February included a Libyan decision to help Turkey solve its foreign exchange problems. Jallūd promised to accord some payment facilities for the 3m tons of oil it was to supply to Turkey annually, and to consider the accumulation of Turkey's oil debt until the end of 1978. However, he said that in view of Libya's prior commitments, there was no possibility of increasing oil supplies to Turkey.[193]

On 2 May, a commercial and financial co-operation agreement was signed between the two countries, under which the Turkish export volume to Libya was to reach $85m annually. Turkish-Libyan joint companies in industry, agriculture and construction were to be established; Libya was to consolidate $47m of Turkey's oil debt; it was to accord Ankara a $450m loan for oil imports in five years; Turkey was to pay for 80% of its oil in cash and 20% by a loan; Libya was to secure credit of $100m for Turkey from international banks.[194] On 17 August, the Turkish Central Bank acting as guarantor, signed a $100m loan agreement with an international banking syndicate, of which the Libyan Bank was a principal manager.[195] This was the first such private loan the government had been able to raise since it came to power, and it undoubtedly marked an important step in strengthening Turkish-Libyan ties.

THE COMMUNIST COUNTRIES
The Turkish-Soviet *rapprochement* (see *MECS 1976-77*, p. 645) continued to develop in 1978, in part by exchanges of visits including that of the Chief of the Soviet General Staff to Turkey (25-29 April). Most important was Ecevit's visit to Moscow (21-25 June 1978), where he signed a "political document" with Premier Kosygin. The agreement bound the two states to develop good-neighbourly relations and co-operation on the basis of respect for each other's sovereignty and territorial integrity, and non-interference in each other's internal affairs. Each

779

agreed to refrain from the use of threats of force and undertook not to allow its territory to be used as a base for attacks on the other. Although the Soviets wanted a non-aggression clause appended, Turkey refused to go beyond a reiteration of the Helsinki Final Act. The final clause of the accord preserved the existing commitments of the two sides under international agreements (i.e. NATO, CENTO and the Warsaw Pact).[196] Despite some early anxiety that the "political document" might reflect a fundamental reversal in Turkey's strategic position,[197] it was in fact similar to accords the USSR had signed with two other NATO members—West Germany and France. The document was in line with Ecevit's concept of a more independent foreign policy—of further improving Turkey's relations with the Eastern bloc (the USSR in particular), while maintaining its Western connections and commitments. However, Ecevit's decision to sign the accord was regarded in the West generally as an attempt to pressure the US to lift the embargo and renew military and financial aid.

Ecevit also secured a Soviet pledge for increased economic and technical aid. The two countries agreed in principle to increase their trade volume from $162m in 1977 to $800m by 1981. Turkey was to buy 3m tons of oil annually against payments of wheat, metals and meat products.[198] A separate agreement was signed during Ecevit's visit delineating the Black Sea continental shelf between the two countries, and agreement was reached on a joint oil exploration venture along Turkey's continental shelf. Upon his return to Ankara, Ecevit said that a new era had opened in Soviet-Turkish relations. Turkey was already one of the largest non-Communist recipients of Soviet economic assistance (see *MECS 1976–77*, pp. 645–46) and stood to gain more by the new economic protocol. Furthermore, previous Turkish efforts to buy oil from the Soviets had met with little success. The new agreement would help Turkey diversify its oil supplies; since the Soviet oil was to be paid for in exports, the financial burden on Turkey's depleted foreign currency reserves would be less.

Ecevit's visit to Moscow came at the end of three months of intensive diplomacy, including visits to other East European countries. His first official visit abroad was to Yugoslavia (13–17 April). The Romanian Prime Minister, Manea Manescu, paid an official visit to Turkey between 24 and 27 April, and Ecevit visited Bulgaria between 3 and 6 May. During these high-level visits it was decided to strengthen friendly relations and speed up economic co-operation. As part of the government's general *Ostpolitik*, it revived trade relations with Albania, signing with it a trade protocol (volume $18m) on 2 June. On 30 May, Turkey renewed diplomatic relations with Cuba, suspended since 1961.

Another dimension to Turkish foreign policy was added by the visit of the Chinese Foreign Minister, Huang Hua, between 12 and 15 June, just before Ecevit left for Moscow. This was the first visit of a high-ranking Chinese leader since the two countries established diplomatic ties in 1972. China was apparently concerned about Turkey's differences with the West and its improved relations with the Soviet Union. However, Huang Hua's disguised attacks on the Soviets were politely ignored by the Turks. Nor was there any immediate response to the hints reportedly dropped by Huang that Turkey would not necessarily have to turn to the USSR for its armaments if the US embargo continued.[199] The two countries agreed to develop their economic and trade relations and a joint Trade Commission drew up an agreement in September for the expansion of trade.

ECONOMIC AFFAIRS ($1 = 25.00 Turkish Liras; £1 = TL 50.10)
Despite registering economic growth in 1977, as measured by a 29.5% jump in Gross National Product (GNP) at current factor cost and a 5.1% increase in GNP at

constant 1968 factor cost, Turkey remained in a prolonged economic crisis throughout the year and in 1978.[200] The indicators of Turkey's economic troubles are many. Unemployment continues to grow, according to most estimates exceeding 20%. One high-ranking Turkish official suggested that the number of unemployed may be as high as 7m. The Prime Minister pointed out that in addition to those regarded as unemployed, a further 20% should be considered as underemployed.[201]

The foreign trade deficit worsened in 1977; although imports appear to have fallen in the first few months of 1978 and government-induced exports to have risen, the trade gap remains a major contributing factor in the economic crisis. Its persistence has drained Turkey's holdings of foreign exchange. An unintended effect of the foreign exchange shortage has been that manufacturers have been less able to purchase imports of factor inputs, with the result that they have been forced to operate at levels as low as 43% of capacity.[202] Under-capacity has resulted in reduced supply which, combined with undiminished demand, has been a major contributor to inflation. Price increases have been variously estimated at levels from 30% to as high as 80%.[203]

Unemployment, under-production, trade deficits and inflation are by no means Turkey's only major economic problems. Energy shortages in the form of cut-backs have become commonplace. The foreign debt has become such a burden that it has had to be re-structured and its servicing partly postponed. The balance of payments position has "worsened sharply" since 1975, according to the IMF. After prolonged negotiations, the IMF finally approved a $450m credit to Turkey in April 1978, conditional on the adoption of a series of austerity measures including a major devaluation of the lira, which took place in March. In August, however, the IMF delayed paying the second tranche of the agreed credit and was reported to have insisted on further austerity measures. Shortly thereafter, the lira was adjusted (i.e. devalued) a series of times.[204] (For details of the political implications of Turkey's economic malaise, see above.)

AGRICULTURE
Agriculture remains the largest single component of Turkey's Gross Domestic Product (GDP), even though its relative share has fallen in the last 15 years from 38% of GDP to 28% of GDP at factor cost. Agriculture also accounts for c. 60% of exports and has played a major role in the series of bilateral trade agreements with Iraq, Iran, Libya and the Soviet Union, which in large part have been wheat-for-crude oil barter deals.[205]

Provisional figures for 1977 show that wheat production, at 16.65m tonnes, rose 1% over 1976 output. Other major crops which registered higher production in 1977 include grapes (+ 3.2%), oil seeds (+ 5.3%), citrus fruits (+ 17.6%) and cotton lint (+ 21%). However, a number of major crops suffered lower outputs in 1977 compared with 1976: sugar beets (-4.3%), barley (-3%), corn (-3.4%) and olives (-63.5%).[206]

In an unpublished survey, the World Bank identified three major problems in the agricultural sector: unco-ordinated policies and programmes; restricted access of small farmers to institutional credit; and insufficient cost recovery in public investment projects.[207]

INDUSTRY
Industries which relied heavily on raw material imports or on intermediate factor inputs suffered severely in 1977–78. The automotive industry, for example, was producing at only 43% of capacity in the second half of 1977, while the figures for basic metal and chemical industries were 51.2% and 53.5% respectively.[208]

Only nine of 16 public sector manufacturing industries registered an increase in production in 1977 over 1976. By comparison, seven of ten private sector, and five of eight combined private and public sector, manufacturing industries realized higher output levels in 1976. Of the more important industries, public sector petrochemicals (+ 19.9% on average), private sector steel mill products (+ 11.9%), and combined sector petroleum products (+ 10%) were among the most prominent gainers in 1977, while public sector cotton fabrics (-13.2%), private sector sheet aluminium (-11.4%), and combined sector pig iron (-10.4%) were notable in suffering decreased production.[209]

MINERALS AND ENERGY

The mining and electricity, gas and water sectors combined to form 3.6% of Turkey's GDP at factor cost in 1977 (cf 2.9% in 1976). In the mineral sector, only crude petroleum (+ 4.5%) and lignite (+ 9.3%) registered increased production in 1977; iron ore (-10.9%), chrome ore (-3.4%) and coal (-4.9%) output all fell. Manganese production remained steady at 34,000 tonnes.[210]

In the energy sector, Turkey is severely hampered by the burden of oil imports which was expected to cost an estimated $1.5 bn for 1978. In 1977, electricity demand exceeded supply, leading to power cuts which became commonplace during the latter part of the year (for details, see above). The energy gap has been labelled "a severe barrier to progress." As late as 1970, domestically-produced oil supplied nearly one-half of Turkey's needs; in 1977, this proportion fell to 19%. At a time when Turkey's foreign exchange shortage is so critical, prices and the growing reliance on foreign oil have hindered manufacturers from importing sufficient quantities of vital supplies to allow them to run their factories at capacity.[211]

Meanwhile, government plans to develop nuclear power-generating complexes and to expand hydroelectric facilities have been restricted by the shortage of foreign exchange.

BALANCE OF PAYMENTS

Turkey's balance of payments deficit, which was first registered in 1974 and has been growing each year since, expanded 76.5% in 1977 to $2,968m (cf $1,682m in 1976). Much of this increase was in the form of the current account deficit which rose from $2,301m in 1976 to $3,425m in 1977. The largest component of the current account deficit was the increase in the foreign trade deficit of $874m, which in turn resulted from the decline in exports combined with the rise in imports.

Other major components of the overall balance of payments deficit in 1977 included foreign debt servicing. Interest payments grew $143m in 1977, while repayment of principal rose $95m. In both cases, debt postponements were excluded.[212]

MONETARY DEVELOPMENTS

On 1 March 1978, the Turkish lira was devalued nearly 30% against the US dollar and slightly more against the SDR (Special Drawing Right or "basket" of the IMF). Less than six months later, in August, the lira was once again devalued against most of the currencies which comprise the SDR, with the notable exception of the falling dollar with which parity was maintained. In this second devaluation, adjustments ranged from 1.9% against the Belgian franc to 18.5% against the Swiss franc; within this range, the value of the lira fell 4.8% against the deutschemark, 3.5% against the pound sterling and 8.8% against the Saudi rial.[213] During September and October 1978, the lira was devalued slightly against most of the currencies in the SDR basket a total of five times, reflecting a policy of frequent adjustment of

exchange rates as opposed to less frequent, but larger scale, devaluations.[214]
 At the end of November 1977, Turkey's international reserves stood at $718m, the lowest total since 1971. From December, however, reserves began to climb, reaching $1,077m at the end of April 1978. During this same period, net foreign assets fluctuated between a low of TL 1.97 bn at the end of November, to a high of TL 11.79 bn the following February, and then fell back to TL 6.07 bn at the end of July 1978. Compared with a peak of TL 31.51 bn at the end of 1973, net foreign assets remained at low levels throughout the first half of 1978.[215]

PUBLIC FINANCE

The draft budget for 1978-79 registered an expenditure growth of 14.9% to TL 256.2 bn (cf TL 222.9 bn actual spending in 1977-78). The Finance Ministry was again given the largest allocation (40.4%), followed by defence (20.6%), education (9.8%) and industry and technology (6.1%). Some of the larger spending increases were allocated to the Prime Minister's office (+45.4%), health (+29.1%) and the general directorate of security (+24.9%). By contrast, rural affairs and co-operatives, and food and agriculture had their respective budgets cut by 28.5% and 20.8%.[216]
 In 1977, revenues rose 29.7% to TL 200.1 bn. The share of the largest component—direct taxes—increased from 38.7% in 1976 to 44.3% in 1977. Over the same period, the share of domestic borrowing in the composition of revenue fell from 7.1% to 6.2%. According to *Türkiye İş Bankası*, the consolidated budget balance fell from a surplus of TL 832m in 1976 to a deficit of TL 37,642 in 1977.[217]

FOREIGN TRADE

Turkey's foreign trade gap widened even further in 1977, as exports fell 10.6% to $1,753m, while imports rose 13% to $5,796m. West Germany consolidated its position as Turkey's leading market for exports (22.2%), and maintained its place as the foremost supplier of Turkish imports (16.3%). Italy (9.3%) became Turkey's second largest market for exports, while the US (6.9%) slid down to third place. Iraq (11.9%) and the US (8.7%) maintained their positions behind West Germany as Turkey's second and third major sources of imports.
 In 1977, the agricultural sector continued to provide a large share of Turkey's exports, with hazelnuts (14.3%), cotton (12.2%) and tobacco (10%) heading the list of commodity exports. This was despite the fact that foreign sales of the latter two fell 51.3% and 30.2% respectively compared with 1976. Turkey's three largest imports in 1977 were liquid fuels (25.4%), machinery (23.3%)' and iron and steel (11.9%).[218]

Aryeh Shmuelevitz and Esther Lidzbarski-Tal
Economic section by Ira E. Hoffman

ARMED FORCES

Total armed forces number 485,000, including 361,000 conscripts. Defence expenditure in 1978-79 was 42.5 bn Turkish liras ($1.7 bn). Military service is compulsory for 20 months. The Army numbers 390,000, including 300,000 conscripts; about half the divisions and brigades are below strength. Formations consist of one armoured division; two mechanized infantry divisions; 14 infantry divisions; five armoured brigades; four mechanized infantry brigades; five infantry brigades; one parachute and one commando brigade; and four surface-to-surface missile battalions with *Honest John*. Equipment consists of 2,800 M-47 and M-48 medium tanks; 1,650 M-113, M-59 and *Commando* armoured personnel carriers; 1,500 75mm, 105mm, 155mm and 203mm howitzers; 265 105mm, 190 155mm, 36 175mm self-propelled guns; 1,750 60mm, 81mm, 4.2-in mortars; 18 *Honest John* surface-to-surface missiles; 1,200 57mm, 390 75mm, 800 106mm recoilless rifles; 85 *Cobra*, SS-11, *TOW* anti-tank guided weapons; 900 40mm anti-aircraft guns; two DHC-2, 18 U-17, three Cessna 421, seven Do-27, nine Do-28, 20 *Beech Baron* aircraft; 100 AB-205/-206, 20 Bell 47G, 48 UH-1D helicopters (193 *Leopard* tanks; *TOW, Milan* anti-tank guided weapon; 56 AB-205 helicopters on order.) Two infantry divisions are deployed in Cyprus; reserves number 500,000.

The Navy numbers 45,000, including 31,000 conscripts. It is equipped with 11 submarines (two Type 209, nine ex-US *Guppy*-class, two on order); 11 destroyers (five ex-US *Gearing*-, five *Fletcher*-, one *Sumner*-class); two frigates; 13 fast patrol boats (14 on order), eight guided-missile fast patrol boats, with *Harpoon* surface-to-surface missiles; 41 large, four coastal patrol craft; 21 coastal, four inshore minesweepers; eight minelayers (seven coastal); four tank landing ships; 25 tank landing craft; 36 landing craft; two anti-submarine warfare squadrons with eight S-2A, 12 S-2E *Tracker*, two TS-2A; three AB-204B, six AB-212 anti-submarine warfare helicopters. (10 AB-212 helicopters, 33 *Harpoon* surface-to-surface missiles on order.) Reserves number 25,000.

The Air Force numbers 50,000 (including 30,000 conscripts) and has 339 combat aircraft; 13 ground-attack fighter squadrons; two with 49 F-4E, four with 100 F-5A and 10 F-5B, two with 32F/TF-104G, two with 30 F-104S, three with 50 F-100C/D/F; one interceptor squadron with 30 F-102A, three TF-102A; two reconnaissance squadrons with 31 RF-5A, four F-5B; four transport squadrons with seven C-130E, 20 Transall C-160, 30 C-47, three C-54, three *Viscount* 794, two *Islander*, six Do-28, three Cessna 421 aircraft; five UH-19, six HH-1H, ten UH-1H helicopters. There are *Sidewinder, Sparrow* and *Falcon* air-to-air missiles and AS.12 *Bullpup* and *Maverick* air-to-surface missiles. Eight surface-to-air missiles with *Nike Hercules*. Trainers include 40 T-33A, 30 T-37, 20 T-34 and 25 T-41 (22 F-4E, 8 RF-4E, 56 *AlphaJet* trainers on order.) Paramilitary forces consist of 110,000 gendarmerie, including three mobile brigades.

Source: *The Military Balance 1978-79* (London: International Institute for Strategic Studies).

BALANCE OF PAYMENTS (million US dollars)

	1975	1976	1977
Current Accounts:			
Exports (fob)	*1,401*	*1,960*	*1,753*
Imports (cif)	*-4,739*	*-5,129*	*-5,796*
Foreign Trade Balance	*-3,338*	*-3,169*	*-4,043*
Invisible Transactions (net)	*1,435*	*853*	*606*
Balance on Current Account	-1,880	-2,301	-3,425
Capital Transactions:			
Balance on Capital Transactions	520	619	457
Overall Balance	**-1,360**	**-1,682**	**-2,968**

Source: Türkiye İş, Bankası, *Economic Indicators of Turkey 1973-77*.

TURKEY

MONETARY SURVEY (billion Turkish liras at approximate end of period)

	1975	1976	1977
Foreign Assets (net)	13.1	15.0	2.0
Domestic Credit	195.7	273.6	387.4
Claims on Government (net)	*35.1*	*48.1*	*95.6*
Claims on Government Enterprises	*21.6*	*43.0*	*62.6*
Claims on Private Sector	*131.9*	*174.9*	*222.2*
Claims on Other Financial Institutions	*7.1*	*7.6*	*7.1*
Money	119.1	152.5	212.0
Quasi-money	30.4	34.2	40.3
Money, Seasonally Adjusted	112.8	144.4	201.1

Source: IMF, *International Financial Statistics.*

PUBLIC FINANCE (billion Turkish liras)

	1975	1976*	1977*
Consolidated Revenues	113.7	154.3	200.1
of which:			
Direct taxes	*44.0*	*59.7*	*88.7*
Indirect taxes	*49.4*	*67.2*	*79.5*
Domestic borrowing	*7.4*	*11.0*	*12.5*
Consolidated Expenditure	113.1	153.4	237.8
Consolidated Budget Balance	+0.6	+0.8	-37.7
Public debts			
Domestic debts	66.5	97.0	134.2
Foreign debts			
1. Due in foreign exchange[1]	3,012	3,822	4,410
2. Due in Turkish Liras[2]	3,412	3,417	3,545

*Provisional.
[1] Million US Dollars.
[2] Million Turkish Liras
N.B. Figures may not total due to rounding.
Source: Türkiye İş Bankası, *Economic Indicators of Turkey, 1973–77.*

BUDGET (million Turkish liras)

	1977–78 (actual)	1978–79 (draft)	% change
Senate	98.8	169.8	+71.9
Chamber of Deputies	403.8	650.0	+61.0
President	37.3	57.2	+53.4
Prime Minister's Office	1,228.6	1,785.9	+45.4
Finance	89,257.0	103,559.7	+16.0
Defence	42,500.0	52,860.0	+24.4
Education	24,115.9	24,997.2	+3.7
Industry and Technology	13,878.5	15,592.6	+12.4
Rural Affairs and Co-operatives	10,807.4	7,732.1	-28.5
Health	6,115.2	7,894.8	+29.1
General Directorate of Security	4,938.5	6,169.5	+24.9
Food and Agriculture	6,241.9	4,946.1	-20.8
Public Works	3,633.9	4,471.1	+23.0
Total (including others)	**222,949.0**	**256,206.9**	**+14.9**

Source: *Middle East Economic Digest.*

GROSS DOMESTIC PRODUCT BY SECTOR (at current factor cost in billion Turkish liras)

	1974*	1975*	1976*	1977*
Agriculture	105.5	136.1	176.3	218.8
Industry	76.7	93.5	115.0	148.0
Public services	38.2	50.5	66.5	101.5
Wholesale and retail trade	52.3	64.8	81.1	102.4
Transportation and communication	35.5	43.3	54.5	69.6
Construction	18.8	24.6	31.0	42.0
Liberal professions and services	19.3	25.0	31.6	40.6
Ownership of dwellings	13.3	17.9	21.9	31.2
Financial institutions	10.1	12.6	16.8	20.5
GDP at factor cost	**369.8**	**468.4**	**594.7**	**774.4**

*Provisional

LABOUR FORCE BY SECTOR (thousands employed)

	1975*	1976*	1977*
Agriculture	9,463	9,280	9,100
Manufacturing	1,507	1,569	1,652
Mining	108	109	115
Energy, water, gas	76	85	90
Construction	501	520	547
Transportation	451	479	497
Wholesale and retail trade	600	621	639
Banking, insurance and real estate	176	182	188
Public and personal services	1,513	1,595	1,686
Unknown activities	273	270	270
Total	**14,668**	**14,710**	**14,784**

*October.

AGRICULTURAL PRODUCTION (thousand tonnes)

	1975	1976	1977*
Wheat	14,750	16,500	16,650
Sugar beets	6,949	9,400	8,995
Barley	4,500	4,900	4,750
Grapes	3,247	3,080	3,180
Potatoes	2,490	2,850	2,800
Oil seeds	1,355	1,437	1,513
Corn	1,200	1,310	1,265
Citrus fruits	958	975	1,147
Cotton (lint)	480	475	575
Olives	561	1,097	400

*Provisional.

PRODUCTION OF MINERALS AND ORES (thousand tonnes)

	1975	1976	1977*
Lignite[2]	6,939	8,252	9,022
Coal[2]	4,813	4,632	4,405
Iron ore[1]	2,359	3,602	3,208
Crude petroleum	3,095	2,595	2,713
Chrome ore[1]	952	945	913
Manganese ore	35	34	34

*Provisional.
[1] Run of mine.
[2] Ready for sale.

SALES OF MAIN INDUSTRIAL PRODUCTS (thousand tonnes)

	1975	1976	1977*
Petroleum products	13,437	14,882	16,937
Electric power (million kwh)	13,492	16,079	17,945
Cement	10,875	12,422	13,865
Lignite	6,866	8,204	8,979
Coal	4,584	4,506	4,242
Sugar	855	943	1,054
Paper	326	337	372
Plate glass	123	140	177
Alcoholic beverages (million litres)	89	108	109

*Provisional.

INDEX OF SELECTED INDUSTRIAL PRODUCTS (1973 = 100)

	1974	1975	1976	1977*
Cotton fabrics[1]	96	97	94	82
Steel ingot[2]	125	125	126	120
Cement[2]	100	121	138	155
Sugar[2]	106	111	136	149
Petroleum products[2]	100	97	96	106
Electric power[2]	108	126	147	166
Cars[3]	128	144	135	124
Tractors[3]	72	84	120	97
Refrigerators[3]	113	139	187	73
Television sets[3]	268	413	447	495

*Provisional.
[1] Public sector.
[2] Public and private sector.
[3] Private sector.

EXPORTS OF SELECTED COMMODITIES (million US dollars)

	1975	1976	1977
Cereals, leguminous seeds	28.2	70.6	128.8
Hazelnuts	154.1	203.2	251.0
Dried grapes	45.5	52.6	75.0
Citrus fruits	25.7	47.8	42.3
Tobacco	183.2	251.3	175.8
Cotton	230.3	438.2	213.6
Mining and quarrying products	105.6	110.0	125.8
Cotton yarn	59.5	159.9	145.7
Leather jackets and coats	64.0	48.1	39.7
Total (including others)	**1,401.1**	**1,960.2**	**1,753.0**

IMPORTS BY MAIN COMMODITY GROUPS (million US dollars)*

	1975	1976	1977
Liquid fuels	811	1,126	1,470
Machinery	1,257	1,344	1,351
Iron and steel	679	546	690
Vehicles	332	518	573
Medicines and dyes	424	459	443
Synthetics, plastics and rubber	152	183	266
Textiles and yarns	118	107	109
Commercial fertilizers	48	98	214
Fats and oils	123	104	21
Others	696	509	557

*Figures exclude grants and imports with waiver.
Source (of eight preceding tables): Türkiye İş Bankası, *Economic Indicators of Turkey, 1973–77.*

DIRECTION OF TRADE (million US dollars)

	1975	1976	1977
Exports to:			
West Germany	304.9	376.7	388.8
Italy	82.1	171.5	163.3
United States	147.1	191.4	121.8
Switzerland	95.8	179.6	108.8
United Kingdom	70.1	137.6	94.3
France	61.9	108.4	94.1
Soviet Union	73.6	81.0	80.4
Netherlands	50.8	63.8	57.5
Belgium	30.3	85.9	56.2
Iraq	45.2	41.1	49.5
Iran	37.1	33.6	48.6
Total (including others)	**1,401.1**	**1,960.2**	**1,753.0**
Imports from:			
West Germany	1,057.7	945.6	944.9
Iraq	504.2	644.4	691.7
United States	425.8	438.2	503.5
Italy	357.9	386.1	454.4
United Kingdom	344.3	409.9	402.8
Switzerland	281.3	280.4	335.5
France	278.7	308.7	327.7
Japan	211.4	227.8	311.2
Libya	78.0	233.7	276.4
Iran	26.1	109.3	165.0
Belgium	129.3	103.3	159.7
Total (including others)	**4,738.7**	**5,128.6**	**5,796.4**

Source: IMF, *Direction of Trade.*

NOTES

1. For the relations between the two parties during their first tenure and the differences between them in domestic and foreign policies, see *MECS 1976–77*, pp. 622–24.
2. Konya was a stronghold of NSP supporters, and Erbakan had promised to turn it into an industrial centre.
3. *Milliyet*, Istanbul; 30 October, 12 November; *Diplomat*, Ankara; 30 November 1977.
4. On political violence before the General Elections, see *MECS 1976–77*, pp. 624–26.
5. R Ankara, 28 December—BBC Summary of World Broadcasts: the Middle East and Africa (BBC), 30 December 1977.
6. See *MECS 1976–77*, pp. 624–25, 625 note 5. Also *The Middle East*, London; February 1978; *The Guardian*, London; 18 May 1978. Other extreme Right-wing youth organizations were rarely involved in violence; see *MECS 1976–77*, p. 624.
7. See *MECS 1976–77*, p. 627.
8. *New York Times (NYT)*, 18 December 1977.
9. *Cumhuriyet*, Istanbul; 2 October 1977.
10. *The Financial Times (FT)*, London; 23 November, 5 December 1977; *Events*, London; 16 December 1977; *The Economist*, London; 19 November 1977; *Outlook*, Ankara; 14 December 1977.
11. *Briefing*, Ankara; 5 April 1978. For details of Erbakan's industrial programme, see *MECS 1976–77*, p. 623.
12. *Milliyet*, 7 November 1977.
13. *Outlook*, 14 December 1977.
14. *FT*, 20 December 1977.
15. The party leader, Ferruh Bozbeyli, had lost his seat in the General Elections in June 1977.
16. For further details on these, see *MECS 1976–77*, pp. 627, 634.
17. *Pulse*, Ankara; 7 October 1977.
18. *Milliyet*, 27 September 1977; *Pulse*, 6 October 1977.
19. Mandalıncı had been Minister of Commerce during the rule of the old Democratic Party in the 1950s.
20. See *MECS 1976–77*, p. 632; *Outlook*, 9 November 1977; *Outlook*, 5 December 1977.
21. *Milliyet*, 31 October 1977.
22. *Cumhuriyet*, 14 November 1977.

23. *Pulse*, 4 December 1977.
24. R Ankara, 24 January—BBC, 27 January 1978.
25. *The Times*, London; 13 December 1977; *Pulse*, 14 December 1977.
26. *Milliyet*, 12 December 1977.
27. R Ankara, 18 December—BBC, 20 December 1977.
28. *Milliyet*, 21 December 1977.
29. *Ibid*, 15 December 1977.
30. R Ankara, 21 December—BBC, 23 December 1977.
31. R Ankara, 19 December—BBC, 21 December 1977.
32. *Pulse*, 26 December 1977; R Ankara, 15 December—BBC, 17 December 1977; *Diplomat*, 21 December 1977.
33. *FT*, 23 December 1977.
34. *Pulse*, 26 December 1977.
35. *Milliyet*, 30 December 1977.
36. *Milliyet*, 29 December 1977; *FT*, 29 December 1977.
37. *Milliyet*, 3 January 1978.
38. *Pulse*, 5 and 6 January 1978.
39. *Milliyet*, 5 January 1978.
40. *Briefing*, 10 May 1978.
41. *International Herald Tribune (IHT)*, Paris; 5 January 1978.
42. For the government's programme, see *Outlook*, 18 January; *Milliyet*, 12 January, R Anatolia, 12 January—BBC, 19 January 1978.
43. *Milliyet*, 2 January 1978; *Tercüman*, Istanbul; 27 December 1978; *Outlook*, 11 January 1978.
44. *Events*, 27 January 1978.
45. See *MECS 1976–77*, p. 626.
46. *Events*, 10 March; *The Times*, 18 January; *Pulse*, 16 January; *Economist*, 7–13 January 1978.
47. *The Times*, 18 January 1978.
48. *The Guardian*, 3 and 13 January; *IHT*, 13 January 1978; *MECS 1976–77*, p. 639.
49. *The Times*, 18 January; *Economist*, 7–13 January 1978.
50. *Foreign Report (FR)*, London; 11 January 1978; *Economist*, 7–13 January 1978.
51. *Pulse*, 5 January 1978.
52. *Outlook*, 18 January 1978.
53. *Briefing*, 5 July 1978.
54. *Cumhuriyet*, 20 January; *Milliyet*, 20 February 1978.
55. *Briefing*, 1 March; *Outlook*, 25 January 1978.
56. *Cumhuriyet*, 24 May; R Ankara, 24 June—BBC, 26 June 1978.
57. *Briefing*, 5 April 1978.
58. *Briefing*, 20 September; *Outlook*, 27 September 1978.
59. *Milliyet*, 10 January 1978.
60. R Ankara, 25 January—BBC, 27 January; *Milliyet*, 12 February; R Ankara, 9 March—BBC, 11 March; R Ankara, 16 July—BBC, 18 July 1978.
61. *Briefing*, 15 February 1978.
62. *Milliyet*, 7 January; *Briefing*, 15 February; R Ankara, 10 February—BBC, 13 February 1978.
63. *Outlook*, 8 February; *Pulse*, 2 February 1978.
64. *Tercüman*, 29 January; R Ankara, 8 March—BBC, 11 March 1978.
65. *Briefing*, 22 March, 28 June; *The Times*, 6 May; *Milliyet*, 8 June 1978.
66. *Briefing*, 22 March 1978.
67. *Ibid*, 26 April, 21 June 1978.
68. *Ibid*, 26 April 1978.
69. R Ankara, 25 April—BBC, 27 April; R Ankara, 19 April—BBC, 20 April 1978.
70. *Pulse*, 20 April 1978.
71. R Ankara, 18 April—BBC, 20 April 1978.
72. *Ibid*.
73. R Ankara, 20 June—BBC, 22 June 1978.
74. *Cumhuriyet*, 24 May 1978.
75. *Ibid*, 16 August 1978.
76. *Briefing*, 28 June; *Milliyet*, 16, 28 March, 8, 24, 29 June 1978.
77. *Outlook*, 19 April; *Pulse*, 12 and 17 May; R Ankara, 17 July—BBC, 19 July 1978.
78. *Briefing*, 5 and 12 April 1978.
79. *Milliyet*, 7 July 1978.
80. R Ankara, 20 March—BBC, 22 March; R Ankara, 21 March—BBC, 23 March 1978.
81. *FT*, 22 July 1978.

82. R Ankara, 28 July—BBC, 29 July 1978.
83. *The Observer*, London; 8 August 1978.
84. R Ankara, 17 July—BBC, 19 July 1978.
85. R Ankara, 16 February—BBC, 18 February 1978.
86. *Briefing*, 26 April 1978.
87. *Milliyet*, 24 May; R Ankara, 9 June—BBC, 12 June 1978.
88. *Pulse*, 24 July; *Briefing*, 16 August 1978.
89. *Tercüman*, 26 March; *Güneydin*, Istanbul; 1 April 1978.
90. *Milliyet*, 30 March, 1 April; *Pulse*, 24 April; *Cumhuriyet*, 2 May 1978.
91. *Cumhuriyet*, 11 July, 23 August 1978.
92. *Briefing*, 6 September 1978.
93. R Ankara, 5 August—BBC, 8 August; *Pulse*, 9 August; *Milliyet*, 15 August 1978.
94. *Milliyet*, 27 November 1978.
95. *Ibid*, 19 February 1978.
96. R Athens, 17 January—BBC, 19 January 1978.
97. R Ankara, 24 January—BBC, 26 January 1978. Since 1974, 14,200 were withdrawn from Cyprus.
98. R Ankara, 8 February—BBC, 10 February 1978.
99. *Milliyet*, 7 April; *Cumhuriyet*, 8 April; R Anatolia, 13 April—BBC, 15 April; *Briefing*, 26 April 1978.
100. *Milliyet*, 16 April; R Nicosia (Greek), 19 April—BBC, 21 April; *The Guardian* , 20 April; Nicosia TV, 20 April—BBC, 22 April 1978.
101. *Briefing*, 26 April; *FT*, 22 April; *Observer*, 23 April 1978.
102. *The Guardian*, 25 April 1978.
103. *FT*, 24 April 1978.
104. R Nicosia, 2 May—BBC, 4 May 1978.
105. R Nicosia, 24 July—BBC, 26 July 1978.
106. *Ibid*.
107. R Bayark, 27 July—BBC, 29 July 1978.
108. R Ankara, 22 January—BBC, 24 January; *Milliyet*, 10 February 1978.
109. *Briefing*, 15 March; *Milliyet*, 10 February 1978.
110. *Milliyet*, 7 January; R Cyprus (Turkish), 7 January—BBC, 9 January 1978.
111. Karamanlis' message to Ecevit dated 23 January 1978.
112. *The Economist*, 7–13 January; *The Christian Science Monitor*, Boston; 9 March 1978.
113. R Ankara, 9 February—BBC, 11 February 1978.
114. *The Times*, 10 February; *Pulse*, 10 February; *Briefing*, 15 February 1978.
115. R Athens, 11 March—BBC, 13 March 1978.
116. R Ankara, 13 March—BBC, 15 March; *Milliyet*, 11, 12 March; *Pulse*, 15 March; *Briefing*, 15 March 1978.
117. *Pulse*, 13 March; *Briefing*, 15 March 1978.
118. *Milliyet*, 11 April 1978.
119. *Pulse*, 3 May; *The Times*, 5 May 1978.
120. R Ankara, 24 April—BBC, 26 April 1978.
121. R Ankara, 30 May—BBC, 31 May; *Milliyet*, 30 May 1978.
122. *Milliyet*, 6 July 1978.
123. *Ibid*, 20 September 1978.
124. R Athens, 20 September—BBC, 22 September 1978.
125. R Ankara, 9 February—BBC, 11 February; *Milliyet*, 13 February 1978.
126. *IHT*, 5 January; *Pulse*, 9 January 1978.
127. *Cumhuriyet*, 21, 22 January; *Milliyet*, 22 January 1978.
128. R Ankara, 23 February—BBC, 25 February 1978.
129. *Milliyet*, 26 January; *Cumhuriyet*, 26 January 1978.
130. *NYT*, 12 March 1978.
131. *The Times*, 14 March; *Milliyet*, 25 March 1978.
132. *IHT*, 21–22 January 1978.
133. R Ankara, 23 March—BBC, 30 March; *Milliyet*, 27, 29 March 1978.
134. Reuter, 6 April; *NYT*, 7 April 1978.
135. *NYT*, 3 April; *Pulse*, 10 April 1978.
136. *NYT*, 4 May 1978.
137. *Milliyet*, 4 May; *Cumhuriyet*, 5 May 1978.
138. *Cumhuriyet*, 14 May 1978.
139. *NYT*, 12 May 1978.
140. *Pulse*, 22 May; *IHT*, 30 May 1978.
141. *Washington Post*, 17 May 1978.
142. *Cumhuriyet*, 31 May 1978.

143. R Ankara, 31 May—BBC, 2 June; *The Times*, 1 June; *Milliyet*, 2 June; *Christian Science Monitor*, 8 June 1978.
144. *Baltimore Sun*, 9 June; *Milliyet*, 15 June, 22 July; *Washington Post*, 29 June; *Pulse*, 3 July; *Events*, 28 July 1978.
145. R Ankara, 26 July—BBC, 27 July 1978.
146. *Milliyet*, 26 July; *The Times*, 27 July 1978.
147. *Milliyet*, 27 July; *Pulse*, 27 July 1978.
148. R Ankara, 2 August—BBC, 3 August 1978.
149. *Ibid.*
150. *The Times*, 16 August 1978.
151. R Ankara, 15 August—BBC, 17 August 1978.
152. *Ibid.*
153. *Jerusalem Post*, 28 September 1978.
154. *Outlook*, 11 October 1978.
155. *Ibid*, 18 January 1978.
156. *Pulse*, 21 January 1978.
157. *Cumhuriyet*, 30 January 1978.
158. *Pulse*, 3 February 1978.
159. *Ibid*, 9 February 1978.
160. *FT*, 25 May 1978.
161. *Ibid; Economist*, 3 June 1978.
162. *Ibid; The Guardian*, 29 June 1978.
163. R Ankara, 17 July—BBC, 19 July 1978.
164. *Milliyet*, 20 July 1978.
165. R Ankara, 10 February—BBC, 21 February 1978.
166. R Ankara, 28 June—BBC, 30 June 1978.
167. Ahmad Feroz, *The Turkish Experiment in Democracy, 1950–1975* (London: C. Hurst Company, 1977), p. 423.
168. *Milliyet*, 10 May; R Ankara, 12 May—BBC, 23 May; *FT*, 13 May 1978.
169. R Ankara, 16 August—BBC, 18 August; *The Guardian*, 17 August 1978.
170. *Milliyet*, 21 November 1977.
171. *Son Havadis*, Istanbul; 18, 21, 26, 27 November; *Milliyet*, 17, 19, 20 November 1977.
172. *Cumhuriyet*, 19, 30 November, 2 December; *Tercüman*, 17, 19, 21 November 1977.
173. *Milliyet*, 22 November 1977.
174. *Ibid*, 27 November 1977.
175. MENA, 3 December—BBC, 13 December; R Ankara, 4 December—BBC, 6 December 1977.
176. *Ibid*, 6 December; R Nicosia, 4 December—BBC, 6 December; *Pulse*, 7 December 1977.
177. *Pulse*, 5, 9 December 1977.
178. *Tercüman*, 11 December 1977.
179. Turkish Legation, Press Release, Tel Aviv, February 1978.
180. *Milliyet*, 5, 18, 23 December 1977; *Cumhuriyet*, 23 July 1978.
181. *Briefing*, 21 June; *Events*, 28 February 1978.
182. *Ibid*, 12 July 1978.
183. See above, Domestic Affairs, Political Opposition and Local Elections; R Ankara, 20 June—BBC, 22 June 1978.
184. *Cumhuriyet*, 8 July; *Milliyet*, 12 July; R Ankara, 4 July—BBC, 11 July 1978.
185. *Cumhuriyet*, 23 July; *Pulse*, 24 July ; *Briefing*, 26 July 1978.
186. *Briefing*, 30 August 1978.
187. *Ibid*; R Ankara, 25 August—BBC, 29 August 1978.
188. *Briefing*, 30 August 1978.
189. R Ankara, 17 January—BBC, 24 January; R Ankara, 24 January—BBC, 31 January; *Cumhuriyet*, 21 February 1978.
190. *Briefing*, 12 July 1978.
191. R Ankara, 4 July—BBC, 11 July 1978.
192. Baykal served as Foreign Minister in 1974, and was partly responsible for the establishment of good relations between the two countries.
193. R Ankara, 24 February—BBC, 27 February; *Milliyet*, 25 February; *Cumhuriyet*, 25 February 1978.
194. *Cumhuriyet*, 7 April; R Ankara, 2 May—Daily Report (DR), 4 May; R Ankara, 2 June—BBC, 13 June 1978.
195. R Ankara, 17 August—BBC, 19 August; *FT*, 18 August 1978.
196. *Briefing*, 28 June 1978.
197. *Cumhuriyet*, 18 June; *NYT*, 24 June 1978.
198. *Events*, 14 July; *Milliyet*, 24 June; R Ankara, 25 June—BBC, 27 June 1978.

199. *The Times*, 16 June 1978.
200. For details of earlier stages of the crisis, see *MECS 1976–77*, pp. 624, 646–49. The GNP figures are from Türkiye İş Bankası (TIB), *Economic Indicators of Turkey 1973–1977 (EIT)*; Ankara, p. 3.
201. *FT*, 13 November 1978.
202. See TIB, *Review of Economic Conditions (REC)*; Ankara, No 3 (1978), pp. 1, 5–6, 14. Also see Economist Intelligence Unit, *Quarterly Economic Review of Turkey (QER)*, London; No 2 (1978), p. 9; and *Middle East Economic Digest (MEED)*, London; 14 July 1978.
203. See *FT*, 13 November 1978; *QER*, No 3 (1978), p. 13; *Briefing*, 4 October 1978, p. 16; and *REC, op. cit.*, p. 1.
204. The sources for reports on Turkey's debt and balance of payments difficulties, and relations with the IMF abound. See, for example, the *FT* survey on Turkey, 13 November 1978; various issues of *MEED* throughout late 1977 and 1978; the first three numbers of *QER* for 1978; and various issues of *Briefing*.
205. See *FT*, 13 November 1977; and *Briefing*, 25 October 1978.
206. TIS, *EIT*, pp. 4–5.
207. *Briefing*, 15 November 1978.
208. *FT*, 13 November 1978, p. 25. Also see *QER*, No 2 (1978), p. 9.
209. TIS, *REC, op. cit.*, p. 11.
210. TIS, *EIT*, p. 7.
211. See *FT*, 13 November 1978; and *Briefing*, 13 September 1978.
212. TIS, *EIT*, p. 10.
213. See *QER*, No 2 (1978), pp. 16–17; *Pulse*, 21 August 1978; and *Briefing*, 23 August 1978.
214. *MEED*, 27 October 1978, p. 44.
215. International Monetary Fund (IMF), *International Financial Statistics*, various issues.
216. *MEED*, 9 December 1977, p. 3.
217. TIB, *EIT*, p. 10.
218. See IMF, *Direction of Trade*, various issues; and TIS, *EIT*, pp. 8–9.

The Yemeni Arab Republic

(Al-Jumhūriyya al-'Arabiyya al-Yamaniyya)

The assassination of the Chairman of the Presidential Council, Aḥmad Ḥusayn al-Ghashmī, in June 1978—the second assassination of a YAR (North Yemeni) Head of State within a year—was one more manifestation of the marked instability prevalent in Yemeni political life.

Like his predecessor, Ghashmī had to manoeuvre—for the most part unsuccessfully—between two conflicting and hostile forces: the northern tribal Zaydī chiefs headed by their powerful leader, 'Abdallah al-Aḥmar, and the coalition of the Shāfi'ī and mainly urban population. (The Zaydīs belong to the Shī'ī branch of Islam; the Shāfi'īs follow one of the four orthodox schools of Sunnī Islam.) Ghashmī's inability to deal with these rival elements was reflected in the establishment in February 1978 of the Constituent People's Assembly, which had been advocated by both sides. However, in practice it failed to satisfy the expectations of either, and served only to exacerbate existing tensions.

Ghashmī's position was further undermined by the internal dissension within the army's high command. His decision to abolish the Military Command Council in April 1978 and to establish a Presidential Council, while retaining the post of Commander-in-Chief, only served to deepen a longstanding rivalry between himself and several high-ranking officers which culminated in an abortive rebellion at the end of the same month.

Ghashmī's assassination in June 1978 caused a further deterioration in the already tense relations between the two Yemens. This was particularly expressed in North Yemen's accusations of PDRY complicity in the assassination, as well as in the border clashes which flared up in its wake.

While relations with PDRY worsened, North Yemen continued to strengthen its relations with Saudi Arabia, which had repercussions in both inter-Arab and international spheres.

POLITICAL AFFAIRS
TRIBAL ZAYDĪS VERSUS LEFTIST SHĀFI'ĪS

Upon Lt-Col Aḥmad Ḥusayn al-Ghashmī's accession to power, in the wake of the assassination of Ibrāhīm Muḥammad al-Ḥamdī on 11 October 1977,[1] he had to contend with the same conflicting forces which had challenged the rule of his predecessor—the northern Zaydī tribal chiefs and the Leftist, mainly urban and Shāfi'ī National Democratic Front (NDF). The first force was headed by the influential leader of the Ḥāshid tribal confederation, 'Abdallah al-Aḥmar, while the second was backed by the People's Democratic Republic of Yemen (PDRY). Basically, each of these two forces demanded a bigger involvement and role in the formulation of domestic and foreign policies. The tribes—who traditionally were closely connected with Saudi Arabia—demanded the implementation of the reconciliation agreement which they had reached with Ḥamdī in September 1977 following a tribal mutiny in the preceding summer.[2] According to this agreement, they were to enjoy a larger representation in the Military Command Council (MCC), in the government and in a Consultative Council which would be formed following general elections. A Consultative Council (*majlis shūrā*)—the supreme legislative body which was responsible for supervising the executive authority and headed by Aḥmar—had been abolished by Ḥamdī after he came to power in June 1974. Since then the tribes persistently demanded its re-establishment.

Ghashmī, who had just ascended to power, was not at all enthusiastic about implementing this agreement. He realized that if he acceded to the demands of the tribal leaders, particularly that of Aḥmar to regain his previous post as chairman of a Consultative Council composed of his followers, he would virtually undo the main achievement of Ḥamdī's 13 June (1974) Corrective Movement[3]—namely, a reduction of Aḥmar's influence (see below).

Not only was Ghashmī faced with the tribal front, but he also had to contend with persistent rivalries among the tribes themselves. Himself a member of the Ḥāshid tribal confederation, Ghashmī had to maintain a delicate balance between 'Ab-dallah al-Aḥmar and the chief of the large Nahm tribe, Sinān Abū Luḥūm, one of the most powerful leaders of the Bakīl tribal confederation located in the central and the southern areas of North Yemen. While this rivalry did not erupt into open conflict, there existed a quiet, but deep internal struggle between the two leaders and their close followers, mainly over senior posts in the armed forces.

Another significant—though less dangerous—source of domestic political tension was the National Democratic Front (NDF), formed in 1976 by six small Leftist organizations.[4] The NDF's constituency was the relatively more advanced urban and Shāfi'ī population of the coastal plain of the Tihāma and the south. Its leadership—civilians and officers alike—was apprehensive about a possible revival of Zaydī predominance which had characterized Yemen's political life before the great civil war of 1960s, thus undercutting the political achievements the Leftists had made through the war and its aftermath. The NDF's main demands, as articulated at the beginning of Ghashmī's rule, called for a more nearly democratic system of government in Yemen: permitting parties and unions to conduct political activities; creating a Consultative Council in which the Leftist forces would also be represented; social and administrative improvements; and the·release of political detainees. In foreign affairs they called for the establishment of unity between the two Yemens and demanded an end to Saudi interference in Yemen's affairs.[5] The NDF demands for administrative and social improvement were generally understood, particularly by the Northern tribes, to mean curtailing the official and unofficial allocations of money dispensed to the tribes by the central authority. These payments constituted a further burden on the Yemeni budgetary deficit. Furthermore, they also entailed prohibiting the tribes' possession of heavy arms—which had enabled them to rise in rebellion whenever they disliked a decision of the central authority. It was clear to Ghashmī from the outset that, while his predecessor had been somewhat successful in curtailing the allocations to the tribes and in inducing them to turn over their heavy arms, this had caused considerable unrest. Ghashmī preferred to resume these allocations and thereby appease the tribes and assure their loyalty, even though he might incur the displeasure of the NDF.

The rivalry between the Zaydī tribes and the Shāfi'ī Leftists, and the competition among the tribes themselves, had repercussions on the power structure within the higher echelons of the civil and military leadership.

GHASHMĪ'S FIRST WEEKS IN POWER

One of Ghashmī's first major decisions as Chairman of the MCC was to retain the post of Commander-in-Chief of the armed forces. In so doing he disappointed the Ḥāshid tribal confederation who preferred Lt-Col (*muqaddam*) Mujāhid Abū Shawārib, a relative of Aḥmar; at the same time, he fuelled the resentment felt by the Paratroops Commander, Maj 'Abdallah 'Abd al-'Ālim, who had coveted the post for himself. (For 'Abd al-'Ālim's subsequent role in leading a rebellion against Ghashmī, see below.)

Moreover, Ghashmī's initial statements, in which he declared his intention to pursue Ḥamdī's domestic and foreign policies,[6] failed to convince the Paratroop and the 'Amāliqa ("Giants") brigades, both of which had been the mainstay of Ghashmī's power. The latter had been commanded by Ḥamdī's brother, Lt-Col 'Abdallah who, together with the Yemeni ruler, was assassinated on 11 October 1977. Indeed, several 'Amāliqa units, some of them members of the Bakīl tribal confederation, had blamed Ghashmī for the assassination of their commander. Others had fled to Aden, which further exacerbated the tense relations between the two Yemens (see chapter on the PDRY). The appointment in October 1977 of 'Abdallah Muḥammad al-Sharīf as their new commander did not have the hoped for effect in reducing tension.[7]

When Ghashmī failed to gain the loyalty of the Paratroops and 'Amāliqa, he turned elsewhere and took the following measures in order to consolidate his authority and power: he visited the various armed forces brigades and the air force units; met with tribal leaders; and appointed his own men to senior military positions.[8] Two officers reported to have been instrumental in Ghashmī's assumption of power were given significant senior appointments: Deputy Chief of Staff, Lt-Col 'Alī al-Shayba, became Chief of Staff;[9] Lt-Col 'Alī 'Abdallah Sālih of the Ḥāshid tribal confederation took command of the Fourth Armoured Battalion based in San'ā as well as of the Reserve Brigade.[10] He was later appointed commander of Ta'izz Province. Ghashmī also carried out purges in the armed forces, mainly of officers considered to be loyal to Ḥamdī. Members of the Yemeni Labour Party (ḥizb al-'amal al-yamanī)—one of the constituent organizations of the NDF—were arrested for advocating rapprochement with the PDRY.[11] However, far from removing the cause of tension, these measures increased restiveness. Daily anti-government demonstrations were reported in Ta'izz and Ḥudayda in November 1977, and there was tribal unrest in the areas bordering the PDRY.

The tense domestic situation, coupled with severe economic problems, led some foreign observers to conclude soon after Ghashmī assumed office that he was "powerless to control" the country.[12] Other observers interpreted the fact that Ghashmī had not reacted either to the NDF demands or to the pressure exerted on him by the tribes as part of a "waiting game" to avoid being caught between the conflicting forces. In November 1977, probably to satisfy both sides, Ghashmī released 307 prisoners, including 135 political detainees.[13]

GHASHMĪ'S CALL FOR NATIONAL RECONCILIATION

Towards the end of October 1977, Ghashmī declared that he had no intention of holding a dialogue with the tribal chiefs as long as they refused to respect the state and the law.[14] This declaration was regarded by the tribes as a breach of their agreement with Ḥamdī which had provided for the enlargement of their political influence. 'Abdallah al-Aḥmar reportedly refused to back Ghashmī's new regime.[15]

By the beginning of December 1977, Ghashmī apparently came to the conclusion that only a measure of participation in the decision-making process would satisfy both Leftist and tribal pressure groups, reduce unrest, and perhaps also ensure the support of 'Abdallah al-Aḥmar and Sinān Abū Luhūm for his regime. Therefore, he announced the convening of a general popular conference which would include "all segments of the people." As a first step, a special preparatory committee composed of "representatives from the co-operatives, expatriates and the state" was formed. At the same time, Ghashmī explained "the future of democracy" in Yemen in these terms:

Democracy is the rule of people for people and in the manner they find suitable to achieve their hopes and aspirations in all fields of life. Our people are by nature practising democracy even in their relations with government officials. Our people are generous, hate oppression and are extremely sensitive about their dignity. Our ancient history testifies to this merit. Since ancient times Yemen has lived in a democratic atmosphere, whereas other nations were living under very difficult conditions. . . . True democracy is not phrases, mottos or shapes void of meaning, but true and practical practice (sic) that aims at making the people rule themselves by themselves and in the manner they choose to preserve their dignity, national sovereignty and total Yemeni identity. Since 13 June [1974] we have been walking in this democratic direction within a fateful framework drawn up by the people and are abiding by its rules and obligations. The idea of holding a general popular conference comprising all factions, [as consistent with] true democracy [had been raised previously]. The idea of holding this conference still exists, for the committee entrusted with the task of convening this conference is working hard to make proper arrangements for it. We are also very careful to provide all guarantees for its success because it will represent all factions of the people without exception. When the committee has finished its task of preparing for the conference and achieved guarantees of success, the location and date of the conference will be fixed.

Ghashmī added that the idea of convening a Consultative Council was not frozen; rather its term had expired. The constitution (i.e. the one proclaimed in June 1974, after Ḥamdī had gained power and had abolished the Permanent Constitution of 1970) was also not frozen, but remained "the legal framework governing our work." [16]

Ghashmī's call for a popular conference was accompanied by an attempt to achieve national reconciliation. In mid-January 1978, Saudi mediation reportedly led to a reconciliation between Ghashmī and the tribal leaders Aḥmar and Sinān Abū Luḥūm. In return for the tribes' pledges of loyalty, Ghashmī ordered the renewal of part of the allocations of funds to them which Ḥamdī had stopped paying after the tribal rebellion of the summer of 1977. [17]

While hinting at the setting up of a Consultative Council, Ghashmī promised the NDF that he would reinstate the parliamentary system. Although he said that this would be done according to the "spirit of the constitution," in fact he continued the policy of restricting party activities. [18]

Also at the beginning of February 1978, Ghashmī increased the pay of every member of the armed forces and security services by YR 150 per month. [19] Another step taken by Ghashmī to reach national reconciliation was to agree to the return of a number of Yemeni exiles. Two military officers, Dirham Abū Luḥūm (former MCC member) and Ḥusayn al-Miswārī (former Chief-of-Staff) were said to have returned to San'ā. On the other hand, negotiations with the former Prime Minister, Muḥsin al-'Aynī (who was regarded as having links with Leftist elements), failed. He was kept under close surveillance in Cairo and later (at an unspecified date) was allowed to leave for Abu Dhabi. [20]

THE ESTABLISHMENT OF A CONSTITUENT PEOPLE'S ASSEMBLY

On 6 February 1978, Ghashmī announced—with the approval of the MCC—the formation of a Constituent People's Assembly (CPA; *majlīs sha'b ta'sīsī*). The Assembly was to be composed of 99 members chosen by the MCC. It would have a term of three years, meeting during six months each year. The Assembly, again with the MCC's approval, would choose a president and two vice-presidents. Its basic functions would be to make recommendations on the authority to be invested in the Presidency, to propose amendments to the Constitution, and to exercise the functions of the Elections Committee and of the Preparatory Committee of the General Popular Conference, as well as of the scientific committee for the codification of the *shari'a* (Islamic religious law). Other functions would include consideration of draft laws and codifications referred to the Assembly by the MCC, reviewing the budget, and studying all subjects referred to it including economic, social, educational, cultural and foreign questions.[21]

During the following two weeks, Ghashmī was occupied in making appointments to the Assembly. Probably hinting at the possibility that free elections might provide the tribal Zaydīs with a majority in the Assembly—a situation which had prevailed before Ḥamdī's 13 June 1974 corrective measures—Ghashmī explained that appointing Assembly members was preferable to electing them because representation of all political trends could be guaranteed. Thus, the preponderance of men of Zaydī faith in the military would not be further enhanced by the majority which they might gain in the Assembly.[22]

The text of Law No 19/1978, including the bylaws of the newly-formed Assembly, was issued on 24 February 1978. It consisted of 65 articles which defined the structure, functions and powers of the Assembly and its various committees.[23] A day later, in his address at the Assembly's inaugural meeting, Ghashmī described it as "a memorable event in the country's history" and spoke of the "return of democracy to public life." Ghashmī added that the biggest mistake the leadership had made since June 1974 was the dissolution of the Consultative Council, "thus disrupting Yemen's constitutional life." He also announced that free elections would be held once the CPA had drafted the elections' law.[24] On 26 February 1978, 'Abd al-Karīm al-'Arshī, a former minister highly respected for his integrity and professional background, was elected the Assembly's chairman.[25]

The formation of the CPA was aimed at satisfying the demands for popular representation made by the conservative tribes as well as by the urban Leftists. However, each side had a different view of the character and purpose of such a body. The Leftists regarded it as a means by which democracy would be enhanced and tribal influence reduced. Aḥmar and the other tribal chiefs regarded the same apparatus as the way to legitimately seize power in the capital. However, Ghashmī's move fell short of the aims of either side. The tribal leaders chosen by Ghashmī did not include 'Abdallah al-Aḥmar, whose wish to be re-elected to his previous powerful post of chairman of the Assembly was thus frustrated. Nor did it include Sinān Abū Luḥūm and Mujāhid Abū Shawārib. However, there was speculation that these three figures would soon be invited by Ghashmī to·participate in a new Presidential Council, which would replace the existing three-member MCC (see below).

While the Ḥāshid and Bakīl tribal confederations were frustrated by the non-inclusion of their prominent representatives, the NDF was also displeased by the inclusion of the conservative tribal leaders in this "hand-picked advisory body."[26]

TRIBAL FIGHTING

At the beginning of March 1978, military clashes with tribes in the northern areas of 'Amrān, Khamir and Rayda were reported, with conflicting explanations provided by observers. According to some commentaries, 'Abdallah al-Aḥmar and Sinān Abū Luḥūm were taking their revenge for not being included in the CPA.[27] According to a different version, the fighting was simply another internal clash between the Ḥāshid and Bakīl tribal confederations. Maj Mujāhid al-Kuḥālī, the Commander of 'Amrān area (on the border of the Ḥāshid territory) and a close associate of previous MCC Chairman Ḥamdī, had seized large quantities of arms and money and incited the Banū Sufyān tribe of the Bakīl confederation to fight against the Ḥāshid. Mujāhid Abū Shawārib was reported to have been wounded in the fighting, which ceased only after the intervention of leaders of the Bakīl. Maj Kuḥālī was arrested by the tribesmen and dispatched to Sanʿā.[28] On 10 March, Kuḥālī was sent to Prague as a Minister Plenipotentiary.[29]

Whatever the reason for the tribal fighting, it threatened Ghashmī's attempts to reach national reconciliation and to win the tribes' support. On 7 March 1978, he visited army units in the northern areas, and the following day received tribal leaders from the Ḥāshid and the Bakīl who had come to declare their allegiance.[30]

In March 1978, Lt-Col ʿAbd al-ʿAzīz Lutfī al-Barātī was appointed Deputy Chief of Staff, and Lt-Col Lutfī Aḥmad ʿAbdallah Sunayn was appointed Commander of the Naval Forces.[31]

THE SADDA CONFERENCE

Widescale arrests of NDF members were reported throughout March 1978. They accused Ghashmī of handing over political power to the tribes—after they had been deprived of that same power by Ḥamdī. A large popular conference reportedly of c. 20,000 people was organized in the central Yemeni town of Sadda in March 1978 by the Leftists, and probably also by some tribal leaders hostile to Ghashmī. The participants denounced Ghashmī's "one-man rule" and the internal disputes within the MCC. They called for the strengthening of all the "national forces" in the two Yemens, demanded political rights and the stoppage of arbitrary arrests and torture. They also called for an independent economy and protested against foreign interference in Yemen's affairs. Yemen was said to be in a "transitional stage" which should last no more than a year. They requested that during this period a new CPA composed of 54 members should be formed to supervise general elections, and that a Presidential Council composed of not less than seven and not more than nine members should be established.[32]

THE ESTABLISHMENT OF THE PRESIDENTIAL COUNCIL

The decree, of February 1978 that one of the basic functions of the CPA would be "to make recommendations on the form of the Presidential Council" (PC, see above) struck a familiar note to many Yemenites, as one of Ḥamdī's first measures when he assumed power in June 1974 was to abolish the PC headed by ʿAbd al-Raḥmān al-Iryānī. Instead, he formed the MCC with himself as its chairman (in addition to his post as Commander-in-Chief). Since that time and in response to pressure exerted by various political forces, Ḥamdī had hinted several times that he might re-establish a PC. No serious measures were taken in this direction, however. In March 1978, Ghashmī said that the issue of setting up a PC required careful study by the CPA, "taking into consideration the existing experiment and what has preceded it."[33]

In the beginning of April 1978, it was speculated that ʿAbdallah al-Aḥmar, Sinān Abū Luḥūm or Abū Shawārib would participate in a PC about to be set up.[34] In the second half of April 1978, the MCC expanded the powers of the CPA, giving it the right to determine the form that the PC should take.[35]

On 22 April 1978, the CPA decided to abolish the MCC and to form a PC comprised of a President and two Vice-Presidents (to be appointed by the President), which would serve for a five-year term. The President would also hold the post of Commander-in-Chief of the armed forces.[36] The 99-member CPA thereupon elected Ghashmī to the presidency: 75 members voted in favour, 18 abstained, and six others were reported to be away on official business.[37]

On 23 April 1978, Prime Minister 'Abd al-'Azīz 'Abd al-Ghanī tendered his government's resignation—a constitutional measure following the reorganization of the executive. The resignation was accepted, but Ghashmī asked 'Abd al-Ghanī to stay on until a new cabinet could be formed.[38] Rumours spread that the announcement of the new government was imminent, but towards the end of April, 'Abd al-Ghanī was still having difficulties with its formation.[39]

At the same time, tribal unrest and disputes within the army were reported.[40] As a result of this and of a rebellion by the Paratroops Commander, Maj 'Ālim, 'Abd al-Ghanī did not succeed in forming a new government until the end of May (see below).

THE REBELLION OF 'ABDALLAH 'ABD AL-'ĀLIM

After the dissolution of the MCC, one of its members, Paratroops Commander Maj 'Abdallah 'Abd al-'Ālim, found himself shunted aside since he was not appointed Commander-in-Chief of the armed forces as he had wished. Instead, Ghashmī was said to have offered him either the post of Vice-President for Military Affairs or of ambassador to France, but 'Abd al-'Ālim rejected both offers. 'Ālim was also known to have been absolutely opposed to Ghashmī's unequivocal commitment to a pro-Saudi orientation rather than continuing along the lines set by Hamdī (i.e. moving towards greater co-operation with the PDRY, while maintaining good relations with Saudi Arabia). On 25 April—just three days after Ghashmī's election—'Abd al-'Ālim and c. 500 adherents from the Paratroops and the 'Amāliqa brigades arrived in 'Abd al-'Ālim's native village of Turba in the al-Hajariyya region of the southern part of Yemen where they staged a rebellion against Ghashmī and seized a stronghold on the border with the PDRY. At first Ghashmī tried to solve the problem peacefully by sending a delegation of notables, including Prime Minister 'Abd al-Ghanī, to mediate. 'Abd al-'Ālim not only refused to negotiate, but he arrested some of the notables and had them killed. Ghashmī then put the army on alert and sent out an expedition headed by the Commander of Ta'izz Province, Lt-Col 'Ali 'Abdallah Sālih, who succeeded in putting down the rebellion. In the second half of May, 'Abd al-'Ālim and a few of his followers fled to the PDRY, but the remainder of his force of c. 100 men was refused entry. According to one report, 'Abd al-'Alim did not request political asylum in the PDRY but continued on to Libya, where he met Qadhdhāfī who promised to assist him.[41]

The North Yemeni authorities denied the existence of an armed uprising, claiming that the situation was "calm and more stable than ever before." However, on 18 May 1978, Maj 'Abdallah Muhammad Sayf was appointed the new Paratroops Commander in place of 'Abd al-'Ālim who, according to official Yemeni sources, was suffering from a nervous illness. Other senior Paratroops commanders were also replaced.[42]

On 22 May 1978, Ghashmī began a five-day tour of the central and southern provinces of Hudayda and Ta'izz, including al-Hajariyya.[43]

Although Ghashmī had succeeded in putting down the rebellion, tension persisted between the central authority and the tribes, as well as within the armed forces. This gave rise to doubts about the ability of such influential forces to coexist within a single balanced system. Referring to the problem, Ghashmī expressed his belief that parliamentary democracy represented the better system:

> Its value, importance or benefit is not diminished by the existence of struggle or differences among the political or social forces over interests and ideas. Such struggle and differences are natural and inevitable. What is important is that the

struggle and differences remain within a framework of objective dialogue and discussion, and [are not] extended to armed clashes or violence. Also, the public interest must dominate the interests of individuals or factions, for democracy will lose the justification of its existence and its meaning if it appears to serve certain citizens to the exclusion of others, or one group or sector to the exclusion of others. . . . In our country . . . the phenomenon of centres of power has disappeared. No specific group can now influence the course of government or direct such a course in accordance with its own interests. How can such a group use government in the service of its interests? Moreover, we do not yet have any organizations, either political or factional. The democracy whose system and foundations we are trying to [introduce] in our country does not belong to any specific person or faction. We will make sure it does not do so, because we believe democracy must belong to every citizen or lose its value.[45]

THE NEW GOVERNMENT (formed 30 May 1978)[44]

Prime Minister	'Abd al-'Azīz 'Abd al-Ghanī
Deputy Prime Minister and Minister of Finance	Muhammad Ahmad al-Junayd
Foreign Affairs	'Abdallah 'Abd al-Majīd al-Asnaj
Interior	Lt-Col Muhsin al-Yūsufī
Communications and Transport	Ahmad Muhammad al-Ansī*
Economy	Ahmad al-Hamdānī*
Information and Culture	Ahmad Sālih al-Ru'aynī*
Supply and Trade	Sālih al-Jamālī*
Development and Chairman of the Central Planning Authority	Muhammad Sālim Bāsindūh
Works and Municipalities	'Abdallah al-Kurshumī
Social Affairs, Labour and Youth	'Abd al-Salām Muqbil
Education	Muhammad al-Khādim al-Wajīh†
Agriculture	'Alī 'Abdallah al-Matarī
Health	Muhammad Ahmad al-Asbahī*
Justice	'Alī al-Sammān
Waqf and Guidance	Muhammad b. Muhammad al-Mansūr
Minister of State and Director of the Mineral Resources Authority	Ahmad Qā'id Barakāt

* New Minister
† Minister in previous government but with different portfolio.

GHASHMĪ'S ASSASSINATION: OFFICIAL ACCOUNT

On the morning of 24 June 1978, Ghashmī was assassinated. The official announcement, issued by the General Command of the armed forces over Radio San'ā revealed that the assassination occurred while Ghashmī was receiving a special emissary in his office who had just flown in from Aden, carrying a letter from the Chairman of the South Yemeni Presidential Council, Sālim 'Alī Rubay'. The moment the emissary opened his briefcase, it exploded, killing himself and Ghashmī. Attributing responsibility for the assassination to "vicious hands in Aden," the announcement blamed the PDRY for committing "the meanest, most outrageous and treacherous operation."

In another statement, Radio San'ā also announced the formation of a new four-man PC. The new Chairman was 'Abd al-Karīm al-'Arshī, Chairman of the Constituent People's Assembly. The three other members were Prime Minister 'Abd al-'Azīz 'Abd al-Ghani, Lt-Col 'Alī al-Shayba, and the Commander of Ta'izz Province, 'Alī 'Abdallah Sālih. The CPA declared that a new President would be elected "according to constitutional procedure as soon as possible."

The first measures taken by the new PC were to empower the government to continue in office; to appoint Lt-Col 'Alī al-Shayba as Commander-in-Chief of the armed forces; and Maj 'Alī 'Abdallah Sāliḥ as Deputy Commander-in-Chief and Chief of Staff. The Council also set up a seven-member investigation committee, which included the Justice, Interior and Foreign Ministers, to inquire into the assassination of Ghashmī.[46] Later that day, Foreign Affairs Minister 'Abdallah al-Asnaj told the heads of foreign missions in San'ā that North Yemen was severing its diplomatic relations with the PDRY. Asnaj also briefed them on developments connected with the assassination. He said that, following a telephone conversation between Ghashmī and Rubay', the former had been expecting the return to San'ā of a number of dissidents who had fled to South Yemen as a result of the rebellion of 'Abdallah 'Abd al-'Ālim. Rubay' called Ghashmī on 23 June 1978 to confirm that he was sending an emissary. On arrival the emissary was not searched because he had been "dispatched by the Head of State with prior agreement." In the President's office he handed Ghashmī the letter which contained the names of those returning from Aden. Minutes later the bomb in the envoy's briefcase exploded. The captain and crew of the special plane which brought the emissary were held in San'ā for investigation but denied any knowledge about him. The official account issued by the investigation committee on 29 June reiterated the versions of the armed forces General Command and of Asnaj. It, too, blamed Aden for the assassination, adding that the emissary carried the names of 20 "kidnapped Yemenis." The explosion was the result of a powerful plastic charge placed in an attaché case with a combination lock which the envoy carried from the time he boarded the plane in Aden until he entered the President's office in San'ā.[47]

Following the assassination, the YAR requested an urgent meeting of the Arab League Council and sent envoys to several Arab countries to explain what had happened.[48] South Yemen denounced the assassination and denied accusations that it was responsible.[49] Later, following Rubay''s execution (see chapter on the PDRY), his opponents in Aden blamed him for having been involved. This accusation was rejected by North Yemen which continued to blame the more radical group of 'Abd al-Fattāḥ Ismā'īl.[50] (For the Arab League Council's decision to freeze relations with the PDRY, see essay on Inter-Arab Relations. For military clashes between the two Yemens in July and August, see chapter on the PDRY.)

GHASHMĪ'S ASSASSINATION: OTHER ACCOUNTS
More details—in some cases conflicting—appeared in the Arab press. A Yemeni source said that the emissary did not carry a letter with names because the original briefcase had been exchanged in Aden.[51] This version was supported by *al-Ahrām's* report that Rubay', after learning that his emissary had been given a second letter in Aden, made another telephone call to Ghashmī, trying to warn him not to receive the emissary and informing him that the new letter contained an explosive device. However, Rubay''s second telephone call was too late.[52]

The Lebanese weekly *al-Diyār* said that no briefcase or letter had been exchanged. According to this version, an explosive device wrapped in a large envelope was put in a briefcase prepared by East German experts. The emissary thought his duty would be restricted to handing over the briefcase, but Ghashmī opened it immediately and both of them were killed.[53] It was reported that secret contacts had been held between Rubay' and Ghashmī during the last few months preceding the assassination, to prepare a plan to overthrow the UPONF in Aden and to set up a new regime in the PDRY that would have closer links with the states in the Arabian Peninsula and the Gulf (for the UPONF, see chapter on the PDRY). According to this version, some of Rubay''s aides who knew about these contacts were UPONF intelligence agents. Rubay''s original emissary to Ghashmī, the South Yemeni Minister of State for Presidential Affairs, 'Alī Sālim La'war, was arrested minutes before he was scheduled to leave for San'ā. The letter he was bearing was confiscated and instead a letter-bomb was sent with a new emissary—a relative of the South Yemeni Minister of Interior. The confiscated letter contained the outlines of a plan to liquidate UPONF in Aden. La'war was later executed along with Rubay' (see chapter on the PDRY).[54] Other sources in Beirut believed that 'Abdallah 'Abd al-'Ālim had masterminded Ghashmī's death.[55]

The most common interpretation of the assassination was that it was a Communist-backed attempt by South Yemen to add to instability in North Yemen, to wean it away from the conservative Saudi regime and to increase the Soviet presence in the Arabian Peninsula.[56] Saudi Arabian sources strongly denounced the assassination, referring to it as an "abominable barbaric crime"; they claimed that Ghashmī was a victim of those who "sold their religion and their homeland to external forces."[57] Arab and foreign observers thought it highly unlikely that Rubay' was involved in the assassination as he had nothing to gain by Ghashmī's death; rather it could only serve to undermine his position, since Ghashmī's removal could tend to discredit him.

THE NEW PRESIDENT: 'ALĪ 'ABDALLAH SĀLIH
From among the four members of the PC formed after Ghashmī's assassination, the Commander of Ta'izz Province, Maj 'Alī 'Abdallah Sālih, emerged as the leading presidential candidate. The other military officer in the PC—Lt-Col 'Alī al-Shayba who became Commander-in-Chief following the assassination—was thought to have no political ambitions.[58] One sign that 'Alī 'Abdallah Sālih had taken precedence was that on 28 June 1978 he was promoted to the rank of Lieutenant-Colonel and started a round of visits of the air force, the military college, the Sixth Armoured Brigade and the Paratroops.[59]

On 17 July 1978, 'Alī 'Abdallah Sālih received 76 votes of the CPA and thus became the new President and Commander-in-Chief of the armed forces (replacing Shayba, see below).[60] Sālih asked the government to remain in office.[61] 'Abdallah al-Ahmar, who had withheld his support from Ghashmī, now declared himself in favour of Sālih (a fellow Hāshid) and called for full co-operation with the new leader.

In his initial statements, President Sālih promised to continue to develop the economy and administration, to strengthen the armed and security forces "within the framework of freedom and democracy . . . in order to build a modern central state, a state of order." With regard to foreign affairs, he spoke of strengthening relations with Saudi Arabia and declared that Aden's "ideological Marxist commitment" and its responsibility for Ghashmī's assassination made it "useless to hold a dialogue" with its leaders.[62]

INITIAL MEASURES OF THE NEW PRESIDENT
The first steps taken by Sālih were to visit the First Armoured and Third Infantry Brigades.[63] A large number of new senior military appointments were also made. On 19 July 1978, Lt-Col 'Alī al-Shayba was appointed as Chief-of-Staff, and Lt-Col 'Abd al-'Azīz Lutfī al-Barātī as his deputy.[64] On 20 July 1978, 'Abd al-Karīm al-'Arshī was appointed Vice-President, while still retaining his position as Chairman of the CPA. Lt-Col Lutfī Ahmad 'Abdallah Sunayn was appointed Secretary of the PC.[65] Through the following weeks, new military commanders were appointed to the Provinces of Ibb and Ta'izz, as well as others for the Reserve Forces and the First Infantry Brigade.[66]

In August 1978, Ṣāliḥ appointed new members to the CPA, among them the Hāshid leader, 'Abdallah al-Aḥmar, and the Bakīl leader, Siddīq Amīn Abū Ra's (son of Amīn Abū Ra's—the powerful chief of the Bakīl who had died in May 1978).[67]

Also in the beginning of August, a trial *in absentia* of former Paratroops Commander, 'Abdallah 'Abd al-Ālim (who had returned from Libya to Aden), and 30 other dissident army officers was held in San'ā. They were found guilty of an attempted coup during which soldiers and civilians were killed in the Provinces of Ta'izz and Ibb "in implementation of the criminal designs issued to them by the ruling clique in Aden." They were sentenced to death.[68]

ATTEMPT TO ASSASSINATE SĀLIḤ

Also in August, armed tribesmen from the Ḥāshid and Bakīl arrived in San'ā. Arab diplomatic sources said that "a coup might be imminent" and that the political climate was similar to that which preceded the assassination of Ḥamdī in October 1977.[69] On 12 September 1978, an attempt to assassinate Ṣāliḥ was reported "to have occurred a few weeks earlier." One of the President's aides was said to have been killed.[70]

FOREIGN AFFAIRS

RELATIONS WITH SAUDI ARABIA

Under Ghashmī's nine-month rule, Yemen continued to draw closer to the Saudi Arabian orbit—a process which had characterized Saudi-Yemeni relations since the beginning of the 1970s.[71] Saudi Arabia's strong influence over Yemen's domestic and external affairs had repercussions on San'ā's relations with other states in the Arabian Peninsula, as well as in wider Arab and international spheres. The fact that Ghashmī was a member of the Ḥāshid tribal confederation further strengthened the good relations which already existed between Saudi Arabia and the northern Zaydī tribes, as well as with pro-Ḥāshid tribal representatives in the government and the armed and security forces. In several statements made throughout 1978, the Yemeni leadership described Saudi-Yemeni relations as strong and vital. Accordingly, relations between North Yemen and the PDRY fluctuated between tense quiet and open border clashes (see chapter on the PDRY).

The conclusion on 13 April 1978 of a four-day visit in San'ā by a high-ranking Saudi Arabian military delegation[72] led to speculation that a defence pact between Saudi Arabia and Yemen would be signed in the near future. But although the new Yemeni President, 'Alī 'Abdallah Ṣāliḥ, praised Saudi-Yemeni fraternal relations, he denied in July and again in August 1978 that any defence agreement had been concluded with Riyadh.[73]

Saudi Arabia continued to pledge substantial economic aid to Yemen's economy. It was reported in December 1977 that the Saudis would give $570m towards the Yemeni $3.6 bn Five-Year Development Plan (1976–81).[74] In March 1978, it was announced that Saudi Arabia would contribute $70.5m to the Yemeni budget in the current fiscal year. The Saudis also agreed to provide Yemen with 50,000 tons of oil, and the Saudi Development Fund (SDF) allocated more than $80m for water, sewage and power projects.[75]

In May 1978, Saudi Arabia paid the YAR's $1m contribution to the Arab Investment Company, thereby enabling it to become a member.[76]

RELATIONS WITH OTHER COUNTRIES

Shortly after assuming power, Ghashmī declared that he would continue to adopt his predecessor's policy of promoting closer co-operation with all Arab states. He stated that "our relations with the Arab countries are excellent" and that Yemen has steered clear of the disagreements that had developed between a number of Arab states. On major all-Arab issues, North Yemen followed the Saudi line. Thus the Yemeni leadership spoke of the necessity of making a "positive contribution to bringing closer Arab views," and of preventing rifts in order to achieve Arab unity with regard to "the fateful issue . . . of our struggle against the Zionist enemy who constitutes a present and future threat to the entire Arab nation." (For Yemen's attitude to Sādāt's initiative, see essay on Inter-Arab Relations.) Like the Saudis, Yemen demanded that the Red Sea area should remain a zone of stability and peace, free from international interference. It urged the Red Sea countries to pay special attention to economic co-operation.[77]

Throughout 1978, Asnaj and 'Abd al-Ghanī made a number of visits to Arab capitals, primarily to get assurances of Arab backing against the PDRY and to solicit economic and financial aid.

RELATIONS WITH THE US
Under Saudi influence, Ghashmī continued Yemen's shift towards the West. The American presence reportedly increased to more than 2,000 experts in various civil and security state organs. San'ā allegedly became a base from which the US monitored South Yemeni activities.[78] In February 1978, the US and North Yemen signed an agreement whereby Washington was expected to give c. $1.5m over a five-year period to help finance technical training for Yemenis.[79] American political delegations visited San'ā in April, June and August 1978.[80] In September 1978, the US was reported to have negotiated with officials in Saudi Arabia and Yemen about the possibility of establishing a military camp in YAR territory close to Bāb al-Mandab.[81]

RELATIONS WITH THE USSR
Yemen's continuing shift towards the West was paralled by worsening relations with the USSR. Since 1976, Soviet military aid and its contingent of experts have been reduced.[82] Nevertheless, attempts were made to avoid a complete severance of relations. On 8 April 1978, the Yemeni Chief of Staff, Lt-Col 'Alī al-Shayba, began a two-week visit in Moscow, where he met the Soviet Chief of Staff and other military officials.[83] The visit was said to be aimed at purchasing modern heavy Soviet military equipment.[84]

In April 1978, two agreements were signed: one granting Yemen a loan of $38.3m to expand its cement factory; a second for training Yemenis in the Soviet Union.[85]

In August 1978, while Yemen was involved in a severe dispute with the PDRY, Asnaj opposed "all types of foreign presence in the area, especially the Soviet presence."[86]

ECONOMIC AFFAIRS ($1 = 4.547 Yemeni rials; £1 = YR 9.531)
The problems and achievements of the development programme were the outstanding features of the economy in 1977–78.[87] In November 1977, representatives from 28 countries attended a conference in San'ā to scrutinize the YAR's development plans and decide on their level of support. In the first quarter of 1978 alone, the Yemeni authorities received $132m in aid, including $80m from Saudi Arabia. Total aid required for the Five-Year Plan was put at $1,400m, of which $1,100m had been committed as of June 1978.[88]

During this same period (mid-1977 to mid-1978), there was a general upsurge in economic activity, accompanied by rising prices. Inflation, estimated at 30%, can be largely attributed to supply bottlenecks, such as congestion in the port of

Hudayda, coupled with growing demand for goods and services. Demand, in turn, has been fuelled by increased remittances from Yemenis working in Saudi Arabia and other Gulf states; by a rise in bank credit to the private sector; and by a deficit in public-sector financial transactions.[89] With workers' remittances steadily increasing, and with the 1978-79 draft budget incorporating a deficit of YR 984m (based on total expenditure of YR 3,177m and revenue of YR 2,193m)—nearly half of total revenues—it is highly unlikely that there will be an easing of demand in the short-term.[90]

BALANCE OF PAYMENTS

The YAR's perennial trade deficit worsened even further in 1977 as imports (and therefore the export gap) leaped c. 50%. Moreover, imports of services jumped 56.9% while exports of services rose by only 22.1%, so that the services deficit also increased. However, North Yemen did profit from transfer payments, as net private unrequited transfers grew 40% to reach nearly $950m. In other words, as a result of private remittances from abroad, which exceeded even the trade deficit by quite a sizeable margin ($244m in 1977), the YAR's payments accounts remained in surplus and even improved by $115m in 1977.[91]

MONETARY DEVELOPMENTS

North Yemen's international reserves rose by two-thirds in 1977 before settling into a slower but steadier pattern of growth during the first half of 1978. At the end of July 1978, these reserves totalled $1,395m, of which 99% were in the form of foreign exchange.

Net foreign assets reached YR 5,675m at the end of the first quarter of 1978—a 51.7% increase during the preceding 12 months. Domestic credit, which hit a peak of YR 679m at the end of March 1977, fell to YR 374m at the end of 1977, before expanding to YR 584m by the end of March.

The money supply grew rapidly throughout 1977 (61% for the year) and continued to grow, though at a slower rate, to reach YR 5,037m at the end of April 1978. The quasi-money supply, on the other hand, registered far less steady growth: it fell 4.2% during March 1978 and then spurted 18.5% to YR 943m during the month of April 1978.[92]

FOREIGN TRADE

Exports, consisting mainly of coffee, cotton and hides and skins, rose from $7.7m in 1976 to $22.6m in 1977. China (24.2%), Taiwan (21.8%) and South Yemen (13.8%) were the YAR's leading markets in 1977.

Imports, by contrast, nearly doubled from $412m in 1976 to $811m in 1977, with the result that the trade gap, too, nearly doubled. Japan (15.2%), Saudi Arabia (12.8%), West Germany (6.8%) and the UK (6.5%) were the main sources for imports in 1977. Classified manufactures (32.6%), machinery and transport equipment (27.2%), and food and live animals (22.3%) remained the three leading commodity groups of imports in the first half of the 1977-78 fiscal year, as they had been for the preceding three years (though not necessarily in the same order).[93]

Haim Shaked and Tamar Yegnes
Economic section by **Ira E. Hoffman**

ARMED FORCES

Total armed forces number 38,000. Defence expenditure in 1977-78 was 360m riyals ($79m). Military service is compulsory for three years. The Army numbers 36,000 in two infantry divisions (ten infantry brigades including three reserve); two armoured brigades; one parachute brigade; two commando brigades; five artillery battalions and two anti-aircraft artillery battalions. Equipment consists of 220 T-34, T-54 medium tanks; 50 *Saladin* armoured, *Ferret* scout cars; 350 BTR-40/-152, *Walid* armoured personnel carriers; 50 76mm, 122mm guns; 50 SU-100 self-propelled guns; 82mm, 120mm mortars; 75mm recoilless rifles; 20 *Vigilant* anti-tank guided weapons and 37mm, 57mm anti-aircraft guns. (Howitzers and anti-aircraft guns on order.) 1,500 men are deployed in the Lebanon with the Arab Peacekeeping Force. The Navy numbers 500 and has four large patrol craft (ex-Soviet *Poluchat*-class) and four motor torpedo boats (ex-Soviet P-4 class). The 1,500-strong Air Force has c. 26 combat aircraft (some believed to be in storage); one light bomber squadron with 14 Il-28; one fighter squadron with 12 MiG-17; three C-47, two *Skyvan* and one Il-14 transport; four F-5B, four MiG-15UTI and 18 Yak-11 trainers; one Mi-4 and two AB-205 helicopters; AA-2 *Atoll* air-to-air missiles. Paramilitary forces consist of 20,000 tribal levies.

Source: The Military Balance 1978–79 (London: International Institute for Strategic Studies).

BALANCE OF PAYMENTS (million US dollars)

	1975	1976	1977
A. Goods, Services and Transfers	129.4	296.6	301.6
Exports of Merchandise, fob	14.2	13.5	14.8
Imports of Merchandise, fob	−245.6	−475.2	−720.1
Exports of Services	37.7	83.2	101.6
Imports of Services	−63.4	−104.4	−163.8
Private Unrequited Transfers, net	270.2	676.8	948.9
Government Unrequited Transfers, net	116.3	102.7	120.3
B. Long-Term Capital, nie	18.0	47.6	47.0
C. Short-Term Capital, nie	−34.3	5.8	34.0
D. Errors and Omissions	39.9	35.4	117.4
E. **Total** (A through D)	**152.9**	**385.4**	**500.0**

INTERNATIONAL LIQUIDITY (million US dollars at end of period)

	1976	1977	(Jan–June) 1978
International Reserves	720.1	1,204.4	1,347.1
Gold	0.1	0.2	0.2
SDRs	2.5	2.6	2.8
Reserves with IMF	2.9	6.5	6.6
Foreign Exchange	714.7	1,231.1	1,337.5
Commercial Banks: Assets	142.2	64.5	97.4*
Liabilities	105.5	74.8	95.4*

*End of April.

MONETARY SURVEY (million Yemeni rials at end of period)

	1976	1977	(Jan–April) 1978
Foreign Assets (net)	3,381.7	5,463.4	5,898.7
Domestic Credit	471.3	374.1	569.3
Claims on Government (net)	*−497.7*	*−984.4*	*−833.5*
Claims on Public Entities	*85.0*	*67.9*	*117.0*
Claims on Private Sector	*884.0*	*1,290.6*	*1,285.8*
Money	2,786.9	4,492.3	5,036.9
Quasi-money	691.0	770.7	942.9
Other Items (net)	375.1	574.6	488.3
Money, Seasonally Adjusted	2,876.1	4,636.0	5,118.8

THE YEMENI ARAB REPUBLIC

NATIONAL ACCOUNTS (million Yemeni rials; year beginning 1 July)

	1973–74	1974–75	1975–76
Exports	204	282	398
Government Consumption	365	517	681
Gross Fixed Capital Formation	472	586	773
Increase in Stocks	158	491	397
Private Consumption	2,991	3,850	4,800
Less: Imports	*–930*	*–1,252*	*–1,868*
Gross Domestic Products (GDP)	**3,260**	**4,474**	**5,181**
Net Factor Income from Abroad	19	25	47
Gross National Expenditure = GNP	3,279	4,499	5,228

Source (of four preceding tables): IMF, *International Financial Statistics*.

IMPORTS BY COMMODITY (million Yemeni rials)

	1974–75	1975–76	1976–77	First half 1977–78
Food and live animals	418.6	741.6	868.4	606.5
Beverages and tobacco	29.1	44.4	49.0	78.4
Raw Materials	3.1	6.6	12.7	9.9
Mineral fuels and lubricants	36.0	81.1	58.9	61.0
Animal and Vegetable Oil	3.6	7.9	11.2	24.6
Chemicals	66.2	82.8	155.3	123.4
Classified Manufactures	193.1	310.7	668.2	885.6
Machinery and Transport Equipment	149.6	289.6	965.7	738.1
Miscellaneous Manufactures	79.6	140.4	243.0	180.6
Goods not Classified	2.0	1.9	2.9	7.6
Total*	**981.0**	**1,706.9**	**3,035.3**	**2,715.6**

*Items may not add to totals due to rounding.
Source: Central Planning Organization, reprinted in *Middle East Economic Digest*, 9 June 1978.

DIRECTION OF TRADE (million US dollars)

	1975	1976	1977*
Exports to			
China PR	5.70	2.56	5.47
Taiwan	...	...	4.91
South Yemen (PDRY)	1.21	2.08	3.12
Italy	1.64	1.38	2.32
Japan	0.31	...	2.00
Saudi Arabia	0.60	1.25	1.24
United States	0.15	0.04	1.05
Total (including others)	**10.89**	**7.66**	**22.56**
Imports from:			
Japan	52.83	41.91	123.32
Saudi Arabia	15.48	47.48	103.46
West Germany	16.38	17.99	54.81
United Kingdom	13.63	26.36	53.00
India	17.86	29.76	43.44
France	7.56	14.19	38.63
United States	5.21	15.46	37.93
Italy	7.28	13.59	35.66
Netherlands	10.34	24.40	30.89
Djibouti	11.24	18.08	29.51
Total (including others)	**293.92**	**412.44**	**810.65**

*Data partly extrapolated and/or derived from partner country.
Source: IMF, *Direction of Trade*.

NOTES
1. See *Middle East Contemporary Survey (MECS) 1976–77*, p. 657.
2. *Ibid*, p. 655.
3. *Ibid*, p. 651.
4. *Ibid*, p. 653.
5. *Al-Nahār al-'Arabī wal-Duwalī (NAD)*, Paris; 19 November 1977.
6. *Rūz al-Yūsuf*, Cairo; 24 October 1977.
7. *Arabia and the Gulf*; London; 7, 14, 19 November 1977.
8. R San'ā, 16 October—British Broadcasting Corporation, Summary of World Broadcasts, Africa and the Middle East (BBC), 18 October 1977; R San'ā, 20 October—Daily Report (DR), 21 October 1977; Middle East News Agency (MENA), Cairo; 19 October 1977.
9. R San'ā, 26 October—DR, 28 October 1977.
10. *Arabia and the Gulf*, 31 October, 7 November 1977.
11. *Ibid*, 7 November 1977, 20 February 1978; *al-Mustaqbal*, Paris; 29 October 1977.
12. *Arabia and the Gulf*, 7, 14 November; *NAD*, 19 November 1977.
13. R San'ā, 17 November—DR, 18 November 1977.
14. *Al-Siyāsa*, Kuwait; 27 October 1977.
15. *Arabia and the Gulf*, 15 December 1977.
16. R San'ā, 3 December 1977, 2 January 1978—DR, 9 December 1977, 3 January 1978.
17. *Al-Wathba*, Abu Dhabi; 14 January 1978.
18. *NAD*, 28 January 1978.
19. R San'ā, 5 February—BBC, 7 February 1978.
20. *Al-Manār*, London; 14 January, 25 February 1978; *Arabia and the Gulf*, 3 April 1978.
21. R San'ā, 6 February—DR, 7 February 1978.
22. *Al-Wathba*, 18 February 1978.
23. R San'ā, 24 February—BBC, 1 March 1978.
24. R San'ā, 25 February—BBC, 1 March 1978.
25. R San'ā, 26 February—BBC, 1 March 1978.
26. *Arabia and the Gulf*, 20 February, 6 March 1978.
27. *Akhbār al-Yawm*, Cairo; 29 April 1978.
28. *Al-Manār*, 11 March 1978; *Arabia and the Gulf*, 13 March 1978.
29. Iraqi News Agency (INA), 12 March—DR, 14 March 1978.
30. R San'ā, 7 March—DR, 10 March 1978; *Thirteenth June*, San'ā; 9 March 1978.
31. R San'ā, 18 March—BBC, 21 March 1978.
32. *Al-Dustūr*, London; 27 March 1978.
33. *Al-Thawra*, San'ā; 18 March 1978.
34. *Arabia and the Gulf*, 10 April 1978.
35. *Al-Thawra*, San'ā; 18, 19 April 1978.
36. R San'ā, 22 April—BBC, 25 April 1978.
37. INA, 22 April—BBC, 25 April 1978; '*Ukāz*, Jidda; 24 April 1978.
38. Reuter, 23 April 1978.
39. *Middle East Economic Digest (MEED)*, London; 28 April 1978.
40. *Akhbār al-Yawm*, 29 April 1978.
41. *Akhbār al-Yawm*, 13 May, 3 June; *al-Siyāsa*, 17, 25 May; *al-Wathba*, 28 May; *al-Sharq al-Jadīd*, Beirut; 28 June; *al-Nahār*, Beirut; 26 July 1978.
42. R San'ā, 18, 20 May—BBC, 20, 22 May 1978.
43. Reuter, 23 May; R San'ā, 27 May—DR, 1 June; *al-Anwār*, Beirut; 11 June 1978.
44. *Al-Thawra*, 31 May 1978.
45. R San'ā, 16 June—DR, 22 June 1978.
46. R San'ā, 24 June—DR, 26, 27 June 1978.
47. INA, 24, 25 June—DR, 26 June; R San'ā, 29 June—DR, 30 June 1978.
48. MENA, 26 June—DR, 27 June; *al-Ra'y al-'Āmm*, Kuwait; 28 June; R San'ā, 29 June—DR, 30 June 1978.
49. R Aden, 25 June—DR, 26 June 1978.
50. *Al-Thawra*, 28 June 1978.
51. *Ibid*, 27 June 1978.
52. *Al-Ahrām*, Cairo; 28 June 1978.
53. *Al-Diyār*, Beirut; 3 July 1978.
54. *Al-Siyāsa*, 10 July 1978.
55. *Financial Times (FT)*, London; 26 June; *Arabia and the Gulf*, 3 July 1978.
56. *The Times*, London; 26 June; *al-Ray al-'Āmm*, 28 June 1978.
57. R Riyadh, 26 June, 2 July—DR, 26 June, 3 July 1978.
58. *Arabia and the Gulf*, 17, 31 July 1978.
59. R San'ā, 28 June—BBC, 30 June 1978.
60. INA, 17 July—BBC, 18 July 1978.

61. R San'ā, 18 July—DR, 19 July 1978.
62. R San'ā, 18 July—DR, 19 July; *al-Anwār, al-Sayyād*, Beirut; 24 July; *al-Bayrāq*, Beirut; 27 July 1978.
63. MENA, 19 July 1978.
64. R San'ā, 19 July—DR, 20 July 1978.
65. R San'ā, 20 July—DR, 21 July 1978.
66. R San'ā, 30 July, 2 September—BBC, 1 August, 5 September 1978.
67. R San'ā, 10 August—BBC, 12 August 1978.
68. R San'ā, 1, 10 August—DR, 2 August; BBC, 12 August 1978.
69. *Al-Siyāsa*, 14 August—DR, 15 August 1978.
70. *Al-Nahār*, 12 September 1978.
71. See *MECS 1976-77*, pp. 659-60.
72. Saudi News Agency (SNA), 13 April—DR, 14 April 1978.
73. *Al-Anwār*, 22 July; *al-Jumhūr*, Beirut; 3-9 August 1978.
74. *MEED*, 9 December 1977; *'Ukāz*, 19 January 1978.
75. *FT*, 15 March; *al-Jumhūr*, 16 March; SNA, 19 May—BBC, 30 May 1978.
76. Gulf News Agency, 30 May—DR, 1 June 1978.
77. R San'ā, 3 December—DR, 9 December 1977; *al-Thawra*, 18 March 1978.
78. *Al-Diyār*, 12 June 1978.
79. Reuter, 27 February 1978.
80. Reuter, 1 April; INA, 27 June—DR, 28 June; Gulf News Agency, 22 August—DR, 23 August 1978.
81. *Al-Sha'b*, Algiers; 10 September 1978.
82. See *MECS 1976-77*, p. 662.
83. INA, 10 April 1978.
84. *Al-Mustaqbal*, 22 April 1978.
85. Gulf News Agency, 20 April—DR, 21 April; TASS, 25 April 1978.
86. *Al-Ittihād*, Abu Dhabi; 28 August 1978.
87. For details on the first stages of the development plan, see *MECS 1976-77*, p. 622.
88. For details of the San'ā conference and its aftermath, see, among others, *Arabia and the Gulf*, 23 January 1978; *The Middle East*, London; January 1978, pp. 28-29; and Economist Intelligence Unit, *Quarterly Economic Review*, London; Nos 4 (1977) and 2 (1978).
89. See *Arab Economist*, London; August 1978, pp. 26-27.
90. Budget figures reported by SNA, 31 July—BBC, 8 August 1978.
91. See International Monetary Fund (IMF), *International Financial Statistics*, October 1978, p. 353.
92. *Ibid*, pp. 400-1.
93. See IMF, *Direction of Trade Annual 1971-77* and *MEED*, 9 June 1978.

INDEX

Index

NOTE

Most political parties, organizations, public bodies and institutions have been indexed by name and not according to country, which appears in parenthesis at the end of the entry.
Page numbers in bold type indicate principal references. The alphabetical order is word-by-word.

INDEX

815

INDEX

INDEX

INDEX

98, 100, 104, 107, 110, 114, 118, 159, 160–2, 163, 166, 586–9, 681, 735
Palestinians, 73–4, 91–2, 100–1, 115, 117, 119, 128–9, 198–201, 254–5, 256, 258, 266, 296, 370, 455, 582, 606, 621–2
Pan-Iranist Party, 476, 488
Paratroop brigades (YAR), 795, 799
Party of the Iranian Nation, 488
Parviz, Amir Husayn Amir, 484, 486
Pasandideh, Morteza, 485
Pathans, 58, 60
Patriotic Union of Kurdistan (PUK), 522
"Peace Now" movement, 397, 553–4
Pejman, Habibollah, 480
People's Democratic Party (Afghanistan), 60
People's Democratic Republic of Yemen (PDRY), 13, 59, 218–21, 241, 367, 655–74, 793, 800–2, 805
  Armed forces, 658, 660–1, 663, 665, 666, 669
  Border clashes, 661, 662, 663
  Economic affairs, 667–72
  Execution of Rubay', 59, 241, 658–60, 800–2
  Government, 656
  Internal power struggle, 655–60
  Internal security forces, 658
  Presidential Council, 660
  Relations with:
    Cuba, 659, 666
    Egypt, 391, 664
    Horn of Africa, 72, 73, 238, 240, 662, 666–7
    N. Yemen, 660, 661, 662–3
    Oman, 664
    Saudi Arabia, 240–1, 656, 660–2
    Soviet bloc, 655, 665–6
    US, 667
People's National Assembly (PNA) (Sudan), 695, 696, 699–700
People's Regional Assembly (PRA) (Sudan), 695, 699–702
Peres, Shimon, 89, 108, 119, 120, 142–4, 170, 175, 177, 397, 544–5, 546
Perim, 665, 666
Perinçek, Dogu, 763
Persian Gulf, 8, 9, 56–60, 343, 492–3, 495, 501, 525, 683–4
Petah Tiqwa, 206
Petroleum Industry Research Foundation (US), 338, 339
Pezeshkpur, Mohsen, 468, 475, 476
Phalangists, 605, 607, 617–18
Pirasteh, Mehdi, 488
Poland, 527, 593, 644
Polisario, 244, 245, 639
Ponomarev, Boris, 37
Ponset, François, 176
Pope John Paul I, 561, 609
Popular Democratic Front for the Liberation of Palestine (PDFLP), 74, 205, 206, 207, 268, 271–2, 275, 581
Popular Front for the Liberation of Oman (PFLO), 436, 437, 641, 664
Popular Front for the Liberation of Palestine (PFLP), 74, 205, 207, 272, 273, 274
Popular Front for the Liberation of Palestine-General Command (PFLP-GC), 269
Popular Liberation Front (PLF), 269
Popular Struggle Front (PSF), (Palestinian), 269
Port Muscat, 437
Port Raysut, 436
Port Sudan, 707, 717
Progressive Patriotic and Nationalist Front (PPNF) (Iraq), 513, 519
Progressive Unionist Socialist Alignment Party (PUSA) (Egypt), 379, 381, 383, 385

Qablān, Aḥmad, 727
Qābūs, Sultan of Oman, 414, 436, 437, 438, 439, 440, 664
Qaddūmī, Fārūq, 265, 266, 588
Qaddūr, Nāzim, 727
Qadhdhāfī, Mu'ammar al-, 13, 14, 57, 71, 215, 219, 220, 234, 244, 260, 391, 588, 628–43, 645–6 passim, 737
Qāḍī, Ḥamdī al-, 290
Qalaq, 'Iz al-Dīn, 277
Qamāta, Ḥusayn, 658
Qansūh, 'Iṣām, 620
Qarār, Bābikr, 707
Qāsim, 'Awn al-Sharīf, 708
Qāsim, Marwān, al-, 580
Qāsimī, Sultān bin Muḥammad al-, 452

Qatar, 413, 414, 446–50
  Armed forces, 446, 448–9
  Economic affairs, 310, 311, 315, 360, 361, 364, 367, 447–8, 449–50
  Immigrant workers, 446–7
  Relations with:
    Egypt, 446–7, 448
    France, 448
    Indonesia, 448
Qatar Development Bank, 75
Qa'ūd, 'Abd al-Majīd al-, 636
Qawāsimī, Fahd al-, 282, 283, 285, 295, 297
Qaysūnī, 'Abd al-Mun'im al-, 369, 372, 400, 401
Qāzimī, 'Abd al-Muttalib al-, 426
Qom, 469, 470, 471, 490
Qudsī, Safwān, 727
Qulay'āt, 607
Qur'ān, 633, 634, 678

Rabbani, 'Ali-Naqi, 500
Rabin, Yitzhak, 86, 87, 96, 169, 545
Radical Movement (Iran), 488
Radio Baghdad, 227
Radio Cairo, 392
Radio of Freedom from Inside South Yemen, 661
Rafiah, 94, 97, 102, 107, 551
Rāfi'ī, 'Abd al-Majīd al-, 619
Rahnema, Mustafa, 488
Rajab, Muḥammad al-Zarūq, 636
Rakah (Israel), 566, 567, 568
Ramaḍān, 'Abd al- 'Azīz, 395
Ramaḍān (al-Jazrāwī), Taha Yāsīn, 218, 516, 524, 748
Rāmallah, 290, 292, 294, 296
Rambod, Hulako, 487
Ra's al-Khaymah, 414–15, 439, 452, 454, 457, 458
Ra's Muḥammad, 103
Ra's Musandan, 414
Ra's al-Nāqūra, 200
Rashīd, Harūn, 257
Rāshid, Shaykh, 414, 451, 452, 453, 454
Rashīdat, Najīb, 581
Rashīdat, Shafīq, 581
Rashmāwī, 'Atā'allah, 293
Rasūl (Bābakr al-Phishdārī), Bakr, 516
Rawābida, 'Abd al-Rā'ūf al-, 580
Rayyis, Zuhayr al-, 288
Razzaz, Munīf al-, 514
Rechtman, Shmuel, 550
Red Sea, 36, 56, 58–60, 72, 237–42, 243, 684, 804
Republican People's Party (RPP) (Turkey), 751, 753, 755–9 passim, 762–6 passim
Republican Reliance Party (RRP) (Turkey), 751, 754, 759, 762, 765
Reunion, 642
Revolutionary Command Council (Iraq), 515, 518–19, 521
Ribicoff, Abe, 25, 26
Ridā, 'Abdallah 'Alī, 687
Rifā'ī, Ghassān al-, 729
Rimalt, Elimelech, 548
Rīmāwī, 'Abdallah al-, 584, 600–1
Rims, 414
Riswat, 436
Riyāḍ, Maḥmud, 230, 239
Riyāḍ, Muḥammad, 373
Riyadh, 344, 394
Riyazi, 'Abdallah, 476
Rohani, Mansur, 489
Romania, 174–5, 500, 561, 780
Rosh Haniqrah, see Ra's al-Nāqūra
Ru'aynī, Aḥmad Sāliḥ al-, 800
Rubay', Sālim 'Alī, 59, 240, 241, 655–9, 800–1, 802
Rubenstein, Amnon, 547

Sabāḥ, Jābir al-Ahmad al-, 424
Sabāḥ, Jābir al-'Alī al-Sālim al-, 424, 426, 427
Sabāḥ, Nawwāf al-Ahmad al-Jābir al-, 426, 427
Sabāḥ, Sabāḥ Sālim al-, 424
Sabāḥ, Sa'd al-'Abdalla al-Sālim al-, 424, 426, 427, 428, 495
Sabbe, Osman, 73, 240
Sa'd, Adīb, 616
Sādāt, Anwar al-, 21–3, 27–31, 83–129 passim, 134–9, 146, 153–4, 157, 162, 169, 175, 176, 177, 214, 217, 231, 234–5, 236, 243, 253–9, 273, 283, 284, 368–97 passim, 523–4, 590

821

INDEX

The Fertile Crescent

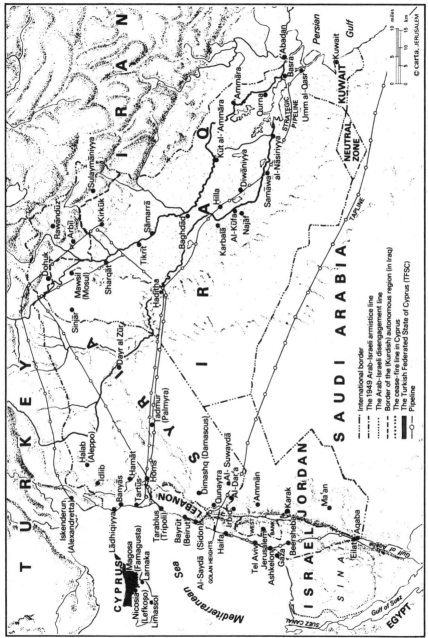

Legend:
- International border
- The 1949 Arab-Israeli armistice line
- The Arab-Israeli disengagement line
- Border of the (Kurdish) autonomous region (in Iraq)
- The cease-fire line in Cyprus
- The Turkish Federated State of Cyprus (TFSC)
- Pipeline

© carta, JERUSALEM

TURKEY

Iskenderun (Alexandretta)
Halab (Aleppo)
Idlib
Banyās
Lādhiqiyya
Tarṭūs
Hamāt
Ḥoms
Tarābulus (Tripoli)
Bayrūt (Beirut)
Al-Saydā (Sidon)
LEBANON

CYPRUS
Nicosia (Lefkoşo)
Magosa (Famagusta)
Larnaka
Limassol

Dohuk
Mawsil (Mosul)
Sharqāṭ
Sinjār
Dayr al-Zūr
Tadmūr (Palmyra)
Ravāndūz
Arbīl
Kirkūk
Sāmarrā
Tikrīt
Ḥadītha

IRAN

IRAQ
Baghdād
Sulaymāniyya
Ammāra
Kūt al-ʿAmmāra
Hilla
Karbalā
Al-Kūfa
Najāf
Dīwāniyya
Samāwa
al-Nāṣiriyya
Qurna
Umm al-Qaṣr
Basra
Abadan

Persian Gulf

Kuwait
KUWAIT
NEUTRAL ZONE

SAUDI ARABIA

STRATEGIC PIPELINE
TAPLINE

SYRIA
Dimashq (Damascus)
Qunaytra
Al-Suwaydā
Al-Darʿa
Ammān
Irbid
GOLAN HEIGHTS

ISRAEL
Haifa
Tel Aviv
Jerusalem
WEST BANK
Ashkelon
Gaza
Beersheba
Karak
Maʿān
JORDAN

SINAI
Eilat
Aqaba
Gulf of Aqaba

Mediterranean Sea

EGYPT
SUEZ CANAL
Gulf of Suez

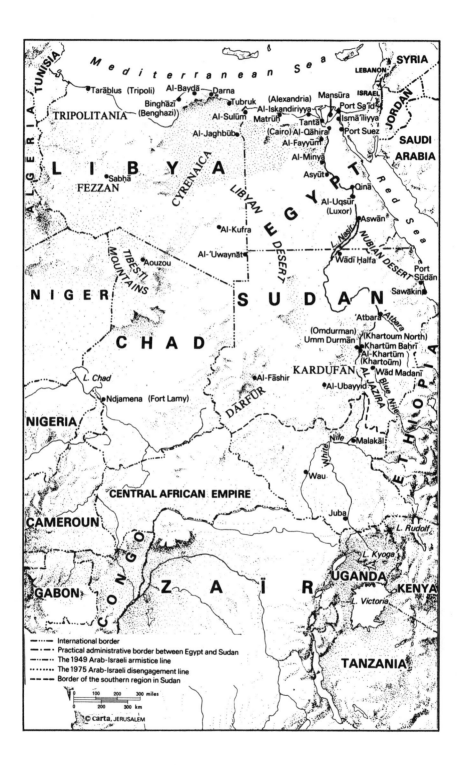

Mediterranean Sea

SYRIA
LEBANON
ISRAEL
JORDAN
SAUDI ARABIA

Tarāblus (Tripoli)
Al-Baydā
Darna
Binghāzī (Benghazi)
Tubruk
(Alexandria)
Mansūra
Al-Iskandiriyya
Port Sa'īd
Al-Sulūm
Matrūḥ
Ismā'īliyya
Tantā
Port Suez
(Cairo) Al-Qāhira
Al-Fayyūm
Al-Minyā
Asyūṭ
Qinā
Al-Uqsur (Luxor)
Aswān
Wādī Ḥalfa
Port Sūdān
Sawākin

TRIPOLITANIA
L I B Y A
FEZZAN
Sabḥā
CYRENAICA
LIBYAN DESERT
E G Y P T
Al-Jaghbūb
Al-Kufra
Al-'Uwaynāt
L. Nasir
NUBIAN DESERT
Red Sea

ALGERIA
TUNISIA

Aouzou
TIBESTI MOUNTAINS
N I G E R
S U D A N
C H A D
'Atbara
Atbara
(Omdurman)
Umm Durmān
(Khartoum North)
Khartūm Bahrī
Al-Khartūm (Khartoūm)
KARDUFĀN
Wād Madanī
AL JAZIRA
Blue Nile
E T H I O P I A

L. Chad
Ndjamena (Fort Lamy)
Al-Fāshir
Al-Ubayyid
DĀRFŪR
NIGERIA

Nile
Malakāl
White
Wau

CENTRAL AFRICAN EMPIRE
CAMEROUN
Juba
L. Rudolf
CONGO
L. Kyoga
GABON
Z A Ï R
UGANDA
KENYA
L. Victoria

TANZANIA

International border
Practical administrative border between Egypt and Sudan
The 1949 Arab-Israeli armistice line
The 1975 Arab-Israeli disengagement line
Border of the southern region in Sudan

0   100   200   300 miles
0   200   300 km

© Carta, JERUSALEM

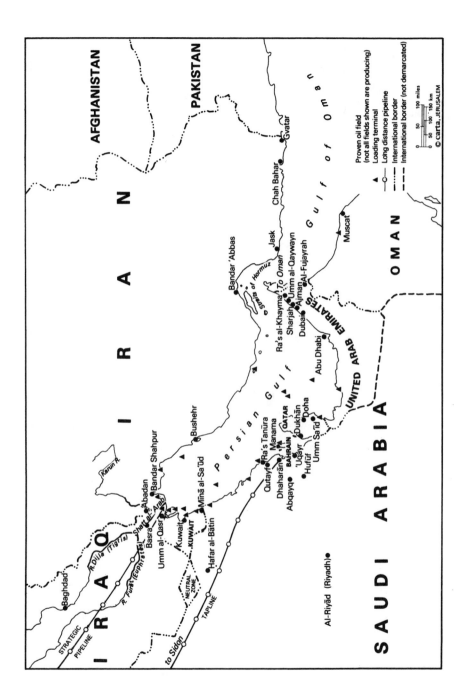

AFGHANISTAN

PAKISTAN

Gulf of Oman

Gvatar

Chah Bahar

Jask

Bandar 'Abbas

Muscat

Straits of Hormuz

To Oman
Umm al-Qaywayn
Al-Fujayrah
Ra's al-Khayma
Sharjah
Ajman
Dubai

UNITED ARAB EMIRATES

OMAN

I R A N

Bushehr

Persian Gulf

Karun R.

Abu Dhabi

Bandar Shahpur

Abadan

Doha

Dukhān

QATAR

Minā al-Saʿūd

Ra's Tanūra
Manama
BAHRAIN
Qutayf
Dhaharān
Abqayq
ʿUdayr
Hufūf
Umm Saʿīd

Basra
Shaṭṭ al-Arab

Umm al-Qasr
Kuwait
KUWAIT

R. Dijla (Tigris)

R. Furāt (Euphrates)

Ḥafar al-Bāṭin

NEUTRAL
ZONE

Baghdad

I R A Q

SAUDI ARABIA

Al-Riyād (Riyadh)

STRATEGIC
PIPELINE

TAPLINE

to Sidon

Proven oil field
(not all fields shown are producing)

Loading terminal

Long distance pipeline

International border

International border (not demarcated)

0   50   100 miles
0   50 100 150 km

© Carta, JERUSALEM

Arabian Peninsula and the Horn of Africa

Turkey and Iran

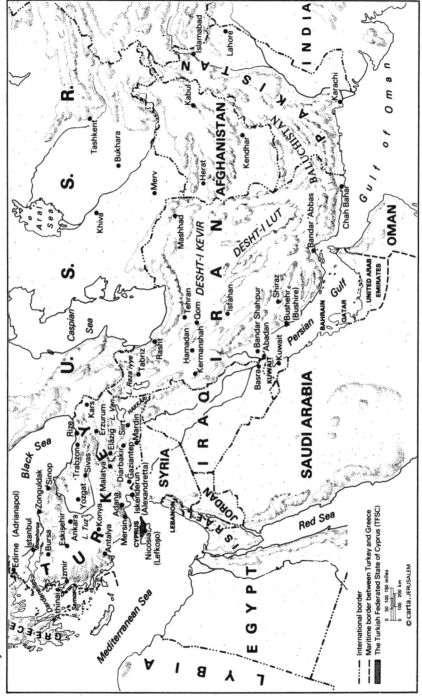

GREECE

Edirne (Adrianapol)
Istanbul
Bosphorus
Dardanelles
Bursa
İzmir
Afhsar
Samsun
Sinop
Zonguldak
Black Sea
Rize
Trabzon
Kars
Erzurum
Sivas
Yozgat
Ankara
Eskişehir
L. Tuz
Konya
Antalya
Mersin
Adana
İskenderun
(Alexandretta)
Gaziantep
Malatya
Elâzig
Diarbakir
Siirt
Mardin
L. Van
HAKKARI
CYPRUS
Nicosia
(Lefkoşa)

T U R K E Y

Mediterranean Sea

LEBANON
ISRAEL
JORDAN
SYRIA
IRAQ
Basra
Baghdad

Rasht
Tabriz
Rezaiyeh
L. Rezaiyeh
Hamadan
Kermanshah
Tehran
Qom
İsfahan
Bandar Shahpur
Abadan
Shiraz
Bushehr
(Bushire)
Mashhad

I R A N

DESHT-I KEVIR

DESHT-I LUT

Bandar 'Abbas
Chah Bahar

Kuwait
KUWAIT
BAHRAIN
QATAR
Persian Gulf
Gulf

UNITED ARAB
EMIRATES
OMAN

Gulf of Oman

SAUDI ARABIA

Red Sea

EGYPT

L Y B I A

Khiva
Merv
Aral Sea
Tashkent
Bukhara

U. S. S. R.

Caspian Sea

Kabul
Kandahar
Herat
AFGHANISTAN
BALUCHISTAN
P A K I S T A N
Islamabad
Lahore
Karachi
INDIA

International border
Maritime border between Turkey and Greece
The Turkish Federated State of Cyprus (TFSC)

0   50 100 150 miles
0   100   200 km

© carta, JERUSALEM

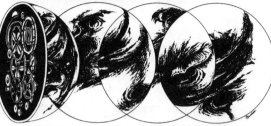

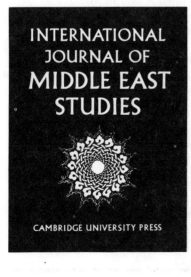

"Of all the many works of reference devoted to Africa, this is the only one worth buying in its latest edition year after year." *The Economist*

AFRICA CONTEMPORARY RECORD

Volume 10, 1977-78
edited by Colin Legum

Combining scholarly accuracy with journalistic timeliness, Volume 10 includes essays on the following topics:
- The Crisis in Southern Africa
- The Crisis in the Horn of Africa
- The United States' Year in Africa: Reinventing the Wheel
- Cuba: The New Communist Power in Africa
- West Germany's Role in Africa in 1977: An Economic Superpower on the Move

as well as:
- 56 country-by-country surveys
- 90 documents relating to political, economic and social developments in Africa.

1472 pp. / ISBN 0-8419-0159-7 / $75

Vols 1-9, covering the years 1968-1977, are available.
Standing orders are invited.

AFRICANA PUBLISHING COMPANY
a division of Holmes & Meier Publishers, Inc.
30 Irving Place, New York, N.Y. 10003